MW00379192

UNIVERSITY CASEBOOK SERIES®

SECURED TRANSACTIONS IN PERSONAL PROPERTY

ELEVENTH EDITION

STEVEN D. WALT

Percy Brown, Jr., Professor of Law

University of Virginia School of Law

FOUNDATION
PRESS

© 1983, 1987, 1992, 1997, 2000, 2004, 2007 Foundation Press
© 2010 Thomson Reuters/Foundation Press
© 2013 LEG, Inc. d/b/a West Academic Publishing
© 2019 LEG, Inc. d/b/a West Academic
© 2023 LEG, Inc. d/b/a West Academic
      860 Blue Gentian Road, Suite 350
      Eagan, MN 55121
      1-877-888-1330

Printed in the United States of America

ISBN: 978-1-68561-435-5

For Maryann

PREFACE

A loan secured by personal property is a prevalent and economically important form of financing. This book describes the law governing secured transactions (or "asset-based" financing). The law here remains largely state law, predominantly Article 9 of the Uniform Commercial Code (UCC). With some exceptions, as enacted Article 9 remains a predominantly uniform statute. Federal law, when applicable, frequently takes Article 9 as its baseline. The Chapters that follow systematically analyze the creation, priority and enforcement of security interests. The book also explores the interface of Article 9 with leases and consignments, specialized areas of financing involving investment securities, intellectual property and letters of credit, and the impact of bankruptcy law on security interests.

The Eleventh Edition takes into account developments in the law of secured transactions since the Tenth Edition. The most important of these has been the 2022 Amendments to the UCC, approved by the American Law Institute and the Uniform Law Commission. The Amendments regulate rights in, and the transfer of, certain digital assets such as virtual currencies, nonfungible tokens and electronic payment rights. Most directly, they add a new Article to the UCC, Article 12 ("Controllable Electronic Records"). In bringing the regulation of certain digital assets within the UCC, the Amendments make changes to almost every Article of the UCC and extensive changes to Article 9. The Amendments also change or clarify some UCC provisions unrelated to digital assets, including select Article 9 provisions.

This Edition describes the impact of the 2022 Amendments on security interests under Article 9 and illustrates their application with problems. In addition, recent decisions interpreting Article 9 and the Bankruptcy Code affect the rights of secured creditors in bankruptcy. Important cases in both areas have appeared since the Tenth Edition, and this Edition reprints some of them. For the significant issues raised by Article 9 that challenge courts or have not come before them, problems are used. They force close consideration of statutory language and pertinent Official Comments, and allow tightly structured class sessions.

The Eleventh Edition contains a fair amount of new text and some new cases, notes and problems. It continues to provide an analysis of relevant provisions and their rationale as background to cases and problems. Against this background, the cases, problems and accompanying notes explore specific applications of provisions. Citations to cases and secondary literature are kept to a minimum. In an area heavily regulated by statute, this streamlined approach seems to me more effective pedagogically than one that approaches the subject primarily through cases or policy. As with previous editions, the book is structured to allow instructors to teach the subject through a mix of cases and problems. It gives them the freedom to select material on which to focus class discussion. New notes and text discuss new cases, regulations and emerging issues; new problems explore application of provisions discussed in the text.

A note about the editing of the cases reproduced in the book. For economy of presentation, some citations in reproduced cases have been removed or shortened without indication. Bracketed references to sections of Article 9 in cases are to sections in the current version of Article 9. Footnotes occasionally have been deleted without indication. Finally, deleted paragraphs are indicated by asterisks and deleted material within a paragraph by an ellipsis.

In preparing this Edition I have missed the advice and wise judgment of my late coauthor, Bill Warren.

STEVEN D. WALT

February 2023

ACKNOWLEDGMENTS

I gratefully acknowledge the permission extended to reprint excerpts from the following works:

The American Law Institute has given permission to reprint the following materials:

Uniform Commercial Code Article 9. Official Text. Copyright © 2012 by The American Law Institute and the National Conference of Commissioners on Uniform State Laws. Selected Sections and Official Comments.

City National Bank. All forms in this book are reprinted with permission of City National Bank, a national banking association, of Los Angeles, California.

Grant Gilmore, Security Interests in Personal Property (1965), Volume 1, page 73. © 1965, Little, Brown and Company, assigned to The Law Book Exchange, Ltd. Reprinted with permission.

Harold R. Weinberg & William J. Woodard, Jr., Legislative Process and Commercial Law: Lessons from the Copyright Act of 1976 and the Uniform Commercial Code, 48 Bus.Law 437, 475 (1993). Copyright © 1993 American Bar Association. Reprinted with permission.

SUMMARY OF CONTENTS

PREFACE...V

ACKNOWLEDGMENTS.. VII

TABLE OF CASES.. XXIII

TABLE OF STATUTES... XXIX

TABLE OF REGULATIONS XLIII

TABLE OF RULES XLV

Chapter 1. Creating a Security Interest...1
A.   Why Secured Credit? 1
B.   Introduction to Article 9 9
C.   Attachment...13

Chapter 2. Perfection 53
A.   Introduction..53
B.   Perfection by Filing..56
C.   The Filing System...102
D.   Perfection by Possession..123
E.   Perfection by Control 129
F.   Security Interests in Consumer Goods..132
G.   Choice of Law 135

Chapter 3. Priority...151
A.   Introduction...151
B.   The First-to-File-or-Perfect Rule 151
C.   Purchase-Money Priority 162
D.   Lien Creditors 182
E.   Buyers and Lessees..184
F.   Rights to Payment 201
G.   Accounts and General Intangibles..218
H.   Controllable Electronic Records and Controllable Payment Rights...225
I.   Chattel Paper and Instruments...228
J.   Deposit Accounts...239
K.   Cash Proceeds 252
L.   Federal Tax Liens 266

Chapter 4. Leases and Consignments 281
A.   Leases 281
B.   Consignments..320

Chapter 5. Security Interests in Intellectual Property 343
A.   Introduction...343
B.   Copyrights 344
C.   Trademarks 369
D.   Patents...374
E.   Restrictions on Assignment of Intellectual Property.................385

Chapter 6. Security Interests in Investment Securities...................389
A.   Introduction..389
B.   What Is a Security?...393
C.   Basic Rules..396
D.   Certificated Securities...397
E.   Uncertificated Securities..422

Chapter 7. Security Interests in Fixtures............................431
A.   What Is a Fixture?...431
B.   Fixture and Other Filings..432
C.   Priority...434
D.   Enforcement..445

Chapter 8. Default and Enforcement..................................455
A.   Introduction..455
B.   Default..456
C.   Enforcement..465

Chapter 9. Security Interests in Bankruptcy.........................525
A.   Overview of Bankruptcy...525
B.   Secured Claims in Bankruptcy..532
C.   Treatment of Secured Claims in Chapters 7, 11 and 13.................537
D.   Avoidance Powers of the Trustee...570
E.   Preferences: BC 547..573
F.   Fraudulent Transfers: BC 548..596

Chapter 10. Letters of Credit...605
A.   Introduction..605
B.   The Letter of Credit Relationship and Types of Credits.................606
C.   Legal Character and Sources of Law.....................................609
D.   Formal Requirements..611
E.   Issuer's Duty to Honor or Dishonor......................................617
F.   Forgery and Fraud..653
G.   Transfer, Assignment and Security Interests.............................664
H.   Letters of Credit in Bankruptcy..671

Appendix I. Accounts Receivable/Loan Agreement.................679

Appendix II. Lockbox Agreement.......................................717

INDEX...723

TABLE OF CONTENTS

PREFACE...V

ACKNOWLEDGMENTS.. VII

TABLE OF CASES...XXIII

TABLE OF STATUTES... XXIX

TABLE OF REGULATIONS XLIII

TABLE OF RULES XLV

Chapter 1. Creating a Security Interest...1
A.   Why Secured Credit? 1
   1.   Rights of Unsecured Creditor...3
   2.   Rights of Secured Creditor 4
   3.   Is Secured Credit Fair or Efficient?......................................6
      Problem 6
B.   Introduction to Article 9 9
   1.   Historical Note 9
   2.   Former Article 9 10
   3.   Article 9 and the 2022 Amendments 12
C.   Attachment..13
   1.   The Security Agreement..13
      Problems 14
   2.   The Composite Document Rule 15
      In re Bollinger Corp. 15
      Notes 21
      Problems 22
   3.   Description of Collateral..23
      In re Hintze...27
      Note 32
      Problems 32
   4.   After-Acquired Collateral 34
      a.   Under 9–204(a)...34
         In re Filtercorp, Inc. 35
      b.   Section 9–204(b)'s Limitations 39
   5.   Value and Rights in Collateral..41
      a.   Value 41
         Problem 41
      b.   Rights in Collateral...42
         In re Jojo's 10 Rest., LLC 44
         Note 47
         Problem 48
   6.   Attachment to Proceeds and Supporting Obligations 49
      Problems 52

Chapter 2. Perfection 53
A.   Introduction..53
      Problem 56

B.   Perfection by Filing..56
    1.   Notice Filing 56
         Problems 58
    2.   Sufficiency of Financing Statement....................................59
         Problems 60
         In re Hergert..60
         Note..66
    3.   Indication of Collateral 67
         a.   Original Collateral 67
              ProGrowth Bank, Inc. v. Wells Fargo Bank, N.A. 69
              Note..74
              Problem 75
         b.   Proceeds 76
              Problem 77
    4.   Name of Debtor 77
         a.   Basic Rules 77
              (1) Individual Debtors...78
              (2) General Partnerships...79
              (3) Registered Organizations...................................79
         b.   Errors or Omissions 80
              In re Nay..81
              1944 Beach Blvd., LLC v. Live Oak Banking Co. 87
              Note...92
         c.   Trade Names 92
              In re EDM Corp...93
              Notes...99
    5.   Financing Statement Authorized by Debtor 100
         Problems 101
C.   The Filing System...102
    1.   Central Filing..102
    2.   Kinds of Records Filed 103
         a.   Financing Statement Records 103
              Problem 106
              In re Motors Liquidation Co. 106
              Note..112
         b.   Safe Harbor Form..113
    3.   When Filing Becomes Effective....................................114
         a.   Filing Office Indexing Errors 114
              Problem 115
         b.   Duty of Filing Office to Accept or Reject................115
    4.   Post-Filing Changes..116
         a.   Transfer of Collateral..116
              Problem 118
         b.   Changes Other Than in Debtor Name or Legal Identity.....118
         c.   Name Change 118
              Problem 119
         d.   Change in Legal Identity 119
              Problem 120
              Problem 122

D. Perfection by Possession..123
    1.   Possession by Agent..123
         In re Rolain 124
         Notes 127
    2.   Possession by Bailee 127
         Problems 128
E. Perfection by Control 129
F. Security Interests in Consumer Goods..132
    1.   Consumer Transactions Under Article 9...........................132
    2.   Perfection of Security Interests in Consumer Goods.........133
         Problems 134
G. Choice of Law 135
    1.   Location of Debtor Governs Tangible and Intangible
        Collateral 136
    2.   Location of the Debtor..137
         In re SemCrude LP...140
    3.   Goods Covered by Certificate of Title 144
        a.   What Law Governs Perfection? 144
        b.   The Basic Rules of Perfection 145
        c.   Change in Debtor's Location..145
         In re Baker..146
         Notes 148
         Problems 148

Chapter 3. Priority..**151**
A. Introduction 151
B. The First-to-File-or-Perfect Rule 151
    1.   Conflicting Security Interests 152
         Problems 153
    2.   Future Advances 153
         Problems 154
         Problem 155
    3.   Financing Statement as an Umbrella................................156
         Problem 156
    4.   Position of First-to-File Secured Party 159
    5.   Operating Under the First-to-File-or-Perfect Rule...........160
         Problems 161
C. Purchase-Money Priority..162
    1.   The Purchase-Money Security Interest 162
         Problems 164
    2.   Priority in Noninventory Goods 167
        a.   Purchase-Money Priority...167
         Brodie Hotel Supply, Inc. v. United States 168
         Notes 170
        b.   The Transformation Rule 172
    3.   Priority in Inventory 174
         Problem 174
         Southtrust Bank v. Borg-Warner Acceptance Corp. 175
         Notes 179

      4.   9–103(h)'s Consumer Goods Exception 181
  D. Lien Creditors 182
      1.   Conflict with an Unperfected Security Interest 182
          Problems 182
      2.   Conflict with a Future Advance 182
  E. Buyers and Lessees 184
      1.   Buyers and Lessees of Non-Inventory Goods 184
      2.   Buyers and Lessees of Inventory Goods 185
         a.   Buyer in the Ordinary Course of Business 185
            Madison Capital Company, LLC v. S & S Salvage,
               LLC 186
             Problems 190
         b.   Goods Subject to Certificate of Title Acts 191
         c.   Waiver 193
      3.   Buyers of Consumer Goods 193
          Problem 193
      4.   When Does a Buyer Buy? 194
      5.   Double Debtors 195
          Bank of the West v. Commercial Credit Financial
             Services, Inc. 195
             Note 201
  F. Rights to Payment 201
      1.   Scope of Article 9 202
      2.   Rights to Payment Under Article 9 202
         a.   Types of Payment Rights: Definitions 202
         b.   Sale of Rights to Payment 204
            Major's Furniture Mart, Inc. v. Castle Credit Corp.,
             Inc. 209
             Notes 216
         c.   Priority in Sold Payment Rights 217
            Problems 218
  G. Accounts and General Intangibles 218
      1.   Priority in Proceeds 218
          Problems 219
      2.   Section 9–309(2)'s Exception 220
         In re Tri-County Materials, Inc. 221
         Notes 224
  H. Controllable Electronic Records and Controllable Payment Rights ... 225
      Problems 227
  I.   Chattel Paper and Instruments 228
      1.   Introduction 228
         Rex Financial Corp. v. Great Western Bank & Trust ... 230
      2.   "Merely as Proceeds" 233
      3.   Instruments 237
      4.   Review Problems 238
          Problems 238
  J.   Deposit Accounts 239
      1.   Introduction 239
      2.   Priority Rules 241

       a.   Control 241
       b.   Security Interests in Deposit Accounts as Proceeds of
            Other Collateral...244
            Problem 245
       c.   Security Interests in Deposit Accounts as Original
            Collateral 245
            Problem 246
       d.   Proceeds of Deposit Accounts: Special Priority Rules..........246
            Problem 249
       e.   Critique 249
K.   Cash Proceeds 252
   1.   Priority..252
       a.   Transferees of Funds Under Section 9–332........................252
            Cortland Sav. & Banking Co. v. Platinum Rapid
               Funding Grp., Ltd. 255
            Note 259
            Problems 261
   2.   Tracing Proceeds 261
       Problems 262
       Notes 263
   3.   Transferees of Instruments Under Section 9–330(d)................265
L.   Federal Tax Liens 266
   1.   Creation and Enforceability of Federal Tax Liens....................268
       In re Spearing Tool and Manufacturing Co., Inc.................270
       Note 273
   2.   The FTLA's General Priority Rule 274
       Problems 276
   3.   Section 6323(c)–(d)'s Exceptions: Post-Lien Transactions 277
       Problems 278
   4.   PMSIs and Post-Lien Proceeds 279
       Problem...280

Chapter 4. Leases and Consignments 281
A.   Leases 281
   1.   Distinguishing Between Lease and Security Interest................283
   2.   Lease with Option to Purchase or Renew: 1–203's Two-Step
      Application...285
       a.   1–203(a) and (b)'s Tests 285
            In re Warne 286
            Problems 297
            Problem 298
       b.   Meaningful Residual Interest....................................299
            Note: Rent-to-Own Leases 300
   3.   Lease Without Option to Purchase or Renew: 1–203(a)'s
      "Test" 301
       In re Pillowtex, Inc. 302
       Notes 311
   4.   Open-End Leases 312
       In re Lightning Bolt Leasing, LLC................................313

    Notes 318
    Problems 320
B. Consignments...320
    1. Common Law Consignments...320
    2. Consignments Under Article 9..321
    3. Security Consignment Exclusion 323
        Problem 324
        In re Georgetown Steel Co., LLC 325
        Note...332
        Problem 333
    4. Exclusion Under 9–102(a)(20)(A)(iii) 333
        In re Downey Creations, LLC 334
        Notes 338
        Problem 339
    5. Non-Article 9 Consignments and Non-Article 9 Law 339
        Problems 341

Chapter 5. Security Interests in Intellectual Property 343
A. Introduction..343
B. Copyrights 344
    In re Peregrine Entertainment, Ltd. 346
    Note...352
    Problem..353
    Notes 354
    In re World Auxiliary Power Co. 358
    Note...368
    Problems 369
C. Trademarks 369
    In re Together Development Corporation 370
    Note...374
D. Patents...374
    In re Cybernetic Services, Inc. 375
    Notes 383
E. Restrictions on Assignment of Intellectual Property 385
    Problem..388

Chapter 6. Security Interests in Investment Securities..........389
A. Introduction..389
    1. Direct and Indirect Holding Systems 389
    2. Security Entitlements and Property Rights....................392
B. What Is a Security?..393
C. Basic Rules 396
D. Certificated Securities 397
    1. Held by Owner...397
        a. Control in Pledge Transactions.............................398
            Problems 399
        b. Dividends 401
            Problem 401
        c. Pledgee's Duty of Reasonable Care 401

Layne v. Bank One, Kentucky, N.A. 402
     Note 408
   2. Certificate in Possession of Securities Intermediary 410
     a. Control Test 410
      Problems 410
     First Nat'l Bank of Palmerton v. Donaldson, Lufkin
      & Jenrette Securities Corp. 414
       Notes 420
     b. Asset Management Accounts 421
      Problem 421
E. Uncertificated Securities 422
   1. Mutual Funds 422
     Problems 423
     In re Pfautz 424
     Note 429
   2. Treasury Securities 429

Chapter 7. Security Interests in Fixtures **431**
A. What Is a Fixture? 431
B. Fixture and Other Filings 432
C. Priority 434
   1. Basic Rules 434
     Problems 435
   2. Construction Mortgages 436
   3. Manufactured Homes 437
     Problem 438
   4. Circular Priorities 438
     Problem 439
     In re Cliff's Ridge Skiing Corp. 441
     Note 444
D. Enforcement 445
   Carmel Fin. Corp. v. Castro 447
   Notes 452

Chapter 8. Default and Enforcement **455**
A. Introduction 455
B. Default 456
   1. Meaning of Default 456
   2. Waiver and Estoppel 458
   Moe v. John Deere Co. 458
     Notes 464
     Problem 464
C. Enforcement 465
   1. Cumulative Remedies 465
   Okefenokee Aircraft, Inc. v. PrimeSouth Bank 467
     Notes 470
   2. Repossession 470
     a. Self-Help Repossession 470
      Problem 471

b. Breach of Peace 471
  Problem 473
  Williams v. Ford Motor Credit Co......................... 474
  Notes 477
  Problem 478
c. Judicial Action 479
  *Cla-Mil East Holding Corp. v. Medallion Funding
    Corp.* 479
  Notes 481
3. Disposition of Collateral 482
  a. Notification Before Disposition 483
    (1) Notification Medium 483
      Problem 484
      Problem 485
      Moore v. Wells Fargo Construction 485
      Notes 490
      Problem 490
    (2) Public or Private Sale 491
    (3) Marshaling 493
  b. Commercially Reasonable Disposition..................... 493
    WM Capital Partners, LLC v. Thornton 495
    Note 500
    Problem 501
  c. Liability for Deficiency.. 501
    Problems 503
    (1) Nonconsumer Transactions 504
    (2) Consumer Transactions 506
      Problems 507
  d. Transfer Statements 508
4. Secondary Obligors 509
  Problem 510
5. Acceptance of Collateral in Satisfaction of Debt................ 511
  a. Strict Foreclosure 511
    Problem 512
    Problem 513
  b. Acceptance In Partial Satisfaction.......................... 513
  c. Default and Consumer Debtor Rules: Assessment 515
6. Effect of Disposition or Acceptance on Third Parties 517
  a. Transferees 517
    Problems 517
  b. Junior Security Interests or Liens 517
    (1) Dispositions... 517
      Problems 518
    (2) Acceptance in Satisfaction 519
7. Collection of Rights to Payment...................................... 520
8. Redemption.. 523

Chapter 9. Security Interests in Bankruptcy............................525
A. Overview of Bankruptcy 525

1. Introduction 525
2. Types of Bankruptcy 526
3. Petition in Bankruptcy and the Automatic Stay 529
4. Trustee in Bankruptcy 529
5. Claims in Bankruptcy 530
6. Distribution of Assets to Unsecured Creditors 531
7. Discharge 532
B. Secured Claims in Bankruptcy 532
1. Meaning of "Secured Claim" 532
   Problem 533
2. The Automatic Stay 534
   Problems 534
3. Effect of Discharge on Secured Claims 535
   Problems 536
C. Treatment of Secured Claims in Chapters 7, 11 and 13 537
1. Consumer Debtors 537
   a. In Chapter 7 537
      In re Jones 539
      Note 542
      Problem 542
   b. In Chapter 13 543
      City of Chicago v. Fulton 544
      Note 551
2. Business Debtors 551
   a. In Chapter 7 552
   b. In Chapter 11: After-Acquired Property and DIP
      Financing 552
      In re Premier Golf Properties, LP 554
      Notes 560
3. Valuing Collateral in Bankruptcy 561
   Associates Commercial Corp. v. Rash 563
   Notes 568
   Problem 570
D. Avoidance Powers of the Trustee 570
1. The Trustee's Strong Arm Power: BC 544(a) 571
   Problems 571
2. Subrogation of Trustee Under BC 544(b) 571
   Problems 573
E. Preferences: BC 547 573
1. Elements of a Preference 573
2. Basic Applications of Preference Law 574
   Problems 574
3. Why Preference Law? 575
4. Effect of Avoidance 577
   Problem 578
5. Preference Period 578
6. Transfers to or for Benefit of a Creditor 579
   a. Transfer of Debtor's Property 579
      Problem 579

      b.   To or for the Benefit of a Creditor 580
  7. Contemporaneous Exchanges 580
      Problems 581
  8. Ordinary Course Payments...582
      In re National Gas Distributors, L.L.C. 583
      Notes 590
  9. Floating Lien as a Preference...591
      Problem 593
  10. False Preferences: Delayed Perfection of Security Interests 594
F. Fraudulent Transfers: BC 548 596
  1. Basic Rules 596
      a.   Actual Fraud 596
      b.   Constructive Fraud 597
  2. Reasonably Equivalent Value 598
      a.   Indirect Benefit 598
      In re Northern Merchandise, Inc.................................598
      b.   Leveraged Buyout 602
      Problems 602
      c.   Securitization 603
      Problem 603

Chapter 10. Letters of Credit **605**
A. Introduction...605
B. The Letter of Credit Relationship and Types of Credits 606
C. Legal Character and Sources of Law...609
D. Formal Requirements...611
  1. Form..611
      Wichita Eagle and Beacon Publishing Co., Inc. v. Pacific
          National Bank of San Francisco...................................612
      Notes 613
      Problems 615
  2. Duration...616
      Problem 616
      Note 617
E. Issuer's Duty to Honor or Dishonor 617
  1. The Strict Compliance Standard...617
      Carter Petroleum Products, Inc. v. Brotherhood Bank &
          Trust Co...619
      Notes 626
  2. Notice of Discrepancies: Waiver and Preclusion..........................632
      Problem..633
      Note..635
      Problems 636
  3. The Independence Principle 638
  4. Issuer's Right to Reimbursement and Other Remedies 640
      a.   Reimbursement 640
      b.   Standard of Compliance..641
      c.   Subrogation, Restitution and Breach of Warranty 642
      JPMorgan Chase Bank v. Cook....................................643

		Note	648
		Note: Restitution and Breach of Warranty	649
		Problems	650
	5.	Damages for Wrongful Dishonor	651
		Problems	652
F.	Forgery and Fraud		653
	Hook Point, LLC v. Branch Banking & Trust Co.		656
	Notes		662
	Problem		664
G.	Transfer, Assignment and Security Interests		664
	1.	Transfer and Assignment	664
	2.	Security Interests	666
		Problem	668
	3.	Letters of Credit as Supporting Obligations	669
		Problem	671
H.	Letters of Credit in Bankruptcy		671
	Form. Letter of Credit Application and Agreement		673

Appendix I. Accounts Receivable/Loan Agreement ... **679**

Appendix II. Lockbox Agreement ... **717**

INDEX ... 723

TABLE OF CASES

The principal cases are in bold type.

1944 Beach Blvd., LLC v. Live Oak Banking Co., 87
Abendroth v. Town of Greenwich, 378
Accessair, Inc., In re, 588
Addison v. Burnett, 293
Adoni Group, In re The, 101
Advo-System, Inc. v. Maxway Corp., 585, 587
AEG Acquisition Corp., In re, 368
Aerocon Engineering Inc. v. Silicon Valley Bank (World Auxiliary Power Co., In re), 382
Aetna Casualty and Surety Company v. Norwalk Foods, 644
Aetna Ins. Co. v. Texas Thermal Indus., 267
AGF Direct Gas Sales & Servicing, Inc., In re, 648
Alaska Statebank v. Fairco, 461
Alaska Textile Co., Inc. v. Chase Manhattan Bank, N.A., 635
Allstate Insurance Co. v. Mazzola, 644
Alphatech Services, Inc., In re, 171
American Airlines, Inc. v. Federal Deposit Ins., 625
American Camshaft Specialties Inc., In re, 591
American Card Co. v. H.M.H. Co., 17
American Coleman v. Intrawest Bank of Southglenn, 624
American Home Mortgage Holdings, Inc., In re, 591
Amex-Protein Development Corp., In re, 18
Amoco Production Co. v. Wilson, Inc., 622
Archer Daniels Midland Corp. v. JP Morgan Chase Bank, N.A., 662
Artists Rights Enforc. Corp. v. King, 356
Associates Commercial Corp. v. Rash, 563
Associates Discount Corporation v. Old Freeport Bank, 233
B. Hollis Knight Co., In re, 223
B.C. Roger's Poultry, Inc., In re, 643
Baker, In re, 146
Banco General Runinahui, S.A. v. Citibank Int'l, 635
Bank Cafetero Panama, United States v., 264
Bank of the West v. Commercial Credit Financial Services, Inc., 195
Bank of Valley v. U.S. Nat'l Bank, 431

Bank One, N.A. v. First National Bank of Baird, 245
Bank Rhode Island v. Mixitforme, Inc., 421
Banknorth, N.A. v. Littlefield, 408
Banner Bank v. First Commercial Bank, 254
Barber v. McCord Auto Supply, Inc. (In re Pearson Industries, Inc.), 329
Bayer CropScience, LLC v. Stearns Bank Nat'l Ass'n, 41
BFC Chemicals, Inc. v. Smith-Douglass, Inc., 329
Billings, In re, 172
Bloomfield State Bank v. United States, 268
BM Electronics Corp. v. LaSalle, 630
Board of Lincoln County Comm'rs v. Nielander, 626
Bolin & Co., LLC, In re, 478
Bollinger Corp., In re, 15
Bombay Indus., Inc. v. Bank of N.Y., 630
BRI Corp., In re, 337
Broadcast Music, Inc. v. Hirsch, 356, 365
Brodie Hotel Supply, Inc. v. United States, 168
Buehne Farms, Inc., In re, 316
Bullard v. Blue Hills Bank, 550
Butner v. United States, 525
Buttke, In re, 22
Cafeteria Operators, L.P., In re, 561
Capos v. Mid-Am. Nat'l Bank, 406
Carmel Fin. Corp. v. Castro, 445, 447
Carter Petroleum Products, Inc. v. Brotherhood Bank & Trust Co., 619
Casco Bank and Trust Co. v. Cloutier, 18
Caterpillar Fin. Servs. v. People's National Bank N.A., 445
Cersey, In re, 181
Chicago, City of v. Fulton, 544
Chrysler Credit Corp. v. Koontz, 477
Chrysler Credit Corp. v. Sharp, 233
Chrysler Credit Corp. v. Superior Court, 262
Citizens Bank of Md. v. Strumpf, 547
Cla-Mil East Holding Corp. v. Medallion Funding Corp., 479
Cliff's Ridge Skiing Corp., In re, 441
Coastal Federal Credit Union v. Hardiman, 542

Cobra Capital, LLC v. Pomp's Servs., Inc., 316

Coin-O-Matic Service Co. v. Rhode Island Hospital Trust Co., 157

Coldwave Systems, L.L.C., In re, 385

Coleman, In re, 438

Colorado National Bank v. Board of County Commissioners, 653

Commercial Money Center, Inc., In re, 207

Community for Creative Non-Violence v. Reid, 348

Compton Corp., Matter of, 673

Consolidated Film Industries v. United States, 222

Coomer, In re, 178

Copeland, In re, 125

Coral Petroleum, Inc., Matter of, 630

Cordova v. City of Chicago, 551

Corland Corporation, Matter of, 580

Cortland Sav. & Banking Co. v. Platinum Rapid Funding Grp., Ltd., 255

Crop Production Services v. Wheeler, 112

Crow-Southland Joint Venture No. 1 v. N. Fort Worth Bank, 451

Cybernetic Services, Inc., In re, 361, 365, 375

D2 Mark LLC v. Orei VI Investments, 492

Dalcon, In re, 47

Daniel v. Bank of Hayward, 194

Danning v. Pacific Propeller, Inc., 349

Darling's Homes, Inc., In re, 195

Days Cal. Riverside Ltd. P'ship, In re, 557

Dean v. Davis, 581

Dean v. Hall, 152

Delbridge v. Production Credit Ass'n, 561

Dena Corp., In re, 316

De-Pen Line, Inc., In re, 208, 522

Dick Warner Cargo Handling Corp. v. Aetna Bus. Credit, Inc., 183

Dixon v. Ford Motor Credit Co., 477

Donald v. Madison Indus., Inc., 280

Dow Corning Corp., In re, 648

Downey Creations, LLC, In re, 334

Dubman v. N. Shore Bank, 409

Duckworth, In re, 22

Dumont, In re, 542

Dynamics Corp. of Am. v. Citizens & S. Nat. Bank, 659

East Girard Sav. Ass'n v. Citizens Nat. Bank & Trust Co. of Baytown, 623

Edison Bros. Stores, Inc., In re, 307

EDM Corp., In re, 93

Educational Dev. Corp. v. Economy Co., 369

EPD Investment Co., In re, 41

Equitable Trust Co. of New York v. Dawson Partners Ltd., 618

Esso Petroleum Canada v. Security Pacific Bank, 633

Everett Home Town Ltd. P'ship, In re, 557

Everex Systems, Inc. v. Cadtrak Corp., 386

Excel Bank v. National Bank of Kansas City, 332

Excello Press, Inc., Matter of, 504

Farmers Bank v. Hubbard, 492

FDIC v. Caliendo, 407, 409

FDIC v. Freudenfeld, 614

Fidelity Bank & Trust Co. v. Production Metals Corp., 407

Fidelity Financial Services, Inc. v. Fink, 595

Filtercorp, Inc., In re, 35

Finova Capital Corp., In re, 492

First Am. Nat'l Bank v. Alcorn, Inc., 614

First Bethany Bank & Trust, N.A. v. Arvest United Bank, 219

First Interstate Bank v. Internal Revenue Service, 279

First National Bank of Black Hills v. Beug, 460

First National Bank of Palmerton v. Donaldson, Lufkin & Jenrette Securities Corp., 414

First National Bank v. Buss, 192

First State Bank v. Diamond Plastics Corp., 631

Ford Motor Credit Co. v. Byrd, 478

Ford Motor Credit Co. v. Herring, 472, 475, 476

Ford Motor Credit Co. v. Solway, 508

Ford v. Feldman, 30

Franchise Pictures LLC, In re, 354, 357

Frazier, In re, 493

Fulton, In re, 545

Gateway Ethanol, L.L.C., In re, 296

Gayler v. Wilder, 381

Gaynor v. Union Trust Co., 464

Gene Express, Inc., In re, 33

Genoa Nat'l Bank v. Southwest Implement, Inc. (In re Borden), 96

Georgetown Steel Co., LLC, In re, 325

GGVXX, Ltd., In re, 557, 558

Giaimo, In re, 22

Gibraltor Financial Corp. v. Prestige Equipment Corp., 312

Globe Holdings, Inc., In re, 591

Golden West Refining Co. v. Suntrust Bank, 617

Grace v. Sterling, Grace & Co., 409

Grain Merchants of Indiana, Inc. v. Union Bank & Savings Co., 592
Griffin, In re, 177
Grogan v. Garner, 549
Gross Mfg. & Importing Co., Inc., In re, 325
Grubbs Construction Co., In re, 311
Gruder's Will, In re Estate of, 158
Grupo Mexicano de Desarrollo, S.A. v. Alliance Bond Fund, Inc., 3
Haley & Steele, Inc., In re, 340
Hamada, In re, 648
Harley-Davidson Credit Corp. v. Galvin, 506
Harman v. First Am. Bank (In re Jeffrey Bigelow Design Group, Inc.), 600
Harper and Row, Publishers v. Nation Enterprises, 367
Hawaiian Telecom Communications, Inc., In re, 242, 433
HB Logistics, LLC, Matter of, 318
Helms v. Certified Packaging Corp., 39
Hendricks v. Bank of America, 662
Henshaw, United States v., 264
Hergert, In re, 60
Hicks, In re, 148
Highland Capital Management, L.P. v. Schneider, 394
Hillbilly Ranch, Inc. v. Kahn (In re Wible), 47
Hillsborough County v. Automated Medical Laboratories, Inc., 348
Hintze, In re, 27
Hitchin Post Steak Co. v. General Electric Capital Corp. (In re HP Distribution, LLP), 288, 313
Hollibush v. Ford Motor Credit Co., 477
Home Owners Funding Corp. of Am. v. Belanger (In re Belanger), 540
Homeplace Stores, In re, 310
Hook Point, LLC v. Branch Banking & Trust Co., 656
Horob Livestock, Inc., In re, 591
Hoskins, In re, 565, 568
Howard, In re, 165
Howell, In re, 84
Hudgins v. IRS (In re Hudgins), 271
Husain, In re, 540
Incredible Auto Sales, In re, 48
International Trade Management, Inc. v. United States, 348
International Trade Relationship & Export v. Citibank, N.A., 664
Intraworld Industries, Inc. v. Girard Trust Bank, 654, 658, 659
Iron Workers District Council of New England Pension v. Baldwin Steel Co., 267

Itek Corp. v. First Nat'l Bank of Boston, 658
ITT Diversified Credit Corp. v. First City Capital Corp., 443
ITT Terryphone Corp. v. Modems Plus, 468
J.H. Rayner & Co. v. Hambros Bank, Ltd., 628
Jim Ross Tires, Inc., In re, 97
John's Bean Farm of Homestead, Inc., In re, 89, 96
Jojo's 10 Rest., LLC, In re, 44
Jones, In re, 539, 540
JPMorgan Chase Bank v. Cook, 643
K.B. Oil Co. v. Ford Motor Credit Co., Inc., 478
Kentucky Highlands Inv. Corp. v. Bank of Corbin, 244
Kimbell Foods, Inc., United States v., 272, 273
Knight v. United States, 341
Kriger, In re, 431
Kroskie, In re, 437
Kuehn, In re, 548
Laminated Veneers Co., Inc., In re, 33
Larimer, In re, 550
Larsen, In the Matter of, 79
Layne v. Bank One, Kentucky, N.A., 402
Levit v. Ingersoll Rand Fin. Corp., 579
Lewis v. Nicholas Fin., Inc., 473
Liberty National Bank & Trust Co. v. Acme Tool Division of Rucker Co., 500
Lightning Bolt Leasing, LLC, In re, 313
Lombardo's Ravioli Kitchen, Inc., In re, 160
Long v. Bullard, 535, 536
M. Fabricant & Sons, In re, 591
Madison Capital Company, LLC v. S & S Salvage, LLC, 186
Major's Furniture Mart, Inc. v. Castle Credit Corp., Inc., 202, 209, 522
Manhattan Credit Co. v. Brewer, 475
Mann v. Clark Oil & Refining Corp., 324
Manuel, In re, 172, 176, 181
Maplewood Bank & Trust v. Sears, Roebuck & Co., 446, 450
Margavitch, In re, 551
Marhoefer Packing Co., Inc., Matter of, 295, 299
Marrama v. Citizens Bank of Mass., 549
Marvin Lumber & Cedar Co. v. PPG Indus., Inc., 330

Mason v. Heller Fin. Leasing, Inc. (In re JII Liquidating, Inc.), 315

Matthews, In re, 172

McCullough v. Mobiland, 468

McDannold v. Star Bank, N.A., 52

McDermott, United States v., 267

McGonigle v. Combs, 52

McGowen v. Nebraska State Bank, 519

McMahan v. Cornelius, 83

Meyer v. United States, 493

Michigan Commerce Bank v. TDY Industries, Inc., 617

Mid-America Tire, Inc. v. PTZ Trading Ltd., 655, 659

Mid-Atlantic Flange, In re, 177

Middle Atl. Stud Welding Co., In re, 36

Miller v. Florida Mining & Materials (In re A.W. & Assocs., Inc.), 588

Miller, In re, 79

Moe v. John Deere Co., 458

Montagne, In re, 67

Moore v. Bay, 572

Moore v. Wells Fargo Construction, 485, 491

Motors Acceptance Corp. v. Rozier, 508

Motors Liquidation Co. Avoidance Trust v. JP Morgan Chase Bank, N.A., 112, 432

Motors Liquidation Co., In re, 106

Music City RV, LLC, In re, 340

National Bank of Alaska v. J.B.L. & K. of Alaska, Inc., 461

National City Bank v. Hotchkiss, 581

National Gas Distributors, L.L.C., In re, 583

National Peregrine, Inc. v. Capitol Federal Savings and Loan Association (In re Peregrine Entertainment, Ltd.), 373, 377

Nay, In re, 81

Network Solutions, Inc. v. Umbro Int'l, Inc., 388

Nevada National Bank v. Huff, 462

New Britain, City of, United States v., 267, 268

Nken v. Holder, 546

Norrell, In re, 176

Northern Merchandise, Inc., In re, 598

Northview Corp., In re, 560

NRP Lease Holdings, In re, 88

Numeric Corp., In re, 18

O'Brien v. Nationwide Mut. Ins. Co., 419

Oakland Police & Fire Retirement Sys. v. Brown, 112

Octagon Gas Systems, Inc. v. Rimmer, 216

Office Depot, Inc. v. Zuccarini, 388

Official Committee of Unsecured Creditors of Motors Liquidation Co. v. JPMorgan Chase Bank, N.A., 106, 110

Okefenokee Aircraft, Inc. v. PrimeSouth Bank, 467

Oswalt, In re, 437

Pactel Fin. v. D.C. Marine Serv. Corp., 307

Page, In re, 671

Pankratz Impl. Co. v. Citizens Nat'l Bank, 96

Park Corrugated Box Corp., In re, 431

Parvez v. Bigelman, 520

Pasteurized Eggs Corp., In re, 383

Pearson v. Salina Coffee House, Inc., 93

Peek v. Spartanburg Reg'l Healthcare Sys., 657

Peregrine Entertainment, Ltd., In re, 346, 354

Perez v. Rent-A-Center, Inc., 300

Pettit Oil Co., In re, 333

Pfautz, In re, 424

Philip Morris Capital Corp. v. Bering Trader, Inc. (In re Bering Trader, Inc.), 556

Pierce, In re, 432

Pillowtex, Inc., In re, 302

Pine Builders, Inc. v. United States, 267

Plymouth Sav. Bank v. Internal Revenue Service, 280

Poynter Investments, Inc. v. Century Builders of Piedmont, Inc., 657

Premier Golf Properties, LP, In re, 554

Pride Hyundai, Inc. v. Chrysler Financial Co., L.L.C., 156

Pristas v. Landaus of Plymouth, Inc., 173

ProGrowth Bank, Inc. v. Wells Fargo Bank, N.A., 69, 96

QDS Components, In re, 295

Rash, In re, 564

Reed v. Central Nat'l Bank, 409

Reeves v. Foutz & Tanner, Inc., 513

Reid v. IRS (In re Reid), 271

Renaud, In re, 438

Reno v. General Motors Acceptance Corp., 478

Republic Nat'l Bank v. Northwest Nat'l Bank, 614

Rex Financial Corp. v. Great Western Bank & Trust, 230

Rhode Island Hospital Trust Nat'l Bank v. Eastern General Contractors, Inc., 635

Rhodes, In re, 542

Riggs Nat. Bank of Washington, D.C. v. Perry, 541

River Valley State Bank v. Peterson, 519

Robinson, In re, 523

Rolain, In re, 124

Roman Ceramics Corp. v. Peoples Nat. Bank, 659

Romani, Estate of, United States v., 267

Rutledge v. Universal C.I.T. Credit Corp., 476

Sanders-Langsam Tobacco Co., Inc., In re, 631

Sarex Corp., In re, 34

Schroeder v. Fageol Motors, Inc., 37

Sears, Roebuck & Co. v. Conry, 23

SemCrude LP, In re, 140

Sharer v. Creative Leasing, Inc., 319

Shelley v. Boothe, 573

Shelton v. Erwin, 18

Silva v. Rent-A-Center, Inc., 300

Simpson, In re, 176

Skagit Pac. Corp., In re, 559

Slamans, In re, 648

Slodov v. United States, 279

Smith v. MCF Capital, LLC, 225

Sniadach v. Family Finance Corp., 470

Solfanelli v. Corestates Bank, N.A., 409

Southtrust Bank v. Borg-Warner Acceptance Corp., 175

Spearing Tool and Manufacturing Co., Inc., In re, 270

Specifin Mgt. LLC v. Elhadidy, 504

Sports, Inc. v. The Sportshop, Inc., 622

Staley, In re, 178

Standard Lumber Company v. Chamber Frames, Inc., 223, 224

Stierwalt v. Associated Third Party Administrators, 253

Stoumbos v. Kilimnik, 36

Stuart, In re, 551

Summit Staffing Polk County, Inc., In re, 89

Suntex Industrial Corp., Ltd. v. The CIT Group/BBC, Inc., 636

Super Feeders, Inc., In re, 296

Sztejn v. J. Henry Schroder Banking Corp., 654, 655, 659

Tabor Court Realty Corp., United States v., 602

Taffi v. United States, 565

Taffi, In re, 565, 567

Taylor, In re, 307

Thet Mah & Assoc., Inc. v. First Bank of N.D., 165

Thompson v. Ford Motor Credit Co., 478

Thompson v. General Motors Acceptance Corp., 546

Thorp Commercial Corp. v. Northgate Indus., Inc., 71

Thummel, In re, 310

Together Development Corporation, In re, 370

Tolona Pizza Products Corp., Matter of, 588

Tony Thornton Auction Serv., Inc. v. United States, 271

Trane Company, The v. CGI Mechanical Inc., 274

Transparent Products Corp. v. Paysaver Credit Union, 615

Transportation Design and Technology, Inc., In re, 373, 380

Traverse County Land Bank Authority v. Verizon Wireless, 432

Tri-County Materials, Inc., In re, 221

Troupe, In re, 135

TSAWD Holdings, Inc., In re, 339

Tudor Development Group, Inc. v. United States Fidelity & Guarantee Co., 644

Tulsa Port Warehouse Co., In re, 313

Tusa-Expo Holdings, Inc. v. Knoll, Inc., In re, 257

Tuscany Energy, LLC, In re, 254

Twyne's Case, 596

U.S. Claims, Inc. v. Flomenhaft, 221

Union Bank v. Wolas, 576, 582, 589

Union Cent. Life Ins. Co., United States v., 271

Union Planters Bank, N.A. v. Peninsula Bank, 145

United Bank Ltd. v. Cambridge Sporting Goods Corp., 664

United Missouri Bank v. Gagel, 511

United States Savings Ass'n v. Timbers of Inwood Forest Assoc., Ltd., 562

Valley Media, Inc., In re, 336

Van Kylen, Matter of, 422

Vaughn, In re, 508

Vic Hansen & Sons, Inc. v. Crowley, 508

Villa v. Alvarado State Bank, 451

Viscount Hill v. Bullock, 432

Voboril, In re, 100

Voest-Alpine Trading USA Corp. v. Bank of China, 629

Warne, In re, 286

Watman, In re, 597

Watson, In re, 154

West v. Office of Ind. Sec. of State, 84

Westfall, In re, 165

Wheeler, In re, 33

Whiting Pools, Inc., United States v., 545, 550

Wichita Eagle and Beacon Publishing Co., Inc. v. Pacific

National Bank of San Francisco, 612
Williams v. Ford Motor Credit Co., 474
Williams v. Walker-Thomas Furniture Co., 133
Williams, In re, 671
Williamson v. Fowler Toyota, Inc., 473
Winthrop Old Farm Nurseries, Inc., In re, 565, 567
WM Capital Partners, LLC v. Thornton, 495
Wombles Charters, Inc. v. Orix Credit Alliance, Inc., 473
World Auxiliary Power Co., In re, 358
WorldCom Inc. v. General Electric Global Asset Management Services (In re WorldCom, Inc), 290
Worthy Lending LLC v. New Style Contractors, Inc., 520
Wright Group, Inc., In re The, 558, 559
Wyoming State Farm Loan Board v. Farm Credit System Capital Corp., 432
XYZ Options, Inc., In re, 666
Yates v. United States, 546
Zaleha, In re, 293
Zeeway Corp., In re, 556
Zenith Productions, Ltd. v. AEG Acquisition Corp. (In re AEG Acquisition Corp.), 365
Zerkle Trucking Co., In re, 293

TABLE OF STATUTES

7 U.S.C. § 1631(d)..........................185
7 U.S.C. § 1631(e)(1) 185
7 U.S.C. § 1631(e)(2) 185
11 U.S.C. § 101...... 361, 528, 575, 579
11 U.S.C. §§ 101 et seq.........327, 525
11 U.S.C. § 101(5)(A)...................580
11 U.S.C. § 101(10).......................530
11 U.S.C. § 101(10)(A)..................580
11 U.S.C. § 101(13A)......................438
11 U.S.C. § 101(13A)(B)..................438
11 U.S.C. § 101(14A).....................531
11 U.S.C. § 101(15).......................530
11 U.S.C. § 101(31).......................575
11 U.S.C. § 101(51D).....................530
11 U.S.C. § 102(a)..........................361
11 U.S.C. § 103(a)..........................146
11 U.S.C. § 109(e)..................527, 549
11 U.S.C. § 201(d)..........................361
11 U.S.C. § 205(a)..........................361
11 U.S.C. § 301..............................529
11 U.S.C. § 303..............................577
11 U.S.C. § 303(h)(1)..............526, 577
11 U.S.C. § 321..............................529
11 U.S.C. § 361..............................567
11 U.S.C. § 362..............................547
11 U.S.C. § 362(a)........ 294, 529, 545, 548
11 U.S.C. § 362(a)(3) 534, 544, 545, 546, 547, 548, 551
11 U.S.C. § 362(a)(4) 548, 551
11 U.S.C. § 362(a)(5) 534
11 U.S.C. § 362(a)(6) 548
11 U.S.C. § 362(b)(3) 571
11 U.S.C. § 362(c)(1)......................534
11 U.S.C. § 362(c)(2)......................534
11 U.S.C. § 362(d)........ 529, 534, 538, 561, 671
11 U.S.C. § 362(h) 539, 541
11 U.S.C. § 362(k)(1) 534
11 U.S.C. § 363..............................546
11 U.S.C. § 363(a)..........................555
11 U.S.C. § 363(c)(2)...............555, 556
11 U.S.C. § 363(d)..........................294
11 U.S.C. § 363(e)..........................550
11 U.S.C. § 363(f) 537
11 U.S.C. § 363(k) 537
11 U.S.C. § 363(p)(2) 556
11 U.S.C. § 364(c)(2).....................553
11 U.S.C. § 365..............................294
11 U.S.C. § 365(10).......................311
11 U.S.C. § 365(d)(2) 294
11 U.S.C. § 365(d)(5) 311
11 U.S.C. § 365(d)(10) 305, 306
11 U.S.C. § 365(f) 387
11 U.S.C. § 365(p)(1) 283, 294
11 U.S.C. § 408(a)..........................361
11 U.S.C. § 501.....................530, 536
11 U.S.C. § 502.....................531, 536

11 U.S.C. § 502(b)..........................531
11 U.S.C. § 502(b)(5)......................536
11 U.S.C. § 502(d)..................531, 577
11 U.S.C. § 502(e) 531, 536
11 U.S.C. § 503..............................531
11 U.S.C. § 506..............................543
11 U.S.C. § 506(a)........563, 564, 565, 566, 568
11 U.S.C. § 506(a)(1)...........241, 531, 537, 562
11 U.S.C. § 506(a)(2)......568, 569, 570
11 U.S.C. § 506(b)..........................562
11 U.S.C. § 506(d)..........................536
11 U.S.C. § 507..............................531
11 U.S.C. § 507(a)(3)–(10) 531
11 U.S.C. § 509..............................648
11 U.S.C. § 509(a)..........................648
11 U.S.C. § 510(a)..........................161
11 U.S.C. § 521(2)(A)...................540
11 U.S.C. § 521(2)(C)....................540
11 U.S.C. § 521(a)..........................541
11 U.S.C. § 521(a)(2).....................539
11 U.S.C. § 521(a)(2)(C)................541
11 U.S.C. § 521(a)(6)......539, 541, 542
11 U.S.C. § 521(a)(6)(A)–(B).........542
11 U.S.C. § 521(d).................541, 542
11 U.S.C. § 522 546
11 U.S.C. § 522(b)..........................560
11 U.S.C. § 522(d).........................527
11 U.S.C. § 522(f)(1)......................180
11 U.S.C. § 522(f)(1)(B) 173, 179, 180, 181
11 U.S.C. § 523(a)..........................532
11 U.S.C. § 524 538
11 U.S.C. § 524(a)..........................535
11 U.S.C. § 524(a)(2)......................542
11 U.S.C. § 524(c) 538, 539, 542
11 U.S.C. § 524(d)..........................542
11 U.S.C. § 524(e) 535, 671
11 U.S.C. § 541 526
11 U.S.C. § 541(a)..........................532
11 U.S.C. § 541(a)(1).....531, 545, 570
11 U.S.C. § 541(a)(3)......570, 572, 577
11 U.S.C. § 542 ......545, 546, 547, 548
11 U.S.C. § 542(a)........546, 547, 548, 549, 551
11 U.S.C. § 542(c) 546
11 U.S.C. § 544 ....45, 123, 125, 327, 435, 571
11 U.S.C. § 544(a)...........45, 125, 146, 359, 360, 525
11 U.S.C. § 544(a)(1)...........5, 53, 182, 333, 334, 335, 338, 339, 374, 376, 383, 435, 570, 571, 596
11 U.S.C. § 544(b).................570, 571
11 U.S.C. § 546(b)..........................571
11 U.S.C. § 546(b)(1).....................571

11 U.S.C. § 547 ..... 573, 575, 576, 577, 579, 583, 596
11 U.S.C. § 547(b) 570, 574, 575, 577, 578, 579, 580, 581, 582, 583, 584, 585, 586, 594
11 U.S.C. § 547(b)(1) 580, 673
11 U.S.C. § 547(b)(2) 575, 580, 673
11 U.S.C. § 547(b)(3) 593
11 U.S.C. § 547(b)(4) 578
11 U.S.C. § 547(b)(4)(A) 578
11 U.S.C. § 547(b)(5) 574, 575
11 U.S.C. § 547(c) 574, 580, 582
11 U.S.C. § 547(c)(1) 581, 582, 594
11 U.S.C. § 547(c)(2) 577, 582, 583, 585, 586, 587, 588, 589, 590
11 U.S.C. § 547(c)(2)(A) 583
11 U.S.C. § 547(c)(2)(B) 583, 585, 587, 591
11 U.S.C. § 547(c)(2)(C) 587, 588
11 U.S.C. § 547(c)(3) 582, 594
11 U.S.C. § 547(c)(3)(B) 595
11 U.S.C. § 547(c)(5) 593, 594
11 U.S.C. § 547(c)(8) 582
11 U.S.C. § 547(e) 592
11 U.S.C. § 547(e)(1) 595
11 U.S.C. § 547(e)(2) 582, 595
11 U.S.C. § 547(e)(2)(A) 595
11 U.S.C. § 547(e)(2)(B) 595
11 U.S.C. § 547(e)(2)(C) 595
11 U.S.C. § 547(e)(3) 582, 593
11 U.S.C. § 547(f) 575
11 U.S.C. § 547(g) 575
11 U.S.C. § 548 ...... 596, 598, 601, 602
11 U.S.C. § 548(a) 570, 600
11 U.S.C. § 548(a)(1) 596, 600
11 U.S.C. § 548(a)(1)(B) 597, 598, 601
11 U.S.C. § 548(a)(1)(B)(i) 602
11 U.S.C. § 548(c) 598, 601
11 U.S.C. § 550 583
11 U.S.C. § 550(a) 182, 360, 570, 572, 574, 577
11 U.S.C. § 550(a)(1) 580
11 U.S.C. § 550(f) 360
11 U.S.C. § 551 578
11 U.S.C. § 552 553
11 U.S.C. § 552(a) 553, 555
11 U.S.C. § 552(b) 553, 556, 557, 559
11 U.S.C. § 552(b)(1) 388, 553, 556
11 U.S.C. § 552(b)(2) 553, 556, 557
11 U.S.C. § 554 536
11 U.S.C. § 554(a) 533, 538
11 U.S.C. § 701 530
11 U.S.C. § 704 529
11 U.S.C. § 704(1) 533
11 U.S.C. § 722 ...... 523, 538, 539, 570
11 U.S.C. § 725 533
11 U.S.C. § 726 531
11 U.S.C. § 727(a) 532
11 U.S.C. § 727(a)(1) 527, 536
11 U.S.C. § 727(b) 532, 535, 542

11 U.S.C. § 1104(a) 530
11 U.S.C. § 1107 ....374, 552
11 U.S.C. § 1107(a) 306, 327, 530
11 U.S.C. § 1108 .... 327, 530
11 U.S.C. § 1121(b) 552
11 U.S.C. § 1121(c) 552
11 U.S.C. § 1121(d) 552
11 U.S.C. § 1129(b) 311
11 U.S.C. § 1129(b)(2)(A) 561
11 U.S.C. § 1141(d) 536
11 U.S.C. § 1181 530
11 U.S.C. § 1183 530
11 U.S.C. §§ 1301–1330 563
11 U.S.C. § 1322(b)(2) 438
11 U.S.C. § 1325 528
11 U.S.C. § 1325(a) 543, 563
11 U.S.C. § 1325(a)(4) 543
11 U.S.C. § 1325(a)(5) ...523, 543, 561, 563
11 U.S.C. § 1325(a)(5)(A) 563
11 U.S.C. § 1325(a)(5)(B) 563, 565, 567, 568
11 U.S.C. § 1325(a)(5)(B)(i) 563
11 U.S.C. § 1325(a)(5)(B)(ii) 564
11 U.S.C. § 1325(a)(5)(B)(iii) 544
11 U.S.C. § 1325(a)(5)(C) 563, 566
11 U.S.C. § 1325(b)(1) 528
11 U.S.C. § 1325(b)(2) 528
11 U.S.C. § 1325(b)(3) 528
11 U.S.C. § 1327(a) 527
11 U.S.C. § 1328(a) 528
11 U.S.C. § 1328(b) 528
15 U.S.C. §§ 78aaa–111 398
15 U.S.C. § 1051(b) 372
15 U.S.C. § 1051(d) 372
15 U.S.C. § 1060 372
15 U.S.C. § 1060(a)(1) 370
15 U.S.C. § 1060(a)(4) 370
17 U.S.C. § 10 346
17 U.S.C. § 28 383
17 U.S.C. § 30 383
17 U.S.C. § 101 ......345, 347, 373, 383
17 U.S.C. § 102(a) 344, 346, 366
17 U.S.C. § 102(b) 344
17 U.S.C. § 106 ....344, 347
17 U.S.C. § 106(5) 355
17 U.S.C. § 201(d)(1) 347, 349
17 U.S.C. § 204(a) 349
17 U.S.C. § 205 ....348, 373
17 U.S.C. § 205(a) 347, 351, 356
17 U.S.C. § 205(c) 344, 348, 349, 351
17 U.S.C. § 205(c)(1) 354
17 U.S.C. § 205(c)(2) 348
17 U.S.C. § 205(d) 345, 349, 350, 354, 357, 361, 362
17 U.S.C. § 302(a) 346
17 U.S.C. § 401 344
17 U.S.C. § 408 ....344, 348
17 U.S.C. § 409 ....348, 362
17 U.S.C. § 410 348
17 U.S.C. § 410(a) 362

17 U.S.C. § 411 348
17 U.S.C. § 411(a) 366
17 U.S.C. § 702 351
26 U.S.C. § 6321 268
26 U.S.C. §§ 6321 et seq 266
26 U.S.C. § 6323 276
26 U.S.C. § 6323(a) 269, 275
26 U.S.C. § 6323(c) 276, 277, 279, 280
26 U.S.C. § 6323(c)–(d) 277
26 U.S.C. § 6323(c)(1) 277
26 U.S.C. § 6323(c)(2)(B) 277
26 U.S.C. § 6323(c)(2)(C) 277
26 U.S.C. § 6323(d) 276, 277, 278, 279
26 U.S.C. § 6323(f) 269
26 U.S.C. § 6323(f)(1)(A) 271
26 U.S.C. § 6323(f)(2)(B) 269
26 U.S.C. § 6323(f)(3) 271
26 U.S.C. § 6323(g) 269
26 U.S.C. § 6323(g)(3)(A) 269
26 U.S.C. § 6323(h)(1) 275, 276
26 U.S.C. § 6323(h)(1)(B) 276
26 U.S.C. § 6334 269
28 U.S.C. § 1291 599
31 U.S.C. § 3713 274
31 U.S.C. § 3713(a) 266, 267
35 U.S.C. §§ 100 et seq 383
35 U.S.C. § 261 ..... 373, 375, 376, 377, 378, 379, 380, 381, 382, 383, 384, 385
42 U.S.C. §§ 5401 et seq 438
49 U.S.C. § 20(c) 383
49 U.S.C. § 1403 383
49 U.S.C. § 11301 383
49 U.S.C. § 44107 383
49 U.S.C. § 44109(b) 134
49 U.S.C. § 44109(c)(2) 134
Pub. L. No. 106–113 382
Bankr. Act § 60a(2) 592
Bankr. Act § 60b 581, 592
Bankr. Act § 70e 572
Bankruptcy Code 506(a)(1) 283
UCC § 1–102 463
UCC § 1–102(1)–(2) 463
UCC § 1–102(2) 463
UCC § 1–103 .... 64, 462, 463, 627
UCC § 1–103(a) 635
UCC § 1–103(a)(1) 198
UCC § 1–103(a)(2) 463
UCC § 1–103(b) 43
UCC § 1–201(26) 65
UCC § 1–201(29) 276
UCC § 1–201(36)(A) 616
UCC § 1–201(37) 213, 288, 306, 307, 310, 318, 328, 336
UCC § 1–201(37)(d)(i) 290
UCC § 1–201(a)(9) 195
UCC § 1–201(a)(30) 104
UCC § 1–201(b)(9) 185, 191, 192, 194
UCC § 1–201(b)(20) 156, 266, 662

UCC § 1–201(b)(24) 13, 24
UCC § 1–201(b)(25) 79, 137
UCC § 1–201(b)(29) ... 48, 49, 104, 400
UCC § 1–201(b)(30) 48, 148, 226, 253, 400, 517
UCC § 1–201(b)(35) 202, 213, 218, 219, 220, 282, 285, 297, 298, 306, 321, 322, 324, 333, 336, 356, 512, 537
UCC § 1–201(b)(36) 511
UCC § 1–201(b)(37) 483
UCC § 1–201(b)(37)(A)–(B) (amended) 14
UCC § 1–201(b)(37)(B) (amended) 100
UCC § 1–201(b)(37)(i)–(iv) 307
UCC § 1–202 511
UCC § 1–203 .... 285, 288, 296, 297, 299, 300, 315, 318, 319
UCC § 1–203(a) 288, 315
UCC § 1–203(b) 285, 288, 289, 299, 301, 302, 306, 315, 316
UCC § 1–203(b)(1) 299
UCC § 1–203(b)(1)–(4) ... 285, 286, 307
UCC § 1–203(b)(3) 295, 299, 311
UCC § 1–203(b)(4) 299
UCC § 1–203(c) 290, 291, 292, 302
UCC § 1–203(c)(1) 302, 311, 312
UCC § 1–203(c)(2) 302
UCC § 1–203(c)(6) 292
UCC § 1–203(d) 295, 297, 298
UCC § 1–203(e) 295, 298
UCC § 1–203, com. 2 ..... 299, 301, 312
UCC § 1–204 .... 41, 49, 276
UCC § 1–204(2) 41, 266
UCC § 1–204(4) 41
UCC § 1–205(b) 629
UCC § 1–207(37) 291
UCC § 1–301 135
UCC § 1–302(b) 611
UCC § 1–303 458
UCC § 1–303(a) 458
UCC § 1–303(d) 458
UCC § 1–304 .... 471, 513
UCC § 1–305(a) 472
UCC § 1–309 457
UCC § 2–102 12
UCC § 2–103(1)(a) 194
UCC § 2–106 .... 12, 194
UCC § 2–106(1) 49, 284
UCC § 2–202 .... 32, 629
UCC § 2–302 629
UCC § 2–326 .... 331, 336
UCC § 2–326(1) 340
UCC § 2–326(1)–(2) 171
UCC § 2–326(2) 331, 340
UCC § 2–326(3) 329, 331
UCC § 2–326(3)(b) 339
UCC § 2–326(d) 336
UCC § 2–326, com. 1 340
UCC § 2–326, com. 6 340
UCC § 2–401(1) 49

UCC § 2–401(2) 48, 49
UCC § 2–401(2)–(3) 194
UCC § 2–403(1) 42, 48, 49, 200
UCC § 2–403(2) 42
UCC § 2–501....................................194
UCC § 2–606....................................194
UCC § 2–716(3) 195
UCC § 2A–102(1)(j) 282
UCC § 2A–301, com. 2...................282
UCC § 2A–307(1)...........................282
UCC § 2A–504(1)...................319, 320
UCC § 3–104....................................609
UCC § 3–104(a) 237
UCC § 3–104(b) 237
UCC § 3–104(j) 239
UCC § 3–302....................................238
UCC § 3–302(a) 265
UCC § 3–302(a)(2) 238
UCC § 3–305.....................................42
UCC § 3–306...........................42, 265
UCC § 3–419....................................509
UCC § 4–104(a)(5) 246
UCC § 4A–202(c) 629
UCC § 5–102(a) 607
UCC § 5–102(a)(1) 652
UCC § 5–102(a)(3) 615
UCC § 5–102(a)(4) 607
UCC § 5–102(a)(6) 615, 616
UCC § 5–102(a)(7) 662
UCC § 5–102(a)(7), com. 3............662
UCC § 5–102(a)(9) 611, 615
UCC § 5–102(a)(10) 605, 611, 614,
   615, 616, 631
UCC § 5–102(a)(12) 616
UCC § 5–102(a)(14) 615
UCC § 5–102, com. 3 662
UCC § 5–102, com. 6 ....614, 615
UCC § 5–102, com. 11 615
UCC § 5–103(c).....610, 611, 627, 638,
   641, 642
UCC § 5–103(d) 611, 638, 651
UCC § 5–103, com. 2 .....611, 627, 642
UCC § 5–104.................611, 614, 635
UCC § 5–104, com. 1 615
UCC § 5–104, com. 3 614
UCC § 5–105....................................609
UCC § 5–106(a) 611, 616
UCC § 5–106(b) 616, 635
UCC § 5–106(c)................................616
UCC § 5–106(d) 611, 616, 617
UCC § 5–106, com. 4 617
UCC § 5–107(a) 607, 664
UCC § 5–107(c)................................607
UCC § 5–107, com. 1 ....616, 664
UCC § 5–108....................................635
UCC § 5–108(a) 618, 619, 627, 628,
   630, 632, 641
UCC § 5–108(b) 633, 636
UCC § 5–108(c)......................633, 636
UCC § 5–108(e)......................619, 627
UCC § 5–108(g) 614
UCC § 5–108(i) 640, 641

UCC § 5–108(i)(1) 663
UCC § 5–108(i)(2) 640
UCC § 5–108(i)(4) 649
UCC § 5–108, com. 1......618, 627, 641
UCC § 5–108, com. 2.....630, 634, 635,
   636
UCC § 5–108, com. 4..............633, 635
UCC § 5–108, com. 7..............630, 636
UCC § 5–108, com. 8...............628
UCC § 5–108, com. 9 614
UCC § 5–109 ....611, 654, 655, 663
UCC § 5–109(a)......649, 653, 654, 655
UCC § 5–109(a)(1) 663
UCC § 5–109(a)(1)(i)–(iv) 663
UCC § 5–109(a)(1)(iv)...................663
UCC § 5–109(a)(2) 662, 663
UCC § 5–109(b)......653, 655, 656, 664
UCC § 5–109(b)(1)–(4) 653
UCC § 5–109(b)(3) 662
UCC § 5–109(b)(4) 662, 663
UCC § 5–109, com. 1..............654
UCC § 5–109, com. 5..............656
UCC § 5–109, coms. 664
UCC § 5–110 ....611, 649, 650, 651
UCC § 5–110(a)...........................650
UCC § 5–110(a)(1) 649
UCC § 5–110(a)(2) 649, 650
UCC § 5–110, com. 2............649, 650
UCC § 5–111 ....611, 651, 652
UCC § 5–111(a)..............651, 652, 653
UCC § 5–111(b) 651
UCC § 5–111(e)......................651, 652
UCC § 5–111, com. 1............652
UCC § 5–111, com. 2............651
UCC § 5–111, com. 4............653
UCC § 5–111, com. 6............652
UCC § 5–112(a)....................664, 665
UCC § 5–112(b)(2) 665
UCC § 5–114 654
UCC § 5–114(a)....................665, 666
UCC § 5–114(c) 666, 668
UCC § 5–114(d)....................611, 666
UCC § 5–114(e)............667, 669, 671
UCC § 5–114(f) 667
UCC § 5–114, com. 1..............666
UCC § 5–114, com. 3..............666
UCC § 5–115, com. 1..............664
UCC § 5–116(a)....................611
UCC § 5–116(c) 610, 611
UCC § 5–117 ....611, 644, 647, 648
UCC § 5–117(a)..............642, 645, 648
UCC § 5–117(d)....................611, 645
UCC § 7–502(a)..........................42, 54
UCC § 8–102(a)(2) 393
UCC § 8–102(a)(4) 393, 397
UCC § 8–102(a)(5) 391, 410
UCC § 8–102(a)(7) 397, 410
UCC § 8–102(a)(8) 390, 420
UCC § 8–102(a)(9) 410
UCC § 8–102(a)(9)(iii)...............395
UCC § 8–102(a)(11) 399, 400
UCC § 8–102(a)(13) 394, 399

UCC § 8–102(a)(14) 397, 410
UCC § 8–102(a)(15) 393, 394, 397, 423
UCC § 8–102(a)(15)(i) 393, 394
UCC § 8–102(a)(15)(ii) 394
UCC § 8–102(a)(15)(iii) 394
UCC § 8–102(a)(16) 54, 399, 410
UCC § 8–102(a)(17) 392, 397, 410, 424
UCC § 8–102(a)(18) 394, 397, 424
UCC § 8–102, com. 13 394
UCC § 8–103 394
UCC § 8–103(a) 394
UCC § 8–103(b) 395, 423, 424
UCC § 8–103(c) 395
UCC § 8–106 .... 130, 396, 400, 413, 416, 426
UCC § 8–106(b) 130, 399, 411, 413
UCC § 8–106(b)(1) 399, 400
UCC § 8–106(c) 397, 399, 413, 424
UCC § 8–106(d) 251, 396, 399, 411, 424
UCC § 8–106(d)(2) 414, 419
UCC § 8–106(d)(2), com. 5 417
UCC § 8–106(d)(3) 411
UCC § 8–106(e) 396, 399, 400, 411
UCC § 8–106(f) 420
UCC § 8–106(f), com. 7 420
UCC § 8–106(g) 414
UCC § 8–106, com. 1 .... 54, 399
UCC § 8–106, com. 3 424
UCC § 8–106, com. 7 ...... 54, 130, 399
UCC § 8–106, com. 7, ex. 11 411
UCC § 8–112(c) 393
UCC § 8–115 254
UCC § 8–115, com. 5 254
UCC § 8–301 .... 400, 420
UCC § 8–301(a) 420
UCC § 8–301(a)(1) 399, 400
UCC § 8–301(b) 424
UCC § 8–301, com. 4 424
UCC § 8–303(b) 42
UCC § 8–501(a) 390, 395, 397, 410, 421
UCC § 8–501(b) 390, 395, 410, 421
UCC § 8–501(c) 392
UCC § 8–501, com. 1 421
UCC § 8–501, com. 2 421
UCC § 8–503(a) 392, 411
UCC § 8–503(b) 393
UCC § 8–503(e) 254
UCC § 8–503, com. 2 392
UCC § 8–505 390
UCC § 8–506 390
UCC § 8–511(a) 411
UCC § 8–511(b) 392
UCC §§ 9–101 to 9–410 213
UCC § 9–101(c), com. 4(c) 144
UCC § 9–101, com. 350
UCC § 9–101, com. 4e 245
UCC § 9–102 213
UCC § 9–102(2) 11

UCC § 9–102(a) 23, 24, 32, 336, 389
UCC § 9–102(a)(1) 163
UCC § 9–102(a)(2) 149, 203, 260, 355
UCC § 9–102(a)(3) 13, 24, 33, 260
UCC § 9–102(a)(5) 55, 75, 152
UCC § 9–102(a)(6) 143
UCC § 9–102(a)(7)(A) (amended) 12, 220
UCC § 9–102(a)(7)(B) 220
UCC § 9–102(a)(8) 239
UCC § 9–102(a)(9) 244, 247
UCC § 9–102(a)(10) 191
UCC § 9–102(a)(11) 149, 203, 206, 207, 228, 231
UCC § 9–102(a)(11)(A) 207
UCC § 9–102(a)(11)(B) 207
UCC § 9–102(a)(12) 152, 321
UCC § 9–102(a)(12)(A) 50, 101
UCC § 9–102(a)(12)(B) 202
UCC § 9–102(a)(20) 322, 323, 324, 331, 332, 333, 334, 335, 336, 337, 338, 339, 340, 341
UCC § 9–102(a)(20)(A)(iii) 333, 336
UCC § 9–102(a)(20)(C) 341
UCC § 9–102(a)(20)(D) 324
UCC § 9–102(a)(23) 11, 135, 341
UCC § 9–102(a)(25)(A) 24
UCC § 9–102(a)(27)(A) (amended) 24
UCC § 9–102(a)(28) 169, 465, 509, 598
UCC § 9–102(a)(28)(A) 117, 169
UCC § 9–102(a)(28)(B) 202
UCC § 9–102(a)(28)(C) 321
UCC § 9–102(a)(29) 149, 239, 260, 421
UCC § 9–102(a)(31)(A) 24
UCC § 9–102(a)(32) 442
UCC § 9–102(a)(33) 11, 33, 149
UCC § 9–102(a)(34) 11
UCC § 9–102(a)(40) 433, 439
UCC § 9–102(a)(41) 431
UCC § 9–102(a)(42) 13, 24, 25, 40, 43, 149, 203, 343, 376, 386, 395, 397
UCC § 9–102(a)(44) 333
UCC § 9–102(a)(47) 149, 203, 204, 237
UCC § 9–102(a)(48) 11, 135, 149
UCC § 9–102(a)(48)(B) 185
UCC § 9–102(a)(49) 130, 421, 426
UCC § 9–102(a)(51) 52, 667
UCC § 9–102(a)(52) 263
UCC § 9–102(a)(52)(A) 3, 385
UCC § 9–102(a)(52)(C) 5, 182
UCC § 9–102(a)(53) 437, 438
UCC § 9–102(a)(54) 438
UCC § 9–102(a)(56) 120, 121
UCC § 9–102(a)(57) 41
UCC § 9–102(a)(59) 465, 509, 598
UCC § 9–102(a)(60) 121

UCC § 9–102(a)(61) 13, 24, 203
UCC § 9–102(a)(62) 40
UCC § 9–102(a)(64) 50, 558, 560
UCC § 9–102(a)(64)(A) 50, 561
UCC § 9–102(a)(64)(B) 50, 401, 561
UCC § 9–102(a)(64)(D) 50
UCC § 9–102(a)(64)(E) 50
UCC § 9–102(a)(64), com. 5(d) 558
UCC § 9–102(a)(65) 204
UCC § 9–102(a)(68)(A) 99
UCC § 9–102(a)(70) 14
UCC § 9–102(a)(71) 79, 80, 137,
   138, 149
UCC § 9–102(a)(72) 509
UCC § 9–102(a)(73) 18
UCC § 9–102(a)(73)(B) 152
UCC § 9–102(a)(73)(C) 321
UCC § 9–102(a)(73)(D) 202
UCC § 9–102(a)(74)(A) 483
UCC § 9–102(a)(76) 343
UCC § 9–102(a)(78) ... 51, 52, 412, 669
UCC § 9–102(a)(79) 203
UCC § 9–102(a)(81) 433
UCC § 9–102(b) 13, 32, 130
UCC § 9–102, com. 2a 117, 509
UCC § 9–102, com. 4b 438
UCC § 9–102, com. 5a 260
UCC § 9–102, com. 5d 204, 343
UCC § 9–102, com. 5e 667
UCC § 9–102, com. 5f 670
UCC § 9–102, com. 9a 15
UCC § 9–102, com. 13a 401
UCC § 9–102, com. 13c 50
UCC § 9–102, com. 14 322
UCC § 9–103 .... 179, 181, 219, 371,
   543
UCC § 9–103(a) 177, 283
UCC § 9–103(a)(1) 163
UCC § 9–103(a)(2) 163, 164
UCC § 9–103(b) 163, 177
UCC § 9–103(b)(1) 144, 179, 283
UCC § 9–103(b)(2) 179
UCC § 9–103(c) 395
UCC § 9–103(d) 322
UCC § 9–103(e) 179, 181
UCC § 9–103(f) 173, 180, 181
UCC § 9–103(f)(2) 179
UCC § 9–103(h) 133, 173, 181
UCC § 9–103, com. 3 .... 165, 171
UCC § 9–103, com. 7a 173
UCC § 9–104 .... 54, 129, 242, 250,
   351, 413
UCC § 9–104(a) 345, 353
UCC § 9–104(a)(1) 244
UCC § 9–104(a)(1)–(3) 131
UCC § 9–104(a)(2) 245, 246, 251,
   252, 260
UCC § 9–104(a)(2)–(3) 131
UCC § 9–104(a)(3) 246, 250
UCC § 9–104, com. 1 352
UCC § 9–104, com. 2 242
UCC § 9–104, com. 3 132

UCC § 9–105 .... 129, 210
UCC § 9–105(1)(b) 231
UCC § 9–105(1)(h) 18
UCC § 9–105(d) 169, 171
UCC § 9–106 .... 129, 411
UCC § 9–106(a) 130, 396, 400
UCC § 9–107 .... 129, 130, 173, 177,
   178, 412, 413, 667, 671
UCC § 9–107(a) 172
UCC § 9–107, com. 2 .... 172, 668
UCC § 9–107A 13, 129, 413
UCC § 9–108 67
UCC § 9–108(a) 23, 343
UCC § 9–108(b) 23, 25
UCC § 9–108(b)(2) 23
UCC § 9–108(b)(3) 23, 32, 67
UCC § 9–108(b)(6) 23
UCC § 9–108(c) 25, 26, 32
UCC § 9–108(d) 410, 411
UCC § 9–108(e) 25, 26, 243
UCC § 9–108(e)(1) 39, 40, 41
UCC § 9–108(e)(2) 11, 39, 173
UCC § 9–108, com. 2 23
UCC § 9–108, com. 3 34
UCC § 9–109 214
UCC § 9–109(a) 202
UCC § 9–109(a)(1) 9, 11, 43, 213,
   322, 324
UCC § 9–109(a)(2) 55, 152
UCC § 9–109(a)(3) 202, 205, 206,
   219, 319, 394, 512
UCC § 9–109(a)(4) 322, 324, 394
UCC § 9–109(c)(4) 668, 671
UCC § 9–109(d)(10) 241
UCC § 9–109(d)(12)–(13) 173
UCC § 9–109(d)(13) 240
UCC § 9–109, com. 1 497
UCC § 9–109, com. 2 .... 11, 26
UCC § 9–109, com. 4 .... 208, 214
UCC § 9–109, com. 5 .... 216, 339
UCC § 9–109, com. 6 324
UCC § 9–109, com. 8 .... 353, 374
UCC § 9–110 29
UCC § 9–115 414
UCC § 9–201 218
UCC § 9–201(a) 5, 53, 151, 573
UCC § 9–201(b)(ii) 47
UCC § 9–202 .... 49, 385
UCC § 9–203 .... 17, 22, 29, 42, 154
UCC § 9–203(1) 197
UCC § 9–203(1)(b) 15, 17, 18, 19,
   20, 21
UCC § 9–203(a) 5, 45, 47, 393
UCC § 9–203(a)(2) 77
UCC § 9–203(b) 13, 41, 45, 46, 47,
   53, 55, 396, 592
UCC § 9–203(b)(2) 40, 42, 393
UCC § 9–203(b)(3) 13, 152, 278
UCC § 9–203(b)(3)(A) ... 13, 15, 17, 18,
   19, 20, 21, 22, 28, 32, 45
UCC § 9–203(b)(3)(B) 15, 124
UCC § 9–203(b)(3)(C) 396, 400

UCC § 9–203(b)(3)(C), com. 4 400
UCC § 9–203(b)(3)(D).... 242, 396, 667
UCC § 9–203(b)(ii)..........................47
UCC § 9–203(d) 120, 121, 123
UCC § 9–203(e) 121
UCC § 9–203(f) 49, 50, 51, 52, 219,
667, 670, 671
UCC § 9–203, com. 1 17
UCC § 9–203, com. 2 32
UCC § 9–203, com. 3 25
UCC § 9–203, com. 4 .... 15, 124
UCC § 9–203, com. 6 42
UCC § 9–203, com. 7 121
UCC § 9–203, com. 9 51
UCC § 9–204...... 36, 41, 343, 351, 591
UCC § 9–204(1) 197, 200
UCC § 9–204(3) 19
UCC § 9–204(a) 34, 42, 200, 537,
553
UCC § 9–204(b) 39
UCC § 9–204(b)(1) 39, 132
UCC § 9–204(b)(1)–(2)....................11
UCC § 9–204(b)(2) 39, 40, 41
UCC § 9–204(b.1)(2) (amended)......41
UCC § 9–204(b.1)(3) (amended)......41
UCC § 9–204(c).... 12, 19, 42, 153, 156
UCC § 9–204(c) (amended) 41
UCC § 9–204(c), com. 5 156
UCC § 9–204, com. 1 200
UCC § 9–205..........................180, 591
UCC § 9–206(a) 412, 413
UCC § 9–207................... 405, 406, 407
UCC § 9–207(a) 402, 408, 469
UCC § 9–207(b)(1) 409
UCC § 9–207(c)(1) 260
UCC § 9–207, com. 2 405
UCC § 9–210................ 57, 58, 59, 162
UCC § 9–210(a) 162
UCC § 9–210(a)(4)..........................59
UCC § 9–301 .... 149, 273
UCC §§ 9–301 to 9–306B 135
UCC § 9–301(1) 136, 137, 142, 143,
144, 343, 374
UCC § 9–301(2) 136
UCC § 9–301(3)(A) 433
UCC § 9–301(3)(C) 136
UCC § 9–301(4) 143
UCC § 9–301, com. 4 .... 136, 137
UCC § 9–302............................222
UCC §§ 9–302 to 9–306.................136
UCC § 9–302(1) 351
UCC § 9–302(1)(e) 222, 225
UCC § 9–302(2) 20
UCC § 9–302(3) 345, 352, 353, 371,
372
UCC § 9–302(3)(a) 351, 352
UCC § 9–302(4) 345, 346, 351, 352
UCC § 9–302, com. 5 223
UCC § 9–302, com. 8 352
UCC § 9–303..............................150
UCC § 9–303(a) 145
UCC § 9–303(b) 148

UCC § 9–303(c).....................144, 145
UCC § 9–303, com. 3 150
UCC § 9–303, com. 6 148
UCC § 9–305.........................125, 126
UCC § 9–306............................231
UCC § 9–306(1)..........................50, 52
UCC § 9–306(2)...............49, 196, 200
UCC § 9–306, com. 3 200
UCC § 9–307........................138, 149
UCC § 9–307(b).............137, 138, 139
UCC § 9–307(c).....................138, 139
UCC § 9–307(e).....137, 138, 142, 273,
343
UCC § 9–307, com. 2 150
UCC § 9–307, com. 4 149
UCC § 9–308........230, 231, 232, 233,
234
UCC §§ 9–308 to 9–316...........53, 237
UCC § 9–308(a)...............45, 46, 197
UCC § 9–308(b)..............................55
UCC § 9–308(d) 670
UCC § 9–308(f) 411
UCC § 9–309.........................53, 222
UCC § 9–309(1).......53, 133, 134, 135,
179, 180, 181, 193
UCC § 9–309(2).....206, 208, 220, 221,
222, 225
UCC § 9–309(3).............202, 205, 217
UCC § 9–309(4).....................206, 217
UCC § 9–310...................20, 55, 667
UCC § 9–310(a)........46, 55, 142, 202,
218, 322, 332, 346
UCC § 9–310(b)..............................55
UCC § 9–310(b)(6) 123
UCC § 9–310(b)(7) 400
UCC § 9–310(c).....................106, 162
UCC § 9–310, com. 4 ....106, 162
UCC § 9–311............55, 134, 145, 150
UCC § 9–311(a)....................345, 374
UCC § 9–311(a)(1) 55, 219, 353,
354, 383, 385
UCC § 9–311(a)(2) 55, 145, 191
UCC § 9–311(a)(2)–(3).................150
UCC § 9–311(b).......55, 145, 345, 346,
353, 374
UCC § 9–311(d) 145, 191, 192
UCC § 9–311, com. 2 353
UCC § 9–311, com. 4 145
UCC § 9–312............................155
UCC § 9–312(3).....................170, 177
UCC § 9–312(4)......165, 168, 169, 170
UCC § 9–312(4), com. 3 170
UCC § 9–312(5)......165, 197, 198, 349
UCC § 9–312(5)(a) 158, 168, 197,
198, 199
UCC § 9–312(5), coms. 4–8 198
UCC § 9–312(a).......55, 129, 150, 251,
396, 398, 400, 410
UCC § 9–312(b)..........................129
UCC § 9–312(b)(1) 54, 131, 242
UCC § 9–312(b)(2) 54, 667, 670
UCC § 9–312(b)(3) 55

UCC § 9–312(b)(4) 13, 54
UCC § 9–312(c) 54
UCC § 9–312(c)–(d) 127
UCC § 9–312(e) 396
UCC § 9–312(g) 396
UCC § 9–312, com. 2 55
UCC § 9–312, com. 5 54
UCC § 9–313 .... 128, 396, 442
UCC § 9–313(a) 54, 124, 127, 150,
      399, 400, 420
UCC § 9–313(c) 127, 128
UCC § 9–313(d) 129
UCC § 9–313(f) 128
UCC § 9–313(f), com. 8.................. 128
UCC § 9–313(g) 128
UCC § 9–313(g)(2) 129
UCC § 9–313(g), com. 8 128
UCC § 9–313(h) 420, 421
UCC § 9–313, com. 3 ..... 124, 127, 499
UCC § 9–313, com. 9 420
UCC § 9–313A(a) 54
UCC § 9–314.................................149
UCC § 9–314(a) 54, 129, 130, 242,
      396, 398, 400, 426
UCC § 9–314A 129
UCC § 9–314A(a) 229
UCC § 9–315.........................55, 219
UCC § 9–315(a) 184, 193, 219
UCC § 9–315(a)(1) 51, 117, 121,
      141, 193, 200
UCC § 9–315(a)(2) 261, 280, 355
UCC § 9–315(b) 280
UCC § 9–315(b)(1) 265
UCC § 9–315(b)(2) 261, 262, 263,
      264, 265
UCC § 9–315(c) 76, 77, 219, 249,
      280
UCC § 9–315(d) 77, 219, 244, 249,
      355
UCC § 9–315(d)(1) 76
UCC § 9–315(d)(1)(C) 220
UCC § 9–315(d)(2) 76, 247
UCC § 9–315(d)(3) 76, 77, 220, 249
UCC § 9–315(e)(1) 76
UCC § 9–315, com. 2 193
UCC § 9–315, com. 3 262
UCC § 9–315, com. 5 220
UCC § 9–316(a) 139
UCC § 9–316(a)(2) 139, 150
UCC § 9–316(a)(3) 117, 139
UCC § 9–316(b) 440
UCC § 9–316(d) 148
UCC § 9–316(d)–(e) 150
UCC § 9–316(d)(2) 247
UCC § 9–316(d), com. 5 148
UCC § 9–316(e)............................148
UCC § 9–316, com. 2 139
UCC § 9–316, com. 3 440
UCC § 9–317................. 152, 276, 336
UCC § 9–317(a) 45, 151, 400, 573
UCC § 9–317(a)(1) 152

UCC § 9–317(a)(2) 53, 182, 183,
      263, 278, 410, 411, 440, 571
UCC § 9–317(a)(2)(A) 5, 276
UCC § 9–317(a)(2)(B) 571
UCC § 9–317(b).............141, 142, 144
UCC § 9–317(d)............................ 384
UCC § 9–317(e)......184, 279, 571, 596
UCC § 9–317, com. 4.................... 182
UCC § 9–318............................... 217
UCC § 9–318(a).............216, 217, 218
UCC § 9–318(b)......................217, 218
UCC § 9–318, com. 2.............216, 217
UCC § 9–319 ....319, 333
UCC § 9–319(a).............323, 336, 340
UCC § 9–319, com. 2.................... 323
UCC § 9–320 193
UCC § 9–320(a).....121, 185, 186, 191,
      193, 194
UCC § 9–320(b)........53, 134, 193, 194
UCC § 9–320(b)(2) 135
UCC § 9–320(e)............................ 185
UCC § 9–320, com. 3......185, 190, 191
UCC § 9–320, com. 5.................... 134
UCC § 9–320, com. 7.................... 143
UCC § 9–321(c) 185
UCC § 9–322...........59, 102, 152, 155,
      162, 247, 249, 431, 434, 591
UCC § 9–322(a).....152, 154, 155, 157,
      198, 219, 247, 248, 411, 413, 439,
      440
UCC § 9–322(a)(1) 102, 122, 123,
      153, 155, 158, 160, 168, 182, 195,
      197, 198, 199, 217, 219, 225, 227,
      228, 234, 246, 248, 440, 671
UCC § 9–322(a)(2) 122, 218
UCC § 9–322(a)(3) 249
UCC § 9–322(b)............................ 219
UCC § 9–322(b)(1) 219, 244, 246,
      249
UCC § 9–322(b)(2) 670
UCC § 9–322(c) 246, 247, 248, 249,
      412, 670
UCC § 9–322(c)(1)........................ 670
UCC § 9–322(c)(2)........................ 249
UCC § 9–322(c)(2)(A)–(C)............. 247
UCC § 9–322(e)......................248, 249
UCC § 9–322(f) 247
UCC § 9–322(f)(1) 162, 412, 413,
      439
UCC § 9–322(g)............................ 152
UCC § 9–322, com. 3.................... 152
UCC § 9–322, com. 4.............152, 155
UCC § 9–322, com. 6.................... 219
UCC § 9–322, coms. 8–9 247
UCC § 9–323 ....59, 155, 183
UCC § 9–323(a)............................ 158
UCC § 9–323(d)............................ 183
UCC § 9–323, com. 3......153, 155, 159
UCC § 9–323, com. 4.................... 183
UCC § 9–324 164
UCC § 9–324(a).....163, 166, 167, 168,
      169, 170, 171, 174

UCC § 9–324(b) 163, 170, 174, 177, 180, 181, 322, 440
UCC § 9–324(g) 165
UCC § 9–324, com. 2 219
UCC § 9–324, com. 3 171
UCC § 9–324, com. 4 174
UCC § 9–324, com. 8 174
UCC § 9–324, com. 13 165
UCC § 9–325(a) 122, 123, 201
UCC § 9–325, com. 6 201
UCC § 9–326 .... 13, 120, 122
UCC § 9–326(a) 122, 123
UCC § 9–326(b) 122, 123
UCC § 9–326A 225, 227, 413
UCC § 9–327 .... 242, 245, 251, 413
UCC § 9–327(1) 244, 247, 249
UCC § 9–327(3) 245
UCC § 9–327(4) 166, 246, 250
UCC § 9–327, com. 4 245
UCC § 9–328 398
UCC § 9–328(1) 166, 396, 400, 411, 413
UCC § 9–328(2) 166, 396, 400, 412
UCC § 9–328(3) 396, 400, 411
UCC § 9–328(6) 166
UCC § 9–328(7) 411
UCC § 9–328, com. 3 .... 401, 414
UCC § 9–328, com. 4 .... 401, 411
UCC § 9–329 .... 412, 413, 669
UCC § 9–329(1) 669, 670, 671
UCC § 9–329, com. 3 669
UCC § 9–329, com. 4 669
UCC § 9–330 ... 41, 230, 231, 232, 236, 237
UCC § 9–330(a) 230, 231, 232, 233, 234, 235, 236, 239
UCC § 9–330(a)(1) 233
UCC § 9–330(b) 230, 233, 235, 236, 239
UCC § 9–330(d) 237, 238, 266
UCC § 9–330(f) 235
UCC § 9–330, com. 3 .... 230, 233
UCC § 9–330, com. 5 234
UCC § 9–330, com. 7 266
UCC § 9–330, com. 11 239
UCC § 9–331(a) 228, 238, 266
UCC § 9–331(c) 227, 265
UCC § 9–331, com. 5 266
UCC § 9–332 .... 252, 253, 254, 261
UCC § 9–332(a) 253
UCC § 9–332(a)(1) 199
UCC § 9–332(b) 253, 255, 260, 261
UCC § 9–332, com. 2A 253
UCC § 9–332, com. 2C 260
UCC § 9–332, com. 3 254
UCC § 9–332, com. 4 254
UCC § 9–334 .... 431, 434, 439, 442
UCC § 9–334(c) 434, 435, 442
UCC § 9–334(d) 435, 453
UCC § 9–334(e) 435
UCC § 9–334(e)(1) 436
UCC § 9–334(e)(1), com. 2 439

UCC § 9–334(e)(2) 434
UCC § 9–334(e)(3) 434, 435
UCC § 9–334(e)(4) 437, 438
UCC § 9–334(f) 437
UCC § 9–334(h) 436, 437
UCC § 9–334, com. 3 431
UCC § 9–334, com. 9 435
UCC § 9–336 265
UCC § 9–336(a) 265
UCC § 9–336(c) 265
UCC § 9–336(e) 265
UCC § 9–336(f)(1) 265
UCC § 9–336(f)(2) 265
UCC § 9–337(1) 148
UCC § 9–338 60
UCC § 9–339 .... 161, 246, 250, 411
UCC § 9–340 .... 241, 245, 249, 251
UCC § 9–340(c) 246
UCC § 9–341 .... 245, 251
UCC § 9–341, com. 3 246
UCC § 9–342 246
UCC § 9–401 385
UCC § 9–401(1)(c) 351
UCC § 9–401(a), com. 1 102
UCC § 9–401, com. 1 348
UCC § 9–402 17
UCC § 9–402(1) 169
UCC § 9–402(5) 440
UCC § 9–402(7) 200
UCC § 9–402(7), com. 5 199
UCC § 9–402, com. 8 199
UCC § 9–404 241
UCC § 9–406 385
UCC § 9–406(a) 520, 522
UCC § 9–406(c) 522
UCC § 9–406(d)–(f) 386
UCC § 9–406(l) 522
UCC § 9–408 ..... 47, 48, 385, 386, 387, 388
UCC § 9–408(a) 386
UCC § 9–408(a)(1) 386
UCC § 9–408(b) 386
UCC § 9–408(c) 48, 386, 388
UCC § 9–408(c)(1) 386
UCC § 9–408(d) 386, 387
UCC § 9–408(d)(1) 386
UCC § 9–408(d)(2) 386
UCC § 9–408(d)(4) 386
UCC § 9–408(e) 48
UCC § 9–408(f) 48
UCC § 9–408, com. 5 386
UCC § 9–408, com. 8 .... 387, 388
UCC § 9–408, com. 9 387
UCC § 9–409 385
UCC § 9–409(a) 667
UCC § 9–409, com. 2 667
UCC § 9–501 213
UCC § 9–501(3)(a) 214
UCC § 9–501(a)(1)(B) 433
UCC § 9–501(a)(2) 56, 102, 433, 435
UCC § 9–501(b) 434

UCC § 9–501(b), com. 5 434
UCC § 9–501, com. 2 102
UCC § 9–501, com. 4 434
UCC § 9–502 .... 95, 99, 215
UCC § 9–502(1) 521
UCC § 9–502(2) 213, 214, 216
UCC § 9–502(a) 59, 64, 96, 100, 276, 343, 433
UCC § 9–502(a)(2) 66
UCC § 9–502(a)(3) 67
UCC § 9–502(b) 114, 433, 439
UCC § 9–502(b)(2) 433
UCC § 9–502(b)(3) 433
UCC § 9–502(c) 433
UCC § 9–502(d) 56, 169
UCC § 9–502, com. 2 56
UCC § 9–502, com. 4 214
UCC § 9–503 ..... 59, 81, 85, 95, 96, 99, 462, 475, 477
UCC § 9–503(a) 77, 81, 85, 95, 97, 100, 118, 273
UCC § 9–503(a)(1) 79, 99
UCC § 9–503(a)(4) 78, 79, 93
UCC § 9–503(a)(4)(A) 79
UCC § 9–503(a)(5) 78
UCC § 9–503(a)(6)(A) 79
UCC § 9–503(a)(6)(B) 79
UCC § 9–503(b)(1) 97
UCC § 9–503(c) 93, 97
UCC § 9–503(g) 79
UCC § 9–503, com. 2 80
UCC § 9–503, com. 2d 79
UCC § 9–503, com. 3 102
UCC § 9–504 .... 59, 96
UCC § 9–504(1) 67, 68, 501
UCC § 9–504(2) 25, 26, 67, 69, 114, 159
UCC § 9–504, com. 2 67
UCC § 9–505 .... 282, 325
UCC § 9–505(a) 297, 325
UCC § 9–505(b) 297, 325
UCC § 9–506 .... 95, 98
UCC § 9–506(a) 66, 80, 95, 96
UCC § 9–506(a)(iii) 98
UCC § 9–506(b) 66, 81, 87, 92
UCC § 9–506(b)–(c) 276
UCC § 9–506(b)–(d) 81
UCC § 9–506(c) 81, 85, 86, 87, 92, 93, 100, 269, 274
UCC § 9–506, com. 2 .... 64, 81
UCC § 9–507(2) 494
UCC § 9–507(a) 117, 118, 121
UCC § 9–507(b) 67, 118
UCC § 9–507(b)–(c) 119
UCC § 9–507(c) 67, 119, 200
UCC § 9–507, com. 3 .... 117, 118
UCC § 9–508 .... 67, 119, 120, 123
UCC § 9–508(a) 121
UCC § 9–508(b) 121
UCC § 9–508(c) 121, 122, 123
UCC § 9–508, com. 3 121
UCC § 9–509 .... 100, 101, 110

UCC § 9–509(a) 100, 103
UCC § 9–509(b) 101, 103
UCC § 9–509(b)(1) 101, 122
UCC § 9–509(c) 101
UCC § 9–509(d) 103
UCC § 9–509(d)(1) 104, 108, 109, 110
UCC § 9–509(d)(2) 105
UCC § 9–509, com. 3 101
UCC § 9–510 110
UCC § 9–510(a) 75, 100, 103, 106
UCC § 9–510(c) 104
UCC § 9–511 104
UCC § 9–511(a) 103, 106
UCC § 9–511(b) 106
UCC § 9–512(a) 103
UCC § 9–512(b) 104
UCC § 9–513 110
UCC § 9–513(a) 105
UCC § 9–513(b) 105
UCC § 9–513(c) 104, 105
UCC § 9–513(c)(4) 101
UCC § 9–513(c), com. 2 105
UCC § 9–514 105
UCC § 9–514(a) 106
UCC § 9–514(b) 106
UCC § 9–515(a) 103
UCC § 9–515(b) 103, 104, 438
UCC § 9–515(c) 103
UCC § 9–515(d) 104
UCC § 9–515(e) 104
UCC § 9–515(f) 103
UCC § 9–516 .... 59, 116
UCC § 9–516(a) 60, 114, 115
UCC § 9–516(b) 59, 60, 115, 116, 276
UCC § 9–516(b)(4) 59, 66
UCC § 9–516(b)(5) 59, 60
UCC § 9–516(d) 60, 115, 116, 276
UCC § 9–516(f)(2) 503
UCC § 9–517 115
UCC § 9–518 .... 102, 105
UCC § 9–518(a) 105
UCC § 9–518(c) 105
UCC § 9–518(e) 105
UCC § 9–520 59
UCC § 9–520(a) 59, 65, 115, 276
UCC § 9–520(c) 59, 116, 276
UCC § 9–521 114
UCC § 9–521(a) 56, 59, 60, 103, 113, 114
UCC § 9–521(b) 103, 114
UCC § 9–521, com. 2 103
UCC § 9–523(a) 115
UCC § 9–523(d) 115
UCC § 9–601 .... 213, 465
UCC § 9–601(a) 456, 468, 479, 535, 537
UCC § 9–601(a)(1) 446, 465
UCC § 9–601(c) 466, 468, 470
UCC § 9–601(e) 465
UCC § 9–601(f) 479

UCC § 9–601(g) 323, 324
UCC § 9–601, com. 5 470
UCC § 9–601, com. 8 479
UCC § 9–602 437
UCC § 9–602(3) 521
UCC § 9–602(5) 214, 216
UCC § 9–602(6) 473
UCC § 9–602(7) 491, 507, 510, 515
UCC § 9–602(10) 514, 516
UCC § 9–603 473
UCC § 9–603(a) 508
UCC § 9–604 453
UCC § 9–604(a) 452
UCC § 9–604(a)(2) 446
UCC § 9–604(b) 446
UCC § 9–604(b)(2) 446, 452, 453
UCC § 9–604(c) 445, 446, 453
UCC § 9–604(d) 445, 480, 481
UCC § 9–605 512
UCC § 9–605, com. 2 512
UCC § 9–607 .... 466, 521
UCC § 9–607(a) 521
UCC § 9–607(a)(1) 520
UCC § 9–607(a)(3) 520, 521
UCC § 9–607(c) 521, 522
UCC § 9–607(c)(2) 522
UCC § 9–607, com. 4 521
UCC § 9–607, com. 9 522
UCC § 9–608(a) 471
UCC § 9–608(a)(4) 209, 213, 216
UCC § 9–608(b)(4) 213
UCC § 9–609 .... 470, 471, 472, 473,
  534
UCC § 9–609(a) 479
UCC § 9–609(a)(1) 468, 475
UCC § 9–609(a)(2) 471
UCC § 9–609(b) 471, 485
UCC § 9–609(b)(1) 479
UCC § 9–609(b)(2) 475, 477
UCC § 9–609(c) 472
UCC § 9–610 .... 408, 466, 469, 503,
  511, 514, 520
UCC § 9–610(a) 401, 446, 483, 494,
  501
UCC § 9–610(b) 470, 491, 492, 494,
  510
UCC § 9–610(c) 402, 491, 492, 508
UCC § 9–610(c)(2) 491
UCC § 9–610(d) 508, 517
UCC § 9–610(d)–(e) 517
UCC § 9–610, com. 2 .... 490, 492
UCC § 9–610, com. 3 .... 408, 514
UCC § 9–610, com. 4 501
UCC § 9–610, com. 5 493
UCC § 9–610, com. 7 .... 491, 514
UCC § 9–610, com. 9 491
UCC § 9–611(a) 510
UCC § 9–611(b) 483
UCC § 9–611(c) 483, 510
UCC § 9–611(c)(1) 517
UCC § 9–611(c)(3) 518
UCC § 9–611(c)(3)(B) 518

UCC § 9–611(d) 402
UCC § 9–611(e) 518
UCC § 9–612(a) 484
UCC § 9–612(b) 484, 485
UCC § 9–612, com. 2 484
UCC § 9–613 483
UCC § 9–613(1) 483, 485
UCC § 9–613(1)(E) 485, 490, 491
UCC § 9–613(2) 483, 485
UCC § 9–613(3)(B) 483
UCC § 9–613, com. 2 490
UCC § 9–614 .... 11, 133, 483, 485
UCC § 9–614(1) 483
UCC § 9–614(1)(B) 484
UCC § 9–614(1)(B)–(D) 515
UCC § 9–614(1)(C) 523
UCC § 9–614(5) 483
UCC § 9–615 .... 466, 503
UCC § 9–615(a) 479, 501, 502, 503,
  518
UCC § 9–615(a)(3)(A) 518
UCC § 9–615(d)(1) 502
UCC § 9–615(d)(2) 502
UCC § 9–615(e) 502
UCC § 9–615, com. 6 .... 502, 503
UCC § 9–616 507
UCC § 9–616(b)(1) 507
UCC § 9–616(b)(2) 507
UCC § 9–616(c) 507
UCC § 9–617 517
UCC § 9–617(a)(1) 508, 517
UCC § 9–617(a)(3) 502, 517, 518
UCC § 9–617(b) 517
UCC § 9–617, com. 2 517
UCC § 9–619 509
UCC § 9–619(c) 509
UCC § 9–620 .... 466, 511, 512, 514,
  520
UCC § 9–620(a) 513
UCC § 9–620(a)(3) 514, 515
UCC § 9–620(b) 512, 513
UCC § 9–620(c)(1) 513, 514
UCC § 9–620(c)(2) 511, 513
UCC § 9–620(d) 520
UCC § 9–620(e) 514, 515
UCC § 9–620(e)–(f) 470
UCC § 9–620(f) 514
UCC § 9–620(g) 133, 173, 514, 515
UCC § 9–620, com. 10 512
UCC § 9–621(a) 519
UCC § 9–622(a) 519
UCC § 9–622(a)(4) 519
UCC § 9–622(b) 520
UCC § 9–623 .... 523, 524, 534
UCC § 9–623(a) 485
UCC § 9–623(b) 485, 537, 570
UCC § 9–624 491
UCC § 9–624(a) 510, 515
UCC § 9–624(b) 516
UCC § 9–625 .... 102, 103
UCC § 9–625(b) 101, 472, 517, 518,
  519, 520

UCC § 9–625(c)(1) 518
UCC § 9–625(c)(2) 472, 506, 507
UCC § 9–625(e)(3) 101
UCC § 9–625(e)(5) 507
UCC § 9–625, com. 3 472
UCC § 9–626(a) 133, 173, 507
UCC § 9–626(a)(2) 505
UCC § 9–626(a)(3) 503, 505
UCC § 9–626(a)(4) 505, 507
UCC § 9–626(a)(5) 503
UCC § 9–626(b) 507
UCC § 9–626, com. 3 ....497, 505
UCC § 9–626, com. 4 505
UCC § 9–627(a) 494
UCC § 9–627(b) 491, 505, 506
UCC § 9–627(b)(3) 494
UCC § 9–627(c) 494
UCC § 9–628 512
UCC § 9–628(d) 507
UCC § 12–102(a)(1)
  (amended) 12, 24, 130
UCC § 12–102(a)(3) 227, 228
UCC § 12–103(a) 228
UCC § 12–104(a) 12, 43, 226
UCC § 12–104(d) 226
UCC § 12–104(e) 43, 226, 227
UCC § 12–104(h) 227
UCC § 12–104, com. 5 33
UCC § 12–105 13
UCC § 12–105(a) 130
UCC § 12–105(a)(1) 130
UCC § 12–105(a)(2) 130
UCC § 12–105(b) 131
UCC § 12–105(c) 131
UCC § 12–105(c)(1)–(2) 131
UCC § 12–106(d) 522
UCC § 12–106(d)(1) 522
UCCC § 1.301(14) 319
UCCC § 3.303 133
UCCC § 5.109 457
UCCC §§ 5.110 to 5.111 471
UCP 500 art. 13b 635
UCP 600 art. 1 610
UCP 600 art. 4a 638
UCP 600 art. 7b 616
UCP 600 art. 8a 632
UCP 600 art. 10a 635
UCP 600 art. 14a 618
UCP 600 art. 14b 634, 635
UCP 600 art. 14d 619, 628
UCP 600 art. 16 634
UCP 600 art. 16b 635
UCP 600 art. 16d.i 636, 637
UCP 600 art. 16d.ii 636, 637
UCP 600 art. 16f 637
UCP 600 art. 38a 665
UCP 600 art. 38b 665
UCP 600 art. 38i 666
UVTA § 1 579
UVTA § 1(8) 579
UVTA § 3(a) 573
UVTA § 4(a)(1) 573

UVTA § 4(b) 597
UVTA § 5(b) 579
UVTA § 9(c) 579
Ala. Code § 7–1–201(37) 328
Ala. Code § 7–2–326(3) 328
Ala. Code § 7–2–326, com. 4 328
Ala. Code § 7–9A–102(a)(20) 328, 329, 331, 332
Ala. Code § 7–9A–102, com. 14 330
Ala. Code § 7–9A–109 328
Ala. Stat. § 01.10.080 170
Cal. C. Civ. Pro. § 514.010............ 481
Cal. C. Civ. Pro. § 697.550............ 79
Cal. Civ. Code § 1812.5................ 506
Cal. Comm. Code § 1201(36) 287
Cal. Comm. Code § 1201(36)(a).... 375
Cal. Comm. Code § 1203.............. 288
Cal. Comm. Code § 9104(a) 362, 377, 383
Cal. Comm. Code § 9106.............. 376
Cal. Comm. Code § 9302(3) 383
Cal. Comm. Code § 9302(3)(a)......363, 382, 383
Cal. Comm. Code § 9302(4) ...363, 382
Del. Code Ann. tit. 6, art. 9 109
Fla. Const., Art. V, § 21.................. 91
Fla. Civ. Prac. & Proc.
  § 55.203(1)(c) 79
Fla. Stat. § 679.1081............28, 29, 30
Fla. Stat. § 679.1081(3) 28, 29
Fla. Stat. § 679.1081, com. 2 29
Fla. Stat. § 679.2031................28, 29
Fla. Stat. § 679.5031(1) 91, 92
Fla. Stat. § 679.5061(2) 87, 88, 92
Fla. Stat. § 679.5061(2)–(3)........... 91
Fla. Stat. § 679.5061(3) 87, 88, 89, 90, 91
I.C. § 28–9–501(b) 62
I.C. § 28–9–502 ....62, 63
I.C. § 28–9–502(a) 63
I.C. § 28–9–502(a)(2) 64
I.C. § 28–9–502(e) 63, 64
I.C. § 28–9–503(a) 64
I.C. § 28–9–506 ....64, 66
I.C. § 28–9–507(b) 66
I.C. § 28–9–507, com. 4 66
I.C. § 28–9–508 66
I.C. § 28–9–511 ....64, 65
I.C. § 28–9–512 65
I.C. § 28–9–515A(4) 105
I.C. § 28–9–516 63
I.C. § 28–9–516(b) 63
I.C. § 28–9–516(b)(4) 63
I.C. § 28–9–516(b)(8) 63
I.C. § 28–9–516, com. 5................... 65
I.C. § 28–9–520 63
I.C. § 28–9–520(a) 63
I.C. § 28–9–520(c) 63
Indiana Code § 7.1–3–1–2 43
Indiana Code
  § 26–1–9.1–102(a)(33)................ 82
Indiana Code § 26–1–9.1–501 83

Indiana Code § 26–1–9.1–503...83, 85
Indiana Code § 26–1–9.1–503(a) 83
Indiana Code § 26–1–9.1–506.........83
Indiana Code § 26–1–9.1–506(c).....83
Indiana Code
   § 26–1–9.1–506, com. 2...............85
Indiana Code § 26–1–9.1–527.........83
Indiana Code § 26–1–9.1–610.......488
Indiana Code § 26–1–9.1–611.......488
Indiana Code § 26–1–9.1–613...... 488,
   489, 490
Indiana Code
   § 26–1–9.1–613(1)(E).................490
Indiana Code
   § 26–1–9.1–624 488
K.S.A. §§ 84–5–101 et seq............621
K.S.A. § 84–5–108 ....621, 622
K.S.A. § 84–5–109 621
K.S.A. § 84–5–113 621
K.S.A. § 84–9–301(1)....................142
K.S.A. § 84–9–339a(o) 143
Ky.Rev.Stat. Ann.
   § 355.1–201(2)(i) 188
Ky.Rev.Stat. Ann.
   § 355.9–207 ....405, 406
Ky.Rev.Stat. Ann.
   § 355.9–315(1)(a) 188
Ky.Rev.Stat. Ann.
   § 355.9–320(1)............................188
La. R.S. § 10: 9–609......................470
Mass. Gen. Law ch. 106 48
Mass. Gen. Law ch. 126, § 23 48
Mass. Gen. Law ch. 138, § 23 44,
   46, 47
MESA § 2.5....................................303
MESA § 4.1(f) 304
MESA § 5.......................................303
MESA § 8.3....................................305
MESA § 9.13(ii) 304
MESA § 11.0..................................304
MESA § 13.2..................................305
MESA § 17.7..................................306
Mich. Comp. Laws
   § 440.9105(1)(g) 442
Mich. Comp. Laws
   § 440.9109(1)(a) 273
Mich. Comp. Laws
   § 440.9313(4)..............................442
Mich. Comp. Laws
   § 440.9313(7)..............................442
Mich. Comp. Laws
   § 440.9503(1)..............................273
Minn. Stat. Ann. § 545.05 105
Minn. Stat. Ann. § 604.17(6).........105
Mo. Rev. Stat. § 400.8–106(c) 429
Mo. Rev. Stat. § 400.9–108 71
Mo. Rev. Stat. § 400.9–310 71
Mo. Rev. Stat. § 400.9–502(a).........71
Mo. Rev. Stat.
   § 400.9–502, com. 2 72
Mo. Rev. Stat. § 400.9–504 ....71, 72
Mo. Rev. Stat. § 400.9–504(2) 72

Mo. Rev. Stat.
   § 400.9–504, com. 2................71, 72
Mo. Rev. Stat. § 400.9–506(a) 71
Mo. Rev. Stat.
   § 400.9–506, com. 2.....................71
Mo. Rev. Stat. §§ 400.9–101 to
   400.9–710..................................71
N.D. Cent. Code § 41–09–92 114
N.J. Stat. § 12A: 9–626..................507
N.Y. Arts and Cult. Affairs Law
   § 12.01(1)(a) 341
N.Y. Arts and Cult. Affairs Law
   § 12.01(1)(a)(v) 341
N.Y. CLS U.C.C.
   § 9–516(b)(5)(C)..........................114
N.Y. U.C.C. § 1–201(37) 306, 307,
   310
N.Y. U.C.C. § 5–108(e) 629
Ohio Rev. Code Ann. § 1309.626...507
47 Pa. Stat. Ann. § 4–468(d) 43
R.C. 1302.44(B)............................257
R.C. 1309.102(A)(2)(a) 258
R.C. 1309.102(A)(29)....................258
R.C. 1309.104(A)(1) 259
R.C. 1309.109(A)(1) 256
R.C. 1309.201(A)....................256, 257
R.C. 1309.203(B)(3)(d) 259
R.C. 1309.315(A)....................257, 259
R.C. 1309.327(C).........................259
R.C. 1309.332....................257, 258
R.C. 1309.332(B)........257, 258, 259
R.C. 1309.332, com. 2 259
S.C. Code Ann. §§ 36–5–101 to
   36–5–119 660
S.C. Code Ann.
   § 36–5–109(b) 660
S.C. Code Ann.
   § 36–5–109(b)(4)..........................661
S.C. Code Ann.
   § 36–9–501(d) 105
Tenn. Code Ann.
   § 47–9–109(a)(1)..........................497
Tenn. Code Ann. § 47–9–601 497
Tenn. Code Ann.
   § 47–9–601(a)(1).................497, 498
Tenn. Code Ann. § 47–9–601(e) 498
Tenn. Code Ann. § 47–9–601(f).....498
Tenn. Code Ann. § 47–9–609(a) 498
Tenn. Code Ann.
   § 47–9–609(b)(2).........................498
Tenn. Code Ann. § 47–9–610 497,
   498, 500
Tenn. Code Ann. § 47–9–610(b)...497,
   498, 499
Tenn. Code Ann. § 47–9–620 497
Tenn. Code Ann. § 47–9–626(1) 499
Tenn. Code Ann. § 47–9–626(2) 499
Tenn. Code Ann. § 47–9–626(3) 497
Tenn. Code Ann. § 47–9–626(4) 497
Tex. Bus. & Com. Code Ann.
   § 1.201(b)(35)..............................449

Tex. Bus. & Com. Code Ann.
§ 9.101 com. 1..............................449
Tex. Bus. & Com. Code Ann.
§ 9.102(a)(12) 449
Tex. Bus. & Com. Code Ann.
§ 9.102(a)(41) 449
Tex. Bus. & Com. Code Ann.
§ 9.102(a)(44) 449
Tex. Bus. & Com. Code Ann.
§ 9.102(a)(74) 449
Tex. Bus. & Com. Code Ann.
§ 9.109(a)...................................449
Tex. Bus. & Com. Code Ann.
§ 9.203 451
Tex. Bus. & Com. Code Ann.
§ 9.301(1)...................................142
Tex. Bus. & Com. Code Ann.
§ 9.334.......................................450
Tex. Bus. & Com. Code Ann.
§ 9.334(d)................... 449, 450, 451
Tex. Bus. & Com. Code Ann.
§ 9.334(d)(1) 450
Tex. Bus. & Com. Code Ann.
§ 9.343(p)...................................143
Tex. Bus. & Com. Code Ann.
§ 9.502 448
Tex. Bus. & Com. Code Ann.
§ 9.502(a)...................................451
Tex. Bus. & Com. Code Ann.
§ 9.504(a)...................................564
Tex. Bus. & Com. Code Ann.
§ 9.504(c) 564
Tex. Bus. & Com. Code Ann.
§ 9.505 564
Tex. Bus. & Com. Code Ann.
§ 9.604 450
Tex. Bus. & Com. Code Ann.
§ 9.604(b)............................449, 450
Tex. Bus. & Com. Code Ann.
§ 9.604(b)(2) 450, 451, 452
Tex. Bus. & Com. Code Ann.
§ 9.604(b), com. 3 .... 450, 452
Va. Code Ann. § 8.9A–9–521.........114
Va. Code Ann. § 46.2–640.1 318
W. Va. Code § 46A–2–106 .....539, 540
Wis. Stat. Ann. § 342.19(6) 146
Wis. Stat. Ann. § 409.301..............147
Wis. Stat. Ann. § 409.301(1) 147
Wis. Stat. Ann. § 409.303..............147
Wis. Stat. Ann. § 409.303(3) 147
Wis. Stat. Ann. § 409.305(3) 147
Wis. Stat. Ann. § 409.306..............147
Wis. Stat. Ann. § 409.316......146, 147
Wis. Stat. Ann. § 409.316(1) 147
Wis. Stat. Ann. § 409.316(1)(b).....147
Wis. Stat. Ann. § 409.316(4) 147
Wis. Stat. Ann. §§ 425.104 to
425.105 471
Wyo. Stat. Ann. § 34.1–5–108(e)...629

TABLE OF REGULATIONS

12 C.F.R. § 7.1016(a)............. 614, 638
16 C.F.R. § 444.2(4)......................... 39
17 C.F.R. § 230.144 403
17 C.F.R. § 230.144(d)–(f) 403
26 C.F.R. § 301.6201–1 269
26 C.F.R. § 301.6203–1 269
26 C.F.R. § 301.6323(c)–1 280
26 C.F.R. § 301.6323(c)–1(c)(1) 277
26 C.F.R. § 301.6323(f)–1(d)(1) 271
26 C.F.R. § 301.6323(f)–1(d)(2) 269, 271
26 C.F.R. § 301.6323(h)–1(a)(3) 276
31 C.F.R. § 306.118(b) 430
31 C.F.R. § 357.11(e) 430
31 C.F.R. part 357 430
37 C.F.R. § 201.4(a)(2) 347
37 C.F.R. § 201.4(c)(1) 351
61 Fed. Reg. § 43626 430

TABLE OF RULES

Admin. Rule 501.1............................84
Admin. Rule 503...............................84
Fed. R. Bkrtcy. P. 7001(1)............550
Fed. R. Bkrtcy. P. 7001(2)............374
Fed. R. Bkrtcy. P. 7056..................28
Fed. R. Civ. P. 12(c).......................81
Fed. R. Civ. P. 56............................28
Fed. R. Civ. P. 56(a) 315
Fed. R. Civ. P. 56(c)........................28
Ariz. R. Civ. P. 56.........................230
ISP 98 Rule 1.01(b) 610
ISP 98 Rule 1.06(a) 616
ISP 98 Rule 1.07...........................638
ISP 98 Rule 4.01...........................618
ISP 98 Rule 4.01(b) 619
ISP 98 Rule 4.09(c).......................627
ISP 98 Rule 5.01...........................635
ISP 98 Rule 5.05...........................636
ISP 98 Rule 5.06(a) 636
Rev. Proc. 2001–28.......................282
Rev. Rul. 68–57 279

SECURED TRANSACTIONS IN PERSONAL PROPERTY

ELEVENTH EDITION

CHAPTER 1

CREATING A SECURITY INTEREST

A. WHY SECURED CREDIT?

Article 9 of the Uniform Commercial Code (UCC) consists of rules governing security interests in personal property. Its rules apply to transactions in which one person makes a loan to another, and both parties agree that, if the borrower defaults, the lender can seize specific personal property of the borrower and sell it to satisfy the loan. The personal property specified in the agreement serves as a source of repayment for the lender. The lender therefore need not rely only on the borrower's cash flow for repayment. In this way the security interest reduces the lender's risk of not being repaid and expands the volume of credit.

A variety of different sorts of transactions can create security interests in personal property. The lender might be a pawnbroker lending money on the security of tangible personal property. It can be a retailer selling goods on credit and retaining a security interest in the goods acquired by the buyer to secure their purchase price. For their part, the borrowers might be consumers or large firms borrowing millions of dollars. The personal property used as collateral can be tangible such as goods, or intangible assets such as accounts receivable, intellectual property or cryptocurrency. It might be specific personal property the borrower currently owns or also specific personal property it acquires subsequently.

Common to secured transactions is the property right a security interest gives the lender: the right to seize specific property of the borrower on its default without having to go to court. This property right is created by the agreement of the parties. By contrast, an unsecured loan lacks a property right in specific assets as a source of repayment. Instead, the unsecured lender relies on the cash flow and creditworthiness of its borrower. Should the borrower default, the lender must enlist the help of the state. It must reduce its claim to a judgment, obtain a writ of execution and levy on property. Unlike a security interest, the unsecured lender can get a property right in specific property only with state aid.

Business lending takes many forms. At the top level are unsecured loans based on the borrower's projected cash flow and creditworthiness. Established companies, usually large publicly traded companies with good credit ratings, avail themselves of this form of lending. Unsecured creditors face risks that the financial position of their borrowers may deteriorate or their borrowers may incur debt from other lenders, including secured debt. To protect against this eventuality, the unsecured loan contract may contain a series of covenants that restrict the borrower's investment activities, including issuing secured debt, limit dividend payments and the sale of certain assets. These loan covenants reduce the risk of a deterioration in the borrower's ability to repay the loan only if the lender monitors the borrower to assure compliance with them. In addition, enforcing these covenants is costly. By comparison, the costs of enforcing a security interest are lower, as the security interest gives the secured creditor the right to foreclose on collateral in the event of the borrower's default. Nonetheless, the issuance of secured debt is not costless, and the risk of a financially sound borrower breaching its loan covenants may be low enough to justify making an unsecured loan.

If the borrower doesn't qualify for unsecured credit, it may be able to obtain credit through asset-based loans. Here the lender takes a first security interest in the borrower's assets, such as equipment, inventory or real estate, as well as intangibles such as rights to payment or intellectual property. The amount of the loan may be based on the value of the borrower's assets. These loans may be used for a wide variety of needs including seasonal cash requirements, business expansion and acquisitions. A major area of asset-based lending is inventory financing in which lenders finance the seller's acquisition of inventory and take security interests in the acquired inventory and its proceeds. Sellers may also finance the acquisition of inventory by securitization, that is, by pooling the proceeds of inventory sales (accounts receivables and other rights to payment) and selling these pools to institutional investors, thus obtaining financing at lower than bank rates. Over 60% of collateralized loans made in the U.S. to small and medium sized firms are collateralized by personal property, usually equipment, inventory and accounts receivable.

Consumer lending has evolved from three traditional forms of financing: (i) personal loans, secured by all the borrower's household goods, (ii) purchase-money credit sales in which the seller takes a security interest in the goods sold to secure the unpaid indebtedness to be repaid in monthly installments, and (iii) unsecured retail charge account credit (open-end credit), in which buyers make monthly payments on balances owed. As will be described later, credit and debit card debt has swallowed up old-fashioned charge accounts, limiting purchase-money secured credit to only big-ticket items like motor vehicles and lessening the need for personal loans. Most credit card debt is unsecured. The paradox is that in business lending only the best credit risks receive unsecured credit, while in consumer financing, owing to competition by card issuers for market share, some of the worst credit risks are accorded unsecured credit with generous balance limits.

The following elementary cases illustrate the advantages of secured credit and its harshness in insolvencies. We compare the rights of unsecured and secured creditors.

1. RIGHTS OF UNSECURED CREDITOR

Case #1. *Seller vs. Debtor.* Debtor operates a winery and buys wine barrels from Seller on credit. When Seller delivered a shipment of barrels, Debtor made a cash down payment and gave Seller its note, promising to pay Seller the balance of the price of the barrels with interest in twelve monthly installments. After Debtor failed to make the third and fourth payments on the note, Seller notified Debtor that it was in default on the note and exercised the right under the terms of the note to declare the entire unpaid balance due. If Debtor is unable or unwilling to pay the balance owing on the note, how can Seller collect from Debtor?

Seller would probably like to reclaim the barrels that Debtor failed to pay for, but they now belong to Debtor, and the historic principle is "that before judgment (or its equivalent) an unsecured creditor has no rights at law or in equity in the property of his debtor." Grupo Mexicano de Desarrollo, S.A. v. Alliance Bond Fund, Inc., 527 U.S. 308, 330 (1999). Thus, for Seller to collect, it must incur the expense and suffer the delay of hiring a lawyer and litigating the case. Seller first must sue Debtor on the promissory note and obtain a money judgment against Debtor. Then it must do whatever is required under state law to authorize the sheriff to seize (levy on) Debtor's assets and sell them in payment of the judgment debt, subject to certain exemptions that allow debtors to protect some of their property from the reach of involuntary creditors. Traditionally the seizure was a physical taking of the property, but in more recent years, the seizure can be symbolic and occur by the public filing of a document. In either case, the seizure results in the transfer from the debtor to the creditor of an interest in the seized property, and that interest is called a judicial lien. Under 9–102(a)(52)(A), Seller is now a "lien creditor" and has rights akin to those of a creditor holding a security interest.

If Debtor chooses to oppose Seller's action, one can scarcely imagine a less efficient, more cumbersome procedure for Seller to collect its debt than that described in the previous paragraph. Unless the sum sought by Seller is large, the cost of collection makes this procedure too expensive to pursue. And if Debtor has no unencumbered, nonexempt assets left that Seller can reach, the judgment may be worthless. Doubtless, the *in terrorem* effect of arming Seller with the power to dismember Debtor's business is substantial and gives Debtor an incentive to pay its debt to Seller. A judgment against Debtor may include not only the balance of the unpaid purchase price of the barrels but also collection costs such as attorney's fees if the note so provides. But, as seen in the following paragraph, even if Debtor wishes to pay Seller to stave off disaster, Debtor's other creditors can deprive it of the means to do so.

Case #2. *Seller vs. Other Unsecured Creditors and Trustee in Bankruptcy.* If Debtor is unable to pay Seller for assets as central to the function of a winery as wine barrels, it may be in financial trouble. If so, there are probably other unpaid creditors pursuing Debtor. Suppose C1 sold grapes to Debtor in September, Seller sold barrels to Debtor in October, and C2 sold equipment to Debtor in November. All the sales were made on unsecured credit and by the end of the year Debtor had defaulted on each debt. In March of the following year, C2 followed the procedures outlined in Case #1 and the sheriff, acting under C2's judgment, seized not only the equipment that it had sold Debtor but also the barrels that Seller had sold Debtor. By the time Seller had obtained a judgment against Debtor in May, the sheriff had already sold both the equipment and the barrels in payment of C2's claim and Debtor had no unencumbered assets left for Seller to reach. Assume that under the law of the state, priority among judgment creditors is based on the time the sheriff seizes the assets; thus, C2 has won the "race to the courthouse," and even though Seller advanced credit to Debtor before C2, it is subordinate to C2's rights as a lien creditor.

Assume that Debtor filed in bankruptcy four months after C2 became a lien creditor but before Seller did so. Seller has only an unsecured claim and will share in the distribution of the assets of Debtor's estate pro rata with other unsecured creditors. But, unless C2's lien creditor status runs afoul of preference law (which it would only if Debtor filed within 90 days after C2 acquired its judicial lien), C2 will be treated as a secured creditor in bankruptcy and prior to the unsecured claims of C1 and Seller.

2. RIGHTS OF SECURED CREDITOR

Case #1. *Seller vs. Debtor.* How would Seller improve its position against Debtor by taking a security interest in the wine barrels that it sold to Debtor to secure the obligation evidenced by the promissory note? By acquiring a property right in the barrels. This property right is called a "lien," and a typical sort of consensual lien is a "security interest." As will become apparent, creating the security interest is quite simple under Article 9. Seller could enter into a written security agreement with Debtor providing for a security interest in the barrels. If the parties are at a distance from each other and desire an immediate security agreement, the agreement may be evidenced by an electronic record, such as an e-mail document, sent by Seller to Debtor and Debtor's signed reply e-mail. When this is done, Seller's security interest in the barrels has "attached," that is, become enforceable against Debtor with respect to the collateral. 9–203(a). Upon Debtor's default in its payment schedule, Seller could retake the barrels from Debtor, usually without going to court, and resell them at an auction sale conducted by Seller at which Seller can bid. Usually, no court proceedings are necessary unless the proceeds of the resale are inadequate to discharge the debt and Seller wishes to collect the amount of the deficiency. If so, it must bring suit against Debtor and obtain a judgment for the deficiency.

Case #2. *Seller vs. Other Creditors and Trustee in Bankruptcy.* How would Seller improve its position against C1 and C2 as described in Case #2 above and Debtor's trustee in bankruptcy by taking a security interest in the wine barrels? So long as C1 and C2 remain unsecured creditors without judicial liens in the barrels, Seller is prior to them under one of the golden rules of secured transactions law, 9–201(a): "Except as otherwise provided [under the Uniform Commercial Code], a security agreement is effective according to its terms between the parties, against purchasers of the collateral, and against creditors." Secured claims trump unsecured claims, unless specific provisions of Article 9 provide "otherwise."

And, in several important instances, Article 9 does provide otherwise. Under 9–317(a)(2)(A), until Seller "perfects" its security interest, it is at risk of having its security interest primed by C1, C2 and Debtor's trustee in bankruptcy, for Article 9 makes an unperfected security interest subordinate to lien creditors. Thus, if either C1 or C2 goes through the process described above to acquire lien creditor status before Seller perfects, Seller's unperfected security interest is subordinate. And since a trustee in bankruptcy acquires lien creditor status from the date Debtor files in bankruptcy (9–102(a)(52)(C)), Seller's unperfected security interest may be avoided by the trustee under BC 544(a)(1). Given the high volume of bankruptcy filings, an important reason creditors seek perfected security interests is to provide protection against the possibility of their debtors' subsequent bankruptcy filings. Bankruptcy proceedings generally leave unaffected property rights covered by perfected security interests.

In the usual commercial case like that described above, perfection is easily achieved by Seller's filing a simple financing statement, giving only minimal information about the secured transaction, in the state's filing office for a minimal fee. The filing may be hastened by use of electronic transmission.

3. IS SECURED CREDIT FAIR OR EFFICIENT?

PROBLEM

Seller sold wine barrels to Debtor on February 1 on unsecured credit. By July, Debtor needed an immediate loan in order to stay in business. After examining Debtor's financial situation, Bank agreed to make the loan only if Debtor granted it a security interest in all its assets, now owned or thereafter acquired, to secure all present and future advances Bank made to Debtor. With no other sources of credit available, Debtor had no choice but to accept Bank's terms and signed a security agreement granting Bank the security interest that it requested. The security agreement described the collateral as including all wine barrels. Bank immediately filed an appropriate financing statement. Although Bank knew about Seller's transaction with Debtor, neither Bank nor Debtor notified Seller of the secured transaction. Based on what you have learned from the Cases above, what is Bank's priority with respect to Seller's rights, inside and outside bankruptcy?

A basic question needs to be raised at the outset: Why does the law allow a debtor to contract with a creditor to award that creditor a priority over the debtor's other creditors, however meritorious their claims and whenever they extended credit, by taking a security interest in the debtor's assets? In short, why have a law of secured credit? As discussed later in this Chapter, Article 9 allows a secured creditor to take a security interest in all of a debtor's personal property then owned or acquired in the future. In addition, the security interest may not only extend to the debtor's tangible assets, such as inventory or equipment, but also to the debtor's stream of earnings or cash flow, that is, the proceeds of sales of inventory or services. It is from this stream of earnings that unsecured creditors like trade creditors and employees expect to be paid. Thus, Article 9, in sweeping away all the historic judicial constraints on the creation of secured credit, makes it easy for secured creditors to take a priority in all of a debtor's assets, present and future, to the exclusion of other creditors. But what justifies having a law of secured credit at all? The answer is not obvious.

It has been argued that secured credit is fair to unsecured creditors. The borrower's grant of a security interest to a creditor increases the risk of other creditors' claims by reducing their expected value should the borrower become insolvent. However, unsecured creditors are aware of the impact of the grant of a security interest on the value of their claims. They therefore can take the impact into account in making lending decisions. A lender can elect not to make an unsecured loan to a borrower which has issued secured debt or insist on a security interest as a condition of the loan. Alternatively, unsecured creditors can increase the interest rate they charge their borrowers to reflect this increased risk, as compensation for bearing it. More generally, unsecured creditors can adjust their interest rates to take into account the likelihood that their

borrowers have granted a creditor a security interest. The defense of
secured credit concludes that it is fair to impose on unsecured creditors
risks of which they are aware and which they can avoid or take into
account. See Thomas H. Jackson & Anthony T. Kronman, Secured
Financing and Priority Among Creditors, 88 Yale L.J. 1143, 1147–1148
(1979).

This argument assumes that unsecured creditors adjust their
interest charges in response to the increased risk resulting from the
debtor's issuance of secured debt. However, the assumption is unsound.
Certain unsecured creditors adjust their interest charges at the prospect
of secured debt and certain other unsecured creditors do not.
Nonconsensual creditors, such as tort, warranty and some statutory
claimants, are not in position to set the terms of their credit in advance.
The interest charge to which these claimants are entitled is not adjusted
in the face of secured debt. Even where the unsecured credit is
consensual, the creditor might have cost-justified reasons for setting a
fixed interest charge. The amount of the unsecured claim might be small,
and the cost of designing a variable interest charge too high, to provide
for an adjustable interest charge in the creditor's loan agreement. See
Lucian A. Bebchuck & Jesse M. Fried, The Uneasy Case for the Priority
of Secured Claims in Bankruptcy, 105 Yale L.J. 857, 882–891 (1996). It
is arguably fair that a consensual creditor bears the increased risk of
nonpayment if it elects not to adjust the terms of its loan agreement to
take the issuance of secured debt into account. However, as a matter of
fairness, it is objectionable to allow secured debt to increase the riskiness
of nonconsensual creditors' claims when the creditors cannot protect
themselves against the issuance of secured debt. The argument that
secured credit is fair to unsecured creditors therefore is inconclusive.

To understand why a law of secured credit might be justified, it is
worth considering why a borrower might issue secured debt even when
all its creditors are adjusting. A lender who is granted a security interest
will reduce the interest rate on its loan to reflect the reduced risk of
nonrepayment. However, the risk of nonrepayment for the borrower's
unsecured lenders is correspondingly increased. These lenders will
increase the interest rate on their loans accordingly. Thus, the gain to
the borrower in the form of a reduced interest rate for secured debt is
offset by the loss to it in the form of increased interest charges for
unsecured debt. The size of the borrower's total debt bill therefore is
unchanged. Because secured debt is costly to issue, the prevalence of
secured debt is puzzling. The problem is not that some lenders will
demand security interests. The puzzle is to explain why borrowers issue
secured debt when doing so is costly and has no effect on the total cost of
the debt they incur.

One explanation is efficiency: secured debt reduces the size of the
debtor's debt bill. There are basically three sorts of efficiency accounts:
monitoring cost, bonding, and signaling. These accounts explain in

different ways how security credit reduces the cost of secured debt without raising the cost of unsecured debt. A security interest in collateral allows the secured creditor to monitor a limited range of assets to protect against the debtor's actions that jeopardize the creditor's repayment prospects. This reduces the monitoring costs the secured creditor incurs in assuring that its loan will be repaid without increasing the monitoring costs incurred by the debtor's other creditors. The reduction in monitoring costs incurred by the secured creditor in turn is reflected in the lower interest rate it demands for making a secured loan. Alternatively, a security interest aligns the debtor and the creditors' interests by giving the secured creditor the right to foreclose on specific assets upon default. Such bonding arrangements enable the debtor to credibly commit not to take actions that affect the secured creditor's repayment prospects, when making a credible commitment is otherwise costly. This commitment increases the prospect that the secured creditor will be repaid, thereby reducing the interest rate of its secured loan. Finally, the grant of a security interest enables the debtor to signal to creditors that its prospects of repaying a loan are good. This is because the right of foreclosure imposes a cost on the debtor which it will bear only if it believes that it will not experience financial difficulties over the term of the loan. The issuance of secured debt reliably conveys this information to creditors when the debtor knows more about its repayment prospects than its creditors. Secured creditors charge a reduced interest rate that reflects the increased likelihood of repayment. The literature has found that none of these efficiency accounts of secured credit are completely adequate. See, e.g., Alan Schwartz, Taking the Analysis of Security Seriously, 80 Va. L. Rev. 2073 (1994); The Continuing Puzzle of Secured Debt, 37 Vand. L. Rev. 1051 (1984).

A nonefficiency explanation of secured debt is redistributional. Security interests reduce repayment risk to secured creditors and therefore the effective interest charge on their loans. However, the repayment risk is shifted to unsecured creditors who do not increase the effective interest rate on their claims accordingly. In this way secured debt reduces the total interest charge debtors incur in issuing debt. LoPucki calls such a redistribution "expropriation." See Lynn M. LoPucki, The Creditor's Bargain, 80 Va. L. Rev. 1887, 1899 (1994). The redistributional account assumes that there are a sufficiently large number of nonadjusting creditors, with large claims, to bias financing in favor of secured credit. In addition, although this account might explain why debtors sometimes grant security interests in their assets, it does not justify the practice or the law that enables secured credit.

Article 9 does not explicitly take a position in the debate over secured credit. However, by increasing the range of collateral and transactions subject to Article 9, as well as reducing the cost of creating and enforcing security interests, Article 9's drafters implicitly assume that security interests are wealth-increasing transactions. This also is the assumption of observers who recommend that developing countries reform their commercial laws to make possible the collateralization of a broad range of personal property. See Heywood Fleisig et al., Reforming Collateral Laws to Expand Access in Finance (2006). The wealth-increasing assumption was endorsed by the Reporters for Revised Article 9, Professors Steven L. Harris & Charles W. Mooney, Jr., in their article, A Property-Based Theory of Security Interests: Taking Debtor's Choices Seriously, 80 Va. L. Rev. 2021 (1994). In their view, "[t]he law should not impair the ability of debtors to secure as much or as little of their debts with as much or as little of their existing and future property as they deem appropriate." Id. at 2021–2022. Harris and Mooney maintain that although secured creditors undeniably enjoy an advantage over unsecured creditors in a debtor's insolvency, most debtors do not become insolvent, and much credit would never be granted unless the grantor could obtain collateral. They note that for years secured creditors battled with courts and legislators to allow them to acquire reliable security interests; Article 9 finally gives secured creditors what they want. Harris and Mooney conclude that until someone can demonstrate empirically that, overall, this is a bad thing, freedom of contract should govern.

B. INTRODUCTION TO ARTICLE 9

1. HISTORICAL NOTE

Section 9–109(a)(1) provides that Article 9 applies to "a transaction, regardless of the form, that creates a security interest in personal property by contract or fixtures by contract." By its terms, 9–109(a)(1) brings within Article 9's scope all secured interests in personal property and fixtures created by contract, "regardless of the form" the transaction takes. This signals a change in the law of secured transactions. Before Article 9's original enactment, "form" mattered. Different laws governed different security devices, depending on the "form" the secured transaction took.

Until the early 19th century, U.S. law recognized only two security devices: the mortgage of real property and the pledge of personal property. The pledge required the secured party to take possession of the collateral. A security interest in the borrower's personal property could not be taken while the property remained in the borrower's hands. The law considered a grant of a security interest in personal property, without a transfer of possession, to be invalid as a fraudulent conveyance. See 1 Grant Gilmore, Security Interests in Personal Property § 2.1 at 24 (1965).

Secured financing in personal property would not become economically significant until a way could be found to allow the debtor to retain possession and enjoyment of personal property collateral while paying off the debt. Two 19th century developments, one statutory and the other common law, legitimized nonpossessory personal property financing. Chattel mortgage acts, first enacted in the 1820s, allowed the creation of a mortgage in chattels in the possession of the mortgagor which was valid against creditors and purchasers so long as the chattel mortgagee filed the mortgage document in designated public records. Meanwhile, the courts were using the complex law of conditions to hold that a seller could retain title to the chattel it sold until the buyer paid the price and retake the property on the buyer's default. Beginning in the 1870s, conditional sales acts made the conditional sales contract enforceable against certain purchasers and creditors only if the conditional sales contract was filed.

Although the chattel mortgage and the conditional sale removed the traditional requirement that possession was required for the validity of secured transactions involving personal property, both security devices were effective only when the collateral was static and the transaction was terminal. Neither device was sufficient when the collateral, as in the case of inventory or accounts receivable, would in the ordinary course of business be converted into cash or other proceeds in the hands of the debtor. In these cases, the creditor needed a security device that would attach automatically to the proceeds resulting from the sale of inventory or the collection of accounts, or the inventory or accounts acquired by the debtor as replacements for the original collateral.

The first half of the 20th century saw the invention of a series of security devices—trust receipts, factors' liens, and assignments of accounts receivable—that gave secured creditors more or less effective security interests in shifting stocks of collateral like inventory and accounts. By the time drafting began on Article 9 in the late 1940s, the leading commercial states had separate and wholly disparate laws on chattel mortgages, conditional sales, trust receipts, factors' liens, and assignments of accounts receivable. The law of chattel security was as provincial and nonuniform then as the law of real estate mortgages is today. Gilmore describes this body of law as one of "extraordinary complexity."

2. FORMER ARTICLE 9

The primary drafters of Article 9, Professors Grant Gilmore and Allison Dunham, began the project resolved to junk the historical and conceptual categories that had characterized chattel security law and to strive for a functional approach to the area. Accordingly, instead of drafting revised and updated chattel mortgage or conditional sales acts, they set out to produce a series of separate statutes on each major type of financing: business equipment, consumer goods, agricultural products, inventory and accounts, and intangibles. As their work progressed, Gilmore and Dunham found that there were more similarities than differences among the various kinds of financing transactions. They therefore decided to draft a unified statute, covering all secured transactions in personal property, that contained different rules for what were functionally different transactions.

Article 9 introduces a unitary security device: the secured transaction. Rather than determining whether a transaction creates a chattel mortgage, conditional sale or other type of security interest, the question under Article 9 is whether the transaction creates a security interest by contract in personal property or fixtures. Accordingly, Article 9's basic notions are "debtor," "secured party," "collateral," "security agreement" and "security interest," not "chattel mortgage" or "conditional sale"—notions which are not found in Article 9's rules. This does not mean that Article 9's unitary security device eliminates all distinctions among different secured transactions. The Article distinguishes types of collateral; see, e.g., 9–102(a)(23), (33), (34), (48). It also distinguishes between different sorts of security interests, such as purchase-money and non-purchase-money security interest. Occasionally, Article 9 has special rules that apply to consumer debtors or types of collateral; see, e.g., 9–614, 9–108(e)(2), 9–204(b)(1)–(2). Nonetheless, Article 9 operates with a single basis for creating a security interest—the secured transaction—whatever the character of the collateral, debtor or type of security interest. If a transaction creates a security interest by contract in personal property or fixtures, Article 9's rules apply unless modified by federal law or inconsistent state law.

Although Article 9 does not abolish the pre-Code security devices, it renders the formal distinctions among them irrelevant. Comment 2 to 9–109 states: "When a security interest is created, this Article applies regardless of the form of the transaction or the name that parties have given to it." Section 9–102(2) of former Article 9 made the same point within Article 9's text: "This Article applies to security interest created by contract including pledge, assignment, chattel mortgage, chattel trust, trust deed, factor's lien, equipment trust, conditional sale, trust receipt, or lien or title retention contract and lease or consignment intended as security." Lawyers and judges may occasionally talk about chattel mortgages or floor-planning, but the old categories have no meaning except as a shorthand way of describing familiar transactions. The overriding statement is found in 9–109(a)(1): "[T]his article applies to a transaction, regardless of its form, that creates a security interest in personal property or fixtures by contract[.]"

Article 9's text has evolved since it appeared as part of the 1952 Official Text of the UCC, the first official text approved. Dissatisfaction with the 1957 and 1958 Official Texts of the UCC (including Article 9) resulted in revisions incorporated into the 1962 Official Text. Although the 1962 Official Text was widely adopted by the states, states enacted a substantial number of nonuniform amendments to Article 9's provisions. To restore uniformity in the enacted version of the Article and to revise some of its problematic provisions, the 1972 Official Text amended the 1962 Official Text of Article 9. Minor amendments to some of Article 9's provisions were made in 1978 and 1994. References in the text to Article 9 prior to its revision in 1999 are prefaced by the word "former," e.g., "former 9–201," without regard to the particular version of former Article 9's Official Text.

3.   ARTICLE 9 AND THE 2022 AMENDMENTS

The 1999 Official Text substantially revised Article 9. The revisions had an effective date of July 1, 2001 in those states that had adopted them. By July 2002 every state as well as Washington D.C. and the Virgin Islands had enacted the 1999 Official Text. Some states adopted nonuniform amendments to Article 9's public filing provisions. Primarily to restore uniformity, as well as to resolve disagreement among courts over certain filing-related matters, amendments to the Official Text were made in 2010. Every state has enacted the 2010 Amendments, as has Washington D.C. and Puerto Rico. (Puerto Rico enacted both revised Article 9 and the 2010 Amendments together, with an effective date of 2013.) The latest revisions to the UCC, including Article 9, were made in July 2022. References in this book to the Official Text of Article 9, which includes the 2010 and 2022 Amendments to it, appear without a preface, e.g., "9–201." References to the Official Text of Article 9 as whole appear as "Article 9" or occasionally "current Article 9" or "revised Article 9" where the context requires it. Where the 2022 Amendments to Article 9 are referred to specifically, they appear with the preface "Amended," e.g., "Amended 9–204."

The 2022 Amendments to the UCC, including significant amendments to Article 9, alter UCC provisions to take account of digital assets. These changes are made in response to the increasing economic importance of digital commerce and uncertainty in the law governing digital assets. A primary purpose of the amendments to the UCC is to define the rights of purchasers (including secured parties) in them. To this end, the Amendments to the UCC add a new Article, Article 12, which governs transactions involving certain digital assets, including cybercurrency such as Bitcoin and Ether, nonfungible tokens, and payment rights embedded in electronic records. Article 12 calls these digital assets "controllable electronic records." Amended 12–102(a)(1). The definition of the term is broad enough to include digital assets created using a distributed ledger or future technology.

To increase the liquidity of digital assets, the 2022 Amendments make them negotiable under prescribed conditions. This allows a purchaser of a controllable electronic record to take free of competing claims to it. 12–104(a), (e). To accommodate technological developments in electronic commerce relating to chattel paper, payments systems, investment property, negotiable instruments and electronic documents of title, the amendments make changes to almost all the Articles of the UCC. Finally, the 2022 Amendments in a few instances take the opportunity to clarify UCC provisions unrelated to digital assets (e.g., 2–102, 2–106) or overrule judicial mistakes in their interpretation (e.g., Amended 9–102(a)(7)(A), 9–204(c)). For a summary of the 2022

Amendments, see Uniform Law Commission, A Summary of the 2022
Amendments to the Uniform Commercial Code (July 21, 2022).

The 2022 Amendments revise Article 9 to facilitate the taking of
security interests in digital assets. They do so primarily by aligning
Article 12's rules governing the purchase (which includes security
interests) of controllable electronic records with Article 9's existing rules
governing security interests. Basically, its rules governing property and
priority rights in personal property generally, and their enforcement, are
adapted to certain digital assets.

Coordinating amendments to Article 9 create three new
classifications of collateral: "controllable electronic records" (Amended
12–102(a)(1); 9–102(b)), "controllable accounts" (Amended 9–
102(a)(27)(A)) and "controllable payment intangibles" (9–102(a)(27B)).
To leave undisturbed existing collateral descriptions, controllable
electronic records count as "general intangibles" (9–102(a)(42)),
controllable accounts count as "accounts" (9–102(a)(3)), and controllable
payment intangibles count as "payment intangibles" (9–102(a)(61)). The
amendments permit the perfection of security interests in these digital
assets by control or filing. "Control" with respect to covered digital assets
(12–105, 9–107A), is the counterpart for intangible assets to possession
of tangible assets. The amendments give priority to the secured party
with a security interest perfected by control over a secured party with a
security interest perfected by filing (9–326). In addition, Article 1 (1–
201(b)(24)) clarifies that, excluding preexisting digital currency, "money"
includes governmentally created or recognized electronic currency.
Under the amendments to Article 9, a security interest in "electronic
money" (9–102(a)(31A) can only be perfected by control (9–312(b)(4)).
This Chapter as well as Chapters 3 and 8 discuss Article 9's treatment of
digital assets in more detail.

C. ATTACHMENT

1. THE SECURITY AGREEMENT

A security interest gives the secured party a property right in
personal property. However, Article 9 does not speak of a party acquiring
a "property right;" instead, it refers to a security interest "attaching."
Article 9 makes creating a security interest easy. Under 9–203(a), a
security interest attaches when it becomes enforceable against the
debtor. The security interest in turn is enforceable against the debtor
under 9–203(b) when the secured party gives value, the debtor has rights
in the collateral or the power to transfer rights in the collateral, and one
of the disjunctive conditions of 9–203(b)(3) is met. The first of 9–
203(b)(3)'s conditions, which applies in the great majority of cases, is that
the debtor has signed a security agreement that provides a description of
the collateral. 9–203(b)(3)(A). "Security agreement" means an agreement
that creates or provides for a security interest. 9–102(a)(74). To "sign"

includes both a written signature and an electronic signature; see Amended 1–201(b)(37)(A)–(B). These are simple, common sense requirements. In the usual case, the secured party gives value either by making a loan or a credit sale to the debtor. The debtor meets the rights-in-collateral requirement because it owns the collateral. And the debtor signs a security agreement that grants to the secured party a security interest in designated collateral.

Article 9 recognizes that business transactions have become national or even international and that persons can do business with each other at a distance swiftly only by electronic communications. Hence, Article 9 is medium-neutral, and the term "record" replaces the terms "writing" and "written" in former Article 9. "Record" includes information in a tangible form such as on paper as well as information in an intangible form that is stored in an electronic or other medium and is "retrievable in perceivable form." 9–102(a)(70). Comment 9a to 9–102 explains that "record" may include "magnetic media, optical discs, digital voice messaging systems, electronic mail, audio tapes, and photographic media, as well as paper."

Before the 2022 Amendments, 9–203(b)(3)(A) required that the debtor authenticate the security agreement. "Authenticate" in turn was defined to include both written and electronic signatures. Amended 9–203(b)(3)(A) replaces the requirement that a security agreement be "authenticated" by the debtor with the requirement that the debtor "sign" the security agreement. As part of the Amendments, the definition of "sign" is expanded to include both written and electronic signatures; Amended 1–201(b)(37)(A)–(B) ("with the present intent to "(A) execute or adopt a tangible symbol; or (B) attach to or logically associate with the record an electronic symbol, sound, or process"). Thus, if the security agreement is written on paper, the debtor signs the writing by adding its signature; if the security agreement is stored in an electronic medium, the debtor signs the record by adding its electronic signature.

PROBLEMS

1.   Patrick, a Chicago businessman, finds himself in negotiations in New York to purchase goods at a favorable price. He can close the deal only by wiring $100,000 to Seller's deposit account in New York Bank (NYB) by the end of the business day. Patrick does not have enough money in his account in Chicago Bank (CB) to make the funds transfer. Although he has borrowed money in the past from that bank, he has no present line of credit outstanding. However, during an extended telephone conversation, Patrick and CB agree that CB will wire the requested funds and, in order to secure the debt, Patrick grants CB a security interest in certain described personal property that he owns. The terms of the loan and security agreement are discussed in detail. CB sends the funds by Fedwire and they are received by NYB and deposited in Seller's account by the end of the day.

(a) Does CB have an enforceable security interest in Patrick's personal property? See Comment 9a to 9–102.

(b) Would CB have an enforceable security interest if it had tape recorded the telephone call in its entirety with Patrick's consent? Would the result change if CB destroyed the recorded tapes after six months?

2. Assume the facts in Problem 1. At the end of their negotiations when agreement had been reached, CB sent a confirmatory e-mail to Patrick's New York hotel room that accurately recited the terms that the parties had orally agreed to. This communication concluded by stating that if Patrick agreed to these terms he should indicate his consent by return e-mail. Patrick immediately replied by e-mail: "I agree to the terms set out in your message. Patrick." Does CB have an enforceable security interest? Would the result change if Patrick's reply did not add his name?

3. Anabel has fallen on hard times and needs money quickly. She has an engagement ring valued at $5,000, all that is left from her disastrous, now-dissolved marriage. Uncle is rich but not generous and when he reluctantly advanced her $3,000, he required that she give him possession of the ring until her debt to him, evidenced by a written promissory note signed by Anabel and due a year later, is paid. Except for the promissory note, which said nothing about a secured interest in the ring, the agreement was entirely oral. Does Uncle have an enforceable security interest in the ring under 9–203(b)(3)(B)? See Comment 4 to 9–203.

2. THE COMPOSITE DOCUMENT RULE

However easy it is to create a security interest, the parties continue to make mistakes of the kind discussed by the case below. Their mistakes can be fatal to the security interest in bankruptcy. In reading the case below, be sure you understand why the bankruptcy court concluded that the note and financing statement, taken together, were not intended to be the security agreement. This opinion is generally considered to contain the classic statement of the composite document rule. The case was decided under former 9–203(1)(b); the provision corresponds to 9–203(b)(3)(A) of the current version of Article 9. Most jurisdictions accept some version of the rule, and revisions to Article 9 make no changes that would affect it.

In re Bollinger Corp.
United States Court of Appeals, Third Circuit, 1980
614 F.2d 924

■ ROSENN, CIRCUIT JUDGE.

This appeal from a district court review of an order in bankruptcy presents a question that has troubled courts since the enactment of Article Nine of the Uniform Commercial Code (U.C.C.) governing secured transactions. Can a creditor assert a secured claim against the debtor when no formal security agreement was ever signed, but where various documents executed in connection with a loan evince an intent to create a security interest? The district court answered this question in the affirmative and permitted the creditor, Zimmerman and Jansen, to assert a secured claim against the debtor, bankrupt Bollinger Corporation in the amount of $150,000. We affirm.

I

The facts of this case are not in dispute. Industrial Credit Company (ICC) made a loan to Bollinger Corporation (Bollinger) on January 13, 1972, in the amount of $150,000. As evidence of the loan, Bollinger executed a promissory note in the sum of $150,000 and signed a security agreement with ICC giving it a security interest in certain machinery and equipment. ICC in due course perfected its security interest in the collateral by filing a financing statement in accordance with Pennsylvania's enactment of Article Nine of the U.C.C.

Bollinger faithfully met its obligations under the note and by December 4, 1974, had repaid $85,000 of the loan leaving $65,000 in unpaid principal. Bollinger, however, required additional capital and on December 5, 1974, entered into a loan agreement with Zimmerman & Jansen, Inc. (Z & J), by which Z & J agreed to lend Bollinger $150,000. Z & J undertook as part of this transaction to pay off the $65,000 still owed to ICC in return for an assignment by ICC to Z & J of the original note and security agreement between Bollinger and ICC. Bollinger executed a promissory note to Z & J, evidencing the agreement containing the following provision:

> *Security.* This Promissory Note is secured by security interests in a certain Security Agreement between Bollinger and Industrial Credit Company. . .and in a Financing Statement filed by [ICC]. . .and is further secured by security interests in a certain security agreement to be delivered by Bollinger to Z & J with this Promissory Note covering the identical machinery and equipment as identified in the ICC Agreement and with identical schedule attached in the principal amount of Eighty-Five Thousand Dollars. ($85,000).

No formal security agreement was ever executed between Bollinger and Z & J. Z & J did, however, in connection with the promissory note, record a new financing statement signed by Bollinger containing a detailed list of the machinery and equipment originally taken as collateral by ICC for its loan to Bollinger.

Bollinger filed a petition for an arrangement under Chapter XI of the Bankruptcy Act in March, 1975 and was adjudicated bankrupt one year later. In administrating the bankrupt's estate, the receiver sold some of Bollinger's equipment but agreed that Z & J would receive a $10,000 credit on its secured claim.

Z & J asserted a secured claim against the bankrupt in the amount of $150,000, arguing that although it never signed a security agreement with Bollinger, the parties had intended that a security interest in the sum of $150,000 be created to protect the loan. The trustee in bankruptcy conceded that the assignment to Z & J of ICC's original security agreement with Bollinger gave Z & J a secured claim in the amount of $65,000, the balance owed by Bollinger to ICC at the time of the assignment. The trustee, however, refused to recognize Z & J's asserted claim of an additional secured claim of $85,000 because of the absence of a security agreement between Bollinger and Z & J. The bankruptcy court agreed and entered judgment for Z & J in the amount of $55,000, representing a secured claim in the amount of $65,000 less $10,000 credit received by Z & J.

Z & J appealed to the United States District Court for the Western District of Pennsylvania, which reversed the bankruptcy court and entered judgment for Z & J in the full amount of the asserted $150,000 secured claim. The trustee in bankruptcy appeals.

II

Under Article Nine of the U.C.C., two documents are generally required to create a perfected security interest in a debtor's collateral. First, there must be a "security agreement" giving the creditor an interest in the collateral. Section 9–203(1)(b) [9–203(b)(3)(A)] contains minimal requirements for the creation of a security agreement. In order to create a security agreement, there must be: (1) a writing (2) signed by the debtor (3) containing a description of the collateral or the types of collateral. Section 9–203, Comment 1. The requirements of section 9–203(1)(b) [cf, 9–203(b)(3)(A)] further two basic policies. First, an evidentiary function is served by requiring a signed security agreement and second, a written agreement also obviates any Statute of Frauds problems with the debtor-creditor relationship. *Id.* Comments 3, 5. The second document generally required is a "financing statement," which is a document signed by both parties and filed for public record. The financing statement serves the purpose of giving public notice to other creditors that a security interest is claimed in the debtor's collateral.

Despite the minimal formal requirements set forth in section 9–203 for the creation of a security agreement, the commercial world has frequently neglected to comply with this simple Code provision. Soon after Article Nine's enactment, creditors who had failed to obtain formal security agreements, but who nevertheless had obtained and filed financing statements, sought to enforce secured claims. Under section 9–402, a security agreement may serve as a financing statement if it is signed by both parties. The question arises whether the converse is true: Can a signed financing statement operate as a security agreement? The earliest case to consider this question was American Card Co. v. H.M.H. Co., 97 R.I. 59, 196 A.2d 150, 152 (1963) which held that a financing statement could *not* operate as a security agreement because there was no language *granting* a security interest to a creditor. Although section 9–203(1)(b) [9–203(b)(3)(A)] makes no mention of such a grant language requirement, the court in *American Card* thought that implicit in the definition of "security agreement" under section 9–105(1)(h) [9–102(a)(73)] was such a requirement; some grant language was necessary to "create or provide security." This view also was adopted by the Tenth Circuit in Shelton v. Erwin, 472 F.2d 1118, 1120 (8th Cir.1973). Thus, under the holdings of these cases, the creditor's assertion of a secured claim must fall in the absence of language connoting a grant of a security interest.

The Ninth Circuit in In re Amex-Protein Development Corp., 504 F.2d 1056 (9th Cir.1974), echoed criticism by commentators of the *American Card* rule. The court wrote: "There is no support in legislative history or grammatical logic for the substitution of the word 'grant' for the phrase 'creates or provides for'." *Id.* at 1059–60. It concluded that as long as the financing statement contains a description of the collateral signed by the debtor, the financing statement may serve as the security agreement and the formal requirements of section 9–203(1)(b) [9–203(b)(3)(A)] are met. The tack pursued by the Ninth Circuit is supported by legal commentary on the issue. See G. Gilmore, Security Interests in Personal Property § 11.4 at 347–48 (1965).

Some courts have declined to follow the Ninth Circuit's liberal rule allowing the financing statement alone to stand as the security agreement, but have permitted the financing statement, when read in conjunction with other documents executed by the parties, to satisfy the requirements of section 9–203(1)(b) [9–203(b)(3)(A)]. The court in In re Numeric Corp., 485 F.2d 1328 (1st Cir.1973) held that a financing statement coupled with a board of directors' resolution revealing an intent to create a security interest were sufficient to act as a security agreement. The court concluded from its reading of the Code that there appears no need to insist upon a separate document entitled "security agreement" as a prerequisite for an otherwise valid security interest.

> A writing or writings, regardless of label, which adequately describes the collateral, carries the signature of the debtor, and establishes that in fact a security interest was agreed upon, would satisfy both the formal requirements of the statute and the policies behind it.

Id. At 1331. The court went on to hold that "although a standard form financing statement by itself cannot be considered a security agreement, an adequate agreement can be found when a financing statement is considered together with other documents." *Id.* At 1332. . . .

More recently, the Supreme Court of Maine in Casco Bank and Trust Co. v. Cloutier, 398 A.2d 1224, 1231–32 (Me.1979) considered the question of whether composite documents were sufficient to create a security interest within the terms of the Code. Writing for the court, Justice Wernick allowed a financing statement to be joined with a promissory note for purposes of determining whether the note contained an adequate description of the collateral to create a security agreement.

The court indicated that the evidentiary and Statute of Frauds policies behind section 9–203(1)(b) [9–203(b)(3)(A)] were satisfied by reading the note and financing statement together as the security agreement.

In the case before us, the district court went a step further and held that the promissory note executed by Bollinger in favor of Z & J, standing alone, was sufficient to act as the security agreement between the parties. In so doing, the court implicitly rejected the *American Card* rule requiring grant language before a security agreement arises under section 9–203(1)(b) [9–203(b)(3)(A)]. The parties have not referred to any Pennsylvania state cases on the question and our independent research has failed to uncover any. But although we agree that no formal grant of a security interest need exist before a security agreement arises, we do not think that the promissory note standing alone would be sufficient under Pennsylvania law to act as the security agreement. We believe, however, that the promissory note, read in conjunction with the financing statement duly filed and supported, as it is here, by correspondence during the course of the transaction between the parties, would be sufficient under Pennsylvania law to establish a valid security agreement.[3]

III

We think Pennsylvania courts would accept the logic behind the First and Ninth Circuit rule and reject the *American Card* rule imposing the requirement of a formal grant of a security interest before a security agreement may exist. When the parties have neglected to sign a separate security agreement, it would appear that the better and more practical view is to look at the transaction as a whole in order to determine if there is a writing, or writings, signed by the debtor describing the collateral which demonstrates an intent to create a security interest in the collateral. In connection with Z & J's loan of $150,000 to Bollinger, the relevant writings to be considered are: (1) the promissory note; (2) the financing statement; (3) a group of letters constituting the course of dealing between the parties. The district court focused solely on the promissory note finding it sufficient to constitute the security agreement. Reference, however, to the language in the note reveals that the note standing alone cannot serve as the security agreement. The note recites that along with the assigned 1972 security agreement between Bollinger and ICC, the Z & J loan is "further secured by security interests in a certain Security Agreement *to be delivered* by Bollinger to Z & J with this Promissory Note. . . ." (Emphasis added.) The bankruptcy judge correctly

---

[3]   The district court held alternatively that the assignment of the 1972 security agreement between Bollinger and ICC to Z & J was sufficient to give Z & J a secured claim in the amount of $150,000. The 1972 security agreement contained a "future advances" clause, allowing ICC to use the collateral for its original loan to Bollinger as security for any future sums advanced by it to Bollinger, as permitted by 9–204(3) [9–204(c)]. . . . Although we have serious reservations whether the "future advances" clause was broad enough to encompass a loan made by a third party, we need not consider this alternative theory offered by the district court because we are convinced that the documents executed between Bollinger and Z & J were sufficient to secure Z & J.

reasoned that "[t]he intention to create a separate security agreement negates any inference that the debtor intended that the promissory note constitute the security agreement." At best, the note is some evidence that a security agreement was contemplated by the parties, but by its own terms, plainly indicates that it is not the security agreement.

Looking beyond the promissory note, Z & J did file a financing statement signed by Bollinger containing a detailed list of all the collateral intended to secure the $150,000 loan to Bollinger. The financing statement alone meets the basic section 9–203(1)(b) [9–203(b)(3)(A)] requirements of a writing, signed by the debtor, describing the collateral. However, the financing statement provides only an inferential basis for concluding that the parties intended a security agreement. There would be little reason to file such a detailed financing statement unless the parties intended to create a security interest.[5] The intention of the parties to create a security interest may be gleaned from the expression of future intent to create one in the promissory note and the intention of the parties as expressed in letters constituting their course of dealing.

The promissory note was executed by Bollinger in favor of Z & J in December 1974. Prior to the consummation of the loan, Z & J sent a letter to Bollinger on May 30, 1974, indicating that the loan would be made "provided" Bollinger secured the loan by a mortgage on its machinery and equipment. Bollinger sent a letter to Z & J on September 19, 1974, indicating:

> With your [Z & J's] stated desire to obtain security for material and funds advanced, it would appear that the use of the note would answer both our problems. Since the draft forwarded to you offers full collateralization for the funds to be advanced under it and bears normal interest during its term, it should offer you maximum security.

Subsequent to the execution of the promissory note, Bollinger sent to Z & J a list of the equipment and machinery intended as collateral under the security agreement which was to be, but never was, delivered to Z & J. In November 1975, the parties exchanged letters clarifying whether Bollinger could substitute or replace equipment in the ordinary course of business without Z & J's consent. Such a clarification would not have been necessary had a security interest not been intended by the parties. Finally, a letter of November 18, 1975, from Bollinger to Z & J indicated that "any attempted impairment of the collateral would constitute an event of default."

From the course of dealing between Z & J and Bollinger, we conclude there is sufficient evidence that the parties intended a security

---

[5]   Z & J would not have had to file a financing statement for the $65,000 covered by the 1972 security agreement between ICC and Bollinger, inasmuch as the assignee of a security interest is protected by the assignor's filing. Section 9–302(2) [9–310].

agreement to be created separate from the assigned ICC agreement with Bollinger. All the evidence points towards the intended creation of such an agreement and since the financing statement contains a detailed list of the collateral, signed by Bollinger, we hold that a valid Article Nine security agreement existed under Pennsylvania law between the parties which secured Z & J in the full amount of the loan to Bollinger.

IV

The minimal formal requirements of section 9–203(1)(b) [9–203(b)(3)(A)] were met by the financing statement and the promissory note, and the course of dealing between the parties indicated the intent to create a security interest. The judgment of the district court recognizing Z & J's secured claim in the amount of $150,000 will be affirmed.

NOTES

1.   A gross characterization of the conflict in the decisions regarding the existence of a valid security agreement follows:

The pro-secured-creditor view: The requirement of a written security agreement is merely evidentiary. If the creditor advances money to a debtor, the debtor signs a promissory note and the financing statement describes the collateral, this is enough to show intent to create a security interest; no additional formal security agreement is needed. Why else would the parties have done this unless they were entering into a secured transaction? *American Card* and its ilk are throwbacks to rigid, formalistic pre-Code thinking. *Bollinger* recognizes the clear intent of the parties even though the creditor was a little careless.

The pro-trustee-in-bankruptcy view: The secured creditor has a very strong position against other creditors in bankruptcy. Recognition of the security interest may clean out the bankrupt's estate, leaving nothing for others. Since the Article 9 requirements for creating an enforceable security agreement are so minimal and the benefits conferred by secured creditor status are so great, we should demand that the creditor who seeks these benefits must comply fully with these simple requirements. *American Card* merely requires that the writing contain some words unequivocally granting a security interest to the creditor. *Bollinger* is wrong in protecting the negligent creditor by finding a security agreement when the promissory note stated that a security agreement would subsequently be delivered to the debtor and none was. Why protect a negligent creditor at the expense of others?

Most courts have adopted the pro-secured-creditor view as indicated in the authorities cited in *Bollinger*. See 4 James J. White & Robert S. Summers, Uniform Commercial Code § 31–3 (6th Prac. ed. 2010).

2.   Under state law, notation of a lien on a vehicle's certificates of title is the exclusive manner by which a security interest is perfected in motor vehicles. But in order for a lender to create a valid security interest in vehicles there must in addition be a security agreement complying with 9–

203(b)(3)(A)'s requirement that the debtor "has signed a security agreement that provides a description of the collateral. . ." In In re Giaimo, 440 B.R. 761 (6th Cir. B.A.P.2010), all the lender could show for a security agreement was the debtor's application for a certificate of title and the certificate of title itself. The court, adopting the composite document view, stated: "We therefore hold that the Debtor's application for certificate of title and the certificate of title indicate that the parties intended to create a security interest and that the written application for certificate of title constitutes a security agreement within the meaning of. . . 9–203. To find otherwise would place undue emphasis on formalism and be contrary to the general principle that the UCC be 'liberally construed and applied to promote [its] underlying purposes and policies[,]' including simplification and modernization of 'the law governing commercial transactions.' " 440 B.R. at 771. The court cites a number of cases supporting its view. Its view is not uniformly shared. Against *Giaimo* is In re Buttke, 2012 WL 529241 (Bankr. D.S.D.2012), which ruled that a certificate of title and certificate of title application, taken together, do not create or provide for a security interest.

PROBLEMS

1. Debtor's security agreement granted Bank a security interest in specified collateral to secure a promissory note dated December 13, 2008. The note referred to in fact was dated and signed on December 15, 2008. When Debtor filed for bankruptcy, Bank claimed that the December 15 note was secured. Among other arguments, Bank contended that the composite document rule allowed it to add the December 15 note to correct the erroneously dated note in the written security agreement. Against this Debtor's bankruptcy trustee contended that the security agreement secured only the nonexistent December 13, 2008 note. Both Bank and Debtor acknowledged that the written security agreement contained a mistaken date and that it was intended to cover the December 15, 2008 note. The facts are based on In re Duckworth, 776 F.3d 453 (7th Cir. 2014). The *Duckworth* court ruled that the composite document rule applied only between Debtor and Bank. It was inapplicable against Debtor's bankruptcy trustee. The rule therefore could not be used to correct an error in the description of the secured debt in the written security agreement. See id. at 457 n.2. Can you reconcile *Duckworth* with *Bollinger*?

2. Store wishes to take security interests in goods purchased by customers using its charge card. When Store issues a charge card to a customer, it includes a copy of a detailed security agreement that purports to grant Store a security interest in goods purchased by customers using Store's charge card. Upon making a purchase by use of the charge card, the customer signs a sales slip that recites: "Purchased under my Store account and security agreement, incorporated by reference. I grant Store a security interest in this merchandise until paid." The sales slip describes the merchandise and is signed by the customer. In litigation about the effect of this transaction, customers have contended that since they never signed the detailed security agreement sent out by Store, there is no enforceable security interest in the goods they have purchased. Does Store have an enforceable security interest in goods purchased pursuant to their charge cards? Do the terms of its security agreement include those in the master agreement? See Sears, Roebuck & Co. v. Conry, 748 N.E.2d 1248 (Ill. Ct. App.2001).

3. DESCRIPTION OF COLLATERAL

Article 9's rules for describing collateral are very forgiving; they offer secured parties a great deal of latitude. For a security interest to be enforceable under 9–203(b)(3)(A), the security agreement must describe the collateral. This requirement makes sense. Because the security agreement defines the security interest, it must identify the assets subject to the security interest. In addition, the description of the collateral in the security agreement provides evidence that specific assets are subject to a security interest. The evidence is useful in determining the debtor's assets against which the secured party can enforce its security interest as well as in settling conflicting claims to the debtor's assets.

Section 9–108 takes a fairly relaxed view of the descriptions that suffice to identify the collateral. Under 9–108(a), a description is sufficient if it merely "reasonably identifies what is described." Section 9–108(b) in turn provides that a description of collateral reasonably identifies the collateral if it does so either specifically, or by category, type (with certain exceptions), or "any other method, if the identity of the collateral is objectively determinable." 9–108(b)(6). Comment 2 to 9–108 states that the test of sufficiency for a description is whether it "make[s] possible the identification of the collateral described." Taking this Comment and the "objectively determinable" test of 9–108(b)(6) together, they state a pliant rule that a description is sufficient if the secured party can show that a reasonable person could identify the collateral from the description given.

Sections 9–108(b)(2) and (3) approve generic descriptions of collateral by "category" or "a type of collateral defined in" the UCC. There is no indication of what is intended by the term "category," but "type" of collateral means the types defined in 9–102(a). Section 9–102(a) defines an array of types and subtypes of collateral. The defined types of collateral are accounts, chattel paper, commercial tort claims, deposit accounts, documents, general intangibles, goods, instruments, investment property, letter-of-credit rights, and money. Section 9–102(a) also defines subtypes of some of these classifications of collateral. Goods, for instance, are subdivided into consumer goods, equipment, farm products and inventory. General intangibles include payment intangibles and software. Some of 9–102(a)'s defined subtypes of collateral reflect the increasing presence of electronic forms of certain types of collateral. So, for example, chattel paper includes both tangible and electronic chattel paper, and documents includes both tangible and electronic documents.

To accommodate the rise in digital assets, the 2022 Amendments add four subtypes of collateral to 9–102(a)'s definitions: "controllable electronic record," a "controllable account," "controllable payment intangible," and "electronic money." A controllable electronic record is a record in electronic form that is subject to control. Amended 12–102(a)(1). Controllable accounts and controllable payment intangibles are specific sorts of electronic payment rights. A controllable account is an account evidenced by an electronic record in which the account debtor undertakes to pay the person in control of the electronic record. Amended 9–102(a)(27)(A). A controllable payment intangible is a payment intangible evidenced by a controllable electronic record in which the account debtor undertakes to pay the person in control of the electronic record. 9–102(a)(25)(A). Controllable electronic records and controllable payment intangibles are subtypes of general intangibles, while controllable accounts are subtypes of accounts. 9–102(a)(3), (42). Unsurprisingly, electronic money is a subtype of money. 9–102(a)(31)(A). Money is currency authorized or adopted by a government—what is often called fiat currency. 1–201(b)(24). Electronic money is virtual fiat currency.

Some controllable electronic records have intrinsic value. Their worth derives from being a medium of exchange and unit of value, or from the value of data in the record. Cryptocurrencies are examples of the former, and nonfungible tokens are examples of the latter. There are no persons obligated on a controllable electronic record, and its value does not derive from evidencing such obligations. By contrast, controllable accounts and controllable payment intangibles evidence the payment obligations of a person. They have value in virtue of the payment obligations they evidence.

Because "controllable electronic record," "controllable account," and "controllable payment intangible" and "electronic money" fall under their respective types, a collateral description by type also describes collateral that falls under the associated subtype. Thus, a practical effect of these newly defined subtypes is to leave undisturbed collateral descriptions in existing security agreements. For instance, a description "all general intangibles" reasonably identifies controllable electronic records as collateral, as the latter is a subtype of general intangibles. Similarly, "all money" reasonably identifies electronic money as collateral, as electronic money is a subtype of money.

The 2022 Amendments create slightly complicated relations between the three defined terms classifying digital assets: "controllable electronic record," "controllable account," and "controllable payment intangible." "Controllable payment intangible" and "controllable account" are mutually exclusive classifications. "Controllable payment intangible" is a subtype of "payment intangible" 9–102(a)(61), and "controllable account" is a subtype of "account" 9–102(a)(3). Thus, because "controllable payment intangible" is a subtype of "payment intangible," which itself is a subtype of "general intangible" 9–102(a)(42), "controllable payment intangible" is a subtype of "general intangible." "Account" and "general intangible" are mutually exclusive classifications 9–102(a)(42) ("any personal property . . . other than accounts . . ."). Thus, because "controllable account" is a subtype of "account," it is not a "general intangible." Finally, "controllable electronic record" is neither a "controllable payment intangible" nor a "controllable account" (12–102(a)(1)). It is a subtype of "general intangible." 9–102(a)(42). Nonfungible tokens and Bitcoins are examples of a controllable electronic record. In sum, the above relations between classifications looks like this:

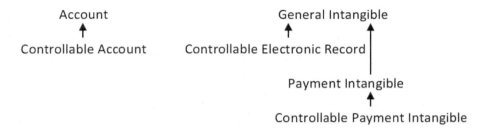

The use of types of collateral for a collateral description is very common in security agreements covering a broad spectrum of a debtor's property. However, 9–108(e) provides that the use of a description only by type is insufficient with respect to commercial tort claims, consumer goods, security entitlements, securities accounts and commodity accounts. The concern is that without a more specific definition, debtors might encumber this property inadvertently. Consumers can't be expected to know what these generic terms include, and the scope of commercial tort claims is probably pretty uncertain to most people.

Descriptions that are generic in nature, such as the subtypes of collateral defined in the UCC (e.g., inventory, accounts, equipment), can be acceptable descriptions under 9–108(b) only if they reasonably identify the collateral. "All equipment" might suffice, even though "equipment" alone might not. A familiar belt-and-suspender's approach is: "all equipment of Debtor, including but not limited to the following: [specific enumeration follows]." Even broader than the use of "types" is the acceptance of "categories," with no indication of what is intended. As illustrated in *Hintze*, reproduced below, 9–108(c) rules out the use of "supergeneric" descriptions, such as "all the debtor's personal property." In contrast, as noted later, 9–504(2) approves a description of collateral in a financing statement if it "covers all assets or all personal property."

There is no convincing justification for banning the use of supergeneric descriptions in the security agreement. To be sure, security agreements and financing statements perform different functions. The security agreement is a bargain between debtor and creditor. Comment 3 to 9–203 states that this agreement must meet evidentiary requirements "in the nature of a Statute of Frauds." A description of the collateral in the record evidencing the agreement reduces proof costs associated with establishing the terms of the parties' agreement. But supergeneric descriptions reliably identify the assets covered by the security agreement. A supergeneric description, such as "all assets of the debtor," provides at least as much evidence that particular assets are covered by the security agreement as a description of the assets by type, such as "all equipment of the debtor," or by category, such as "all crops." Supergeneric descriptions therefore reduce the cost of establishing the scope of the security agreement at least as much as descriptions by type or category.

Section 9–108(c) disagrees with this view. It is not clear why. The function of the financing statement is to put third parties on notice about the possibility of a security interest granted by the debtor to a creditor and to establish priority. The description of collateral in that record serves part of the notice and priority function in ways discussed below. For this purpose, supergeneric descriptions are adequate, as in 9–504(2). Granted, the purpose of the security agreement is not to provide notice to third parties or establish priority. But it is not apparent why a supergeneric description cannot serve both to reduce proof costs and provide notice and contribute to establishing priority. Why would a supergeneric description be adequate for notice or priority purposes but inadequate to reduce the proof costs of establishing the terms of the security agreement? Article 9 has no good answer. Comment 2 to 9–109 merely notes that 9–108(c) follows prevailing case law on the matter.

The requirement of a more specific description of collateral in the security agreement can serve functions other than reducing proof costs. An additional function might be to induce creditors to disclose information to their debtors about the precise nature of the assets the security agreement is to cover where debtors otherwise would remain ignorant. Section 9–108(e) acknowledges this disclosure function by refusing to recognize generic descriptions of certain sorts of collateral, such as commercial tort claims and consumer goods. Section 9–108(c) also could have a similar disclosure function. However, a concern with uninformed debtors might be a reason for refusing to give effect to supergeneric descriptions in specific sorts of security agreements. But this concern isn't a reason for a blanket ban on their use to describe collateral in all security agreements. More generally, it is not apparent that the benefits resulting from the ban offset the increased costs 9–108(c)'s ban imposes on both informed and uninformed debtors. In sum, it is not at all obvious that the case against allowing supergeneric collateral descriptions in the security agreement is compelling.

In re Hintze

United States Bankruptcy Court, N. D. Florida, 2015
525 B.R. 780

■ **Opinion by:** KAREN K. SPECIE.

THIS MATTER came before the Court for hearing on November 4, 2014, on the Plaintiff's Motion for Summary Judgment and Defendant's Opposition to the Motion. Having reviewed the pleadings and heard argument of counsel, the Court finds that no material issues of fact remain and that the Plaintiff is entitled to Summary Judgment in her favor as a matter of law.

Factual History

The material facts are not in dispute. Matthew Bruce Hintze and Larina K. Hintze (the "Debtors") delivered a promissory note in the principal amount of $375,000 to Christopher James, the Defendant, on November 10, 2010. The promissory note included the following language: "As security for the payment of the principal, interest and other sums due under this Note, Maker hereby grants to Holder a security interest in all of Maker's assets." About nineteen months later, on June 11, 2012, a UCC-1 Financing Statement was recorded with the Florida Secretary of State listing the Defendant as the secured party and the Debtors as the obligors. The financing statement described the collateral as: "All personal property owned by the Debtors, including cash or cash equivalents, stocks, bonds, mutual funds, certificates of deposit, household goods and furnishings, automobiles, and watercraft."

The Debtors filed their Chapter 7 petition on November 1, 2012. Before filing bankruptcy one of the Debtors, Matthew Hintze, was the Managing Member and owner of a business called TutoringZone, LC ("TZ I"). By agreement effective as of June 4, 2012, TZ I transferred its intellectual property to TutoringZone II, LLC ("TZ II"), an entity formed, and apparently owned, by the Defendant.

The Debtors listed the Defendant on their Schedule D as a secured creditor with a "UCC-1—Security Interest" on "[a]ll personal property of the Debtors." On their Amended Schedule B, in answer to question 13 they listed, among other things, "100% interest in TutoringZone, LC" as an asset. In September of 2013 the Trustee, here the Plaintiff, filed and served a notice of intent to sell the "[n]on-exempt equity" in "Debtors' 100% membership interest in TutoringZone, LC" for $10,000.00. Claiming a perfected security interest in this asset, the Defendant objected to the proposed sale and demanded the right to credit bid; he further complained that the Trustee had improperly rejected his $25,000 credit bid. In response, the Trustee objected to the Defendant's proof of claim. After the Defendant moved to strike the objection, claiming that the Trustee could only attempt to invalidate his security interest via an adversary proceeding, the Plaintiff commenced this action.

The Plaintiff requests summary judgment declaring that the Defendant does not have a valid security interest in the Debtors' assets, including the 100% membership interest in TZ I. She alleges that under Florida law the collateral description of "all of Maker's assets" is legally insufficient to have created a security interest. The Defendant's response is that summary judgment is not appropriate because the intent of the parties governs, insisting that the Court must take parol evidence on the meaning of this collateral description. The Defendant also argues that the Plaintiff has stepped into the Debtors' shoes for purposes of this adversary proceeding, and so therefore has waived her right to challenge the validity of the security interest or, alternatively, is estopped from doing so.

Summary Judgment Standard

Summary judgment is governed by Federal Rule of Civil Procedure 56, made applicable by Federal Rule of Bankruptcy Procedure 7056. A court may grant summary judgment where "there is no genuine dispute as to any material fact and the movant is entitled to judgment as a matter of law." Fed. R. Civ. P. 56(c). The moving party has the burden of establishing the right to summary judgment. . . .

The undisputed facts in this case show that the Defendant does not have, and has never had, a valid security interest in the Debtors' assets. The Defendant has not proven that his affirmative defenses apply to bar summary judgment for the Plaintiff. No material issues of fact remain that might affect this outcome under the governing law.

Statutory Analysis

Under Section 679.2031 of Florida's Uniform Commercial Code ("UCC"), a security interest attaches and is enforceable against the debtor and third parties if 1) the secured party has given value; 2) the debtor has rights in the collateral; and 3) there is an authenticated security agreement that describes the collateral.[1] Florida Statutes § 679.1081 governs sufficiency of descriptions of collateral for creation of a security interest; its requirement is clear: "a description of personal or real property is sufficient, whether or not it is specific, if it *reasonably identifies* what is described." With limited exceptions, a description reasonably identifies the collateral if it contains the UCC's defined categories, quantity, computational or allocational formulas or procedures, or any other method "if the identity of the collateral is *objectively determinable*" [emphasis added]. The combination of Fla. Stat. §§ 679.1081(3) and 679.2031 makes it clear that because the Defendant and Debtors described the collateral as "all of Maker's assets," the promissory note was insufficient to create a security interest in favor of the Defendant that attached and is enforceable against the Debtor or the Plaintiff. Fla. Stat. §§ 679.1081(3) provides:

---

[1] [Ed.—The 2022 Amendment to 9–203(b)(3)(A) requires that the debtor has signed a security agreement describing the collateral.]

A description of collateral as "all the debtor's assets" or "all the debtor's personal property" or using words of similar import does not reasonably identify the collateral for purposes of the security agreement.

The Defendant argues that language in one sentence of Official Comment 2 to Fla. Stat. § 679.1081 should alter this outcome: "The purpose of requiring a description of collateral in a security agreement under Section 9–203 is evidentiary." Focusing on the word "evidentiary," the Defendant asserts that a super-generic description like the one here does not, by itself, render a security agreement invalid or unenforceable. The fallacy of this argument is apparent upon a reading of all of Comment 2, rather than the single sentence selected by the Defendant. Comment 2 to § 679.1081, in its entirety, states:

> The purpose of requiring a description of collateral in a security agreement under Section [679.2031] is evidentiary. The test of sufficiency of a description under this section, as under former Section 9–110, is that the description do the job assigned to it: *make possible the identification of the collateral described* [emphasis added]. This section rejects any requirement that a description is insufficient unless it is exact and detailed (the so-called "serial number" test).

Official Comment 2 serves its purpose, which is to clarify. It does not even imply that a description such as "all of Maker's assets" is sufficient under the UCC, or that such a description makes identification of the collateral possible.

Under § 679.2031, an enforceable security interest is created *only if* all elements are present, including an authenticated security agreement *with a description of the collateral*. If the description is explicitly insufficient under § 679.1081, it is axiomatic that the description cannot meet the requirements of § 679.2031. Because the Defendant does not have an authenticated security agreement with a description of the collateral that is enforceable under Florida's UCC, the third requirement for creation of a security interest is missing. Because no security interest was created, the Defendant has no security interest to enforce.

Parol Evidence

Despite the clarity of Fla. Stat. § 679.1081(3), the Defendant maintains that the first sentence of Official Comment 2 requires this Court to permit him to introduce parol evidence to prove that he and the Debtors intended for him to have a security interest in the Debtors' personal property, including TZ I. He cites a number of cases in support of this argument. But none of those cases involved a super-generic description of collateral. Rather, each case cited by the Defendant involved a collateral description that was sufficient under the UCC's minimal requirements. * * *

. . . None of the cases cited by the Defendant support a ruling that the description "all of Maker's assets" is adequate, nor do they support allowing him to introduce parol evidence to explain what was meant by this description.

A case argued by the Defendant at the hearing, *Ford v. Feldman*, 177 B.R. 374 (Bankr. M.D. 1994), provides no support for allowing Defendant to introduce parol evidence under the facts here. In *Ford v. Feldman*, John Wilson convinced a medical doctor to invest in a joint venture for importing "Tegue" lizard skins from Paraguay, tanning them, and then selling them at a profit; the joint venture business was incorporated and became the debtor. The debtor borrowed money from a third party. In conjunction with that loan the debtor executed a promissory note, security agreement and financing statement; the signed security agreement referenced an exhibit that set forth lot numbers, pack numbers, tanner identification numbers, and the number of skins but did not specify that the skins were Tegue lizard skins. The debtor went out of business, defaulted on its obligations and filed bankruptcy. The bankruptcy trustee challenged the security interest on the basis that the collateral description was insufficient: it did not specify what *type* of lizard skins. The court held that the description was adequate to describe the collateral pledged because it was "without any doubt . . . that all parties to the security agreement . . . knew that the Debtor's one and only asset which was intended to be the collateral were [sic] the Tegue lizard skins."

Unlike here, the collateral description in *Ford v. Feldman* was very detailed, and the loan documents were executed contemporaneously. Against this factual backdrop the bankruptcy court recognized that by requiring an adequate description of collateral the UCC discourages parol evidence:

> [The Florida UCC] provides that for the purpose of the Statute any description of personal property is sufficient, whether or not it is specific, as long as it *reasonably identifies* what is described
>
> . . .
>
> These formal requisites to enforceability are in the nature of a Statute of Frauds. It is designed to document the intent of the parties concerning the creation of the security interest and to *eliminate parol evidence to prove the intent* [emphasis added].

The First Circuit Court of Appeals, analyzing the Massachusetts equivalent of Fla. Stat. § 679.1081, ruled similarly:

> The draftsmen of the UCC ascribed two purposes to [the] requirement [for a formal security agreement]. One purpose was evidentiary, to prevent disputes as to precisely which items of property are covered by a secured interest. . . . The second purpose of the signed-writing requirement is to serve as a

Statute of Frauds, preventing the enforcement of claims based on wholly oral representations.

. . . .

A writing or writings, regardless of label, which *adequately describes the collateral*, carries the signature of the debtor, and establishes that in fact a security interest was agreed upon, would satisfy both the formal requirements of the statute and the policies behind it [emphasis added].

It is difficult, if not impossible, to imagine how an independent third party could ascertain what was to be included in "all of Maker's assets" without parol evidence. Undoubtedly, that is why the UCC discards such a description as insufficient. At minimum, parol evidence would be needed to prove what the "Maker," here the Debtors, owned as of the date the document was signed. This is contrary to the purpose and effect of the UCC. The Defendant seeks to introduce parol evidence to *create*, ex post facto, a legally sufficient description of the collateral, not to clarify what assets were covered by a description that was legally sufficient to begin with. This the Defendant cannot do.

The Composite Document Rule

Defendant argues in the alternative that his security interest is valid and enforceable because the collateral description of "all of Maker's assets" in the promissory note should be read in conjunction with the unsigned financing statement filed more than a year and a half later. Although it is true that under certain circumstances multiple documents may be combined to create a valid security interest under the composite document rule, case law does not support the application of the composite document rule under these facts. * * * The Defendant has cited no case in which a court applied the composite document rule to salvage a super-generic collateral description, or where loan documents were executed more than eighteen months apart. * * *

Conclusion

The description of "all of Maker's assets," in the promissory note, without more, was insufficient to create an enforceable security interest. There is no support for combining that language with a financing statement recorded nineteen months later. Without a sufficient description of the collateral, no valid security interest (or lien) was ever created. Since no lien was created, there is no lien to avoid. The Plaintiffs only course of action was to seek a declaratory judgment, which she did using her status under § 544. The Defendant has not met his burden of proving that the affirmative defenses of estoppel and waiver apply. There being no disputed material issues of law or fact, for the reasons stated it is

ORDERED: Plaintiffs Motion for Summary Judgment is GRANTED.

NOTE

The court maintains that 9–108(c) deems supergeneric descriptions in the security agreement not to reasonably identify the collateral because, without parol evidence, the collateral could not be identified. The explanation is unpersuasive. Once the debtor's personal property is identified, a supergeneric description avoids the need for parol evidence. A third party can easily and reliably identify an item of the debtor's personal property as collateral because all items of its personal property are collateral. It does not require parol evidence to construe which of the debtor's personal property is covered by the security agreement. Even if a supergeneric description required parol evidence for its application, the UCC limits but does not bar its use in other contexts; see, e.g., 2–202. Nothing in Article 9 prevents reliance on parol evidence to construe the scope of the security agreement. Against the court's claim, the use of parol evidence is not contrary to the UCC's purposes.

A more persuasive rationale for 9–108(c)'s ban on supergeneric descriptions is 9–203(b)(3)(A)'s Statute of Frauds requirement. Section 9–203(b)(3)(A)'s requirement that there be a signed security agreement describing the collateral is in the nature of the Statute of Frauds, as Comment 2 to 9–203 notes. Considered together with 9–203(b)(3)(A), 9–108(c) adds that a supergeneric description of collateral in a signed security agreement does not describe the collateral. Section 9–203(b)(3)(A)'s Statute of Frauds requirement is a requirement for the enforceability of a security agreement, not the evidence admissible to prove the terms of the security agreement. Accordingly, a security agreement with a supergeneric description of the collateral is unenforceable. The question as to the evidence that is admissible to prove the terms of the security agreement therefore does not arise.

PROBLEMS

1. Friends Corp. processes and sells feed for farm animals. It stores in warehouses feed for sale along with face masks its employees use in processing feed. An innovator in genetically modified feed, Friends uses its sophisticated microscopes to inspect the genetically modified feed it produces. It also holds patents for genetically modified animal food, several of which have been licensed to other feed producers. Friends is owed royalties on the patents it has licensed. Finally, Friends has in its digital wallet 10 Bitcoins. Friends offers these assets as collateral for a loan.

(a)   Describe the collateral by type and subtype. 9–108(b)(3), 9–102(a), (b), Amended 12–102(a)(1).

(b)   Assume that the debtor is Friends University, which processes animal feed only for purposes of research. Describe the collateral by type and subtype.

2. Debtor provides plumbing services to commercial buildings under long-term service contracts with their owners. It bills the owners semiannually for services provided during the billing period. Debtor maintains a written ledger for small invoice amounts and computer files for larger invoice amounts. The computer files are accessible only with a password for each invoice. To secure a loan from Secured Party, Debtor grants Secured Party a security interest in the amounts due as stated in all its outstanding invoices. Describe Secured Party's collateral by type and subtype? 9–102(a)(3), Amended 12–102(a)(1). Does the collateral include the computer files themselves or the passwords for the computer files? See Comment 5 to 12–104 (Example 2). State the assumptions you are making.

   3.   Debtor leased a store from Landlord. The written lease agreement set rent and provided in relevant part that "Debtor grants to Landlord a security interest in all of its personal property on the leased premises, now owned or hereafter acquired, to secure Debtor's obligation to Landlord pay the rent set." Later, Debtor fails to pay rent due and files for bankruptcy. Debtor's bankruptcy trustee maintains that Landlord does not have a security interest in Debtor's personal property because the language of the lease agreement does not reasonably identify the collateral. Is the trustee correct? Compare In re Wheeler, 410 P.3d 483 (Colo. Ct.App.2013) with In re Gene Express, Inc., 2013 Bankr. LEXIS 1721 (Bankr. E.D.N.C. April 26, 2013).

   4.   The following fact situations are based on two cases that were decided by the same court with opinions by the same judge. He upheld the validity of the collateral description in one case and rejected it in the other. In your view which is the more vulnerable description? Can you distinguish the cases?

   (a)   The security agreement granted a security interest in certain specifically described items, including an International Truck, and contained the following omnibus clause:

> In addition to all the above enumerated items, it is the intention that this mortgage shall cover all chattels, machinery, equipment, tables, chairs, work benches, factory chairs, stools, shelving, cabinets, power lines, switch boxes, control panels, machine parts, motors, pumps, electrical equipment, measuring and calibrating instruments, office supplies, sundries, office furniture, fixtures, and all other items of equipment and fixtures belonging to the mortgagor, whether herein enumerated or not, now at the plant of [Debtor] located at 115–02 15th Ave. College Point, New York, and all chattels, machinery, fixtures, or equipment that may hereafter be brought in or installed in said premises or any new premises of the mortgagor, to replace, substitute for, or in addition to the above mentioned chattels and equipment with the exception of stock in trade.

The issue was whether the omnibus clause covered two Oldsmobile automobiles used in Debtor's business. The clause covered "equipment," defined in 9–102(a)(33). The two automobiles clearly are within the UCC definition. See In re Laminated Veneers Co., Inc., 471 F.2d 1124, 1125 (2d Cir.1973).

   (b)   The security agreement described the collateral as the following:

Items

Machinery, equipment and fixtures; Molds, tools, dies, component parts including specifically the 1×1 two cavity cassette cover and base mold, 2×2 four cavity cassette cover and base mold, One twenty-four cavity roller mold, One sixteen cavity hub mold

Location, etc.

To be located either at the Debtor's plant in North Bergen, New Jersey; and in the case of the molds also at the plants of contractors who may be using said molds in the manufacture of products for the Debtor

The issue was whether the security agreement covered only the specifically described molds or whether it also covered other machinery and tools of the Debtor. If it were held to apply to other machinery and tools, could one identify which articles of machinery and tools were covered? See In re Sarex Corp., 509 F.2d 689 (2d Cir.1975).

4.   AFTER-ACQUIRED COLLATERAL

a.   UNDER 9–204(a)

Under Article 9 a security interest may not only apply to the collateral the debtor owns at the time the security interest is granted but also to later-acquired collateral. Under 9–204(a), no new security agreement is necessary when the collateral is acquired later if the security agreement provides that it applies to after-acquired collateral. In transactions like inventory financing in which goods are sold and replaced, or accounts financing in which accounts are collected and replaced, it is important that the security agreement cover later-acquired inventory or accounts, lest the collateral liquidate over time leaving the secured creditor with a claim only to proceeds. In the usual inventory or accounts financing transactions the description of the collateral will include a phrase like "now owned or hereafter acquired." When the parties have left out after-acquired property clauses in situations like inventory or accounts financing transactions in which it is likely that they intended to include them, the courts have been divided on whether to imply them. The drafters of Article 9 decided to take no position on this issue: "This question is one of contract interpretation and is not susceptible to a statutory rule (other than a rule to the effect that it is a question of contract interpretation). Accordingly, this section contains no reference to descriptions of after-acquired collateral." Comment 3 to 9–108. Hence, case law under former Article is still guiding precedent. The following case inventories the authorities and takes the majority view of the case law on the issue.

In re Filtercorp, Inc.

United States Court of Appeals, Ninth Circuit, 1998
163 F.3d 570

■ SCHWARZER, SENIOR DISTRICT JUDGE.

We must decide whether under Washington law a security agreement that grants an interest in "inventory" or "accounts receivable," without more, presumptively includes after-acquired inventory or accounts receivable. The bankruptcy court and Bankruptcy Appellate Panel (BAP) held that to secure after-acquired property, an express after-acquired property clause is required. We reverse, holding that Washington law would presume security interests in "inventory" and "accounts receivable" to include after-acquired property, absent evidence of intent to the contrary. Applying this rule to the security agreement at issue between Henry Paulman and Filtercorp, Inc., we hold that Paulman had a security interest in after-acquired accounts receivable, but not in after-acquired inventory because the security agreement demonstrated an intent to limit the inventory collateral by referencing an attached inventory listing. * * *

I.   Paulman's Loans to Filtercorp, Inc.

Filtercorp, Inc. was a Washington corporation which developed and distributed carbonated pads used in the food service industry to filter cooking oils. Beginning in November 1991, the company took out a series of loans from Paulman, an individual salesman, to help fund further development and meet large orders. The loans were short term, ranging from two to three months, and memorialized by promissory notes drafted by Paulman's attorney. The final note—the subject of this litigation—was a three-month note, executed on June 30, 1992, and due September 30, 1992.

The June 1992 note provided for the following security:

> This note is secured by 75,000 shares of Filter Corp. [sic] stock owned by Robin Bernard, the accounts receivable and inventory of Filter Corp. [sic] (See UCC-1 filing and attached inventory listing.) and John Gardner personally.

The parties never executed a separate security agreement. However, Paulman perfected his security interest by filing a UCC-1 financing statement on October 5, 1992. The UCC-1 statement identified the collateral as (1) accounts receivable and (2) materials inventory. Despite the note's reference to an inventory listing, none was ever attached to the note or the financing statement.

There is no contemporaneous evidence shedding light on whether the parties intended to secure after-acquired inventory or accounts receivable with the June 1992 note. In the course of this litigation, the parties presented conflicting versions of their intent. Paulman claimed that he and Filtercorp, Inc. understood the security interest to attach to future rather than presently-held inventory and accounts receivable so as not to interfere with the company's ability to raise additional capital. Hence, he did not attach the inventory listing. In contrast, Robin Bernard, President of Filtercorp, Inc., stated that in light of the short, three-month term of the loan he did not contemplate an ongoing security interest. * * *

I.   Summary Judgment Ruling on Paulman's Security Interest
* * *

A.   Principles Governing Security Interests in Inventory and Accounts Receivable

Whether a security agreement creates a lien on particular assets is a question of state law. Because no reported decisions of Washington courts or federal courts interpreting Washington law have answered the question whether a security agreement that grants an interest in "inventory" or "accounts receivable," without more, extends to after-acquired property, we must determine how Washington's highest court would resolve the issue. * * *

Whether security interests in "inventory" presumptively include after-acquired property under Washington law came before us in Stoumbos v. Kilimnik, 988 F.2d 949, 954–56 (9th Cir.1993). We acknowledged the existence of a split of authority on whether a security interest in inventory or receivables automatically extended to after-acquired inventory or receivables despite the absence of an after-acquired property clause, but, on the facts of the case, did not have to decide the issue. See *id.* at 955–56. We now hold that if the issue came before the Washington Supreme Court, it would hold that security interests in "inventory" and "accounts receivable" presumptively include after-acquired inventory and receivables, subject to rebuttal by evidence that the parties intended otherwise.

Courts disagree over what terms are required in a security agreement to cover after-acquired inventory and accounts receivable. A minority of jurisdictions require express language evidencing the parties' intent to cover after-acquired inventory or accounts receivable. See, e.g., In re Middle Atl. Stud Welding Co., 503 F.2d 1133, 1135–36 (3d Cir.1974) (applying Delaware law). . . . These courts view the Uniform Commercial Code provision concerning after-acquired property, U.C.C. § 9–204, as contemplating express after-acquired property clauses. . . . They reason that it is "neither onerous nor unreasonable to require a security agreement to make clear its intended collateral." Middle Atlantic, 503 F.2d at 1136. To do so simplifies the interpretation of security agreements and provides more precise notice to third parties of the extent of a perfected security interest in the debtor's property. See *id.* (noting that a "subsequent lender might expect the parties to make explicit an intention to include this kind of property, both for precision and because of the [pre-U.C.C.] law's historic hostility" to floating liens). In these jurisdictions, a grant of a security interest in "inventory" or "accounts receivable," without more, is insufficient to include after-acquired property.

However, we find more persuasive the contrary position, adopted by the majority of jurisdictions, that a security interest in inventory or accounts receivables presumptively includes an interest in after-acquired inventory or accounts receivables, respectively. . . . The rationale for this position rests on the unique nature of inventory and accounts receivable as "cyclically depleted and replenished assets." Stoumbos, 988 F.2d at 956. . . . Because inventory and accounts receivable are constantly turning over, "no creditor could reasonably agree to be secured by an asset that would vanish in a short time in the normal course of business." Stoumbos, 988 F.2d at 955. . . . Essentially, a floating lien on inventory and accounts receivable is presumed because the collateral is viewed in aggregate as a shifting body of assets. * * *

Commentators support the majority position. See, e.g. Barkley Clark, The Law Of Secured Transactions Under The Uniform Commercial Code ¶ 2.09 [5][b] at 2–98 n. 338 (1993) ("The best rule for the courts is to excuse any reference to after-acquired property in the financing statement, but to draw the line in the security agreement according to real expectations in the commercial world; inventory, accounts, and farm products should not require inclusion of after-acquired property clauses in the security agreement, while equipment or general intangibles should."). . . .

> [T]he majority of courts and commentators reason that the presumption of a floating lien on inventory and accounts receivable is not created by particular language but rather springs from an appreciation of the cyclical nature of the collateral itself. . . .

The presumption that a grant of a security interest in inventory or accounts receivable includes after-acquired property is of course rebuttable. For example, the presumption would be overcome where the security agreement language itself manifests an intent to limit the collateral to specific identified property, where a party presents clear evidence of contemporaneous intent to limit the collateral, or where the debtor can demonstrate that it was engaged in a type of business where the named collateral, whether inventory or receivables, does not regularly turn over so that the rationale for the presumption does not apply. . . .

We conclude that were the issue to come before the Washington Supreme Court, it would hold that after-acquired collateral is presumptively covered by a security agreement referencing "inventory" or "accounts receivable." Because Washington has recognized that "the Uniform Commercial Code was promulgated in order to develop uniformity in commercial transactions," Schroeder v. Fageol Motors, Inc., 86 Wash.2d 256, 544 P.2d 20, 24 (Wash.1975) (en banc), it can be expected to follow the rule adopted by a majority of the jurisdictions that have addressed the issue and that conforms to commercial practice and common sense.

B.   Security Agreement Between Paulman and Filtercorp

Applying the foregoing analysis to the security agreement between Paulman and Filtercorp, we reach different results with respect to accounts receivable and inventory. The note (which serves as the security agreement) states that it was secured by "the accounts receivable and inventory of Filter Corp. [sic] (see UCC-1 filing and attached inventory listing.)." While the presumption that after-acquired property is included stands unrebutted as to accounts receivable, it is rebutted for inventory by the reference to the attached inventory listing.

Under the approach we adopt, the reference to "accounts receivable" presumptively includes after-acquired accounts receivable. The bankruptcy court found the opposing declarations of Paulman and Filtercorp, Inc.'s President as to their contemporaneous intent to be inconclusive. That finding of fact is not clearly erroneous. There is no other evidence of intent in the record. Therefore, we hold that Paulman has a security interest in after-acquired accounts receivable of Filtercorp. That security interest was perfected when Paulman filed a UCC-1 financing statement before other creditors and before Filtercorp filed for bankruptcy.

With respect to the security interest in inventory, the note referenced an "attached inventory listing" which, however, was never attached to either the note or the financing statement. Paulman claims that he did not attach the listing because he agreed with Filtercorp, Inc.'s President Bernard to create a security interest in inventory in general, including after-acquired inventory. Bernard, in contrast, claims that after-acquired inventory was never discussed by the parties prior to entering into the loan agreement and that he did not intend to attach after-acquired property given the short[-]term nature of the loans. The bankruptcy court's finding that this conflicting evidence is inconclusive is not clearly erroneous. Thus, we are left with the language of the note itself.

When, as in this case, a security interest in inventory is described by reference to a list, it suggests an intent to limit the collateral rather than cover inventory as a floating mass including after-acquired inventory. . . . Yet, reference to an attached list does not preclude securing after-acquired collateral when the agreement or the listing demonstrate an intent to do so. . . .

Here, the Paulman-Filtercorp note referenced an inventory listing, which rebuts the presumption that after-acquired inventory is attached, and failed to demonstrate any particular intent to cover after-acquired inventory. The note's ambiguity regarding the security interest in inventory must be construed against Paulman, the drafter of the note. . . . We conclude that Paulman does not have a security interest in after-acquired inventory of Filtercorp.

Accordingly, we reverse the summary judgment with respect to Paulman's lien on accounts receivable, including after-acquired accounts receivable, of Filtercorp, and affirm with respect to his lien on inventory. . . .

b.   SECTION 9–204(b)'S LIMITATIONS

The policy of making it easy for creditors to take security interests in after-acquired property does not extend to consumer goods collateral. In a step toward consumer protection, 9–204(b)(1) provides that an after-acquired property clause is generally not effective with respect to consumer goods, and 9–108(e)(2) bars descriptions of kinds of consumer goods only by types. When a consumer buys a stove from a retailer on secured credit, the retailer's security interest should not extend to consumer goods purchased subsequently. Consumers should not be held to understand the consequences of such a transaction on their future purchases from that retailer. Federal regulations generally prohibit lenders from taking security interests in the consumer's household goods. 16 C.F.R. § 444.2(4).

Under 9–204(b)(2), after-acquired property clauses are also ineffective with respect to commercial tort claims. In Helms v. Certified Packaging Corp., 551 F.3d 675 (7th Cir.2008), Debtor granted a security interest to Lender to secure loans made to Debtor. The collateral described in the security agreement included equipment of Debtor that was subsequently damaged by fire, creating a tort claim. Debtor received a settlement from an insurance broker for business loss it incurred from the fire after the broker negligently failed to include the debtor's plant in the debtor's business loss coverage. Business loss is loss of revenue from Debtor having to shut its plant down, and the claim against the broker for this loss is a commercial tort claim. The question was whether Lender's security interest extended to the proceeds of the settlement. The court held that it did not. The security agreement said that the collateral included "Commercial Tort Claims listed on Schedule B" of the agreement, but Schedule B was blank except for its title "SCHEDULE B: Commercial Tort Claims." Although the claim against the insurance broker was a commercial tort claim, 9–204(b) provides that an after-acquired property clause does not apply. Nor, under 9–108(e)(1), would use of the "type" of collateral, "commercial tort claim," properly describe the specific claims in question. Since an after-acquired property clause would not automatically extend Lender's security interest to cover the damages when they arose, the security agreement authorized Lender to amend the security agreement by adding any specific commercial tort claims when they were acquired. But it failed to do so after Debtor notified Lender of the damage. Thus, the security agreement was not amended to cover the specific tort claims that subsequently arose against the insurance broker.

Lender contended that failure to specify the claims was an innocent mistake that harmed no one. The financing statement included "commercial tort claims," and any third party seeing this would have called Lender and learned of the kinds of claims involved. Judge Posner replied: "Well, that is not true. A prudent potential creditor would have requested a copy of the security agreement because that, and not what an employee of an existing creditor might tell the potential creditor over the phone, is the security interest that the parties to the security agreement had agreed to create. The prudent potential creditor would have read the relevant portion of the agreement, seen that Schedule B was blank, and concluded—and would have been reasonable in concluding—that [Lender] had no security interest in [Debtor's] tort claims." Id. at 680. Would a prudent creditor care about the security agreement or its content even if the creditor has read it? See Chapter 3.B. Why does Article 9 make it so difficult to take a security interest in commercial tort claims? What policy is furthered by the provisions discussed? Should not business creditors know what the term means and be on guard when examining a debtor's financing statement or security agreement containing such a description of collateral?

Commercial tort claims are treated similarly under 9–108(e)(1) and 9–204(b)(2). Section 9–108(e)(1) imposes a heightened description requirement on commercial tort claims as original collateral: a description of the collateral only as a "commercial tort claim" ("only by type") is insufficient. For its part, 9–203(b)(2) in effect requires that commercial tort claims as original collateral be in existence. The latter requirement prevents a security interest from attaching to a commercial tort claim under an after-acquired property clause. Both 9–108(e)(1)'s heightened description requirement and 9–203(b)(2)'s limitation on after-acquired coverage apparently have the same purpose: to protect the commercial debtor from inadvertently encumbering its commercial tort claims with security interests.

The proceeds of a commercial tort claim can fall within an after-acquired property clause. For instance, the settlement of a commercial tort claim constitutes proceeds of the claim. The settlement likely gives the debtor a payment right against the defendant, which also likely creates a payment intangible. 9–102(a)(62). At the same time, a security agreement might cover after-acquired general intangibles, which include payment intangibles. 9–102(a)(42). Does the heightened description requirement and the limitation on after-acquired coverage, which applies to commercial tort claims as original collateral, also apply to proceeds of commercial tort claims that fall within an after-acquired property clause covering collateral other than commercial tort claims? If they do, 9–108(e)(1)'s heightened description requirement and 9–204(b)(2)'s limitation on after-acquired coverage prevent a security interest from attaching to after-acquired payment intangibles (the likely result of settlement of a commercial tort claim).

Some courts have wrongly drawn this conclusion. They have ruled that rights under a tort settlement fall outside the scope of an after-acquired general intangibles clause. See, e.g., In re EPD Investment Co., 2020 WL 6937351 (Bankr. C.D. Cal. Oct. 29, 2020); Bayer CropScience, LLC v. Stearns Bank Nat'l Ass'n, 837 F.3d 911 (8th Cir. 2016). There is no basis in Article 9 for the ruling. By their terms, 9–108(e)(1) only requires additional specificity in the description of collateral, and 9–204(b)(2) limits after-acquired coverage only to collateral ("after-acquired collateral"). Neither provision applies to the proceeds of collateral. Rights under a settlement of a commercial tort claim are general intangibles (likely payment intangibles), not commercial tort claims. Thus, as proceeds of a commercial tort claim, general intangibles are not subject to the enhanced description requirement and the limitation on after-acquired coverage. The 2022 Amendments to 9–204 agree. Amended 9–204(c) overrules cases that have concluded otherwise. Amended 9–204(b.1)(3) in relevant part provides that 9–204(b)'s limitation on after-acquired coverage does not prevent a security interest from attaching to proceeds of a commercial tort claim. For its part, Amended 9–204(b.1)(2) provides that the limitation does not prevent a security interest from attaching to commercial tort claims as proceeds of collateral.

5. VALUE AND RIGHTS IN COLLATERAL

a. VALUE

Under 9–203(b), a security interest does not attach in collateral until value has been given and the debtor has rights in the collateral. In the simple case, the secured party gives value in a loan transaction when it makes the loan, and in credit sales when it makes the sale. This is value under 1–204(4): "any consideration sufficient to support a simple contract." It is also "new value" under 9–102(a)(57) as money, property or new credit given up front. As will become apparent later, new value plays a role in Article 9, e.g., 9–330, but, for the purpose of attachment of a security interest, only the general definition of value in 1–204 is relevant. Under 1–204(2), a creditor gives value by taking a security interest "for, or in total or partial satisfaction of, a preexisting claim." The importance of this provision to the operation of the "floating lien" in inventory and accounts financing is seen in the elementary Problem below.

PROBLEM

Debtor, a wholesale furniture dealer, entered into a revolving credit agreement with Bank, under which Bank made advances to Debtor from time to time, which Debtor used to purchase new inventory. Debtor and Bank concluded a written security agreement, signed by Debtor, in which Debtor granted Bank a security interest in all its inventory and accounts, now owned or thereafter acquired (9–204(a)), to secure all present indebtedness and future advances (9–204(d)). On January 1, Debtor owed Bank $1 million; Bank made no further advances to Debtor. On February 1, Debtor received a shipment of inventory from Manufacturer for which Debtor paid cash. Does Bank have a security interest in the February shipment of furniture that is enforceable against Debtor under 9–203? If so, when did it attach?

b.   RIGHTS IN COLLATERAL

Under 9–203(b)(2), a security interest does not attach unless the debtor has "rights in the collateral or the power to transfer rights in the collateral." As far as the phrase "rights in the collateral" goes, 9–203(b)(2) may be stating only the obvious. The phrase is not defined and it is doubtful if any precise definition is possible. In the usual case, due diligence will show that the debtor owns the collateral outright and there is no issue of rights in collateral. In the fraud case in which the debtor is a thief who stole the collateral, the secured party whose diligence failed to discover the debtor's deception takes the loss.

However, the rights-in-collateral concept goes far beyond the simple full title/no title cases in at least two respects. First, under 9–203(b)(2), a debtor may have rights in collateral in cases in which it has less than the full bundle of ownership rights in the collateral. Comment 6 to 9–203 explains that: "A debtor's limited rights in collateral, short of full ownership, are sufficient for a security interest to attach. . .to whatever rights a debtor may have, broad or limited as those rights may be." For instance, a lessee of personal property doesn't own the leased property but may create a security interest in its valuable rights under the lease. Courts sometimes ask whether the debtor has sufficient rights in the collateral for purposes of 9–203(b)(2). Their inquiry is directed at determining the minimum quantum of rights needed for a security interest to attach. Strictly, this inquiry is unnecessary. A security interest can attach to whatever rights the debtor has in the collateral, however "minimal" those rights might be. The value of the debtor's rights is a separate question, with which 9–203(b)(2)'s rights-in-collateral requirement is not concerned. Second, 9–203(b)(2) goes beyond the rights-in-collateral requirement by allowing a security interest to attach when the debtor has the "power to transfer rights in the collateral to a secured party." As the subsection recognizes, the debtor need not actually have rights in the collateral; it need only have the power to transfer rights. Comment 6 says that this language enables a "debtor to transfer, and a security interest to attach to, greater rights than the debtor has."

Law other than Article 9 creates this power with respect to specific sorts of assets; see 2–403(1), (2) (sale of goods), 3–305, 3–306 (negotiable instruments), 7–502(a) (negotiable document of title), 8–303(b) (investment securities). Article 12 of the UCC enables a person to transfer greater rights than it has in certain electronic payment rights.

Under 12–104(e), a controllable electronic record can be transferred, under prescribed conditions, to a qualified purchaser free of claims or property rights in the controllable electronic record. Section 12–104(a) gives the same power to transfer a controllable account or controllable payment intangible free of claims or property rights in them. This enables a debtor to grant greater rights in a controllable account or controllable payment intangible than it has to a secured creditor, as long as the secured creditor is a qualified purchaser.

For example, assume that the debtor remains in control of a controllable account it previously sold. The debtor grants its secured creditor a security interest in the account. The previous sale leaves the debtor with no rights in the account it can offer as collateral. However, 12–104(a) gives the debtor the power to transfer the controllable account free of the buyer's property right in it. This includes the power to transfer rights in the account to the secured creditor, to which the creditor's security interest can attach, as long as the secured creditor is a qualified purchaser.

Some case law finds that some of the traditional bodies of law mentioned in 1–103(b) give the debtor the power to transfer rights. Section 1–103(b) states that "the principles of law and equity, including the law merchant and the law relative to the capacity to contract, principal and agent, estoppel, fraud, misrepresentation, duress, coercion, mistake, bankruptcy, and other validating or invalidating cause" may supplement the provisions of the UCC. The rights-in-collateral issue is significantly involved in the priority contests treated in Chapter 3, which addresses it further.

The following case involves the application of the rights-in-collateral requirement to a liquor license. State statutes and decisional law differ as to whether a liquor license is personal property or a personal privilege. Compare, e.g., 47 Pa. Stat. Ann. § 4–468(d) (2020) (property as between licensee and third parties) with Ind. Code Ann. § 7.1–3–1–2 (2022) (not property). For Article 9 to govern a secured transaction in a liquor license, the license must be personal property; see 9–109(a)(1). Similarly, a liquor license is classified as a general intangible only if the license is personal property; see 9–102(a)(42). If the license is a personal privilege, the licensee cannot grant a right in the license that is enforceable against the licensor.

The trend in state law is to consider a liquor license to be personal property. However, even if applicable state statute or other law deems the license to be personal property, the debtor-licensee might not have rights in the license in which it can grant a security interest. This is because it is for the state issuing the license to determine whether the debtor-licensee has the rights (or power to) grant a security interest in it. Property rights usually come with restrictions, and a restriction on the transfer of the license can prevent the licensee from creating a security interest in it. In the following case the court had to decide whether

Massachusetts law gave a licensee a limited property right that in the circumstances of the case prevented a security interest from attaching to the license. The Note following the case describes the impact of Article 9's rules on legal restrictions on the assignment of a license, including those of Massachusetts law.

In re Jojo's 10 Rest., LLC

United States Bankruptcy Court for the District of Massachusetts, 2011
455 B.R. 321

■ **Opinion by:** MELVIN S. HOFFMAN

Factual Background

The relevant facts are not in dispute. On May 15, 2009, the debtor and Devin entered into, among other agreements, a commercial lease agreement, an asset purchase agreement, a bill of sale, a promissory note and a pledge agreement by which the debtor leased space and purchased assets in order to operate a restaurant in Devin's building in Maynard, Massachusetts. The equipment sold by Devin to the debtor had been acquired by Devin in connection with a prior restaurant operating at the premises. Devin financed the asset purchase transaction.

Pursuant to the asset purchase agreement, the debtor agreed to pay $285,000 to purchase all of Devin's assets used in the former restaurant including inventory, furniture, fixtures and equipment (the "Physical Assets"). The agreement also provided for the transfer to the debtor of all transferable licenses issued in Devin's name, including the former restaurant's liquor license issued by the town of Maynard.

In accordance with the asset purchase agreement, the parties executed a bill of sale through which the debtor acquired the assets listed on a schedule similar to the one attached to the asset purchase agreement. In payment of a portion of the purchase price, the debtor gave Devin a non-interest bearing promissory note dated May 15, 2009 in the amount of $225,000, payable within sixty months of execution. The promissory note refers to "collateral given to the Lender to secure this Note," thereby indicating that the parties understood that the loan was to be collateralized. The note does not, however, identify specific collateral or contain any language affirmatively granting to Devin a security interest.

The parties signed a pledge agreement whereby the debtor agreed to pledge its liquor license to Devin as security for its obligations under the promissory note. The parties agree that neither party received approval of the pledge in accordance with Mass. Gen. Laws ch. 138, § 23.

Section 5 of the asset purchase agreement, entitled "Security Documents," referring to the promissory note, commercial lease and liquor license, provides that "said Note and Commercial Lease Agreement shall be secured by a standard form UCC Security Agreement and perfected by a standard form UCC Financing Statement [and] a pledge against the Full Beverage Liquor License approved by the Town of Maynard. . . ." No agreement purporting to be a "UCC Security Agreement" or any similarly-titled document was introduced into the record of this case nor has there been any allegation that such an agreement was entered into. Devin prepared a financing statement in accordance with Mass. Gen. Laws ch. 106, the Massachusetts version of the Uniform Commercial Code (the "UCC"), signed by Donna L. Cunningham, the manager of Devin, which contained a rider listing as collateral many of the debtor's assets, including its "licenses, permits and approvals." Devin recorded the financing statement on May 19, 2009 with the secretary of the Commonwealth of Massachusetts. * * *

Position of the Parties

Devin argues that the agreements summarized above, when taken as a whole, served to create a security interest in its favor in those assets listed in the rider to the financing statement, which security interest was duly perfected upon the recording of the financing statement with the secretary of the commonwealth. The trustee argues that the debtor failed to grant Devin a security interest in any of its assets other than the liquor license and that with respect to the liquor license Devin failed to properly perfect its security interest. The trustee asserts his status as a hypothetical lien creditor under Bankruptcy Code § 544 to seek to avoid Devin's security interest.

Applicable Statutes

Bankruptcy Code § 544 endows a trustee with so-called "strong-arm" powers that enable the trustee to avoid certain prepetition liens against property of the debtor. Section 544(a) confers on a trustee the right to seek to avoid any transfer of property or obligation incurred by a debtor that is voidable by the holder of a judicial lien or execution against the debtor or a bona fide purchaser for value of real estate as of the date of case commencement.

The UCC governs the creation of security interests. To be effective, a security interest must have attached to the collateral in question. UCC § 9–308(a). Unless an agreement between the parties provides otherwise, a security interest attaches to collateral only when it becomes enforceable against a debtor with respect to the collateral. § 9–203(a). A security interest in a debtor's assets becomes enforceable when (i) value has been given, (ii) the debtor has rights in the collateral or the power to transfer the rights and (iii) the debtor has authenticated a security agreement that provides a description of the collateral.[1] § 9–203(b). In order for a security interest to have priority over subsequent secured creditors, it must be perfected. § 9–317(a). An attached security interest is perfected

---

[1]   [Ed.—The 2022 amendment of 9–203(b)(3)(A) requires that the debtor has signed the security agreement.]

upon the filing of a financing statement in the appropriate centralized registry. §§ 9–308(a) and 9–310(a).

With respect to the liquor license, Mass. Gen. Laws. ch. 138, § 23 permits a licensee to pledge its interest in the license as collateral for a loan "provided approval of such loan and pledge is given by the local licensing authority and the [Massachusetts Alcoholic Beverage Control Commission (the "ABCC")]."

Discussion

Whether the trustee may avoid Devin's security interest in the debtor's property requires a determination as to whether the security interest is enforceable with respect to the collateral under the three-part test of UCC § 9–203(b). There is no dispute that by loaning money to the debtor, Devin gave value to the debtor in exchange for a security interest in both the Physical Assets and the liquor license, thereby satisfying the first test for enforceability. Applying the remaining tests under § 9–203(b) requires examining the Physical Assets and liquor license separately.

With respect to the Physical Assets, there is no dispute that having acquired those assets by way of the bill of sale, the debtor had sufficient "rights in the collateral" to satisfy the second requirement for enforceability under § 9–203(b). It is the third requirement, for an authenticated security agreement, that underpins the trustee's position that Devin's security interest in the Physical Assets is unenforceable.

The drafters of the UCC included the requirement to authenticate a security agreement to prevent disputes from arising over which assets are intended to serve as collateral. Massachusetts law does not require that an agreement be entitled security agreement as long as it contains a description of the collateral and it evidences an intent to create a security interest in that collateral. In fact, the security agreement may consist of several different documents that "collectively establish an intention to grant a security interest" in the collateral identified in the documents. If one such document lists the collateral to be secured, it must contain some granting language expressing the debtor's intent to create a security interest.

None of the transaction documents in the present case (except the pledge agreement, which applies only to the liquor license) contains language in which the debtor grants a security interest to Devin. The asset purchase agreement and the related bill of sale identify the assets purchased by the debtor, but neither contains a grant of a security interest or indicates which, if any, of those assets are intended to become collateral for Devin's loan. In fact, the asset purchase agreement states that the relevant grant will be by means of a separate security agreement. No such agreement has been produced. The only document in the record that identifies collateral is the financing statement, but it was signed by Devin only and cannot possibly be construed to reflect the debtor's intent to grant a security interest in such collateral. Without an authenticated security agreement, the secured transaction between the debtor and Devin fails the third test for enforceability under § 9–203(b). Accordingly Devin's security interest in the Physical Assets never attached as required by § 9–203(a).

With respect to the pledge of the liquor license, the debtor authenticated the pledge agreement by signing it, thus satisfying the third requirement for enforceability under § 9–203(b). It does not appear, however, that the debtor had sufficient rights in the liquor license to satisfy the second test of the statute. Mass. Gen. Laws. ch. 138, § 23 requires that a debtor must receive approval from both the local licensing authority and the state ABCC before a liquor license may be pledged. In *In re Dalcon*, 120 B.R. 620 (Bankr. D. Mass. 1990), the court held that a debtor must comply with both the UCC and ch. 138, § 23 in order to effectuate an enforceable pledge of a liquor license. The court in *Hillbilly Ranch, Inc. v. Kahn (In re Wible)*, 42 B.R. 622 (Bankr. D. Mass. 1984) determined that the alleged security interest in a liquor license was invalid when the debtor failed to obtain the necessary governmental approvals even though the parties did everything required under the UCC to create and perfect the security interest in the liquor license.

These and other cases on this subject rely on a 1976 amendment to Mass. Gen. Laws ch. 138, § 23. Prior to that amendment, it was accepted that the holder of a liquor license had no property rights in the license. So for example, the state could revoke an outstanding liquor license without violating the licensee's due process rights. The 1976 amendment created a limited property right in favor of a liquor licensee by permitting the licensee to pledge the license as collateral for a loan, but only with the approval of the licensing authorities. Thus a debtor never acquires independent rights in a Massachusetts liquor license for purposes of satisfying UCC § 9–201(b)(ii) unless and until there is a pledge and that pledge has been approved by the required authorities under Mass. Gen. Laws ch. 138, § 23. As the debtor in this case failed to secure the necessary governmental approvals to pledge the liquor license to Devin, it did not acquire "rights in the collateral" within the meaning of § 9–203(b)(ii). Devin's security interest in the liquor license was, therefore, never enforceable against the debtor, and thus did not attach to the collateral. * * *

Conclusion

In light of the foregoing, I will deny Devin's motion for summary judgment and grant in part the trustee's motion for summary judgment determining that Devin has no security interest in the debtor's assets.

NOTE

The court's analysis fails to take into account 9–408 and its impact on Massachusetts law's restriction on the licensee's ability to pledge its liquor license. Massachusetts Gen. Law ch. 126, § 23 allows a licensee to pledge its liquor license only with the approval of the Massachusetts Alcoholic Beverage Control Commission ("Commission"). The court concludes that, because the Commission did not approve the debtor's pledge, the debtor had no rights in the license to which Devin's security interest could attach. However, 9–408(c) provides that a ". . . statute that requires the consent of a . . . governmental body . . . to the . . . creation of a security interest in [a]. . . general intangible, including a . . . license . . . is ineffective to the extent that the . . . statute . . . (1) would impair the creation, attachment or perfection of a security interest." As personal property under Massachusetts law, a liquor license is a general intangible. Section 9–408(c) therefore overrides (renders "ineffective") the requirement of Mass. Gen. Law ch. 126 § 23 that the licensee obtain the Commission's approval for it to pledge its liquor license. Given this override, the debtor would have rights in the license to the extent that it could create a security interest in the license without obtaining the Commission's approval.

Section 9–408(c)'s override is subject to a limitation imposed by 9–408(e). However, the limitation does not apply. Massachusetts' nonuniform version of 9–408(e) provides that except as provided by 9–408(f), which is inapplicable the creation of a security interest, 9–408 "prevails over any inconsistent provision of an existing or future statute, . . . unless the provision is contained in a statute of the commonwealth, refers expressly to [9–408] and states that the provision prevails over [9–408]." Mass. Gen. Law ch. 106, § 9–408(e). Section 9–408(c) is inconsistent with Mass. Gen. Law ch. 126, § 23, as the latter requires the licensee obtain the Commission's approval to pledge a liquor license while the former renders the requirement ineffective. In addition, Massachusetts Gen. Law ch. 126, § 23 does not refer to 9–408. Thus, under Massachusetts' nonuniform version of 9–408(e), 9–408(c)'s override prevails: the requirement that the licensee can pledge its license only with the Commission's approval is ineffective. Accordingly, the debtor therefore had rights in the liquor license to which Devin's security interest could attach. Section 9–408 is discussed in more detail in Chapter 5.E.

PROBLEM

Wholesaler agreed to sell 10 new cars to Drive. Drive paid for the cars by check, which it gave Wholesaler on the date it took delivery of them. The terms of the sale agreement prohibited Drive from selling the cars delivered or giving any interest in them to another person until Drive's bank paid the check. Wholesaler had no reason to know that Drive previously had granted Lender a security interest in its existing and after-acquired inventory of cars. Drive's bank account contained insufficient funds to pay the check, and Wholesaler's bank returned it to Wholesaler. At the time it made its arrangement with Wholesaler, Drive knew that the check would not be honored by its bank. When Wholesaler tried to retrieve the cars it had delivered, Lender claimed a superior right in them. Wholesaler claimed that it is entitled to the cars. What result? See 2–401(2), 2–403(1), 1–201(b)(29), (30); In re Incredible Auto Sales, 62 UCC Rep. Serv.2d 357 (Bankr.

Mont.2007). Could Wholesaler retrieve the cars from a car dealer to which Drive had turned them over as a favor, to increase the dealer's inventory? See 2–403(1), 1–201(b)(29), 1–204. Assume that Wholesaler had not delivered the cars to Drive when Drive's bank refused to honor the check. What result if Wholesaler and Drive's sales agreement provided that a sale occurred only if Drive's bank paid the check? See 1–201(b)(35), 2–106(1), 2–401(1), (2), 9–202

6. ATTACHMENT TO PROCEEDS AND SUPPORTING OBLIGATIONS

Proceeds are discussed in detail elsewhere in this book. For discussion of the security agreement, it is sufficient to make two points. First, Article 9 continues the rule that the description of collateral in the security agreement automatically covers proceeds. Second, 9–102(a)(64) significantly expands the scope of the definition of "proceeds."

The parties to the security agreement presumptively intend it to cover proceeds unless otherwise agreed. Otherwise, the secured party risks losing its security interest if the debtor disposes of the collateral. Article 9 gives effect to this presumed intent. Taken together, 9–203(f) and 9–315(a)(2) provide that a security interest that has attached to collateral automatically attaches to any identifiable proceeds of the collateral. Thus, the description of collateral in a security agreement need not say anything about proceeds. See Comment 8 to 9–203. Although this is entirely clear under Article 9, in many descriptions of collateral that will cross your desk, there will be a specific reference to proceeds. It's easy to do and drafters are always concerned about independent-minded federal courts that may be somewhat selective in their application of state law to bankruptcy.

The definition of proceeds has always been a work in progress: as new issues arise, the definition has been amended to resolve them. Under former Article 9, the term "proceeds" was limited to whatever was received when collateral was "sold, exchanged, collected or otherwise disposed of." "Collected" refers to payments received by the debtor from obligors on accounts or other rights to payment. In other cases, the emphasis on disposition of collateral left many unanswered questions. For example, are insurance proceeds from loss or damage to collateral covered? What about dividends from investment securities? At the time of the original draft of Article 9, equipment and consumer goods leasing were far less popular than they are now, and disputes arose over whether leasing of the collateral was a disposition that gave the secured creditor rights in the rental payments. Similar problems arose with respect to the royalties arising from licensing of intellectual property. A 1994 amendment to Article 9 answered some of these questions, by providing that "proceeds" includes payments or distributions made with respect to investment property collateral (see former 9–306(2)). Dividend distributions, therefore, clearly are proceeds. However, former Article 9's definition still left uncertain the status of insurance, lease and royalty payments.

Section 9–102(a)(64) expands the definition of "proceeds." It broadens the scope of the term in two ways. First, the definition eliminates the former restriction that the debtor receive what is yielded from the disposition of the collateral. Second, it broadens the scope of the term. As under former Article 9, "proceeds" includes what is "acquired upon the sale, lease, license, exchange, or other disposition of collateral." 9–102(a)(64)(A). "Proceeds" also includes cash or stock dividends that are covered by whatever is "distributed on account of, collateral." 9–102(a)(64)(B). Claims arising from loss or damage to the collateral are covered by 9–102(a)(64)(D). Insurance payments arising from such loss or damage are also "proceeds" to the extent of the value of the collateral. 9–102(a)(64)(E); see Steven Walt, When Are Insurance Payments Recoverable Proceeds Under Revised Article 9?, 38 UCC Law J. 159 (2005). The expanded scope of "proceeds" means that the results of dispositions of collateral for which the proceeds status previously was uncertain now are covered by the term.

The definition of "proceeds" has a specific application where proceeds of collateral are used to obtain other assets. For example, suppose the collateral is inventory, which the debtor sells for cash. The debtor in turn uses the cash to purchase more inventory. The question is whether the new inventory purchased with the cash is proceeds of the collateral. The cash is often referred to as first-generation proceeds and the new inventory second-generation proceeds. This terminology reflects former Article 9's definition of "proceeds," which defined the term to include "proceeds of proceeds" (see former 9–306(1)). Under former Article 9's definition, the cash is proceeds of the original inventory and the new inventory, as proceeds of the cash, also is proceeds. Revised Article 9 takes a different approach. It also considers the new inventory to be proceeds, but on a different basis. Section 9–102(a)(12)(A) defines "collateral" to include proceeds. Thus, in the ongoing example, the cash realized from the sale of the original inventory is "proceeds." When the new inventory is purchased with the cash, both the original inventory and the cash are considered "collateral," and the new inventory "proceeds." Thus, as under former Article 9, the final-generation proceeds are considered "proceeds" under 9–102(a)(64). However, earlier generations of proceeds are "collateral" under 9–102(a)(12)(A). Comment 13c to 9–102 recognizes that the final generation proceeds are proceeds and states: "No change in meaning is intended." Note however, an important qualification: security interests in collateral attach only to "identifiable proceeds" (9–315(a)(2)), and, as will be discussed later, identifying proceeds can be problematic.

Section 9–203(f) provides that a security interest that attaches to collateral automatically attaches to obligations supporting the collateral. Thus, Article 9 treats supporting obligations in the same way it treats proceeds. Comment 9 to 9–203 states that the same treatment of supporting obligations was "implicit" under former Article 9. Section 9–203(f) makes that treatment explicit.

To understand supporting obligations and their role in secured transactions, recognize why some sorts of collateral are backed or "supported" by obligations of third parties. Where the value of certain sorts of collateral depends on the financial condition of a person, that person's financial difficulties can diminish the value of the collateral. For instance, where the collateral is an account, the account debtor's financial troubles can leave it unable or willing to honor its payment obligations. This risk affects the value of the account. For other sorts of collateral, such as investment securities, exogenous changes in market conditions can diminish their value. In both instances the value of the collateral is enhanced by the obligations of third parties that support the collateral. This is because the obligations of third parties give the secured party an additional source of repayment. If the debtor defaults and the value of the collateral is impaired, the secured party can obtain payment from the third party whose payment obligation backs the collateral. For instance, guarantees frequently are issued to back account receivables. The guarantees increase the accounts' value because the obligee of the accounts can obtain payment due on the accounts from the guarantor if the account debtors refuse or are unable to pay.

Section 9–102(a)(78)'s definition of "supporting obligation" includes a list of collateral which the obligation can support. Included in that list are accounts, chattel paper and instruments, which give certain payment rights. The value of these payment rights as collateral can vary dramatically depending on the financial condition of the obligors on the receivables. Documents of title and investment property also are included in 9–102(a)(78)'s list of collateral, presumably because their value too can be volatile. Section 9–102(a)(78) defines a "supporting obligation" to mean a letter-of-credit right or secondary obligation, such as a guarantee, which supports an account, chattel paper, document, general intangible, instrument or investment property.

The rationale for 9–203(f)'s rule providing for automatic attachment to supporting obligations is the same as the rationale for 9–315(a)(1)'s rule providing for automatic attachment to proceeds of collateral: the presumed intention of the parties to the security agreement. The secured party prefers and would likely insist that the agreement cover obligations that support certain sorts of collateral. Otherwise, it risks loss if on the debtor's default the value of the collateral is impaired and it cannot obtain payment from the third party whose payment obligation backs the collateral. Section 9–203(f) saves the parties to the security agreement the cost of providing for attachment of the security interest to supporting obligations.

PROBLEMS

1. Debtor pledged stock with Creditor. When Debtor's stock became worthless, Debtor sued the promoters of the stock for security fraud and recovered a sum of money almost equaling the market value of the stock at the time the stock was pledged. Creditor claimed the money as proceeds as a substitute for the stock but Debtor objected on the ground that there was no disposition of the stock. Under the definition of proceeds under former 9–306(1), courts were divided on this issue. Compare McGonigle v. Combs, 968 F.2d 810 (9th Cir.1992) (amount recovered was proceeds), with McDonnold v. Star Bank, N.A., 261 F.3d 478 (6th Cir.2001) (not proceeds). How would this be decided under 9–102(a)(64)?

2. Debtor is the named beneficiary of a letter of credit ("LC1") that undertakes to pay it a fixed sum of money. The issuance of LC1 was unrelated to Debtor's sales activities. Debtor is also owed payment from a number of customers for goods it sold them. Guarantor has agreed to pay Debtor amounts owed it by these customers if they fail to pay Debtor. In order to maintain Debtor's high credit rating, Bank issues a letter of credit ("LC2") undertaking to pay Debtor if Debtor presents to it a certificate stating that its credit customers have failed to pay for their purchases. Debtor grants Creditor a security interest in its right in "all account receivables, existing or hereafter acquired, arising from its sales of goods." Does Creditor's security interest attach to Guarantor's obligation? To Debtor's rights to payment under LC1 and LC2? See 9–102(a)(51), (78), 9–203(f).

CHAPTER 2

PERFECTION

A. INTRODUCTION

If a security interest has "attached," it is enforceable against the debtor (9–203(b)) as well as unsecured creditors (9–201(a)). In general, a secured party's security interest attaches when the secured party has given value, the debtor has rights in the collateral and the debtor has signed a security agreement that provides a description of the collateral. However, for a security interest to have the most favorable status with respect to third party claimants, such as other secured parties, buyers and lien creditors, it must be perfected. "Perfection" is a legal conclusion indicating that a security interest is enforceable against a third party.

It is somewhat misleading to say that a security interest that has attached but has not been perfected is enforceable against unsecured creditors. The statement is true only outside of bankruptcy. In bankruptcy, unperfected security interests can be avoided by the debtor's bankruptcy trustee, who represents the unsecured creditors. As noted in the previous Chapter, under Bankruptcy Code 544(a)(1), the trustee in bankruptcy has the rights of a hypothetical lien creditor and under 9–317(a)(2), an unperfected security interest is generally subordinate to the rights of a lien creditor. If the security interest is avoided in bankruptcy, the former secured party is demoted to the status of an unsecured creditor and must share the assets of the estate pro rata with the other unsecured creditors.

A security interest is perfected if it has attached and, with limited exceptions, public notice of the security interest is given in a prescribed way. See 9–308(a). Sections 9–309 through 9–316 describe methods for perfecting a security interest. These methods are summarized below and discussed in detail in this Chapter.

Section 9–309 sets out the instances in which security interests are automatically perfected when they attach. Public notice of the security interest is not required. For instance, the traditional rule that purchase-money security interests in consumer goods require no filing is continued in 9–309(1). If a retailer retains a security interest in goods sold to a consumer, its unfiled security interest is good as against other secured parties and trustees in bankruptcy, but not against a subsequent consumer who buys the property from the first consumer. 9–320(b). A consumer's purchase at a garage or yard sale is an example.

The oldest form of security interest in personal property is the "pledge," in which the secured party takes possession of the collateral. The traditional rationale of the pledge is that the secured party's possession, which leaves the debtor without possession, gives third parties notice that the pledged assets might be subject to a security interest. Section 9–313(a) states that possession of the collateral by the secured party constitutes perfection with respect to goods, instruments (promissory notes, checks), negotiable tangible documents (bills of lading, warehouse receipts), tangible money (currency) and certificated securities (stocks, bonds). Section 9–313A(a) permits the secured party to perfect its security interest in tangible chattel paper by taking possession. Common to these types of collateral is that they are capable of being possessed. Goods and tangible money are tangible items of collateral. Instruments and tangible chattel paper are rights to payment that are represented by writings whose delivery operates to transfer the rights to payment to another. Tangible negotiable documents are writings that represent rights to goods being shipped or stored. 7–502(a), 9–312(c). Certificated securities represent interests in the issuer or the payment obligations of the issuer. 8–102(a)(15), (16). Both instruments, tangible negotiable documents and certificated securities are semi-intangible items of collateral, and they too can be possessed. Items of collateral such as general intangibles and accounts are not represented by essential writings. As pure intangibles, security interests in them cannot be perfected by possession.

Perfection can be achieved by control for certain types of collateral. In general, "control" is the ability to dispose of collateral unilaterally without the cooperation of the debtor. See Comments 1 and 7 to 8–106. It does not require that the debtor be unable to access the collateral. Control only requires the ability to dispose of the collateral without action by the debtor or its consent. Where perfection by control is permitted for an item of collateral, the means of obtaining control are specifically defined. Control is a permissible method of perfection for letter-of-credit rights, investment property, electronic chattel paper, and deposit accounts. 9–314(a). The 2022 Amendments also permit control as a method of perfection for controllable electronic records, controllable accounts, controllable payment intangibles and electronic money 9–314(a).

For some types of collateral, control is the exclusive method of perfection. For example, under 9–312(b)(2) and (4), the only method of perfecting a security interest in a letter-of-credit right and electronic money is by control. Likewise, under 9–312(b)(1), control is the exclusive method of perfecting a security interest in a deposit account (checking or savings accounts maintained with a bank) as original collateral. "As explained in Section 9–104, 'control' can arise as a result of an agreement among the secured party, debtor, and bank, whereby the bank agrees to comply with instructions of the secured party with respect to disposition of the funds on deposit, even though the debtor retains the right to direct disposition of the funds." Comment 5 to 9–312. But if the funds added to a deposit account are proceeds, a security interest perfected in those proceeds by other means follows into the account to the extent the proceeds are traceable. 9–315.

Section 9–311 provides that security interests subject to other law can be perfected only in compliance with that law; filing under Article 9 is neither necessary nor effective. For instance, security interests in motor vehicles are perfected by notation of the lien on the certificate of title pursuant to the state vehicle code. 9–311(a)(2). Security interests in registered copyrights must be recorded in the Copyright Office in Washington D.C. 9–311(a)(1). Compliance with these laws is the equivalent of filing under Article 9. 9–311(b).

Section 9–310(a) sets out the basic rule that perfection must be by filing a financing statement. Section 9–310(b) enumerates the cases discussed above in which filing is not necessary to perfect a security interest. In most of the cases in which a security interest can be perfected by possession, it can also be perfected by filing. This is true for goods, instruments, negotiable tangible documents, tangible chattel paper, and certificated securities. 9–312(a). But security interests in tangible money can be perfected only by possession, owing to the negotiability of currency. 9–312(b)(3). Under former Article 9 the same was true of instruments but, for the reasons set out in Comment 2 to 9–312, Revised Article 9 allows perfection by filing even though instruments are highly negotiable: purchasers for value who take possession of an instrument without knowledge of a security interest in the instrument usually take free of a security interest perfected by filing. Security interests in accounts and payment intangibles can be perfected only by filing.

Article 9's rules on perfection apply not just to security interests. They also apply to agricultural liens, as defined in Article 9. Unlike security interests, agricultural liens are not created by contract. They instead are created by operation of law. As defined under 9–102(a)(5), an agricultural lien is a nonpossessory statutory lien on farm products securing payment or performance for goods or services provided, or leased real estate, in connection with the debtor's farming operation. Article 9 brings agricultural liens fitting this definition within its scope. 9–109(a)(2). However, it regulates agricultural liens separately from security interests. In addition, Article's 9 regulation of agricultural liens is limited. Its rules on attachment, for instance, do not apply to agricultural liens. Cf. 9–203(b). Nonetheless, agricultural liens are subject to Article 9's perfection rules. Under 9–308(b), an agricultural lien is perfected if it has become effective and 9–310's perfection requirements are met. Non-Article 9 law determines whether an agricultural lien becomes effective. To perfect an agricultural lien, the lienor must file a financing statement. 9–310(a).

The following illustrative Problem presents the sequence of events involved in perfecting a security interest.

PROBLEM

On September 1, Debtor requested a loan from SP. After examining Debtor's financial condition, SP agreed to make the loan. Debtor signed a security agreement on September 3 covering certain described collateral of Debtor. On that date, SP initiated a search of the records in the state filing office, and, when it discovered that no other financing statements were on record, filed its financing statement on September 5 and advanced the requested funds to Debtor on September 6. When did SP's security interest attach? When was SP's security interest perfected? See 9–308(a), 9–502(d). Assume that Debtor purchased an asset on September 6 covered by the collateral description in SP's filed financing statement. When was SP's security interest in it perfected?

B. PERFECTION BY FILING

1. NOTICE FILING

Reform of the filing system was one of the most important contributions of former Article 9 to personal property financing. Before the UCC, filing with respect to chattel mortgage and conditional sale transaction followed the archaic patterns set by real estate mortgage recordings: the chattel mortgage document or the conditional sale contract was recorded in the local county recorder's office. Some state laws required filing of the chattel mortgage document in a different office than the filing of a conditional sale contract. Article 9 changes the document that must be filed, the information required in it, and the place where the document is to be filed. The Article implements a regime under which notice filing and central filing are fully operative. Notice filing means that the only record filed is a financing statement that merely gives notice that a security interest may exist in the debtor's collateral. Turn to 9–521(a) and examine the UCC Financing Statement Form (UCC-1), the written initial financing statement form. The Form UCC–1 (field 4) does not state that the secured party filing the financing statement has a security interest in the collateral described there, Central filing means that the financing statement is to be filed in a single office designated by the state enacting Article 9. Under 9–501(a)(2), central filing is required in most instances.

The Article 9 filing system has two purposes: to allow the filing party to establish a priority in the debtor's collateral and to provide information to the searching party about security interests in this property. It has been reasonably successful in serving the first of these purposes, but less so with respect to the second. The authoritative statement on notice filing is found in Comment 2 to 9–502:

> This section adopts the system of "notice filing." What is required to be filed is not, as under pre-UCC chattel mortgage and conditional sales acts, the security agreement itself, but only a simple record providing a limited amount of information

(financing statement). The financing statement may be filed before the security interest attaches or thereafter. See subsection (d). See also Section 9–308(a) (contemplating situations in which a financing statement is filed before a security interest attaches).

The notice itself indicates merely that a person may have a security interest in the collateral indicated. Further inquiry from the parties concerned will be necessary to disclose the complete state of affairs. Section 9–210 provides a statutory procedure under which the secured party, at the debtor's request, may be required to make disclosure. However, in many cases, information may be forthcoming without the need to resort to the formalities of that section.

What is striking about Article 9's notice filing system is how little information the filer's financing statement discloses to searchers. The only public document in an Article 9 secured transaction is the financing statement. The security agreement is not open to public scrutiny. Unless the debtor or secured creditor is willing to allow a searcher to see the security agreement or to reveal to the searcher the details of the secured transaction, only the fragmentary statements in the financing statement are available to the searcher. See 9–210.

What is the justification for allowing secured parties to perfect a security interest in collateral by filing a public statement that gives searching parties so little information? If you were interested in a debtor's financial position, wouldn't you like to know the amount of the credit the collateral secured, where the collateral is located, whether the creditor intended to make further advances, and so forth? The law of real estate mortgages typically requires the filing of the mortgage document, a detailed description of the mortgaged real estate, and, in a number of jurisdictions, requires a description of the debt secured. Because Article 9's notice filing system requires secured parties to provide far less information, searchers have to invest in acquiring the information from sources other than the filed records. The expense and delay of this off-record search may be great.

To understand why Article 9's system of notice filing might be justified, recognize that requiring information in a filed public statement has two effects: one on the filing creditor and the other on prospective creditors consulting the filings to learn whether its debtor might have granted a security interest in specific assets. The requirement that the financing statement contain certain information creates disclosure costs for the filing creditor: the expense of collecting and supplying the required information. For their part, prospective creditors incur costs in searching the filings to discover whether its debtor's assets might be subject to a security interest. In general, requiring more information in the financing statement increases the filing creditor's disclosure costs while reducing the prospective creditors' search costs. Requiring less information in the financing statement generally has the opposite effect: it reduces the filing creditor's disclosure costs while increasing prospective creditors' search costs. Where the debtor does not seek secured financing from third party creditors, the filing creditor's cost of supplying more information in its filed financing statement is not offset by a benefit to prospective secured creditors. A further consideration is that technological advances in information collection have significantly reduced prospective creditors' search costs. Article 9's drafter's make the implicit judgment that, taking these "wasted" filings and their associated disclosure costs into account, notice filing optimally minimizes the sum of disclosure and search costs. To date there are no studies that investigate the size of creditors' disclosure and search costs.

The obvious source of information about the extent to which the debtor has collateralized its assets is the debtor. If the debtor is seeking credit from the searcher, it can be expected to cooperate by showing the searcher the security agreement and other documents. But the searcher may not feel safe until it confirms the information with the secured creditor of record, who may have no incentive beyond business comity to make any disclosure to the searcher. If the searcher is a judgment creditor of the debtor who is looking for assets to seize to satisfy the judgment, not even the debtor is likely to be a willing source of information.

Section 9–210 is the only provision of Article 9 that addresses the informational deficiency facing a person searching the filing office records. Read that section and the Comment following and apply it to the following Problems.

PROBLEMS

1.   Debtor, Medicorp, operates a health maintenance organization (HMO) and contracts with a partnership of physicians, Doctors LLP, to provide the required medical services to members of the HMO. Medicorp is having financial problems. It has fallen $500,000 behind in its payments to Doctors, which has consulted your firm about collecting the money by a lawsuit against Medicorp. You have searched the UCC records and discovered a financing statement filed by Lender against Medicorp covering "medical equipment, proceeds thereof and replacements thereof." Doctors' personnel have informed you that they believe Lender financed Medicorp's purchase of some of the expensive diagnostic equipment used for patients. The financing statement indicates to you that Lender probably took purchase-money security interests in this equipment to secure Medicorp's loan. Doctors has no information about which items of equipment are covered by Lender's security interest or how much Medicorp owes on the loan. You need to have this information in order to evaluate the desirability of your client's initiation of a lawsuit against Medicorp. What help does 9–210 give you? What help would it give Medicorp if it were trying to ascertain the extent of Lender's claims against it?

2. In January, Lender took a perfected security interest in all Debtor's personal property to secure the present advance of $1 million and all future advances made by Lender. In July, Bank took a perfected security interest in the same collateral to secure an advance of $500,000. In doing so, Bank relied on a statement of account (9–210(a)(4)) approved by Lender in July that Debtor owed Lender only $1 million. But in August, Lender advanced another $500,000 to Debtor, which, as shown later, under Article 9 priority rules primed Bank's intervening security interest. 9–322 and 9–323. Bank contended that Lender's approval of the statement of account in July implied that it would not be making further advances to Debtor. Otherwise, 9–210 statements of account are misleading and worthless in any case in which the prior security interest covers future advances. Does Bank have a case?

2. SUFFICIENCY OF FINANCING STATEMENT

Section 9–502(a) provides that a financing statement is "sufficient" only if it provides the names of the debtor and secured party or its representative (9–503) and indicates the collateral covered (9–504) by the financing statement. Section 9–520(c) states that if the financing statement contains this information, it is "effective." What does this mean? Article 9's answer is complicated.

The three basic requirements in 9–502(a) do not include some information that is important to the operation of a filing system, such as the addresses of the debtor and secured party and whether the debtor is an individual or an organization. The Financing Statement Form in 9–521(a) has space for all this information, Prior to the 2010 Amendments, where the debtor is an organization, the Financing Statement Form required entry of the type and jurisdiction of the organization. Some states have adopted nonuniform financing statement forms that continue to require this information.

Section 9–516(b) provides that filing does not occur if the filing office refuses to accept a record that lacks the information required by the subsection. This means that filing does not occur if the filing office rejects a sufficient financing statement lacking the information. Notice that the information that must be supplied does not have to be accurate; see, e.g., 9–516(b)(4) ("provide a name and mailing address of the secured party of record"), 9–516(b)(5) ("provides a name of the debtor"). Section 9–516(b) only requires the financing statement to contain specified information; it doesn't require that the information supplied be accurate. For good reason, 9–516(b) doesn't demand accuracy. Filing officers have neither the time nor the expertise in most cases to vet the accuracy of the contents of financing statements submitted to them. Section 9–516(b) therefore considers them automata with respect to their decision to accept or reject a financing statement. Section 9–520(a) in turns requires the filing office to reject a financing statement that lacks the information required by 9–516(b), and permits the office to reject a financing statement only if it lacks this information. Thus, 9–516 and 9–520, taken together, effectively compel 9–516(b)'s additional information to be included in a financing statement.

It is clear that if the financing statement doesn't contain the information stated in 9–516(b), the financing office can reject it and it does not become effective. But what happens if the filing office accepts the financing statement without such information? See 9–516(a). Is the financing statement legally sufficient even if it omits the information specified in 9–516(b)(5)?

PROBLEMS

1.   Debtor, Inc. (D) granted a security interest to Secured Party (SP) in business machinery, properly described in the security agreement. SP filed a written financing statement using the form set out in 9–521(a). The filing office accepted the financing statement and duly indexed it. Later, D defaulted on its obligation to SP and filed in bankruptcy. T, D's trustee in bankruptcy, combed through D's case file in the hope of finding some basis for avoiding SP's security interest and discovered that although all of the other relevant blanks in the form were properly filled in, SP had not entered a mailing address for D. Can T avoid SP's security interest on the grounds that it was not perfected? Cf. 9–516(d).

2.   Harold Kim (D), an individual, granted Lender a security interest in identified personal property. Lender filed a written financing statement using the form set out in 9–521(a) but filled in the mailing address of another Harold Kim. The filing office accepted the financing statement and duly indexed it. Later, after D had fallen into default on his loan transaction with Lender, he applied for an unsecured loan from Bank to finance a real property purchase. Bank's loan department made the loan because it confused D with the Harold Kim whose address was on the filed financing statement and whose credit report showed him to be an excellent credit risk. Bank contends that it would never have made the loan to D had it not been misled by the incorrect address. Does Bank have rights against Lender under 9–338?

In the following case, at the time of the debtor's bankruptcy, a searcher would find that both the name and address on the financing statement were incorrect. How did the court find that the financing statement was sufficient and effective?

In re Hergert

United States Bankruptcy Court, D. Idaho, 2002
275 B.R. 58

■ TERRY L. MYERS, BANKRUPTCY JUDGE.

    * * *

II.   Relevant Facts

The Debtors' farming business was originally financed through Pacific One Bank ("Pacific"). As part of a merger in 1998, all of the assets of Pacific were acquired by the Bank.

These assets included three secured loans of the Debtors: (i) a commercial loan with an outstanding amount of principal, interest and late fees as of trial on January 8, 2002 of $182,051.68; (ii) a commercial loan with an outstanding amount of principal, interest and late fees as of January 8, 2002 of $51,595.44; and (iii) a consumer loan with an outstanding balance of $45,395.12 as of the Petition Date, August 9, 2001.

The two commercial loans are secured under an Agricultural Security Agreement and two Commercial Security Agreements. By their terms, these security agreements cross-collateralize the commercial loan obligations. The consumer loan is secured by an interest in the Debtors' manufactured home.

In connection with the Agricultural Security Agreement, and to perfect the security interest granted thereunder, Pacific filed a UCC-1F (farm products) financing statement. See Exhibit H. In connection with the Commercial Security Agreements, and to perfect the security interests described therein, Pacific filed a UCC-1 financing statement, Exhibit G, and obtained notation of its lien on certificates of title to several vehicles. In regard to the consumer loan, Pacific is shown as a lienholder on the certificate of title ("Title") to the Debtors' manufactured home.

Both the UCC-1 and the Title identify the secured party as "Pacific One Bank" with a mailing address of P.O. Box 40108, Portland, Oregon, 97240 (the "Portland Address"). The UCC-1 lists an additional address of P.O. Box 9344, Nampa, Idaho 83652–9344 (the "Nampa Address") as the address to which the Secretary of State should return its "acknowledgment" copy of the filing.

The UCC-1F also identifies "Pacific One Bank" as the secured party, with the Nampa Address shown as the address of the secured party. The Debtors do not dispute that the names and addresses on the UCC-1 and UCC-1F were accurate when the documents were created and filed. *See* Pre-trial Stipulation, at p.2, ¶ 6.[1]

After origination of the Debtors' loans, and before the chapter 12 filing, Pacific was merged into the Bank. The Bank has never amended

---

[1]   For additional clarity, the Court notes that the Debtors do not dispute the creation of security interests as described in the documents. Pre-Trial Stipulation, at p.2, P 4. Rather, the Debtors dispute only that the Bank's perfection remained valid at the Petition Date. In turn, this dispute relates solely to the issue regarding the accuracy of the names and addresses shown for the secured party on that date. No other issues concerning the sufficiency of the financing statements on the Petition Date are alleged.

the secured party's name or address(es) in any of the above-described documents.

The Bank has maintained and continues to use the Portland Address. The Bank has been receiving mail there since the merger, and today still is, even if the mail is addressed to Pacific.

At some point subsequent to the merger, the Nampa Address expired and the Bank no longer received mail there. This was the situation at the time of Debtors' chapter 12 petition on August 9, 2001.

Ann Ybarguen, a special credits representative of the Bank, testified regarding this situation. The Nampa Address was for a post office box within the main building of the Karcher Mall, a retail shopping facility in Nampa, Idaho. Mail sent there after the Nampa Address had expired would be marked as undeliverable. Pacific's old physical address inside the Karcher Mall was also an invalid address. However, at times the local postman would take mail improperly addressed to Pacific's old physical address to the Bank's new physical location, which happened to be on a retail pad in the parking lot of the Karcher Mall. This method of delivery was inconsistent and unpredictable. * * *

III. Analysis and Disposition

* * *

B.   The Commercial Loans

3.   The UCC-1F

* * *

To evaluate the effectiveness of the UCC-1F on the Effective Date, reference is first made to revised I.C. § 28–9–502, which establishes the prerequisites for effective financing statements. In pertinent part, it provides:

(a)   Subject to subsection (b) of this section, a financing statement is sufficient only if it:

(1)   Provides the name of the debtor;

(2)   Provides the name of the secured party or a representative of the secured party; and

(3)   Indicates the collateral covered by the financing statement.

(b)   Except as otherwise provided in section 28–9–501(b), to be sufficient, a financing statement that covers as-extracted collateral or timber to be cut, or which is filed as a fixture filing and covers goods that are or are to become fixtures, must satisfy subsection (a) of this section and also:

(1)   Indicate that it covers this type of collateral;

(2)   Indicate that it is to be filed in the real property records;

    (3) Provide a description of the real property to which the collateral is related sufficient to give constructive notice of a mortgage under the law of this state if the description were contained in a record of the mortgage of the real property; and

    (4) If the debtor does not have an interest of record in the real property, provide the name of a record owner. . . .

  (e) A financing statement covering farm products is sufficient if it contains the following information:

    (1) The name and address of the debtor;

    (2) The debtor's signature;

    (3) The name, address and signature of the secured party;

    (4) The social security number of the debtor, or in the case of a debtor doing business other than as an individual, the debtor's internal revenue service taxpayer identification number;

    (5) A description by category of the farm products subject to the security interest and the amount of such products, where applicable;

    (6) A reasonable description of the real estate where the farm products are produced or located. This provision may be satisfied by a designation of the county or counties, and a legal description is not required.

Under revised I.C. § 28–9–520(a), a filing officer shall refuse to accept a financing statement if it is not in compliance with revised I.C. § 28–9–516(b). Revised I.C. § 28–9–516(b)(4) indicates that a filing officer is entitled to reject a financing statement if it lacks a name or mailing address for the secured party. Revised I.C. § 28–9–516(b)(8) indicates that the filing officer may reject a farm products financing statement if it does not contain all the information specified in revised I.C. § 28–9–502(e) or conform to the official form of the Idaho secretary of state.

However, revised I.C. § 28–9–520(c) protects improper statements so long as they are in fact filed and contain certain essential information. That section states:

A filed financing statement satisfying section 28–9–502(a) and (b) is effective, even if the filing office is required to refuse to accept it for filing under subsection (a) of this section.

Id.; see also, revised I.C. § 28–9–516, Official Comment 9 (Effectiveness of Rejectable but Unrejected Record); revised I.C. § 28–9–520, Official Comment 3 (Consequences of Accepting Rejectable Record).

Note that under revised I.C. § 28–9–520(c), the filed statement need only meet the requirements of subsections (a) and (b) of revised I.C. § 28–9–502 in order to benefit from the protection which actual filing affords.

Unlike revised I.C. § 28–9–502(e), those two subsections do not contain a requirement for the secured party's address or signature, only its name. See revised I.C. § 28–9–502(a)(2).

i.   Name

The name of the secured party shown on the UCC-1F on the Effective Date was Pacific, not the Bank. To determine whether this is sufficient identification of the secured party, the Court looks to several provisions of New Article 9.

First, revised I.C. § 28–9–506 provides in part:

(a) A financing statement substantially satisfying the requirements of this part is effective, even if it has minor errors or omissions, unless the errors or omissions make the financing statement seriously misleading.

(b) Except as otherwise provided in subsection (c) of this section, a financing statement that fails to sufficiently provide the name of the debtor in accordance with section 28–9–503(a) is seriously misleading.

Subsection (b) makes a failure to sufficiently provide the name of the debtor a seriously misleading error. Negative inference would indicate that an error in the name of the secured party is not of the same magnitude. At a minimum, it is not automatically or *per se* seriously misleading.

Second, Official Comment 2 to revised I.C. § 28–9–506 states, in part:

In addition to requiring the debtor's name and an indication of the collateral, Section 9–502(a) requires a financing statement to provide the name of the secured party or a representative of the secured party. Inasmuch as searches are not conducted under the secured party's name, and no filing is needed to continue the perfected status of a security interest after it is assigned, an error in the name of the secured party or its representative will not be seriously misleading. However, in an appropriate case, an error of this kind may give rise to an estoppel in favor of a particular holder of a conflicting claim to the collateral. See Section 1–103.

Id.[9]

Third, revised I.C. § 28–9–511 indicates that the secured party identified in the financing statement is the "secured party of record" and

---

[9]   However, to give rise to such an estoppel, the name error would have to actually result "in prejudice to a particular searcher that reasonably relied to its detriment on the error and would be harmed unfairly if the filer who committed the error were allowed to assert its priority." Harry C. Sigman, Twenty Questions About Filing Under Revised Article 9: The Rules of the Game, 74 Chi.-Kent L.Rev. 861, 866 (1999) (addressing UCC § 9–506, Official Comment 2).

will remain such until the situation is altered by amendment. Official Comment 3 to revised I.C. § 28–9–511 recognizes:

> Application of other law may result in a person succeeding to the powers of a secured party of record. For example, if the secured party of record (A) merges into another corporation (B) and the other corporation (B) survives, other law may provide that B has all of A's powers. In that case, B is authorized to take all actions under this Part that A would have been authorized to take. Similarly, acts taken by a person who is authorized under generally applicable principles of agency to act on behalf of the secured party of record are effective under this Part.

While amendments of financing statements can be made, *see* revised I.C. §§ 28–9–511, 28–9–512, nothing in those sections appears to indicate that they must be made. It is particularly relevant here that revised I.C. § 28–9–511 does not require an amendment of the financing statement to reflect a succession in interest such as by merger, but instead addresses the question as one of the actor's authority.

ii. Address

Closely related to questions under New Article 9 regarding the name of the secured party are questions of that party's address. New Article 9 recognizes that a limited function is served by the inclusion on the financing statement of the secured party's address; it only indicates a place to which others can send any required notifications. See revised I.C. § 28–9–516, Official Comment 5:

> 5. Address for Secured Party of Record. Under subsection (b)(4) and Section 9–520(a), the lack of a mailing address for the secured party of record requires the filing office to reject an initial financing statement. The failure to include an address for the secured party of record no longer renders a financing statement ineffective. See Section 502(a). The function of the address is not to identify the secured party of record but rather to provide an address to which others can send required notifications, e.g., of a purchase money security interest in inventory or of the disposition of collateral. Inasmuch as the address shown on a filed financing statement is "an address that is reasonable under the circumstances," a person required to send a notification to the secured party may satisfy the requirement by sending a notification to that address, even if the address is or becomes incorrect. See Section 9–102 (definition of "send"). Similarly, because the address is "held out by [the secured party] as the place for receipt of such communications [i.e., communications relating to security interests]," the secured party is deemed to have received a notification delivered to that address. See Section 1–201(26).

For all these reasons, the errors in name or address on the UCC-1F cannot be viewed as rendering the filing of that statement ineffective to perfect the security interest in farm products as of the Effective Date. The structure of New Article 9 makes the absence of a name or address grounds for the filing officer to reject the statement, but if accepted for filing it will be effective.[10] Errors in the secured party's name or address as shown are, by virtue of the structure of New Article 9, not seriously misleading, and do not vitiate the effectiveness of the filing.[11] * * *

IV. Conclusion

The Effective Date of New Article 9 was July 1, 2001. This preceded the filing of the Debtors' chapter 12 petition on August 9, 2001. On the date this bankruptcy case commenced, both the UCC-1 and UCC-1F financing statements of record were sufficient to perfect the security interests granted the Bank.

Based upon the foregoing, the Court finds and concludes that the Bank has a valid, perfected security interest in the property described in the UCC-1 and in the UCC-1F, and in the manufactured home shown on the Title. These are the sole questions posed by the parties' pleadings and stipulations. Counsel for the Bank shall prepare a form of Judgment consistent with this Decision.

NOTE

The court states that 9–506(b) "makes a failure to provide the name of the debtor a seriously misleading error. Negative inference would indicate that an error in the name of the secured party is not of the same magnitude. At a minimum it is not automatically or *per se* seriously misleading." Part of the statement is mistaken. Section 9–506(a) does not allow the negative inference, because the provision supposes that a failure to substantially comply with the provisions of Part 5—not just 9–506(b)—can render the financing statement seriously misleading. This includes an error in the secured party's name. Beyond 9–506(a), the court's statement to the effect that errors in the secured party's name aren't *per se* seriously misleading is trivially true: no error in the financing statement is *per se* seriously misleading, even an error in the debtor's name. See 9–506(b) ("Except as

---

[10] Additionally, revised I.C. § 28–9–507(b) states that:

(b) Except as otherwise provided in subsection (c) of this section and section 28–9–508, a financing statement is not rendered ineffective if, after the financing statement is filed, the information provided in the financing statement becomes seriously misleading under section 28–9–506.

As Official Comment 4 to revised I.C. § 28–9–507 makes clear, post-filing changes that render a financing statement inaccurate—and even seriously misleading—do not render that financing statement ineffective.

[11] See also Sigman, supra, at 868: "The secured party's address is not an element of sufficiency under [revised] Section 9–502[(a)(2)]. Failure to provide an address for the secured party is a ground for rejection under [revised] Section 9–516(b)(4), but if the financing statement is nevertheless accepted by the filing office, it is effective. Since a filed financing statement that lacks a secured party address would be effective, a filed financing statement with an erroneous address or an address that was correct when filed but is no longer correct must surely remain effective."

otherwise provided in [9–506](c) . . .). Comment 2 (final paragraph) to 9–506 shares the *Hergert* court's view that an error in the secured party's name does not render the financing statement seriously misleading. But it immediately adds that in an "appropriate case" the error may give rise to estoppel in favor of a secured party with a conflicting secured claim. How could the filing creditor whose financing statement contained an error in its own name be estopped unless such an error can render the financing statement seriously misleading?

The post-filing event of Pacific's merger with Bank rendered the information in the financing statement erroneous with respect to the name and address of the secured party. However, 9–507(b) doesn't allow information in an initially effective financing statement to render the statement ineffective by post-filing events, however seriously misleading the information becomes, subject to 9–507(c) (change in debtor's name) and 9–508 (difference in name between original and new debtors). Shouldn't 9–507(b)'s "once effective, always effective" rule govern cases involving post-filing events such as a different secured creditor or secured creditor's address, as in this case? This analysis would reach the same result as the court in *Hergert*, but is cleaner. In re Montagne, 417 B.R. 214 (Bankr. D. Vt.2009), the secured party was held to have a perfected security interest in the proceeds of the collateral even though the collateral had already been sold before the secured party filed some two years after its security interest attached. The court noted that there is no time limit imposed by the Code under which the secured party is required to perfect its security interest in either the collateral or the proceeds.

3. INDICATION OF COLLATERAL

a. ORIGINAL COLLATERAL

Section 9–502(a)(3)'s requirement that the financing statement indicate the collateral covered by the financing statement is met by either a description of the collateral pursuant to 9–108 or "an indication that the financing statement covers all assets or all personal property." 9–504(1), (2). Under a regime of notice filing, a financing statement indicates the collateral covered if it provides notice that the person identified as the secured party may have a security interest in the collateral claimed. Generic descriptions by types of collateral (e.g., inventory, accounts, equipment) suffice under 9–108(b)(3). The previous Chapter addressed the issue as to why a supergeneric description is satisfactory for the financing statement but not for the security agreement. Comment 2 to 9–504 justifies the supergeneric description in the financing statement:

> Debtors sometimes create a security interest in all, or substantially all, of their assets. To accommodate this practice, paragraph (2) expands the class of sufficient collateral references to embrace "an indication that the financing statement covers all assets or all personal property." If the

property in question belongs to the debtor and is personal property, any searcher will know that the property is covered by the financing statement.

As 9–504(1) suggests, a sufficient description of collateral in the security agreement may be used to indicate the collateral in the financing statement, and often drafters use the same description in both records. But the secured party may wish to use a broader indication in the financing statement than in the security agreement. Consider the following two cases.

Case #1.   D's security agreement grants SP a security interest in all D's equipment, inventory and accounts. The financing statement covers inventory and accounts.

Case #2.   D's security agreement grants SP a security interest in inventory and accounts. The financing statement covers equipment, inventory and accounts. In what collateral does SP have a perfected security interest in Case #1? In Case #2?

A notice filing regime in which filers need only describe collateral in terms of broad generic types is a huge convenience to secured parties. By use of simple, easy-to-draft generic descriptions in their financing statements, they can establish reliable priority for many years in a wide spectrum of collateral, including after-acquired property, to secure a multitude of future credit extensions, some of which may have been unforeseen at the time the financing statement was filed. Thus, in "floating lien" cases involving shifting collateral like inventory or accounts, additional supplementary financing statements need be filed only in unusual cases in which the identities of the parties change or the nature of the collateral changes radically. For secured parties, the system not only offers priority over unsecured creditors and subsequent secured creditors but is also effective insurance against the debtor's potential bankruptcy.

On the face of it, for a relatively small filing fee, a secured party can establish its priority against all claimants in a broad spectrum of a debtor's collateral for many years in the future. For the most part, filers are also searchers since a filer must determine who else has an interest in the debtor's property before it can safely claim a priority. The financing statement reveals so little that much of the information a searcher seeks is off record. Which items of a debtor's property are covered by a generic description like "inventory" or "equipment"? Where are they located? Are they in more than one jurisdiction? What is the amount of the debt the property secures? Does the property secure future advances as well as present debts?

Whether the searcher's costs would be significantly reduced by requiring more information in financing statements is the subject of endless debate. Compare Peter A. Alces, Abolish the Article 9 Filing

System, 79 Minn. L. Rev. 679, 701 (1995) ("Do we know enough to say with any confidence that the benefits of relying on the system to provide broader credit information would exceed the costs of such a model?"), with Lynn M. LoPucki, Computerization of the Article 9 Filing System: Thoughts on Building the Electronic Highway, 55 Law and Contemp. Probs. 5, 37 (1992) ("The need for some additional types of data will be apparent."). It is ironic that the party who most frequently litigates the validity of the secured party's financing statement is the debtor's trustee in bankruptcy who, as a hypothetical creditor, never actually relies on the filing system.

Some commentators contend that since Article 9 does not require that the financing statement give enough information to searchers to determine whether specific items of property are encumbered, the requirement of a collateral description should be abolished. They believe that if this were done, in most instances, the diligence required of searchers to determine the scope of the filer's security interest would not be appreciably greater and losses resulting from errors in describing collateral in the financing statement would be obviated. Carl S. Bjerre, Bankruptcy Taxes and Other Filing Facts: A Commentary on Professor Bowers, 79 Minn. L. Rev. 757, 762–765 (1995). The same arguments support the supergeneric or one-size-fits-all indications that Article 9 approves in 9–504(2).

Allowing supergeneric descriptions in the financing statement has proved to be one of the most controversial changes made to Article 9. A supergeneric description is seen as making it even easier for creditors to perfect a security interest in all the debtor's assets, to the disadvantage of creditors who later perfect security interests in specific assets of the debtor. This policy issue is discussed in the introductory material in Chapter 1.

ProGrowth Bank, Inc. v. Wells Fargo Bank, N.A.

United States Court of Appeals, Eighth Circuit, 2009
558 F.3d 809

■ BYE, CIRCUIT JUDGE.

Wells Fargo Bank, N.A. ("Wells Fargo") and Global One Financial, Inc. ("Global One") (collectively, the "Defendants") appeal from the district court's grant of summary judgment in favor of ProGrowth Bank, Inc. ("ProGrowth") on its claim for a declaratory judgment. We reverse.

I

This case concerns separate and unrelated loans made by Global One and ProGrowth to Christopher Hanson ("Hanson") and/or the Christopher Hanson Insurance Agency (the "Agency"). On September 8, 2005, Global One and the Agency entered into a Promissory Note and a Security Agreement, pursuant to which Global One loaned the Agency one million dollars. As security for the loan, Hanson assigned his interests in two separate annuity contracts, both issued by Fidelity and Guaranty Life Insurance Company ("Fidelity and Guaranty"). The two annuity contracts were valued at one million dollars, and they were identified as "L9E00015" and "L9E00016," respectively.

That same day, Wells Fargo, acting as a collateral agent for Global One, filed a financing statement with the Secretary of State of Missouri. The financing statement identifies the "Debtor" as "Christopher J. Hanson," and it describes the collateral as follows:

> All of Debtor's right, title, and interest in and to, assets and rights of Debtor, wherever located and whether now owned or hereafter acquired or arising, and all proceeds and products in that certain Annuity Contract No.: LE900015 issued by Lincoln Benefit Life in the name of Debtor. . . .

Of importance in the instant appeal, the financing statement identifies the contract number as "LE900015" instead of "L9E00015," and it identifies the issuer as "Lincoln Benefit Life" instead of Fidelity and Guaranty. On September 16, 2005, Wells Fargo, again acting as a collateral agent for Global One, filed an additional financing statement. This statement identifies the "Debtor" as "Christopher J. Hanson" and provides the following description of collateral:

> All of Debtor's right, title, and interest in and to, assets and rights of Debtor, wherever located and whether now owned or hereafter acquired or arising, and all proceeds and products in that certain Annuity Contract No.: L9E00016 issued by Lincoln Benefit Life in the name of Debtor. . . .

Although this financing statement correctly identifies the contract number, it once again mistakenly refers to the issuer of this contract as "Lincoln Benefit Life" instead of Fidelity and Guaranty. During this same time period, Wells Fargo filed financing statements regarding at least two other annuity contracts, which are not involved in this lawsuit, owned by Hanson and issued by Lincoln Benefit Life.

On February 9, 2006, Hanson obtained a loan from ProGrowth. As security for the loan, Hanson assigned his interests in the Fidelity and Guaranty annuity contracts to ProGrowth. On February 14, 2006, ProGrowth filed two financing statements with the Secretary of State of Missouri. They identify Hanson and the Agency as the debtor, and they accurately describe the collateral as: "Fidelity and Guaranty Life Insurance Annuity Contracts Number L9E00015 and Number L9E00016[.]"

ProGrowth then filed this lawsuit against Global One and Wells Fargo asserting a claim for a declaratory judgment decreeing that its perfected security interests in the Fidelity and Guaranty annuity contracts are prior to and superior to any perfected security interests claimed by the Defendants. . . . ProGrowth argued that the Defendants' security interests are not perfected because the financing statements filed with respect to those interests are seriously misleading. The district court granted ProGrowth's motion for summary judgment.... This appeal followed.

II

* * *

Both ProGrowth and the Defendants have security interests in the Fidelity and Guaranty annuity contracts. The parties agree the priority of the Defendants' security interests is dependent upon whether their interests are perfected in accordance with Article 9 of the Missouri Uniform Commercial Code ("Missouri UCC"), Missouri Revised Statute § 400.9–101–400.9–710. Under the circumstances involved in this case, Defendants' security interests in the annuity contracts are perfected only if the financing statements they filed with respect to those interests are sufficient under Missouri law. *See id.* § 400.9–310. "[A] financing statement is sufficient only if it: (1) [p]rovides the name of the debtor; (2) [p]rovides the name of the secured party or a representative of the secured party; and (3) [i]ndicates the collateral covered by the financing statement." Id. § 400.9–502(a). The parties dispute whether the Defendants' financing statements satisfy the third requirement.

A financing statement "sufficiently indicates the collateral that it covers if the financing statement provides: (1)[a] description of the collateral pursuant to section 400.9–108; or (2)[a]n indication that the financing statement covers all assets or all personal property." Id. § 400.9–504. Under section 400.9–108, a "description of personal or real property is sufficient, whether or not it is specific, if it reasonably identifies what is described." Finally, "[a] financing statement substantially satisfying the requirements of this part is effective, even if it has minor errors or omissions, unless the errors or omissions make the financing statement seriously misleading." *Id.* § 400.9–506(a).

.... [T]he financing statement "serves the purpose of putting subsequent creditors on notice that the debtor's property is encumbered." *Thorp Commercial Corp. v. Northgate Indus., Inc.*, 654 F.2d 1245, 1248 (8th Cir.1981). Its function is not to "identify the collateral and define property which the creditor may claim, but rather to warn other subsequent creditors of the prior interest." *Id.* Thus, we view the validity of the financing statement in terms of whether "it provides notice that a person *may* have a security interest in the collateral claimed." Mo.Rev.Stat. § 400.9–504 (UCC cmt. 2) (emphasis added). The UCC allows for imperfect financing statements, and it recognizes that sometimes "[f]urther inquiry from the parties concerned will be necessary to disclose the complete state of affairs." *Id.* Therefore, errors or omissions in the description of collateral do not render financing statements ineffective unless they are seriously misleading, which "is designed to discourage the fanatical and impossibly refined reading of statutory requirements in which courts have occasionally indulged themselves." *Id.* § 400.9–506 (UCC cmt. 2).

ProGrowth argues the Defendants' financing statements are seriously misleading because they identify the annuity contracts as issued by Lincoln Benefit Life instead of Fidelity and Guaranty, and because contract no. L9E00015 is identified as no. LE900015. Were this the only language contained in the Defendants' financing statements, we may be inclined to agree. These provisions of the financing statements, however, cannot be read in isolation. The financing statements describe the collateral as:

> All of Debtor's right, title, and interest in and to, assets and rights of Debtor, wherever located and whether now owned or hereafter acquired or arising, *and* all proceeds and products in that certain Annuity Contract No.: LE900015 [or L9E00016] issued by Lincoln Benefit Life in the name of Debtor. . . . (Emphasis added).

It is necessary to analyze the financing statements in their entirety because, under the Missouri UCC, a financing statement sufficiently identifies the collateral it covers if it provides an "indication that the financing statement covers all assets or all personal property." Mo.Rev.Stat. § 400.9–504. By identifying the collateral as all assets or all personal property, the filer ensures that if "the property in question belongs to the debtor and is personal property, any searcher will know that the property is covered by the financing statement." *Id*. § 400.9–504 (UCC cmt. 2). While such a broad, generic description is insufficient to describe collateral in a security agreement, it is sufficient to describe collateral in a financing statement because it puts subsequent searchers on notice that any item of collateral owned by the debtor *may* be encumbered, which is the purpose of the filing system. When faced with a financing statement purporting to cover "all assets" of a debtor, it is then incumbent upon the subsequent creditor to investigate whether the collateral at issue is in fact covered by a security agreement. *See id*. § 400.9–502 (UCC cmt. 2) ("Further inquiry from the parties concerned will be necessary to disclose the complete state of affairs.").

We conclude the Defendants' financing statements satisfy the filing provisions of the Missouri UCC because they indicate coverage over all of Hanson's assets. The first clause of the financing statements identify the collateral as "[a]ll of Debtor's right, title, and interest in and to, assets and rights of Debtor, wherever located and whether now owned or hereafter acquired or arising. . . ." This language sufficiently describes the collateral under section 400.9–504(2) because it gives an indication that all of Hanson's assets may be covered. Thus, any inaccuracies in describing the specific annuity contracts at issue are immaterial and do not render the statements seriously misleading.

ProGrowth argues—and the district court agreed—the financing agreements should be interpreted to cover only "assets and rights of Debtor" "acquired or arising" in the "certain Annuity Contract[s]." The district court construed the "all assets" clause as simply referring to rights contained in, or derived from, the annuity contracts. We think this interpretation, however, is unduly restrictive and ignores the plain language of the statements. The statements contain two distinct phrases separated by the word "and," which indicates the descriptive clauses are independent from each other. . . . The first part covers all "assets and rights of Debtor," while the second part covers "proceeds and products in that certain Annuity Contract[s]." Because the two phrases are separated by a comma and the word "and," the most natural reading of the financing statements is that the statements' identification of the collateral as "[a]ll of Debtor's right, title, and interest in and to, assets and rights of Debtor" is *in addition to* the identification of the collateral as "all proceeds and products in the Annuity Contract[s]." *See id.*

Moreover, even if it is reasonable to construe the "all assets" language as simply referring to rights contained in the annuity contracts, it is equally reasonable to construe it as a separate, independent phrase covering all of Hanson's assets. Where a description can reasonably be interpreted in one of two ways—one of which may cover the collateral at issue and one of which does not—notice filing has served its purpose of alerting subsequent creditors to the possibility that a piece of collateral may be covered; the burden is then on the subsequent creditor to inquire further. *See Thorp,* 654 F.2d at 1252–53 ("Even assuming the words 'assignment accounts receivable' could be interpreted narrowly. . . the words also have an obvious broader meaning; in the present case notice filing has served its purpose of alerting subsequent creditors to the need for further inquiry. The UCC puts the burden on the subsequent creditor to seek clarification."). Additionally, the UCC does not require a *perfect* description that the financing statement covers all of a debtor's assets, but simply an "indication" of such coverage.

ProGrowth makes two final arguments in support of its contention that the financing statements do not sufficiently indicate coverage over all of Hanson's assets. First, it argues Defendants must not have intended the financing statements to cover all of Hanson's assets because doing so would render the subsequent descriptions of the annuity contracts superfluous. Additionally, ProGrowth argues, it would have been redundant for Defendants to have filed multiple other financing statements asserting security interests in other property owned by Hanson. This is immaterial, however, because nothing in the UCC prevents a creditor from filing redundant or precautionary financing statements, nor does the UCC prevent financing statements from setting forth alternative means of describing collateral. Further, we have previously rejected an attempt to impugn a filer's intent in filing one financing statement based on the fact that subsequently filed statements would have been redundant, holding the "standard for evaluating intent is the notice given to subsequent creditors. . . ." *Id.* at 1248 n. 5.

Second, ProGrowth argues—and the district court again agreed— that even if the financing statements do sufficiently identify the collateral as all of Hanson's assets, such a broad statement cannot cure the seriously misleading descriptions given for the specific annuity contracts at issue.[1] We think this fails to comprehend the structure of the UCC. The UCC gives two methods for identifying collateral in a financing statement: a description of the collateral, or an indication that the financing statement covers all of the debtor's assets. It then provides that errors or omissions do not render the statements ineffective unless they are seriously misleading. The relevant question is whether the statements—judged in their entirety—are seriously misleading, not whether one alternative, and ultimately unnecessary, means of describing the collateral contained therein is seriously misleading. While Defendants' specific descriptions of the annuity contracts contain errors, the statements themselves are not seriously misleading because a subsequent creditor should reasonably understand that the financing statements may cover all of Hanson's assets. It was then incumbent upon subsequent creditors to inquire whether specific collateral owned by Hanson is the subject of a prior security agreement. Therefore, we hold the Defendants' financing statements are not seriously misleading, and, as such, they are sufficient to perfect Defendants' security interests. The district court erred in granting summary judgment in favor of ProGrowth on its claim for a declaratory judgment.

III

Accordingly, the decision of the district court granting summary judgment in favor of ProGrowth is reversed, and the case is remanded to the district court for further proceedings consistent with this opinion.

NOTE

How far does this holding go? In effect, the court uses a supergeneric clause in the financing statement to cure errors in a specific description of collateral that standing alone might have been found to be seriously misleading. Although this seems harmless, the court's analysis is provocative. It breaks the indication of collateral statement in the financing statement into two separate and independent parts: "The first part covers all 'assets and rights of Debtor,' while the second part covers 'proceeds and products in that certain Annuity Contracts[s].' Because the two phrases are separated by a comma and the word 'and,' the most natural reading of the financing statements is that the statements' identification of the collateral as '[a]ll of the Debtor's right, title, and interest in and to, assets and rights of Debtor' is *in addition* to the identification of the collateral as 'all proceeds and products in the Annuity Contract[s].'" 558 F.3d at 814. Thus, the

---

[1]   The district court noted that it was unable to find a single case in which a seriously misleading description of a specific item of collateral was "cured" by a generic reference in a financing statement to all of a debtor's assets. While true, neither is there a case holding that a valid identification of collateral under the "all assets" provision is rendered invalid because a financing statement subsequently provides a description of a specific item that is deemed seriously misleading.

misleading description of the collateral drops away and only the generic clause is operative.

Would this mean that if the generic clause, "all Debtor's assets," were used in a case in which an additional clause might mistakenly describe entirely different collateral from that covered in the security agreement, the financing statement indication of collateral—though entirely misleading— would be adequate because of the curative powers of the supergeneric indication of collateral? The district court thought not but the Eighth Circuit court says without remorse that, if a generic clause is present, inaccuracies in describing the collateral are immaterial and do not render the financing statement seriously misleading. "The UCC puts the burden on the subsequent creditor to seek clarification." Id. Should the burden be this heavy? The teaching of this case apparently is that lenders' lawyers are safe if they print their financing statements with a simple supergeneric "all Debtor's assets" indication in all cases. If so, why require any "indication of collateral" in financing statements?

In considering these questions, note that the debtor is not helpless. For the financing statement to be effective, the debtor must authorize its filing. 9–510(a). A filed financing statement that indicates the collateral as "all Debtor's assets" along with a potentially misleading collateral description likely increases the debtor's cost of obtaining loans from other creditors. This is because borrowing costs include the burden prospective creditors incur in clarifying the scope of the indication of the collateral in a financing statement. Thus, the debtor must calibrate the costs and benefits of a collateral indication that combines a supergeneric description with a potentially misleading description of collateral. The debtor will authorize the filing of the financing statement that indicates the collateral in this way only if doing so is a net benefit to it.

PROBLEM

Debtor, which sold agricultural products, granted Bank a security interest in specific assets. Bank filed a financing statement covering all of the Debtor's equipment. The financing statement included the statement: "This filing filed as agricultural lien." However, Bank did not check the "Ag Lien" box on the Alternative Designations part of the UCC-1 form (box 6b). Later, in connection with a secured loan made by Finance, Debtor granted Finance a security interest in its equipment and farm products. At the same time, Finance filed a financing statement covering this collateral. Finance challenged the adequacy of Bank's financing statement on the grounds that the statement included in Bank's financing statement rendered it seriously misleading. An agricultural lien covers only farm products (9–102(a)(5)). Because farm products are not equipment, the statement "This filing filed as agricultural lien" in Bank's financing statement makes the collateral description in the financing statement ambiguous. Bank's position is that, although the statement leaves the collateral description ambiguous, the ambiguity does not render its financing statement seriously misleading. Which side is correct? See Winfield Solutions, LLC v. Success Grain, Inc., 2018 U.S. Dist. LEXIS 55684 (E.D.Ark. April 2, 2018).

b.   PROCEEDS

Chapter 1 discussed the creation of security interests in proceeds, and priorities in proceeds is treated in the next chapter. Perfection of security interests in proceeds is briefly discussed here. The basic rules are easily stated. A perfected security interest in the original collateral automatically continues in the proceeds, whether or not the financing statement mentions proceeds. 9–315(c). However, the security interest in proceeds is perfected automatically only temporarily. It becomes unperfected on the 21st day after the security interest attaches to the proceeds unless one of the three following conditions is met. (1) If a filed financing statement covers the original collateral, the security interest in the proceeds continues until the financing statement either lapses or is terminated (9–315(e)(1)), as long as (a) the proceeds are collateral in which a security interest may be perfected by filing in the office in which the financing statement is filed, and (b) the proceeds are not acquired with cash proceeds. 9–315(d)(1).

(2) If the proceeds are identifiable cash proceeds, the security interest in them continues past 20 days after the security interest attaches to the proceeds. 9–315(d)(2). (3) If the security interest in proceeds is perfected other than temporarily within 20 days after the security interest attaches to the proceeds, the security interest continues past 20 days after the security interest attaches to the proceeds. 9–315(d)(3). The failure to perfect the security interest in the proceeds within this 20-day period leaves the security interest unperfected on the 21st day after the security interest attached to the proceeds. For instance, if the filed financing statement covers only inventory but the proceeds are equipment, the financing statement does not afford adequate public notice of the security interest in the equipment. The same is true if, for example, the filed financing statement covered only inventory but the debtor uses cash proceeds to buy equipment. In both cases, to continue perfection past 20 days after the security interest attaches to the equipment, the security interest in the equipment must be perfected within this 20-day period.

Two innovations in Article 9 tend to assure that in the ordinary commercial case a security interest perfected by filing will continue in the proceeds until the filing lapses or is terminated. The first is that filing for registered organizations must be made in the place of registration. This means that for most tangible collateral there need be no concerns about the movement of the collateral from one jurisdiction to another, or, with respect to intangible collateral, worries about changes in the location of the debtor's chief executive office. Hence, a financing statement covering the original collateral belonging to a corporation is almost always filed in the correct place to cover the kinds of collateral represented by the proceeds. The second innovation is Article 9's controversial embrace of the supergeneric identification of collateral discussed in the previous section. If the financing statement covers "all personal property of the debtor," it will be an appropriate indication of most kinds of collateral purchased by cash proceeds, and 9–315(d)(3) poses no problems. Of course, if none of 9–315(d)'s conditions are satisfied, the secured creditor must take action to continue its security interest in proceeds past 20 days after its security interest attached to them.

Article 9's limited regulation of agricultural liens is important with respect to proceeds. Agricultural liens are not security interests. Thus, 9–203(a)(2), which provides that a security interest that attaches to collateral automatically attaches to the identifiable proceeds of the collateral, does not apply to agricultural liens. Similarly, 9–315(c)'s rule, under which a security interest in collateral is automatically perfected in the proceeds of the collateral, also does not apply to agricultural liens. This means that an attached or perfected agricultural lien does not attach or be perfected in the proceeds of an agricultural lien. Non-Article 9 law governing agricultural liens determines whether an agricultural lien extends to its proceeds.

PROBLEM

On February 1, SP perfected a security interest in all of Debtor's existing and after-acquired inventory by properly filing a financing statement. SP's security agreement also covered Debtor's deposit accounts, and SP took control of them on February 1. On March 1, Debtor sold some of its inventory on an unsecured credit basis and other items of inventory for cash. Debtor kept the cash separate in marked envelopes in its safe. Also on March 1, Debtor had its depository bank issue a cashier's check in its favor and debit its account in the amount of the check. Debtor retained possession of the check.

By April 14, SP had not taken any action with respect to any of the items above. Does SP have a perfected security interest in (a) Debtor's rights arising from the March 1 credit sales of its inventory, (b) the cash Debtor received from the March 1 cash sales, and (c) the cashier's check in Debtor's possession? Suppose Debtor purchased accounts with the cash it received from the March 1 sales?

4. NAME OF DEBTOR

a. BASIC RULES

Financing statements are indexed under the name of the debtor. If a financing statement contains an incorrect name for the debtor, searchers will be misled and may not find the financing statement. Such a financing statement does not provide notice. The basic rules are set out in 9–503(a) stating when a financing statement "sufficiently provides the name of the debtor."

(1) Individual Debtors

Courts have had considerable difficulty in deciding what an individual debtor's correct name is for purpose of a financing statement under 9–503(a)(4). Is it the debtor's "legal name"? If so, what is the debtor's legal name: the one on a birth certificate, a driver's license, a social security card, a passport? In drafting the 2010 Amendments, creditors sought a definition of an individual debtor's name that they could rely on for a financing statement with some certainty. After years of wrangling, the drafters of the 2010 Amendments compromised. They agreed that for a debtor who is an individual, 9–503(a)(4) and (5) should provide alternatives—Alternative A and B—to determine the individual's name. Jurisdictions that have enacted Article 9 select between the Alternatives. The term "individual debtor" includes not only consumers but also sole proprietorships. Since no filing is required for perfection in a number of consumer finance transactions, as discussed below, most individual debtor filings involve business debtors.

Under Alternative A, if the debtor is an individual to whom the state of her principal residence has issued an unexpired driver's license, a financing statement sufficiently provides the name of the debtor only if it provides the name of the individual as shown on the license. If the debtor does not hold such an unexpired driver's license, the financing statement is sufficient if (i) it either provides the "individual name" of the debtor or (ii) provides the debtor's surname (i.e. family name) and first personal name (i.e., first name other than the surname). The colloquial term, "last name" that appeared in the former statute was confusing. In the 2010 amendments, "surname" is used in place of "last name" to accommodate cultures in which the family name appears first or in a location in which it is neither first nor last. Alternative A is sometimes referred to as the "only if" Alternative: if an individual debtor has an unexpired driver's license the financing statement sufficiently provides the name of an individual "only if" the name on the driver's license appears on the financing statement. If the individual does not have an unexpired license, the individual's name or the surname, first name and middle initial must be provided. Forty four states have enacted Alternative A's "only if" rule for 9–503(a)(4).

Under Alternative B, the financing statement may sufficiently provide the name of an individual who is a debtor in three different ways: (i) by providing the "individual name" of the debtor; (ii) by providing the surname and first personal name of the debtor; or (iii) by providing the name of the individual which is indicated on an unexpired driver's license to whom the state of principal residence has issued to the individual. The term "individual name" of the debtor is not defined by Article 9. Unlike registered organizations, there is no public organic record to which reference can be made and from which the name and its components can be definitively determined as the name of a debtor. Since "individual name" was generally required by the law prior to 2013 (the effective date of the 2010 Amendments), an extensive body of case law has grown up around it. Alternative B is sometimes referred to as offering creditors a "safe harbor."

Difficulties can arise under both alternatives. Section 9–503(g) provides that if a state has issued more than one driver's license to an individual, the one that was issued most recently is the one to which subsection (a)(4) refers. To be safe, creditors must ascertain the debtor's name as it appears on the most recently driver's license issued by the resident state. In addition, Alternative A effectively forces creditors to conduct dual searches. This is because federal tax lien filings require the taxpayer's name. For their part, judgment liens filings in some states require judgment debtor's legal name. See, e.g., Cal. C. Civ. Pro. § 697.550 (2019); Fla. Civ. Prac. & Proc. § 55.203(1)(c) (2018). The taxpayer's name and its legal name may both differ from the debtor's name as it appears on the debtor's most recently issued driver's license. Thus, to be safe, a prospective creditor searching UCC and tax or judgment lien filings must search potentially under different names.

Alternative B has its own troubles. Suppose that in an Alternative B jurisdiction the Debtor's individual name, described by the court as his "legal name," was Michael D. Larsen, but the secured party filed a financing statement under the name of Mike D. Larsen. In the Matter of Larsen, 72 UCC Rep. Serv.2d 187 (Bankr. S.D. Iowa 2010), held that the use of a "nickname" in this case was seriously misleading. See Comment 2d to 9–503. A different result was reached in In re Miller, 78 UCC Rep. Serv.2d 296 (C.D Ill.2012). Noting that 9–503(a)(4)(A) requires the individual's "name," not its "legal name," the court ruled that a nickname appearing in official documents was part of the debtor's individual name.

(2) General Partnerships

If the debtor is a general partnership, the financing statement sufficiently provides the name of the debtor by giving the name of the partnership, not that of the partners. This is explained by the use of the term "organizational name of the debtor" in 9–503(a)(6)(A). Under the broad definition of "organization" in 1–201(b)(25), all partnerships are organizations, and if the partnership has a name it must be used. Of course, the enterprise may not have a name. If Thomas Jones and Robert Wagner, without any formal agreement, operate a restaurant that has a sign out in front saying "Tom and Rob's Cafe," their business has no name and a financing statement would have to provide the names of the two individuals. 9–503(a)(6)(B).

(3) Registered Organizations

If the debtor is a "registered organization," the organization's name is the name that appears in its public organic record most recently filed with a state or federal government. 9–503(a)(1). The key terms here have specific definitions. Under 9–102(a)(71) "registered organization" is an organization that is formed or organized solely under the law of a state or federal government by the filing of a public organic record with, issuance of a public organic record by, or the enactment of legislation by the state or the United States. "Public organic record" in turn is defined in 9–102(a)(68). As defined, it is a record that is available to the public for inspection. In addition, the record must be one which is (a) initially filed with or issued by a State or the United States to form or organize an organization and any such record which amends or restates the initial record, (b) an organic record of a business trust be filed with the State if the State requires the filing, or (c) a record consisting of legislation enacted by the legislature of a State or the Congress of the United States which forms or organizes an organization and any record amending the legislation and any record which amends or restates the name of the organization.

Among the registered organizations are corporations, limited liability companies and statutory trusts. A business trust also is a registered organization if it is formed or organized under the law of a State, where state statute requires that the trust's organic record be filed with the State. General partnerships are not registered organizations. Comment 2 to 9–503. Comment 2 to 9–502 mistakenly counts a limited partnership as a registered organization. Because limited partnerships are created by the agreement of the partners, not the filing of a certificate of partnership (even if state law requires the filing), a limited partnership is not a registered organization under 9–102(a)(71).

A registered organization might file publicly available records in which different organizational names appear. For example, the name of a corporation in its registration of intellectual property and state annual reports can differ. And the name of the corporation in these records in turn can differ from the name as it appears in the corporation's articles of incorporation filed with the state or federal government. Although intellectual property registrations and annual reports are records, they are not filed to form or organize the corporation. Thus, these records are not public organic records, and the name that appears in them therefore is not the name of the corporation. Instead, the name that appears in the corporation's most recently filed articles of incorporation is the corporation's name.

b.   ERRORS OR OMISSIONS

Article 9 does not require that the contents in the financing statement be accurate in every respect. The financing statement may be effective even if it contains errors. Under 9–506(a), a financing statement that substantially complies with the provisions of Part 5 ("this part") is effective, even if contains minor errors or omissions, unless the errors or omissions render the financing statement seriously misleading. As Comment 2 says, minor mistakes will occur and this section is in line with the policy of discouraging fanatical and impossibly refined reading of the statute that some courts have indulged in. But 9–506(a) applies only to errors or omissions other than in the debtor's name. Sections 9–506(b)–(d) apply to errors in the debtor's name.

Under 9–506(b), a financing statement that fails sufficiently to provide the debtor's name in accordance with 9–503(a) is seriously misleading as a matter of law. However, a safe harbor exception is stated in 9–506(c): if the financing statement nevertheless would be discovered in a search under the debtor's "correct name," using the filing office's standard search logic, if any, then as a matter of law the incorrect name does not make the financing statement seriously misleading. Comment 2 of 9–506 adds: "For purposes of subsection (c), any name that satisfies Section 9–503(a) at the time of the search is a 'correct name.'"

Comment 2 to 9–506 explains 9–506(b) and (c)'s operation "This section and Section 9–503 balance the interests of filers and searchers. Searchers are not expected to ascertain nicknames..., and the like by which the debtor may be known and then search under each of them. Rather, it is the secured party's responsibility to provide the name of the debtor sufficiently in a filed financing statement. Subsection (c) sets out the only situation in which a financing statement that fails sufficiently to provide the name of the debtor is not sufficiently misleading. As stated in subsection (b), if the name of the debtor provided on a financing statement is insufficient and subsection (c) is not satisfied, the financing statement is seriously misleading. Such a financing statement is ineffective even if searchers know or have reason to know that the name provided on the financing statement refers to the debtor. Any suggestion to the contrary in a judicial opinion is incorrect."

In re Nay
United States Bankruptcy Court, S.D. Indiana, 2017
563 B.R. 535

■ **Opinion by:** BASIL H. LORCH III.

This matter comes before the Court on the Motion for Judgment on the Pleadings filed by the Plaintiff, MainSource Bank ("MainSource") on October 27, 2016 and the Defendant's opposition thereto. Supplemental briefs were filed by both parties on November 14, 2016. MainSource seeks a determination of the validity, priority, or extent of the competing lien interests between itself and LEAF Capital Funding, LLC ("LEAF"). MainSource has moved for a ruling under Fed.R.Civ.P. 12(c) based upon a single determinative matter of law, that is, whether LEAF's inadvertent omission of the letter "t" from the Debtor's middle name invalidates LEAF's UCC Financing Statements. For the reasons set forth herein below, the Court finds that it does.

Undisputed Facts

The Debtors are indebted to MainSource pursuant to various debt instruments, including, but not limited to, a certain Promissory Note, dated May 5, 2015, in the original principal amount of $1,200,000.00 (the "Note"). The amount outstanding on the Note, including accrued interest and fees as of the Petition Date was $1,218,453.50. To secure repayment of the Note, among other collateral, the Debtors executed and delivered Agricultural Security Agreements, dated July 23, 2014, and May 11, 2015, whereby the Debtors granted to MainSource a security interest in personal property owned by the Debtors, including, but not limited to, all present or future inventory, chattel paper, accounts, equipment, general intangibles, crops, farm products, livestock, farm equipment and instruments and all proceeds, profits, replacements and substitutions related thereto (the "Security Agreements"). The security interests granted to MainSource by virtue of the Security Agreements were properly perfected by the filing of a financing statement with the Indiana Secretary of State, as Filing Number 201400000945368, on February 4, 2014.

On or about December 17, 2015, LEAF made a loan to Debtor, Ronald Markt Nay ("Nay") to finance the purchase of a Terex TA400 Dump Wagon (the "TA400"), evidenced by a Finance Agreement of that same date in the original principal amount of $41,000.00. LEAF claims that it has a first priority security interest in the TA400 by virtue of the filing of a financing statement the Indiana Secretary of State, as Filing Number 201500009761152, and filed on December 21, 2015. LEAF also made a loan to Nay to finance the purchase of a Terex 3066C Dump Wagon (the "3066C"), evidenced by a Finance Agreement dated December 10, 2015, in the original principal amount of $36,950.00. LEAF claims that it holds a first priority security interest in the 3066C by virtue of the filing of a financing statement with the Indiana Secretary of State, as Filing Number 201500009472787 (together with the aforesaid financing statement, the "LEAF UCCs"), and filed on December 10, 2015. The TA400 and the 3066C constitute "equipment" as that term is defined under applicable Indiana law. IC 26–1–9.1–102(a)(33). The LEAF UCCs each identify the Debtor's name as "Ronald Mark Nay" while the Debtor's actual name listed on his most recently issued unexpired Indiana driver's license, is "Ronald Markt Nay".

Nay and his wife, Sherry L. Nay, commenced a Chapter 11 bankruptcy case in this court on May 13, 2016. On September 21, 2016, MainSource initiated this adversary proceeding alleging causes of action against LEAF for declaratory judgment and as an objection to LEAF's proof of claim. The Complaint seeks a declaration that MainSource has a first priority security interest in the TA400 and the 3066C and further requests that the Court sustain MainSource's objection to LEAF's proof of claim.

Discussion

When a motion for judgment on the pleadings is asserted in an attempt to dispose of a case based upon the underlying substantive merits, the appropriate standard is that which is applicable to summary judgment, except that the court may consider only the contents of the pleadings. As such, the Court "must view as true the non-movant's allegations of fact, although it is not bound by the non-movant's legal conclusions." *McMahan v. Cornelius*, 756 F.Supp. 1156, 1157 (S.D.Ind. 1991). In order to prevail on its Motion, therefore, MainSource must establish that there are no material issues of fact to be resolved and that it is entitled to judgment as a matter of law.

In considering whether the LEAF UCCs are valid as a matter of law, the Court turns to the following pertinent language of Indiana Code § 26–1–9.1–506 regarding the effect of errors or omissions on the validity of financing statements:

> (a) A financing statement substantially satisfying the requirements of IC 26–1–9.1–501 through IC 26–1–9.1–527 is effective, even if it has minor errors or omissions, unless the errors or omissions make the financing statement seriously misleading.

> (b) Except as otherwise provided in subsection (c), a financing statement that fails sufficiently to provide the name of the debtor in accordance with IC 26–1–9.1–503(a) is seriously misleading.

> (c) If a search of the records of the filing office under the debtor's correct name, using the filing office's standard search logic, if any, would disclose a financing statement that fails to sufficiently provide the name of the debtor in accordance with IC 26–1–9.1–503(a), the name provided does not make the financing statement seriously misleading.

Admittedly, LEAF's financing statement contained a minor error in the misspelling of the Debtor's name. Whether that defect makes the filing "seriously misleading" is dependent upon section 503(a). In 2010, the language of IC 26–1–9.1–503 was extensively modified. The statute as amended, effective July 1, 2013, now provides that if the debtor is an individual to whom a driver's license has been issued, a financing statement sufficiently provides the name of the debtor *only if* it "provides the name of the individual which is indicated on the driver's license" (emphasis added). Prior to the 2010 Amendment, the statute required only the individual name of the debtor.

Based upon the plain language of the amended statutory language, it would appear that LEAF's financing statement containing the Debtor's misspelled name is insufficient or "seriously misleading" in that it does not provide the name of the Debtor as indicated on his Indiana driver's license. The financing statement is fatally defected unless LEAF can establish, under the safe harbor provision of 26–1–9.1–506(c), that its financing statement was otherwise discoverable by searching under the Debtor's correct name using the standard search logic promulgated by the Indiana Secretary of State.

Standard search logic is that logic used by a filing office to determine which filings will appear on an official UCC search. Model Administrative Rules were developed by the International Association of Commercial Administrators (IACA) in an effort to set the framework for state filing offices and those rules have been adopted in large part by the Indiana Secretary of State. The Indiana Secretary of State's "standard search logic" is found in Administrative Rule 503. That rule begins with a notation that "[s]earch results are created by applying standardized search logic to the name presented to the filing officer by the person requesting the search" and goes on to set out the parameters utilized by the search engine in gathering search results for the particular name presented in the query. The standard search logic in Rule 503 establishes how words or things such as punctuation, spaces, initials, case of letters, and similar details are interpreted in generating a report. As regards the "correct name" to be searched, however, Rule 503 provides no authority.

Nay suggests that Administrative Rule 501.1 addresses that question. It provides that:

> A search request must set forth the full correct name of a debtor or the name variant desired to be searched and must specify whether the debtor is an individual or an organization. The full name of an individual shall consist of a first name or initial, a middle name or initial, and a last name. A search request may be submitted with no middle name or initial. If only a single name is presented (e.g. "Cher") it will be treated as a last name and will return only names having the same last name which have no first name and no middle initial. A search request will be processed using the name in the exact form it is submitted.

MainSource responds that the "full correct name" is not necessarily the "correct name" but, more importantly, whether the "full correct name" or some alternate name is *permissible* in conducting a search, MainSource contends that it is not *required* because the statute itself provides that the "correct name" of the Debtor is the name set out on his Indiana driver's license. The Court is inclined to agree. Should the Court adopt Nay's reasoning, it would seem to contravene the language and the intent behind the statutory amendment.

To the extent a Court is called upon to interpret the language of a statute, it must begin "with the plain language of the statute, giving its words their ordinary meaning and considering the structure of the statute as a whole." *West v. Office of Ind. Sec. of State*, 54 N.E.3d 349, 353 (Ind. 2016). Furthermore, the Court must "generally presume that all statutory language is used intentionally, so that each word should be given effect and meaning where possible, and not treated as mere surplusage." *In re Howell*, 27 N.E.3d 723, 726 (Ind. 2015) (internal cites and quotes omitted). In this case, considering the plain language of the statute, given its ordinary meaning, and reading section 503 together with section 506, it seems clear that the "only" correct name of the Debtor under section 503 is the name on his Indiana driver's license, Ronald Markt Nay. Section 506 provides relief to LEAF only inasmuch as a search of the debtor's "correct" name (as established by section 503), using standardized search logic, would reveal its financing statement. It does not.

Official Comment to 26–1–9.1–503 lends credence to the Court's conclusions. It notes quite simply that "[s]ubsection (a) explains what the debtor's name is for purposes of a financing statement." Uniform Commercial Code Comment 2 to Section 506 goes on to provide:

> . . . For purposes of subsection (c), any name that satisfies Section 9–503(a) at the time of the search is a "correct name."

> This section and Section 9–503 balance the interests of filers and searchers. Searchers are not expected to ascertain nicknames, trade names, and the like by which the debtor may be known and then search under each of them. Rather, it is the secured party's responsibility to provide the name of the debtor sufficiently in a filed financing statement. Subsection (c) sets forth the only situation in which a financing statement that fails sufficiently to provide the name of the debtor is not seriously misleading. As stated in subsection (b), if the name of the debtor provided on a financing statement is insufficient and subsection (c) is not satisfied, the financing statement is seriously misleading. Such a financing statement is ineffective even if the debtor is known in some contexts by the name provided on the financing statement and even if searchers know or have reason to know that the name provided on the financing statement refers to the debtor. Any suggestion to the contrary in a judicial opinion is incorrect.

While the result in this case seems harsh, the Court is constrained to interpret the statute in a manner consistent with legislative intent, which is "to simplify formal requisites and filing requirements. It is designed to discourage the fanatical and impossibly refined reading of statutory requirements in which courts occasionally have indulged themselves." *See*, Official Comment 2 to I.C. 26–1–9.1–506.

Based upon all of the foregoing, the Court hereby finds that MainSource is entitled to Judgment as a matter of law and a separate Judgment shall issue forthwith. The Motion for Judgment on the Pleadings is, accordingly, GRANTED. The Court, having found that the security interests of LEAF Capital Funding, LLC are unperfected, does now SUSTAIN the Objection to LEAF's Proof of Claim.

IT IS SO ORDERED.

Section 9–506(c)'s safe harbor for the most part states a clear and easily administrable test: If a search using the debtor's correct name and conducted in accordance with the applicable filing office's standard search logic, if any, would yield the financing statement containing an error in the debtor's name, the error makes the financing statement seriously misleading; otherwise, not. However, by its terms, the test applies only if the applicable filing office employs a standard search logic ("if any"). What counts as a standard search logic therefore is important. Article 9 does not define what constitutes a "standard search logic." Although the term might connote a computer search according to software algorithms, nothing in the term limits its application to computerized algorithms. Any set of search procedures, whether or not computerized, in principle can count as a "standard search logic."

In rare cases, the absence of a definition of the term can create controversy over 9–506(c)'s application. Consider an unusual but possible example. Assume that the applicable filing office's search procedures are regularly used by the office to conduct searches. They are in this sense "standard." Also assume that these search procedures, when operating on the debtor's correct name, do not identify a set of financing statements as "hits." Instead, the search procedures return a web page containing the entire index of debtor names. The search locates within that index 20 entries that range from the exact matches to the less exact matches of the debtor's correct name. From that location, the website allows a search forward and backward through the entire index of debtor names. The search procedure in this example closely resembles Florida's search procedure, as described in *1944 Beach Boulevard LLC v. Live Oak Banking Co.*, reproduced below. Is the search procedure described in the example a "standard search logic"?

Two different views can be taken as to what constitutes a "standard search logic." One view looks only at the search procedures in use in the applicable filing office, not the results produced by those procedures. If those procedures are regularly used by the office, they count as a standard search logic. This practice-based view would find the search procedure described in the example to be a standard search logic. Another view requires that the search procedure identify certain results as hits; results not identified as hits are not considered by the procedure to be an exact or close match of the debtor's correct name. The view is functional because it determines what counts as a standard search logic by whether the search procedure allows the identification of some financing statements as hits and others as not hits. See Kenneth C. Kettering, Standard Search Logic Under Article 9 and the Florida Debacle, 66 U. Miami L. Rev. 907 (2012). Because the search procedure in the example does not designate certain results as hits, the functional view does not count the procedure as a standard search logic. In *1944 Beach Boulevard LLC v. Live Oak Banking Co.*, the Eleventh Circuit implicitly relies on the first view while the Florida Supreme Court relies on the second, functional view.

The two different views of what counts as a standard search logic have different consequences for the application of 9–506(c)'s safe harbor to the example above. Under the practice-based view, because the applicable filing office's search procedure is a standard search logic, 9–506(c) would apply if a search in accordance with that procedure would reveal the financing statement with the incorrect debtor name (it would eventually). Because the functional view finds that the filing office has no standard search logic ("if any"), 9–506(c)'s safe harbor is inapplicable to the example. The exception to 9–506(b) therefore does not come into play. This means that under 9–506(b) an error in the debtor's name renders the financing statement seriously misleading.

1944 Beach Blvd., LLC v. Live Oak Banking Co.

Supreme Court of Florida, 2022
346 So.3d 587

■ **Opinion by:** LAWSON, J.

This case is before the Court for review of three questions of Florida law certified by the United States Court of Appeals for the Eleventh Circuit that are determinative of a cause pending in that court and for which there appears to be no controlling precedent. We have jurisdiction.

The certified questions concern the interpretation of section 679.5061(3), Florida Statutes (2021), which creates a safe harbor for financing statements that are otherwise ineffective to perfect a security interest because they fail to correctly name the debtor as required by Florida law. The safe harbor applies when a financing statement that fails to correctly name the debtor is disclosed by "a search of the records of the filing office under the debtor's correct name, using the filing office's standard search logic, if any." § 679.5061(3). Collectively, the Eleventh Circuit's questions ask us to delineate the proper scope of the "search" of the filing office's records as that term is used in the safe harbor provision.

However, as explained below, we find dispositive a threshold question that was not expressly addressed or certified by the Eleventh Circuit, namely: "Is the filing office's use of a 'standard search logic' necessary to trigger the safe harbor protection of section 679.5061(3)?" Reading section 679.5061 in its entirety, our answer is yes. Because Florida's filing office, the Florida Secured Transaction Registry, does not employ a "standard search logic," we hold that the safe harbor cannot apply, which means that a financing statement that fails to correctly name the debtor as required by Florida law is "seriously misleading" and therefore ineffective. § 679.5061(2). Accordingly, it is unnecessary to reach the Eleventh Circuit's three certified questions concerning the proper scope of the "search" under the safe harbor provision.

BACKGROUND

1944 Beach Boulevard, LLC (Beach Boulevard), is a limited liability company organized and existing under the laws of Florida.

Beach Boulevard and its affiliates were jointly and severally indebted to Live Oak Banking Company (Live Oak) in the approximate amount of $3,000,000 on account of two loans, each in the original principal amount of $2,500,000. The two loans purport to be secured by a blanket lien on all of Beach Boulevard's assets. To perfect its claimed security interests, Live Oak filed two UCC-1 Financing Statements with the Florida Secured Transaction Registry (Registry). However, the financing statements filed by Live Oak improperly name the debtor as "1944 Beach *Blvd.*, LLC" instead of "1944 Beach *Boulevard*, LLC." (Emphasis added.)

On December 5, 2019, Beach Boulevard and its affiliates filed voluntary petitions for reorganization under Chapter 11 of the United States Bankruptcy Code. When Beach Boulevard's manager conducted a search of the Registry, Live Oak's financing statements did not appear on the page of twenty results generated by the Registry. Live Oak's financing statements did, however, appear on the immediately preceding page.

Beach Boulevard filed a complaint in the bankruptcy court, which asserted that Live Oak's financing statements failed to correctly name the debtor as required by Florida law, making the statements "seriously misleading" within the meaning of section 679.5061(2) and therefore ineffective to perfect Live Oak's security interest. Seeking the statutory safe harbor protection provided by section 679.5061(3) for financing statements that would otherwise be ineffective for failing to correctly name the debtor, *see* § 679.5061(2), Live Oak asserted in its answer to Beach Boulevard's complaint the affirmative defense that "its financing statements substantially complied with Florida law and that abbreviating 'Boulevard' to 'Blvd.' was a minor error or omission that does not render the financing statements defective or seriously misleading." *In re NRP Lease Holdings*, 20 F.4th at 751. Live Oak also "claimed that the filing statements were not 'seriously misleading' because they can be found within one page of the initial search results." *Id.* In support, Live Oak explained that "while its liens do not appear on the first page of results for a search in the Registry under '1944 Beach Boulevard, LLC,' the search results are displayed in alphabetical order and 'merely clicking the blue "<<PREVIOUS" tab one time' will reveal the existence of its liens." *Id.*

Beach Boulevard and Live Oak filed cross-motions for summary judgment. The bankruptcy court denied Beach Boulevard's motion and granted Live Oak's motion, concluding that Live Oak's financing statement fell within the statutory safe harbor "because the Registry's standard search logic discloses the financing statements on the page immediately preceding the initial page on the Registry's website." Id. The bankruptcy court, therefore, ruled that the financing statements filed by Live Oak were "not seriously misleading and [were] effective to perfect [Live Oak's] security interest in all of [Beach Boulevard's] assets." Id.

Beach Boulevard appealed the bankruptcy court's decision to the federal district court, which reviewed the bankruptcy court's legal conclusions de novo and its factual findings for clear error. Applying these standards, the district court affirmed the bankruptcy court's decision, writing only that "the bankruptcy court committed no errors of law and made no clearly erroneous factual findings." Beach Boulevard appealed the district court's decision to the Eleventh Circuit.

On appeal, the Eleventh Circuit identified "two competing interpretations" in the case law regarding the scope of the search that is necessary to determine whether the safe harbor of section 679.5061(3) applies. It cogently explained the split as follows:

> The *In re John's Bean Farm* [*of Homestead, Inc.*, 378 B.R. 385 (Bankr. S.D. Fla. 2007),] court concluded that the statutorily-established "standard search logic" generates "a single page on which [twenty] names appear" and that page constitutes the entirety of the "search" for purposes of the safe harbor. *Id.* Under that court's logic, if a financing statement with the debtor's incorrect name does not appear on that page, it is ineffective. In contrast, the *In re Summit Staffing* [*Polk County, Inc.*, 305 B.R. 347 (Bankr. M.D. Fla. 2003),] court concluded that the initial page of twenty names does not constitute the entirety of the "search"; instead, the "search" consists of the entirety of the Registry, which can be scrolled to from the initial page of twenty names. And that court determined the searcher "must reasonably examine the results of the search" to determine whether it discloses a financing statement with the debtor's incorrect legal name.

In re NRP Lease Holdings, 20 F.4th at 756.

Faced with substantial doubt as to how this Court would resolve the split, which it found to be a matter of state law dispositive of the case before it, the Eleventh Circuit certified to this Court the following questions:

> (1) Is the "search of the records of the filing office under the debtor's correct name, using the filing office's standard search logic," as provided for by Florida Statute § 679.5061(3), limited to or otherwise satisfied by the initial page of twenty names displayed to the user of the Registry's search function?

> (2) If not, does that search consist of all names in the filing office's database, which the user can browse to using the command tabs displayed on the initial page?

> (3) If the search consists of all names in the filing office's database, are there any limitations on a user's obligation to review the names and, if so, what factors should courts consider when determining whether a user has satisfied those obligations?

Id. at 758.

ANALYSIS

The certified questions present issues of statutory interpretation concerning the scope of the search necessary to determine whether a financing statement that would otherwise be ineffective because it fails to correctly name the debtor falls within the safe harbor established by section 679.5061(3). . . . Thus, we begin with the statute's text. * * *

The safe harbor exception codified in section 679.5061(3) provides that a financing statement with errors or omissions in naming the debtor will still be effective to perfect a security interest so long as "a search of the records of the filing office under the debtor's correct name, using the filing office's standard search logic, if any, would disclose" the financing statement. § 679.5061(3).

As evinced by the Eleventh Circuit's certified questions, section 679.5061(3) does not define the scope of the search of the filing office's records that is necessary to determine whether the safe harbor applies. Its only direction is to conduct the search "using the filing office's standard search logic, if any," with no explanation of what "standard search logic" means. *Id.*

However, the meaning of "standard search logic" as used in Article 9 of the Uniform Commercial Code, which governs secured transactions and which Florida has adopted, is well understood within the industry. Within the industry, "standard search logic" is reasonably accepted to mean a procedure that "identif[ies] the set (which might be empty) of financing statements on file that constitute hits for the search," or stated differently, that produces an "[u]nambiguous identification of hits." Kenneth C. Kettering, *Standard Search Logic under Article 9 and the Florida Debacle*, 66 U. Miami L. Rev. 907, 913 (2012). This is because "[t]he whole point of the 'standard search logic rule' is to establish an objective procedure for determining whether a given financing statement is sufficient. A procedure that does not identify which financing statements are hits and which are not is alien to the purpose of the rule." *Id.*

The problem in Florida—as cogently explained by the amicus—is that although the Registry offers an option for searching its records, that option is not a "standard search logic." Instead of returning a finite list of hits when a search is conducted, the Registry returns a list of twenty names starting with the name that most closely matches the name entered. That list of names is but a point from which the user can navigate forward and backward through all of the names indexed in the Registry. In other words, "a search" of the Registry returns an index of all of the financing statements in the Registry. The Registry's current search option also produces inconsistent results depending upon the date a search is conducted. This is true because as financing statements are filed, amended, and removed, the position of a financing statement on the

Registry's index changes, which means that a financing statement included in a list of twenty today might not be on the same list tomorrow.

We agree with Professor Kettering that a "search procedure that returns as hits, for any search string, all financing statements in the filing office's database cannot rationally be treated as a 'standard search logic.'"

In certifying its questions concerning the proper scope of the search required to determine whether the safe harbor of section 679.5061(3) applies, the Eleventh Circuit recognized these problems with the Registry's current search option, but it nevertheless determined that the Registry employs a "standard search logic." In addressing the certified questions, we cannot accept the Registry's search option as the "standard search logic" contemplated by the statute; rather, the Florida Constitution requires us to decide de novo what "standard search logic" means. *See* art. V, § 21, Fla. Const.

We adopt the definition of "standard search logic" accepted in the secured transactions industry, which requires the search to identify specific hits, if any, and hold that under this definition the search option offered by the Registry, which returns the entire index, is not a "standard search logic." Moreover, because we read section 679.5061(2)–(3) as conditioning the safe harbor's application on the ability to search the Registry's records using a "standard search logic," it is unnecessary for us to address the Eleventh Circuit's certified questions. Instead, we hold that section 679.5061(3) provides one way and one way only to search the filing office's records for purposes of determining whether the safe harbor applies to a financing statement that incorrectly names a debtor—i.e., "using the filing office's standard search logic, if any." Because the Registry lacks a "standard search logic," the search contemplated by section 679.5061(3) is impossible, which means that filers are left with the zero-tolerance rule of section 679.5061(2).

This interpretation is further bolstered by reading section 679.5061(2)–(3) together with section 679.5031(1), which plainly places the burden to correctly name the debtor on the filer of a financing statement. By interpreting section 679.5061(2)–(3) as being intolerant of any errors or omissions in naming the debtor—no matter how minor— unless and until the Registry implements a "standard search logic" necessary to determine whether the safe harbor applies, we faithfully adhere to the text of section 679.5061(2)–(3), keep the burden on the filer consistent with section 679.5031(1), and avoid imposing requirements on the searcher that are not specified in the statute.

CONCLUSION

The Eleventh Circuit's certified questions ask us to define the scope of the search required to determine whether a financing statement that fails to correctly name the debtor is nevertheless deemed effective under the safe harbor of section 679.5061(3). However, because we hold that the

Florida Secured Transaction Registry's failure to employ a "standard search logic" precludes the safe harbor from applying in the first instance, we find it unnecessary to reach the certified questions. Unless and until the Registry employs a standard search logic, under the zero-tolerance rule of section 679.5061(2), any financing statement that fails to correctly name the debtor as required by section 679.5031(1) is "seriously misleading" and therefore ineffective. Having explained why our interpretation of section 679.5061 makes it unnecessary to reach the certified questions, we return this case to the United States Court of Appeals for the Eleventh Circuit.

It is so ordered.

NOTE

Florida's optional search procedure is pathological. The functional view adopted by the Florida Supreme Court probably gives the better understanding what makes a search procedure a "standard search logic." However, in Florida's case, both the practice-based and functional views described above have unwelcome consequences. The view that a standard search logic is determined only by regularly observed or recognized official search rules would find the optional search procedure available in Florida's filing offices to be a standard search logic. But because the optional search rules offered by Florida's filing offices effectively yield the entire debtor index (which includes the financing statement with the debtor's incorrect name), 9–506(c)'s standard search logic test always will be satisfied. No incorrect debtor name therefore can be seriously misleading under 9–506(b). As a result, the practice-based view would construe 9–506(c)'s safe harbor to be a rule of maximum tolerance of errors in the debtor's name. On the other hand, under the functional view Florida's optional search procedure is not a standard search logic, as it does not yield a set of hits. Section 9–506(c)'s standard search logic test therefore never applies, and any error in the debtor's name is seriously misleading. Although 9–506(c) allows for the possibility that a filing office does not have a standard search logic ("if any"), it is unlikely that a filing office uses or recognizes a search procedure that, without indication, is not a standard search logic. In sum, Florida's legislature, in enacting 9–506(c) likely would be surprised to learn that, given the optional search procedure in force in Florida's filing offices, 9–506(c)'s standard search logic test is either always met or always inapplicable.

c.   TRADE NAMES

Suppose that Debtor's legal name is Beacon Realty Investment Co., a general partnership, but everyone in the business community calls it "Hilton Inn." Assume also that that nobody in that community has ever heard it called anything but "Hilton Inn" because that is the name Debtor itself uses on all it correspondence, contracts and checks, and this is the name that Secured Party (SP) used in its financing statement. Later, Debtor is in bankruptcy and its trustee in bankruptcy, examining the documentation of SP's security interest, contends that SP used the wrong name under 9–503(a)(4) for a general partnership. But SP responds with the common sense argument that everyone in the financial community interested in Debtor's credit record would search under the name "Hilton Inn" and they would find the financing statement. If it were filed under Debtor's correct name, they wouldn't have found the financing statement. Should not an exception be made for cases in which the debtor is known to its creditors and to the public at large only by its trade name? The facts just described are based on those in Pearson v. Salina Coffee House, Inc., 831 F.2d 1531 (10th Cir.1987). Under former Article 9, a number of cases held that the use of a trade name in the financing statement in a case like this was appropriate. How would this case be decided under 9–503(c)? Is there a sound policy basis for this resolution? Which party should have the burden of discovering the debtor's correct name, the secured party or the searchers? Why?

The following opinion treats in detail two important issues that arise under the Article 9 filing provisions: The first is the use of a trade name along with the organizational name of a debtor in financing statements. The other is the application of 9–506(c)'s safe harbor rule.

In re EDM Corp.

United States Bankruptcy Appellate Panel, Eighth Circuit, 2010
431 B.R. 459

■ **Opinion:** FEDERMAN, BANKRUPTCY JUDGE.

Hastings State Bank appeals from the Order of the Bankruptcy Court declaring that its lien against the Debtor's assets was not properly perfected due to the manner in which Hastings State Bank listed the debtor's name on its financing statement filed with the Nebraska Secretary of State. For reasons that follow, we AFFIRM.

Debtor EDM Corporation is a Nebraska corporation which sold and leased emergency vehicles. It was incorporated in 1991, and its official name of record at the Nebraska Secretary of State's office is "EDM Corporation." The Debtor routinely did business as "EDM Equipment," and was commonly known by that name, although it had no registered trade names with the Nebraska Secretary of State. At issue here is the priority of liens in the proceeds of a particular ambulance (the "Ambulance") which had been owned by EDM. Hastings State Bank, TierOne Bank, and Huntington National Bank each assert a lien against the Ambulance. As stated, the sole issue here is priority.

Over the years, Hastings State Bank made several loans to EDM, in excess of $4.5 million. Hastings filed a financing statement on June 10, 2003, with the Nebraska Secretary of State. Its financing statement identified the debtor as "EDM CORPORATION D/B/A EDM EQUIPMENT." Neither TierOne Bank nor Huntington National Bank disputes that, but for an alleged defect in the way EDM's name appears as the debtor on the financing statement, Hastings would be first in priority because its lien was created, and its financing statement was filed, first.

On December 30, 2005, TierOne Bank extended a $3.0 million line of credit to EDM. TierOne ran three UCC searches, using the standard search logic, over several months around the time of its loan, none of which revealed Hastings' financing statement. To perfect its lien, TierOne filed a financing statement on January 6, 2006, listing the debtor as "EDM Corporation." On or about November 21, 2007, Huntington National Bank made a $250,000 revolving line of credit loan to EDM. Huntington conducted a UCC search on the Nebraska Secretary of State's search engine, using the standard search logic, under the debtor name "EDM Corporation." The search did not reveal Hastings' financing statement, but did reveal TierOne's. To perfect its security interest, Huntington filed a financing statement with the Nebraska Secretary of State on December 13, 2007, identifying the debtor as "EDM Corporation." That financing statement also contained a broad description of collateral, including inventory and equipment. On December 13, 2007, Huntington made an advance on the line of credit directly to the manufacturer of the Ambulance, to pay for EDM's purchase of the Ambulance. TierOne and Huntington had entered into an intercreditor agreement whereby TierOne agreed to subordinate any interest that it may have in the Ambulance to Huntington's interest, so there is no dispute that Huntington's interest trumps TierOne's in the Ambulance, even though TierOne's was filed before Huntington's.

Neither TierOne nor Huntington conducted a lien search under the d/b/a of EDM Equipment. One of the issues in this appeal is whether they were obligated to do so. Despite conducting lien searches using the debtor's organizational name (EDM Corporation), neither TierOne nor Huntington was advised by those searches of the existence of the prior lien to Hastings; and, neither had actual knowledge of such lien.

EDM filed a voluntary Chapter 7 case on April 10, 2008, and Hastings subsequently filed an adversary proceeding to determine the validity, extent, and priority of the liens in various of EDM's assets, including the Ambulance. The parties agreed that Huntington could obtain relief from the stay, sell the Ambulance, and deposit the proceeds with an escrow agent, pending a determination as to priority in the Ambulance and its proceeds. The Bankruptcy Court ultimately held that Hastings' financing statement was not validly perfected because a search of the Nebraska Secretary of State's U.C.C. records, using the office's standard search logic, did not reveal the financing statement identifying the debtor as "EDM Corporation d/b/a EDM Equipment." Therefore, the Court held that Huntington was in first position due to the purchase-money subordination agreement with TierOne.

We review findings of fact for clear error, and legal conclusions *de novo*.

Discussion

Nebraska adopted Revised Article 9 of the Uniform Commercial Code, effective July 1, 2001. To put the relevant statutory provisions in context, in practice, a creditor wishing to perfect its lien files with the appropriate governmental authority a financing statement, typically on a standardized form, listing the name of the debtor, the name of the creditor, and a description of the collateral. Once a financing statement is filed, a government employee enters the data from the financing statement into a computerized indexing system. If a potential lender wants to determine for itself whether there are existing liens on the borrower's property, that lender can submit a request to the authority for a lien search (sometimes by conducting its own search on-line). More than 40 states that have adopted Revised Article 9 have also adopted administrative regulations which guide both the governmental authority in entering data from financing statements, as well as the public in conducting searches. Parts of the regulations are often referred to as "search logic." As relevant here, the Nebraska search logic requires that data be entered into the system and indexed based on the exact name listed in the field on the financing statement reserved for the debtor's name. The purpose of this system is to put subsequent creditors on notice of asserted liens and, if everything is done correctly, the search should reveal any financing statements filed.

With that background, we turn to the relevant provisions of Nebraska's version of Revised Article 9. Section 9–506(a) provides:

> (i) ... A financing statement substantially satisfying the requirements of this part is effective, even if it has minor errors or omissions, unless the errors or omissions make the financing statement seriously misleading.

> (ii) Except as otherwise provided in subdivision (iii) of this subsection, a financing statement that fails sufficiently to provide the name of the debtor in accordance with section 9–503(a) is seriously misleading.

> (iii) If a search of the records of the filing office under the debtor's correct name, using the filing office's standard search logic, if any, would disclose a financing statement that fails sufficiently to provide the name of the debtor in accordance with section 9–503(a), the name provided does not make the financing statement seriously misleading.

Hastings asserts that, contrary to the Bankruptcy Court's ruling, a court should not consider § 9–506's "seriously misleading" analysis unless the financing statement does not sufficiently provide the debtor's name in accordance with §§ 9–502 and 9–503. And, Hastings asserts that its financing statement did sufficiently provide EDM's name in accordance with §§ 9–502 and 9–503 because the words "EDM Corporation" were included in the name provided. We hold both that its financing statement did not provide the name of the debtor, and also that it was seriously misleading.

The Eighth Circuit has emphasized that the purpose of filing a financing statement is to put subsequent creditors on notice that the debtor's property is encumbered. In *Pro Growth v. Wells Fargo Bank*, 558 F.3d 809 (8th Cir. 2009), in interpreting §§ 9–502(a), 9–504 (relating to the description of the collateral on a financing statement), and 9–506(a), the Eighth Circuit stated:

> The requirements of the UCC concerning filing, notice and perfection all are intended to provide to those dealing with commercial activities knowledge of the status of the commodity with which they are dealing so that they may protect their interests and act in a commercially prudent manner. To that end, the financing statement serves the purpose of putting subsequent creditors on notice that the debtor's property is encumbered. Its function is . . . to warn other subsequent creditors of the prior interest.

Id. at 812. * * *

We find it significant that the Eighth Circuit emphasized that the purpose of the filing requirements is to let other creditors know of the existence of the lien. The very first step in that process for creditors is *finding* the UCC statement in the first place, and the way to do that is by searching the records under the debtor's organizational name. In other words, complete accuracy is even more important with the debtor's name than it is with the description of collateral. As one court has stated, with regard to the debtor's name, the legislative language and purpose of the revised UCC "evidenced an intent to shift the responsibility of getting the debtor's name right to the party filing the financing statement. This approach would enable a searcher to rely on that name and eliminate the need for multiple searches using variants of the debtor's name, all leading to commercial certainty."[14] And, according to another court, "[p]ost-revision case law is fairly well settled that the burden is squarely on the creditor [filing the financing statement] to correctly identify the name of the debtor."[15]

Hastings points out that the official comments to § 9–503 state that, "[t]ogether with subsections (b) and (c), subsection (a) reflects the view prevailing under former Article 9 that the actual individual or organizational name of the debtor on a financing statement is both necessary and sufficient, *whether or not the financing statement provides trade or other names of the debtor . . . .*" (emphasis added). Thus, Hastings

---

[14] *Genoa Nat'l Bank v. Southwest Implement, Inc. (In re Borden)*, 353 B.R. 886, 890 (Bankr. D. Neb. 2006) (quoting *Pankratz Impl. Co. v. Citizens Nat'l Bank*, 281 Kan. 209, 130 P.3d 57, 63 (Kan. 2006)).

[15] *In re John's Bean Farm of Homestead, Inc.*, 378 B.R. 385, 390 (Bankr. S.D. Fla. 2007).

asserts, the comment implies that trade names can be included in addition to the organizational name of the debtor.

While official comments to the UCC are not binding, they are persuasive in matters of interpretation. However, when considered in conjunction with the rest of the rules and regulations, and keeping in mind the critical importance of accuracy in the debtor's name under Revised Article 9, we do not interpret this comment to endorse the practice of adding superfluous information to a registered organization's *name* in the name field on a financing statement. Rather, it is clear from the language of the statute itself that § 9–503 requires that, as to registered organizations, the debtor's name (as listed in the name field on the form) must be "the name of the debtor indicated on the public record of the debtor's jurisdiction of organization." Viewed with § 9–503(b)(1), which provides that "[a] financing statement that provides the name of the debtor in accordance with subsection (a) is not rendered ineffective by the *absence of* . . . a trade name or other name of the debtor," and § 9–503(c), which provides that "[a] financing statement that provides *only* the debtor's trade name does not sufficiently provide the name of the debtor," we interpret the comment to mean that trade or other names may be added as *other* or *additional* names on a financing statement, but not in place of, or as part of, the debtor's organizational name.

In *In re Jim Ross Tires, Inc.*, 379 B.R. 670 (Bankr. S.D. Texas 2007), the Bankruptcy Court for the Southern District of Texas was presented with facts which are, for all practical purposes, identical to those here. In that case, the name of the debtor on the records of the Texas Secretary of State was "Jim Ross Tires Inc." The debtor also had previously had an "assumed name" of "HTC Tires & Automotive Centers" but that name had expired in 2000, and was not renewed. In 2002, a creditor filed a financing statement listing the debtor as "JIM ROSS TIRES, INC. dba HTC TIRES & AUTOMOTIVE CENTERS." The trustee in Jim Ross Tires Inc.'s bankruptcy case asserted that the creditor's financing statement had not been properly perfected because the debtor's name had not been properly listed.

As here, the creditor in *Jim Ross* relied on the official comment to § 9–503 and argued, as does Hastings here, that it had correctly listed the legal name, and that the addition of the DBA information after the correct name should be considered superfluous and ignored in the analysis. The court disagreed, however, finding that:

> While it is clear that the legislature considered certain effects of dba usage in satisfying § 9–503(a), the Court finds that the interpretation [the creditor] applies is overly broad and inoperable in application when considered with other sections of the Code. Specifically, [the creditor's] asserted interpretation, if applied, conflicts with the purposes of the indexing system when evaluated against the administrative procedures for indexing

and searching UCC records filed with the Texas Secretary of State.

Id. at 676.

As discussed above, we agree with that analysis.

In sum, we interpret § 9–503 to mean exactly what it says: if the debtor is a registered organization, then a financing statement "provides the name of the debtor" only if it "provides the name of the debtor indicated on the public record of the debtor's jurisdiction of organization"—nothing more and nothing less. Trade names may be added, but not as part of the organizational name itself. Consequently, because Hastings' UCC statement added superfluous information to EDM's organizational name, it did not sufficiently provide the name of the debtor.

Thus, having correctly determined that Hastings' financing statement did not sufficiently provide the name of the debtor, the Bankruptcy Court then turned to § 9–506's safe harbor, to determine whether the error rendered the filing seriously misleading. Again, § 9–506(a)(iii) provides that, if a search of the records of the filing office under the debtor's correct name, using the filing office's standard search logic, would disclose a financing statement, then the erroneous name provided does not make the financing statement seriously misleading. The undisputed evidence was that a search of the Nebraska Secretary of State's records, using the debtor's correct name, "EDM Corporation," and using the office's standard search logic, did not disclose Hastings' financing statement. Hastings asserts, in effect, that there must be some flaw in Nebraska's search logic and that the Bankruptcy Court allowed the technological deficiencies of the state's search engine to trump a properly filed financing statement. Indeed, at oral argument, Hastings counsel contended that the search logic is contrary to the statute, and so should not serve as the basis for striking down its perfection.

In essence, Hastings asserts that the standard search logic should have found its UCC statement because it should have ignored everything in the field for the debtor's name except the very words "EDM Corporation." The Administrative Code provides that organization names are to be entered into the system by the Secretary of State's filing officer exactly as set forth in the financing statement; that the full name of a corporation shall consist of the name as stated on the articles of incorporation; and that a search request will be processed using the name in the exact form submitted. The Administrative Code contains a standardized list of "noise words" (*e.g.*, company, limited, incorporation, corporation) which are ignored in the search process. That list does not include "d/b/a" or names used as a d/b/a. These administrative provisions are not unique to Nebraska. They set out clear rules which were in place when all parties here filed their financing statements. While Huntington and TierOne were aware that EDM Corporation did business as EDM

Equipment, they filed financing statements which would be found using the standard search logic, listing the debtor only as EDM Corporation.

As to Hastings, the addition of "d/b/a EDM Equipment" to the debtor's name field on the financing statement made the document seriously misleading as to the name of the debtor. As the Bankruptcy Court said, it simply cannot be the rule that a financing statement should be deemed effective as long as words constituting the legal name of the debtor appear somewhere in the string of words listed as the debtor's name, and regardless of whatever additional words are tacked on to the end.

Finally, we should point out that the strict filing requirements as to corporations and other registered organizations do not necessarily apply to debtors who are human beings. Prior to enactment of Revised Article 9, the question in all cases was whether a "reasonably diligent search" would locate the lien under the name used. However, as shown, Revised § 9–503(a) provides that, as to registered organizations only, the financing statement must contain the name of the debtor as indicated on the public record of its jurisdiction of organization. Admittedly, §§ 9–502 and 9–503 may well leave some room for judgment in the search process as to human beings. Thus, if a person is widely known by a name different from that on his or her birth certificate, or does business under a different name, a searcher might be expected to look under those names as well. But as to registered organizations, the name on the "birth certificate" (*e.g.*, the articles of incorporation) controls. And, this makes sense: in contrast to registered organizations such as corporations, there is no public "registry" of people from which a creditor can ascertain a person's correct legal name.

Conclusion

We agree with the Bankruptcy Court that Hastings' financing statement was insufficient due to the addition of the d/b/a information as part of EDM's name. Accordingly, we affirm.

NOTES

1.   The *EDM* court held that a financing statement that includes the debtor's d/b/a name as part of the debtor's registered organization's name does not provide the name of the debtor. Because the case was decided before enactment of the 2010 Amendments, the court didn't have the benefit of relevant amendments to 9–503(a)(1). On the same facts, the court's ruling now has express statutory support. Section 9–503(a)(1) states that "[a] financing statement sufficiently provides the name of the debtor: (1) . . .if the debtor is a registered organization. . . only if the financing statement provides the name that is stated to be the registered organization's name on the public organic record most recently filed with or issue or enacted by the registered jurisdiction of organization. . ." As noted above, a public organic record in turn is a record available to the public, filed or issued by the state or United States, to form or organize an organization. 9–102(a)(68)(A). Thus,

unless the d/b/a name appears in the registered organization's formation documents as part of its name, the debtor's name does not include its d/b/a name.

2. Section 9–506(c)'s safe harbor rule protects filings using the debtor's incorrect name if a search in the applicable filing office, under the debtor's correct name and using that office's "standard search logic," would disclose the financing statement containing the debtor's incorrect name. Although undefined, a "standard search logic" likely consists of the regular and reproducible procedures (manual or computer) used by the filing office to conduct searches. Included in a standard search logic is the database in which the filing office searches if presented with a name. In re Voboril, 568 B.R. 797 (Bankr. E.D.Wisc.2017), the creditor entered the individual debtor's name ("Stephen R. Vorobil") on the financing statement in the field reserved for a debtor's organizational name. In accordance with Wisconsin's filing office rules, the financing statement was filed in the index containing the names of organizational debtors. Wisconsin's filing office rules required a lien searcher to designate whether the name to be searched is the name of an individual or an organization. The designation apparently was needed because financing statements were stored in two different databases: one for individuals and the other for organizations. Finding that the creditor's financing statement did not sufficiently provide the debtor's name when the name appeared in the wrong place (9–503(a)), the court turned to 9–506(c). The creditor's financing statement was seriously misleading unless a search under the debtor's correct name, using the filing office's standard logic, would disclose the creditor's financing statement. Because a search in the database for individual names would not disclose the creditor's financing statement, the court concluded that its financing statement was seriously misleading and therefore ineffective.

5. FINANCING STATEMENT AUTHORIZED BY DEBTOR

Article 9 does not require that a financing statement be signed by the debtor. All states permit filing to be done electronically and an increasing number require it. Although an electronic record may be signed (Amended 1–201(b)(37)(B)), a sufficient financing statement need not be signed. See 9–502(a). Its filing need only be authorized. Section 9–510(a) states that a "filed record is effective only to the extent that it was filed by a person that may file it under Section 9–509." And 9–509 in turn allows the authorization to file to take different forms. Section 9–509(a)(1) provides for express authorization. Under it a person (usually the secured party) may file an initial financing statement only if the "debtor authorizes the filing in a signed record." Thus, although the debtor doesn't have to sign the financing statement, it must authorize the filing of the financing statement in a signed record. The convenience to the secured party is evident: at any point in the process of granting the credit, the secured party may have the debtor sign a record authorization empowering the secured party to file an initial financing statement. The secured party may then file the financing statement electronically or in writing at the appropriate time without further consent from the debtor.

In most cases, the debtor's express authorization need not be sought. This is because 9–509 contains rules that relieve the secured party of the burden of obtaining from the debtor an authorization to file. According to 9–509(b)(1), by signing the security agreement, the debtor automatically authorizes the secured party to file an initial financing statement covering the collateral described in the security agreement. This is called "ipso facto authorization." The same rule applies with respect to proceeds of collateral: by signing a security agreement covering described collateral, the debtor automatically authorizes the secured party to file a financing statement covering the proceeds of the collateral. Finally, by acquiring collateral in which a security interest continues, the acquirer (which 9–102(a)(12)(A) deems a "debtor") automatically authorizes the secured party to file an initial financing statement covering the collateral. 9–509(c). In that financing statement the acquirer will be named as the debtor. These rules, which allow for ipso facto authorization, are transaction cost-saving devices.

The secured party's failure to obtain an authorization to file a financing statement not only renders its filing ineffective. It also exposes the secured creditor to liability. If the secured party files a financing statement without the requisite authorization by the debtor, 9–625(b) allows the debtor to collect damages in the amount of the loss caused by the secured party's act and 9–625(e)(3) provides for a $500 penalty recoverable by the debtor. Moreover, in such a case, 9–513(c)(4) gives the debtor the right to demand a termination statement from the secured party that must be sent within 20 days after it receives the demand.

PROBLEMS

1. In a signed written security agreement, Debtor granted Secured Party a security interest in all its medical equipment now owned or thereafter acquired, and Secured Party advanced funds. Subsequently, Secured Party filed a financing statement naming Debtor and describing the collateral as "all Debtor's personal property." Has Debtor authorized Secured Party to file the financing statement? 9–509(b).

2. On January 1, Secured Party filed a financing statement naming Debtor and covering machine XYZ. On that date, Debtor and Secured Party were negotiating the terms of a security agreement. On February 1, they came to terms and executed a written security agreement covering machine XYZ, which Debtor signed. Two weeks before, Debtor signed a security agreement with Bank covering machine XYZ, and on the same day Bank filed a proper financing statement. Both Secured Party and Bank made loans to Debtor as part of their respective security agreements. (a) Is Secured Party's filing authorized? If so, on what date? See Comment 3 to 9–509; In re The Adoni Group, 530 B.R. 592 (Bankr. S.D.N.Y.2015). For the bearing of the question on Secured Party and Bank's respective rights in machine XYZ, see Comment 3 (fourth paragraph) to 9–503; 9–322(a)(1); Comment 4 (second paragraph) to 9–322. (b) If Secured Party and Debtor do not reach an agreement and no security interest attaches, Secured Party liable for sanctions under 9–625 for unauthorized filing of the financing statement? Does Debtor have other recourse? See 9–518.

C. THE FILING SYSTEM

1. CENTRAL FILING

Section 9–501(a)(2) designates the state's central filing office, usually the office of the Secretary of State, as the place of filing a financing statement in all cases except those involving certain real property-related collateral. In the latter case, filing must occur locally in the office where real property mortgages are recorded. This provision finally abolishes the wasteful practice of requiring filing both centrally and locally that prevailed in several states. The belief that it is more convenient to have the files in the courthouse downtown than on an easily accessible central database is an illusion. Comment 2 to 9–501.

When former Article 9 was in force, estimates are that the requirement of dual filing in a number of states produced a system of more than 4300 UCC filing offices. Lynn M. LoPucki, Why the Debtor's State of Incorporation Should Be the Proper Place for Article 9 Filing: A Systems Analysis, 79 Minn. L. Rev. 577, 579 (1995). The increased costs of a system requiring dual filing are obvious: filing creditors have more records to file, filers have more chances for error and more fees are paid.

The professed reason for requiring local filing was stated in Comment 1 to former 9–401(a): "[I]t can be said that most credit inquiries about local businesses, farmers and consumers come from local sources; convenience is served by having the files locally available and there is not great advantage in centralized filing." This statement assumes a business world that no longer exists. It is difficult to believe that today it is more convenient for a filer or searcher to go to the county courthouse and hunt around in the paper records there than it is to deal with a central, electronically accessible database. In truth, it is likely that the statement quoted above is little more than a rationalization of the political reality that in many states the county recorders were a powerful force that demanded as much local filing as possible as a condition to removing their opposition to the Code. Dual filing generated filing revenue for localities and states in which local filing offices were located. In moving from a dual filing to a central filing requirement, localities and states lost this revenue. Opposition to abandoning the requirement of dual filing therefore might be expected, at least in states receiving significant revenue from local filings. Anecdotal evidence shows that the UCC's initial enactment would have been blocked in some of the early adopting states if the county recorders had not been placated. Apparently there no opposition to Article 9's regime of central filing or, if present, the opposition was overcome.

2.   KINDS OF RECORDS FILED

a.   FINANCING STATEMENT RECORDS

Section 9–102(a)(39) defines "financing statement" as meaning "a record or records composed of an initial financing statement and any filed record relating to the initial financing statement." This definition includes amendments, continuation statements and termination statements.

Initial Financing Statement. When a "financing statement" is referred to, the initial financing statement usually is meant. Such a financing statement is effective for five years (9–515(a)). In the case of a public financing or manufactured-home transaction, the financing statement is effective for 30 years. 9–515(b). If the debtor is a transmitting utility, the financing statement's duration is perpetual. 9–515(f). The initial financing statement lapses at the end of the relevant period of effectiveness unless before that time a continuation statement is filed (9–515(c)).

The UCC Financing Statement (Form UCC1) in 9–521(a) is the safe harbor written form for an initial financing statement that must be accepted by all filing offices. Comment 2 to 9–521. If more than two debtors or one secured party are involved in the transaction or more space is needed for the description of collateral, the Addendum form (Form UCC1Ad) may be used as a supplement to the financing statement. As noted above, a person is entitled to file an initial financing statement only if the debtor has authorized the filing in a signed record. 9–509(a). But the debtor's authentication of a security agreement automatically authorizes the filing of a financing statement covering the collateral described in the security agreement and the proceeds of that collateral. 9–509(b). An unauthorized filing of a financing statement is ineffective (9–510(a)), and the filer is liable under 9–625 for actual and statutory damages.

Amendment. Under 9–512(a), "amendment" is a generic term that includes continuation or termination of an existing financing statement, adding or deleting collateral, or otherwise changing the information provided in a financing statement. The amendment must identify by its file number the initial financing statement to which it relates. UCC Financing Statement Amendment (Form UCC3Ad) set out in 9–521(b) is the safe harbor written amendment form. If the amendment adds collateral or an additional debtor to a financing statement, the debtor must authorize the filing. 9–509(a). Otherwise, under 9–509(d), amendments usually may be authorized by the secured party of record, defined in 9–511(a).

Continuation Statement. The effectiveness of a financing statement may be extended by the filing of a continuation statement. In the case in which the initial financing statement is effective for five years, the financing statement is made effective for an additional five years by the filing of a continuation statement (line 4 of Form UCC3) before lapse of the financing statement. 9–515(e). The new five-year period runs from the time the financing statement would have become ineffective if no continuation statement had been filed. Additional continuation statements may be filed, but the filer cannot achieve ten years' protection by filing a continuation statement the day after filing the initial financing statement. Under 9–515(d), a continuation statement may be filed only within six months before expiration of the financing statement. A continuation statement that is not filed within the six-month period is ineffective. 9–510(c). The filing of an amendment other than a continuation statement does not extend the period of effectiveness of the financing statement. 9–512(b). The secured party of record (9–511) may authorize the filing of a continuation statement without further authorization by the debtor if some part of the obligation secured by the security interest is still owing. 9–509(d)(1).

The effect of the lapse of a financing statement is a bit tricky. Although the financing statement ceases to be effective upon lapse, it remains effective with respect to certain parties. Under 9–515(b), a security interest that was perfected by the lapsed financing statement becomes unperfected. It remains unperfected as against all parties acquiring interests in the collateral after the date of lapse. However, 9–515(b) also provides that if the security interest becomes unperfected upon lapse, "it is deemed never to have been perfected as against a purchaser of the collateral for value." Implicit in the quoted language is a limitation on the effect of lapse. A security interest that becomes unperfected upon lapse in the effectiveness of the financing statement remains unperfected against a purchaser of the collateral for value, even if the purchaser acquired an interest in the collateral before the effectiveness of the financing statement lapsed. However, the negative implication of the quoted language is that the security interest that becomes unperfected upon lapse in a financing statement remains perfected as against one other than a purchaser of the collateral for value before lapse. A lien creditor is not a purchaser. See 1–201(b)(29), (30). Likewise, a donee does not give value for the collateral. Thus, the security interest remains perfected as against these two sorts of parties.

Termination Statement. Line 2 of UCC3 applies to termination statements. In commercial cases, when the obligation secured by the collateral covered by the financing statement is paid in full, the debtor may demand that, within 20 days, the secured party either send the debtor a termination statement that debtor may file or file the termination statement itself. 9–513(c). Since secured parties have no desire to pay additional filing fees, the common practice is to send the statement to the debtor for filing. The requirement of 9–513(c) means that the secured party has no duty to send debtor a termination statement until debtor demands one. Comment 2 to 9–513(c) assures us that even if debtors forget, the files will not be cluttered with financing statements covering defunct transactions because they automatically lose effectiveness after five years unless they are continued. Sections 9–513(a) and (b) recognize that it would be unrealistic to expect consumer debtors to request termination statements and place the burden on the secured party to file a termination statement within one month after the obligation secured by the financing statement is paid. If the secured party fails to comply with 9–513(a) or (c), the debtor may authorize the filing of a termination statement. 9–509(d)(2). A filed termination statement, if authorized, ends the effectiveness of the financing statement to which it relates.

Information Statement. A secured creditor or debtor may believe that a filed financing statement is inaccurate or filed without authorization. The believed inaccuracies or unauthorized filing may be an initial financing statement or a record relating to it, such as an amendment or termination statement. Section 9–518 allows a nonjudicial means of indicating that the information in the financing statement is believed to be inaccurate, by a filing an information statement. Form UCC5. The secured party of record as well as the debtor may file an information statement. 9–518(a), (c).

The filing of an information statement has no effect on the effectiveness of the initial financing statement or record relating to it. So, for example, an information statement declaring that a financing statement is terminated has no effect on whether the financing statement is terminated. 9–518(e). An information statement does not purge an inaccurate or unauthorized filing from the filing records, and Article 9 has no procedure for doing so. This is a problem because filings that have no legitimate basis—"bogus filings"—can harm a debtor or even a non-debtors' creditworthiness, or burden a filing creditor with the expense of establishing the continued effectiveness of its financing statement. Although the party harmed by a bogus filing likely will have a cause of action for defamation or slander of title, recovering from a judgment proof bogus filer is another matter. In response, a number of states have enacted statutes that allow for civil and criminal liability for bogus filings. See Fraudulent UCC Filing Remedies by State: 2019 Edition (2019). Some nonuniform amendments to Article 9 or separate statutes authorize the purge of inaccurate or unauthorized filings. See, e.g., Idaho Code § 28–9–515A(4), Minn. Stat. Ann. §§ 604.17(6), 545.05, S.C. Code Ann. § 36–9–501(d). Some states give their filing offices the authority to remove bogus filings from the public record. Others give the same authority to their Secretaries of State.

Assignment. Security interests are frequently assigned. Section 9–514 prescribes the methods for reflecting assignments in the filing records. Line 3 of the UCC3 applies to assignments. Consider two sorts of cases involving the assignment of a security interest. **Case #1.** A common transaction is for a dealer to take a security interest in goods sold and, almost immediately, assign the security interest to a financer. 9–514(a). In cases of this sort, the initial financing statement is commonly filed by the assignee with its name and address as the secured party. The assignee becomes the secured party of record and only it can authorize amendments. 9–511(a). It is not apparent to a searcher that the security interest has been assigned. **Case #2.** Another familiar transaction is for the original secured party to become the secured party of record by filing the original financing statement. Later, the secured party may assign the security interest to an assignee and reflect this by filing an amendment to the initial financing statement that provides the name and address of the assignee. 9–514(b). The person named in the amendment is the secured party of record. 9–511(b).

PROBLEM

What are the consequences in Case #2 if no amendment reflecting the assignment to the assignee is ever filed? The security interest is now owned by the assignee with no public notice given that the secured party of record (the original secured party) no longer owns the security interest. If the debtor goes into bankruptcy, is the assignee left with an unperfected security interest? See 9–310(c) and Comment 4 to 9–310.

As with any record, a filed record is effective only if its filing is authorized. See 9–510(a). But what has to be authorized: the filing of a record or the filing of a record that has the effect intended by the filer? For example, suppose a creditor, having filed an initial financing statement, authorizes another to file a continuation statement on its behalf. The creditor approves the filing of a record it mistakenly believes to be a continuation statement. In fact, the statement approved is a termination statement, which is later filed. Has the creditor authorized the filing of termination statement when it intended to have filed a continuation statement? The case that follows addresses this question in connection with slightly different facts involving a mistakenly filed termination statement.

In re Motors Liquidation Co.

United States Court of Appeals, Second Circuit, 2015
777 F.3d 100

■ PER CURIAM.

We assume familiarity with our prior certification opinion, *Official Committee of Unsecured Creditors of Motors Liquidation Co. v. JP Morgan Chase Bank, N.A. (In re Motors Liquidation Co.)*, 755 F.3d 78 (2d Cir. 2014), and the resulting decision of the Delaware Supreme Court,

Official Committee of Unsecured Creditors of Motors Liquidation Co. v. JPMorgan Chase Bank, N.A., 103 A.3d 1010, 2014 Del. LEXIS 491, 2014 WL 5305937 (Del. Oct. 17, 2014). We restate the most salient facts.

BACKGROUND

In October 2001, General Motors entered into a synthetic lease financing transaction (the "Synthetic Lease"), by which it obtained approximately $300 million in financing from a syndicate of lenders including JPMorgan Chase Bank, N.A. ("JPMorgan"). General Motors' obligation to repay the Synthetic Lease was secured by liens on twelve pieces of real estate. JPMorgan served as administrative agent for the Synthetic Lease and was identified on the UCC-1 financing statements as the secured party of record.

Five years later, General Motors entered into a separate term loan facility (the "Term Loan"). The Term Loan was entirely unrelated to the Synthetic Lease and provided General Motors with approximately $1.5 billion in financing from a different syndicate of lenders. To secure the loan, the lenders took security interests in a large number of General Motors' assets, including all of General Motors' equipment and fixtures at forty-two facilities throughout the United States. JPMorgan again served as administrative agent and secured party of record for the Term Loan and caused the filing of twenty-eight UCC-1 financing statements around the country to perfect the lenders' security interests in the collateral. One such financing statement, the "Main Term Loan UCC-1," was filed with the Delaware Secretary of State and bore file number "6416808 4." It "covered, among other things, all of the equipment and fixtures at 42 GM facilities, [and] was by far the most important" of the financing statements filed in connection with the Term Loan.

In September 2008, as the Synthetic Lease was nearing maturity, General Motors contacted Mayer Brown LLP, its counsel responsible for the Synthetic Lease, and explained that it planned to repay the amount due. General Motors requested that Mayer Brown prepare the documents necessary for JPMorgan and the lenders to be repaid and to release the interests the lenders held in General Motors' property.

A Mayer Brown partner assigned the work to an associate and instructed him to prepare a closing checklist and drafts of the documents required to pay off the Synthetic Lease and to terminate the lenders' security interests in General Motors' property relating to the Synthetic Lease. One of the steps required to unwind the Synthetic Lease was to create a list of security interests held by General Motors' lenders that would need to be terminated. To prepare the list, the Mayer Brown associate asked a paralegal who was unfamiliar with the transaction or the purpose of the request to perform a search for UCC-1 financing statements that had been recorded against General Motors in Delaware. The paralegal's search identified three UCC-1s, numbered 2092532 5, 2092526 7, and 6416808 4. Neither the paralegal nor the associate realized that only the first two of the UCC-1s were related to the

Synthetic Lease. The third, UCC-1 number 6416808 4, related instead to the Term Loan.

When Mayer Brown prepared a Closing Checklist of the actions required to unwind the Synthetic Lease, it identified the Main Term Loan UCC-1 for termination alongside the security interests that actually did need to be terminated. And when Mayer Brown prepared draft UCC-3 statements to terminate the three security interests identified in the Closing Checklist, it prepared a UCC-3 statement to terminate the Main Term Loan UCC-1 as well as those related to the Synthetic Lease. No one at General Motors, Mayer Brown, JPMorgan, or its counsel, Simpson Thacher & Bartlett LLP, noticed the error, even though copies of the Closing Checklist and draft UCC-3 termination statements were sent to individuals at each organization for review. On October 30, 2008, General Motors repaid the amount due on the Synthetic Lease. All three UCC-3s were filed with the Delaware Secretary of State, including the UCC-3 that erroneously identified for termination the Main Term Loan UCC-1, which was entirely unrelated to the Synthetic Lease.

A.   General Motors' Chapter 11 Bankruptcy Filing

The mistake went unnoticed until General Motors' bankruptcy in 2009. After General Motors filed for chapter 11 reorganization, JPMorgan informed the Committee of Unsecured Creditors (the "Committee") that a UCC-3 termination statement relating to the Term Loan had been inadvertently filed in October 2008. JPMorgan explained that it had intended to terminate only liens related to the Synthetic Lease and stated that the filing was therefore unauthorized and ineffective.

On July 31, 2009, the Committee commenced the underlying action against JPMorgan in the United States Bankruptcy Court for the Southern District of New York. The Committee sought a determination that, despite the error, the UCC-3 termination statement was effective to terminate the Term Loan security interest and render JPMorgan an unsecured creditor on par with the other General Motors unsecured creditors. JPMorgan disagreed, reasoning that the UCC-3 termination statement was unauthorized and therefore ineffective because no one at JPMorgan, General Motors, or their law firms had intended that the Term Loan security interest be terminated. On cross-motions for summary judgment, the Bankruptcy Court concluded that the UCC-3 filing was unauthorized and therefore not effective to terminate the Term Loan security interest.

B.   Prior Certification Opinion

On appeal to this Court, the parties offered competing interpretations of UCC § 9–509(d)(1), which provides that a UCC-3 termination statement is effective only if "the secured party of record authorizes the filing." JPMorgan reasoned that it cannot have "authorize[d] the filing" of the UCC-3 that identified the Main Term Loan

UCC-1 for termination because JPMorgan neither intended to terminate the security interest nor instructed anyone else to do so on its behalf. In response, the Committee contended that focusing on the parties' goal misses the point. It interpreted UCC § 9–509(d)(1) to require only that the secured lender authorize the act of filing a particular UCC-3 termination statement, not that the lender subjectively intend to terminate the particular security interest identified for termination on that UCC-3. The Committee further argued that even if JPMorgan never intentionally instructed anyone to terminate the Main Term Loan UCC-1, JPMorgan did literally "authorize[ ] the filing"—even if mistakenly— of a UCC-3 termination statement that had that effect.

In our prior certification opinion we recognized that this appeal presents two closely related questions. First, what precisely must a secured lender of record authorize for a UCC-3 termination statement to be effective: "Must the secured lender authorize the termination of the particular security interest that the UCC-3 identifies for termination, or is it enough that the secured lender authorize the act of filing a UCC-3 statement that has that effect?" *In re Motors Liquidation Co.*, 755 F.3d at 84. Second, "[d]id JPMorgan grant to Mayer Brown the relevant authority—that is, alternatively, authority either to terminate the Main Term Loan UCC-1 or to file the UCC-3 statement that identified that interest for termination?" *Id.*

Recognizing that the first question—what is it that the UCC requires a secured lender to authorize—seemed likely to recur and presented a significant issue of Delaware state law, we certified to the Delaware Supreme Court the following question:

> Under UCC Article 9, as adopted into Delaware law by Del. Code Ann. tit. 6, art. 9, for a UCC-3 termination statement to effectively extinguish the perfected nature of a UCC-1 financing statement, is it enough that the secured lender review and knowingly approve for filing a UCC-3 purporting to extinguish the perfected security interest, or must the secured lender intend to terminate the particular security interest that is listed on the UCC-3?

The second question—whether JPMorgan granted the relevant authority—we reserved for ourselves, explaining that "[t]he Delaware Supreme Court's clarification as to the sense in which a secured party of record must authorize a UCC-3 filing will enable us to address . . . whether JPMorgan in fact provided that authorization."

C.   *The Delaware Supreme Court's Answer*

In a speedy and thorough reply, the Delaware Supreme Court answered the certified question, explaining that if the secured party of record authorizes the filing of a UCC-3 termination statement, then that filing is effective regardless of whether the secured party subjectively intends or understands the effect of that filing:

> [F]or a termination statement to become effective under § 9–509 and thus to have the effect specified in § 9–513 of the Delaware UCC, it is enough that the secured party authorizes the filing to be made, which is all that § 9–510 requires. The Delaware UCC contains no requirement that a secured party that authorizes a filing subjectively intends or otherwise understands the effect of the plain terms of its own filing.

Official Comm. of Unsecured Creditors of Motors Liquidation Co., 2014 Del. LEXIS 491, 2014 WL 5305937, at *5. That conclusion, explained the court, follows both from the unambiguous terms of the UCC and from sound policy considerations:

> JPMorgan's argument that a filing is only effective if the authorizing party understands the filing's substantive terms and intends their effect is contrary to § 9–509, which only requires that "the secured party of record authorize[ ] the filing."
>
> . . .
>
> Even if the statute were ambiguous, we would be reluctant to embrace JPMorgan's proposition. Before a secured party authorizes the filing of a termination statement, it ought to review the statement carefully and understand which security interests it is releasing and why. . . . If parties could be relieved from the legal consequences of their mistaken filings, they would have little incentive to ensure the accuracy of the information contained in their UCC filings.

2014 Del. LEXIS 491, [WL] at *3–4 (first alteration in original) (footnote omitted).

DISCUSSION

The Delaware Supreme Court has explained the sense in which a secured party must "authorize[ ] the filing" of a UCC-3 termination statement. What remains is to answer the question we reserved for ourselves in our prior certification opinion: Did JPMorgan authorize the filing of the UCC-3 termination statement that mistakenly identified for termination the Main Term Loan UCC-1?

In JPMorgan's view, it never instructed anyone to file the UCC-3 in question, and the termination statement was therefore unauthorized and ineffective. JPMorgan reasons that it authorized General Motors only to terminate security interests related to the Synthetic Lease; that it instructed Simpson Thacher and Mayer Brown only to take actions to accomplish that objective; and that therefore Mayer Brown must have exceeded the scope of its authority when it filed the UCC-3 purporting to terminate the Main Term Loan UCC-1. JPMorgan's and General Motors' aims throughout the Synthetic Lease transaction were clear: General Motors would repay the Synthetic Lease, and JPMorgan would terminate its related UCC-1 security interests in General Motors' properties. The Synthetic Lease Termination Agreement provided that, upon General

Motors' repayment of the amount due under the Synthetic Lease, General Motors would be authorized "to file a termination of any existing Financing Statement relating to the Properties [of the Synthetic Lease]." J.A. 2151. And, to represent its interests in the transaction, JPMorgan relied on Simpson Thacher, its counsel for matters related to the Synthetic Lease. No one at JPMorgan, Simpson Thacher, General Motors, or Mayer Brown took action intending to affect the Term Loan.

What JPMorgan intended to accomplish, however, is a distinct question from what actions it authorized to be taken on its behalf. Mayer Brown prepared a Closing Checklist, draft UCC-3 termination statements, and an Escrow Agreement, all aimed at unwinding the Synthetic Lease but tainted by one crucial error: The documents included a UCC-3 termination statement that erroneously identified for termination a security interest related not to the Synthetic Lease but to the Term Loan. The critical question in this case is whether JPMorgan "authorize[d] [Mayer Brown] to file" that termination statement.

After Mayer Brown prepared the Closing Checklist and draft UCC-3 termination statements, copies were sent for review to a Managing Director at JPMorgan who supervised the Synthetic Lease payoff and who had signed the Term Loan documents on JPMorgan's behalf. Mayer Brown also sent copies of the Closing Checklist and draft UCC-3 termination statements to JPMorgan's counsel, Simpson Thacher, to ensure that the parties to the transaction agreed as to the documents required to complete the Synthetic Lease payoff transaction. Neither directly nor through its counsel did JPMorgan express any concerns about the draft UCC-3 termination statements or about the Closing Checklist. A Simpson Thacher attorney responded simply as follows: "Nice job on the documents. My only comment, unless I am missing something, is that all references to JPMorgan Chase Bank, as Administrative Agent for the Investors should not include the reference 'for the Investors.' "

After preparing the closing documents and circulating them for review, Mayer Brown drafted an Escrow Agreement that instructed the parties' escrow agent how to proceed with the closing. Among other things, the Escrow Agreement specified that the parties would deliver to the escrow agent the set of three UCC-3 termination statements (individually identified by UCC-1 financing statement file number) that would be filed to terminate the security interests that General Motors' Synthetic Lease lenders held in its properties. The Escrow Agreement provided that once General Motors repaid the amount due on the Synthetic Lease, the escrow agent would forward copies of the UCC-3 termination statements to General Motors' counsel for filing. When Mayer Brown e-mailed a draft of the Escrow Agreement to JPMorgan's counsel for review, the same Simpson Thacher attorney responded that "it was fine" and signed the agreement.

From these facts it is clear that although JPMorgan never intended to terminate the Main Term Loan UCC-1, it authorized the filing of a UCC-3 termination statement that had that effect. "Actual authority . . . is created by a principal's manifestation to an agent that, as reasonably understood by the agent, expresses the principal's assent that the agent take action on the principal's behalf." Restatement (Third) of Agency § 3.01 (2006). JPMorgan and Simpson Thacher's repeated manifestations to Mayer Brown show that JPMorgan and its counsel knew that, upon the closing of the Synthetic Lease transaction, Mayer Brown was going to file the termination statement that identified the Main Term Loan UCC-1 for termination and that JPMorgan reviewed and assented to the filing of that statement. Nothing more is needed.

CONCLUSION

For the foregoing reasons, we REVERSE the Bankruptcy Court's grant of summary judgment for the Defendant and REMAND with instructions to the Bankruptcy Court to enter partial summary judgment for the Plaintiff as to the termination of the Main Term Loan UCC-1.

NOTE

Other courts reach the same conclusion as the Delaware Supreme Court, on which the Second Circuit relied: the operative authorization is the authorization to file a specific record. See Crop Production Services v. Wheeler, 580 B.R. 719 (Bankr. W.D.Ky.2017). Although the filed record in *Motors Liquidation* was a termination statement, there seems no reason to limit the sort of authorization required to terminate other sorts of filed statements. For a filed financing statement to be effective, it is sufficient that the proper party authorize its filing; whether that party intended the filing to have a particular effect is irrelevant to the authorization. In a later phase of the litigation, JP Morgan argued that the lending syndicate held a perfected security interest in various fixtures because fixture filings had been made. See Motors Liquidation Co. Avoidance Trust v. JP Morgan Chase Bank, N.A., 2017 WL 4280934 (Bankr. S.D.N.Y. Sept. 26, 2017). The litigation is described in Chapter 8, infra. In an epilogue to *Motors Liquidation*, JP Morgan and the members of its lending syndicate, frustrated by the result in the case, sued General Motors' counsel, Mayer Brown, to recover damages resulting from the mistaken termination of the wrong financing statement. Their theories of recovery were legal malpractice and negligent misrepresentation. Affirming the district court's dismissal of the suit, the Seventh Circuit found that Mayer Brown, as General Motors' counsel, owed no duty of care to JP Morgan and the other lenders, who were not its clients. See Oakland Police & Fire Retirement Sys. v. Brown, 861 F.3d 644 (7th Cir.2017).

b.   SAFE HARBOR FORM

UCC FINANCING STATEMENT
FOLLOW INSTRUCTIONS

| A. NAME & PHONE OF CONTACT AT FILER (optional) |
| B. E-MAIL CONTACT AT FILER (optional) |
| C. SEND ACKNOWLEDGMENT TO: (Name and Address) |

THE ABOVE SPACE IS FOR FILING OFFICE USE ONLY

1. DEBTOR'S NAME: Provide only one Debtor name (1a or 1b) (use exact, full name: do not omit, modify, or abbreviate any part of the Debtor's name); if any part of the Individual Debtor's name will not fit in line 1b, leave all of item 1 blank, check here ☐ and provide the Individual Debtor information in item 10 of the Financing Statement Addendum (Form UCC1Ad)

1a. ORGANIZATION'S NAME			
OR 1b. INDIVIDUAL'S SURNAME	FIRST PERSONAL NAME	ADDITIONAL NAME(S)/INITIAL(S)	SUFFIX
1c. MAILING ADDRESS	CITY	STATE / POSTAL CODE	COUNTRY

2. DEBTOR'S NAME: Provide only one Debtor name (2a or 2b) (use exact, full name: do not omit, modify, or abbreviate any part of the Debtor's name); if any part of the Individual Debtor's name will not fit in line 2b, leave all of item 2 blank, check here ☐ and provide the Individual Debtor information in item 10 of the Financing Statement Addendum (Form UCC1Ad)

2a. ORGANIZATION'S NAME			
OR 2b. INDIVIDUAL'S SURNAME	FIRST PERSONAL NAME	ADDITIONAL NAME(S)/INITIAL(S)	SUFFIX
2c. MAILING ADDRESS	CITY	STATE / POSTAL CODE	COUNTRY

3. SECURED PARTY'S NAME (or NAME of ASSIGNEE of ASSIGNOR SECURED PARTY): Provide only one Secured Party name (3a or 3b)

3a. ORGANIZATION'S NAME			
OR 3b. INDIVIDUAL'S SURNAME	FIRST PERSONAL NAME	ADDITIONAL NAME(S)/INITIAL(S)	SUFFIX
3c. MAILING ADDRESS	CITY	STATE / POSTAL CODE	COUNTRY

4. COLLATERAL: This financing statement covers the following collateral:

5. Check only if applicable and check only one box: Collateral is ☐ held in a Trust (see UCC1Ad, item 17 and Instructions)	☐ being administered by a Decedent's Personal Representative
6a. Check only if applicable and check only one box: ☐ Public-Finance Transaction ☐ Manufactured-Home Transaction ☐ A Debtor is a Transmitting Utility	6b. Check only if applicable and check only one box: ☐ Agricultural Lien ☐ Non-UCC Filing
7. ALTERNATIVE DESIGNATION (if applicable): ☐ Lessee/Lessor ☐ Consignee/Consignor ☐ Seller/Buyer	☐ Bailee/Bailor ☐ Licensee/Licensor
8. OPTIONAL FILER REFERENCE DATA:	

UCC FINANCING STATEMENT (Form UCC1) (Rev. 04/20/11)

A National Form. Throughout the drafting of Article 9, the goal was to find a safe harbor financing statement form acceptable to filing offices all over the nation. American business is increasingly national in operation, and secured parties may file in a number of states. Uniformity in filing office requirements therefore is desirable. Acceptance of the UCC Financing Statement Form (UCC1), set out in 9–521(a), achieves that goal, and enacting states require their filing offices to accept the Form.

Additional Debtor Information. About half the states require use of 9–521's safe harbor financing statement form. The other states either allow submission of a record that contains the same information as 9–521's form or mandate the exclusive use of a financing statement form promulgated by the designated state authority (e.g., N.D. Cent. Code § 41–09–92, Va. Code Ann. § 8.9A–9–521). The forms promulgated by the latter states generally require the same information as 9–521's form. The exception is for organization type, jurisdiction of organization and organizational identity numbers. Although the safe harbor form does not require this information, some states require the financing statement to provide it. In those states the safe harbor form includes Box 1e. "type of organization," Box 1f. "jurisdiction of organization," and Box 1g. "organizational ID, if any." The availability of the organization ID number, coupled with disclosure of the jurisdiction or organization, make identification of registered entities much easier. States whose financing statements require organizational information also direct their filing offices to refuse to accept financing statements that do not provide it; e.g., NY CLS UCC § 9–516(b)(5)(C) (2021).

Financing Statement Addendum. Form UCC1Ad. 9–521(a). Most filers will not need an addendum, but some will. An addendum should be filed when there are more than two debtors or more than one secured party of record. These are relatively rare occurrences. Box 12 provides space for additional collateral descriptions in cases in which the space on the financing statement is inadequate. Some of the need for lengthy collateral descriptions has been removed by the decision in 9–504(2) to allow as an adequate description a statement that the financing statement "covers all assets or all personal property." The addendum must be used if collateral is real property-related collateral such as timber to be cut or goods that are or are to become fixtures. Section 9–502(b) requires a financing statement covering such collateral to indicate that it is to be filed in the real property records and provide a description of the real property. See Boxes 13 and 14.

Financing Statement Amendment. Form UCC3Ad. 9–521(b) is the Swiss Army Knife of UCC forms. It allows the secured party to (1) terminate the effectiveness of the financing statement, (2) continue the effectiveness of the financing statement, (3) give the name of an assignee of the security interest, (4) change debtors or secured parties of record, and (5) add or delete collateral. The Form has an addendum for additional information.

3.   WHEN FILING BECOMES EFFECTIVE

a.   FILING OFFICE INDEXING ERRORS

Section 9–516(a) continues the rule that filing occurs either when a financing statement is presented to the filing office with tender of the filing fee, or the filing office accepts the record. But what if the filing office does not correctly index the record after it is received? Section 9–517 provides that the failure of the filing office to index a record correctly does not affect the effectiveness of the filing. A secured party that has presented an appropriate financing statement does not bear the risk that the filing office will not perform its duties even though no public notice is given. How far does this protection of the secured party extend?

PROBLEM

SP-1 filed with the proper filing office a written financing statement that meets all requirements of Article 9. SP-1 availed itself of its right under 9–523(a) to furnish a copy of the financing statement to the filing office with a request that it note on the copy a file number and the date and time of the record and send the copy to SP-1. Under 9–523(d), the filing office is obliged to send the copy to SP-1 not later than two business days after it received the record in question. SP-1's practice is to file another financing statement in any case in which it has not received the copy from the filing office within ten calendar days after it dispatched the financing statement to the filing office. Although SP-1 can prove that the filing office received the financing statement, for unknown reasons the office never indexed it. Owing to staff error, SP-1 failed to note that the copy had not been returned; hence, it did not refile with the filing office. Has SP-1 made an effective filing in this case? See 9–516(a). Assume that the filing office indexed SP-1's financing statement under a name other than the debtor's name as it appears in the financing statement. Assume also that another creditor, SP-2, made a secured loan to the debtor after its filing search failed to disclose SP-1's financing statement. Is SP-1's financing statement effective as against SP-2? See 9–517; cf. 9–516(d).

b.   DUTY OF FILING OFFICE TO ACCEPT OR REJECT

Former Article 9 prescribed the requirements for a "sufficient" financing statement but was silent on what a filing office could or should do if presented with a document that did not meet these requirements. The assumption was that the filing office could reject such documents but nothing in the statute said that it must do so. There was no uniformity among filing offices on the extent to which, in deciding whether to accept a financing statement, a filing office's duties were merely ministerial (e.g., no mailing address for debtor) or whether some discretion could be exercised in interpreting the statutory requirements (e.g., adequacy of description of collateral).

Current Article 9 is decisive on these issues. Under 9–520(a), "[a] filing office shall refuse to accept a record for filing for a reason set forth in Section 9–516(b) and may refuse to accept a record for filing only for a reason set forth in Section 9–516(b)." Thus, as noted earlier, a filing office's discretion is curbed; it must reject any financing statement that lacks the information prescribed in 9–516(b), and it may reject only if it lacks this information. Hence, a filing office is not permitted to impose conditions or requirements other than those stated in 9–516(b). But what if it wrongfully rejects a record on an extra-9–516(b) ground? Section 9–516(d) provides that such a record is effective as a filed record "except as against a purchaser of the collateral which gives value in reasonable reliance upon the absence of the record from the files." The consequence of when a filing office wrongfully accepting a record that does not contain the information set out in 9–516 was described earlier in this Chapter. See 9–520(c).

Article 9 does not address the liability of a filing officer to those harmed by the officer's acts. State tort law normally applies to hold the filing officer liable for its negligence resulting in harm to filing or searching parties. Of course, wrongful rejection by the officer of a financing statement for reasons other than those stated in 9–516(b) does not cause harm to the filing party because 9–516(d) considers the statement effective as a filed record except as against relying purchasers. There is no negligence liability. In other cases, such as the negligent issuance of a certification where no financing statement was filed, filing office acts might cause harm. Jurisdictions generally take one of three positions on the matter: (1) allow recovery against the filing officer, usually based on negligence, subject to standard tort defenses; (2) insulate the officer from personal liability through coverage by liability insurance; or (3) insulate the officer from personal liability through state sovereign immunity.

4. POST-FILING CHANGES

Events occurring after a financing statement has been filed can affect the accuracy of information contained in the financing statement. Examples include changes in the debtor's name, transfers of collateral, changes in the use of the collateral, and changes in the legal identity of the debtor. Whether a post-filing change has an impact on the effectiveness of a filed financing statement depends on the particular sort of post-filing change. Former law never adequately dealt with all the changes that can take place after the filing of a financing statement, particularly changes in the name or business structure of the debtor. Article 9 deals extensively with post-filing changes. This section identifies four different kinds of post-filing changes and describes how the Article treats them.

a. TRANSFER OF COLLATERAL

Consider the following example. D granted a security interest to SP in all its equipment, and the security agreement contained a provision forbidding D to sell the equipment without SP's express written consent. SP filed a financing statement covering equipment with D named as the debtor. In violation of the security agreement, D sold some of the equipment to Buyer, who had no actual knowledge of SP's security interest or financing statement. Six months after the transfer of property, Buyer filed a bankruptcy petition. (a) Does SP retain a perfected security interest in the equipment that Buyer obtained from D? (b) Would your answer change if it can be shown that SP learned of the unauthorized sale shortly after it was made but did nothing to assert its rights in the collateral until it learned of Buyer's bankruptcy?

Perfection of a nonpossessory security interest requires two things: filing of an effective financing statement and a security interest that has attached. Accordingly, D's transfer of equipment to Buyer could affect either the continued effectiveness of SP's financing statement or its attached security interest. The two possibilities are independent of each other. See Comment 3 to 9–507. If either eventuality occurred, SP's security interest would be unperfected. Section 9–507(a) deals with the effect of a transfer of collateral on the continued effectiveness of a financing statement. Section 9–315(a)(1) addresses the effect of a disposition of collateral on a security interest in it.

The issue present in the ongoing example is one that has long been debated. What is the duty of a secured party to monitor its debtor with respect to post-filing changes? Section 9–315(a)(1) states the general rule that a security interest continues in collateral after the debtor transfers it to another person unless the secured party "authorized the disposition free of the security interest." Section 9–315(a)(2) says that the security interest attaches to "any identifiable proceeds of collateral." Thus, in this case, SP has a security interest both in the equipment in the possession of Buyer as well as the proceeds of that collateral, i.e., consideration that Buyer gave D for the equipment. Proceeds issues are discussed later. Focusing discussion on collateral, 9–507(a) provides that SP's financing statement remains effective with respect to the collateral that D sold Buyer "even if the secured party knows of or consents to the disposition."

Sections 9–507(a) and 9–315(a)(1)s' rules, taken together, work to save the secured creditor monitoring costs and impose search costs on third parties dealing with transferees of collateral. But this is true only within a range of transfers of collateral. For transfers outside this range, Article 9 indirectly imposes monitoring costs on the secured creditor. This is true where the debtor transfers collateral to a transferee-debtor located in another jurisdiction. Section 9–316(a)(3) provides in this case that the security interest remains perfected for one year after the transfer. Thus, to remain perfected, the secured creditor must perfect its security interest in the transferee-debtor's jurisdiction within that time.

Given this consequence of collateral transfers, prudent secured creditors must monitor their collateral to some extent. Note that 9–102(a)(28)(A) defines a "debtor" to include "a person having an interest. . . in the collateral." In the ongoing example, Buyer therefore is a "debtor" because, as the transferee of collateral, it acquired such an interest. See Comment 2a to 9–102. However, 9–316(a)(3)'s one-year limitation doesn't apply in the ongoing example to render SP's security interest unperfected: Buyer filed a bankruptcy petition six months after Debtor transferred the collateral to it. Buyer's location therefore has no effect on the result.

Is the result in this example fair? Or perhaps more to the point, doesn't the result depress the price buyers are willing to pay for assets, reflecting the risk that the assets they purchase turn out to be collateral in which a security interest continues? Don't these rules also mislead searchers attempting to assess the extent of Buyer's financial resources? SP has what amounts to a secret lien in property in the possession of Buyer that searchers may believe is unencumbered. No search of filings in Buyer's name is likely to turn up SP's interest. In considering these questions, recognize that 9–507(a)'s transfer rule, by preserving the effectiveness of the filing creditor's financing statement, reduces the interest rate the filing creditor otherwise will demand to make a secured loan. Thus, a complete assessment of 9–507(a)'s transfer rule has to consider both the cost it creates for the debtor (a reduced sale price) and the benefits it provides the debtor (a reduction in the interest charge of secured loans it obtains).

PROBLEM

If you are representing a creditor planning to make a secured loan to a person like Buyer in the previous discussion, what steps do you have to take in exercise of due diligence? See Comment 3 to 9–507.

b. CHANGES OTHER THAN IN DEBTOR NAME OR LEGAL IDENTITY

Into this category fall post-filing changes other than changes in the debtor's name or legal identity. A change in the secured party's name, the addresses of the debtor or secured party, and the debtor's changed use of the collateral are examples. As an illustration of changed collateral use, assume that the proper classification of the debtor's machinery initially is "equipment." The financing statement filed by the secured party accurately described the collateral accordingly. Later, the debtor puts its machinery up for sale. The machinery now has become inventory and third parties would treat it as such. The change in use therefore clearly renders the financing statement seriously misleading. Nonetheless, 9–507(b) provides that financing statement remains effective, even if the information in it has become seriously misleading. Just as 9–507(a) puts the burden of prospective creditors to trace the chain of title of their debtor's assets, 9–507(b)'s "once effective, always effective" rule puts the burden on them to determine whether the information in the filed financing statement other than the debtor's name was accurate at the time the financing statement was filed.

c. NAME CHANGE

This category covers instances in which the filed financing statement provides a name that, at the time of filing, satisfies the requirements of Section 9–503(a) with respect to the named debtor but, at later time, no longer does so. The individual or business entity has not changed, only its name has. This is sometimes called a "pure" name change. Section 9–507(c) addresses this sort of post-filing change.

PROBLEM

Shannon and Patricia Scott own all the stock of K.C. of Camden, Inc., which entered into a security agreement granting a security interest in all its inventory, accounts, machinery, equipment, furniture, and fixtures, now owned or thereafter acquired, to Bank as security for a loan. Bank promptly filed a financing statement naming K.C. of Camden, Inc. as the debtor. A year later the Scotts decided to change the name of their company to "Camden Audio and Video, Inc." They did not inform Bank of the change. The newly renamed company applied for a loan from Lender, which advanced the funds after finding no financing statement on record in the name of Camden Audio and Video, Inc. Lender took a security interest in the same assets covered by Bank's security interest and filed a financing statement naming Camden Audio and Video, Inc. as the debtor. Which secured party is prior as to the described collateral acquired by the debtor before and after the name change? Would you get the same result if the new name were "K.C. of Camden Audio and Video, Inc."? See 9–507(b)–(c) and Comment 4 to 9–507.

d.   CHANGE IN LEGAL IDENTITY

Section 9–508 deals with certain changes in the business structure of the debtor. These changes occur, for example, when the original debtor is an individual proprietor who incorporates, a corporate debtor that merges into another corporation, or a corporation that is incorporated in one state incorporates in another state. The changes in business structure creates a new legal entity. In the case of a legal person, the original entity does not survive under the same or different name. As a result, security agreements to which the original entity is a party might not bind the new legal entity, leaving the secured creditor of the original debtor without a security interest in the new entity's assets.

A change in legal identity presents a risk to a secured creditor of the original debtor. Although the secured creditor's security agreement with the original debtor typically prohibits such changes without the secured party's consent, the original debtor may breach this covenant. As with any covenant, it is costly for the secured creditor to ascertain that its debtor is complying with the covenant against unauthorized changes in identity. Determining whether the debtor has changed its legal identity requires access to the documents and resolutions, which are costly to obtain on an ongoing basis, as these items are in the debtor's control. As a result, the cost of monitoring the debtor to ascertain whether the debtor has changed its legal identity can be high. Article 9's "new debtor" rules, described below, allocate the risk of the debtor's change in legal identity between secured creditors of the original debtor and secured creditors of the entity with the changed legal identity. By doing so these rules affect the monitoring costs of both sorts of creditors.

The debtor's change in legal identity presents legal issues not present when a debtor changes its name without changing its legal identity. Does a security interest in the collateral of the original debtor continue when the collateral is transferred to the entity with a changed business structure? Does the security interest in the original debtor's assets also extend to assets acquired by the entity after the change in business structure? If the security interest of the original debtor's secured party extends to assets acquired by the entity with a changed business structure, does the secured party's security interest have priority over security interests in the same assets held by secured parties of the entity?

Article 9's "new debtor" rules address these questions. The somewhat complex rules can be briefly summarized. The Article defines an entity as a "new debtor" if it is bound by the terms of the original debtor's security agreement. 9–102(a)(56). It becomes bound by contract or law either when the security agreement is effective to create a security interest in the entity's property or the entity is generally liable for the original debtor's obligations and acquires all or substantially all of the original debtor's assets. 9–203(d). In this way the security interest of the original debtor's secured party can attach to assets had or acquired by the new debtor. Additional rules make the financing statement of the original debtor's secured party effective with respect to collateral had or acquired by the new debtor, subject to limitations. 9–508. These rules enable the security interest of the original debtor's secured party to be perfected in collateral owned or acquired by the new debtor. A final set of rules determine priority as between the original debtor's secured party and secured parties of the new debtor in collateral had or acquired by the new debtor. 9–326. The two Problems below implicate the new debtor rules. A more detailed discussion of some of them follows the first Problem. Discussion of the special priority rules for new debtors follows the second Problem.

PROBLEM

Shannon and Patricia Scott, as individuals, bought a business in May 2018. They granted a security interest to Bank in all of the business' inventory, accounts, equipment, and fixtures to secure a loan. Bank perfected its security interest by filing. The security agreement included an after-acquired property clause, and the financing statement described this collateral and identified the debtors as Shannon and Patricia Scott "d/b/a K/C Audio/Video Center of Camden." In July 2018, the Scotts incorporated the business as "KC of Camden, Inc." (or "Corporation") and transferred all their business assets to Corporation, which assumed all their business debts. Bank knew nothing about these events. In August 2018, Borg-Warner (BW) made a loan to Corporation. To secure the loan, granted BW a security interest in all Corporation's inventory in a security agreement containing an after-acquired property clause. BW's filed financing statement identified the debtor as "KC of Camden, Inc." In 2019, Corporation defaulted on all its debts. Bank sued to foreclose on the inventory that the Scotts had transferred to Corporation, which Corporation still had on hand.

(a) Does Bank have a perfected security interest in the transferred inventory? See 9–507(a), 9–508(c); cf. 9–315(a)(1), 9–320(a).

(b) Assume that Corporation purchased inventory in September and December 2018. Both purchases remain in Corporation's hands on its default. Does Bank have an attached security interest in both purchases? Is Bank's security interest perfected in the purchased inventory? See 9–508(a), (b).

Using the facts of the above Problem, KC of Camden, Inc. (or "Corporation") is a "new debtor" under 9–102(a)(56) if it "becomes bound as debtor under 9–203(d) by a security agreement previously entered into by another person." Section 9–203(d), in turn, provides that a person may become bound as a debtor on a security agreement entered into by another person either by contract or by operation of law. A common way for a successor entity to become bound as a debtor is for it to agree to become liable for all debts of its predecessor at the time its predecessor's assets are transferred to it. This general liability would include liability on the predecessor's security agreement. Another way of becoming bound as a debtor is by operation of law. In some cases, such as mergers, state corporate law renders successor entities liable for the debts of the old entities. State law generally does not make a corporation liable for the debts of its incorporator. However, if state law holds the corporation liable for the incorporator's debts, KC Camden, Inc. is a "new debtor." See Comment 7 to 9–203 and Comment 3 to 9–508. The Scotts in that case become the "original debtor" under 9–102(a)(60).

Section 9–203(e)(1) provides that if KC of Camden, Inc. is a new debtor, bound by the security agreement of the Scotts with Bank, there is no requirement that the new debtor enter into a new security agreement with Bank. Bank's security interest attaches to all the existing or after-acquired property of the new debtor (Corporation) to the property as described in the security agreement with the original debtor. Comment 7 to 9–203.

Now consider the financing statement of the original debtor's secured party. Section 9–508(a) provides that a financing statement naming the original debtor is effective to perfect a security interest in collateral of the new debtor to the extent that the financing statement would have been effective had the original debtor acquired the collateral. This includes existing collateral held by the new debtor covered by the original debtor's security agreement, not just the collateral acquired from the original debtor. Section 9–508(b) states an exception to this rule in cases in which the difference between the names of the original debtor and the new debtor causes the financing statement to be "seriously misleading." If the financing statement has become seriously misleading, it is effective to perfect a security interest only in collateral had or acquired by the new debtor before, and within four months after, the new debtor becomes bound unless a financing statement naming the new debtor is filed before expiration of the four-month period. Section 9–508(a) and (b)'s rules do not apply to collateral transferred from the original debtor to the new debtor in which a security interest continues; see 9–508(c).

Thus, if the financing statement is not seriously misleading with respect to Corporation, Bank does not have to re-file against Corporation. If it has become seriously misleading, Bank does not have a perfected security interest in collateral acquired by Corporation more than four months after Corporation becomes bound unless it files an initial financing statement before the expiration of that time. Section 9–509(b)(1)'s ipso facto rule for authorization applies to new debtors ("[b]y becoming bound as a debtor by a security agreement, a. . . new debtor authorizes the filing. . ."). On re-filing, the new debtor will be named as the debtor.

So far, the effect of the elaborate provisions described in a new debtor case is to benefit the secured creditor of the original debtor. This is because the new debtor is bound by the original debtor's security agreement, and the creditor of the original debtor's security interest remains perfected in existing and newly acquired collateral without the filing of a new financing statement, at least for four months. However, priority is a different matter. In the Problem above both Bank and BW have perfected security interests in Corporation's existing and after-acquired inventory. The Problem below implicates 9–326's priority rule in priority contests involving a new debtor.

PROBLEM

In settlement negotiations arising from the facts described in the previous Problem, Bank argues that the analysis above establishes its priority with respect to the collateral acquired by Corporation. BW disagrees, contending that under 9–326(a) Bank's security interest is subordinated to that of BW in collateral acquired by Corporation.

(a) Who has priority in the inventory the Scotts transferred to Corporation: Bank or BW? 9–325(a), 9–326(a) and (b) .

(b) Who has priority in the inventory Corporation acquired in September 2018? 9–326(a).

(c) Who has priority in the inventory Corporation acquired in December 2018? 9–322(a)(2).

(d) Assume that Bank filed a financing statement in September naming Corporation as the debtor. Who has priority in the inventory acquired by Corporation in September and December? What result if Bank, learning of Corporation's status as a new debtor, filed a financing statement in July naming Corporation as the debtor? 9–322(a)(1).

You might wonder whether Article 9's new debtor rules are worth the statutory effort expended to draft and apply them. The rules work: they give the secured party of the original debtor well defined rights in the new debtor's assets. However, the original debtor's secured party seldom will benefit from the new debtor rules. This is because applicable priority rules usually will subordinate that party's security interest to the security interest of the new debtor's secured party. Section 9–326(a)'s special priority rule subordinates the security interest of the original debtor's secured party to the security interest of the new debtor's secured parties, and Article 9's other priority rules, where applicable, usually do so too. Under 9–326(a), it does not matter whether the secured party of the original debtor filed its financing statement before the secured party of the new debtor filed its financing statement. The secured party of the original debtor has priority in the new debtor's assets only if it files a financing statement naming the new debtor as debtor before the new debtor's secured party file its own financing statement. See 9–326(b), 9–322(a)(1). As to collateral transferred to the new debtor, the new debtor rules don't apply, including its special priority rule. See 9–508(c), 9–325(a).

So where might the new debtor rules play a more useful role? Perhaps in bankruptcy against the new debtor's bankruptcy trustee. Under 544(a)(1) of the Bankruptcy Code, the bankruptcy trustee the power to avoid unperfected security interests in the debtor's property. Section 9–203(d) and 9–508, in combination, ensure that the secured party of the original debtor has a perfected security interest in collateral had or acquired by the new debtor for at least four months after it becomes a new debtor. Thus, if the new debtor files for bankruptcy within four months of becoming a new debtor, the new debtor's bankruptcy trustee cannot exercise its 544(a)(1) powers to avoid the secured party's security interest in these assets.

As is apparent in this section on post-filing changes, Article 9 is kind to filers and tough on searchers. In cases of transfer of assets, the burden is on prospective lenders or other searchers to ascertain whether a prospective debtor has acquired property that is subject to a prior security interest. Article 9 does not force a secured party that has perfected by filing to monitor its debtor to learn whether it has transferred collateral to another. In name-change cases, the secured party that has filed has four months to learn of the change and to file an amended financing statement containing the new name. Four months should be enough for a secured party to become aware of the fact that the debtor's checks in payment and correspondence bear a different name. In new debtor cases, the secured party that has filed on the property of the original debtor need take no action to protect itself against creditors of the new debtor unless the name change has made the financing statement seriously misleading. Even in this circumstance the four-month rule applies. But 9–326(a)'s special priority rule in effect compromises the consequence of this rule for priority.

D. PERFECTION BY POSSESSION

1. POSSESSION BY AGENT

The transaction in which perfection occurs by the secured party's possession is often called a pledge. Section 9–310(b)(6) follows traditional law in empowering secured parties to perfect security interests by taking possession of goods, instruments (promissory notes) and documents of title (bills of lading, warehouse receipts). The role of possession in the perfection of security interests in investment securities (stocks and bonds) will be more fully discussed in Chapter 6. These items have in common the fact that they can be physically possessed. Although a promissory note is a promise to pay money, the promise is exclusively embodied in a piece of paper and can be enforced only by the holder of the note. This is not true of a contract to build a house; one gains no rights by being in possession of the written contract. Nor is it true of accounts, such as rights to payment arising from the credit sale of inventory, or general intangibles such as copyrights; intangibles cannot be possessed.

If the secured party physically possesses an article of collateral belonging to the debtor, the debtor's other creditors should be on notice and have reason to investigate. Thus, both attachment (9–203(b)(3)(B)) and perfection (9–313(a)) occur when a secured party takes possession of collateral pursuant to the agreement of the debtor. No signed security agreement is required. See the discussion on this point in Comment 4 to 9–203.

Modern commercial affairs are conducted by organizations that must operate through their agents, and possession by an agent of the secured party for the purpose of possessing on behalf of the secured party is perfection. See the important discussion of possession in Comment 3 to 9–313. The following case discusses the limits of perfection by possession of an agent.

In re Rolain

United States Court of Appeals, Eighth Circuit, 1987
823 F.2d 198

■ EUGENE A. WRIGHT, CIRCUIT JUDGE.

We are asked to apply Minnesota law in this appeal arising from bankruptcy proceedings. The trustee in bankruptcy contends that the creditor bank has no perfected security interest in a negotiable instrument entrusted by the bank to an attorney agent. We find that there was a perfected security interest and affirm the judgment of the district court.

Norwest Bank loaned $163,000 to Rolain and a corporation of which he was president, United Wisconsin Properties. United Wisconsin executed a promissory note that was later partially guaranteed by United Corporations of Minnesota (UCM), its parent company. UCM's guarantee was secured by a note of one of its debtors, Owen. The Owen note was the collateral pledged by UCM to Norwest to secure the loan.

Norwest wished to perfect its security interest in the Owen note, which would require the bank or its agent to hold the document. Rolain was reluctant to let Norwest hold the note, however, because its terms were subject to a confidentiality agreement between himself and Owen.

The parties agreed that the note would be held by Rolain's attorney, Mannikko, under a written agency agreement.

In November 1981, in consideration for Norwest extending the note's due date, UCM increased its guarantee of the note between Norwest and United Wisconsin. The agency agreement was amended accordingly. Rolain later filed for bankruptcy under Chapter VII and that proceeding was consolidated with those of the corporations owned by Rolain, including UCM and United Wisconsin.

Norwest moved in the bankruptcy court for a partial summary judgment that it had perfected its security interest in the Owen note. Bergquist, the trustee in bankruptcy, filed a cross-motion for summary judgment. The bankruptcy court granted the bank's motion and denied Bergquist's, and the district court affirmed. * * *

A trustee may avoid transfers or encumbrances on property of the bankrupt estate. 11 U.S.C. § 544(a) (1982). The [Bankruptcy] Code vests him with the rights of a bona fide purchaser of real property from the debtor or a creditor having a judicial lien or an unsatisfied execution. *Id.* The trustee's rights under section 544 are derivative. They are those of a creditor under state law. Here the applicable law is Minn. St. 336.9–305:

When Possession By Secured Party Perfects Security Interest Without Filing.

> A security interest in letters of credit and advice of credit. . . goods, instruments (other than certificated securities), money, negotiable documents, or chattel paper may be perfected by the secured party's taking possession of the collateral. If such collateral other than goods covered by a negotiable document is held by a bailee, the secured party is deemed to have possession from the time the bailee receives notification of the secured party's interest. . . .

Comment 2 to this provision states:

> [p]ossession may be by the secured party himself or by an agent on his behalf: it is of course clear, however, that the debtor or a person controlled by him cannot qualify as such an agent for the secured party. . . .

The issue is whether Mannikko was under such control by Rolain that he could not serve as a bailee/agent under § 9–305.

The leading case on the issue of bailee/agent possession is In re Copeland, 531 F.2d 1195 (3d Cir.1976). The court held that an escrow agent, acting for the benefit of both parties, was a "bailee with notice" within the meaning of § 9–305 and that his possession perfected the creditor's security interest. *Id.* at 1203–04. *Copeland* and subsequent cases explained that the purpose of the perfection requirement is to give notice to all current and potential creditors that the property was being used as collateral and could not be repledged. . . .

Copeland noted that if the debtor or "an individual closely associated" with him holds the collateral, this would not sufficiently alert prospective creditors that the debtor's property is encumbered. *Copeland,* 531 F.2d at 1204. However, the holder of the document need not be under the sole control of the creditor. "[P]ossession by a third party bailee, who is not controlled by the debtor, which adequately informs potential lenders of the possible existence of a perfected security interest" satisfies the notice requirements of § 9–305. *Id.*

Once the parties have designated an agent with no interest in the collateral. . .and the collateral is delivered to him, the debtor no longer has unfettered use of the collateral and the notice function of section 9–305 is served by the agent's possession. . . .

Mannikko is a third party who asserts no interest in the collateral. Because the Owen note was delivered to him under a written agency agreement, Rolain would not have unfettered use of it and could not repledge it. If he did so, his lack of possession would notify the third party creditor that the note was encumbered.

Bergquist argues that a debtor's attorney may never be a suitable bailee because the attorney-client relationship necessarily means that the attorney is under the control of the client. However, courts have held explicitly that attorneys may act as valid § 9–305 agents. In *O.P.M. Leasing,* the debtor deposited money with its firm of lawyers to be held in escrow as security for performance under a lease contract. 46 B.R. at 664. The court found that the law firm was a valid bailee. *Id.* at 670.

The lawyers' possession of the security served " 'to provide notice to prospective third party creditors that the debtor no longer has unfettered use of [his] collateral.' " *O.P.M. Leasing,* 46 B.R. at 670 (quoting *Ingersoll-Rand,* 671 F.2d at 844–45). Because the debtor's attorneys had their client's consent and were acting as a fiduciary to the secured creditor, they were bound by the terms of the escrow agreement. 41 Bus. Law. at 1478. Possession of the negotiable documents served notice to third parties that the documents were encumbered. *Id.*

The same may be said here. With Rolain's consent, Mannikko signed an agency agreement, promising to act as Norwest's agent in holding the note and perfecting Norwest's security interests. He acted as a fiduciary to Norwest, was bound to respect the agency, and did so.

Bergquist argues that, even if a debtor's attorney may serve as a creditor's § 9–305 agent, the personal relationship between Rolain and Mannikko was so close that there was debtor control of the agent. He says that the two engaged in business ventures, vacationed together, and confided in each other about personal matters. Therefore, says Bergquist, Rolain controlled Mannikko and that Norwest and others were aware of that control. The argument concludes that Mannikko's possession of the note did not put others on notice of the note's encumbrance.

This is unpersuasive. Except for Rolain's claims, the record indicates nothing unusual about selecting Mannikko as Norwest's agent. All parties agreed to the arrangement. Indeed, it was desirable because Mannikko was one of the few persons whom both parties could trust to hold the note without disclosing its confidential terms. There is no remaining question of material fact.

Norwest's security interest in the Owen note was perfected.

AFFIRMED.

NOTES

1. Article 9 does not define "possession." See Comment 3 to 9–313. Thus, the term must be defined by the purpose of the requirement of perfection by possession. If the purpose of possession by a secured creditor is to put third parties on notice that the creditor might have an interest in the debtor's possessed asset, then a secured creditor or its agent has possession when the debtor lacks unrestricted control of the asset. When does that occur? When the debtor no longer has exclusive control over the asset? Or when the secured creditor or its agent has exclusive control?

2. Can possession by an agent of both the debtor and secured party perfect a security interest in the secured party? Should entrustment of possession of the collateral, a note, by the secured party, Bank, to Mannikko, the debtor's lawyer, be enough to perfect Bank's security interest under 9–313(a)? Isn't Mannikko the debtor's agent? How does this act give the debtor's other creditors notice of Bank's security interest in the note? Wouldn't creditors assume that Rolain still controls the note? See Comment 3 to 9–313. Would *Rolain* be decided under 9–313(a) or (c)?

3. The *Copeland* case, discussed in *Rolain*, involves the pledge of corporate stock. Chapter 7 discusses perfection of security interests in investment securities.

2.   POSSESSION BY BAILEE

Under former Article 9, if the debtor's property was in possession of a non-agent bailee, the debtor and secured party could create a perfected security interest in the property. How perfection could be achieved depended on the nature of the bailment. If the bailee had issued a negotiable document of title covering the goods, perfection could occur either in the document or the goods. In all other bailments, perfection could occur if the secured creditor had the bailee issue a document of title in its name, notified the bailee of its security interest, or filed as to the goods. These "other" cases are bailments in which the bailee either issues a non-negotiable document of title or issues no document at all. Article 9 retains these rules in the case of bailments in which negotiable and nonnegotiable documents of title covering the goods are issued. See 9–312(c)–(d). It alters the perfection requirements when the bailee has not issued a document of title.

Section 9–313(c) makes an abrupt change in law. Under former Article 9 (former 9-305), the secured creditor could perfect in the bailed property simply by notifying the bailee that it holds the property for the secured creditor's benefit. The bailee's agreement was not required, and the question of its duties under such an arrangement was never clearly resolved by case law. Under 9–313(c), a secured party does not have a perfected security interest in property in possession of a third person unless the person acknowledges that it holds possession of the collateral for the secured party and does so in a signed record. And if a third party is instructed by the debtor and secured party to acknowledge that it holds possession for the secured party, the person may decline; it is not required to acknowledge that it holds the property for the secured party. 9–313(f). Comment 8 notes that there are many reasons why a third person may possess debtor's goods, e.g., storage, repair, use by a lessee, that may be inconsistent with holding for the secured party.

If the third person does acknowledge that it holds possession for the secured party, the nature of its duties and responsibilities is left to the agreement of the parties or other applicable law. 9–313(g). Comment 8 states: "For example, by acknowledging, a third party does not become obliged to act on the secured party's direction or to remain in possession of the collateral unless it agrees to do so or other law so provides." Because the bailee has no duties with respect to collateral unless imposed by applicable law, the secured party must bargain for any duties assumed by the bailee. This prevents the bailee from being forced to subsidize the secured party's costs in perfecting its security interest.

In summary, under 9–313, a secured party cannot perfect a security interest in property in possession of a non-agent third party unless the party agrees in a signed record to hold possession of the goods for the secured party and further agrees as to the nature of the duties and responsibilities under which it holds the property. An issue on which former Article 9 law was particularly unsettled was whether a junior secured party could take a security interest in collateral already in the possession of a senior secured party without the consent of that party. How would the following Problems be decided under 9–313?

PROBLEMS

Debtor, the payee of a negotiable promissory note for the amount of $100,000, borrowed $10,000 from Bank and pledged the note to Bank to secure the loan. Debtor indorsed the note and delivered it to Bank. The pledge agreement provided that upon payment by Debtor of its debt to Bank, the note would be returned to Debtor with Bank's indorsement. The agreement also provided that if Debtor defaulted, Bank could either collect from the maker of the note if the note was due or sell the note to the highest bidder. If collection or sale of the note brought more than the amount of Debtor's debt, Bank was required to return the surplus to Debtor. Later, Lender agreed to lend Debtor $15,000, and, to secure the loan, Debtor executed a security agreement granting Lender a junior security interest in the note which was in Bank's possession. Debtor and Lender jointly sent a letter to Bank directing Bank to hold the note for the benefit of the Lender and, if the note was collected from the maker or sold, (1) deliver the note to Lender if the debt to Bank was paid and (2) pay any surplus over $10,000 to Lender, to the extent needed to pay Debtor's debt to Lender, with the remaining surplus going to Debtor.

1.   Bank did not reply to the letter from Debtor and Lender. Does Lender have a perfected security interest in the note?

2.   Bank promptly replied by letter stating that it agreed to hold the note on Lender's behalf according to the conditions described in Lender and Debtor's letter. When Debtor repaid the $10,000 loan, Bank indorsed and returned the note to Debtor without notification to Lender. Did Lender have a perfected security interest before Bank returned the note to Debtor? Did it have a perfected security interest after Bank returned the note to Debtor? 9–313(d).

3.   As in Problem 2 by return letter Bank agreed to hold the note on Lender's behalf. After Debtor had repaid $5,000 of Bank's $10,000 loan, the note was stolen. Is Bank liable to Lender for any loss Lender suffered as a result? 9–313(g)(2); cf. 9–207.

4.   When Bank failed to reply to the letter, Lender decided to file a financing statement describing the note as collateral. What are Lender's rights with respect to the collateral? Recall that 9–312(a) provides that security interests in instruments may be perfected by filing.

E. PERFECTION BY CONTROL

Control will be discussed more fully in the context of the materials on deposit accounts in Chapter 3 and investment securities in Chapter 6. At this point, it is worth noticing the increasingly important part played in Article 9 by the control concept. As mentioned above, Article 9 expands the role of perfection by control. The 2022 Amendments expand its role further by defining new classifications of digital assets and allowing perfection in them by control. Control is a way of perfecting a security interest in the following types of collateral: controllable accounts (9–107A), controllable electronic records (9–107A), controllable payments intangibles (9–107A), deposit accounts (9–104), electronic documents (7–106)), electronic money (9–105A), investment property (9–106) and letter-of-credit rights (9–107). See 9–314(a). Control also is a permissible means of perfection for chattel paper where all the authoritative copies of the chattel paper are in an electronic form. 9–314A. (Where the authoritative copies are in both tangible and electronic form, perfection can be achieved by possession of tangible copies and control of the electronic copies. 9–314A.) In the case of deposit accounts and electronic money as original collateral and letter-of-credit rights other than as supporting obligations, control is the only means of perfection. 9–312(b). The notion of control at work throughout Article 9 closely follows its use in Article 8 with respect to investment property. Comment 7 to 8–106 identifies the characteristic feature of control: "The key to the control concept is that the purchaser has the present ability to have the securities sold or transferred without further action by the transferor."

Article 9 defines the requirements for control for each type of collateral. The requirements differ. For instance, control of a letter-of-credit right requires the issuer of a letter of credit to "consent" to the assignment of proceeds of the letter of credit. 9–107. On the other hand, control of a certificated security—a type of investment property (9–102(a)(49))—requires control as provided by 8–106. See 9–106(a). According to 8–106(b), control of a certificated security occurs when the certificate is delivered and endorsed to the purchaser or in blank or registered by the issuer in the purchaser's name. Delivery and endorsement or registration are more onerous requirements than "consent."

The method of perfection by control can be illustrated in the case of a controllable electronic record. Under 9–314(a), a security interest in a controllable electronic record may be perfected by control of the record. A controllable electronic record is a record in electronic form that is susceptible of control. See Amended 12–102(a)(1); 9–102(b). For a person to have control of a controllable electronic record, three conditions must be met: (1) the person must have the power to enjoy substantially all the benefit of the controllable electronic record; (2) The person must have the exclusive power to exclude others from enjoying substantially all of that benefit; (3) the person must have the exclusive power to transfer control or to cause another person to obtain control of the controllable electronic record. In addition, the person must be readily able to identify itself to a third party as the person having these powers. 12–105(a)(1), (2) .

A non-fiat cryptocurrency, such as a Bitcoin, is a controllable electronic record. Suppose a lender holds a digital wallet that contains the debtor's Bitcoins. Assume also that the lender has the public and private keys to the Bitcoins, which are collateral for lender's loan to the debtor. The public and private keys give the lender the power to enjoy substantially all the benefits of the Bitcoin in the wallet. (The lender probably does not have the right to do so.) Because the lender has the private key to the Bitcoin in its wallet, it has the exclusive power to exclude others from enjoying that benefit and can transfer control of the Bitcoin to others. In addition, the lender's possession of the private and public keys to the Bitcoin allow it to identify itself to third parties as the person with these powers. The lender therefore meets 12–105(a)'s conditions and therefore has control of the Bitcoins in the lender's wallet. The lender has perfected its security interest in the debtor's Bitcoins by control.

Although 12–105(a)'s conditions for control require that the power to exclude others from enjoying substantially all the benefits of the Bitcoin and to transfer control of the Bitcoin be exclusive, "exclusive" has a technical, nonordinary meaning. The ordinary meaning of "exclusive" is something like "limited to the person; not available to another person or shared." However, according to 12–105(b), the powers to exclude and transfer are exclusive even when the power is shared. Powers that are not exclusive in the ordinary meaning of the word therefore can be exclusive under 12–105(b). For example, suppose that two secured lenders both have the private and public keys to the debtor's Bitcoins, the Bitcoins serving as collateral for their respective loans. This gives each lender independently the power to exclude and transfer. Their powers to exclude and transfer are exclusive under 12–105(b) even though the lender has the same powers. This is because the exercise of each lender's relevant powers does not depend on the exercise of the other person. Their powers can be exercised unilaterally and independently of each other's powers.

Section 12–105(c) limits subsection (b)'s allowance that the relevant powers be shared. Subsection (c) provides a shared power is not exclusive if the person can exercise the power only if the other person exercises the power and either the other person can exercise the power without the person exercising the power or the other person is the transferor of the interest in the controllable electronic record. 12–105(c)(1)–(2). However, in the example just given, each secured lender has the independent powers to exclude and transfer. Thus, 12–105(c)'s limitation does not apply. Although in any ordinary sense their powers are not "exclusive," 12–105(b) counts them as exclusive.

As a method of perfection, control is open to criticism. The purpose of a requirement of perfection is to cure the ostensible ownership problem: the inference of unencumbered ownership that third parties draw from the debtor's possession of collateral. A filed financing statement provides information that prevents third parties from wrongly drawing the inference. Obviously, a pledge does too because the pledged collateral no longer remains in the debtor's possession. The control concept in Articles 7, 8, 9 and 12 does not always cure the ostensible ownership problem; it sometimes doesn't serve as an informational substitute for filing or possession.

For instance, control is the exclusive means of perfecting a security interest in deposit accounts as original collateral. 9–312(b)(1). Control in a deposit account can be obtained in three different ways: (i) when the secured party is the depository bank at which the account is held; (ii) when the debtor, secured party and bank agree in a signed record that the bank will comply with the secured party's instructions with respect to the deposit account; or (iii) when the secured party becomes the bank's customer with respect to the deposit account. 9–104(a)(1)–(3). On the other hand, control by a secured creditor other than the depository bank requires it to either obtain the depository bank's "signed agreement" or become the bank's customer with respect to the deposit account. 9–104(a)(2)–(3). Where there is a qualifying three-party signed agreement, third parties are on notice that a deposit account might be subject to a security interest. Record evidence provided by the signed agreement signals that further inquiry might be warranted. The same is true, of course, when the secured party is the bank's customer with respect to a deposit account because the secured party is the owner of record of the deposit account. No notice at all is provided to third parties when the depository bank is the secured party. Although Comment 3 to 9–104 says that in this case "[n]o other form of public notice is necessary," in fact, no public notice is given. Perfection instead occurs automatically, by virtue of the depository bank's status as a secured creditor having a security interest in the debtor's deposit account. The ostensible ownership problem remains uncured. Earlier drafts of Article 9 allowed filing of a financing statement to perfect in deposit accounts. Filing would have given notice of the depository bank's possible security interest. The final version of the Revision eliminated filing as a permissible perfection method.

F. SECURITY INTERESTS IN CONSUMER GOODS

1. CONSUMER TRANSACTIONS UNDER ARTICLE 9

Most of Article 9's provisions apply to both business and consumer debtors. Relatively few apply only to consumer transactions. This probably reflects the fact that creditors' lawyers are closely involved in Article 9's drafting and revision while consumer groups are more diffuse and less actively involved in the process. At the same time, the risk that Article 9 or its revisions will not be enacted by states, or enacted with nonuniform amendments, if its provisions do not take consumer interests into account induces the incorporation of select consumer rules into Article 9. This political dynamic, which has operated since the drafting of former Article 9, has resulted in a compromise of sorts between creditors groups and consumer advocates. The compromise (1) subordinates Article 9's rules to applicable state consumer law rules, (2) leaves unaddressed certain rules in consumer goods transactions and (3) incorporates a limited number of consumer rules incorporated into Article 9.

Section 9–201(b) subordinates Article 9 to consumer protection rules under applicable state law. The provision effectively leaves consumer rules to state law without impairing the uniformity of Article 9 as enacted. To the same effect is 9–403(e), which leaves to enacting states the determination of the validity of defenses clauses in consumer credit transactions.

Another instance of the compromise in favor of subordination is 9–204(b)(1). With a limited exception, the provision prevents a security interest from attaching to consumer goods under an after-acquired property clause. Section 9–204(b)(1)'s purpose is to prevent a credit seller from adding new sales to the balances of old ones merely by use of an after-acquired property clause in the original security agreement. But all a seller has to do to avoid this provision is to require the buyer to sign new security agreements at the time of subsequent sales. Nothing in Article 9 then prevents the seller from consolidating the sales and subjecting all the goods sold to the buyer to a security interest securing the combined balances of all the sales. This leaves the unfortunate consumer buyer in the position, described in Williams v. Walker-Thomas Furniture Co., 350 F.2d 445 (D.C.Cir.1965), of being subjected to a lien on all property purchased until the last dollar of the consolidated balance is paid off. Some applicable state law prevents this abuse. The Uniform Consumer Credit Code 3.303 (1974) and other state statutes allocate the debtor's payments entirely to discharging the debts first incurred. As a result, the seller's security interest in each item sold is released as soon as the debtor's payments equal the debt arising from that sale.

The compromise in favor of leaving certain consumer rules unaddressed by Article 9 is reflected in 9–103(h) and 9–626(b). Section 9–103(f) adopts a "dual status" rule with respect to purchase-money security interests, under which securing purchase-money debt with non-purchase-money collateral, for instance, does not destroy the purchase-money status of the security interest. However, this treatment of purchase-money security interests is limited to non-consumer goods. Section 9–103(h) leaves to the courts the proper rule to apply in the case of consumer goods. Similarly, 9–626(a) limits the rebuttable presumption rule, applicable to calculate the deficiency, to nonconsumer transactions. Section 9–626(b) leaves to the courts the determination of the proper rule to calculate the deficiency in a consumer transaction.

Finally, the compromise produced a limited number of consumer rules. During the drafting process of Revised Article 9, a raft of pro-consumer provisions were proposed. These included limits on deficiency judgments, the award of attorney's fees for the successful debtor-plaintiff and the right to cure defaults. See Report of the Consumer Issues Subcommittee of the U.C.C. Article 9 Drafting Committee (1996). The proposals were not adopted. Nonetheless, Article 9 contains some consumer rules, primarily with respect to default and foreclosure discussed in Chapter 8. These include the mandatory disposition of consumer goods in prescribed circumstances (9–620(e)), statutory damages for failure to comply with provisions on default in consumer transactions (9–625(c)(2)), a ban on partial satisfaction in consumer transactions (9–620(g)) and enhanced notification requirements before disposition of consumer goods collateral (9–614).

2. PERFECTION OF SECURITY INTERESTS IN CONSUMER GOODS

Under 9–309(1) a purchase-money security interest in consumer goods is automatically perfected at the time of attachment. No filing is required. . The reasons for this exception are: (1) consumer transactions are frequently small, so the expense of filing can significantly add to the price that the consumer will have to pay; (2) consumer transactions are very numerous and they would unduly burden the filing system; (3) the pre-Code rule in most states did not require filing in conditional sale transactions; and (4) parties to consumer transactions are less likely to search the records. See 2 Grant Gilmore, Security Interests in Personal Property § 19.4 (1965). However, filing is necessary to perfect a nonpurchase-money security interest in consumer goods and, as will be seen later, is required for priority in consumer-to-consumer sales under 9–320(b). Comment 5 to 9–320.

Two circumstances reduce the importance of 9–309(1) today. The first is that automatic perfection does not apply to some of the most valuable kinds of consumer goods: motor vehicles, boats and the like. Under certificate of title laws, perfection of security interests in these items must usually be accomplished by listing the security interest on the certificate of title. 9–311. Security interests in airframes and jet engines must be recorded in both the FAA registry and designated international registry. See 49 U.S.C. § 44109(b), (c)(2); Convention on International Interests in Mobile Equipment and Protocol on Matters Specific to Aircraft Equipment (2001). The second reason is the advent of credit and debit cards, which have almost entirely taken over the credit purchase of "small ticket" consumer goods; most of these purchases are unsecured. However, some retailers who issue their own credit cards retain security interests in sales made pursuant to these cards. Except for the use of secured credit card transactions by a few retailers, the purchase-money security interest in "small ticket" consumer goods sales is a thing of the past. Problem 1 below helps illustrate the operational problems with 9–309(1) but it is dated because Music Center probably got rid of its credit department years ago and has been allowing Visa, MasterCard, American Express, Discovery, etc. to deal with its customers' payments problems.

The following two elementary Problems show that the same article of goods can be defined differently in different transactions with very different legal consequences.

PROBLEMS

1. Your client, Music Center, sells musical instruments of all kinds: strings (electric guitars are its best seller), pianos, brasses, and woodwinds. Music Center reserves a security interest in goods sold on credit. Some items run in excess of $5,000 in price but most sales are between $250 and $1,000. Among its customers are amateur musicians: high school band and orchestra members, and adults who play instruments for their own pleasure. Perhaps a fourth of Music Center's credit sales are made to professional musicians: members of professional performing groups and teachers who use their instruments in giving lessons. Your client complains that some customers sell their instruments at swap meets to raise money before they have paid

for them; others file in bankruptcy when they lose their jobs. Advise him how to set up workable operating procedures that will protect its security interest in goods sold. 9–309(1) and 9–320(b)(2). Assume that in the jurisdiction, filing fees are $25 for a written financing statement and $20 for an electronic filing. Would your advice change if some of Music Center's amateur musicians become so proficient at their purchased instruments that they later become professional musicians? What if a buyer signs a written representation in the contract that she intends to use the goods for a consumer purpose but, in fact, uses them for a business purpose? See In re Troupe, 340 B.R. 86 (Bankr. W.D. Okla.2006).

    2. Manufacturer sold furniture to Retailer on credit, reserving a security interest in the furniture and its proceeds after it had been sold. Retailer sold furniture to numerous consumers, reserving a security interest in the furniture. Neither Manufacturer nor Retailer filed financing statements covering the furniture they sold. Does Manufacturer have a perfected security interest in the furniture that it sold to Retailer which is still in Retailer's possession? Does Retailer have a perfected security interest in furniture sold to consumers? See the definitions of "consumer goods" in 9–102(a)(23) and "inventory" in 9–102(a)(48).

G. CHOICE OF LAW

    The discussion so far has supposed that the law governing a secured transaction is the same wherever the debtor or collateral is located. The assumption has been that the Official Text of Article 9 applies to the transaction. This of course is an unrealistic assumption, even within the United States. The Official Text of Article 9 by itself is not law. Article 9 is state law only as enacted, and some states have enacted Article 9 with nonuniform amendments. Even where states have enacted identical versions of the Article, nonuniform case law construing its provisions can develop. For both reasons, which state's version of Article 9 governs a secured transaction needs to be determined. The rules that select the law governing issues that arise in the transaction are choice of law rules. Choice of law rules are rules that control the judicial or nonjudicial forum's selection of applicable law—in this case, which state's law governs issues that arise in a secured transaction.

    Article 9 contains its own choice of law rules. These rules select the law applicable to just three issues that might arise from a secured transaction: perfection, the effect of perfection or nonperfection, and priority. See 9–301–9–306B. A secured transaction might implicate other issues. In this case the UCC's general choice of law rules contained in 1–301 select the law governing them. For instance, suppose an issue arises concerning the enforcement of a security interest or validity of a security agreement. Because enforcement and validity are not matters of perfection, the effect of perfection or nonperfection or priority, 1–301's rules select the law applicable to them.

Article 9's provisions on choice of law radically simplify the law and make it much easier to apply. Moreover, choice of law issues are often somewhat less important under Article 9. This is true because all 50 states enacted the same version of the Article (although with some variations). All jurisdictions have virtually identical provisions on perfection and enforcement of security interests in personal property, with isolated instances of minor variations in priority rules. So if Article 9 is in effect in every state, why the concern with deciding which state's law controls perfection, the effect of perfection or nonperfection and priority?

One reason, of course, is nonuniform case law and amendments addressing these issues. But there is a more important reason. There is no national filing office for UCC financing statements. Therefore, if perfection is by filing, the filing must be done in the filing office of some state. Which state? Where would the debtor's prospective creditors be most likely to look for financing statements filed against the debtor: where the debtor resides, where the debtor does business, where the collateral is located, or where a corporate debtor is chartered? These are questions to which Article 9's choice of law rules provide answers.

1.   LOCATION OF DEBTOR GOVERNS TANGIBLE AND INTANGIBLE COLLATERAL

9–301(1), which is Article 9's general choice of law rule. Under 9–301(1), the law of the location of the debtor governs issues of perfection, the effect of perfection, and priority with respect to both tangible and intangible collateral, whether perfected by filing or automatically. Comment 4 to 9–301. This rule is subject to the exceptions set out in 9–301, as well as exceptions for particular sorts of collateral such as deposit accounts, controllable electronic records, investment property and letter-of-credit rights described in other sections. See 9–302 to 9–306.

Section 9–301(2) provides that with respect to *possessory* security interests, the issues of perfection, the effect of perfection and priority are governed by a situs test: the location of the collateral controls, not the debtor's location. A rather confusing exception is found in paragraph (3)(C), which provides that, with respect to nonpossessory perfection of security interests in tangible property, the law of the situs of the collateral governs the effect of perfection and the priority of the security interest. The subsection leaves the issue of perfection to be determined by the law of the location of the debtor. Comment 7 explains the reason for this bifurcation between perfection and the effect of perfection and priority:

> For example, assume a security interest in equipment located in Pennsylvania is perfected by filing in Illinois, where the debtor is located. If the law of the jurisdiction in which the debtor is located were to govern priority, then the priority of an execution

lien on goods located in Pennsylvania would be governed by rules enacted by the Illinois legislature.

The bifurcation between the law governing perfection and priority will be discussed later. At this point the question is where and how to perfect and not the priority of a perfected security interest.

In summary, 9–301 states the rule that the location of the debtor governs the perfection, effect of perfection, and priority of security interests in intangible collateral, for intangible collateral has no location. For tangible collateral in which perfection is by possession, the law of the location of the collateral governs perfection, the effect of possession, and priority. But for tangible property in which perfection is by filing, the law of the location of the debtor governs perfection, while the law of the location of the collateral governs the effect of possession and priority.

2. LOCATION OF THE DEBTOR

As noted, 9–301(1)'s general rule is that with respect to nonpossessory security interests, the law of the debtor's location governs questions of perfection, the effect of perfection and priority. Under 9–307(b), a debtor that is an organization is located at its place of business if it has one, at its chief executive office if it has more than one place of business, and at the debtor's residence if the debtor is an individual. "Organization" is defined broadly to include every legal or commercial entity other than an individual. 1–201(b)(25).

Subsection 9–307(b) is somewhat misleading because it is subject to an exception that devours the rule in most business cases. The exception is contained in 9–307(e), which states that a "registered organization" organized under state law is located in the state of organization. "Registered organization" is defined in 9–102(a)(71) as "an organization formed or organized solely under the law of a single state or the United States by the filing of a public organic record with, the issuance of a public organic record by, or the enactment of legislation by the State or the United States." This definition is broad enough to include limited liability companies and business trusts in addition to corporations. For convenience, the discussion below refers to the guiding rule for the location of corporations and other registered organizations simply as the "place-of-incorporation" rule. Section 9–307(b) locates an individual debtor at its principal residence and an unregistered partnership at the debtor's chief executive office.

The seminal article recommending and justifying the place-of-incorporation test is Lynn M. LoPucki, Why the Debtor's State of Incorporation Should be the Proper Place for Article 9 Filing: A Systems Analysis, 79 Minn. L. Rev. 577, 595–597 (1995). Article 9 Drafting Committee was persuaded by his reasoning and adopted the test. Professor LoPucki's thesis is that the two principal bases for attacking the validity of financing statements, errors in the debtor's name and filing in the wrong office, can both be largely removed by adoption of the place-of-incorporation test. A corporation can have but a single state of incorporation and that place is discoverable from public incorporation records with relatively little expense and effort, either by a telephone call or on the Internet. This is in contrast to a location-of-collateral rule or a chief-executive-office rule, neither of which is based on a matter of public record or verifiable by computer and both of which will often require multiple filings. Since the place-of-incorporation rule will drive filers and searchers to consult public incorporation records to verify where the debtor is incorporated, errors with respect to the debtor's name should be reduced because these records will show the correct name of the debtor. This development will allow the Code to require that the debtor's exact name and state of incorporation be used on financing statements.

Article 9 does not reflect LoPucki's reasoning completely. LoPucki's thesis would locate the debtor at its place of registration, wherever the place of registration. The thesis would direct prospective creditors to search records at that location, whether the location is domestic or foreign. Section 9–307, however, does not locate foreign registered organizations at the place of their registration. Section 9–102(a)(71) limits "registered organizations" to state or federally registered organizations. Hence, 9–307(e)'s registration-locus rule doesn't apply to foreign registered organizations. Further, 9–307(c) contains an exception (a "limitation" according to the subsection's title) to 9–307(b)'s location-of-debtor rule for debtors located in jurisdictions other than the United States. The exception makes 9–307(b)'s location rule applicable to non-United States debtors only when the foreign jurisdiction's law generally requires public record notice of nonpossessory security interests as a condition of priority. If the foreign jurisdiction's law does not generally do so, 9–307(c) locates the foreign debtor in the District of Columbia. In this case, creditors are to direct their searches to Washington D.C., not to the place of registration. The actual location of the foreign debtor (place of business or chief executive office) is irrelevant.

Section 9–307(c)'s exception to 9–307(b)'s location-of-debtor rule is difficult to justify for two reasons. First, as a comparative matter, a creditor can determine its debtor's location, wherever the location, at less cost than it can determine whether 9–307(c) deems the debtor to be located in the District of Columbia. Arguably, it is also less costly to determine where the debtor's chief executive office or its place of business is located. Second, and related, in order to know whether 9–307(b)'s location-of-debtor test is inapplicable to foreign debtors, a creditor must know a fair amount about applicable foreign substantive law. It must know whether foreign law "generally" subordinates nonpossessory security interests which have not been made public through record notice. The creditor needs to know this in order to know the proper place to file or search. The only safe (and costly) alternative is to file and search in two jurisdictions: the foreign location of the debtor and the District of

Columbia. By requiring a fair amount of knowledge of foreign law, 9–307(c) requires creditors to make a significant initial investment in vetting their prospective debtors.

It is worth asking whether 9–307(c)'s exception to 9–307(b)'s location-of-debtor rule yields benefits that justify the additional costs imposed on creditors. It's also worth asking whether a simple place-of-registration test for registered debtors, domestic or foreign, wouldn't be less costly for filing and searching creditors. Section 9–316(a) continues perfection for different periods when the debtor or collateral moves to another jurisdiction. Section 9–316(a)(2) provides that when the debtor changes its location to another jurisdiction, the secured party has four months after removal to file in the state of removal. Strictly speaking, a corporation doesn't change its place of incorporation; it must incorporate in the state of removal, or merge with or be acquired by a corporation in the other state. Because a corporation does not retain its legal status when it reincorporates or merges, reincorporation or merger cannot constitute "a change of the debtor's location to another jurisdiction" for 9–316(a)(2)'s purposes. Instead, 9–316(a)(3) applies so that the secured creditor's security interest remains perfected for "one year after a transfer of collateral to a person that thereby becomes a debtor and is located in another jurisdiction." See Example 4, Comment 2 to 9–316. Monitoring will always be required in these situations, but a corporation is probably less likely to change its place of incorporation than its chief place of business, and it is certainly less likely to do so than to move its goods around.

At first glance, a place-of-incorporation rule might seem to direct a disproportionate number of filings to Delaware, where over half of large U.S. corporations are incorporated. But Professor LoPucki found that there is a 93% chance that a corporation is incorporated in the state where it operates. LoPucki, 79 Minn. L. Rev. at 600. With respect to the large corporations that do incorporate in Delaware, some have no secured debt and, for those that do, their creditors are likely to be sufficiently sophisticated to know to file in Delaware. The location of a company's chief place of business is only important for businesses that are not registered organizations, e.g., sole proprietorships and general partnerships.

The choice of law governing perfection is decisive in the case below. The dispute there was between two downstream purchasers of oil (J. Aron and BP) and their remote sellers (the Kansas and Texas Producers). The Producers contended that they had a continuing security interest in the oil J. Aron and BP purchased from their immediate seller. J. Aron and BP disagreed. Under 9–317(b) a buyer takes free of a security interest if the buyer gives value and takes delivery of the collateral without knowledge of the security interest and before it is perfected. Whether the Producers were perfected depends on the applicable state law governing perfection of their security interests.

In re SemCrude LP

United States Court of Appeals for the Third Circuit, 2017
864 F.3d 280

■ **Opinion by:** AMBRO

I.   BACKGROUND

SemGroup's Two Businesses

SemGroup L.P. and its subsidiaries (jointly and severally referred to as "SemGroup") provided "midstream" oil services. It purchased oil from producers and resold it to downstream purchasers. It also traded financial options contracts for the right to buy or sell oil at a fixed price on a future date. At the end of the fiscal year preceding bankruptcy, SemGroup's revenues were $13.2 billion.

Two of SemGroup's operating companies, SemCrude, L.P. and Eaglwing, L.P., purchased oil from thousands of wells in several states and from thousands of oil producers, including from Appellants, producers located in Texas, Kansas, and Oklahoma. The producers act on behalf of many parties who have interests in the oil at the wellhead. These interest owners include the person or entity who owns the land in fee simple, and thus owns the rights to the minerals. That person or entity transfers the mineral rights to an oil company through a lease. The company holds the "working interest"—the right to drill and sell the oil from the leased land. The working-interest owners appoint an operator to work the well. Most of the producers in this appeal are owners of working interests or operators.

After purchase, SemGroup moved the oil via trucks and pipelines and stored it in major aggregation centers in Oklahoma, Kansas, and elsewhere. Per industry custom, SemGroup purchased the oil on credit, paying for it on the 20th day of the month following the sale. For example, oil purchased in January would be paid for on February 20.

SemGroup always paid the producers for the oil in full until the bankruptcy filing. It then resold the product to downstream purchasers, including to Appellees, J. Aron & Company and BP Oil Supply Co., both large oil distributors. . . . Again, per industry custom the downstream purchasers bought the oil on credit, with payment due the 20th of the following month. * * *

Until the bankruptcy filing, J. Aron and BP paid in full for the oil they bought. BP also sold oil to SemGroup, so when payment was due they would net out their obligations—*i.e.*, if BP bought $10 million from SemGroup and SemGroup bought $8 million from BP, then BP would just pay $2 million to SemGroup. * * *

Bankruptcy Proceedings

Following its Chapter 11 filing, more than a thousand oil producers were unpaid. Oil producers, purchasers, and SemGroup's lending banks inundated the Bankruptcy Court with adversary proceedings and motions to distribute SemGroup's assets. The Court established omnibus procedures to determine the producers' rights and priorities versus the banks, with a single adversary proceeding for each state where the producers sold product. The relative priority of the producers and downstream purchasers was preserved for later rulings. * * *

Meanwhile, J. Aron and BP filed separate adversary proceedings where they sought to tender the amount they owed to the bankruptcy estate in exchange for a release from all liability. The producers also filed nearly 30 separate lawsuits against J. Aron and BP in state and federal courts. These suits were transferred to the Bankruptcy Court for resolution. . . .

After a discovery process involving more than 100 parties, over 150 depositions, and millions of pages of documents, J. Aron and BP moved for summary judgment against the Appellant-Producers (hereafter, the "Producers"). The Bankruptcy Court filed proposed findings of facts and conclusions of law recommending summary judgment in favor of J. Aron and BP. It concluded in exceptional depth and easily understood language that . . . that J. Aron and BP purchased the oil from SemGroup free of any purported security interest either as (1) buyers for value, or (2) as buyers in the ordinary course. * * *

IV. ANALYSIS

[T]he Texas and Kansas Producers rely on their states' nonuniform amendments to the Uniform Commercial Code, which they argue give them automatically perfected security interests in the oil they sold to SemGroup that J. Aron and BP ultimately received. We first conclude that the Producers do not have a perfected security interest even if Texas or Kansas law applied. Accordingly, J. Aron and BP purchased the oil from SemGroup free of any lien as buyers for value. U.C.C. § 9–317(b). * * *

A.   *The U.C.C. Claim*

* * * The Producers contend that they sold the oil to SemGroup on credit subject to a security interest—that is, they retained a lien in the oil as long as SemGroup had not paid them for that oil, and if SemGroup did not pay for the oil the Producers could hypothetically repossess it. The oil they sold here is the "collateral," and SemGroup, who purchased the oil, is the "debtor." The Producers further assert that their security interests continued in the oil even after SemGroup resold it to J. Aron and BP. *See* U.C.C. § 9–315(a)(1) ("a security interest or agricultural lien continues in collateral notwithstanding sale"). Thus, J. Aron and BP received the oil subject to the security interest, and, because SemGroup did not pay the Producers in full, the Producers had the right to reclaim the oil from J. Aron and BP. Accordingly, J. Aron and BP would have to return to the Producers the value of the oil used to set off options debt with SemGroup.

J. Aron and BP, however, contend that they took the oil as buyers for value and thus free of any security interest. *See* U.C.C. § 9–317(b) ("[A] buyer, other than a secured party, of . . . goods . . . takes free of a security interest . . . if the buyer gives value and receives delivery of the collateral without knowledge of the security interest . . . and before it is perfected."). This defense is simple: if a security interest is not perfected, a buyer takes the property free of that security interest unless the buyer actually knew of the security interest. As discussed below, we conclude that J. Aron and BP qualify as buyers for value. To do so, we address whether (1) the security interests were perfected, (2) J. Aron and BP actually bought the oil or acquired it as secured parties, and (3) they knew the Producers' security interests even existed.

1.   Security interests were not perfected.

To perfect a security interest, in most instances a party must file a financing statement in the appropriate state office. *See* U.C.C. § 9–310(a) ("[A] financing statement must be filed to perfect all security interests."). Here, the Texas and Kansas Producers did not file a financing statement or take any other steps to perfect their security interests. Instead, they urge us to apply their states' versions of the U.C.C. because they contain nonuniform amendments that the Producers argue give oil producers an automatically perfected security interest in the oil they produced. But the Producers miss that, even if we were to apply Texas or Kansas law,[5] we apply those states' versions of Article 9, not just their nonuniform amendments in isolation.

Texas and Kansas, along with every other state, adopted a key feature of revised U.C.C. Article 9: its uniform choice-of-law provision. So even starting with Texas's or Kansas's U.C.C., we begin with this rule, which states that "while a debtor is located in a jurisdiction, the local law of that jurisdiction governs perfection, the effect of perfection or nonperfection, and the priority of a security interest in collateral." U.C.C. § 9–301(1); *see* Tex. Bus. & Com. Code § 9.301(1) (same); Kan. Stat. § 84–9–301(1) (same).

Here, as noted above, SemGroup is the debtor because it purchased the oil on credit subject to the Producers' security interests. SemGroup and its affiliates are registered in Delaware or Oklahoma. U.C.C. § 9–307(e) ("A registered organization that is organized under the law of a State is located in that State."). Accordingly, the "local law of [Delaware or Oklahoma] governs perfection," not Texas or Kansas law. U.C.C. § 9–301(1). Oklahoma and Delaware require perfection by filing a financing statement. Because it is undisputed that the Producers never made such a filing, their interests are unperfected.

---

[5]   The Bankruptcy and District Courts applied Delaware's U.C.C. choice-of-law rules because that is the forum state. We need not reach this issue for the purposes of this appeal because, regardless of the state, each has the same choice-of-law rule, U.C.C. § 9–301.

The only potential exception to § 9–301(1)'s debtor-location rule is for as-extracted collateral. See U.C.C. § 9–301(4) ("The local law of the jurisdiction in which the wellhead or minehead is located governs perfection, the effect of perfection or nonperfection, and the priority of a security interest in as-extracted collateral."). The Producers' oil does not qualify for this exception because, for oil to be as-extracted collateral, a debtor must have a preexisting interest in the oil *before* it is extracted at the wellhead. *See* U.C.C. § 9–102(a)(6) ("'As-extracted collateral' means (A) oil, gas, or other minerals that are subject to a security interest that: (i) is created by *a debtor having an interest in the minerals before extraction*; and (ii) attaches to the minerals as extracted; or (B) accounts arising out of the sale at the wellhead or minehead of oil, gas, or other minerals in which *the debtor had an interest before extraction*.") (emphases added). Here, SemGroup had no interest in the oil while it was in the ground. Only after the Producers extracted and sold it did SemGroup become involved.

The Producers nonetheless argue that these automatic perfection laws "necessarily displace" the choice-of-law rule. *See* Tex. Bus. & Com. Code § 9.343(p) ("The rights of any person claiming under a security interest or lien created by this section are governed by the other provisions of this chapter except to the extent that this section *necessarily displaces* those provisions.") (emphasis added); Kan. Stat. § 84–9–339a(*o*) (same). But nothing about these automatic perfection laws "necessarily displace[s]" the rest of Article 9. Rather, these local laws apply when the debtor is located in Texas or Kansas, or where the debtor is so closely involved at the wellhead that it has some preexisting interest in the oil before it is extracted from the ground so that the oil constitutes as-extracted collateral. U.C.C. §§ 9–301(1), (4). * * *

The Producers also argue that Delaware or Oklahoma perfection laws incorporate the automatic-perfection oil lien laws. They rely on an Official Comment to a separate section of Article 9 (on buyer defenses) that generally mentions the existence of nonuniform amendments. *See* U.C.C. § 9–320 cmt.7 ("Several [states] have adopted special statutes and nonuniform amendments to Article 9 to provide special protections to mineral owners."). This Comment recognizes that certain states might adopt special provisions to protect mineral owners; it does not automatically incorporate unspecified local laws. Beyond that, a Comment to the U.C.C. does not supersede statutory text, and the Comment says nothing about overriding Article 9's choice-of-law rules.

All told, the Producers misunderstand the burdens and uncertainty their U.C.C. interpretation would create. SemGroup resold oil from thousands of producers located in eight different states. The downstream purchasers, including J. Aron and BP, had no dealings with this diverse group of producers, did not even know who these producers were, and were buying oil in bulk from storage centers, so they did not know which producers' oil they received. To determine possible conflicting security interests, instead of merely checking the filing records of the states of the entities they purchase from, downstream purchasers would have to discover the identities and locations of potentially thousands of producers with whom they have no contact.

Eliminating this type of uncertainty was of foundational importance to the U.C.C.'s simplified notice system. Prior to the 2001 revisions of the U.C.C., parties normally had to search for financing statements wherever a debtor had collateral to know if anything was encumbered. *See* U.C.C. § 9–103(b)(1) (1995) ("Except as otherwise provided in this subsection, perfection and the effect of perfection or non-perfection of a security interest in collateral are governed by the law of the jurisdiction where the collateral is when the last event occurs on which is based the assertion that the security interest is perfected or unperfected."). Now the U.C.C. requires that a party check for filings in the debtor's location and understand that locale's secured transactions laws. *See* U.C.C. § 9–101 cmt.4(c) ("This Article changes the choice-of-law rule governing perfection (i.e., where to file) for most collateral to the law of the jurisdiction where the debtor is located."). If the oil producers want to encumber the oil they sell to an out-of-state first purchaser, all they need to do is comply with the rules uniformly applicable throughout the country to all sellers of goods—file a financing statement in the state where that first purchaser is located.

In conclusion, under U.C.C. § 9–301(1), Delaware and Oklahoma law govern perfection. Texas and Kansas's nonuniform amendments to Article 9 do not save the Producers. J. Aron and BP thus may qualify as buyers for value because the security interests the Producers may have claimed were not perfected. See U.C.C. § 9–317(b) (buyer-for-value defense only applies "before [the security interest] is perfected").

[The court went on to find that J. Aron and BP took free of the Producer's unperfected security interest under 9–317(b).]

3.   GOODS COVERED BY CERTIFICATE OF TITLE

a.   WHAT LAW GOVERNS PERFECTION?

The choice of law rule for goods covered by a certificate of title is an exception to 9–301(1) general choice of law rule. Section 9–303(c) states: "The local law of the jurisdiction under whose certificate of title the goods are covered governs perfection, the effect of perfection or nonperfection, and the priority of a security interest in the goods covered by a certificate of title from the time the goods become covered by the certificate of title until the goods cease to be covered by the certificate of title." Unlike 9–301(1)'s general choice of law, 9–303(c)'s choice of law rule is not a debtor or collateral locus rule. The law of the jurisdiction that has issued the certificate of title covering the goods governs perfection, the effect of perfection or nonperfection and priority of a security interest. Because 9–

303(c)'s states a place-of-issuance rule, the debtor need have no connection with the state issuing the certificate of title. 9–303(a).

b. THE BASIC RULES OF PERFECTION

Filing a financing statement is neither necessary nor effective to perfect a security interest in goods in which a certificate-of-title law provides for a security interest to be indicated on the certificate as a condition or result of perfection. 9–311(a)(2). Compliance with such a statute is the equivalent to filing a financing statement and a security interest in such property may be perfected only by compliance. 9–311(b). "[A] security interest so perfected remains perfected notwithstanding a change in the use or transfer of possession of the collateral." 9–311(b).

A special rule is for goods held in inventory for sale or lease by a dealer who sells goods of that kind. Ordinarily, no certificate of title for a motor vehicle is issued by the state until the vehicle is sold or leased by the dealer. The manufacturer sends a certificate of origin to the dealer and when the vehicle is sold, the dealer sends the certificate of origin along with the buyer's application for a certificate of title to the state's department of motor vehicles (DMV). If the sale is being financed, the certificate of title issued must indicate the security interest of the financer as a condition of perfection. Hence, during the time the dealer holds the vehicles for sale or lease, no certificate of title has yet been issued, and 9–311(d) provides that during this time 9–311 does not apply. A secured party financing the dealer's inventory may perfect its security under normal rules applying to inventory, that is by filing a financing statement. Section 9–311(d) does not apply to dealers who only lease goods; even though they eventually sell the goods, they should not be considered to be "in the business of selling goods of that kind." Comment 4 to 9–311. See Union Planters Bank, N.A. v. Peninsula Bank, 897 So.2d 499 (Fla. Dist.Ct.App.2005) (debtor is car rental company).

c. CHANGE IN DEBTOR'S LOCATION

Because 9–303(c) is a place-of-issuance rule, the debtor's change of location cannot affect the law governing a security interest in a good covered by a certificate of title. Typically, state laws require that motor vehicles have certificates of title and that perfection of security interests in goods covered by certificates of title occurs either upon indication of a security interest on a certificate of title or upon receipt by a state's department of motor vehicles (DMV) of a properly tendered application for a certificate of title on which the security interest is to be indicated. See Legislative Note at end of 9–311. In the following case Baker bought a car in New Mexico and obtained a certificate of title in that state when she registered the car. The certificate of title listed Primus as the lienholder. She moved to Wisconsin and registered the car there but did not obtain a Wisconsin certificate of title. Three years after her move to Wisconsin Baker filed in bankruptcy. Must Primus take action to perfect its security interest in Wisconsin? Since anyone buying the car from Baker or lending money on the security of the car would demand to see the certificate of title and would learn about Primus's security interest, why should Primus have to take any action in Wisconsin at all?

In re Baker

United States Court of Appeals, Seventh Circuit, 2005
430 F.3d 858

■ TERENCE T. EVANS, CIRCUIT JUDGE.

In 2001, Judith K. Baker purchased a 2000 Oldsmobile Alero. Financing was provided by Primus Financial Services, and the State of New Mexico issued a certificate of title listing Primus as the lienholder. Soon after the deal was made, Baker moved to Wisconsin. Although she registered her vehicle in Wisconsin after the move, Baker never obtained a Wisconsin certificate of title. The New Mexico certificate of title, however, remained in place.

In 2004, some 3 years after her move to Wisconsin, Baker filed a Chapter 7 petition in the bankruptcy court. Claire Ann Resop was appointed trustee of Baker's bankruptcy estate. As bankruptcy trustee, Resop enjoys "strongarm" powers and may seek to avoid unperfected liens, assert a superior interest in assets, and distribute the value of those assets to other creditors. See 11 U.S.C. § 103(a); 11 U.S.C. § 544(a). This means she could, for example, challenge the validity of the lien Primus holds on Baker's vehicle, seek to gain control over it, sell it, and use the funds it yields to pay off general creditors to whom Baker owes money. That is what the trustee wanted to do in this case, but her efforts were thwarted by both the bankruptcy court and the district court. Today we resolve her appeal from the final judgment of the district court.

This appeal requires that we interpret several Wisconsin statutes. Under her reading of these statutes, the trustee argues that within 4 months of Baker's move to Wisconsin, Primus was required to reperfect its security interest in her vehicle there. Since Primus did not do so, the trustee believes that Primus's lien may be avoided.

Primus counters that this argument misreads Wisconsin law and that it had no duty to reperfect its interest simply because Baker moved herself and her vehicle to a different state but neglected to apply for a new title when she got there. Under Wisconsin law, Primus argues, the lien recorded on the New Mexico title remained valid.

The bankruptcy court examined the relevant statutes and agreed with Primus, as did the district court on appeal. . . .

Our starting point is the Wisconsin motor vehicle code. Wis. Stat. § 342.19(6) provides: "If a vehicle is subject to a security interest when brought into this state, § 409.316 states the rules which apply to determine the validity and perfection of the security interest in this state."

In turn, § 409.316, which is part of the state's codification of the Uniform Commercial Code, tells us in relevant portion: "A security interest perfected pursuant to the law of the jurisdiction designated in § 409.301(1) or 409.305(3) remains perfected until the earliest of: . . . (b) The expiration of 4 months after a change of the debtor's location to another jurisdiction." § 409.316(1). Finally, we consult § 409.301(1), which instructs us that "while a debtor is located in a jurisdiction, the local law of that jurisdiction governs perfection, the effect of perfection or nonperfection, and the priority of a security interest in collateral."

The trustee urges us to stop here and conclude that Primus's security interest in the vehicle became unperfected when Baker moved to Wisconsin and 4 months passed without Primus doing anything to reperfect its interest. And that might be a reasonable reading were it not for the fact that, as the district court explained, § 409.301(1) cannot be read without reference to the limiting language in the introduction to § 409.301. That limiting language tells us that the subsections provide the rules governing perfection *"[e]xcept as otherwise provided* in §§ 409.303 to 409.306." (Emphasis added.)

And so, turning to § 409.303, as the statutory guideposts tell us we must, we find the reason why the trustee's attempt to avoid the lien must fail. Section 409.303 provides the relevant law on the perfection and priority of security interests for "goods covered by a certificate of title." Specifically, § 409.303(3) states: "The local law of the jurisdiction under whose certificate of title the goods are covered governs perfection, the effect of perfection or nonperfection, and the priority of a security interest in goods covered by a certificate of title from the time the goods become covered by the certificate of title until the goods cease to be covered by the certificate of title." In nonlawyer speak, the 4-month period for reperfection provided by § 409.316(1)(b) does not apply to titled goods. Under Wisconsin law, as long as the New Mexico title continued in force, it was sufficient to protect Primus's interest. . . .

. . . . The rule that a security interest must be reperfected within 4 months after a debtor moves to a new jurisdiction makes sense in the context of untitled goods. But it is unreasonable to suggest that a lienholder's interest can become undone simply because an owner neglects her duty to apply for a new title when she changes states. Finance companies do not title vehicles, owners do. Had Baker retitled her vehicle in Wisconsin, Primus would have had to reperfect when its interest became unperfected under New Mexico law. Wis. Stat. § 409.316(4). But we know of no authority for the notion, suggested by the trustee at oral argument, that a secured creditor is obligated to keep track of the domiciles of its debtors. An important function of a title is to record a secured creditor's interest, regardless of where the payments come from, or where the debtor and vehicle may roam. In this case, the

New Mexico title is the only record available, and the Wisconsin statutes yield the sensible result that, under that valid title, the creditor's interest remains perfected. The judgment of the district court is AFFIRMED.

NOTES

1.   States usually require owners to register their vehicles in the state where the owner is located and pay regulatory fees in order to obtain license plates or tags. When a debtor moves from State A to State B, she usually has a limited time within which to register the auto in that state and obtain State B license plates or tags before traffic police start issuing citations. The purpose of the registration statutes is identification and revenue, and the sooner the owner registers, the sooner the state gets its money. When the debtor registers the auto in State B, DMV will demand to see the certificate of title issued by State A as proof of her ownership. Typically, the law of State B will require the surrender of the State A title before State B will issue a new one. DMV is required to indicate SP's security interest on the new State B title. If this is done, SP's security interest continues perfected in the auto pursuant to the new certificate of title and the former certificate of title is no longer effective because the auto has become covered by a certificate of title issued by another jurisdiction. 9–303(b). As Comment 6 to 9–303 states: "Ideally, at any given time, only one certificate of title is outstanding with respect to particular goods." Although in most cases this is true, things sometimes can go wrong, as in *Baker*. We are not told why the Wisconsin DMV did not take up the New Mexico certificate of title and issue a Wisconsin certificate of title when Baker registered the car in Wisconsin.

2.   (a) Assume that Baker had obtained a Wisconsin certificate of title when she registered her car in Wisconsin. Also assume that the Wisconsin DMV neglected to list Primus's lien on the certificate of title. Later, Ms. Baker sold the car to a consumer buyer who had no knowledge of Primus's security interest. Does the buyer take free of Primus's security interest? See 9–316(e), 9–337(1).

(b)   Assume the same facts as in (a) except that instead of selling the car, Baker filed for bankruptcy two months after she moved to Wisconsin and obtained the certificate of title. Is Baker's bankruptcy trustee prior to Primus? What if Baker filed six months after issuance of the new title? See 9–316(d) and Comment 5. Does 9–316(e) apply in this case? See the definition of "purchaser" in 1–201(b)(30); In re Hicks, 491 F.3d 1136 (10th Cir.2007) (secured party's lien omitted owing to filing office error).

PROBLEMS

1.   Ace Gaming Supplies, Inc. ("AGS") is a Delaware corporation that sells slot machines, gaming tables, billiard tables, and related products, to casinos and other end-users, as well as to some retail dealerships that resell these goods. The headquarters of AGS is in Century City in Los Angeles. All marketing, financial and accounting services are conducted in this office. AGS maintains warehouses in Reno and Las Vegas, Nevada, and in Phoenix, Arizona, where gaming products are stored pending sale. The founder, Ace

Goodman, is the Chief Executive Officer of AGS, and his son, Gerald, is the Chief Operating Officer. Ace has an apartment in Century City but spends most of the year in Aspen, Colorado, where, as his son puts it, he still "calls the shots." Gerald lives in Beverly Hills the year round. The years 2020–2021 have not been kind either to the company or Ace personally. AGS's sales declined and Ace's personal investment portfolio suffered heavy losses. Bank had been financing the company from its inception entirely on the basis of unsecured loans that were personally guaranteed by Ace. In late 2021, the company needed a major cash infusion to meet some of the mounting bills that it owed its suppliers and other impatient creditors but when Bank examined Ace's personal financial situation to determine the value of his guarantee, it decided that any new loan to the company would have to be secured.

In what jurisdiction should Bank perfect security interests in the assets of the company listed below and how should perfection be accomplished? In answering these questions, consider 9–301 through 9–307's rules. Also consult the definitions of some kinds of collateral: "account" 9–102(a)(2); "chattel paper" 9–102(a)(11); "deposit account" 9–102(a)(29); "equipment" 9–102(a)(33); "general intangible" 9–102(a)(42); "instrument" 9–102(a)(47); "inventory" 9–102(a)(48); and "promissory note" 9–102(a)(65). The next Chapter deals with these definitions in more detail, but for now you need a general idea of their meaning. See also "registered organization" 9–102(a)(71) and Comment 4 to 9–307.

(a)   The goods located in the warehouses in Nevada and Arizona.

(b)   The proceeds of the sale of these goods. These proceeds may consist of the following: (1) Checks received from cash buyers and buyers making payments on credit contracts. These checks are deposited daily in the AGS's deposit account in Bank in its Los Angeles office. We will discuss methods of perfecting security interests in deposit accounts (9–314) in more detail in the next chapter. (2) For those buyers who are better credit risks, the unsecured obligations, set out in written contracts, that arise upon the credit sale of the goods to casinos or dealers who agree to pay in cash the entire amount within 90 days of the sale. (3) For less creditworthy buyers, the secured obligations, set out in written contracts, that arise upon the credit sale of the goods to casinos or dealers who agree to pay the purchase price in monthly installments over a period of one or two years and to grant the company a security interest in the goods they buy to secure the unpaid portion of the purchase price.

(c)   The business machines: (1) computers, printers, scanners, copiers, etc., located at both the Century City office and at the warehouses; and (2) the heavy loading machines located at the three warehouses in Nevada and Arizona.

(d)   Several promissory notes, totaling over $250,000, which are made payable to the order of AGS "on demand" and held by the company in its safe in Century City. These notes result from AGS's practice of demanding that buyers delinquent more than 60 days on an unsecured debt give AGS a note as evidence of their indebtedness until they can come up with the money. See 9–312(a) and 9–313(a).

2.   Assume that AGS is a general partnership in which the only partners are Ace and Gerald Goodman. Also assume that Ace has a 75% share and Gerald, the remaining 25%. The name of the partnership is "Ace Gaming Supplies." Under these changed facts, what are the results in Problem 1(a)–(d)? See Comment 2 to 9–307.

3.   What action would Bank have to take to safeguard its security interests if: (1) AGS Inc. in Problem 1 subsequently moved the company headquarters to Dallas, Texas, in order to take advantage of the more favorable tax climate in Texas? or (2) the partnership in Problem 2 made the same move? Assume in each case that Ace and Gerald moved their personal residences to Texas as well. See 9–316(a)(2).

4.   Assume that AGS Inc. owns 20 trucks and cars. All of the trucks and most of the cars are located at the warehouses. A few cars are at the Century City office. How should Bank perfect its security interest in these motor vehicles? And in what jurisdiction? See 9–303, Comment 3 to 9–303, 9–311(a)(2)–(3), and 9–316(d)–(e). You may assume that all the states involved have laws similar to that described in the italicized Legislative Note appended to 9–311.

CHAPTER 3

PRIORITY

A. INTRODUCTION

Attachment of a security interest gives the secured party a property right in specific assets of the debtor. If the security interest is perfected, the security interest is enforceable against other creditors. This Chapter deals with the priority among claimants to the same property. The claimants can be secured parties, consignors, lessors, buyers, lessees, lien creditors or transferees. Article 9's rules rank their competing claims and determine the order in which claimants can satisfy their claims from the same property. Article 9's rules usually are stated in terms of "priority." A few of them, however, rank competing claims to specific assets less directly, by "subordinating" a security interest or allowing a party to "take free" of a security interest. These are priority rules in everything but name. If B's security interest is subordinate to A's claim A's claim has priority over B's security interest. Similarly, if A takes free of B's security interest, A's interest in the property is not subject to B's security interest. A's interest therefore has priority.

Section 9–201(a) proclaims the primacy of security interests: "Except as otherwise provided in [the UCC], a security agreement is effective according to its terms between the parties, against purchasers of the collateral, and against creditors." According to this provision, unless the UCC provides otherwise, even an unperfected security interest is prior to the rights of unsecured creditors and to any other purchaser or creditor. Article 9's priority rules frequently, and other Articles of the UCC sometimes, provide otherwise. Hence, the study of priorities under Article 9 is the examination of the provisions in Subpart 3 of Part 3 that are the "exceptions" referred to in 9–201(a). By and large, Article 9 works well, but whether its priority rules operate fairly raises policy questions that will be addressed throughout this Chapter. In greatly strengthening the position of the first party to file, has the Code been overly protective of banks and other institutional creditors at the expense of other meritorious claimants, or has the Code in fact succeeded in constructing an efficient system of priority allocation, the benefits of which outweigh the hardship that some of its rigid rules occasion? The classic tension between efficiency and fairness is evident in this area. There is also disagreement as to which priority rules are efficient.

B. THE FIRST-TO-FILE-OR-PERFECT RULE

The key provisions in any study of UCC priority law are:

Section 9–317(a): A security interest or agricultural lien is subordinate to the rights of:

(1)   a person entitled to priority under Section 9–322; and

(2)   except as otherwise provided in subsection (e) [with respect to purchase-money security interests], a person that becomes a lien creditor before the earlier of the time:

    (A)   the security interest or agricultural lien is perfected; or

    (B)   one of the conditions specified in Section 9–203(b)(3) is met and a financing statement covering the collateral is filed.

Section 9–322(a): Except as otherwise provided in this section, priority among conflicting security interests and agricultural liens in the same collateral is determined according to the following rules:

(1)   Conflicting perfected security interests and agricultural liens rank according to priority in time of filing or perfection. Priority dates from the earlier of the time a filing covering the collateral is first made or the security interest or agricultural lien is first perfected, if there is no period thereafter when there is neither filing nor perfection.

The first thing to notice is that the priority rules in both sections apply to agricultural liens as well as security interests. As noted in Chapter 2, agricultural liens are essentially statutorily created property rights in farm products that secure obligations incurred by the debtor in connection with its farming operations. 9–102(a)(5). Although agricultural liens are not consensually created security interests, Article 9 deems the holder of an agricultural lien to be a "secured party" and the farm products subject to the lien "collateral." 9–102(a)(73)(B), 9–102(a)(12). Under 9–109(a)(2), Article 9 covers agricultural liens. Except for proceeds of farm products subject to an agricultural lien and the place of filing, the same rules that apply to security interests generally apply to agricultural liens. Although extra-Code law governs the creation of agricultural liens, Article 9 governs issues of their perfection and priority. See Dean v. Hall, 50 UCC Rep. Serv.2d 618 (E.D. Va.2003). Section 9–317 and 9–322s' priority rules control unless the statute creating the agricultural lien gives the lien priority over a conflicting security interest. 9–322(g). The material below focuses only on security interests.

1.   CONFLICTING SECURITY INTERESTS

Section 9–317(a)(1) cedes to 9–322 the first issue that we address: the priority with respect to conflicting Article 9 security interests in the same collateral. Under traditional law, the basic priority rule was "first in time, first in right," but we see in the following problems that this dictum is too imprecise to deal with a notice filing system in which filing and attachment of a security interest can happen at different times. In Problem 1, Bank is first to file but Lender is first to perfect. In Problem 2, Bank is first to perfect and Lender is first to file. See Comments 3 and 4 to 9–322. What is the justification for the results in these problems?

PROBLEMS

1. Debtor applied to Bank for a loan. On February 2, Bank filed a financing statement authorized by Debtor covering all Debtor's equipment, along with a search request for information about any other financing statements on file under Debtor's name. Debtor also applied to Lender for a loan. On February 5, Debtor signed a written security agreement covering all its equipment; Lender advanced the proceeds of the loan to D and electronically filed a financing statement covering the equipment. On February 9, the filing office notified Bank that there were no other financing statements on Debtor on file on February 2. Bank advanced the loan proceeds to Debtor on that date and Debtor signed the security agreement. Which creditor is prior under 9–322(a)(1) with respect to the collateral in which each party claims a perfected security interest?

2. Debtor applied to Bank for a loan. When Bank asked for collateral, Debtor entrusted a valuable jewel to Bank under a pledge agreement that allowed Bank to retain possession of the jewel until Debtor repaid the loan with interest. Bank advanced the funds. Later, Debtor borrowed money from Lender and granted Lender a security interest in various items of its property in a security agreement, including the jewel. Lender perfected its security interest by filing a financing statement. Which creditor is prior under 9–322(a)(1)?

The basic rule of Article 9's priority scheme is usually referred to as the "first-to-file rule." The Problems above demonstrate that this is a misnomer and, as Comment 3 to 9–323 suggests, the correct designation is "the first-to-file-or-perfect rule." However, the great preponderance of nonpossessory secured transactions over possessory secured transactions justifies the usual description of the rule. Perfection by possession is usually infeasible in cases of inventory or equipment financing and impossible for most types of intangibles. We therefore often follow predominant practice and refer to 9–322(a)(1)'s rule as the "first-to-file rule."

2. FUTURE ADVANCES

Any debt can be secured. Some security agreements cover all obligations owed by the debtor to the creditor, however they arise. Such agreements accomplish this through the use of what are called "all obligations" clauses. Frequently, security agreements cover a more limited type of obligation: "future advances." Section 9–204(c) permits a security agreement to cover them. Article 9 doesn't define an "advance." However, the term generally connotes value given by the creditor to the debtor or from which the debtor benefits.

In understanding Article 9's treatment of future advances, future advances clauses must be distinguished from after-acquired property clauses. Future advances clauses concern the type of debt (future advances) secured by the debtor's assets. After-acquired property clauses concern the collateral (after-acquired) that secures the debt. The two clauses deal with different things and have different effects. For instance, future advances could be secured only by existing collateral and, conversely, after-acquired collateral could secure only existing debt. Security agreements often cover both future advances and after-acquired property. Earlier it was established that if a security agreement includes an after-acquired property clause and future advances clause, the security interest automatically attaches to any after-acquired property at the time when the debtor acquires rights in this collateral, and the collateral secures all future advances made by the secured party to the debtor. See 9–203 and 9–204. Thus, if the secured party has perfected its security interest in the original collateral, its security interest becomes perfected in the after-acquired collateral when it attaches. The issue we consider in this section is whether the priority of the secured party's future advances dates from the time the secured party first perfected or from the time it made the future advances.

A contractual device frequently used to secure future advances is a dragnet clause. A dragnet clause is a provision in a security agreement that secures both a specific loan as well as future loans made by the creditor to the debtor with the same collateral. To do so, the clause provides for cross-collateralization: collateral securing the specific loan also secures future advances. For example, suppose a creditor makes a secured loan to a debtor as part of a security agreement listing particular items of the debtor's personal property as collateral. The agreement contains a dragnet clause securing "all loans" made by the creditor to the debtor, whenever made. Later, the creditor makes an unsecured loan to the debtor. With the dragnet clause, the later loan is secured by the same collateral securing the earlier secured loan. Although some courts find dragnet clauses in an adhesion contract unenforceable if part of a secured loan to a consumer, most courts enforce them. Dragnet clauses generally are considered valid unless specific grounds for invalidating them exist. See In re Watson, 286 B.R. 594 (Bankr. D. N.J.2002).

PROBLEMS

1.   Bank lent Debtor $100,000 and took a security interest in Debtor's equipment to secure the obligation. On October 1, Bank filed a financing statement covering the equipment. The security agreement stated that the collateral covered not only the original advance but any future advances that Bank made to Debtor. Later Lender advanced $75,000 to Debtor on the same equipment and filed a financing statement on November 1. On December 1, Bank made an additional advance of $100,000 to Debtor pursuant to the future advances clause. When Debtor defaulted on all debts, the collateral was found to be worth only $150,000. (a) How should this sum be divided between Bank and Lender? (b) Would your answer change if Lender had notified Bank of its loan before Bank made its subsequent advance? See 9–322(a) and Comment 4. (c) Would it matter if Bank's financing statement said nothing about future advances? Why reward Bank, which is arguably in bad faith, with priority as to the subsequent advance? In some states, the pre-UCC law was contrary, and, with respect to real estate transactions,

notice to the senior mortgagee is still important. Restatement of the Law (Third) Property: Mortgages § 2.3 (1996). What interest was Article 9 furthering by omitting the notice rule?

2. On October 1, Bank lent Debtor $100,000 and took possession of a painting, known as "Red Square," pursuant to a pledge agreement that provided that Bank could retain the painting until Debtor repaid its obligations. The agreement contained a future advances clause. On November 1, Debtor borrowed $75,000 from Lender pursuant to a security agreement that granted Lender a security interest in several works of art, including "Red Square." Lender perfected its security interest by filing. On December 1, Bank advanced an additional $100,000 to Debtor. When Debtor defaulted on all its debts, "Red Square" was found to be worth only $150,000 and Lender's remaining collateral was valueless. How should this sum be divided between Bank and Lender? See 9–322(a)(1) and Comment 4.

In Problems 1 and 2, in order to determine the priority of future advances, only 9–322(a) and Comment 4 to 9–322 were considered. Why isn't 9–323, which is entitled "Future Advances," relevant? Do you find any provisions in 9–323 that pertain to the above Problems? Comment 3 to 9–323 is helpful in explaining the relationship of 9–322 and 9–323:

> Under a proper reading of the first-to-file-or-perfect rule of Section 9–322(a)(1). . . it is abundantly clear that the time when an advance is made plays no role in determining priorities among conflicting security interests except when a financing statement was not filed and the advance is the giving of value as the last step for attachment and perfection. Thus, a secured party takes subject to all advances secured by a competing security interest having priority under Section 9–322(a)(1). This result generally obtains regardless of how the competing security interest is perfected and regardless of whether the advances are made 'pursuant to commitment' (Section 9–102). . . . Thus, an advance has priority from the date it is made only in the rare case in which it is made without commitment and while the security interest is perfected only temporarily under 9–312.

PROBLEM

In 2012, Dealer and Financer entered into a retail finance agreement containing the terms under which Financer would purchase the retail installment contracts entered into by buyers who bought cars from Dealer on credit. These contracts granted Dealer a security interest in the cars securing the unpaid portion of the obligations owed by buyers to Dealer for the purchase of the cars. Financer purchased these agreements from Dealer coincident with or shortly after the sale of the cars and thereafter buyers made their monthly installment payments to Financer, which now held security interests in the buyers' cars and a right to repossess upon default.

The retail finance agreement between Dealer and Financer set up a "charge-back" account, common in the retail finance industry, in which Dealer agreed to maintain an account with Financer of 1.5% of the value of the outstanding installment contracts that Dealer had assigned to Financer. The agreement gave Financer the right to charge back against this account for any losses it suffered upon defaults by buyers on their retail installment contracts. The retail finance agreement did not grant Financer a security interest in Dealer's assets to secure Dealer's obligation to contribute to this account.

In 2013, Dealer and Financer entered into a wholesale finance agreement under which Financer would lend Dealer the funds to buy new cars from the manufacturer. This inventory financing transaction is sometimes described as "floor-planning." The agreement provided that Financer would maintain a security interest in all cars it financed under the wholesale finance agreement, and this inventory lien would secure the full payment of all advances made, interest, all costs and expenses incurred by Financer in the collection or enforcement of the obligations under the agreement, and "each and every other indebtedness or obligation now or hereafter owing by [Dealer] to [Financer] including any collection or enforcement costs and expenses or monies advanced on behalf of [Dealer] in connection with any such other indebtedness or obligations." The agreement also gave Financer a security interest in almost all of Dealer's other assets.

When relations between Dealer and Financer became strained, the question arose whether under 9–204(c) the quoted provision in the 2013 wholesale finance agreement granted Financer a security interest in almost all Dealer's assets to secure Dealer's obligation established by the 2012 retail finance agreement to contribute to the charge-back account. Dealer argued that the retail and wholesale agreements were separate transactions and that the industry norm was that the terms of retail finance agreements do not provide for a security interest in a dealership's general assets. Financer contended that under 9–204(c) the quoted provision swept in any obligation that Dealer owed Financer under the retail finance agreement as well as under the wholesale agreement. Which party is correct? The facts are based on Pride Hyundai, Inc. v. Chrysler Financial Co., LLC., 369 F.3d 603 (1st Cir.2004). See Comment 5 to 9–204(c), 1–201(b)(20).

3.   FINANCING STATEMENT AS AN UMBRELLA

The following Problem examines how far the priority of the first party to file extends in a case in which there was no future advances clause in the original security agreement and the later advance was made pursuant to a subsequent security agreement for which a new financing statement had been filed.

PROBLEM

Transaction One. Bank lent Debtor $20,000 in January to buy First Combine. To secure the obligation, Bank took a security interest in the combine, which it perfected by filing a financing statement that described the collateral as "Allis-Chalmers Combine, Model G, Serial No. 77665533." The security agreement did not contain a future advances clause.

Transaction Two. Lender lent Debtor $15,000 in June and secured the obligation by taking a security interest in the First Combine that it perfected by filing a financing statement describing the combine in the same manner as in Transaction One. The security agreement did not contain a future advances clause. Lender knew nothing about Transaction One.

Transaction Three. In December, Debtor bought Second Combine with money borrowed from Bank. Since Debtor had not fully paid its obligation to Bank for First Combine, in a new security agreement Bank took a security interest in both First and Second Combines as security for both the unpaid balance on the first transaction and the amount of the loan advanced to enable Debtor to buy Second Combine. Bank filed a new financing statement that described each combine by the same "serial number" description as used in the first transaction. Bank cancelled the contract used to finance the purchase of First Combine but forgot to terminate the financing statement filed in January.

When Debtor defaulted on all debts, Lender claimed a priority to the extent of $15,000 in First Combine under the first-to-file rule. Before entering into the second contract with Debtor, Bank had failed to check the filings and was chagrined to learn of Lender's claim of priority. However, its analysis of these transactions convinced Bank that its January financing statement, still on file, gave Bank a priority over Lender in First Combine even though the first security agreement had been cancelled. Lender replied that the absence of a future advances clause in the first security agreement precluded Bank from making such a claim; Bank should not enjoy a windfall from a prior financing statement inadvertently left on file and arising from an earlier transaction that had been cancelled. How would this case be decided under 9–322(a)?

Controversy in the financial community on the issue raised in this Problem caused further amendments to former Article 9 on future advances and shaped somewhat the view taken by Revised Article 9 on that subject. The first decision on facts like those in the Problem, Coin-O-Matic Service Co. v. Rhode Island Hospital Trust Co., 3 UCC Rep.Serv. 1112 (R.I.Super.Ct.1966), held that Lender was prior. For Bank to enjoy priority for future advances based on its January financing statement, the January security agreement must have contained a future advances clause and the advances must be made pursuant to that contract. Bank's January financing statement is not an "umbrella" giving Bank a priority with respect to advances made pursuant to subsequent security agreements covering the same collateral between the same parties.

Courts and commentators rejected *Coin-O-Matic*'s holding. A future advances clause in a security agreement is a transactions-cost saving device for securing subsequent advances. By covering later advances, the clause does not require the secured creditor and debtor to incur the contracting costs of securing them. However, a future advances clause is not the exclusive means of securing later advances. The same result can be achieved by a series of security agreements, with each advance secured under its respective security agreement. If the lender has filed a financing statement covering the collateral described in each security agreement, the filing perfects the lender's security interest in the collateral with respect to both the initial advance and subsequent advances. See James Talcott, Inc. v. Franklin National Bank, 194 N.W.2d 775 (Minn.1979). Courts generally refused to follow *Coin-O-Matic*'s ruling that, to enjoy the priority of the initial advance, subsequent advances must be covered by a future advances clause in the initial security agreement.

See In re Estate of Gruder's Will, 392 N.Y.S.2d 203 (N.Y. Sur.1977), summarizes the rationale for rejecting *Coin-O-Matic*'s holding, quoting James J. White & Robert S. Summers, Uniform Commercial Code § 25–4, at 908 (1972), as follows:

"We reject the *Coin-O-Matic* holding for three reasons. First, it provides little protection against overreaching, for a creditor can avoid the holding simply by including a future advance clause in his security agreement. Second, we suspect that the *Coin-O-Matic* court misunderstands commercial practice. We suspect that it is a rare banker who will lend against the same collateral which secures a prior loan; in our experience the commercial practice is for the second lender to pay off the first and so take a first priority as to all of the collateral. Finally, *Coin-O-Matic* conflicts with the most obvious and we think intended meaning of 9–312(5)(a) [9–322(a)(1)]; if the draftsmen had wished to qualify the rule as the *Coin-O-Matic* court did, they could have done so."

Id. at 206.

Revised Article 9 leaves unchanged former Article 9's treatment of future advance priority. However, the drafting of its provisions to reach this result is opaque. Section 9–322(a)(1)'s general first-to-file-or-perfect priority rule applies to "conflicting perfected security interests." Since a security interest can be perfected by a future advance, the general rule governs the priority of future advances too. Under 9–322(a)(1), the time at which value is given doesn't determine the priority of the security interest, unless a financing statement hasn't been filed and the giving of value is the final perfection event. When a financing statement has been filed, priority is determined by the date of its filing. The same goes for secured future advances as well. When the advance was made, therefore, generally is irrelevant for purposes of priority.

Section 9–323(a) states a limited exception to this rule. Under this limited exception, for 9–322(a)(1)'s purposes, the priority of an advance dates from the time it was made. Here, timing matters. The exception only applies when a security interest is perfected automatically or temporarily, and is not made pursuant to a commitment while the security interest was perfected by some other method. See 9–323(a).

These are somewhat unusual circumstances. When they don't obtain, 9–323(a)'s exception is inapplicable, and 9–322(a)(1)'s general priority rule controls. Under 9–322(a)(1), when a financing statement has been filed, the timing of an advance is irrelevant for priority purposes.

4. POSITION OF FIRST-TO-FILE SECURED PARTY

Now all the pieces are in place for an understanding of the position of the first party to file with respect to after-acquired property and future advances under Article 9. Notice filing allows a secured party to file a financing statement that will be effective for five years and may be continued so long as debt is still outstanding. The financing statement may indicate the collateral covered by a supergeneric indication: "all personal property." See 9–504(2).

> **Case #1.** Assume that Debtor authorizes Bank to file a financing statement covering "all personal property," and the security agreement contains after-acquired property and future advances clauses. Now Bank takes a perfected security interest in all personal property acquired by Debtor pursuant to that security agreement and all subsequent advances made by the secured party pursuant to that agreement are secured by that collateral. Bank has priority over competing secured parties with respect to the after-acquired property to the full extent of the advances made.

> **Case #2.** Assume that over a period of several years Debtor buys items of heavy equipment with money borrowed from Bank. Each time Bank finances a purchase, it enters into a new security agreement with Debtor granting Bank a security interest in the specifically described equipment purchased. The security agreement does not contain after-acquired property or future advances clauses. Before the first of these transactions, Debtor authorized Bank to file a financing statement covering "all personal property." No subsequent financing statement was filed by Bank. Bank has priority over competing secured parties with respect to the collateral covered by each of the discrete security agreements over the five-year life of the financing statement. Comment 3 to 9–323, in discussing a case similar to Case #1, says that in Case #2, Bank would have priority even if the subsequent advance "was not made under the original agreement with the debtor, but was under a new agreement."

Thus, a creditor can take a security interest in all the personal property a debtor now owns or ever will own to secure all extensions of credit for so long as a financing statement is effective, which can be forever, and, with certain exceptions, this security interest is prior as to competing secured parties. This allows a secured creditor to clean out a debtor's bankruptcy estate without a penny for either the unsecured creditors or junior secured creditors. Moreover, it allows the first-to-file creditor to monopolize the debtor's credit; subsequent creditors cannot afford to take junior security interests. The explanation for the primacy accorded first-to-file creditors given in Comment 4 to 9–322 is on efficiency grounds: "The justification for determining priority by order of filing lies in the necessity of protecting the filing system—that is, of allowing the first secured party who has filed to make subsequent advances without each time having to check for subsequent filings as a condition of protection." For an opinion by a veteran bankruptcy judge that applies the first-to-file-or-perfect rule to a complex financing transaction, see In re Lombardo's Ravioli Kitchen, Inc., 2009 WL 3257492 (Bankr. D. Conn.2009).

5. OPERATING UNDER THE FIRST-TO-FILE-OR-PERFECT RULE

The preceding Problems have examined in detail the consequences of the first-to-file-or-perfect rule with respect to competing secured parties. The characteristic features of Article 9's priority rules are apparent there: precise, sharp-edged and ruthless. However, their importance should not be overemphasized. The lesson to be learned from an understanding of the 9–322(a)(1)'s first-to-file-or-perfect rule is that secured creditors should never allow themselves to become involved in a conflict with another secured creditor who has filed first unless they have taken the precautions discussed below. The presence of junior secured creditors in each of the hypothetical cases posed in these Problems is the result of classroom license to illustrate a point. In the real commercial world, there would be no junior creditors involved in these cases unless they were terribly uninformed.

One reason that cases involving junior creditors are scarce is the custom of including covenants in loan agreements prohibiting the debtor from granting security interests in the collateral to other parties or incurring additional debt from other lenders without the consent of the secured party. The purpose of these covenants is to prevent the debtor from impairing its ability to repay its loan. Its breach constitutes an event of default that results in the debt becoming immediately due and payable. Hence, in practice a debtor may grant a security interest to a junior creditor only at the sufferance of the senior creditor.

Assuming that the senior creditor does not object to the creation of a junior security interest, the situations in which a creditor can safely deal with a debtor with respect to collateral in which another creditor has a senior security interest are: (i) the junior creditor has a purchase-money security interest; (ii) the senior creditor has agreed to subordinate its security interest in part or in whole to that of the junior creditor; or (iii) the junior creditor has bought out the senior creditor. The next section discusses purchase-money priority. In the last two situations, the junior creditor in effect becomes the senior creditor in part or whole.

There are circumstances in which it is in the senior secured creditor's interest to allow a junior creditor to make advances to the debtor. For example, the debtor may need further advances to keep afloat that the senior creditor does not wish to make. However, the senior creditor may be willing to agree to subordinate its security interest to that of the junior creditor in some of the debtor's collateral. The law is very accommodating to subordination agreements. Section 9–339 states: "This article does not preclude subordination by agreement by a person entitled to priority." And Bankruptcy Code 510(a) provides that subordination agreements are enforceable in bankruptcy to the same extent as under nonbankruptcy law.

If the prior secured creditor will not agree to subordination or allow further the debtor to incur further debt, a subsequent creditor who wishes to deal with a debtor has no choice but to pay off the prior creditor. To do so it can proceed in two different ways. The subsequent creditor can pay off the debtor's debt to the secured creditor or supply the debtor with the funds to repay the debt. The principle of equitable subrogation generally allows a person who discharges the debt of another to succeed to the rights of the creditor with respect to the claim paid. As applied, the principle enables the subsequent creditor who pays off the prior secured creditor to succeed to that creditor's rights against the debtor, including its security interest. See Restatement (Third) of Restitution and Unjust Enrichment § 57(1) (2011). Alternatively, the subsequent creditor can purchase the prior creditor's secured claim, taking an assignment of the creditor's security interest. Consider these two different ways of paying off a prior secured creditor in Problem 1 below.

A junior creditor sometimes is willing to provide financing even without the senior creditor agreeing to subordinate its lien. If the debtor requires additional short-term financing, for instance, a junior secured loan is an attractive option. The loan allows the debtor to avoid obtaining a low-cost loan from the senior creditor, who might insist on a longer term loan than the debtor prefers or on unfavorable loan terms, or a high-cost unsecured loan. The market for second lien financing responds to the debtor's need for this "intermediate" sort of financing. The senior secured creditor often does not object to a second lien because the second lien is subordinate to its security interest and the short-term nature of the loan does not permanently increase the debtor's debt-servicing costs. For the same reason, the senior secured creditor sometimes will agree to allow the debtor to make interest payments to the second lien lender on the lender's loan. In this second lien arrangement the second lien lender subordinates its security interest but not its payments rights on the debt.

PROBLEMS

1.   Bank One and Lender have security interests perfected by filing in Debtor's collateral. Bank One, who was first to file, refused to extend further credit to Debtor and wished to terminate its credit relationship with Debtor.

Bank Two agreed with Debtor to replace Bank One and, in time, to advance more funds to Debtor.

Case #1. Bank Two agreed to advance funds to Debtor to be used to pay off Debtor's remaining obligation to Bank One on condition that Bank One send Debtor a termination statement, which would then be filed. Debtor granted Bank Two a security interest in its collateral and Bank Two advanced the funds. Debtor paid Bank One and Bank Two filed a financing statement on Debtor.

Case #2. Bank Two agreed to pay off Bank One and to take an assignment of Bank One's security interest in Debtor's collateral. Bank Two paid Bank One and received the requested assignment. What is Bank Two's priority with respect to Lender in these two cases? What is the result in Case #1 if Bank One's financing statement is not terminated? See 1–103(b). What if Bank Two neglected to file a financing statement in Case #2? See 9–310(c) and Comment 4.

2.   On February 1, Bank advanced $50,000 on the security of Debtor's equipment and filed a financing statement covering the equipment. When Bank refused to grant more credit, Debtor induced Lender to advance $40,000 on the security of Debtor's equipment. Lender filed a financing statement on June 15. Before advancing the funds to Debtor, Lender had noted Bank's filed financing statement and had requested that Debtor submit to Bank under 9–210(a) a "request for an accounting" asking Bank's approval of the fact that only $50,000 was owed by Debtor to Bank. When the request was made, Bank promptly approved the statement. Lender examined Debtor's security agreement with Bank and found that it did not contain a future advance clause. Lender assumed from the 9–210 statement and the fact that neither Bank's financing statement nor security agreement mentioned future advances that Bank would not be lending Debtor more money on the security of Debtor's equipment. Lender advanced the funds. But Lender's assumption was wrong, for in July Bank advanced another $60,000 to Debtor pursuant to a new security agreement granting Bank a security interest in Debtor's equipment. Debtor's equipment is worth $100,000. What is the priority of Lender in this case? Does Lender have rights against Bank based on 9–210?

C. PURCHASE-MONEY PRIORITY

1.   THE PURCHASE-MONEY SECURITY INTEREST

Section 9–322's first-to-file-or-perfect rule is a temporal priority rule: priority is awarded according to the order in time in which a financing statement is filed or the security interest is perfected. "First in time, first in right," as the rule is sometimes summarized. Nonetheless, Article 9 recognizes exceptions to the first-to-file-or-perfect priority rule. 9–322(f)(1). The exceptions state nontemporal priority rules. Among the most important of them gives priority, under prescribed conditions, to a purchase-money security interest over an earlier or simultaneously perfected security interest in the same collateral.

Simply put, a purchase-money security interest (PMSI) is a security interest in an asset that secures the financing needed to enable the debtor to acquire the asset. Perhaps unsurprisingly, Article 9's definition is more complex. Under 9–103(b), a security interest is a purchase-money security interest to the extent that the goods or software are purchase-money collateral with respect to the security interest. Section 9–102(a)(1) in turn defines purchase money collateral as goods or software that secures a purchase-money obligation. Finally, 9–103(a)(2) defines a purchase-money obligation as one incurred (i) as all or part of the price of collateral (seller sells goods to buyer and takes a security interest in the goods to secure the unpaid price), or (ii) for value given to enable the debtor to acquire rights in or the use of the collateral if the value is in fact so used (lender lends money to debtor to enable it to buy goods). These obligations sometimes are referred to as seller purchase-money and lender purchase-money obligations, respectively, and the respective security interests created as a seller's PSMI and lender's PMSI. Unlike under former Article 9, a PMSI is limited to goods and software. See 9–103(a)(1).

Under 9–324(a), a PMSI in goods other than inventory or livestock has priority over a conflicting security interest in the same goods and their identifiable proceeds if the PMSI is perfected when the debtor receives possession of the collateral or within 20 days thereafter. Section 9–324(b) grants PMSI priority in inventory under prescribed conditions having to do with notice.

Although purchase-money priority has long been a part of the law of secured transactions and mortgages, its justification is elusive. Perhaps the most plausible justification relies on the idea of risk alteration. A later secured loan might change the debtor's behavior, increasing the risk that it will default on earlier secured loans. See Hideki Kanda & Saul Levmore, Explaining Creditor Priorities, 80 Va. L. Rev. 2113 (1995). This is because the later loan might enable the debtor to undertake riskier projects than it has previously undertaken. The failure of these projects could leave the debtor unable to satisfy its earlier secured obligations. Purchase-money priority limits the purchase-money creditor's priority to the purchase-money collateral, so that the purchase-money loan enables the debtor to put at risk at least the purchase-money collateral. If the purchase-money loan does not also increase the risk to the nonpurchase-money collateral securing earlier obligations, earlier secured lenders remain unaffected by purchase-money priority. Id. At 2138–2142. Purchase-money priority is justified where the PMSI brings in new financing without impairing the collateral of existing secured creditors, including risk to its value.

Crucial to this risk-alteration rationale for purchase-money priority is the assumption that purchase-money loans do not put at risk the collateral of earlier lenders. Whether, and how frequently, purchase-money loans enable the debtor to undertake projects that increase risk to nonpurchase-money collateral is an empirical question. However, there is reason to doubt that purchase-money loans always leave the risk to nonpurchase-money collateral unaffected. This is because a PMSI need not be limited to replacement equipment or isolated inventory: acquisitions that do not usually allow the debtor to enter a new line of business. The financed purchase of equipment or a new line of inventory could allow the debtor to undertake a novel project. (Former 9–107 allowed a PMSI in non-goods collateral. Its broader scope enabled debtors to acquire intangible assets such as intellectual property or accounts on a PMSI basis.) Acquisition of these assets easily could allow a debtor to enter into a new business or offer a new product line. These new projects could affect the risk nonpurchase-money collateral. It might be significant that many security agreements contain covenants prohibiting or limiting the extent to which the debtor can issue purchase-money debt. See, e.g., Accounts Receivable/Loan Agreement ¶ 7.1, Appendix I. This is consistent with the belief among nonpurchase-money lenders that PMSIs risk jeopardizing their collateral.

By their terms, 9–324's purchase-money priority rules give the security interest priority only if the security interest is a PMSI. Problems 1–3 below ask whether the security interest described in each problem is a PMSI. Problem 4 asks about priority among PMSIs.

PROBLEMS

1. On July 1, Seller sold goods to Debtor on unsecured credit. On July 7, Debtor borrowed $50,000 from Bank to pay Seller. Bank wrote the check to Seller and Debtor as joint payees and Debtor indorsed the check to Seller. Did Bank have a purchase-money security interest when Debtor granted Bank a security interest in the goods to secure the debt? 9–103(a)(2). Suppose Debtor has sufficient funds to purchase goods from Seller on a cash basis but its financial position does not allow it to buy from Seller and continue operating unless it can subsequently borrow the amount of the price from Bank. Debtor pays Seller in cash on July 7 and later obtains a loan from Bank, granting Bank a security interest in the goods purchased earlier from Seller. Does Bank have a purchase-money security interest in the goods purchased on July 7?

2. Debtor borrowed $10,000 from Bank on July 1 for the purpose of buying a machine. Bank advanced the money by immediately crediting Debtor's checking account. Debtor granted Bank a security interest in the machine on July 1 and Bank immediately filed a financing statement. Debtor purchased the machine on July 3 and paid Seller by a check for $10,000 drawn on the checking account in Bank. The balance in Debtor's account just before Bank credited the account was $15,000. When Debtor's check to Seller was paid the balance was $22,000. Does Bank have a purchase-money security interest in the machine? 9–103(a)(2).

3. Debtor wanted to buy a new car. At the time she owed a bank $14,000 secured by her existing car with a value of $10,000. She therefore had "negative equity" of $4,000 in her car. Lacking the means to pay off the bank or pay the $18,000 purchase price for the new car she wanted, Debtor and Dealer reached an agreement. Dealer would finance the entire price of the new car it would sell Debtor. To do so, Dealer would pay off Debtor's $14,000 loan from the bank and take her existing car as a $10,000 trade-in (the bank releasing its security interest in the trade in). The $4,000 "negative equity" trade-in would be added to Dealer's $18,000 financing of the purchase price of the new car, and the resulting $22,000 loan would be secured by the new car. If Debtor buys the new car from Dealer on the terms described, to what extent does Dealer have a PMSI in it? See Comment 3 to 9–103; In re Westfall, 599 F.3d 498 (6th Cir.2010); In re Howard, 597 F.3d 852 (7th Cir. 2010).

Alter the facts as follows: Suppose Debtor owed $4,000 in parking tickets that had to be paid and would be unable to purchase a new car if she paid them. If Dealer paid the parking tickets and secured the $4,000 paid with the new car, as agreed, would Dealer's PMSI include this amount? See Comment 3 (second paragraph) to 9–103.

4. At the beginning of the year Debtor granted Bank a security interest in all of Debtor's equipment then owned or after acquired. Bank filed a financing statement covering equipment. In March, Seller agreed to sell Debtor equipment for a price of $100,000 on terms calling for 20% down. Bank agreed to advance $20,000 to enable Debtor to buy the equipment. Bank wrote a check for $20,000 to Debtor and Seller as joint payees and Debtor indorsed it to Seller. Seller retained a security interest in the equipment which it perfected by filing upon delivery of the equipment to Debtor. What are the priorities as to the equipment between Bank and Seller? See Thet Mah & Assoc., Inc. v. First Bank of N.D., 336 N.W.2d 134 (N.D.1983); 2 Grant Gilmore, supra, § 29.2, at 784 (1965). Section 9–324(g), discussed below, resolves the matter.

At issue in Problem 4 is priority among multiple purchase-money security interests. There are three possible resolutions: (i) priority goes to the first purchase-money security interest to file, (ii) priority goes to a favored type of purchase-money security interest, or (iii) the purchase-money security interests rank equally and priority is awarded on a pro rata basis. Although former 9–312(4) favored (iii), a pro rata distribution, and former 9–312(5) favored (i), the first PMSI to file, neither provision clearly has the stronger statutory case. Section 9–324(g) endorses (ii) and awards priority to Seller.

The policy reason for doing so, recited in Comment 13 to 9–324, relies on justifications given in the Restatement (Third) of the Law of Property, Mortgages § 7.2(c) (1997). One justification is that "equities favor the vendor" and that purchase-money vendors would not agree to extend credit unless they were given a priority. As to the equities, they are at least as much with the enabling lender as with the purchase-money seller. After all, the lender also has provided a valuable financial input into the debtor's acquisition of the collateral. The fact that cash rather than a specific asset purchased is provided is unimportant. Both are needed for the debtor's acquisition of the asset. As to the terms of the secured interest, the lender also might not make a loan unless it was given a purchase-money security interest. Focusing on the terms of the credit agreement does not favor the credit seller over the lender. A second justification, which the Restatement finds decisive, is the law's "sympathy" for the vendor. The descriptive observation about existing law does not justify continuing to favor the purchase-money seller over purchase-money creditors. The question is whether the "sympathy" is appropriate or misplaced.

Article 9 also is inconsistent in its commitment to awarding priority among multiple purchase-money security interests. Sometimes it awards priority to the purchase-money seller and sometimes not. Priority in investment property under 9–328(1) is given to the secured party who has control over the collateral. Cf. 9–327(4) (security interest in deposit account perfected by control enjoys priority over security interest held by bank). If two or more secured parties have control, 9–328(2) priority is determined by the order in time in which they obtained control. Section 9–328(6) awards priority on a pro rata basis among claimants when perfection occurs without control and the debtor is a broker, securities intermediary or commodities intermediary. None of these priority rules favors a particular type of security interest. In fact, none recognize purchase-money priority at all. Cf. 9–324(a) (purchase-money priority applies where the collateral is goods).

A more convincing way of settling priority among multiple purchase-money creditors perhaps is the following. A creditor with a security interest in collateral has a property right in it, and multiple secured creditors in effect have joint property rights in collateral. Joint property rights generally create inefficiencies in use. For example, some of the benefits of monitoring an item of collateral by one creditor flow to other creditors who have security interests in the same item. Because the monitoring creditor does not capture the full benefit of its monitoring efforts, it will invest suboptimally in monitoring. The same is true for the other secured creditors. Allocating priority to one or another purchase-money creditor creates an exclusive property right (up to the amount of the secured debt held by the creditor) and allows a creditor to capture the full benefits of its monitoring activities. This is a reason for not ranking purchase-money security interests equally and distributing collateral on a pro rata basis between them. The next question is which among the remaining ways of assigning priority are preferred. Article 9 prefers the purchase-money seller over other purchasers. Doing so creates an exclusive property right and is defensible for that reason. However, the same would be true if the purchase-money lender were preferred. The law's sympathy for the purchase-money seller provides a certain salience to Article 9's preference. But the preference at bottom is arbitrary; some means of creating an exclusive property right is needed. The particular means used is less important and probably lacks a compelling justification.

2. PRIORITY IN NONINVENTORY GOODS

a. PURCHASE-MONEY PRIORITY

Section 9–324(a) restates the traditional rule that a PMSI has priority over conflicting security interests in the same collateral. If the priority of the first party to file is justified by its effect in lowering monitoring costs or realizing economies of scale in secured lending, thereby encouraging the greater extension of credit at lower interest rates, how can the purchase-money priority exception to the first-to-file rule be accounted for? Assume that a first-to-file lender has a security interest in all of the debtor's now owned or after-acquired equipment. Seller sells the debtor additional equipment and reserves a PMSI in the new equipment. The lender claims a priority in the new equipment under its after-acquired property clause by virtue of its status as the first party to file but 9–324(a) accords Seller's PMSI priority as to the new equipment. The effect is to impose a burden on the lender of monitoring the records for subsequently filed financing statements and tracing the origin of the debtor's after-acquired equipment to be sure that it is not collateral in which a seller has a PMSI. Does not the purchase-money priority undercut the very basis for the first-to-file rule? Note 3 following *Brodie* below cites other justifications for PMSI priority. For now, in light of the discussion of the first-to-file-or-perfect rule in the previous section, it is enough to note that the purchase-money priority is sometimes pointed to as a welcome means of allowing debtors to break the monopoly of the first party to file over the debtor's credit supply.

Courts sometimes have difficulty deciding when the debtor has received possession of the collateral for the purpose of 9–324(a). See Note 2 following *Brodie*. An example is the following case, decided under former Article 9 at a time when the period within which to perfect was ten days. Restaurants are among the leading candidates for bankruptcy, and, when the inevitable happens, unpaid suppliers of the restaurant equipment, like Brodie, would prefer having the new tenant of the restaurant, Lyon, buy the equipment in place rather than to rip it out and try to sell it on the used goods market. But Lyon takes a while to make up his mind. Does this delay cost Brodie his purchase-money priority?

Brodie Hotel Supply, Inc. v. United States

United States Court of Appeals, Ninth Circuit, 1970
431 F.2d 1316

■ HAMLEY, CIRCUIT JUDGE.

Brodie Hotel Supply, Inc. (Brodie), brought this action against the United States to determine which of the parties had priority, under their respective chattel mortgages, to the proceeds of the sale of certain restaurant equipment. The facts were stipulated and the property was sold and proceeds impounded by agreement. The district court granted summary judgment for Brodie and the United States appeals.

In 1959, Brodie sold the restaurant equipment to Standard Management Company, Inc., for use in a restaurant at Anchorage, Alaska. Standard Management went bankrupt. Brodie repossessed the equipment but left it in the restaurant. With the consent of Brodie, James Lyon took possession of the restaurant and began operating it on June 1, 1964. Throughout the summer of 1964, Brodie and Lyon negotiated over the price and terms under which Lyon was to purchase the equipment.

On November 2, 1964, Lyon borrowed seventeen thousand dollars from the National Bank of Alaska and, as security for the loan, which was evidenced by a promissory note, executed a chattel mortgage covering the restaurant equipment. This equipment consisted of 159 separate types of items, including a refrigerator, a dishwasher, an ice cream cabinet, spoons, forks, cups, ladles, pots, pans, and assorted glassware and chinaware. The bank assigned its mortgage to the Small Business Administration (SBA), represented in this action by the United States. On November 4, 1964, the bank filed a financing statement, showing the SBA as assignee.

On November 12, Brodie delivered to Lyon a bill of sale covering the equipment. On the same day Lyon executed a chattel mortgage on the equipment, naming Brodie as mortgagee. This mortgage was given to secure the unpaid purchase price of the equipment. Brodie filed a financing statement on November 23, 1964.

Alaska has adopted the Uniform Commercial Code (Code). Under § 9–312(5)(a) [9–322(a)(1)], the general rule of priority, if both interests are perfected by filing, is that the secured party who first files a financing statement (in this case SBA as assignee of the bank) prevails, regardless of when his security interest attached. However, there is a special exception for purchase-money security interests in collateral other than inventory. Brodie had such an interest. Under this exception, the purchase-money security interest prevails over conflicting interests in non-inventory collateral if "the purchase money security interest is perfected [i.e., here it was perfected by filing a financing statement] at the time the debtor receives possession of the collateral or within 10 days [20 days] after the debtor receives possession." § 9–312(4) [9–324(a)].

On the basis of these stipulated facts, Brodie moved for summary judgment. Brodie contended that although Lyon received possession of the restaurant equipment on June 1, 1964, over five months before Brodie's financing statement was filed, Lyon did not become a "debtor," and the equipment did not become "collateral" until November 12, 1964, when Lyon received the bill of sale and executed Brodie's chattel mortgage. Accordingly, Brodie contended, it was not until November 12, that "the debtor [Lyon] receive[d] possession of the collateral" within the meaning of the statute referred to above. As already indicated, Brodie's financing statement was filed within ten days of that date. The district court agreed with this analysis in granting summary judgment for Brodie.

If the term "debtor" is given the meaning ascribed to it in § 9–105(d), Brodie was entitled to priority.[1] It was not until November 12, 1964, that Lyon purchased the equipment and became obligated to pay the purchase price. Until that obligation came into being, Lyon was not Brodie's debtor with power to mortgage the restaurant equipment as collateral for the unpaid purchase price.

But the United States argues that in the context of this case the priority statute, § 9–312(4) [9–324(a)], is ambiguous as to whether "debtor" is used in the sense defined in § 9–105(d) [9–102(a)(28)], or whether it is used merely to identify an individual in possession, who ultimately becomes indebted to the purchase-money mortgagee. In contending that this "ambiguity" should be resolved in favor of the latter construction, the United States refers to the history and underlying purposes and policies of the Code, the assertedly different language of the prior Uniform Conditional Sales Act, and the fact that, under § 9–402(1) [9–502(d)] a financing statement may be filed before a security agreement is made or a security interest otherwise attaches, notwithstanding the fact that this section refers to "debtor," "secured party," and "security interest."

We are not persuaded that either recourse to the history or consideration of the underlying purposes of the Code supports the Government's position. In our view, the term "debtor" as it is used in this particular priority statute, § 9–312(4) [9–324(a)], means "the person who owes payment or other performance of the obligation secured." § 9–105(d) [9–102(a)(28)]. Although Lyon might have been liable for the reasonable rental of the equipment or for its return to Brodie, he did not owe performance of an "obligation secured" by the collateral in question until November 12, 1964, and therefore was not a "debtor" for purposes of § 9–

---

[1]   " '[D]ebtor' means the person who owes payment or other performance of the obligation secured, whether or not he owns or has rights in the collateral, and includes the seller of accounts, contract rights, or chattel paper; where the debtor and the owner of the collateral are not the same person, the term 'debtor' means the owner of the collateral in any provision of the article dealing with the collateral, the obligor in any provision dealing with the obligation, and may include both where the context so requires." § 9–105(d) [9–102(a)(28)(A)].

312(4) [9–324(a)]. Brodie's filing was therefore within the ten-day period and Brodie has priority over the conflicting security interest held by SBA.

The Government has urged us to look at the policy and the purposes of the Code to resolve what it considers to be the ambiguous meaning of "debtor." The Code has granted a specially favored position to the holder of a purchase-money security interest in non-inventory collateral. The holder of such an interest need not follow the notice procedures which are prescribed for the holders of purchase-money interests in inventory. § 9–312(3) [9–324(b)]. Such a holder is also given a special priority position. His interest, perfected second, but within the ten-day grace period, will prevail over any previously perfected security interest. This priority exists even though the framers of the Code knew that the holder of the conflicting security interest would be relying on the possession of the collateral and upon the absence of a prior filing. Similarly, the holder of a purchase-money security interest in non-inventory collateral will have priority over a previously perfected security interest which includes the collateral by virtue of an after-acquired property clause. § 9–312(4) [9–324(b)], Official Comment 3. Such a holder therefore is not required to search the files to determine the existence of such a conflicting interest in order to be sure of his priority.

The protection which the Code confers upon a purchase-money interest in non-inventory collateral is not unduly extended by a decision giving priority to Brodie's interest. Although it is true that Brodie could have filed a financing statement as soon as Lyon went into possession and thus protected itself, it is also true that the bank, SBA's assignor, could have protected itself by inquiring into Lyon's interest in the equipment before accepting his chattel mortgage. Due to the favored status given by the Code to the holder of a purchase-money interest in non-inventory collateral, we are not convinced that the trial court erred in refusing to impose this burden on Brodie.

Affirmed.

NOTES

1.   You might wonder how Brodie could come within former 9–312(4)'s ten-day period: Brodie seemingly would have to file by November 22, ten calendar days after November 12 but Brodie filed on November 23. The answer is contained in Alaska's general statute controlling the computation of time. Under that statute, in effect when *Brodie* was decided, "[t]he time in which an act provided by law is required to be done is computed by excluding the first day and including the last, unless the last day is a holiday, and then it is also excluded." Alaska Stat. § 01.10.080 (2002). In *Brodie*, former 9–312(3)'s ten-day period therefore began to run on November 13, and Brodie filed within ten days of that date.

2.   Section 9–324(a) awards a creditor a purchase-money priority if the creditor perfects within 20 days after "the debtor receives possession of the collateral." Courts have had difficulty applying this language to cases like

Brodie in which the goods have been in possession of a person for more than 20 days without any indication on the record of the existence of a security interest in them. The possibility that third parties, like the bank in *Brodie*, could be misled by the ostensible ownership of a person like Lyon is obvious. Nonetheless, the court decided the case on the ground that the possession must be that of a debtor and the possessor did not become a debtor until it agreed to buy the goods. Not until then was an obligation incurred and a security interest created. Comment 3 to 9–324 approves the *Brodie* analysis. Brodie might have prevented the bank's loss by filing as soon as possession passed to Lyon; the bank might have avoided loss by inquiring of Lyon about its rights in the goods. The court places the burden on the bank. But if a seller sells and delivers goods to a buyer on unsecured credit and more than 20 days later converts the transaction into a secured transaction by taking a security interest in the goods sold, the buyer incurred an obligation to pay at the outset and the 20-day period commences then. See Comment 3 (second paragraph) to 9–103.

Brodie imposes on prospective creditors the burden of inquiring into the nature of the obligations acquired by their debtors as well as the dates on which those obligations were acquired. It does so by closely parsing former 9–105(d)'s definition of "debtor." In re Alphatech Services, Inc., 317 F.3d 1267 (11th Cir.2003), on facts similar to those presented in *Brodie*, concludes that the person receiving the goods becomes a debtor from the date it takes possession. Otherwise, according to the court, purchase-money priority is "extremely susceptible to manipulation by debtors and creditors." Id. at 1269. Statutory provisions aside, is the burden placed on prospective creditors justified? Would the same analysis be made under Revised Article 9?

Suppose 9–324(a) were read so that the 20-day period begins to run from the date at which a person obtains possession of the collateral, even if it becomes a debtor subsequently. What costs would this create for secured sellers who wanted to retain purchase-money priority? Consider in this regard three things the creditor could do. (1) Require her debtor to buy prior to taking possession. Alternatively, if the person is already in possession and wants to purchase the asset on a secured basis, require her to relinquish it and redeliver the collateral later. (2) File a financing statement covering the goods delivered prior to delivery, even if a sale ultimately is not concluded. (3) Deliver the goods on a "sale on approval" basis. Goods delivered on this basis are not subject to the claims of the buyer's creditors until the goods are accepted. See 2–326(1)–(2). Significant transaction costs can be produced by each of these devices. As to (1), buyers might not agree to purchase prior to taking delivery and examining the goods. As to (2), a prospective buyer might not want a financing statement filed if it decides not to buy, given the possibly adverse effects a filing might have on its credit standing. As to (3), "sales on approval" allow a buyer to return even conforming goods prior to acceptance, and a seller might not want to continue to bear this risk.

3. Since the seller or lender granting credit in a purchase-money transaction gives the debtor new value—goods, in seller credit, or loans, in lender credit—how has the security interest of the prior secured party been impaired by awarding the seller or lender a priority in the new collateral that it enabled the debtor to acquire? Purchase-money priority is justified only if nonpurchase-money security interests are not impaired by the issuance of a purchase-money security interest. Evidence from contracting practice suggests that they might be harmed. As noted above, many security agreements either prohibit or restrict the debtor's issuance of purchase-money debt. See, e.g., infra Accounts Receivable/Loan Agreement ¶ 7.1, Appendix I. The frequency of these contractual provisions suggests that purchase-money security interests might impair the security interests of nonpurchase-money secured creditors. Otherwise, nonpurchase-money secured creditors would rarely if ever prohibit or restrict purchase-money debt in their security agreements. The justification of purchase-money priority remains unsettled. For different efficiency justifications of purchase-money priority, see Hideki Kanda & Saul Levmore, Explaining Creditor Priorities, 80 Va. L. Rev. 2103 (1994); Alan Schwartz, A Theory of Loan Priorities, 18 J. Legal Stud. 209 (1989); Robert E. Scott, A Relational Theory of Secured Financing, 86 Colum. L. Rev. 901 (1986). For doubt about the efficiency or fairness of purchase-money priority, see James J. White, Reforming Article 9 Priorities in Light of Old Ignorance and New Filing Rules, 79 Minn. L. Rev. 529, 560–563 (1995).

b.   THE TRANSFORMATION RULE

Seller sold goods to Debtor who granted Seller a security interest in the goods sold to secure the unpaid portion of the price. Does Seller's security interest remain, in whole or in part, a purchase-money security interest in the following cases?

Case #1. Debtor found it difficult to make the required monthly payments. Seller accommodated Debtor's needs by reducing the amount of the monthly payments and extending the duration of the debt. The refinancing was done by canceling the old security agreement and entering into a new security agreement embodying the new terms. In re Matthews, 724 F.2d 798 (9th Cir.1984), treated this transaction as a new loan, the proceeds of which were not used to acquire rights in the collateral; hence, the security interest was no longer purchase-money. The court believed that this result was supported by the last sentence of Comment 2 to former 9–107. In re Billings, 838 F.2d 405 (10th Cir.1988), disagreed, holding that the refinancing did not extinguish the old obligation and create a new one.

Case #2. Seller sold additional goods to Debtor. The parties entered into a new security agreement in which the old and new debts were consolidated and were secured by both the old and new collateral (cross-collateralization). In re Manuel, 507 F.2d 990 (5th Cir.1975), held that as to the old collateral, Seller's security interest lost its purchase-money character because under former 9–107(a), the security interest in that property was not retained solely to secure "all or part of its price." The same principle would invalidate the purchase-money nature of Seller's security interest in the new collateral as well. This view has come to be known as the "transformation" rule in which a security interest in any item securing more than its own price is transformed into a nonpurchase-money security interest. Pristas v. Landaus of Plymouth, Inc., 742 F.2d 797 (3d Cir.1984), rejected the transformation rule in favor of a "dual status" doctrine, which holds that the presence of a nonpurchase-money security interest does not destroy the purchase-money aspect. A purchase-money security interest can remain such "to the extent" (former 9–107) that it secures the price of the goods even though it secures the price of other items as well.

Section 9–103(f) adopts the "dual status" rule for nonconsumer goods transactions: "a purchase-money security interest does not lose its status as such, even if: (1) the purchase-money collateral also secures an obligation that is not a purchase-money obligation; (2) collateral that is not purchase-money collateral also secures the purchase-money obligation; or (3) the purchase-money obligation has been renewed, refinanced, consolidated, or restructured." See Comment 7a. to 9–103.

Matthews, Manuel and *Pristas* involve consumer transactions. Section 9–103(h) provides that the dual status rule of 9–103(f) does not apply to consumer-goods transactions and prevents courts in such transactions from relying on 9–103(f) to characterize them. It doesn't disturb relevant existing case law and leaves to courts the fashioning of the proper rules in consumer-goods transactions. Of course, 9–103(h)'s exclusion does not prevent a court from deciding on independent grounds to apply the "dual status" rule to consumer-goods transactions.

Section 9–103(h) reflects a compromise between consumer and commercial interests to retain, for the most part, the status quo concerning consumer protection. Consumer advocates wished to preserve the transformation rule in consumer cases because some bankruptcy courts used it to broaden the scope of the kinds of nonpurchase-money security interests subject to avoidance under BC 522(f)(1)(B). This issue is discussed in section 3 on purchase-money priority in inventory, immediately below. The compromise means that Article 9's provisions either exclude consumer transactions from their scope or restrict particular rules to commercial transactions. See, e.g., 9–108(e)(2), 9–109(d)(12)–(13), 9–620(g), 9–626(a). For a description of the consumer interests implicated in the drafting of Revised Article 9, see Jean Braucher, Deadlock: Consumer Transactions Under Revised Article 9, 73 Am. Bankr. L.J. 83 (1999); Gail Hillebrand, The Uniform Commercial Code Drafting Process: Will Articles 2, 2B and 9 be Fair to Consumers?, 75 Wash. U.L.Q. 69, 119–147 (1997). In Charles W. Mooney Jr., The Consumer Compromise in Revised U.C.C. Article 9: The Shame of It All, 68 Ohio St. L.J. 215 (2007), the author, one of the Co-Reporters of Revised

Article 9, is critical of the compromise as an expedient measure to gain consumer support at the cost of leaving some important issues unresolved. The matter is further discussed in Note 2 following *Southtrust Bank* below.

3. PRIORITY IN INVENTORY

Section 9–324(b) states requirements for establishing a purchase-money priority in inventory quite different from those found in 9–324(a) for other types of collateral. The first major difference is the requirement that the purchase-money secured party must notify any prior holders of security interests in the debtor's inventory who have filed financing statements that it intends to engage in purchase-money financing of the debtor's inventory. The notice is good for a five-year period, and the PMSI does not begin to run for goods delivered until the purchase-money secured party perfects. The notice requirement for inventory collateral contrasts with non-inventory financing under 9–324(a), which has no notice requirement; the purchase-money secured party does not have to search for prior filings. The notice requirement is explained in Comment 4 to 9–324 as necessary because inventory financing typically requires the secured party to make periodic advances against incoming inventory or periodic releases of old inventory as new inventory is received. The inventory financer is entitled to notice before it makes further advances that are secured by incoming inventory in which a creditor has taken a PSMI.

The second important difference is 9–324(b)'s treatment of proceeds. Under 9–324(a), the purchase-money priority carries over to the proceeds of the original collateral, but under 9–324(b), with certain exceptions with respect to chattel paper and instruments, it is limited to identifiable cash proceeds received on or before delivery of the inventory to the buyer, i.e., cash down payments. This effectively deprives purchase-money creditors of priority in all the usual proceeds from credit sales of inventory, such as goods traded-in, accounts, and cash payments on accounts received after delivery of the goods to a buyer. Comment 8 attempts to explain the line-drawing in this complex section as reflecting the expectations of the parties engaged in inventory financing. We are comforted to learn: "Many parties financing inventory are quite content to protect their first-priority security interest in the inventory itself." Comment 8. Thus, in bankruptcy, all the purchase-money secured party receives is what is left of the inventory it financed. It is shut out of the obligations of and collections from buyers of inventory previously sold.

PROBLEM

On January 1, Ace makes a loan to Debtor secured by Debtor's existing and after-acquired inventory. At the same time, Ace files a proper financing statement. On March 1, Bank lends Debtor funds to purchase new inventory and Debtor grants it a security interest in the inventory purchased with

Bank's funds. On the same date, Bank sends Ace notice by letter of the interest in the new inventory it intends to obtain, which Ace receives on March 5. Bank files a proper financing statement covering the new inventory on March 1. Later, Debtor defaults on its obligations to both Ace and Bank.

(a) If Debtor receives the new inventory on March 2, who has priority in Debtor's inventory purchased with Bank's funds: Ace or Bank?

(b) What result if Debtor received the inventory on March 10?

(c) Suppose Debtor sold 5 items of the new inventory to buyers, who paid a total of $500 in cash and another 5 items to buyers, each of whom promises to pay $110 per item. The buyers later pay Debtor in full so that Debtor receives a total of $1050 for the 10 items of new inventory. The money is traceable to each item of inventory sold. Who has priority in the $500: Ace or Bank? In the $550 Debtor eventually receives?

(d) Would the result in (c) change if 5 buyers executed promissory notes and granted Debtor security interests in the items purchased? Would the result change if Debtor delivered the notes to Bank?

(e) Would the result in (c) change if Debtor had granted Bank a security interest in new machinery to be used in its factory, to be purchased with Bank's funds?

The following case, decided under former Article 9, challenges whether the purchase-money financer even has a priority in the remaining inventory. How does Article 9 change the result in the case?

Southtrust Bank v. Borg-Warner Acceptance Corp.

United States Court of Appeals, Eleventh Circuit, 1985
760 F.2d 1240

■ TUTTLE, SENIOR CIRCUIT JUDGE.

Borg-Warner Acceptance Corporation ("BWAC") appeals from a decision of the district court denying its motion for summary judgment and granting summary judgment to Southtrust Bank ("the Bank") in a diversity suit. The Bank filed a declaratory judgment action to ascertain which of the parties has priority in the inventory of four debtors, Molay Brothers Supply Company, Inc., Gulf City Distributors, Inc., Standard Wholesale Supply Company and Crest Refrigeration, Inc. These debtors, which are no longer in existence, defaulted on obligations they owed to one or the other party.

Both the Bank and BWAC have perfected security interests in the inventory of the debtors. In each case, the Bank filed its financing statement first. BWAC contends that as a purchase money lender it falls within the purchase money security interest exception to the first to file rule and therefore is entitled to possession of the inventory. The Uniform

Commercial Code (UCC) as adopted in both Alabama and Georgia, provides in pertinent part:

A security interest is a "purchase money security interest" to the extent that it is:

(a) Taken or retained by the seller of the collateral to secure all or part of its price; or

(b) Taken by a person who by making advances or incurring an obligation gives value to enable the debtor to acquire rights in or the use of collateral if such value is in fact so used.

BWAC engages in purchase money financing. Here, BWAC purchased invoices from vendors who supplied inventory items to the debtors in question. The security agreements between BWAC and each of the debtors contained the following provision:

In order to secure repayment to Secured Party of all such extensions of credit made by Secured Party in accordance with this Agreement, and to secure payment of all other debts or liabilities and performance of all obligations of Debtor to Secured Party, whether now existing or hereafter arising, Debtor agrees that Secured Party shall have and hereby grants to Secured Party a security interest in all Inventory of Debtor, whether now owned or hereafter acquired, and all Proceeds and products thereof.

The term "Inventory" was defined as "all inventory, of whatever kind or nature, wherever located, now owned or hereafter acquired. . . when such inventory has been financed by Borg-Warner Acceptance Corporation."

BWAC and the debtors employed a scheduled liquidation arrangement to reduce the debt owed BWAC. Under this arrangement a debtor was permitted to pay a percentage of the invoice each month, without regard to whether the item was actually sold. If an unpaid item was sold, then the remaining inventory served as collateral to secure the unpaid balance.

The key issue for decision by this Court is whether inclusion of an after-acquired property clause and a future advances clause in BWAC's security agreements converted its purchase money security interest (PMSI) into an ordinary security interest.

The district court held that inclusion of after-acquired property and future advances clauses ("the clauses") in the security agreement converted BWAC's PMSI into an ordinary security interest. The court relied on In re Manuel, 507 F.2d 990 (5th Cir.1975) (holding, in a consumer bankruptcy context, that PMSI must be limited to the item purchased at time of the agreement and cannot exceed the price of that item); In re Norrell, 426 F.Supp. 435 (M.D.Ga.1977) (same); and In re

Simpson, 4 U.C.C.Rep.Serv. 243 (Bankr.W.D.Mich.1966) (inclusion of future advances clause in security agreement for farm equipment destroys PMSI).

BWAC argues that the cases relied on by the court are distinguishable. First, BWAC notes that almost all the cases following the "transformation" rule (i.e., inclusion of the clauses transforms a PMSI into an ordinary security interest) are consumer bankruptcy cases. It argues that the rationale of those cases, which is to protect the consumer, does not apply in commercial cases such as the case at bar. See In re Mid-Atlantic Flange, 26 U.C.C.Rep.Serv. 203, 208 (E.D.Pa.1979). BWAC argues that the policy considerations in a commercial setting, promoting commercial certainty and encouraging credit extension, do not support the application of the transformation rule. According to BWAC, applying the transformation rule to inventory financiers would require them to police inventory constantly and to see that inventory corresponds on an item-by-item basis with debt.

The Bank argues that the transformation rule is not a product of special bankruptcy considerations, and that if the drafters had intended to limit the rule to consumer transactions, they would have said so, as they did in other sections of the Code. The Bank contends that a holding that inclusion of the clauses destroys a PMSI would not have a serious negative effect on inventory financiers. It points out that such financiers could retain priority by obtaining a subordination agreement from the first-to-file creditor.

We see no reason to limit the holding of *In re Manuel* to consumer bankruptcy cases. In that case, the Fifth Circuit stated:

> A plain reading of the statutory requirements would indicate that they require the purchase money security interest to be in the item purchased, and that, as the judges below noted, the purchase money security interest cannot exceed the price of what is purchased in the transaction wherein the security interest is created. . . .

Id. at 993. Nothing in the language of U.C.C. § 9–312(3) [9–324(b)] or § 9–107 [9–103(a) and (b)] distinguishes between consumer and commercial transactions or between bankruptcy and nonbankruptcy contexts. We see no policy reasons for creating a distinction where the drafters have not done so.

Second, BWAC contends that the cases supporting the transformation rule involve situations in which the clauses were actually exercised, e.g., *Manuel* (agreement covered pre-existing debt); *Simpson* (future advances actually made). BWAC argues that mere inclusion of the clauses does not void a PMSI. In re Griffin, 9 B.R. 880 (Bankr.N.D.Ga.1981) (when creditor is seller, mere existence of unexercised future advances clause does not destroy PMSI); *Mid-Atlantic Flange* (same). We need not reach the issue of whether mere inclusion of unexercised future advances and after-acquired property clauses voids a PMSI because we find that BWAC exercised the clauses here. After entering the security agreements with the debtors, BWAC regularly purchased inventory for the debtors and now claims that the debtors' BWAC-financed inventory secures these purchases. This is an exercise of the future advances clause. Similarly, BWAC claims as collateral not only the inventory purchased at the time the security agreements were entered, but all BWAC-financed inventory. This is an exercise of the after-acquired property clause. We hold, therefore, that BWAC's exercise of the future advances and after-acquired property clauses in its security agreements with the debtors destroyed its PMSI.

We note, as did the district court, that BWAC retains a security interest in the goods. It merely loses its priority status as a purchase money secured lender. The concept of the floating lien under the U.C.C. remains intact. We hold, merely, that such a floating lien is inconsistent with a PMSI. A PMSI requires a one-to-one relationship between the debt and the collateral.

BWAC's final argument is that the court should adopt a "to the extent" rule, based on the literal language of UCC, § 9–107:

> A security interest is a "purchase money security interest" to the extent that it is. . . (b) Taken by a person who by making advances or incurring an obligation gives value to enable the debtor to acquire rights in or the use of collateral if such value is in fact so used.

Some courts have held that the clauses, even if exercised, do not invalidate a PMSI if there is some method for determining the extent of the PMSI. For example, in In re Staley, 426 F.Supp. 437 (M.D.Ga.1977), the court held that the PMSI was valid because the security agreement specified that payments be allocated first to items bought first. Thus, it was easy for the court to ascertain which items had been fully paid for and hence no longer served as collateral. Here, however, nothing in the contract or in state law allocates payments to particular items of inventory. BWAC, in fact, claims all BWAC-financed inventory as its collateral without regard to payments made by the debtors. We agree with the court in In re Coomer, 8 B.R. 351, 355 (Bankr.E.D. Tenn.1980), that

> Without some guidelines, legislative or contractual, the court should not be required to distill from a mass of transactions the extent to which a security interest is purchase money.

Unless a lender contractually provides some method for determining the extent to which each item of collateral secures its purchase money, it effectively gives up its purchase money status.

Because we hold that BWAC's exercise of the after-acquired property and future advances clauses in its security agreements voided its PMSI, we need not reach the other issues raised by the Bank. We also do not reach the issue raised by BWAC concerning the district court's reference to proceeds from sales of the inventory being held "in trust." Whether the proceeds are held "in trust" is relevant only to the issue of damages. The district court entered final judgment only on the claim for declaratory relief and referred the damage claim to a magistrate. Because no final judgment has been entered as to damages, that issue is not properly before this Court.

AFFIRMED.

NOTES

1. Section 9–103 changes the result in *Southtrust*. Subsection (f)(2)'s "dual status" rule preserves a PMSI even if purchase-money collateral also secures nonpurchase-money obligations. Thus, cross-collateralization does not destroy PMSI status. Section 9–103(f)(2) therefore statutorily overrules *Southtrust*'s requirement that there be a "one-to-one relationship between the debt and the collateral." Section 9–103(b)(2) in particular alters the outcome in *Southtrust*. Subsection (b)(2) defines a security interest in goods as a PMSI "if the security interest is in inventory that is or was purchase-money collateral, also to the extent that the security interest secures a purchase-money obligation incurred with respect to other inventory in which the secured party holds or held a purchase-money security interest." Each item of inventory covered by BWAC's security agreement is purchase-money collateral for the purchase-money obligation it secured, and the security agreement's cross-collateralization clause secures all of BWAC's other purchase-money obligations with each item of inventory. Thus, 9–103(b)(2) considers all of BWAC's security interests in its debtors' inventory to be PMSIs.

Since under 9–103's rules a security interest may be purchase-money to some extent and nonpurchase-money to some extent (see 9–103(b)(1)), some method is required for allocating payments between purchase-money and nonpurchase-money obligations. Section 9–103(e) supplies a mechanism for allocating payments that the court in *Southtrust* found lacking. Under 9–103(e)'s mechanism, in nonconsumer goods transactions payments are applied according to a "reasonable method" agreed upon by the parties. Absent such an agreement, in accordance with the debtor's manifested intent. If there is neither a reasonable method of allocation agreed upon nor the relevant intent manifested by the debtor, payments are allocated to unsecured obligations first. As between secured obligations, payments are allocated to purchase-money obligations in the order in which they occurred. In *Southtrust*, this final allocational method would apply to BWAC's purchase-money and nonpurchase-money obligations.

2. Whether a security interest is purchase-money under 9–103 is relevant in two other situations in addition to cases arising under 9–324. Under 9–309(1), a purchase-money security interest in consumer goods is perfected without possession or filing, and BC 522(f)(1)(B) allows a trustee in bankruptcy to avoid a nonpossessory, nonpurchase-money security

interest in certain consumer goods. The great bulk of litigation on the meaning of purchase-money has occurred in bankruptcy courts under BC 522(f)(1)(B). The distinction drawn in BC 522(f)(1)(B) between purchase-money credit (e.g., retailer retains a security interest in household goods sold to the debtor) and nonpurchase-money credit (e.g., a personal loan company takes a security interest in household goods the debtor had already purchased to secure a loan made to the debtor) is based on Congressional hostility toward the personal finance business. Congress considers consumer financers to be lenders of last resort, whose security interests are in terrorem collection devices used to coerce necessitous debtors into paying the loan company in preference to other creditors or reaffirming debts discharged in bankruptcy. The impact of 522(f)(1) on the price of consumer credit for all consumer debtors apparently is not a decisive consideration for Congress.

Although the consumer context of both Bankruptcy Code 522(f)(1)(B) and 9–309(1) is wholly foreign to the issue raised by 9–324(b) of determining priorities between two sophisticated commercial financers, the court in *Southtrust* relies on these consumer bankruptcy cases for guidance and adopts the rigid rule that cross-collateralization destroys the purchase-money nature of a transaction. As the court says, "[a] PMSI requires a one-to-one relationship between the debt and the collateral." Thus, *Southtrust* allows a reliable purchase-money priority only if each sale is treated as a separate transaction. This, of course, is totally infeasible in any but big-ticket items like motor vehicles. Even in these cases, *Southtrust* seems inconsistent with both former and Revised 9–205, which allows the debtor to deal with the collateral without the treatment being fraudulent as to its creditors.

3. In *Southtrust*, the court suggests that a purchase-money financer should protect its priority by an intercreditor subordination agreement with the first-to-file creditor. This is still good advice even though 9–103(f) statutorily overrules *Southtrust*. A subordination agreement avoids costly litigation over priority issues if negotiating one is cost-justified. There is still another barrier to recognition of an effective purchase-money priority in inventory under 9–324(b). The following is a covenant of the debtor, generally known as a "negative pledge clause," taken from a standard loan and security agreement used in inventory financing by a leading financial institution:

> The Borrower is, and as to inventory to be acquired after the date hereof, shall be, the owner of all inventory and shall neither create nor suffer to exist any lien or encumbrance thereon or security interest therein. . . in favor of any person other than the Lender.

See Accounts Receivable/Loan Agreement ¶ 7 (Negative Covenants), Appendix I, which contains a negative pledge clause (§ 7.6) as well as a covenant on the borrower's part not to incur additional debt without Bank's consent (§ 7.1).

Since breach of these covenants constitutes an event of default, which results in the debt secured by the inventory becoming immediately due and payable, the first-to-file creditor may call its loan if the debtor even attempts to enter into purchase-money financing with another creditor. Query: does

9–324(b) have any commercial significance today? Would you counsel a client to rely on it for a priority without the consent of the prior secured party?

4.   9–103(h)'S CONSUMER GOODS EXCEPTION

As discussed in Note 2 above, there are advantages to a secured party in having its security interest qualify as purchase-money. A PMSI cannot be avoided under BC 522(f)(1)(B), and no financing statement need be filed to perfect a PMSI in consumer goods. 9–309(1). Hence, in consumer goods transactions trustees in bankruptcy for consumer debtors have attacked the purchase-money status of secured interests reserved by sellers in add-on sales and revolving charge account transactions. They have enjoyed some success. In the add-on sale transaction described in Case #2 in the section on the transformational rule above, In re Manuel, 507 F.2d 990 (5th Cir.1975), held that a seller has a purchase-money-security interest in goods purchased only when the security interest is taken *solely* to secure all or part of its price. Since in that case, the security agreement provided that the security interest in the goods purchased also secured debts arising from previous sales, the court held the security interest could not be purchase-money.

Even more important to retailing than add-on sales is the revolving charge account in which the consumer opens an account with a retailer and is permitted to charge purchases, often pursuant to the retailer's credit card, to be paid for in monthly installments. If *Southtrust*'s "one-to-one" limitation is applied to this transaction, an attempt by a seller to retain a purchase-money security interest in goods sold to secure the running balance of the account would fail. Moreover, even if the seller attempted only to retain a security interest in each item sold to secure only the price of that item, the security interest could not be purchase-money unless the agreement or presumably the law of the state prescribed an allocation formula for the consumer's payments. Such an allocation provision is set out in In re Cersey, 321 B.R. 352 (Bankr. M.D. Ga.2004).

The provisions of 9–103(e) (allocation of payments) and (f) (dual status) would, if they were applied to the consumer goods transactions described above, overturn *Manuel*. In earlier drafts of 9–103, these provisions applied to consumer goods as well as commercial transactions. However, in the final draft, consumer goods transactions were excepted from subsections (e) and (f). Subsection (h) also was added, which provides that in consumer goods transactions the courts are free to make their own rules about the desirability of the dual status and payment allocations rules. Presumably they can embrace *Manuel*. Hostility of consumer groups toward security interests in low-priced goods was reflected in the National Bankruptcy Review Commission's recommendation to abolish in bankruptcy purchase-money security interests in household goods worth less than $500. 1 National Bankruptcy Commission, Bankruptcy: The Next Twenty Years 169

(1997) (Recommendation 1.3.4). Doubtless, the same pressure from consumer groups that resulted in this recommendation played a role in persuading the Article 9 Drafting Committee to leave retailers to the mercy of the bankruptcy courts without a statute establishing their rights in add-on and charge account sales transactions.

D. LIEN CREDITORS

1. CONFLICT WITH AN UNPERFECTED SECURITY INTEREST

Section 9–317(a)(2) states the rule that, with the exception set out in (2)(B), an unperfected security interest is subordinate to the rights of a lien creditor. Since a trustee in bankruptcy is a lien creditor under 9–102(a)(52)(C), this provision, together with BC 544(a)(1) and BC 550(a), allows a trustee in bankruptcy to avoid an unperfected security interest. Thus, these provisions constitute the statutory anvil on which Article 9 security interests are tested in bankruptcy.

PROBLEMS

1. On February 1, Debtor granted a nonpurchase-money security interest in described collateral to SP in a signed security agreement; SP advanced value to Debtor on that date. On February 5, Creditor's judicial lien attached to the same collateral. On February 9, SP filed a financing statement covering the collateral. Who is prior under 9–317(a)(2)?

2. On February 1, Debtor granted a nonpurchase-money security interest in described collateral to SP in a signed security agreement; SP filed a financing statement covering Debtor's collateral on that date. On February 5, Creditor's judicial lien attached to the same collateral. On February 9, SP advanced value to Debtor. Who is prior under 9–317(a)(2)? How can you reconcile the result in Problem 2 with that in Problem 1? See Comment 4 to 9–317. Are you persuaded by the explanation given in the Comment for the change in law in 9–317(a)(2)?

2. CONFLICT WITH A FUTURE ADVANCE

The previous section discusses perhaps the most important conflict treated by Article 9; the conflict discussed in this section is much less significant. As described earlier, in a case of conflicting Article 9 security interests, 9–322(a)(1) protects the priority of the first party to file or perfect with respect to future advances even though the advances were made after that party had knowledge of a subsequent security interest in the same collateral. Comment 4 to 9–322 justifies this rule on efficiency grounds: the rule allows the first secured party who has filed to make subsequent advances without each time having to check for subsequent filings as a condition of protection. But when the conflict is between an advance made pursuant to an Article 9 security interest and a subsequent lien creditor's rights, a different rule controls. Under 9–323(b), the secured future advance has priority (i) if the advance is made or committed within 45 days after the lien arises even with knowledge of the lien and (ii) if the advance is made or committed after the 45-day period, so long as the secured party is without knowledge of the lien at the time of the advance or commitment.

Thus, monitoring costs to the secured party are only slightly increased with respect to competing judicial liens: only if the secured party has actual knowledge of the lien must it hold up on future advances, and not even then if less than 45 days have gone by. It is highly improbable that any secured party will make an optional future advance, even within the 45-day window, if it knows that the collateral is subject to a judicial lien. In some instances, a judicial lien may be obtained only by seizing the property, and property in the possession of a sheriff is not attractive collateral. So the question must be asked why the statute protects the priority of a secured party who makes a future advance with knowledge of the lien during the 45-day period after the lien arises—an advance no sensible secured creditor will ever make. The provision is particularly difficult to justify given 9–323(d), which cuts off advance priority against a buyer when the advance is made with actual knowledge of the purchase, even within the 45-day period. Comment 4 to 9–323 reveals that it is important for purposes of the Federal Tax Lien Act to establish under state law an absolute priority for a future advance over a lien creditor for 45 days even if made with knowledge of the lien. No one expects any UCC cases to arise under it.

Notice a final implication of 9–323(b). Because the subsection only deals with the subordination of future advances under prescribed conditions, it has no effect on the priority of *non*advance obligations incurred by the debtor after a lien attaches. In short, 9–323(b) doesn't address priority contests between a creditor whose nonadvance obligations are secured and the rights of a lien creditor. As Comment 4 to 9–323 reinforces, "[s]ubsection (b) of this section [9–323] provides that a security interest is subordinate to those rights to the extent that the specified circumstances occur." Priority contests pitting nonadvance secured obligations against a lien creditor's rights aren't among those "specified circumstances." Instead, 9–317(a)(2) controls them, and under 9–317(a)(2), aside from 9–317(a)(2)(B), the secured nonadvances are protected when made by a creditor perfected on or before the lien attaches. The date on which the nonadvance is made does not affect its priority. See Dick Warner Cargo Handling Corp. v. Aetna Bus. Credit, Inc., 746 F.2d 126 (2d Cir.1984). Nonadvances can include items ranging from collection and interest charges to attorney's fees. Unlike advances, nonadvance obligations easily can be incurred by a debtor after a lien attaches.

E. BUYERS AND LESSEES

1.   BUYERS AND LESSEES OF NON-INVENTORY GOODS

Secured parties are in a very strong position with respect to persons who buy or lease goods from their debtors. Section 9–315(a) provides that the security interest continues in the goods sold or leased and in any identifiable proceeds, unless the secured party authorizes the disposition free of its security interest or an Article 9 rule or one recognized by it cuts off the security interest. This continuation rule increases the value of collateral to the secured party, because it preserves the party's security interests, while reducing its value to the person to whom the collateral is transferred, because it takes the asset subject a continuing security interest. Under 9–317(b), buyers and lessees take subject to perfected security interests. Section 9–317(e) under prescribed conditions grants unperfected purchase-money secured parties a 20-day relation-back period after the debtor has received delivery of the collateral in which to perfect by filing. Even unperfected security interests are prior to the rights of buyers and lessees other than those who give value and receive delivery without knowledge of the security interest.

> **Case #1.** Debtor, a manufacturer, granted Lender a security interest in its equipment to secure a loan of $100,000 on February 1. Debtor contracted to sell two pieces of equipment to Buyer on March 1 in violation of a provision in the security agreement forbidding sale of collateral without Lender's written permission. Buyer, who knew nothing of Lender's security interest, paid Debtor $10,000 at the time of the contract and agreed to pay the remaining $15,000 owing at the time of delivery. Lender discovered that it had failed to file before the sale and corrected its error by filing on March 15. Buyer paid the $15,000 balance on April 1 and Debtor delivered the equipment at that time. Is Lender's security interest prior to Buyer's rights in the equipment?

> **Case #2.** Assume the facts are the same as those in Case #1 except that Debtor delivered the equipment to Buyer, who paid the remaining balance of the price on March 10. Before Buyer made its final payment, it searched the record and found no financing statement on record under Debtor's name. (i) Is Lender's security interest prior to Buyer's rights in the equipment? (ii) What would the result be if Lender had lent money to Debtor that enabled Debtor to buy the equipment that it later sold to Buyer? Assume that Debtor itself had taken delivery of the equipment on March 5.

2.   BUYERS AND LESSEES OF INVENTORY GOODS

a.   BUYER IN THE ORDINARY COURSE OF BUSINESS

A major exception to the basic rule that buyers and lessees from a debtor take subject to perfected security interests is the traditional rule that buyers and lessees of inventory collateral take free of inventory security interests. Inventory is meant to be sold or leased (9–102(a)(48)(B)) with the secured party looking to the proceeds of the disposition for security rather than pursuing the goods in the hands of the buyer or lessee. This rule is stated in 9–320(a): "[A] buyer in ordinary course of business, other than a person buying farm products from a person engaged in farming operations, takes free of a security interest created by the buyer's seller, even if the security interest is perfected and the buyer knows of its existence." A comparable rule for lessees is found in 9–321(c). Section 1–201(b)(9) provides in part: " 'Buyer in ordinary course of business' means a person that buys goods in good faith, without knowledge that the sale violates the rights of another person in the goods, and in the ordinary course from a person. . .in the business of selling goods of that kind." As Comment 3 to 9–320 notes, 9–320(a)'s rule is restricted primarily to inventory collateral.

Section 9–320(a)'s "takes free" rule is subject to three restrictions. Two are apparent on the face of 9–320(a). One restriction is that the rule allows the buyer to take free only of security interests created by its seller. By its terms, 9–320(a) prevents a buyer from taking free of a security interest created by a remote seller. The second restriction is that the rule does not apply to the buyer of farm products from a seller engaged in food production. Thus, as far as 9–320(a) goes, the buyer of farm products from this seller takes subject to a security interest created by her seller in the farm products. This is not a significant restriction because federal law protects the buyer. Under the Food Security Act, a buyer of farm products from a producer in the ordinary course of business takes free of a security interest created by its seller unless the seller has given the requisite notice of its security interest. 7 U.S.C. § 1631(d). Notice can be given either directly, by sending the buyer written notice, or by filing notice where possible. 7 U.S.C. § 1631(e)(1), (2) . Filing notice is possible only in states that have a system for registering security interests in farm products ("a central filing system"). To date, 19 states have a central filing system. Even in these states, the "central filing system" for giving notice of a security interest in farm products is separate from the centralized filing system for recording UCC financing statements. In addition, the required content of the filing notice for farm products differs from that of a UCC financing statement. The third restriction on 9–320(a)'s "take free" rule, added by 9–320(e), is that the secured party not be in possession of the goods. Accordingly, a buyer of goods in which a secured party has a possessory security interest takes subject to the security interest, unless the secured party authorizes the sale free of its security interest.

The following case has disputed facts. Assume the following: Smith Companies (Smith) were engaged in mining. Smith borrowed money from CTB, a bank, and granted a security interest in underground mining equipment to secure the loan. Included in this equipment were 85 "Shields," underground roof supports, which Smith attempted to sell. Unable to find a buyer, Smith contends that it sold the Shields as scrap to S & S Salvage (S & S), which in turn sold them to River Metals Recycling. S & S contends that it merely acted on Smith's behalf in hauling the equipment to River Metals and receiving payment. What is clear is that River Metals bought the equipment from S & S without any knowledge of Smith. Eventually, Madison Capital purchased CTB's position as a secured creditor of Smith and sued S & S and River Metals in conversion. The issue is whether River Metals is a buyer in ordinary course of business under 9–320(a).

Madison Capital Company, LLC v. S & S Salvage, LLC

United States District Court, W.D. Kentucky, 2011
765 F.Supp.2d 923

■ JOSEPH H. McKINLEY, JR., DISTRICT JUDGE.

This matter is before the Court on cross motions for summary judgment by Plaintiff Madison Capital Company, LLC, Defendant River Metals Recycling, LLC, and Defendant S & S Salvage, LLC. Fully Briefed, this matter is ripe for decision. * * *

II.   Background

In February 2005, Community Trust Bank (CTB) issued a $1,500,000 term loan and a $350,000 revolving loan to three coal companies owned by Timothy P. Smith; American Mining and Manufacturing Corporation, American Engineering and Construction Corporation, and United States Coal Corporation (the "Smith Companies"). Smith signed a security agreement in connection with the loan pledging several pieces of the three companies' equipment as collateral for the loan as well as personally guaranteeing the loan. CTB promptly recorded and perfected its security interest in the collateral equipment.

The collateral for the loan included a Joy Longwall Mining System which contained various pieces of underground mining equipment. The Longwall System was comprised of numerous parts including eighty-five (85) Hemscheidt Shields (the "Shields"), which were mechanized underground roof supports made of various metals that weighed approximately fifteen (15) tons per shield.

One month after securing the loan with CTB, Smith contacted Brett Keene, a commercial loan officer at CTB, to discuss selling portions of the Longwall System to C.W. Mining Company. These portions did not include the Shields. Smith already had a purchase agreement with C.W. Mining and was requesting that CTB allow the sale and release its lien on the equipment. Keene and CTB denied Smith's request to sell any portion of the Longwall System and refused to release its lien. Nevertheless, Smith sold portions of the Longwall System to C.W. Mining.

After this unauthorized sale to C.W. Mining, Smith sought out a buyer for the eighty-five Shields. In December 2005, unable to find a buyer for the Shields, Smith agreed to sell the Shields as scrap metal. The terms of the agreement to sell the Shields are disputed. Smith contends that he sold the Shields to S & S Salvage, LLC who in turn sold them to River Metals Recycling, LLC. S & S contends that it agreed to transport the Shields to River Metals for Smith and use its open account at River Metals to process the weighing of the scrap and payment. In return, S & S would receive a fee based upon the tonnage hauled to River Metals. Regardless of the nature of the transfer to S & S, River Metals bought the Shields from S & S over several days without any knowledge of Smith or the Smith Companies. River Metals issued a series of checks to S & S between December 22, 2005, and December 29, 2005, for the Shields. S & S deposited the checks in its own account, calculated and retained its fee, and remitted the remainder back to Smith in the form of two checks dated December 27, 2005, and December 31, 2005. One check was written to Smith personally and the other was written to American Mining.

In November 2005, Smith convinced Madison Capital Company, LLC to help his cash-strapped companies by loaning American Mining $3,750,000. In January and February of 2006, Madison issued additional loans of $300,000 and $1,200,000 to Smith companies. On May 30, 2006, Madison, Smith, the Smith Companies, and CTB entered into a contribution and company interests purchase agreement, whereby the Smith Companies transferred all of their assets to a newly formed entity, American Mining & Manufacturing LLC (AMM, LLC), in exchange for a 25% equity interest in the new company and Madison contributed $4,000,000 in capital in exchange for a 75% equity interest in the new company. As part of this agreement, AMM, LLC was added as an additional borrower on the CTB bank loan and Smith reaffirmed his absolute and unconditional personal guarantee of the original bank loans. Smith was retained as CEO of the new LLC, and shortly after the creation of AMM, LLC, he requested additional capital from Madison. On July 11, 2006, AMM, LLC terminated Smith's employment with the company.

In September 2006, Madison purchased CTB's position as a secured creditor of the Smith Companies by way of an assignment, which included a mutual general release of all claims against one another. Madison, as the assignee of CTB's interests, then pursued Smith through litigation for his personal guarantee of the CTB bank loans, eventually obtaining a judgment against him on August 26, 2008 in the amount of $1,200,000. After securing its judgment against Smith, Madison filed suit against S & S, in November 2008, for its part in the sale of the Shields and then amended its complaint to include River Metals on February 13, 2009.

III. Discussion

Madison has filed suit against S & S and River Metals, jointly and severally, alleging claims of conversion. . . based on the respective Defendants' actions in relation to the Shields. The Defendants have denied these allegations and alleged various defenses including statute of limitations and laches. River Metals has also claimed that it is a buyer in the ordinary course of business, which severs Madison's security interest. The parties have filed cross motions for summary judgment. Madison has moved for summary judgment on its conversion. . . claims, while S & S and River Metals has each moved for summary judgment on all of Madison's claims.

A.   Buyer in the Ordinary Course of Business

River Metals motion for summary judgment revolves around the contention that it bought the Shields as a buyer in the ordinary course of business, and, therefore, took good title to the Shields. River Metals contends that if it had good title to the Shields then the claims asserted against it by Madison should be dismissed. As a matter of Kentucky law, a perfected security interest "continues in collateral notwithstanding sale, lease, license, exchange, or other disposition thereof unless the secured party authorized the disposition free of the security interest." Ky.Rev.Stat. Ann. § 355.9–315(1)(a) (West 2010). However, "a buyer in ordinary course of business. . . takes free of a security interest created by the buyer's seller, even if the security interest is perfected and the buyer knows of its existence." Ky.Rev.Stat. Ann. § 355.9–320(1) (West 2010). Kentucky statute defines a buyer in the ordinary course as "a person that buys goods in good faith, without knowledge that the sale violates the rights of another person in the goods, and in the ordinary course from a person, other than a pawnbroker, in the business of selling goods of that kind." Ky.Rev.Stat. Ann. § 355.1–201(2)(i) (West 2010). To successfully claim protection as a buyer in the ordinary course River Metals must prove that it bought the Shields from the entity that created the security interest, and that that entity sells equipment like the Shields in its ordinary course of business.

Madison contends that S & S Salvage bought the Shields from Smith and then sold them in a separate transaction to River Metals. Under this scenario, River Metals would not qualify as a buyer in the ordinary course because it would have bought from a seller who did not create the security interest. River Metals claims it bought the Shields from Smith through

S & S, who was acting as the undisclosed agent of Smith. River Metals contends that Smith was the seller, and because he created the security interest, River Metals qualifies as a buyer in the ordinary course. However, even if River Metals recitation of the facts is accurate it would still fail to qualify as a buyer in the ordinary course because Smith is not in the business of selling mining equipment, he is in the business of mining. Smith's earlier sale of the Joy Longwall Mining System and his subsequent sale of the Shields do not make him a seller of mining equipment in the ordinary course of business.

River Metals argues, in the alternative, that if Smith is not in the business of selling mining equipment that River Metals is still entitled to protection under the buyer in the ordinary course exception because it bought the Shields as scrap from Smith's agent, S & S, who sells scrap in the ordinary course of business. River Metals contends that the buyer in the ordinary course exception should be examined from the buyer's perspective, and that River Metals should be protected because it bought the goods through a dealer of those types of goods. The Court disagrees.

The buyer in the ordinary course exception is designed to protect buyers in the very limited set of circumstances where a lender takes a security interest in goods and then leaves the goods in the possession of a debtor who sells goods of that kind. Such an action by the lender confers apparent authority on the debtor to sell the goods. William H. Lawrence, *The "Created by His Seller" Limitation of Section 9–307(1) of the U.C.C.: A Provision in Need of an Articulated Policy,* 60 Ind. L.J. 73, 80–81 (1984–85). When a lender gives its debtor the apparent authority to sell the collateralized goods in the debtor's ordinary course of business, it is appropriate that the lender bear the risk that the debtor will make unauthorized sales. However, when the lender leaves non-inventory goods in the possession of a debtor who does not sell goods of that kind, the lender does not confer authority to the debtor to sell the goods. It is the "absence of apparent authority to sell [which] is the justification for continuing the validity of the security interest in such situations even against a buyer in ordinary course of business." *Id.* at 87.

A lender who takes a security interest in non-inventory and properly files a financing statement disclosing that interest has done all that is required to protect its interest. When a debtor transfers the collateralized property to a dealer of such goods, such as happened here, who in turn sells that property to an unsuspecting buyer, the security interest remains attached. While this result is a harsh one given the buyer's innocence, the unsuspecting buyer still has a remedy; he can sue the transferor under a warranty of title claim. *Id.* at 94–95. In the instant case, it is not appropriate to consider Smith the seller of the goods for purposes of the created by the seller limitation and then consider S & S as the seller for purposes of the ordinary course of business limitation. Either Smith was the seller for all purposes of the analysis or S & S was, but River Metals cannot mix and match the parties to create protection under the exception.

River Metals final contention is that sound public policy requires that it be protected under the buyer in the ordinary course exception because it was an innocent buyer. However, CTB was also an innocent party to this transaction, and the law does not protect buyers simply because they are innocent. Merchants who unknowingly buy from a thief or individuals who unknowingly buy goods through a wrongful sale by a bailee do not receive good title. *Id.* at 89. Similarly, River Metals innocence alone does not require a finding that it should receive good title under the buyer in the ordinary course exception.

Regardless of who was the actual seller of the Shields, the fact remains that CTB left non-inventory mining equipment with Smith who was not a seller of mining equipment. CTB did not confer apparent authority on Smith to sell the Shields, so it should not bear the risk of Smith's unauthorized sale. Accordingly, CTB's security interest in the Shields remained attached even after the sale to River Metals. * * *

IV. Conclusion

For the reasons set forth above, IT IS HEREBY ORDERED that Plaintiff Madison's Motion for Summary Judgment as to the conversion. . . claims is DENIED.

PROBLEMS

1.   Lender perfected a security interest in Debtor's equipment by filing. The equipment is business machines used in Debtor's accounting firm. In violation of a provision in the security agreement, Debtor sold some of the machines to Dealer without Lender's knowledge or consent. Dealer buys and sells used business machines and sold the machines in question to Buyer for cash. Buyer bought the machines for use in his business. Neither Dealer nor Buyer knew about Lender's security interest in the machines.

   (a)   Is Dealer a buyer in the ordinary course of business?

   (b)   Is Buyer a buyer in the ordinary course of business?

   (c)   What are Lender's rights with respect to the machines now in Buyer's possession? See Comment 3 to 9–320.

2.   Lender has been financing Dealer's inventory for some time but it recently placed Dealer on "credit watch" with new restrictions on Dealer's operations. One of these limitations is that Dealer must obtain Lender's consent to the sale of any machine with a sale price exceeding $5,000. In violation of this limitation, Dealer sold and delivered to Buyer a machine for $10,000 cash. Buyer is a sophisticated person who was well aware that Dealer's inventory was very likely to be subject to a security interest in favor of a financial institution. Buyer also knew that Dealer was having financial problems and took this into consideration in negotiating for a low price for the machine. You may assume that Lender's security interest was perfected

by filing. What are Lender's rights with respect to the machine now in Buyer's possession? See Comment 3 to 9–320.

b.   GOODS SUBJECT TO CERTIFICATE OF TITLE ACTS

One of the most valuable articles of goods are motor vehicles. These are covered by state motor vehicle acts, which, given their anti-theft origin, usually provide that no one can acquire ownership without receiving a "certificate of title," which may consist of tangible records, electronic records or a combination of both, 9–102(a)(10), or, in the case of new motor vehicles never sold at retail, the manufacturer's certificate of origin. But, as discussed in the previous section, 9–320(a) gives a buyer in the ordinary course of business priority over a security interest created by the buyer's seller. Which party has priority when a secured party obtains a security interest in a car by having its lien indicated on a certificate of title covering the car and the owner sells the car to a buyer in the ordinary course of business without being able to deliver a clean certificate of title to the buyer?

Given that the dollar volume of motor vehicle sales must exceed that of any other article of personal property sold at retail, one might expect that the conflict between Article 9 and the state's motor vehicle act would be resolved in the provisions of Article 9. However, there is no explicit treatment of the issue in Article 9. Three of Article 9's sections provide information relevant to a priority contest between the security party and a buyer of motor vehicle covered by a certificate of title which is not delivered to it: (1) In 9–320(a), that a buyer in ordinary course of business takes free of a security interest created by the buyer's seller even if the security interest is perfected and the buyer knows of its existence. (2) In 9–311(a)(2), that, except as provided in 9–311(d), the exclusive method of perfecting a security interest in certain kinds of goods, which include motor vehicles, is by indicating the secured party's lien on the certificate of title. However, (d) excepts goods held in a dealer's inventory from certificate of title perfection. In such cases, the secured party can perfect by filing. (3) In 1–201(b)(9), the definition of "buyer in ordinary course of business" requires that such a buyer buys in good faith, without knowledge that the sale violates the rights of another person in the goods, and in ordinary course from a person in the business of selling goods of that kind. How do these provisions deal with the following cases involving desperate dealers?

Case #1. Buyer purchased a new car from Dealer who was in financial trouble. Buyer paid cash. Among the numerous papers Buyer was required to sign at the time of sale was an application for issuance of title by the state department of motor vehicles (DMV). Dealer assured Buyer that the application and fee would be forwarded to DMV and Buyer would receive the certificate of title within a few weeks. Financer, who had perfected a security interest in Dealer's inventory of new cars by filing a financing statement under 9–311(d), had retained possession of the manufacturer's certificate of origin for all new vehicles. Financer obtained these certificates of origin by advancing to Manufacturer the price of each car sold to Dealer. By retaining possession of the certificates of origin, Financer expected to safeguard itself against Dealer's fraud because no one could obtain issuance of a certificate of title for a new car from DMV without presenting Manufacturer's certificate of origin. Financer's agreement with Dealer was that Financer would not surrender a certificate of origin to Dealer without receipt of the proceeds of Dealer's sale to a buyer. When Buyer did not receive the certificate of title within a reasonable time, inquiry disclosed that Dealer had not sent the proceeds of the sale to Financer, the application had not been sent to DMV, the certificate of origin was still in the possession of Financer, and Dealer had absconded with the proceeds of the sale. Who is entitled to the car, Financer or Buyer? Is Buyer a buyer in the ordinary course of business when he bought a car without receiving the certificate of title? Some states amended their motor vehicle acts at the time of enactment of the UCC to provide that Article 9 governs the priority of security interests.

Case #2. Buyer purchased for cash a used car from Dealer who was in financial trouble. When Dealer took the car as a trade-in, the previous owner delivered the certificate of title to Dealer with the owner's name signed as transferor. The space for designating the name of the transferee was left blank. The practice was for a dealer to fill in as transferee the name of the buyer of the used car when sale occurred and to send the old title along with the buyer's application to DMV for issuance of a new title in the buyer's name. Dealer appeared to be following this practice when it asked Buyer to sign an application for a new title and assured Buyer that the new title would arrive in a few weeks. But Dealer had no intention of obtaining a new title for Buyer. Bank had an arrangement with Dealer that it would lend money on Dealer's used car inventory and would take from Dealer as security the certificate of title of each vehicle in the inventory when dealer obtained the car. When the used car was sold, Dealer could obtain the certificate of title only by paying Bank the proceeds of the sale. Bank had also filed a financing statement covering Dealer's used car inventory. Dealer absconded with the proceeds of the sale to Buyer who, consequently, never received a title. Who is entitled to the car, Bank or Buyer? Everyone knows that ownership of a used car is represented by an existing certificate of title. Can a buyer of a used car who doesn't receive a certificate of title qualify as a buyer in ordinary course of business within 1–201(b)(9)? See First National Bank v. Buss, 143 S.W.3d 915 (Tex. App.2004), which collects the authorities. What if the buyer is another dealer?

c. WAIVER

Section 9–315(a)(1)'s continuation rule provides in relevant part: "[A] security interest. . . continues in collateral notwithstanding sale, lease, license, exchange, or other disposition thereof unless the secured party authorized the disposition free of the security interest. . . ." Since the purpose of inventory is to be sold, the inventory financer may expressly authorize the dealer to sell the inventory free of its security interest while safeguarding its interest by imposing controls over the proceeds received by the dealer for the goods sold, such as requiring the dealer to deposit the proceeds in a lockbox account under the control of the secured party. In such cases, buyers take free of the financer's security interest without having to rely on 9–320.

A large body of conflicting case law concerned the question of when courts would find the existence of a secured party's authorization to sell free of a security agreement, particularly in farm products financing in which there is no buyer-in-ordinary-course-of-business exception. See 9–320(a). For instance, the security agreement might give the debtor the right to sell without prior consent but only conditional on the proceeds of the sale being deposited in a designated account. Is this an authorization to sell even if the debtor violated the agreement and did not deposit the proceeds in that account? Section 9–315(a) requires that a secured party's waiver authorize disposition free of its security interest. Authorization to sell without more is insufficient. Other cases with additional facts will be more difficult. Comment 2 to 9–315 reports that Article 9 "leaves the determination of authorization to the courts, as under former Article 9."

3. BUYERS OF CONSUMER GOODS

As noted in Chapter 2, 9–309(1) provides for automatic perfection of purchase-money security interests in consumer goods, defined as meaning goods that are used or bought for use primarily for "personal, family, or household purposes." Thus, a retailer who reserves security interests in the consumer goods it sells but does not file in such transactions has a perfected security interest in those goods and, therefore, is prior to the rights of the buyer's trustee in bankruptcy. But problems for a nonfiling retailer arise under 9–320(b) if its buyer sells the goods to other buyers. The following Problem examines Article 9's treatment of this issue.

PROBLEM

Wholesaler sells household appliances to Retailer who markets these goods to buyers who buy for their personal, family, or household purposes. Wholesaler reserves a security interest in the goods sold to Retailer and perfects its security interest by filing. Retailer reserves a security interest in the goods it sells to buyers but does not perfect by filing.

(a) If Retailer defaults on its secured obligation to Wholesaler, what rights does Wholesaler have against goods in the possession of consumer buyers who bought from Retailer? Since consumer goods are involved, which provision governs, 9–320(a) or (b)?

(b) If Buyer bought household goods from Retailer but sold them to Neighbor at a garage sale, what rights does Retailer have in the goods in Neighbor's possession if Buyer moved away and defaulted on its obligation to Retailer? See 9–320(b).

(c) How would your answer to question (b) change if Retailer had perfected by filing? Do you know any garage sale buyers who search the UCC records before buying?

4. WHEN DOES A BUYER BUY?

Determining when someone becomes a buyer can be important for purposes of 9–320(a) and (b). It can make the difference between taking subject to and taking free of a security interest in goods purchased. Assume that Bank lends to Manufacturer on a secured basis, taking a security interest in all of Manufacturer's existing and after-acquired inventory, and files an effective financing statement. The security agreement defines a violation of the agreement to include default. Manufacturer both makes and sells custom desks, and Buyer orders a custom desk to be produced, paying the purchase price in advance. The sales contract calls for Buyer to take delivery of the desk at Manufacturer's place of business. Six months later, after the desk has been completed but before delivery, Manufacturer defaults on its payments to Bank and Bank seizes all of Manufacturer's inventory, including its desks. At the same time it informs Buyer of Manufacturer's violation of the security agreement. Is Buyer entitled to take delivery of the desk or must it satisfy Manufacturer's debt to Bank as a condition of doing so? The answer depends on whether Buyer became a buyer in the ordinary course. This in turn depends on when Buyer became a buyer.

Section 1–201(b)(9) defines a "buyer in ordinary course of business" to require that he buy "without knowledge that the sale violates the rights of another person in the goods." It does not specify the point in time at which someone buys and therefore the point at which the buyer's knowledge is relevant. Possible dates include (1) the execution of the sales contract (2–103(1)(a), 2–106); (2) identification of the goods under it (2–501); (3) passage of title in the goods (2–401(2)–(3)); (4) delivery of the goods, and (5) acceptance of them (2–606). The issue has arisen in contexts pitting consumer buyers against inventory financers of defaulting debtors. Most courts have sided with the consumer buyer, accelerating the date of purchase to the point at which the goods are identified to the contract. See, e.g., Daniel v. Bank of Hayward, 425

N.W.2d 416 (Wis.1988); In re Darling's Homes, Inc., 46 B.R. 370 (Bankr. D.Del.1985).

UCC provisions outside Article 9 make dating the purchase more definite by requiring that a "buyer in ordinary course" take possession or have a possessory remedy available to it. Section 1–201(a)(9) provides that "[o]nly a buyer that takes possession of the goods or has a right to recover the goods from the seller under Article 2 may be a buyer in ordinary course." Section 2–716(3) in turn gives a consumer buyer a right of replevin when it acquires a special property in the goods, which occurs upon their identification to the contract: "In the case of goods bought for personal, family or household purposes, the buyer's right of replevin vests upon acquisition of a special property. . . ." Thus, a consumer buys when it has a right of replevin.

5. DOUBLE DEBTORS

Consider the following facts: Debtor 1 granted SP-1 a security interest in business equipment and SP-1 filed a financing statement covering the equipment in 2020. Debtor 1 sold the equipment to Debtor 2, which is not a buyer in ordinary course of business, and Debtor 2 took the equipment subject to SP-1's security interest. Previously, in 2019, Debtor 2 had granted a security interest in all its equipment, now owned or thereafter acquired, to SP-2 who promptly filed a financing statement. Who is prior with respect to the equipment that Debtor 1 sold to Debtor 2? SP-1 and SP-2 have conflicting security interests in the same collateral created by different debtors. SP-2 claims priority in the equipment as after-acquired property under the first-to-file rule of 9–322(a)(1). SP-1 contends that SP-2 took a security interest only to the extent that Debtor 2 had rights in the collateral, and the rights acquired from Debtor 1 were merely the equity that Debtor 1 may have had in the equipment over and above the amount of SP-1's security interest.

This conundrum has fascinated scholars. For years litigants were quite uncooperative and failed to bring the problem before the appellate courts for resolution. *Bank of the West* finally resolved what is called the "double debtor" or "dual debtor" problem. Section 9–325, which is a priority rule applicable to security interests created by different debtors, adopts the view of *Bank of the West*. The case explains the rationale behind 9–325's resolution of the "double debtor" problem.

Bank of the West v. Commercial Credit
Financial Services, Inc.

United States Court of Appeals, Ninth Circuit, 1988
852 F.2d 1162

■ THOMPSON, CIRCUIT JUDGE.

[Ed.—In 1982, Bank of the West made a loan to Allied and was granted a security interest in all of Allied's existing and after-acquired inventory and accounts as well as proceeds of that collateral. The bank promptly filed a financing statement that perfected that security interest. In 1984 CCFS entered into a factoring agreement with BCI, which owned a beverage business. Under the agreement CCFS made loans to BCI. To secure the loans, BCI granted to CCFS a security interest in all of its existing and after-acquired inventory and accounts as well as proceeds of that collateral. CCFS promptly filed a financing statement that perfected that security interest. Later in 1984, BCI sold its beverage business to Allied. As part of the sale, BCI transferred assets to Allied. Among the assets were inventory and accounts in which CCFS had a perfected security interest. Both Bank of the West and CCFS claim priority with respect to the inventory and accounts transferred by BCI to Allied and to proceeds of that collateral, including accounts that arose as the result of sales of inventory by Allied after its purchase of the beverage business from BCI.] * * *

B.   The Post-Transfer Security Interests

1.   The Bank's Security Interest

Bank of the West's security agreement with Allied granted the Bank a security interest in Allied's future-acquired inventory, accounts, and proceeds. . . . Bank of the West's security interest became perfected at the moment of attachment as a result of the Bank's financing statement naming Allied as its debtor, which was filed with the California Secretary of State on April 7, 1982. . . . In addition to its perfected security interest in assets actually transferred from BCI to Allied, because of the after-acquired property clause in its security agreement, Bank of the West had a perfected security interest in all inventory, accounts, and proceeds thereafter acquired by Allied.

2.   CCFS'S Security Interest

In its opinion, the district court concluded that it was unnecessary for it to determine whether CCFS's security interest remained perfected after the transfer. *Bank of the West,* 655 F.Supp. at 814. In light of our resolution of the priority dispute, we must address this question.

Two provisions of the commercial code are relevant to deciding whether CCFS's security interest continued after the transfer of the beverage business to Allied. We begin with section 9–306(2), which provides in pertinent part:

> Except where this division . . . otherwise provides, a security interest continues in collateral notwithstanding sale, exchange or other disposition thereof unless the disposition was authorized by the secured party in the security agreement or otherwise, and also continues in any identifiable proceeds including collections received by the debtor.

Neither the factoring agreement nor the related security agreement expressly authorized BCI to transfer its assets to another corporation. There is no evidence to show that CCFS otherwise authorized this disposition of its collateral. California courts have made clear that implied authorizations of sales of the debtor's collateral will not be found absent clear evidence based on the prior conduct of the parties. . . . Because there is no evidence that CCFS authorized BCI's disposition of the collateral, CCFS's security interest in the collateral actually transferred (inventory and accounts) and its proceeds continued after the transfer.

C. Resolving the Priority Dispute

Having concluded that both Bank of the West and CCFS had perfected security interests in the inventory and accounts actually transferred from BCI to Allied/BIBCO, as well as the inventory and accounts acquired by Allied/BIBCO after the July 1, 1984 transfer, we must decide which of these security interests is entitled to priority. The district court resolved this question by looking to section 9–312(5). . . .

By applying section 9–312(5)(a) [9–322(a)(1)] according to its literal language, the district court concluded that Bank of the West's security interest prevailed over that of CCFS. When BCI transferred the beverage business to Allied/BIBCO, Bank of the West's security interest attached under the after-acquired property clause in its security agreement. See § 9–203(1) and § 9–204(1). When Bank of the West's security interest attached, it automatically became perfected pursuant to the earlier filed financing statement naming Allied as its debtor. See § 9–303(1) [9–308(a)]. Bank of the West's financing statement was filed on April 7, 1982. CCFS's financing statement was filed January 5, 1984, and its security interest became perfected on January 10, 1984 when BCI executed the factoring and related security agreements. Section 9–312(5) [9–322(a)(1)] sets forth a "first to file or first to perfect" rule of priority. Because Bank of the West's financing statement was filed first, the district court concluded that the Bank's security interest prevailed over that of CCFS. *Bank of the West*, 655 F.Supp. at 817.

The situation we have described above has until this case been regarded by the commentators as only a hypothetical scenario. It is a scenario offered by the commentators, however, to illustrate a failure of the commercial code to resolve a priority dispute properly. See, e.g., B. Clark, The Law of Secured Transactions Under the Uniform Commercial Code ¶ 3.8[4] (1980); Harris, The Interaction of Articles 6 and 9 of the Uniform Commercial Code: A Study in Conveyancing, Priorities, and Code Interpretation, 39 Vand. L. Rev. 179, 222–25, 225 n. 182 (1986). The difficulty noted by these commentators is this: Before the transfer from BCI to Allied, CCFS (the transferor's creditor) had a perfected security interest in the collateral. After the transfer, CCFS's perfected security interest suddenly is subordinated to the perfected security interest of Bank of the West (the transferee's creditor). CCFS, which had taken all steps required of it by the commercial code to announce its interest in the collateral *to potential creditors of the transferor* (BCI), now finds its security interest subordinated to that of the *transferee's* (Allied's) *creditor,* (Bank of the West), whose security interest came into play only because BCI made an unauthorized disposition of the collateral to which the Bank's security interest attached solely by operation of an after-acquired collateral clause. * * *

We agree with the commentators that applying section 9–312(5) to resolve this priority dispute produces an unsatisfactory result. The principal reason that section 9–312(5) [9–322(a)(1)] fails to produce a proper result is that it does not appear the drafters contemplated what Professor Clark calls the "dual debtor dilemma." See B. Clark, supra, ¶ 3.8[4]. Certainly the official comments to the Uniform Commercial Code, which offer several illustrations of the operation of section 9–312(5) [9–322(a)(1)], do not address the situation in which the competing security interests are between creditors of *different* debtors. See § 9–312(5) [9–322(a)(1)] Uniform Commercial Code Comments 4–8. In Mr. Coogan's seminal article, *The New UCC Article 9,* 86 Harv. L. Rev. 477 (1973), no mention of the dual debtor scenario is made in the thoughtful portion of the article addressing the drafters' reasons for adopting section 9–312(5) [9–322(a)(1)]. See id. at 507–11. Because section 9–312(5) [9–322(a)(1)] does not contemplate the dual debtor scenario, we must resolve this priority dispute by returning to first principles.

As a general rule of construction, the commercial code "shall be liberally construed and applied to promote its underlying purposes and policies." § 1–102(1) [1–103(a)(1)]. The commercial code is intended to be flexible. "It is intended to make it possible for the law embodied in this Act to be developed by the courts in the light of unforeseen and new circumstances and practices. However, the proper construction of the Act requires that its interpretation and application be limited to its reason." Id. Uniform Commercial Code Comment 1. There are two reasons behind the rule of section 9–312(5)(a) [9–322(a)(1)]. First, the "first to file or first to perfect" rule serves to modify the common law notion of "first in time, first in right." Harris, supra, 39 Vand. L. Rev. at 222. Section 9–312(5) [9–322(a)] places a premium on prompt filing of financing statements as a means of protecting *future* creditors of the debtor. The financing statement alerts potential creditors that collateral against which they are contemplating making a loan already is encumbered. Thus, section 9–312(5)(a) [9-322(a)(1)] penalizes a creditor who has a security interest but who does not promptly file a financing statement by awarding priority to a later creditor who acquires a security interest in the same collateral and who more promptly files a financing statement. The "first to file or first to perfect" rule of § 9–312(5)(a) [9–322(a)(1)] thus addresses the problem of secret security interests that so concerned pre-Code courts. See id. But in the present case, the notice giving function of § 9–312(5)(a) [9–322(a)(1)] does not apply. Bank of the West is a creditor of another debtor entity, and the Bank's interest in the collateral arises solely out of an after-acquired property clause. Bank of the West cannot claim that it has relied to its detriment on the absence of a filed financing statement by CCFS.

A second purpose behind section 9–312(5)(a) [9–322(a)(1)] is an implied commitment to a secured creditor who has filed a financing statement that, absent special considerations such as a purchase money security interest. . . no subsequent creditor will be able to defeat the complying creditor's security interest. This notion finds support in comment 5 to section 9–402(7), which reads in pertinent part: "The justification for this rule lies in the necessity of protecting the filing system—that is, of allowing the secured party who has first filed to make subsequent advances without each time having, as a precondition of protection, to check for filings later than his.". . . This has been described as the "claim staking" function of the financing statement. See F. Stephen Knippenberg, Debtor Name Changes and Collateral Transfers Under 9–402(7): Drafting From the Outside-In, 52, 52 Mo. L. Rev. 57, 61 &n. 22 (1987). What this means is that by filing a proper financing statement in the proper place, a secured creditor has staked a claim to its collateral and knows that, absent special considerations, its claim will prevail against *subsequently arising* interests in the same property. By complying with the Code, the creditor is relieved of much of the responsibility of monitoring its debtor's collateral—the Code has allocated the burden of discovering prior filed financing statements to later lenders. Cf. § 9–402 [9–507] Uniform Commercial Code Comment 8 [3] ("[A]ny person searching the condition of ownership of a debtor must make inquiry as to the debtor's source of title, and must search in the name of a former owner if the circumstances seem to require it.").

Applying section 9–312(5)(a) [9–322(a)(1)] to the present case serves neither of the rationales behind the "first to file or first to perfect" rule. The notice giving function is irrelevant because the creditor of a different debtor whose sole interest in disputed collateral arises from an after-acquired property clause has no incentive to check for financing statements against the property of another debtor. Certainly the burden is on a transferee's creditor to search the title to property, but this duty arises only when the transferee's creditor first appears on the scene after the transfer. Likewise, it makes no sense to use section 9–312(5)(a) [9–322(a)(1)] to defeat CCFS's perfected security interest when CCFS has taken all steps required of it by the Code to proclaim its interest in the collateral. CCFS is entitled to rely on the Code's promise that a creditor who fully complies usually may expect its security interest to be given priority in a dispute with another secured creditor. To apply section 9–312(5)(a) [9–322(a)(1)] to this case would produce an undesirable result that does not follow from the principles that the section is meant to promote.[8]

---

[8]   It is possible to argue, of course, that our analysis does violence to the interest of the transferee's creditor, whose security interest has been perfected by filing just the same as the transferor's creditor. But it is important to remember that the situation we consider is one in

We think the correct result is reached in this case by applying the common sense notion that a creditor cannot convey to another more than it owns. Put another way, the transferee, Allied, cannot acquire any greater rights in the beverage business's assets than its transferor, BCI, had in them. Cf. § 2–403(1) ("A purchaser of goods acquires all title which his transferor had or had power to transfer except that a purchaser of a limited interest acquires rights only to the extent of the interest purchased."). Our analysis also finds direct support in the California Commercial Code. Section 9–312(1) [cf. 9–322(f)(1)] provides, "The rules of priority stated in other sections of this chapter. . . shall govern where applicable." And section 9–306(2) [9–315(a)(1)] provides that a security interest follows collateral into the hands of a transferee when there is an unauthorized disposition by the transferor. . . . The drafters tell us that "[i]n most cases when a debtor makes an unauthorized disposition of the collateral, the security interest, under. . . this Article, continues in the original collateral in the hands of the purchaser or other transferee. That is to say, . . .the transferee *takes subject to the security interest.* . . . Subsection 9–306(2) [9–315(a)(1)] codifies this rule." § 9–306 Uniform Commercial Code Comment 3. If the transferee (Allied) takes the transferred collateral subject to the transferor's creditor's (CCFS's) security interest, certainly the transferee's creditor (Bank of the West) can have no greater rights in the collateral than does its debtor (Allied). Because section 9–402(7) preserves CCFS's perfected security interest in the collateral actually transferred as well as in the property acquired in the four months after the transfer, CCFS's security interest continues to be superior to Bank of the West's interest during this period, even though Bank of the West's interest also is perfected. This result is consistent with the principles of the filing system that we have previously discussed. If the notice giving function does not apply because Bank of the West has no reason to check for filings against BCI, the claim-staking function that protects CCFS should be enforced. CCFS has done all that the Code asks

---

which the transferee's creditor's security interest attaches to the transferred collateral solely by operation of an after-acquired property clause. Although the Uniform Commercial Code expressly validates after-acquired property clauses, § 9–204(1) [9–204(a)], these "floating liens" still have not been whole-heartedly accepted by the drafters.

Subsection 1 makes clear that a security interest arising by virtue of an after-acquired property clause has equal status with a security interest in collateral in which the debtor has rights at the time value is given under the security agreement. That is to say: security interest in after-acquired property is not merely an "equitable" interest; no further action by the secured party * * * is required. This does *not* mean however *that the interest is proof against subordination or defeat* * * *.

§ 9–204 Uniform Commercial Code Comment 1 (emphasis added). To the extent our opinion results in holders of after-acquired property clauses not being able to prevail against the perfected security interest of a transferor's secured creditor, this is consistent with the drafters intention in validating after-acquired property clauses but not granting them an assurance of absolute priority in all cases.

For an excellent analysis of the monitoring burdens placed on creditors as they relate to the second sentence of section 9–402(7) [9–507(c)] and after-acquired property clauses, see Knippenberg, supra, 52 Mo. L. Rev. at 92–97.

of it to protect its interest. Absent some countervailing consideration, CCFS should be entitled to rely on its perfected security interest. * * *

NOTE

Comment 6 to 9–325 suggests that 9–325's resolution of the "double debtor" problem can be extended in appropriate circumstances, even if the section's conditions aren't satisfied. The following might be one such circumstance. Assume that Creditor 1 has a purchase-money security interest in a piece of inventory acquired by Debtor on day 1. Creditor 1 files a financing statement covering the inventory on day 15. On day 10 Debtor sells the piece of inventory to Buyer out of the ordinary course. Buyer had previously granted Creditor 2 a security interest in all its existing and after-acquired inventory, and Creditor 2 had filed a proper financing statement a year before. Section 9–325(a) does not subordinate Creditor 2's security interest in the piece of inventory to Creditor 1's interest because (a)(2) isn't satisfied: Creditor 1's purchase-money security interest was unperfected when Buyer acquired the inventory. Perfection occurred five days later when it filed. Still, the rationale underlying 9–325 (and *Bank of the West*) continues to apply. Creditor 2 has a comparative advantage at determining the value of the security interest it is obtaining in the piece of inventory. At the time Creditor 1 obtains its purchase-money security interest, it has no reason to expect that Debtor will sell the purchase-money collateral out of the ordinary course. Nor does it know to whom the sale will be made. Creditor 2, however, could adjust the terms of its loan ex ante to reflect the probability that its debtor, Buyer, will purchase collateral out of the ordinary course. Although Creditor 1 also could adjust its loan terms to reflect the corresponding risk of Debtor's behavior, 9–325 is premised on Creditor 2 being in a better position to do so in dealing with Buyer, its debtor.

F. RIGHTS TO PAYMENT

In the past century, the dollar volume in asset-based personal property financing has shifted from tangible to intangible collateral. Among the most important kinds of intangible collateral are rights to payment, such as accounts, payment intangibles, chattel paper and instruments. These are often referred to as "receivables." What began humbly as lending to distressed sellers on the security of their accounts has burgeoned into a trillion dollar industry in which receivables of every conceivable kind are pooled and securitized, making up the collateral for the issuance of bonds and other investment securities. By financial alchemy, the obligation of a consumer to pay her credit card debt to a retailer is transformed into security for highly rated bonds. One of the challenges facing Article 9's drafter was to come to grips with the kinds of intangibles financing that were unimaginable when the 1962 UCC was promulgated.

Before dealing with priority rules for rights to payment, sections 1 and 2 below discuss Article 9's coverage, categorization and reordering of payment rights. Section 3 describes the priority rules for payment rights.

1.   SCOPE OF ARTICLE 9

With respect to rights to payment, the basic scope provision, 9–109(a), provides that Article 9 applies to:

(1)   a transaction, regardless of its form, that creates a security interest in personal property or fixtures by contract; [and]

. . . .

(3)   a sale of accounts, chattel paper, payment intangibles, or promissory notes;

It is a baseline principle that Article 9 applies to security interests in personal property and not to outright transfers. For instance, sales and leases of goods are treated in Articles 2 and 2A of the UCC, not in Article 9. Why did the drafters deviate from this rule with respect to sales of the rights to payment enumerated in 9–109(a)(3)? Among the reasons is the difficulty in distinguishing between transactions creating security interests in rights to payment and those making outright transfers, often referred to as assignments. See Major's Furniture Mart, Inc. v. Castle Credit Corp., 602 F.2d 538, 542–43 (3d Cir.1979). Moreover, the Article 9 provisions for perfection by filing and priority under the first-to-file-or-perfect rule for security interests in rights to payment are equally appropriate for sales of these rights. In sum, with respect to rights to payment, it is convenient to cover two conceptually different transactions—secured loans and sales—in one statute: problems of distinguishing between the two transactions are lessened and the provisions for perfection and priority are appropriate for both.

Article 9 implements its extension to sales of payment rights by what might be called terminological assimilation: it applies to these sales for purposes of perfection and priority the nomenclature of secured transactions. Thus, the interest acquired by the buyer of a payment right is a "security interest" (1–201(b)(35)), the buyer is the "secured party," the seller the "debtor" (9–102(a)(28)(B), (73)(D)), and the payment right sold is "collateral" (9–102(a)(12)(B)). As the holder of a security interest, the buyer of a payment right "perfects" its ownership interest either automatically in the case of a sale of payment intangibles and promissory notes, and by filing or by possession in the case of sales of other payment rights, depending on their type. 9–310(a), 9–309(3).

2.   RIGHTS TO PAYMENT UNDER ARTICLE 9

a.   TYPES OF PAYMENT RIGHTS: DEFINITIONS

Rights to payment consist of accounts, chattel paper, payment intangibles, and promissory notes. The extent to which Article 9 covers security interests in and outright transfers of rights to payment is determined by the definitions of the different kinds of rights to payment.

Former Article 9 restricted its definition of accounts to rights to payment arising out of the sale or lease of goods or for services rendered. The definition of "account" in 9–102(a)(2) greatly expands the definition to include rights to payment arising from the disposition of any kind of property, including real property and intellectual property, as well as the rendering of services. The term includes healthcare receivables, lottery winnings, and credit and charge card obligations. However, it does not include rights to payment evidenced by chattel paper or instruments or those for loan advances (the lender's right to repayment for money or funds advanced or sold) or commercial tort claims. In short, "account" includes most *unsecured* obligations arising from the disposition of property or the rendering of services that are not evidenced by negotiable instruments.

"Chattel paper," defined in 9–102(a)(11), is a right to payment of a monetary obligation secured by specific goods if the right to payment and security agreement are evidenced by a record. The term also includes a right to payment of a monetary obligation owed under a lease agreement if the right to payment and the lease agreement are evidenced by a record, as long as the predominant purpose of the lease transaction was to give the lessee possession and use of the goods. Chattel paper may be either tangible) or in an electronic form. Installment sale contracts and leases of goods are common examples of chattel paper. A promissory note along with a security agreement can be chattel paper. In this case the promissory note does not count as an instrument for purposes of Article 9; see 9–102(a)(47).

"General intangible," defined in 9–102(a)(42), is a residual category, meaning any personal property other than "accounts, chattel paper, commercial tort claims, deposit accounts, documents, goods, instruments, investment property, letter-of-credit rights, letters of credit, money and oil, gas, or other minerals before extraction. The term includes controllable electronic records, payment intangibles and software." The definition of general intangible covers important kinds of intangible property that are not rights to payment, such as rights in software, copyrights, trademarks, patents and characterization rights, but it also covers rights to payment that arise in transactions other than those expressly excluded from the definition of general intangibles. These rights to payment are described as "payment intangibles."

"Payment intangible," defined in 9–102(a)(61), is a subset of a general intangible under which the account debtor's principal obligation is a monetary obligation. Since the expanded definition of "account" broadly includes rights to payment arising from the disposition of almost any kind of property, what is left to fall within the payment intangibles category? An important example of a payment intangible is a bank loan. When the repayment obligation isn't evidenced by an instrument, it is a payment intangible. As we see below, obligations to repay bank loans form the basis for the loan participation industry and are important elements in asset securitization.

The adjective "principal" in the definition should be noticed. There are some circumstances in almost any transaction under which the account debtor would owe a monetary obligation. For instance, a breach of contract giving rise to damages or a tort both would create an obligation to pay money. Cf. Comment 5d. to 9–102. This doesn't create a payment intangible. A payment intangible requires that the obligation to pay money be the main or primary obligation. Article 9 does not define when an obligation is "principal" and when ancillary, and the determination can turn on how the obligation arose. If the right to receive payment from the account debtor alone is assigned, the obligation to pay money is the main part of the transaction. If an entire contract is assigned, where the contract contains covenants and imposes duties of performance on the account debtor, the nature of the obligation to pay is less clear. A wrong guess can leave the creditor's security interest unperfected.

"Promissory note," as defined in 9–102(a)(65), is an instrument that evidences a promise to pay money. The definition excludes checks and certificates of deposit. Section 9–102(a)(47)'s definition of "instrument" excludes writings that evidences chattel paper. The latter exclusion means that a promissory note, when part of chattel paper, is not an instrument. "Chattel paper" and "instrument" therefore are mutually exclusive categories of payment rights.

b. SALE OF RIGHTS TO PAYMENT

Although former Article 9 applied to both security interests in and sales of accounts and chattel paper, it applied only to security interests in general intangibles. Thus, sales of general intangibles fell outside the UCC, and were subject to the vagaries of the statutes and common law of each enacting state. Lending on the security of general intangibles has remained significant, but in the past half-century its importance has been dwarfed by the vast financial industries involving the outright sales of intangibles. These are the loan participation and asset securitization markets. Thus, the careful distinctions in Article 9 between accounts, general intangibles and payment intangibles are drawn for a very practical reason having to do with important patterns of financing and the preferences of financers. In fact, the desire on the part of the financial community to redraw these boundaries was a major impetus for enactment of revised Article 9.

Asset securitization involves the sale of assets to an entity usually created for that purpose and called a "special purpose vehicle" or "special purpose entity." The assets sold can be any money-generating item, from royalty rights from intellectual property to franchise fees to accounts, chattel paper and payment intangibles. To fund the purchase, the special purpose vehicle issues securities that are payable from the stream of revenues produced by the assets transferred to it, such as collections on the accounts or other money-generating item. The transferor of the assets is paid in cash raised from the sale of securities. Securitization offers the transferor access to financial markets that allows raising capital at a lower cost than that offered by bank loans or from alternative sources. See Steven L. Schwarcz, Structured Finance: A Guide to the Principles of Asset Securitization (3d ed. 2002). The lower cost of capital is due primarily to the elimination of financial intermediaries between investors and borrowers and the reduced business risk presented by the special purpose vehicle.

Under former Article 9, some rights to payment acquired for securitization purposes were covered by the UCC and some were not. A case in which a retail chain sells its accounts to a securitization entity would be covered as sales of accounts but if the receivables sold were obligations on loans, former Article 9 did not apply because this was a sale of general intangibles. The rapidly growing asset securitization industry wanted the certainty of knowing that all the receivables it dealt with were covered by the UCC. Article 9 gave the industry what it wanted by broadening the definition of accounts and adding the new category of payment intangibles. Section 9–109(a)(3) includes virtually all the rights to payment, including promissory notes, that this industry deals with. But sales of other kinds of personal property falling within the definition of general intangibles that are not rights to payment, such as copyrights, trademarks and software are not covered by Article 9. See Paul M. Shupack, Preferred Capital Structures and the Question of Filing, 79 Minn. L. Rev. 787, 800–01 (1995).

The interest of parties in the loan participation market sharply diverged from those in the asset securitization business with respect to UCC coverage. The loan participation business, in which a bank sells participations in a debtor's obligation to repay a loan, had grown up outside former Article 9 because the transaction involved was the sale of general intangibles. Hence, parties were unaccustomed to filing financing statements and dealing with the complexities of the UCC filing system. As a flourishing mature industry, they could see no reason why they should have to incur the new transaction costs that the filing requirement would entail when the old system provided enough certainty at less cost.

Current Article 9 settles on a compromise between the preferences of the two industries. Section 9–109(a)(3) extends Article 9 to cover the sale of payment intangibles. By implication, sales of other sorts of general intangibles are excluded. This satisfies the demand of parties operating in the market for asset securitization for legal certainty. (Neither industry thought that bringing all sales of general intangibles within Article 9 was desirable.) Section 9–309(3) provides that the sale of a payment intangible is perfected without filing. By eliminating the need to file and the attendant transaction costs, the provision satisfies the concerns of parties in the loan participation market. This sophisticated industry had operated without the requirement of public notice, and the Drafting Committee saw nothing to be gained by requiring filing. The statutory term "perfection" in 9–309(3) with respect to sales of loan participation shares is somewhat inartful. A creditor "perfects" a security interest; strictly, a buyer does not "perfect" the ownership interest it purchased. Still, the effect of automatically perfecting the buyer's interest in a payment intangible is clear: the buyer gets the benefit of Article 9's perfection and priority rules and is protected in its seller's bankruptcy proceeding. Section 9–309(4) provides that sales of promissory notes are also automatically perfected.

Thus, the controversy over whether sales of general intangibles should be covered by Article 9 has been resolved by the Solomonic decision to break the former Article 9 category of general intangibles into three parts. One part, the large volume of rights to payment arising from the disposition of real property and intellectual property, are brought within the definition of "account" and the sale of these rights is treated accordingly. A second part, rights to payment that fall within the attenuated definition of general intangibles but are principally monetary obligations, are treated differently as payment intangibles, the sale of which is covered by Article 9. The third part, other intangible property that is not rights to payment such as software, other intellectual property, and other personal property that is not goods, is retained in the definition of general intangibles, and its sale is not covered by 9–109(a)(3), which provides that Article 9 applies to "a sale of accounts, chattel paper, payment intangibles, or promissory notes."

Article 9's handling of the sale of payment intangibles does not solve all problems. Two problems remain. One is whether a right to payment, once separated from the chattel paper of which it is a part, remains chattel paper. Assume that a payment right is secured by specific goods and that both the payment right and security interest are evidenced by a record. This record constitutes chattel paper; 9–102(a)(11). Later, the payment right is separated from the security interest and sold, the secured party retaining the security interest. Once the payment right has been separated from the security interest, does it become a payment intangible or does the payment right retain its character as chattel paper? This question matters in asset securitizations in which payments are stripped and sold while the chattel paper of which it was a part is retained. As noted, in a sale of a payment intangible, the buyer's interest is automatically perfected under 9–309(2). By contrast, there is no automatic perfection in a sale of chattel paper. Thus, the buyer must file to protect its interest if payment rights, although stripped and sold, remains tangible chattel paper. Does the classification of the payment right change when it is separated from chattel paper and sold without the chattel paper of which it is a part?

The question was raised by the facts in In re Commercial Money Center, Inc., 350 B.R. 465 (9th Cir. B.A.P. 2006), an important case for the securitization industry. There the payment rights under the lease were "stripped" from the lease and sold. The *Commercial Money Center* court ruled that the "stripped" payment rights were payment intangibles, not chattel paper. Comment 5d to 9–102 disapproves of the ruling. It states: "If. . . the lessor's rights to payment and with respect to the leased goods are evidenced by chattel paper, then, contrary to *In re Commercial Money Center, Inc.* . . . an assignment of the lessor's right to payment constitutes an assignment of the chattel paper." The Comment adds: "In classifying intangible collateral, a court should begin by identifying the particular rights that have been assigned. The account debtor (promissor) under a particular contract may owe several types of monetary obligations as well as other, nonmonetary obligations. If the promissee's right to payment of money is assigned separately, the right is an account or payment intangible, *depending on how the account debtor's obligation arose*" (emphasis added). A fair implication of the Comment is that if the lessee's payment obligations arose from a lease evidenced by a record, the payment obligation is part of chattel paper, not a payment intangible. The subsequent separate sale of the payment obligation does not affect the classification of the collateral as chattel paper.

The 2022 Amendments alter the wording in the definition of chattel paper to prevent an argument made by the *Commercial Money Center* court that stripped payment rights could not be chattel paper. Prior to the 2022 Amendments, 9–102(a)(11) defined chattel paper in relevant part as "a record or records that evidence both a monetary obligation" and a security interest or lease in specific goods." Reasoning from this definition, the court concluded that a stripped payment right is a monetary obligation, not a record that evidence a monetary obligation and therefore cannot be chattel paper. The 2022 Amendments modify 9–102(a)(11)'s definition in relevant part to provide that "chattel paper" means "a right to payment of a monetary obligation secured" if the payment right and security interest is evidenced by a record. A similar modification is made for "a right to payment of a monetary obligation owed by a lessee." 9–102(a)(11)(A), (B). This slight change in wording does not allow the *Commercial Money Center* court's argument. Because chattel paper is defined to mean "a right to payment of a monetary obligation" evidenced by the relevant record, stripped payment rights remain monetary obligations evidenced by a record. They therefore remain chattel paper.

This still leaves the second, more basic problem of how to distinguish a sale from a security interest. Because an interest in the sale of a payment intangible is automatically perfected while a security interest in a payment intangible is not, perfection of a security interest in a payment intangible may require filing. (Filing is required if the security interest is not perfected automatically under 9–309(2).) Thus, a sale must be distinguished from a security interest. Article 9 provides no help in characterizing a transaction, even on the order of a list of factors to consider. It instead leaves the matter to the courts. See Comment 4 to 9–109.

Distinguishing a sale of payment rights from a security interest in them can be difficult. A sale transfers ownership; a security interest does not. However, the notion of ownership itself can be as difficult to ascertain as the difference between a sale and a secured transaction. Ownership is easily determined in two simple cases: the case where the transferor continues to bear all upside and downside risks associated with the asset transferred and the case where it bears none of these risks. Examples of upside risk are increases in the value of the asset or beneficial changes in the suitability of the asset for particular uses. Decreases in asset value or damage or risk of loss are examples of downside risk. In the case of payment rights, the upside risk might be that the account debtor pays in full while the downside risk is that it defaults on its payment obligations. A good indication of ownership is the bearing of all upside and downside risk around the asset. Where the transferor continues to bear them, as in the first simple case, no change in ownership and therefore no sale has occurred. In the second simple case, where the transferee bears both upside and downside risks, ownership has changed and therefore a sale has occurred.

However, the hallmarks of ownership are elusive even in slightly more complex transactions. The trouble is that upside and downside risks can be split and divided even within themselves between the transferor and transferee. In these cases it can be indeterminate as to whether the transfer or transferee owns the financial asset. For instance, a right of recourse places the risk of the account debtor's default ("collectibility risk") on the assignor, not the assignee. It is the equivalent of a warranty given by the seller in the ordinary sale of goods, the warranty allocating the risk of nonconformity in the goods to the seller. See, e.g., In re De-Pen Line, Inc., 215 B.R. 947 (Bankr. E.D.Pa.1997). In both cases, the transferor bears the risk of the asset not performing according to the terms of the underlying contract. A limited right of recourse divides the collectibility risk between the assignor and assignee; it corresponds to a restricted warranty or remedy limitation in the case of the sale of goods. Thus, the allocation of downside risk through a right of recourse does not by itself identify ownership in the account assigned. This is why in *Major's Furniture Mart*, reproduced below, the court observes that "[g]uarantees of quality alone, or even guarantees of collectability alone, might be consistent with a true sale," 602 F.2d at 545, and that it is the "nature of the recourse" that distinguishes a sale from a financing transaction. Id at 544.

The allocation of upside risks also does not decisively determine ownership. A paradigmatic owner derives revenues directly from the asset it owns, while a lender's return typically is fixed and unrelated to the asset's performance. Fixed returns or returns unrelated to the account debtor's actual payment under the account or chattel paper therefore might appear to mark the transferee of the account or chattel paper as a lender. See Peter V. Pantaleo et al., Rethinking the Role of Recourse in the Sale of Financial Assets, 52 Bus. Law. 159 (1996). However, these revenue streams can be split to give the transferee a fixed or variable share. For instance, amounts collected from the account debtor above a stipulated sum can be divided between the assignor and assignee. Alternatively, the assignor and assignee can agree to readjust the "price" of an account to reflect the account debtor's performance over time. In both cases, the transaction can be characterized either as a sale of a divisible portion of an account or as a loan with a floating rate of interest. The notion of ownership probably is not up to the job of distinguishing sales from secured loans in such transactions. Rather, characterization must be based directly on efficiency gains in the form of transaction cost savings or risk reduction produced by transfers of accounts or chattel paper with recourse, holdbacks, divisible interests and the like.

The distinction between a sale and a security interest matters not just for purposes of perfection. It also is important for determining who is entitled to the proceeds from the collection of payment when the security interest is enforced. Section 9–608(a)(4) requires the secured party to remit to the debtor amounts above the amount of the secured debt ("surplus") realized on a sale of collateral. However, the debtor does not have a right to the surplus if the payment right has been sold. 9–608(b). Thus, the debtor's right to the surplus turns on whether the transfer of payments right is a sale or a security interest. In the influential case below the court relies on the transferee's right of recourse against the transferor to determine the character of the transfer of payment rights. Enforcement of a security interest against collateral consisting of payment rights is discussed in Chapter 9.

Major's Furniture Mart, Inc. v. Castle Credit Corp., Inc.

United States Court of Appeals, Third Circuit, 1979
602 F.2d 538

■ GARTH, CIRCUIT JUDGE.

This appeal requires us to answer the question: "When is a sale not a sale, but rather a secured loan?" The district court held that despite the form of their Agreement, which purported to be, and hence was characterized as, a sale of accounts receivable, the parties' transactions did not constitute sales. Major's Furniture Mart, Inc. v. Castle Credit Corp., 449 F.Supp. 538 (E.D.Pa.1978). No facts are in dispute, and the issue presented on this appeal is purely a legal issue involving the interpretation of relevant sections of the Uniform Commercial Code. . .and their proper application to the undisputed facts presented here.

The district court granted plaintiff Major's motion for summary judgment. Castle Credit Corporation appeals from that order. We affirm.

I

Major's is engaged in the retail sale of furniture. Castle is in the business of financing furniture dealers such as Major's. Count I of Major's amended complaint alleged that Major's and Castle had entered into an Agreement dated June 18, 1973 for the financing of Major's accounts receivable; that a large number of transactions pursuant to the Agreement took place between June 1973 and May 1975; that in March and October 1975 Castle declared Major's in default under the Agreement; and that from and after June 1973 Castle was in possession of monies which constituted a surplus over the accounts receivable transferred under the Agreement. Among other relief sought, Major's asked for an accounting of the surplus and all sums received by Castle since June 1, 1976 which had been collected from the Major's accounts receivable transferred under the Agreement.

The provisions of the June 18, 1973 Agreement which are relevant to our discussion provide: that Major's shall from time to time "sell" accounts receivable to Castle, and that all accounts so "sold" shall be with full recourse against Major's. Major's was required to warrant that each account receivable was based upon a written order or contract fully performed by Major's.[3] Castle in its sole discretion could refuse to "purchase" any account. The amount paid by Castle to Major's on any particular account was the unpaid face amount of the account exclusive of interest less a fifteen percent "discount"[5] and less another ten percent of the unpaid face amount as a reserve against bad debts.[6]

Under the Agreement the reserve was to be held by Castle without interest and was to indemnify Castle against a customer's failure to pay the full amount of the account (which included interest and insurance

---

[3]   The parties do not dispute that their rights are governed by the law of Pennsylvania. The Pennsylvania Uniform Commercial Code, and in particular § 9–105 [9–102(a)(11)], classifies the accounts receivable which are the subject of the agreement as "chattel paper."

[5]   The 15% "discount" was subsequently increased unilaterally by Castle to 18% and thereafter was adjusted monthly to reflect changes in the prime rate (Appellee's Supplemental Appendix 3b–4b).

[6]   It becomes apparent from a review of the record that the amount which Castle actually paid to Major's on each account transferred was the unpaid face amount exclusive of interest *and* exclusive of insurance premiums less 28% (18% "discount" and 10% reserve).

In its brief on appeal, Castle sets out the following summary of the transactions that took place over the relevant period. It appears that the face amount of the accounts which were "sold" by Major's to Castle was $439,832.08, to which finance charges totaling $116,350.46 and insurance charges totaling $42,304.03 were added, bringing the total amount "purchased" by Castle to $598,486.57. For these "purchases" Castle paid Major's $316,107. Exclusive of any surplus as determined by the district court Castle has retained $528,176.13 which it has received as a result of customer collections and repurchases by Major's. Collection costs were found by the district court to be $1,627.81.

premiums), as well as any other charges or losses sustained by Castle for any reason.

In addition, Major's was required to "repurchase" any account "sold" to Castle which was in default for more than 60 days. In such case Major's was obligated to pay to Castle

> an amount equal to the balance due by the customer on said Account plus any other expenses incurred by CASTLE as a result of such default or breach of warranty, less a rebate of interest on the account under the "Rule of the 78's". . . .[7]

Thus essentially, Major's was obligated to repurchase a defaulted account not for the discounted amount paid to it by Castle, but for a "repurchase" price based on the balance due by the customer, plus any costs incurred by Castle upon default.

As an example, applying the Agreement to a typical case, Major's in its brief on appeal summarized an account transaction of one of its customers (William Jones) as follows:

> A customer Jones of Major's (later designated Account No. 15,915) purchased furniture from Major's worth $1700.00 (or more). [H]e executed an installment payment agreement with Major's in the total face amount of $2549.88, including interest and insurance costs. . . . Using this piece of chattel paper, . . . Major's engaged in a financing transaction with Castle under the Agreement. . . . Major's delivered the Jones' chattel paper with a $2549.88 face amount to Castle together with an assignment of rights. Shortly thereafter, Castle delivered to Major's cash in the amount of $1224.00. The difference between this cash amount and the full face of the chattel paper in the amount of $2549.88, consisted of the following costs and deductions by Castle:

1. $180.00 discount credited to a "reserve" account of Major's.

2. $300.06 "discount" (actually a prepaid interest charge).

3. $30.85 for life insurance premium.

4. $77.77 for accident and health insurance premium.

5. $152.99 for property insurance premium.

6. $588.27 interest charged to Jones on the $1700 face of the note.

---

[7]   The Rule of 78 is "the predominant method used to determine refunds of unearned finance charges upon prepayment of consumer debts." Hunt, James H., "The Rule of 78: Hidden Penalty for Prepayment in Consumer Credit Transactions," 55 B.U. L. Rev. 331, 332 (1975). That article points out that the Rule of 78 allocates a disproportionately large portion of finance charges to the early months of a credit transaction which produces a hidden penalty for prepayment, although the extent of the penalty diminishes as the term of the debt nears expiration.

Apparently a rebate of insurance premiums was provided as well as a rebate of interest.

Thus, as to the Jones' account, Castle received and proceeded to collect a piece of chattel paper with a collectible face value of $2549.88. Major's received $1224.00 in cash.

As we understand the Agreement, if Jones in the above example defaulted without having made any payments on account, the very least Major's would have been obliged to pay on repurchase would be $1,700 even though Major's had received only $1,224 in cash on transfer of the account and had been credited with a reserve of $180. The repurchase price was either charged fully to reserve or, as provided in the Agreement, 50% to reserve and 50% by cash payment from Major's. In the event of bankruptcy, default under the agreement or discontinuation of business, Major's was required to repurchase all outstanding accounts immediately. . . .

Under the Agreement, over 600 accounts were transferred to Castle by Major's of which 73 became delinquent and subject to repurchase by Major's. On March 21, 1975, Castle notified Major's that Major's was in default in failing to repurchase delinquent accounts. Apparently to remedy the default, Major's deposited an additional $10,000 into the reserve. After June 30, 1975, Major's discontinued transferring accounts to Castle. On October 7, 1975 Castle again declared Major's in default.

Major's action against Castle alleged that the transaction by which Major's transferred its accounts to Castle constituted a financing of accounts receivable and that Castle had collected a surplus of monies to which Major's was entitled. We are thus faced with the question which we posed at the outset of this opinion: did the June 18, 1973 Agreement create a *secured interest* in the accounts, or did the transaction constitute a *true sale* of the accounts? The district court, contrary to Castle's contention, refused to construe the Agreement as one giving rise to the sales of accounts receivable. Rather, it interpreted the Agreement as creating a security interest in the accounts which accordingly was subject to all the provisions of Article 9 of the U.C.C. It thereupon entered its order of June 13, 1977 granting Major's' motion for summary judgment and denying Castle's motion for summary judgment. This order was ultimately incorporated into the court's final judgment entered May 5, 1978 which specified the amount of surplus owed by Castle to Major's. It was from this final judgment that Castle appealed.

Castle on appeal argues (1) that the express language of the Agreement indicates that it was an agreement for the sale of accounts and (2) that the parties' course of performance and course of dealing compel an interpretation of the Agreement as one for the sale of accounts. Castle also asserts that the district court erred in "reforming" the Agreement and in concluding that the transaction was a loan. In substance these contentions do no more than reflect Castle's overall position that the Agreement was for an absolute sale of accounts.

II

Our analysis starts with Article 9 of the Uniform Commercial Code which encompasses both *sales* of accounts and *secured interests* in accounts. Thus, the Pennsylvania counterpart of the Code "applies. . . (a) to any transaction (regardless of its form) which is intended to create a security interest in. . . accounts. . . ; and also (b) to any sale of accounts. . ." § 9–102 [9–109(a)(1)]. The official comments to that section make it evident that Article 9 is to govern *all* transactions in accounts. Comment 2 indicates that, because "[c]ommercial financing on the basis of accounts. . . is often so conducted that the distinction between a security transfer and a sale is blurred," that "sales" as well as transactions "intended to create a security interest" are subject to the provisions of Article 9. Moreover, a "security interest" is defined under the Act as "any interest of a buyer of accounts." § 1–201(37) [1–201(b)(35)]. Thus even an outright buyer of accounts, such as Castle claims to be, by definition has a "security interest" in the accounts which it purchases.

Article 9 of the Pennsylvania Code is subdivided into five parts. Our examination of Parts 1–4, §§ 9–101 to 9–410, reveals no distinction drawn between a sale and a security interest which is relevant to the issue on this appeal. However, the distinction between an outright sale and a transaction intended to create a security interest becomes highly significant with respect to certain provisions found in Part 5 of Article 9. That part pertains to default under a "security agreement." § 9–501 [9–601], et seq.

The default section relevant here, which distinguishes between the consequences that follow on default when the transaction *secures an indebtedness* rather than a *sale,* provides:

> A secured party who by agreement is entitled to charge back uncollected collateral or otherwise to full and limited recourse against the debtor and who undertakes to collect from the account debtors or obligors must proceed in a commercially reasonable manner and may deduct his reasonable expenses of realization from the collections. *If the security agreement secures an indebtedness, the secured party must account to the debtor for any surplus,* and unless otherwise agreed, the debtor is liable for any deficiency. But, *if the underlying transaction was a sale of accounts,* contract rights, or chattel paper, *the debtor is entitled to any surplus* or is liable for any deficiency *only if the security agreement so provides.*

§ 9–502(2) (emphasis added) [9–608(a)(4) and (b)].

Thus, if the accounts were transferred to Castle *to secure Major's indebtedness,* Castle was obligated to account for and pay over the surplus proceeds to Major's under § 9–502(2) [9–608(a)(4)], as a debtor's (Major's) right to surplus in such a case cannot be waived even by an express agreement. § 9–501(3)(a) [9–602(5)]. On the other hand, if a *sale of accounts* had been effected, then Castle was entitled to all proceeds received from all accounts because the June 18, 1973 Agreement does not provide otherwise.

However, while the Code instructs us as to the consequences that ensue as a result of the determination of "secured indebtedness" as contrasted with "sale," the Code does not provide assistance in distinguishing between the character of such transactions. This determination, as to whether a particular assignment constitutes a sale or a transfer for security, is left to the courts for decision. § 9–502, Comment 4 [9–109, Comment 4]. It is to that task that we now turn. . . .

IV

The comments to § 9–502(2) [9–109] (and in particular Comment 4) make clear to us that the presence of recourse in a sale agreement without more will not automatically convert a sale into a security interest.[2] Hence, one of Major's arguments which is predicated on such a *per se* principle attracts us no more than it attracted the district court. The Code comments however are consistent with and reflect the views expressed by courts and commentators that "[t]he determination of whether a particular assignment constitutes a [true] sale or a transfer for security is left to the courts." § 9–502, Comment 4 [9–109, Comment 4]. The question for the court then is whether the *nature* of the recourse, and the true nature of the transaction, are such that the legal rights and economic consequences of the agreement bear a greater similarity to a financing transaction or to a sale.

[The court's discussion of other cases is omitted.]

Hence, it appears that in each of the cases cited, despite the express language of the agreements, the respective courts examined the parties' practices, objectives, business activities and relationships and determined whether the transaction was a sale or a secured loan only after analysis of the evidence as to the true nature of the transaction. We noted earlier that here the parties, satisfied that there was nothing other than the Agreement and documents bearing on their relationship. . . . , submitted to the court's determination on an agreed record. The district court thereupon reviewed the Agreement and the documents as they reflected the conduct of the parties to determine whether Castle treated the transactions as sales or transfers of a security interest. In referring

---

[2]   [Ed.—The sentence in Comment 4 to former 9–502 to which the court is referring reads as follows: "The last sentence of [former 9–502(2)] therefore preserves freedom of contract, and the subsection recognizes that there may be true sale of accounts or chattel paper although recourse exists." This sentence does not appear in Comment 4 to 9–109 or elsewhere in revised Article 9.]

to the extremely relevant factor of "recourse"[12] and to the risks allocated, the district court found:

> In the instant case the allocation of risks heavily favors Major's claim to be considered as an assignor with an interest in the collectability of its accounts. It appears that Castle required Major's to retain all conceivable risks of uncollectibility of these accounts. It required warranties that retail account debtors—e.g., Major's customers—meet the criteria set forth by Castle, that Major's perform the credit check to verify that these criteria were satisfied, and that Major's warrant that the accounts were fully enforceable legally and were "fully and timely collectible." It also imposed an obligation to indemnify Castle out of a reserve account for losses resulting from a customer's failure to pay, or for any breach of warranty, and an obligation to repurchase any account after the customer was in default for more than 60 days. Castle only assumed the risk that the assignor itself would be unable to fulfill its obligations. Guaranties of quality alone, or even guarantees of collectability alone, might be consistent with a true sale, but Castle attempted to shift all risks to Major's, and incur none of the risks or obligations of ownership. It strains credulity to believe that this is the type of situation, referred to in Comment 4, in which "there may be a true sale of accounts... although recourse exists." When we turn to the conduct of the parties to seek support for this contention, we find instead that Castle, in fact, treated these transactions as a transfer of a security interest.

449 F.Supp. at 543.

Moreover, in looking at the conduct of the parties, the district court found one of the more significant documents to be an August 31, 1973 letter written by Irving Canter, President of Castle Credit, to Major's. As the district court characterized it, and as we agree:

> This letter, in effect, announces the imposition of a floating interest rate on loans under a line of credit of $80,000 per month, based upon the fluctuating prime interest rate. The key portion of the letter states:

---

[12] Gilmore, in commenting on the Code's decision to leave the distinction between a security transfer and a sale to the courts, would place almost controlling significance on the one factor of recourse. He states:

> If there is no right of charge-back or recourse with respect to uncollectible accounts and no right to claim for a deficiency, then the transaction should be held to be a sale, entirely outside the scope of Part 5. If there is a right to charge back uncollectible accounts (a right, as § 9–502 puts it, of "full or limited recourse") or a right to claim a deficiency, then the transaction should be held to be for security and thus subject to Part 5 as well as the other Parts of the Article.

II Gilmore, Security Interests in Personal Property, § 44.4 at 1230.

Here, of course, the Agreement provided Castle with full recourse against Major's.

Accordingly, your volume for the month of September cannot exceed $80,000. Any business above that amount will have to be paid for in October. I think you'll agree that your quota is quite liberal. The surcharge for the month of September will be 3% of the principal amount financed which is based upon a 9 1/2% prime rate. On October 1, and for each month thereafter, the surcharge will be adjusted, based upon the prime rate in effect at that time as it relates to a 6 1/2% base rate. . . .

This unilateral change in the terms of the Agreement makes it obvious that Castle treated the transaction as a line of credit to Major's—i.e., a loan situation. Were this a true sale, as Castle now argues, it would not have been able to impose these new conditions by fiat. Such changes in a sales contract would have modified the price term of the agreement, which could only be done by a writing signed by all the parties.

449 F.Supp. at 543.

It is apparent to us that on this record none of the risks present in a true sale is present here. Nor has the custom of the parties or their relationship, as found by the district court, given rise to more than a debtor/creditor relationship in which Major's debt was secured by a transfer of Major's customer accounts to Castle, thereby bringing the transaction within the ambit of § 9–502 [9–608(a)(4)]. To the extent that the district court determined that a surplus existed, Castle was obligated to account to Major's for that surplus and Major's right to the surplus could not be waived, § 9–502(2) [9–602(5)]. Accordingly, we hold that on this record the district court did not err in determining that the true nature of the transaction between Major's and Castle was a secured loan, not a sale. * * *

The judgment of the district court will be affirmed.

NOTES

1. *Major's Furniture Mart* assumes that under Article 9 the debtor can either transfer absolute ownership of, or create a security interest in, accounts and chattel paper. This commonly held (and correct) premise was challenged in Octagon Gas Systems, Inc. v. Rimmer, 995 F.2d 948 (10th Cir.1993). Relying on Article 9's designation of a buyer of accounts as a "secured party," the accounts seller as a "debtor," and the accounts sold "collateral," *Octagon* holds that an outright sale of accounts leaves a residual interest in the transferor-debtor. Section 9–318(a) rejects *Octagon* by making it clear that the debtor's sale transfers all its interests in the accounts or chattel paper sold. See Comment 2 to 9–318 and Comment 5 to 9–109. The debtor's sale of payment rights is discussed in the next part.

2. The court maintains that recourse provided in a purported sales agreement doesn't by itself create a security interest. This suggests that an assignment of accounts could be a sale under some circumstances even if it provided for recourse against the assignor if the account debtors defaulted.

How would this work? The court found the assignment in *Major's Furniture Mart* was a security interest because it gave the assignee full recourse against the assignor. But suppose the assignment had allowed only for limited recourse against the assignor. The court determined that it is the nature of the recourse, not its extent, that distinguishes a sale from a security interest. What is the nature of the recourse that could make an assignment with limited recourse a sale?

c.   PRIORITY IN SOLD PAYMENT RIGHTS

The sale of a payment right can give rise to competing claims to the payment right sold. This creates a priority conflict either between buyers of the right or between a buyer of the right and a secured creditor claiming a security interest in the payment right sold. Because Article 9 covers sales of accounts, chattel paper, payment intangibles and promissory notes, its priority rules apply to their sale. Most important among these rules is 9–322(a)(1)'s first-to-file-or-perfect rule.

Section 9–318 adds special rules that are implicated in the resolution of priority contests involving the sale of certain payment rights. Section 9–318(a) provides that, subject to 9–318(b)'s exception, the debtor (seller) of an account, chattel paper, payment intangible or promissory note retains no legal or equitable interest in it. This states the obvious consequence of an outright sale; see Comment 2 to 9–318. Under 9–318(b), for purposes of determining the rights in accounts and chattel paper sold, while the buyer is unperfected, the debtor (seller) is deemed have the rights and title to the accounts and chattel paper it sold. This gives the seller an interest it otherwise would not have: the rights and title to the accounts or chattel paper it sold. By "deeming" the seller to retain the rights and title it sold to an unperfected buyer of accounts or chattel paper, 9–318(b) enables the seller to re-sell these payment rights to another buyer or encumber them with a security interest. This unwelcome consequence for the initial buyer encourages it to perfect its "security interest" in accounts or chattel paper purchased. By its terms, 9–318(b) has no application to payment intangibles and promissory notes because buyers of these payment rights are perfected automatically in them. 9–309(3), (4).

Two examples illustrate 9–318's application to competing claims to a sold payment right. Example 1: On January 1 Debtor sold a payment intangible it owns to Bank. Bank did not give public notice of its interest in the payment intangible. On February 1 Debtor sold the same payment intangible to Finance. Section 9–318(b)'s "deeming" exception to 9–318(a) is inapplicable because, by its terms, 9–318(b) applies only to a sale of accounts and chattel paper, not to a sale of payment intangibles. (In addition, 9–318(b) applies only while the buyer of accounts or chattel paper is unperfected in them; Bank is automatically perfected in the payment intangible it bought. 9–309(3).) Thus, under 9–318(a), Debtor retains no legal or equitable interest in the payment intangible it sold to

Bank on January 1. As a result, Debtor retained no interest in the payment intangible it could sell to Finance on February 2. Bank holds a perfected security interest in the payment intangible it bought, while Finance's holds merely an unsecured claim against Debtor. Section 9–201 gives priority to a security interest in collateral over an unsecured claim. Bank therefore has priority over Finance.

Example 2: On January 1 Debtor sold the only account it owned to Bank. Bank did not file a financing statement covering the account it bought. On February 1 Debtor granted Finance a security interest in its accounts, including the account sold to Bank, and Finance properly filed a financing statement covering Debtor's accounts. Section 9–318(a), which leaves the seller with no legal or equitable interest in an account it sold, is subject to 9–318(b)'s exception. Because Bank failed to file as to the account it bought, it has an unperfected security interest in the account. Cf. 1–201(b)(35); 9–310(a). Section 9–318(b) therefore deems Debtor to have the rights and title in the account that it sold to Bank on January 1. This gives Debtor rights in the account in which it can create a security interest. Debtor granted Finance a security interest in the account it sold to Bank, which Finance perfected by filing a proper financing statement. As between a perfected security interest and unperfected security in the same collateral, 9–322(a)(2) gives the perfected security interest priority. Financer therefore has priority over Bank in the account.

PROBLEMS

Who has priority in account XYZ in the circumstances described below?

1.   On January 1 Bank, with Debtor's authorization, filed a financing statement covering Debtor's accounts. On February 1 Debtor granted Finance a security interest in account XYZ, which it owns, and Finance filed an effective financing statement covering the account. Debtor sold account XYZ to Bank on March 1.

2.   On January 1 Bank, with Debtor's authorization, filed a financing statement covering Debtor's accounts. On February 1 Finance bought account XYZ from Debtor and filed an effective financing statement covering the account. On March 1 Debtor granted Bank a security interest in account XYZ.

G. ACCOUNTS AND GENERAL INTANGIBLES

1. PRIORITY IN PROCEEDS

This section and the ones following it examine the priority rules applicable to specific kinds of rights to payment: accounts and general intangibles, chattel paper, deposit accounts, and cash proceeds.

As a general rule, accounts and general intangibles can be perfected only by filing (9–310(a)): possession is not a means of perfection for intangibles such as these. Priority between conflicting security interests in accounts and general intangibles is determined by the first-to-file rule of 9–322(a). Exceptions to the general rule for perfection found with respect to payment intangibles, discussed above, and security interests subject to other law, such as rights in registered copyrights (9–311(a)(1)), discussed in Chapter 6. Purchase-money security interests can be created only in goods and software and not in accounts. See 9–103, Comment 2 to 9–324 and First Bethany Bank & Trust, N.A. v. Arvest United Bank, 77 P.3d 595 (Okla.2003).

Since accounts are often the proceeds of collateral, such as inventory, consideration of the provisions on proceeds in 9–315 is essential in determining priorities in accounts. Relevant here also is 9–322(b)(1)'s general priority rule for proceeds. Under 9–322(b)(1), for purposes of priority under 9–322(a)(1)'s first-to-file-or-perfect rule, the time of filing or perfection as to a security interest in the collateral is the time of filing or perfection as to a security interest in the proceeds of the collateral. In other words, the time of filing or perfection as to the security interest in the collateral carries over to the time of filing or perfection of the security interest in the proceeds. How do these provisions apply in Problem 1 below?

PROBLEMS

1.   Debtor sells goods to retailers who agree to pay Debtor for the goods within 90 days after delivery. Bank periodically advances funds to Debtor to allow it to buy new inventory while awaiting payment from the retailers.

(a) Debtor secured these advances by granting Bank a security interest in "all inventory now owned or hereafter acquired," which was perfected by filing. Later, Lender made advances to Debtor, which Debtor secured by granting Lender a security interest in "all accounts now owned or hereafter acquired." Lender promptly filed a financing statement. No reference was made to proceeds in the security agreements and financing statements of either Bank or Lender. Who is prior with respect to the accounts arising from the sale of items from Debtor's inventory, Bank or Lender? See 9–203(f), 9–315(a), (c) and (d), and 9–322(b)(1). See also Comment 6 to 9–322.

(b) Debtor secured these advances by granting Bank a security interest in "all inventory and accounts now owned or hereafter acquired," which was perfected by filing. The retailers were not told of Bank's security interest. Later, Debtor made an outright sale of all its accounts to Factor, falsely assuring Factor that Bank's loan would be paid off with the funds received from Factor. Factor immediately filed a financing statement covering all Debtor's accounts now owned or thereafter acquired and notified the account debtors that it now owned the accounts and that all payments were to be made to it. Who is prior with respect to Debtor's accounts, Bank or Factor? See 9–109(a)(3) and 1–201(b)(35) (definition of security interest), in addition to the provisions mentioned in (a) above.

2. In a written security agreement, Debtor granted SPA a security interest in all its inventory now owned or thereafter acquired and all the proceeds thereof. SPA advanced value and filed a financing statement indicating the collateral as "inventory." Subsequently, in a written security agreement, Debtor granted SPB a security interest in all its equipment and replacements now owned or thereafter acquired, and the proceeds thereof. SPB filed a financing statement indicating the collateral as "equipment." Debtor sold items of its inventory on 30-day unsecured credit and deposited the checks received in payment in a special account in Bank, which held nothing but the proceeds of the sale of Debtor's inventory. Debtor drew checks on this account to purchase new equipment from Supplier.

(a) Is SPA's security interest prior to that of SPB in the newly acquired equipment? 9–315(d)(1)(C) and (3). See Comment 5.

(b) Would your answer change if SPA's financing statement indicated "all personal property of Debtor"?

2. SECTION 9–309(2)'S EXCEPTION

Section 9–309(2) allows for automatic perfection in certain assignments of accounts. Under 9–309(2) a security interest is perfected when it attaches if the assignment of accounts or payment intangibles, individually or collectively to the same assignee, does not transfer "a significant part of the assignor's outstanding accounts or payment intangibles." The assignment may be an outright assignment of ownership or an assignment of payment rights as security. See Amended 9–102(a)(7)(A), (B) . With respect to an outright assignment, recall that 1–201(b)(35)'s definition of "security interest" includes the interest acquired by the buyer of accounts.

The rationale for 9–309(2)'s exception to Article 9's general filing requirement is the cost effectiveness of not requiring filing. Prospective creditors are unlikely to make their lending decisions based on information about their debtor's isolated or comparatively few assignments of its accounts or payment intangibles. Thus, the benefit to them from public notice of these "insignificant" assignments is at best modest. The assignee's cost of filing, which is fixed, therefore arguably exceeds the limited benefit filing provides. A filing requirement for "insignificant" assignments is not cost effective. On the other hand, prospective creditors contemplating collateralizing their loans with the debtor's accounts or payment intangibles care whether the debtor has assigned a significant portion of these assets. The benefit to them from public notice of the assignments therefore is likely to be large. In this case the assignee's filing cost arguably is less than the benefit filing produces. Requiring filing where a significant portion of accounts is assigned is cost effective.

Section 9–309(2) limits the automatic perfection of assignments of accounts or payment intangibles to assignments, individually or collectively to the same assignee, that do not constitute a "significant part" of the assignor's accounts or payment intangibles. This limitation states a quantitative standard, not a precise quantitative rule. Courts understand the "significant part" standard to state a test based on the percentage in value of the accounts assigned in relation to the total outstanding accounts held by the assignor. See U.S. Claims, Inc. v. Flomenhaft, 2008 Phila. Ct. Comm. Pl. LEXIS 119 (May 14, 2008); *In re Tri-County Materials, Inc.* Further complicating 9–309(2)'s application is `Comment 4 to 9–309, which purports to explain 9–309(2)'s purpose: "The purpose of paragraph (2) is to save from *ex post facto* invalidation casual or isolated assignments—assignments which no one would think of filing. Any person who regularly takes assignments of any debtor's accounts or payment intangibles should file." A number of courts understand this part of the Comment to state an independent test. According to this test, an assignment is perfected automatically under 9–309(2) only if the assignment is "casual and isolated."

Consider both 9–309(2) and Comment 4 to 9–309 in connection with the following hypothetical and the case below. Your brother-in-law, a small-time painting contractor, borrows $10,000 from you to deal with what he describes as an emergency. You are skeptical both about the existence of an emergency and, in the light of his credit history with you, his likelihood of repaying the money within two months as he said he would. But, in the interest of family harmony, you give him the money. However, in order to impress upon him that you expect to get your money back fairly soon, you extract from him as security for the loan a written assignment of his right to be paid under the contract he has with the owner of the building that he is now working on. When he finishes his work he will be owed $12,000 on that contract. Neither you nor he has ever been involved with the assignment of an account before and neither of you has ever heard about Article 9 or its filing requirements. Does 9–309(2) exempt you from filing in this case?

In re Tri-County Materials, Inc.

United States District Court, C.D. Illinois, 1990
114 B.R. 160

■ MIHM, DISTRICT JUDGE.

* * *

FACTS

Tri-County Materials, the Debtor below, operated a sand and gravel pit. Ladd Construction Company was a general contractor which had a contract with the State of Illinois to construct a portion of Interstate 39. Ladd and Tri-County entered into a contract according to which Tri-County would supply Ladd with 100,000 tons of sand and gravel at $2.50 per ton. In order to complete its contractual obligations, Tri-County needed certain equipment to process the sand and gravel from the land it leased. As a result, KMB, Inc. leased equipment to Tri-County for that purpose. The leased equipment was used only at the gravel pit. Once the material was processed, a trucking firm hired by Ladd transported the material to the construction site, some eight to ten miles from the gravel pit.

Although initially the agreement between Tri-County and KMB for the lease of the equipment was oral, that agreement was reduced to writing in June of 1988. In the agreement, Tri-County assigned part of its account with Ladd Construction Company to KMB for the purpose of securing the rental charges which Tri-County owed to KMB. Ladd was notified of the assignment and received bi-weekly notification of the amount due to KMB by Tri-County. KMB did not file a Uniform Commercial Code financing statement regarding the assignment.

Tri-County filed a voluntary petition for bankruptcy under Chapter 11 in October of 1988. At that time, Ladd owed Tri-County $43,413.71 for previously supplied material while Tri-County owed KMB $30,484.

The bankruptcy court found that KMB did not have a security interest in the funds due from Ladd because they had failed to perfect that interest as required under Article 9 of the Uniform Commercial Code. . . .

PERFECTION OF SECURITY INTEREST

Tri-County owed KMB $30,484 at the time of filing bankruptcy. KMB claims that, because Tri-County assigned its right to receive payments from Ladd to the extent that it owed money to KMB, it had a security interest in the money owed to Tri-County.

§ 9–302 [9–309] provides as follows:

> (1) [(2)] a financing statement must be filed to perfect all security interests except the following: . . . (e) an assignment of accounts which does not alone or in conjunction with other assignments to the same assignee transfer a significant part of the outstanding accounts of the assignor.

KMB takes the position that it is entitled to rely on § 9–302(1)(e) [9–309(2)] because it is not regularly engaged in accounts receivable financing, thus making this a casual and isolated transaction, and because the amount which Tri-County owed to KMB, when compared to the $250,000 which Tri-County was entitled to receive from Ladd was a mere 12%, thus making it an insignificant transfer. Appellant argues that because KMB fails to meet either test it did not have a perfected security interest in the Ladd account.

The burden of proving the applicability of § 9–302(1)(e) [9–309(2)] rests on the party asserting the exception. See, Consolidated Film Industries v. United States, 547 F.2d 533 (10th Cir.1977). Although the Code does not define "significant part," case law has developed two tests.

The first test is referred to as the percentage test. This test focuses on the size of the assignment in relation to the size of outstanding accounts. In re B. Hollis Knight Co., 605 F.2d 397 (8th Cir.1979); Standard Lumber Company v. Chamber Frames, Inc., 317 F.Supp. 837 (E.D.Ark.1970).

The second test is the "casual or isolated" test. This test is suggested by the language of Comment 5 to UCC § 9–302 [Comment 4 to 9–309] which states that:

> The purpose of the subsection (e)(1) exemptions is to save from ex post facto invalidation casual or isolated assignments: some accounts receivable statutes have been so broadly drafted that all assignments, whatever their character or purpose, fall within their filing provisions. Under such statute many assignments which no one would think of filing may be subject to invalidation. The subsection (1)(e) exemptions go to that type of assignment. Any person who regularly takes assignments of any debtor's accounts should file.

The totality of circumstances surrounding the transaction determines whether an assignment was casual or isolated. If the transaction was not part of a regular course of commercial financing then under this test filing is not required. The rationale appears to be the reasonableness of requiring a secured creditor to file if assignment of debtor's accounts is a regular part of business and the corresponding unreasonableness of a filing requirement for casual or isolated transactions.

There is no authoritative determination of whether both tests must be met in order to claim the exemption or whether either by itself is sufficient. The bankruptcy court agreed with the *Hollis Knight* court which held that both tests must be met. This Court agrees with that assessment. The statutory language specifically requires that the assignment be an insignificant part of the outstanding account. Thus, at the very least, this test must be met in every instance. A showing of a casual or isolated assignment of a significant part of outstanding accounts would not be entitled to the exemption given this clear statutory requirement. On the other hand, given the comments to the UCC regarding the purpose of this exemption, in a case involving the transfer of an insignificant part of outstanding accounts to a creditor whose regular business is financing, such accounts should not fall within this exemption. Thus it is a logical result of the language and purpose of this section to require that both tests be met. * * *

The Debtor's bankruptcy schedules indicate that Tri-County had ten accounts at the time of the Chapter 11 filing, of which the largest by far was the Ladd contract for $250,000. The assignment to KMB permitted KMB to:

request that the Ladd Construction Company. . . make any and all payments to [Tri-County] by including on said check payment the name of [KMB] who shall have said check negotiated and endorsed by [Tri-County] and said check shall be deposited in [KMB's] account with [Tri-County's] endorsement, at which time [KMB] shall issue a check to [Tri-County] for the difference between the amount of the check issued and the rental payment owed to [KMB].

It is thus clear that the assignment was not of the entire Ladd account but only of that portion of the account necessary to cover the balance due to KMB. At the time the parties entered into the Agreement, the total rental amount was estimated at $30,000; the actual figure turned out to be $30,484. The ratio of the amount assigned to the total account, even assuming that the Ladd contract was the *only* account, is approximately 12%.

Although there is no bright line marking the division between significant and insignificant, the 12% figure is surely on the "insignificant" side. See, Standard Lumber Co. v. Chamber Frames, Inc., 317 F.Supp. 837 (D.C.Ark.1970) (16% insignificant). Thus, the first test, contrary to what the bankruptcy court found, has been satisfied. The bankruptcy court based its finding on the assumption that Tri-County had assigned the entire Ladd account to KMB, an assumption that is not supported by the record.

The record also shows without contradiction that KMB was not in the business of accepting contract assignments, nor had either party to the assignment engaged in such a transaction at other times. The bankruptcy court found that despite the "isolated" nature of this assignment, it was "a classic secured transaction," and thus failed to fall within the "casual and isolated" exception to the filing requirement.

This Court agrees with that assessment. This is not the type of "casual" transaction in which reasonable parties would fail to see the importance of filing. Rather, it was evidenced by a formal, written agreement between two corporations; notice of the agreement was sent to Ladd, and other conduct engaged in by KMB indicates the degree of formality attached to it. This is the type of transaction for which the UCC requires filing in order to perfect.

Because KMB failed to perfect its security interest, this Court affirms the bankruptcy court's ruling. * * *

NOTES

1. Although Comment 4 to 9–309 refers to a "casual or isolated" assignment, the test *Tri County* and other courts extract from the Comment asks whether the assignment is "casual and isolated." This is a more demanding test than one which requires that the assignment be "casual or

isolated." How would the court in *Tri-County* apply the exception from filing in 9–309(2), as interpreted in Comment 4, to the following cases?

Case #1. The brother-in-law hypothetical in the text preceding *Tri-County* in which an assignment of all of the assignor's accounts, amounting to $12,000, was made to a noncommercial assignee who knew nothing about how to perfect a security interest in accounts.

Case #2. A large corporation assigns accounts amounting to $500,000 to a commercial bank. Both the assignor and assignee regularly engage in accounts financing. The accounts assigned amounted to less than 1% of the assignor's total accounts. Bank failed to file because of an oversight of a clerk.

2. Courts have had so much difficulty trying to make sense of former 9–302(1)(e), 9–309(2)'s predecessor, that the issue has generated more case law than almost any other aspect of accounts financing. Section 9–309(2), together with Comment 4, clears up none of the problems. Probably the most serious problem is the proper understanding of 9–309(2)'s "significant part" limitation in light of Comment 4 to 9–309. Courts continue to use a percentage test, a "causal and isolated" test, or a combination of the two tests. See Smith v. MCF Capital, LLC, 2019 WL 13217125 (S.D.Miss. 2019). For criticism of the practice of treating UCC Comments as a source of law, see Steven D. Walt, Presumptuous Official Comments and Their Place in Article 9, 47 UCC L.J. 259 (2017).

H. CONTROLLABLE ELECTRONIC RECORDS AND CONTROLLABLE PAYMENT RIGHTS

Although a security interest in controllable electronic records (CERs) and controllable account and payment intangibles (collectively, "controllable payment rights") can be perfected by filing or control, the UCC has special priority rules that apply when the secured party is perfected by control. These control priority rules are contained in both Article 9 and Article 12. Under 9–326A, a security interest in a controllable electronic record, controllable account or controllable payments intangible perfected by control has priority over a conflicting security interest not perfected by control. As with other control priority rules, 9–326A is a nontemporal priority rule: the security interest perfected by control has priority, without regard to when control was obtained. However, 9–326A's control priority rule is limited in its scope. Unlike the control priority rules for deposit accounts and investment property, 9–326A does not order priority when conflicting security interests are both perfected by control. In this case Article 9's other priority rules establish priority, including 9–322(a)(1)'s first-to-file-or-perfect rule.

Article 12's priority rules are potentially more significant for security interests in CERs and controllable payment rights perfected by control. As background, there is a simple but important distinction between the record evidencing rights and the rights evidenced by the record. As a result, the transfer of the record may or may not also transfer the rights evidenced by it. For example, the sale of a writing evidencing a lease agreement transfers the writing. But the sale may or may not transfer rights under the lease. The law governing leases determines whether it does so. With one exception, law other than Article 12 determines whether the transfer of a record transfers the rights it evidenced. This is true with respect to the purchase of a CER. Section 12–104(d) provides that a purchaser of a CER acquires all the rights in the CER its transferor had or had the power to transfer. For its part, under 12–104(e) a qualified purchaser of a CER acquired its rights free of claims or property rights in the CER. Both provisions are limited to rights in the CER. Law other than Article 12 determines whether the purchaser acquires the rights evidenced by the CER it purchased. For example, a nonfungible token is a CER. Suppose the digital content linked to the token is subject to copyright law. Under 12–104(d), the purchaser of the nonfungible token acquires its transferor's rights in the token, and under 12–104(e), if the purchaser is a qualified purchaser, it takes those rights free of claims or property rights to the token. However, copyright law determines whether the purchaser acquires rights in the digital content linked to the nonfungible token.

The single exception to Article 12's deference to other law is with respect to controllable accounts and controllable payment intangibles. Transfer of control of the CER evidencing these payment rights also transfers control of the payments rights evidenced by the CER. Section 12–104(a) provides that its provisions apply to the purchase of rights in a controllable account or controllable payment intangible in the same way the section applies to a CER. This tethers payment rights to the CER evidencing them, so that they travel with the CER, as it is sometimes put. A purchaser acquires the rights in the CER its transferor had or had the power to transfer. 12–104(d). And 12–104(e) provides that a qualified purchaser of a CER takes free of previous claims or property rights in the CER. Thus, under 12–104(a), a purchaser of the CER acquires the payment rights its transferor had or had the power to transfer. If the purchaser is a qualified purchaser, the purchaser also acquires payment rights evidenced by the CER free of previous claims or property right in them.

Section 12–104(e)'s "take free" rule is a priority rule for CERs. Section 12–104(a) extends this rule to controllable payment rights. Under 12–104(a) the purchaser of controllable payment rights has the same rights in them that it has in the CER evidencing the payment rights. Accordingly, a qualified purchaser of controllable payment rights takes the payment rights free of claims or property rights in them. A secured party is a purchaser; see 1–201(b)(30). Thus, if the secured party is a qualified purchaser of controllable payment rights, it takes free of competing claims or property interests in them. A qualified purchaser in turn is defined as a purchaser who obtains control of a CER for value, in good faith and without notice of a claim or property right in the CER. 12–102(a)(3). The filing of a financing statement is not notice of a claim or property right in the CER. 12–104(h). As a result, a security party who obtains control over controllable payment rights takes free of an existing security interest in these rights perfected by filing or control, if the secured party is a qualified purchaser.

Care needs to be taken in understanding what it means for a secured party to "take free" under 12–104(e). The phrase suggests that the transfer of controllable payment rights to a qualified purchaser eliminates previous claims or property rights in them. That is correct when the qualified purchaser buys the payment rights. The buyer acquires ownership without previous claims or property rights encumbering its interest. However, a security interest is not an ownership interest; it is a limited interest. When the qualified purchaser is a secured party, the purchase does not eliminate existing security interests in the controllable payment rights purchased. They continue. It is just that the purchaser's security interest is not subject to existing security interests, including their priority. As a qualified purchaser, the secured party "takes free" of these security interests, to the extent of the interest purchased—its security interest. This gives the secured party priority in the controllable payment rights purchased to the extent of its security interest.

PROBLEMS

1. On January 1 Bank perfected its security interest in Debtor's controllable accounts by filing a financing statement covering them. On March 1 Lender perfected a security interest in certain of Debtor's controllable accounts by taking control of them. At the time, Lender knew nothing about Debtor's dealings with Bank. The accounts are among the controllable accounts covered by Bank's security agreement with Debtor. On May 1, as part of another financing arrangement with Bank, Debtor gave Bank control over the controllable accounts in which it had a security interest. These include the accounts in which Lender is perfected by control. Who has priority in the controllable accounts in which Lender is perfected by control? Would the result change if Lender had learned of Bank's filed financing statement at the time it took control? 9–326A, 9–322(a)(1); 12–102(a)(3), 12–104(e).

2. On January 1 Bank perfected its security interest in certain of Debtor's nonfungible tokens of portraits by R. Mutt by taking control of the tokens. On March 1 Lender also perfected its security interest in the same nonfungible tokens by taking control of them. Who has priority in these nonfungible tokens? 9–326A, 9–322(a)(1). Would the result change if Lender did not know of Bank's security interest at the time it took control of Debtor's nonfungible tokens? 12–104(e), 9–331(c).

3. On January 1 Bank perfected its security interests in certain of Debtor's controllable accounts by taking control of them. On March 1 Lender perfected its security in the same accounts by also taking control of them. As

in Problem 1, Lender knew nothing of Debtor's dealings with Bank on the date it took control of the controllable accounts Bank controlled. Who has priority in these accounts? 9–322(a)(1), 12–102(a)(3), 9–331(a), 12–103(a).

I. CHATTEL PAPER AND INSTRUMENTS

1. INTRODUCTION

The growth in consumer goods financing after World War II created a need for retailers to use the assets generated by their consumer credit sales to finance their own operations. These assets were the payment rights the retailers had against their credit buyers and the security interests in the goods sold to them. The payment rights gave the retailer both a payment right against its buyer and a security interest in the goods sold to secure the buyer's payment obligation. A retailer of course could sell or collateralize the payment obligation as an account along with the security interest backing it. However, purchasers or secured creditors would have to determine the rights they were acquiring without the benefit of information contained in a tangible document. Merging the payment right represented by an account and the security interest with a document—"paperizing" it—allows parties to determine payment rights from the paper. It enables the transfer of a payment right and security interests backing it by transferring the paper representing them. This reduces the cost of obtaining payment rights either by sale or as collateral for a loan. See Thomas A. Jackson, Embodiment of Rights in Goods and the Concept of Chattel Paper, 50 U. Chi. L. Rev. 1051, 1058–59 (1983). Article 9 creates a separate type of collateral for paperized payment rights, "chattel paper," with special priority rules sometimes applicable to them.

Gilmore observes: " 'Chattel paper' is a novel term coined by the Code draftsmen to describe a species of property which had previously managed to exist without a name." 1 Grant Gilmore, supra, § 12.5, at 378 (1965). In general terms, chattel paper is a right to payment of a monetary obligation secured by specific goods, where evidenced by a record, or a right to payment of a monetary obligation under a lease agreement, where evidenced by a record. See 9–102(a)(11). As explained earlier, a security interest in accounts and general intangibles in a non-electronic form can be perfected only by filing; there is no physical embodiment of the right to payment of which a creditor can be given possession. However, with respect to instruments and tangible chattel paper, the right to payment or performance is sufficiently embodied in written agreements so that possession of these writings, gives the possessor control over the obligation. Hence, these writings are pledgeable, as it is sometimes put. Two simple examples of chattel paper are leases of goods and purchase-money security agreements which either contain an obligation to pay, usually in installments, or less commonly a promissory note.

The trend in the commercial context is from paper to electronic storage and transmission. In line with this trend, chattel paper increasingly is evidenced by records in an electronic form or in both electronic and tangible form. Occasionally chattel paper in a tangible form is converted to an electronic form, and vice versa. Recognizing the trend towards electronic transmission, the 2022 Amendments alter the definition of chattel paper to include both chattel paper in a tangible form and chattel paper in an electronic form. Under 9–314A(a), where records evidencing the monetary obligation are in both tangible and electronic form, perfection in chattel paper is achieved by taking possession of the tangible records and obtaining control of each authoritative electronic copy of the electronic record. Accordingly, if chattel paper consists only of tangible records, perfection can be achieved by taking possession of the records. If the paper consists only of electronic records, perfection occurs when the secured party has control of all the authoritative electronic copies of the electronic record. What constitutes an "authoritative" copy is undefined, its interpretation presumably left to the courts.

Key to understanding the value of chattel paper as collateral is to notice that the secured party's rights are derivative: they are based on the rights that chattel paper gives the debtor against the account debtor (the party the obligated to pay). Chattel paper gives the debtor a payment right against the account debtor secured by the account debtor's specific goods. Thus, as collateral chattel paper gives the secured party the contingent right to receive payment from the account debtor secured by specific goods of the account debtor. Accordingly, if the debtor defaults on its own payment obligations to the secured party, the secured party can realize on its collateral, which is chattel paper. This gives the secured party the debtor's rights in the chattel paper: the right to receive payment from the account debtor secured by the account debtor's specific goods. However, because the debtor cannot foreclose on these goods unless the account debtor defaults on its own payment obligations to the debtor, neither can the secured party. The secured party can do so only if both the debtor and account debtor default on their respective payment obligations. Similarly, because the secured party's rights derive from the debtor's rights in the chattel paper, the secured party's rights are correspondingly limited. Thus, if the debtor's payment right and security interest are subordinate to those of the account debtor's other creditors, so too is secured party's payment right against the account debtor and the security interest securing it.

A debtor in financial difficulty might grant a security interest in its chattel paper to two creditors at different times. Alternatively, the debtor initially might have granted a security interest in its inventory to a creditor. When the debtor sells its inventory to buyers on credit, it receives chattel paper in exchange. Later, the debtor sells the paper or grants a security interest in the paper. The chattel paper in this case is proceeds of the inventory financer's collateral and original collateral for the purchaser. In both situations a priority conflict arises. Section 9–330 states a nontemporal priority rule that is applicable when its conditions are satisfied. The rule applies to both chattel paper in both tangible and electronic form. If 9–330's conditions are not satisfied, Article 9's other priority rules apply, including its first-to-file-or-perfect rule. In the following classic case, decided under former Article 9, an inventory financer with a proceeds interest in chattel paper is pitted against a chattel paper purchaser. To determine the result under current Article 9, consult 9–330(a) and (b), Comment 3 to 9–330 and the material following the case.

Rex Financial Corp. v. Great Western Bank & Trust

Court of Appeals of Arizona, 1975
532 P.2d 558

■ DONOFRIO, JUDGE.

This is an appeal from a judgment in favor of the appellee, Great Western Bank & Trust, on a motion to dismiss which was treated by the trial court as a motion for summary judgment under Rule 56 of the Arizona Rules of Civil Procedure, 16 A.R.S. The trial court considered all of the pleadings, affidavits, other matters of record, and the oral arguments of counsel and determined that there was no genuine issue of material fact, in reaching its judgment. For the reasons given below we affirm the judgment of the trial court.

The relevant facts are undisputed. In December of 1971 appellant entered into an agreement with Liberty Mobile Home Centers, Inc., a dealer in mobile homes, under which appellant agreed to finance this dealer's inventory of mobile homes. The dealer delivered to appellant certain manufacturer's certificates of origin on mobile homes to secure repayment of the loans, and gave appellant a security interest in the vehicles by way of a security agreement between the parties. This appeal concerns four of those mobile homes. The four mobile homes were sold by the dealer in the regular course of his business to certain individuals on security agreement contracts. These four security agreement contracts were then sold and assigned to the appellee, Great Western, in the ordinary course of its business for a certain sum which was paid to the dealer. Unfortunately, the dealer did not use these funds to pay off its outstanding loans owed to the appellant.

The basis for attacking a Rule 56 summary judgment ruling is that there were material factual issues disputed by the parties. All facts considered by the trial court appear in the pleadings, affidavits, depositions, and of course, oral arguments of the parties. On reviewing the record we are compelled to agree with the trial court that there were no material issues of fact, and that this was a question of law concerning the construction and application of U.C.C. § 9–308 [9–330] concerning the priority between certain secured creditors and purchasers of chattel paper.

§ 9–308 [cf. 9–330(a)] states:

"A purchaser of chattel paper or a nonnegotiable instrument who gives new value and takes possession of it in the ordinary course of his business and without knowledge that the specific paper or instrument is subject to a security interest has priority over a security interest which is perfected under § 9–304 (permissive filing and temporary perfection). *A purchaser of chattel paper who gives new value and takes possession of it in the ordinary course of his business has priority over a security interest in chattel paper which is claimed merely as proceeds of inventory subject to a security interest (§ 9–306), even though he knows that the specific paper is subject to the security interest.*" (Emphasis added.)

Since it was established that Great Western Bank had knowledge of the security interest claimed by Rex Financial Corporation in the four mobile homes, the second sentence of the foregoing section is the critical one for our purposes.

Appellant's first argument concerns the definition of "chattel paper" used in the above-mentioned sentence of § 9–308 [9–330]. Appellant argues that the manufacturer's certificates of origin, which remained in its possession, were a part of the chattel paper and were necessary ingredients along with the security agreements purchased by Great Western to make up the "chattel paper" which must be possessed by the purchaser. We do not agree. § 9–105(1)(b) [cf. 9–102(a)(11)] defines "chattel paper" as:

" 'Chattel paper' means a writing or writings which evidence both a monetary obligation and a security interest in or a lease of specific goods. When a transaction is evidenced both by such a security agreement or a lease and by an instrument or a series of instruments, the group of writings taken together constitutes chattel paper."

Appellant asserts that. . .the Motor Vehicle Code contemplate[s] that a manufacturer's certificate of origin is a part of the "transaction" where chattel paper is purchased as in § 9–105(1)(b) [cf. 9–102(a)(11)] above. We do not think that such comparison is relevant here. "Chattel paper" clearly must evidence "both a monetary obligation and a security interest in or a lease of specific goods." The manufacturer's certificates of origin do not meet this definition, and the trial court's construction of § 9–105(1)(b) [cf. 9–102(a)(11)] was correct in the application to this factual situation. It was undisputed that Great Western gave "new value" for the four security agreements it purchased from the dealer, all in accordance with § 9–308 [9–330].

The next requirement of § 9–308 [9–330] which is attacked by appellant is the requirement that the purchase of the chattel paper be "in the ordinary course of *his* business." (emphasis added) Appellant maintains that this refers to a practice which "should have been followed" and not to the practice of this particular purchaser of chattel paper. Again we do not agree. The plain language of the statute refers to *"his business"* (meaning the purchaser of the chattel paper). It is undisputed that this purchase was the normal means used at Great Western to obtain this type of chattel paper. As was stated in the deposition of Mr. McFadden, a representative of Great Western, he expected the *dealer* to disburse funds to appellant to pay off the loans for the "floor plan" financing that the dealer had obtained from appellant. The term "buyer in the ordinary course of business" with its requirements of good faith, as used elsewhere in the Uniform Commercial Code, is to be distinguished from the use here of "[buyer] in the ordinary course of *his* business." In fact, § 9–308 (second sentence) [9–330(a)] allows the purchaser of the chattel paper to have priority even if he has knowledge of a prior security interest in the collateral. As noted by White and Summers in their Treatise on the Uniform Commercial Code, ". . . the later party is favored on the assumption that chattel paper is his main course but merely the frosting on the cake for the mere proceeds claimant." White and Summers, Uniform Commercial Code, Sec. 25–17, p. 951 (1972 Edition).

This brings us to the final issue raised by appellant: the fourth requirement of the second sentence of § 9–308 [9–330], that the security interest claimed by appellant is claimed "merely as proceeds of inventory subject to a security interest." We find Comment 2 to this section of the U.C.C. (as found in the Final Report of the Permanent Editorial Board for the Uniform Commercial Code, Review Committee for Article 9, April 25, 1971) instructive on this issue. There it is stated:

> "Clause (b) of the section deals with the case where the security interest in the chattel paper is claimed merely as proceeds—i.e., on behalf of an inventory financer who has not by some new transaction with the debtor acquired a specific interest in the chattel paper. In that case a purchaser, even though he knows of the inventory financer's proceeds interest, takes priority provided he gives new value and takes possession of the paper in the ordinary course of his business."

We take this language to mean that the drafters of the Code contemplated a situation such as the instant one where the inventory financer, Rex Financial Corp., had a security interest in the collateral (mobile homes) and the proceeds upon sale. The record before us does *not* indicate that Rex entered into any new transaction with the debtor/dealer. The trial court had before it the security agreement between Rex and the dealer as well as the affidavit of Rex's president, and found that Rex's claim was merely to the proceeds of the inventory when sold. We do not find error in this construction and application of the term "mere proceeds of inventory" by the trial court. We think it is a reasonable interpretation of the record that the appellant, Rex, did *not* place a substantial reliance on the chattel paper in making the loan, but rather relied on the collateral (mobile homes) and the proceeds when the collateral was sold. The proceeds of the sale of these four mobile homes included the chattel paper sold by the dealer to Great Western. Rex could have protected itself by requiring all security agreements executed on sale of the mobile homes to be turned over immediately to Rex, or if sold, that all payments for the security agreements (chattel paper) be made to itself.

A case that aptly illustrates the operation of U.C.C. § 9–308 [9–330] is Associates Discount Corporation v. Old Freeport Bank, 421 Pa. 609, 220 A.2d 621 (1966). In that case a finance company which purchased chattel paper from an auto dealer (in a factual situation somewhat similar to ours) prevailed over a bank which had "floor planned" the inventory of the dealer. The court found that the bank's claim was a mere proceeds claim to the chattel paper and that U.C.C. § 9–308 (second sentence) [9–330(a)(1)] would operate to give priority to the purchaser of the chattel paper. The inventory financer's interest in the "proceeds" of the sale of the inventory had been shifted to the money paid by the purchaser of the chattel paper to the dealer. Another case in which the same result was obtained was Chrysler Credit Corporation v. Sharp, 56 Misc.2d 261, 288 N.Y.S.2d 525 (1968), a New York case, which again applied U.C.C. § 9–308 [9–330] and held that the purchaser of an installment contract from an automobile dealer would prevail over a secured inventory financer. * * *

Affirmed.

2. "MERELY AS PROCEEDS"

Whether subsection (a) or (b) of 9–330 applies depends on whether the chattel paper is claimed "merely as proceeds of inventory" or "other than merely as proceeds of inventory." Those coming to 9–330 for the first time find this distinction difficult to understand, and well they might. The distinction simply isn't clear. There is no definition of these phrases in either the text of the statute or its Comments, nor is there a statement of any underlying principle on which the distinction is founded. For an "elaboration" of the term, Comment 3 to 9–330 refers to PEB Commentary No. 8. As an aid to understanding the distinction between "merely proceeds" and "not merely proceeds," consider the three prototypic Illustrations below that are based on the Commentary.

In the following two Illustrations, General Motors Acceptance Corporation (GMAC) finances the new car inventory of a Chevrolet Dealer (Dealer). This is sometimes called "floor-planning," meaning that GMAC lends Dealer money to buy cars from the manufacturer, General Motors, and takes a security interest, perfected by filing, in the inventory and its proceeds. When Dealer sells a car, it must account to GMAC for the amount loaned against the car; if the car is not sold within 90 days, Dealer must account for it at the end of the period.

Illustration #1.   Dealer sells a car to Buyer who pays 20% down and signs an installment sale contract in which she agrees to pay the balance of the price ($20,000) plus a finance charge in 36 monthly payments. The contract grants Dealer a security interest in the car to secure the unpaid balance. Dealer sells and delivers possession of the contract to Finance Company (Finance) for $20,000 in cash. Finance buys automobile paper in the ordinary course of its business and is well aware that GMAC is floor-planning Dealer's inventory. Dealer deposited the $20,000 check in its general operating deposit account and failed to account to GMAC for the proceeds of the sale to Finance. GMAC did not require Dealer to deposit cash proceeds in any form of restricted or blocked deposit account that would have given GMAC a measure of control over the account. Hence, it was easy for Dealer to use the funds for purposes other than accounting to GMAC. When GMAC discovered Dealer's failure to account, it asserted a priority interest in the chattel paper, as proceeds of its inventory collateral, in the possession of Finance. Finance is prior under 9–330(a).

This is the paradigm case under 9–330(a) in which GMAC is claiming its security interest in the contract *merely as proceeds*. Finance is giving new value in ordinary course of its business. Although Finance has not searched the filings, it knows that virtually every new car inventory is financed and that Chevrolet dealers are usually financed by GMAC. As Comment 5 to 9–330 points out with respect to 9–330(a), "[A] purchaser who meets the possession or control, ordinary course and new value requirements takes priority over a competing security interest unless the chattel paper itself indicates that it has been assigned to an identified assignee other than the purchaser. . . . This approach, under which the chattel paper purchaser who gives new value in ordinary course can rely on possession of unlegended, tangible chattel paper without any concern for other facts that it may know, comports with the expectations of both inventory and chattel paper financers."

A possible justification for this exception to the first-to-file-or-perfect rule of 9–322(a)(1) is that the position of GMAC has not worsened because of the sale of the paper to Finance. In place of the chattel paper, Dealer has the $20,000, and, if GMAC has maintained prudent controls over Dealer's handling of cash proceeds that allows it to trace the proceeds of the check, it has a secured claim in the cash proceeds. Common law cases typically awarded priority to purchasers of the chattel paper against the secured party who financed the inventory. 2 Grant Gilmore, supra, § 27.3 (1965). Former 9–308 and present 9–330(a) continue this traditional priority. This rule is benign: it allows dealers to sell their paper to purchasers who offer better deals than the inventory financer and, in doing so, encourages competition.

GMAC's problem in this case is its failure to impose controls over the cash proceeds in Dealer's possession. It shouldn't matter to GMAC whether the car was sold for $25,000 cash or for $5,000 down with the balance represented by chattel paper that was sold to Finance for $20,000. In both cases, Dealer ends up with $25,000 in cash, an agreed portion of which should have been paid over to GMAC. Prudent inventory financers shouldn't find the priority preference of 9–330(a) unsettling. In Illustration #1, carefully monitored cash management controls, such as blocked or lockbox accounts into which cash proceeds must go, imposed by GMAC on its dealers, protects GMAC against any damage stemming from 9–330(a)'s awarding priority to Finance.

Illustration #2.   Dealer sells a car to Buyer who pays $5,000 down and signs a contract agreeing to pay the balance of $20,000 plus interest in monthly installment payments over a three-year period. The contract granted a security interest in the car to Dealer to secure the unpaid balance. Dealer sold the contract to GMAC for $20,000. GMAC allowed Dealer to retain possession of the contract in order to serve as GMAC's agent in making collections under the contract. Dealer was in financial difficulties and wrongfully sold the contract to Finance for $20,000 in cash. Dealer did not account to GMAC for the cash. Finance is in the business of purchasing automobile paper from Dealers and is aware of the likelihood that GMAC may claim a security interest in the contract, but Finance has no knowledge that GMAC had bought the paper. When GMAC discovered Dealer's fraud, it asserted its priority over the chattel paper in Finance's possession. Finance is prior under 9–330(b).

Although the meaning of "merely as proceeds" is unclear, this is an easy case for finding that GMAC is claiming a security interest in the chattel paper "other than merely as proceeds of the inventory" because in a subsequent transaction it bought the paper from Dealer. Whatever else "merely as proceeds" means, GMAC clearly took the chattel paper out of the merely-as-proceeds category in this case by giving new value against the chattel paper in a new transaction. It is claiming the paper as the purchaser of it, not as proceeds of Dealer's inventory in which GMAC had a security interest.

The possibility of this case occurring in modern automobile financing is remote in the extreme. First, GMAC can preclude any fraudulent double financing by a dealer merely by taking possession of the chattel paper, and this is the practice in the industry. Second, even though there is no pattern in automobile financing of purchasers of paper leaving possession of the paper with dealers, if GMAC were to do so it could establish its priority over Finance by stamping a legend on the paper indicating that it had been assigned to GMAC. In a 9–330(b) case Finance cannot prevail unless it is "without knowledge that the purchase violates the rights of the secured party." Under 9–330(f), an indication on the paper that it had already been assigned to GMAC would have given Finance the requisite knowledge of violation of GMAC's rights.

According to PEB Commentary No. 8, there was a practice in the 1950s when Article 9 was being drafted of chattel paper purchasers leaving possession of the paper with the dealers for collections. Department stores liked this practice because it often brought customers who bought goods on installment sale contracts back to the store to make their payments. The location of the credit department usually required the customer to walk past as much merchandise as possible, as a lure to impulse buyers, on the way to the credit department. Since the drafters of the original Article 9 did not want to disrupt these practices, they allowed such purchasers to perfect a security interest in chattel paper by filing and introduced the ungainly "other than merely as proceeds" distinction to protect such purchasers from subsequent buyers of the paper from the fraudulent dealer who knew about the purchaser's security interest. Legending the paper would be particularly useful to these chattel purchasers. In an age when most small goods purchases are done on credit or debit cards on an unsecured basis rather than on installment sale contracts, the practices described by the Commentary seem hopelessly dated; nonetheless, the distinction based on the "merely as proceeds" test was carried over into 9–330 and remains a trap for unwary lenders.

Illustration #3 involves different facts. Dealer sells appliances and furniture. Smaller items are sold on an unsecured basis, larger items are sold on installment credit contracts in which security interests are taken. Bank finances Dealer's operations by taking a floating lien on all Dealer's inventory and receivables (accounts and chattel paper). Bank has filed a financing statement. Dealer is allowed to borrow as much as requested up to an agreed percentage of the value of Dealer's inventory and receivables. In violation of its agreement with Bank, Dealer sells chattel paper having a face value of $200,000 to Financer for $150,000 in cash. Financer takes possession of chattel paper in the ordinary course of its business. If Financer's knowledge becomes an issue, is this case governed by subsection (a) or (b) of 9–330?

PEB Commentary No. 8 takes the view that Bank has more than a mere proceeds interest in the chattel paper in this case because it is part of the collateral on which the lending formula is based; therefore, the chattel paper is primary collateral. The Commentary observes: "The structure of the deal is such that the chattel paper is part of the primary collateral for the debt. That interest extends to any chattel paper subsequently generated by a sale of inventory whether or not at any particular time the existing inventory is adequate security for the debt actually outstanding." It is not clear how Financer is supposed to recognize whether Bank is relying on chattel paper as primary collateral in cases of this sort.

A strong argument can be made that Article 9 should have dropped the "merely as proceeds" rule. Not only is it confusing but the rule rests on a false distinction between "merely as proceeds" and other than "merely as proceeds." No inventory financer claims chattel paper "merely as proceeds" of inventory. They always rely on chattel paper in setting loan terms, including the interest rate. This is because the inventory financer must consider a future contingency in which the debtor is insolvent or close to it. In these circumstances, debtors have an incentive to take risks with collateral or proceeds in order to avoid default. The limit of debtor's risk-taking, of course, is to dissipate money received from the sale of chattel paper. Inventory financers, knowing of this possible contingency, must look primarily to the paper for repayment of their loans. They will adjust the interest charge of the loans if they cannot do so. Thus, the lenders are always looking substantially to the chattel paper at the time the loan is made. If the test is one of substantial reliance on the paper in making the loan, as followed by the court in *Rex Financial*, all inventory financers qualify. The financer who ignores the possibility of having to reach the paper does not exist. Chattel paper is always part of the cake and never the frosting for inventory financers. This conclusion might explain why a definition of "mere proceeds" interest eludes 9–330's drafters: none is consistent with the plausible pricing of loans by inventory financers.

Commentary No. 8 does not try to justify the distinction between "mere proceeds" and "other than mere proceeds" interests. Instead, it takes the distinction as given by former 9–308 and tries to describe it based on case law that relies on former 9–308. The Commentary offers as comfort the observation that the problem is of only "limited importance since, even if the security interest is more than a mere proceeds interest, the chattel paper financer under 9–330 will take free of the interest unless it has knowledge that the purchase violates the rights of the secured party." So, why didn't 9–330's drafters write it that way?

3. INSTRUMENTS

Suppose Bank takes a security interest in Debtor's inventory and all the proceeds thereof, including accounts, chattel paper and instruments. Bank perfected its security interest by filing a financing statement covering all Debtor's personal property. When Debtor sells some items of its inventory, it accepts promissory notes from buyers in which they promise to pay to the order of Debtor a stated sum of money at a stated future time. Under 3–104(a), these notes are classified as "negotiable instruments" and under 3–104(b), are "instruments." But for Article 9 purposes "instruments" is broadened to include not only negotiable instruments but also other written promises to pay money that are, in effect, treated similarly in the marketplace. 9–102(a)(47). The question addressed by 9–330(d) is the priority between Bank and one who purchases an instrument from Debtor. This provision likens instruments to chattel paper for priority purposes. The purchaser of the instrument prevails if it gives value (not just new value) and takes possession of the instrument in good faith and without knowledge that the purchase violates the rights of the secured party.

The question arises how to reconcile 9–330(d) with 9–331(a), which says that nothing in Article 9 limits the rights of a holder in due course of a negotiable instrument. If the purchaser of the instrument in the previous paragraph took delivery of the note for value in good faith and without notice of claims or defenses, it becomes a holder in due course who takes free of claims or defenses under 3–302. It is accepted negotiable instruments law that a holder in due course takes free of a prior security interest in the instrument (a claim of ownership) but a holder who knows of the security interest cannot qualify as a holder in due course. See 3–302(a)(2). Thus, if the purchaser knew about the existence of Bank's security interest, it would be subject to Bank's security interest under Article 3. But under 9–330(d), the purchaser would be prior to Bank even though it knew of the security interest so long as it had no knowledge that the purchase violated Bank's rights. The Article 9 priority rule found in 9–330(d) would prevail. Section 9–330(d) provides that its rule applies "except as otherwise provided in Section 9–331(a)," and nothing in that section provides otherwise. Article 3 determines who is a holder in due course but whether the purchaser is a holder in due course is irrelevant to the purchaser's rights under 9–330(d).

4. REVIEW PROBLEMS

PROBLEMS

1.   ZBest is an appliance dealer. Bank advanced $250,000 operating capital to ZBest and took a security interest in all its inventory then owned or thereafter acquired including all proceeds from the disposition of that collateral. Bank filed a financing statement, with ZBest's consent, indicating the collateral as "all ZBest's personal property."

    a.   ZBest sold a radio-CD player to A for $200. A used a ZBest credit card to pay for the merchandise.

    b.   ZBest sold a refrigerator to B for $1,000 and in a written contract reserved a security interest in the refrigerator for the unpaid price plus the finance charge to be paid in 12 equal monthly installments.

    c.   ZBest sold a washing machine and dryer unit to C for $1,000 and accepted C's negotiable promissory note, payable to the order of ZBest, for the balance of the price plus interest.

    d.   ZBest in a written agreement leased a large-screen television set to D for one year at $100 per month rental. D has the right to renew the lease for an additional year at the same monthly rental price. At the expiration of the lease, D was obliged to return the set to ZBest at its own expense.

ZBest, desperate to survive the recession, sold all its receivables to Factor who paid $100,000 cash. Factor knew that Bank had a security interest in the inventory but knew nothing of the terms of Bank's security agreement with ZBest. In effectuating the sale, Factor took possession of all credit card slips, installment sale contracts, promissory notes (bearing ZBest's indorsement), and lease agreements.

(a) Which party has priority with respect to the receivables of ZBest arising out of the transactions with A, B, C and D?

(b) Which party has priority with respect to the ZBest's residual interest in the television set? See Comment 11 to 9–330.

2. Debtor granted Bank a security interest in all of its inventory and chattel paper, now owned or thereafter acquired, and the proceeds thereof. Bank perfected by filing. Later, Debtor sold all its receivables, including its chattel paper, to Financer who paid cash and took possession in good faith. After Debtor failed, both Bank and Financer claimed priority in the chattel paper sold to Financer. Assume that Bank can prove that Financer took the paper with knowledge that its purchase violated the rights of Bank. Financer asserted that this issue was irrelevant because 9–330(a) governed and knowledge is not a factor under that provision. Bank replied that 9–330(b) governed because the description of collateral in its security agreement mentioned chattel paper as primary collateral and not as proceeds; hence, its claim to the chattel paper was not "merely as proceeds." Which subsection governs, (a) or (b)?

J. DEPOSIT ACCOUNTS

1. INTRODUCTION

Section 9–102(a)(29) defines a "deposit account" as a "demand, time, savings, passbook or similar account maintained with a bank." "Bank" includes "savings banks, savings and loan associations, credit unions, and trust companies." 9–102(a)(8). The definition of "deposit account" does not include accounts evidenced by negotiable certificates of deposit; these are covered in Article 3 as instruments. Section 3–104(j) defines a CD as an instrument issued to a depositor by a bank acknowledging that a sum of money has been deposited in the bank that the bank promises to repay. The depositor can pledge the CD, which amounts to a promissory note of the bank, as security for a loan in the same manner as any other instrument. Nor does the definition include "investment property," meaning money market funds or mutual fund accounts, even if redeemable by check.

The broad definition of "deposit account" sweeps in everything from simple checking accounts on through savings and trust accounts. Customers of commercial and savings banks maintain deposit accounts in these institutions amounting to enormous sums of money. The question of how the holders of these accounts, which contain great wealth, can effectively use them as collateral for debt has long puzzled courts and legislatures. This section addresses the response to this question offered by Article 9.

Article 9 covers security interests in deposit accounts taken as original collateral as well as its proceeds. This step contributes greatly to the commendable goal of bringing uniformity and consistency into what had been a confusing area of law. However, attainment of this goal is somewhat frustrated by the exclusion in 9–109(d)(13) of security interests in deposit accounts as original collateral in consumer transactions, which leaves this area to the vagaries of prior law. This exclusion can be circumvented by turning the consumer's deposit account into either a certificate of deposit or investment property, such as a money market account. A few states have adopted nonuniform amendments to 9–109(d)(13) that bring within Article 9 security interests in deposit accounts in consumer transactions.

Section 9–109(d)(13)'s exclusion of security interests in deposit accounts as original collateral in consumer transactions apparently is a response to the concerns of consumer advocates. They took seriously the risk that consumers are prone to inadvertently grant security interests in their savings or retirement accounts. In their defense, there exists some experimental evidence that decision makers in some settings systematically make erroneous probability judgments or inferences. See Eldar Shafir & Robyn A. LeBoeuf, Rationality, 53 Ann. Rev. Psychol. 491 (2002); Choices, Values, and Frames (Daniel Kahneman & Amos Tversky eds. 2000). These judgments or inferences can result in misestimates of the probability of events or overconfidence or underconfidence in predictions. A consumer's estimate of its prospects of default or repayment might be subject to such errors. However, even if consumers often are subject to such misjudgments or misestimates, 9–109(d)(13)'s exclusion isn't responsive to the problem. This is because 9–109(d)(13)'s exclusion doesn't prevent consumers from granting security interests in deposit accounts as original collateral; it only prevents the transaction from being governed by Article 9. Common law or extra-Article 9 statutory law controls instead. Further, as noted above, the exclusion in any case can be circumvented by having the consumer-debtor turn its deposit account into original collateral covered by Article 9, such as a certificate of deposit or investment property. In that case, parties can "transact into" Article 9—with additional transaction costs. Thus, 9–109(d)(13)'s exclusion apparently only increases the costs of taking security interests in deposit accounts in consumer transactions.

Two factors unique to deposit accounts complicate their use as collateral. When customers deposit money in banks, they enter into a debtor-creditor relationship with the banks in which the deposits are maintained. A deposit represents a liability of the depository bank to its depositor. The depositor therefore becomes a creditor of the bank and has a right to payment from the bank in the amount of the deposit. The customer may use this payment right as collateral, but the most common secured transaction in deposit accounts is one in which the security interest in the right to payment is created in favor of the depositary bank itself. Hence, the bank finds itself as, in effect, both the account debtor and the secured party.

A second complication is the existence of the bank's traditional right of setoff. Under the common law, a bank that has lent money to a customer has the right to offset the amount owing on a loan in default against a deposit account of the customer maintained in that bank. Since banks rarely loan money to debtors who do not have deposit accounts in the lender bank, the bank's right of setoff usually parallels any rights the bank may have under a security interest in the account. The bank's setoff right can be exercised against both a secured party with security interest in the deposit account and creditors garnishing the account. A common practice is for a lending bank to require the debtor to maintain a "compensating balance" in its deposit account equal to a fixed percentage of the amount of the loan, against which the bank may offset if the debtor defaults on the loan. Setoff may be accomplished informally by the bank's merely debiting the deposit account for the amount owed the bank. In everything but name, the amount of the deposit account subject to setoff is collateral and the bank's setoff right against it a security interest. Thus, the bank's setoff right is so similar in function to a security interest that Bankruptcy Code § 506(a)(1) classifies the right of a creditor to offset as a "secured claim."

Section 9–109(d)(10) excludes setoff rights from Article 9's scope, with two exceptions. The first is 9–340, which allows the depositary bank to exercise setoff against a bank account in which a secured party holds a security interest. This gives the bank exercising its setoff right priority in the deposit account, to the extent of the amount setoff, as against the secured party. Section 9–340 does not create the depository bank's setoff rights; these setoff rights are created under non-Article 9 law or by contract. Instead, 9–340 recognizes these setoff rights and allows the depository bank to exercise them. The second exception to 9–109(d)(10)'s exclusion relates to defenses or claims of an account debtor. Section 9–404 basically subjects the assignee to defenses available to the account debtor against the assignor, unless a rule of law provides otherwise. Strictly, this rule doesn't apply to a bank's right of setoff. Nonetheless, courts speak of 9–404 as giving the account debtor a right of setoff against the assignee's security interest.

2. PRIORITY RULES

a. CONTROL

As noted in Chapter 7, when Revised Article 8 was drafted a few years before current Article 9, the drafters adopted the concept of control as the method for both attachment and perfection of security interests in investment property. Article 8's drafters, for reasons explained in Chapter 7, thought necessary for the systemic safety of stock and bond markets that a single entity be in a position of full control over the transfer of securities without having to seek the consent of the debtor or other secured parties to liquidate the collateral expeditiously. Article 9 has taken the control concept out of its original context of securities markets and applied it to deposit accounts, perhaps on the rationale that security interests in deposit accounts could have an impact on the structural security of the banking system. Thus, the attachment (9–203(b)(3)(D)), perfection (9–312(b)(1), 9–314(a)), and priority (9–327) of a security interest in a deposit account depends on whether the secured party has "control" under 9–104.

Section 9–104 provides in part:

(a)   A secured party has control of a deposit account if:

    (1)   the secured party is the bank with which the deposit account is maintained;

    (2)   the debtor, secured party, and bank have agreed in a signed record that the bank will comply with instructions originated by the secured party directing disposition of the funds in the account without further consent by the debtor;

    (3)   the secured party becomes the bank's customer with respect to the deposit account; or

    (4)   another person, other than the debtor:

        (A) has control of the deposit account and acknowledges that it has control on behalf of the secured party; or

        (B) obtains control of the deposit account after having acknowledged that it will obtain control of the deposit account on behalf of the secured party.

Hence, a third-party lender obtains control in three circumstances: when, with the debtor's consent, the lender and debtor obtain the depositary bank's agreement to act on the lender's instructions, when the account is placed in the name of the lender, making it the depositary bank's customer, or someone who has or obtains control of the account acknowledges that it has control on the lender's behalf. On the other hand, a depositary bank gains control merely by obtaining a security interest in the deposit account. Simpler methods of establishing perfection and priority in a third-party lender, such as filing a finance statement or notification of the bank where the deposit is held, are rejected. Control is the sole method of perfection for security interests created in deposit accounts as original collateral. See 9–312(b)(1) and Comment 2 to 9–104. See In re Hawaiian Telecom Communications, Inc., 2009 WL 2575663 (Bankr. D.Haw.2009).

Why perfection by control rather than by filing? The answer isn't clear. Security interests in deposit accounts resemble those in investment securities, and somewhat analogous laws apparently seemed appropriate to the drafters. However, the resemblance isn't telling: the drafters have allowed filing as an alternative method of perfection for investment property, controllable electronic records and controllable payment rights. Another factor favoring control over filing in the minds of the drafters was their concern about making it too easy to create security interests in deposit accounts. Under a filing regime, secured parties might sweep deposit accounts into the coverage of their security interests as a matter of course by boilerplate clauses without actually relying on them in extending credit. Secured parties might enjoy windfalls and debtors might suffer the unexpected loss of their bank balances. The view taken was that if creditors have to exercise control over the deposit accounts in order to effect perfection and to enjoy priority, they will do so only if they are in fact relying on the deposit account in granting the credit. Thus, the drafters treat deposit accounts very differently from other types of personal property. For other types of personal property, Article 9 makes it very easy to perfect security interests in property now owned or hereafter acquired, without caring much about what the secured party relied upon.

The drafters' justification for the special treatment of deposit accounts is weak, for three reasons. First, the justification applies equally to every type of collateral. Filing always carries the risk of a financing statement covering collateral that the secured party isn't relying upon and of which a debtor may be unaware. The risk isn't peculiar to deposit accounts. Thus, if the risk of "windfall" or "unexpected" coverage is enough to prevent filing as a perfection method for deposit accounts, it should also be enough to prevent filing as a perfection method for all types of collateral. Second, it's unclear whether the total costs associated with perfection are reduced by requiring control. When filing isn't a permissible perfection method, the generally increased cost of control over filing is borne only by relying secured creditors (and ultimately the debtor). Secured creditors who otherwise would rely on collateral described in a financing statement take control; creditors who would not rely remain unperfected with respect to deposit accounts. The increased cost of taking control per creditor, summed over the number of relying secured creditors, could increase the total costs of perfecting security interests in a deposit account. Whether total perfection costs are increased by requiring control depends on the size of the increased cost for each relying secured creditor and the number of such creditors in the population of secured creditors. The drafters make no estimate of these numbers. Third, a better response to the risk of "windfall" or "unexpected" coverage is more disclosure, not preventing filing as a perfection method. Requiring more detailed collateral descriptions in financing statements, for instance, is a low-cost means of preventing unexpected loss by debtors. Section 9–108(e) already treats as insufficient collateral descriptions only by type with respect to certain items or in consumer transactions. This works to require increased disclosure in the areas covered by 9–108(e), and the same could be extended to deposit accounts.

b. SECURITY INTERESTS IN DEPOSIT ACCOUNTS AS PROCEEDS OF OTHER COLLATERAL

The priority provisions of Article 9 with respect to deposit accounts are complex. They are best considered in two prototypic cases. The first case is the common one in which third-party lenders have security interests in deposit accounts as proceeds of other collateral in which a lender has a security interest. The second case is one in which both a third-party lender and a depository bank have security interests in the deposit account the bank maintains as original collateral.

Case #1. Debtor, a retailer, granted SP a security interest in its inventory and proceeds, which SP perfected by filing a financing statement covering "all Debtor's personal property." Buyers of goods from Debtor's inventory usually paid either by check or by use of unsecured credit cards issued by Debtor. Debtor deposited the checks and payments received on the credit card accounts, usually checks, in the deposit account it maintained in Bank. At the time Debtor opened its account with Bank, it granted a security interest in the account to Bank to secure all its existing and future obligations to Bank. Bank subsequently granted credit to Debtor but did not file a financing statement. At the time Debtor defaulted on its debt to SP, the deposit account held $100,000, all identifiable proceeds of the disposition of the inventory collateral. SP claimed the amount of the deposit account as cash proceeds (defined in 9–102(a)(9) as including deposit accounts) in which it had a perfected security interest under 9–315(d), the priority of which dated from the time it filed on the inventory. 9–322(b)(1). Who has priority in the contents of the deposit account?

Bank prevails in this priority dispute under 9–327(1), which provides that a security interest held by a secured party having control has priority over the security interest of a secured party that does not have control. SP's perfected security interest in the account does not give it control, but Bank has control under 9–104(a)(1), which provides that if the bank in which the deposit account is maintained has a security interest in the account, it has control. Did Bank rely on its security interest in Debtor's deposit account in granting credit to Debtor? The most valuable lesson to be learned from Article 9's provisions on deposit accounts is that once proceeds are deposited in a deposit account in which the depositary bank has a security interest, the security interest in the proceeds is likely to be subordinated to the bank's security interest. See Kentucky Highlands Inv. Corp. v. Bank of Corbin, 217 S.W.3d 851 (Ky. Ct.App.2006). The advice universally given to banks after enactment of current Article 9 is to take security interests as a matter of course upon opening a commercial deposit account to secure existing balances and future advances. Now you know why.

PROBLEM

Change the facts of Case #1 in one respect. Owing to the negligence of Bank's counsel, Bank failed to take a security interest in Debtor's deposit account before it learned of SP's claim. (i) Can Bank gain priority by taking a security interest from Debtor in the deposit account after SP's claim arose? That is, is there any temporal requirement in 9–327? (ii) Can Bank invoke its state-law right of setoff to gain priority over SP's security interest in the proceeds? See 9–340, 9–341, and Bank One, N.A. v. First National Bank of Baird, 2003 WL 22137171 (N.D. Tex. Sept. 16, 2003).

c.   SECURITY INTERESTS IN DEPOSIT ACCOUNTS AS ORIGINAL COLLATERAL

Case #2. Debtor, an entrepreneur, maintained a substantial savings account in Bank, which Debtor wished to use as collateral for a loan from Lender. Lender's due diligence inquiry uncovered the information that Bank had taken a security interest in Debtor's account at the time it was opened and subsequently advanced funds to Debtor, but Lender could find no financing statement on record. Ultimately, Lender refused to advance the funds to Debtor unless it could perfect its security interest in the account by control. Lender obtained control under 9–104(a)(2) by obtaining an agreement from Bank, with the consent of Debtor, that Bank would act on the Lender's instructions without further consent by Debtor. At the time Debtor defaulted on her obligation to Lender, Debtor was in default on a loan that Bank had previously made to Debtor. (i) Which creditor is prior with respect to the deposit account, Lender or Bank? (ii) Can Bank refuse to enter into such an agreement? (iii) Would the result in this Illustration differ if Debtor and Bank had agreed that the savings account be placed in Lender's name?

In order of the questions raised about Case #2: (i) Bank is prior under 9–327(3) even if it agrees to grant Lender control over the account under 9–104(a)(2). This result must seem extraordinary to Lender, given the consent on the part of Bank to Lender's assertion of control. The result is explained in Comment 4 to 9–327: "A rule of this kind enables banks to extend credit to their depositors without the need to examine either the public record or their own records to determine whether another party might have a security interest in the deposit account." One might ask why perfection under 9–104(a)(2) by agreement with a depositary bank is in the statute. It gives third-party lenders no reliable protection against depositary banks. True, it would allow third-party lenders to prevail against other secured creditors or trustees in bankruptcy, but depositary banks would presumably prevail over third-party lenders who have perfected by agreement under 9–104(a)(2) even though the depositary bank's security interest wasn't even created until after the lender had advanced funds. There are no temporal conditions to the application of 9–327(3). See Comment 4e. to 9–101.

(ii)   Section 9–342 allows Bank to refuse to enter into a 9–104(a)(2) agreement like the one in this Illustration.

(iii) Lender is protected against Bank in only two instances. First, when Lender acquires control under 9–104(a)(3) by becoming the bank's "customer" with respect to the account. "Customer" is defined in 4–104(a)(5) as meaning "a person having an account with a bank." Thus, if the account is placed in the name of Lender, it becomes the customer of Bank and, as such, would have the right to withdraw funds from or close the account. Under 9–327(4), Lender would be prior to Bank. The statute is not clear on whether this result would follow if Lender had merely become a joint holder of the account with Debtor. The second means Lender can use to protect itself is to enter into a subordination agreement with Bank under 9–339 in which the rights of Lender and Bank are spelled out in detail. The standard deposit account control agreement lenders use provides for the subordination to the secured party's security interest of any interest the depository bank acquires in the customer's deposit account. See Model Deposit Account Control Agreement § 4 Prac. L. Inst. (No. 8706, 2006).

PROBLEM

Change the facts in Case #2 to these: Debtor owed Bank a substantial sum on an unpaid loan. Lender entered into an agreement with Debtor in which Debtor agreed to place her account in Bank in Lender's name in order that Lender would have control under 9–104(a)(3), and Lender agreed that if this were done, it would hold the account for Debtor's benefit, subject to Lender's rights to collect from the account if Debtor defaulted on its loan to Lender. Debtor requested Bank to place the account in Lender's name. You may assume that banks have the discretion to decline to accept persons as customers and to close unwanted accounts. (i) If Bank made the name change, would it retain the right of setting off against the deposit account the amount of Debtor's debt to Bank? See 9–340(c) and Comment 3 to 9–341. (ii) Would you advise Bank to make the name change?

d.   PROCEEDS OF DEPOSIT ACCOUNTS: SPECIAL PRIORITY RULES

Article 9 has special priority rules for proceeds of deposit accounts and other collateral in which a security interest has control priority. As noted above, the general priority rule for proceeds is that, for purposes of priority under 9–322(a)(1)'s first-to-file-or-perfect rule, the time of filing or perfection in the collateral is the time of filing or perfection in proceeds of the collateral. 9–322(b)(1). The priority in collateral carries over to the priority in proceeds of the collateral. However, 9–322(c) and (d) are special priority rules for proceeds of collateral such as deposit accounts in which a security interest has priority by control. These rules are Article 9 at its most intricate—or most frustrating depending on one's point of view. The rules, which also apply to types of collateral other than deposit accounts, are briefly described below with reference to examples below involving deposit accounts. Other examples appear in Comments 8 and 9 to 9–322. To keep discussion focused on 9–322's special proceeds priority rules, the description below ignores the yet further complication that 9–322(f) makes 9–322(c) and (d)'s rules subject to certain other priority rules.

Section 9–322(c)'s special priority rule for proceeds applies to certain proceeds of collateral in which a security interest has nontemporal temporal priority, including control priority. The rule basically carries over the nontemporal priority of the security interest in collateral to these proceeds of the collateral. Under 9–322(c), the security interest with priority in the collateral by control also has priority in the cash proceeds of collateral if the security interest is perfected in them. The priority extends to noncash proceeds if they are of the same type as the collateral. Finally, the priority in proceeds also extends to proceeds of proceeds of the collateral if all intervening proceeds are cash proceeds, proceeds of the same type as the collateral or an account relating to the collateral. 9–322(c)(2)(A)–(C). If 9–322(c)'s special priority rule for proceeds does not apply, the priority of security interests in proceeds is determined either by 9–322(d)'s special priority rule or 9–322(a) and (b)(1)'s general priority rule for proceeds.

Consider the following example: SP perfects its security interest in Debtor's deposit account by control and Finance has perfected its security interest in Debtor's inventory by filing a financing statement covering it. Later, Debtor sells a piece of inventory for cash and deposits the cash in its deposit account, which contains only the proceeds of this sale of inventory. Still later, Debtor withdraws cash from the deposit account and retains it in a manner that makes the cash traceable to the deposit account.

The deposit account is original collateral for SP and proceeds of collateral for Finance. Because the deposit account is identifiable cash proceeds of Finance's collateral, Finance is continuously perfected in the account. 9–316(d)(2), 9–102(a)(9). The cash Debtor withdrew from its deposit account, because traceable to it, also is identifiable cash proceeds of the deposit account. Thus, both SP and Finance are continuously perfected in the cash from the deposit account under 9–315(d)(2). SP has priority over Finance in the deposit account under 9–327(1) because it has control of the deposit account while Finance does not. SP's security interest in the cash proceeds meets 9–322(c)'s requirements: SP's security interest has priority over Finance's security interest in the deposit account by control, the cash is proceeds of the account, and SP's security interest is perfected in the cash. Accordingly, under 9–322(c) SP's security interest in the cash proceeds has priority over Finance's security interest in the cash proceeds. It doesn't matter whether Finance filed its financing statement covering Debtor's inventory before SP took control of Debtor's deposit account. Section 9–322(c) extends SP's priority over Finance from Debtor's deposit account to the cash proceeds of that account.

Section 9–322(d)'s special priority rule for proceeds applies when the security interest in deposit accounts, negotiable documents, investment property or letter-of-credit rights is perfected either by control or possession ("by a method other than filing"). Under 9–322(d), conflicting security interests in the proceeds of this collateral according to priority in time of filing. This is a first-to-file priority rule, not a first-to-file-or-perfect priority rule, for proceeds. However, 9–322(e) limits the types of proceeds to which (d)'s priority rule applies. It makes subsection (d)'s first-to-file rule inapplicable to cash proceeds, chattel paper, instruments, negotiable documents, investment property or letter-of-credit rights.

As is probably apparent, 9–322(d) and (e) are not drafted in a reader-friendly manner. Comments 7 and 9 have a somewhat helpful shorthand description of 9–322(d) and (e)'s limitation on 9–322(d). Comment 7 calls collateral in which perfection can be achieved other than by filing "non-filing collateral," and Comment 9 refers proceeds in which perfection can be achieved by other than filing as "proceeds that are non-filing collateral." These sorts of proceeds can be called "non-filing proceeds" for short. The types of proceeds listed in 9–322(e) are non-filing proceeds. Filing proceeds, which are not on that list, are accounts, commercial tort claims, goods, and general intangibles including payment intangibles and nonnegotiable documents of title ("the proceeds of the collateral are not. . ."). Put in these terms, 9–322(e) limits 9–322(d)'s first-to-file rule to filing proceeds of non-filing collateral. If the proceeds of collateral are non-filing proceeds of non-filing collateral, priority in them is determined either by 9–322(c)'s special rule or 9–322(a) and (b)(1)'s's general rule for priority in proceeds.

Comment 7 and 9's description of "non-filing collateral" is potentially confusing because a security interest in some of the items of collateral identified by the term, such as chattel paper and investment property, can be perfected by filing. Probably a simpler description of 9–322(d), together with (e), is that its first-to-file rule displaces 9–322(a)(1)'s first-to-file-or-perfect rule for proceeds that themselves are not collateral subject to the control and possession priorities for the types of collateral listed in 9–322(d). It would have been better had 9–322(d) simply listed the types of proceeds to which its first-to-file priority does apply.

A variant of the example presented above illustrates 9–322(d)'s application. Suppose Debtor did not withdraw cash from its deposit account. Instead, assume that Debtor purchased a piece of inventory with funds from its deposit account. Assume also that Debtor immediately delivered the inventory to SP on SP's demand. The facts are otherwise those of the previous example.

The acquired inventory is proceeds of the deposit account. In addition, both SP and Finances' security interests in the inventory are continuously perfected under 9–315(d)(3): SP because it took possession of the acquired inventory, and Finance because its financing statement covered the acquired inventory. Although SP has priority over Finance with respect to its security interest in Debtor's deposit account under 9–327(1), the acquired inventory is not cash proceeds of the deposit account or proceeds of the same type as SP's collateral (the deposit account). Thus, 9–322(c)(2) does not apply to give SP's security interest priority over Finance's security interest with respect to acquired inventory. Instead, either 9–322(d)'s special priority rule or 9–322(b)(1)'s general priority rule for proceeds applies. On the facts of the example, 9–322(d) determines SP and Finance's priority in Debtor's acquired inventory. Because inventory is not among the types of proceeds to which 9–322(e) makes 9–322(d) inapplicable, 9–322(d) governs priority in the inventory as proceeds of Debtor's deposit account. Only Finance filed its financing statement covering Debtor's inventory. Thus, under 9–322(d)'s first-to-file rule, Finance's security interest in the acquired inventory has priority over SP's security interest in the acquired inventory. The fact that SP was perfected in the inventory by possession (and temporarily perfected automatically) is irrelevant under the first-to-file rule.

Consider 9–322's proceeds priority provisions with respect to the priority of security interests in proceeds in connection with the following Problem.

PROBLEM

SP obtained control of Debtor's deposit account in May in accordance with its security agreement with Debtor. In June, in accordance with its security agreement with Debtor, Finance obtained control of the same deposit account. Debtor purchased equipment with funds from the deposit account on July 5. Today is December 1. Debtor continues to use the equipment and neither SP nor Finance have taken any further action. Who has priority in the equipment Debtor purchased? See 9–315(c) and (d), 9–322(a)(3), 9–322(c) and (d) .

e. CRITIQUE

The principal accomplishment of Article 9's provisions on security interests in deposit accounts is to provide for the first time a coherent legal structure governing a subject area that had been uncertain and confused. Given the strongly held and contradictory views of the participants in the drafting process, this is no small achievement. The deposit account provisions have been most successful in delineating and clarifying priority rules respecting conflicting security interests in cash proceeds. Now it is finally clear that if a third-party lender allows its debtor to deposit proceeds with a bank, the bank's interest will almost always take priority over the lender's interest, either because of the bank's inevitable security interest in the deposit account or its right to set off against that account. 9–327(1), 9–340. The lender can protect itself only by proceeding under 9–104(a)(3) and becoming the customer of the account, a step that presumably must be approved by the bank. 9–327(4). Non-bank lenders must value their rights in cash proceeds in light of this severe limitation, which reverses most of the pre-revision law on the subject.

Article 9 is less successful in dealing with its major innovation: extending coverage to security interests in deposit accounts as original collateral. One might have hoped that in providing a legal framework for creating security interests in deposit accounts as original collateral, the drafters had taken some steps toward unlocking the great wealth in deposit accounts in a way that would enable debtors to use this value as security for needed credit extensions. But instead of making it easier for debtors to use their deposit accounts as security for needed credit, Article 9 makes it very difficult—sometimes impossible—for creditors to take reliable security interests in deposit accounts.

The indelible message of Article 9 is that debtors cannot create reliable security interests in deposit accounts as original collateral without the consent of the depositary bank. Only by obtaining control by becoming the bank's customer can a third-party lender enjoy priority over the bank's security interest or offset rights (9–327(4)) and, presumably, that can be done only with the bank's acquiescence. Article 9's provisions on security interests in deposit accounts as original collateral probably will languish as unused default provisions, ignored by informed participants who will proceed under 9–339 to work out a subordination agreement with the bank that will clear up the details that Article 9's provisions omit. If a depositary bank is willing to give up its priority rights in a deposit account by agreeing to accept the lender as a customer under 9–104(a)(3), it should be even more willing to enter into an agreement that allows the parties, rather than the sparse provisions of Article 9, to adjust their rights. Private ordering likely will preempt the field, leaving the Code provisions for the unwary.

Surprisingly, a risk of relying on a subordination agreement to work out the priorities between lenders and depository banks in deposit accounts is the possible bankruptcy of the debtor. If the third-party lender does not perfect its rights by taking control under 9–104, its security interest can be avoided in bankruptcy. This is true because control is the exclusive method for perfection of security interest in deposit accounts as original collateral; filing is of no effect. Thus, even though the parties enter into a subordination agreement, the lender must be sure that it also obtains control under 9–104 so that the lender's interest survives bankruptcy.

The draconian effect of these provisions is that if the bank withholds its consent to the lender's obtaining control, the lender's security interest is not only unperfected, it is *unperfectable*. This poses a unique situation under Article 9: a debtor and a creditor cannot perfect a security interest in a right to payment owed to the debtor by the bank without the consent of the account debtor, the bank. Even when the bank is not a creditor of the debtor, if it wishes to preserve debtor's deposit account as a source that it may setoff against for future claims, it has the arbitrary power to block secured parties from perfecting a security interest in the debtor's deposit account by withholding its consent to control.

It is not clear why Article 9 does not allow lenders to perfect their security interest against lien creditors and trustees in bankruptcy by filing. The Article 8 control concept for investment property, 8–106(d), is accompanied by perfection by filing. A broker holding a securities account can prevent a secured party from gaining control by withholding its consent but the secured party can perfect by filing without the consent of the broker. 9–312(a). Article 9's drafters probably borrowed the control concept from Article 8 because some investment property, like money market accounts, is so similar to deposit accounts. Why then should a lender be able to safeguard its security interest in a money market account against lien creditors and trustees in bankruptcy by filing a financing statement if it cannot do the same with respect to a bank account?

A depositary bank's complete power over perfection of a security interest by a lender in a deposit account is unnecessary to protect the bank. Under 9–341, without regard to perfection, depositary banks have no duties to secured parties with respect to deposit accounts that they don't agree to. The depositary bank's own priority is unaffected by a lender's perfection in the same account under 9–327 and 9–340. Thus, to the extent the control rule is intended to obviate the need for depositaries to search for filings, it is not needed. Since lenders can have a security interest that is perfected by filing in a deposit account as proceeds of other collateral, there seems little reason to deny perfection by filing for a security interest in a deposit account as original collateral.

Allowing perfection only by control is inefficient: it increases the cost of issuing secured credit without yielding a corresponding benefit. By requiring the depository bank's signed agreement, 9–104(a)(2) adds another party to the bargain between the debtor and secured creditor. Perfection of a security interest in favor of someone other than the depository bank requires concluding an agreement between the debtor, secured creditor and depository bank. The additional party creates an additional transaction cost. The cost of obtaining the bank's agreement may be substantial. (Some banks in Louisiana apparently include anti-pledge clauses in their standard deposit account contracts. See PEB Study Group, Uniform Commercial Code—Article 9: Appendices to Report 341 (1992). Altering a term in a standard contract requires negotiation.) Even if the depositor decides not to deal with its depository bank and instead transfers its deposit account to a compliant bank, an additional transaction cost is incurred. By comparison, perfection by filing only requires a bargain between debtor and secured creditor, and one fewer transaction. Because filing is a cheaper substitute than requiring the depository bank's agreement for control, 9–104(a)(2) increases the debtor's costs in using deposit accounts as collateral and reduces its net benefit from issuing debt secured by them.

Before revised Article 9, very few deposit accounts apparently were used as original collateral. It therefore is unclear whether most depositors would prefer to use their accounts as collateral with a change in law. See Eldon H. Reiley & Tom Stieber, Proposals to Expand the Scope of Article 9: Should Deposit Accounts, as Original Collateral, be Included?, 30 UCC L.J. 82 (1997); PEB Study Group, Uniform Commercial Code—Article 9: Appendices to Report 332 (1992). However, given uncertainty about depositors' preferences and the presence of higher transaction costs under Article 9 than under a rule allowing for perfection by filing, Article 9 arguably sets the rule for perfection incorrectly.

K. CASH PROCEEDS

1. PRIORITY

This Chapter has traced the priority of the first-to-file-or-perfect secured party against conflicting interests in the original collateral and in the proceeds of its disposition. The previous section considered the priority of the secured party in proceeds deposited in a deposit account. This section describes the priority of the secured party with respect to those to whom the debtor has made payments from the deposit account. What happens to the secured party's interest in the proceeds in the account if the debtor pays its bills by drawing on the account? If the secured party could recover money paid by the debtor from its deposit account to its employees or trade creditors, the value of the debtor's payments to them would decline. If the secured party cannot recover the debtor paid money paid to its employees or trade creditors, the secured party will increase the interest charge on its loan accordingly to reflect the increased risk that it won't recover the outstanding amount of the loan. It is not hard to predict which of these alternatives Article 9 selects.

a. TRANSFEREES OF FUNDS UNDER SECTION 9–332

Section 9–332 clarifies the law on this subject. It provides:

(a) A transferee of money takes the money free of a security interest if the transferee receives possession of the money without acting in collusion with the debtor in violating the rights of the secured party.

(b) A transferee of funds from a deposit account takes the funds free of a security interest in the deposit account if the transferee receives the funds without acting in collusion with the debtor in violating the rights of the secured party.

(c) A transferee of electronic money takes the money free of a
security interest if the transferee obtains control of the
money without acting in collusion with the debtor in
violating the rights of the secured party.

The section gives exceptional protection to the transferee not often found
in commercial law. It does so by stating a nontemporal priority rule with
few restrictions on the rule's application. With one limitation, under 9–
332(a) a transferee that receives money (i.e., tangible currency) takes free
of a security interest in the money. Also subject to the limitation, the
same rule applies to transferees who get control of electronic money or
receive funds from a deposit account. By "taking free" of the earlier
security interest, the transferee has priority in money or funds from a
deposit account received, or electronic money over which it gets control.

The breadth of 9–332's protection is the result of the wide scope of
its terms and the absence of restrictions usually present in comparable
rules in commercial law. Although "transferee" is undefined, a transferee
does not have to be a purchaser. A purchaser is a party to a voluntary
transaction with the debtor (1–201(b)(30)), while a transferee may be a
party to an involuntary transaction. A lien creditor levying on the
debtor's property, although not purchaser, therefore can be a transferee.
The debtor, however, is not a transferee; see Comment 2A to 9–332.
Further, 9–332's protection does not require the transferee to give value
or act in reliance on the money or funds from a deposit account received
from the debtor. Nor does its protection require the transferee to take in
good faith. Section 9–332 only requires that the transferee receive
possession of the tangible money or receive funds from a deposit account,
or get control of electronic money. This requirement, added by the 2022
Amendments, resolves uncertainty in the case law as to when a transfer
to the transferee occurs. The "receipt" requirement overrules cases that
have ruled that a transferee takes free before funds have been dispersed
to the transferee. See, e.g., Stierwalt v. Associated Third Party
Administrators, 2016 U.S. Dist. LEXIS 68744 (N.D. Cal. May 25, 2016).

Tangible money, funds from a deposit account and electronic money
are transferred when the transferee acquires an interest in them.
However, neither 9–332 nor any of Article 9's other provisions determine
when a transferee acquires this interest. Non-Article 9 law instead
dictates when the transferee acquires the relevant property interest. See
Comment 2A to 9–332. Nonetheless, some generalizations safely can be
made as to when a transfer occurs. If a depositor withdraws currency
from a deposit account in which proceeds are deposited that is subject to
a security interest and delivers it to another person, tangible money has
been transferred to the recipient. Accordingly, 9–332(a) protects the
recipient against the claim of a secured party. For its part, 9–332(b)
protects the transferee of funds from a deposit account who receives the
funds. Funds in a deposit account represent a claim the depositor has
against the depository bank in the amount of the account balance. A

transfer of funds involves a transfer of credits to deposit accounts. If the transferee and debtor bank at the same depository institution, a transfer of funds from the debtor's deposit account occurs when the depository bank credits the transferee's deposit account and debits the debtor's deposit account in the amount of the credit. At that point the transferee receives the funds. If the debtor draws a check on its checking account in favor of another person, the payee who has deposited the check with its own bank receives the funds when its deposit account is credited in the amount of the check. In both cases 9–332(b) protects the recipient of the funds.

Section 9–332's single limitation is that the transferee who receives money, gets control of electronic money or receives funds from a deposit account not collude with the debtor to violate the secured party's rights. As Comment 4 to 9–332 explains: "To deal with the question of the 'bad actor,' this section borrows "collusion" language from Article 8 [8–115, 8–503(e)]. . . . This is the most protective (i.e. least stringent) of the various standards now found in the UCC." The noncollusion limitation requires that the transferee not collude at the time it receives tangible money or funds from a deposit account, or obtains control over electronic money.

Neither 9–332 nor Comment 4 elaborate on the sort of behavior that makes for collusion. Apart from Comment 4's reference to the "bad actor," 9–332 does not say when a transferee's behavior counts as collusive, thereby preventing the transferee from taking free of a security interest in money or funds from a deposit account. Pretty clearly, collusion requires some sort of coordination between the debtor and the transferee. Comment 4 agrees, stating that the collusion standard is a more demanding standard than "without knowledge." As a result, a transferee who knows its action violates the rights of a secured party, but is not coordinating its behavior with the debtor to do so, has not colluded. See In re Tuscany Energy, LLC, 581 B.R. 681 (Bankr. S.D. Fla.2018); but cf. Banner Bank v. First Commercial Bank, 854 F.Supp.2d, 846, 857 (D. Mont.2012) ("willful ignorance" satisfies 9–332's collusion standard). Beyond coordinated behavior, what more does 9–332's collusion standard require? Article 8 of the UCC, whose "collusion" language 9–332 borrows, states that the principles in the Restatement (Second) of Torts 876 (1979) govern the collusion standard. Comment 5 to 8–115. According to Section 876 of the Restatement (Second), there is collusion if two parties act in concert for a purpose that is illegal, fraudulent or otherwise wrongful to the injured party.

Comment 3 to 9–332 states the policy basis for 9–332's unusually broad protection of transferees:

> Broad protection for transferees helps to ensure that security interests in deposit accounts do not impair the free flow of funds. It also minimizes the likelihood that a secured party will enjoy a claim to whatever the transferee purchases with the funds. Rules concerning recovery of payments traditionally have

placed a high value on finality. The opportunity to upset a completed transaction, or even to place a completed transaction in jeopardy by bringing suit against the transferee of funds, should be severely limited. . . .

In giving broad protection to transferees, 9–332 increases the value to transferees of money or funds transferred to them. This is because previous security interests do not continue in the money or funds transferred. But 9–332's broad protection comes with a cost: it diminishes the value of collateral or it proceeds in the form of money, electronic money or deposit accounts by cutting off previous security interests in them. Section 9–332's drafters apparently judge that the 9–332's broad protection increases the value of the money or funds to transferees more than it diminishes their value as collateral or proceeds to secured parties.

In addition to its failure to articulate the standard of collusion, 9–332 leaves unresolved other questions that might arise over its application. One concerns when a transfer occurs for purposes of 9–332. As noted above, 9–332 leaves this matter to non-Article 9 law, and that law might itself be unclear in particular cases as to when a recipient acquires a property interest in tangible money, funds from a deposit account or electronic money. Another unaddressed matter concerns 9–332(c)'s reference to a transferee of "funds from a deposit account." Under 9–332(c) a transferee in receipt of the funds takes free of a security interest in the deposit account. Does the transferee thereby take free of a security interest in the funds in the account? Article 9 does not deal explicitly with the relationship between the deposit account and funds in it. By allowing a transferee of "funds from a deposit account" to take free, 9–332(b) seems to suggest that a deposit account contains funds. As a perhaps inevitable result, courts disagree as to whether a transfer that cuts off a security interest in the deposit account also cuts off a security interest in the funds in the deposit account. The case below asks whether a deposit account contains funds at all.

Cortland Sav. & Banking Co. v. Platinum Rapid Funding Grp., Ltd.

Ohio Court of Appeals, 2021
106 UCC Rep. Serv.2d 886

■ **Opinion by:** THOMAS R. WRIGHT.

Platinum Rapid Funding Group, Ltd. ("Platinum") appeals the decision denying its motion for summary judgment and granting partial summary judgment to The Cortland Savings and Banking Company ("Cortland Bank"). We reverse and remand.

Cortland Bank is a community bank in Northeastern Ohio. On March 19, 2018, Cortland Bank, 21st Century Concrete Construction, Inc. ("21st Century"), and Patrick J. Butler as president of 21st Century, entered into a written business loan agreement, whereby Cortland Bank loaned 21st Century $1,000,000 pursuant to a promissory note and a commercial security agreement. The commercial security agreement granted Cortland Bank a security interest in numerous assets owned by 21st Century, including its accounts. Pursuant to the business loan agreement, 21st Century maintained a deposit account with Cortland Bank ("the checking account"). Cortland Bank filed a UCC-1 Financing Statement with the Ohio Secretary of State identifying the collateral involved in the transaction.

Platinum is a "New York corporation engaged in the business of providing businesses with working capital funding for operating expenses by virtue of purchasing future business receivables and sales proceeds from merchants at a discount." In April, June, and October 2018, Platinum and 21st Century entered into three merchant agreements, whereby Platinum agreed to make two advances of $250,000 and one advance of $846,000 to 21st Century in exchange for a percentage of 21st Century's future receivables in the total amount of $1,526,000. 21st Century authorized Platinum to withdraw weekly payments from its checking account maintained at Cortland Bank until the amount owed to Platinum was paid in full. Between March 2018 and March 2019, $869,250 was transferred from the checking account to Platinum.

21st Century defaulted on its loan with Cortland Bank. On April 29, 2019, Cortland Bank received a judgment against 21st Century and Butler in the approximate amount of $1,000,000. Thereafter, Cortland Bank filed a complaint against 21st Century, Butler, and Platinum. Subsequently, Cortland Bank amended its complaint, removing 21st Century as a named defendant. With respect to Platinum, Cortland Bank sought return of all funds transferred to Platinum from the checking account prior to 21st Century defaulting on the Cortland Bank loan. Cortland Bank alleged claims of conversion, unjust enrichment, impairment of a security interest, and tortious interference with contract. Cortland Bank and Platinum filed competing summary judgment motions. The trial court denied Platinum's motion and granted Cortland Bank's motion on its claims for conversion, impairment of security interest, and tortious interference with contract and certified that there was no just cause for delay pursuant to Civ.R. 54. * * *

Here, the trial court's decision turns largely upon statutory construction. . . .

This matter involves Article 9 of the Uniform Commercial Code ("UCC") as adopted in Ohio Revised Code Chapter 1309, as it applies to "[a] transaction, regardless of its form, that creates a security interest in personal property or fixtures by contract[.]" R.C. 1309.109(A)(1). Pursuant to R.C. 1309.201(A), "[e]xcept as otherwise provided . . ., a security agreement is effective according to its terms between the parties, against purchasers of the collateral, and against creditors."

There does not appear to be any dispute that Cortland Bank held a security interest in 21st Century's accounts receivable and deposit account effective against Platinum pursuant to R.C. 1309.201(A). In addition, Cortland Bank's interest in the accounts receivable attached to proceeds from the accounts receivable pursuant to R.C. 1309.315(A), which provides:

Except as otherwise provided in this chapter and in division (B) of section 1302.44 of the Revised Code:

(1) A security interest or agricultural lien continues in collateral notwithstanding sale, lease, license, exchange, or other disposition thereof unless the secured party authorized the disposition free of the security interest or agricultural lien; and

(2) A security interest attaches to any identifiable proceeds of collateral.

However, the parties dispute the meaning of R.C. 1309.332, which provides:

(A) A transferee of money takes the money free of a security interest [if the transferee receives possession of the money without acting] in collusion with the debtor in violating the rights of the secured party. * * *

(B) A transferee of funds from a deposit account takes the funds free of a security interest in the deposit account [if the transferee receives the funds without acting] in collusion with the debtor in violating the rights of the secured party.

Neither party argues that subsection (A) applies. However, based upon R.C. 1309.332(B), Platinum maintains that the funds it received from 21st Century's account at Cortland Bank were transferred free of Cortland Bank's interest.

The trial court disagreed, concluding that because the "funds from a deposit account" are different than the "deposit account" itself, R.C. 1309.332(B) strips a secured party's interest in "the deposit account," leaving intact its interest in the "funds." In reaching this conclusion, the trial court relied on the Fifth Circuit's decision in *In re Tusa-Expo Holdings, Inc. v. Knoll, Inc.*, 811 F.3d 786, 798 (5th Cir.2016). There, the court found that the plain language of Texas' adoption of this UCC provision (identical to that adopted in Ohio) does not "even address, must less strip, a security interest that encumbers *the funds contained in the deposit account*." (Emphasis added.) *Id.* at 796.

However, the Fifth Circuit did not consider the definition of an "account" under Article 9. Despite ordinary parlance, a "deposit account" under Article 9 *is not* a device containing funds. *See* Merriam-Webster Dictionary, https://merriam-webster.com/dictionary/deposit%20account (defining a deposit account as "a bank account in which people keep money that they want to save: savings account.") (accessed August 5, 2021). Instead, Article 9 defines a "deposit account" as "a demand, time, savings, passbook, or similar *account* maintained with a bank but does not include investment property or accounts evidenced by an instrument." (Emphasis added.) R.C. 1309.102(A)(29). The UCC defines an "account" as, with certain exclusions,

> *a right to payment of a monetary obligation*, whether or not earned by performance, (i) for property that has been or is to be sold, leased, licensed, assigned, or otherwise disposed of, (ii) for services rendered or to be rendered, (iii) for a policy of insurance issued or to be issued, (iv) for a secondary obligation incurred or to be incurred, (v) for energy provided or to be provided, (vi) for the use or hire of a vessel under a charter or other contract, (vii) arising out of the use of a credit or charge card or information contained on or for use with the card, or (viii) as winnings in a lottery or other game of chance operated or sponsored by a state, governmental unit of a state, or person licensed or authorized to operate the game by a state or governmental unit of a state.

(Emphasis added.) R.C. 1309.102(A)(2)(a).

Accordingly, for purposes of Article 9, a deposit account is by statutory definition a right to payment from a bank of the money that was deposited by the customer. Pursuant to this definition, the deposit of funds in an account is the equivalent of exchanging the funds for a promise to pay. Therefore, we disagree with *In re Tusa-Expo* insofar as the court based its decision on the premise that a deposit account *contains* funds. Instead, the funds are transformed to a right to payment, i.e. the deposit account, to which the security interest attaches. However, the security interest does not attach from the deposit account to the funds ordered paid, absent collusion, pursuant to R.C. 1309.322(B).

Although we reach this conclusion based upon the statutory definition of "account," this reading of the statute is also consistent with the policy underlying R.C. 1309.332, as set forth in Official Comment 3, which provides:

> Broad protection for transferees helps to ensure that security interests in deposit accounts do not impair the free flow of funds. It also minimizes the likelihood that a secured party will enjoy a claim to whatever the transferee purchases with the funds. Rules concerning recovery of payments traditionally have placed a high value on finality. The opportunity to upset a completed transaction, or even to place a completed transaction in jeopardy by bringing suit against the transferee of funds, should be severely limited. * * *

Applying the above Article 9 provisions and definitions to this case, Cortland Bank's interest in 21st Century's accounts receivable attached to the proceeds of the accounts receivable upon payment. *See* R.C.

1309.315(A). When the proceeds were deposited to the checking account, Cortland Bank's interest attached to the deposit account, i.e. the right to payment. *See id.* Cortland Bank also had an original interest in the deposit account, i.e. the right to payment, superior to Platinum's, due to Cortland Bank's position as a secured creditor that is also the depository bank. *See* R.C. 1309.203(B)(3)(d) (security interest in a deposit account enforceable pursuant to security agreement where creditor has control of the account); R.C. 1309.104(A)(1) ("A secured party has control of a deposit account if * * * [it] is the bank with which the deposit account is maintained[.]"); and R.C. 1309.327(C) ("[e]xcept as otherwise provided * * *, a security interest held by the bank with which the deposit account is maintained has priority over a conflicting security interest held by another secured party"). However, when the funds were transferred to Platinum, R.C. 1309.332(B) operated to transfer the funds free of the interest in the right to payment, i.e. the deposit account, if there was no collusion.

Therefore, Platinum's first assigned error has merit insofar as we agree that R.C. 1309.332(B) permits Platinum, as the transferee, to take the funds free of Cortland Bank's security interest in the deposit account absent collusion, and that the trial court erred in its determination that a security interest in the funds remained intact. This is the outcome precisely contemplated by Comment 2 to R.C. 1309.332, as illustrated by Example 1 to that Comment:

> **Example 1**: Debtor maintains a deposit account with Bank A. The deposit account is subject to a perfected security interest in favor of Lender. Debtor draws a check on the account, payable to Payee. Inasmuch as the check is not the proceeds of the deposit account (it is an order to pay funds from the deposit account), Lender's security interest in the deposit account does not give rise to a security interest in the check. Payee deposits the check into its own deposit account, and Bank A pays it. Unless Payee acted in collusion with Debtor in violating Lender's rights, Payee takes the funds (the credits running in favor of Payee) free of Lender's security interest. This is true regardless of whether Payee is a holder in due course of the check and even if Payee gave no value for the check.

Although the parties raised arguments regarding collusion in their summary judgment filings, the trial court did not reach that issue, as it was unnecessary due to its construction of the statute. However, the issue of collusion is now determinative, and this matter is remanded to the trial court to address that issue in the first instance. * * *

NOTE

The court's conclusion that a deposit account does not contain funds is correct. A deposit account, as the court notes, gives the depositor a right against the depository bank to payment of the amount of the funds it deposited. Accordingly, the account balance represents the sum of the amount of money the depositor has a right to be paid by the depositor bank resulting from funds deposited at different times. The depositor's right is only against the depository bank: it isn't a right to the bank's assets. As a result, as a legal matter the deposit account doesn't contain funds. However, the court is on weaker ground when it bases its argument for this conclusion on Article 9's definition of "account" (9–102(a)(2)). Although both an account and a deposit account give a right to payment of money, their respective definitions run in parallel rather than the latter being defined in terms of the former. The definition of "deposit account" does not refer to the definition of "account;" see 9–102(a)(29). In addition, it is only an accident of language that, in Article 9's classification of collateral, "account" appears in "deposit account." To prevent an inference from the definition of "account" to "deposit account," the 2022 Amendments amend 9–102(a)(3) to provide that the term "account" applies except as used inter alia in "deposit account." See Comment 5a. to 9–102. The court's correct conclusion that a deposit account does not contain funds is reached more directly by recognizing the legal nature of a deposit account.

The trouble in 9–332(b)'s interpretation is created by 9–332(b)'s reference to "funds from a deposit account." The phrase wrongly suggests that a deposit account contains funds. Otherwise, funds can't come "from" the deposit account. Although Article 9 refers to "funds" elsewhere (e.g., 9–104(a)(2), 9–207(c)(1), Comment 5a to 9–102), it does not define or elaborate on the term. For this reason, it is hard to understand how funds can come from a deposit account without being in some way "contained in" the account. The 2022 Amendments could have avoided the trouble in 9–332(b)'s relevant phrase by reformulating the provision to eliminate the confusing expression. At a minimum, the Amendments might have explained how the phrase is to operate. Instead, Comment 2C to Amended 9–332 explains that "[t]he depositor's creditors (whether secured parties or lien creditors) do not have any interest in any *funds* from the deposit account as a result of having an interest in the deposit account (the right to payment of the bank's obligation)." The drafters of the 2022 Amendments missed the opportunity to put an end to the difficulty in understanding the appearance of "funds from a deposit account" in 9–332(b).

A better understanding of 9–332(b)'s reference to "funds from a deposit account" recognizes the legal nature of a deposit account. Funds from the deposit account are credits the depository bank issues to honor its obligations to the depositor to return what the depositor has paid the bank (plus interest). Accord Comment 2C to 9–332 (Example 2). A credit is "from" the deposit account only in the sense that the credit the depository bank issues corresponds to the bank's promise of repayment it made to the depositor when the bank took in funds from the depositor. For example, a $10 credit issued by the depositor bank in favor of a payee discharges the bank's earlier promise to repay the depositor $10 (or more) when the depositor deposited $10 (or more). Given the proximity in time between the $10 credit in the payee's favor and the bank's debit of the depositor's deposit account in the amount of $10, the $10 credit to the payee's account is the same $10 credit previously to the drawer-depositor's deposit account. The $10 credit in the payee's favor therefore represents funds "from" the depositor's account. Allowing the transferee to take the credit in its favor free of a security interest in the deposit account is 9–332(b)'s awkward way of saying that a security interest does not attach to the credit. It would have been better had 9–332(b) said just this.

PROBLEMS

Assume that SPA and SPB both have security interests in Debtor's inventory and their proceeds. Both are perfected by filing proper financing statements, and SPA filed first. Debtor deposited the cash proceeds of the sale of inventory and the collection of accounts in its deposit account in Bank, which held only proceeds from these sales and collections.

1.   Debtor drew a check on Bank payable to SPB for $100,000 and delivered it to SPB, who deposited the check in its deposit account in another bank and eventually withdrew all of the funds from that account. SPB knew about SPA's senior security interest when it received the payment. Does SPB take free of SPA's prior security interest in the funds received?

2.   Assume the facts in the first sentence of Problem 1. Debtor was in financial trouble and both SPA and SPB knew it. SPB urged Debtor to pay him before SPA because of SPB's willingness to advance credit to Debtor earlier when SPA had refused to do so. Debtor agreed to do so even although both Debtor and SPB knew that they were violating SPA's rights and that payment to SPB would probably mean that SPA would not be paid from Debtor's diminishing assets. Can SPB keep the money when SPA claims priority?

2.   TRACING PROCEEDS

A security interest in proceeds in a deposit account is a risky matter for the secured party. As described above, the debtor may drain an account by payments to transferees who take free of the security interest under 9–332. Or the debtor may commingle the proceeds in the account with nonproceeds, making it difficult for the secured party to identify the proceeds in compliance with 9–315(a)(2)'s requirement that for a security interest to continue in proceeds the proceeds must be identifiable. Although Gilmore's view was that a security interest in proceeds is lost when they are commingled with nonproceeds, 2 Gilmore, supra, § 27.4, at 736 (1965), the courts have not agreed. Section 9–315(b)(2) clarifies the law by providing that nongoods proceeds that are commingled with nonproceeds are identifiable proceeds "to the extent that the secured party identifies the proceeds by a method of tracing, including application of equitable principles, that is permitted under law other than this article with respect to commingled property of the type involved."

Of course, tracing rules are fictional. They do not really identify proceeds when proceeds are commingled with nonproceeds in an account.

They cannot because commingling makes identifying proceeds impossible. Rather, a tracing rule is a way of defining property rights in a commingled account. Section 9–315(b)(2) allows the use of tracing principles to designate the portion of a commingled account as proceeds of a security interest, to which the secured party is entitled. Priority in the proceeds, as identified by applicable tracing rules, is determined by Article 9's priority rules.

Most cases decided under former Article 9 permitted the use of the lowest intermediate balance rule (LIBR) as a method of tracing, and Comment 3 to 9–315 approves the use of this rule. The LIBR, borrowed from the law of trusts, has two parts. One part provides that where a trustee withdraws funds from a single account into which trust funds and personal funds have been wrongfully commingled, trust funds remain on deposit to the extent that the amount withdrawn is less than the amount of trust funds deposited. See Restatement (Second) of Trusts § 202, comms. j & k (1959). In other words, the trustee is presumed to withdraw its own funds first until the personal funds in the commingled account are dissipated. The second part is the presumption that the trustee's subsequent deposit of personal funds does not replenish trust funds previously withdrawn. See Restatement (Third) of Restitution and Unjust Enrichment § 59(2)(b) (2011). Although some case law recognizes an exception to the presumption against replenishment, the exception has been held not to apply in tracing proceeds of collateral; see Chrysler Credit Corp. v. Superior Court, 17 Cal. App.4th 1303, 1317 (Cal. Ct. App.1993). Applied to a deposit account into which proceeds of collateral are commingled with nonproceeds, the LIBR provides that the proceeds are identifiable to the extent of the lowest account balance between when the debtor deposited the proceeds and when the secured creditor claims the account balance as proceeds, provided that the proceeds thus identified cannot exceed the amount of proceeds deposited.

In practice the LIBR can be hard to apply when there are multiple deposits and withdrawals over time from the commingled account. Its application requires determining the time and amount of proceeds deposited and the lowest intermediate balance at the time of each withdrawal. This can be particularly challenging when multiple deposits and withdrawals are made over the course of a day. If the debtor deposits proceeds from different collateral into a commingled account, the LIBR identifies the portion of the account that represents proceeds. However, a tracing principle other than the LIBR is needed to identify the portion of the proceeds attributable to the different collateral. In the latter case, courts tend to supplement the LIBR with a pro rata rule to attribute portions of the proceeds to different security interests.

PROBLEMS

On May 1, Lender loaned Debtor $10,000 and perfected a security interest in all of Debtor's existing and after-acquired accounts. The loan was effectuated by Lender having Debtor's general operating account held at Bank credited in the amount of the loan. At the time, the account had a balance of $5,000. Debtor deposited cash it received from its sales activities into that account. Debtor's activity in its account is as follows.

Date	Transaction	Balance
May 1	$10,000 loan proceeds	$15,000
May 20	$1,000 deposit from accounts paid	$16,000
May 22	$2,000 withdrawn	$14,000
June 1	$13,500 withdrawn	$500
June 4	$100 withdrawn	$400
June 10	$500 deposit from inventory sold	$900
June 15	$3,000 deposit from accounts paid	$3,900

1. As of June 15, to what extent is Lender's security interest in the account balance identifiable as proceeds of its collateral?

2. On June 15, Debtor defaulted on all of its loan obligations without repaying Lender. Finance, one of Debtor's creditors, later garnished Debtor's deposit account. As between Lender and Finance, who has priority in the balance in Debtor's account? See 9–317(a)(2), 9–102(a)(52). Would the result change had Debtor not defaulted on its loan obligations to Lender?

3. Would the result change if the June 10 deposit had not been made?

4. Would the result change if Lender's security agreement granted it a security interest in "all of Debtor's existing accounts"?

5. Assume that Bank had made the $10,000 secured loan to Debtor secured by Debtor's existing and after-acquired accounts, and credited Debtor's account held at Bank in the amount of the loan. Also assume that Bank is unable to trace the proceeds of its collateral into the account into which they were deposited. On June 15, Debtor defaulted on its loan obligations to both Bank and Finance, a creditor who garnished Debtor's bank account. At the time Debtor continued to owe Bank $10,000. What are the relative priorities of their claims?

NOTES

1. Although 9–315(b)(2) clarifies the law by expressly allowing the use of tracing principles applicable under non-Article 9 law, the subsection still leaves some uncertainty. In particular, it appears to allow the use of any tracing rule to identify commingled non-goods as long as the rule is found in non-Article 9 law. The qualifying language in (b)(2), "permitted under law other than this article," places no restriction on the area of non-Article 9 law that recognizes a tracing rule. Thus, 9–315(b)(2)'s language appears to allow the secured party to choose the tracing rule that will benefit it from any area of non-Article 9 law that allows tracing. For instance, the law of civil forfeiture recognizes the government's right to trace the proceeds of illegal

drug sales into a commingled bank account using either the lowest intermediate balance rule, a pro rata share rule or a "drugs-in, first out" rule. See United States v. Bank Cafetero Panama, 797 F.2d 1154, 1160 (2d Cir. 1986). In cases of conversion, courts have allowed a LIFO method of tracing; see United States v. Henshaw, 388 F.3d 718 (10th Cir. 2004). Could the secured party, using the LIBR to trace its proceeds, now make a decent argument that (b)(2) allows it to rely on an exception to the presumption against replenishment applicable under trust law? Or on a tracing rule other than the LIBR recognized under non-Article 9 law?

2. As a policy matter, Gilmore's view that a security interest in proceeds is lost when they are commingled with nonproceeds is defensible. The LIBR's application in Article 9 cases involve a priority contest among two or more creditors, where the debtor has "misbehaved" and the loss is allocated among two or more creditors, her "victims." Allowing tracing in this intra-creditor case imposes a cost on the other creditors: commingled proceeds that can be traced are unavailable to satisfy their claims. Allowing a creditor to trace proceeds arguably produces inefficient behavior. This is because tracing saves the creditor some of the cost of monitoring collateral. If the debtor by commingling proceeds, tracing preserves the creditor's security interest in commingled funds. However, the secured creditor might be in a better position to monitor the debtor's assets than any of the other creditors. An optimal allocation of monitoring effort would assign the responsibility to monitor to the creditor. Tracing reduces the secured creditor's incentive to monitor her collateral. Its effect is to shift part or all of the responsibility to creditors who might be in an inferior position to undertake monitoring. Section 9–315(b)(2)'s drafters apparently disagree with this conclusion.

3. As should be apparent, the position of a secured party claiming commingled proceeds in a deposit account is precarious. In some instances, secured parties may write off any commingled proceeds because of the litigation costs of identification. The means by which these creditors could have protected themselves are well known and frequently used. They involve removing the debtor from control over the deposit account, usually by the use of some form of what is known as a "lockbox account." The device is described in 2 Barkley Clark & Barbara Clark, The Law of Secured Transactions Under the Uniform Commercial Code § 10.04[3] (3d ed. 2010). Under this device, account debtors are instructed to direct their payments to the debtor to a postal box directly controlled by the secured party who removes the checks daily, indorses them with the name of the debtor-payee, and deposits them in an account of the debtor in a bank. Restrictions can be imposed on such an account which preclude the debtor from either making deposits or withdrawals without the consent of the secured party. When the debtor needs advances, the secured party will move funds from the account into the debtor's operating account. Since the debtor cannot deposit nonproceeds in the account, there can be no commingling; since the debtor cannot draw on the account, no third parties can receive payments to the detriment of the secured party. The account is entirely proceeds, and if the debtor defaults, messy problems of tracing proceeds through an active checking account are avoided. See Lockbox Agreement, Appendix II, for a basic cash management arrangement showing the manner in which checks are processed.

4. Section 9–315(b)(2) permits the tracing of commingled proceeds where the proceeds are not goods. Where the proceeds are commingled goods, 9–315(b)(1) allows proceeds to be identifiable only in accordance with 9–336. Section 9–336 contains its own tracing rules. Under 9–336(a), commingled goods are goods physically united with other goods such that "their identity in a product or mass is lost." Section 9–336 in turn does not allow the tracing of the proceeds into the commingled product or mass. Instead, the security interest attaches to the product or mass as a whole. 9–336(c). If two or more security interests attach to the commingled product or mass, under 9–336(f)(1) the security interest that was perfected before the proceeds became commingled has priority over the security interest that was not perfected before the goods became commingled. If the security interests were perfected before the collateral became commingled, 9–336(f)(2) provides that they rank equally in proportion to the value of the collateral at the time it became commingled goods. Notice that this is a pro rata rule, not a priority rule: competing security interests are treated equally. Finally, Article 9's priority rules other than those in 9–336 apply to priority contests between a security interest in commingled goods and a security interest in the product or mass. 9–336(e).

3. TRANSFEREES OF INSTRUMENTS UNDER SECTION 9–330(d)

Assume these facts: Debtor granted a security interest in its inventory and proceeds to SPA who perfected by filing. Subsequently, Debtor granted a junior security interest in the same collateral to SPB who also perfected by filing. When Debtor sells items of its inventory it receives checks payable to Debtor, which, under its agreement with SPA, is required to negotiate to SPA by indorsement and delivery without depositing them in a deposit account. Debtor violated the agreement by negotiating the checks to SPB who knew of SPA's prior security interest.

This is a familiar method of inventory control. By requiring a debtor who has received a check from an account debtor to indorse the check to the secured party, in specie, without running it through the debtor's bank account, the secured party can be sure that payments are actually being received from account debtors. Questions of priority in checks involve the law of negotiable instruments, found in Article 3, as well as Article 9.

Under 3–306, if a holder takes an instrument in which there is a security interest, it takes subject to that security interest (a claim of ownership) unless it is a holder in due course. Under 3–302(a), a holder is a holder in due course if it takes an instrument for value, in good faith and without notice of claims or defenses. Does SPB have notice of SPA's claim because of SPA's filed financing statement? Section 9–331(c) answers this question definitively by providing that filing under Article 9 does not constitute notice of a claim or defense to the holders or purchasers of instruments. But in this case, SPB had actual knowledge of the earlier security interest of SPA and SPB, therefore, cannot be a holder in due course.

There are two other Article 9 provisions that bear on this question. The first, 9–331(a), provides that Article 9 "does not limit the rights of a holder in due course of a negotiable instrument" and that such a holder takes priority over an earlier security interest, even if perfected, to the extent provided in Article 3. Thus, if SPB qualified as a holder in due course under Article 3, it would take free of SPA's security interest, but SPB does not qualify because of its knowledge of the claim of ownership. See Comment 5 to 9–331.

The second relevant provision, 9–330(d), provides:

> Except as otherwise provided in Section 9–331(a), a purchaser of an instrument has priority over a security interest in the instrument perfected by a method other than possession if the purchaser gives value and takes possession of the instrument in good faith and without knowledge that the purchase violates the rights of the secured party.

Since there are no facts showing that SPB knew that purchasing the checks violated the rights of SPA, SPB should prevail under this section. See Comment 7 to 9–330. SPB has given value by reason of its outstanding loans (1–204(2)); new value is not required. There is no reason to believe that SPB was other than in good faith: 1–201(b)(20) requires honesty in fact and observance of reasonable commercial standards. The good faith requirement does not impose on SPB a general duty of inquiry and not enough facts are given to evaluate its observance of reasonable commercial standards. Comment 5 to 9–331. Hence, the rights of a purchaser of instruments are roughly comparable to those of purchasers of chattel paper, except that the new value and ordinary course of business requirements are omitted.

L. FEDERAL TAX LIENS

Debtors often owe tax obligations to the federal government: in the case of individual debtors, income or estate taxes, and in the case of employers, payroll taxes. Since a debtor in default on a secured loan sometimes also is in default on its obligations to other creditors, the government competes with other creditors for priority in the debtor's assets. Federal law, not Article 9 or other state law, determines the priority of the federal government against the debtor's other creditors. Two federal statutes potentially affect the priority of unpaid tax obligations to the United States government: the general federal priority statute (31 U.S.C. § 3713(a)) and the Federal Tax Lien Act (FTLA) contained in the Internal Revenue Code (26 U.S.C. § 6321 et seq. (2022)).

The general federal priority statute provides that the federal government "shall be paid first" when a bankruptcy case hasn't been filed and the debtor is insolvent. Section 3713(a) applies to any indebtedness owed to the federal government, not just to indebtedness arising from taxes. More important, the statute is absolute in its terms, making no exceptions in which the government "shall" not have priority. Section 3713(a) therefore seems to give the federal government unrestricted priority as against other claimants of the taxpayer.

Prior to the FTLA's passage in 1966, courts created an exception which subordinated the federal government's claim to an earlier consensually or nonconsensually created property right (a lien) if the lien was "choate." A lien is choate when the identity of the lienor, the property subject to the lien and the amount of the lien are definite. See United States v. City of New Britain, 347 U.S. 81, 85–86 (1954). Although courts have understood a lien to be choate when the lien is perfected, they have often used the choateness doctrine in unpredictable ways to disadvantage competing liens. The FTLA is much more restrictive than the general federal priority statute, subordinating federal tax liens under prescribed conditions described below. None of the FTLA's provisions say anything about "choateness."

Two questions therefore arise about the relation of the general federal priority statute and the FTLA: does the FTLA implicitly repeal § 3713(a) when the two conflict?; and does the choateness doctrine apply to competing liens under the FTLA? In United States v. Estate of Romani, 523 U.S. 517 (1998), the Supreme Court held that Congress intended the FTLA, a more recent, detailed and comprehensive statute, to apply when it conflicts with § 3713(a). *Romani*'s holding implicitly repeals the general federal priority statute by limiting its application to instances when it is compatible with the FTLA.

The fate of the choateness doctrine under the FTLA is uncertain. Some courts have doubted that the doctrine survives the FTLA; e.g., Aetna Ins. Co. v. Texas Thermal Indus., 591 F.2d 1035, 1038 (5th Cir.1979); Pine Builders, Inc. v. United States, 413 F.Supp. 77 (E.D. Va.1976). Other courts disagree, including the Supreme Court. See, e.g., United States v. McDermott, 507 U.S. 447 (1993); Iron Workers District Council of New England Pension v. Baldwin Steel Co., 2001 WL 1555539 (D. Mass.2001). These courts apparently require that liens, such as security interests, both prime a tax lien under the FTLA *and* be choate at the time the tax lien attaches. The continued existence of the choateness doctrine under the FTLA is questionable. Congress enacted the FTLA as "an attempt to conform the lien provisions of the internal revenue laws to the concepts developed in this Uniform Commercial Code." S. Rep. No. 89–1708, at 1, reprinted in 1966 U.S.S. CAN. 3722. The FTLA, according to *Romani*, is a "specific" and "comprehensive" priority statute. 523 U.S. at 532. If neither the UCC nor the FTLA mentions choateness, isn't the safer inference that the choateness doctrine doesn't apply under the FTLA?

Judge Posner comments on the choateness doctrine under the FTLA as follows:

> The "existence" condition for a creditor's lien to trump a federal tax lien is known in tax-speak (and to a lesser extent in bankruptcy when priority between two security interests is disputed) as "choateness." The word "choate," used as it is in law to mean "in existence" (its usage outside of law is essentially nonexistent), is a barbarism, albeit a venerable one. Its earliest known appearance is in 2 R.S. Donnison Roper & Henry Hopley White, *A Treatise on the Law of Legacies* 358 (3d ed. 1829); it first appeared in a U.S. Supreme Court opinion in United States v. City of New Britain, 347 U.S. 81, 84, 74 S. Ct. 367, 98 L. Ed. 520 (1954). "*Choate*, a back-formation from *inchoate*, is a misbegotten word, for the prefix in *inchoate* is intensive and not negative. . . The word derives from the Latin verb *inchoare* 'to hitch with; to begin.' Yet, because it was misunderstood as being a negative (meaning 'incomplete'), someone invented a positive form for it, namely *choate* (meaning 'complete')." Bryan Garner, *A Dictionary of Modern Legal Usage* 152 (2d ed. 1995); see also Ben Zimmer, "On Language—Choate," *N.Y. Times*, Jan. 3, 2010, p. MM16. The "in" in "inchoate" is no more a negative than the "in" in "incipient" or "into" or "ingress" or "inflammable." Imagine thinking that because "inflammable" means "catches fire," "flammable" must mean fireproof. "Inchoate" means vague, unformed, or undeveloped. If there were a word "choate," it would mean approximately the same thing. Garner adds that "although the word is etymologically misbegotten, it is now fairly well ensconced in the legal vocabulary. . . [and] is used even by those who deprecate its origins." Garner, *supra*, at 152–53. For the law's use of "choate" is not only a sign of ignorance but also a source of confusion. The requirement of being in existence does not apply to the lien; no one doubts that the *lien* exists—if it didn't the taxpayer couldn't get to first base. Yet beginning with *City of New Britain* the cases invariably state the question as whether the *lien* is "choate." What must exist is the *property* that the lien is on. The statute could not be clearer.

Bloomfield State Bank v. United States, 644 F.3d 521, 523–24 (7th Cir.2011).

1. CREATION AND ENFORCEABILITY OF FEDERAL TAX LIENS

The FTLA doesn't speak of a tax lien attaching or being perfected. It instead refers to a tax liability being "assessed" and the tax lien being "valid." Section 6321 provides that the United States government has a lien on all real and personal property of the taxpayer if the taxpayer neglects or refuses to pay after demand. The lien isn't restricted to property owned by the debtor at the time of the taxpayer's neglect or refusal; it reaches after-acquired property as well. Section 6322 in turn provides that the tax lien "arise[s]" in favor of the government when the tax is assessed. Treasury Department regulations determine that assessment occurs when the tax liability is noted in the records by the appointed IRS assessment officer. 26 C.F.R. §§ 301.6201–1, 301.6203–1 (2022). Thus, the tax lien is enforceable against the debtor upon assessment. Because assessment doesn't require filing, the lien is secret. Although § 6334 exempts limited types of property or dollar amounts from a tax levy, the tax lien still attaches to all of the taxpayer's property.

Once the tax lien arises, it is enforceable against both the taxpayer and everyone else except "any purchaser, holder of security interest, mechanic's lienor, or judgment lien creditor." 26 U.S.C. § 6323(a). To make its lien effective against these excepted classes, the IRS must file a notice of the lien. Thus, notice is the FTLA's counterpart to perfection. Under § 6323(f), state law controls where notice must be given. The most recent uniform state law on the subject is the Uniform Federal Lien Registration Act, promulgated in 1978, which has widely been adopted. 7A Uniform Laws Annotated 336 (2022). In the case of real property, the IRS must file notice in the office designated by the state in which the property is located. For personal property, filing must be in the state of the taxpayer's residence. Where the taxpayer is a corporation or partnership, its residence is its principal executive office. § 6323(f)(2)(B). If the state hasn't designated an office for tax lien filings, filing is in the federal district court for the judicial district in which the real or personal property is located. Section 6323(g) makes a tax lien filing effective for ten years and 30 days after the date the tax is assessed. In a provision similar to 9–515(d)'s "refiling window," § 6323(g)(3)(A) allows refiling within one year of the end of the effectiveness period.

Treasury Department regulations prescribe the form and content of a notice of tax lien. They require the notice to provide the name of the taxpayer. 26 C.F.R. § 301.6323(f)–1(d)(2). A notice of a tax lien is the counterpart of a financing statement covering a security interest. As with a financing statement identifying the debtor, the tax lien notice might provide the incorrect name of the taxpayer. In this case the question is whether the error in the taxpayer's name renders the notice insufficient. Federal law ultimately answers the question, and it need not give the same answer as Article 9 gives with respect errors in the debtor's name in the financing statement. Where a financing statement provides an erroneous debtor name, 9–506(c)'s standard search logic test requires a search under the debtor's correct name. The case produced below describes the federal standard governing errors in the taxpayer's name in the tax lien notice and the precedents applying it. The Note following the case evaluates the standard.

In re Spearing Tool and Manufacturing Co., Inc.

United States Court of Appeals, Sixth Circuit, 2005
412 F.3d 653

■ COOK, CIRCUIT JUDGE.

In this case arising out of bankruptcy proceedings, the government appeals the district court's reversal of the bankruptcy court's grant of summary judgment for the government. For the following reasons, we reverse the district court, and affirm the bankruptcy court.

I.   Background and Procedural History

In April 1998, Spearing Tool and Manufacturing Co. and appellee Crestmark entered into a lending agreement, which granted Crestmark a security interest in all of Spearing's assets. The bank perfected its security interest by filing a financing statement under the Uniform Commercial Code, identifying Spearing as "Spearing Tool and Manufacturing Co.," its precise name registered with the Michigan Secretary of State.

In April 2001, Spearing entered into a secured financing arrangement with Crestmark, under which Crestmark agreed to purchase accounts receivable from Spearing, and Spearing granted Crestmark a security interest in all its assets. Crestmark perfected its security interest by filing a UCC financing statement, again using Spearing's precise name registered with the Michigan Secretary of State.

Meanwhile, Spearing fell behind in its federal employment-tax payments. On October 15, 2001, the IRS filed two notices of federal tax lien against Spearing with the Michigan Secretary of State. Each lien identified Spearing as "SPEARING TOOL & MFG. COMPANY INC.," which varied from Spearing's precise Michigan-registered name, because it used an ampersand in place of "and," abbreviated "Manufacturing" as "Mfg.," and spelled out "Company" rather than use the abbreviation "Co." But the name on the IRS lien notices was the precise name Spearing gave on its quarterly federal tax return for the third quarter of 2001, as well as its return for fourth-quarter 1994, the first quarter for which it was delinquent. For most of the relevant tax periods, however, Spearing filed returns as "Spearing Tool & Manufacturing"—neither its precise Michigan-registered name, nor the name on the IRS tax liens.

Crestmark periodically submitted lien search requests to the Michigan Secretary of State, using Spearing's exact registered name. Because Michigan has limited electronic-search technology, searches disclose only liens matching the precise name searched—not liens such as the IRS's, filed under slightly different or abbreviated names.[2] Crestmark's February 2002 search results came back from the Secretary of State's office with a handwritten note stating: "You may wish to search

---

[2]   The search engine ignores various "noise words" and their abbreviations, including "Incorporated" and "Company," but not "Manufacturing" or "and."

using Spearing Tool & Mfg. Company Inc." But Crestmark did not search for that name at the time, and its exact-registered-name searches thus did not reveal the IRS liens. So Crestmark, unaware of the tax liens, advanced more funds to Spearing between October 2001 and April 2002.

On April 16, 2002, Spearing filed a Chapter 11 bankruptcy petition. Only afterward did Crestmark finally search for "Spearing Tool & Mfg. Company Inc." and discover the tax-lien notices. Crestmark then filed the complaint in this case to determine lien priority. The bankruptcy court determined the government had priority; the district court reversed. The questions now before us are whether state or federal law determines the sufficiency of the IRS's tax-lien notices, and whether the IRS notices sufficed to give the IRS liens priority.

II.   Federal Law Controls Whether the IRS's Lien Notice Sufficed

Crestmark argues Michigan law should control the form and content of the IRS's tax lien with respect to taxpayer identification. The district court, though it decided in favor of Crestmark on other grounds, rightly disagreed.

When the IRS files a lien against a taxpayer's property, it must do so "in one office within the State. . . as designated by the laws of such State, in which the property subject to the lien is situated." 26 U.S.C. § 6323(f)(1)(A). The Internal Revenue Code provides that the form and content "shall be prescribed by the [U.S. Treasury] Secretary" and "be valid *notwithstanding any other provision of law regarding the form or content of a notice of lien.*" 26 U.S.C. § 6323(f)(3) (emphasis added). Regulations provide that the IRS must file tax-lien notices using IRS Form 668, which must "identify the taxpayer, the tax liability giving rise to the lien, and the date the assessment arose." 26 C.F.R. § 301.6323(f)–1(d)(2). Form-668 notice "is valid notwithstanding any other provision of law regarding the form or content of a notice of lien. For example, omission from the notice of lien of a description of the property subject to the lien does not affect the validity thereof even though State law may require that the notice contain a description of property subject to the lien." § 301.6323(f)–1(d)(1); *see also United States v. Union Cent. Life Ins. Co.,* 368 U.S. 291 (1961) (Michigan's requirement that tax liens describe relevant property "placed obstacles to the enforcement of federal tax liens that Congress had not permitted.").

The plain text of the statute and regulations indicates Form-668 notice suffices, regardless of state law. We therefore need only consider how much specificity federal law requires for taxpayer identification on tax liens.

III.   The Notice Here Sufficed

An IRS tax lien need not perfectly identify the taxpayer. . . . *See, e.g., Hudgins v. IRS (In re Hudgins),* 967 F.2d 973, 976 (4th Cir.1992); *Tony Thornton Auction Serv., Inc. v. United States,* 791 F.2d 635, 639 (8th Cir.1986); *Reid v. IRS (In re Reid),* 182 B.R. 443, 446

(Bankr.E.D.Va.1995). The question before us is whether the IRS's identification of Spearing was sufficient. We conclude it was.

The critical issue in determining whether an abbreviated or erroneous name sufficiently identifies a taxpayer is whether a "reasonable and diligent search would have revealed the existence of the notices of the federal tax liens under these names." *Tony Thornton,* 791 F.2d at 639. In *Tony Thornton,* for example, liens identifying the taxpayer as "Davis's Restaurant" and "Daviss (sic) Restaurant" sufficed to identify a business correctly known as "Davis Family Restaurant." *Id.* In *Hudgins*, the IRS lien identified the taxpayer as "Hudgins Masonry, Inc." instead of by the taxpayer's personal name, Michael Steven Hudgins. This notice nonetheless sufficed, given that both names would be listed on the same page of the state's lien index. 967 F.2d at 977.

Crestmark argues, and we agree, that those cases mean little here because in each, creditors could search a physical index and were likely to notice similar entries listed next to or near one another—an option which no longer exists under Michigan's electronic-search system. So the question for this case becomes whether Crestmark conducted a reasonable and diligent electronic search. It did not.

Crestmark should have searched here for "Spearing Tool & Mfg." as well as "Spearing Tool and Manufacturing." "Mfg." and the ampersand are, of course, most common abbreviations—so common that, for example, we use them as a rule in our case citations. Crestmark had notice that Spearing sometimes used these abbreviations, and the Michigan Secretary of State's office *recommended* a search using the abbreviations. Combined, these factors indicate that a reasonable, diligent search by Crestmark of the Michigan lien filings for this business would have disclosed Spearing's IRS tax liens.

Crestmark argues for the unreasonableness of requiring multiple searches by offering the extreme example of a name it claims could be abbreviated 288 different ways ("ABCD Christian Brothers Construction and Development Company of Michigan, Inc."). Here, however, only two relevant words could be, and commonly are, abbreviated: "Manufacturing" and "and"—and the Secretary of State specifically recommended searching for those abbreviations. We express no opinion about whether creditors have a general obligation to search name variations. Our holding is limited to these facts.

Finally, we note that policy considerations also support the IRS's position. A requirement that tax liens identify a taxpayer with absolute precision would be unduly burdensome to the government's tax-collection efforts. Indeed, such a requirement might burden the government at least as much as Crestmark claims it would be burdened by having to perform multiple lien searches. "The overriding purpose of the tax lien statute obviously is to ensure prompt revenue collection." *United States v. Kimbell Foods, Inc.,* 440 U.S. 715, 734–35 (1979). "[T]o attribute to Congress a purpose so to weaken the tax liens it has created would require very clear language," which we lack here. *Union Central,* 368 U.S. at 294. Further, to subject the federal government to different identification requirements—varying with each state's electronic-search technology—"would run counter to the principle of uniformity which has long been the accepted practice in the field of federal taxation." *Id.*

Crestmark urges us to require IRS liens to meet the same precise-identification requirement other lien notices now must meet under Uniform Commercial Code Article 9. *See* Mich. Comp. Laws § 440.9503(1) ("A financing statement sufficiently provides the name of [a] debtor [that is] a registered organization, only if the financing statement provides the name of the debtor indicated on the public record of the debtor's jurisdiction of organization which shows the debtor to have been organized."). We decline to do so. The UCC applies to transactions "that create[ ] a security interest in personal property or fixtures *by contract.*" Mich. Comp. Laws § 440.9109(1)(a) (emphasis added). Thus, the IRS would be exempt from UCC requirements even without the strong federal policy favoring unfettered tax collection.

More importantly, the Supreme Court has noted that the United States, as an involuntary creditor of delinquent taxpayers, is entitled to special priority over voluntary creditors. *See, e.g., Kimbell Foods,* 440 U.S. at 734–35, 737–38. Thus, while we understand that a requirement that the IRS comply with UCC Article 9 would spare banks considerable inconvenience, we conclude from Supreme Court precedent that the federal government's interest in prompt, effective tax collection trumps the banks' convenience in loan collection.

IV. Conclusion

We reverse the district court and affirm the bankruptcy court's grant of summary judgment for the government.

NOTE

As described in Chapter 2, Article 9's rules with respect to debtor-name errors on financing statements provide that (i) financing statements for debtors that are "registered organizations" (corporations) must be filed in the organizing jurisdiction (the state of incorporation) of the debtor (9–301 and 9–307(e)), and (ii) the debtor must be identified on the financing statement by the name found in the public records of that jurisdiction (9–503(a)). Since technology has made it easy to discover the correct name of debtors from public records, these rules allow a searcher to conduct one search in the correct name of the debtor in the proper jurisdiction and be sure of finding every effective UCC filing. In many states, federal tax liens and UCC financing statements are included in the same file. In such a case, if the IRS rules for the taxpayer's name were like those under revised Article 9, a single search under the correct name would turn up all the liens, consensual and nonconsensual, state and federal, against a corporate debtor-taxpayer's property.

After *Spearing Tool*, this is not possible. Federal court precedent adopts the reasonably diligent search rule, and the Sixth Circuit embraced the traditional interpretation of this rule as meaning that an incorrect version of the taxpayer's name on the notice is acceptable so long as a reasonably diligent search would have turned up the filing. This interpretation of the reasonably diligent searcher rule rejects 9–506(c)'s "standard search logic" standard. The indeterminate nature of this rule may require multiple searches under different versions of the debtor's name to look for a federal tax lien on the debtor's property, with no certainty that there is not another financing statement filed under another variation of the debtor's name yet undiscovered. *Spearing Tool* effectively undermines Congress' intent to make the FTLA consistent with Article 9.

If *Spearing Tool* is bad, The Trane Company v. CGI Mechanical Inc., 2010 WL 299516 (D.S.C. July 28, 2010), is worse. Purporting to rely on *Spearing Tool*, the court held that the notice of the tax lien listing the taxpayer by its *former* name properly identified the taxpayer because a reasonable and diligent search would have disclosed the tax liens.

The reasonably diligent searcher rule is a relic of the pre-digital past. A diligent searcher today can rather easily find the correct name of a corporation by calling up its incorporation records. If it finds nothing under this name, it is a waste of time and money to require the searcher to speculate on what erroneous name the IRS may have used. The teaching of this case is that the IRS can pretty well get away with filing under the name the taxpayer used on its tax returns without looking further for its correct name. Ironically, since tax returns are not public documents, the searcher, even one who has learned the taxpayer's correct name, has no sure way of finding this name, however diligent its search. The court had the opportunity to recognize how anachronistic the reasonably diligent search concept is after the Internet and to do something about it in this case, but it failed.

Professor Lynn LoPucki observes that the IRS is so adroit in preventing cases that might overturn *Spearing Tool* from coming before other courts of appeal that the Sixth Circuit holding may prevail for many years. See Lynn M. LoPucki, The *Spearing Tool* Filing System Disaster, 68 Ohio St. L.J. 281, 313 (2007). It is most likely that reform can come only through legislative or administrative intervention. One palliative sometimes discussed is the establishment by the IRS of a national filing system for tax liens in Washington. Another is to amend Treasury Department regulations to expressly require notice of a tax lien to supply the debtor's correct name.

2. THE FTLA'S GENERAL PRIORITY RULE

Federal law could have made the tax lien valid against both the taxpayer and all competitors whenever it arises. Such a rule would have given the federal tax lien complete priority. Section 3713, the general federal priority rule, in effect is such a rule. However, the FTLA doesn't adopt a "government always wins" rule. It instead determines priority essentially according to the order in time in which a competing interest in the taxpayer's property is obtained. In general, interests obtained before notice of the tax lien is filed prevail against the tax lien; interests obtained after filing notice of the tax lien occurs are subordinated to the tax lien. Although the FTLA's terminology differs from that of Article 9, the FTLA's general priority rule gives priority only to security interests perfected before notice of a tax lien is filed.

Section 6323(a) states the FTLA's general priority rule. It provides in relevant part that the tax lien "shall not be valid as against any purchaser, holder of a security interest, mechanic's lienor, or judgment lien creditor until notice thereof which meets the requirements of subsection (f) has been filed" by the IRS. As is often noted, § 6323(a) can't be read literally. Read literally, the subsection states that the federal tax lien has priority over the enumerated competitors when proper notice of the lien is filed. So read, a filed tax lien has retroactive effect: competitors lose to the federal tax lien once notice of the tax lien has been filed even if the competing interests attached before filing notice was given. Because the literal reading conflicts with the FTLA's purpose to coordinate tax liens with other liens, § 6323(a) is understood nonliterally. Read nonliterally, § 6323(a)'s general priority rule is that the federal tax lien primes the interests of purchasers, security interests, mechanic's liens, and judgment liens that come into existence after proper notice of the tax lien has been filed; these competitors have priority when their interests exist before filing notice of the tax lien occurs. Section 6323(a)'s general rule is subject to exceptions, discussed below. However, unless an exception applies, interests in the taxpayer's property that come into existence after the tax lien filing are subordinate to the tax lien.

Security interests are among the competing interests enumerated in § 6323(a). In order for a secured creditor to have priority over the tax lien under § 6323(a), the secured creditor must be a "holder of a security interest" at the time of the tax lien filing. Section 6323(h)(1) in turn defines "security interest." This important definition provides in relevant part that "[a] security interest exists at any time (A) if, at such time, the property is in existence and the interest has become protected under local law against a subsequent judgment lien arising out of an unsecured obligation, and (B) to the extent that, at such time, the holder has parted with money or money's worth." Thus, to hold a security interest at the time of the tax lien filing, three requirements must be met: the collateral must exist, the security interest must be protected under local law against a subsequent judgment lien on an unsecured claim, and the creditor must have parted with money or money's worth. Failure to meet one or more of these requirements means that the claimant doesn't hold a "security interest" for purposes of the FTLA. As such, it loses to the federal tax lien under § 6323(a)'s general rule.

Two points about § 6323(h)(1)'s definition should be noted. First, because (A) requires that collateral be in existence at the time of the tax lien filing, § 6323(a)'s general rule doesn't protect perfected security interests in after-acquired property against a tax lien. Security interests in after-acquired property are protected, if at all, under one or more exceptions to § 6323. See § 6323(c). Second, (h)(1) uses the rights of a lien creditor under local law (i.e., non-FTLA law) as a baseline of sorts. If a security interest doesn't have priority over a lien creditor under local law, it isn't a "security interest" under the FTLA. If the security interest has priority under local law, it's a "security interest" under the FTLA as long as the other requirements of (h)(1) are satisfied. Article 9, of course, is a prominent sort of local law. Section 9–317 determines the priority of a security interest against a lien creditor's rights. The problems below test an understanding of § 6323(a)'s general priority rule.

PROBLEMS

1. On January 1, SP made a loan to D Corporation and D granted SP a security interest in its equipment in use in its factory in Virginia to secure the loan. The same day, SP filed a financing statement in the proper office identifying D as "Dee Corp." On February 1, after D refused to pay payroll taxes it owed the federal government, the IRS properly filed notice of a tax lien in Virginia.

(a)   In a contest between the IRS and SP over D's equipment in use, who prevails? 9–317(a)(2)(A), 9–502(a), 9–506(b)–(c).

(b)   Assume that SP's filed financing statement is such that under 9–317 SP is subordinated to the IRS. Is SP the "holder of a security interest" under § 6323(h)(1)? Under Article 9?

(c)   Assume that on January 1 the financing statement SP filed omitted D Corporation's address. Does the result in (a) change? 9–502(a), 9–516(b), 9–520(a), (c).

(d)   Assume that on January 1 SP's financing statement identified D as "D Corporation" and included its address. The filing officer, however, rejected SP's financing statement when SP presented it along with a filing fee. Does the result in (a) change? 9–502(a), 9–516(d), 1–201(29).

2. On January 1, SP had D execute a security agreement covering D's equipment in use and at the same time properly filed a financing statement. The security agreement gave SP the right to refuse to make loans to D. On February 1, the IRS properly filed notice of a tax lien covering D's equipment. The next day, SP loaned D funds.

(a)   If a contest arises between SP and the IRS over D's equipment, who will prevail under § 6323(a)? § 6323(h)(1)(B), 9–317(a)(2)(B), 26 C.F.R. § 301.6323(h)–1(a)(3) (2003); cf. § 6323(d), 9–323(b).

(b)   Would the result under § 6323(a) change if on January 1 SP agreed to loan D funds on February 2, which it subsequently did? § 6323(h)(1)(B), 1–204, 26 C.F.R. § 301.6323(h)–1(a)(3) (2003).

3. On January 1, D Corporation purchased from Seller on credit a piece of equipment for its factory. To secure the purchase price owed, D executed on that date a security agreement granting Seller a security interest in the equipment purchased as well as in equipment it owned at the time. Seller delivered the piece of equipment to D on January 8. On January 10, the IRS properly filed a tax lien arising from unpaid payroll taxes owed by D. Seller filed a valid financing statement covering D's equipment on January 15. In a contest between the IRS and Seller over D's equipment, who has priority?

3. SECTION 6323(c)–(d)'S EXCEPTIONS: POST-LIEN TRANSACTIONS

Sections 6323(c) and (d) contain important exceptions to § 6323(a)'s general priority rule. Section 6323(c) addresses both future advances and floating liens, and § 6323(d) concerns future advances. By its terms, § 6323(a) only gives priority to holders of security interests at the time filing notice of the tax lien is given. A post-notice advance creates a security interest not in existence at the time of the tax lien filing. Similarly, a post-notice acquisition by the debtor of collateral covered by an after-acquired property clause creates a security interest that didn't exist at the time of the filing of the tax lien. Without §§ 6323(c) or (d), all post-notice advances and post-notice acquisitions of collateral, therefore, would be subordinate to the IRS's tax lien under § 6323(a). Section 6323(c) protects a secured creditor's future advances and after-acquired property against subordination to a tax lien, and § 6323(d) also protects its future advances from subordination. Both sections prescribe the conditions under which the tax lien is "invalid" against a security interest.

Section 6323(c)(1) protects a range of security interests that come into existence within 45 days after the tax lien filing through the taxpayer's acquisition of collateral. To be protected, the collateral acquired must be "qualified property" covered by a pre-notice "commercial transactions financing agreement," and protected under local law against a judgment lien creditor. Section 6323(c)(2)(B) defines "qualified property" as "commercial financial security" acquired by the taxpayer within 45 days after the date of the tax lien filing. Section 6323(c)(2)(C) in turn defines "commercial financial security" to include commercial paper, accounts receivable, real property mortgages and inventory. (Treasure Department regulations have extended the category of commercial paper to include commercial documents evidencing contract rights. 26 C.F.R. § 301.6323(c)–1(c)(1).) Thus, in plain English, § 6323(c)(1) protects security interests in certain types of after-acquired property when the property is collateral acquired by the taxpayer within 45 days of a tax lien filing.

Section 6323(d) gives priority against a tax lien to prescribed future advances. Under (d), the tax lien is subordinate to security interests that come into existence "by reason of a disbursement made" within 45 days of the tax lien filing. Future advances are disbursements. To have priority, the secured party must make the advance without actual knowledge of the tax lien filing, the advance must be secured by collateral existing at the time of the filing, and the advance must be protected under local law against the rights of judgment lien creditors. The first condition means that § 6323(d) treats future advances less favorably than under Article 9. Under 9–317(a)(2) and 9–323(b), advances by a secured creditor who is perfected or has filed a financing statement and satisfied one of 9–203(b)(3)'s conditions has priority over a lien creditor when made within 45 days of the lien. The secured creditor's knowledge of the intervening lien does not affect the advance's priority. By contrast, under § 6323(d) the secured creditor's actual knowledge of the tax lien filing cuts off the advance's priority over the intervening tax lien even if the advance is made within the 45-day period.

Sections 6323(c) and (d) overlap to some extent. By defining a "commercial transactions financing agreement" to cover advances under such agreements made within 45 days of the tax lien filing without knowledge of the filing, subsection (c) also protects some post-lien advances. However, the subsections generally give different protections. Section 6323(c) protects qualifying after-acquired collateral, (d) protects only future advances. Unlike (c), § 6323(d) does not restrict the type of collateral securing protected future advances. For its part, (c)'s protection of qualifying after-acquired property is unaffected by a secured creditor's actual knowledge of the tax lien filing.

PROBLEMS

1.   On January 1, SP and Debtor executed a security agreement covering Debtor's factory machinery in use, and on January 2, SP properly filed a valid financing statement. The IRS on January 3 properly filed notice of a tax lien against Debtor. On January 4, SP made a secured loan to Debtor knowing of the tax lien filing.

   (a)   If Debtor defaults on its obligations to SP under the security agreement, who has priority in the collateral described in SP and Debtors' security agreement: SP or the IRS?

   (b)   Suppose SP had loaned Debtor $1,000 on a secured basis on January 2. It also made another $5,000 secured loan to Debtor on January 4 knowing of the IRS's tax lien filing. Who as priority in the collateral described in SP and Debtors' security agreement: SP or the IRS?

2.   On January 1, SP and Debtor executed a security agreement covering Debtor's existing and after-acquired inventory. On January 2, SP loaned Debtor funds covered by the security agreement and properly filed a valid financing statement listing the collateral as inventory. On January 3, the IRS properly filed notice of its tax lien against Debtor. Debtor, with SP's knowledge, acquired two pieces of inventory, one on February 1 and the other on May 1.

   (a)   In a priority dispute between the IRS and SP, who has priority in the two pieces of inventory?

(b)   Suppose the collateral had been Debtor's machinery in use in its factory, Debtor acquiring one piece of machinery on February 1 and the other on May 1. Would the result in (a) change?

4.   PMSIS AND POST-LIEN PROCEEDS

Courts and the Internal Revenue Service have created exceptions to the FTLA protecting purchase-money security interests and post-lien proceeds. Consider the exceptions in turn. In some circumstances, the FTLA gives a PMSI priority over an intervening tax lien. For instance, suppose a creditor and debtor execute a security agreement on day 1, the creditor delivers the collateral the same day, and the creditor's security interest is a purchase-money security interest. On day 2, the IRS files notice of its tax lien against the debtor, and on day 15, the creditor files a financing statement covering the collateral. Under § 6323(h)(1), the creditor "holds a security interest" on day 1. This is because (h)(1)'s conditions are satisfied as of that date: the purchase-money collateral is in existence as of the date notice of the tax lien is given since it was delivered on day 1; the creditor's purchase-money security interest is protected under 9–317(e) against an intervening lien creditor's rights; and the creditor has parted with "money or money's worth." As the holder of a security interest, the purchase-money creditor's security interest is "valid" against the tax lien and therefore has priority under § 6323(a).

However, in other circumstances PMSIs aren't protected. For instance, assume that a tax lien is filed on day 1 covering all of taxpayer's assets. On day 5, a purchase-money creditor delivers the purchase-money collateral to the taxpayer. The creditor has the taxpayer execute a security agreement and files a financing statement on day 8. The creditor isn't a "holder of a security interest" at the time the tax lien was filed. See § 6323(h)(1). Although it later became a holder of a security interest, neither § 6323(c) nor (d) allows the creditor priority over the tax lien because both sections require that a written security agreement be executed prior to the filing of the tax lien.

Under a judicially created exception to the FTLA, the purchase-money creditor nonetheless has priority over the previously filed tax lien. This is so regardless of whether the security agreement creating the PMSI occurred before or after the tax lien was filed. See Slodov v. United States, 436 U.S. 238, 258 n.23 (1978); First Interstate Bank v. Internal Revenue Service, 930 F.2d 1521 (10th Cir.1991); Rev. Rul. 68–57, 68–1 C.B. 553. In Slodov, the Supreme Court's justification is that the purchase-money creditor's priority "reflects his contribution of property to the taxpayer's estate and therefore does not prejudice creditors who are prior in time." 426 U.S. at 258 n. 23. Affected noncreditors, such as the taxpaying public, may feel differently when the reduction in tax revenues collected increases their tax rates. If the Court is right, why does 9–317(e) restrict purchase-money priority over intervening lien creditors in the way it does? If the Court is wrong and there is prejudice, why isn't the judicially created exception tailored more precisely to the circumstances in which creditors are likely to be prejudiced?

The other judicially created exception to tax lien priority concerns proceeds of collateral. The FTLA doesn't address the priority in proceeds. Treasury Department regulations instead deal with the matter; 26 C.F.R. § 301.6323(c)–1 (2022). Obviously, pre-notice identifiable proceeds of pre-notice collateral don't cause a problem. If the proceeds are identifiable under 9–315(b), a security interest attaches to them under 9–315(a)(2). Further, under 9–315(c), a perfected security interest in collateral carries over to proceeds. Thus, a secured creditor with a pre-notice perfected security interest in proceeds is a "holder of a security interest" for § 6323(h)(1)'s purposes. Its security interest in proceeds therefore is "valid" against a tax lien filing under § 6323(a). However, the FTLA is silent about the priority treatment of proceeds in two other circumstances: when post-notice proceeds are realized from disposal of pre-notice collateral and when post-notice proceeds are realized from the disposal of post-notice collateral that is "qualifying property" under § 6323(c). In the former circumstance, the proceeds are not "in existence" as required by (h)(1) at the time notice of the tax lien is filed. In the latter case, both the collateral and its proceeds are not "in existence" at that time as required by (h)(1). Faced with the latter circumstance, Plymouth Sav. Bank v. Internal Revenue Service, 187 F.3d 203 (1st Cir.1999), proceeds of post-notice collateral is protected by § 6323(c) if the collateral is "qualifying property" under that subsection.

PROBLEM

Debtor manufactures truck trailers. Bank loaned money to Debtor and took a duly perfected security interest in "all items of personal property, wherever situated, including but not limited to: cars, trucks, inventory, accounts receivable, equipment used in connection with manufacturing, tools, finished products, work in progress, now owned or purchased as a replacement, or purchased as new equipment in the future." Later, the IRS filed a tax lien against the Debtor in the appropriate place. On the 45th day after the filing of the tax lien, Debtor had in its possession some finished and some unfinished truck trailers. After this date, it sold some of the finished trailers and took in exchange trade-ins and cash which it segregated in a deposit account. Debtor expended labor and added parts after the 45th day to complete the unfinished trailers. The added parts were acquired by the Debtor after the 45th day. What are the priorities of Bank and the IRS in (1) the deposit account holding the proceeds, (2) the trailers traded-in, and (3) the trailers finished after the 45-day period? See Donald v. Madison Indus., Inc., 483 F.2d 837 (10th Cir.1973).

CHAPTER 4

LEASES AND CONSIGNMENTS

This Chapter discusses two transactions that are used as alternatives to secured transactions. Leases compete with secured transactions as methods for financing equipment and consumer goods. Consignments are a traditional method of inventory financing. Although both transactions raise troubling issues of ostensible ownership, Article 9 deals with the two in very different ways. Leases are governed by law outside Article 9, but commercial consignments are brought into Article 9.

A. LEASES

A lease and a secured transaction are different arrangements. A lease gives a right of possession and use of goods for a period of time in exchange for consideration. By contrast, a secured transaction creates a property right in an asset that secures an obligation. In the case of a secured sale, the sale transfers ownership of the goods to the buyer and the security interest secures the buyer's obligation to pay the purchase price. The distinction between a lease and sale in which the seller reserves a purchase-money security interest has long perplexed American commercial law.

There are accounting, tax and legal differences between leases and sales, including secured sales, and some are significant. Accounting standards distinguish between two sorts of leases: capital and operating leases. See Financial Accounting Standards Board (FASB), Accounting Standards No. 13: Accounting for Leases (1976). The distinction basically turns on whether the lessee enjoys the risks and benefits of ownership for most of the asset's useful life. A capital lease makes the lessee the owner of the assets, and the transaction is a financed sale to her. An operating lease leaves the important incidents of ownership with the lessor.

Until 2018, lease accounting rules required different treatment of capital and operating leases. Capital leases are required to be recognized on the lessee's balance sheet, where the lease is to be recorded as both an asset and a liability. A capital lease in effect is considered a financed purchase of the leased asset. However, prior to 2018, operating leases did not have to be recognized on the lessee's balance sheet. They were disclosed instead in notes to the lessee's financial statements. This treatment of operating leases allowed the lessee to show a more favorable debt-to-equity ratio on its balance sheet than if the lease had to be recognized.

In 2016 FASB revised its accounting standards for leases. Effective December 15, 2018, the new standards eliminate the distinction between capital (now called "finance") and operating leases for leases with a term of a year or more, for purposes of the lessee's balance sheet. See FASB, Accounting Standards Update (Topic 842) (February 2016). The revised standards leave the accounting treatment of capital leases unchanged. However, operating leases must be recorded on the lessee's balance sheet as both an asset and a liability. This treatment reflects the fact that all leases create an asset (the right of use during the lease term) and a liability (the present value of the total rent owed over the lease term). Nonetheless, FASB takes the position, with which others might disagree, that rental liabilities on operating leases are operating obligations, not debt. If accepted, this view has the intended effect that bringing operating lease liabilities onto the lessee's balance sheet won't affect debt covenants to which the lessee might be subject.

For tax purposes, a lessee may deduct rent payments as ordinary business expenses. By contrast, the buyer of a good may not deduct the purchase price paid at the time of the purchase. Instead, the price may be deducted as an expense through a prescribed depreciation schedule. The allowable depreciation schedule usually is based on an estimate of the economic life of the asset that is shorter than the asset's actual useful life. Thus, the periodic depreciation expense allowed to a buyer usually is greater than the deductible rental payments allowed to the lessee. Tax law has its own criteria for determining when a transaction is a lease. See Rev. Proc. 2001–28 C.B. 1156 (2001). Because accounting standards, sales law and tax law each use different criteria to determine the character of a lease, a transaction can be a lease for accounting purposes or sales law but not for tax purposes, and vice versa.

Current law treats leases, sales and security interests very differently. Each occupies its own legal space: Article 2A applies to leases, Article 2 to sales and Article 9 to secured transactions. A lease is not a sale or a security interest; 2A–102(1)(j), 1–201(b)(35), Nonetheless, third parties might reasonably infer from the lessee's possession of the leased asset that it owns the asset free of security interests. Despite the lessee's ostensible ownership of the leased asset, the lessor need give no public notice of its interest, and third party claimants of the lessee—creditors, trustees in bankruptcy and buyers—are subject to the lessor's prior interest in the property. Section 2A–307(1), Comment 2 to 2A–301. Although the lessor can file a financing statement in case the transaction later is determined to create a security interest (9–505), it need not do so to protect its leasehold interest. By contrast, a secured party must perfect its security interest usually by giving public notice of its interest, typically by filing. If it does not, its security interest may be subject to third party claimants of the debtor.

Bankruptcy law deals with leases very differently than security interests. If an agreement is a true lease, the lessee's bankruptcy trustee must assume or reject the lease within a reasonable time fixed by the bankruptcy court. Assumption requires the trustee to honor the lessee's obligations under the lease, including curing most defaults. Rejection is the trustee's decision not to perform the lease. The lessor can retrieve leased property under a lease that the lessee's trustee rejects. See BC 365(p)(1). If an agreement creates a security interest, the debtor may be permitted to remain in possession of the equipment under a plan approved by the court. The secured party will be entitled only to payment or other compensation for loss in the value of its collateral while the debtor remains in possession.

In bankruptcy creditors usually prefer to have their transaction with the debtor characterized as a lease rather than as a security interest. This is because rejection of the lease entitles the lessor to retrieve the leased goods and redeploy or dispose of them. The lessor also will have an unsecured claim against the debtor's bankruptcy estate for damages resulting from the trustee's rejection of the lease, which typically will not be paid in full. However, retrieving and redeploying the goods reduces the lessor's loss from rejection. By contrast, under the Bankruptcy Code a security interest gives the secured creditor a secured claim in the amount of the judicially determined value of the collateral and an unsecured claim for the deficiency. Bankruptcy Code 506(a)(1). Courts make errors in valuation, and undersecured creditors are not compensated for the loss from being deprived of access to their collateral during the bankruptcy case. For both reasons, the secured creditor tends to suffer greater loss than the lessor.

1. DISTINGUISHING BETWEEN LEASE AND SECURITY INTEREST

Distinguishing between a lease and a security interest can be difficult. This is particularly true when the security interest is part of a sale. In a secured sale the seller frequently finances the buyer's purchase of the good. In exchange the buyer grants the seller a security interest in the good purchased to secure its price. 9–103(a) and (b)(1). Objectively, there is no observable difference between the obligations under a lease and a secured sale. For instance, assume that a transaction calls for the transferee of the good to make monthly payments of $100 to the transferor for one year. The $100 periodic payments may be characterized as rental payments under a one-year lease with $1,200 in total lease payments due. Alternatively, the $100 payments may be deemed installment payments on a $1,200 purchase price. If the lessee fails to make the rental payments, the lessor can retrieve the leased good. Correspondingly, if the buyer-debtor fails to make its installment payments on the purchase price, the seller-secured creditor can repossess the good. Obligations to maintain the good or pay taxes and insure it affect only the size of the periodic payments, not their character as rental or installments payments. The lessor, for instance, could make the lessee responsible for these expenses or incur the expenses and increase the monthly rental payments due in their amount. The seller can do the same in the case of an installment sale, adjusting the amount of the installment payments accordingly.

Whether a transaction creates a lease or a security interest requires a judgment about who owns the goods when the terms of the agreement have been performed. In the paradigmatic lease, the lessor retains a residual interest in the goods and is entitled to get them back at the end of the term of the lease. It remains the owner of the good. In a sale, the buyer becomes the owner of the good. See 2–106(1). If the sale is secured, when the buyer pays the purchase price to the seller, the security interest ends and the buyer owns the good unencumbered. If a transaction transfers possession for the useful life of a good having no salvage value, the transferee gets the benefits and bears the risks of fluctuations in the value of the good during that time. Because an owner gets the benefits and bears the burdens of an asset, the transferee effectively owns the good. Regardless of whether this transaction is described as a lease with a purchase option price of $0 or an installment sale, the transferee owns the good. In substance the transaction is a secured sale, even if the parties label their agreement a "lease."

Purchase options complicate judgments about the character of a transaction as a lease or a security interest. This is because purchase options make the determination of ownership difficult. By splitting the risks normally associated with ownership, a purchase option sometimes makes it hard to identify the owner of the good. Suppose an agreement gives the transferee the option to purchase the good at the end of a specified term. If the price at which the purchase option may be exercised is less than the current market value of the good, the optionee will exercise the option and own the good. An optionee who doesn't have the funds needed to do so can borrow them on the strength of the option, which has value. If the purchase option price is more than the current market value, the optionee will not exercise the option. In that case the optionor will continue to own the good. Thus, there is no answer to the question as to who will be the owner of the good at the end of the specified term of the transaction. The only accurate answer is "it depends."

In the case of purchase options the test of ownership requires asking whether the transferee is likely to become the owner of the good at the end of the term. If the transferee likely will exercise the purchase option, it will come to own the good and the transaction is a sale. If not, the transferor will continue to own the good and the transaction is a lease. Whether the transferee likely will exercise the purchase option depends on the price at which the purchase option can be exercised and the market value of the good (ignoring interest rates). For the ownership test to be serviceable with purchase options, the market value of the good must be the market value of the good at the time the option can be exercised, as estimated at the inception of the agreement. Otherwise, the result of the ownership test would change over time according to when the estimate of market value is made. Judgments about the character of a transaction in that case would be difficult for the parties to ascertain ex ante.

2. LEASE WITH OPTION TO PURCHASE OR RENEW: 1–203'S TWO-STEP APPLICATION

a. 1–203(a) AND (b)'S TESTS

The UCC does not explicitly distinguish between a lease and a security interest according to ownership at the end of the term of the transaction. It instead does so indirectly by relying on factors that are proxies for ownership. Section 1–201(b)(35), which defines "security interest," states that "[w]hether a transaction in the form of a lease creates a 'security interest' is determined pursuant to Section 1–203." Section 1–203, in turn provides standards for determining when a transaction creates a security interest rather than a lease.

Section 1–203 describes two different tests for determining whether a transaction creates a security interest. One test states a sufficient condition for a lease being a disguised security interest. The test is stated in 1–203(b) and is often called a "bright-line" or "per se" test. According to this test, a transaction structured as a lease creates a security interest if the lease cannot be terminated and (1) the term of the lease equals or exceeds the remaining economic life of the asset leased, (2) the lessee is obligated to renew the lease for the remaining economic life of the asset leased, (3) the lessee has the option to renew the lease for the asset's remaining economic life for no additional consideration or nominal consideration, or (4) the lessee has the option of becoming the owner of the leased asset for no additional consideration or nominal consideration. It is fair to say that 1–203(b)(1)–(4)'s disjunctive conditions describe circumstances in which the lessee is or is likely to become the owner of the asset.

Section 1–203(a) states a different test. According to 1–203(a), whether the transaction in the form of a lease creates a lease or security interest is determined by "the facts of each case." To describe 1–203(a) as stating a "test" is generous. It does no such thing. The subsection neither sets a standard nor gives guidance as to which facts determine whether the transaction creates a security interest. At best determination by "the facts of each case" states the obvious truth that facts determine the character of the transaction. As a result, 1–203(a) leaves to the courts the identification of the facts that determine whether a transaction creates a lease or a security interest. As described below, courts look to whether the lessor retains a meaningful economic interest in the asset. This too is a proxy for ownership.

Section 1–203's structure requires the provision to be applied in two steps. Because 1–203(b) states a sufficient condition for a transaction creating a security interest, its bright-line test must be applied first. If the lease cannot be terminated and one or more of 1–203(b)'s four conditions are met, the transaction creates a security interest. Application of 1–203(a)'s test therefore is unnecessary. However, if the transaction is subject to termination or none of 1–203(b)(1)–(4) conditions are met, the transaction still might create a security interest. In this case, as a second step, 1–203(a)'s test must be applied. Whether the transaction creates a security interest is determined under 1–203(a)'s "facts of each case" test. The agreement in the form of a lease in the case below contained a purchase option. Accordingly, the court relies on 1–203's two-step application to determine whether the transaction created a security interest.

In re Warne

United States Bankruptcy Court, D. Kansas, 2011
2011 WL 1303425

■ ROBERT E. NUGENT, BANKRUPTCY JUDGE.

The matter before the Court is the Motion to Compel Assumption or Rejection of Executory Contract (hereafter "Motion") filed by Dakota Financial, L.L.C. (hereafter "Dakota"). Prepetition Debtor, as lessee, and Dakota, as lessor, entered into an Equipment Lease Agreement for Debtor's use of a 2007 Volvo semi-tractor for 61 months (hereafter "Agreement"). Payments under the Agreement were in default when Debtor filed for relief under Chapter 13. Dakota requests that the Court determine that the Agreement is a true lease and requests the Court to fix a reasonable time for Debtor to assume or reject and, if Debtor rejects, to grant relief from stay. Debtor opposes the Motion, asserting that because the Agreement should be re-characterized as a secured sale, he should be permitted to remain in possession of the semi-tractor while making payment in full of Dakota's secured claim through his Chapter 13 plan.

The issue of whether the Agreement is a true lease was submitted for decision on stipulations of fact and briefs. The Court, having carefully considered the stipulated facts, reviewed the Agreement, and studied the authorities submitted, is now ready to rule.

Findings of Fact

The Court makes the following findings of fact based upon the stipulation and review of the Agreement (filed with the stipulation) and the Payment Schedule Addendum (filed with the Debtor's brief).

In August 2008, Debtor and Dakota executed an Equipment Lease Agreement, lease #2473, pursuant to which Debtor leased a 2007 Volvo, VNL64T880, VIN #* * 57 (hereafter "Semi-tractor). The Semi-tractor was at all times owned by Dakota. The Agreement states it is to be interpreted under California law and in paragraph 1, states, "It is the intent of Lessor and Lessee that this Lease is a true lease and not a lease

intended as security pursuant to Cal. Com.Code Section 1201(36)."
Debtor was required to make an initial rental payment of $20,000 and 60
rental payments of $2,185, due on the first day of every month. Pursuant
to paragraph 5 of the Agreement, Debtor also paid a security deposit of
$31,100 upon execution of the Agreement. The present value of the lease
payments, excluding the security deposit, does not equal or exceed the
purchase price of the Semi-tractor. The signature page of the Agreement
states in bold face, large type that "THIS LEASE IS NON-
CANCELLABLE. . . ."

The Debtor assumed the risk of loss of the tractor. Paragraph 11 of
the Agreement, entitled "Risk of Loss," states, "Lessee shall bear the
entire risk of loss, theft, destruction, damage or disrepair of the
Equipment or any part thereof for any cause whatsoever." The transfer
of this risk to the Debtor is reinforced by paragraph 7 of the Agreement,
which states, "Lessee bears all risk that the Equipment may become
unusable for any reason. . . . Debtor also agreed to pay taxes, insurance,
license and registration fees, and all service or maintenance costs.

The $31,100 security deposit is available to Dakota to secure
payment "for potential damages or excessive wear" to the Semi-tractor.
If Debtor performs every obligation under the Agreement, the security
deposit, or so much of it as has not been applied by Dakota, shall be
returned to the Debtor.

Debtor is not required to renew the Agreement at the end of the term
and does not have an option to do so. At the end of the term, the Semi-
tractor shall be returned to Dakota, unless Debtor exercises the purchase
option. As to return, the Agreement, paragraph 13 states, "Upon the
expiration or earlier cancellation or termination of this Lease, Lessee
shall, at Lessee's sole cost, expense and risk promptly return the
Equipment by delivering it, pack and ready for shipment, to such place
or carrier as Lessor may specify in good condition as received, less
reasonable wear and tear." As to Debtor's purchase option, the
Agreement, paragraph 19, states, "Provided that the Lease has not been
terminated or cancelled and that no default or Event of Default has
occurred and is continuing, on the last day of the Term, Lessee shall have
the option of to purchase the Equipment for a price equal to the following
'Purchase Option Price': $31,100. Lessor and Lessee acknowledge and
agree that such price represents the estimated fair market value of the
Equipment as of the date of the Lease."

There is no evidence that the rental payments required by the
Agreement were excessive as compared to typical lease payments. Debtor
contends the residual value of the subject Semi-tractor after expiration
of the lease term will be between $20,000 and $40,000. There is no
evidence that the Debtor was required to pay a substantial,
nonrefundable security deposit.

Debtor filed for relief under Chapter 13 on November 30, 2009.
Dakota is listed on Debtor's schedules as a secured creditor with a lien

on the Semi-tractor. Debtor's proposed plan treats Dakota's claim under the Agreement as a secured claim up to the value of the Semi-tractor. Through the Motion, Dakota objects to this treatment of its claim, contending that the Agreement is a true lease which Debtor should be compelled to assume or reject.

Analysis

A. The Equipment Lease Agreement is a True Lease

Much ink has been spilt over the intriguing question of what is a true lease. This Court recently examined the significant distinctions between a true lease and a security agreement in *HP Distribution, LLP*.[8] This opinion will not be prolonged by re-plowing that ground.

Determination of the question whether the August 2008 Equipment Lease Agreement is a true lease requires the Court to apply § 1–203 of the UCC, the relevant portions of which have been adopted without amendment in California.[9] As the party contending that the Agreement is not what it purports to be, the Debtor has the burden of proof.[10] An often cited law review article states the following as the guiding principles of the UCC amendments distinguishing leases from security interests that were initially codified in UCC § 1–201(37) and are now found in UCC § 1–203:

> The important principle recognized in amended section 1–201(37) is that lessors under a true lease are economic investors possessing a real economic stake in the residual value of the leased goods. . . . The original agreement in a true lease cannot contain an economically irresistible option, which the parties expect from the outset will be exercised by the lessee to purchase the goods or renew the lease for the remaining economic life of the goods. *To have a true lease, the original agreement must leave the lessor with some meaningful economic interest in the residual.*[11]

Under the UCC § 1–203(a), "[w]hether transaction in the form of a lease creates a lease or a security interest is determined by the facts of each case." Subsection (b) sets forth a "bright line" test of when a transaction in the form of a lease creates a security interest as a matter of law based upon the terms of the transaction. If the agreement in issue does not create a security interest per se under the bright line test, the Court then considers the "facts of each case" to determine if an

---

[8]   *Hitchin Post Steak Co. v. General Electric Capital Corp. (In re HP Distribution, LLP),* 436 B.R. 679 (Bankr.D.Kan.2010).

[9]   Cal. Com.Code § 1203.

[10]   *In re HP Distribution, LLP,* 436 B.R. at 682.

[11]   Edwin E. Huddleson, III, Old Wine in New Bottles: UCC Article 2A—Leases, 39 Ala. L.Rev. 615, 632 (1988) (Emphasis added).

economically meaningful interest was reserved to the lessor at the end of the lease term.[12]

The Bright-Line Test

The parties agree that the bright line test is not satisfied. As stated in U.C.C. § 1–203(b), the test is as follows:

(b) A transaction in the form of a lease creates a security interest if the consideration that the lessee is to pay the lessor for the right to possession and use of the goods is an obligation for the term of the lease and is not subject to termination by the lessee, and:

(1) The original term of the lease is equal to or greater than the remaining economic life of the goods;

(2) the lessee is bound to renew the lease for the remaining economic life of the goods or is bound to become the owner of the goods;

(3) the lessee has an option to renew the lease for the remaining economic life of the goods for no additional consideration or for nominal additional consideration upon compliance with the lease agreement; or

(4) the lessee has an option to become the owner of the goods for no additional consideration or for nominal additional consideration upon compliance with the lease agreement.[13]

The Court agrees with the parties that the facts of this case do not satisfy the bright line test. The test requires that the agreement cannot be terminated by the lessee and one of four other elements be present. As to termination, the Agreement expressly states on the signature page, in bold face large capitals, "THIS LEASE IS NON-CANCELLABLE. . . ." Therefore, the initial requirement is present.

The first three of the four alternative additional requirements clearly are not present. The original term of the lease is approximately five years. Debtor provides no direct evidence as to the remaining economic life of the Semi-tractor. However, based upon the Debtor's stipulation that the Semi-tractor will have a residual value between $20,000 and $40,000 at the end of the lease term, the Court finds that the economic life of the Semi-tractor exceeds the lease term. Debtor is not bound to renew the lease, and the Debtor does not have an option to renew the lease for the remaining economic life of the goods.

The fourth additional factor also is not satisfied. It asks whether the Debtor has an option to become the owner of the goods (1) for no additional consideration or (2) for nominal consideration. The agreement

---

[12] *Id.* at 625.

[13] UCC § 1–203(b).

provides that Debtor may purchase the Semi-tractor at the end of the term by the payment of $31,100. Although Debtor has stipulated that he "does not have the option to become the owner... for no additional consideration upon completion of the lease agreement," in his arguments he appears to assert that by applying the security deposit he could acquire the Semi-tractor for no additional consideration. Since the $31,100 option price is equal to the security deposit paid by Debtor at the inception of the lease, Debtor suggests that no additional consideration would be required to exercise the option. The Court rejects this argument. The Agreement specifies the expenses which are covered by the security deposit, and such expenses do not include the exercise of the purchase option. The Agreement provides for the payment of $31,100 additional consideration. Further, the full $31,100 security deposit would be available to apply to the option price only if at the end of the term no other expenses are deductible from the deposit, an event which Debtor has not shown to be likely. The Court concludes that additional consideration is required to exercise the purchase option.

The Court also finds the purchase price of $31,100 is not nominal. UCC § 1–201(37)(d)(i) provides that additional consideration is *not* nominal "when the option to become the owner of the goods is granted to the lessee, the price is stated to be the fair market value of the goods determined at the time the option is to be performed." Here the parties have stipulated that the option "price represents the estimated fair market value of the Equipment as of the date of the Lease." The fourth alternative of the bright line test is not satisfied.

The Economic Realities Test

Because the Court cannot conclusively presume that the Agreement is a security interest after applying the bright-line test, it must consider the economic realities of the transaction to determine if the Agreement is a true lease. The fundamental question is "whether the lessor retains a 'meaningful reversionary interest' in the property." The inquiry looks beyond the form of the Agreement and examines the nature and extent of the reversionary interest retained by Dakota, whether it retained a meaningful upside or downside risk. Stated somewhat differently, did Dakota relinquish its reversionary interest in the Semi-tractor under the terms of the Agreement?

Although the UCC directs courts to examine the "facts of each case," it "does not provide any standard for determining which facts are relevant or how relevant facts should be weighed in the final determination"[21] of whether the lessor retained a meaningful reversionary interest. Instead, UCC § 1–203(c) enumerates six factors which, if present, do not create a security interest "merely because" of

---

[21] *WorldCom Inc. v. General Electric Global Asset Management Services (In re WorldCom, Inc),* 339 B.R. 56, 71 (Bankr.S.D.N.Y.2006) (applying California law).

their presence.[22] The Court finds that four of the conditions are present and three are not. The second, third, fourth, and sixth factors are respectively shown as follows. The second factor is shown because the Debtor has assumed the risk of loss of the tractor. The third factor appears because the Debtor agreed to pay taxes, insurance, license and registration fees, and all service or maintenance costs. The Debtor has the option to become the owner of the Semi-tractor by paying Dakota $31,100 at the end of the term of the Agreement, demonstrating the fourth factor. The sixth factor is shown because the fixed price of $31,100 "represents the estimated fair market value of the Equipment as of the date of the" Agreement.

Three of the "merely because" factors, the first, fifth, and seventh, are not present. As the parties have stipulated that "the present value of the lease payments, excluding the security deposit, does not equal or exceed the purchase price of the subject Semi-tractor," the first is not present. Neither is the fifth because Debtor has stipulated that he does not have the option to renew the Agreement. Finally, the seventh factor is absent because the Agreement does not provide for increase or decrease in the rental payments.

However many factors appear, White and Summers suggest that these factors were included in the statute to overrule a series of bad decisions under the pre-1987 version of section § 1–207(37) and that generally, with the possible exception of condition (a), which is not present in this case, the factors are not only "not enough" to indicate a security agreement, and are "generally irrelevant."[26] One court has stated that the list "provides no guidance in determining what fact or set of facts would justify the court concluding that an agreement created a security interest."[27]

---

[22]   UCC § 1–203(c) provides:

(c) A transaction in the form of a lease does not create a security interest merely because:

    (1)   The present value of the consideration the lessee is obligated to pay the lessor for the right to possession and use of the goods is substantially equal to or is greater than the fair market value of the goods at the time the lease is entered into;

    (2)   the lessee assumes risk of loss of the goods;

    (3)   the lessee agrees to pay, with respect to the goods, taxes, insurance, filing, recording, or registration fees, or service or maintenance costs;

    (4)   the lessee has an option to renew the lease or to become the owner of the goods;

    (5)   the lessee has an option to renew the lease for a fixed rent that is equal to or greater than the reasonably predictable fair market rent for the use of the goods for the term of the renewal at the time the option is to be performed; or

    (6)   the lessee has an option to become the owner of the goods for a fixed price that is equal to or greater than the reasonably predictable fair market value of the goods at the time the option is to be performed.

[26]   4 J. White and R. Summers, Uniform Commercial Code § 30–3(c)(2) (2009).

[27]   In re WorldCom, Inc., 339 B.R. at 71.

California case law provides that two features of a lease must be examined in light of the question whether the lessor has relinquished its reversionary interest: "(1) any option to purchase and (2) any provision for the lessee's acquisition of equity in the goods." As to the option to purchase, the Agreement states:

> Provided that the Lease has not been terminated or cancelled and that no default or Event of Default has occurred and is continuing, on the last day of the Term, Lessee shall have the option to purchase the Equipment for a price equal to the following "Purchase Option Price": $31,100. Lessor and Lessee acknowledge and agree that such price represents the estimated fair market value of the Equipment as of the date of the Lease.[29]

UCC § 1–203(c)(6) "validates certain fixed price options as clearly consistent with true lease status."[30] It states:

> (c) A transaction in the form of a lease does not create a security interest merely because:
>
> . . .
>
> (6) the lessee has an option to become the owner of the goods for a fixed price that is equal to or greater than the reasonably predictable fair market value of the goods at the time the option is to be performed.[31]

This "safe harbor defines the classic case where the lessor retains a real, economically meaningful interest in the residual."[32]

In this case, the purchase option is within the safe harbor. The parties have stipulated that the $31,100 payment required by Debtor to become the owner at the end of the lease term represents the estimated fair market value of the Semi-tractor at that time, as determined on the date of the lease. However, a lessor can be found to have not retained a meaningful reversionary interest even though the purchase option is within safe harbor UCC § 1–203(c)(6).[34] The Court therefore considers Debtor's argument that this safe harbor does not control because of the $31,100 security deposit. As to the security deposit, the Agreement provides,

> Any security deposit paid by Lessee. . . shall be held by Lessor to secure payment for potential damages or excessive wear and performance of the obligations of Lessee hereunder. In the event Lessee performs each and every obligation under the

---

[29] Agreement ¶ 19, Dkt.74–1, p. 6.
[30] Edwin E. Huddleson, III, Old Wine in New Bottles, 39 Ala. L.Rev. at 633.
[31] UCC § 1–203(c).
[32] Edwin E. Huddleson, III, Old Wine in New Bottles, 39 Ala. L.Rev. at 633.
[34] *In re Grubbs Construction Co.*, 319 B.R. at 718 ([T]here is substantial authority that if the 'economic realities' dictate otherwise, the inclusion of a fair market value option . . . does not require the finding that the agreement is a true lease").

terms of his Lease, such security deposit or so much thereof that has not been applied by Lessor shall be returned to Lessee.

Based upon the security deposit provision, Debtor contends at the end of the term, if there were no charges against the deposit, "Dakota would not have a meaningful reversionary interest because either way the Debtor would either be paid the value of the semi-tractor [through return of the security deposit] or would have the semi-tractor returned." Debtor cites *Grubbs* and *Zerkle*[38] in support.

This argument ignores the function of a security deposit. The deposit operates to protect Dakota in the event of Debtor's default of his lease obligations, and at the end of the term any remaining balance shall be refunded to Debtor. The security deposit does not operate to negate Dakota's reversionary interest. The calculation of the refund is independent of the purchase option. If Debtor wishes to retain possession of the Semi-tractor at the end of the term, he must pay the purchase option price without regard to the amount of the security deposit refund. If Debtor does not wish to purchase the Semi-tractor, he may return it to Dakota and will also receive his refund. It is only if there are no charges against the security deposit that these transactions are economically neutral or offsetting. The Debtor does not argue, and there is no evidence, that the security deposit was set at the amount of the purchase option because of an expectation that Debtor would exercise the option and there would be no charges against the deposit. *Zerkle*, one of the cases relied upon by the Debtor, finds that refundable security deposits are consistent with true leases.[39] *Grubbs*, also cited by the Debtor, does not consider security deposits. Examination of the option to purchase indicates that the Agreement is a true lease.

When considering whether Dakota relinquished its reversionary interest in Semi-tractor, California case law also directs consideration of whether the lessee has acquired an equity in the leased goods.[40] "If a lessee develops equity in the leased property such that the only sensible decision economically for the lessee is to exercise the option. . . it suggests that the lessor did not expect the return of the leased goods."[41] As one court explained the test, "In asking whether the lessee has an equity interest, the Court is essentially examining whether the contractual option price was set lower than the predicted FMV of the goods in order to reflect the equity interest in the goods that the lessee had previously accumulated, presumably by paying more in 'rent' than the parties would have agreed to in the absence of an intent to allow the lessee to accumulate such equity."[42]

---

[38] *In re Zerkle Trucking Co*, 132 B.R. 316 (Bankr.S.D.Va.1991).

[39] *In re Zerkle*, 132 B.R. at 320.

[40] *Addison v. Burnett*, 41 Cal.App.4th at 1296, 49 Cal. Rprt.2d at 137.

[41] *Id., quoting In re Zaleha*, 159 B.R. 581, 585 (Bankr. D.Idaho 1993).

[42] *In re WorldCom, Inc.*, 339 B.R. at 73.

Debtor relies exclusively upon the security deposit in support of his argument that he has acquired equity in the Semi-tractor. He asserts that the security deposit should be recharacterized as "a potential down payment that could merely become applicable at the tail-end of the Agreement." If the down payment is only "potential," the Debtor has acquired no equity. Debtor stipulated that the security deposit is refundable and that "there is no evidence that the debtor was required to pay a substantial, nonrefundable security deposit." Further, Debtor stipulated that "the present value of the lease payments, excluding the security deposit, does not equal or exceed the purchase price of the subject semi-tractor" and "there is no evidence that the rental payments required by the lease were excessive as compared to typical lease payments." The $31,100 option price set at the commencement of the lease is in the middle of the $20,000 to $40,000 range which Debtor now contends to be the residual value of the Semi-tractor of the end of the lease term. Clearly the evidence precludes the Court from concluding that the only economically sensible option for the Debtor would be to exercise the option at the end of the term. Because the Debtor has not acquired equity in the Semi-tractor, Dakota has retained a meaningful reversionary interest.

For the foregoing reasons, the Court finds that the Agreement is a true lease. The bright line test is not satisfied. The economic realities evidence that Dakota retained a significant reversionary interest in the semi-tractor and Debtor does not have equity in the Semi-tractor.

B.   Debtor's Obligation to Assume or Reject the Lease

Since the 2008 Agreement is a true lease with a five year term and it had not expired as of the date of filing, the Agreement is subject to § 365 of the Code. Pursuant to § 365(d)(2), in a Chapter 13 case, the trustee, may assume or reject an unexpired lease of personal property of the debtor at any time before the confirmation of the plan, but, on request of the lessor, the court "may order the trustee to determine within a specified time whether to assume or reject the such lease or contract." Section 1303 provides that the debtor shall have the rights and powers of the trustee under § 363(d).

Dakota requests in its Motion that Debtor be compelled to assume or reject the Agreement, but states no suggested deadline. The Court therefore ORDERS that Debtor file a pleading electing to assume or reject within 30 days of the docketing of this Memorandum Opinion. Such election, in conjunction with the applicable Code sections, shall determine the rights and obligations of the parties relating to the Agreement and the Semi-tractor. Pursuant to § 365(p)(1), if Debtor rejects the Agreement or it is not timely assumed, the Semi-tractor will no longer be property of the estate, and the stay of § 362(a) will be automatically lifted.

Conclusion

For the foregoing reasons, the Court finds that the Equipment Lease Agreement between Debtor as lessee and Dakota as lessor whereby Debtor acquired possession of the Semi-tractor is a true lease. The terms of the Agreement do not satisfy the bright line test when a purported lease is a security agreement. The economic realities of the transaction evidence that Dakota retained a significant reversionary interest in the Semi-tractor and Debtor does not have equity in the Semi-tractor.

Dakota Financial, LLC's Motion to Compel Assumption or Rejection of Executory Contract is hereby granted. Within 30 days of the docketing of this Memorandum Opinion, Debtor shall file a pleading stating his intent to assume or reject the Agreement.

Sections 1–203(b)(3) and 1–203(b)(4)'s terms are in important respects underspecified. Section 1–203(b)(3) provides that a security interest is created if the agreement contains "an option to renew the lease for the remaining economic life of the goods for no additional consideration or nominal additional consideration upon compliance with the lease agreement." Section 1–203(b)(4) provides that a security interest is created if the lessee has an "option to become the owner of the goods for no additional consideration or nominal additional consideration upon compliance with the lease agreement."

Crucial to the application of 1–203(b)(3) and (4) is the meaning of "nominal consideration." Under 1–203(d), "[a]dditional consideration is nominal if it is less than the lessee's reasonably predictable cost of performing under the lease agreement if the option is not exercised." One aspect of the issue is clear: Matter of Marhoefer Packing Co., Inc., 671 F.2d 1139 (7th Cir. 1982) established that in determining whether an option price is nominal, the proper figure to compare it with is not the actual fair market value of the leased goods at the time option is exercised but the value anticipated at the time the lease was signed. If because of inflation or other matters the lessee's option became more favorable than either party anticipated at the time of signing, the character of the transaction is not changed. Section 1–203(e) codifies this result by stating that the remaining economic life of the goods or the reasonably predictable fair market value or cost of performing "must be determined with reference to the facts and circumstances at the time the transaction is entered into."

The meaning of "less than the lessee's reasonably predictable cost of performing if the option is not exercised" has perplexed courts and commentators. The determination of the "cost of performing" is intensely factual and poses a "definitional nightmare both for those attempting to structure a lease transaction and those subsequently called upon to interpret it." See In re QDS Components, 292 B.R. 313, 341 (Bankr. S.D. Ohio 2002). Some see this language as merely reviving the traditional "economic realities" test: is the option price so low that the lessee will certainly exercise it and leave no meaningful reversion for the lessor? See In re Gateway Ethanol, L.L.C., 415 B.R. 486, 500 (Bankr. D. Kan.2009). The court in *QDS Components* concluded, with resignation, that there are "nearly as many different approaches to determining the existence of a meaningful residual interest as there are reported decisions." *QDS Components*, at 342.

More important is the lack of a definition of "nominal consideration" in 1–203. The absence of a definition allows courts to construe the term differently. In In re Super Feeders, Inc., 236 B.R. 267 (Bankr. D. Neb.1999), the court held that an option to buy for $46,250 was nominal when the purchase price was $925,000, the total rental payments were $1,281,987, and the predicted value at the end of the seven-year lease was $225,000. The option purchase price was five percent of the predicted value of the asset. According to the court, the percentage made the option price "nominal." In *Marhoefer*, the court characterized an option purchase price of almost 50 percent of the estimated value of the asset as "not nominal." Suppose the relevant percentage had been 23, 50 or 75 in these cases. At what point does the percentage of purchase option price to predicted value make the option price "nominal"?

Some commentators favor a percentage test of "nominal consideration." White and Summers, for example, advocate this test: "We would allow a substantial deviation from that value [value that goods are expected to have at the time the option is to be exercised] and yet conclude the amount is not 'nominal.' We believe that any option price less than 50% of the predicted fair market value (predicted at signing as the value at the option date) is nominal and anything above 50% should normally be accepted as not nominal." 4 James J. White and Robert S. Summers, Uniform Commercial Code § 30–3 at 37 (6th Prac. ed. 2010). Percentage tests in general are problematic. Apart from the trouble of settling on a particular percentage, the more basic difficulty is to justify why any percentage of estimated asset value makes an option price not nominal.

Section 1–203's drafters tried to agree on a percentage formula to define what is nominal consideration, e.g., no greater than 10 percent of the original value of the goods or less than 75 percent of the reasonably predictable fair market value of the goods at the time the option was to be exercised. See Edwin E. Huddleson III, Old Wine in New Bottles: UCC Article 2A—Leases, 39 Ala. L. Rev. 615, 628–631 (1988). Eventually, efforts to arrive at a percentage formula were abandoned. By comparison, the efforts of accountants have been more successful. by the Financial Standards Board, Accounting Standards Update No. 2016–02, Leases (Topic 842) (2016), includes percentage tests among its tests for distinguishing capital (or "finance") leases from operating leases. For example, a lease must be treated as a finance lease if the net present value of minimum lease payments equal or exceed 90 percent of the fair market value of the leased asset as of the lease's inception. The court in *QDS Components* infers from 1–203's failure to mention a percentage test of nominal consideration that such a test is inapplicable to 1–203.

Although 1–203 does not define "nominal consideration," a defensible position is that, as a first approximation, a purchase option price is nominal if it is less than the fair market value of the asset at the time the purchase option can be exercised, as forecast at the inception of the transaction., More precise notions of nominal consideration will take into account the cost of not exercising the option. For example, if the optionee must return the asset and forfeit its deposit should the purchase option not be exercised, and the sum of the cost of returning the asset and the amount of deposit is greater than the purchase option price, the price is nominal. 1–203(d)'s first sentence confirms this result. Although "nominal consideration" conjures up ideas of a minimal or very small amount, the suggested definition of "nominal consideration" fits with the notion that a purchase option is likely to be exercised if it is a bargain price. A purchase option price in turn is a bargain price if it is less than fair market value, as estimated when the transaction is entered into, at the time the option can be exercised. Whether the purchase option price is minimal or very small does not matter. The rough definition seems appropriate in an inquiry to determine whether the lessor will retain a meaningful residual interest in the asset at the end of the transaction.

Article 9 takes into account the difficulties in applying 1–203 to characterize a transaction as creating a lease or a security interest. Section 9–505(a) permits the lessor to file a financing statement using the terms "lessor" and "lessee." Under 9–505(b), the filing cannot be used by itself to determine whether the transaction creates a security interest. The lessor's filing protects its interest if the lease transaction later is found to create a security interest. Nonetheless, lessors often do not make a protective filing because their lessees refuse to allow it (filing can have an adverse impact on a lessee's finances), they do not believe that a court will heed 9–505(b)'s injunction or they are confident that the transaction will be characterized as a lease.

PROBLEMS

Characterize the transactions described below by consulting 1–201(b)(35) and 1–203. In doing so, assume where relevant that a straight line rate of depreciation accurately reflects reduction in the value of the machine referred to below. A straight-line rate allocates depreciation per period by the formula:

$$\text{Per period depreciation} = \frac{\text{Cost of asset} - \text{Salvage value}}{\text{Useful life of asset}}$$

Assume also that the machine involved in the transactions below has no salvage value at the end of its useful life.

1.   Susan and Bill concluded a written agreement concerning a machine with a useful life of ten years. Machines of the type subject to their agreement normally sell for $100,000. The terms of the agreement recited that "Susan agrees to lease the machine to Bill for ten years at an annual rent of $10,000. At the end of that time, Bill is required to return the machine to Susan. Neither Bill nor Susan have the right to cancel this lease." Lease or security interest? Would the characterization change if the agreement recited that "Susan retains title to the machine throughout the lease term"? 1–201(b)(35) (sixth sentence).

2.   Assume that the agreement in Problem 1 is for five years. The agreement gives Bill the right to purchase the machine at the end of the third year for $40,000. In light of Bill's extraordinary care of the machine, the machine has a value of $70,000 at the end of the third year. Lease or security interest? See 1–203(d)(2) and (e).

3.   Bill leased a machine from Susan for five years. Their agreement calls for Bill to make annual payments as rent and does not allow either party to cancel the arrangement. Neither party is entitled to cancel the lease. Machines of the sort Bill leased can be purchased for $20,000 and have a six-year useful life, and no scrap value. The industry has a strong preference for new machines, so that the machine Bill leased will decline in value to $12,000 on delivery. The machine's value declines by $2,000 in each subsequent year. For instance, at the end of the first year after delivery the machine's value is $10,000. Bill's agreement with Susan gives him the right to purchase the machine at the end of each year of the five-year arrangement. The purchase price is set by a schedule calculated according to a straight line rate of depreciation over the five-year period of the transaction. For example, at the end of the first year Bill could purchase the machine for $16,000. Lease or security interest? Would the result change if the machine turns out to have no value after the third year? 1–203(d). Would the result change if Bill had the right to purchase the machine at the end of the first four years of the five-year arrangement according to the calculated purchase prices?

PROBLEM

Supplier offered to sell or lease a food processing machine to Customer. For a cash sale, the purchase price was $33,225. For a credit sale, the terms were $7,225 down and 24 monthly installments of $1,224, for a total purchase price of $36,601. However, Customer chose a third alternative that was designated a lease. The terms were that Lessor leased the machine to Lessee for four years at $665 per month for a total of $31,920. At the end of the four-year term, Lessee had the option of (1) returning the machine to Lessor, (2) purchasing the machine for $9,968, or (3) renewing the lease for four more years at an annual rental of $2,990. If Lessee chose the third option, it could purchase the machine for $1 at the end of the second four-year term. The useful life of the machine was eight to ten years. The $9,968 option price was arrived at by estimating that at the end of four years the machine would have a market price of 30% of its original $33,225 cash price.

Lessee filed for bankruptcy only a year after the lease was entered into. Since Lessor did not file a financing statement, the trustee in bankruptcy moved to sell the property free of Lessor's interest. The issue was whether the lease created a security interest or whether it was a true lease which would be valid in bankruptcy without a filing. At the hearing on Lessor's motion, the trustee introduced expert testimony that the value of the machine at the end of four years would be $18,000 to $20,000. On this basis, the trustee contended that the option to buy for $9,968 was actually nominal consideration. The facts are based on Matter of Marhoefer Packing Co., Inc., 674 F.2d 1139 (7th Cir.1982). Comment 2 (final paragraph) to 1–203 states: "[T]his section could have stated a rule to govern the facts of In re Marhoefer Packing Co. . . . This was not done because it would unnecessarily complicate the definition. Further development of this rule is left to the courts."

(a)   Does this "lease" create a security interest under 1–203?

(b)   In the above "lease," the purported lessee is not obligated to renew the lease for a second four-year period. Therefore, it is not obligated to make payments necessary to exercise the $1 purchase option. On the same facts, the *Marhoefer* court found this decisive in characterizing the transaction as a true lease; see *Marhoefer*, Id. at 1143. Do you agree? Suppose the "lessee" were obligated to renew the "lease" for a second four-year term, but it also had the right to terminate the "lease" one day prior to the end of the second period. Would the transaction still be a true lease? What statement would express a defensible rule to govern both the facts above as well as the altered facts concerning termination?

b.   MEANINGFUL RESIDUAL INTEREST

The distinguishing feature of a lease is that it grants the lessee the right to use the property for a period less than its economic life with the concomitant obligation to return the property to the lessor while it retains some substantial economic life. Accordingly, the lessor retains an economically meaningful residual interest in the leased property. Because the lessor retains this residual interest, it continues to own the property at the end of the lease. Both 1–203(b) and 1–203(a), the latter as applied, test whether the lessor retains a residual interest in the goods—whether the lessor remains the owner—at the end of the lease term. Section 1—203(b)'s four disjunctive conditions all relate to the purported lessor's retention of a residual interest. One goes to the term of the lease and the other three conditions relate to options to purchase or renew the lease. If the duration of the lease is equal to or greater than the economically useful life of the asset, so that 1–203(b)(1) applies, the lessor has no residual interest in the asset of value at the end of the lease term. Similarly, if a purchase or renewal option price is nominal, so that the lessee likely will exercise the option, the lessor also will not retain a meaningful residual interest in the leased asset. 1–203(b)(3) and (4) . The lessee therefore likely will acquire the residual interest. As noted below, in applying 1–203(a) courts inquire into whether the lessor retains a meaningful residual interest at the end of the lease term. *Warne* is representative. In applying 1–203(a), the court states that the "fundamental question" to be whether the lessor retains a meaningful reversionary interest in the goods.

NOTE: RENT-TO-OWN LEASES

A rent-to-own contract is a terminable lease with an option to purchase. No down payment or security deposit is required and the credit history or financial state of the lessee is not checked. The term of the lease is typically short, from one week to a month, and the rent for the period is paid in advance. The lease permits the lessee to renew the lease for an additional term simply by paying in advance for the term. If the lessee continues to rent the asset for a stipulated period (usually about 78 weeks), it becomes the owner at the end of the period. RTOs typically also include an option allowing the lessee to purchase the asset within the period for a cash price determined in part by the amount of rental payments previously made. Small rental payments are usually required; the effective exercise price of becoming the owner under an RTO lease often is two to four times the retail cash price. The assets rented are mostly new and used furniture, appliances and electronic equipment. Although the RTO industry reports that most RTO customers do not end up owning the assets rented, an FTC survey finds that 70 percent of RTO customers purchase the merchandise. Federal Trade Commission Bureau of Economics Staff Report, Executive Summary (2000).

RTOs have become the focus of legislative efforts, pitting consumer groups and bankruptcy trustees against the RTO industry. At the federal level, the National Bankruptcy Review Commission in 1997 recommended that the Bankruptcy Code be amended to characterize RTOs as installment sales contracts. See 1 National Bankruptcy Review Commission, Bankruptcy: The Next Twenty Years 174–178 (1997) (Recommendation 1.3.5). The recommendation was not adopted. The RTO industry has been influential at the state level. Almost all states have enacted statutes providing that RTOs terminable by the lessee are "true leases," not installment sales contracts. Even in the few states that have not enacted such legislation, 1–203 arguably does not consider a terminable RTO a "security interest." In Perez v. Rent-A-Center, Inc., 892 A.2d 1255 (N.J. 2006), the New Jersey Supreme Court relied on its finding that a vast majority of RTO customers purchase the merchandise rented to conclude that a terminable RTO contract is a type of conditional sales contract. Although the *Perez* court did not consider 1–203, its "conditional sale" characterization commits it to characterizing the transaction as creating a security interest. Other courts disagree, finding that the absence of an obligation of the RTO customer to renew the lease or purchase the goods makes the transaction a true lease. See, e.g., Silva v. Rent-A-Center, Inc., 454 Mass. 667 (2009).

3. LEASE WITHOUT OPTION TO PURCHASE OR RENEW: 1–203(a)'S "TEST"

As described in the previous section, the functional difference between a lease and a security interest is that the lessor retains a meaningful reversionary interest in the goods. By contrast, a seller of goods backed by a security interest does not retain a meaningful residual interest in the goods sold. A sale passes ownership in the goods to the buyer while the lessor continues to own the leased property at the end of the lease term. If a nonterminable lease does not contain a purchase or renewal option and its duration is less than the economic life of the leased goods, 1–203(b)'s bright-line test does not apply. By its terms, 1–203(b)'s test also is inapplicable where the lease is terminable. In both cases 1–203(a) instead determines whether the transaction creates a security interest. Under 1–203(a), whether a transaction in the form of a creates a security interest is determined by "the facts of each case."

As noted above, 1–203(a) describes a "test" in name only. The subsection does not state a standard, much less one related to the lessor's retention of a meaningful residual interest. Instead, it leaves to courts to determine which facts determine whether the transaction creates a security interest. Most courts follow *Warne* and *Pillowtex* (the latter reproduced below) in finding that the most significant fact for purposes of 1–203(a)'s test is whether, given the economic realities, the lessor retains a meaningful residual interest in the leased asset at the end of the lease term.

Comment 2 to 1–203 potentially adds to the uncertainty in 1–203(a)'s "facts of each case" test. The Comment in relevant part states: "A fixed price purchase option in a lease does not of itself create a security interest. This is particularly true if the fixed price is equal to or greater than the reasonably predictable fair market value of the goods at the time the option is to be performed. A security interest is created only if the option price is nominal. . . . There is a set of purchase options whose fixed price is less than fair market value but greater than nominal that must be determined on the facts of each case to ascertain whether the transaction in which the option is included creates a lease or a security interest." The Comment is reasonable enough as far as it goes: 1–203(a) requires resort to relevant facts to determine whether a nonnominal purchase option price which is below fair market value creates a security interest. But without a definition of when consideration is nominal, 1–203(a) leaves the inquiry into relevant facts completely unguided. In such cases the only fact that is apparent is that fair market value is greater than the purchase option price. It makes no sense to ask whether a nonnominal purchase option price falls within a specific range of prices without a definition of what makes a purchase option price nominal.

Section 1–203(c) sets out six common provisions in leases that do not by themselves or in combination ("merely because") create a security interest. According to 1–203(c)(1), a lease under which the lessee is obligated to pay an amount whose present value is equal to or greater than the fair market value of the goods at the time the lease is entered into alone does not create a security interest. Thus, a full payout lease does not per se create a security interest. Sections 1–203(c)(2) and (3) overrule some bad caselaw by providing that whether a lessee assumes the risk of loss of the goods or agrees to pay taxes, insurance, or services costs does nothing to distinguish a lease from a security transaction.

In addition, 1–203(c) provides in relevant part that a transaction in the form of a lease does not create a security interest merely because: (4) it provides that a lessee has an option to renew or buy, or (5) that the lessee has an option to renew the lease for a fixed rent equal to or greater than the reasonably predictable fair market rent for the term of the renewal at the time the option is to be performed, or (6) that the lessee has an option to buy for a fixed price that is equal to or greater than the reasonably predictable fair market value of the goods at the time of exercise of the option is to be performed. If a lease provides that the lessee has the option to renew or buy at the fair market price determined at the time of exercise of the option, the risk of the market is entirely on the lessor and the transaction does not create a security interest. But by predicting the fair market rent or value at the inception of the transaction, paragraphs (5) and (6) place some of the risk on the lessee but not enough to justify a finding of a security transaction.

Section 1–203(c)'s purpose is prophylactic. It prevents a court from characterizing a transaction as creating a security interest only because one or more provisions are on subsection (c)'s list. As a result, in determining whether a transaction to create a security interest under 1–203(a), the court must rely at least in part on provisions in the agreement other than those described in 1–203(c). Although 1–203(c) in principle can apply to transactions tested by 1–203(b)'s bright-line test, subsection (c)'s application there is unnecessary: If the bright-line test determines that the transaction creates a security interest, it does not matter whether one of more of the security agreement's provisions are on subsection (c)'s list.

In re Pillowtex, Inc.

United States Court of Appeals, Third Circuit, 2003
349 F.3d 711

■ Fuentes, Circuit Judge.

Duke Energy Royal LLC ("Duke") appeals from an order of the District Court denying a motion to compel Pillowtex Corporation ("Pillowtex" or "debtor") to make lease payments owing under the Master Energy Services Agreement ("MESA"), an agreement its predecessor entered into with Pillowtex. The District Court denied Duke's motion on the grounds that the MESA was not a true lease, but rather a secured financing arrangement. The sole issue in this appeal is whether the District Court correctly determined that the MESA entered into between Pillowtex and Duke prior to Pillowtex's bankruptcy filing was a secured financing arrangement rather than a true lease. We affirm because we agree with the District Court that, based on the economic realities of the underlying transaction, the MESA was a secured financing arrangement.

I.   Facts and Procedural Background

Because the nature of the MESA is at issue, we first turn to its provisions and the transaction underlying the agreement. Pillowtex and Duke entered into the MESA on June 3, 1998. Pursuant to the MESA, Duke agreed to install certain equipment "for the purpose of improving the efficiency of energy consumption or otherwise to reduce the operating costs" incurred by Pillowtex at its facilities. (MESA § 2.5, App. at 299). The MESA covered two different sets of energy services projects, one involving production equipment and the other energy-savings equipment. The production equipment was provided to Pillowtex by Duke pursuant to separate stand-alone agreements, which were recorded as true leases on Pillowtex's books, and which the parties agree constituted true leases. Therefore, only the nature of the parties' arrangements concerning the energy-savings equipment is at issue in this appeal.

The energy-savings equipment included certain lighting fixtures, T8 lamps and electronic ballasts (collectively the "lighting fixtures"), which were installed in nine of Pillowtex's facilities and a new wastewater heat recovery system that included hot water heating equipment (the "wastewater system" and together with the lighting fixtures, the "energy fixtures"), which was installed at Pillowtex's Columbus, Georgia plant. The lighting fixtures were selected, and the wastewater system was constructed, specifically for Pillowtex's facilities.

In order to induce Pillowtex to enter into the energy services projects, Duke offered to originate funding for the production equipment "on a two-to-one basis (*i.e.,* for every $1 million of energy projects Duke would originate $2 million for funding of equipment) with a minimum of $28 million in funding for equipment leasing or financing." Another incentive Pillowtex had for entering into the agreement was "that the energy projects would be cost neutral to Pillowtex for the term of the agreement; that is, Pillowtex's payments to Duke would be equivalent to Pillowtex's actual savings. . . and Pillowtex would then reap the benefits from the cost savings after the end of the term of the project." (App. at 153). In keeping with this arrangement, Pillowtex accounted for its payments to Duke under the MESA as a utility expense.

The MESA provided that the cost of acquiring and installing the energy fixtures would be paid by Duke, which incurred total costs of approximately $10.41 million. (MESA § 5, App. at 302; 339). Of this amount, approximately $1.66 million was for material and labor costs for the wastewater system. Approximately $4.46 million was for labor to install the lighting fixtures and $4.29 million was for material costs for the lighting fixtures, which is to say that the cost of labor to install the fixtures was higher than the cost of the actual materials themselves. Also, Duke paid approximately $223,000 to dispose of light fixtures and related equipment that it removed from Pillowtex's facilities.

In exchange, Pillowtex was to pay Duke on a monthly basis one-twelfth of Pillowtex's annual energy savings, in an amount the parties agreed to in advance, until the end of the MESA's 8 year term. (MESA § 7.0). In addition, the parties agreed that the simple payback of all of Duke's costs was not to exceed 5 years. (MESA § 4.1(f)). "Simple payback" is synonymous with "payback period," an accounting term which refers to "[t]he length of time required to recover a venture's initial cash investment, without accounting for the time value of money." BLACK'S LAW DICTIONARY 1150 (7th ed. 1999). In other words, the payments were structured to ensure that Pillowtex would make predetermined, equal monthly payments and that Duke would recover its costs 3 years prior to the end of the term of the MESA. Although the MESA was for an 8 year term, the parties agree that the useful life of the energy fixtures was 20–25 years.

It is undisputed that Duke and Pillowtex intended to structure the MESA to have the characteristics of a lease and that the parties were trying to create a true lease. Indeed, Pillowtex's counsel conceded during oral argument before the District Court, "I don't disagree that [the MESA] was structured to have those characteristics for tax purposes and, you know, to [the] extent they could, the parties were trying to create a true lease, I would admit that." The parties intended for the MESA to be structured as a true lease, in large part, because Pillowtex was subject to capital expenditure limitations under its senior credit facility and did not wish to have the energy-savings equipment count as capital expenditures under that facility. Nevertheless, the MESA is not labeled a lease and it does not refer to the parties as lessee and lessor. * * *

In keeping with their intent to structure the transaction as a lease, the MESA provides that title to the equipment would remain with Duke. (MESA § 11.0). Also, Pillowtex agreed not to claim ownership of the equipment for income tax purposes, (MESA § 9.13(ii)), and Pillowtex was not obligated to purchase the equipment at the end of the term of the MESA. Rather, the MESA provided the following four options to Duke at the conclusion of its term, if Pillowtex was not then in default:

(i) remove the Equipment installed and replace those [sic] Equipment with equipment comparable to those originally in place, provided that no such replacement shall be required with respect to Production Equipment; or,

(ii) abandon the Equipment in place; or,

(iii) continue this Agreement until the expiration of the term hereof and then extend the term of this Agreement for such additional period(s) and payment terms as the parties may agree upon; or,

(iv) [g]ive the Customer the option of purchasing all (but not less than all) of the Equipment at a mutually agreed upon price.

(MESA § 8.3). If Duke elected to exercise option (I), it was bound to "be responsible for all costs and expenses in removing such Equipment, including costs to repair any damage to [Pillowtex's] Facility caused by such removal." (*Id.*)[2] Despite the existence of the option for Duke to repossess the equipment, Pillowtex's Vice President for Engineering, Michael Abba, testified that in his understanding, there was no chance of that option being exercised:

> It was clearly my understanding that Duke would abandon the Lighting Fixtures and the Wastewater System at the conclusion of the MESA and in fact statements were made to me by Duke sales personnel to that effect. Moreover, because the energy projects were of no economic benefit to Pillowtex until the end of the term when Pillowtex would reap the energy savings going forward, I would not have signed off on the projects if the Lighting Fixtures and Wastewater System were not to be abandoned. I also believe that, based on the prohibitive cost of removing and replacing the Lighting Fixtures and the Wastewater System for Pillowtex, Duke [had] no choice but to abandon the Lighting Fixtures and the Wastewater System at the end of the term of the MESA.

[Ed.—After Duke and Pillowtex executed the MESA, Duke made a collateral assignment agreement with General Electric Capital Corporation (GECC) under which GECC agreed to finance Duke's purchase of lighting fixtures it installed at four of the nine Pillowtex facilities. Duke in exchange granted GECC a security interest in all its rights and interests under the MESA, including Duke's right to payment under the MESA. Later, GECC assigned all its rights under the MESA to Southtrust.]

On November 14, 2000, Pillowtex and certain of its subsidiaries filed petitions for relief under Chapter 11 of the Bankruptcy Code. Thereafter, Pillowtex stopped making payments due under the MESA. On February 21, 2002, Duke filed a motion under section 365(d)(10) of the Bankruptcy Code to compel Pillowtex to make lease payments on the equipment it had provided to Pillowtex under the MESA. Section 365(d)(10) requires debtors-in-possession, such as Pillowtex, to "timely perform all of the obligations of the debtor. . . first arising from or after 60 days after the order for relief in a case under Chapter 11. . . under an unexpired lease of personal property. . . until such lease is assumed or rejected. . . ."

---

[2] In the event of a default by Pillowtex, Duke would have the right to remove the equipment at Pillowtex's expense, without being obligated to replace it, and could terminate the MESA. (MESA § 13.2, App. at 309).

§ 365(d)(10).[3] In response to Duke's motion, Pillowtex filed an objection in which it argued that Duke was not entitled to payment of post-petition monthly obligations, which Pillowtex represented amounted to $1.8 million, because the MESA was not a true lease. After a hearing on the matter, the District Court, sitting in Bankruptcy, denied Duke's motion. Duke timely appealed. * * *

III. Analysis

Whether an agreement is a true lease or a secured financing arrangement under the Bankruptcy Code is a question of state law. . . . In this case, the parties agreed that the MESA would be interpreted, performed, and enforced in accordance with the laws of the State of New York. (MESA, Appendix A, § 17.7). Accordingly, we turn to New York law in order to resolve whether the MESA constitutes a secured financing arrangement or a lease. * * *

Section 1–201(37) [1–201(b)(35)] of the U.C.C. provides that a security interest "means an interest in personal property or fixtures which secures payment or performance of an obligation." N.Y. U.C.C. § 1–201(37). After defining the term "security interest," section 1–201(37) sets out a test for determining whether a transaction creates a lease or a security interest. Section 1–201(37) [1–203(a)] begins by noting that whether a transaction creates a lease or a security interest is to be determined on a case-by-case basis. After indicating that courts are to examine the facts of each case in order to characterize a transaction, the statute sets out a bright-line test, sometimes referred to as a per se rule, for determining whether a transaction creates a security interest as a matter of law. Specifically, section 1–201(37) [1–203(a) and (b)] provides:

(a)   Whether a transaction creates a lease or security interest is determined by the facts of each case; however, a transaction creates a security interest if the consideration the lessee is to pay the lessor for the right to possession and use of the goods is an obligation for the term of the lease not subject to termination by the lessee, *and:*

(i)   the original term of the lease is equal to or greater than the remaining economic life of the goods,

(ii)   the lessee is bound to renew the lease for the remaining economic life of the goods or is bound to become the owner of the goods,

(iii) the lessee has an option to renew the lease for the remaining economic life of the goods for no additional consideration or nominal additional consideration upon compliance with the lease agreement, *or*

---

[3]   Although § 365(d)(10) refers to the obligation of a trustee to make lease payments, its provisions apply to Pillowtex because the Bankruptcy Code provides that debtors-in-possession, such as Pillowtex, are to perform all of the functions and duties of a Chapter 11 trustee. *See* 11 U.S.C. § 1107(a).

(iv) the lessee has an option to become the owner of the
goods for no additional consideration or nominal additional
consideration upon compliance with the lease agreement.

N.Y. U.C.C. § 1–201(37) [1–203(a) and (b)] (emphasis added). Thus,
under the two-part test set out in New York's U.C.C., if Pillowtex did not
have the right to terminate the MESA prior to the end of its term, *and*
any of the four factors set out in section 1–201(a)(37)(i)–(iv) are met, then
the MESA would be considered to create a security interest as a matter
of law. *See In re Owen,* 221 B.R. at 60–61. If, on the other hand, it is
determined that "the transaction is not a disguised security agreement
per se, [we] must then look at the specific facts of the case to determine
whether the economics of the transaction suggest such a result." *In re
Taylor,* 209 B.R. 482, 484 (Bankr.S.D.Ill.1997) (citation omitted). In this
case, the District Court went directly to the economic realities of the
transaction memorialized in the MESA. In doing so the Court seems to
have implicitly held that the MESA was not a disguised security
agreement under the bright-line test of section 1–201(37). We agree.

[Ed.—The court determined that none of the four factors set out in
former 1–201(b)(37)(i)–(iv) [1–203(b)(1)–(4)] was met.]

The parties agree that, where none of the four factors set out in
section 1–201(37) are present, courts are to consider the economic reality
of the transaction in order to determine, based on the particular facts of
the case, whether the transaction is more fairly characterized as a lease
or a secured financing arrangement. They also agree that the District
Court applied the correct standard for evaluating the economic reality of
their transaction. As the District Court explained:

Under relevant case law, courts will look to various factors in
evaluating the "economic reality of the transaction... in
determining whether there has been a sale or a true lease,"
Pactel Fin. v. D.C. Marine Serv. Corp., 136 Misc.2d 194, 518
N.Y.S.2d 317, 318 (N.Y.Dist.Ct.1987), including the following:
"[a] whether the purchase option is nominal; [b] whether the
lessee is required to make aggregate rental payments having a
present value equaling or exceeding the original cost of the
leased property; and [c] whether the lease term covers the total
useful life of the equipment." *In re Edison Bros. Stores, Inc.,* 207
B.R. 801, 809–10 and n. 8, 9, 10 (Bankr.D.Del.1997). *See also*
[N.Y. U.C.C.] § 1–201(37) (McKinney Supp.1996). "In this
regard, courts are required to examine the intent of the parties
and the facts and circumstances which existed at the time the
transaction was entered into." *In re Edison,* 207 B.R. at 809.

The District Court found that the MESA was substantively better
characterized as a security agreement than a true lease because the
second *Edison Bros.* factor clearly weighed in Pillowtex's favor, and the
first and third factors were largely neutral. We agree with the District
Court's conclusion in this regard.

Specifically, with respect to the second factor, Duke concedes that the aggregate rental payments owing by Pillowtex under the MESA had a present value equal to or exceeding the cost of the energy fixtures. The *Edison Bros.* court cogently explained the importance of such a fact in showing the existence of a security agreement:

> The rationale behind this second factor is that if the alleged lessee is obligated to pay the lessor a sum equal to or greater than the full purchase price of the leased goods plus an interest charge over the term of the alleged lease agreement, a sale is likely to have been intended since what the lessor will receive is more than a payment for the use of the leased goods and loss of their value; the lessor will receive a consideration that would amount to a return on its investment.

Edison Bros., 207 B.R. at 814 (*quoted in Owen,* 221 B.R. at 61–62). Applying that logic to this case, Duke has already been well-compensated for the transferral of the lighting fixtures to Pillowtex, undercutting the proposition that the fixtures were merely leased.

Like the District Court, we are unpersuaded by Duke's attempt to rely on the first and third *Edison Bros.* factors. With respect to the first factor, Duke points out that the MESA provides that it "has the option to. . . give [Pillowtex] the option of purchasing all (but not less than all) of the Equipment at a *mutually agreed price."* App. at 304 (emphasis added). Based on this provision of the MESA, Duke asserts that "Pillowtex does not have the option to purchase the Equipment unless Duke offers it such option, and even then only if Pillowtex agrees on a satisfactory price with Duke." Duke's Br. at 21. Duke concludes that, therefore, the first economic realities factor weighs in favor of a finding that the MESA is a lease. We agree, however, with Pillowtex's contention that, although the MESA nominally required Pillowtex to bargain for an option price, Pillowtex could essentially ensure a nominal option price by refusing to bargain. This refusal would "effectively compel Duke to abandon the [e]nergy [f]ixtures to avoid the exorbitant expense of acquiring and installing replacements." Pillowtex's Br. at 28. Thus, as an economic reality the option price at the end of the MESA was illusory, nullifying the weight of this factor.

With respect to the third factor, Duke observes that the useful life of the energy fixtures is longer than the term of the MESA, and cites to *Edison Bros.* for the proposition that the long life of the fixtures is indicative of a true lease. In relevant part, the *Edison Bros.* court explained that:

> An essential characteristic of a true lease is that there be something of value to return to the lessor after the term. Where the term of the lease is substantially equal to the life of the lease property such that there will be nothing of value to return at the end of the lease, the transaction is in essence a sale. Conversely, if the lessor expected a remaining useful life after the expiration

of the lease term, it can be reasonably inferred that it expected to retain substantial residual value in the leased property at the end of the lease term and that it therefore intended to create a true lease.

207 B.R. at 818 (citations omitted). We agree that under certain circumstances, the fact that transferred goods have a useful life extending beyond the term of the transferring agreement could reveal the transferor's expectation of retaining residual value in those goods. Such an inference would only be proper, however, where the evidence showed a plausible intent by the transferor to repossess the goods.

The economic realities of the particular transaction in this case belie any such intent. Although the useful life of the lighting fixtures is 20–25 years, eclipsing the MESA's 8-year term, it would be unreasonable for Duke to incur the high costs necessary to repossess the fixtures: namely, the costs associated with removing, scrapping, and replacing the fixtures. Also, the uncontroverted evidence in this case establishes that there is little (if any) market value for used lighting fixtures. In short, it would have made no economic sense for Duke to spend large amounts of money to reclaim the fixtures, especially in the face of poor resale prospects. We therefore conclude that the District Court did not err by discounting the significance of the useful life of the lighting fixtures as compared to the length of the MESA when conducting its analysis of the economic realities of the transaction underlying the MESA. On balance, then, applying the three *Edison Bros.* factors to this case leads us to conclude that the MESA was not a true lease.

Beyond reiterating its arguments on the three factors, Duke argues that (1) the mutual subjective intent of the parties was to structure the MESA as a lease; (2) Pillowtex's accounting for the MESA payments as a utility expense is evidence that it did not treat the MESA as a repayment of debt incurred to purchase the energy fixtures; (3) it is of no consequence that the MESA is not labeled a lease; and (4) Duke maintained a meaningful reversionary interest in the fixtures at the end of the MESA's term. None of these arguments is persuasive to us.

First, Duke argues that the District Court erred by failing to analyze the intent of the parties. Duke asserts that the record shows that the parties structured the MESA so that it would qualify as a lease under relevant accounting standards. That way, Pillowtex would not reduce the amount of credit available to it under its senior credit facility. Duke also cites a statement that counsel for Pillowtex made to the District Court, which Duke characterizes as a concession: "I don't disagree that it was structured to have that, those characteristics for tax purposes and, you know, to the extent that they could, the parties were trying to create a lease, I would admit that."

Duke's intent argument fails, however, because the New York U.C.C. no longer looks to the intent of the drafting parties to determine whether a transfer is a lease or a security agreement. Specifically, the

1992 version of § 1–201(37) directed courts to determine "[w]hether a lease *is intended* as security" (emphasis added); this language was amended in 1995 to read "[w]hether a transaction *creates* a lease or security interest" (emphasis added). In this way, the reference to parties' intent was explicitly omitted. The Official Comment to the amended version confirms the importance of the changed language:

> Prior to this amendment, [s]ection 1–201(37) provided that whether a lease was intended as security (i.e., a security interest disguised as a lease) was to be determined from the facts of each case. . . Reference to the intent of the parties to create a lease or security agreement has led to unfortunate results. In discovering intent, courts have relied upon factors that were thought to be more consistent with sales or loans than leases. Most of these criteria, however, are as applicable to true leases as to security interests. . . Accordingly, amended section 1–201(37) [1–203(a)] deletes all references to the parties' intent.

U.C.C. § 1–201(37), Official Cmt.

Duke relies on *Edison Bros.,* 207 B.R. at 809, for the proposition that "[c]ourts are required to examine the intent of the parties and the facts and circumstances which existed at the time the transaction was entered into." *Edison Bros.,* however, explicitly relied on the 1992 version of the statute in looking at intent, and therefore has been superseded by the 1995 version of the U.C.C. Indeed, Judge Walsh, the author of *Edison Bros.,* noted in a later opinion: "I am persuaded by th[e] clear weight of authority that the intent of the parties, no matter how clearly spelled out in the parties' representations within the agreement, cannot control the issue of whether the agreement constitutes a true lease or a security agreement." *In re Homeplace Stores,* 228 B.R. 88, 94 (Bankr.D.Del.1998). Judge Walsh observed that the shift away from intent had been remarked upon by various commentators. * * *

Duke goes on to insist that it had a "meaningful residual interest" in the fixtures, such an interest being "the fundamental characteristic distinguishing a lease from a security interest." *E.g., In re Thummel,* 109 B.R. 447, 448 (Bankr.N.D.Okla.1989). As discussed earlier, however, Duke only has a nominal residual interest, not a *meaningful* one: the combination of the cost of retrieving the fixtures and their poor market value renders the residual interest negligible. Duke claims that we should not "speculate" as to what it might do for economic reasons at the end of the MESA's term, and instead look to the parties' intent at the time of drafting the agreement. As we have mentioned above, however, Duke's argument is backwards: the Court must subordinate the parties' intent to the economic reality that Duke would not have plausibly reclaimed the fixtures at the end of the MESA's term. This is not mere speculation on our part. The uncontroverted evidence shows that removal of the fixtures would be prohibitively expensive, and that the fixtures' value on the market would not make it worth Duke's while to reclaim them. In short, the economic realities analysis not only permits, but *requires* us to examine the state of affairs at the end of the MESA's term. * * *

IV. Conclusion

After carefully considering the arguments discussed above and all other arguments advanced by appellant, we conclude that the District Court correctly determined that the MESA was not a lease and, therefore, that Duke was not entitled to lease payments under 11 U.S.C. § 365(10). We will remand this case to the District Court so that it may determine whether Duke is entitled to adequate protection.

NOTES

1. The court in *Pillowtex* decided that the facts to which 1–203(a) refers are those that bear on whether the purported lessor retains a meaningful reversionary interest in the leased goods. And in order to determine the existence of such a reversionary interest, the court goes back to one of the earliest tests used to distinguish leases from security interests: an economic realities analysis. At the inception of the transaction, it was understood by both Duke and Pillowtex that at the end of the 8-year lease the economic reality was that Duke had no choice but to abandon the equipment even though it had many more years of useful life. Thus, Duke had no meaningful reversionary interest in the equipment. The bankruptcy consequences of this holding are that Duke could not compel Pillowtex within 60 days of filing either to reject or to assume the lease by making all payments due on the lease under BC 365(d)(5). Hence, Duke's security interest became vulnerable to cramdown under Pillowtex's Chapter 11 plan under BC 1129(b).

2. In re Grubbs Construction Co., 319 B.R. 698 (Bankr. M.D. Fla. 2005), is a particularly ardent embrace of the economic realities test. There, the court goes so far as to state in the course of the opinion that a transaction may create a security interest notwithstanding the inclusion of a fair value purchase option if the economic realities otherwise indicate. It is as though 1–203(b)(3) and (d)(2) had not been adopted. The case collects the authorities and cites *Pillowtex* with approval. It notes that the economic realities test has been known colloquially as the "no sensible person" or "no person in its right mind" test. In *Pillowtex* the court believed that no sensible person in Duke's position would have exercised any option other than abandonment of the equipment in Pillowtex's possession. Hence, under the economic realities test, Duke had no meaningful reversionary interest.

3. The lease in *Pillowtex* contained a "full payout" clause. A "full payout" lease is a lease in which the lessor recovers the entire price of the leased asset, including profit, in lease payments from the lessee. Leases in which the present value of total lease payments is equal to or greater than the fair market value of the leased assets are full payout leases. The *Pillowtex* court considered the full payout clause in the lease agreement to "undercut[ ] the proposition that the fixtures were merely leased." Section 1–203(c)(1) disagrees. A full payout clause by itself ("merely because") does not create a security interest. Thus, an agreement in the form of a lease does not create a secured transaction merely because it contains a full payout term. See Comment 2 (paragraph 8) to 1–203.

Some courts are hostile to (c)(1)'s limited protection of full payout leases. The *Warne* court says that, "with the possible exception" of (c)(1), the factors listed in 1–203(c) are not enough to indicate a security agreement. See also Gibraltor Financial Corp. v. Prestige Equipment Corp., 949 N.E.2d 314, 325 n.11 (Ind. 2011). For these courts, a full payout clause is a hallmark of a security interest. Where the present value of the lessee's payments equals the fair market value of the leased property, the lessor is paid the purchase price. Any amount by which the present value of payments exceeds fair market value represents interest on the purchase price owed. Section 1–203(c)(1) disagrees.

A full payout clause has an economic justification consistent with a lease. A lessee might agree to a full payout term for either of two reasons. First, it might be operating under liquidity constraints. In this case the lessee could have insufficient free cash to purchase the asset. It might have only enough funds to make period lease payments, even if the sum of those payments equals or exceeds the fair market value of the asset. Second, a lessee's inferior bargaining power might compel it to agree to a full payout term. For instance, an immediate need for goods sold in a thin market could force a lessee to lease them under a full payout term rather than having to wait to find suitable goods to buy. Thus, the lessee's illiquidity or inferior bargaining power does not transform an otherwise true lease into a security interest.

4. OPEN-END LEASES

Equipment and consumer leasing is a huge industry with innumerable legal problems. The brief treatment of leases above has concentrated on how to distinguish true leases from credit sales. But even in this relatively narrow segment of the field, there are variations found in leasing contracts. This is nowhere more evident than with respect to the issue raised by what has come to be known as the "terminal rent adjustment clause" or TRAC. The issue here is whether a lease with a TRAC creates a security interest or whether the clause leaves unaffected the character of a lease as a true lease.

A TRAC creates an open-end lease. In a closed-end lease the lessees' entitlements and obligations under the lease end at the end at the lease term. In an open-end lease its entitlements and obligations continue when the lease term ends. Leases with TRACs are particularly common in commercial car and truck leases. The typical TRAC contains an estimate of the projected residual value of the vehicle at the end of the lease term. The actual value of the vehicle is determined after the vehicle has been returned to the lessor, usually by sale to a third party or appraisal. The TRAC requires an upward or downward adjustment of rent depending on the vehicle's actual value. In the case of an unlimited TRAC, if the estimated value of the vehicle exceeds its actual value, the lessee receives a downward adjustment of its rent to the extent of this difference. If the estimated value of the vehicle is greater than its actual value, the lessee's rent is adjusted upward to the extent of this difference and the lessee must pay it. A TRAC lease may or may not give the lessee a purchase option.

Courts divide on the characterization of a lease with a TRAC. On the one hand, the lease transaction could be described as a secured sale. The lessor receives the purchase price of the vehicle, part of which is paid by the lessee in installment payments (called "rent") and the rest paid by a third-party buyer on the vehicle's sale. The purchase price includes interest paid for the seller's financing of the buyer's purchase. See In re Tulsa Port Warehouse Co., 690 F.2d 809 (10th Cir. 1982). The arrangement assures that the lessor doesn't bear any of the market risk around the vehicle's value. On the other hand, the transaction could be described as a true lease. The lease agreement obligates the lessee to make period rental payments plus a balloon rental payment at the end of the lease term, calculated by the TRAC. The payments are for the use of the vehicle during the lease term, the final payment taking into account the actual mileage and condition of the vehicle at the end of the lease. Although the agreement's call for the vehicle's sale at the end of the lease term assures that the vehicle doesn't revert to the lessor (unless the TRAC calls for a vehicle appraisal only), the lessor's receipt of the sale proceeds assures that it retains the vehicle's value. See In re HP Distribution, LLP, 436 B.R. 679 (Bankr. D. Kan. 2010).

In re Lightning Bolt Leasing, LLC

United States Bankruptcy Court, M.D. Florida, 2016
Case No. 3:15–bk–05173–JAF

■ **Opinion:** JERRY A. FUNK.

The case is before the Court upon competing motions for summary judgment filed by creditor, Central Truck Finance, LLC, f/k/a/ Central Truck Finance, Inc. f/k/a/ CIT Equipment Finance, Inc. (the "Creditor") and the Debtor. The Debtor filed a Response in Opposition to the Creditor's Motion for Summary Judgment. For the reasons stated herein, the Creditor's Motion for Summary Judgment will be denied while the Debtor's Motion for Summary Judgment will be granted.

BACKGROUND

The Creditor claims that it is an entity which is in the business of leasing trucks. On October 23, 2013, the parties entered into an agreement entitled "Equipment Lease Agreement" (the "Agreement") whereby the Debtor agreed to make 48 consecutive monthly payments to the Creditor in the amount of $5,676.41 for the use of the following equipment: 1) a 2014 Kenworth, Model T680, VIN No. 1XKYDP9X9EJ413217 and a 2013 Dynasis, Model APU, Serial No. 13722 (the "Kenworth"); and 2) a 2014 Volvo, Model VNL64T780, VIN

No. 4V4NC9EH2EN168334 and a 2013 Dynasis, Model APU, Serial No. 14159 (the "Volvo") (collectively, the "Equipment"). The Agreement contains the following provisions outlining the interests of the Parties in the Equipment during the term of the Agreement:

- The Equipment was to be titled "at all times" in the Creditor's name and that "[n]o right, title or interest in or to the Equipment shall pass to the [Debtor], except for the [Debtor]'s rights to possession, quiet enjoyment and use of the Equipment. . . ."

- The Debtor has no option to purchase the Equipment "at any time," however, the Debtor "may have an opportunity to purchase the Equipment upon the expiration of the Lease for an amount equal to the Residual Value."

- The Debtor "expressly understands that [the Debtor] shall have absolutely no equity or other ownership rights in the Equipment unless and until [the Debtor] purchases said Equipment" pursuant to the terms of the Agreement.

The Agreement contains the following provisions regulating the disposition of the Equipment at the end of the Agreement's term:

- Upon the expiration of the term of the Agreement, the Debtor "shall return" the Equipment to the Creditor.

- If the Debtor fails to return the Equipment upon the expiration of the Agreement term, the Debtor must continue to make payments in the same amount that was in effect at the end of the Agreement term.

- Upon the expiration of the Agreement, the Debtor may (at the sole discretion of the Creditor) have the opportunity to purchase the Equipment for an amount equal to the Residual Value (as set forth in the Schedule(s) to the Agreement).

The Agreement also includes the Terminal Rental Adjustment Clause (the "TRAC"), which provides that the Debtor agreed to the adjustment of the "rental price" and that the adjustment will take place upon the sale or other disposition of the Equipment. Specifically, if upon the sale or other disposition after expiration of the Agreement term, the net proceeds received by the Creditor are less than $47,500.00 for the Kenworth and $47,000.00 for the Volvo (the "TRAC value"), the Debtor "immediately" must pay the Creditor the amount of such deficiency as additional rent. If, however, the net proceeds are in excess of the TRAC value, then the excess will be returned to the Debtor. On March 6, 2015, the Kenworth was involved in an accident, which resulted in a total loss of the Kenworth. The Debtor is in possession of and uses the Volvo in the operation of its business.

The Debtor defaulted on the terms of the Agreement by failing to make payments as they became due. On November 25, 2015, the Debtor filed a petition requesting relief under Chapter 11 of the Bankruptcy Code. On January 11, 2016, the Creditor filed a second amended motion for relief from the automatic stay requesting that the Court lift the automatic stay so that the Creditor could repossess the Volvo and pursue collection of the insurance proceeds from the losses sustained to the Kenworth (the "motion for relief from stay"). On January 11, 2016, the Creditor filed its second amended motion to compel assumption or rejection of unexpired leases and for post-petition lease payments (the "motion to compel"). The Debtor filed its response to the motion to compel claiming that the Agreement constitutes a disguised security interest agreement rather than a lease agreement and therefore the Debtor cannot be compelled to assume or reject the Agreement (the "response").

Thus, the Debtor requested that the Court deny both the motion for relief from stay and the motion to compel. The Court held a hearing on the matter on January 21, 2016. At the hearing the Court granted in part the Creditor's motion for relief from stay and lifted the automatic stay to allow the Creditor to pursue its efforts to collect the insurance proceeds for the loss of the Kenworth. The Court directed the parties to submit simultaneous motions for summary judgment on the issues raised by the motion to compel and the response thereto.

In their respective motions for summary judgment, the parties agree that there are no facts in dispute and that Illinois law applies; the parties dispute whether the Agreement is a lease or a disguised security agreement only. The Creditor asserts the Agreement represents a lease of personal property between the parties, which must be assumed or rejected by the Debtor. The Debtor, by contrast, asserts the Agreement is a disguised security interest agreement.

ANALYSIS

Under Federal Rule of Civil Procedure 56(a), "[t]he court shall grant summary judgment if the movant shows that there is no genuine dispute as to any material fact and the movant is entitled to judgment as a matter of law." * * * As no dispute exists as to any material fact in issue, the sole issue before the Court is whether the Agreement is a lease agreement or a disguised security agreement under Illinois Law.

"[T]o determine whether an agreement that contends to be a lease is a true lease or a security agreement, the Court must look to state law." Mason v. Heller Fin. Leasing, Inc. (In re Jll Liquidating, Inc.), 341 B.R. 256, 267 (Bankr. N.D. Ill. 2006). Under Illinois law, "[w]hether a transaction in the form of a lease creates a 'security interest' is determined pursuant to [Uniform Commercial Code §] 1–203." Pursuant to § 1–203(a), "[w]hether a transaction in the form of a lease creates a lease or security interest is determined by the facts of each case." Furthermore, pursuant to § 1–203(b)

A transaction in the form of a lease creates a security interest if the consideration that the lessee is to pay the lessor for the right to possession and use of the goods is an obligation for the term of the lease and is not subject to termination by the lessee, and:

(1) the original term of the lease is equal to or greater than the remaining economic life of the goods;

(2) the lessee is bound to renew the lease for the remaining economic life of the goods or is bound to become the owner of the goods;

(3) the lessee has an option to renew the lease for the remaining economic life of the goods for no additional consideration or for nominal additional consideration upon compliance with the lease agreement; or

(4) the lessee has an option to become the owner of the goods for no additional consideration or for nominal additional consideration upon compliance with the lease agreement.

Section 1–203(b) sets forth the *per se* test. "If an agreement is found to be a security agreement as a matter of law under the *per se* test, the Court's inquiry is over." In re Buehne Farms, Inc., 321 B.R. 239, 243 (Bankr. S.D. Ill. 2005). "However, if it is determined that a transaction is not a disguised security agreement *per se,* the Court must then examine the facts particular to the case to determine whether the 'economics of the transaction' point to such a result." Id. Here, it is undisputed that the Agreement is not a security agreement as a matter of law under the *per se* test. Thus, the Court turns to the economics of the transaction test. The threshold issue of the economics of the transaction test "is how the agreement allocates risk of ownership (if a lease) or credit (if a form of loan)." In re Dena Corp., 312 B.R. 162, 169 (Bankr. N.D. Ill. 2004). "There cannot be a true lease where the 'lessor' has no ownership interest at the end of the lease term." Id. "This is because the lessee has effectively purchased the property through the mechanism of the lease, and so the lessee, not the lessor, has the benefit or burden of changes in the value of the property when the lease terminates." Id. (internal quotations omitted). "Similarly, if the lease lasts for the economic life of the property being leased, the lessee, not the lessor, bears the risk of changes in value." Id. "Where it is the lessor that retains the meaningful reversionary interest at the end of the term, 'the parties have signed a lease, not a security agreement.'" Cobra Capital, LLC v. Pomp's Servs., Inc., No. 08 C 6884, 2010 WL 680947, at *4 (N.D. Ill. Feb. 23, 2010) (quoting James J. White & Robert S. Summers, Uniform Commercial Code § 30–3.d (6th ed. 2009)).

The Debtor argues that, in the instant case, the Creditor did not retain any meaningful reversionary interest due to the applicability of the TRAC. As mentioned before, the TRAC provides that the Debtor agreed to the adjustment of the "rental price" and that the adjustment will take place upon the sale or other disposition of the Equipment after the expiration of the Agreement term. Specifically, if upon the sale or other disposition after expiration of the Agreement term, the net proceeds received by the Creditor are less than $47,500.00 for the Kenworth and $47,000.00 for the Volvo, the Debtor "immediately" must pay the Creditor the amount of such deficiency as "additional rent." If, however, the net proceeds are in excess of the TRAC value, then the excess will be returned to the Debtor. Based on the foregoing, the Debtor claims that the Debtor has the true "up-side right" and "downside risk" after the term of the agreement expires. The Court agrees. The purpose of the "TRACs" has been described as follows:

> TRACs are used when the parties anticipate that the lessor will sell the leased goods at the end of the lease term. The parties set a value for the residual interest in the goods. If the goods are sold or appraised for more than this value at the end of the lease, then the lessee gets the gain; if the goods are worth less, the lessee is liable for the difference. The question, then, is how much of the risk associated with this sale is retained by the lessor. At times, a clause of this sort merely protects the lessor against excessive mileage or wear and tear. It may be defensible as a true lease. Most of these clauses, though, effectively divest the lessors of any real residual interest in the leased goods. If the lessee insures the lessor against any downside market risk, and retains any upside gain, then the lessee effectively has taken the full risk of any market change. This sounds like a classic security interest, because the lessor has handed off its real residual right in the goods. It is guaranteed a certain amount—the lease payments, plus a lump-sum payment at sale. The lessee is thus, in essence, the economic owner of the goods.

Larry T. Ga[r]vin, The Changed (and Changing) Uniform Commercial Code, 26 Fla. St. U. L. Rev. 285, 310 n.151 (1999).

After a close review of the TRAC language set forth in the Agreement, the Court concludes that it effectively divests the Creditor of any real residual interest in the Equipment as the Creditor retains no risk associated with the sale or other disposition of the Equipment. Nevertheless, the Creditor claims that the Agreement does not end upon the useful life of the Equipment as reflected by the agreed-by-the-parties TRAC Values of $47,500.00 and $47,000.00 respectively. As such, the Creditor asserts that the TRAC value represents a meaningful reversionary interest and shows that the Creditor is concerned about the return of the Equipment at the end of the Agreement term. This argument does not, however, address the fact that the TRAC at issue shifts entirely the benefit and burden of changes in the value of the property after the expiration of the Agreement term [to] the Debtor. The Creditor also argues that the Illinois Legislature has enacted a TRAC neutral statute, § 625 ILCS 5/3–201.1, which provides that "a transaction does not create a sale or security agreement merely because it provides that the rental price is permitted or required to be adjusted under the agreement either upward or downward by reference to the amount realized upon the sale or other disposition of the motor vehicle or trailer." Unfortunately, this argument is also unpersuasive. The Court cannot overlook the fact that the statutory language specifically states that a mere adjustment upward or downward of the rental price is not determinative. It is economically prudent to allow certain adjustments based on the amount of wear and tear because motor vehicles are easily damaged, destroyed, overused or abused. Nevertheless, shifting the entire risk of ownership, as opposed to agreeing to a certain adjustment, as is the case here, is not within the protection of the statute. For this reason, the Court concludes that the Agreement at issue is a disguised security agreement. Accordingly, the Debtor's motion for summary judgment will be granted while the Creditor's motion for summary judgment will be denied.

Accordingly, it is **ORDERED:**

1.   Debtor's motion for summary judgment is granted. 2. Creditor's motion for summary judgment is denied. 3. The Creditor's motion to compel is denied. 4. The Creditor's motion for relief from the stay, to the extent it was not already ruled by the Court, is denied.

NOTES

1.   Although industry representatives wanted former 1–201(37) (current 1–203) to provide that open-end leases are true leases, Article 2A's drafters decided not to include special provisions on TRAC leases. Edwin E. Huddleson III, Old Wine in New Bottles: UCC Article 2A—Leases, 39 Ala. L. Rev. 615, 638–641 (1988).

Motor vehicle and trailer lessors are a compact interest group whose activities are significantly affected by 1–203. They have successfully lobbied in every state for a nonuniform amendment to 1–203. Sometimes the amendment appears in a state's certificate of title rules, not the UCC. A typical nonuniform amendment provides that in the case of motor vehicles or trailers, "a transaction does not create a sale or security interest merely because it provides that the rental price is permitted or required to be adjusted under the agreement either upward or downward by reference to the amount realized upon sale or other disposition of the motor vehicle or trailer." See, e.g., Va. Code Ann. § 46.2–640.1 (2020). The operative language is "merely because." The language is intended to make characterization turn on factors other than the rent adjustment clause. A purported lessor's hope is that, without the clause taken into account, the TRAC lease will be characterized as a true lease. The statute is discussed in detail and upheld in Matter of HB Logistics, LLC, 2011 WL 4625198 (Bankr. N.D.Ala.2011). The language of typical nonuniform legislation doesn't require courts to ignore the rent adjustment clause; it only prevents them from treating a TRAC lease as a sale or security interest "merely" because of the TRAC clause's presence. The legislation assures TRAC-neutrality. Nonetheless, a number of courts have construed the legislation as effectively creating a safe harbor and concluded that a TRAC lease is a true lease.

2.   The majority of nonbankruptcy cases recognize the true lease character of leases with TRACs. See Edwin E. Huddleson, TRAC Vehicle Leasing, 33 J. Equip. Lease Fin. 1 (Fall 2015). The results in bankruptcy cases are more mixed. *In re Lightning Bolt* is representative of bankruptcy cases that rule that a TRAC lease creates a security interest. In Sharer v. Creative Leasing, Inc., 612 So.2d 1191 (Ala.1993), a nonbankruptcy case, the court held an open-end lease to be a true lease. The court maintained that in order to create a security interest, a lease must give the lessee some ownership in the leased property. An open-end lease does not transfer an ownership interest or create equity in the lessee but merely shifts the risk of fluctuations in market value to the lessee. "Therefore, it cannot be said that such a shifting of the risk of loss in value of the item alone is sufficient to hold that any lease agreement containing such a clause necessarily was intended to create a security interest." Id. at 1196. Is there any important analytical difference between owning an asset and bearing the downside and upside risks with respect to it? A better defense of the true lease status of TRAC leases maintains that the TRAC shifts the risk of the lessee's overuse of the asset without shifting its ownership to the lessee. See *HP Distribution, LLP.*, 436 B.R. at 694. The TRAC functions as a liquidated damages clause to compensate the lessor for the lessee's unpredictable depreciation of the asset through use during the lease term. It leaves the lessor with the market risk around the residual value of the asset at the end of the lease term. A TRAC should be enforceable, as are other liquidated damages clauses in leases (e.g., 2A–504(1)), without the TRAC by itself effecting the true lease status of the lease.

3.   Almost every year new cases decide whether a lease creates a security interest. Has the UCC taken the correct approach in making the determination depend on the sometimes-difficult issue of when a lease creates a security interest under 1–203? With respect to consignments, as discussed in the next section, Article 9 requires filing in most cases to protect the consignor's interest against the consignee's creditors even though no security interest is created. 9–102(a)(20), 9–319. Article 9 covers in a similar manner both security interests in and outright sales of accounts and other rights to payment. 9–109(a)(3). Should the same approach be taken in the leasing area with filing required for all leases of personal property in which the term of the lease exceeds a certain period of time? See the Uniform Consumer Credit Code definition of "consumer lease" as a "lease of goods. . .which is for a term exceeding four months." UCCC § 1.301(14) (1974). The issue was extensively debated in the course of drafting Article 2A and the decision was made not to require filing for true leases. See Charles W. Mooney, Jr., The Mystery and Myth of "Ostensible Ownership" and Article 9 Filing: A Critique of Proposals to Extend Filing Requirements to Leases, 39 Ala. L. Rev. 683 (1988). The PEB Study Group Report recommended no change in the current law on this issue and the Drafting Committee proposed none.

PROBLEMS

1. Drive and Smith entered into an agreement described as a "lease" which calls for Smith to lease a car from Drive for a period of two years. The lease payments are based on the difference between the car's estimated residual value at the end of the period and the original purchase price. (The estimated value is based on the figures given in the current Industry Standards Manual.) At the end of the two-year period, Drive is required to sell the vehicle in a commercially reasonable manner. The car has a useful life of 10 years. If the sale proceeds are less than the car's estimated residual value, Smith must pay Drive the deficiency. If the sale proceeds exceed the estimated residual value, Drive must credit Smith for the surplus. Smith doesn't have the right to cancel or extend the agreement, or purchase the car from Drive. Is this transaction a lease or a disguised secured sale?

2. Assume that Drive and Smith enter into a different agreement. This agreement contains an estimated number of miles the car is to be driven over the two-year period. Drive is to retain the car at the end of the term. If the car is driven more than the estimated miles, the excess mileage is charged to Smith at a per mile charge of 25 cents. If fewer miles are driven than the estimate, Smith is given a credit on the same per mile basis. The mileage charge is called a "rent readjustment" and the credit a "rent rebate." Lease or disguised secured sale?

3. Assume that Drive and Smiths' agreement states an estimated residual value of the car at the end of the two-year period. It also provides that at the end of the period, Drive is to retain the car and obtain a commercially reasonable appraisal of its fair market value at that time. Smith is liable for any deficiency between the estimated and appraised values of the car and is to be credited for any surplus. Lease or disguised secured sale? See 2A–504(1).

4. Assume that Drive and Smith's agreement requires Drive to sell the car in a commercially reasonable manner at the end of the two-year term. If the proceeds of sale exceed the estimated residual value of the car, Drive is to receive from that excess a maximum stated amount called "rent" and Smith is entitled to the remainder, which the agreement calls a "rent rebate." If sale proceeds are below the car's estimated residual value, Smith is liable for one half the deficiency. The agreement calls Smith's share of the deficiency a "rent adjustment," which Smith is to pay Drive. True lease or security interest? What result if the agreement divided the sales proceeds above the estimated residual value of the car equally between Drive and Smith?

B. CONSIGNMENTS

1. COMMON LAW CONSIGNMENTS

Commercial consignments have long been used as an alternative to secured transactions in financing merchant inventories. The basic consignment is a simple transaction that is described in the following quotation.

> Under a "true" consignment, the owner of goods delivers them to a consignee for sale. If the consignee sells them, he must account to the owner-consignor for the proceeds of sale less his commission. If he does not sell the goods, he must return them, but he does not in any case become liable to the consignor for the price of the goods if they are not sold. Title to the goods remains in the consignor during the consignment and passes, when the goods are sold, directly to the purchaser. . . . The consignment was never thought of as a security device, and indeed, since there is no obligation to be secured, it is not. . . . [A]s a matter of common law the consignor was protected against the consignee's creditors and on insolvency was entitled to reclaim the goods from the consignee's trustee in bankruptcy.

1 Grant Gilmore, Security Interests in Personal Property § 3.5, at 73–74 (1965).

In short, at common law a consignment was a bailment for the purpose of sale. The bailee-consignee did not own the goods and its creditors could not reach the ownership interest of the bailor-consignor. Consignments were used for a variety of purposes, among them, to induce dealers to stock inventory untested in the marketplace, maintain the supplier's control of the dealer's resale prices, or, in most cases, make it possible for dealers to stock merchandise by allowing them to acquire inventory without having to invest their own capital.

2. CONSIGNMENTS UNDER ARTICLE 9

Since commercial consignments function as a form of purchase-money financing, they create an ostensible ownership problem for the consignee's creditors and purchasers. Potential lenders may assume that the merchant owns the inventory that it possesses. A consignee's senior inventory financer might rely on the consignee's unencumbered ownership of incoming consigned goods to extend subsequent credit to it. Article 9 has addressed the ostensible ownership problem by terminological assimilation. According to Article 1 and Article 9's definitions, a commercial consignment creates a "security interest" in consigned goods, the consigned goods are "collateral," the consignor is a "secured party" and the consignee is a "debtor." See 1–201(b)(35), 9–102(a)(12), (73)(C), (28)(C). By extending the terminology of a secured transaction to a commercial consignment, Article 9 effectively forces consignors to file financing statements in the broad category of cases falling within the definition of "consignment" in 9–102(a)(20) below. The rationale for assimilating commercial consignments to security interests for limited purposes is functional. These consignments create the same problem of ostensible ownership created by nonpossessory security interests. Accordingly, Article 9 cures the ostensible ownership problem created by commercial consignments in the same way it cures the ostensible problem created by nonpossessory security interests: by requiring filing notice.

Section 9–102(a)(20) defines "consignment" as follows: "Consignment" means a transaction, regardless of its form, in which a person delivers goods to a merchant for the purpose of sale and:

    (A) the merchant:

        (i)   deals in goods of that kind under a name other than the name of the person making the delivery;

        (ii) is not an auctioneer; and

        (iii) is not generally known by its creditors to be substantially engaged in selling the goods of others;

    (B) with respect to each delivery, the aggregate value of the goods is $1,000 or more at the time of the delivery;

    (C) the goods are not consumer goods immediately before delivery; and

    (D) the transaction does not create a security interest that secures an obligation.

If the transaction falls within this definition, it is covered by Article 9 under 9–109(a)(4). Whenever the term "consignment" is used in Article 9, it refers only to the transaction described in 9–102(a)(20). Comment 14 to 9–102 explains: "The definition of 'consignment' excludes, in subparagraphs (B) and (C), transactions for which filing would be inappropriate or of insufficient benefit to justify the costs. . . . The definition also excludes, in subparagraph (D), what have been called 'consignments intended for security'. These 'consignments' are not bailments but secured transactions. Accordingly, [under 9–109(a)(1)] all of Article 9 applies to them."

Section 1–201(b)(35) provides: " 'Security interest' includes any interest of a consignor. . .that is subject to Article 9." Accordingly, this provision treats consignments defined in 9–102(a)(20) ("consignments") as security interests within Article 9 even though they do not meet the test of the first sentence of 1–201(b)(35) of securing an obligation. Since an Article 9 consignment creates a security interest, it must be perfected by filing under 9–310(a). The consignor's failure to file a financing statement leaves it vulnerable in its consignee's bankruptcy. In addition, because 9–103(d) treats the consignor's security interest as a purchase-money security interest in inventory, the consignor must comply with the filing and notification requirements of 9–324(b) for protection against a prior filed security interests and lien creditors.

Thus, the common law view that a consignor's interest was not subject to creditors of the consignee has been radically changed. Under a common law consignment, title to the goods remained in the consignor and the consignee was only a bailee of the goods for the purpose of sale.

Since the bailee-consignee has no ownership rights in the consigned goods, how can creditors of, or purchasers from the consignee, reach the owner-consignor's rights in these goods? Section 9–319(a) deals with this by legislative fiat: "for purposes of determining the rights of creditors of, and purchasers for value of goods from, a consignee, while the goods are in the possession of the consignee, the consignee is deemed to have rights and title to the goods identical to those the consignor had or had power to transfer." Thus, creditors of and purchasers from the consignee can take judicial liens and security interests in the consigned goods even though they belong to the consignor. Comment 2 to 9–319.

To summarize, the effect of Article 9's provisions is to bring substantially all commercial consignments within Article 9 and to assimilate them to purchase-money security interests. Accordingly, consignors must file financing statements to protect their interest against lien creditors and other claimants, as well as meet the notification requirements of purchase-money financing with respect to prior inventory security interests. Exclusions from the sweeping definition of consignments in 9–102(a)(20) are for the most part commercially insignificant: consumer goods, goods under $1,000 in value, and auctioneer merchants. Later discussion addresses (i) the exclusions regarding transactions securing an obligation and (ii) merchants generally known by creditors to be substantially engaged in selling the goods of others.

Article 9 determines rights only between the consignee's creditors and purchasers and the consignor with respect to goods in the possession of the consignee. It does not deal with the relationship between the consignor and consignee. In keeping with this, 9–601(g) states "this part imposes no duties upon a secured party that is a consignor. . . ." The "part" mentioned is Part Six that governs the enforcement rights of secured parties upon default by a debtor. The remedies of an Article 9 consignor against a consignee are left to the agreement of the parties or other law. There is no requirement that upon default by the consignee the consignor dispose of the collateral or collect obligations in a commercially reasonable manner, nor are there deficiency limitations. Section's 9–601(g)'s rationale is that the consignee's other claimants and lien creditors have no interest in an Article 9 consignment that is protected against them. As a result, the consignor's exercise of its enforcement rights with respect to consigned goods can have no impact on the consignee's creditors. Thus, the only limitations on the consignor's remedies against the defaulting consignee, if any, are set by agreement between the consignor and consignee.

3. SECURITY CONSIGNMENT EXCLUSION

Article 9 applies to two different transactions that may be referred to by the parties as consignments. The first of these is what Article 9 calls a "consignment," as defined in 9–102(a)(20). This is a transaction that satisfies 9–102(a)(20)'s conditions. Under 9–102(a)(20)(D), a security interest securing an obligation cannot be a consignment. Thus, however the parties label the arrangement, a transaction that is a consignment under Article 9 does not create a security interest. The second arrangement is a transaction in the form of a consignment that secures an obligation. This is sometimes called a "security consignment" because the consignment secures an obligation and therefore creates a security interest under the first sentence of 1–201(b)(35). Section 1–201(b)(35)'s second sentence expressly provides that this transaction creates a security interest. A security consignment is not a genuine consignment. This transaction is never referred to in Article 9 as a consignment and is treated merely as creating a security interest in inventory. See Comment 6 to 9–109. Thus, Article 9 applies to two kinds of transactions that the parties may have labeled "consignments." Under 9–109(a)(4), Article 9 applies to "consignments," as defined in 9–102(a)(20), but, because of 9–601(g), only the first five Parts of Article 9 apply to them. However, under 9–109(a)(1) all of Article 9 applies to transactions in which the consignment secures an obligation. Does 9–102(a)(20) apply to the transaction in the following Problem?

PROBLEM

In an agreement termed a "consignment," Manufacturer (M) entrusted his new line of road bicycles ("Roadsters") to Dealer for sale at his Bicycle Shop. Demand for Roadsters is strong, and the deal M and Dealer reached was: (i) Dealer must account to M at the end of each month for the agreed wholesale price of M's bikes sold that month; (ii) in the unlikely case that a bike fails to sell within a six-month period, at the end of this period Dealer must account to M for the wholesale price of the bike and can then deal with the bike in any way it wishes. Does this transaction create a security interest that secures an obligation? See 9–102(a)(20)(D), 1–201(b)(35) "security interest."

———————————

Case law on the differences between true consignments and security consignments was confusing and unsatisfactory under former Article 9. Article 9 helps somewhat by having a clear definition of a "consignment" in 9–102(a)(20), but nothing in the text of 1–201(b)(35) offers assistance on when a consignment secures an obligation. Gilmore sensibly believed that for a transaction labeled a consignment to create a security interest, the consignee must owe an obligation to pay the consignor for the goods after a period of time, whether they were sold or not. But the cases have gone far beyond that. For instance, in Mann v. Clark Oil & Refining Corp., 302 F.Supp.1376 (E.D.Mo.1969), an oil company consigned gasoline to a dealer; if it failed to sell the gasoline it had to return the gasoline to the oil company. The court found the existence of a security interest: reservation of title to the gasoline secured the payment for the gasoline that was delivered. If the court held that a security interest is created if the consignment agreement reserves title to the consigned goods and requires the consignee to pay for the goods when sold, then every consignment creates a security interest. In In re Gross Mfg. & Importing Co., Inc., 328 F.Supp. 905 (D.N.J.1971), the agreement required the consignee either to sell the goods and pay for them within 30 days or return the unsold goods. The court found a security interest even though there was no obligation to pay for the goods in any event.

How do consignors cope with this uncertainty? With respect to attachment, perfection and priority, it usually doesn't matter whether there is a true consignment or security consignment if the consignor has filed an appropriate financing statement. Section 9–505 allows the consignor to make a protective filing. The consignor's filed financing statement can use the terms "consignor" and "consignee" instead of "secured party" and "debtor." 9–505(a). Perhaps more important, the filing of a financing statement cannot be used as a factor in determining whether the transaction is a true consignment or a security consignment, and, if the transaction is found to secure an obligation, a financing statement using consignment terminology is effective to perfect the security interest. 9–505(b). But filing does not solve the consignor's problem of whether, on default, it must comply with Part 6 by disposing of the consigned goods in a commercially reasonable manner. Whether the consignment is a security consignment or a true consignment usually does not arise in what is probably most likely default case, that of the bankruptcy of the consignee. If the trustee in bankruptcy undertakes to liquidate the collateral, Part 6 does not matter. In other disposition cases, consignors may find some comfort in giving the consignee notification of intent to sell by a private sale before disposition.

The following case demonstrates the application of the consignment provisions of Article 9.

In re Georgetown Steel Co., LLC

United States Bankruptcy Court, D. South Carolina, 2004
318 B.R. 352

■ JOHN E. WAITES, BANKRUPTCY JUDGE.

This matter comes before the Court upon cross Motions for Summary Judgment filed by Georgetown Steel Company, LLC ("Georgetown Steel" or "Debtor") and Progress Rail Services Corporation ("Progress Rail" or "Defendant"). The controversy in this matter is the determination of which party is entitled to the proceeds of certain inventory that was in Debtor's possession on the date of the bankruptcy filing. After examining the record of the case and considering the arguments of counsel, the Court believes that before it can rule on the ultimate issue of which party is entitled to the proceeds of the inventory, it must first determine the nature of the transaction between the Debtor and Progress Rail. After reviewing the parties' pleadings and arguments, the Court makes the following findings of fact and conclusions of law relating to the nature of the transaction between the Debtor and Progress Rail.

Findings of Fact

1. Hot briquetted iron, also known as HBI in the steel industry, is a raw material commodity used in the production of steel. Debtor processed HBI in order to produce steel.

2. Progress Rail supplied HBI and other raw materials to Debtor.

3. On October 10, 2003, Debtor and Progress Rail entered into an agreement titled "Consignment Agreement" (the "Agreement").

4. During the period between October 10, 2003 and October 20, 2003, Progress Rail delivered HBI to Debtor at its facility in Georgetown, South Carolina as required by the Agreement.

5. Pursuant to the terms of the Agreement, Progress Rail maintained title to the HBI delivered to Debtor. Debtor stored the HBI in a segregated location from its other inventory, and removed and used the HBI from the location on an as-needed basis. Once a week Debtor reported the HBI usage to Progress Rail and paid Progress Rail for the HBI that it consumed during the prior week.

6. The parties do not dispute that Progress Rail did not file a UCC-1 financing statement to evidence its interest in the inventory of HBI in Debtor's possession.

7. It is also undisputed that on October 20, 2003, Progress Rail sent a written notice to Debtor stating that it was terminating the Agreement and sent an additional written notice demanding reclamation of certain goods in Debtor's possession. Progress Rail's written notice terminating the Agreement advised Debtor that the Agreement was to be terminated effective October 21, 2003, and Debtor was directed to immediately stop withdrawing and consuming HBI.

8. Progress Rail's reclamation demand provided that the demand was for all goods received by Debtor from Progress Rail within the applicable reclamation period, regardless of whether such goods were included in the exhibit to the reclamation demand.

9. On October 21, 2003 (the "Petition Date"), Debtor filed its voluntary petition for relief under Chapter 11 of the Bankruptcy Code. Debtor is operating its business and managing its properties as debtor-in-possession pursuant

to Sections 1107(a) and 1108 of title 11 of the United State Code, 11 U.S.C. § 101, *et seq.* (the "Bankruptcy Code").

10. After the Petition Date, Debtor no longer had an immediate use for the HBI because of the closure of the mill.

11. On the Petition Date, the CIT Group/Business Credit Inc. ("CIT") claimed a first priority perfected security interest in Debtor's entire inventory, including the HBI, based on its loan documents with Debtor and as further set forth in the Cash Collateral Orders entered by the Court in the bankruptcy case. MidCoast Industries, Inc. ("MidCoast") claimed a second perfected security interest in Debtor's inventory.

12. After the Petition Date, Debtor and Progress Rail entered into a Stipulation (the "Stipulation"), which provided for the sale of HBI in Debtor's possession. Both Debtor and Progress Rail wanted to liquidate the inventory of HBI because the market price of HBI at that time was high and was expected to decrease in the near future.

13. Furthermore, the Stipulation provided that this Court would resolve all claims and disputes concerning ownership of the proceeds generated by the sale of the HBI. Moreover, Debtor and Progress Rail also agreed that the sale would not affect any party's interest in the HBI and that any interest in the HBI would attach to the proceeds produced from the sale.

14. The HBI was sold in December 2003 pursuant to the terms of the Stipulation. The sale of the HBI generated $1,381,435.01 in proceeds. The proceeds of the sale are currently being held in trust pending the outcome of this adversary proceeding.

15. On December 22, 2003, Debtor filed a Complaint seeking a declaratory judgment that Debtor's interest in the HBI is superior and senior to Progress Rail's interests in the HBI and asserting its rights as a lien creditor pursuant to 11 U.S.C. § 544.

16. Debtor contends that the Agreement is a consignment pursuant to Article 9 of the Uniform Commercial Code ("UCC") as enacted by the state of Alabama under Title 7 of the Alabama Code (the UCC provisions enacted under Title 7 of the Alabama Code shall generally be referred to as the "Alabama Commercial Code"). However, Progress Rail contends that the Agreement represents a sales transaction governed by the provisions of Article 2 of the Alabama Commercial Code. In light of the parties' competing views,

the Court must determine which alternative best describes this transaction.

Conclusions of Law

The question before the Court, as stipulated by the parties, is whether the Agreement is a consignment governed under Article 9 of the Uniform Commercial Code (Article 9A of Title 7 of the Alabama Code) or is more in the nature of a sale or transaction in goods in which Article 2 expressly applies.

I.   Article 9 Consignment

Prior to the 1999 revisions to the UCC, most of the law concerning consignment transactions was governed by Article 2 of the UCC. Following the revisions, most provisions governing consignments are now contained in Article 9. White and Summers, Uniform Commercial Code, § 30–4 (5th ed., 2002); Official Comment 4 to Ala. Code § 7–2–326. Additionally, the definition of a "security interest" under the revised UCC now includes an interest of a consignor pursuant to Article 9. *See id.;* UCC § 1–201(37); Ala. Code § 7–1–201(37) (West, WESTLAW through 2004 Legis. Sess.). Alabama has adopted the 1999 revisions to the UCC.

In order to determine whether the Agreement is a consignment governed by Article 9, it is necessary to examine whether the transaction between Debtor and Progress Rail meets the definition of consignment under the Alabama Commercial Code. If the transaction falls outside the definition, it is likely governed by Article 2. *See* White and Summers, Uniform Commercial Code, § 30–4 (5th ed., 2002).

Section 7–9A–109 of the Alabama Commercial Code states that Article 9A (Alabama's enactment of revised 1999 version of Article 9 of the UCC) applies to:

(1)   a transaction, regardless of its form, that creates a security interest in personal property or fixtures by contract; . . . [and]

(4)   a consignment.

According to the changes in the Alabama Commercial Code, the provisions describing a consignment under former § 7–2–326(3) are now largely incorporated into the definition of consignment pursuant to Ala. Code § 7–9A–102(a)(20). Section 7–9A–102(a)(20) of the Alabama Commercial Code defines a consignment as follows:

"Consignment" means a transaction, regardless of its form, in which a person delivers goods to a merchant for the purpose of sale and:

(A)   the merchant:

(i)   deals in goods of that kind under a name other than the name of the person making delivery;

(ii)   is not an auctioneer; and

(iii) is not generally known by its creditors to be substantially engaged in selling the goods of others;

(B) with respect to each delivery, the aggregate value of the goods is $1,000 or more at the time of delivery;

(C) the goods are not consumer goods immediately before delivery; and

(D) the transaction does not create a security interest that secures an obligation.

In order to be a consignment agreement solely governed by Article 9A of the Alabama Commercial Code, the transaction at issue must fall within the definition set forth above. Debtor contends that the Agreement meets all of the elements of a consignment pursuant to Ala. Code § 7–9A–102(a)(20). Progress Rail concedes that the transaction meets most of the above criteria but argues that the Agreement is not a consignment because (A) the goods were not delivered to a merchant "for the purpose of sale"; (B) Debtor does not "deal in goods of that kind;" and (C) the Agreement creates a security interest that secures an obligation.

A. Did Progress Rail Deliver the HBI to Debtor "For the Purpose of Sale"?

The goods under a "consignment" transaction as defined by § 7–9A–102(a)(20) must be delivered "for the purpose of sale." The Agreement between Debtor and Progress Rail provides that title to the HBI shall remain with Progress Rail and that Debtor "[s]hall purchase [HBI] only for its own use." While there is no evidence indicating that Debtor sold HBI as a commodity to others, the Agreement contemplates the processing and incorporation of HBI into Debtor's manufactured steel products, which Debtor sells to its customers. Thus, the issue here is whether Debtor must sell HBI in its raw and unadulterated form to others in order to find that Progress Rail's delivery of HBI was "for the purpose of sale."

This issue is not new. When determining whether goods were delivered "for sale" under the provisions of former UCC § 2–326(3), the courts in *Pearson Industries, Inc.* and *BFC Chemicals, Inc.* rejected similar arguments to that made by Progress Rail in the matter before the Court. The court in *Pearson Industries* concluded that manufacturers selling component goods incorporated into products are delivered for sale as "component parts" of the product that the manufacturer sold to its customers. *Barber v. McCord Auto Supply, Inc. (In re Pearson Industries, Inc.)*, 147 B.R. 914, 928 (Bankr.C.D.Ill.1992). In addressing the same issue, the Court in *BFC Chemicals, Inc.* concluded that in order to apply former UCC § 2–326(3), debtor-consignee is not required to sell the raw form of goods delivered by a vendor for such goods to be delivered "for sale." *BFC Chemicals, Inc. v. Smith-Douglass, Inc.*, 46 B.R. 1009, 1019 (E.D.N.C.1985).

Further, the current version of the Alabama Commercial Code and commentary on the UCC lend support to Debtor's argument that the delivery was "for the purpose of sale." Official Comment 14 to Ala. Code § 7–9A–102, the statutory provision that defines a "consignment," provides that:

> The definition of "consignment" requires that goods be delivered "to a merchant for the purpose of sale." If the goods are delivered for another purpose as well, *such as milling or processing,* the transaction is a consignment nonetheless because a purpose of delivery is "sale."

(emphasis added). Finally, the leading commentary on the Uniform Commercial Code contemplates transactions such as that between Debtor and Progress Rail and concludes:

> If despite their processing and commingling the goods are to be returned to the owner and not sold to a third person, the transaction is not a consignment under the 1999 Article 9. . . . If, on the other hand, the goods are to be processed and then sold by the processor to persons to be selected by him, *the transaction is a consignment even though the processor is both processing and selling.*

White and Summers, Uniform Commercial Code, § 30–5 (5th ed., 2002) (emphasis added). In the matter before the Court, Debtor processed the HBI delivered by Progress Rail and incorporated the HBI into steel. The HBI is an integral component of the steel that Debtor sells to its customers. Therefore, this Court concludes that Progress Rail delivered HBI to Debtor "for the purpose of sale."

B.   Does Debtor "Deal in Goods of that Kind"?

The Alabama Commercial Code does not specifically provide for the precise meaning of "dealing in goods of the kind." Additionally, the Court was unable to find, and the parties did not cite, Alabama case law specifically defining the phrase "deals in goods of the kind." However, a survey of other jurisdictions provided some measure of guidance. In *Marvin Lumber & Cedar Co. v. PPG Indus., Inc.,* 223 F.3d 873, 883–84 (8th Cir.2000), the Eighth Circuit, in determining whether Minnesota's economic loss doctrine applied to a specific transaction, addressed the issue of whether a manufacturer that incorporated a component good into its end product may be considered a merchant that deals in that particular component good. Under the facts of *Marvin Lumber & Cedar Co.,* a manufacturer and seller of customized wooden windows and doors incorporated a wood preservative into his final products. In light of the manufacturer's expertise in selling the wooden products and incorporating the wood preservative into those products, the Eighth Circuit held that the manufacturer dealt in wood preservatives. *Id.* In so holding, the Eighth Circuit stated that "[w]here a manufacturer with sophisticated knowledge of a component purchases and incorporates that component into its product, the manufacturer is a [sic] not merely a dealer with respect to finished product, but with respect to the component part as well." *Id.*

In *Pearson Industries, Inc.,* the debtor received tires and incorporated them into machinery that it manufactured and then sold. The vendor that supplied the tires argued that former UCC § 2–326, as adopted by the state of Illinois, did not apply to the transaction because the debtor did not sell the tires individually. The court in that case rejected the vendor's argument and concluded that debtor maintained a place of business at which it dealt with the tires delivered by vendor by incorporating the tires into the equipment that debtor manufactured and sold. The Court went on to conclude that despite the fact that debtor did not retail the component tires individually and apart from its manufactured product, former UCC §§ 2–326(2) and (3) applied nonetheless. 147 B.R. at 928.

In *BFC Chemicals,* as in this case, a debtor-consignee purchased goods from the creditor-consignor, processed and transformed the goods, and then resold the processed and transformed goods. 46 B.R. at 1019. The Court in *BFC Chemicals* noted that the goods that were the subject of the consignment agreement between debtor-consignee and creditor-consigner would normally be in the inventory of a manufacturer such as the debtor-consignee. Notwithstanding the transformation of the purchased goods, the court in *BFC Chemicals* held that the buyer dealt in the goods of the kind involved in the transaction. *Id.*

In this case, Debtor received the HBI from Progress Rail, and through its manufacturing process, combined it with other materials to produce steel. HBI is a processed metal used to manufacture Debtor's product and, in fact, is an integral component part of Debtor's final product. Moreover, HBI appears to be a raw material normally maintained in the inventory of manufacturers such as Debtor. Despite the fact that further processing of HBI is required to incorporate HBI into the steel that Debtor sells, HBI is a component of the steel produced and sold by Debtor; thus, it appears that Debtor deals in goods of the kind delivered by Progress Rail. Therefore, the Court finds that Debtor "deals in goods of the kind" for purposes of applying § 7–9A–102(a)(20) to the transaction between Debtor and Progress Rail.

C.   Did the Agreement Create a Security Interest "that Secures an Obligation?"

In determining the last element of Article 9's definition of a consignment, a distinction can be made between a "conventional" commercial consignment—as defined in UCC § 9–102(a)(20)—and an "unusual" commercial consignment. *See* White and Summers, Uniform Commercial Code, § 30–4 (5th ed., 2002). The "conventional" commercial consignment is also typically a security interest, while the "unusual" commercial consignment creates a security interest "that secures an obligation." *Id.* The latter is still treated under Article 9 (even though it does not meet part D of UCC § 9–102(a)(20)), but is restricted to the recovery rules set forth in Part 6 of Article 9. *Id.*

Whether an interest "secures an obligation" has been described as dependent upon whether there is a duty to pay for unsold goods. *Id.* In the matter before the Court, it is clear that Debtor only owed Progress Rail a debt for the goods it consumed. The Agreement does not reference any accompanying broader debt or obligation Debtor owes to Progress Rail. Although the Agreement states, "[t]o the extent it may be necessary or appropriate under applicable law or regulation, [Debtor] grants [Progress Rail] a security interest in the [HBI]," the conditional nature of the language indicates that the terms of the Agreement do not create a clear and express grant of a security interest *that secures an obligation* in the HBI to Progress Rail. Thus, the Court concludes that the Agreement does not create a security interest that secures an obligation. Accordingly, the transaction meets all of the elements of the definition of a consignment set forth in § 7–9A–102(a)(20) of the Alabama Commercial Code. * * *

IV. Conclusion

In light of the provisions of the Agreement and the definition of "consignment" provided by Ala. Code § 7–9A–102(a)(20), the Court determines that the Agreement between Debtor and Progress Rail is a consignment transaction as defined by the provisions of Article 9A of the Alabama Commercial Code.

Therefore, for the reasons set forth hereinabove, it is hereby

ORDERED that the Agreement between Debtor and Progress Rail is a consignment transaction pursuant to Ala. Code § 7–9A–102(a)(20). . . .

NOTE

In Excel Bank v. National Bank of Kansas City, 290 S.W.3d 801 (Mo. Ct.App.2009), Bank delivered vehicles to a used car dealer ("Dealer") for sale under terms strictly prescribed by Bank with respect to price, repairs, choice of buyers, etc. Although Bank did not file a financing statement covering Dealer's inventory, it did retain possession of the original certificates of title for all the vehicles which showed Bank as owner; however, none of the vehicles on Dealer's lot were identified as being subject to any claim or interest by Bank. Later GAAC, a finance company, made a loan to Dealer, took a security interest in its inventory and filed a financing statement covering the inventory. When Dealer went into default, GAAC seized a portion of Dealer's inventory. Bank filed a petition of replevin to recover the vehicles from GAAC. Were the relationship between Bank and Dealer a consignment, Bank would lose because it failed to file a financing statement as required under 9–310(a). But Bank contended that the relationship was a simple bailment of the vehicles to which GAAC's security interest could not attach; Dealer wasn't holding the vehicles for sale; the relationship was more like a "parking garage" than a consignment because Bank retained the certificates of title which listed Bank as the owner; Dealer did not have authority to transfer title without Bank's approval but was only procuring offers for purchase. The court concluded: "Both Excel and GAAC are sophisticated parties with access to expert advice on the requirements of the UCC. Excel could easily have filed a financing statement to protect its interest in the vehicles, but took no steps whatsoever to inform third parties that it retained any interest in the vehicles, other than retaining the certificates of title in its possession. Although GAAC could have checked the motor vehicle registry in addition to the UCC filings, it was not required to do so. Point denied." 290 S.W. 3d at 809.

PROBLEM

Consignor delivered fuel to Consignee under a consignment arrangement whereby Consignee sold the fuel to its own customers. When a customer paid cash for the fuel, Consignee was required to remit the proceeds to Consignor. If a customer bought the fuel on credit, Consignee informed Consignor of the amount the customer owed for the purchase. Consignor did not file a financing statement covering the consigned fuel. Later, at the time Consignee filed for bankruptcy, Consignee has cash received from its paying customers as well as outstanding amounts owed by its credit customers. In Consignee's bankruptcy, Consignor takes the position that, even if its interest in the consigned fuel is subordinate to Consignee's bankruptcy trustee, its interest in the cash and accounts receivable proceeds from the sale of consigned fuel is superior to the trustee. Is Consignor's position persuasive? See 1–201(b)(35) ("security interest"), 9–102(a)(44) ("goods") and (12) ("collateral"), 9–319; In re Pettit Oil Co., 917 F.3d 1130 (9th Cir. 2019).

4. EXCLUSION UNDER 9–102(a)(20)(A)(iii)

If the consignee is generally known by its creditors to be "substantially engaged in selling the goods of others," there is no ostensible ownership problem and, presumably, its creditors and purchasers will not rely on the consignee's ownership of the goods. Therefore, 9–102(a)(20)(A)(iii) excludes the transaction from the definition of consignments. The case below, *In re Downey Creations, LLC*, probes the scope and meaning of this briefly stated exclusion. Consignment cases are disputes between suppliers of goods to merchants for sale and the merchants' creditors. Most of these cases are heard in bankruptcy courts. The basic issue in these cases is whether the transaction involved is a consignment within 9–102(a)(20). If so, the consignor's security interest in the goods can be avoided by the merchant's trustee in bankruptcy under the "strong arm" clause of BC § 544(a)(1) unless the consignor has filed a financing statement. In most Chapter 11 cases, there is no bankruptcy trustee and the avoiding powers of the hypothetical lien creditor reside in the debtor in possession (DIP), as in *Downey Creations*.

In *Downey Creations*, Plaintiffs are the parties who entrusted jewelry for sale to the merchant, Downey Creations. Defendants are

Downey Creations in its role as DIP and Regions Bank, a secured creditor of Downey Creations. Since most of the Plaintiffs did not file financing statements, their interests can be avoided by the DIP exercising the powers of a hypothetical lien creditor under BC 544(a)(1) if the transaction is a consignment under 9–102(a)(20). Plaintiffs contend that the exclusion under (A)(iii) applies in this case because Downey Creations was generally known by its creditors to be substantially engaged in selling the goods of others; therefore, the transaction was not a consignment but some form of "commercial bailment" and Plaintiffs could get their goods back even though they had not filed financing statements. They sued to reclaim their goods. The DIP, representing Downey Creations' creditors, contends that the transaction is a consignment under 9–102(a)(20) because the exclusion under (A)(iii) does not apply. Thus, the non-filing Plaintiffs are not entitled to retake the goods.

In re Downey Creations, LLC

United States Bankruptcy Court, S.D. Indiana, 2009
414 B.R. 463

■ JAMES K. COACHYS, BANKRUPTCY JUDGE.

This matter comes before the Court on Defendant Downey Creations, LLC's ("Downey") Motion for Partial Summary Judgment (the "Motion") against Plaintiffs French Design Jewelry, Inc., Disons Gems, Inc., Wear the Passion, Inc., J.I.I.C., Inc. d/b/a South American Imports, Levine Design, Inc., Indigo Jewelry, Inc., Chatham Created Gems, Inc., and Classic Colors, Inc. (collectively, the "Plaintiffs") on their Complaint to Recover Certain Property in Possession of the Debtor and Any Money Generated from the Sale Thereof (the "Complaint") against Downey and Regions Bank, N.A. ("Regions").

Procedural History

On August 11, 2008, the Plaintiffs filed an involuntary Chapter 7 petition against Downey. On September 29, 2008, Downey filed its Consent to Entry of Order for Relief, along with a Motion to Convert Involuntary Chapter 7 Case to One Under Chapter 11 of the Bankruptcy Code. On September 30, 2008, the Court entered an Order for Relief and converted the case to Chapter 11. On October 2, 2008, the Plaintiffs sought relief from the automatic stay to recover certain goods that they had delivered to Downey pre-petition "on memorandum" pursuant to what they alleged were common law bailments. In discussing the various matters heard by the Court on October 2, 2009, Downey and Regions outlined their response to the Plaintiffs' stay motion, arguing that the subject transactions were "consignments" under Revised Article 9 of the Uniform Commercial Code (the "U.C.C.") and that the Plaintiffs' failure to file financing statements rendered their interests in the subject goods subordinate to Regions' blanket lien. * * *

On October 8, 2009, the Plaintiffs filed their Complaint against Downey and Regions in compliance with the Court's instruction. The Complaint essentially asserts a claim for replevin for the goods the Plaintiffs delivered to Downey. Downey asserts on summary judgment that the Plaintiffs' interests in the subject goods are unperfected and, thus, avoidable under BC. § 544(a)(1).

Findings of Fact

Downey is a limited liability company organized and existing under the laws of Indiana. Downey buys and sells diamonds and colored stones, mountings, semi-mountings, and finished goods. Through contractual agreements with retail jewelers, Downey conducts special event trunk shows, selling goods to the retailers' customers and invoicing the retailer for the wholesale cost of the goods sold. With the exception of Levine Design, Inc., the Plaintiffs directly delivered goods to Downey to be sold to Downey's customers at these trunk shows (the "Contested Transactions").

On May 1, 2006, to secure its obligations under a Promissory Note dated May 1, 2006, in the amount of $4,000,000 given by Downey to Regions, Downey granted Regions a security interest in substantially all of Downey's assets, including all then-owned and after-acquired inventory and the proceeds therefrom. On June 14, 2006, Regions filed U.C.C. financing statement number 200600005725168 with the Indiana Secretary of State against Downey, thereby perfecting a security interest in substantially all of Downey's assets.

All but two of the Plaintiffs did not file financing statements with respect to the Contested Transactions. The two that did—Disons Gems, Inc. ("Disons Gems") and J.I.I.C., Inc., d/b/a South American Imports ("SAI")—filed financing statements, but only after Regions' filed its financing statement.

Conclusions of Law

* * *

This case turns on whether the Contested Transactions are "consignments" for purposes § 9–102(a)(20). Both Downey and the Plaintiffs agree that in order to settle this dispute on summary judgment, the Court must first determine which party bears the burden of proof under § 9–102(a)(20) of the U.C.C. The Court agrees.

Section § 9–102(a)(20) provides:

"Consignment." A transaction, regardless of its form, in which a person delivers goods to a merchant for the purpose of sale and all of the following apply:

(A) The merchant:

. . . .

(iii) is not generally known by its creditors to be substantially engaged in selling the goods of others.

. . . .

Section 1–201(37) [1–201(b)(35)] of the U.C.C. further states that any consignment-as that term is defined above-is a "security interest." Accordingly, to protect their security interests from competing claims and from avoidance under BC § 544(a)(1), consignors must perfect them like any other security interest. *See* U.C.C. § 9–317.

As indicated above, to determine whether the Contested Transactions meet § 9–102(a)(20)'s definition of "consignment," the Court must first determine who bears the burden of proving its applicability. The parties agree that the only element of the definition at issue on summary judgment is § 9–102(a)(20)(A)(iii), i.e., whether Downey is "generally known by its creditors to be substantially engaged in selling the goods of others." * * *

The Court must. . .reject the Plaintiffs' argument that the burden of proof rests on the party seeking the protection of § 9–102(a)(20). . . . In the Court's opinion, placing the burden on the party seeking the protection of § 9–102(a)(20). . .does little to serve the underlying purpose of the provision. As explained below, the Court finds that it makes much more sense to place the burden on the party who bears the risk under § 9–102(a)(20), i.e., the consignor. . . .

While § 9–102(a)(20) does not explicitly assign the burden of proof as former § 2–326 did, the purpose behind the provision suggests to the Court that the burden nevertheless remains on the consignor. In their treatise on the Uniform Commercial Code, White and Summers explain:

> The definition [of "consignment" in Revised U.C.C. § 9–102(a)(20)] incorporates most of the conditions of former 2–326. In a second important definitional change, section 1–201(37) states that any consignment (as that term is defined in 9–102(a)) is a "security interest." This means that all consignors not explicitly excluded by the definition in 9–102(a)(20) hold security interests that are subject to subordination by lien creditors and others under 9–317 if their interests are unperfected. *To protect their interests, consignors will have to perfect them like any other security interest. The combination of 9–102(a)(20) and 1–201(37) has moved almost all commercial consignments into Article 9—at least for most purposes.*

4 WHITE & SUMMERS, UNIFORM COMMERCIAL CODE § 30–4 (5th ed) (italics added).

[T]he purpose of former 2–326(d) and now revised 9–102(a)(20) and 9–319(a) is to protect general creditors of the consignee from secret liens in the consignee's inventory. *In re Valley Media,* Inc., 279 B.R. 105, 125 (Bankr. D. Del. 2002). . . .

. . .[I]t makes little sense to place the burden of proving § 9–102(a)(20) on a consignee's creditors (or, as in this case, a debtor in possession sitting in the shoes of a hypothetical lien creditor by virtue of BC § 544(a)(1)). As between a consignee's creditors and the consignor, only the consignor is in a position to determine whether its transaction with the consignee falls under the U.C.C.'s definition of "consignment" and to file a financing statement to perfect its interest if it does. It stands to reason, then, that if a consignor chooses not to file a financing statement, it must then bear the burden of proving that the transaction is not subject to Article 9 if and when a dispute arises. In the Court's opinion, placing the burden of proof on the consignor provides some incentive for the consignor to file a U.C.C. financing statement to protect its interest simply out of an abundance of caution. That, in turn, not only discourages "secret liens," but also provides more predictability, thereby reducing the need for costly litigation such as the case at hand.

Accordingly, the Court must conclude that the burden of proof rests with the Plaintiffs to ultimately prove that Downey's creditors generally knew that Downey was substantially engaged in selling the goods of others. To satisfy the "generally known" element of 9–102(a)(20), the Plaintiffs must prove that a majority of Downey's creditors were aware that Downey was substantially engaged in selling the goods of others. *See Valley Media*, 279 B.R. at 125 (citing *In re BRI Corp.*, 88 B.R. 71, 75 (Bankr.E.D.Pa.1988)). That majority is determined by the number of creditors, not by the amount of creditors' claims. *Id.* Testimony as to general knowledge in the industry is insufficient to prove knowledge by a majority of creditors.

In its response to Downey's summary judgment motion, the Plaintiffs contend that fifty of Downey's creditors knew that Downey was substantially engaged in selling the goods of others.

The Court disagrees with many of the inferences upon which the Plaintiffs' arguments are based. Even if a given creditor knew-by virtue of its own transactions with Downey—that Downey was engaged in selling the goods of others, it does not necessarily follow that the creditor knew that Downey was *substantially* engaged in selling others' goods. . . . As already stated, evidence of general knowledge within an industry is insufficient. . . .

As indicated above. . .the Plaintiffs must show that a majority of the 91 creditors listed on Downey's bankruptcy schedules knew that Downey was substantially engaged in selling the goods of others. The Plaintiffs urge the Court to adopt a different standard-one that is based on the dollar amount of the creditors' claims, rather than the number of creditors. Plaintiffs' argument is simply not supported by the plain language of 9–102(a)(20). *See Wicaco*, 49 B.R. at 344 ("Webster's Third New Dictionary" defines generally as "on the whole" and "as a rule" and substantial as "an important or material part."). Accordingly, the Court concludes that the Plaintiffs have failed to establish a genuine issue of material fact regarding whether Downey's creditors generally knew that Downey was substantially engaged in selling the goods of others.

Conclusion

Based on the foregoing, the Court concludes that the Plaintiffs have failed to establish a genuine issue of material fact as to whether the Contested Transactions are "consignments" under 9–102(a)(20). Thus, the Court grants Downey's summary judgment motion against those Plaintiffs whose security interests in the goods they delivered to Downey were not perfected. Because Disons Gems and SAI's security interest were perfected, Downey is not entitled to judgment against them. . . .

Thus. . .the Court finds that Downey is entitled to avoid the Plaintiffs' security interests—to the extent such interests are unperfected—under BC 544(a)(1). A judgment order consistent with this opinion will be entered contemporaneously herewith.

NOTES

1.   Does the 9–102(a)(20)(A)(iii) exclusion make sense? Assume that when Merchant files in Chapter 7 bankruptcy, its bankruptcy schedules show ten consignors with claims amounting to $500,000 and 50 unsecured creditors with claims totaling $25,000. None of the consignors filed financing statements. The consignors produced irrefutable evidence that all the parties in the consignment business knew that Merchant was engaged in selling goods of others. There is no evidence that any of the 50 unsecured creditors— various utilities, contractors engaging in refurbishing Merchant's premises, credit card issuers, newspaper advertisers, and the like—knew that Merchant was selling the goods of others. Merchant's trustee in bankruptcy seeks to avoid consignor's security interest as unperfected by failure to file; the majority of Merchant's creditors did not know that Merchant was engaged in selling the goods of others. The consignors argue that the relevant group of creditors were those in the consignment business and all of them knew the nature of Merchant's business. Thus, filing was needless. The trustee is confronted by the statements made in *Downey Creations*: "Plaintiffs must prove that a majority of Downey's creditors were aware that Downey was substantially engaged in selling the goods of others." "That majority is determined by the number of creditors, not by the amount of creditors' claims." 414 B.R. at 471. What action should the trustee take with respect to the rights of the consignors?

If the holding of *Downey Creations* is followed, the exclusion would not apply because the majority of the consignee's creditors did not know that it was substantially engaged in selling the goods of others. This would be true even though all the consignors involved knew that the consignee was substantially engaged in selling goods of others. Since the definition of consignment under 9–102(a)(20) would apply to the consignors in this case, they would have a security interest, which, because it was unfiled, the trustee could set aside under its 544(a)(1) strong arm power.

If the facts were that the consignee had no creditors other than the consignors, the exclusion would apply because the consignee was generally known by its creditors to be substantially engaged in selling the goods of others. Section 9–102(a)(20) would not apply and the case would have to be decided on extra-UCC law.

2.   Whether the views expressed in *Downey Creations* are right or wrong, the results in the hypothetical cases stated above are retrograde. The thrust of the revision of consignments law under the 1999 version of Article 9 was to recognize consignments as purchase-money security interests and to deal with them accordingly, requiring filing and notice to prior inventory financers. Actual knowledge of creditors was ruled out as an element of priority determinations with respect to security interests in the original version of the UCC in the 1950s. The revision of Article 9 in 1999, which pulled consignments law from Article 2 (former 2–326(3)(b)) and placed it in Article 9, was the opportunity to get rid of rules based on actual knowledge of creditors. The (A)(iii) knowledge-of-creditors provision is a vestige of its Sales law origin; it has no place in Article 9.

PROBLEM

Assume that a merchant is substantially engaged in selling the goods of others on a consignment basis. Suppose too that 99 of the merchant's 100 creditors are ignorant of this fact. One of its creditors, however, knows that the merchant is substantially engaged in selling consigned goods. Are Article 9's rules concerning perfection and priority in consigned goods applicable against this creditor? In re TSAWD Holdings, Inc., 595 B.R. (Bankr. Del. 2018), held that a lender's security interest is subordinate to a consignor's interest when the lender knows that the consignee is substantially engaged in consignment sales. Does 9–102(a)(20) support the court's ruling?

5.   NON-ARTICLE 9 CONSIGNMENTS AND NON-ARTICLE 9 LAW

Not all genuine consignments are Article 9 consignments. Consignments that do not satisfy 9–102(a)(20)'s conditions are not regulated by Article 9 and therefore are not subject to its perfection and priority rules. A transaction not satisfying 9–102(a)(20)'s conditions inevitably raises three questions: (1) does the transaction describe a true consignment?; (2) if so, what law governs the consignment?; and (3) what does that law provide with respect to the rights of the consignor against the consignee's creditors? As to the first question, an arrangement that isn't an Article 9 consignment still may be a consignment. A non-Article 9 consignment is a genuine consignment that does not satisfy all of 9–102(a)(20)'s requirements. See Comment 5 to 9–109. In a true consignment the consignor retains the risk of fluctuations in market price around the asset. It continues to own the goods while they are in the consignee's possession. The consignee has the right to return the goods if unable to sell them. As a non-Article 9 consignment, none of Article 9's filing requirements apply to the non-Article 9 consignor, and the rights of the consignee's creditors against the consigned goods are not controlled by Article 9 (e.g., 9–319(a)). Of course, an arrangement that is not an Article 9 consignment might not be a consignment at all. It instead may be another sort of bailment, such as a bailment for services. As with a non-Article 9 consignment, Article 9's filing requirements do not apply to a bailment that is not a consignment.

As to the question of applicable non-Article 9 law, some courts and commentators maintain that UCC Article 2 governs the consignment or at least will be treated as governing it. Section 2–326(2) provides that goods held on sale or return are subject to the claims of the buyer's creditors while in the possession of the buyer. Comment 1 to 2–326 describes a "sale or return" transaction: "A 'sale or return'. . .typically is a sale to a merchant whose unwillingness to buy is overcome by the seller's engagement to take back the goods. . .in lieu of payment if they fail to be resold. A sale or return is a present sale of goods which may be undone at the buyer's option." In a footnote in *Georgetown Steel* not reproduced above, the court states: "In essence, if a transaction satisfied UCC § 9–102(a)(20) A through C, the consignor's interest is a security interest treated under Article 9. Those transactions that fall outside of the scope of 9–102(a)(20) by failing to satisfy 9–102(a)(20) A through C will likely be treated under revised Article 2–326(1) [as a sale or return]. White and Summers, Uniform Commercial Code § 30–4 (5th ed. 2002)." *Georgetown Steel*, 318 B.R. at n.10. The proposed treatment is inappropriate. Because a consignment is not a sale, it cannot be a "sale or return" under 2–326(1), and 2–326 has been amended so that it no longer regulated a consignment as a sale or return. Comment 6 to 2–326; PEB Commentary No. 20: Consignments 4 (2019). Thus, because a non-Article 9 consignment isn't covered by Article 2, the applicable state's non-Code law on the subject of consignments controls.

This raises the third question: what does the applicable state's controlling extra-Code law governing non-Article consignments generally provide? There are three possible positions that can be taken on the matter. One position is that the pre-Code common law of bailments applies. Under it, the consignor prevails against the consignee's creditors even when it fails to give public notice of its consignment interest. A second position is that non-Code common law developed while former Article 9 was in effect applies, and under it the consignor might lose to the consignee's creditors. See In re Music City RV, LLC, 304 S.W.3d 806 (Tenn.2010); In re Haley & Steele, Inc., 58 UCC Rep. Serv.2d 394 (Mass.Super.Ct.2005). The third position is that courts will mistakenly consider non-Article 9 consignments "sale or return" transactions and treat them accordingly under 2–326(2).

Some state legislation displaces Article 9's rules on consignments even when an arrangement is a consignment under 9–102(a)(20). For example, under a New York statute an artist's delivery of her own artwork to a gallery ("an art merchant") for the purpose of sale establishes a consignment. See N.Y. Arts and Cultural Affairs Law § 12.01(1)(a). The statute makes Article 9's consignment provisions inapplicable to artist consignments within the law's scope ("notwithstanding. . . any provision of the uniform commercial code. . . to the contrary"). § 12.01(1)(a). The legislation provides that the artwork delivered as well as its proceeds are trust property for the consignor's benefit. It also provides that the consigned artwork and its proceeds are not subject to or subordinate to security interests or liens of the consignee's creditors. § 12.01(1)(a)(v).

PROBLEMS

1.   Knight was broke and needed to raise money to pay her taxes. She took her valuable gold charm bracelet to The Alamo, a store that sold western clothing and accessories. The agreement was that the bracelet was on consignment from Knight and that the store would attempt to sell it for her for no less than $1,200; if it sold it for more than that amount the store could keep the surplus. The Alamo did very little consignment selling, and both Knight and The Alamo were ignorant of any filing requirements regarding consignments. But, The Alamo hadn't been paying its taxes, and the IRS seized the store's inventory, including the bracelet, under a jeopardy assessment and levy. The facts are based on Knight v. United States, 838 F.Supp. 1243 (M.D.Tenn.1993). See 9–102(a)(20)(C); 9–102(a)(23) ("consumer goods"). Is this case within 9–102(a)(20)? Should Knight get her bracelet back?

2.   Ace needed drones and Delta, which was stretched financially, was unable to purchase the components required to produce them. Accordingly, Ace and Delta reached an agreement labeled a "Consignment Agreement." Under its terms Ace would purchase the required components from third party suppliers, which they would deliver to Delta. Delta in turn would assemble drones with these components and deliver them to Ace. It would receive a "commission" for each drone it delivered. The agreement acknowledged that Ace retained title to the components and allowed Ace to retrieve them from Delta. Unknown to Ace, Lender had a security interest in Delta's inventory, existing and after-acquired, which it perfected by filing a proper financing statement. Ace filed nothing. On Delta's default on its obligations to Lender, Lender claims that it is entitled to the components on Delta's premises to be used to assemble Ace's drones. For its part, Ace asserts that it is entitled to retrieve these components. Is Ace entitled to do so?

CHAPTER 5

SECURITY INTERESTS IN INTELLECTUAL PROPERTY

A. INTRODUCTION

Intellectual property usually falls within the definition of "general intangible" in 9–102(a)(42). Obvious examples are copyrights, trademarks, patents and trade secrets. Comment 5d. to 9–102 notes that the reference to "things in action" in the definition of general intangible includes rights that arise under a license of intellectual property, including the right to exploit the intellectual property without liability for infringement. The definition specifically includes "software," which is defined under 9–102(a)(76) as meaning a computer program, when software isn't embedded in goods.

As described in Chapter 2, the perfection and priority rules under Article 9 with respect to general intangibles are simple. In order to perfect a security interest in general intangibles, the secured creditor need only reasonably identify the collateral in the security agreement (9–108(a)) and file a financing statement indicating the collateral covered (9–502(a)). Creditors will usually be safe if they describe the collateral in both the security agreement and the financing statement as "all general intangibles." The secured creditor can enjoy the benefits of the floating lien by including after-acquired property and future advances clauses. 9–204. Moreover, the secured creditor need file in only one jurisdiction, that of the location of the debtor (9–301(1)), which, if the debtor is a registered organization, such as a corporation, is its state of organization (9–307(e)). Hence, only the filing records of that jurisdiction need be searched preparatory to the credit extension.

Federal statutes regulate copyrights, trademark and patents. They significantly alter the rights of secured creditors with security interests in intellectual property collateral. To coordinate Article 9 with federal law, Article 9 contains provisions that defer to federal law or "step-back" when federal law applies. The Article 9 "step-back" provisions this Chapter discusses coexist uneasily with federal statutes on copyrights, trademarks and patents. These statutes appear to have been drafted with no regard to state laws like the UCC and its precedent statutes. Courts have had a great deal of difficulty in deciding the extent to which the federal statutes on intellectual property preempt the UCC provisions on general intangibles. The difficulties have been highlighted in recent years by the astonishing growth in the value of intellectual property.

In today's high-tech world, it is quite common for a firm's intellectual property—copyrights, patents, trademarks and trade secrets—to be worth vastly more than its tangible assets. In the last 25 years intellectual property has become an increasingly important sort of collateral for large secured loans. Moreover, the increased internationalization of business has greatly enhanced the value of trade names like Marlboro, Coca-Cola or Sony, trade secrets like Coke's secret formula, character rights like "Winnie the Pooh," or software like Microsoft's Windows. If businesses cannot reliably use their intellectual property as collateral for loans, their ability to finance their operations is greatly curtailed, for one of the greatest sources of wealth today is intellectual property. The following section shows that, with respect to the use of intellectual property as collateral for loans, the law is critically deficient; reform is badly needed. To date there is little prospect that federal statutes dealing with security interests in intellectual property will be reformed.

B. COPYRIGHTS

The simple question is how to perfect a security interest in a copyright and the proceeds stemming from the exploitation of the copyright. Since 1978, a copyright arises automatically when a work is "fixed in any tangible medium of expression," and not when it is later registered or published. 17 U.S.C. § 102(a). The copyright "notice" (the letter C in a circle or the word "Copyright") need not be placed on the work until publication. 17 U.S.C. § 401. Thus copyrights abound. You have a copyright in your seminar papers as well as in your novel of law school life that the publishers have been so unreasonable about. These garden variety copyrights are called unregistered copyrights. But under U.S.C. § 102(b), facts and ideas cannot be protected by copyright law. For the most part, the basic protections of the Copyright Act apply without respect to whether the copyright is registered, e.g., the exclusive right of the copyright owner to copy, publish, or, in the case of dramatic works, to perform the work. 17 U.S.C. § 106. But in some instances, benefits accrue from registration, an act that can be accomplished at any time during the life of the copyright by sending to the Copyright Office an application, fee, and the requisite number of copies of the work. 17 U.S.C. § 408. For instance, registration gives the copyright owner the ability to obtain a nation-wide injunction against copyright infringement and statutory damages. Registration is necessary when a security interest is granted in a copyright because a copyright must be registered before a security interest can be recorded in the Copyright Office and become effective against third parties. 17 U.S.C. § 205(c). In 2008, the Copyright Office implemented an electronic system for registration, but since many applications are still in paper form, Copyright Office staff were backed up for six months in processing electronic applications. Lyndsey Layton, © 2009? Wishful Thinking, Perhaps, as Backlog Mounts, Wash. Post, May 19, 2009, at A01.

The relevant provisions of the Copyright Act are:

Section 205(d). "As between two conflicting transfers, the one executed first prevails if it is recorded, in the manner required to give constructive notice under subsection (c), within one month after its execution in the United States or within two months after its execution outside the United States, or at any time before recordation in such manner of the later transfer. Otherwise the later transfer prevails if recorded first in such manner, and if taken in good faith, for valuable consideration or on the basis of a binding promise to pay royalties, and without notice of the earlier transfer."

Section 101. "A 'transfer of copyright ownership' is an assignment, mortgage, exclusive license, or any other conveyance, alienation, or hypothecation of a copyright or of any of the exclusive rights comprised in a copyright, whether or not it is limited in time or place, of effect but not including a nonexclusive license."

The following case, *Peregrine Entertainment,* decided when former Article 8 was in effect, shook the world of intellectual property financing to its foundation. Former Article 9 contained two "step-back" provisions: 9–104(a) and 9–302(3), (4). By their terms, Article 9 deferred to federal law ("stepped back") when the provisions applied. Section 9–109(c)(1), 9–311(a) and (b) replace former 9–104(a) and 9–302(3), (4) respectively. Set out below are the former Article 9 "step-back" provisions that were in force at the time of both this decision and the next case, *World Auxiliary.* After each provision, Article 9's replacement to it is set out.

Former 9–104(a): "[This Article does not apply] to a security interest subject to any statute of the United States, to the extent that such statute governs the rights of parties to and third parties affected by transactions in particular types of property."

Current 9–109(c)(1): "This article does not apply to the extent that a statute, regulation, or treaty of the United States preempts this article."

Former 9–302(3): "The filing of a financing statement otherwise required by this Article in not necessary or effective to perfect a security interest in property subject to (a) a statute or treaty of the United States which provides for a national or international registration. . .or which specifies a place of filing different from that specified in this Article for filing of the security interest."

Current 9–311(a): "[T]he filing of a financing statement is not necessary or effective to perfect a security interest in property subject to: (1) a statute, regulation, or treaty of the United States whose requirements for a security interest's obtaining priority over the rights of a lien creditor with respect to the property preempt Section 9–310(a) [requiring filing of a financing statement]."

Former 9–302(4): "Compliance with a statute or treaty described in subsection (3) is equivalent to the filing of a financing statement under this Article, and a security interest in property subject to the statute or treaty can be perfected only by compliance therewith. . . ."

Current 9–311(b): "Compliance with the requirements of a statute, regulation, or treaty described in subsection (a) for obtaining priority over the rights of a lien creditor is equivalent to the filing of a financing statement under this article. . . ."

In re Peregrine Entertainment, Ltd.

United States District Court, C.D. California, 1990
116 B.R. 194

■ KOZINSKI, CIRCUIT JUDGE.

This appeal from a decision of the bankruptcy court raises an issue never before confronted by a federal court in a published opinion: Is a security interest in a copyright perfected by an appropriate filing with the United States Copyright Office or by a UCC-1 financing statement filed with the relevant secretary of state?

I

National Peregrine, Inc. (NPI) is a Chapter 11 debtor in possession whose principal assets are a library of copyrights, distribution rights and licenses to approximately 145 films, and accounts receivable arising from the licensing of these films to various programmers. NPI claims to have an outright assignment of some of the copyrights; as for the others, NPI claims it has an exclusive license to distribute in a certain territory, or for a certain period of time.[1]

In June 1985, Capitol Federal Savings and Loan Association of Denver (Cap Fed) extended to American National Enterprises, Inc., NPI's predecessor by merger, a six million dollar line of credit secured by what is now NPI's film library. Both the security agreement and the UCC-1 financing statements filed by Cap Fed describe the collateral as "[a]ll inventory consisting of films and all accounts, contract rights, chattel

---

[1] According to NPI, valid copyrights exist in all of the motion pictures in its library by virtue of either (1) originality and fixation with respect to the works created after January 1, 1978, the effective date of the Copyright Act of 1976, or (2) publication and notice with respect to films created prior to 1978, and, thus governed by the Copyright Act of 1909. See Brief of Appellants at 6 n. 6 (citing 17 U.S.C. § 10 (1909 Act); 17 U.S.C. §§ 102(a), 302(a) (1976 Act)). Cap Fed, however, contends that NPI failed to offer any proof in its motion for summary judgment that any of these works were protected under either Act. The court need not resolve this dispute, however. For purposes of presenting the legal issues raised by this appeal, it is sufficient if at least one of the films in NPI's library is the subject of a valid copyright. Cap Fed has stipulated that there is at least one such film, the unforgettable "Renegade Ninjas," starring Hiroki Matsukota, Kennosuke Yorozuya and Teruhiko Aoi, in what many consider to be their career performances. . . .

paper, general intangibles, instruments, equipment, and documents related to such inventory, now owned or hereafter acquired by the Debtor." Although Cap Fed filed its UCC-1 financing statements in California, Colorado and Utah, it did not record its security interest in the United States Copyright Office.

NPI filed a voluntary petition for bankruptcy on January 30, 1989. On April 6, 1989, NPI filed an amended complaint against Cap Fed, contending that the bank's security interest in the copyrights to the films in NPI's library and in the accounts receivable generated by their distribution were unperfected because Cap Fed failed to record its security interest with the Copyright Office. NPI claimed that, as a debtor in possession, it had a judicial lien on all assets in the bankruptcy estate, including the copyrights and receivables. Armed with this lien, it sought to avoid, recover and preserve Cap Fed's supposedly unperfected security interest for the benefit of the estate.

The parties filed cross-motions for partial summary judgment on the question of whether Cap Fed had a valid security interest in the NPI film library. The bankruptcy court held for Cap Fed. . . . NPI appeals.

II

A.   Where to File

The Copyright Act provides that "[a]ny transfer of copyright ownership or other document pertaining to a copyright" may be recorded in the United States Copyright Office. 17 U.S.C. § 205(a); see Copyright Office Circular 12: Recordation of Transfers and Other Documents (reprinted in 1 Copyright L.Rep. (CCH) ¶ 15,015) [hereinafter "Circular 12"]. A "transfer" under the Act includes any "mortgage" or "hypothecation of a copyright," whether "in whole or in part" and "by any means of conveyance or by operation of law." 17 U.S.C. §§ 101, 201(d)(1); see 3 Nimmer on Copyright § 10.05[A], at 10–43C10–45 (1989). The terms "mortgage" and "hypothecation" include a pledge of property as security or collateral for a debt. See Black's Law Dictionary 669 (5th ed. 1979). In addition, the Copyright Office has defined a "document pertaining to a copyright" as one that has a direct or indirect relationship to the existence, scope, duration, or identification of a copyright, or to the ownership, division, allocation, licensing, transfer, or exercise of rights under a copyright. That relationship may be past, present, future, or potential. 37 C.F.R. § 201.4(a)(2); see also Compendium of Copyright Office Practices II ¶¶ 1602–1603 (identifying which documents the Copyright Office will accept for filing).

It is clear from the preceding that an agreement granting a creditor a security interest in a copyright may be recorded in the Copyright Office. See G. Gilmore, Security Interests in Personal Property § 17.3, at 545 (1965). Likewise, because a copyright entitles the holder to receive all income derived from the display of the creative work, see 17 U.S.C. § 106, an agreement creating a security interest in the receivables generated by a copyright may also be recorded in the Copyright Office. Thus, Cap Fed's security interest *could* have been recorded in the Copyright Office; the parties seem to agree on this much. The question is, does the UCC provide a parallel method of perfecting a security interest in a copyright? One can answer this question by reference to either federal or state law; both inquiries lead to the same conclusion.

1. Even in the absence of express language, federal regulation will preempt state law if it is so pervasive as to indicate that "Congress left no room for supplementary state regulation," or if "the federal interest is so dominant that the federal system will be assumed to preclude enforcement of state laws on the same subject." Hillsborough County v. Automated Medical Laboratories, Inc., 471 U.S. 707, 713, 105 S.Ct. 2371, 2375, 85 L.Ed.2d 714 (1985) (internal quotations omitted). Here, the comprehensive scope of the federal copyright act's recording provisions, along with the unique federal interests they implicate, support the view that federal law preempts state methods of perfecting security interests in copyrights and related accounts receivable.

The federal copyright laws ensure "predictability and certainty of copyright ownership," "promote national uniformity" and "avoid the practical difficulties of determining and enforcing an author's rights under the differing laws and in the separate courts of the various States." Community for Creative Non-Violence v. Reid, 490 U.S. 730 (1989); H.R.Rep. No. 1476, 94th Cong., 2d Sess. 129 (1976), U.S.Code Cong. & Admin.News 1976, p. 5659. As discussed above, section 205(a) of the Copyright Act establishes a uniform method for recording security interests in copyrights. A secured creditor need only file in the Copyright Office in order to give "all persons constructive notice of the facts stated in the recorded document." 17 U.S.C. § 205(c).[7] Likewise, an interested third party need only search the indices maintained by the Copyright Office to determine whether a particular copyright is encumbered. . . .

A recording system works by virtue of the fact that interested parties have a specific place to look in order to discover with certainty whether a particular interest has been transferred or encumbered. To the extent there are competing recordation schemes, this lessens the utility of each; when records are scattered in several filing units, potential creditors must conduct several searches before they can be sure that the property is not encumbered. . . . UCC § 9401, Official Comment ¶ 1. It is for that reason that parallel recordation schemes for the same types of property are scarce as hens' teeth; the court is aware of no others, and the parties have cited none. No useful purposes would be served—indeed, much confusion would result—if creditors were permitted to perfect security

---

[7] For a recordation under section 205 to be effective as against third parties, the copyrighted work must also have been registered pursuant to 17 U.S.C. §§ 408, 409, 410. See 17 U.S.C. § 205(c)(2). Of course, registration is also a prerequisite to judicial enforcement of a copyright, except for actions for infringement of copyrights in foreign works covered by the Berne Convention. 17 U.S.C. § 411; International Trade Management, Inc. v. United States, 553 F.Supp. 402, 402–03, 1 Cl.Ct. 39 (1982).

interests by filing with either the Copyright Office or state offices. See G. Gilmore, Security Interests in Personal Property § 17.3, at 545 (1965); see also 3 Nimmer on Copyright § 10.05[A] at 10–44 (1989) ("a persuasive argument. . . can be made to the effect that by reasons of Sections 201(d)(1), 204(a), 205(c) and 205(d) of the current Act. . . Congress has preempted the field with respect to the form and recordation requirements applicable to copyright mortgages").

If state methods of perfection were valid, a third party (such as a potential purchaser of the copyright) who wanted to learn of any encumbrances thereon would have to check not merely the indices of the U.S. Copyright Office, but also the indices of any relevant secretary of state. Because copyrights are incorporeal—they have no fixed situs—a number of state authorities could be relevant. . . . Thus, interested third parties could never be entirely sure that all relevant jurisdictions have been searched. This possibility, together with the expense and delay of conducting searches in a variety of jurisdictions, could hinder the purchase and sale of copyrights, frustrating Congress's policy that copyrights be readily transferable in commerce.

This is the reasoning adopted by the Ninth Circuit in Danning v. Pacific Propeller, Inc. [620 F.2d 731 (9th Cir.1980)]. *Danning* held that 49 U.S.C.App. § 1403(a), the Federal Aviation Act's provision for recording conveyances and the creation of liens and security interests in civil aircraft, preempts state filing provisions. 620 F.2d at 735–36. According to *Danning*,

> the predominant purpose of the statute was to provide one central place for the filing of [liens on aircraft] and thus eliminate the need, given the highly mobile nature of aircraft and their appurtenances, for the examination of State and County records.

620 F.2d at 735–36. Copyrights, even more than aircraft, lack a clear situs; tangible, movable goods such as airplanes must always exist at some physical location; they may have a home base from which they operate or where they receive regular maintenance. The same cannot be said of intangibles. As noted above, this lack of an identifiable situs militates against individual state filings and in favor of a single, national registration scheme.

Moreover, as discussed at greater length below. . . , the Copyright Act establishes its own scheme for determining priority between conflicting transferees, one that differs in certain respects from that of Article Nine. Under Article Nine, priority between holders of conflicting security interests in intangibles is generally determined by who perfected his interest first. UCC § 9312(5). By contrast, section 205(d) of the Copyright Act provides:

> As between two conflicting transfers, the one executed first prevails if it is recorded, in the manner required to give

> constructive notice under subsection (c), *within one month after
> its execution in the United States or within two months after its
> execution outside the United States*, or at any time before
> recordation in such manner of the later transfer. . . .

17 U.S.C. § 205(d) (emphasis added). Thus, unlike Article Nine, the
Copyright Act permits the effect of recording with the Copyright Office
to relate back as far as two months.

Because the Copyright Act and Article Nine create different priority
schemes, there will be occasions when different results will be reached
depending on which scheme was employed. The availability of filing
under the UCC would thus undermine the priority scheme established
by Congress with respect to copyrights. This type of direct interference
with the operation of federal law weighs heavily in favor of
preemption. . . .

The bankruptcy court below nevertheless concluded that security
interests in copyrights could be perfected by filing either with the
copyright office or with the secretary of state under the UCC, making a
tongue-in-cheek analogy to the use of a belt and suspenders to hold up a
pair of pants. According to the bankruptcy court, because either device is
equally useful, one should be free to choose which one to wear. With all
due respect, this court finds the analogy inapt. There is no legitimate
reason why pants should be held up in only one particular manner:
Individuals and public modesty are equally served by either device, or
even by a safety pin or a piece of rope; all that really matters is that the
job gets done. Registration schemes are different in that the *way* notice
is given is precisely what matters. To the extent interested parties are
confused as to which system is being employed, this increases the level
of uncertainty and multiplies the risk of error, exposing creditors to the
possibility that they might get caught with their pants down.

A recordation scheme best serves its purpose where interested
parties can obtain notice of all encumbrances by referring to a single,
precisely defined recordation system. The availability of parallel state
recordation systems that could put parties on constructive notice as to
encumbrances on copyrights would surely interfere with the effectiveness
of the federal recordation scheme. Given the virtual absence of dual
recordation schemes in our legal system, Congress cannot be presumed
to have contemplated such a result. The court therefore concludes that
any state recordation system pertaining to interests in copyrights would
be preempted by the Copyright Act.

2.   State law leads to the same conclusion. Article Nine of the
Uniform Commercial Code establishes a comprehensive scheme for the
regulation of security interests in personal property and fixtures. By
superseding a multitude of pre-Code security devices, it provides "a
simple and unified structure within which the immense variety of
present-day secured financing transactions can go forward with less cost
and greater certainty." UCC § 9101, Official Comment. However, Article

Nine is not all encompassing; under the "step back" provision of UCC § 9104, Article Nine does not apply "[t]o a security interest subject to any statute of the United States to the extent that such statute governs the rights of parties to and third parties affected by transactions in particular types of property."

For most items of personal property, Article Nine provides that security interests must be perfected by filing with the office of the secretary of state in which the debtor is located. See UCC §§ 9302(1), 9401(1)(c). Such filing, however, is not "necessary or effective to perfect a security interest in property subject to. . . [a] statute or treaty of the United States which provides for a national or international registration. . . or which specifies a place of filing different from that specified in [Article Nine] for filing of the security interest." UCC § 9302(3)(a). When a national system for recording security interests exists, the Code treats compliance with that system as "equivalent to the filing of a financing statement under [Article Nine,] and a security interest in property subject to the statute or treaty can be perfected only by compliance therewith. . . ." UCC § 9302(4).

As discussed above, section 205(a) of the Copyright Act clearly does establish a national system for recording transfers of copyright interests, and it specifies a place of filing different from that provided in Article Nine. Recording in the Copyright Office gives nationwide, constructive notice to third parties of the recorded encumbrance. Except for the fact that the Copyright Office's indices are organized on the basis of the title and registration number, rather than by reference to the identity of the debtor, this system is nearly identical to that which Article Nine generally provides on a statewide basis.[10] And, lest there be any doubt,

---

[10] Moreover, the mechanics of recording in the Copyright Office are analogous to filing under the UCC. In order to record a security interest in the Copyright Office, a creditor may file either the security agreement itself or a duplicate certified to be a true copy of the original, so long as either is sufficient to place third parties on notice that the copyright is encumbered. See 17 U.S.C. §§ 205(a), (c); 37 C.F.R. § 201.4(c)(1). Accordingly, the Copyright Act requires that the filed document "specifically identif[y] the work to which it pertains so that, after the document is indexed by the Register of Copyrights, it would be revealed by a reasonable search under the title or registration number of the work." 17 U.S.C. § 205(c); see also Compendium of Copyright Office Practices II and 1604–1612; Circular 12, at 8035–4.

That having been said, it's worth noting that filing with the Copyright Office can be much less convenient than filing under the UCC. This is because UCC filings are indexed by owner, while registration in the Copyright Office is by title or copyright registration number. See 17 U.S.C. § 205(c). This means that the recording of a security interest in a film library such as that owned by NPI will involve dozens, sometimes hundreds, of individual filings. Moreover, as the contents of the film library changes, the lienholder will be required to make a separate filing for each work added to or deleted from the library. By contrast, a UCC-1 filing can provide a continuing, floating lien on assets of a particular type owned by the debtor, without the need for periodic updates. See UCC § 9204.

This technical shortcoming of the copyright filing system does make it a less useful device for perfecting a security interest in copyright libraries. Nevertheless, this problem is not so serious as to make the system unworkable. In any event, this is the system Congress has established and the court is not in a position to order more adequate procedures. If the mechanics of filing turn out to pose a serious burden, it can be taken up by Congress during its oversight of the Copyright Office or, conceivably, the Copyright Office might be able to ameliorate the problem through exercise of its regulatory authority. See 17 U.S.C. § 702.

the drafters of the UCC specifically identified the Copyright Act as establishing the type of national registration system that would trigger the section 9302(3) and (4) step back provisions:

Examples of the type of federal statute referred to in [UCC § 9302(3)(a)] are the provisions of [Title 17] (copyrights). . . .

UCC § 9302, Official Comment ¶ 8; see G. Gilmore, Security Interests in Personal Property § 17.3, at 545 (1965) ("[t]here can be no doubt that [the Copyright Act was] meant to be within the description of § 9–302(3)(a)").[11]

The court therefore concludes that the Copyright Act provides for national registration and "specifies a place of filing different from that specified in [Article Nine] for filing of the security interest." UCC § 9302(3)(a). Recording in the U.S. Copyright Office, rather than filing a financing statement under Article Nine, is the proper method for perfecting a security interest in a copyright. . . .

Conclusion

The judgment of the bankruptcy court is reversed. The case is ordered remanded for a determination of which movies in NPI's library are the subject of valid copyrights. The court shall then determine the status of Cap Fed's security interest in the movies and the debtor's other property. To the extent that interest is unperfected, the court shall permit NPI to exercise its avoidance powers under the Bankruptcy Code.

NOTE

In Footnote 10 of *Peregrine* Judge Kozinski comments that filing with the Copyright Office "can be much less convenient than filing under the UCC. This is because UCC filings are indexed by owner, while registration in the Copyright Office is by title or copyright registration number. . . .This means that the recording of a security interest in a film library such as that owned by NPI will involve dozens, sometimes hundreds, of individual filings. Moreover, as the contents of the film library changes, the lienholder will be required to make a separate filing for each work added to or deleted from the library. By contrast, a UCC filing can provide a continuous, floating lien on assets of a particular type owned by the debtor, without the need for periodic updates."

---

[11] Cap Fed points to a portion of the official commentary that suggests the contrary conclusion:

> Although the Federal Copyright Act contains pro visions permitting the mortgage of a copyright and for the recording of an assignment of a copyright [Title 17] such a statute would not seem to contain sufficient provisions regulating the rights of the parties and third parties to exclude security interests in copyrights from the provisions of this Article.

UCC § 9104, Official Comment and 1. . . .

PROBLEM

In *Peregrine*, the court states that step-back under former 9–302(3) depends on whether a federal statute "provides for a national or international registration. . .or which specifies a place of filing different from that specified in this Article for filing of the security interest." 116 B.R. at 202. And whether the federal statute also provides a priority scheme different from that in Article 9 is a separate issue. "Compliance with a national registration scheme is necessary for perfection regardless of whether federal law governs priorities." Id. at 204. How does current 9–311(a)(1) and (b) affect the court's holding?

Article 9's "step-back" provisions are different from former Article 9's counterpart provisions, and potentially affect the law governing the perfection of security interests in copyrights. Under the predominant understanding of former 9–104(a) and 9–302(3), state law filing requirements applied unless federal law either preempted state law or state law otherwise deferred to federal filing requirements. Current Article 9's "step-back" provisions do not otherwise defer to federal law. Rather, Article 9 and its filing requirements are inapplicable only when federal law preempts them. See 9–109(c)(1), Comment 8 to 9–109, and Comment 2 to 9–311. In other words, Article 9 makes state filing unnecessary and ineffective only when it has to: when federal law preempts state filing requirements. Article 9 therefore makes irrelevant *Peregrine's* inquiry into whether Article 9 defers to federal law even if it does not preempt state filing requirements. Of course, it remains a matter of federal law as to when preemption occurs.

Under current 9–311(a)(1), a UCC filing is neither necessary nor effective to perfect a security interest only when the relevant federal statute requires a federal filing in order to obtain priority over a lien creditor. The standard is one of federal preemption against a baseline of a lien creditor's rights. Section 9–311(a)(1) is unclear in one detail: the explicitness with which federal law must preempt state filing requirements. The subsection's terms refer to the "requirements" of the relevant federal law, and the question is whether federal filing "requirements" must expressly displace state filing requirements or whether less explicit displacing provisions are sufficient. If the former, the Copyright Act doesn't preempt a UCC filing requirement because it doesn't expressly deal with the priority of lien creditors or displace state filing requirements. If the latter, the Act's priority provisions might be sufficiently explicit for 9–311(a)(1)'s purposes. Section 9–311(a)(1) seemingly doesn't require explicit displacement of state filing requirements. It can't. After all, federal preemption is a matter of federal law over which state law, including Article 9, has no say. This is required by the Supremacy Clause of the Constitution. If federal law filing requirements preempt state filing requirements, state filing is neither necessary nor effective even if federal law doesn't explicitly say so. This is simply a consequence of preemption.

The question now is how 9–311(a)(1) applies in the case of the Copyright Act. Arguably, the Act's filing requirements make UCC filings neither necessary nor effective. Section 9–311(a)(1) makes state filing requirements inapplicable when the relevant federal statute's filing requirements preempt state filing requirements for priority over a lien creditor's rights. The preemptive effect of the Copyright Act's priority rule (section 205(d)), therefore, is at issue. The rule doesn't expressly mention the rights of lien creditors. While the Act's definition of "transfer" (section 101) doesn't mention involuntary conveyances, section 201(d)(1) allows a transfer of ownership by "operation of law." Courts have read the definition broadly to include involuntary conveyances such as liens. See In re Franchise Pictures LLC, 389 B.R. 131 (Bankr. C.D.Cal.2008); In re Peregrine Entertainment Ltd., 116 B.R. 194, 205–06 (C.D.Cal.1990). More important, the Act doesn't expressly preempt state filing requirements for priority over a lien creditor. It says nothing about state filing requirements. However, the Act's priority rule (section 205(d)) is sufficiently comprehensive in its ordering of interests that it's unlikely that the rule doesn't apply against a lien creditor's rights as well. Why would the Act include liens as transfers while allowing unrecorded security interests to prevail against liens recorded in the Copyright Office? And 9–311(a)(1) seemingly doesn't require relevant federal law filing requirements to expressly preempt state filing requirements. Thus, following *Peregrine's* preemption analysis, under 9–311(a)(1), UCC filings are neither necessary nor effective with respect to copyrights.

NOTES

1.   Recordation of a document in the Copyright Office gives notice only if "the document. . .specifically identifies the work to which it pertains. . ." 17 U.S.C. § 205(c)(1). Hence, recording a security agreement, even one that purports to cover after-acquired copyrights, gives constructive notice only with respect to the work as it was at the time it was registered and not future copyrights. See Footnote 10 of *Peregrine* and Paul Heald, Resolving Priority Disputes in Intellectual Property Collateral, 1 J. Intell. Prop. L. 135 (1993). In short, although state law has recognized after-acquired property clauses for more than 100 years, they are ineffective under federal law for security interests in copyrights.

> . . .[In the 1976 Copyright Act] Congress temporally expanded federal copyright back from the point of publication under the 1909 Copyright Act to the point in time where the work was "fixed in a tangible medium of expression" under the Copyright Act. If as we believe, Peregine and AEG Acquisition are correct interpretations of congressional intent, much of the copyright financing that used to be controlled by state law and Article 9 of the UCC is now controlled by federal law and, therefore, by more primitive principles. . . .

[O]ne result of this expansion may be to sharply reduce or eliminate the possibility of using creative work in progress as collateral for a loan. Consider, for instance, a debtor that creates valuable intellectual property in stages, for example, an author whose work is produced over time or through different drafts, or a movie studio that produces a film from daily shootings.

Harold R. Weinberg & William J. Woodward, Jr., Legislative Process and Commercial Law: Lessons from the Copyright Act of 1976 and the Uniform Commercial Code, 48 Bus. Law. 437, 475 (1993). But see the next case.

2. In a second holding, equally as important as the first, *Peregrine* decided that a Copyright Office recording is also the exclusive method for perfecting a security interest with respect to copyright receivables, that is, the proceeds from licensing the showing of the debtor's films. Though the court was on solid ground in deciding that recording pursuant to the federal Copyright Act is the exclusive means of perfecting a security interest in a copyright, the basis for its holding on proceeds is not as clear. The court describes the debtor's right to collect these fees as "accounts receivable." This is correct under 9–102(a)(2) ("accounts"). Under 9–315(a)(2) and (d), a security interest in these proceeds would be perfected by perfecting a security interest in the films. Certainly a security interest in a copyright is much less valuable if it doesn't cover the return from the exploitation of the copyrighted work. The Copyright Act has no specific provisions on proceeds. Judge Kozinski based his holding on § 106(5) which doesn't mention proceeds but gives a copyright owner the exclusive right to display the copyrighted work. Thus "a copyright entitles the holder to receive all income derived from the display of the creative work. . . ." 116 B.R. at 199. He apparently reasons from this that since the receivables flow from the copyrighted work, the manner of perfecting a security interest in the copyrighted work should control for the receivables as well.

The implications of this holding for lenders who rely on receivables for collateral are ominous. Suppose a lender finances the operations of a retailer who sells computers together with copyrighted software by taking a security interest in the receivables that arise from the sale of the computers (inventory) and software (general intangibles). The software developer has registered a copyright in the software; retail customers receive a diskette and are licensed to make limited use of the program that it contains. Lender complies with Article 9 with respect to perfecting its security interest in all present and future accounts of the retailer. What additional burdens does *Peregrine* impose on the lender to perfect a security interest in the software receivables? Since these receivables are proceeds of a copyrighted software program, must the lender file its security interest in the Copyright Office to perfect as to these receivables? If so, given the inapplicability of after-acquired property clauses in copyright law, must it refile each time it acquires a security interest in additional receivables? Until the law is clarified, these problems may dissuade lenders from relying on receivables arising out of the marketing of copyrightable intellectual property. These issues are discussed in Patrick R. Barry, Note, Software Copyrights as Loan Collateral: Evaluating the Reform Proposals, 46 Hastings L.J. 581, 594–98

(1995); Alice Haemmerli, Insecurity Interests: Where Intellectual Property and Commercial Law Collide, 96 Colum. L. Rev. 1645, 1694–1695; Steven Weinberger, Perfection of Security Interests in Copyrights: The *Peregrine* Effect on the Orion Pictures Plan of Reorganization, 11 Cardozo Arts & Ent. L.J. 959, 980 (1992).

3. Arguably, *Peregrine*'s holding discussed in Note 2 has been overruled by Broadcast Music, Inc. v. Hirsch, 104 F.3d 1163 (9th Cir.1997). In that case, Debtor, a songwriter, received royalties on his compositions through BMI, which licenses performances of copyrighted musical compositions and collects and pays royalties to composers. In payment of debts he owed to Creditors, Debtor assigned his rights to future royalties to them to satisfy his debts. They neither recorded the assignments with the Copyright Office nor, apparently, did they attempt to perfect under the UCC. Before the debts were paid, the IRS asserted a tax lien for Debtor's unpaid taxes. The Ninth Circuit, interpreting the Copyright Act and New York assignment law, held that the Creditors' rights in the royalties were superior to those of the IRS. No recording in the Copyright Office was required because there was no "transfer of copyright ownership or other document pertaining to a copyright." 17 U.S.C. § 205(a). An assignment of royalties is not, the court opined, an assignment of a copyright or an interest in a copyright. The court distinguished *Peregrine* on the ground that this case does not involve the creation of a security interest; it is a case of "outright assignments of a right to receive royalties for the purpose of satisfying a debt." Id. at 1166. Other courts agree with the Ninth Circuit; see, e.g., Artists Rights Enforc. Corp. v. King, 2017 WL 2063988 (S.D.N.Y. 2017).

Where does *Broadcast Music* leave the law on security interests in rights to payment, like royalties or license fees, arising from the exploitation of copyrighted works? Distinguishing *Broadcast Music* from *Peregrine* on the ground that a security interest was created in the latter while an outright assignment was present in the former is too glib. It's also inaccurate. Under the definition of a security interest in 1–201(b)(35) (an interest in personal property that secures payment of an obligation), in a case in which a debtor grants a creditor the right to collect payments due the debtor from an account debtor until the obligation is paid, it seems extremely unlikely that a court would distinguish between a debtor's granting a security interest in the payments to the creditor and the debtor's assigning the payments. In each case, the creditor would have only the right to collect until its debt is paid; it doesn't "own" the future payments. Thus, a security interest has been created. Restatement (Third) of Property, Mortgages, § 4.2, Reporters' Notes to Comment a. (1997) takes the position that an "absolute" assignment of rents to a creditor that will terminate upon satisfaction of the debt is merely security for an obligation and does not confer absolute ownership in the creditor.

A more fundamental distinction between *Peregrine* and *Broadcast Music* is that the court in the latter case reads the statute narrowly to say that recordation in the Copyright Office is necessary only in the case of transfers (assignments and security interests) in ownership of the copyright itself. Recordation indicates to prospective creditors and buyers who own rights in the copyright itself. Transfer of royalties resulting from licensing of the copyright has nothing to do with ownership of the copyright itself; therefore, recordation is unnecessary. If this interpretation were to be accepted in the future, it could be the basis for a regime in which federal law recordation would apply to assignments of and security interests in copyrights, but Article 9 would apply to receivables arising out of copyright exploitation, thus greatly diminishing the operational problems discussed in Note 2. Alice Haemmerli, supra Note 2, at 1692, contends that requiring Copyright Office recording for copyright receivables is not defensible under either federal or state law. 4 Melville B. and David Nimmer, Nimmer on Copyright § 19A.04[C][5] (2007), concludes that *Broadcast Music* "undercuts, if not overrules, *Peregrine*'s holding with respect to receivables."

4. Although some secured lenders apparently continue to make UCC filings, the *Peregrine* decision has greatly increased the number of recordings of security interests in intellectual property in the Copyright Office. It has also focused critical attention on the antiquated system prescribed by federal law for protection of security interests in copyrights. The "tract" system of recording security interests in copyrights, described by Judge Kozinski in Footnote 10 of the opinion noted above, in which the security interests are indexed not by the name of the debtor but by the registration number or title of the copyright, has been improved in recent years by the practice of cross-indexing in the name of the debtor. But the cross-indexing has not been done for older copyrights. Even when the searcher ascertains that no security agreement has been recorded regarding a given copyright, the relation-back provisions of 17 U.S.C. § 205(d) (one month after execution of the security agreement if executed within the U.S. or two months if executed outside the U.S.) may still allow a later recorded interest to take priority over an earlier recorded one. Matters have been hopelessly complicated in past years by the practice of the Copyright Office of delaying recording documents submitted to it for a period of months. See 4 Melville B. and David Nimmer, Nimmer on Copyright § 7.18 (2007).

5. In re Franchise Pictures LLC, 389 B.R. 131 (Bankr. C.D.Cal.2008), involved litigation between Franchise, a producer of films, and Morgan Creek, a distributor that contracted to distribute eight films to be made by Franchise. Copyrights on the films were registered and Morgan Creek recorded a copyright mortgage on the films. A dispute between the parties led Morgan Creek to sue Franchise and obtain a judicial lien that under California law extended to all its personal property. The court relied on *Peregrine* to hold that the judicial lien was a transfer subject to the Copyright Act that could only be perfected by recording in the Copyright Office. Hence, the judicial lien was unperfected and unenforceable with respect to the registered copyrights.

The following decision is a welcome clarification of the law on security interests in unregistered copyrights.

In re World Auxiliary Power Co.

United States Court of Appeals, Ninth Circuit, 2002
303 F.3d 1120

■ KLEINFELD, CIRCUIT JUDGE.

In this case we decide whether federal or state law governs priority of security interests in unregistered copyrights.

Facts

Basically, this is a bankruptcy contest over unregistered copyrights between a bank that got a security interest in the copyrights from the owners and perfected it under state law, and a company that bought the copyrights from the bankruptcy trustees after the copyright owners went bankrupt. These simple facts are all that matters to the outcome of this case, although the details are complex.

Three affiliated California corporations—World Auxiliary Power, World Aerotechnology, and Air Refrigeration Systems—designed and sold products for modifying airplanes. The FAA must approve modifications of civilian aircraft by issuing "Supplemental Type Certificates." The three companies owned copyrights in the drawings, technical manuals, blue-prints, and computer software used to make the modifications. Some of these copyrighted materials were attached to the Supplemental Type Certificates. The companies did not register their copyrights with the United States Copyright Office.

The companies got financing from Silicon Valley Bank, one of the appellees in this case. Two of the companies borrowed the money directly, the third guaranteed the loan. The security agreement, as is common, granted the bank a security interest in a broad array of presently owned and after-acquired collateral. The security agreement covered "all goods and equipment now owned or hereafter acquired," as well as inventory, contract rights, general intangibles, blueprints, drawings, computer programs, accounts receivable, patents, cash, bank deposits, and pretty much anything else the debtor owned or might be "hereafter acquired." The security agreement and financing statement also covered "[a]ll copyright rights, copyright applications, copyright registrations, and like protections in each work of authorship and derivative work thereof, whether published or unpublished, now owned or hereafter acquired."

The bank perfected its security interest in the collateral, including the copyrights, pursuant to California's version of Article 9 of the Uniform Commercial Code, by filing UCC-1 financing statements with the California Secretary of State. The bank also took possession of the Supplemental Type Certificates and the attached copyrighted materials. But the copyrights still weren't registered with the United States Copyright Office, and the bank did not record any document showing the transfer of a security interest with the Copyright Office.

Subsequently, the three debtor companies filed simultaneous but separate bankruptcy proceedings. Their copyrights were among their major assets. Aerocon Engineering, one of their creditors (and the appellant in this case), wanted the copyrights. Aerocon was working on a venture with another company, Advanced Aerospace, and its President, Michael Gilsen, and an officer and director, Merritt Widen (all appellees in this case), to engineer and sell aircraft modifications using the debtors' designs. Their prospective venture faced a problem: Silicon Valley Bank claimed a security interest in the copyrights. To solve this problem, Aerocon worked out a deal with Gilsen, Widen, and a company named Erose Capital (not a party in this case) to buy the debtors' assets, including their copyrights, from the bankruptcy trustees along with the trustees' right to sue to avoid Silicon Valley Bank's security interest. Once Aerocon owned the copyrights, it planned to exercise the trustees' power to avoid Silicon Valley Bank's security interest[7] so that the venture would own the copyrights free and clear.

The transaction to purchase the copyrights and the trustees' avoidance action worked as follows. First, Aerocon paid the bankruptcy trustees $90,000, $30,000 for each of the three bankruptcy estates. Then, the trustees, with the bankruptcy court's approval, sold the estates' assets and avoidance action to Erose Capital, Gilsen, and Widen. Gilsen and Widen then sold their two-thirds interest to their company, Advanced Aerospace.

After this transaction was completed, for reasons not relevant to this appeal, Aerocon's planned joint venture with Advanced Aerospace and Gilsen and Widen fell through. In the aftermath, Erose Capital sold its one-third interest to Aerocon and Advanced Aerospace sold its two-thirds interest to Airweld. These transactions meant that Aerocon and Airweld owned the debtors' copyrights and the trustees' avoidance action as tenants in common.

Meanwhile, Silicon Valley Bank won relief from the bankruptcy court's automatic stay and, based on its security interest, foreclosed on the copyrights. Then the bank sold the copyrights to Advanced Aerospace (Gilsen's and Widen's company) which then sold the copyrights to Airweld. Had Aerocon's joint venture with Gilsen and Widen gone through, buying off the trustees' and the bank's interests in the copyrights would have been a sensible, if expensive, way to ensure that the venture owned the copyrights free and clear. But, of course, the venture did not go through, and Gilsen and Widen's affiliations had changed. Thus Gilsen and Widen's purchase from the bank and sale to Airweld meant that Aerocon, which had paid $90,000 for the copyrights and had owned them as a tenant in common with Airweld, now had a claim adverse to Airweld's, which purportedly owned the copyrights in fee simple.

---

[7] *See* 11 U.S.C. § 544(a) (2000).

Aerocon brought an adversary proceeding in each of the three bankruptcy proceedings against Silicon Valley Bank, Advanced Aerospace, Gilsen, Widen, and Airweld. (These adversary proceedings were later consolidated.) Aerocon sued to avoid Silicon Valley Bank's security interest and to recover the copyrights or their value from subsequent transferees Advanced Aerospace, Gilsen, Widen, and Airweld.[9] The bankruptcy court granted the subsequent transferees' motion to dismiss Aerocon's claims against them as time-barred.[10] The bankruptcy court then granted summary judgment to Silicon Valley Bank on all of Aerocon's claims on the ground that the bank had perfected its security interest in the copyrights under California's version of Article 9 of the Uniform Commercial Code. Aerocon appealed to the Ninth Circuit Bankruptcy Appellate Panel. Silicon Valley Bank objected, and the appeal was transferred to the district court, which affirmed the bankruptcy court. Aerocon appeals from the district court's order.

Analysis

Copyright and bankruptcy law set the context for this litigation, but the legal issue is priority of security interests. The bankruptcy trustees sold Aerocon their power to avoid any security interest "that is voidable by a creditor that extends credit to the debtor at the time of the commencement of the case, and that obtains, at such time and with respect to such credit, a judicial lien. . . ."[15] Under this "strong-arm" provision, Aerocon has the status of an "ideal creditor" who perfected his lien at the last possible moment before the bankruptcy commenced, and if this hypothetical creditor would take priority over Silicon Valley Bank's lien, then Aerocon may avoid the bank's security interest.

Whether Aerocon's hypothetical lien creditor would take priority turns on whether federal or state law governs the perfection of security interests in unregistered copyrights. The bank did everything necessary to perfect its security interest under state law, so if state law governs, the bank has priority and wins. The bank did nothing, however, to perfect its interest under federal law, so if federal law governs, Aerocon's hypothetical lien creditor arguably has priority, although the parties dispute whether Aerocon might face additional legal hurdles.

We are assisted in deciding this case by two opinions, neither of which controls, but both of which are thoughtful and scholarly. The first is the bankruptcy court's published opinion in this case, *Aerocon Engineering Inc. v. Silicon Valley Bank (In re World Auxiliary Power Co.)*, which we affirm largely for the reasons the bankruptcy judge gave. The second is a published district court opinion, *National Peregrine, Inc. v. Capitol Federal Savings & Loan Association (In re Peregrine*

---

[9]   *See id.* § 550(a).

[10]   *See id.* § 550(f).

[15]   *See* 11 U.S.C. § 544(a).

Entertainment, Ltd.), the holdings of which we adopt but, like the bankruptcy court, distinguish and limit.

Our analysis begins with the Copyright Act of 1976. Under the Act, "copyright protection subsists. . . in original works of authorship fixed in any tangible medium of expression. . . ."[20] While an owner must register his copyright as a condition of seeking certain infringement remedies, registration is permissive, not mandatory, and is not a condition for copyright protection.[22] Likewise, the Copyright Act's provision for recording "transfers of copyright ownership"[23] (the Act's term that includes security interests)[24] is permissive, not mandatory: "Any transfer of copyright ownership or other document pertaining to copyright may be recorded in the Copyright Office. . . ."[25] The Copyright Act's use of the word "mortgage" as one definition of a "transfer"[26] is properly read to include security interests under Article 9 of the Uniform Commercial Code.[27]

Under the Copyright Act,

[a]s between two conflicting transfers, the one executed first prevails if it is recorded, in the manner required to give constructive notice. . . within one month after its execution. . . or at any time before recordation. . . of the later transfer. Otherwise the later transfer prevails if recorded first in such manner, and if taken in good faith, for valuable consideration. . . and without notice of the earlier transfer.[28]

The phrase "constructive notice" refers to another subsection providing that recording gives constructive notice but only if—

(1) the document, or material attached to it, specifically identifies the work to which it pertains so that, after the document is indexed by the Register of Copyrights, it would be revealed by a reasonable search under the title or registration number of the work; and

---

[20] *Id.* § 102(a).

[22] *Id.* § 408(a) ("[T]he owner of copyright . . . may obtain registration of the copyright claim. . . . Such registration is not a condition of copyright protection.").

[23] *Id.* §§ 101, 205(a).

[24] *See id.* §§ 101, 201(d).

[25] *Id.* § 205(a) (emphasis added).

[26] *Id.* § 101 ("A 'transfer of copyright ownership' is an assignment, mortgage, exclusive license, or any other conveyance, alienation, or hypothecation of a copyright. . . .").

[27] *See* Grant Gilmore, 1 *Security Interests in Personal Property* § 13.3, at 415 (1965) ("The phrase 'may be mortgaged' in [the Copyright Act of 1909] should be read as equivalent to 'may be transferred for security.' . . . A copyright would not in any case seem to be within the category of intangible property which can be pledged; under Article 9 of the [Uniform Commercial] Code it would be a 'general intangible.' "). *See also In re Cybernetic Services, Inc.,* 252 F.3d 1039, 1056 (9th Cir.2001) ("[T]he Copyright Act, by its terms, governs security interests."); *National Peregrine, Inc.,* 116 B.R. at 199 ("It is clear . . . that an agreement granting a creditor a security interest in a copyright may be recorded in the Copyright Office.").

[28] 17 U.S.C. § 205(d) (emphasis added).

(2)   registration has been made for the work.[29]

A copyrighted work only gets a "title or registration number" that would be revealed by a search if it's registered.[30] Since an unregistered work doesn't have a title or registration number that would be "revealed by a reasonable search," recording a security interest in an unregistered copyright in the Copyright Office wouldn't give "constructive notice" under the Copyright Act, and, because it wouldn't, it couldn't preserve a creditor's priority. There just isn't any way for a secured creditor to preserve a priority in an unregistered copyright by recording anything in the Copyright Office. And the secured party can't get around this problem by registering the copyright, because the secured party isn't the owner of the copyright, and the Copyright Act states that only "the owner of copyright. . . may obtain registration of the copyright claim. . . ."[31]

Aerocon argues that the Copyright Act's recordation and priority scheme exclusively controls perfection and priority of security interests in copyrights. First, Aerocon argues that state law, here the California U.C.C., by its own terms "steps back" and defers to the federal scheme. Second, whether or not the U.C.C. steps back, Aerocon argues that Congress has preempted the U.C.C. as it applies to copyrights. We address each argument in turn.

A.   U.C.C. Step Back Provisions

Article 9 of the Uniform Commercial Code, as adopted in California, provides that unperfected creditors are subordinate to perfected, and as between perfected security interests, the first perfected interest prevails. The bank perfected first under state law by filing a financing statement with the California Secretary of State on existing and after-acquired copyrights. The U.C.C. treats copyrights as "general intangibles." Security interests in general intangibles are properly perfected under the U.C.C. by state filings such as the one made by the bank in this case.

To avoid conflict with the federal law, the U.C.C. has two "step-back provisions," by which state law steps back and out of the way of conflicting federal law. The first, more general "step-back" provision says that Article 9 "does not apply. . . [t]o a security interest subject to any statute of the United States to the extent that such statute governs the rights of parties to and third parties affected by transactions in particular types of property. . . ."[35] As applied to copyrights, the relevant U.C.C. Official Comment makes it clear that this step-back clause does not exclude all security interests in copyrights from U.C.C. coverage, just

---

[29]   *Id.* § 205(c) (emphasis added).

[30]   *See id.* § 409 ("The application for copyright registration shall . . . include . . . the title of the work. . . ."); *id.* § 410(a) ("When . . . the Register of Copyrights determines that . . . the material deposited constitutes copyrightable subject matter . . . the Register shall register the claim and issue . . . a certificate of registration. . . . The certificate shall contain the information given in the application, together with the number and effective date of the registration.").

[31]   *Id.* § 408(a).

[35]   Cal. Comm.Code § 9104(a).

those for which the federal Copyright Act "governs the rights" of relevant parties:

> Although the Federal Copyright Act contains provisions permitting the mortgage of a copyright and for the recording of an assignment of a copyright such a statute would not seem to contain sufficient provisions regulating the rights of the parties and third parties to exclude security interests in copyrights from the provisions of this Article.[36]

The second step-back provision[37] speaks directly to perfection of security interests. It exempts from U.C.C. filing requirements security interests in property "subject to. . . [a] statute. . . of the United States which provides for a national. . . registration. . . or which specifies a place of filing different from that specified in this division for filing of the security interest."[38] Compliance with such a statute "is equivalent to the filing of a financing statement. . . and a security interest in property subject to the statute. . . can be perfected only by compliance therewith. . . ."[39]

Under the U.C.C.'s two step-back provisions, there can be no question that, when a copyright has been registered, a security interest can be perfected only by recording the transfer in the Copyright Office. As the district court held in *Peregrine,* the Copyright Act satisfies the broad U.C.C. step-back provision by creating a priority scheme that "governs the rights of parties to and third parties affected by transactions" in registered copyrights and satisfies the narrow step-back provision by creating a single "national registration" for security interests in registered copyrights. Thus, under these step-back provisions, if a borrower's collateral is a registered copyright, the secured party cannot perfect by filing a financing statement under the U.C.C. in the appropriate state office, or alternatively by recording a transfer in the Copyright Office. For registered copyrights, the only proper place to file is the Copyright Office. We adopt *Peregrine*'s holding to this effect.

However, the question posed by this case is whether the U.C.C. steps back as to unregistered copyrights. We, like the bankruptcy court in this case, conclude that it does not. As we've explained, there's no way for a secured creditor to perfect a security interest in unregistered copyrights by recording in the Copyright Office. The U.C.C.'s broader step-back provision says that the U.C.C. doesn't apply to a security interest "to the extent" that a federal statute governs the rights of the parties. The U.C.C. doesn't defer to the Copyright Act under this broad step-back provision because the Copyright Act doesn't provide for the rights of secured parties to unregistered copyrights; it only covers the rights of

---

[36] *Id.* Official Comment 1.

[37] *Id.* § 9302(3)(a).

[38] Cal. Comm.Code § 9302(3)(a).

[39] *Id.* § 9302(4).

secured parties in *registered* copyrights. The U.C.C.'s narrow step-back provision says the U.C.C. doesn't apply if a federal statute "provides for a national. . . registration. . . or which specifies a place of filing different from that specified in this division for filing of the security interest." The U.C.C. doesn't defer to the Copyright Act under this narrow step-back provision because the Copyright Act doesn't provide a "national registration": unregistered copyrights don't have to be registered, and because unregistered copyrights don't have a registered name and number, under the Copyright Act there isn't any place to file anything regarding unregistered copyrights that makes any legal difference. So, as a matter of state law, the U.C.C. doesn't step back in deference to federal law, but governs perfection and priority of security interests in unregistered copyrights itself.

B.   Federal Preemption

It wouldn't matter that state law doesn't step back, however, if Congress chose to knock state law out of the way by preemption. Federal law preempts state law under three circumstances. The first is "express preemption," where Congress explicitly preempts state law. The second is "field preemption," where Congress implicitly preempts state law by "occupy[ing] the entire field, leaving no room for the operation of state law" The third is "conflict preemption," where we infer preemption because "compliance with both state and federal law would be impossible, or state law stands as an obstacle to the accomplishment and execution of the full purposes and objectives of Congress." We presume that federal law does not preempt "state law in areas traditionally regulated by the States."

Aerocon argues, relying on *Peregrine,* that Congress intended to occupy the field of security interests in copyrights. Aerocon also argues that the U.C.C. actually conflicts with the Copyright Act's text and purpose.

Because Aerocon relies so heavily on *Peregrine* and its progeny, we will briefly review the facts and holding of that case. In *Peregrine,* a bank had secured a loan with the debtor's copyrights in a library of films licensed out for exhibition and related accounts receivable and attempted to perfect its security interest by filing a U.C.C. financing statement. The debtor later filed for bankruptcy and, as debtor-in-possession, sued in the bankruptcy court to avoid the bank's lien on the ground that the bank had failed to perfect its lien by failing to record it with the Copyright Office. The bankruptcy court held for the bank, and the debtor-in-possession appealed to the district court. The district court reversed, holding that "the comprehensive scope of the Copyright Act's recording provisions, along with the unique federal interests they implicate, support the view that federal law preempts state methods of perfecting security interests in copyrights. . . ." The district court reasoned that federal law preempts state law because "the Copyright Act establishes a uniform method for recording security interests in copyrights" and creates a different priority scheme than state law, and because "competing recordation schemes. . . lessen [ ] the utility of each."

Although *Peregrine* did not specify whether the copyrights at issue were registered, it is probably safe to assume that they were, and that the *Peregrine* court did not have a case involving unregistered copyrights, because the collateral at issue was a movie library that got licensed out to exhibitors[57] and, in the ordinary course, copyrights in such films would be registered. Also, as the bankruptcy judge in the case at bar pointed out, *Peregrine*'s "analysis only works if the copyright was registered." The district court in *Peregrine* held that Congress had preempted state law because of "the comprehensive scope of the Copyright Act's recording provisions." As applied to registered copyrights, the Act's recording scheme is comprehensive; it doesn't exclude any registered copyright from its coverage. But as applied to unregistered copyrights, the Act doesn't have comprehensive recording provisions. Likewise, *Peregrine* notes that "[t]o the extent there are competing recordation schemes, this lessens the utility of each." This holds true for registered copyrights. But there aren't two competing filing systems for unregistered copyrights. The Copyright Act doesn't create one. Only the U.C.C. creates a filing system applicable to unregistered copyrights. *Peregrine* reasoned that creditors could get conflicting results under the U.C.C. and the Copyright Act, because each provides a different priority scheme. That's true only for registered copyrights. The Copyright Act wouldn't provide a conflicting answer as to unregistered copyrights because it wouldn't provide any answer at all. *Peregrine*'s holding applies to registered copyrights, and we adopt it, but as the bankruptcy court reasoned in the case at bar, it does not apply to unregistered copyrights.

We accordingly reject two other lower court opinions, *Zenith Productions, Ltd. v. AEG Acquisition Corp. (In re AEG Acquisition Corp.)*[63] and *In re Avalon Software Inc.*,[64] that extended *Peregrine*'s holding to unregistered copyrights. No circuit court has come to that erroneous conclusion.[66] In both cases, the courts held that security interests in unregistered copyrights may not be perfected under the U.C.C.; perfection could be obtained only by registering the copyrights and recording the security interest with the Copyright Office. We reject these opinions because they miss the point made by the bankruptcy judge in this case, and discussed above, that *Peregrine*'s analysis doesn't work if it's applied to security interests in unregistered copyrights. Moreover,

---

[57] *Id.* at 197.

[63] 161 B.R. 50 (9th Cir.BAP 1993), *affirming* 127 B.R. 34 (Bankr.C.D.Cal.1991).

[64] 209 B.R. 517 (D.Ariz.1997).

[66] In *In re Cybernetic Services, Inc.*, 252 F.3d 1039 (9th Cir.2001), we held that state law governs perfection of security interests in patents. *Id.* at 1059. We distinguished *Peregrine* because the Patent Act, unlike the Copyright Act, doesn't contemplate the recordation of security interests. *See id.* at 1056. We neither approved nor disapproved *Peregrine* because patent law, not copyright law, was at issue. *Id. See also Broadcast Music, Inc. v. Hirsch*, 104 F.3d 1163, 1166 (9th Cir.1997) (distinguishing *Peregrine* on the ground that an assignment of royalties was not a "transfer" of an interest in copyright).

such extensions of *Peregrine* to unregistered copyrights would make registration of copyright a necessary prerequisite of perfecting a security interest in a copyright. The implication of requiring registration as a condition of perfection is that Congress intended to make unregistered copyrights practically useless as collateral, an inference the text and purpose of the Copyright Act do not warrant.

In the one instance where the Copyright Act conditions some action concerning a copyright on its registration—the right to sue for infringement—the Act makes that condition explicit.[70] Nowhere does the Copyright Act explicitly condition the use of copyrights as collateral on their registration. Second, the Copyright Act contemplates that most copyrights will not be registered. Since copyright is created every time people set pen to paper, or fingers to keyboard, and affix their thoughts in a tangible medium,[71] writers, artists, computer programmers, and web designers would have to have their hands tied down to keep them from creating unregistered copyrights all day every day. Moreover, the Copyright Act says that copyrights "may" be registered, implying that they don't have to be, and since a fee is charged and time and effort is required, the statute sets up a regime in which most copyrights won't ever be registered.

Though Congress must have contemplated that most copyrights would be unregistered, it only provided for protection of security interests in registered copyrights. There is no reason to infer from Congress's silence as to unregistered copyrights an intent to make such copyrights useless as collateral by preempting state law but not providing any federal priority scheme for unregistered copyrights. That would amount to a presumption in favor of federal preemption, but we are required to presume just the opposite. The only reasonable inference to draw is that Congress chose not to create a federal scheme for security interests in unregistered copyrights, but left the matter to States, which have traditionally governed security interests.

For similar reasons, we reject Aerocon's argument that congressional intent to preempt can be inferred from conflict between the Copyright Act and the U.C.C. There is no conflict between the statutory provisions: the Copyright Act doesn't speak to security interests in unregistered copyrights, the U.C.C. does.

Nor does the application of state law frustrate the objectives of federal copyright law. The basic objective of federal copyright law is to "promote the Progress of Science and useful Arts"[75] by "establishing a marketable right to the use of one's expression" and supplying "the

---

[70] *See* 17 U.S.C. § 411(a).

[71] *See id.* § 102(a) ("[C]opyright protection subsists . . . in original works of authorship fixed in any tangible medium of expression. . . .").

[75] U.S. Constitution, article 1, section 8.

economic incentive to create and disseminate ideas."[76] Aerocon argues that allowing perfection under state law would frustrate this objective by injecting uncertainty in secured transactions involving copyrights. Aerocon conjures up the image of a double-crossing debtor who, having gotten financing based on unregistered copyrights, registers them, thus triggering federal law, and gets financing from a second creditor, who then records its interest with the Copyright Office and takes priority. We decline to prevent this fraud by drawing the unreasonable inference that Congress intended to render copyrights useless as collateral unless registered.

Prudent creditors will always demand that debtors disclose any copyright registrations and perfect under federal law and will protect themselves against subsequent creditors gaining priority by means of covenants and policing mechanisms. The several *amici* banks and banking association in this case argue that most lenders would lend against unregistered copyrights subject to the remote risk of being "primed" by subsequent creditors; but no lender would lend against unregistered copyrights if they couldn't perfect their security interest. As we read the law, unregistered copyrights have value as collateral, discounted by the remote potential for priming. As Aerocon reads the law, they would have no value at all.

Aerocon's argument also ignores the special problem of copyrights as after-acquired collateral. To use just one example of the multi-industry need to use after-acquired (really after-created) intangible intellectual property as collateral, now that the high-tech boom of the 1990s has passed, and software companies don't attract equity financing like tulips in seventeenth century Holland, these companies will have to borrow more capital. After-acquired software is likely to serve as much of their collateral. Like liens in any other after-acquired collateral, liens in after-acquired software must attach immediately upon the creation of the software to satisfy creditors. Creditors would not tolerate a gap between the software's creation and the registration of the copyright. If software developers had to register copyrights in their software before using it as collateral, the last half hour of the day for a software company would be spent preparing and mailing utterly pointless forms to the Copyright Office to register and record security interests. Our reading of the law "promote[s] the Progress of Science and useful Arts" by preserving the collateral value of unregistered copyrights, which is to say, the vast majority of copyrights. Aerocon's reading of the law—which would force producers engaged in the ongoing creation of copyrightable material to constantly register and update the registrations of their works before obtaining credit—does not.

---

[76] *Harper and Row, Publishers v. Nation Enterprises*, 471 U.S. 539, 558, 105 S.Ct. 2218, 85 L.Ed.2d 588 (1985).

Conclusion

Regarding perfection and priority of security interests in unregistered copyrights, the California U.C.C. has not stepped back in deference to federal law, and federal law has not preempted the U.C.C. Silicon Valley Bank has a perfected security interest in the debtors' unregistered copyrights, and Aerocon, standing in the bankruptcy trustees' shoes, cannot prevail against it.

AFFIRMED.

NOTE

The importance of *World Auxiliary* is shown in the fluid context of a field like film making. Take the elementary case in which a shell corporation (Production) is set up to make a single feature film to be distributed by Studio. Bank is willing to finance the picture solely because Studio has given Production an iron-clad agreement (the negative pick-up agreement) to buy the film (the negative) at an agreed purchase price when the film is completed. Bank is covered in case the film is not finished by a completion bond from Insurer payable to Bank. Although Studio is functionally the debtor in this transaction, Studio doesn't want the loan on its balance sheet, and the deal is structured so that Bank makes its loan to Production, which assigns to Bank its right to be paid the purchase price by Studio when the film is completed. The purchase price will equal the amount of the loan made by Bank to Production plus interest. Thus, if the film is completed and Studio honors the negative pick-up agreement, Bank is paid; if the film is not completed, Bank is paid by Insurer. Clearly, Bank's credit risk is Studio's solvency; if it files in bankruptcy before paying the purchase price of the film, Bank is going to have collection problems.

If Bank doesn't get paid by Studio, it at least wants possession of the film from Production. Banks usually aren't happy about involuntarily becoming equity participants in the entertainment business, but having a completed film may be better than having a claim in Studio's bankruptcy. Hence, before Bank disburses the loan proceeds to Production, Bank will take a security interest in whatever rights it can get in the as yet unmade film. For what it is worth, it will perfect a security interest under Article 9 in all Production's assets, now owned or hereafter acquired, including all the existing and future intellectual property such as the script and the eventual film. Under *Peregrine*, Bank must also perfect under the Copyright Act. But at the inception of the transaction, there may be at most a script; Bank may require registration of a copyright in the script and any other copyrightable property that Production has at that time so that it can promptly record its security agreement. But, as the film progresses, each new version of the script and each new print of the film would be "fixed in a tangible medium of expression" and covered by the 1976 Copyright Act. Under *Peregrine* the Copyright Office is the place to record a security interest in such rights and the recording can have no effect until the copyright is registered. In re AEG Acquisition Corp., 161 B.R. 50 (9th Cir. B.A.P.1993). But Alice Haemmerli, in Insecurity Interests: Where Intellectual Property and Commercial Law

Collide, 96 Colum. L. Rev. 1645, 1695 (1996), points out that obtaining registration "is a matter of many months." Since the copyright for the film is usually not registered until the film is ready for release, Bank's security interest in the film could be jeopardized if Production filed in bankruptcy before the copyright was registered and recorded; moreover, preference law might be implicated if registration and recording took place within 90 days before Production filed. *World Auxiliary* solves Bank's problems by allowing it to take an effective Article 9 security interest in the unregistered copyrighted material that is created before the film is finished. This security interest is valid in Production's bankruptcy and against subsequent buyers or secured parties.

PROBLEMS

1. Assume the facts in the preceding Note. Under *World Auxiliary*, Bank can take an Article 9 security interest in all of the unregistered copyright material involved in the film that will protect Bank until it has Production register the completed film and Bank records its security interest, if it has not been paid by then. But suppose Production, after it has registered the film, fraudulently grants a security interest in the film to Lender who records its security interest in the Copyright Office before Bank. Before making the loan to Production, Lender searched the Copyright Office records and found nothing. When Bank is ready to record its security interest, it discovers that Lender had recorded three months earlier. Is Lender prior to Bank with respect to the intellectual property associated with the film?

2. In *Peregrine* the court held that a Copyright Office recording is the exclusive method for perfecting a security interest in copyright receivables, the proceeds of the exploitation of the copyright. How does *World Auxiliary* affect this holding?

C. TRADEMARKS

A trademark is a distinctive mark, symbol or emblem used by a producer or manufacturer to identify and distinguish that person's products from those of others. Edu. Dev. Corp. v. Economy Co., 562 F.2d 26 (10th Cir.1977). The name "Coke" distinguishes one soft drink from another soft drink, "Pepsi," which looks and tastes almost the same. Trademark protection arises from either federal or state law. The owner of a trademark may register it at the U.S. Patent and Trademark Office (PTO), and certain benefits flow from such registration. But federal registration is permissive, and the owner can also register the trademark in the states where it is used or can choose not to register the trademark at all and rely on a common law trademark based on its status as a first user.

The Lanham Act provides: "A registered mark or mark for which application to register has been filed shall be assignable with the good will of the business in which the mark is used, or with that part of the goodwill of the business connected with the use of and symbolized by the mark. . . . An assignment shall be void against any subsequent purchaser for valuable consideration without notice, unless the prescribed information reporting the assignment is recorded in the United States Patent and Trademark Office within three months after the date of the assignment prior to the subsequent purchase." 15 U.S.C. § 1060(a)(1) and (4). Thus, for federally registered trademarks, recording of assignments is mandatory, but, unlike the Copyright Act, nothing is said about security interests. In the comprehensive revision of the Lanham Act in 1988, consideration was given to providing that recording a security interest in a trademark in the PTO would establish the secured party's priority against subsequent claimants. But this proposal was not enacted.

Working with a fragmentary federal statute and a somewhat ambiguous UCC, the court in the following case decides the issue of how to perfect a security interest in a trademark.

In re Together Development Corporation

United States Bankruptcy Court, D. Massachusetts, 1998
227 B.R. 439

■ JAMES F. QUEENAN, BANKRUPTCY JUDGE.

This case presents the question of the proper method of perfecting a security interest in trademarks. The subject involves a trap for the unwary.

By previous order, the court authorized Together Development Corporation (the "Debtor") to sell substantially all its assets, including its trademark "Together Dating Service", free of the security interest of Horace Trimarchi ("Trimarchi"). The order attached the security interest to the sales proceeds. The order also set down an evidentiary hearing so the court could adjudicate the validity and perfection of Trimarchi's security interest. Set forth here are my findings of fact and conclusions of law following that hearing.

The case was submitted on agreed exhibits and an oral stipulation of facts. Trimarchi is a former shareholder of the Debtor. By agreement dated May 13, 1986, the Debtor purchased all its shares owned by Trimarchi (and two others). The price for Trimarchi's shares was $200,000, which was represented by the Debtor's promissory note in that amount bearing interest at 10% per annum and payable in 780 weekly installments of $500. In consideration of other indebtedness owed Trimarchi, the Debtor gave him its promissory note in the sum of $30,372.12, also bearing interest at 10% and payable in 780 weekly installments. Both notes were secured by the Debtor's "accounts receivable, it's [sic] Trademark, Franchise Fees and Royalties." In furtherance of that security interest, the Debtor executed and delivered to Trimarchi a separate assignment which described the assigned property as the Debtor's "Trademark (Together Dating Service). . . which is registered under Certificate Number 1,145,365 in the United States Patent Office transfer said mark [sic], along with the goodwill of the business connected with that mark. . . ." The Debtor also gave to Trimarchi a signed financing statement (UCC-1) covering the following described collateral: "All fixtures, office furniture, files, etc., accounts receivable, Franchise Fees, Royalties, License Fees, Franchise Agreements, License Agreements, and 'TOGETHER' Trademark-Registration number 1,145,365."

Trimarchi did not make a filing with the Secretary of State of Connecticut, where the Debtor's principal office was then located, nor with any other state. Instead, he filed the financing statement by mail with the United States Patent and Trademark Office ("PTO"), which sent back a written acknowledgment of the filing. There is no dispute that Trimarchi's security interest in items of property other than the trademark is unperfected for lack of recording with the appropriate state authority. The question is whether the filing with the PTO was sufficient to perfect his security interest in the trademark.

The parties' agreement provides that it "shall be interpreted under the Laws of the State of New York. . . ." The agreement does not state it shall be "governed" by New York law. Because there is no essential difference among the states on the point at issue, I assume, as urged by Trimarchi, that the agreement is governed by New York law in all respects. If a federal statute contains filing requirements for particular collateral, U.C.C. § 9–302(3) defers to the federal statute. As in effect in New York, § 9–302(3) provides as follows:

> (3) The filing of a financing statement otherwise required by this Article is not necessary or effective to perfect a security interest in property subject to
>
> > (a) a statute or treaty of the United States which provides for a national or international registration or a national or international certificate of title or which specifies a place of filing different from that specified in this Article for filing of the security interest
>
> . . .
>
> (4) Compliance with a statute or treaty described in subsection (3) is equivalent to the filing of a financing statement under this Article, and a security interest in property subject to the statute or treaty can be perfected only by compliance therewith except as provided in Section 9–103 on multiple state transactions. Duration and renewal of perfection of a security interest perfected by compliance with the statute or treaty are governed by the provisions of the statute or treaty; in other respects the security interest is subject to this Article.

The "Lanham Act," chapter 22 of Title 15 of the United States Code, governs trademarks. Its provision on the transfer of an interest in a trademark reads in relevant part as follows:

> A registered mark or a mark for which application to register has been filed shall be assignable with the goodwill of the business in which the mark is used, or with that part of the goodwill of the business connected with the use of and symbolized by the mark[,]. However, no application to register a mark under section 1(b) [15 U.S.C. § 1051(b)] shall be assignable prior to the filing of the verified statement of use under section 1(d) [15 U.S.C. § 1051(d)], except to a successor to the business of the applicant, or portion thereof, to which the mark pertains, if that business is ongoing and existing. . . . An assignment shall be void as against any subsequent purchaser for a valuable consideration without notice, unless it is recorded in the Patent and Trademark Office within three months after the date thereof or prior to such subsequent purchase. . . .

15 U.S.C. § 1060.

The Lanham Act contains no definition of "assignment," thereby casting doubt on whether the term includes the grant of a security interest. The question therefore is this: Is its provision on transfer a statute which, in the words of § 9–302(3), "specifies a place of filing different from that specified in this Article for filing of the security interest"?

I have been directed to no pertinent legislative history. In the abstract, the term "assignment" is broad enough to include the granting of a consensual lien. See BLACK'S LAW DICTIONARY 1342 (5th ed. 1979) (defining term as "[a] transfer. . . of the whole of any property. . . or any estate or right therein."). It is helpful, however, to have some history in mind. The Lanham Act was passed in 1946, prior to the general passage by the states of the Uniform Commercial Code, which uses the phrases "security agreement" and "security interest" to describe the granting of a consensual lien in personal property. In 1946, a "chattel mortgage" or "conditional sale" was the vehicle through which most consensual personal property liens were granted. Outside the sales context, to describe the grant of a security interest it was then common to refer to the grant of a "mortgage" rather than an "assignment," the term used in the Lanham Act. The term "hypothecation" was often used with respect to receivables. Thus ordinary language usage points away from treating the grant of a security interest as an "assignment" under the Lanham Act.

Two other considerations indicate the statute does not apply to security interest filings. First, its reference to the "successor to the business" suggests Congress had in mind an outright assignment in the context of the sale of an entire business of which the trademark is a part. Second, and perhaps more persuasive, Congress has expressly included consensual liens in the copyright recording system, thereby demonstrating its awareness of the possibility of such liens and its inclination to make manifest an intention to require their recording when that intention is present. See 17 U.S.C.S. § 205 (providing for recording of "transfer" of copyright); 17 U.S.C.S. § 101 (defining "transfer" to include "mortgage" or "hypothecation").

I therefore conclude that Trimarchi's security interest in the trademark is unperfected. The case law appears to be in uniform agreement. . . .

Pointing to the national filing requirement for security interests in copyrights, Trimarchi suggests that a similar requirement for trademarks makes a great deal of sense. He cites a copyright case, National Peregrine, Inc. v. Capitol Federal Savings and Loan Association (In re Peregrine Entertainment, Ltd.), 116 B.R. 194 (C.D.Cal.1990). In that case, in the process of holding that filing with the United States Copyright Office is the proper method for perfection of security interests in copyrights, the district court espoused the virtues of mandatory national filing of such security interests. Those virtues may also be present as to trademarks. A proposed purchaser or lender might well find it more convenient and reliable to have just one filing office at which to ascertain both the registered ownership of a trademark and the existence of encumbrances on it. But my job is to apply the statute as Congress has written it. The *Peregrine* court was careful to point out the absence of any reference to security interests in the trademark statute and the consequent irrelevance of trademark cases. See 116 B.R. at 204, n. 14. See also In re Avalon Software Inc., 209 B.R. 517 (Bankr.D.Ariz.1997) (holding PTO proper place for filing for security interest in copyright).

It is of course unfortunate that the trademark statute is sufficiently vague to require judicial interpretation. This produced the understandable mistake made here. Security interests in patents present the same difficulty. See 35 U.S.C. § 261 (requiring recording for "assignment" of patents without furnishing definition of "assignment"); In re Transportation Design and Technology, Inc., 48 B.R. 635 (Bankr.S.D.Cal.1985) (ruling that filing with state, not PTO, perfects security interest in patents against subsequent lien creditor, but not against subsequent bona fide purchaser). Not even the copyright statute is totally consistent with the Uniform Commercial Code. All three statutes should be amended to place them in better harmony with the Code. See Alice Haemmerli, Insecurity Interests: Where Intellectual Property and Commercial Law Collide, 96 Colum. L. Rev. 1645 (1996) (noting difficulties and various proposals for reform). The problem was emphasized long ago in a leading treatise. See 1 Grant Gilmore, Security Interests in Personal Property § 13.1 (1965) (stating statutes such as copyright and patent statutes "pose intricate and difficult problems with respect to the interrelationship of state and federal law and the jurisdiction of state and federal courts—problems which remain largely unsettled and indeed unexplored.").

Being unperfected, Trimarchi's security interest is "subordinate" to a "person who becomes a lien creditor before the security interest is perfected." § 9–301(1). As debtor in possession, the Debtor has the "rights" and "powers" of a trustee. 11 U.S.C.S. § 1107. A trustee, in turn, has the "rights and powers of, or may avoid any transfer of property of the debtor. . . that is voidable. . . by a [lien creditor]." 11 U.S.C.S. § 544(a)(1). Hence Trimarchi's security interest is subordinate to the Debtor's rights as a lien creditor, and the Debtor may avoid that security interest. Avoidance should normally be accomplished through an adversary proceeding. Fed. R. Bankr.P. 7001(2). For the sake of simplicity, however, at the hearing on the Debtor's sales motion, to which Trimarchi was an objecting party, I dispensed with the necessity of further pleadings. Trimarchi has not objected to this procedure.

An order has accordingly issued declaring Trimarchi's security interest in the trademark (as well as other collateral covered by the parties' agreement) invalid by reason of lack of perfection.

NOTE

Notwithstanding an unbroken line of precedent taking the same view as *Together Development*, commentators recommend, as a precaution, filing a copy of a security agreement and the requisite cover sheet in the PTO for security interests in registered trademarks. Morris W. Hirsch, Taking Security Interests in Personal Property 26 (Cal. CEB Action Guide 1993). In George C. Yu, Security Interests in Federally Registered Trademarks: The Double Filing Problem and a Proposal for a State-Based Perfection System (1996) (unpublished paper on file with the Editors), the author found that double filing was the norm. Alice Haemmerli, Insecurity Interests: Where Intellectual Property and Commercial Law Collide, 96 Colum. L. Rev. 1645, 1719 (1996), views the trademark scene and sees that "the potential for trouble lurks just beneath the surface."

D. PATENTS

Federal statutes on copyrights, trademarks and patents are not so comprehensive as to completely exclude coverage of security interests in these kinds of collateral from the provisions of Article 9. Section 9–109(c)(1) aggressively states that Revised Article 9 defers to federal law only when and to the extent that federal law preempts it. See Comment 8 to 9–109. But whether filing under the federal statute is the exclusive manner of perfection under 9–311(a) and (b) is answered differently with respect to each of the federal statutes. A federal filing is the exclusive method of perfecting a security interest in copyrights, and Article 9 filing is the exclusive manner of perfecting a security interest in trademarks. In the case of patents, federal and state law offer parallel systems governing perfection of security interests: for one set of claimants the secured party can perfect under Article 9; for another it must perfect under federal law. The relevant federal statute is set out in the following opinion.

In re Cybernetic Services, Inc.

United States Court of Appeals, Ninth Circuit, 2001
252 F.3d 1039

■ GRABER, CIRCUIT JUDGE.

As is often true in the field of intellectual property, we must apply an antiquated statute in a modern context. The question that we decide today is whether 35 U.S.C. § 261 of the Patent Act, or Article 9 of the Uniform Commercial Code (UCC), as adopted in California, requires the holder of a security interest in a patent to record that interest with the federal Patent and Trademark Office (PTO) in order to perfect the interest as against a subsequent lien creditor.[1] We answer "no"; neither the Patent Act nor Article 9 so requires. We therefore affirm the decision of the Bankruptcy Appellate Panel (BAP).

The parties stipulated to the relevant facts: Matsco, Inc., and Matsco Financial Corporation (Petitioners) have a security interest in a patent developed by Cybernetic Services, Inc. (Debtor). The patent is for a data recorder that is designed to capture data from a video signal regardless of the horizontal line in which the data is located. Petitioners' security interest in the patent was "properly prepared, executed by the Debtor and timely filed with the Secretary of State of the State of California," in accordance with the California Commercial Code. Petitioners did not record their interest with the PTO.

After Petitioners had recorded their security interest with the State of California, certain creditors filed an involuntary Chapter 7 petition against Debtor, and an order of relief was granted. The primary asset of Debtor's estate is the patent. Petitioners then filed a motion for relief from the automatic stay so that they could foreclose on their interest in the patent. The bankruptcy Trustee opposed the motion, arguing that Petitioners had failed to perfect their interest because they did not record it with the PTO.

The bankruptcy court ruled that Petitioners had properly perfected their security interest in the patent by following the provisions of Article 9. Furthermore, the court reasoned, because Petitioners had perfected their security interest before the filing of the bankruptcy petition, Petitioners had priority over the Trustee's claim in the patent and deserved relief from the stay. Accordingly, the bankruptcy court granted Petitioners' motion. The BAP affirmed.

---

[1] A "security interest" is an interest in personal property that secures a payment or the performance of an obligation. Cal. Com.Code § 1201(36)(a). We refer to a person who holds a security interest in property but who does not hold title to that property as a "lien creditor."

Petitioners then filed this timely appeal.

Discussion

Article 9 of the UCC, as adopted in California, governs the method for perfecting a security interest in personal property. Article 9 applies to "general intangibles," a term that includes intellectual property. Cal. Com.Code § 9106 [9–102(a)(42)]. The parties do not dispute that Petitioners complied with Article 9's general filing requirements and, in the case of most types of property, would have priority over a subsequent lien creditor. The narrower question in this case is whether Petitioners' actions were sufficient to perfect their interest when the "general intangible" to which the lien attached is a patent. The parties also do not dispute that, *if* Petitioners were required to file notice of their security interest in the patent with the PTO, then the Trustee, as a hypothetical lien creditor under 11 U.S.C. § 544(a)(1), has a superior right to the patent.

The Trustee makes two arguments. First, the Trustee contends that the Patent Act preempts Article 9's filing requirements. Second, the Trustee argues that Article 9 itself provides that a security interest in a patent can be perfected only by filing it with the PTO. We discuss each argument in turn. . . .

A.   Preemption

1.   The Analytical Framework

. . .The Trustee argues that the recording provision found in 35 U.S.C. § 261 requires that the holder of a security interest in a patent record that interest with the PTO in order to perfect as to a subsequent lien creditor. Section 261 provides:

Ownership; assignment

Subject to the provisions of this title, patents shall have the attributes of personal property.

Applications for patent, patents, or any interest therein, shall be assignable in law by an instrument in writing. The applicant, patentee, or his assigns or legal representatives may in like manner grant and convey an exclusive right under his application for patent, or patents, to the whole or any specified part of the United States.

A certificate of acknowledgment under the hand and official seal of a person authorized to administer oaths within the United States, or, in a foreign country, of a diplomatic or consular officer of the United States or an officer authorized to administer oaths whose authority is proved by a certificate of a diplomatic or consular officer of the United States, or apostle of an official designated by a foreign country which, by treaty or convention, accords like effect to apostles of designated officials in the United States, shall be prima facie evidence of the execution of an assignment, grant or conveyance of a patent or application for patent.

> *An assignment, grant or conveyance shall be void as against any subsequent purchaser or mortgagee for a valuable consideration, without notice, unless it is recorded in the Patent and Trademark Office* within three months from its date or prior to the date of such subsequent purchase or mortgage.

(Emphasis added.)

If the Trustee's reading of the relevant portion of § 261 is correct, then to the extent that Article 9 allows a different method of perfection, it would be preempted under either a "field" or "conflict" preemption theory. That is because recording systems increase a patent's marketability and thus play an integral role in the incentive scheme created by Congress. Recording systems provide notice and certainty to present and future parties to a transaction; they work "by virtue of the fact that interested parties have a specific place to look in order to discover with certainty whether a particular interest has been transferred." *Nat'l Peregrine, Inc. v. Capitol Fed. Savs. & Loan Ass'n (In re Peregrine Entm't, Ltd.)*, 116 B.R. 194, 200 (C.D.Cal.1990). . . If, as the Trustee argues, the Patent Act expressly delineates the place where a party must go to acquire notice and certainty about liens on patents, then a state law that requires the public to look elsewhere unquestionably would undercut the value of the Patent Act's recording scheme. If, on the other hand, § 261 does not cover liens on patents, then Article 9's filing requirements do not conflict with any policies inherent in the Patent Act's recording scheme.

Article 9 itself recognizes the existence of preemption principles. California Commercial Code § 9104(a) expressly subordinates Article 9's requirements to those of federal law. That section provides that Article 9 does not apply to any "security interest subject to any statute of the United States to the extent that such statute governs the rights of parties to and third parties affected by transactions in particular types of property." Section 9104(a) may be broader than federal preemption doctrine under the Patent Act. The text of § 9104(a) implies that Article 9's requirements are inapplicable to the extent that a federal law *governs* the rights of a party to a secured transaction, with or without a *conflict* between the state law and the scheme created by Congress in the Patent Act. . . .

This possible difference in scope does not affect the result in the present case, however. As noted, the Trustee argues that § 261 *required* Petitioners to record their interest with the PTO. If that is true, then the Trustee has priority to the patent's proceeds, either because there is a clear conflict between the state and federal schemes and the state scheme is preempted, or because the Patent Act "governs the rights of parties" to the transaction and § 9104(a) operates to nullify Article 9's filing requirements. We turn to that issue now.

2.   The Patent Act Requires Parties to Record with the PTO Only Ownership Interest in Patents.

As noted, the Patent Act's recording provision provides that an "assignment, grant or conveyance shall be void as against any subsequent purchaser or mortgagee for a valuable consideration, without notice, unless it is recorded in the [PTO]." 35 U.S.C. § 261. In order to determine whether Congress intended for parties to record with the PTO the type of interest that is at issue in this case, we must give the words of the statute the meaning that they had in 1870, the year in which the current version of § 261 was enacted. . . .

With that history in mind, we must determine whether Congress intended to include the kind of transaction at issue in this case within the scope of 35 U.S.C. § 261. The first phrase in § 261's recording provision—"assignment, grant or conveyance"—refers to different types of transactions. The neighboring clause—"shall be void as against any subsequent purchaser or mortgagee"—refers to the status of the party that receives an interest in the patent. Therefore, for the Trustee to prevail in this case, (1) Petitioners' transaction with Debtor must have been the type of "assignment, grant or conveyance" referred to in § 261, and (2) the Trustee, who has the status of a hypothetical lien creditor, must be a "subsequent purchaser or mortgagee." We hold that neither condition is met.

As we will discuss next, our conclusion finds support in the text of § 261, keeping in view the historical definitions of the terms used in the recording provision; the context, structure, and policy behind § 261; Supreme Court precedent; and PTO regulations. We will begin by analyzing the statute's text and context, as interpreted by the Supreme Court. For the sake of clarity, we will discuss the two relevant phrases in the recording provision of § 261 separately.

a.   The phrase "assignment, grant or conveyance" concerns transfers of ownership interests only.

The historical meanings of the terms "assignment, grant or conveyance" all involved the transfer of an ownership interest. A patent "assignment" referred to a transaction that transferred specific rights in the patent, all involving the patent's title. . . .

A "grant," historically, also referred to a transfer of an ownership interest in a patent, but only as to a specific geographic area. . . .

Although older cases defining the term "conveyance" in the context of intangible property are sparse, and its historic meaning tended to vary, the common contemporaneous definition was "to transfer the legal title. . .from the present owner to another." *Abendroth v. Town of Greenwich,* 29 Conn. 356 (1860). . . .

In summary, the statute's text, context, and structure, when read in the light of Supreme Court precedent, compel the conclusion that a security interest in a patent that does not involve a transfer of the rights of ownership is a "mere license" and is not an "assignment, grant or conveyance" within the meaning of 35 U.S.C. § 261. And because § 261 provides that only an "assignment, grant or conveyance shall be void" as against subsequent purchasers and mortgagees, only transfers of ownership interests need to be recorded with the PTO. . . .

In the present case, the parties do not dispute that the transaction that gave Petitioners their interest in the patent did not involve a transfer of an ownership interest in the patent. Petitioners held a "mere license," which did not have to be recorded with the PTO.

b.   The phrase "subsequent purchaser or mortgagee" does not include subsequent lien creditors.

The Trustee's argument fails not only because a security interest that does not transfer ownership is not an "assignment, grant or conveyance," but also because he is not a subsequent "purchaser or mortgagee." Congress intended for parties to record their ownership interests in a patent so as to provide constructive notice only to subsequent holders of an ownership interest. Again, we derive our conclusion from the historical definitions of the words, from the context and structure of § 261, and from Supreme Court precedent.

The historical meaning of "purchaser or mortgagee" proves that Congress intended for the recording provision to give constructive notice only to subsequent holders of an ownership interest. For the sake of convenience, we begin with the definition of "mortgagee."

Historically, a "mortgagee" was someone who obtained title to property used to secure a debt. . . . A "mortgage" must be differentiated from a "pledge," a term that is absent from the Patent Act. Professor Gilmore, in his treatise, Security Interests in Personal Property § 1.1, at 8, notes that the historical distinction between a pledge and a mortgage was that "the mortgagee got title or an estate whereas the pledgee got merely possession with a right to foreclose on default."

That the Patent Act refers to securing a patent through a "mortgage" but not through a "pledge" is significant, for both were common methods of using a patent as collateral. . . . Generally, the inclusion of certain terms in a statute implies the exclusion of others. . . . It seems then, that by using the term "mortgagee," but not "lien" or "pledge," Congress intended in 1870 for the Patent Act's recording provision to protect only those who obtained title to a patent.

The term "purchaser" does not detract from this conclusion. Section 261 instructs that an unrecorded "assignment, grant or conveyance" shall be void as against a subsequent "purchaser. . . for a valuable consideration, without notice." The historical definition of a "purchaser for value and without notice" was a *bona fide* purchaser. A purchaser. . .who takes a conveyance purporting to pass the entire title, legal and equitable," who pays value and does not have notice of the rights of others to the property. Bouvier's Law Dictionary 1005 (Baldwin's Century ed.1926). . . .

Congress, by stating that certain transactions shall be void as against a subsequent "purchaser or mortgagee" intended for the words to be read together: A "purchaser" is one who buys an ownership interest in the patent, while a "mortgagee" is one who obtains an ownership interest in a patent as collateral for a debt.

Our previous comments about the context and structure of § 261 support our conclusion that Congress intended to protect only subsequent holders of an ownership interest. As noted, the title of § 261 is "Ownership; assignment," which suggests that the recording provision is concerned only with ownership interests.

Similarly, the second paragraph delineates the types of transactions that § 261 covers—(1) the assignment of a patent, and (2) the grant or conveyance of an exclusive right in the patent to the whole or any specified part of the United States—each involving the transfer of an ownership interest in a patent. It follows that, when Congress referred to a "subsequent purchaser or mortgagee," it was simply describing the future recipients of those transactions. In one case the recipient bought the interest (purchaser), while in the other the recipient loaned money and received the interest as collateral (mortgagee). In either case, an ownership interest was transferred.

Precedent confirms our reading of the statute. The Supreme Court has endorsed the view that Congress intended to provide constructive notice only to subsequent recipients of an ownership interest in a patent. In *Waterman,* the Court observed, as we do, that the Patent Act refers to a "mortgage" but not to a "pledge."

In summary, the historical definitions of the terms "purchaser or mortgagee," taken in context and read in the light of Supreme Court precedent, establish that Congress was concerned only with providing constructive notice to subsequent parties who take an ownership interest in the patent in question. *See In re Transp. Design & Tech., Inc.,* 48 B.R. 635, 639–40 (1985) (interpreting *Waterman* as holding that the Patent Act is concerned only with transactions that transfer title). . .

The Trustee is not a subsequent "mortgagee," as that term is used in § 261, because the holder of a patent mortgage holds title to the patent itself. . . . Instead, the Trustee is a hypothetical lien creditor. The Patent Act does not require parties to record documents in order to provide constructive notice to subsequent lien creditors who do not hold title to the patent.

3.   Public Policies that Underlie Recording Provisions Cannot Override the Text of the Patent Act.

The Trustee argues that requiring lien creditors to record their interests with the PTO is in line with the general policy behind recording statutes. It may be, as the Trustee argues, that a national system of filing security interests is more efficient and effective than a state-by-state system. However, there is no statutory hook upon which to hang the Trustee's policy arguments. Moreover, we are not concerned with the policy behind recording statutes generally but, rather, with the policy behind § 261 specifically.

. . .[Section] 261, as we have demonstrated and as its label suggests, is concerned with patent ownership. In that provision Congress gave patent holders the right to transfer their ownership interests, but only in specific ways. The congressional policy behind that decision was to protect the patent holder and the public for, as the Supreme Court put it,

> it was obviously not the intention of the legislature to permit several monopolies to be made out of one, and divided among different persons within the same limits. Such a division would inevitably lead to fraudulent impositions upon persons who desired to purchase the use of the improvement, and would subject a party who, under a mistake as to his rights, used the invention without authority, to be harassed by a multiplicity of suits instead of one, and to successive recoveries of damages by different persons holding different portions of the patent right in the same place.

Gayler v. Wilder, 51 U.S. (10 How.) 501, 519–20 (1850). . . . The recording provision, if read to include ownership interests only, is perfectly aligned with that policy. By contrast, a security interest in a patent does not make "several monopolies. . .out of one. . .divided among different persons within the same limits." 51 U.S. at 519.

We must interpret § 261 in the light of the purposes that Congress was seeking to serve. . . . Congress simply was not concerned with nonownership interests in patents, and this limitation was well understood at the time. As explained in a venerable treatise on the law of patents:

> A license is not such a conveyance of an interest in the patented invention as to affect its ownership, and hence is not required to be recorded. . . . The value of the patented invention to the vendee may be impaired by such outstanding licenses, but of this he must inform himself at his own risk as best he may. The record of a license, not being legally required, is not constructive notice to any person for any purpose.

2 Robinson § 817, at 602–03 (footnotes omitted).

> The Patent Act was written long before the advent of the "unitary" Article 9 security interest. But we must interpret § 261 as Congress wrote it. The Constitution entrusts to Congress, not to the courts, the role of ensuring that statutes keep up with changes in financing practices. It is notable that Congress has revised the Patent Act numerous times since its

enactment, most recently in 1999, *see* Pub.L. 106–113, but it has not updated the Act's recording provision. We decline the Trustee's invitation to do so in Congress' place. . . .

6.   There is no Conflict Between the Patent Act and Article 9 in this Case.

Because the Patent Act does not cover security interests or lien creditors at all, there is no conflict between 35 U.S.C. § 261 and Article 9. Petitioners did not have to file with the PTO to perfect their security interest as to a subsequent lien creditor.

B.   Article 9's Step-Back Provision

The Trustee's second major argument is that Article 9 itself requires that a creditor file notice of a secured transaction with the PTO in order to perfect a security interest. California Commercial Code § 9302(3)(a) states that the filing of a financing statement pursuant to Article 9 "is not necessary or effective to perfect a security interest in property subject to. . .[a] statute. . . which provides for a national or international registration. . .or which specifies a place of filing different from that specified in" Article 9. If § 9302(3)(a) applies, then a party *must* utilize the federal registration system in order to perfect its security interest. Cal. Com.Code § 9302(4).

The question, then, is whether the Patent Act is "[a] statute. . .which provides for a national or international registration. . .or which specifies a place of filing different from that specified in" Article 9. Cal. Com.Code § 9302(3)(a). The Patent Act is clearly a statute that provides for a national registration. But that begs the more focused question: a national registration *of what?* Courts have tended to use the context of the statute to amplify the bare text and to answer the focused question: a national registration *of security interests.* For example, in *Aerocon Engineering, Inc. v. Silicon Valley Bank (In re World Auxiliary Power Co.),* 244 B.R. 149, 155 (1999), the bankruptcy court observed that § 9302(3)(a), if read literally, would be absurd. It would provide that, whenever a particular type of collateral may be registered nationally, regardless of whether the federal statute specifies a place for filing a security interest different than that provided by the UCC, filing a UCC-1 financing statement would be neither necessary nor effective to perfect a security interest in the collateral.

Courts have thus read § 9302(3)(a) as providing that federal filing is necessary only when there is a statute that "provides for" a national registration *of security interests.* . . . We agree with that interpretation.

Under that more restrictive definition, it is clear that the Patent Act is outside the scope of § 9302(3)(a). As we have explained, a transaction that grants a party a security interest in a patent but does *not* effect a transfer of title is *not* the type of "assignment, grant or conveyance" that is referred to in 35 U.S.C. § 261. The transaction in this case did not transfer an ownership interest. Therefore, § 9302(3)(a) did not require that Petitioners record their security interest with the PTO.

The Comments to Article 9 of the UCC support this view. Comment 8 states that § 9302(3)

> exempts from the filing provisions of this Article transactions as to which an adequate system of filing, state or federal, has been set up outside this Article and subsection (4) makes clear that when such a system exists perfection of a relevant security interest can be had only through compliance with that system.

The Comments instruct that "17 U.S.C. §§ 28, 30 (copyrights), 49 U.S.C. § 1403 (aircraft), [and] 49 U.S.C. § 20(c) (railroads)" are examples of the "type of federal statutes" referred to in § 9302(3). Each of the statutes listed in the Comments refers expressly to security interests. *See* 17 U.S.C. § 101; 49 U.S.C. § 44107; 49 U.S.C. § 11301. The Patent Act is not among them.

C. Conclusion

Because § 261 concerns only transactions that effect a transfer of an ownership interest in a patent, the Patent Act does not preempt Article 9, and neither California Commercial Code § 9104(a) nor § 9302(3) applies. Consequently, Petitioners perfected their security interest in Debtor's patent by recording it with the California Secretary of State. They have priority over the Trustee's claim because they recorded their interest before the filing of the bankruptcy petition.

AFFIRMED.

NOTES

1. The court justly refers to § 261 as an "antiquated statute," but in a major revision of patent law, referred to as the America Invents Act (AIA), 35 USC §§ 100 et seq, (2011), § 261 was retained with almost no change.

2. **Case #1.** Debtor is a patent holder. It granted a security interest in the patent to SP to secure a debt owed by Debtor to SP, who filed an Article 9 financing statement in the filing office of the State of Debtor's residence. Later, Debtor filed in bankruptcy and its trustee (T) asserted that, in its capacity as a hypothetical lien creditor, it was entitled to avoid SP's security interest under BC 544(a)(1). *Cybernetic Services* held that SP would prevail even though it had not recorded its interest under section 261, which applies only to assignments of ownership to the patent (not present here) and protects only purchasers and mortgagees (not present here) against unrecorded assignments. Hence, former Article 9 applies and protects SP with a perfected security interest against T because its step-back provisions do not apply. The same would be true under 9–311(a)(1). See In re Pasteurized Eggs Corp., 296 B.R. 283 (Bankr. D. N.H.2003).

Case #2. If SP files only an Article 9 financing statement, how safe is it in cases having facts different from those in Case #1? (i) Before SP filed its financing statement, Debtor sold the patent to Buyer (B) who recorded the assignment with the PTO? Or failed to record with the PTO? (ii) After SP filed its financing statement, Debtor sold the patent to B who recorded in the PTO. (iii) After SP made an Article 9 filing, Debtor granted Finance a security interest in the patent in a "collateral assignment": ownership of the patent was transferred to Finance, reverting to Debtor on full payment of Finance's loan. Finance recorded the assignment with the PTO. Does SP have an enforceable security interest it can enforce against the patent in cases (i)–(iii)?

Section 261 has nothing to say about SP's security interest in these cases because, in the court's view, an Article 9 security interest does not affect ownership in the collateral and SP is not a subsequent purchaser or mortgagee within the court's understanding of those terms. Section 9–317(d) has something to say about cases (i) and (ii). The section's apparent assumption is that state law governs the matter. However, it is not clear that Article 9, including 9–317(d), governs the contests described in cases (i)–(iii).

3.   Unease about the questions raised by the cases in Case #2 has driven creditors taking security interests in patents to record in the PTO as well as file under Article 9. The obstacle they face in attempting to record a security interest is the prevailing assumption in patent law that the terms "assignment, grant or conveyance" do not contemplate the bare grant of a security interest. Shreen Danamraj, Note, *Priority Disputes Involving Security Interests in Patents: Case Law and Current Proposals*, 2 Tex. Intell. Prop. L.J. 257 (1994). The practice today is to cast a security agreement covering a patent in the form of an assignment, either a "collateral assignment" (absolute present assignment defeasible by repayment of the debt) or a "conditional assignment" (assignment worded as a present transfer that takes effect only on the happening of a future event). But some forms we have seen merely say: "Grantor does hereby collaterally assign and grant to Grantee a lien and security interest in all of Grantor's right, title and interest to [the described patent]." Or: "Assignor assigns and grants to Assignee a security interest in and mortgage on [rights in the patent] to secure payment of the obligations." Such language can be dangerous. According to *Cybernetic Services*, the grants create "mere licenses," not a security interest created by assignment or mortgage. Because the grants don't transfer an ownership interest, the Patent Act doesn't govern the secured interests created. Alice Haemmerli, *Insecurity Interests: Where Intellectual Property and Commercial Law Collide*, 96 Colum. L. Rev. 1645, 1696–1716 (1996), has an extensive discussion of patents and the many difficulties associated with perfecting a reliable security interest in them. In the course of her discussion she comments on the issues raised by use of the various kinds of assignments. Id. at 1710–16. She concludes that under the present law one can never be completely confident that perfection has been achieved and that reform is essential.

4. The lien creditor test of step-back under 9–311(a)(1) supports the holding of *Cybernetic Services*. Section 261 is not a statute that deals with priority with respect to lien creditors. But the court's opinion raises eyebrows with its definition of lien creditors in footnote 1: "We refer to a person who holds a security interest in property but who does not hold title to that property as a 'lien creditor.' 252 F.3d at 1044, n.1." Compare this with 9–102(a)(52)(A): "a creditor that has acquired a lien on the property involved by attachment, levy, or the like. . . ." Recall that under 9–202 title is immaterial under Article 9. One wonders whether the court's misconception of the meaning of "lien creditor" will come home to roost someday.

5. In re Coldwave Systems, L.L.C., 368 B.R. 91 (Bankr. D. Mass.2007), is the opposite of *Cybernetic Services*. The issue in that case was not what rights a trustee has against a party who did not file in the PTO, but against one who did so. *Coldwave Systems* is a solid holding that the federal statute does not protect holders of security interests in patents.

E. RESTRICTIONS ON ASSIGNMENT OF INTELLECTUAL PROPERTY

A debtor generally can grant a security interest in its assets, and if it defaults the secured creditor can enforce its security interest by foreclosing on the assets. Restrictions in the security agreement limiting the debtor's power to transfer its rights in the assets do not prevent their transfer. 9–401. This rule reflects a broader principle operative in much of commercial law: the free assignability of contract rights. The free assignability of rights treats as ineffective restraints on alienation, including contractual restrictions on assignment.

A different principle underlies the law governing intellectual property and certain other intangible rights: freedom of contract. Under patent and copyright law, for instance, the licensee can assign its rights under the license only with the licensor's consent. This means that an assignee cannot enforce these rights against the licensor unless the licensor consents to the assignment. The principles of free assignability and freedom of contract obviously conflict. If the licensee's transfer of a right requires the licensor's consent, the transfer is restrained. If the right is freely transferable, notwithstanding a contractual restriction on transfer, the parties' freedom of contract is compromised. Article 9's slightly complicated provisions governing restrictions on the assignment of intangible rights involve a compromise between free assignability and freedom of contract.

Sections 9–406 through 9–409 regulate the assignment of different sorts of intangible rights. The most frequently applicable sections are 9–406 and 9–408. Both sections endorse free assignability by rendering contractual and noncontractual restrictions on assignments "ineffective" in most instances. The basic difference between 9–406 and 9–408 is the extent to which the two sections render ineffective ("override") restrictions on assignments. Section 9–406's override is complete while

9–408's override is limited. Section 9–406's override rule applies to assignments of chattel paper, payment intangibles, promissory notes and accounts (other than health-care receivables). The rule also applies to sales of chattel paper and accounts (other than health-care receivables). 9–406(d)–(f). The section makes ineffective contractual or legal restrictions or prohibitions, or that require consent, inter alia for the creation, attachment perfection or enforcement of a security interest in the assets listed. In extending the override to enforcement, 9–406's override rule is complete.

Section 9–408's override is limited. The override applies to assignments of general intangibles (other than payment intangibles) as security interests and heath care-insurance receivables as well as to sales of promissory notes. It also extends to the license of a general intangible. 9–408(a), (b). Section 9–408(a)(1) and (c)(1) render "ineffective" contractual and legal restrictions on assignments "to the extent" that they "impair the creation, attachment or perfection of a security interest." Given these subsections, antiassignment provisions don't prevent attachment of a security interest in the listed assets. However, under 9–408(d), the security interest is unenforceable against the licensor, the licensee's security agreement doesn't impose any obligations on the licensor, and the secured creditor cannot use the license. 9–408(d)(1), (2) and (4). This limits 9–408's override.

Intellectual property such as patents, copyrights, trademarks and trade secrets are general intangibles. 9–102(a)(42). Thus, 9–408 applies to contracts that create a security interest in these intangible assets. As applied to licenses of intellectual property, 9–408 uses the terms "account debtor" and "debtor." Section 9–408(a) and 9–408(c)s' override enables the "debtor" to grant a security interest in the assets described in 9–408. In the case of a license of a general intangible—a patent or copyright license, for instance—the licensor is the "account debtor" and the licensee the "debtor," and the licensee's interest is a general intangible. Comment 5 to 9–408 explains that even though the licensee will be obligated to pay royalties to the licensor, the licensor is the account debtor for purposes of applying 9–408 because it is obligated to render performance in exchange for payment.

As noted above, under intellectual property law an assignment, including the creation of a security interest, is ineffective without the consent of the owner. Unless federal law applies, 9–408(a)(1) renders the restriction on assignment ineffective to the extent that it prevents the attachment or perfection of a security interest in intellectual property. Nonetheless, 9–408's override is limited: the secured party cannot enforce its security interest against the collateral (without the debtor's consent). Further, the qualification just entered, "unless federal law applies," is important. Federal law holds that a nonexclusive licensee with a federal created intellectual property right may not assign its rights without the licensor's consent. See, e.g., Everex Systems, Inc. v.

Cadtrak Corp., 89 F.3d 673 (9th Cir. 1996)(patents); 3 Melville B. and David Nimmer, Nimmer on Copyright § 10.02[B][4] (1998) (copyrights). Because federal law preempts inconsistent state law, 9–408's override is inapplicable in the case of intellectual property governed by federal law. Comment 9 recognizes this significant limitation on 9–408's application, offering 9–408 as a "template for future federal law reform."

Even if federal law is inapplicable to intellectual property collateral, so that 9–408's override enables a security interest to attach to an intellectual property license, there remains a basic practical question: what good is a security interest that cannot be enforced without the debtor's consent? Professor Mann reports that secured creditors believe that they have enough protection if they have the right to terminate the debtor-licensee's power to use the license. Ronald Mann, Secured Credit and Software Financing, 85 Cornell L. Rev. 134, 173, 177 (1999). He maintains that this might be accomplished by including terms in the loan agreement that give the secured party the right to stop the licensee from further use of the license by court order or by installing a self-help termination switch on the computers. This is uncharted territory, and prediction about how courts will treat a "stop use" provision in a security agreement is hazardous. Such provisions might run afoul 9–408(d). Uncertainties in the free assignment of intangibles are described in Steven D. Walt, Uncertainty about Free Assignment: Payment Rights and General Intangibles Under Article 9, 2006 J. Payment Sys. L. 4.

What, then, is the value of having a security interest that cannot be enforced on default? That is, how does 9–408 increase the value of intangible assets as collateral above zero? To understand how, realize that the value of collateral to the secured party is a function of the expected distributions on the collateral it receives either outside or inside the debtor's bankruptcy. Given 9–408(d)'s elimination of enforcement rights, the value of the intangible collateral to the secured party outside of bankruptcy is very close to zero. Example 5 in Comment 8 to 9–408 is unrealistically optimistic in its assessment. The Example proposes a non-debtor franchisor who consents to the debtor-franchisee's assignment of its rights to create a security interest. Consent, of course, overrides a default rule against assignability, and one wonders why the franchisor wouldn't have consented to the assignment initially. The scenario, although possible, isn't likely or frequent. It certainly isn't likely or frequent enough to justify a new Code section.

The value to the secured creditor instead comes from expected distributions on the collateral in the debtor's bankruptcy. Under prescribed conditions, Bankruptcy Code 365(f) allows the bankruptcy trustee to assign the debtor's rights under an executory contract, notwithstanding nonbankruptcy restrictions on its assignment. Essentially, this means that anti-assignment provisions in executory contracts generally are invalid in bankruptcy. A copyright, patent or other intellectual property license is a type of executory contract, and 9–

408(c) enables a security interest to attach to the licensee's rights in the license. BC 365(f) allows the licensee's trustee to sell the licensee's interest, overriding relevant attendant anti-assignment provisions. The sale yields proceeds, and the licensee's secured party is entitled to them under BC 552(b)(1) as postpetition proceeds of prepetition collateral. Comment 8 to 9–408 recognizes this outcome. A debtor's prospects of bankruptcy can be substantial and expected to change over the life of a loan. Thus, while the secured party might receive nothing on the debtor's default outside of bankruptcy, it might well receive a distribution from liquidation of the debtor's license interest in the debtor's bankruptcy. Section 9–408(c), therefore, increases the ex ante value of the debtor's intangible assets above zero. The prospect of a bankruptcy payout from these assets provides the added value.

PROBLEM

Lender has financed the operations of certain retailers on a secured basis for several years. In response to the substantial revenues these retailers earn from their online sales, Lender is considering offering a new lending program. Under the program it will make loans to qualified retailers secured by the web domain names registered to them with a third party domain name registry. The domain names, particularly generic or easy to remember ones, are potentially valuable to retailers to which they are registered. They are potentially valuable collateral to Lender only if it can use the domain names or otherwise transfer them to another firm in the event the retailer defaults on its obligations to Lender. The service agreements between the registering retailers and their registrars contain an anti-assignment clause that provides that "your rights under this agreement are not assignable or transferable." Lender is concerned about this clause.

Assume that the domain names registered to the retailers are not subject to trademark law or otherwise subject to federal law. There is a division of opinion as to whether a web domain name is a property right or a contract for the use of a service; compare Office Depot, Inc. v. Zuccarini, 596 F.3d 696 (9th Cir. 2010) (property right). with Network Solutions, Inc. v. Umbro Int'l, Inc., 529 S.E.2d 80 (Va. 2013) (contractual right of use). You may assume that applicable law deems a domain name to be a property right. What advice do you offer Lender in light of 9–408 and other relevant law?

As part of its new lending program, Lender also is considering accepting as collateral nonexclusive licenses retailers hold in copyrighted tee shirts. Advise Lender.

CHAPTER 6

SECURITY INTERESTS IN INVESTMENT SECURITIES

A. INTRODUCTION

This Chapter describes Article 9's rules governing security interests in investment securities. Federal and state securities law regulates the issuance of securities and financial information relating to them, and the exchanges on which securities are traded and participants in the securities industry. Article 8 of the UCC governs a different subject: the ownership and transfer of investment securities. Because a secured transaction in securities creates a security interest in them, Article 9's rules are coordinated with those of Article 8. For illustrations this Chapter uses simple transactions, familiar to commercial law generalists, in which individuals or industry nonprofessionals use their stocks, bonds, mutual funds and the like, as collateral for loans. In business these are called retail transactions. This section describes the background for understanding Article 9's rules governing security interests in securities.

1. DIRECT AND INDIRECT HOLDING SYSTEMS

Section 9–102(a) defines "investment property" as meaning "a security, whether certificated or uncertificated, security entitlement, securities account, commodity contract, or commodity account." The terms "security" and "security entitlement" and "securities account" reflect a difference in the way securities are held. Investors hold securities either directly or indirectly in what are called direct and indirect holding systems, respectively. In a direct holding system, the investor is registered as the owner of the security on the books of the issuer of the security. It has an interest in the security. The relationship between the investor and issuer of the security is direct, as depicted below.

As the owner of 10 securities, each investor has rights, including the right to dividends and voting rights, where the securities are shares of stock, and a right to interest payments where the securities are bonds. Whether the 10 securities held by the investors are certificated or uncertificated has no effect on the investors' ownership of the securities or the rights ownership gives them.

In an indirect holding system, investors do not have a direct relationship with the issuer of the securities. The investors are not listed on the issuer's books as owners of securities. Instead, they hold securities through intermediaries. Only the intermediary with a direct relationship with the issuer owns the securities issued and is registered on the issuer's books as the owner. The investors instead have a beneficial interest in the securities in securities accounts maintained for them by intermediaries with which they are in a direct relationship. These interests give the investors certain economic and legal benefits. See, e.g., 8–505, 8–506. The relationship between the investor and the security held is indirect, as depicted below.

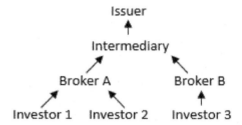

In the above illustration, neither the investors nor their respective intermediaries, Brokers A and B, are in a direct relationship with the issuer of the securities. Only Intermediary is in a direct relationship with Issuer and is listed on Issuer's books as owning 20 securities. Investors 1–3 each has a beneficial interest—"beneficial ownership" as the interest is sometimes called—in 10 securities issued by Issuer in the securities accounts maintained for them by their respective brokers. The holders of beneficial interests in the securities are not recorded on Issuer's books. Article 8 describes Intermediary and Brokers as "financial intermediaries," the accounts maintained for their respective customers as "securities accounts," and the 10 shares credited to the respective securities accounts as "financial assets." See 8–102(a)(8), (9) and (14), 8–501(a). Investors 1–3 hold a "security entitlement" against their respective Brokers with respect to 10 shares issued by Issuer. 8–501(b). The same descriptions apply to entities in Brokers' position in further downward tiers between Broker A and B and Investor 1–3, if any, in the holding system.

An indirect holding system produces significant efficiencies in the trading of securities. Key to these efficiencies is the reduction in the cost of trading securities resulting from "immobilizing" them and making book entry changes in securities accounts to reflect trades. If securities held directly are traded, the transfer of ownership must be recorded on the issuer's books, and security certificates, where issued, physically delivered to the buyer. By comparison, if the securities are held indirectly, their trade can be accomplished without physical delivery of the shares traded. The securities are immobilized by remaining in the custody of a depository and the trade effected by book entries on the records of the relevant intermediaries. This considerably reduces the transaction costs of trading securities. Further costs are saved where, as in many instances, neither the issuer nor the intermediary with which it is in a direct relationship need reflect trades on their respective records. As a result, the book entry system of settlement in an indirect holding system reduces the number of transactions that need to be accomplished to settle trades. This increases the liquidity of indirectly held securities.

For example, if Investor 1 sells its 10 shares to Investor 2, the trade can be settled on Broker A's records by Broker A debiting Investor 1's securities account in the amount of 10 securities of Issuer and crediting Investor 2 securities account in the same amount. Neither Issuer's nor Intermediary's records need reflect the trade, since the net positions of their respective account holders (Intermediary and Broker A) remain unchanged. If Investor 1 sells its 10 shares to Investor 3, the trade is settled by Intermediary debiting Broker A's securities account and crediting Broker B's securities account with it, Investor 1 and Investor 3's own respective securities accounts with Broker A and Broker B being adjusted accordingly. Issuer's records remain unchanged, as there is no change in Intermediary's net position on Issuer's books.

In the United States, most publicly traded shares issued by large corporations are issued in certificated form to Cede & Co. as the shareholder of record for its customers. Cede & Co. is in the position of Intermediary in the illustration above. It is the nominee of The Depository Trust Company (DTC), a trust company owned by a consortium of major broker-dealers and banks. Most brokers and large U.S. banks are participants in the DTC. The DTC, which holds the physical certificates in its vaults, offers clearance and settlement services to its customers through book entry changes on its own records. It provides these services for almost all corporate equity and debt securities, and money market securities in the United States. (The DTC also offers direct registration services through which an investor can register on the issuer's books as the owner of securities, the DTC retaining custody of the security certificates.) By dealing with their trades over a single depository, the DTC's participating broker-dealers and banks avoid having to deliver security certificates or have issuers of securities adjust their own records to reflect trades. See James Steven Rogers, Policy Perspectives on Revised Article 8, 43 UCLA L. Rev. 1431, 1444 (1996). Article 8 considers the DTC to be both a "clearing corporation" and a "securities intermediary;' see 8–102(a)(5) and (a)(14). As Professor Rogers explains, much of the impulse for revising Article 8 stemmed from the need to deal with the current practice of having most securities held by intermediaries rather than the beneficial owners of the securities. A more detailed description of indirect holding systems and their regulation by Article 8 appears in id.; see also Uniform Commercial Code Revised Article 8 Prefatory Note 1.A–1.D (1994).

2. SECURITY ENTITLEMENTS AND PROPERTY RIGHTS

The indirect holding system is not just a way of owning and transferring securities. It also determines what participants in the system own. The description of the system as a way of owning securities indirectly through a securities intermediary might suggest that investors own specific securities indirectly. Strictly, this is inaccurate. There is a difference between a security and a security entitlement. A security gives its owner a property right in a specific item as well as certain contractual rights against the issuer. By comparison, a security entitlement with respect to a particular security gives the entitlement holder (the owner) a combination of a property right in certain securities held by the security intermediary and rights against the security intermediary with respect to the securities. See 8–102(a)(17). A security and a security entitlement therefore describe different property rights. The entitlement holder owns a security entitlement; it does not own the financial assets underlying the entitlement.

As Comment 2 to 8–503 states: "A security entitlement is not a claim to a specific identifiable thing; it is a package of rights and interest that a person has against the person's securities intermediary and the property held by the intermediary." Because a security and a security entitlement are different, an investor can acquire a security entitlement to a specific security even if its securities intermediary does not acquire the security. Section 8–501(c) allows for this possibility. Under 8–501(c), a person who acquires a security entitlement through a securities intermediary has the entitlement even if the securities intermediary does not itself hold the financial asset (e.g., the security).

The entitlement holder does not have a property right in specific financial assets. Rather, it has a pro rata property right in certain of the security intermediary's financial assets. Article 8 separates property of the securities intermediary from property of the entitlement holders. Section 8–503(a) provides that the underlying financial assets held by the securities intermediary for its entitlement holders are not property of the securities intermediary or its creditors, to the extent necessary to satisfy all security entitlements respect to a particular financial asset. Thus, if the securities intermediary has insufficient underlying financial assets to satisfy these security entitlements, only entitlement holders have a property right in underlying financial assets held by their securities intermediary corresponding to the securities to which the holders are entitled. (An exception to this rule applies where a creditor of the securities intermediary has control of the underlying financial asset; see 8–511(b). Control is discussed in section D. below.)

However, Article 8 does not separate property rights in underlying financial assets held by the securities intermediary as between entitlement holders. Instead, under 8–503(b) the entitlement holder has a pro rata property right in particular financial assets held by the securities intermediary, without regard to whether the intermediary has identified specific securities as belonging to a entitlement holder. As a result, the entitlement holder has a pro rata property right in a fungible bulk of financial assets rather than in specific financial assets. For example, assume that Broker's books credit Smith with 8 shares and Jones with 2 shares issued by the same issuer. Broker has not credited shares issued by the issuer to any of its other customers' financial accounts. Assume also that Broker owns only 5 of the issuer's shares. Smith has a property interest in 4 shares (80% x 5) and Jones has a property interest in 1 share (20% x 5).

The entitlement holder's property right in the securities intermediary's financial assets has an immediate consequence for security interests in investment securities held through the indirect holding system. Under 9–203(a) a security interest is created when it attaches. Attachment in turn requires, among other conditions, that the debtor have rights in the collateral or the power to transfer such rights. 9–203(b)(2). Where the debtor holds securities in an indirect holding system, the debtor's security entitlement to a particular financial asset gives it a pro rata property right in the securities intermediary's corresponding financial assets. Thus, when the security entitlement is collateral, the secured party's security interest attaches to this right. Because the debtor does not own the underlying security, the secured party's security interest does not attach to it. In addition, the secured party generally can enforce its security interest against the collateral only by proceeding against the debtor's securities intermediary. 8–112(c).

B. WHAT IS A SECURITY?

The brief treatment of investment securities in this Chapter does not probe the fringes of investment securities. Its focus is on familiar examples of securities: stocks and bonds. These are "securities" as defined under 8–102(a)(15). Section 8–102(a)(15)'s definition states four requirements for an item to be security. The first requirement (stated in the introductory language of 8–102(a)(15)'s definition) is that the item must be an obligation of the issuer or an interest in the issuer. Bonds are obligations of the issuer, and shares are a type of interest in the issuer.

The second requirement concerns the form the item must take. Section 8–102(a)(15)(i) requires that it take one of three forms. Two of the forms involve a certificated security. A certificated security is a security represented by a writing, such as a stock certificate. 8–102(a)(4). Certificated securities can be in either bearer or for or registered form. As the term "bearer" suggests, to be in bearer form the certificate must state that the security is payable to the bearer of the certificate. 8–102(a)(2). Bearer certificates are rare. To be in registered form, the certificate must specify a person entitled to the security. The transfer must also be capable of being registered on the issuer's transfer books. 8–102(a)(13). The third form an item can take is an uncertificated security. An uncertificated security is not represented by a certificate. 8–102(a)(18). Because an uncertificated security is not represented by a certificate, its transfer cannot occur by transfer of a certificate. Instead, an uncertificated security can be transferred only by entries on issuer's books or on the books of maintained for the issuer. 8–102(a)(15)(i).

The requirement that certificated securities other than those in bearer form be in "registered form" has been a source of dispute. To be in "registered form," the form must be one in which the transfer "may be registered upon books maintained for that purpose" by or on the issuer's behalf. Highland Capital Management, L.P. v. Schneider, 866 N.E.2d 1020 (N.Y. 2007) ruled that the registrability requirement is met as long as a transfer of an obligation could be registered on the issuer's books, even if the issuer does not record transfers of the obligation on its books and its books are not maintained for the purpose of registering these transfers. This ruling matters because, if *Highland Capital*'s reading of "registered form" is correct, a promissory note could be a security. As a security, its sale would not be governed by Article 9, including Article 9's rule of automatic perfection for sales of promissory notes. See 9–109(a)(3), 9–109(4). Comment 13 to 8–102 rejects *Highland Capital*'s understanding of 8–102(a)(13)'s registrability requirement. According to the Comment, it's not enough that the issuer *could* register a transfer on its books. It is necessary that the issuer must in fact be maintaining its books for the purpose of registering the particular sort of transfer. To date Article 8 has not amended its definition of "registered form" to reflect this understanding.

The third requirement is that the item be divided or divisible into a class of shares or obligations. 8–102(a)(15)(ii). Thus, two or more issued instruments in the same class are "divided" into a class. A single instrument is "divisible" if, by its terms, it can be divided into two or more instruments in a class. For instance, a single bond that cannot be divided into two or more bonds doesn't satisfy the "divisibility" test. On the other hand, although a single certificate (e.g., a jumbo certificate) may be issued, the underlying intangible interest, by the terms of certificate, may be divided. The divisibility clause serves to distinguish debt securities from negotiable instruments. The fourth requirement, appearing in 8–102(a)(15)(iii), states a "functional" test: the item either must be of a type that is traded on securities exchanges or markets or must expressly provide that it is governed by Article 8.

Article 8 effectively extends the definition of "security" past 8–102(a)(15). Section 8–103 deems certain investment products to be securities even if they don't satisfy 8–102(a)(15)'s functional test. Under 8–103(a), the shares of a corporation, business trust, joint stock company or similar entities are securities. Their shares are securities even if the shares are traded over the counter and not on securities exchanges. For its part, 8–103(b) provides that an equity interest issued by an entity registered under federal investment company laws is a security. These laws include the Investment Company Act of 1940, under which companies issuing mutual funds register. Thus, under 8–103(b), shares of mutual funds, which are not traded over exchanges, are securities. Finally, 8–103(c) provides that an interest in a partnership or limited liability company is not a security unless the interest is traded on securities exchanges or its express terms the interest is made subject to Article 8.

Interests in limited liability companies (LLCs) are usually not securities under 8–103(c)'s "traded on" language because members' interests are commonly uncertificated and rarely traded on securities markets. However, under 8–103(c) they are securities if the interests expressly provide for coverage under Article 8, a treatment that the LLC's organizational rules or operating agreement control. Accordingly, 8–103(c)'s flexibility in coverage allows for strategic behavior by debtors with LLC interests. Interests in LCCs are classified as general intangibles. See 9–102(a)(42). Thus, a secured party can perfect its security interest in the debtor's LLC interests by a security agreement and filed financing statement that describes the collateral as "general intangibles." Later, if the LCC rules are amended to expressly opt-in to Article 8, the debtor can grant a security interest in its LCC interests now properly described as securities or investment property. As a security, the later secured party can perfect in the debtor's LLC interests by control. The later secured party has priority in these interests if it does so, as described in the next section. Breach of a covenant in a security agreement prohibiting an express "opt-in" to Article 8 might not be worth much where the debtor is insolvent.

Article 8 governs not just securities. It also governs financial assets in a securities account that are not securities. A string of definitions establishes this more expansive coverage. A "security entitlement" arises when a "securities intermediary" credits a person's "securities account" with a "financial asset" on its books. 8–501(b). A "securities account" in turn is an account in which a financial asset may be credited in accord with the agreement between the securities intermediary maintaining the account and its customer. 8–501(a). Although "financial asset" includes securities, it is not restricted to them. 8–102(a)(9). Section 8–102(a)(9)(iii) counts as a financial asset any property held in a securities account if the securities intermediary maintaining the account expressly agreed to treat the property as a financial asset under Article 8. As far as 8–102(a)(9)(iii) goes, there is no restriction on the sort of property maintained in a securities account. Accordingly, a membership interest in an LLC counts as a financial asset if the securities intermediary expressly agrees to treat it as such. This is so even if the membership interest has not opted-in to Article 8, in accordance with 9–103(c). As another example, a digital asset such as cryptocurrency or other digital assets is a financial asset if the securities intermediary expressly agrees that the cryptocurrency or other digital assets in the securities account is subject to Article 8.

C. BASIC RULES

The following is a simplified summary of the UCC rules governing security interests in investment securities. These rules are discussed in in more detail in subsequent sections in this Chapter. Attachment, perfection and priority of security interests in investment securities are governed by Article 9, although important rules and definitions are found in Article 8. If the other requirements of 9–203(b) are met, attachment occurs with respect to certificated securities when delivered to the secured party (9–203(b)(3)(C)) and with respect to other investment property when the secured party has control (9–203(b)(3)(D)).

The permissible methods of perfection differ according to whether the debtor holds securities directly or through an indirect holding system. In the case of securities held directly, perfection occurs by control (9–314(a)), filing (9–312(a)) or delivery if the securities are certificated (9–313). A security interest in a certificated security is perfected automatically under 9–312(e) and 9–312(g)'s restrictive conditions. Where the debtor holds uncertificated securities, perfection occurs by filing or control. In the case of securities held through an indirect holding system, perfection in security entitlements and securities accounts can be achieved by filing or control (9–314(a), 9–312(a)). A security interest in investment property is perfected automatically when it attaches if the debtor is a broker or securities intermediary (9–309(10)).

Under 9–106(a), a person has control of a certificated security, uncertificated security or security entitlement as stated in 8–106. A security interest perfected by control is prior to one perfected by filing whether or not the party with control had knowledge of the filing. 9–328(1). Priority among security interests perfected by control is on a first-in-time basis. 9–328(2). Security interests held by brokers or banks in securities held by them (the common margin loan situation) are prior to security interests held by other parties. 8–106(e), 9–328(3).

Article 8's drafters conceived the control doctrine to meet the problems raised both by indirect holding of securities by securities intermediaries and by uncertificated securities. For a secured party to gain control with respect to a security interest in certificated securities held by a securities intermediary, it must either become the entitlement holder or enter into a three-party agreement with the debtor and the broker or bank holding the securities that gives the secured party the power to have the securities sold or transferred without further action by the debtor. 8–106(d). Control is automatic where the debtor is the entitlement holder and grants its securities intermediary a security interest in the security entitlement. 8–106(e). For control with respect to a security interest in an uncertificated security, such as a mutual fund, the secured party must either become the registered owner or reach an agreement with the debtor and the issuer that gives the secured party the power to sell or transfer without the consent of the owner. 8–106(c).

Understanding Article 8's bearing on security interests in security requires a familiarity with some of its basic terms and their definitions. Several of Article 8's terms were used in the section A. in describing the indirect holding system for investment securities. Section B. discussed Article 8's definition of "security." Working definitions of some of the terms dealt with in this Chapter follow:

A "certificated security" is one that is represented by a certificate. 8–102(a)(4). An "uncertificated security" is one that is not. 8–102(a)(18).

A "financial asset" is a (i) security, (ii) an obligation or other interest in a person or property or an enterprise which is of type deal in or traded in financial markets or (iii) any property that is held by a securities intermediary for another person in a securities account if the intermediary has expressly agreed with the person that the property is to be treated as a financial asset under Article 8. 8–102(a)(9).

A "securities account" is an account to which financial assets such as stocks, bonds, and mutual funds are credited. 8–501(a).

A "securities intermediary" means a broker or bank that maintains securities accounts for others. 8–102(a)(14).

A "security entitlement" means the rights of a customer of the brokers or banks with respect to a financial asset in its securities account. 8–102(a)(17). The customer is described as an "entitlement holder." 8–102(a)(7).

"Investment property" is defined in 9–102(a)(49) to include securities, whether certificated or not, security entitlements and securities accounts. This catch-all phrase is used throughout Article 9 as a convenient way to refer to the kinds of property that are subject to the special rules set out above with respect to security interests. This collateral would otherwise fall within the definition of general intangible, from which they are specifically excluded. 9–102(a)(42).

The "issuer" of a bond is the obligor. The "issuer" of stock is the enterprise or property whose equity interest the shares of stock represent. 8–102(a)(15), 8–201.

D. CERTIFICATED SECURITIES

1. HELD BY OWNER

Most investors do not choose to be listed on the company's books as the registered owner with a stock or bond certificate issued to them. They instead elect to have their certificated securities in publicly traded companies held by an intermediary such as a broker-dealer or bank.

Stock certificates for shares in close corporations are usually held by owners. The probable explanation for the greater popularity of the indirect holding method is its convenience. The intermediary provides consolidated records of all sales, purchases, margin loans, dividends and interest payments, reinvestments, and the like. Tax reporting information is given. When sales are made there is no need to hunt around for the securities certificates which must be promptly delivered to the broker. There are no certificates to be lost or stolen. In addition, many intermediaries offer an asset management service, to be discussed later, which automatically sweeps all of the dividends, interest and sale proceeds into a money market account on which the investor can draw by check or credit card.

But there are some advantages in possessing stock or bond certificates. Under the indirect holding system, the investor is locked into one broker when it wishes to sell the securities, but an investor who holds the certificates can call a number of brokers to see which offers the most favorable commission rate. Lenders can make loans immediately if a debtor has a stock certificate to pledge; under an indirect holding system it will take more time to arrange a loan on the security of the debtor's brokerage account from any lender other than the intermediary itself. Moreover, some companies offer investors dividend reinvestment plans in which investors are allowed to reinvest their dividends in additional shares without having to pay a brokerage commission. In order to participate in one of these plans, the investor must have the stock registered in its name. A growing number of companies now sell their shares directly to investors; the advantage to the investor is that there is no brokerage commission to pay. Another reason given to explain why investors are willing to endure the inconvenience of holding certificates is that they are concerned about the safety of securities left with brokerage houses. Since the Securities Investor Protection Corporation now insures customers against loss owing to the failure of intermediaries up to $500,000, this concern has been allayed in most instances. Securities Investor Protection Act, 15 U.S.C. §§ 78aaa–111.

a.   CONTROL IN PLEDGE TRANSACTIONS

As noted above, there are two alternative methods for perfecting a security interest in investment securities: filing a financing statement and controlling the collateral. 9–312(a), 9–314(a). Perfecting by control rather than by filing has advantages (and costs) for the secured party. One is ease in gaining access to the collateral in the event of the debtor's default. In general, the secured party with control over securities is in a position to enforce its security interest against them without requiring the debtor's cooperation. The secured party doesn't require judicial assistance or risk breaching the peace in liquidating the securities. The other advantage control gives the secured party is a special priority rule favorable to it. See 9–328.

There is a generic notion of control that underlies the different forms control takes. This is the notion that a party has control when it can dispose of the collateral without further action by the debtor. See Comments 1 (second paragraph) and 7 (second paragraph) to 8–106. Possession of a security, even where possible, by itself does not give control. It does not enable the party in possession to liquidate the security without further action by the debtor. For instance, consider a certificated security registered in the debtor's name. A secured party can perfect its security interest in a certificated security by taking delivery of the certificate. 9–313(a). Delivery in this case consists in taking possession of the certificate. 8–301(a)(1). However, delivery alone doesn't give the secured party control, because it doesn't put the secured party in a position to dispose of the certificated security without the debtor's cooperation. To be able to dispose of the security, the debtor must endorse the certificate in blank or in the name of the secured party. Cf. 8–106(b)(1).

How control of securities is obtained depends on the way the debtor holds the securities and the form of the security. Section 8–106(b) and (c) describe the control requirements where the debtor holds securities directly. Subsection (b) states the requirements for control of directly held certificated securities, and subsection (c) states the control requirements for directly held uncertificated securities. For its part, 8–106(d) states the control requirements for securities held indirectly by the debtor through a securities intermediary. Section 8–106(e) has a special control rule for the securities intermediary whose customer grants it a security interest in a security entitlement held against the intermediary. The following Problems concern a lending transaction involving a pledge of securities the debtor holds directly. In the first Problem Bank, the secured party, takes delivery of certain of the debtor's securities; in the second Problem Lender takes delivery of them.

PROBLEMS

1. Eleanor owns 1,000 shares of Amalgamated, Inc., worth approximately $200,000, and possesses a security certificate (8–102(a)(16)) registered on the books of the company in her name (8–102(a)(13)). She wishes to borrow $100,000 from Bank as a short term loan to allow her to make a down payment on a new residence while awaiting the sale of her old residence. Bank required security for the loan and, pursuant to an agreement, she delivered possession of the stock certificate to Bank to secure the loan on the date Bank advanced the funds to her. The stock certificate contained her indorsement (8–102(a)(11)), that is, she signed the transfer form on the back of the certificate, leaving the name of the transferee blank. Although her indorsement entitled Bank to have the shares registered in its name on the books of the company, it merely retained possession of the certificate without acting to have the registration changed to its name or notifying Amalgamated of its security interest. What are Bank's rights with respect to the stock pledged as against Eleanor's creditors and, if she

subsequently files in bankruptcy, her trustee in bankruptcy? Work your way through the following provisions. 9–203(b)(3)(C) (attachment) and Comment 4 to that section; 9–313(a) (perfection by delivery under 8–301); 8–301(a)(1) (possession is delivery to purchaser); a pledgee is a purchaser under 1–201(b)(29), (30); 9–314(a) (perfection by control); 9–106(a) (control) refers to 8–106(b)(1) which defines control of a certificated security as delivery of indorsed certificate to purchaser; and 9–310(b)(7) (no filing required to perfect if certificated security delivered to secured party).

Although the facts stated above are adequate to raise the issue to be decided in this Problem, the elementary manner in which Eleanor indorsed the certificate by signing the transfer form is not the usual way of proceeding. Lenders anticipate that pledges will be redeemed by the debtors and the stock certificate will be returned to the debtor. If this happened in this case, Eleanor would find herself holding a certificate indorsed with her name but blank as to the transferee. The effect would be a blank indorsement creating a situation in which any bearer of the certificate, including a thief, could claim ownership. The preferred method is to have Eleanor sign a separate stock power appointing the pledgee as attorney to transfer the stock certificate if there is default; however, the name of the person to act as attorney is usually left blank to be filled in by the transferee if transfer is called for. The definition of "indorsement" in 8–102(a)(11) includes a signature on a separate stock power. See John F. Dolan, Commercial Law: Essential Terms and Transactions § 14.3 (2d ed. 1997).

2. Change the facts in Problem 1 to these: Bank did not take possession of the certificate but did require Eleanor to sign a security agreement and authorize a financing statement describing the stock as collateral. Bank promptly filed the financing statement.

(a) If Eleanor files in bankruptcy, what are Bank's rights against her trustee in bankruptcy? See 9–312(a) (perfection by filing); 9–317(a) (priority of security interest against lien creditor).

(b) While her debt to Bank was still unpaid, Eleanor indorsed and delivered the certificate to Lender as security for a loan of $120,000 which Lender made to her. There is good reason to believe that Lender knew of Eleanor's transaction with Bank. What are Bank's rights with respect to the stock as against Lender? See 8–106(b)(1) (control by possession); 9–328(1) (priority).

The basic priority rule in Article 9 with respect investment securities is that a secured party who obtains control (8–106) has priority over other claimants who do not obtain control. 9–328(1). If each secured party has control, priority is determined by the order in time in which the secured parties obtained control. 9–328(2). A security interest of a securities intermediary in a securities account or security entitlement it maintains has priority over a conflicting security interest, even if the conflicting security interest is perfected by control. 9–328(3). Although this last rule might appear to be inconsistent with control priority, it is not. A security intermediary has control of a security entitlement in which its entitlement holder has granted it a security interest. 8–106(e). Thus, 9–328(3) gives priority to a securities intermediary perfected by control over a competing security interest also perfected by control. Comment 4 to 9–328. In the case of a certificated security, the control principle is consistent with the traditional rule that a secured party with possession of the certificate has a perfected security interest that is prior to other claims. Comment 3 to 9–328 elaborates on the character of a control priority rule:

> The control priority rule does not turn on either temporal sequence or awareness of conflicting security interests. Rather, it is a structural rule, based on the principle that a lender should be able to rely on the collateral without question if the lender has taken the necessary steps to assure itself that it is in a position where it can foreclose on the collateral without further action by the debtor. . . . As applied to the retail level, the control priority rule means that a secured party who obtains control has priority over a conflicting security interest perfected by filing without regard to inquiry into whether the control secured party was aware of the filed security interest. . . . The priority rules are not based on the assumption that parties who perfect by the usual method of obtaining control will search the files. Quite the contrary, the control priority rule is intended to ensure that, with respect to investment property, secured parties who do obtain control are entirely unaffected by filings. To state the point another way, perfection by filing is intended to affect only general creditors or other secured creditors who rely on filing.

b.   DIVIDENDS

The facts in the following Problem raised difficulties under former Article 9. How does current Article 9 deal with cash and stock dividends in pledge cases?

PROBLEM

Change the facts in Problem 1 above so that while the certificate was still in the possession of Bank and Eleanor's debt was unpaid, Amalgamated declared its usual quarterly cash dividend and sent a check for the amount to Eleanor. Does Bank's security interest cover the cash dividend? Would your answer be the same if Amalgamated declared a stock dividend and sent Eleanor a certificate for 1,000 additional shares? See 9–102(a)(64)(B) and Comment 13a. to 9–102.

c.   PLEDGEE'S DUTY OF REASONABLE CARE

The pledgor will ordinarily be required by the pledgee to execute a stock power which allows the pledgee to transfer the stock represented by the certificate held by the pledgee if it forecloses. The pledgee may sell the stock if the pledgor is in default. 9–610(a). If the stock "is of a kind that is customarily sold on a recognized market or the subject of widely distributed standard price quotations," the pledgee may buy the stock at a private sale or sell it to another, without prior notification to the pledgor of the time and place of sale. 9–610(c), 9–611(d). This allows pledgees to move quickly in realizing on shares listed on stock exchanges.

Section 9–207(a) imposes on a pledgee the duty to use reasonable care in the custody and preservation of collateral in its possession. The question has arisen about the nature of pledgee's duty in cases in which the value of the stock is declining. Does the pledgee have a duty to take reasonable measures merely to physically care for the stock pledged or does it require taking reasonable measures to preserve the stock's value? In the case of pledged stock certificates, for instance, the former duty of physical care usually is minimal. The latter duty can be more demanding. If the pledgee is undersecured, it will take reasonable measures to preserve the value of pledged stock (up to amount of the debt secured), because doing so will be in its own interest. The measures undertaken will preserve or decrease the creditor's undersecured position: the amount by which the secured debt exceeds the value of the pledged stock. If the pledgee is oversecured, it will not always undertake measures to preserve the value of pledged stock. This is because, within a range of declining prices, the amount by which the value of the pledged stock exceeds the debt secured. Within that range, a decline in the price of pledged stock still leaves the stock price at an amount sufficient to satisfy the secured debt in full. On the other hand, if the pledgee sells pledged stock declining in price, it risks disturbing the diversification the debtor has chosen for its investment portfolio. The pledgee also risks the debtor's charge ex post that the sale came too early or too late. The pledgee of stock in the following case was oversecured.

Layne v. Bank One, Kentucky, N.A.

United States Court of Appeals, Sixth Circuit, 2005
395 F.3d 271

■ MOORE, CIRCUIT JUDGE.

Plaintiff-Appellant, Charles E. Johnson, Jr. ("Johnson"), appeals the district court's grant of summary judgment in favor of Defendants-Appellees, Bank One, Kentucky, N.A. and Banc One Securities Corporation (collectively, "Bank One"). The district court found that under Kentucky law, Bank One was not liable for the depreciation in value of the shares it held as collateral for a loan to Johnson. Furthermore, the district court found that by selling the stock on a national stock exchange, Bank One acted in a commercially reasonable way in disposing of the collateral. On appeal, Johnson asserts that the district court erred in these findings. . . . We conclude that the district court did not err on any of these issues, and thus, the grant of summary judgment to the defendants is AFFIRMED.

I.   Background

This case arises out of two loan transactions made by Bank One to plaintiffs Johnson and Geoff Layne ("Layne"). Johnson was the founder and CEO of PurchasePro.com, Inc. ("PurchasePro"); Layne served as the national marketing director of the company. Following a successful initial public offering, both Johnson and Layne had considerable net worth, though their PurchasePro shares were subject to securities laws restricting their sale.[2] To increase their liquidity, Johnson and Layne entered into separate loan agreements with Bank One for an approximately $2.8 million and $3.25 million line of credit respectively, secured by their shares of PurchasePro stock. The loan agreements included a Loan-to-Value ("LTV") ratio, which conditioned default on the market value of the collateral stock. The LTV ratio was calculated as the outstanding balance on the line of credit over the market value of the collateral stock. Specifically, Layne's loan agreement had a 50% LTV ratio, which meant that the market value of the collateral stock must be at least twice the outstanding balance on the line; Johnson's loan agreement had a 40% LTV ratio, which meant that the market value must remain two and a half times the outstanding balance.[4] The credit agreements provided that if the LTV ratio exceeded those specified percentages, Johnson and Layne had five days to notify Bank One and either increase the collateral or reduce the outstanding balance such that the target LTV ratios were met. Failure to remedy the situation would be an immediate default and Bank One "*may exercise* any and all rights and remedies" including, "*at Lender's discretion,*" selling the shares (emphasis added). If Bank One intended to sell the shares, it had to give Johnson written notice ten days prior to the sale. Pursuant to these agreements, Johnson and Layne entered into trade authorization agreements that enabled Bank One to sell the shares without their consent. Though Bank One had the option of selling the collateral shares if the LTV ratios were not met, nothing in the loan agreements obligated it to do so.

In February 2001, along with the rest of the Internet sector, the stock price of PurchasePro fell considerably, such that both loans exceeded their respective LTV ratios.[5] Rather than selling the collateral stock, Bank One entered into discussions with Johnson and Layne to pledge more collateral. The record reveals that Layne and Johnson repeatedly stated their intentions to pledge additional collateral to meet the LTV requirements. On March 6, 2001, Layne wrote that he had "been able to hold [Bank One] off from calling it in because of additional collateral that

---

[2]   Johnson and Layne were considered "affiliates" of PurchasePro as defined under SEC Rule 144 and therefore, their shares in the company were restricted. 17 C.F.R. § 230.144. Pursuant to Rule 144, an affiliate may not sell restricted securities unless certain conditions are met, including a minimum holding period, a limitation on the amount to be sold, and the manner of the sale. 17 C.F.R. § 230.144(d)–(f).

[4]   For example, if Johnson utilized the entire line of credit, approximately $2.8 million, the market value of his collateral stock would need to be approximately $6.9 million to comply with the required LTV ratio of 40%.

[5]   Because the loans were over-collateralized, though the market value of the stock was below the required LTV level, it was still greater than the outstanding loan balances. Thus, Bank One could have sold the stock in February, recouped the value of the loans, and returned the surplus proceeds to Layne and Johnson.

I have pledged." (Email from Layne to Lichtenberger). On March 19, 2001, Johnson sent an email to Layne inquiring about whether Bank One was "hanging in there." (Email from Johnson to Layne). On March 22, 2001, Bank One sent a letter to Layne informing him that the loan was in default. (Letter from Holton to Layne). That same day, in a conversation with Bank One, Layne stated that "[you] guys have been great. . . holding on for this long," but he indicated he would like to begin selling some of the collateral stock. (Tr. of call between Layne and Thompson). After this conversation, Bank One began taking steps to liquidate the collateral stock for both loans. Later that same day, however, Johnson sent an email to Layne under the subject heading "Bank 1" which stated "they want to sell our shares and I want to stop it with additional collateral-pls call." (Email from Johnson to Layne). Later that night, Layne sent an email to Burr Holton ("Holton"), Bank One's loan officer, under the heading "[h]old off on selling" which stated that "[Johnson] is putting together a collateral package (real estate, additional shares, etc.) to secure the note at acceptable levels." (Email from Layne to Holton). Early the next morning, Layne left a voicemail for Doug Thompson, Bank One's senior trader, stating "[i]t's a possibility that. . . [Johnson]'s gonna put up some additional securities to secure his note and my note and maybe we don't sell right now. So I just wanna put a hold on any. . . trading activity until [Johnson] talks with [the loan officer]." (Voice Message from Layne to Thompson). On April 3, 2001, Layne called Holton and stated that "he was ready to sell his [collateral] stock as soon as possible" and that "he has decided not [to work] with Mr. Johnson on combining their loans and adding additional collateral, which would have cured their default." (Memo. from Holton to File). The next day, April 4, 2001, Layne faxed a letter to Holton which stated that he would not be able to provide additional collateral to satisfy the loan agreement. (Letter from Layne to Holton); 634 (Layne Dep.). The following day, however, Layne changed his mind again and faxed Holton a letter which stated:

> [Johnson] and myself are putting together a collateral package to secure our notes with Bank One. I DO NOT wish for the bank to proceed with any liquidation whatsoever of my PurchasePro stock at this time. I believe we have a strong company and that market conditions will improve, thus enabling the stock to recover to a price that allows me to pay my debt to Bank One in it's [sic] entirety. And that is certainly in everybody's best interest.

(Letter from Layne to Holton). The same day, Layne sent an email to Holton which stated "[Johnson] will be back this afternoon and we will firm the plan then. I would like to have time to discuss this [sic] him before we start liquidation." (Email from Layne to Holton). The record reveals that Johnson and Bank One were involved in discussions in the end of April and May to pay down the balance or pledge additional collateral including his house in Las Vegas. At the end of May, the proposed deal fell through and Bank One sent letters to Johnson notifying him of his continued default on the loans. Throughout the entire time from February to May 2001, Layne and Johnson continued to make principal and interest payments under the terms of the agreement, but both loans significantly exceeded their respective LTV ratios. Bank One finally sold Johnson's PurchasePro shares over four days in July, recovering $524,757.39 in net proceeds to pay down his debt, leaving approximately a $2.2 million unpaid balance.[6]

Layne and Johnson separately filed suit against Bank One in the United States District Court for the Eastern District of Kentucky on a number of counts. On January 30, 2002, the cases were consolidated. Bank One filed counterclaims against Johnson and Layne, seeking payment for the deficiencies on the loans. On November 1, 2002, Bank One filed a motion for summary judgment on all counts as well as its counterclaims. On March 26, 2003, the district court granted Bank One's motion. Johnson appeals from that ruling.

II. Analysis

* * *

B. Duty to Preserve Collateral

We first consider Johnson's argument that Bank One violated a duty under Kentucky law to preserve the value of the collateral held in its possession. With respect to the regulation of secured transactions, Kentucky has adopted the Uniform Commercial Code ("U.C.C."), which states that "a secured party shall use reasonable care in the custody and preservation of collateral in the secured party's possession. In the case of chattel paper or an instrument, reasonable care includes taking necessary steps to preserve rights against prior parties unless otherwise agreed." Ky.Rev.Stat. Ann. § 355.9–207. Whether a secured party's duty to preserve collateral applies to pledged shares is an issue of first impression in Kentucky. . . . As the district court noted below, although Kentucky courts have not reviewed the matter, several courts around the country have addressed the issue of whether § 9–207 applies to pledged stock. Before analyzing their holdings, however, we begin our analysis with the U.C.C. itself.

The comment to § 9–207 states that the provision "imposes a duty of care, similar to that imposed on a pledgee at common law, on a secured party in possession of collateral," and cites to §§ 17–18 of the Restatement of Security. U.C.C. § 9–207 cmt. 2. Section 17 of the Restatement is essentially identical to the first sentence of § 9–207, and its accompanying explanatory comment states that "[t]he rule of

---

[6]   If the full $2.8 million credit line was used, the market price of the 410,000 shares would need to be approximately $16.89 in order to maintain an LTV ratio of 40%. In July, the shares were sold at an average price of $1.28 over the four-day period. The LTV ratio at the time the collateral was sold was approximately 530%.

reasonable care expressed in this Section is confined to the *physical care* of the chattel, whether an object such as a horse or piece of jewelry, or a negotiable instrument or document of title." Restatement of Security § 17 cmt. a (1941) (emphasis added). Section 18 of the Restatement mirrors the second sentence of § 9–207 and addresses "instruments representing claims of the pledgor against third persons." Restatement of Security § 18. Though it deals with negotiable instruments rather than equity investments, § 18 sheds light on the topic of preserving collateral value. Specifically, the explanatory comment accompanying the section states "[t]he pledgee is not liable *for a decline in the value* of pledged instruments, even if timely action could have prevented such decline." Restatement of Security § 18 cmt. a (1941) (emphasis added). In the context of pledged stock, courts have used this language from the Restatement to hold that "a bank has no duty to its borrower to sell collateral stock of declining value." *Capos v. Mid-Am. Nat'l Bank,* 581 F.2d 676, 680 (7th Cir.1978). As the Seventh Circuit stated, "[i]t is the borrower who makes the investment decision to purchase stock. A lender in these situations merely accepts the stock as collateral, and does not thereby itself invest in the issuing firm." *Capos,* 581 F.2d at 680. "Given the volatility of the stock market, a requirement that a secured party sell shares. . . held as collateral, at a particular time, would be to shift the investment risk from the borrower to the lender." *Air Atl., Inc.,* 452 N.E.2d at 1147.

We agree with the reasoning of these courts and believe that the Kentucky Supreme Court would adopt a similar approach with regards to Ky.Rev.Stat. Ann. § 355.9–207. Specifically, we conclude that under Kentucky law a lender has no obligation to sell pledged stock held as collateral merely because of a market decline. If the borrower is concerned with the decline in the share value, it is his responsibility, rather than that of the lender, to take appropriate remedial steps, such as paying off the loan in return for the collateral, substituting the pledged stock with other equally valued assets, or selling the pledged stock himself and paying off the loan.

In his brief, Johnson attempts to distinguish his case from the several cases outlined above, by arguing that in the situation where a loan is *over-secured,* the pledgee has a duty to preserve the surplus. Johnson argues that where a loan is over-secured, the amount of collateral greater than the loan value belongs to the borrower and a duty should be imposed on the secured party to protect that surplus because the secured party has no incentive to do so on its own. By contrast, Johnson argues, where a loan is *under-secured,* the secured party's incentive is the same as that of the borrower, and thus no statutory duty to preserve the value of the collateral is necessary. In support of his argument, Johnson cites to two district court opinions which distinguish between over-secured and under-secured loans. Unfortunately, his theory is neither supported by these cases nor compelling on its own.

Generally, the dual purpose of collateral is to secure financing for the borrower and hedge against credit risk for the lender. Where a lender extends credit solely on the basis of *over-secured* collateral, it is because of perceived heightened risk, and therefore over-collateralization provides the lender with more flexibility. In this case, Bank One agreed to loan Johnson $2.8 million dollars only if he pledged two-and-a-half times that value in PurchasePro stock, or $6.9 million. The underlying rationale was that unless the surplus value was included, the collateral may be insufficient at the time of any default. The LTV ratio was to provide a cushion so that Bank One could either wait for the stock to rebound, restructure the loan, solicit additional collateral, or call the loan with enough time to sell the stock to recoup the value. If accepted, Johnson's argument would bifurcate the collateral amount between the actual value of the loan and the surplus value, and impose a duty upon the lender to preserve the latter. Requiring preservation of the surplus value, however, leaves only the actual value of the loan to serve as collateral and wipes out any flexibility for the lender. Under Johnson's theory, Bank One would have had only $2.8 million worth of stock as collateral for the $2.8 million loan and would have been required to preserve the remaining $4.1 million of surplus. On the first day the market value of the stock fell below the LTV requirement, Bank One would have called the loan or risked liability under § 9–207. Imposing automatic liability for the decreased value of the surplus defeats the inherent purpose of requiring over-collateralization in the first place.

The two cases Johnson cites for support do not stand for the proposition that over-collateralization necessarily implies a duty of the lender to preserve, but rather suggest that the borrower does have a valid interest in the surplus value and therefore his wishes should not be ignored in over-collateralized situations. In *Fidelity Bank & Trust Co. v. Production Metals Corp.*, 366 F.Supp. 613, 618 (E.D.Pa.1973), the district court found that "where the value of the collateral exceeds the amount of the debtor's entire obligation. . . there is no justification for a rule authorizing the pledgee to disregard [the pledgor's] interest in the collateral and deprive him of the right to control its disposition for the benefit of both parties." The district court noted that where the pledgee, "*upon request of the pledgor* "fails to take steps to preserve the value of the collateral, "a question should properly be raised as to whether the pledgee has exercised reasonable care under the circumstances." *Id.* (emphasis added). The *Fidelity* court noted, however, that "where the entire obligation of the pledgor exceeds the value of the collateral held by the pledgee. . . the pledgee's refusal to sell the collateral upon request of the pledgor would not, as a matter of law, constitute a breach of his duty to preserve its value." *Id.* at 619. Similarly, in *FDIC v. Caliendo*, 802 F.Supp. 575, 583–84 (D.N.H.1992), the district court, citing *Fidelity Bank,* ruled that a pledgor could bring a claim under § 9–207, where there is an over-collateralized loan, a default by the pledgor, and "the receipt of a reasonable request by the pledgor/borrower to either sell or have the stock redeemed." These two cases do not provide any support for Johnson's argument that a duty to preserve collateral arises simply because of an over-collateralized situation; rather, where there is over-collateralization *and the pledgor has requested liquidation,* the pledgee should respect the pledgor's interest in the surplus value. These two cases are inapposite to Johnson's case, because the record is clear that he never made a request to the bank to sell the collateral to preserve his surplus, but rather urged Bank One as late as May 1, 2001, to do the opposite.

In sum, we conclude that, under Kentucky law, a lender is not under any duty or obligation to sell collateral in its possession merely because the collateral is declining in value, regardless of whether the loan is over-collateralized. Therefore, the district court's grant of summary judgment on this issue is affirmed. . . .

III. Conclusion

In summary, we conclude that none of issues Johnson raises on appeal are compelling, and therefore we AFFIRM the grant of summary judgment in favor of Bank One.

NOTE

In a deleted portion of *Layne*, the court considered Pledgors' claim that pledgee bank had failed to conduct a commercially reasonable disposition of the collateral under 9–610 because of its delay in selling the stock. Comment 3 to 9–610 says: "[I]f a secured party. . .holds collateral for a long period of time without disposing of it, and if there is no good reason for not making a prompt disposition, the secured party may be determined not to have acted in a 'commercially reasonable' manner." The court held that the time of the sale was commercially reasonable under the circumstances in this case: the parties were still negotiating until the end of May; Pledgee had to make sure that Rule 144 was complied with; and the timing of the sale was influenced by the thin market volume. Moreover, Johnson never demanded a sale. The opinion noted that courts have been reluctant to second-guess the timing of stock dispositions; pledgees, like pledgors, may reasonably believe that the market price of the stock may revive and both parties have an incentive for getting the highest price for the stock on resale. See the discussion below.

Banknorth, N.A. v. Littlefield, 2005 WL 5895220 (Super.Ct.Vt. Dec. 1, 2005), discusses and approves *Layne*.

———————

Section 9–207(a) leaves unspecified the precise content of the pledgee's duty with respect to collateral, and the case law does not help to specify the duty. In specifying the pledgee's duty of reasonable care, two factors are present: disparities in information about the value of the collateral and the extent to which the secured debt is collateralized. Consider them in turn. With tangible assets, the pledgor and pledgee usually have the same knowledge about its value and what measures would preserve or increase value. Both parties know that leaving a pledged piece of equipment unattended or maintained, for example, is likely to diminish its value. With intangible assets such as investment securities, there is asymmetric information: the pledgor knows about its own investment goals and strategies, and the effect of market changes in a security on the value of its investment portfolio; the pledgee often does not have the same knowledge. Requiring the pledgee to take measures to preserve or increase the value of intangible collateral imposes a duty on the party in an inferior informational position. Thus, the predominant rule that a pledgee's duty with respect to pledged securities is limited to taking physical care of pledged assets.

The few cases in which courts find that the pledgee's duty of care extends to preserving or increasing their value are cases in which the asymmetry in information has been eliminated. These are instances in which the pledgor has demanded that the securities be sold or kept. See Reed v. Central Nat'l Bank, 421 F.2d 113 (10th Cir.1970); cf. Grace v. Sterling, Grace & Co., 289 N.Y.S.2d 632 (N.Y. App. Div.1968) (demand not required; even without communication from pledgor, pledgee knew consequences of failure to convert debentures). The demand conveys to the pledgee information about the pledgee's valuation of the collateral.

The extent of collateralization also is crucial to the pledgee's duty. This is because it affects the secured creditor's incentives to take action that preserves the value of collateral. Where the creditor is overcollateralized, there is sufficient collateral to satisfy the secured debt held. Since the creditor's interest in the collateral is limited by the amount of its debt, any benefit produced by preserving collateral value above that amount goes to the debtor; the creditor receives none of it. Thus, as noted above, when the loan is overcollateralized, within a range of declining prices, the creditor has no incentive to take value-preserving measures with respect to the collateral. In these circumstances, the debtor and creditor's interests diverge. True, under 9–207(b)(1), amounts expended by the creditor in preserving the collateral are chargeable to the debtor and are secured by the collateral. However, this at most makes the creditor indifferent between taking or not taking action to do so.

Case law imposing a duty with respect to maintaining or increasing collateral value has done so only when the creditor is overcollateralized and the debtor requests liquidation of the collateral. See Solfanelli v. Corestates Bank, N.A., 203 F.3d 197 (3d Cir.2000); Dubman v. North Shore Bank, 271 N.W.2d 148 (Wis. Ct.App.1978) (dicta). The court in FDIC v. Caliendo, 802 F.Supp. 575 (D. N.H.1992), expressly conditioned the creditor's duty on this fact. Where a creditor is undercollateralized, the creditor and debtor's incentives are aligned: the benefit of preserving or increasing collateral value (up to the amount of the secured debt held) flows to the creditor because it can avoid looking to the debtor to satisfy the debt. The debtor too benefits because the outstanding deficiency it owes is reduced or at least not increased. There is therefore no need to impose a duty on the pledgee to preserve collateral value and case law does not impose one.

2. CERTIFICATE IN POSSESSION OF SECURITIES INTERMEDIARY

a. CONTROL TEST

By a wide margin, the most common form in which securities are held today is by an intermediary such as a broker or a bank. The control concept was conceived to deal with security interests in certificates held by intermediaries. The following Problems illustrate how control operates in this case. In completing these Problems, consider why more familiar priority rules, such as first-to-file or first-to-notify the intermediary, were abandoned in favor of the novel and complicated control test.

PROBLEMS

1. Seth opened a securities account (8–501(a)), designated Account Number 987654321, with a broker-dealer firm (Firm), a securities intermediary (8–102(a)(14)) that buys, sells and holds securities on behalf of its customers, as well as for its own account. Seth placed a buy order with Firm for 1,000 shares of Consolidated, Inc. When the trade was completed, Firm credited the stock to Seth's account, giving Seth a security entitlement (8–102(a)(17), 8–501(b)) with respect to the stock. Seth is now an entitlement holder (8–102(a)(7)). All of Consolidated's shares are represented by security certificates (8–102(a)(16)), most of which are in the possession of Depository Trust Company (DTC), a clearing corporation (8–102(a)(5)) and a securities intermediary, as registered owner. Firm is one of DTC's many customers, and the trade in question was cleared through DTC, which holds the shares in Firm's account. Settlement through DTC was on a net basis by book entries. At the time Seth opened his account, he granted Firm a security interest in his account and all of the financial assets (8–102(a)(9)) held in the account to secure any future advances made by Firm to Seth. Later, Seth borrowed $10,000 from Bank. He executed a security agreement describing the collateral as "1,000 shares of Consolidated, Inc. stock."

(a) Bank promptly filed a financing statement containing the description of the collateral in the security agreement. Subsequently, Seth filed in Chapter 7 bankruptcy. In a contest between Bank and Seth's trustee in bankruptcy with respect to the stock, who is prior? See 9–108(d) (sufficiency of description); 9–312(a) (perfection by filing); and 9–317(a)(2) (priority of lien creditor).

(b) Bank promptly filed a financing statement containing the description of the collateral in the security agreement. Subsequently, Seth borrowed $30,000 from Lender and executed a security agreement granting Lender a security interest in "Acct. No. 987654321 held by Firm." Lender promptly filed a financing statement authorized by Seth containing that description of the collateral. If Seth defaults on both loans, which creditor is prior with respect to the stock, Bank or Lender? See 9–308(f) (perfection of security interest in securities account); 9–328(7) (priority of security interests in investment property); and 9–322(a) (residual priority rule). See also 9–108(d) referred to in Problem (a) above.

(c)   Bank promptly filed a financing statement containing the description of the collateral in the security agreement. In addition, Bank sent Firm a copy of the security agreement and financing statement, as well as the number of Seth's account.

(i)   Subsequently, Firm advanced Seth a margin loan of $15,000 in exchange for a security interest in the securities account it maintained for Seth. Firm took no further action. If Seth defaults on both loans, which creditor is prior with respect to the stock, Bank or Firm? See 8–106(e) (control by securities intermediary); 9–106 (control); 9–328(1) (priority of secured party having control) and (3) (priority of securities intermediary).

(ii)   With Seth's authorization, Firm agreed to comply with any orders by Bank regarding transfer or redemption of the stock without further consent by Seth. Subsequently Firm advanced Seth $15,000. If Seth defaults on both loans, which creditor is prior with respect to the stock, Bank or Firm? See 8–106(d) (control by purchaser) and (e); 9–106 (control); and 9–328(3) (priority of securities intermediary.) See Comment 4 to 9–328. How could Bank ever be prior to Firm? See 9–339.

2.   Debtor grants Bank One a security interest in an account Debtor holds with Broker containing 1,000 shares of ABC stock. Bank One and Debtor agree that Bank's attorney can foreclose on the account only if Debtor defaults on the terms of the loan. Broker agrees to the arrangement. Later, Debtor grants Bank Two a security interest in the same account with Broker. Bank Two and Debtor's agreement allows Bank Two to foreclose on Debtor's account only if Debtor has defaulted on Bank Two's loan. Again Broker agrees to the arrangement. In both cases Debtor retains the right to trade the assets in its account. Neither Bank One nor Two files a financing statement covering Debtor's account with Broker. If Debtor files a petition in bankruptcy and its trustee alleges that it has priority in Debtor's account over both Bank One and Two, who will prevail? See 8–106(d)(3); Comment 7 to 8–106, Example 11; 9–317(a)(2).

3.   Broker maintains accounts for its customers to which it has credited 100 shares of ABC Corporation. Recently, in need of funds, Broker borrowed from Bank on a secured basis. As part of the arrangement, Broker granted Bank a security interest in 100 shares of ABC stock, endorsing and delivering to Bank the stock certificates for them. Broker is insolvent and has defaulted on its obligations to both its customers and Bank. Among its listed assets are the 100 shares of ABC stock it has pledged to Bank. As between Broker's customers and Bank, who is entitled to the shares? 8–503(a), 8–511(a) and (b), 8–106(b).

4. Debtor holds an account with Broker containing bonds issued by the ABC Corporation. The bonds are backed by a letter of credit issued by a bank. The bank undertakes in the letter of credit to pay to the owner of the bond the face amount of the bond plus accrued interest in the event ABC fails to do so when the bond matures. On January 1 Debtor grants SP-1 a security interest in the account administered by Broker. At the same time, SP-1 files a proper financing statement covering the account and has the bank agree to pay over to it proceeds of the letter of credit if the letter is drawn upon. On February 1, SP-2 obtains a security interest in Debtor's account with Broker. SP-2, Debtor and Broker agree that SP-2 can dispose of the assets in the account only if Debtor defaults on the terms of the loan. As between SP-1 and SP-2, if Debtor defaults on its loan obligations to SP-1 and SP-2, who has priority in Debtor's account? 9–328(2). In the proceeds from the letter of credit? 9–102(a)(78), 9–107, 9–322(c), 9–322(f)(1), 9–329.

Why have a control priority rule? Professor Rogers, Reporter for Revised Article 8, explains, that the impetus for the 1994 revision was growing concern about the adequacy of the existing system of securities clearance and settlement. See Rogers, Policy Perspectives on Revised U.C.C. Article 8, 43 UCLA L. Rev. (1996) at 1437–1449. What if, owing to an unanticipated excess in trading volume or the failure of a major brokerage house, sellers do not get paid and buyers do not receive the securities they have purchased? In short, trades do not clear and settlements are not made. The failure of some trades to clear might, in a chain reaction, prevent others from clearing; the failure of one brokerage firm might have a knock-on effect on the solvency of other firms unpaid in their trades with that firm; systemic collapse might result that would bring stock exchanges to a stop. Liquidity is essential to the securities market; an investor's nightmare is being unable to unload securities in a rapidly falling market like the one-day 1987 crash. In a systemic crisis, the value of the stocks and bonds in which trillions of dollars are invested would be at great risk.

Control and control priority reduces the risk of knock-on effects caused by defaults in securities markets. Assume that Bank buys shares on behalf of Broker, one of its customers, and pay for them. There is a gap in time between Bank's purchase of the shares and its reimbursement by Broker. Although Broker is obligated to reimburse Bank for its payment, Broker might be unable or unwilling to do so. Because Bank is a securities intermediary (8–102(a)(14)(ii)), with its own obligations to its other customers, and others, Bank might be unable to honor its obligations to them as a result of Broker's default. Article 9's control and control priority rules eliminates this risk. Article 9 gives Bank a perfected security interest in the shares purchased on Broker's behalf that is entitled to priority over competing claimants in Broker's shares. Under 9–206(a), Bank has a security interest in the shares it purchased on Broker's behalf, which attaches automatically. Bank will be holding the shares in a way that enables it to sell them without Broker's cooperation. Accordingly, under 8–106, Bank has control of them. See 8–106(b) and (c). Thus, under 9–328(1), Bank has priority over competing security interest in the shares perfected other than by control. It can therefore sell the shares and recover its payment. Broker's default on reimbursement obligation to Bank therefore will not cause Bank to default on its own obligations to others.

The same result holds at the level of retail securities transactions in which the risk of knock-on effects is absent. Assume that Broker purchases shares on Individual's behalf in advance of Individual's payment of them. Broker is obligated to pay for the shares whether or not Individual reimburses it. As above, Article 9 gives Broker an automatically attached security interest in the shares it purchased. 9–206(a). Broker almost inevitably will be in a position to sell the shares purchased without Individual's cooperation. As a result, Broker is perfected in the shares by control. 8–106(b) and (c). It therefore has priority over competing security interests in the shares not perfected by control. 9–328(1). Accordingly, because Broker's security interest enables Broker to recover the purchase price of the shares if Individual doesn't reimburse it for them, Broker can without risk purchase shares for Individual in advance of receiving Individual's payment. See Rogers, at 1438. This is so even though the Broker-Individual transaction presents no risk of producing knock-on effects in the event of Individual's default. Although Broker's priority position benefits Broker, it reduces the chance that Individual's other creditors with security interests in Individual's purchased shares can look to the shares for repayment. These creditors presumably adjust the interest rate they charge the debtor accordingly.

Article 9 expands the role of control in perfection and priority beyond just investment property. Sections 9–104 to 9–107 respectively define when control occurs with respect to deposit accounts as original collateral, electronic chattel paper, investment property, and letter-of-credit rights. The 2022 Amendments extend role of control further to allow perfection by control in controllable electronic records, controllable accounts and controllable payment intangibles. 9–107A. Section 9–322(a)'s basic priority rules are made subject, via 9–322(f)(1), to the control priority rules of 9–326A, 9–327 to 9–329 governing respectively controllable electronic records, controllable accounts, and controllable payment intangibles, deposit accounts, investment property, and letter-of-credit rights.

Why current Article 9, including the 2022 Amendments covering certain digital assets, expands the role of control priority is uncertain. As indicated above, security interests in investment property at the retail level don't appear to have the potential to produce externalities on the order of meltdowns in the clearance and settlement network. Even if they did, the same isn't true of assets other than investment property such as deposit accounts and letter-of-credit rights. Digital assets regulated by

Article 9 may or may not have the potential to produce significant externalities, depending on whether and how a securities intermediary maintains security accounts containing them. Comment 3 to 9–328 justifies control priority for investment property by settled practice: before 1994 filing was not a permissible method of perfection, and control priority preserves the expectations of parties who perfect by taking control of investment property. Again, even if so, this doesn't warrant expanding control priority to types of collateral in which control wasn't a perfection method under former Article 9.

Although 8–106(d)(2) does not require the control agreement to be in a signed record, it does require the securities intermediary's agreement. Section 8–106(g) does not obligate the intermediary to enter into a control agreement. Accordingly, a secured party does not obtain control when the securities intermediary maintaining the debtor's securities account does not respond on receipt of a proposed control agreement sent by the secured party. Silence without more is not agreement. See United Hudson Bank v. PNC Bank New Eng., 58 UCC Rep. Serv.2d 984 (Conn. Super. Ct. 2006). An interesting case on whether a secured party has achieved control of investment property follows. This case was decided before current Article 9 was enacted, and the references to former 9–115 are now found in several provisions of Article 9 considered above.

First Nat'l Bank of Palmerton v. Donaldson, Lufkin & Jenrette Securities Corp.

United States District Court, E.D. Pennsylvania, 1999
1999 WL 163606

■ YOHN, J.

Plaintiff First National Bank of Palmerton ('the bank') has brought suit against Donaldson, Lufkin & Jenrette Securities Corporation ('DLJ'), claiming negligence, breach of fiduciary duty, and fraud. The suit arises out of a security interest taken by the bank in marketable securities held for the debtor in a DLJ brokerage account. Pending before the court is defendant's motion to dismiss. The court finds that the bank has failed to plead the necessary elements to state a cause of action for negligence, breach of fiduciary duty, or fraud. Therefore, plaintiff's complaint will be dismissed.

On May 15, 1996, the bank entered into a loan agreement with Pankesh Kadam and Alka Patel ('first loan'). As part of this agreement, Kadamand Patel signed a promissory note in the amount of $50,000. The parties to the loan agreement also signed a security agreement in which the borrowers granted the bank a security interest in, among other things, marketable securities registered in Patel's name and held by DLJ in Account Number 219-141298. The securities were valued at $56,350.

On the same day that Patel and Kadam entered into the loan agreement, the bank sent a letter to DLJ explaining that Patel had "pledged the marketable securities" and "she agreed to have the bank perfect its interest in the stocks." In the letter, the bank requested that DLJ either "forward the stock certificates or an agreement from [DLJ] that the securities will remain in the account until notification from the bank." At the end of the letter, Patel had signed an acceptance and acknowledgment whereby she "consented to the stock certificates being forwarded to The First National Bank of Palmerton." DLJ forwarded the stock certificates to the bank.

Sometime after the Bank received the certificates from DLJ, Patel allegedly requested that the stocks be returned to her brokerage account to enable her to trade them. The bank agreed and on August 20, 1996, sent the stock certificates back to DLJ. Accompanying the stocks was a transmittal letter in which the bank's vice-president stated, "The stocks are being returned to you to be retained in Ms. Patel's account. It is our understanding that she will trade the stocks, however, maintain the principal balance in her account #219-141298." The complaint contains no allegation that DLJ ever responded to this letter.

On June 6, 1997, Patel individually executed a second promissory note for $25,000 ('second loan'). Collateral for the loan consisted of the DLJ brokerage account Number 219-141298 then valued at $60,520.52. Patel signed a security agreement and a collateral pledge agreement which granted the bank an assignment and security interest in the account. On May 22, 1997, prior to the execution of the promissory note and security agreement, the bank sent DLJ a copy of the collateral pledge agreement. The bank also requested that DLJ sign and return an acknowledgment form whereby it would agree that the bank, as the secured party, would have the sole right to make withdrawals from the collateral. The acknowledgment form was signed by the bank's vice-president and Patel. DLJ, however, did not sign the form or return it to the bank.

Seven months later, on December 15, 1997, Kadam and Patel defaulted on the first loan. At the same time, Patel defaulted on her payments under the second loan. When the bank tried to liquidate the securities in the collateral brokerage account in order to apply the funds toward the borrowers' outstanding debt, it learned that Patel had liquidated the account the previous month. Plaintiff alleges that Patel liquidated the account without obtaining express written consent from the bank. In an effort to recover its loss, the bank has brought suit against DLJ claiming that by allowing Patel to liquidate the brokerage account, DLJ was negligent, breached its fiduciary duty, and committed fraud. * * *

DLJ argues that the bank has failed to plead facts sufficient to state a cause of action for negligence, breach of fiduciary duty, or fraud. With regard to the negligence and breach of contract claims, DLJ asserts that it had no duty to act on behalf of the bank. . . . As such a duty is a required element of the claims of negligence and breach of fiduciary duty, DLJ contends that plaintiff's complaint is deficient with regard to these causes of action. * * *

A. Negligence and Breach of Fiduciary Duty Claims

To state a cause of action for either breach of fiduciary duty or negligence, the bank must allege the existence of a duty owed to it by DLJ. . . . DLJ claims that the bank did not perfect its security interest in the securities held in the DLJ account in accordance with the Pennsylvania Uniform Commercial Code. Because the bank failed to perfect its security interest, defendant asserts that it "had no duty under the UCC to act for the benefit of the Bank." Absent this duty, DLJ contends, the allegations in the complaint do not support the bank's claims of negligence and breach of fiduciary duty.

Sections eight and nine of the Uniform Commercial Code [as revised 1994] ("UCC"), as codified in the Pennsylvania statutes, set forth the rights and duties of parties participating in secured transactions involving marketable securities such as those maintained in Patel's account with DLJ. For purposes of the UCC, the collateral at issue here falls into the category of investment property, which includes certificated and uncertificated securities, security entitlements, and security accounts. The term "security entitlement" is defined as "the rights and property interest of a person who holds securities or other financial assets through a securities intermediary." Title 13, section 8102(a), UCC Comment ¶ 17. The UCC defines a "securities intermediary" as "a bank or broker. . . . that in the ordinary course of its business maintains securities accounts for others and is acting in that capacity." Title 13, section 8102(a). Both parties agree that DLJ qualifies as a securities intermediary who maintained Patel's securities in her brokerage account. Patel's interest in these securities in her account constituted a security entitlement and Patel was the entitlement holder or the "person identified in the records of a securities intermediary as the person having a security entitlement against the securities intermediary." Title 13, section 8102(a).

In the instant case, Patel granted to the bank a security interest in her security entitlements. In and of itself, this transaction did not establish a duty between DLJ, the securities intermediary, and the bank, the secured party. Although Pennsylvania courts do not appear to have considered this issue yet, the drafters of the Uniform Commercial Code have stated that a "securities intermediary owes no duties to the secured party, unless the intermediary has entered into a 'control' agreement in which it agrees to act on entitlement orders originated by the secured party." Uniform Commercial Code § 8–507, 2C U.L.A. 147 (Supp.1998) (citing to UCC § 8–106). A "control agreement" is created when "the securities intermediary has agreed that it will comply with entitlement orders originated by the purchaser without further consent by the entitlement holder." Id. § 8106(d). Thus, the legal duty owed by DLJ to the bank that is necessary to support claims of negligence and breach of fiduciary duty, could arise only if the bank, Patel, and DLJ all agreed that the bank had the power "to have the securities sold or transferred without further action by [Patel]." Title 13, section 8106(d)(2), UCC Comment 7.

Control of a security entitlement can be achieved in one of two ways: through a control agreement or by having the secured party become the entitlement holder. See Title 13, section 8106(d). To acquire a securities entitlement and thus become the entitlement holder, the bank would have needed to establish a separate securities account to which DLJ would credit Patel's securities. See id. § 8501(b). Plaintiff does not allege that this occurred and, thus, it cannot claim to be the entitlement holder. This leaves a control agreement as the sole means by which the bank could have perfected its security interest.

Consequently, in this particular case, whether the bank perfected its security interest and whether DLJ owes any duty to the bank both depend on whether the bank controlled the securities and account by means of a control agreement.

To obtain control through an agreement in conformance with section 8106(d)(2), a secured party cannot simply notify the intermediary of the secured party's interest and the debtor's willingness to allow entitlement orders to issue from the secured party—"it is essential that the. . . . securities intermediary. . . . actually be a party to the agreement." Title 13, section 8106(d)(2), UCC Comment 5; see William D. Hawkland et al., Uniform Commercial Code Series § 8–106:04 (Main Volume 1996) (stating that sending notice of security interest to intermediary is insufficient to establish control through agreement). While the intermediary must "specifically agree" to allow the secured party to issue entitlement orders, the statute does not require that the intermediary agree in writing. See Title 13, section 8106(d)(2), UCC Comment 5; Hawkland, supra (noting that asserting existence of unwritten agreement likely would occur as "a rescue effort in litigation for a transaction in which someone made some fairly obvious blunders in practical planning"). The bank acknowledges that no written control agreement exists in this case. Instead, the bank claims that DLJ's conduct in response to three separate letters from the bank evidences its assent to follow entitlement orders from the bank without concurrence from Patel.

The first of these letters sent to DLJ on May 15, 1996, stated in relevant part:

> As per our prior discussions, Alka P. Patel has pledged the marketable securities in Account #219-141298 to the First National Bank of Palmerton for a loan. As a result, she agreed to have the bank perfect its interest in the stocks. Please forward the stock certificates or an agreement from your firm that the securities will remain in the account until notification from the bank.

Below the closing and signature of the bank's vice-president, the letter included the following paragraph:

> ACCEPTANCE: I acknowledge that I have pledged the securities in my stock Account #219-141298 and hereby consent to the stock certificates being forwarded to the First National Bank of Palmerton.

Patel's signature appeared beneath this paragraph. In response to this letter, DLJ sent the stock certificates to the bank.

The bank claims that "it clearly thought that [DLJ's forwarding of the stock certificates to the bank] implied DLJ's agreement to the terms of the security arrangement generally." The complaint, however, contains no allegation that DLJ was in possession of or had knowledge of the security agreement such that it could have agreed with all or any of its terms. Furthermore, DLJ's conduct evidences only that it complied with Patel's explicit authorization which extended exclusively to delivering the stock certificates to the bank. Thus, despite what the bank says it "thought", the complaint contains no evidence of a control agreement having been entered into at this point.

On August 20, 1996, the bank sent the certificates back to DLJ accompanied by a transmittal letter in which the bank stated:

Enclosed please find the following stock certificates in the name of Alka Patel:

2000 shares Hospitality Properties Trust

1175 shares Q Sound Labs, Inc.

> The stocks are being returned to you to be retained in Ms. Patel's account. It is our understanding that she will trade the stocks, however, maintain the principal balance in her account #219-141298.

DLJ credited Patel's account with the securities.

In its memorandum in opposition to DLJ's motion to dismiss, the bank states that "when [it] returned the certificates to DLJ. . . . , it relied on its understanding that DLJ would be bound by the terms of the parties' agreement, which was that, in the absence of a possessory pledge, DLJ would undertake to see that the principal balance in the account would remain in its custody." Plaintiff's claim appears somewhat disingenuous, however, given that the complaint contains no allegations that any agreement to that effect between DLJ and the bank actually existed at the time the bank sent the certificates to DLJ. Perhaps in the alternative, the bank also contends that DLJ's acceptance of the returned certificates demonstrated its agreement to maintain the balance in the account.

Neither the UCC nor Pennsylvania contract law require that acceptance of an offer be in writing or even be an express oral acknowledgment—conduct can suffice. Whatever form the acceptance takes, however, it must be "unconditional and absolute." O'Brien v. Nationwide Mut. Ins. Co., 689 A.2d 254, 258 (Pa.Super.Ct.1997). DLJ's "conduct" in receiving the returned certificates and crediting them to Patel's account does not meet this standard. * * *

DLJ contends that, as with the first loan and security interest, no agreement existed between DLJ, Patel, and the bank such that the bank had control of the account pursuant to § 8106(d)(2). In response, the bank argues that, because a security agreement was already in place with respect to the securities, and the bank had agreed to maintain the principal balance regardless of which securities were held in the account, the bank "perfected" its security interest in the account when it "forwarded to DLJ the collateral pledge agreement signed by the debtor." In essence, the bank seems to be arguing that a control agreement existed with respect to the entire contents of the account as a result of DLJ's having accepted the securities back from the bank, and consequently, a control agreement was in place with regard to the account itself.

If a control agreement had already existed between the parties and Patel, plaintiff's argument would have some merit. See Title 13, [former] section 9115 (stating that with regard to control, "a secured party has control over a securities account. . . . if the secured party has control over all security entitlements. . . . in the securities account"). As discussed above, however, no control agreement was in place at the time the bank negotiated the second loan.

Taken individually, the actions of DLJ do not support a finding that a control agreement existed pursuant to section 8106(d)(2). Nevertheless, the bank argues that DLJ became "obligated to recognize the security interest because of the pattern of dealings among the parties during the whole course of the transactions." DLJ's alleged conduct during this period amounts to the following: (1) not creating and forwarding a written agreement regarding the certificates pursuant to the bank's first letter on May 15, 1996; (2) placing the stock certificates into the brokerage account of Patel, the registered owner and entitlement holder; (3) not signing and returning to the bank an acknowledgment of Patel's assignment of a second interest in her account; (4) following Patel's order to liquidate the account. None of these alleged actions, viewed individually or as a whole, evidence an intent to enter into an agreement with the bank and Patel such that DLJ would accept entitlement orders emanating solely from the bank. As no agreement existed, no duty arose between DLJ and the bank. Because the bank cannot allege the existence of a duty, I must dismiss plaintiff's negligence and breach of fiduciary duty claims. * * *

IT IS HEREBY ORDERED that the motion to dismiss is GRANTED and plaintiff's complaint is dismissed with prejudice.

NOTES

1.   Suppose Patel, DLJ and Bank had agreed that DLJ would comply with Bank's orders to sell without further consent by Patel, but the agreement also allowed Patel to continue to trade the stock held by DLJ. This means that if Patel issued an "entitlement order" (8–102(a)(8)) to DLJ directing it to transfer stock, it would have to comply. Would Patel's power to transfer stock without further consent of Bank invalidate Bank's control status? How can Bank be said to have control if Patel can order DLJ to sell the property Bank supposedly controls? See 8–106(f) and Comment 7. How does this practice differ from what happened in the principal case?

2.   Control agreements with security intermediaries usually are detailed documents, not the somewhat skeletal agreement alleged by the bank in *First National Bank of Palmerton*. Common clauses include the intermediary's obligation not to agree to comply with entitlement orders by third parties without the secured creditor's consent, a subordination of specific existing and after-acquired liens in favor of the intermediary, specification of the conditions under which the creditor can exercise control and the means of doing so, and the indemnification of the intermediary against liability arising from its compliance with the control agreement. Control agreements typically insulate the intermediary from liability for complying with its customer's entitlement orders received before the intermediary has an opportunity to act on the secured creditor's instructions. Even if the bank in *First National Bank of Palmerton* had a control agreement with DLJ, DLJ likely would not have been liable to the bank for allowing Patel to liquidate its brokerage account maintained with DLJ. Form control agreements appear in Sandra M. Rocks & Robert A. Wittie, Getting Control of Control Agreements, 31 UCC L.J. 318 (1999).

3.   At Bank's request DLJ forwarded to Bank Patel's stock certificates it held in Patel's account. Bank later redelivered the certificates to DLJ. An apparent ambiguity in 9–313(h) allows Bank to argue on these facts that it remained perfected even after redelivery to DLJ. Under 9–313(a) Bank was perfected in the certificated securities when DLJ delivered them to it in accordance with 8–301. Section 8–301(a) in turn deems delivery to occur when DLJ, a purchaser, obtains possession of the certificates. Section 9–313(h) in relevant part provides that a secured party doesn't lose possession by delivering "the collateral" to a person other than the debtor if the secured party has instructed the person to hold the collateral for it. Bank, the secured party, redelivered the certificates ("the collateral") to DLJ, a person other than Patel, the debtor. Subsection (h) deems Bank nonetheless to remain in possession and therefore perfected if Bank instructed DLJ to hold the certificates for its benefit.

Section 9–313(h) appears to contain an ambiguity in its reference to "the collateral." "The collateral" seemingly refers to any asset subject to a security interest capable of being delivered by transfer of possession. However, Comment 9 to 9–313 restricts its reference to mortgage notes. According to the Comment, 9–313(h)'s intent is to protect mortgage lenders who as a practical matter sometimes must relinquish mortgage notes to prospective purchasers. Subsection (h) operates to protect these lenders under prescribed conditions. Because stock certificates were collateral delivered in *First National Bank of Palmerton*, not mortgage notes, Comment 9 would make 9–313(h) inapplicable to continue Bank's perfection in them. On the other hand, 9–313(h)'s reference to "the collateral" is broad enough to cover tangible and semi-intangible assets in addition to mortgage notes. Code comment and statute therefore conflict. At least one court has applied 9–313(h)'s "delivery without relinquishing possession" rule to collateral other than mortgage notes; see Bank Rhode Island v. Mixitforme, Inc., 2007 R.I. Super. LEXIS 9 (Jan. 11, 2007) (funds in an escrow account). Even if applicable, 9–313(h) does Bank no good in *First National Bank of Palmerton* because Bank's suit against DLJ is based on breach of contract, not its perfected status.

b. ASSET MANAGEMENT ACCOUNTS

Asset management accounts, like the one in the Problem below, have become a common feature of brokerage accounts. The fact that they resemble a bank account is no accident. They contain a great deal of wealth, but there have been problems on how to categorize them. Are they "deposit accounts" (9–102(a)(29)) or "investment property" (9–102(a)(49))? See 8–501(a) and (b), and Comments 1 and 2.

PROBLEM

Customer holds stocks and bonds in an account with Royce Hall Securities (RHS), a broker-dealer and securities intermediary. The account also contains a Liquid Asset Fund (LAF), a money market fund that RHS maintains in the accounts of each of its customers. Customers may acquire shares (each share is maintained at the price of $1) in their LAFs by depositing cash in the fund; moreover, all bond interest and stock dividends, as well as all proceeds from sales of securities, are automatically poured over into the fund. The cash flowing into the LAF is invested by RHS for Customer's benefit in corporate commercial paper (obligations of corporations with 90 to 120 day maturities) and short term U.S. Treasuries; hence, the return on the fund is at relatively low money market rates. Money may be withdrawn by Customer at any time by (i) a written order or an oral order made through authorized telephone access, (ii) a check drawn on RHS Bank & Trust, a subsidiary of RHS, or (iii) use of a Visa card issued by RHS Bank & Trust. Customer has found the account extremely convenient. Not only may it be used to "park" cash but it also obviates the need to have a local bank account. The return on the LAF is always higher than the interest paid on checking accounts by commercial banks, and no per-check charges are made. At times between securities transactions, Customer has very large sums of money in the LAF. How would Bank perfect a security interest in the LAF and of what use would a security interest be in an asset management account, the proceeds of which Customer can withdraw by writing a check anytime it wishes? The definition of "deposit account" in 9–102(a)(29) excludes "investment property." See 8–501(a) and (b) and Comments 1 and 2.

Asset management accounts, the generic term for the arrangement described in the Problem, are discussed in Matter of Van Kylen, 98 B.R. 455 (Bankr. W.D.Wis.1989), at 459, n.2:

> 2. Cash management accounts have been noted as an instance of competition from non-bank financial institutions with conventional banking entities.
>
> Other non-bank financial institutions also compete with commercial banks and savings institutions to some extent. In the recent period of high interest rates, competition from money-market funds for the savings of depositors who otherwise would use the services of commercial banks and savings institutions has been intense. Moreover, there appears to be a growing tendency for these non-bank institutions to offer services similar to those offered by banks and savings institutions. Major brokerage houses offer their customers diverse financial services. For example, Merrill Lynch, Pierce, Fenner and Smith has a Cash Management Account in which the customer receives interest on balances maintained, checking facilities, a charge card, and lending privileges.

Frederick K. Beutel, Bank Officer's Handbook of Commercial Banking Law 5–45 (5th ed. 1982). Merrill Lynch pioneered these accounts in the 1970s, and "Cash Management Account" is their registered trademark.

E. UNCERTIFICATED SECURITIES

1. MUTUAL FUNDS

The movement of investors, particularly individual investors, away from holding individual securities and into mutual funds has been pronounced for several years. In the 1990s, it became a tidal wave. Traditional brokerage houses like Merrill Lynch, which 40 years ago did not offer mutual funds, have fought competition from giant mutual fund providers like Fidelity and Vanguard by offering a full range of mutual funds. Today trillions of dollars are invested in American mutual funds.

There are two types of mutual funds. By far the most common is the open-end fund which will issue as many shares as investors wish to purchase, except in unusual cases in which the fund is temporarily closed to new investors because of a perceived lack of attractive securities in which to invest new funds. Open-end fund issuers will redeem shares from their shareholders at net asset value as a matter of right. Closed-end funds are much less popular. They issue a fixed number of shares at the inception of the fund and do not redeem shares from shareholders. Thus, shareholders who wish to liquidate must find buyers for their shares; by the same token, new investors must find shareholders willing to sell. However, since closed-end funds are usually listed on securities exchanges, thereby creating a secondary market for them, trading shares in closed-end funds is usually as simple as trading other listed securities. A characteristic of closed-end funds is that after the initial issuance of shares, the shares tend to trade at a discount to the net asset value of the securities held by the fund. Sometimes the discount is a substantial one. Open-end funds are securities under 8–103(b), and 8–102(a)(15) considers close-end funds securities.

Mutual funds are almost entirely uncertificated and corporate bonds are also mostly held in electronic book entry form. Issuance of corporate stock in an uncertificated form through a direct registration system would offer investors a third option, in addition to the traditional ones of having a certificate issued directly to the investor or having stock held in the street name of a securities intermediary. Historically, state corporate law frequently has prevented the practice by requiring that shares be represented by certificates; see Study of the Securities Industry: Hearings, 92nd Cong., First [and Second] Sessions 2259 (1972). Most state corporate statutes now permit issuance of uncertificated shares. This option would allow the investor to have its name registered on the issuer's records as the owner but instead of sending the investor a stock certificate, the issuing company would make an electronic book entry in its records and send the investor the kind of statement that mutual fund investors now receive. This method offers the investor both the convenience of having the issuing company (through its transfer agent) do all of the record keeping that investors who have their securities held in a street name or who hold mutual funds now enjoy, as well as the advantages of being the registered owner and having (i) the power to select the broker through which the stock is sold, and (ii) the opportunity to participate in corporate dividend reinvestment programs open only to registered owners. If the issuer is a close corporation, an uncertificated share relieves the investor of having to keep track of a stock certificate.

The posture of the direct registration stockholder is similar but not identical to that of the mutual fund investor. The rules that apply for security interests in uncertificated mutual fund securities would apply in direct registration cases. However, a major difference between mutual funds and direct registration systems is that mutual fund investors, at least with respect to open-end funds, do not need to sell their shares in order to withdraw their investment because mutual funds agree to redeem the owner's shares at any time. Stock issuers make no such agreement. A direct registration investor who wishes to sell would instruct the issuing company's transfer agent to route the shares to a broker of the investor's choice who would sell them for the investor. Transfers would be by electronic book entries and the investor could engage in whatever negotiations it chooses with the broker about the terms of the sale. Presumably, such a system would result in more competition between brokers and better service and rates to investors.

PROBLEMS

Barbara wearied of attempting to pick the right stock for her investment portfolio and decided to make all her investments in the future through mutual funds. "Let the experts pick the stock," became her creed. Her procedure was to scan financial publications for information on well managed, "no load" (no sales commission charged) stock and bond funds. When she had made her selection, she would call the fund and ask for a prospectus and an application to purchase. She followed this course with the Oak Growth Fund, a member of the Oak Family of Funds, whose portfolio included mostly mid-cap growth stocks. She sent the application, along with her check for $25,000, to this fund. In her application she agreed that all dividends would be reinvested. She received a document informing her that she was the owner of 2,280 shares of the Oak Growth Fund and that her account number was 123456789. Periodic statements of her account would be sent to her quarterly.

Barbara applied for a loan from Bank. In the past, when Barbara had invested in stocks or bonds, she always insisted on having the securities registered in her name with the stock or bond certificate in her possession. When she wished to borrow money from Bank, it was a simple matter to take the certificate out of her safe deposit box and pledge it with Bank. But when she wished to borrow money on the security of her position in the Oak Growth Fund, she had nothing to offer Bank for security but the document referred to above. Before making the loan, Bank had Barbara sign a security agreement granting Bank a security interest in "all debtor's shares of the Oak Growth Fund, now owned and hereafter acquired, in Account Number 123456789 of the Oak Family of Funds." Bank promptly filed a financing statement.

1.   How would Bank perfect by control in this case? See 8–103(b); 8–106(c); 8–301(b); Comment 3 to 8–301 (discussing "delivery").

2.   How would Bank perfect by control if instead of buying the mutual funds directly from the issuer, Barbara bought them through her broker who held them as a securities intermediary in her securities account? Does Bank obtain control pursuant to 8–106(c) for an uncertificated security (8–102(a)(18)) or under 8–106(d) for a security entitlement (8–102(a)(17))? See Comment 3 to 8–106.

The following case illustrates the mechanics of perfecting a security interest in a mutual fund and the function of the transfer agent.

In re Pfautz
United States Bankruptcy Court, W.D. Missouri, 2001
264 B.R. 551

■ ARTHUR B. FEDERMAN, CHIEF JUDGE.

The Chapter 7 trustee (the Trustee) filed a motion to compel Liberty Bank to turn over certain uncertificated securities, owned by debtors Jerry and Suzanne Pfautz, in which Liberty Bank claims a security interest. . . .

Debtors granted Liberty Bank a security interest in uncertificated securities. Liberty Bank and the debtors established a loan collateral account to hold the securities. The loan collateral account is administered by a transfer agent designated by the issuer of the securities. The transfer agent will only release the securities upon instructions from Liberty Bank. In order to perfect a security interest in uncertificated securities under Missouri law the secured party must exercise control over the securities. Control is defined as having the power to sell the securities without the consent of the owners. The Third Party Pledge Agreement grants Liberty Bank the authority to dispose of the securities in the event of default, but does not specifically say that Liberty Bank can sell the securities without the consent of the debtors. Did debtors agree to allow Liberty Bank to sell the securities without their consent when they signed the Third Party Pledge Agreement, thus granting Liberty Bank control of the securities?

The language in the Third Party Pledge Agreement authorizes the secured party to dispose of the collateral in the event of default. By signing the Agreement, the debtors agreed to allow Liberty Bank to sell the uncertificated securities without their consent. Thus, Liberty Bank properly perfected its security interest.

Sometime prior to January of 1998, debtors acquired 289.786 shares of Guardian Park Avenue Fund-A (Guardian), Account Number 52576–3, in the form of uncertificated securities (the Uncertificated Securities). On January 14, 1998, debtors executed a "Third Party Pledge Agreement" in which they granted Liberty Bank a security interest in the Uncertificated Securities. On May 1, 1998, debtors, Liberty Bank, and State Street Bank and Trust Company (State Street), as the transfer agent for Guardian, established a separate Loan Collateral Account by executing a Loan Collateral Account Establishment Request for Recording of Assignment as Security (The Request). The debtors, a vice-president of Liberty Bank, and the Client Relations Officer for State Street signed the Request.

On January 23, 2001, debtors filed a Chapter 7 bankruptcy petition. As of December 31, 2000, the Uncertificated Securities had a market value of $11,933.39. On February 14, 2001, Liberty Bank filed a motion to lift the automatic stay to allow it to foreclose its security interest in the Uncertificated Securities. The Trustee filed a response in which he claimed that Liberty Bank had failed to prove its security interest was perfected. On March 21, 2001, this Court held a hearing on Liberty Bank's motion, which it then continued at the request of the parties to allow counsel for Liberty Bank to obtain additional documentation of perfection. . . . On June 6, 2001, the Trustee and counsel for Liberty Bank deposed Traci Connery. Ms. Connery is a division manager for National Financial Data Services (NFDS), a subsidiary of State Street, and the servicing agent, or recordkeeping agent, for Guardian. Ms. Connery testified that NFDS maintains Guardian's mutual fund accounts. Ms. Connery also testified as to the procedures NFDS uses to establish a loan collateral account, and the procedure for redeeming any uncertificated securities subject to a security interest. Ms. Connery stated that NFDS transferred the Uncertificated Securities into the loan collateral account on June 9, 1998, and that, since that time, the loan collateral account has contained a "stop transfer," which freezes the assets. Ms. Connery also testified that NFDS would only act upon instructions from Liberty Bank to release the collateral held in the account. She further stated that the release does not require the signature of the debtors. The Trustee objected to some of Ms. Connery's replies. On June 11, 2001, counsel for Liberty Bank submitted the transcript, and this Court is now prepared to rule.

Uncertificated securities are securities that are not represented by certificates. Pursuant to the Uniform Commercial Code, uncertificated securities are defined as investment property:

> (f) "Investment property" means:
>
> (i) A security, whether certificated or uncertificated. [Rev. 9–102(a)(49)]

A secured party perfects its security interest in uncertificated securities by controlling the securities:

> (4) Perfection of a security interest in investment property is governed by the following rules:
>
> (a) A security interest in investment property may be perfected by control. [Rev. 9–314(a)]

A purchaser, or secured party, has control of an uncertificated security if it has accepted delivery, or if the issuer agrees to comply with the purchaser's instructions without consent from the registered owner:

> (c) A purchaser has "control" of an uncertificated security if:
>
> (1) The uncertificated security is delivered to the purchaser; or
>
> (2) The issuer has agreed that it will comply with the instructions originated by the purchaser without further consent by the registered owner. [8–106]

Liberty Bank does not contend that it has accepted delivery of the Uncertificated Securities by becoming the registered owner. The issue, therefore, is whether Liberty Bank can demand that Guardian, or its transfer agent, redeem or dispose of the Uncertificated Securities without regard to the Pfautzes' wishes. The Trustee contends that neither the Third Party Pledge Agreement nor the Loan Collateral Account contains a provision wherein the issuer agrees to comply with instructions from Liberty Bank without consent of the debtors. Liberty Bank argues that it controls the loan collateral account and is, therefore, perfected, since the issuer will respond only to its instructions.

I begin with the exhibits from both the trial and the deposition. The Third Party Pledge Agreement is signed by Jerry and Suzanne Pfautz, and it purports to grant Liberty Bank a security interest in "MUTUAL FUND ACCT #52576." No one disputes that Mutual Fund Acct. #52576 is the Guardian Fund Account. The Pledge Agreement spells out the rights of Liberty Bank as the secured party and provides that:

> Pledgor agrees that Secured Party may at any time, whether before or after the occurrence of an Event of Default and without notice or demand of any kind, (i) notify the obligor on or issuer of any Collateral to make payment to Secured Party of any amount due or distributable thereon, (ii) in Pledgor's name or Secured Party's name enforce collection of any Collateral by suit or otherwise, or surrender, release or exchange all or any part of it, or compromise, extend or renew for any period any obligation evidenced by the Collateral, (iii) receive all proceeds of the Collateral, and (iv) hold any increase or profits received from the Collateral as additional security for the Obligations, except that any money received from the Collateral shall, at Secured Party's option, be applied in reduction of the Obligations, in such order of applications as Secured Party may determine, or be remitted to Debtor.

In this document the debtors grant to Liberty Bank alone the right to instruct Guardian, as the issuer of the collateral, to sell the Uncertificated Securities.

Ms. Connery testified that in order to perfect a security interest in Uncertificated Securities, both the registered owner and the secured party must request the establishment of a loan collateral account. It is undisputed that Liberty Bank and the Pfautzes made such a Request. The Request identifies the collateral as the Guardian Park Avenue Fund, Account Number 52576–3. In the Request, the Pfautzes instruct State Street, as the Fund's transfer agent, to record the Guardian shares pledged, along with Liberty Bank's security interest, on the books and records of the Fund and on the initial transaction statement. The Request also contains the following instructions:

Transfer such shares into separate Loan Collateral Account. . . registered on the books and records of the Fund in the following manner:

1) LOAN COLLATERAL ACCOUNT

2) LIBERTY BANK PLEDGEE

3) JERRY A. PFAUTZ AND SUZANNE PFAUTZ Sharehold(s)/Pledgor(s)

4) 4133 N HAVEN SPRINGFIELD MO 65803

The Request states that the instructions contained within the Request cannot be amended or terminated without the prior written consent of Liberty Bank, and that Liberty Bank's rights shall be in accordance with the procedures established and in effect between the Fund and State Street. The Request directs the issuer to distribute the

Uncertificated Securities to a Loan Collateral Account. Finally, the Request provides that "[e]xecution and return of this Request of Assignment as Security by State Street shall serve as notice that State Street has recorded the Pledge and security interest herein referenced on the books and records of the Fund as required under the applicable provisions of the Uniform Commercial Code." The Request contains the signature of one Wilma Collado, Client Relations Officer for State Street.

During Ms. Connery's deposition, she testified that Wilma Collado is her manager at NFDS, and that Ms. Collado is also a vice-president of Boston Financial Services, a parent company of NFDS. She also testified that NFDS follows the written procedures of their parent company, Boston Financial, when establishing a loan collateral account. . . .

At Ms. Connery's deposition, Liberty Bank offered a document titled "ASSIGNMENT OF ACCOUNT AND ESTABLISHMENT OF LOAN COLLATERAL ACCOUNT." Part I of this document sets forth the procedure for assigning an account or establishing a loan collateral account. It provides as follows:

> The shareholder(s) and account officer of the lending institution. . . [shall] complete three copies of the *Assignment of Securities Account and Control Agreement* and the *Request for Recording of Assignment as Security,* Section One, and return three signed originals to Boston Financial. These forms serve as a request from the shareholder to transfer the indicated number of shares into a separate Loan Collateral Account and to record the security interest on the books and records of the Fund. All signatures must be guaranteed.

[T]he issuer's transfer agent apparently recognizes the procedures established by Boston Financial, as Ms. Connery testified that the loan collateral account is frozen, and only Liberty Bank can release the freeze. According to the procedure set forth, the Request must identify the account, the name of the pledgee, the shareholder's name, and the shareholder's address. I find that Trial Ex. #1 contains this information. Finally, upon receipt of the documents, the issuer shall:

1a) Establish a Loan Collateral Account.

1b) Reinvest distributions to the Loan Collateral Account or establish a special mail file to the shareowner as indicated on the Request for Recording form.

1c) No privileges are carried over or established.

1d) Transfer shares from the assignor's account to the Loan Collateral Account.

1e) Place a Stop Transfer on the Loan Collateral Account.

1f) Code the assignor's original account Non Purge Y so that it will be available for transfer deposit when the collateral shares are released.

Ms. Connery testified that NFDS followed all of these procedures. She stated, "[W]e transferred the account into the loan collateral account on June 9, 1998, and we have had a stop transfer, which freezes the assets in that account since that time, and have not removed it." She further testified that NFDS would only release the collateral in the loan collateral account upon instructions of Liberty Bank. Based upon the language in the Request and the Third Party Pledge Agreement, I find that the Pfautzes granted Liberty Bank the right to sell the Uncertificated Securities upon their default, and, thus, they consented to the possibility of such a sale. That constitutes control pursuant to section 400.8–106(c) of Missouri's Revised Statutes. I, therefore, find that Liberty Bank properly perfected its security interest in the Uncertificated Securities, and I will deny the Trustee's motion for turnover.

An Order in accordance with this Memorandum Opinion will be entered this date.

NOTE

Liberty Bank was fortunate that the court resolved any doubts in its favor as to whether Liberty Bank had control over the Pfautzs' mutual funds shares. The court relies on two documents to find control: the Third Party Pledge Agreement and the Request to Guardian through its transfer agent to create a loan collateral account. The Third Party Pledge Agreement is an agreement only between Liberty Bank and the Pfautzs. Guardian wasn't a party to it and therefore could not have agreed in it to comply with Liberty Bank's orders with respect to the Pfautzs' mutual fund shares. Acting on the Request made jointly by Liberty Bank and the Pfautzs, Guardian placed the Pfautzs' shares in a separate loan collateral account. An employee of Guardian's transfer agent testified that the transfer agent would release the shares in the account only on Liberty Bank's instructions. The court appeared to take the employee's testimony, together with the Request, to indicate that Guardian agreed to comply with Liberty's orders to release the Pfautzs' shares to it on their default without their consent.

Liberty Bank could have avoided this expensive litigation on the issue of perfection of the security interest by filing a finance statement. Filing is cheap bankruptcy insurance. Alternately, it could have defeated the trustee's case by having Guardian's transfer agent become a party to a formal control agreement or at least have the transfer agent agree in clearly stated documentation to act on orders from Liberty Bank without further consent by the debtor. Such a statement shows control. The expense of presenting testimony by employees of the transfer agent may have exceeded the $12,000 market value of the uncertificated securities account.

2. TREASURY SECURITIES

The debt of the United States is evidenced by debt securities issued by the Treasury ranging from 30-year government bonds to very short term Treasury bills or notes. All of these securities are uncertificated, with ownership rights shown on the "books" of the Federal Reserve Banks in favor of "participants," typically banks, that have a securities account relationship directly with a Federal Reserve Bank. In turn, broker-dealers and banks hold Treasuries entitlements in securities accounts with the participants, and individual holders have Treasuries entitlements in securities accounts with the broker-dealers or banks. Under this system, participants, broker-dealers and banks, and individual holders have securities entitlements and are entitlement holders. Federal Reserve Banks, participants, and broker-dealers and banks are securities intermediaries. Transfers of Treasury securities are done on a book-entry basis. In short, federal law creates an indirect holding system for Treasuries.

Federal law governs the creation of security interests in Treasury securities. Treasury rules effectively incorporate Revised Article 8 as the federal law governing the creation of security interests in Treasury securities. 61 Fed. Reg. 43626 (1996), 31 C.F.R. pt. 357. They do this by providing that state law governs in states that have already adopted Revised Article 8 and in states that have not yet adopted it, the official text of Article 8 applies "as though the State had adopted Revised Article 8." 31 C.F.R. § 357.11(e). All states have adopted Article 8.

Although mutual funds and Treasuries are both uncertificated securities, there is an important difference in the manner in which they are held. A very substantial percentage of mutual funds are directly held by individual holders and as to these, the provisions of Article 8 and 9 on the perfection and priority of security interests in uncertificated securities apply. In contrast, only a very small percentage of Treasury securities are directly held by beneficial owners; these are called Treasury Direct accounts. These are held on the records of the Treasury through its agents the Federal Reserve Banks in a direct account relationship between the beneficial owner of the Treasury security and the Federal Reserve Bank. The vast majority of Treasury securities are held by securities intermediaries under the system described in the first paragraph of this section, and perfection and priority of security interests in these securities are determined by the rules concerning security interests in securities accounts. See 31 C.F.R. § 306.118(b).

CHAPTER 7

SECURITY INTERESTS IN FIXTURES

A. WHAT IS A FIXTURE?

Section 9–102(a)(41) states: "'Fixtures' means goods that have become so related to particular real property that an interest in them arises under real property law." Related how? Article 9 does not go beyond a definition that refers us to local real property law for the answer. Comment 3 to 9–334 observes: "[T]his section recognizes three categories of goods: (1) those that retain their chattel character entirely and are not part of the real property; (2) ordinary building materials that have become an integral part of the real property and cannot retain their chattel character for the purpose of finance; and (3) an intermediate class that has become real property for certain purposes, but as to which chattel financing may be preserved." Using a simple residential example, a lamp plugged into a wall socket would probably be in class 1; bricks and mortar used in the walls of the house would surely be in class 2; a heating and air-conditioning unit may be in either class 3 or class 1. Goods falling in class 3 are called fixtures, and priorities with respect to claims in fixtures are determined by 9–334 rather than by 9–322, as for class 1 goods, or by the law of real property for property in class 2.

Although 9–334's priority rules for fixture claimants are uniform across the states, the key variable in applying these rules is whether the collateral is a fixture under the law of the applicable state. The courts of the different states have varied wildly on what they find to be a fixture. For instance, a five-room house built by a lessee is personal property in Nebraska, Bank of Valley v. U.S. Nat'l Bank, 341 N.W.2d 592 (Neb.1983). But carpets and pads, nailed to the floor and easily removable, are fixtures in Pennsylvania, In re Kriger, 169 B.R. 336 (Bankr. W.D. Pa.1994). A machine weighing 45,000 pounds, 124 inches wide by eight feet in length, anchored securely by leg screws and connected by a 220 volt electric line, which could "easily be removed in one hour without material physical damage to the building" (by how many people we are not told), is personal property in New Jersey, In re Park Corrugated Box Corp., 249 F.Supp. 56 (D. N.J.1966).

These differences have been so great and unpredictable that commentators question whether any universal, one-size-fits-all definition is possible or perhaps even desirable. Before the 1962 Code was enacted, Professor Harold W. Horowitz pointed out, prophetically, in The Law of Fixtures in California—A Critical Analysis, 26 S. Cal. L. Rev. 21, 22 (1952): "There is no separate universe of the law in which objects are either fixtures or not. . . . Terms such as 'realty,' 'personalty' and 'fixtures' should be recognized to be not only descriptions of fact but also convenient but confusing descriptions of the nature of legal relations between persons in various factual situations." In short, the term "fixture" is a legal conclusion about who should win a lawsuit, not a description of an object. However uncertain the meaning of this term, courts must decide the cases before them. As Lord Lindley said in Viscount Hill v. Bullock, (1897) 2 Ch. 482, in which it was claimed that certain stuffed birds were fixtures: "[A]fter all there is such a thing as common sense, and it must be brought to bear upon the question whether these birds are or are not fixtures." Quoted in Wyoming State Farm Loan Board v. Farm Credit System Capital Corp., 759 P.2d 1230, 1241 n.5 (Wyo. 1988).

Courts have tended to coalesce around some formulaic criteria, however vague, that they can cling to for guidance. They often require three elements for the recognition of a fixture: (1) physical annexation to the land; (2) adaptation for use with the land; and (3) annexation made with the intention to make a permanent addition to the land. See, e.g., In re Pierce, 621 B.R. 434 (Bankr. Ind. 2020); Traverse County Land Bank Authority v. Verizon Wireless, 2017 Mich. App. LEXIS 753 (Mich. Ct. App. May 4, 2017). However common the use of this three-prong "test," the legal standard governing fixtures remains unsettled and nonuniform in result.

This is well illustrated in litigation in connection with General Motors' 2009 bankruptcy. There a bankruptcy court had to decide whether 200,000 assets located in GM plants in 26 counties were fixtures. See Motors Liquidation Co. Avoidance Trust v. JP Morgan Chase Bank, N.A., 2017 WL 4280934 (Bankr. S.D.N.Y. Sept. 26, 2017). The assets ranged from huge stamping presses and machining equipment to robotic arms and conveyer systems. Noting that it was impractical to determine the fixture status of each asset, in pretrial proceedings the court directed the parties to select 40 "representative" assets. In analyzing the three-prong test under different applicable state law governing fixtures, the court discerned two principles in relevant case law that help determine whether an asset is a fixture. One was that "concrete pits, trenches, slabs, or specialized foundations are strong indications that an asset is a fixture." Id. at *97. The other principle was that the intention for the asset to remain in place indefinitely is reinforced where the asset is "closely integrated, assimilated or interlocked" with other assets. Id. at *101. Relying on these principles and on-site visits to two GM plants, the court made different determinations about each representative asset.

B. FIXTURE AND OTHER FILINGS

A good that becomes a fixture retains its character as a type of collateral defined under the UCC. A factory machine bolted to the floor is still equipment even if it also becomes a fixture. Fixture status simply means that a real estate interest in the good can arise. Correspondingly, an ordinary filed financing statement that perfects a security interest in a good continues to perfect the security interest after the good becomes a fixture. These filings are often called "UCC" or "chattel" filings. A security interest in a fixture also can be perfected by making a "fixture filing." Section 9–102(a)(40) defines a fixture filing as "the filing of a financing statement covering goods that are or are to become fixtures and satisfying Section 9–502(a) and (b)." Article 9 doesn't require that a fixture filing be made to perfect a security interest in fixtures. See 9–501(a)(1)(B) ("the financing statement is filed as a fixture filing"). A UCC filing suffices. Finally, a security interest in a fixture can be perfected under applicable realty law, usually by recording a mortgage that covers the fixture. An appurtenances clause or similar language in the mortgage instrument is enough to extend the mortgage to fixtures. Section 9–502(c) refers to the recorded mortgage as "effective" as a fixture filing. Thus, there are three sorts of filings that can perfect security interests in goods that are fixtures: a UCC filing, a fixture filing, and a recorded mortgage.

A fixture filing differs from a UCC filing both in the information required in the financing statement and the place at which the financing statement must be filed. As to required information, in addition to the information demanded by 9–502(a), the financing statement must contain the information described by 9–502(b). 9–102(a)(40). Section 9–502(b) requires, among other information, a description of the realty to which the collateral is or will be affixed as well as the somewhat formalistic demand that the financing statement "indicate" that it is being filed in the realty records. 9–502(b)(2), (3). These requirements necessitate use of a UCC-1 Addendum to accompany the financing statement. The Addendum has designated fields for a description of the realty (Box 16) and an indication that the financing statement is being filed as a fixture filing (Box 14). UCC filings need not satisfy 9–502(b)'s informational demands.

As to the place of filing, 9–501(a)(1)(B) requires a fixture filing in the office designated for the filing of mortgages on realty. This is typically the register of deeds. (Section 9–301(3)(A) selects as the applicable law for perfecting security interests in fixtures the local law of the jurisdiction in which the affixed good is located.) For its part, a UCC filing is made centrally, usually in the office of the secretary of state. 9–501(a)(2). A filing in the office where mortgages are recorded saves realty interests the cost of conducting a dual search: one search to detect UCC filings and another to detect mortgage interests in fixtures. Transmitting utilities, defined in 9–102(a)(81), like the telecommunications network involved in In re Hawaiian Telecom Communications, Inc., 430 B.R. 564 (Bankr. D.Haw.2009), are subject to different rules for mortgage filings to avoid the requirement for filing with legal descriptions in every county in which debtors have property. A fixture filing for a transmitting utility must be made in a designated central office, usually that of the secretary of state, in each state in which the debtor has fixtures. See 9–501(b) and Comment 5.

A secured party has an option in filing a financing statement covering goods that are or will become fixtures. It may make a UCC filing in the Article 9 records. Alternatively, the secured party may file its financing statement as a fixture filing. Comment 4 to 9–501. In this case the filing is made in the applicable realty records. Both sorts of filings suffice to perfect the secured party's security interest in fixtures. A fixture filing or UCC filing are both good against a secured creditor who has made a UCC filing. However, for purposes of priority against realty interests in fixtures, a fixture filing is necessary. A UCC filing has limited effect against realty interests.

To obtain priority over realty interests, in most cases a fixture filing is needed. However, a UCC filing is effective against certain realty interests. It is good against a lien creditor's rights in the fixture arising from its lien on the real estate. 9–334(e)(3). A UCC filing also is effective as to fixtures that fall within the restricted class of readily removable goods described by 9–334(e)(2). In all other cases, the UCC filing is ineffective against realty interests. Thus, to be protected against both realty and competing security interests in most goods that are or will become fixtures, a prudent secured creditor must at least make a fixture filing covering the goods. Of course, if the goods described in the mortgage records aren't fixtures, recording the mortgage is not a filing with respect to the goods. The priority problems below describe the protection given by UCC and fixture filings.

C. PRIORITY

1. BASIC RULES

Section 9–334 provides the priority rules governing contests between secured creditors and realty interests in goods that have become fixtures. Contests between secured creditors over the goods continue to be governed by 9–322's basic priority rules. The classic conflict addressed by 9–334 is between the holder of a security interest in goods that are attached to real property and the mortgagee of the real property to which the goods are attached. Typically, the security agreement will provide that the goods remain personal property even though attached to realty, and the mortgage will cover all fixtures and other appurtenances to the realty. The thrust of 9–334 is to subordinate a security interest in fixtures to the conflicting interest of the real property mortgagee unless the secured party brings its interest into the real property recording system by making a "fixture filing." 9–334(c).

The following Problems implicate the priority rules set out in 9–334.

PROBLEMS

1. Seller sold Debtor a heating/cooling unit that was installed in Debtor's building by attaching pipes, vents, and electrical conduits. Seller took a security interest in the unit in a written security agreement that specifically provided that the unit remained personal property after installation and that Seller had a right to remove it upon default by Debtor. Mortgagee (M) recorded a record of a mortgage covering Debtor's real property and all fixtures and appurtenances attached to the property in the county recorder's office. You may assume that the unit is a fixture under the law of the relevant jurisdiction.

(a) Assume that M's mortgage was on record when Seller sold the unit to Debtor. What steps must S take to protect its interest from subordination to the interest of the mortgagee under 9–334(c)? See 9–334(d) and (e).

(b) At the time Seller took its security interest in the unit, there was no mortgage on Debtor's property. What steps should Seller take to be sure that no subsequent mortgage on D's land could subordinate Seller's interest in the unit? See 9–334(e).

(c) At the time Seller took its security interest in the unit, there was no mortgage on Debtor's property. Seller made a regular filing covering the unit in the central filing office of the State. Subsequently, Debtor filed a bankruptcy petition and its bankruptcy trustee sought to avoid Seller's interest under BC 544(a)(1) as a hypothetical lien creditor. Should the trustee succeed? See 9–334(e)(3) and 9–501(a)(2). See Comment 9 to 9–334. See Mark S. Scarberry, Fixtures in Bankruptcy, 16 Cap. U.L. Rev. 403, 441–478 (1987), for a general treatment of the subject.

2. Assume the facts are those in In re Park Corrugated Box Corporation, cited above, in which the Seller made a fixture filing with respect to a machine it believed, with some justification, was a fixture. The machine weighed 45,000 pounds, was 124 inches wide by eight feet in length and was anchored securely by leg screws and connected by a 220 volt electric line. Subsequently, Debtor, the buyer of the machine and owner of the structure to which the machine was affixed, filed a bankruptcy petition. Its trustee in bankruptcy sought to avoid Seller's interest under BC 544(a)(1) as a hypothetical lien creditor. The court held that the machine was not a fixture. Should the trustee succeed? See 9–334(e)(3).

3. First Mortgagee (M1) held a duly recorded mortgage on Debtor's real property and fixtures securing Debtor's obligation to M1. After M1 recorded its mortgage, Seller sold a heating unit to Debtor on credit and took a security interest in the unit to secure the unpaid purchase price. You may assume that the unit fell within the definition of a fixture in the relevant jurisdiction. Six weeks after Seller installed the unit, it made a fixture filing covering the unit. Subsequently, interest rates were falling and Debtor wished to refinance its mortgage through Second Mortgagee (M2). The refinancing was carried out by M2's advancing the money to Debtor, Debtor paying off M1, M1's returning Debtor's promissory note, marked "paid," to

Debtor and recording a satisfaction statement that terminated its mortgage. Debtor in turn signed a new promissory note payable to M2 and granted M2 a mortgage on the real property and the fixtures, which M2 promptly recorded. Is Seller's security interest in the unit subordinated to M2's mortgage? See 9–334(e)(1).

2. CONSTRUCTION MORTGAGES

Construction lending often involves an agreement by a lender to advance money to a developer in a series of "progress payments" to be made at various stages in the construction of a project. The lender customarily records its mortgage on the premises before the work of improvement commences. If the developer buys goods on credit which may become affixed to the improvement and the seller retains a security interest in the goods sold, a priority contest may arise upon the developer's default between the lender, claiming a prior security interest in the entire improvement, and the seller, who seeks to remove the attached goods.

Pre-UCC law favored the construction lender over the fixture financer, but the 1962 version of Article 9 omitted this priority. Having been told that Article 9 had no effect on real property law, the powerful real property finance industry was not much involved in the drafting of Article 9. When it discovered this omission, fears arose that the new UCC would allow a supplier of air-conditioning units for a housing development in Arkansas to remove the units in mid-summer and render the development unmarketable. The industry lobbied for restoration of the old rule and prevailed in the 1972 version of Article 9. The revision continues this rule in 9–334(h).

This following example illustrates this priority: Bank agreed to advance $5 million to Developer (D), the owner of the real property, to enable D to build a structure on the land. The money was to be paid out under a schedule that allowed D to receive advances as the work of improvement reached certain stages of completion. Before construction began, Bank recorded a record of the mortgage, which included fixtures, securing D's obligations, which stated that it was a construction mortgage. Instead of paying cash for the heating and cooling equipment for the structure out of the proceeds of the construction loan, as the loan agreement required, D induced Seller to sell D the equipment on credit, secured by a purchase-money security interest in the equipment that was perfected by a fixture filing. Assume that under the law of the jurisdiction this equipment would be classified as a fixture. Under 9–334(h), Seller's interest is subordinated to that of Bank.

(a) What is the policy basis justifying the traditional priority rule that protects the Bank in this case? Do construction lenders need this priority?

(b) Once Seller learns that Bank is advancing funds to D pursuant to a construction mortgage, how can Seller take a security interest in fixtures it sells to D on credit that will be protected against Bank's 9–334(h) priority? See 9–334(f) and 9–602.

3. MANUFACTURED HOMES

Courts have had difficulties in classifying mobile homes for fixtures purposes. When wheels are placed under them, they are, indeed, mobile. Personal property? But when they come to rest they are placed on foundations, hooked up to water pipes and power wires, telephone and cable connections, and they stay put. Fixtures? Over time, with more built-ons and attachments, they become more and more a part of the real property. How do they differ from prefabricated or modular homes that are assembled on the owner's land? Real property?

Article 9 has undertaken to clarify the status of mobile homes as collateral. See 9–334(e)(4). The term "manufactured home" is ambiguous. Was it intended to mean what used to be called "trailer homes" and for several decades has been known as "mobile homes"? These are small, relatively inexpensive housing boxes that are usually restricted by zoning to trailer parks and are occupied by people who can't afford traditional housing. Or is the intention to cover prefabricated homes, now called "modular homes," that are manufactured in components in factories and shipped to the building site where they are assembled? Prefabs started with the Sears' build-your-own-home kit in 1908—the Goldenrod, three rooms, no bath (outhouse sold separately) cost $445 in 1925—and have progressed to modern modular homes that have architectural pretensions and $200,000 price tags. See Daniel Akst, The Very Model of a Modern Modular House, Wall St. J., May 29, 2003 at D8. Now the Sears' homes are collectors' items. A large version advertised in Sears' catalog in the 1920s for $3,727 sold in 2016 for $1.06 million. Nancy Keates, Kit Homes: An Appreciation, Wall St. J., Sept. 21, 2017 at M1. The definition of "manufactured home" in 9–102(a)(53) makes clear that the term means a mobile home and not a modular home.

Although judicial opinions under former Article 9 differed on their nature for purposes of perfection of security interests, the likelihood that mobile homes would be classified as either fixtures or real property led financers to be sure to record their security interest in the real property records. But the quest of state governments for revenue has led to widespread inclusion of mobile homes in certificate-of-title statutes, with the requirement that security interests be indicated on the certificate. Under such a statute, is indication of a security interest on the certificate the exclusive means of perfection of security interests in mobile homes? In re Kroskie, 315 F.3d 644 (6th Cir.2003), held that it is, and banks stopped financing mobile homes in Michigan. The legislature promptly responded by providing that recording in real property records is an alternative method of perfection. See In re Oswalt, 318 B.R. 817 (Bankr. W.D. Mich.2004). Some states continue to provide that perfection under their certificate-of-title law is the exclusive method of perfection. See, e.g., In re Renaud, 302 B.R. 280 (Bankr. E.D. Ark.2003).

Section 9–334(e)(4) gives a security interest in a manufactured home perfected under a state certificate-of-title statute priority over conflicting interests of encumbrancers or owners of the real property if the security interest is created in a manufactured-home transaction. The detailed definition of "manufactured home" in 9–102(a)(53) is taken from the federal Manufactured Housing Act, 42 U.S.C. §§ 5401 et seq. See Comment 4b. to 9–102. It means a structure of 320 or more square feet, "which is built on a permanent chassis and designed to be used as a dwelling with or without a permanent foundation. . . ." This definition excludes smaller trailer-type units, but the limits of its meaning may puzzle participants in mobile home financing for years to come.

A "manufactured-home transaction" is defined in 9–102(a)(54) to mean a purchase-money security interest in a manufactured home or a security interest in which the manufactured home is the primary collateral. It excludes manufactured homes held in inventory. Under 9–515(b), an initial filing with respect to a manufactured home transaction is effective for 30 years if it indicates that it is filed in connection with a manufactured-home financing.

PROBLEM

BC 1322(b)(2) provides that a Chapter 13 plan may "modify the rights of holders of holders of secured claims, other than a claim secured only by a security interest in real property that is the debtor's principal residence. . . ." BC 101(13A)(B) defines the term "debtor's principal residence" as including "a mobile or manufactured home, or trailer." Debtor's Chapter 13 plan modifies the amount of the secured claim in her manufactured home, which is her principal residence. Since her home is not permanently attached to the land, it is classified as personal property in Missouri where she lives. The secured creditor contends that Debtor cannot modify its claim because BC 1322(b)(2) applies to "the debtor's principal residence" and the definition of that term in BC 101(13A) includes manufactured homes. Debtor argues that BC 1322(b)(2) applies to manufactured homes only when they are classified as real property under the law of the state where they are located. Who is right? See In re Coleman, 392 B.R. 767 (8th Cir. B.A.P.2008).

4. CIRCULAR PRIORITIES

Priority rules are intended to rank competing claims to the same assets, no matter how many claimants there are to the assets. However, Article 9's priority rules, including its fixture priority rules, rank one claimant's claim over another claimant's claim. They state a two-party ranking, as it were. The priority rules give a consistent ranking of claims where only two parties have claims against the same assets. However, where three or more parties have claims against the assets, Article 9's priority rules sometimes may not yield a consistent ranking of claims.

This occurs when their application produces a circular priority in which A has priority over B, B has priority over C, and C has priority over A. A circular priority frustrates the purpose of priority rules. Consider circular priorities in connection with the following Problem.

PROBLEM

Debtor operated a plant on a piece of land it owned. The plant contains a spare sprinkler system housed in concrete struts. Requiring working capital for the plant, Debtor obtained a loan from M Bank secured by a mortgage on the land and plant. The mortgage instrument contained the usual appurtenances clause, and M Bank recorded its mortgage interest in the proper registry of deeds. A year before, Debtor had granted First Bank a security interest in the sprinkler system in the plant to secure a loan First Bank made to it. First Bank filed a valid Article 9 financing statement in both the proper location for filing Article 9 financing statements and the registry of deeds. The financing statement, however, filed in the registry of deeds did not recite that it was filed as a fixture filing. Two months later, Second Bank made a loan to Debtor also secured by Debtor's sprinkler system and filed a valid financing statement in both places. Second Bank's statement filed in the registry of deeds recited that it was being filed as a fixture filing. Debtor subsequently defaulted on the loans from the three banks. Assuming that the spare sprinkler system is worth $100,000 and Debtor owes each bank $100,000, who has priority in the system? See 9–102(a)(40), 9–322(a), (f)(1), 9–334, Comment 2 to 9–334(e)(1), and 9–502(b).

———

This Problem involves a circular priority in a fixture: First Bank has priority over Second Bank; Second Bank has priority over Mortgage Bank; and Mortgage Bank has priority over First Bank. Article 9's relevant priority rules apply in pairwise contests among First Bank, Second Bank and Mortgage Bank. The final result of combining them is an intransitive order of priority of their claims. Since a circular priority describes an intransitive ordering of claimants, the scheme of priority rules does not give a consistent sequence in which claims are to be paid. This creates a serious practical problem because a priority scheme must determine who is paid first. Circular priorities, although rarely found in case law controlled by Article 9, are possible in contexts other than priority contests over fixtures. In general, circular priorities are possible when a priority rule contains a "knowledge" component or when different priority schemes, such as the Bankruptcy Code, the Federal Tax Lien Act or realty law, apply to different claimants. There are solutions to them, ranging from a pro rata share to "equitable" devices for subordinating one creditor to the others, see 2 Gilmore, Security Interests in Personal Property 1120–46 (1965); M. Stuart Sutherland, Note, Circular Priority Systems Within the Uniform Commercial Code, 61 Tex. L. Rev. 517 (1982), but they are controversial and not compelled by Article 9's provisions. At the very least, it is wise not to create a circular priority that needs resolving in the first place.

Article 9 gets mixed marks on this score. Its priority rules allow circular priorities in assets other than fixtures. One instance is a priority contest involving purchase-money and non-purchase-money security interests in inventory in which the purchase-money financer gives proper notice to only one of the non-purchase-money secured creditors. See 9–324(b), 9–322(a)(1). Another is a priority contest involving a lapsed financing statement. Section 9–316(b) provides that, when a financing statement becomes ineffective under stipulated conditions, it is deemed never to have been effective "against a purchaser of the collateral for value." The negative implication is that the statement remains effective against nonpurchasers such as lien creditors. Thus, because a financing statement can be ineffective against a secured creditor but still effective against a lien creditor, Article 9 allows the following priority order: Secured Creditor 1 over Lien Creditor via 9–317(a)(2) and 9–316(b)'s negative implication; Lien Creditor over Secured Creditor 2 via 9–317(a)(2); and Secured Creditor 2 over Secured Creditor 1 via 9–316(b) and 9–322(a). .

Article 9's drafters are fairly sanguine about allowing circular priorities to continue, estimating that the bankruptcy consequences of not doing so are more serious. See Comment 3 to 9–316 (another approach would create significant and unjustifiable preference risks). Their estimate can be questioned. Adverse bankruptcy consequences faced by a creditor give it an additional incentive to maintain perfection, by monitoring the location of collateral and updating the financing statement. This might not be a bad thing. At least the creditor then can calculate accurately the marginal benefits and costs of updating the statement or monitoring the collateral. Because resolutions of circular priorities are nonuniform, controversial and have no explicit statutory basis, circular priorities can create a good deal of legal uncertainty. Creditors incur socially wasteful costs in planning transactions to avoid the uncertainty of the prospect of circularity.

An intransitive ranking of claims also can be produced where relevant priority rules otherwise give a consistent ranking of claims. In the following case, a private agreement between two of the three competing creditors produces a circular priority. Strictly, contrary to what the *Cliff Ridge* court maintains, the result is not a true circular priority, because Article 9's priority rules produce a consistent ranking of claims. The circularity in priority instead is the result of a private agreement between two of the three parties. Nonetheless, the private agreement gives one party to it the right to satisfy its claim from an asset before the other party satisfies its claim from the same asset. As a result, the agreement, in combination with Article 9's priority rules, produces the intransitive ranking described in the case. Unlike a true circular priority, however, interpretation of the private agreement provides a means of establishing a consistent ranking of claims.

In re Cliff's Ridge Skiing Corp.

Bankr. W.D. Mich. 1991
123 B.R. 753

■ JAMES D. GREGG, UNITED STATES BANKRUPTCY JUDGE.

In this contested matter, three creditors are fighting over sale proceeds from a ski chairlift. Although the parties have attempted to settle this matter, this has not been possible. The Court will therefore grapple with the issues and render a decision.

The issues presented are many. ... What is the priority of the creditors' respective interests? Did one creditor validly subordinate its interest to another creditor? Is there a circular priority problem? If so, how should it be resolved?

PROCEDURAL BACKGROUND

On October 28, 1987, Cliff's Ridge Skiing Corporation, ("Debtor"), filed for relief under chapter 11 of the Bankruptcy Code. On January 4, 1988, the case was converted to a chapter 7 case. The Debtor's assets were sold, after notice and hearing, pursuant to a court order dated July 28, 1988. The sale proceeds were distributed to secured creditors, or retained by the estate, pursuant to a court order dated December 27, 1988. One of the assets sold was a Riblet chairlift-2 place, No. 6470, 75 HP electric drive ("chairlift"). The sale proceeds received from the chairlift were $ 22,500.00. These proceeds were placed in an interest-bearing escrow account pending a court determination as to creditors' entitlement to the proceeds.

Three creditors, First National Bank & Trust Company of Marquette ("First National"), Cliffs Ridge Development Co. ("Cliff's Ridge Dev."), and First of America Bank-Marquette, N.A., formerly known as Union National Bank & Trust Company of Marquette ("FOA"), each assert they are legally entitled to the escrowed proceeds and the interest earned therefrom. * * *

[Ed.—In 1980 Cliff's Ridge Dev. mortgaged certain of its real property to FOA, including all fixtures then owned or after-acquired attached to it. FOA recorded its mortgage on August 1, 1980. Debtor purchased a chairlift on August 1, 1982 and affixed it to the realty some time before November 22, 1982. On November 22, 1982, Cliff's Ridge Dev. conveyed the real property to Debtor, subject to FOA's mortgage. Debtor in exchange granted Cliff's Ridge Dev. a mortgage on the realty the same day, which Cliff's Ridge Dev. recorded on November 23, 1982. The mortgage covered appurtenances to the real estate, including the chairlift. On December 13, 1982, Debtor granted First National's assignor a security interest in the chairlift, which First National perfected by making a fixture filing the next day. The court determined that the chairlift was a fixture.]

If these were the only facts and law to be applied, the court would now easily apply the U.C.C. priority rules and determine entitlement to the sale proceeds. Unfortunately, sorting out commercial security transactions is not always so simple. * * *

Subordination by FOA to First National.

FOA agreed to subordinate its interest in the chairlift to First National pursuant to the Subordination Agreement on December 13, 1982. * * *

Under Michigan law, the court concludes that the Subordination Agreement between FOA and First National is valid and enforceable between those parties. However, Cliff's Ridge Dev. was not a party to the Subordination Agreement and there exists no fact in the record which supports a conclusion that Cliff's Ridge Dev. validly subordinated its interest in the chairlift to First National. Therefore, the Subordination Agreement does not affect Cliff's Ridge Dev.'s interest in the chairlift or its relative priority in the sale proceeds from the chairlift.

Resolution of Priority to Chairlift Proceeds.

Priority of competing or conflicting interests in a fixture is governed by the U.C.C. In certain specified instances, a holder of a perfected security interest in a fixture will have priority over a prior encumbrancer under real estate law. Mich. Comp. Laws Ann. § 440.9313(4) [9–334(e)]. An encumbrancer includes the holder of a real estate mortgage. Mich. Comp. Laws Ann. § 440.9105(1)(g) [9–102(a)(32)]. In other instances, a holder of a perfected security interest in a fixture will be subordinate to a conflicting interest of an encumbrancer of the related real estate. Mich. Comp. Laws Ann. § 440.9313(7) [9–334(c)].

A leading commentator has succinctly stated the U.C.C. fixture priority general rule which is germane to this dispute. This court sees no need to attempt to improve the comment or restate the general rule. "The first-in-time-first-in-right rule runs throughout Article Nine, and 9–313 [9–334] is no different . . . . If the fixture lender perfects by a fixture filing before the real estate creditor files a mortgage on the real estate to which the goods have become affixed, the fixture lender has priority. If the mortgagee files first, he wins." White & Summers, *Uniform Commercial Code* 1156 (3rd ed. 1988).

In accordance with this court's factual findings, the general fixture priority rule initially governs. First National does not hold a perfected purchase money security interest in the chairlift. Cliff's Ridge Dev., as an encumbrancer, did not consent in writing to First National's security interest or disclaim its interest in the chairlift as a fixture. No other specific exception to the general fixture priority rule is applicable. Therefore, *absent* FOA's *subordination*, the priority of the parties' interests in the chairlift would be: First, FOA as a real estate encumbrancer; second, Cliff's Ridge Dev. as a real estate encumbrancer; and third, First National as holding a perfected security interest.

As a result of the Subordination Agreement between FOA and First National, the respective initial priorities have been consensually altered. However, Cliff's Ridge Dev.'s priority has not been affected because it was not a party to the subordination. Based upon the subordination, the priority is altered as follows: (1) FOA is prior to Cliff's Ridge Dev.; (2) Cliff's Ridge Dev. is prior to First National; and (3) First National is prior to FOA. The classic circular priority conundrum (of the kind briefly addressed, but seldom resolved, in law school) therefore exists. How should the circular priority be resolved? The parties and the court have been unable to discover any Michigan reported cases discussing circular priorities.

FOA urges the court to divide the proceeds among the three parties on an equitable basis. If FOA requests this court to split the proceeds among the three competing claimants in a fashion the court arbitrarily deems to be "fair," this court declines such an invitation. However, if the applicable U.C.C. priority statute does not resolve the circular priority dispute (and it does not), this court agrees with FOA that non-bankruptcy case law and equitable principles may be utilized to establish the appropriate priorities of the parties.

The court believes that the effect of the Subordination Agreement should be construed as FOA and First National having "traded places" to the extent of the money advanced by First National to the Debtor for the chairlift loan which remains unpaid or the remaining mortgage balance owed to FOA by the Debtor, whichever is less. By so doing, Cliff's Ridge Dev.'s interest and its original priority position will not be adversely or beneficially affected by the other parties' subordination agreement.

After a careful review of the case law cited by the parties and after conducting independent research, this court has determined to follow the circular priority formula set forth in *ITT Diversified Credit Corp. v. First City Capital Corp.*, 31 Tex. Sup. Ct. J. 10, 737 S.W.2d 803, 804, 4 U.C.C.R. Serv. 2d(Callaghan) 927, 929 (1987):

For example, A, B and C have claims against the debtor which are entitled to priority in alphabetical order. "A" subordinates his claim to "C." After foreclosure of the secured interest, the resulting fund is insufficient to satisfy all three claims. The proper distribution of the fund is as follows.

1.   Set aside from the fund the amount of "A"'s claim.

2.   Out of the money set aside, pay "C" the amount of its claim, pay "A" to the extent of any balance remaining after "C"'s claim is satisfied.

3.   Pay "B" the amount of the fund remaining after "A"'s claim has been set aside.

4.   If any balance remains in the fund after "A"'s claim has been set aside and "B"'s claim has been satisfied, distribute the balance to "C" and "A."

See Gilmore, *Security Interests in Personal Property § 39.1 at 1021 (1965).*

Thus, "C", by virtue of the subordination agreement, is paid first, but only to the amount of "A"'s claim, to which "B" was in any event junior. "B" receives what it had expected to receive, the fund less "A"'s prior claim. If "A"'s claim is smaller than "C"'s, "C" will collect the balance of its claim, in its own right, only after "B" has been paid in full. "A", the subordinator, receives nothing until "B" and "C" have been paid except to the extent that its claim, entitled to first priority, exceeds the amount of "C"'s claim, which, under its agreement, is to be first paid.

Cliff's Ridge Dev. argues that the subordination by FOA to First National mandates that FOA's initial first priority status should be entirely relegated to a third position behind *both* Cliff's Ridge Dev. and First National. . . If this argument is accepted, Cliff's Ridge Dev. would be beneficially elevated to the first priority and become entitled to receive the chairlift sale proceeds.

This court declines to follow those cases cited by Cliff's Ridge Dev. and rejects its argument. FOA did not subordinate its entire real estate mortgage to First National; FOA only subordinated its mortgage interest to the extent it covered the chairlift to be attached as a fixture. The partial subordination by FOA is more akin to the facts of *ITT Diversified* rather than those cases relied upon by Cliff's Ridge Dev. More importantly, this court strongly believes that the better reasoned resolution of the circular priority dilemma mandates that Cliff's Ridge Dev.'s initial priority should not be altered, either beneficially or adversely, as a result of a subordination agreement to which it was not a party.

FOA, Cliff's Ridge Dev. and First National each hold claims in amounts in excess of the proceeds realized from the sale of the chairlift. Applying the circular priority formula set forth in *ITT Diversified,* after paying "C" (First National) a portion of the amount of its claim, the fund is completely exhausted. No remaining funds are available for distribution to either "A" (FOA) or "B" (Cliff's Ridge Dev.).

CONCLUSION

The court holds First National has priority to all proceeds from the sale of the chairlift, and the interest earned therefrom, which are now being held in escrow. An order shall be entered accordingly.

NOTE

In resolving the circular priority, the *Cliff's Ridge* court describes two different interpretations of the subordination agreement in the case. The "complete subordination" rule construes the subordination agreement to be an agreement in which one party undertakes not to assert its claim against collateral until the other party's claim has been satisfied from the collateral. The subordinated party agrees to move in line behind the party to whom it subordinated, as it's sometimes put. This is the rule understandably urged by Cliff's Ridge, which the court rejects. The "partial subordination" rule construes the subordination agreement as one party's undertaking to transfer its priority position to the other party. This gives the other party the benefit of the subordinated party's priority position, to the extent of that party's priority. Under the parties' agreement the parties trade places in line. The rule described in the excerpts from *ITT Diversified Credit* and Gilmore, 2 Security Interests in Personal Property (1965), and adopted by the court, is the "partial subordination" rule. The majority of courts adopt this rule; see Caterpillar Fin. Servs. v. People's National Bank N.A., 710 F.3d 691 (7th Cir. 2013). Which rule is more likely to accord with the intentions of the parties to the subordination agreement?

D. ENFORCEMENT

If a creditor's security interest in fixtures has priority over encumbrancers and owners of real property, 9–604(c) allows the secured party to remove the fixture from the real property. However, under 9–604(d), the secured party must reimburse an encumbrancer or owner of the real property "for the cost of repair of any physical injury caused by the removal," and the person entitled to reimbursement may demand adequate assurance of reimbursement as a condition of its permission to remove. The difficulties facing the fixture financer in using the removal remedy are obvious. Removing the fixture can be costly. These costs, which include the expense of reimbursing the encumbrancer or owner for physical injury to the realty, might well exceed the second-hand value of the fixture removed. Tearing out built-in fixtures will inevitably leave damage to walls and floors as well as enrage home owners not likely to welcome the repossessors into their kitchen. Haggling over the amount of injury caused by the removal and the adequacy of the reimbursement proffered by the fixture financer seems inevitable.

If the fixture financer cannot share in the proceeds of foreclosure of the real property, it may well choose to write off the debt unless it can make a deal with the encumbrancer or owner of the realty. The basis for the deal would be that the encumbrancer or owner's interest in the realty probably is more valuable with the fixture left in than with them removed. This is because, to maintain the value of the realty, removal of the fixtures might require installation of new fixtures. As suggested in Note 2 following *Carmel Fin. Corp. v. Castro*, the fixture financer has a bargaining position that might lead to a settlement with the encumbrancer or owner of realty to which the fixture is attached. Presumably the deal struck would give the fixture financer at least the net amount the financer would receive if it removed and resold the fixture (the least the financer will accept) and at most an amount equal to the diminution in value of realty were the fixture removed (the most the encumbrancer or owner will offer).

The deal just described can be struck without the remedies Article 9 makes available to the fixture financer. Nonetheless, 9–604(b) gives the fixture financer remedies if the debtor defaults. Section 9–604(b) provides: "Subject to subsection (c), if a security agreement covers goods that are or become fixtures, a secured party may proceed (1) under this part; or (2) in accordance with the rights with respect to real property, in which case the other provisions of this part do not apply." Subsection (1) allows the fixture financer to proceed against the defaulting debtor and collateral under Article 9's enforcement provisions ("this part") while subsection (2) allows it to proceed against the collateral under real property law. The Article 9 remedies include suing the debtor for a personal judgment under 9–601(a)(1) and removal of the fixture under 9–604(c). However, the right to foreclose and dispose of collateral under 9–610(a) surely would not entitle the fixture claimant to foreclose on the real property to which the fixture is attached, and foreclosure and disposition of the fixture in place hardly seems a feasible remedy.

Section 9–604(b)(2) is less clear as to the remedies it makes available to the fixture financer. The subsection allows the fixture claimant to proceed "in accordance with the rights with respect to real property." However, we are not told what this means. The real property law of the relevant jurisdiction is likely to have provisions on the right of a real property mortgagee to proceed in a case in which its mortgage lien covers fixtures as well as land. However, it may have no provisions governing the rights of a fixture financer to proceed against its fixture collateral, and it almost surely will have no law allowing such a claimant to compel the sale of the real property to which the fixture is appurtenant.

Comment 3 to 9–604 offers very little help in clarifying 9–604(b)(2)'s meaning: "[9–604(b)] makes clear that a security interest in fixtures may be enforced either under real-property law or under any of the applicable provisions of Part 6, including sale or other disposition either before or after removal of the fixtures (see subsection (c)). Subsection (b) also serves to overrule cases holding that a secured party's only remedy after default is the removal of the fixtures from the real property. See, e.g., Maplewood Bank & Trust v. Sears, Roebuck & Co., 625 A.2d 537 (N.J.Super.App.Div.1993)." In *Maplewood*, decided under former Article 9, the court found that the fixture financer's exclusive remedy was to foreclose on the fixture. In doing so it denied the fixture financer the right to share in the proceeds of the foreclosure sale of the real property. By expanding the available remedies to include enforcement against the fixture in accordance with real property law, 9–604(b)(2) overrules *Maplewood*.

But the Comment does not say which part of *Maplewood*'s holding 9–604(b)(2) overrules. Does it merely overrule *Maplewood*'s holding limiting the fixture financer's remedies to foreclosure on the fixture? If so, 9–604(b)(2) leaves to real property law the other remedies available to the financer. Those remedies may or may not include a right to share in the proceeds of a foreclosure sale of the realty. Or does 9–604(b)(2) overrule *Maplewood*'s denial of the fixture financer's right to share in the proceeds of the foreclosure sale of the realty? If so, 9–604(b)(2) gives the financer the right to share in the proceeds of the foreclosure sale of the realty. In this case the courts have to decide how this can be done. The fixture financer may be allowed to join in a judicial foreclosure and, depending on the priority of the security interest in the fixtures, to share in the proceeds of the foreclosure according to the ratio between the values of the fixtures and the real property without the fixtures. If the mortgage lien is prior to the fixture security interest, the fixture interest would share only after the mortgage lien is satisfied. Some mechanism would have to be worked out for fixture financers to participate in the non-judicial foreclosures that predominate in many states. The right of the fixture party to share in the proceeds of foreclosure of the real property is meaningless if the mortgagee is not foreclosing. Here the fixture financer seems to be left with the right of removal, imperfect as that remedy may be. Although perhaps not decisive, 9–604(b)(2)'s language ("in accordance with the rights with respect to real property") seems to favor the former, more limited overruling of *Maplewood*. The following case is one of the very few to construe 9–604(b)(2).

Carmel Fin. Corp. v. Castro

Tex. Ct. App., 2016
514 S.W.3d 291

■ **Opinion by:** WILLIAM J. BOYCE.

Carmel Financial Corporation, Inc. appeals from the trial court's orders on cross-motions for summary judgment. The orders arise from claims against Shaun Donovan in his official capacity as Secretary of Housing and Urban Development ("HUD") and Stephanie Dickson in connection with Carmel's judicial foreclosure and declaratory judgment action.

This dispute focuses on the reach of a Texas Uniform Commercial Code (UCC) fixture filing and subsequent efforts to foreclose on a lien arising from Carmel's financing of a water treatment system installed in a house. Carmel contends that its security interest and the accompanying lien extended to the real property. According to Carmel, it has "a super-priority lien on the Property" that became "superior to the existing mortgage on the property and was not extinguished" by a subsequent foreclosure. According to HUD and Dickson, Carmel's fixture filing did not create a lien on real property; they contend the fixture filing only entitled Carmel to repossess the water treatment system.

Because we agree with HUD and Dickson that Carmel's fixture filing did not create a lien on real property under the circumstances presented here, we affirm the trial court's summary judgment orders.

Background

Carmel financed the purchase and installation of a $5,990 water treatment system in April 2008, for a house in Katy, Harris County, Texas. The governing contract is a consumer credit document with a revolving charge agreement. This agreement provides as follows:

> 13. Security Agreement: This agreement is a Security Agreement covering the purchased products and/or services and title thereto shall not pass to you until all payments hereunder, including collection charges, and attorney's fees, if any, are fully paid. You further agree that all purchased products shall be kept and or installed on the premises described herein and shall not be removed therefrom without our written consent or our assignee's written consent and that you shall not make any material change therein without our consent.

The "product" is identified as "New Water Treatment System, Aqua Tech USA."

In the event of default, the agreement gives Carmel "the right to demand the entire amount owed on your account and be paid immediately. If we begin collection proceedings, you agree to pay all collection costs, court fees and attorney's fees in the amount permitted by law."

Carmel perfected its purchase money security interest in the water treatment system through an April 2008 fixture filing recorded in the real property records in Harris County. *See* Tex. Bus. & Com. Code Ann. § 9.502 (Vernon Supp. 2016). The fixture filing states as follows: "This Financing Statement covers the following collateral—New Whole House Water Treatment System Model: Aqua Tech USA Serial # 280023." Carmel recorded no other lien to secure payment for the water treatment system. At the time Carmel recorded its fixture filing, Bank of America held a first-mortgage lien on the house.

The homeowner subsequently defaulted on payment for the water treatment system. He also defaulted on his mortgage. Bank of America foreclosed in September 2010 and transferred its rights in the property to HUD in May 2013.

HUD notified Carmel in September 2013 that it would not pay the full amount owed to Carmel for the water treatment system; instead, HUD offered $1,000. Carmel declined the offer. HUD then removed the water treatment system from the house. Carmel refused to accept delivery when HUD attempted to return the system. HUD sold the house to Dickson in January 2014; at that time, the water treatment system no longer was attached to the house.

Carmel sued HUD in December 2013, seeking judicial foreclosure and a declaratory judgment; Carmel added Dickson as a defendant in 2014, after she bought the house from HUD. Carmel alleged that its fixture filing lien attached to the real property and so allowed Carmel to judicially foreclose on the real property to obtain payment for the water treatment system. Carmel asserted that Dickson took possession of the property subject to Carmel's lien. Carmel also maintained that HUD's removal of the water treatment system did not eliminate the lien because Carmel's lien already had attached by the time HUD removed the system.

The parties filed cross-motions for traditional summary judgment. The trial court decided all issues in favor of Dickson and HUD, and dismissed Carmel's claim against HUD. The trial court further ordered that Carmel take nothing on its claims against Dickson, and denied Carmel's request for a declaration that Carmel is "authorized to foreclose on the subject property." Additionally, the trial court awarded Dickson attorney's fees. This appeal timely followed. * * *

Analysis

In a single issue on appeal, Carmel argues that the trial court erred in granting summary judgment because (1) the fixture filing perfected Carmel's security interest and created a super-priority lien; (2) the fixture filing extended to the real property; (3) removing the fixture did not extinguish the lien; (4) Carmel's remedies are not limited to repossession of the fixture; and (5) homestead protection may not be asserted against a prior lien holder. Dickson and HUD argue that Carmel's fixture security interest applies only to the water treatment system itself as collateral.

Article 9 of the Texas Uniform Commercial Code (UCC) establishes a "comprehensive scheme for the regulation of security interests in personal property and fixtures." *See* Tex. Bus. & Com. Code Ann. § 9.101 cmt. 1 (Vernon 2011). It applies to transactions creating a "security interest in personal property or fixtures by contract." *Id.* § 9.109(a) (Vernon Supp. 2016).

A "security agreement" is "an agreement that creates or provides for a security interest." *Id.* § 9.102(a)(74) (Vernon Supp. 2016). "Security interest means an interest in personal property or fixtures which secures payment or performance of an obligation." *Id.* § 1.201(b)(35) (Vernon Supp. 2016). "Collateral" is "the property subject to a security interest . . . ." *Id.* § 9.102(a)(12). "Fixtures" are "goods that have become so related to particular real property that an interest in them arises under the real property law of the state in which the real property is situated." *Id.* § 9.102(a)(41). "Goods" are "all things that are movable when a security interest attaches. The term includes . . . fixtures." *Id.* § 9.102(a)(44).

The parties do not dispute that the water treatment system at issue here is a fixture under section 9.102(a)(41).

Carmel looks to sections 9.334(d) and 9.604(b) in arguing that its fixture filing securing payment for the water treatment system created a "super-priority lien" that attached not just to the fixture itself but also to the real property to which the fixture was attached.

Section 9.334 is entitled "Priority of Security Interests in Fixtures and Crops." Section 9.334(d) provides:

[A] perfected security interest in fixtures has priority over the conflicting interest of an encumbrancer or owner of the real property if the debtor has an interest of record in or is in possession of the real property and:

> (1) the security interest is a purchase-money security interest;

> (2) the interest of the encumbrancer or owner arises before the goods become fixtures; and

> (3) the security interest is perfected by a fixture filing before the goods become fixtures or within 20 days thereafter.

See Tex. Bus. & Com. Code Ann. § 9.334(d) (Vernon 2011). Carmel cites section 9.334(d)(1) for the proposition that "the fixture filing attached to the real property and obtained priority."

Section 9.604 is entitled "Procedure if Security Agreement Covers Real Property or Fixtures." Section 9.604(b) provides:

(b) Subject to Subsection (c), if a security agreement covers goods that are or become fixtures, a secured party may proceed:

> (1) under this subchapter; or

> (2) in accordance with the rights with respect to real property, in which case the other provisions of this subchapter do not apply.

(c) Subject to the other provisions of this subchapter, if a secured party holding a security interest in fixtures has priority over all owners and encumbrancers of the real property, the secured party, after default, may remove the collateral from the real property.

Tex. Bus. & Com. Code Ann. § 9.604(b) (Vernon 2011). Section 9.604(b) was added in 2001. According to the official UCC comment, "Subsection (b) . . . serves to overrule cases holding that a secured party's only remedy after default is the removal of the fixtures from the real property." *See id.* § 9.604(b) cmt. 3 (citing *Maplewood Bank & Trust v. Sears, Roebuck & Co.*, 265 N.J. Super. 25, 625 A.2d 537 (N.J. Super. Ct. App. Div. 1993)).

According to Carmel, section 9.604(b)(2) means its fixture filing allows it to enforce its interest under real property law against third parties. Carmel further asserts that "[s]uch real property remedy can only be judicial foreclosure because to hold otherwise would be to assume that there is no real property remedy."

Carmel's contentions bypass a threshold issue: What was the nature of the security interest established by Carmel's security agreement with the homeowner for the purchase and installation of the water treatment system?

"The security agreement defines the collateral to enable the debtor and other interested persons to identify the property that the creditor may claim as security." *Crow-Southland Joint Venture No. 1 v. N. Fort Worth Bank*, 838 S.W.2d 720, 723–24 (Tex. App.—Dallas 1992, writ denied). "Accordingly, the security agreement must describe the collateral." *Id.*; *see also* Tex. Bus. & Com. Code Ann. § 9.203 (Vernon 2011). "The financing statement is the instrument designed to notify third parties . . . that there may be an enforceable security interest in the property of the debtor." *Villa v. Alvarado State Bank*, 611 S.W.2d 483, 486–87 (Tex. Civ. App.—Waco 1981, no writ). "A proper security agreement is a requisite for attachment of the security interest . . . and a proper financing statement is a requisite for perfection of the security interest; both attachment and perfection are necessary for the enforcement of the . . . security interest against a third party . . . ." *Id.*

Carmel did not contract with the homeowner to create a security interest in real property in connection with the water treatment system; instead, Carmel contracted to create a security interest in the system itself. Carmel contends that its security agreement with the homeowner "merely references the [water treatment system] for contractual purposes" and does not limit Carmel's security interest "to only the [water treatment system]." This contention fails because the underlying security agreement contained no authorization to give the fixture lien holder a security interest in real property. Paragraph 13 states: "This agreement is a Security Agreement covering the purchased products and/or services and title thereto shall not pass to you until all payments hereunder, including collection charges, and attorney's fees, if any, are fully paid." The "purchased product[ ]" is the water treatment system.

Neither section 9.334(d) nor section 9.604(b)(2) operates independently to create a security interest in real property that the underlying security agreement did not authorize. These provisions address mechanisms for pursuing the security interest that the creditor and debtor agreed to create.

Section 9.334(d) addresses the priority of fixture liens when encumbrancers of real property have conflicting liens. Moreover, section 9.334(d) references a security interest in "fixtures," which, in turn, contemplates a financing statement that sets forth the requirements for goods that are to become fixtures. *See, e.g.*, Tex. Bus. & Com. Code Ann. § 9.502(a), (b) (A financing statement for goods that are to become fixtures must provide, among other information, "a description of the real property to which the collateral is related sufficient to give constructive notice of a mortgage under the law of this state if the description were contained in a record of the mortgage of the real property.") (Vernon Supp. 2016).

Carmel also misplaces its reliance on section 9.604(b)(2). This provision addresses the right of a holder of a fixture lien to utilize appropriate remedies, if any, available under state real property law to obtain payment. *See* Tex. Bus. & Com. Code Ann. § 9.604(b) cmt. 3 (Subsection (b) "makes clear that a security interest in fixtures may be enforced either under real-property law or under any of the applicable provisions of Part 6, including sale or other disposition either before or after removal of the fixtures . . . .). Section 9.604(b)(2) does not operate independently to expand the collateral covered by a Texas UCC fixture lien to include the whole of the real property to which the fixture is attached, and it does not itself create a security interest in the real property.

We overrule Carmel's issue insofar as it challenges the propriety of the trial court's grant of Dickson's summary judgment motion. . . .

NOTES

1.   *Castro* is an easy case and its interpretation of 9–604(b)(2) uncontroversial as far as it goes. Section 9–604(b)(2) allows the fixture financer with priority in the fixture to enforce its security interest against the fixture under real property law. It does not give the financer enforcement rights against assets other than the fixture. In particular, 9–604(b)(2) does not permit enforcement against the reality to which the fixture is attached. The subsection only gives the fixture financer access, as it were, to the enforcement rights that real property law gives it ("in accordance with the rights with respect to real property"). As the *Castro* court notes, 9–604(b)(2) "does not operate independently to expand the collateral covered by a Texas UCC fixture lien to include the whole of the real property to which the fixture is attached. . . " For the financer to have enforcement rights against the realty, its security agreement must cover the realty in addition to the fixture. Carmel's security agreement with the homeowner debtor didn't cover the realty to which the water treatment system was attached.

Section 9–604(b)(2)'s limited reach is confirmed by 9–604(a), which allows enforcement of the security interest against realty when the security agreement extends to both personal property and real property. The dispute over 9–604(b)(2)'s interpretation is over whether the subsection gives the fixture financer rights to share in the proceeds of a foreclosure sale of the realty to which the fixture has attached. Carmel had no rights in the reality that entitled it to compel a sale. Because Carmel sought to judicially foreclose on the realty to which the water treatment system once was attached, it was not asking to share in the proceeds of a foreclosure sale initiated by the mortgagee. Thus, the *Castro* court could deny Carmel's application without taking part in the controversy over 9–604(b)(2)'s interpretation.

2.   Another way of viewing the plight of the fixture claimant in a more favorable light is to recognize that its right to remove fixtures gives the claimant a bargaining position that might enable it to share in the proceeds of foreclosure without overcoming the limits on remedies provided by real estate law. Consider the position of a fixture financer with a security interest

in fixtures that is prior to a mortgagee under 9–334(d). Since the financer perfected its security interest by a fixture filing in the real estate records, a title examiner will note the fixture security interest and a purchaser at the foreclosure sale will take subject to the fixture financer's right to remove the fixture. See 9–604(c). If the mortgagee finds it more advantageous to sell a house with the fixture rather than the house without it, either the mortgagee and fixture financer or the mortgagee and the prospective purchaser may well find some basis for compromise. Section 9–604 can affect the compromise reached.

To see this, notice that 9–604 gives the fixture financer the right to remove the fixture or proceed "in accordance with [its] rights with respect to real property." 9–604(c), (b)(2). These are remedies provided by Article 9. However, 9–604 does not require the fixture financer to pursue legal remedies in order to satisfy its claim. An obvious alternative "remedy" is contractual: the mortgagee and the fixture financer can bargain ex post to allocate a portion of the proceeds of a foreclosure sale to the financer. Sections 9–604(b)(2) and (c) together, therefore, in effect create a default rule, which the parties can alter by agreement. The default rule is that the fixture financer can remove the fixture or proceed against the realty in accordance with real property law unless the parties agree otherwise.

This default rule may or may not be a good one. It depends on an estimate of the costs associated with operating under 9–604 as compared to feasible alternative rules. In estimating these costs, understand that the fixture financer and mortgagee's situation describes a bilateral monopoly. In order to obtain some of the foreclosure proceeds of a sale without removing the fixture or wrestling with mysteries of unresponsive real property law, the fixture financer has to reach agreement with the mortgagee. Correspondingly, to sell the realty with the fixture, the mortgagee must purchase the fixture financer's right to remove the fixture. Neither party can obtain its requirements from an alternative source. The trouble is that the transaction costs of reaching agreement are high where a bilateral monopoly exists, because competition isn't present to provide credible information about price. They may exceed the surplus realized from selling the realty with the fixture.

For instance, assume that a dual default occurs: the debtor defaults on its obligations to both its fixture financer and its mortgagee. Suppose too that the realty with the fixture can be sold for $100,000 and for $80,000 without it. Suppose too that the fixture, if removed, can be sold for $10,000 and that there are no costs associated with its removal. A $10,000 surplus therefore is realized if the parties can agree to sell the realty with the fixture ($100,000 less the sum of $80,000 if the realty is sold without the fixture plus $10,000 realized by the fixture financer from the sale of the fixture alone), but to do so the distributional issue of how it will be split must be solved. $80,000 plus one cent makes the mortgagee better off than if the realty is sold without the fixture, the fixture financer receiving $9,999.99 of the surplus. Alternatively, $10,000 plus one cent gives the fixture financer more than it would receive if it removes the fixture, $9,999.99 going to the mortgagee. Thus, the possible distributions that can be bargained for range between one cent and

$9,999.99. The allocation actually agreed to apparently depends on factors such as the relative bargaining positions of the parties, the psychological salience of a particular allocation and the likelihood of repeated bargains of a similar sort in the future. See generally Alvin E. Roth, Bargaining Experiments, in The Handbook of Experimental Economics 253–348 (John H. Kagel & Alvin E. Roth eds. 1995); Sidney Siegel & Lawrence E. Fouraker, Bargaining and Group Decision Making: Experiments in Bilateral Monopoly (1960). The transaction costs of negotiating a particular allocation can exceed $10,000.

CHAPTER 8

DEFAULT AND ENFORCEMENT

A. INTRODUCTION

A secured party has formidable remedies to enforce its security interest against a defaulting debtor under Part 6 of Article 9. It can take possession of tangible collateral such as equipment, sell it to satisfy the secured debt and hold the debtor for any deficiency. In the case of rights to payment such as accounts and chattel paper, it can collect directly from the account debtors the amounts they owe the debtor or sell the rights to payment. Thus, the secured party may deprive the business debtor of assets that it must have to operate its business and the consumer debtor of property essential to her lifestyle. In short, Article 9 allows a secured party to put a defaulting business debtor out of business in most cases and to lower the consumer debtor's standard of living by depriving her of such necessities of contemporary life as automobiles, furniture and appliances. Deficiency judgments allow the creditor to take the consumer debtor's unencumbered property and future earnings to the extent the property and earnings are nonexempt.

Frequently, when business and consumer debtors are threatened by secured parties with enforcement action, they turn to bankruptcy for protection. Chapter 9 of the casebook examines the impact of bankruptcy on secured transactions. Suffice it to say at this point that the Bankruptcy Code provides an alternative body of law on the enforcement of secured transactions.

Once the debtor files in bankruptcy, all creditor action to enforce a security interest is automatically stayed and brought under the control of the bankruptcy court. The secured party is no longer free to repossess collateral and conduct its own foreclosure sale; it must seek the approval of the court before doing so. In a liquidation bankruptcy, the trustee in bankruptcy will sell the debtor's assets and distribute proceeds of the sale to creditors having claims against the estate, with secured claims receiving priority. When the debtor has no equity in property subject to a secured claim, the bankruptcy court may abandon the property to the debtor and allow the secured party to proceed to foreclose under Article 9 rules. If the debtor is proceeding under Chapter 11 to reorganize a business, under Chapter 12 to adjust the debts of a farm family, or under Chapter 13 to rehabilitate an individual, the secured party may be completely barred from retaking its collateral. If the debtor's reorganization or rehabilitation plan calls for the collateral to be retained, the plan will promise payments to the secured party, subject to court approval, that compensate it for the loss of its right to repossess and foreclose on the collateral. Thus, the debtor's petition in bankruptcy changes the rules of enforcement of security interests drastically. This

Chapter describes the rules governing the enforcement of a security interest outside of bankruptcy.

B. DEFAULT

1. MEANING OF DEFAULT

The event that triggers a secured party's rights to enforce its security interest under 9–601(a) is the debtor's default. Article 9 does not define default. The definition of default instead is left to the parties' agreement. See Comment 3 to 9–601. This makes sense. The range of secured transactions suitable for different debtors and their lenders is wide, as are their terms. A statutory definition of default that could accommodate the variety of secured transactions therefore is likely to be either so abstract as to be vacuous or, if more specific, inefficient for some of them. In addition, the information needed to verify whether a statutorily defined event of default occurred might be unavailable to a court or other third party. For both reasons, as with the other terms in a security agreement, the parties to it are best positioned to define the events that constitute default.

The great variety of commercial and consumer transactions falling within Article 9's broad scope yields almost infinite variations in the kinds of events that the security agreement may define as defaults. In all instances, agreements make failure to meet required payments a default. Other commonly found events of default are the death, dissolution, insolvency or bankruptcy of the debtor, and the debtor's breach or failure to perform any of the agreements, covenants, representations, or warranties contained in the agreement. See Accounts Receivable/Loan Agreement ¶ 9.1 (Events of Default), Appendix I. If the collateral is tangible personal property, the debtor will typically agree to insure the collateral, maintain it in good condition, not remove or transfer the collateral, and not permit its loss, theft, damage, or destruction, or levy, seizure, or attachment. See Accounts Receivable/Loan Agreement ¶ 6.5 (Taxes and Premiums), ¶ 6.6 (Insurance), and ¶ 7 (Negative Covenants), Appendix I. If the collateral is accounts, the debtor may affirm that it owns all accounts free and clear of any claims of others, that the account debtor has accepted delivery of the goods giving rise to the account, and that all accounts are binding obligations of the account debtor. See Accounts Receivable/Loan Agreement ¶ 1.21 (Eligible Accounts), Appendix 1. In commercial lending transactions, events of default may include the debtor's failure to maintain net worth or working capital ratios or any other material adverse change in the debtor's financial position. See Accounts Receivable/Loan Agreement ¶ 6.11 (Financial Tests), Appendix I.

If the creditor is concerned that its enumeration of specific events of default is not adequate to protect against unforeseen occurrences that might impair the debtor's prospect of payment, it may contract for the right to declare a default whenever it deems itself insecure. See 1–309. The CNB form provides: "Notwithstanding any other provisions of this Agreement, upon the occurrence of any event, action or inaction by Borrower, or if any action or inaction is threatened which CNB reasonably believes will materially affect the value of the Collateral, CNB may take such legal actions as it deems necessary to protect the Collateral, including, but not limited to, seeking injunctive relief and the appointment of a receiver, whether an Event of Default or Potential Event of Default has occurred under this Agreement." Accounts Receivable/Loan Agreement ¶ 9.4 (Additional Remedies), Appendix I.

A provision frequently included in loan agreements is an "acceleration clause." The clause makes the entire principal and accrued interest due on default. The Loan Agreement ¶ 9.3 (CNB's Remedies) gives CNB the right on an event of default to declare the principal and accrued interest due. Acceleration clauses alter the legal rule otherwise applicable to the parties' rights on default. Unless the parties agree otherwise, that rule gives the lender the right to recover only for its loss resulting from the debtor's failure to make the required interest payment. The debtor's breach does not give the lender the right to the immediate payment of the outstanding principal. Because the debtor's failure to make an interest payment or other breach increases the risk that it will not pay the principal when due, lenders often reserve the right to call the entire loan due on an event of default. Some acceleration clauses make the entire loan in these circumstances due automatically. A lawyer risks legal malpractice by omitting an acceleration clause in a loan agreement.

In failing to define default, Article 9 leaves for resolution by agreement the crucial issue of when a creditor may proceed against the collateral. As mentioned, in commercial transactions seizure of the collateral may effectively close the debtor's business. In consumer cases, repossession of the debtor's automobile, furniture, or appliances may alter drastically the debtor's standard of living. In most instances, economic considerations restrain creditors from proceeding against collateral as other than a last resort, utilized only after all other collection efforts by way of workout arrangements have failed. Creditors understandably prefer payment from debtors, even though delayed, to the expense of foreclosing on collateral.

In leaving the definition of default to the agreement of the parties, Article 9 assumes that debtors and creditors can best look after their own interests. However, the consumer movement of the 1960s and 1970s rejected this assumption in consumer transactions on the ground that there was a disparity in bargaining position between creditors and consumer debtors. For example, § 5.109 of the Uniform Consumer Credit Code (1974) defines default as follows:

An agreement of the parties to a consumer credit transaction with respect to default on the part of the consumer is enforceable only to the extent that:

(1) the consumer fails to make a payment as required by agreement; or

(2) the prospect of payment, performance, or realization of collateral is significantly impaired; the burden of establishing the prospect of significant impairment is on the creditor.

Only a dozen states have adopted the UCCC, either in its original or revised versions. State consumer protection legislation has for the most part not regulated contractual definitions of default.

2. WAIVER AND ESTOPPEL

A secured party's enforcement remedies arise only after the debtor's default. But what if the secured party has not insisted on the debtor's compliance with the terms of the agreement? The secured party's post-default conduct can be interpreted in two ways, both adverse to it. One interpretation is that the debtor's actions were part of a course of dealing, understood under 1–303 as an element of the parties' agreement. 1–303(a), (d). As part of a course of dealing, the debtor's actions don't constitute a default. The other, more plausible interpretation is that the secured party's post-default conduct constitutes waiver of the debtor's default. Litigation on the waiver issue has flourished and secured parties have attempted to deal with the problem by including nonwaiver clauses in the agreement like the one quoted in the case below. Comment 3 to 9–601 states that Article 9 takes no position on the kind of conduct that constitutes waiver or the effect of nonwaiver clauses. Hence, case law under former Article 9 is still good precedent. The following case is a good example of the trend of authority on this issue.

Moe v. John Deere Co.

Supreme Court of South Dakota, 1994
516 N.W.2d 332

■ MOSES, CIRCUIT JUDGE.

This is an appeal by Ted Moe (Moe) from a summary judgment granted by Third Judicial Circuit Court in favor of John Deere Company (Deere) and Day County Implement Company (Implement). We reverse.

Facts

On September 29, 1983, Moe bought a farm tractor from Day County Equipment in Watertown, South Dakota. He purchased a John Deere D8850 for a cash price of $121,268. In financing the transaction, Moe traded in two old tractors for the amount of $77,543 and agreed to pay the $59,802 difference in five equal installments of $11,960 each due on

October 1st for the years 1984, 1985, 1986, 1987 and 1988. After the contract was completed it was assigned to Deere on September 30, 1983.

Moe was two months late in paying his first installment. Rather than paying $11,960 on October 1, 1984, Moe paid $12,212 on December 3, 1984. On October 1, 1985, Moe was again unable to timely pay his second installment. Deere waived full payment and extended the time in which Moe was to make this payment. On January 13, 1986, Moe made a partial payment in the amount of $6,200, over three months late. Moe and Deere agreed that Moe was to pay a second amount on March 1, 1986 in the amount of $6,350 to complete the second installment. On March 10, 1986, Deere sent a notice to Moe indicating that Moe's second installment was past due and that he had until March 20, 1986 to pay $6,389 to bring his account current. Again Moe missed this payment deadline.

Deere did not follow up on the delinquent payment until a representative from Deere contacted Moe sometime in May or the first part of June 1986, over seven months after the second installment was originally due. Deere's representative and Moe agreed that Moe would pay $2,000 of the $6,389 plus interest owing to Deere and Deere would allow Moe to pay the balance when he started to harvest. Deere's representative and Moe failed to specify the due date for either the $2,000 payment or when the balance was due. Moe had no further conversations with the representative from Deere about the $2,000 until after Deere repossessed the tractor on July 30, 1986.

Moe, who was in Oklahoma at the time of repossession, did not receive any notice from Deere's representative that the tractor was going to be repossessed because his payments were delinquent. Deere reassigned Moe's contract to Implement following the repossession. On August 1, 1986, Deere mailed from Minneapolis, Minnesota a certified letter dated July 31, 1986 to Moe which indicated that Deere "[found] it necessary to gain possession of the equipment involved." This letter apparently was returned to Deere undelivered to Moe. Thus, Deere hand-addressed a new letter and sent it to Moe who picked it up on August 18, 1986. The letter indicated:

> We intend to reassign your contract to the above named dealer. Once we reassign it, two weeks from the date of this letter, you will contact them on all matters concerning the disposition of the equipment or the amount owed under the contract. They intend to dispose of said collateral by public or private sale. If you wish to redeem this equipment, you must pay to John Deere Company $37,591 plus any expenses incurred from this repossession, in cash certified funds, before we reassign the contract.

> We hope you will be able to pay this amount within the prescribed period. If you have any questions regarding this matter please contact us. M.K. Mehus, Manager Financial Services.

Implement sold the tractor on August 19, 1986 for $44,000. Implement paid Deere in full on the contract and applied the proceeds to the debt and turned over the excess proceeds to Moe's lender by mailing two (2) checks totaling $2,616 to the Farmers and Merchants Bank on December 1, 1986.

Moe sued Deere and Implement on the following causes of action: (1) wrongful repossession; (2) fraudulent repossession; (3) commercially unreasonable sale; and (4) failure to account for the surplus.

Deere moved for partial summary judgment on the third and fourth issues of commercially unreasonable sale and failure to account for surplus. The trial court granted Deere's motion. Then, Deere moved for summary judgment on the first and second issues of wrongful repossession and fraudulent repossession. On February 5, 1993, the trial court issued an order granting Deere's summary judgment motion on both issues. Moe appeals. * * *

We recognized in First Nat. Bank of Black Hills v. Beug, 400 N.W.2d 893, 896 (S.D.1987), that "[t]he term 'default' is not defined in the Uniform Commercial Code, thus we must look to other sources for a definition." Id. At 895. Then, we turned to hornbook law for a definition of default:

> "Default" triggers the secured creditor's rights under Part Five of Article Nine. But what is "default?" Article Nine does not define the word; instead it leaves this to the parties and to any scraps of common law lying around. Apart from the modest limitations imposed by the unconscionability doctrine and the requirement of good faith, default is "whatever the security agreement says it is."

Id. At 896 (quoting J. White and R. Summers, Uniform Commercial Code § 26–22 at 1085–86 (2d ed. 1980)). . . .

Here, the promissory note provided a definition of default:

> The borrower shall be in default upon the occurrence of any one or more of the following events: (1) the Borrower shall fail to pay, when due, any amount required hereunder, or any other indebtedness of the borrower to the Lender of any third parties; (2) the Borrower shall be in default in the performance of any covenant or obligation under the line of credit or equivalent agreement for future advances (if applicable) or any document or agreement related thereto; (3) any warranty or representation made by the Borrower shall prove false or misleading in any respect; (4) the Borrower or any Guarantor of this promissory note shall liquidate, merge dissolve, terminate its existence, suspend business operations, die (if individual), have a receiver appointed for all or any part of its property, make an assignment for the benefit of creditors, or file or have filed against it any petition under any existing or future

bankruptcy or insolvency law; (5) any change that occurs in the condition or affairs (financial or otherwise) of the Borrower or any Guarantor of this promissory note which, in the opinion of the Lender, impairs, the Lender's security or increases its risk with respect to this promissory note or (6) an event of default shall occur under any agreements intended to secure the repayment of this promissory note. Unless prohibited by law, the Lender may, at its option, declare the entire unpaid balance of principal and interest immediately due and payable without notice or demand at any time after default as such term is defined in this paragraph.

Technically, there was a breach of the security agreement and the promissory note when Moe did not make his payment on October 1, 1984, but instead paid it on December 3, 1984. One could find Moe in default, and under § 9–503, Deere would have had a right to repossess the tractor. However, Deere's right to a default or remedies under breach of contract can be modified or waived by the conduct of the parties.

The trial court's memorandum opinion indicated that "The terms of the written contract should control. Further the 'course of dealing' between the parties is not persuasive." However, here there is a question of fact. Did the oral statements and conduct of the parties modify the written agreement? In Alaska Statebank v. Fairco, 674 P.2d 288 (Alaska 1983), the issue was if the parties' oral statements and conduct between September 15, 1978 and November 6, 1978 modified the written agreement so that pre-possession notice was required. The court held:

[M]odification of a written contract may be effected either through subsequent conduct or oral agreements. Whether a modification has occurred is a question of fact. The superior court found that the parties had agreed to such modification, "[g]iven the course of dealings between the parties. . . ."

Id. At 292 (quoting Nat. Bank of Alaska v. J.B.L. & K. of Alaska, Inc., 546 P.2d 579, 586–87 (Alaska 1976)). * * *

The record reveals through affidavits and depositions that the oral statements and conduct of the parties herein between October 1, 1984 and July 30, 1986 appear to modify the written agreement. Deere sent notice to Moe that he had until March 20, 1986 to pay $6,389 including late charges. Moe admits that in May or the first week of June 1986 he agreed to pay the March installment in two parts. He agreed to pay $2,000 with the balance due in August 1986 when he commenced his wheat harvest. There was no date certain by which Moe was to pay the $2,000. In determining if there was a default on the part of Moe in complying with this contract, all statements and conduct of the parties are essential in determining whether there was an oral modification or waiver of the promissory note or security agreement by John Deere. * * *

The second issue that needs to be addressed is whether the "non-waiver clause" is enforceable in this contract. Deere's brief refers to this clause as an "anti-waiver" clause but we will refer to it as a "non-waiver" clause. . . . The security agreement between Moe and Deere contained the following provisions:

> In the event of default (as defined on the reverse side hereof), holder may take possession of the Goods and exercise any other remedies provided by law.

> This contract shall be in default if I (we) shall fail to pay any installment when due. . . .

> In any such event (default) the holder may immediately and without notice declare the entire balance of this contract due and payable together with reasonable expenses incurred in realizing on the security interest granted hereunder, including reasonable attorney's fees.

> Waiver or condonation of any breach or default shall not constitute a waiver of any other or subsequent breach or default.

We now turn to other jurisdictions' interpretations of the "non-waiver" clause. Courts have adopted two basic rules for interpreting situations where repeated late payments have been accepted by a creditor who has the contractual (i.e., "non-waiver" clauses) and the statutory right (i.e., § 9–503) to repossess the collateral without notice. Some courts have held that the acceptance of late payments does not waive or otherwise affect the right of a creditor to repossess without notice after subsequent late payment defaults. . . . Other courts have imposed a duty on the creditor to notify the debtor that strict compliance with the time for payment will be required in the future or else the contract remedies may be invoked. . . .

Deere urges us to adopt the position that the acceptance of late payments does not waive or otherwise affect the right of a creditor to repossess without notice after subsequent late payment defaults stating to do so would mean that the "non-waiver" clause is a nullity.

A majority of states who have considered the issue adhere to the general rule that "a secured party who has not insisted upon strict compliance in the past, who has accepted late payments as a matter of course, *must*, before he may validly rely upon such a clause to declare a default and effect repossession, *give notice* to the debtor. . . that strict compliance with the terms of the contract will be demanded henceforth if repossession is to be avoided." [Nevada National Bank v.] Huff, 582 P.2d 364, 369 [Nev.1978] (citations omitted) (emphasis in original).

The basis for imposing this duty on the secured party is that the secured party is estopped from asserting his contract rights because his conduct has induced the debtor's justified reliance in believing that late payments were acceptable. § 1–103[(b)] preserves the law of estoppel. The acts which induced reliance are the repeated acceptance of late payments. The reliance is evidenced by the continual pattern of irregular and late payments.

The debtor has the right to rely on the continuation of the course of performance and that right to rely is sufficient to satisfy the reliance element. This right to rely is supported by the policy of the Uniform Commercial Code which encourages the continual development of "commercial practices through, custom, usage, and agreement between the parties." See § 1–102(2) [1–103(a)(2)]. South Dakota's adaptation of the Uniform Commercial Code is found in Title 57A of the South Dakota Code. The purpose of Title 57A is found in § 1–102 [1–103] and states in pertinent part as follows:

> (1) This title shall be liberally construed and applied to promote its underlying purposes and polices.
>
> (2) Underlying purposes and polices of this title are
>
> > (a) To simplify, clarify and modernize the law governing commercial transactions;
> >
> > (b) To permit the continued expansion of commercial practices, through custom, usage and agreement of the parties;

§ 1–102(1)–(2) [1–103(a)(1)–(2)]. The Uniform Commercial Code should be liberally construed and applied to promote its underlying purposes and policies.

Adopting the rule that a creditor must give pre-possession notice upon modification of a contract results in both the debtor and the creditor being protected. The debtor would be protected from surprise and from a damaging repossession by being forewarned that late payments would no longer be acceptable. Likewise, the creditor would be protected utilizing the device of "one letter." The creditor can totally preserve his remedies so that if the account continues in default, repossession could be pursued as provided in the contract without further demand or notice. It is recognized that this rule does place the creditor in a slightly worse position because if a creditor sends out a letter to preserve his rights and then once again accepts late payments another notice would be required. The second notice would be required because the acceptance of the late payment after the initial letter could again act as a waiver of the rights asserted in the letter.

We hold that the repeated acceptance of late payments by a creditor who has the contractual right to repossess the property imposes a duty on the creditor to notify the debtor that strict compliance with the contract terms will be required before the creditor can lawfully repossess the collateral.

The dispositive issue is if the plaintiff was in default. Whether a default exists is a factual question not properly resolved on a motion for summary judgment. . . . We reverse this order and the judgment of the circuit court and remand for trial.

NOTES

1. In Gaynor v. Union Trust Co., 582 A.2d 190 (Conn.1990) (Peters, C.J.), the court enforced a nonwaiver clause in a consumer repossession case. In this case, the debtors had repeatedly been late with their payments. In April, the secured party warned the debtors by letter that their defaults put them at the risk of repossession. In early July, the debtors agreed to make payments of $300 at the beginning of each month to make their account current. They made the July payment but missed the payment due on August 1; the secured party repossessed on August 15. The contract said: "Waiver of Notice. If you do not repay this loan when it becomes due or do not keep your other promises in this agreement, we do not have to make a protest or give you any notice." Another clause said: "Delay in Enforcement. We can delay enforcing any of our rights without losing them. If on any occasion we should waive one of our rights, it does not necessarily mean that we will waive that right in the future. We will still have that right." In holding for the secured party, the court said:

> The essence of the [debtors'] contention is that no creditor should be allowed to invoke formal contractual provisions that a consumer debtor had reason to believe would not be enforced. Whatever the merits of this legal principle might be in the abstract, it cannot prevail in the light of two crucial findings of fact by the trial court in this case. One finding is that the repossession was precipitated by the [secured party's] failure to receive a $300 payment that the [debtors] had expressly agreed to pay on August 1, 1987, in accordance with the work-out plan to make their indebtedness more current. This case therefore cannot be characterized as one in which a creditor without warning retakes goods following its silent acceptance of one or more belated installment payments on the part of the debtor. The second finding is that the [debtors] were not lulled into any misapprehensions about the jeopardy that they faced because of their lateness in making payments. We conclude, accordingly, that the defendant had the contractual authority to repossess the plaintiff's car.

Id. at 196.

2. See the nonwaiver clause in Accounts Receivable/Loan Agreement ¶ 10.3 (Cumulative Rights and No Waiver), Appendix I.

PROBLEM

Your creditor client has heard about decisions like *Moe* but she finds it hard to turn down late payments from financially stressed debtors. Something is better than nothing. She asks you to suggest a procedure for dealing with such debtors that will not result in the kind of trouble in which Deere found itself. What is your advice?

C. Enforcement

1. Cumulative Remedies

Most overdue debts are collected—if they are collected at all—without litigation through negotiation and settlement. But it is fair to assume that debtors are more amenable to voluntary repayment because of the existence of powerful legal remedies that creditors can inflict on them if they refuse payment. And, increasingly, in an information world the ability of unpaid creditors to affect the credit score of debtors by reporting defaults is a powerful stimulant to voluntary repayment.

If voluntary payments are not forthcoming, Article 9 offers secured parties a broad array of enforcement remedies that are summarized in 9–601. Section 9–601(a)(1) recognizes that the secured party can disregard its in rem rights against its collateral and proceed outside Article 9 to obtain an in personam judgment against the debtor as though the debt were unsecured. "Debtor" is defined as the person who owns the collateral in 9–102(a)(28); "obligor" is defined as the person who owes the debt in 9–102(a)(59). In most cases the debtor and the obligor are the same person. Accordingly, for convenience, this person is referred to as the "debtor" unless the reference is only to the obligor.

The secured party may sue the debtor on the obligation and obtain a judgment for the amount of the debt, and may collect the judgment by whatever means available under state law. For instance, as a judgment creditor the secured party may obtain a writ of execution on the debtor's nonexempt assets, real or personal, selling the property at a public sale presided over by a judicial officer, and applying the sale proceeds to satisfaction of the judgment. Other common judgment satisfaction remedies are levying on the debtor's deposit accounts and garnishing an individual debtor's wages. If a secured creditor levies on the collateral pursuant to its judgment against the debtor, 9–601(e) provides that the lien of the levy relates back to the earlier of the date of filing or perfection of the security interest. Thus, the secured party enjoys the priority of the first-to-file-or-perfect rule with respect to property that is collateral.

The disadvantage of using judicial process is that court proceedings may be expensive and time-consuming. The advantage is that all of the debtor's nonexempt property can be levied on, not just the collateral, and the judgment obtained will allow the judgment creditor to sell off the debtor's property piecemeal without further court proceedings until the judgment debt is satisfied, with any deficiency remaining serving as the basis for further executions against the debtor's subsequently obtained property. Foreclosure by judicial sale avoids having to comply with the commercial reasonableness standard applicable to all Article 9 dispositions. Moreover, the judgment creditor can buy at its own judicial sale, as can foreclosing creditors in most nonjudicial dispositions.

In the great majority of cases, secured parties choose to proceed against the collateral by the extra-judicial procedures authorized by Article 9, which are cheap and fast. These procedures fall within two general categories: sale or other disposition of the collateral and collection of rights to payment. The two prototypic cases are: (1) under 9–610 the secured party may make a commercially reasonable sale of collateral consisting of goods at either a public or private sale and, under 9–615, apply the proceeds of the sale to satisfaction of the obligation secured by the security interest, with any surplus going to the debtor; or (2) in the case of a right to payment, such as an account, the secured party may proceed in a commercially reasonable manner under 9–607 to collect the amount owing by notifying the account debtor to make payment to the secured party. In the alternative, instead of disposing of the collateral, the secured party may opt to accept the collateral in full or partial satisfaction of the amount owing under 9–620 but only if the debtor consents to the acceptance in the manner prescribed by the statute.

It is worth emphasizing that secured parties can proceed to repossess and sell collateral or collect rights to payment without going to court. The secured party, not judicial officers, conducts the sale of property or collects the payments on accounts and other rights to payment. Not until the secured party has established that the debtor is liable for a deficiency does it have to bring a lawsuit in order to obtain a judgment for the amount of the deficiency. An advantage of control as a method of perfection, where possible, is that enforcement of the security interest on the debtor's default does not require judicial assistance or the debtor's cooperation. To repossess the collateral, the secured party in control need only order the relevant third party to act on its instructions with respect to the collateral.

A question that has traditionally arisen in both real and personal property security law is whether a creditor can use both avenues of recovery—money judgment and extra-judicial sale—simultaneously so long as only one satisfaction is obtained, or whether, once the creditor chooses one track it has, by the doctrine of election of remedies, waived any right to proceed by the other. Courts, and to some extent legislatures, have sometimes reasoned that if a creditor has encumbered a debtor's asset with a security interest, fairness requires that it must proceed first against that asset in a single action instead of levying on the debtor's unencumbered assets which are available to satisfy the claims of the debtor's other creditors. Or, if a secured creditor has proceeded by the money judgment route, it waives its security interest in the debtor's assets. These are called variously "one action," "security first," or "election of remedies" rules for enforcement. The rules, where codified by statute, usually are limited to real property collateral. Most courts find that the election of remedies doctrine does not apply to personal property. Article 9 addresses this question in 9–601(c): "The rights under subsections (a) and (b) are cumulative and may be exercised simultaneously." State law "election of remedies" rules therefore do not apply where Article 9 governs the enforcement of security interests.

Okefenokee Aircraft, Inc. v. PrimeSouth Bank

Court of Appeals of Georgia, 2009
676 S.E.2d 394

■ BERNES, JUDGE.

Okefenokee Aircraft, Inc. ("OAI") and Joseph E. Rimes III appeal from a grant of summary judgment to PrimeSouth Bank (the "Bank"), a secured creditor that brought an action for money judgment on the note while holding the collateral pledged by appellants. We conclude that a secured creditor can retain a debtor's collateral while seeking an independent action for money judgment and therefore affirm.

The following facts are undisputed. On or around September 9, 2005, the Bank issued a loan to OAI for the purchase of an airplane. OAI executed a promissory note (the "Note") in favor of the Bank in the principal amount of $161,306.25 plus interest. Rimes executed a personal guarantee on the Note, guaranteeing the payment of sums due according to the terms set forth in the Note. The Note was secured by the airplane being purchased.

OAI defaulted on the Note. The Bank made a demand for payment on both appellants, but neither paid the sums due. The Bank then repossessed the airplane securing the Note. Instead of first disposing of the collateral and seeking a deficiency judgment, however, the Bank held the collateral and sued appellants to enforce the Note, seeking a money judgment for the loan principal and interest, plus attorney fees.

The Bank moved for summary judgment, arguing that the facts of the case were undisputed and that the only issue for the trial court's consideration was OAI's admitted default and non-payment of the indebtedness under the Note; therefore, the Bank argued that it was entitled to the relief sought as a matter of law. The Bank considered irrelevant its repossession of the collateral to the fact that it was entitled to a money judgment against the appellants for the amount due under the Note.

In response, appellants did not deny defaulting on the Note nor did they dispute the amount due under the Note. Instead, they argued that the Bank was not entitled to a money judgment while it remained in possession of the collateral securing the Note. They further argued that any proceeds from the sale of the airplane must be applied toward the underlying debt and that the Bank's failure to dispose of the airplane once it had been repossessed created a genuine issue of material fact as to whether the Bank acted in a commercially reasonable manner as required by the Uniform Commercial Code.

The trial court agreed with the Bank and, given that the existence of the loan, the default, and the guarantee were undisputed, granted its motion for summary judgment. The trial court specifically held that "[t]he potential breach of [the Bank's] obligations with regard to the collateral is not a defense to a suit on the [Note]." This appeal followed.

Appellants contend that the trial court erred in granting summary judgment to the Bank for two reasons. First, they assert that a genuine issue of material fact exists as to whether the Bank's conduct in repossessing the collateral and failing to dispose of it was commercially reasonable. Second, they argue that a genuine issue of material fact exists as to the amount of appellants' indebtedness until such time as the Bank sells or otherwise lawfully disposes of the collateral and credits the net proceeds of the sale to the indebtedness.

Appellants' arguments are misplaced. The present lawsuit dealt only with the Note that OAI signed and that Rimes guaranteed; the undisputed facts established both the appellants' default in payment and the amount of the underlying debt. Appellants did not file a counterclaim or otherwise present any evidence that the Bank's handling or disposition of the airplane was commercially unreasonable beyond asserting that the Bank's act of repossessing and not disposing of the collateral itself gave rise to a factual issue as to the reasonableness of its conduct. But, as illustrated below, the applicable statutory and case law authorizes the Bank to simultaneously repossess and retain its collateral while at the same time seeking a money judgment for the full amount of the outstanding debt.

The Uniform Commercial Code provides that once default has occurred, a secured creditor is authorized to take or retain possession of the collateral. 9–609(a)(1). The secured creditor may then "reduce a claim to judgment, foreclose, or otherwise enforce the claim, security interest, or agricultural lien by any available judicial procedure." 9–601(a). Indeed, "[n]othing in the Code prohibits the creditor in possession of the goods from proceeding in a judicial action on the note." *McCullough v. Mobiland,* 139 Ga.App. 260, 263(2), 228 S.E.2d 146 (1976). See *ITT Terryphone Corp. v. Modems Plus,* 171 Ga.App. 710, 711–712(2), 320 S.E.2d 784 (1984). To the contrary, the Code expressly states that the rights and remedies afforded a secured creditor "are cumulative and may be exercised simultaneously." 9–601(c).

As we have previously held:

> It is of course basic law that the purpose of collateral is to secure the creditor and increase his chance of recovery in the case of default. The existence of a security interest in no way affects the existence of the debt. It merely provides the secured party with an immediate source of recovery in addition to the standard remedies of an unsecured creditor. The intent of the [C]ode was to broaden the options open to a creditor after default rather than to limit them under the old theory of election of remedies.

(Citation and punctuation omitted.)

Here, the Bank is attempting to reduce its claim to judgment; it is not seeking to recover a deficiency judgment. . . . As stated above, the law allows a secured creditor in possession of a debtor's collateral to employ a number of different remedial steps until the debt is satisfied. Consequently, "[the Bank's] election to repossess the collateral and then to file suit on the [Note] without first disposing of the collateral was not improper under the terms of the [Note] or of the Uniform Commercial Code." *ITT Terryphone Corp.*, 171 Ga.App. at 712(2), 320 S.E.2d 784. Nor did the Bank's repossession of the collateral impact the amount of the OAI's outstanding debt under the Note.

OAI is absolutely correct that the Uniform Commercial Code imposes certain duties upon a secured creditor in possession of collateral, including a mandate that the creditor act in a commercially reasonable manner.[3] As this Court has previously explained:

> It would be unfair to allow a creditor to deprive the debtor of the possession and use of the collateral for an unreasonable length of time and not apply the asset or the proceeds from its sale toward liquidation of the debt. Moreover, it would be equally unfair to allow a creditor to take possession at all, if the creditor never intended to dispose of the security. For during the period that the debtor is deprived of possession he may have been able to make profitable use of the asset or may have gone to far greater lengths than the creditor to sell. Once a creditor has possession he must act in a commercially reasonable manner toward sale, lease, proposed retention, where permissible, or other disposition. If such disposition is not feasible, the asset must be returned, still subject, of course, to the creditor's security interest. *To the extent the creditor's inaction results in injury to the debtor, the debtor has a right of recovery.*

(Citation and punctuation omitted; emphasis in original.) *ITT Terryphone Corp.*, 171 Ga.App. at 712(3), 320 S.E.2d 784.

Thus, if the Bank fails to proceed in a commercially reasonable manner with respect to its handling of the repossessed collateral, OAI may have a viable cause of action for damages. But the questions of whether the Bank acted commercially reasonable and/or whether and in what amount OAI will owe the Bank in deficiency if and when the Bank disposes of the collateral are not presently before us. . . . The only issue before this Court is whether the Bank is entitled to a money judgment in the full amount of the indebtedness of the Note, and the above-cited

---

[3] See, e.g., 9–207(a) ("[A] secured party shall use reasonable care in the custody and preservation of collateral in the secured party's possession."); 9–610 (if a secured party chooses to dispose of collateral, "[e]very aspect of a disposition of collateral, including the method, manner, time, place, and other terms, must be commercially reasonable.").

statutory and case law directs us to answer that question in the positive. . . . Accordingly, we affirm the judgment of the trial court.

NOTES

1. The court decides that Bank can sue on the note after it has taken possession of the collateral. 9–601(c). But what if Bank's action on the note drags on for months; can debtor get its airplane back? Surely it is depreciating. See 9–610(b). Comment 5 to 9–601 explains that "[p]ermitting the simultaneously exercise of remedies under subsection (c) does not override any non-UCC law, including the law of tort and statutes regulating collection of debts, under which the simultaneous exercise of remedies in a particular case constitutes abusive behavior or harassment giving rise to liability." Conversion?

2. In the unusual case in which at the time of repossession a debtor has paid over 60% of an obligation secured by consumer goods, the secured party must dispose of the collateral within 90 days after repossession. 9–620(e)–(f).

2. REPOSSESSION

a. SELF-HELP REPOSSESSION

A secured creditor has a property right in collateral. The property right includes the right to repossess the collateral upon the debtor's default without judicial assistance. The right of extra-judicial self-help repossession set out in 9–609 is a traditional remedy in the United States. It is less often found in civil law systems and legal systems influenced by civil law. Louisiana law, for instance, does not permit self-help and has enacted 9–609 without a self-help option. La. R.S. § 10: 9–609. The prohibition on self-help is partly due to a concern about the risk of violence from its exercise. The risk of violence aside, the prohibition enhances judicial control over the transfer of property rights. To this extent the prohibition takes the transfer of property out of the hands of private parties and the agreements they reach. This legal difference with respect to self-help may reflect as much a political difference about the extent of state power as a difference in the assessment of the risk of violence accompanying extra-judicial self-help.

The revolution in creditor's remedies law occasioned by Sniadach v. Family Finance Corp., 395 U.S. 337 (1969) ("due process for debtors"), threatened the legality of self-help repossession. Since creditor groups cherished the remedy as one of their most important weapons—probably for its *in terrorem* effect on debtors—and debtor groups detested it as being subject to abuse, both sides threw maximum resources into a series of test cases that raged across the country throughout the 1970s. But the courts could find no state action in self-help repossessions and the creditors won all the battles in the federal appeals courts. The great debtor-creditor issue of the decade never reached the Supreme Court. See

William M. Burke & David J. Reber, State Action, Congressional Power and Creditors' Rights: An Essay on the Fourteenth Amendment, 47 S. Cal. L. Rev. 1 (1973); James R. McCall, The Past as Prologue: A History of the Right to Repossess, 47 S. Cal. L. Rev. 58 (1973).

PROBLEM

Debtor granted a security interest in its fishing boat to Bank to secure a loan. Bank was aware that Debtor was a lobster fisherman and that it was his practice to leave lobster pots at sea for several days. Debtor was behind in his payments, and Bank notified him in writing that he must come in and discuss with his loan officer at Bank ways of bringing his account current. When Debtor failed to respond to this notice, Bank repossessed the boat without notifying Debtor of its intent to do so. Debtor had several lobster pots at sea that were never recovered. Debtor sued Bank for conversion on the ground that the repossession was wrongful because he was entitled to notice of Bank's intention to repossess. Bank had not referred to the possibility of repossession in any of its prior communications with Debtor. Had he been given notice of the repossession he would have voluntarily surrendered possession after recovering his lobster pots. Is there any basis in 9–609 for a court to impose a duty on Bank to give notice of intention to repossess? Since there was no risk that Debtor would abscond with the fishing boat—such boats are hard to hide and slow to flee—should 1–304 be read to require that notice of repossession be given in any case in which there is no danger of a debtor's removing, concealing, or dissipating the collateral?

Some consumer protection statutes prevent the creditor from accelerating or repossessing until the debtor is notified of the right to cure a default within a stated number of days. See, e.g., Uniform Consumer Credit Code §§ 5.110–5.111 (1974); Wis. Stat. Ann. §§ 425.104–425.105 (1998).

b. BREACH OF PEACE

Under 9–609(b) a secured party may repossess without judicial process only if it can do so "without breach of the peace." The phrase is neither defined nor elaborated. The breadth and uncertainty of the meaning of this language, coupled with the potential for significant liability, have severely limited the use of self-help repossession by secured parties. In the great majority of cases in which the secured party retakes possession, it does so with the expressed consent of the debtor, who knows it is in default and wishes to avoid the heavy costs of judicial actions for possession. If the secured party cannot take possession without risking a breach of the peace, and the debtor will not voluntarily relinquish possession, it may have judicial officers seize possession under a replevin action or the like, with the costs passed on to the debtor under 9–608(a).

Under 9–609(a)(2), a secured creditor need not take possession of the collateral in order to sell it; it may render the collateral unusable and sell it on the debtor's premises. This procedure may be necessary in cases in which the collateral is bulky and removal is impractical or unduly expensive. See Comment 6. Section 9–609(c) authorizes a secured party to require a debtor in default to "assemble the collateral and make it available to the secured party at a place to be designated by the secured party which is reasonably convenient to both parties." Loan agreements invariably include provisions covering the right of self-help repossession, sale without removal, and assembly of the collateral. In reality, no matter what the statute or agreement says about the secured party's right to require the debtor to assemble the collateral at another place, the debtor's cooperation is needed; if the debtor is recalcitrant, it may have incurred further liability but the secured party may have to go to court to enforce its rights. The same may be true with respect to the secured party's efforts to conduct a sale on the debtor's premises.

If a breach of the peace occurs in a self-help repossession case, 9–625(b) subjects the secured party to liability for damages in the amount of any loss suffered by the debtor. In consumer transactions, 9–625(c)(2) provides for statutory damages "not less than the credit service charge plus 10 percent of the principal amount of the obligation or the time-price differential plus 10 percent of the cash price." The time-price differential is difference between the cash price and the credit price (the price charged for paying at a later date). It is the interest on the loan. In cases in which the consumer goods are expensive automobiles or boats, these damages can be substantial. As statutory minimum damages ("not less than"), they are available whether or not the consumer is injured by repossession that breaches the peace. Anecdotal evidence tends to show that a comparable provision under former Article 9 has rarely been used.

Debtors may seek recovery outside Article 9 for repossessions that result in a breach of the peace. Wrongful repossession is the tort of conversion, and Comment 3 to 9–625 recognizes that tort law supplements recovery for a breach of the peace under 9–609. The typically more generous statute of limitations in tort is attractive to debtors. More important, the potential for punitive damages is present if the repossessing party's conduct falls within whatever the law of the jurisdiction requires, e.g., malice, oppression, or fraud. Section 1–305(a) states that "penal damages" are not recoverable under the UCC unless specifically provided "or by other rule of law." Presumably, every jurisdiction has a body of law, whether judge-made or statutory, on punitive damages.

Case law has struggled with the meaning of the ancient term "breach of the peace." Courts note that the standard includes a risk of violence. See, e.g., Ford Motor Credit Co. v. Herring, 589 S.W.2d 584 (Ark.1979). The difficulty in the cases, of course, is to identify the circumstances in which the risk exists. Actual violence obviously breaches the peace. A risk of violence is harder to determine in two other circumstances. One involves trespass on the debtor's property. Case law finds that trespass by itself is insufficient to breach the peace. Case outcomes suggest that the proximity of the trespass to the home or business and whether the debtor has taken measures to secure the area are important factors in determining whether the trespass breaches the peace. The large body of case law on the subject finds that a secured party breaches the peace by entering an enclosed area without consent, such as a house, apartment, garage, office or enclosed area. No breach occurs with respect to unattended vehicles parked on streets or driveways. More difficult and unpredictable are instances in which the secured party recovers collateral on the debtor's property outside the debtor's house. The other, more frequent circumstance involves a verbal objection by the debtor to the removal of the collateral. Courts divide over whether, and what the sort of, objection is enough to forecast an ensuing risk of violence.

A growing body of case law finds that a secured creditor cannot avoid liability for breach of the peace by employing an independent contractor to serve as the repo agent. Its rationale is that the duty not to breach the peace is nondelegable. See, e.g., Lewis v. Nicholas Fin., Inc., 686 S.E.2d 468 (Ga. App.2009). And if the agent or independent contractor misbehaves, the secured party has even been held liable for punitive damages, e.g., Williamson v. Fowler Toyota, Inc., 956 P.2d 858 (Okla.1998). Hence, self-help repossession is used most commonly with respect to unattended motor vehicles parked on streets or in unenclosed areas. In other instances, if the debtor's consent to the retaking cannot be obtained, the creditor must proceed by judicial process.

PROBLEM

SP repossessed a bus in which it had a purchase-money security interest from Debtor who was in default. Debtor sued SP for wrongful repossession and alleged that: (i) the bus was parked in a fenced-in area with a "No Trespassing" sign in plain view; and (ii) In order to enter the lot, SP broke the lock on the entry gate. SP countered by stating that even if these allegations were true, its conduct was protected by a provision in the security agreement that said: "It shall be lawful for [SP] to take possession of the [collateral] at any time where it may be and to enter any premises without liability for trespass." The repossession took place at night and there was no threat of violence to any person. Does SP's conduct amount to a breach of the peace under 9–609? See 9–602(6) and 9–603. These facts are based on Wombles Charters, Inc. v. Orix Credit Alliance, Inc., 46 UCC Rep. Serv.2d 599 (S.D. N.Y.1999).

The following case addresses the issue of the legality of repossession of a vehicle when the owner is present.

Williams v. Ford Motor Credit Co.
United States Court of Appeals, Eighth Circuit, 1982
674 F.2d 717

■ BENSON, CHIEF JUDGE.

In this diversity action brought by Cathy A. Williams to recover damages for conversion arising out of an alleged wrongful repossession of an automobile, Williams appeals from a judgment notwithstanding the verdict entered on motion of defendant Ford Motor Credit Company (FMCC). In the same case, FMCC appeals a directed verdict in favor of third party defendant S & S Recovery, Inc. (S & S) on FMCC's third party claim for indemnification. We affirm the judgment n.o.v. FMCC's appeal is thereby rendered moot.

In July, 1975, David Williams, husband of plaintiff Cathy Williams, purchased a Ford Mustang from an Oklahoma Ford dealer. Although David Williams executed the sales contract, security agreement, and loan papers, title to the car was in the name of both David and Cathy Williams. The car was financed through the Ford dealer, who in turn assigned the paper to FMCC. Cathy and David Williams were divorced in 1977. The divorce court granted Cathy title to the automobile and required David to continue to make payments to FMCC for eighteen months. David defaulted on the payments and signed a voluntary repossession authorization for FMCC. Cathy Williams was informed of the delinquency and responded that she was trying to get her former husband David to make the payments. There is no evidence of any agreement between her and FMCC. Pursuant to an agreement with FMCC, S & S was directed to repossess the automobile.

On December 1, 1977, at approximately 4:30 a.m., Cathy Williams was awakened by a noise outside her house trailer in Van Buren, Arkansas.[2] She saw that a wrecker truck with two men in it had hooked up to the Ford Mustang and started to tow it away. She went outside and hollered at them. The truck stopped. She then told them that the car was hers and asked them what they were doing. One of the men, later identified as Don Sappington, president of S & S Recovery, Inc., informed her that he was repossessing the vehicle on behalf of FMCC. Williams explained that she had been attempting to bring the past due payments up to date and informed Sappington that the car contained personal items which did not even belong to her. Sappington got out of the truck, retrieved the items from the car, and handed them to her. Without further complaint from Williams, Sappington returned to the truck and drove off, car in tow. At trial, Williams testified that Sappington was polite throughout their encounter and did not make any threats toward her or do anything which caused her to fear any physical harm. The automobile had been parked in an unenclosed driveway which plaintiff shared with a neighbor. The neighbor was awakened by the wrecker

_____
[2] Cathy Williams testified that the noise sounded like there was a car stuck in her yard.

backing into the driveway, but did not come out. After the wrecker drove off, Williams returned to her house trailer and called the police, reporting her car as stolen. Later, Williams commenced this action.

The case was tried to a jury which awarded her $5,000.00 in damages. FMCC moved for judgment notwithstanding the verdict, but the district court, on Williams' motion, ordered a nonsuit without prejudice to refile in state court. On FMCC's appeal, this court reversed and remanded with directions to the district court to rule on the motion for judgment notwithstanding the verdict. The district court entered judgment notwithstanding the verdict for FMCC, and this appeal followed.

§ 9–503 [cf. 9–609(a)(1), (b)(2)] provides in pertinent part:

> Unless otherwise agreed, a secured party has on default the right to take possession of the collateral. In taking possession, a secured party may proceed without judicial process if this can be done without breach of the peace. . . .[4]

In Ford Motor Credit Co. v. Herring, 27 U.C.C.Rep. 1448, 267 Ark. 201, 589 S.W.2d 584, 586 (1979), which involved an alleged conversion arising out of a repossession, the Supreme Court of Arkansas cited § 9–503 and referred to its previous holdings as follows:

> In pre-code cases, we have sustained a finding of conversion only where force, or threats of force, or risk of invoking violence, accompanied the repossession. . . .

The thrust of Williams' argument on appeal is that the repossession was accomplished by the risk of invoking violence. The district judge who presided at the trial commented on her theory in his memorandum opinion:

> Mrs. Williams herself admitted that the men who repossessed her automobile were very polite and complied with her requests. The evidence does not reveal that they performed any act which was oppressive, threatening or tended to cause physical violence. Unlike the situation presented in Manhattan Credit Co. v. Brewer, supra, it was not shown that Mrs. Williams would have been forced to resort to physical violence to stop the men from leaving with her automobile.

In the pre-Code case Manhattan Credit Co. v. Brewer, 232 Ark. 976, 341 S.W.2d 765 (1961), the court held that a breach of peace occurred when the debtor and her husband confronted the creditor's agent during the act of repossession and clearly objected to the repossession, 341 S.W.2d at 767–68. In *Manhattan,* the court examined holdings of earlier

---

[4] It is generally considered that the objectives of this section are (1) to benefit creditors in permitting them to realize collateral without having to resort to judicial process; (2) to benefit debtors in general by making credit available at lower costs. . . ; and (3) to support a public policy discouraging extrajudicial acts by citizens when those acts are fraught with the likelihood of resulting violence. . . .

cases in which repossessions were deemed to have been accomplished without any breach of the peace, id. In particular, the Supreme Court of Arkansas discussed the case of Rutledge v. Universal C.I.T. Credit Corp., 218 Ark. 510, 237 S.W.2d 469 (1951). In *Rutledge,* the court found no breach of the peace when the repossessor acquired keys to the automobile, confronted the debtor and his wife, informed them he was going to take the car, and immediately proceeded to do so. As the *Rutledge* court explained and the *Manhattan* court reiterated, a breach of the peace did not occur when the "Appellant [debtor-possessor] did not give his permission but he did not object." *Manhattan,* supra, 341 S.W.2d at 767–68; *Rutledge,* supra, 237 S.W.2d at 470.

We have read the transcript of the trial. There is no material dispute in the evidence, and the district court has correctly summarized it. Cathy Williams did not raise an objection to the taking, and the repossession was accomplished without any incident which might tend to provoke violence. . . .

Appellees deserve something less than commendation for the taking during the night time sleeping hours, but it is clear that viewing the facts in the light most favorable to Williams, the taking was a legal repossession under the laws of the State of Arkansas. The evidence does not support the verdict of the jury. FMCC is entitled to judgment notwithstanding the verdict.

The judgment notwithstanding the verdict is affirmed.

■ HEANEY, CIRCUIT JUDGE, dissenting.

The only issue is whether the repossession of appellant's automobile constituted a breach of the peace by creating a "risk of invoking violence." See Ford Motor Credit Co. v. Herring, 267 Ark. 201, 589 S.W.2d 584, 586 (1979). The trial jury found that it did and awarded $5,000 for conversion. Because that determination was in my view a reasonable one, I dissent from the Court's decision to overturn it.

Cathy Williams was a single parent living with her two small children in a trailer home in Van Buren, Arkansas. On December 1, 1977, at approximately 4:30 a.m., she was awakened by noises in her driveway. She went into the night to investigate and discovered a wrecker and its crew in the process of towing away her car. According to the trial court, "she ran outside to stop them. . . but she made no *strenuous* protests to their actions." (Emphasis added.) In fact, the wrecker crew stepped between her and the car when she sought to retrieve personal items from inside it, although the men retrieved some of the items for her. The commotion created by the incident awakened neighbors in the vicinity.

Facing the wrecker crew in the dead of night, Cathy Williams did everything she could to stop them, short of introducing physical force to meet the presence of the crew. The confrontation did not result in violence only because Ms. Williams did not take such steps and was otherwise powerless to stop the crew.

The controlling law is the UCC, which authorizes self-help repossession only when such is done "without breach of the peace. . . ." § 9–503 [9–609(b)(2)]. The majority recognizes that one important policy consideration underlying this restriction is to discourage "extrajudicial acts by citizens when those acts are fraught with the likelihood of resulting violence." Supra, at 719. Despite this, the majority holds that no reasonable jury could find that the confrontation in Cathy Williams' driveway at 4:30 a.m. created a risk of violence. I cannot agree. At a minimum, the largely undisputed facts created a jury question. The jury found a breach of the peace and this Court has no sound, much less compelling, reason to overturn that determination.

Indeed, I would think that sound application of the self-help limitation might require a directed verdict in favor of Ms. Williams, but certainly not against her. If a "night raid" is conducted without detection and confrontation, then, of course, there could be no breach of the peace. But where the invasion is detected and a confrontation ensues, the repossessor should be under a duty to retreat and turn to judicial process. The alternative which the majority embraces is to allow a repossessor to proceed following confrontation unless and until violence results in fact. Such a rule invites tragic consequences which the law should seek to prevent, not to encourage. I would reverse the trial court and reinstate the jury's verdict.

NOTES

1.   What would the court have Cathy Williams do to show her lack of consent? In Hollibush v. Ford Motor Credit Co., 508 N.W.2d 449 (Wis. Ct.App.1993), when the repo man hooked the debtor's Bronco up to his tow truck, the debtor's fiancé, in debtor's presence, said: "You are not going to take the Bronco." Despite this admonition, the tow truck drove off with the Bronco. The court held that a breach of the peace had taken place and stated: "Cases interpreting [former] § 9–503 also support [debtor's] assertion that 'no means no.'" Id. at 454. In Dixon v. Ford Motor Credit Co., 391 N.E.2d 493, 497 (Ill. App.1979) (citing James J. White & Robert S. Summers, Uniform Commercial Code § 26–6, at 972 (1st ed. 1972)), the court said: "When a creditor repossesses in disregard of the debtor's unequivocal oral protest, the repossession may be found to be in breach of the peace."

Chrysler Credit Corp. v. Koontz, 661 N.E.2d 1171 (Ill. Ct.App.1996), the case of the demure debtor, rejects the "just-say-no" rule. Koontz, fearing repossession, parked his car in his front yard so that he could see it by the porch light. When the repossessor arrived, Koontz ran out and shouted, "Don't take it." The repossessor made no verbal or physical response while removing the vehicle. Koontz testified that although he was close enough to the repossessor to run over and get into a fight, he elected not to do so because he was in his underwear. The court stated that the term breach of the peace "connotes conduct which incites or is likely to incite immediate public turbulence, or which leads to or is likely to lead to an immediate loss of public order and tranquility." Id. at 1173. The probability of violence is sufficient to constitute a breach of the peace, the court stated, but nothing Koontz did would indicate to the repossessor that violence was likely to ensue if he continued to repossess the vehicle. Thus, the court found no breach of the peace: "We note that to rule otherwise would be to invite the ridiculous situation whereby a debtor could avoid a deficiency judgment by merely stepping out of his house and yelling once at a nonresponsive repossessor. Such a narrow definition of the conduct necessary to breach the peace would, we think, render the self-help repossession statute useless. Therefore, we reject Koontz's invitation to define 'an unequivocal oral protest,' without more, as a breach of the peace." Id. at 1174. Presumably, if Koontz had not been so modest and had duked it out with the repossessor, a breach of the peace would have occurred. Does the court wish to encourage such conduct?

2.   The secured party's use of trickery or fraud to recover collateral has generated a line of inconsistent case outcomes. In Thompson v. Ford Motor Credit Co., 550 F.2d 256 (5th Cir.1977), the automobile sought by the seller was found in a repair garage. The garageman refused to allow the seller to take the vehicle unless he had obtained the debtor's consent. The seller lied in telling the garageman that he had the debtor's consent. The court stated that "[m]erely to connive to repossess does not make [the seller] liable. . . ." Id. at 258. On similar facts, the same result was reached in K.B. Oil Co. v. Ford Motor Credit Co., Inc., 811 F.2d 310 (6th Cir.1987). In Reno v. General Motors Acceptance Corp., 378 So.2d 1103 (Ala.1979), the finance company repossessed an automobile from the parking lot of a grocery supermarket where the debtor worked by use of a duplicate key obtained from the dealer who had sold the installment contract to the finance company. The court held that there was no breach of the peace because possession was obtained without fraud, artifice, stealth, or trickery. The same court found a breach of the peace when the repo agent induced the debtor to drive his car to the dealer's office to discuss whether his payments were in arrears. While the debtor was inside discussing the account, his car was removed. See Ford Motor Credit Co. v. Byrd, 351 So.2d 557 (Ala.1977).

PROBLEM

Lender provided financing on a secured basis to Debtor that enabled it to purchase a vehicle. After Debtor purchased the vehicle it never paid the balance owing on the loan which the vehicle secured. Lender, through one of its agents, repossessed the vehicle while it was parked on the street in front of the Debtor's house. This was done while Debtor's son came out of the house and saw a tow truck parked in front of the vehicle and a police car parked across the street in front of a neighbor's house. The police were present at the request of Lender's agent, who had asked for a police escort because the repossession was to occur in a high crime neighborhood. The officers intervened with Debtor's son, telling him to lower his voice after he had called out to Lender's agent several times. They did nothing more. Although the police officers present did not encourage or direct Lender's agent, they had arrived with Lender's agent. Is Lender liable for wrongful repossession or in conversion? See Albertorio-Santiago v. Reliable Financial Services, 612 F.Supp.2d 159 (Dist. P.R. 2009). In In re Bolin & Co., LLC, 437 B.R. 731 (D.

Conn.2010), the presence of a peace officer did not prove a breach of the peace when it was shown that the officer was not present to compel the debtor to relinquish possession of the collateral.

c. JUDICIAL ACTION

As described in the previous section, self-help repossession is problematic owing to the liability a secured party may incur in cases in which the debtor will not consent to the repossession. Under 9–609(a), the secured party is entitled to take possession of the collateral when the debtor defaults, and it may do so by judicial action under 9–609(b)(1). Depending on state law outside Article 9, it may bring an action in replevin or, in some states, claim and delivery, and obtain a writ of possession. The levying officer (sheriff or marshal) may seize the property and deliver it to the secured party, who may then dispose of the property pursuant to Article 9. Another course of action is for the secured party to reduce its claim to judgment, levy on the collateral, and execute on its judgment by a judicial sale under 9–601(a). The sale is conducted by judicial officers under the same rules that govern other execution sales pursuant to a money judgment in the jurisdiction. Section 9–601(f) and Comment 8 make clear that an execution sale is an appropriate method of foreclosure.

Still another alternative is for the secured creditor to bring a judicial foreclosure proceeding in which a court sells the collateral under a judicial sale, similar to the execution sale on a money judgment. If the collateral is either repossessed or sold by judicial officers, Article 9 limitations do not apply to the removal or sale. The requirements of a commercially reasonable disposition are inapplicable, and whether a secured party may bid at the judicial sale is governed by other state law. Comment 8 to 9–601. Judicial sales that meet the procedural requirements of state statutes as to notice, location, bidding and the like are virtually invulnerable to debtor attack. Of course, judicial actions may be costly and the fact that these costs can be shifted to the debtor's obligation (9–615(a)) is no guaranty that they will be collectible.

An important advantage to secured parties in opting for judicial action is revealed in the following case.

Cla-Mil East Holding Corp. v. Medallion Funding Corp.

Court of Appeals of New York, 2006
6 N.Y.3d 375

■ ROSENBLATT, J.

A secured creditor, Medallion Funding Corp., obtained a court order directing the New York City marshal to recover collateral located on property belonging to Cla-Mil East Holding Corp. Cla-Mil, the judgment debtor's landlord, has alleged that the marshal negligently damaged its real estate, and has sued Medallion and its law firm under a variety of theories. The only one it seriously argues here is that it was entitled to reimbursement under UCC 9–604(d).* We must now decide whether Medallion's court-ordered use of the marshal, rather than self-help, insulates it from Cla-Mil's claim. We hold that it does.

The present dispute began when a tenant of Cla-Mil's who had operated a laundromat on his leased space defaulted on his rent. About the same time, the tenant defaulted on payments he owed Medallion, which had provided him with a loan to purchase the laundry equipment, including large washers and dryers. The loan was secured by the equipment itself as collateral. Cla-Mil evicted the tenant. Medallion then obtained a judgment against its debtor (the tenant) and an ex parte order from Supreme Court, based on that judgment, directing the city marshal to recover possession of the collateral.

Pursuant to the Supreme Court decree and without notice to Cla-Mil, the marshal broke the landlord's seal on the premises (which, perhaps ironically, had also been placed there by the city marshals) and removed the washers, dryers and associated equipment. To accomplish the removal, the marshal severed air vents, unplugged power lines, and disconnected hot and cold water pipes.

Cla-Mil has sued Medallion and its law firm, alleging that the damage to the premises was caused by the marshal's negligence in performing these disconnections. Cla-Mil alleged trespass, abuse of process and negligence. Supreme Court denied Medallion's motion for summary judgment and granted Cla-Mil partial summary judgment on the question of liability, reasoning in part that Medallion had an obligation to notify Cla-Mil before sending the marshal to repossess the collateral. The Appellate Division reversed and granted summary judgment in Medallion's favor. We now affirm.

UCC 9–604(d) specifies that "[a] secured party that removes collateral shall promptly reimburse" the owner of real property damaged by the removal (other than the debtor). Here, the party that "remove[d] collateral" was not the secured party, nor any employee, contractor, or agent of the secured party. The New York City marshals are government officers appointed by the Mayor (CCA 1601), neutral and free of any conflict of interest concerning the removal of collateral (CCA 1601–a [a]), and subject to discipline by appropriate authorities (id.). Marshals do not owe allegiance to or take orders from the secured creditors whose collateral they recover; rather, they act under the direction of a court, as the marshal did here.

(1) The marshal's actual and legal independence from the secured party suggests to us that the UCC reference to a "secured party that removes collateral" does not include secured parties who arrange for

---

* The Appellate Division correctly awarded Kramer and Shapiro, P.C. summary judgment. The firm acted properly in seeking a court order on behalf of its client.

marshals to remove collateral under court order. Policy reasons support a distinction between marshals and secured parties, and we see no reason to conflate their identities under the UCC. If the marshal here damaged the real property, as Cla-Mil alleges, Cla-Mil should have brought an action against the marshal, rather than against Medallion. Indeed, marshals are bonded for just that purpose (*see* CCA 1604), and the Legislature has expressly authorized such actions in the New York City Civil Court (CCA 1605). We see no link between Medallion and the marshal sufficient to make Medallion liable for the marshal's alleged negligence.

(2) Furthermore, we reject Cla-Mil's claims to the extent they allege any direct wrongdoing by Medallion. Medallion obtained a judgment against the debtor, returned to court to get an order executing the judgment, and brought the order to a marshal to carry out the execution. At each stage, Medallion avoided self-help and appropriately relied on the legal system to recover its collateral with no breach of peace. Far from abusing legal process, Medallion submitted to legal authority at every step. Such conduct is consistent with public policy disfavoring parties taking matters into their own hands.

Accordingly, the order of the Appellate Division should be affirmed, with costs.

Chief Judge Kaye and Judges G.B. Smith, Ciparick, Graffeo, Read and R.S. Smith concur.

Order affirmed, with costs.

NOTES

1. Removal of collateral may cause damage either to the collateral or to the premises where the collateral is located. As noted in the previous section, a secured party cannot avoid liability by employing an agent. However, the *Cla-Mil East* court ruled that the secured party is not liable for the damage caused by judicial officers in a removal. Here the Marshals allegedly damaged the real property of the debtor's landlord in removing the washers and dryers and related equipment by severing air vents, unplugging power lines and disconnecting water pipes. The debtor's landlord brought suit against the secured party, Medallion, for damage to its property, for which it relied on 9–604(d) for reimbursement. The debtor was not involved. Crucial to the court's ruling is its finding that the Marshals were not acting as the secured party's agent or contractor. The collateral in this case is classified under Article 9 as fixtures, which is discussed in Chapter 8.

2. The court's advice to the landlord is to sue the Marshals, who are bonded. If liability is to fall on the judicial officers, there will be resistance on the part of these officers to making removals that will cause damage. Note how the California provisions set out below deal with this issue. The following provisions are found in the California Code of Civil Procedure § 514.010:

(c) If the specified property or any part of it is in a private place, the levying officer shall at the time he demands possession of the property announce his identity, purpose, and authority. If the property is not voluntarily delivered, the levying officer may cause any building or enclosure where the property may be located to be broken open in such a manner as he reasonably believes will cause the least damage and may call upon the power of the county to aid and protect him, but, if he reasonably believes that entry and seizure of the property will involve a substantial risk of death or serious bodily harm to any person, he shall refrain from seizing the property and shall promptly make a return to the court from which the writ issued setting forth the reasons for his belief that the risk exists. In such case, the court shall make such orders as may be appropriate.

(d) Nothing in this section authorizes the levying officer to enter or search any private place not specified in the writ of possession or other order of the court.

3. DISPOSITION OF COLLATERAL

The law has long struggled with the problem of how to strike a fair balance between the interest of the foreclosing creditor in being able to realize on collateral quickly and cheaply and the rights of the defaulting debtor in having a disposition of the property that brings a fair price. The traditional view was to require a public auction sale to the highest cash bidder after public notice of the sale. As in the foreclosure of real estate mortgages, if the creditor complied with all the procedural requirements, the sale was a valid termination of all the debtor's rights in the collateral even though the price obtained for the property might be only a fraction of what the debtor thought the property was worth. The old Uniform Conditional Sales Act was an example of the assimilation of the procedures for disposition on default of personal property to the rigid procedures long used in the foreclosure of real property mortgages.

Article 9's drafters wanted something better than a "sale on the courthouse steps" held before a listless audience of courthouse loiterers or, still worse, before a conniving group of professional public sale bidders colluding to keep the bids down. In Part 6 of Article 9, they strove to relax the disposition process and make it more businesslike in order to get a better return. They encourage the creditor to resell in private sales at market prices. But as a balance to this freedom of action, the creditor is held to an ex post standard of "commercial reasonableness" in all aspects of the realization process with strict accountability for failure to meet this flexible standard. The adoption of the commercially reasonable standard and the introduction of dispositions by private sale by the 1962 version of Article 9 constituted a revolution in foreclosure of security interests and raised many issues unresolved by the language of the rather terse provisions of the Act. Article 9 moved to address these issues and, in doing so, has posed a new set of questions.

Section 9–610(a) allows the foreclosing creditor to "sell, lease, license or otherwise dispose" of the collateral. Since most dispositions are by sale of the collateral, we usually use this form of disposition in the discussion in the following sections on disposition of collateral.

a.   NOTIFICATION BEFORE DISPOSITION

(1) Notification Medium

Debtors usually know whether they are in default; what they don't know is what the secured party intends to do about it. Although creditors have very likely communicated with defaulting debtors about the range of remedies available, the UCC does not require creditors to inform debtors of their intentions until they decide either to foreclose on the collateral or to accept it in satisfaction of the debt. If the secured party chooses to foreclose by extra-judicial sale, 9–611(b) and (c) provide that the secured party "shall send. . . a reasonable signed notification of disposition" to the debtor, any secondary obligor, such as a guarantor, and, in nonconsumer cases, to certain other enumerated parties. The signature requirement (1–201(b)(37)) resolves the question under former Article 9 whether oral notice sufficed. Use of the term "send" (9–102(a)(74)(A)) continues the rule that the secured party need only prove the signed notice was dispatched, not that it was received. Section 9–613 prescribes the contents of the notification in nonconsumer goods transactions and offers secured creditors a safe harbor notification form. Section 9–614 does the same for consumer goods transactions.

Both 9–613 and 9–614 require the information contained in 9–613(1): the method of intended disposition must be stated, as well as the time and place of a public disposition or the time after which any other disposition is to be made, such as a private sale. The differences in the information required by the two sections show that creditors are cut more slack in commercial transactions than in consumer transactions. The major differences are:

(i)   Section 9–613(2) provides that whether a notification that lacks any of the information required by paragraph (1) is sufficient is a question of fact. Section 9–614(1) provides that for a notification to be sufficient, it must contain all the information stated in that subsection.

(ii)   Section 9–613(3)(B) provides that a notification may be sufficient even though it includes "minor errors that are not seriously misleading." No such provision is found in 9–614. Section 9–614(5) excuses errors only with respect to information not required by paragraph (1).

(iii) In consumer goods transactions, 9–614(1)(B) requires a description of any liability of the debtor for a deficiency.

One of the aspects of former Article 9 that particularly irritated creditors was the absence of any specific directions on the timeliness of notice of disposition. Pre-UCC statutes had always set definite deadlines. Article 9 responds to creditor complaints. Section 9–611(b) requires the secured party to send a "reasonable signed notification of disposition." Comment 2 explains that this includes timeliness ("a reasonable time before the disposition is to take place"). Section 9–612(a) states that whether a notification is sent within a reasonable time "is a question of fact." But 9–612(b) gives creditors in commercial cases the safe harbor protection they had long sought by providing that a notification of disposition sent after default and at least 10 days before the earliest time of disposition is sent within a reasonable time.

It is important to note that the safe harbor provision does not apply to consumer transactions. Here the only guidance provided secured parties is that the notice must be sent within a reasonable time under 9–612(a). Section 9–612's drafters offer no justification for the different treatment of consumer transactions and only scant assistance in determining what they mean by a reasonable time. Comment 2 to 9–612 states: "A notification that is sent so near to the disposition date that a notified person could not be expected to act on or take account of the notification would be unreasonable." Does this quotation require secured parties to anticipate what kind of action the debtor wishes to take? Not much notice is needed to allow the debtor to attend the sale and observe whether all goes well; more might be required if the debtor intends to attempt to raise the money to redeem before the sale.

PROBLEM

Store held a security interest in Jones' computer to secure its price when Jones bought the computer from Store on credit. On May 1, Store repossessed the computer after Jones defaulted on its payment obligations to it. Store was able to do so after Jones left the computer in her driveway while cleaning her garage. Store sent Jones an email that read in relevant part:

May 5, 2022

Dear Jones,

As you have no doubt learned by now, we repossessed our collateral in light of your failure to honor your payment obligation to us in connection with your credit purchase of the computer. We will sell the computer at a sale sometime after May 20, 2022.

We will apply the proceeds of the sale to the outstanding debt you owe us and hold you responsible for any deficiency that remains after the application. Of course, to the extent that the sale proceeds exceed the amount of the outstanding debt you owe us, we will pay you this sum.

You can contact us by telephone at (434) 935-0241 or at our mailing address at 123 Oak Street, Charlottesville, VA 22903.

Sincerely,

Store

Store sold Jones' computer for $200 at an auction it conducted on May 21, 2022. Although Store used Jones' email address to send the email message, for some reason Jones never received Store's email.

(a)   Did Store's seizure of Jones' computer comply with Article 9's requirements governing repossession? 9–609(b).

(b)   Did Store's email comply with Article 9's notification requirements? Does it matter whether Jones uses the computer for her everyday purposes or uses it in her home office as part of her business? See 9–612(b), 9–613(1), (2), 9–614.

PROBLEM

If a secured party fails to give timely notice before the foreclosure sale or fails to give notice at all, how is the debtor injured? What can the debtor do to protect its interests if it receives timely notification? Hustle up prospective bidders? (Hasn't the debtor in a commercial case probably been trying to sell the collateral since it learned that it would have to default on its loan with no success?) Redeem from the secured party before the sale? See 9–623(a). How much would it have to pay to do so? See 9–623(b) and the description of the right to redeem found in the safe harbor form in 9–614 ("You can get the property back. . . ."). How often do you believe redemption is used by defaulting debtors?

As noted above, there is a major difference between the notification of disposition requirement with respect to public sales and private sales: 9–613(1)(E) requires notification of disposition of the "time and place of a public disposition" but only "the time after which" any private disposition is to be made.

Moore v. Wells Fargo Construction

Court of Appeals of Indiana, 2009
903 N.E.2d 525

■ NAJAM, JUDGE.

Richard Moore appeals from the trial court's judgment in favor of Wells Fargo Construction ("Wells Fargo"), formerly known as The CIT Group/Equipment Financing, Inc. ("CIT"), on its complaint to recover a deficiency owed under a personal guaranty. Moore raises two issues for review:

1.   Whether the evidence is sufficient to support the trial court's finding that Wells Fargo conducted the sale of a repossessed excavator in a commercially reasonable fashion.

2.   Whether Wells Fargo provided adequate notice to Moore of the sale of the excavator.

We affirm.

McCawith Energy, Inc. ("McCawith") was a mining corporation that operated a mine in Parke County, Indiana. George McGuire, Gerald Carr, Donald Wile, and Moore were principals of McCawith, though Moore had a minority interest. On June 14, 2000, McCawith refinanced a 1998 Liebherr R984B excavator ("the Excavator") through CIT for $557,918.28. In return for the refinancing, Moore and the other principals executed and delivered to CIT a security agreement and a personal guaranty for the indebtedness. The security agreement provides, in relevant part:

> Upon Debtor's default and at any time thereafter, Secured Party [CIT] shall have all the rights and remedies of a secured party under the Uniform Commercial Code and any other applicable laws, including the right to any deficiency remaining after disposition of the Collateral for which Debtor hereby agrees to remain fully liable. Debtor agrees that Secured Party, by itself or its agent, may without notice to any person and without judicial process of any kind, enter into any premises or upon any land owned, leased or otherwise under the real or apparent control of Debtor or any agent of Debtor where the collateral may be or where Secured Party believes the Collateral may be, and disassemble, render unusable and/or repossess all or any item of the Collateral, disconnecting and separating all Collateral from any other property. . . .

> Secured Party may sell or lease the Collateral at a time and location of its choosing provided that the Secured Party acts in good faith and in a commercially reasonable manner. Secured Party will give Debtor reasonable notice of the time and place of any public sale of the Collateral or of the time after which any private sale or any other intended disposition of the Collateral is to be made. Unless otherwise provided by law, the requirement of reasonable notice shall be met if such notice is mailed, postage paid, to the address of Debtor shown herein at least ten days before the time of the sale or disposition. Expenses of retaking, holding, preparing for sale, selling and the like shall include reasonable attorneys' fees and other legal expenses. Debtor understands that Secured Party's rights are cumulative and not alternative.

Moore and the principals also executed a single personal guaranty ("the Guaranty") on the indebtedness. The Guaranty provides, in relevant part: "Each of us waives. . . the failure to notify any of us of the disposition of any property securing the obligations of [McCawith and] the commercial reasonableness of such disposition or the impairment, however caused, of the value of such property. . . ."

McCawith defaulted on the loan from CIT in 2003, and CIT took possession of the Excavator. McCawith then filed for bankruptcy, as did all of the principals of McCawith except Moore. CIT sent a Notice of Disposition of Collateral ("First Notice") to Moore and McCawith on December 2, 2003. The First Notice apprised Moore that CIT planned to "sell the Liebherr R984B S/N: 409-2002 and any and all attachments privately sometime after Tuesday, December 16, 2003. You are hereby put on notice that CIT Group, Inc. intends to pursue a deficiency action against you for any deficiency that might exist after the sale of the collateral." On October 5, 2005, CIT sent a second Notice of Disposition of Collateral ("Second Notice") to Moore. The Second Notice provides, in relevant part:

We will sell the One (1) 1998 Liebherr model R984B Excavator a/n [sic] 409-2002 in public as follows:

Day and Date: Wednesday, October 19, 2005

Time: 8 a[.]m[.] till sold

Place: www. salvagesales. com

Salvage Sale, Inc.

1001 McKinney

Houston, TX 77002

(713) 286-4660

You are hereby put on notice that CIT intends to pursue a deficiency action against you for any deficiency that might exist after the sale of the collateral.

CIT was unable to sell the Excavator through the auction website. As a result, CIT again offered the equipment for sale privately. In January 2006, Bramer & Son of Louisville, Kentucky ("Bramer") offered to purchase the Excavator for $48,000. CIT counter-offered, and Bramer agreed to buy the Excavator for $54,000. After deducting $3434 for locating and making minimal repairs to the Excavator, CIT applied $50,566 to McCawith's indebtedness, leaving a balance of $251,696.39.

In June 2006, CIT filed a deficiency action against Moore. On August 2, 2007, Wells Fargo was substituted as the plaintiff and real party in interest. A bench trial was held on March 31, 2008, and on July 3, the court entered its findings of fact and conclusions thereon in favor of Wells Fargo ("Judgment"). . . . Moore now appeals.

Issue One: Commercial Reasonableness of Sale

* * *

Here, the Guaranty that Moore executed contains the following provision: "[e]ach of us waives. . . any and all defenses based on suretyship or any other applicable law, including without limitation all rights and defenses arising out of. . . the commercial reasonableness of

[the] disposition or the impairment, however caused, of the value of [the Excavator.]" Moore does not contend that the Guaranty's waiver provision is ambiguous, nor does he maintain that he executed the Guaranty under economic duress, fraud, or mistake. And Moore does not contest the trial court's finding that the "Guaranty contains provisions including. . . [a] waiver of the guarantor basing a defense of liability on the commercial reasonableness of CIT's disposition of the collateral, or CIT's failure to notify of the disposition of collateral." In fact, Moore does not address the waiver provision in his brief at all. Instead, he argues only that Indiana Code Section 26–1–9.1–610 requires all sales of collateral to be conducted in a commercially reasonable manner and that the instant sale did not meet that standard.

We agree with Moore that Section 26–1–9.1–610 requires sales such as the instant one to be commercially reasonable. But the plain language of the Guaranty shows that Moore intended to waive any claim regarding the commercial reasonableness of a sale of the Excavator. Thus, under the Guaranty, Moore has waived that claim.

Issue Two: Notice of Sale

Moore also contends that CIT did not provide proper notice of the sale of the Excavator. As an initial matter, we note that the Guaranty contains a waiver of the failure to notify any guarantor of the disposition of the Excavator. But, under Indiana Code Section 26–1–9.1–624, a debtor or secondary obligor may waive the right to notification of the sale of collateral as defined by Indiana Code Section 26–1–9.1–611 only by a post-default authenticated agreement. Here, Moore signed the Guaranty before McCawith defaulted on its payments to CIT. Thus, the waiver of notice in the Guaranty is ineffective.

. . . . Indiana Code Sections 26–1–9.1–611 and –613 govern the notification required before a secured creditor may sell collateral. Thus, we consider whether the Second Notice sent by CIT to Moore satisfies those statutes.[5]

Indiana Code Section 26–1–9.1–611 provides, in relevant part:

(a)   As used in this section, "notification date" means the earlier of the date on which:

     (1)   a secured party sends to the debtor and any secondary obligor an authenticated notification of disposition; or

     (2)   the debtor and any secondary obligor waive the right to notification.

(b)   Except as otherwise provided in subsection (d), a secured party that disposes of collateral under IC 26–1–9.1–610 shall send to the persons specified in subsection (c) a reasonable authenticated notification of disposition.

---

[5]   Moore limits his argument to the adequacy of the Second Notice. He does not assert an argument regarding the adequacy of the First Notice.

(c) *To comply with subsection (b), the secured party shall send an authenticated notification of disposition to*:

    (1) the debtor; [and]

    (2) *any secondary obligor. . . .*

(Emphases added). And Indiana Code Section 26–1–9.1–613 provides, in relevant part:

    (1) The contents of a notification of disposition are sufficient if the notification:

        (A) describes the debtor and the secured party;

        (B) describes the collateral that is the subject of the intended disposition;

        (C) states the method of intended disposition;

        (D) states that the debtor is entitled to an accounting of the unpaid indebtedness and states the charge, if any, for an accounting; and

        (E) *states the time and place of a public disposition* or the time after which any other disposition is to be made [emphasis in original].

    (2) Whether the contents of a notification that lacks any of the information specified in subdivision (1) are nevertheless sufficient is a question of fact.

    (3) The contents of a notification providing substantially the information specified in subdivision (1) are sufficient, even if the notification includes:

        (A) information not specified by that subdivision; or

        (B) minor errors that are not seriously misleading.

    (4) A particular phrasing of the notification is not required. . . .

Here, the lower court found that CIT issued the Second Notice to McCawith and Moore. That notice informed Moore that CIT intended to sell the Excavator through a public internet auction website on October 19, 2005. The court also found that CIT gave Moore notice of CIT's intention to resell the Excavator in mitigation of the McCawith debt and that CIT would hold Moore liable for any deficiency.

Moore does not contest these findings. Nevertheless, he argues that he "did not receive proper notice about the location for the sale of the [E]xcavator[.]" Specifically, Moore contends that CIT did not inform him of the physical location for the proposed sale of the Excavator through the internet auction website. But, aside from stating simply that a *physical* location is required when the sale is to be conducted through an internet auction, Moore does not support his argument with cogent reasoning and, therefore, he has waived it.

Nevertheless, again, the relevant statute provides that the notice shall state the "time and place of a public disposition." Ind.Code § 26–1–9.1–613. The Second Notice informed Moore that CIT intended to sell the Excavator in a public auction over the internet. The notice listed the date and web address for the auction and the physical address of the auction company. An internet auction has no physical location and is not a situs in the traditional sense. But the web address of the auction and the physical address of the auction company adequately apprised Moore where the auction would be held, allowing him to monitor or even participate in the auction. Thus, we conclude that the Second Notice, containing the web address of the auction and the physical address of the auction company, satisfies the location requirement in Indiana Code Section 26–1–9.1–613(1)(E). As such, Moore's argument that the Second Notice was inadequate must fail.

Affirmed.

■ FRIEDLANDER, J., and VAIDIK, J., concur.

NOTES

1. The court apparently views a sale made pursuant to the Second Notice as a public sale; hence, the "time and location" had to be stated under 9–613(1)(E). The court's holding is that even if the location had to be stated, the "web address" satisfied this requirement. This is the first case that involved an Internet auction in a public sale context. The practice now is popular. The court's interpretation of the "place of a public disposition" language to include the web address makes these sales legally feasible. The 2010 Amendments amended Comment 2 to 9–613 to provides: "This section applies to notification of public dispositions conducted electronically. A notification of an electronic disposition satisfies paragraph (1)(E) if it states the time when the disposition is scheduled to begin and states the electronic location. For example, under the technology current in 2010, the Uniform Resource Locator (URL) or other Internet address where the site of the public disposition can be accessed suffices as an electronic location."

2. Secured parties have long used the Internet to advertise private dispositions. Internet auctions of repossessed cars by eBay are popular. See Richard Nowka, eBay Auctions of Repossessed Motor Vehicles—A Template for Commercial Reasonableness Under Revised Article 9, 31 S. Ill. U. L.J. 281 (2007). The notice of sale states that the auction will be held over a period of specified days and the place of the auction is eBay's Internet address. Comment 2 to 9–610 has been amended to read: "Although subsection (b) permits both public and private dispositions, *including public and private dispositions conducted over the Internet,*. . . 'every aspect of a disposition. . . must be commercially reasonable' " (emphasis added).

PROBLEM

The court in the preceding case properly held that the guaranty agreement's waiver of the right to notification of disposition on the part of the guarantor was invalid under 9–624. Did it err in its holding that waiver by the guarantor of the right to a commercially reasonable sale is valid? See 9–602(7) and 9–610(b), Moore v. Wells Fargo Construction, 907 N.E. 2d 1038 (Ind. Ct.App.2009) (judgment modified).

(2) Public or Private Sale

If the secured party decides to dispose of the collateral, it may do so either by "public or private proceedings" so long as every aspect of the method of disposition selected is commercially reasonable. See 9–610(b); 9–627(b). There are two procedural consequences of the secured party's choice. First, as noted above, if a public sale is selected, the notification must state the time and place of the public sale, but if a private sale is chosen, only the time after which the sale will be made. See 9–613(1)(E). The second is that in most instances a secured party may not purchase at a private sale but it may do so at a public sale. See 9–610(c). The term "public or private proceeding" is not defined in the text of Article 9, but Comment 7 to 9–610 speaks to the issue: "[A]s used in this Article, a 'public disposition' is one at which the price is determined after the public has had a meaningful opportunity for competitive bidding. 'Meaningful opportunity' is meant to imply that some form of advertisement or public notice must precede the sale (or other disposition) and that the public must have access to the sale (disposition)." The requirements of public notice and opportunity to participate are consistent with the understanding under former Article 9; see William E. Hogan, The Secured Party and Default Proceedings Under the UCC, 47 Minn. L. Rev. 205, 226–27 (1962).

The only case in which a secured party is allowed to buy at a private sale is one in which the collateral is of a kind that is "customarily sold on a recognized market or the subject of widely distributed standard price quotations." 9–610(c)(2). According to Comment 9 to 9–610, a recognized market is one in which inter alia the items sold are fungible. Given the existence of Kelley Blue Books and Internet sources, the issue has arisen whether automobile "car barn" auctions of used cars fall within this provision. Such sales are not public sales because they are not available to the general public and courts have generally held that there is not a "recognized market" involved that would allow the secured party to buy at a private sale. The scope of the exception has been narrowed to the private sale of securities and the like.

Section 9–610(b) requires that every aspect of the disposition of collateral be commercially reasonable. Is it possible that in some instances a disposition by public sale cannot be commercially reasonable? Since secured creditors generally cannot purchase at their own private disposition, they have strong incentive to get the highest bids obtainable. But secured parties can buy at their public sales and, like all buyers, their incentive is to bid as little as possible. If there are no higher bids, the secured creditor may acquire the property without laying out any cash, merely by credit-bidding (offsetting) the amount of the debt. See In re Finova Capital Corp., 356 B.R. 609 (Bankr. D. Del.2006). The creditor may then dispose of the property in any manner. Although Comment 2 to 9–610 states that 9–610(b) "encourages private dispositions on the assumption that they frequently will result in higher realization on collateral for the benefit of all concerned," the option granted to secured parties by 9–610(c) to buy at their public sales encourages secured parties to choose public dispositions. In fact, creditors are often the purchasers at their own public sales, sometimes because they are the only bidder.

If Article 9 allows, in fact encourages, the creditor to opt for a public sale, isn't this a return to the situation before the Code: a funereal auction on the courthouse steps with the only people present being the local public-sale vultures and the secured creditor prepared to bid the amount of the debt? Not if courts take seriously 9–610(b)'s admonition that "[e]very aspect of a disposition of collateral, including the method, manner, time, place, and other terms must be commercially reasonable." In D2 Mark LLC v. Orei VI Investments, LLC, 2020 N.Y. Misc. LEXIS 19445 (Supr. Ct., June 23, 2020), the court closely scrutinized a proposed sale of collateral for its commercial reasonableness in light of the COVID-19 pandemic. It issued a preliminary injunction (later vacated) stopping the sale of equity interests in the Mark Hotel in New York City. Relying on expert testimony, the court found defects in the process of the proposed sale. The expert's submission included the finding that the proposed sale failed to accommodate New York's "stay at home" orders in response to COVID-19. The court also credited the debtor's claim that the secured creditor's notice of 36 days prior to auction was unreasonable when the hotel was closed for 27 of the 36 days. Finally, the court found that an executive order banning mortgage foreclosure sales temporarily in light of COVID-19 pandemic supported the general proposition that normally reasonable business practices may be unreasonable during a pandemic. In light of the fear over COVID-19 infection, it ordered that the secured party's auction notice be consistent with CDC guidelines and allow bidders to participate virtually.

Place of sale also is scrutinized for its commercial reasonableness. In Farmers Bank v. Hubbard, 276 S.E.2d 622 (Ga.1981), the creditor sold a tractor and trailer at public sale after advertisement and notice. The creditor sued for a deficiency judgment. The court said:

> In passing, however, we note that it was not shown that selling a tractor-trailer on the courthouse steps was commercially reasonable, where there was no evidence that tractor-trailers are customarily sold on the courthouse steps where the sale occurred. We note further that there was no evidence as to what a dealer in used tractor-trailers would have paid for the tractor-trailer or what an auctioneer would have been able to sell it for. That is to say, courthouse sales may not be commercially reasonable as to all types of collateral, especially where there

are better recognized means of marketing the particular collateral involved.

Id. at 627. See also In re Frazier, 93 B.R. 366 (Bankr. M.D.Tenn.1988) (public sale inappropriate for sale of Lear Jet). But if the sale is held at a place convenient for bidders who are interested in collateral of the type sold, and if adequate publicity has been given about the sale, a public sale can be commercially reasonable.

(3) Marshaling

The equitable doctrine of marshaling, applicable via 1–103(b), sometimes can prevent a secured party from disposing of collateral. Disposing of an item of collateral generally harms other creditors in that they can no longer satisfy their claims from the item. For instance, when a senior secured party disposes of collateral in which a junior secured party has a security interest, the junior party must look to other assets from which to satisfy its claim. The junior party might be unsecured with respect to these assets. The doctrine of marshaling allows a junior secured creditor to require a senior secured party to proceed against collateral other than assets in which the junior secured party has a security interest. The doctrine applies when three conditions are satisfied: (1) the two parties are creditors of the same debtor; (2) two funds are owned by debtor; and (3) one of the creditors can satisfy its entire claim from either or both funds, while the other creditor can satisfy its claim from only one of the funds. See Meyer v. United States, 375 U.S. 233, 237 (1963).

Marshaling is permitted only when the creditor wouldn't be prejudiced or inconvenienced by being required to proceed against one of the funds. In addition, the doctrine only applies to creditors with liens on assets, such as secured parties. It also can't be used by one junior secured creditor having another junior secured creditor. Some bankruptcy courts have extended the doctrine to allow the bankruptcy trustee, representing unsecured creditors, to require marshaling against secured creditors. A few other courts relax the "debtor ownership" requirement, allowing marshaling as long as a creditor has the right to proceed against two or more funds (whoever owns them). Comment 5 to 9–610 leaves to courts the determination as to when marshaling is appropriate.

b.   COMMERCIALLY REASONABLE DISPOSITION

As explained earlier, one of the principal goals of the 1962 Code was to increase the return on dispositions of collateral. The drafters strove to make the disposition process more "business-like" and to get away from the rigidities of the old "sale on the courthouse steps" methods of foreclosing on collateral. The 1962 Code encouraged creditors to sell by private negotiations rather than at public sales. The thrust was to have collateral disposed of in the same manner as other property of the same kind so that something approaching market value could be obtained.

Current Article 9 carries on this policy: 9–610(a) provides broadly that disposition may be by sale, lease, license or otherwise, and 9–610(b) allows either a public or private disposition.

The tradition in secured transactions in both real and personal property law had been that the defaulting debtor was entitled to a public sale in order to protect its "equity" in the property. That is, the property might be worth more than the debt, and a public sale was necessary to test the value of the property. If the sale price was greater than the amount of the debt plus the expenses of the disposition, the surplus would go to the debtor, but if the price was less than the amount of the debt, the interest of the secured party was protected by allowing it a judgment for the amount of the deficiency. Old fashioned statutes like the Uniform Conditional Sales Act prescribed rigid procedures for the disposition of collateral modeled on those governing judicial foreclosures. Everyone agreed that these statutes didn't work for debtors, but how could the flexibility needed to sell collateral in a business-like manner at near market prices be achieved without giving up the protections the debtor had under the old statutes? The drafters of the 1962 Code attempted to solve this problem by introducing to secured transactions law the overriding concept of commercial reasonableness. The secured party should be allowed to dispose of the collateral in almost any manner so long as "[e]very aspect of a disposition of collateral, including the method, manner, time, place, and other terms, must be commercially reasonable." 9–610(b).

When former Article 9 was being drafted in the 1950s, creditors were appalled by this new-fangled idea of commercial reasonableness. The old foreclosure statutes may not have been perfect, but for creditors they provided a safe harbor: if the creditor met all the notice and sale requirements, it was very difficult for debtors to attack the legality of the sale, however paltry the price paid for the collateral. Now, under the commercial reasonableness rubric, every disposition was open to attack. Creditors noted that debtors will always contend that the proceeds of a sale do not represent the true value of the property. There will be many lawsuits, they predicted. And they were right: there were many lawsuits about the meaning of commercial reasonableness under former Article 9.

Section 9–627(b)(3) offers a safe harbor definition of the crucial term similar to that in former 9–507(2): a disposition is commercially reasonable if it is "in conformity with reasonable commercial practices among dealers in the type of property that was the subject of the disposition." The safe harbor focuses on procedure rather than the price obtained at the disposition, which is what debtors are most interested in. Section 9–627(a) spells this out: the fact that a higher price could have been obtained at a different time or in a different method from that selected by the secured party "is not of itself sufficient to preclude the secured party from establishing that the. . .disposition. . .was made in a commercially reasonable manner." Section 9–627(c) offers secured parties another safe harbor of sorts by providing that a disposition is commercially reasonable if it has been approved by a court or creditors' committee.

WM Capital Partners, LLC v. Thornton

Court of Appeals of Tennessee, 2016
525 S.W.3d 265

■ **Opinion:** W. NEAL MCBRAYER, JUDGE.

I. FACTUAL BACKGROUND

The facts are largely undisputed. Anthony and Elizabeth Thornton owned and operated Bowling Green Freight, Inc., a trucking company that derived significant income from transporting parts to General Motors Corporation's Corvette plant in Bowling Green, Kentucky. Over time, Tennessee Commerce Bank (the "Bank") made several loans to Bowling Green Freight. In connection with these loans, Bowling Green Freight granted the Bank a security interest in, among its assets, equipment. Mr. and Mrs. Thornton also unconditionally guaranteed payment of the loans to the Bank.

General Motors' financial difficulties during the last decade put corresponding financial pressure on Bowling Green Freight. After defaulting on its loans to the Bank, Bowling Green Freight and the Bank entered into a forbearance agreement, in which Bowling Green Freight acknowledged that it was in default and that it had no claims or defenses to the Bank's right to pursue its legal and contractual remedies. In return, the Bank agreed not to exercise its rights if Bowling Green Freight cured its default by February 28, 2011. When Bowling Green Freight was unable to do so, the Bank and Bowling Green Freight entered into amended forbearance agreements, which ultimately extended the forbearance period to July 5, 2011.

Because Bowling Green Freight had lost the General Motors business and Mr. Thornton realized that Bowling Green Freight could no longer make payments on the loans, he asked the Bank to repossess Bowling Green Freight's collateral, sell it, and apply the proceeds to the outstanding loans. When this request was made on June 23, 2011, the value of the collateral exceeded the outstanding balance of the loans. Despite this fact, the Bank declined the offer and instead directed Bowling Green Freight to continue to use the collateral, including the equipment. Subsequent requests to repossess the collateral were made, but in each instance, the Bank declined.

On August 17, 2011, the Bank demanded payment in full of the loans, and in January 2012, the Bank filed suit against Bowling Green Freight and the Thorntons. But, the same day it filed suit, the Bank, facing financial difficulties of its own, was placed into a receivership with the Federal Deposit Insurance Corporation ("FDIC"). While the suit was pending, on August 9, 2012, the FDIC, as receiver for the Bank, sold three of the loans involved, identified as Notes 184900, 18107, and 18224, to WM Capital Partners, LLC ("WMCP"). WMCP moved and received leave to intervene in the suit originally filed by the Bank. By this point, the case had been removed to federal district court, and the FDIC had been substituted as plaintiff for the Bank. Unfortunately for WMCP, the suit originally filed by the Bank did not include a claim against the Thorntons for breach of their guaranty relative to Note 184900, the loan with the largest outstanding balance. WMCP moved to add the claim to the suit, but the district court denied the motion. The district court did permit WMCP to dismiss its other claims without prejudice, which led to the present action. At some point, WMCP finally repossessed the collateral securing all three of the loans. WMCP sold the collateral at auction on July 11, 2013. WMCP applied the net proceeds of the sale to the principal owed on Note 184900.

II. PROCEDURAL HISTORY

The following year in the Chancery Court for Davidson County, Tennessee, WMCP filed suit against the Thorntons seeking a deficiency judgment based on their personal guarantees. WMCP later amended its complaint to add a breach of contract claim against Bowling Green Freight. WMCP moved for summary judgment. In support of its motion, WMCP submitted a statement of undisputed material facts and the affidavit of Jim Barr Coleman. Mr. Coleman recounted the history of the loans, the purchase of the loans from the FDIC, and WMCP's repossession and sale of the collateral securing the loans. He explained the application of the net proceeds from the sale to the debt and attested to the amount owed by Bowling Green Freight on each of the three loans as of December 1, 2014. In opposition to the motion for summary judgment, Bowling Green Freight and the Thorntons filed the affidavits of Mr. Thornton and his attorney and their own interrogatory responses. In his affidavit, Mr. Thornton recounted his requests to the Bank to repossess the collateral securing the loans and the Bank's refusals. The attorney's affidavit described the federal lawsuit. The affidavit also included a copy of an affidavit filed in the federal case on behalf of WMCP, which contained statements allegedly inconsistent with the affidavit of Mr. Coleman.

The chancery court granted the motion for summary judgment. The court found that Bowling Green Freight executed the documents evidencing its indebtedness under the loans and defaulted on its obligations. The court also found that the Thorntons had unconditionally guaranteed Bowling Green Freight's indebtedness to the Bank. WMCP established that it was the successor to the rights of the Bank under the loan documents. The court also determined that WMCP's disposition of the collateral was commercially reasonable. The court awarded a judgment in favor of WMCP and against Bowling Green Freight and the Thorntons in the amount of $6,507,435.10.

III. ANALYSIS

On appeal, Bowling Green Freight and the Thorntons identify six issues for review. But they acknowledge, and we agree, that there are two primary issues. First, whether the delay between the date the Bank was first asked to repossess its collateral and the date of the auction of the collateral by WMCP rendered the disposition commercially unreasonable. Second, whether WMCP met its burden of production with respect to the amount of damages. * * *

B. DISPOSITION OF THE COLLATERAL

Article 9 of the Uniform Commercial Code as adopted by Tennessee governs a transaction, such as the one between the Bank and Bowling Green Freight, "that creates a security interest in personal property." Tenn. Code Ann. § 47–9–109(a)(1) (2013). Article 9 "provides a comprehensive scheme for the regulation of security interests in personal property and fixtures." U.C.C. § 9–109 cmt. 1 (2014). It regulates everything from the creation and attachment of the security interest to rights after default and the enforcement of the security interest. Our focus in this case is on the steps taken by both the Bank and WMCP after default. Upon default, the secured creditor "may reduce a claim to judgment, foreclose, or otherwise enforce" its claim or security interest. Tenn. Code Ann. § 47–9–601(a)(1) (2013). In addition, the secured creditor "may take possession" of any collateral after default. *Id.* § 47–9–609 (2013).

1. The Requirement of a Commercially Reasonable Disposition

After taking possession of the collateral after default, the secured creditor has the option of proposing to accept the collateral in full or partial satisfaction of the debt or of disposing of the collateral. *Id.* §§ 47–9–620, –610 (2013). If the secured creditor chooses to dispose of the collateral, then "[e]very aspect of [the] disposition of collateral, including the method, manner, time, place, and other terms, must be commercially reasonable." *Id.* § 47–9–610(b).

The failure to conduct a commercially reasonable disposition is significant for both the secured creditor and parties obligated on the debt. If the issue is raised in an action to recover a deficiency judgment, a presumption arises that "the amount of proceeds that would have been realized [in a commercially reasonable disposition] is equal to the sum of the secured obligation, expenses, and attorney's fees unless the secured party proves that the amount is less than that sum." *Id.* § 47–9–626(4) (2013). Under this "Rebuttable Presumption Rule," the secured party may be denied a deficiency judgment. *Id.* § 47–9–626(3), (4); U.C.C. § 9–626 cmt. 3 (2014).

Bowling Green Freight and the Thorntons complain that the time aspect of the disposition of the collateral securing the loans at issue was not commercially reasonable. They note that over two years lapsed between Mr. Thornton's request that the Bank repossess its collateral and the date WMCP finally auctioned the collateral. For purposes of summary judgment, WMCP also agreed that "[the Bank's] refusal to accept the tender was commercially unreasonable and caused the value of the collateral to plummet due to inescapable depreciation of the equipment in question." The trial court concluded that this fact was not material to the outcome of this case.

We agree that the Bank's refusal to repossess the collateral standing alone did not render the disposition commercially unreasonable for purposes of Article 9. Bowling Green Freight and the Thorntons would have us interpret Article 9 to require a secured creditor to repossess collateral after default upon request of the debtor or an obligor. But the statutory language includes no duty on the part of a secured party to accede to such a request or right on the part of a debtor or obligor to make such a request.

Default engenders rights in the secured party, but these rights are optional. As a result, a secured party must consider, not only what options to pursue, but when and how to pursue them. One consideration is whether to make use of self-help remedies or to resort to the courts. As noted above, in addition to any rights provided by the agreement of the parties, the secured party "[*m*]*ay* reduce a claim to judgment, foreclose, or otherwise enforce the claim, security interest, or agricultural lien by any available judicial procedure." Tenn. Code Ann. § 47–9–601(a)(1) (emphasis added). Although the rights may be exercised simultaneously, no particular sequence for exercise of the secured party's rights is mandated. Article 9 specifically contemplates that a secured party might reduce its claim to judgment before resorting to any collateral. *See id.* § 47–9–601(e), (f). After deciding to resort to collateral, a secured party "*may* take possession," but a secured party also, "without removal, *may* render equipment unusable and dispose of collateral on the debtor's premises." *Id.* § 47–9–609(a) (emphasis added). The use of the word "may" in referencing each of these rights and the context confirms that the secured party has discretion in choosing which rights to exercise and when.

Article 9 does place limits on the secured party's rights. For instance, after deciding to resort to collateral, a secured party may not repossess the collateral or render equipment unusable without judicial process if doing so would result in a "breach of the peace." Tenn. Code Ann. § 47–9–609(b)(2). The disposition of the collateral must also be "commercially reasonable." *Id.* § 47–9–610(b). Even if they cannot dictate when collateral should be repossessed and sold, Bowling Green Freight and the Thorntons argue that the delay in auctioning the collateral was nonetheless "commercially unreasonable." They interpret the commercial reasonable disposition requirement found in Tennessee Code Annotated § 47–9–610 as, in effect, imposing a time limit on the secured party to dispose of collateral after default. In support of this interpretation, they cite two prior decisions of this Court. * * *

Consistent with our prior precedent, we conclude that the requirement for a commercially reasonable disposition applies only once the secured party has possession, either actual or constructive, of the collateral. We note courts in other states, in interpreting Article 9's commercially reasonable disposition requirement, have reached the same conclusion. . . . Whether a secured party has possession of collateral is a question of fact. In some instances, although the collateral is in the possession of another, the secured party may nonetheless have possession, for example when the party in actual possession acts as the agent of the secured party. *See* U.C.C. § 9–313 cmt. 3 (2014).

Constructive possession is a more difficult concept than actual possession. We have previously described constructive possession as having a "sufficient 'right to control'" the collateral. But such a description is too broad in that any secured party will have a right to control collateral by both agreement with the debtor and operation of Article 9. A more precise description or definition of constructive possession is the exercise of "[c]ontrol or dominion over a property without actual possession or custody of it." Black's Law Dictionary 1351 (10th ed. 2014). . . . [W]e conclude that declining a request to repossess collateral does not, without more, amount to constructive possession. The only evidence of the Bank exercising any control or dominion over the property after default is its direction to Bowling Green Freight to continue its use of the collateral. Under these facts, we also conclude that this direction falls short of constructive possession. However, rejecting the date that Bowling Green Freight and the Thorntons propose for the commencement of the commercial reasonableness requirement does not end our inquiry.

2. Compliance with the Commercially Reasonable Disposition Requirement

Unless the secured party's compliance is placed in issue, "[a] secured party need not prove compliance with the provisions of [Article 9] relating to collection, enforcement, disposition, or acceptance." Tenn. Code Ann. § 47–9–626(1) (2013). Here Bowling Green Freight and the Thorntons placed WMCP's compliance with the disposition requirements of Article 9 in issue, specifically, the time aspect of the disposition. As a result, WMCP bore the burden of proving that the time aspect of the disposition was commercially reasonable. *Id.* §§ 47–9–626(2), –610(b).

Meeting this burden required a showing that the time between possession (or constructive possession) of the collateral and its ultimate disposition was commercially reasonable. The record reveals that the collateral was disposed of on July 11, 2013, but we do not know when WMCP asserts it took possession. Presumably WMCP contends this occurred on the date of repossession of the collateral, but the proof presented by WMCP does not establish this date. Further, WMCP failed to offer any proof showing that the time between repossession and disposition was commercially reasonable. Because WMCP failed to meet its burden of production, the trial court should have denied the motion for summary judgment.

C. DAMAGES

Bowling Green Freight and the Thorntons also take issue with WMCP's proof of its damages. However, our resolution of the previous issue renders review of this issue unnecessary.

IV. CONCLUSION

We conclude that the requirement for a commercially reasonable disposition found in Tennessee Code Annotated § 47–9–610 applies only once the secured party has possession, either actual or constructive, of the collateral. The Bank had no obligation to agree to the debtor's request to repossess the collateral, and the Bank's actions in refusing the request did not render the subsequent disposition of the collateral commercially unreasonable as a matter of law. But, we conclude that WMCP failed to satisfy its burden of production, and therefore, we reverse the grant of summary judgment.

NOTE

It is difficult to generalize about how courts construe the commercially reasonable test. Some courts have imposed standards of conduct on secured creditors that would have been unthinkable under pre-UCC procedure-oriented foreclosure laws. An example is Liberty National Bank & Trust Co. v. Acme Tool Division of Rucker Co., 540 F.2d 1375 (10th Cir.1976), referred to in the principal case. The court there described Liberty Bank's actions in selling an oil rig as follows:

> It had no previous experience in selling an oil rig and so the officers inquired or investigated as to the usual manner of such sales. Liberty was told that the ordinary method for selling a drilling rig was to employ an auctioneer to move the rig to a convenient location to clean and paint it and then notify interested persons and, in addition, advertise the sale in trade journals and newspapers. The bank followed none of these suggestions. Indeed, it sold the rig without any professional help. Notices were sent to 16 creditors, including Taurus, and to some 19 other companies. Mrs. Bailey did not receive notice except information furnished by her son-in-law. The rig was neither cleaned, painted nor dismantled. Liberty did not move it to a convenient site, but sold it at the place where it had been near Perryton, Texas. The sale was conducted by an attorney for Liberty who had never conducted an auction of an oil rig or oil field equipment and who lacked experience in the oil business. The attorney was assisted by a Liberty Bank officer who knew something about oil production but was not acquainted with the drilling of wells. Some 40 or 50 people appeared for the sale, but few made bids. In fact, after the price reached $37,000, there were only two bidders. The final sale price, $42,000, was sufficient to pay off the Taurus note and pay the expenses of the sale but left little

for the other creditors. The rig had been appraised at $60,000 to $80,000.

The successful bidder was Raymond Hefner of Bonray Oil Company and Miller & Miller Auctioneers. In June 1972, Miller & Miller sold the equipment for $77,705.50.

Id. at 1377–78.

In deciding that the sale was not conducted in a commercially reasonable manner (it was held in a snowstorm in Perryton, Texas), the court quoted the District Court's finding of fact:

> The proper way to sell the rig and related equipment would have been to contract with a professional auctioneer, or to follow the same steps and procedures a professional auctioneer follows in disposing of equipment of this type which is to clean and paint the equipment, prepare a brochure and mail it to the proper people; advertise in trade journals, regional newspapers and the Wall Street Journal; move the equipment to a convenient location, and offer the equipment on a piece by piece basis as well as in one lot. The Court finds that the rig and related equipment were not sold by Liberty Bank in the usual manner in a recognized market, nor in conformity with reasonable commercial practices among oil field equipment dealers.

Id. at 1378 n.1.

PROBLEM

In the paragraph quoted immediately above, the court in *Liberty Bank* said that one of the aspects of conducting a commercially reasonable sale of the equipment in question is to clean and paint it. But former 9–504(1) seemed to give secured parties an option whether to refurbish or not, and Section 9–610(a) merely paraphrases former 9–504(1) ("in its present condition or following any commercially reasonable preparation or processing"). However, Comment 4 is new. How would you advise a creditor client with respect to refurbishing in light of 9–610(a) and Comment 4?

c.   LIABILITY FOR DEFICIENCY

Section 9–615(a) states the order in which the secured party disposing of the collateral is to distribute the cash proceeds from the disposition. The order of distribution describes a "payment waterfall": the cash proceeds are applied to amounts due to those at the higher rung before amounts due to those at the rung below it are paid anything. Section 9–615(a) provides the following order in which cash proceeds from the disposition are to be applied: (1) to the secured party's expenses incurred in disposing of the collateral; (2) to satisfy the obligation secured by the security interest under which the disposition is made; (3) to satisfy the obligations secured by subordinate security interests; and (4) to satisfy the consignor of the collateral's demand for proceeds before the disposition is complete. The remaining surplus, if any, is to be paid to the debtor. 9–615(d)(1). Correspondingly, under 9–615(d)(2) the debtor is liable for any deficiency that remains after the cash proceeds have been distributed in accordance with 9–615(a).

Of course, if the underlying transaction is an outright sale of, rather than a security interest in, accounts, chattel paper, payment intangibles or promissory notes, 9–615(e) provides that the debtor receives no surplus and the obligor is not liable for a deficiency. A secured party with a security interest senior to that of the secured party disposing of the collateral is not entitled to payment under 9–615(a). This is because the senior security interest survives disposition of the collateral. See 9–617(a)(3).

The deficiency under 9–615(d) usually is calculated as the difference between the amount of the secured debt that remains unpaid and the amount of proceeds distributed to the secured party in accordance with 9–615(a). Section 9–615(f) provides an exception. It specifies a way of calculating the deficiency when the disposition is to the secured party disposing of the collateral or a party related to the secured party. As background, 9–615(f) grew out of method of curtailing deficiency judgments in real property mortgage financing during the economic depression of the 1930s. The purpose of the method was to limit the amount of the deficiency to the difference between the amount of the debt and the "fair value" of the land sold on foreclosure. No definition of fair value was stated in these laws, and courts tended to find that the fair value of the land and the amount of the debt were the same, thus protecting mortgagors from both losing their land and being burdened by large deficiency judgments. The traditional safeguards of a noticed public auction were unsuccessful in protecting mortgagors from socially and politically unacceptably large deficiency judgments in those years of economic crisis.

Section 9–615(f) has a similar purpose. It is intended to protect debtors by limiting deficiency judgments in cases in which the foreclosure sale (i) is made either to the secured party conducting the sale, a person related to the secured party (such as an affiliate), or a secondary obligor (such as a guarantor of the debt), and (ii) the price obtained at the sale is "significantly below the range of proceeds that a complying disposition to a person other than the secured party. . .would have bought." The underlying assumption of 9–615(f) is that a secured party or its affiliates lack the incentive to bid at a price that equals the value of the collateral. Apparently the idea is that even in a commercially reasonable foreclosure sale the winning credit bid can be less than the collateral's fair market value. See Comment 6 to 9–615. In such cases, the deficiency is based on the amount of proceeds that would have been realized by a commercially reasonable disposition to a person other than the secured party, a related person or a secondary obligor. As calculated under 9–615(f), the deficiency is equal to the difference between the amount of the secured debt that remains unpaid and the amount that would have been received in this disposition. The debtor bears the burden of establishing the deficiency as calculated according to 9–615(f). 9–626(a)(5).

Section 9–615(f)'s method of calculating the deficiency applies only when the disposition is commercially reasonable. True, subsection (f) does not say so explicitly. It refers only to a "disposition" in relevant part, which might be commercially reasonable or unreasonable as far as the subsection goes. However, 9–615, of which subsection (f) is a part, describes the order in which the proceeds of commercially reasonable dispositions ("dispositions under 9–610") are to be distributed and allows for a deficiency under such dispositions. See 9–615(a) and (d). In addition, Comment 6 to 9–615, by rejecting the notion that a "low price" disposition referred to in 9–615(f) is necessarily commercially unreasonable, suggests that the "low price" disposition referred to there is commercially reasonable. Finally, if the disposition is not commercially reasonable, 9–626(a)(3) and (4), discussed below, calculates the deficiency, not 9–615(f). For these reasons, 9–615(f)'s method of calculating the deficiency applies only when the disposition is commercially reasonable.

From the standpoint of efficiency, 9–615(f) has three defects. First, the secured party in effect can shift back to the debtor ex ante by higher interest charges the risk of an "excessively low" price yielded ex post in a procedurally correct sale. In a world of adjusting secured creditors, 9–615(f) therefore doesn't produce efficiency-gains. Second, the subsection induces transaction costs by encouraging litigation over prices yielded even in some procedurally correct sales. Third, 9–615(f) lacks a workable standard of price disparity. It requires determining the price that a person other than the secured party or one related to it would have paid in a complying disposition. To which set of counterfactual complying dispositions and purchasers does the subsection refer? It is often easy enough to determine whether an actual disposition was commercially reasonable and the price that was yielded by it. After all, the actual disposition occurred. However, there are potentially many alternative feasible commercially reasonable dispositions that could but did not occur. These potential dispositions can yield different prices. To which among these counterfactual commercially reasonable dispositions is 9–516(f)(2) referring? Section 9–615(f) does not say ("in a disposition complying with this part"). Without a specification of this "reference" disposition, it is impossible to determine whether the price yielded in the actual disposition is "significantly below" the price that would be yielded in the counterfactual disposition. As a result, 9–516(f)'s calculation of the deficiency is impossible to make in a nonarbitrary way.

PROBLEMS

Debtor granted Creditor a security interest in its medical receivables in exchange for a loan. When Debtor later defaulted by closing its business, Creditor terminated the security agreement, gave Debtor proper notice of the intended disposition and held a public auction of Debtor's outstanding medical receivables. At the time Debtor owed $300,000 on Creditor's secured loan. Creditor purchased the receivables, which had a face amount of $673,000, at the public auction with its $50,000 credit bid. The credit bid was the only bid made. Debtor can prove that 40% of the face amount of receivables is recoverable from the account debtors.

(a)   What is the amount of Debtor's deficiency, if any? How does 9–615(f) apply to this case? See Specifin Mgt. LLC v. Elhadidy, 158 N.Y.S.3d 366 (N.Y. Ct. App. 2021). Does it apply to any case? Section 9–615(f) applies to commercially reasonable dispositions. Is it possible to have a commercially reasonable disposition if its proceeds are "significantly below the range of proceeds that a complying deposition to a person other than the secured party. . .would have brought"? The court in Matter of Excello Press, Inc., 890 F.2d 896, 905 (7th Cir.1989) (Easterbrook, J.), opined: "The price obtained in a commercially reasonable sale is not *evidence* of the market value. . . . It *is* the market value."

(b)   How do we know when a sale price is "significantly below the range of proceeds" when neither the Code nor the Comments provide guidance on the issue? Could a debtor establish this fact in a sale of collateral to the secured party if: (1) the secured party bid the full amount of the obligation and resold the collateral for twice the price two months later; (2) some other bidders made bona fide bids at the sale; or (3) other people attending the sale testified that they would have bid but that they assessed the collateral's value below the amount of the secured party's bid?

(1) Nonconsumer Transactions

Prudent creditors think twice before seeking deficiency judgments. A secured party can conduct an extra-judicial foreclosure sale without hiring lawyers and going to court but it can obtain a deficiency judgment only through a lawsuit, and lawsuits and lawyers are expensive. This means the debtor will also have to hire counsel who may challenge the commercial reasonableness of the foreclosure or assert lender liability claims. Another question is whether a judgment obtained against a debtor who has defaulted on a significant debt is worth anything. The debtor's other assets, if any, may be hard to reach or already encumbered by others. Then too, in the case in which the debtor is an individual, as in guarantor cases discussed later, a deficiency judgment is dischargeable in bankruptcy. But if after weighing all these factors, the secured party wishes to pursue a deficiency, the provisions of Article 9 offer reasonably clear guidance.

What is the debtor's remedy if the secured party seeking the deficiency fails to comply with the disposition provisions of Article 9? The only remedy, other than injunction, set out in former Article 9 for noncompliance in nonconsumer cases was recovery of damages from the secured party for any loss caused by the failure to comply. Former 9–507(1). But merely awarding compensatory damages for failure of the secured party to give notification before sale, for example, was likely to be of small benefit to debtors because actual damages of any significance were hard to prove and of little deterrence to secured parties. Hence, courts almost unanimously viewed the damages remedy under former Article 9 as inadequate in cases in which the secured party sought a deficiency, and imposed their own sanctions that limited the secured party's right to a deficiency judgment.

The decisions were divided among three rules: the "absolute bar," "rebuttable presumption" and "setoff" rules. See Comment 4 to 9–626. The "absolute bar" rule denied the noncomplying secured party a deficiency judgment altogether. It was easy to apply and gave secured creditors the maximum incentive to comply strictly with the statute. It was also grossly unfair in cases in which the secured party's transgression was minor and the deficiency amount was large. Other courts limited the liability of the secured party to the amount by which debt exceeded the amount that would have been recovered at the sale of the collateral had it been disposed of in compliance with the statute. This was called the "rebuttable presumption" rule. The presumption was that the proceeds of the sale were equal to the amount of the debt, leaving no deficiency, unless the secured party could rebut the presumption by proving that a complying sale of the collateral would have brought less than the debt. A majority of courts adopted this rule. A minority followed the "setoff" rule. The rule allows the debtor to deduct from the deficiency owed the amount of its loss caused by the secured party's transgression.

In 9–626(a)(3) and (4), Article 9 adopts the rebuttable presumption rule in nonconsumer transactions. Comment 3 to 9–626 states the rule:

> Unless the secured party proves that compliance with the relevant provisions would have yielded a smaller amount, under paragraph (4) the amount that a complying collection, enforcement, or disposition would have yielded is deemed to be equal to the amount of the secured obligation, together with expenses and attorney's fees. Thus, the secured party may not recover any deficiency unless it meets this burden.

Thus, if the debtor places in issue the secured party's compliance with Part 6 of Article 9, under 9–626(a)(2), the secured party has the burden of establishing that it has complied with the requirements of Part 6. Its failure to meet its burden creates the presumption that the value of the collateral at the time of the disposition was equal to the amount of the outstanding debt. But, even if the secured party cannot prove, for example, that it gave the required notification before sale, it can still recover a deficiency judgment by proving that the price obtained at the sale was that which would have been produced at a commercially reasonable resale. The secured party's proof consists of showing that the disposition complied with 9–627(b): that it was made in the usual manner on a recognized market, at the price current in that market, and conformed to reasonable commercial practices among dealers in the type of property sold.

In *Harley-Davidson Credit Corp. v. Galvin*, 807 F.3d 407 (1st Cir. 2015), the court found that the repossessing creditor had not established that its disposition met 9–627(b)'s standards of commercial reasonableness. There the secured creditor sold the repossessed aircraft through a dealer. The aircraft, which had been vandalized while in the creditor's possession, was sold without being repaired. The court ruled that the use of a dealer was not enough to establish that the sale was commercially reasonable. It concluded that the secured creditor had failed to establish that the sale of an unrepaired aircraft met the standard of reasonable commercial practices among dealers. *WM Capital Partners*, reproduced above, is an instance in which the secured party did not meet its burden of proving that the time between its repossession and disposition was commercially reasonable.

(2) Consumer Transactions

Both the rebuttable presumption and the absolute bar rules demonstrate judicial hostility toward deficiency judgments. Perhaps one of the unspoken reasons why courts were so willing to curtail deficiency judgments under case law interpreting former Article 9 is the harshness of deficiency judgments in cases in which there is no ready secondhand market for the goods. This is particularly true in the case of used consumer goods such as furniture, appliances, and clothing, with respect to which the price on resale may be so low in relation to the value of the item to the debtor and the expenses of resale so high that the embittered debtor ends up without the property but owing a deficiency in excess of the original price. The relatively low balances owing in cases of most consumer goods other than motor vehicles often mean that the cost of resale may be disproportionately great in relation to the amount owing on the contract. No wholly satisfactory solution to the deficiency judgment problem has been worked out. Some states prohibit deficiency judgments in all consumer sales except those of motor vehicles for which the used market is usually good. See, e.g., Cal. Civ. Code § 1812.5.

Deficiency judgments in consumer transactions are problematic for creditors as well because they are likely to pose collection problems. The debtor's other assets, if any, may be exempt from judgment under state exemption law, and attempts to garnish the debtor's earnings may drive the debtor into Chapter 7 bankruptcy in which judgments are dischargeable. Moreover, pursuing deficiency judgments against a consumer debtor forces the consumer to hire counsel who may, if noncompliance is found, recover statutory damages under 9–625(c)(2) not less than the amount of the finance charge plus 10 percent of the principal amount, which can be a considerable. These statutory damages are easy for debtors to prove.

If, in spite of all this, the secured party seeks a deficiency, 9–626(a) (preamble) and (b) leave to the courts the determination of the proper deficiency rules in consumer transactions. The exclusion of consumer transactions was done at the request of consumer advocates, presumably, to allow courts to continue to apply the absolute bar rule in the many jurisdictions that applied that rule before revised Article 9 was enacted. Section 9–626(b) reflects the compromise reached between advocates for consumers and secured parties. See Charles W. Mooney, Jr., The Consumer Compromise in Revised U.C.C. Article 9: The Shame of It All, 68 Ohio St. L.J. 215 (2007), for a critical assessment of the compromise by one of the Reporters for revised Article 9. It prohibits courts from drawing a negative inference in consumer transactions from 9–626(a)'s rebuttable presumption rule to nonconsumer transactions. The prohibition still allows courts to rely on other law to determine the appropriate deficiency rule in consumer transactions. Section 9–626(b)'s requirement of forced neutrality remains controversial. A significant minority of states have not enacted 9–626(b). See. e.g., Ohio Rev. Code Ann. § 1309.626; N.J. Stat. § 12A: 9–626. In those states 9–626(a)(4)'s rebuttable presumption rule applies to calculate the deficiency in both nonconsumer and consumer transactions.

Section 9–616 is a commendable attempt to tell the hapless consumer who has lost her goods by repossession what her rights are after foreclosure. Under 9–616(b)(1), in consumer goods transactions, if after disposition the debtor is either entitled to a surplus or liable for a deficiency, the secured party may have to give the debtor a detailed explanation of how the surplus or deficiency was calculated. 9–616(c). However, if the debtor or obligor is neither entitled to a surplus nor liable for a deficiency, this explanation need not be made, and even if the obligor is liable for a deficiency, the explanation need not be made if the secured party sends the consumer obligor a record waiving its right to a deficiency. 9–616(b)(2). Section 9–628(d) goes easy on the secured party who fails to comply with 9–616. It insulates the secured party from liability for the statutory minimum amount of damages for noncompliance set by 9–625(c)(2). The security party still remains liable in the more modest amount of $500 in statutory damages in addition to damages recoverable for loss resulting from its failure to give the debtor the required explanation; see 9–625(e)(5).

PROBLEMS

1. Debtor is a retail automobile dealer and Secured Party finances Debtor's inventory. The following clause appears in the security agreement: "Debtor further agrees that if Secured Party shall solicit bids from three or more other dealers in the type of property repossessed by Secured Party hereunder, any sale by Secured Party of such property to the bidder submitting the highest cash bid therefore shall be deemed to be a commercially reasonable means of disposing of the same." Debtor contends the clause is an invalid attempt at a waiver barred by 9–602(7). Secured

Party asserts that it is a valid exercise of 9–603(a). Who is right? See Ford Motor Credit Co. v. Solway, 825 F.2d 1213 (7th Cir.1987).

2. On August 1, Debtor purchased a used car from Dealer for $1,595 plus finance charges, payable under an installment sale contract under which Dealer was granted a security interest in the car. The car immediately developed mechanical problems and Debtor had to return the car several times for repairs. On August 25, after paying only one partial installment, Debtor refused to make additional payments and surrendered the car to Dealer. After making a demand for payment which was ignored, Dealer sent written notice to Debtor that after October 15 the car would be sold at private sale. The car was purchased by Dealer at a private sale to itself on October 16. The sale took place by means of an interoffice exchange of papers by which Debtor was credited with $900, the proceeds of the sale. Debtor was also credited with the amount of the down payment and first installment payment totaling $95. Dealer then brought an action against Debtor for a deficiency judgment of $600 ($1,595–$995).

Dealer testified that the $900 value was based on the wholesale value for used cars of the same model, year and condition stated in the then-current market reporter or "blue book" used by used car dealers in the area. Dealer resold the car to a retail customer for $1,495 a few weeks after Debtor surrendered the car.

How much is Dealer entitled to recover from Debtor? Would your answer differ if Dealer had sold the car surrendered by Debtor to another used car dealer for $900 and used that sale as the basis for its deficiency judgment claim? See Vic Hansen & Sons, Inc. v. Crowley, 203 N.W.2d 728 (Wis.1973).

d.   TRANSFER STATEMENTS

If foreclosure sales are to bring something approximating the value of the collateral, the secured party who conducts the sale must be able to pass good title to the transferee (the purchaser at the sale). But the secured party doesn't own the collateral. In Motors Acceptance Corp. v. Rozier, 597 S.E.2d 367, 367 (Ga.2004), the court stated: "The question. . .in this case is whether, under Georgia law, ownership of collateral passes from a debtor to a creditor upon repossession. . . . [W]e hold that ownership remains with the debtor until the creditor disposes of or elects to retain the collateral in accordance with the procedures of the" UCC; accord In re Vaughn, 2006 WL 44261 (E.D. Mich. Jan. 6, 2006) (majority of courts follow Rozier). However, 9–617(a)(1) empowers the selling secured party to pass "all of the debtor's rights in the collateral" to the transferee, and warranties of title, possession, quiet enjoyment, and the like, are made unless disclaimed. See 9–610(c) and (d).

Problems arise if the collateral, such as a motor vehicle, is subject to a certificate of title statute, and the name on the title is that of a buyer as the record owner who won't voluntarily indorse the title and deliver it to the secured creditor. This precludes the transferee from having a new certificate of title issued to it by the state DMV. Before current Article 9, some states addressed this problem by allowing the secured party to obtain a title-clearing transfer statement vesting title in either the secured party or the transferee, which the transferee at the disposition sale could submit with its application for issuance of title in its name. Section 9–619 brings this title-clearing solution into Article 9. It contemplates a transfer of title to the secured party if the statement is sought before disposition, or to the transferee if obtained after disposition. Former Article 9 cases had been divided on whether a title-clearing transfer was a disposition under Article 9. Section 9–619(c) makes clear that it is not; the secured party retains its duties under Article 9.

4. SECONDARY OBLIGORS

Under 9–102(a)(28) "debtor" includes "a person having an interest, other than a security interest or other lien, in the collateral, whether or not the person is an obligor." Typically, the interest would be an ownership interest. "Obligor" under 9–102(a)(59) includes a person who "owes payment or other performance" of the secured obligation. Usually the obligor is also the debtor. Section 9–102(a)(72) defines "secondary obligor" as meaning an obligor to the extent that "the obligor's obligation is secondary" or "the obligor has a right of recourse with respect to an obligation secured by collateral against the debtor, another obligor, or property of either." See the brief discussions of these terms in Comment 2a to 9–102. The Restatement (Third) of Suretyship and Guaranty § 1 (1996), in general terms, speaks of a secondary obligation as one in which the secondary obligor is liable to the obligee but, as between the principal obligor and the secondary obligor, it is the principal obligor who is ultimately liable. Under § 17 of the Restatement, when a secondary obligor has paid the obligee, it is subrogated to all rights of the obligee against the principal obligor. Guarantors and sureties are secondary obligors. There is no definition of "guarantor" and the word is not used in Article 9.

> **Case #1.** D grants a security interest to SP in its equipment to secure a loan made by SP to D. D is a debtor and an obligor. This is the most common case. If D's equipment secures a loan SP made to O and D is not obligated to repay SP, D is the debtor and O is the obligor.

> **Case #2.** D grants a security interest to SP in its equipment to secure a loan made by SP to D, and G signs a separate agreement promising to pay D's debt if D defaults. D is a debtor and obligor. G is a secondary obligor.

> **Case #3.** D grants a security interest in its equipment to SP to secure a loan by SP to D, and G cosigns D's promissory note, which evidences D's obligation to SP as an accommodation party under 3–419. G is a secondary obligor.

Two issues concerning guarantors were widely litigated before enactment of current Article 9. First, whether a guarantor was entitled to receive notification before disposition. Under former Article 9, this turned on whether a guarantor was a debtor. The majority view was that guarantors were debtors for these purposes. Current Article 9 expressly provides in 9–611(c) that secondary obligors as well as debtors are entitled to notification of disposition.

The second issue was whether guarantors could make effective pre-default waiver of their rights under Article 9 to notification and a commercially reasonable disposition. The traditional rule is that guarantors may make effective waivers of their defenses, and the PEB Study Group Report, Recommendation 31.B, at 226–27, favored validating a guarantor's pre-default waiver of the right to notification of disposition of the collateral. Although early drafts of Article 9 followed the PEB's recommendation, Article 9's final draft does not. The concern was with the impact of an individual guarantor's waiver on the secured party's incentive to maximize the collateral's resale value on the debtor's default. The guarantor is liable for the deficiency left after the secured party has disposed of the collateral. As a result, the secured party is not encouraged to get the highest price for the sale of collateral after the debtor's default. Commercial guarantors have the resources and knowledge to assure that the secured party maximizes the price yielded as a result of the disposition. Individual guarantors, such as small business owners guaranteeing the secured obligations of their business, arguably do not. The worry is that, knowing this, secured parties might demand that their individual guarantors, as part of the guarantee contract, waive their right to notice of the disposition and defenses based on the disposition.

Section 9–602(7) removes the secured party's incentive to make the demand. It provides that neither debtors nor obligors may waive the right to a commercially reasonable disposition under 9–610(b) or notification of disposition under 9–611(a) unless the waiver was agreed to post-default. After the debtor's default the guarantor arguably might be better armed with information about a forthcoming disposition of the collateral so as to effectively monitor the process. Alternatively, 9–624(a) puts the guarantor in a position to insist on a concession from the secured party as the price of a post-default waiver of its right to receive notice of disposition of the collateral. In the latter case, it is not clear why Article 9 should favor the guarantor over the secured party.

PROBLEM

Section 9–611(c) requires the secured party to send notification of disposition to "any secondary obligor" as well as to the debtor. Has notification been sent to the guarantor in the following common fact situation? Bank sent a notification of sale to Debtor, a corporation, giving adequate notice of the time after which Bank would conduct a private sale of

Debtor's collateral. Volpe was Debtor's chief executive officer and a guarantor of Debtor's obligations to Bank. Although no such notice was sent to Volpe, was shown the notice as soon as it arrived at Debtor's place of business and clearly had actual knowledge of the contents of the notice. Volpe contends that these facts do not comply with the statutory requirement that notification of the sale must be sent to her. Is she correct? United Missouri Bank v. Gagel, 815 F.Supp. 387 (D.Kan.1993). See 1–201(b)(36) ("Send"), 1–202 ("Notice; Knowledge"). If she is correct? Why allow Volpe to benefit from the notice requirement when she is not harmed by Bank's failure to comply with it?

5. ACCEPTANCE OF COLLATERAL IN SATISFACTION OF DEBT

a. STRICT FORECLOSURE

Article 9 provides a secured party alternate procedures for cutting off the debtor's rights in the collateral after default: disposition under 9–610 and acceptance by the secured party of the collateral in satisfaction of the secured obligation under 9–620. The latter procedure is known as "strict foreclosure." Article 9's drafters made expansion and clarification of this procedure one of their goals. It may be mutually advantageous to the secured party and the debtor to choose strict foreclosure. Under this procedure, the secured party receives the collateral without the expense and delay of a foreclosure sale as well as the uncertainties of complying with the commercially reasonable standard in disposing of the collateral. The secured creditor can then market the returned collateral in any manner it wishes. The defaulting debtor, who concedes that it cannot pay the secured debt, escapes any further liability for a deficiency, which would be even greater with addition of the expenses of disposition. This procedure may be especially attractive to secured parties in the all-too-frequent case in which recovery of a deficiency from the defaulting debtor is unlikely. Thus, the drafters promote strict foreclosure as a cheaper and faster way of realizing on collateral.

Secured parties can enjoy the benefits of strict foreclosure only if after default the debtor consents to the acceptance in satisfaction. With respect to cases in which the secured party is offering full satisfaction, the debtor may consent by expressly agreeing to the terms of the acceptance in a record signed after default. 9–620(c)(2). Alternatively, it may consent by its silence. The secured party may send the debtor a proposal to accept the collateral in full satisfaction of the secured obligation. If the secured party has not received a signed notification of the debtor's objection within 20 days after the proposal is sent, the debtor is deemed to have accepted the secured party's proposal. 9–620(c)(2).

In real property law, if the parties wish to avoid a foreclosure sale, a common practice is for the mortgagor and mortgagee to expressly agree that the mortgagor will deed the property to the mortgagee who will then release the debtor from any further liability on the debt. This is commonly referred to as a "deed in lieu of foreclosure." Real property law has never embraced acceptance by silence as a method of agreement, and one might ask why Article 9 does so. Certainly, acceptance by silence under Article 9 has raised problems.

Former Article 9 allowed strict foreclosure only with respect to collateral in the possession of the secured party. This called into question any attempt at strict foreclosure in cases involving intangibles, such as accounts. The restriction is unjustified in commercial transactions, as the debtor's estimate of the value of the collateral will not vary according to whether the secured party is in possession of the collateral. Section 9–620 does not have a possession requirement except in the case of consumer goods collateral covered by 9–620(a)(3). Comment 10 to 9–620 explains that a consequence of allowing satisfaction by acceptance of collateral such as accounts, chattel paper, payment intangibles and promissory notes is that the secured party's acceptance is a sale to the secured party that would normally give rise to a new security interest in that party under 1–201(b)(35) and 9–109(a)(3).

Sections 9–605 and 9–628 are exculpation provisions that protect foreclosing secured parties from liability to unknown persons. Comment 2 to 9–605 explains: "[A] secured party may be unaware that the original debtor has sold the collateral subject to the security interest and that the new owner has become the debtor. If so, the secured party owes no duty to the new owner (debtor) or to a secured party who has filed a financing statement against the new owner." Accordingly, 9–628 provides that the secured party is not liable to these persons.

The most litigated issue in case law under former Article 9 in the area of acceptance in satisfaction involves what is called "constructive" acceptance in satisfaction. The question was whether a secured party's retention of possession of repossessed collateral for a long period without either foreclosing by sale or proposing acceptance in satisfaction amounted to a "constructive" acceptance in satisfaction, which deprived the secured party of the right to a deficiency. This issue focused on the nature of the secured party's interest in the collateral after repossession but before sale. The Problem below tests 9–620(b)'s view of "constructive acceptance."

PROBLEM

Debtor's motorboat, which Debtor inherited and occasionally used for recreation, secured a loan SP made to Debtor. After Debtor defaulted on the loan, Debtor delivered the motorboat to SP. SP, who dealt in recreation watercrafts, knew that Debtor's motorboat had a value far in excess of the amount of outstanding amount of the loan due. Intending to sell the motorboat, SP made a written proposal to Debtor in which SP offered to retain the motorboat in full satisfaction of Debtor's secured obligation to SP. Debtor agreed to SP's proposal by return post, and SP later sold the motorboat for an amount substantially above what Debtor owed. After learning of the sale, Debtor contests SP's retention of the motorboat on two grounds. One is that SP cannot retain the motorboat in full satisfaction of Debtor's secured debt when it intends to dispose of the motorboat. The other ground is that, even if SP can retain the motorboat in full satisfaction of Debtor's secured debt, SP's proposal to do so was made in bad faith. Is Debtor likely to prevail on either ground? The facts of the Problem are loosely based on Reeves v. Foutz & Tanner, Inc., 617 P.2d 149 (N.M.1980). See 9–620(a), Comment 11 to 9–620, 1–304.

Yes, good faith

PROBLEM

Seller sold his appliance business, including all inventory, receivables, and furnishings, to Buyer for $300,000. Buyer paid $50,000 down, signed a note to Seller for the remaining $250,000 secured by a security interest in all the property acquired from Seller, and took possession of these assets at the place of business. The note was payable in monthly installments over a period of five years. Seller perfected his security interest in the collateral by filing. After six months, Buyer found that she was unable to make her payments; she called Seller and told him that she "would have to ask him to call off the deal and take back his business." Soon after, she vacated the premises and enrolled in business school. Seller went back into possession, where he found to his dismay that the assets were currently worth no more than $200,000. After brooding about the matter for several months, Seller sent Buyer a demand that she pay him the difference, $50,000, between the value of the assets that he had sold her (less her down payment) and the value of the goods that she returned to him. Buyer replied that she thought the deal was that Seller would keep the $50,000 down payment and take back his collateral, and that she was released from any further liability. (i) What are Seller's rights with respect to the collateral after repossession? Does Seller own the collateral or must he cut off Buyer's rights in the collateral by either disposition or acceptance in satisfaction? (ii) Some pre-Revision cases held that Seller in this case would have no right to a deficiency judgment because, owing to Seller's delay, there has been a "constructive" acceptance in satisfaction by Seller. Would this be true under 9–620(b)?

b. ACCEPTANCE IN PARTIAL SATISFACTION

A debtor may consent to the secured party's acceptance of collateral in partial satisfaction of the secured debt. In this case the debtor gets credit for an amount agreed upon and remains liable for the remainder of the debt. A partial satisfaction is effective only if the debtor expressly agrees to the terms of the acceptance in a record signed after default. 9–620(c)(1). Acceptance by silence is not allowed. Consider the following two cases.

> **Case #1.** Debtor is in default on a $100,000 obligation owing to SP that is secured by an interest in Debtor's equipment now in SP's possession. Debtor is unsure how much the collateral would bring at a foreclosure sale. Under 9–620(c)(2), Debtor can

consent to SP's proposal that it agrees to accept the collateral in full satisfaction by failing to object within 20 days after the proposal is sent.

Case #2. Same facts except that SP's proposal is that it agrees to accept the collateral in satisfaction of $50,000 of the debt. In this case, Debtor can consent only by an express agreement under 9–620(c)(1).

Why is Debtor's silence considered adequate evidence of its best interest in the case of full satisfaction but not in the case of partial satisfaction? In both cases Debtor's decision will rest on its assessment of the value of the collateral. Debtor should object to SP's proposal in Case #1 if it believes the collateral is likely to bring more than $100,000 on a commercially reasonable disposition. In Case #2, it should object if it believes the collateral would bring more than $50,000. What's the difference? Is it that if Debtor underestimates the value of the collateral, in Case #1, it can only lose a surplus, but in Case #2, it may be liable for a greater deficiency? Section 9–620(g) forbids a secured party from accepting collateral in partial satisfaction of the obligation it secures in a consumer transaction. Nor is acceptance in satisfaction of consumer goods effective if possession of the collateral is still with the debtor. 9–620(a)(3). Apparently the thought behind the latter limitation is that, if the consumer is not in possession of the collateral, it will not take acceptance-in-satisfaction notices seriously.

Out of an abundance of caution, 9–620(e) requires that a secured party in possession of consumer goods collateral must foreclose by disposition under 9–610 if the debtor has paid either 60 percent of the cash price of the collateral or 60 percent of the obligation secured by the goods. The belief is that if the debtor has paid this much, it is entitled to have the possibility of a surplus tested by a disposition. Section 9–620(f) requires the mandated disposition to take place within 90 days after taking possession. Both mandated dispositions and the ban on partial strict foreclosure are mandatory terms that can't be altered by agreement. 9–602(10). However, Comment 3 to 9–610 allows the parties to "settle" claims arising from breach of these mandatory terms. A settlement for breach effectively makes an ostensibly mandatory term requiring a disposition a term the parties can contract around ex post.

May a secured party foreclosing on consumer goods collateral purchase the collateral at a private disposition? The purchase has the same result as the secured party's acceptance of the consumer goods collateral in satisfaction of the obligation: the secured party retains the collateral and the debt is discharged. If permitted, this in effect would avoid a mandatory disposition under 9–620(e). Section 9–620 does not address the possibility. Nonetheless, Comment 7 to 9–610, which considers the sale to the foreclosing creditor at a private disposition to be the equivalent of a strict foreclosure, makes 9–620 applicable to the foreclosure sale. Section 9–620(e) in turn requires a secured party foreclosing on consumer goods collateral securing debt of which the debtor has paid at least 60 percent of the obligation to do so by disposition. Thus, in this case the foreclosing creditor must dispose of consumer goods collateral in a public disposition or in a private disposition to a third party purchaser. Under 9–624(b), the debtor can waive the right to this mandatory disposition by a post-default agreement with the secured party.

c. DEFAULT AND CONSUMER DEBTOR RULES: ASSESSMENT

The picture of the defaulting consumer debtor that emerges from Article 9's provisions regulating strict foreclosure and disposition of collateral is complex. It supposes that with respect to some decisions after default the consumer debtor is ignorant and incapable of processing relevant information proficiently while with respect to other decisions after default the debtor is sufficiently knowledgeable and capable. Article 9's defaulting consumer debtor is assumed to make informed or uninformed choices depending on the context within which the decision is made. This view of the consumer debtor ultimately relies on testable propositions about consumer decision-making with respect to certain post-default decisions. Although these propositions may be accurate, Article 9's drafters don't rely on empirical evidence to support them.

For example, the notice of disposition required in a consumer goods transaction must contain additional information not required if the debtor is not a consumer or if the debtor is a consumer but the collateral is not consumer goods. See 9–614(1)(B)–(D). Presumably this is because the debtor in a consumer goods transaction lacks certain information that it has or can feasibly obtain with respect to collateral other than consumer goods, such as investment securities or general intangibles. However, after default the consumer debtor can waive its right to receive notification of disposition of collateral, including consumer goods. 9–624(a), 9–602(7). Permitting this post-default waiver is justified only if consumer debtors are knowledgeable about the legal consequences of their waivers and capably can assess them.

Other consumer debtor rules also assume that the consumer debtor's decision-making capacity is sensitive to context. The secured party's retention of the collateral in partial satisfaction of the debt is ineffective in the case of a consumer transaction. 9–620(g). Even an agreement to retain consumer goods collateral in full satisfaction of the debt is ineffective if concluded before the secured party has repossessed the collateral. 9–620(a)(3). And the secured party foreclosing on consumer goods collateral in its possession must dispose of it if the debtor has already paid 60 percent or more of the cash price in the case of a purchase-money security interest or percent of the amount of the secured obligation in the case of a non-purchase money security interest. 9–620(e). The ban on acceptance in partial satisfaction makes sense only if the consumer debtor cannot accurately value the collateral to it, either overestimating or underestimating the value. The ban on full satisfaction while the debtor remains in possession of consumer goods collateral is defensible if the consumer debtor underestimates the value of the collateral or misunderstands the secured party's proposal for a full satisfaction only while the collateral remains in the debtor's possession. This tendency to underestimate value or misunderstand the secured party's proposal is assumed not to operate when the secured party has possession of the collateral.

The mandatory disposal of consumer goods collateral is a ban on full satisfaction of the debt too when the debtor has already paid at least 60 percent of its obligation secured by consumer goods collateral. The justification for this ban is obscure. Consumer goods rapidly depreciate in value and their disposition is costly, so that a sale of the collateral is unlikely to yield a surplus to be turned over to the debtor. Nonetheless, a required disposition could be defensible if the consumer debtor tends to inaccurately assess the value of the collateral to it when the secured party is in possession of the collateral. But the consumer debtor's inaccurate assessment of the value of consumer goods collateral isn't assumed when the debtor has paid less than 60 percent of its obligation secured by the collateral before default, even when the debtor retains the collateral. This seems unlikely. More important, the consumer debtor can waive its right to the mandatory disposition in an agreement with secured party concluded after it has defaulted. 9–624(b), 9–602(10). The agreement is effective whether or not the secured party has the collateral. Allowing a waiver is justified only if the consumer debtor can accurately forecast the value of its collateral, however much of the cash price is already paid. The supposition underlying the right to waive disposition of the collateral is that the consumer debtor has the information and capacity to accurately value collateral after its default.

The assumptions about consumer decision-making underlying Article 9's enforcement provisions might be accurate with respect to consumer debtors in different contexts. For instance, consumer debtors might tend to be poorly informed about collateral value or their rights with respect to it, or have difficulty in effectively processing this information before they default. At the same time, consumer debtors might be sufficiently knowledgeable after their default to waive their right to notification of a disposition of the collateral. As another example, it is possible (although improbable) that the consumer debtor is insufficiently informed about the value of collateral to warrant the ban on partial satisfaction while being sufficiently informed to allow full satisfaction. In these and other instances, the decision-making capacities of consumer debtors could vary according to the type of decision they make. Whether defaulting consumer debtors are poorly informed with respect to a particular financial decision is a testable proposition.

Some studies suggest that circumstances can bias the financial decisions of consumer so that they make suboptimal choices. See generally CFPB Symposium: Behavioral Law and Economics, and Consumer Financial Protection (September 19, 2019). The significance and implications of these studies for the regulation of consumer finance are controversial. The consumer debtor provisions of Article 9, which were contested, are the result of a compromise of sorts between consumer and creditor groups. Against this background, it would be surprising if all the nuanced and testable assumptions Article 9's consumer debtor provisions make about the cognitive limits of the consumer debtor in default are accurate.

6.   EFFECT OF DISPOSITION OR ACCEPTANCE ON THIRD PARTIES

a.   TRANSFEREES

A person who buys at a foreclosure sale is called a transferee by 9–617. The popular usage of "purchaser" for such a person is not technically correct. This is because the transfer is not voluntary with respect to the debtor. The transferee therefore cannot be a "purchaser," according to 1–201(b)(30)'s definition of the term. Although the selling secured party does not "own" the collateral after repossession, 9–617(a)(1) empowers it to make a transfer of all the debtor's rights to the transferee. Unless disclaimed by the secured party, such a transfer includes warranties relating to title, possession, quiet enjoyment and the like. 9–610(d)–(e).

PROBLEMS

1.   SP, who held the only security interest in Debtor's collateral, on Debtor's default sold the collateral for value to Transferee at a public auction. SP failed to give Debtor the notification required by 9–611(c)(1). At the time of the sale Transferee knew of this fact. May Debtor undo the sale? See 9–617(a)(1) and (c)(1), 9–625(b) and (c)(1). What rights does Transferee have against SP? See 9–610(d).

2.   SP sold Debtor's collateral to Transferee for value at a public auction sale that met all the requirements for a commercially reasonable disposition. However, SP gave Debtor no notification of sale. Transferee had no knowledge of SP's error. What are Debtor's rights against Transferee and SP? See 9–617(b), Comment 2 to 9–617, and 9–625(b).

b.   JUNIOR SECURITY INTERESTS OR LIENS

(1)   Dispositions

If buyers are to be induced to bid at a foreclosure sale, they must be able to buy the property free of any security interests or liens that are junior to the security interest that is being foreclosed. Section 9–617(a)(3) affords them this protection. Since foreclosure sales cut off the rights of junior lien holders in the collateral sold, these parties have a strong interest in having the sale made for a price that will leave a surplus to be distributed to them under 9–615(a), for if there is no surplus, they are relegated to the status of being unsecured creditors of the debtor. Thus, they want notification of sale and a method of claiming any surplus resulting from the disposition.

Under former Article 9, the duty of senior secured parties to notify junior secured parties was controversial. Should notice be given only to those who gave written request for notice or should the secured party have the duty to notify any junior secured party whose security interest was on file? Current Article 9 requires that notification must be given to both. Under 9–611(c)(3), the secured party disposing of the collateral by sale must give notice of sale (i) to a person who has given the secured party before sale notification of a claim to the collateral, and (ii) any other secured party or lienholder whose interest was perfected by a filing statement indexed in the debtor's name in the proper filing office. Hence, the burden is placed on the secured party to search the files. Some of the difficulties likely to arise under this requirement are ameliorated by 9–611(e). It provides a safe harbor period within which the secured party did not receive a response after requesting information concerning filed financing statements. Even though a junior secured party whose financing statement is properly filed is entitled to notification of the disposition, this person is entitled to share in any surplus from the sale only if the foreclosing secured party receives from the junior "a signed demand for proceeds before distribution of the proceeds is completed." 9–615(a)(3)(A).

PROBLEMS

1. SPA, who held the senior security interest in Debtor's collateral, sold the collateral to Transferee for value at a public auction sale that met all the requirements for a commercially reasonable sale. However, SPA failed to give the notification of sale required by 9–611(c)(3)(B) to SPB, who held a junior security interest in the same collateral that had been perfected by filing several months before the sale. Transferee knew of SPB's interest but had no knowledge that SPA had failed to give the requisite notice to SPB. (i) Does Transferee take the property subject to SPB's security interest? See 9–617(a)(3). (ii) What are SPB's rights against SPA? See 9–625(b) and (c)(1).

2. SP-1 perfected a security interest in Debtor's machinery on January 1 to secure its $100,000 loan. SP-2's $500,000 loan to Debtor was secured by a security interest in the same machinery, perfected on February 1. On March 1 Debtor granted SP-3 a security interest also in the same machinery to secure SP-3's $200,000 loan to it. Later, Debtor defaulted on its obligations to SP-2 and SP-3, and SP-2 repossessed Debtor's machinery. Both SP-1 and SP-3 notified Debtor by email of their demand for their share of the proceeds of SP-2's sale of the machinery. The machinery brought $750,000 at SP-2's properly conducted foreclosure sale. SP-2 retained $500,000 in satisfaction of its own debt, distributed $200,000 to SP-3, and paid over the remaining $50,000 to Debtor. Unfortunately, the machinery no longer has any value. Is SP-2 liable to SP-1? Is SP-1 entitled to the $50,000 Debtor still has in its possession?

What is the loss that must be shown in order for a junior secured party to recover damages under 9–625(b)? In McGowen v. Nebraska State Bank, 427 N.W.2d 772 (Neb.1988), the senior secured party failed to notify the junior secured party of the sale of the collateral. The junior contended that it was damaged by the lack of notice because it was deprived of the profit that could have been realized by buying the collateral at the senior's sale and subsequently selling it at a higher price. The court decided in favor of the senior:

> We hold that the "loss" envisioned by [former] 9–507(1), as to junior lienholders, refers to the loss of any surplus proceeds due to an improper disposition of the collateral. Surplus proceeds in this case means the difference between the fair market value of the collateral, if sold at a proper sale, and the amount required to satisfy the senior lien. Thus, a junior lienholder can only be said to suffer a loss due to lack of notice if a commercially reasonable sale would have produced an amount in excess of the senior lien.

Id. at 775. River Valley State Bank v. Peterson, 453 N.W.2d 193 (Wis. Ct.App.1990), is in accord.

(2) Acceptance in Satisfaction

Article 9's most ambitious reform in this area is to state the effect of acceptance in satisfaction on the rights of others. Section 9–622(a) provides that a secured party's acceptance of collateral in full or partial satisfaction of debt not only transfers to the secured party all of the debtor's rights in the collateral but also cuts off all rights of junior lienors and other subordinate interests. This resolves for Article 9 purposes a controversy that has cast a cloud over real property deed-in-lieu transactions. That is, if the debtor deeds the property to the mortgagee in satisfaction of the mortgage debt, does the mortgagee take the property subject to any junior liens under the nefarious doctrine of merger, which holds that the mortgagee's lien is discharged by merging into ownership? Ann M. Burkhart, Freeing Mortgages of Merger, 40 Vand. L. Rev. 283 (1987). After all, the junior lienors didn't consent to the transfer and no court order has foreclosed their interests. In consequence, real property mortgagees will usually not enter into a deed-in-lieu transaction if there are junior lienors.

Since 9–622(a)(4) allows an acceptance of collateral by the secured party with the consent of the debtor to cut off all junior liens, fairness requires that junior parties be allowed to prevent this from happening by objecting. Accordingly, 9–621(a) provides that the secured party must send notification of its proposal not only to parties who notify the secured party that they claim an interest but also to holders of security interests who have perfected by filing financing statements or who have otherwise perfected by compliance with certificate of title acts. These parties can halt the secured party's attempt at strict foreclosure by objecting within the periods set out in 9–620(d). Even though no proposal need be sent to the debtor if it agrees to an acceptance in a signed record, a proposal must be sent to third parties entitled to notification, whether or not there was agreement between the secured party and debtor, allowing them to object to the acceptance in satisfaction. Comment 4 to 9–620. What if the secured party fails to notify junior lienors or otherwise fails to comply with the Act? Section 9–622(b) provides that the secured party still takes the property free of their interests, but these parties may sue for damages pursuant to 9–625(b) for any loss resulting from the secured party's noncompliance with this section.

7. COLLECTION OF RIGHTS TO PAYMENT

Creditors have an advantage in realizing on collateral consisting of rights to payment over creditors whose collateral is tangible property. As is apparent from the discussion above, secured parties encounter difficulties in realizing on tangible personal property. The creditor using self-help to repossess the collateral has to worry that a court might find that the creditor violated 9–609(b) by breaching the peace. Separately, the selling creditor must be concerned about refurbishing or repairing the property, selling it in the proper market, and getting a decent price even though the liquidation value of used goods may be disproportionately low compared to their original cost. In short, the selling creditor must make sure that goods were disposed of in a manner that a reviewing court years later will find commercially reasonable.

Contrast the position of a creditor having a security interest in accounts, chattel paper, payment intangibles or promissory notes. If the financing arrangement calls for account debtors to pay the secured party directly, the secured party continues to collect after the default of the debtor assignor. Security agreements invariably allow the secured party to notify account debtors to make payment to the secured party. See Accounts Receivable/Loan Agreement ¶ 8.2 (Notification of Account Debtors), Appendix I; 9–607(a)(3). If the security agreement does not call for account debtors to pay the secured party, 9–607(a)(1) allows the secured party after the debtor's default to notify the account debtors to make their payments directly to the secured party in the future. Under 9–406(a), the account debtors must comply or they may have to pay twice, as in Worthy Lending LLC v. New Style Contractors, Inc., 2022 N.Y. LEXIS 2384* (N.Y. Ct. App. Nov. 22, 2022). There is no requirement that the secured party must notify the debtor before it collects directly from the account debtors. If the accounts are good, the secured party collects one hundred cents on the dollar and does so with very little additional expense. If the secured party does not choose to collect the accounts, it may dispose of the collateral by sale under 9–610.

In Parvez v. Bigelman, 2005 WL 3479824 (Mich. Ct.App. Dec. 20, 2005), after the apparent default of the debtor-assignor, the secured party sent letters to the account debtors stating that the secured party had a perfected security interest in all debtor's accounts and that, owing to the debtor's default, the account debtors were to pay to the secured party any amounts owing to debtor. Debtor sued the secured party for tortuous interference with its business relationship, alleging it was not in default and that the secured party had acted in bad faith by sending the letters without investigating whether default had occurred and without first obtaining a judgment of default. Debtor claimed that as a result of the letters, debtor's customers assumed that debtor was going into bankruptcy and ceased doing business with debtor. The court granted the secured party summary judgment; the debtor had come forward with no evidence contravening secured party's assertions that it had only legitimate business purposes in mind when it distributed the letters. It held that if default had occurred, the secured party had no duty to investigate the existence of the default or to obtain a judgment of default before sending the letters to the account debtors. If the debtor's business was disrupted, so be it. Although the case was decided under former 9–502(1), 9–607(a) confirms the court's decision.

Under 9–607(a)(3), the secured party may actively enforce the obligations of the account debtor or obligor to pay the debtor and exercise the rights and remedies of the debtor with respect to these obligations. Thus, a secured party may collect whatever is owed on the collateral directly from the account debtor or obligor whether the security agreement provides for the account debtor or obligor to pay the debtor, as in "nonnotification" financing, or to pay the secured party, as in "notification" financing. Section 9–607 also gives the secured party collection rights against the account debtor, even if the debtor has not defaulted, where allowed by the security agreement. Comment 4 to 9–607.

What duties does the secured party owe the debtor in the collection process? Under 9–607(c), whether a secured party must proceed in a commercially reasonable manner in collecting from account debtors depends on whether the assignee of the right to payment has a right of recourse against the debtor. A secured party must collect in a commercially reasonably manner only if it has a right of recourse against the debtor. The debtor's right to a commercially reasonable collection under 9–607(c) may not be waived. 9–602(3). In all cases in which the assignment secures a debt there will be a right of recourse. However, in most true sales the assignee will have no right of recourse against the debtor.

The right of recourse explains the secured party's duty to proceed in a commercially reasonable manner. Because recourse against the assignor leaves the assignor with the risk of the account debtor's default, how the assignee collects from the account debtor affects the assignor's liability to the assignee. However, the assignee has no incentive to maximize the amount it collects from the account debtor, as it can recover its loss on the receivable from the assignor. The secured party's obligation to collect in a commercially reasonable manner forces the assignee to take the assignor's interests into account when it otherwise would not do so. Comment 9 to 9–607 notices this point: "The obligation to proceed in a commercially reasonable manner arises because the collection process affects the extent of the seller's recourse liability, not because the seller retains an interest in the sold collateral (the seller does not)." By contrast, where the assignee has no recourse against the assignor, as in most true sales of payment rights, the assignee of the payment rights bears the risk that the account debtor will refuse or be unable to pay. Accordingly, the assignor retains no interest that needs to be protected, and 9–607(c) imposes no obligation on the assignee to the assignor. See 9–607(c)(2). In fact, the existence of the right of recourse is a strong factor that many courts invoke to characterize a transaction as a security assignment rather than an outright sale. See In re De-Pen Line, Inc., 215 B.R. 947 (Bankr. E.D.Pa.1997); Major's Furniture Mart, Inc. v. Castle Credit Corp., Inc., 602 F.2d 538 (3d Cir. 1979), Chapter 3, section F. discusses the role of recourse in the characterization.

Finally, the assignee has duties to the account debtor if the debtor has assigned its payment rights to the secured party or third party, even when the debtor has not defaulted. Most important to the account debtor in this case is that its payment to the assignee discharges its obligation to the debtor. Discharge avoids having to pay twice. Nonetheless, the debtor's assignment of a payment right can leave the account debtor uncertain about whom to pay. Under 9–406(a), the account debtor on an account, chattel paper, or a payment intangible may discharge its obligation by paying the assignor until it receives signed notification of the assignment and an instruction to make payment to the assignee. On receipt of this notification, the account debtor is discharged only by paying the assignee.

Some account debtors still might remain uncertain that an assignment has been made, even after receiving notice. In this case the account debtor may ask for proof of the assignment. Section 9–406(c) requires the assignee (which might be the secured party or the buyer) seasonably to provide reasonable proof. Here the way in which reasonable proof must be provided to the account debtor on demand is more stringent for controllable accounts and controllable payment intangibles. For these payment rights, 12–106(d)(1) requires that the method of providing reasonable proof must have been agreed to by the account debtor and the debtor in a signed record. By comparison, 9–406(c) does not have a similar requirement for payment rights not evidenced by an electronic record. Section 9–406(c)'s less stringent demand of reasonable proof of assignment does not apply to controllable accounts and controllable payment intangibles. 9–406(l). Although 12–106(d) doesn't by its terms require that the "signed record" be the controllable electronic record evidencing the payment right, presumably the agreed method of proof, if any, in most cases will be stated in this record. Without this agreed method of supplying reasonable proof of the assignment stated in a signed record, notification of the assignment is ineffective. Accordingly, the account debtor's continued payment to the debtor discharges its debt.

8. REDEMPTION

Section 9–623 recognizes the debtor's traditional right to redeem the collateral by paying the secured party before foreclosure the full amount owing on the debt plus the expenses incurred by the secured party in repossessing and preparing the property for sale. In consumer goods transactions, the debtor must be given information about its right to redeem. See 9–614(1)(C) and safe harbor notification form. A safe assumption is that by the time the secured party is ready to foreclose, it has accelerated the debt and the whole amount is due. The debtor probably doesn't need a statute to force the secured party to take full payment; creditors will always make this deal. But if the debtor could afford to pay the total debt owed, it probably wouldn't have defaulted on the installment payments that are now overdue.

Bankruptcy offers some help. Under BC 722, a Chapter 7 debtor can redeem consumer goods in some cases by paying the secured party in full the value of the collateral; any deficiency remaining becomes an unsecured claim of the creditor and is discharged. This is a better deal than that offered by 9–623, which requires the debtor to pay the secured party the full amount of its outstanding obligation. However, BC 722 still requires the debtor to come up with the cash in a lump sum at the time of redemption ("in full"). The basic shortcoming of both 9–623 and BC 722 is that the defaulting debtor is broke and at best can pay the amount necessary to redeem only in installments. But if the debtor is an individual who is eligible for Chapter 13, BC 1325(a)(5) allows the debtor to do what a debtor cannot do under 9–623 or BC 722: redeem the property by paying the creditor its present value in installments. See In re Robinson, 285 B.R. 732 (Bankr. W.D. Okla.2002). However, as discussed in Chapter 9 of the casebook, the Bankruptcy Code places limits on BC 1325(a)(5) in purchase-money transactions involving motor vehicles.

Why should a consumer have to go into Chapter 13 bankruptcy in order to reinstate a loan in default? Earlier drafts of Article 9 provided that in a case in which 60% of the cash price has been paid, a consumer debtor or guarantor could cure a default by paying the amount due at the time of tender, without acceleration, plus a performance deposit or percentage of the total unpaid obligation, whichever is less. Tender of this payment restores the parties to their rights as if the default had not occurred. This provision, along with a number of other pro-consumer provisions that had caused controversy, was dropped in the last year of the drafting process. The only substantive change in 9–623 is to grant to the holders of nonconsensual liens the right to redeem.

CHAPTER 9

SECURITY INTERESTS IN BANKRUPTCY

A. OVERVIEW OF BANKRUPTCY

1. INTRODUCTION

No lawyer can competently advise on the planning of secured transactions or on the enforcement of security interests arising from these transactions without a detailed understanding of the Bankruptcy Code's impact on Article 9 security interests. This Chapter's coverage of security interests in bankruptcy is divided into two parts. First, the Chapter briefly discusses how Article 9 security interests are treated by the Bankruptcy Code. It presents an overview of bankruptcy law, noting the effect of the automatic stay on the enforcement of security interests, and discussing the status of secured claims under Chapters 7, 11 and 13 of the Bankruptcy Code. Second, the Chapter describes the trustee's avoiding powers and the effect of bankruptcy on secured interests. Here the "strong arm" powers of the bankruptcy trustee, preferences and fraudulent transfers are discussed.

Bankruptcy law is federal law. The applicable statute is the Bankruptcy Reform Act of 1978, 11 U.S.C. §§ 101 et seq., which went into effect in 1979, replacing the Bankruptcy Act of 1898. The 1978 Act is referred to as the "Bankruptcy Code," and its provisions are cited as, for example, BC 544(a). Amendments to the Bankruptcy Code occur frequently. The most significant amendment to the 1978 Act is the Bankruptcy Abuse Prevention and Consumer Protection Act (BAPCPA), enacted in 2005. The Bankruptcy Code is supplemented by the Bankruptcy Rules that govern procedures in the United States Bankruptcy Courts.

Although bankruptcy is federal law, the rights in bankruptcy of debtors and creditors are governed by nonbankruptcy law, in large part by rights under applicable state law. Butner v. United States, 440 U.S. 48 (1979), established that the substantive rights of the parties are ordinarily determined by otherwise applicable non-bankruptcy law unless a specific bankruptcy rule or principle alters these rights. Liens, which are created by state law, are of paramount importance in bankruptcy. The creditor whose debt is secured by a lien in the debtor's property has absolute priority with respect to that property over other creditors who have no liens or whose liens are of lower priority. Usually bankrupts are insolvent, i.e., the value of their assets is less than their debts, and the debtor's property is often encumbered. The result in many of these cases is that the bulk of the bankrupt's assets are applied to the payment of secured debts. Much of bankruptcy law is concerned with striking an equitable balance between the rights of secured and unsecured creditors to the debtor's assets. Toward this end, bankruptcy law allows some liens that are valid outside bankruptcy to be invalidated in a bankruptcy proceeding, thus demoting the lienholder from the status of a secured creditor to that of an unsecured creditor. Sometimes bankruptcy law recognizes the validity of a lien but the rights of the lienholder are restricted in some fashion in order to enhance the rights of unsecured creditors.

Under the early law, bankruptcy was exclusively a creditor's remedy, and in modern times bankruptcy is still an important, though little used, creditor's remedy. Some creditors who would receive little or nothing in payment of their claims outside bankruptcy may be able to obtain substantial payment if the debtor is in bankruptcy. Creditors can, under some circumstances, force a debtor into bankruptcy by filing a involuntary bankruptcy petition against a debtor. The most common ground for an involuntary bankruptcy is that "the debtor is generally not paying such debtor's debts as such debts become due. . . ." BC 303(h)(1). Involuntary bankruptcy, however, is uncommon. Bankruptcy today is most important as a debtor's remedy. The overwhelming majority of bankruptcies are initiated by voluntary filing by debtors who are seeking immediate relief from the demands of their creditors.

Outside of bankruptcy there is often little relief for a debtor unable to pay its creditors. Creditors with security interests may be threatening to sell collateral. Other creditors may have obtained, or are threatening to obtain, judicial liens in the debtor's property. Although state law may allow the debtor to protect exempt property from execution or attachment, that law may not apply to some property that the debtor vitally needs. Most debtors that are not natural persons are not allowed to protect any property from creditors though exemptions. For debtors beset by creditors, bankruptcy can provide instant and dramatic relief. The paragraphs that follow provide a brief description of the principal characteristics of bankruptcy proceedings.

2. TYPES OF BANKRUPTCY

The debtor can choose two types of bankruptcy. The first, and most simple, is liquidation under Chapter 7 of the Bankruptcy Code. In a liquidation bankruptcy, all of the property of the debtor owned at the date of bankruptcy becomes part of the bankruptcy estate. BC 541. A debtor who is an individual is entitled to exempt certain property from the bankruptcy estate. The exempt property is released to the debtor by the trustee in bankruptcy. The property that may be exempted is, in most cases, determined by the law of the state of the debtor's domicile and consists of property that is exempt from judicial liens in that state. In some cases, the debtor has the option of electing to exempt property listed in BC 522(d). The trustee must also dispose of property in which a lienholder or other person, such as a co-owner, has a property interest. In some cases that property is abandoned by the trustee to the debtor. In other cases, the property is sold by the trustee and the property interest of the lienholder or other person is satisfied from the proceeds of sale. Any remaining property of the estate is sold by the trustee and the proceeds are applied to payment of claims of the debtor's creditors and the expenses of the bankruptcy proceedings.

A debtor who is an individual normally will be discharged of personal liability on all or most prebankruptcy debts. The ability of an individual to obtain a discharge of prebankruptcy debts is one of the most important characteristics of modern bankruptcy law. The overextended debtor can get a "fresh start" by having personal liability on prebankruptcy debts wiped out while being allowed to retain all exempt property. Debtors other than individuals, such as corporations and partnerships, do not need this fresh start. An insolvent organization can simply be dissolved and liquidated by distributing all its assets to creditors. Thus, in Chapter 7, only an individual can be discharged. BC 727(a)(1). The Bankruptcy Abuse Prevention and Consumer Protection Act (BAPCPA) limits an individual debtor's access to Chapter 7. Individuals whose income prior to the bankruptcy exceeded applicable state median family income are subject to a "means test" that is designed to compel individuals who are deemed to have sufficient future income to obtain relief in Chapters 13 or 11 rather than Chapter 7. Close to two thirds of bankruptcy filings are in Chapter 7 and over ninety percent of these are individual bankruptcy filings.

In the second type of bankruptcy the assets of the debtor need not be liquidated. This type of bankruptcy is usually referred to as reorganization or rehabilitation bankruptcy and is governed by Chapter 11, Chapter 12, or Chapter 13 of the Bankruptcy Code. Chapter 13 can be used only by a debtor who is an individual with regular income and noncontingent and liquidated debts which, at the filing of the petition, total less than $2,750,000. BC 109(e). This debt limit, which increased the previous debt thresholds in Chapter 13 cases, is temporary and expires on July 21, 2024. The advantage of Chapter 13 is that the debtor can get the benefits of discharge without losing nonexempt property.

The debtor is required to formulate a plan under which the debtor proposes to pay, in whole or in part, some or all prebankruptcy debts over a period of time, usually five years. Creditors are paid in accordance with the plan, normally from postbankruptcy earnings, although the plan can provide for a liquidation of some assets. The plan need not be approved by creditors. If the plan is confirmed by the bankruptcy court, creditors are bound by its terms. BC 1327(a). But a plan cannot be confirmed over the objection of a creditor unless certain requirements are met. If the plan does not propose payment in full of unsecured claims, the plan must provide for all of the debtors "projected disposable income" for the period of the plan. BC 1325(b)(1). In most cases, disposable income means total income received by the debtor less the amount reasonably necessary for the maintenance or support of the debtor and the debtor's dependents. BC 1325(b)(2). But for debtors whose incomes exceed applicable state family medians, this amount is limited by certain standards that rely on statistical medians published by the Internal Revenue Service and the Bureau of the Census. BC 1325(b)(3). When all payments are completed, the debtor is entitled to a discharge of those debts (with some exceptions) that are provided for in the plan. BC 1328(a). Under some circumstances, the debtor can obtain a discharge even if payments under the plan have not been completed if the failure to complete the plan is not the fault of the debtor. BC 1328(b). The treatment of secured claims in Chapter 13 will be discussed in detail later in this chapter when we take up the BAPCPA amendments to BC 1325.

Although Chapter 11 can be used by both individuals and organizations, whether or not the debtor is engaged in business, it is designed primarily for business organizations. It resembles Chapter 13 in that the debtor is normally allowed to retain its assets and to continue operating its business. However, there is an important difference between a Chapter 11 reorganization for firms and a Chapter 13 debt adjustment for individuals. The Chapter 13 debt adjustment plan proposes to repay some or all of the individual debtor's prepetition debts from her future income. By contrast, in Chapter 11 the debtor's prebankruptcy debts are restructured by cancelling and replacing them with new obligations and interests. The reorganization plan defines and distributes new claims or interests to prebankruptcy creditors on account of their old claims. In the typical Chapter 11 reorganization, the holders of prebankruptcy debt are given equity interests in the reorganized firm or claims against it, or both. The shares of stockholders of the insolvent firm are cancelled, so that, unlike the Chapter 13 debtor, the stockholders no longer "own" the firm or its assets.

The debtor usually proposes a plan of reorganization. Unlike Chapter 13, confirmation of a plan in Chapter 11 is usually made only after it has been accepted by the various classes of creditors and stockholder interests of the debtor. Acceptance by a class is accomplished by a vote of members of the class in specified majorities. Under some circumstances, a plan can be confirmed even though not all classes accept the plan. Upon confirmation of the plan, the debtor, whether an individual or an organization, is normally given a discharge of all preconfirmation debts. In return, creditors and stockholder interests have rights that are given to them by the plan. There are various provisions in Chapter 11 designed to protect the interests of creditors and stockholder interests who do not accept the plan.

Chapter 12 was added to the Bankruptcy Code in 1986 to provide for the rehabilitation of "family farmers" defined in BC 101. Chapter 12 is similar to Chapter 13, but it incorporates some elements of Chapter 11.

It is specifically designed to make it easier for family farmers who are threatened with loss of their farms to restructure their debts in bankruptcy while continuing to operate their farms. Chapter 9 governs bankruptcy relief of municipalities, and Chapter 15 governs the recognition of bankruptcy proceedings initiated in foreign countries. Although bankruptcy filings under Chapters 9, 12 and 15 account for a very small percentage of annual bankruptcy filings, the value of assets involved in these filings can be significant.

3. PETITION IN BANKRUPTCY AND THE AUTOMATIC STAY

Voluntary bankruptcy, or a "voluntary case" as it is called in the Bankruptcy Code, is commenced by the debtor's filing a petition in bankruptcy in the Bankruptcy Court. BC 301. In addition to the petition, the debtor must file various statements and schedules of information, including a statement of assets and liabilities with descriptions of each and a list of creditors identified by name and address.

This filing operates as an automatic stay against a variety of acts taken against the debtor or with respect to property of the bankruptcy estate. BC 362(a). Among the most important acts that are stayed are the following: the commencement or continuation of judicial proceedings against the debtor to recover a prebankruptcy claim; the enforcement of any prebankruptcy judgment against the debtor or against property of the estate; any act to obtain possession of property of the estate or property held by the estate; and any act to create, perfect or enforce any lien against property of the estate. The stay applies even to informal acts to collect a prebankruptcy debt such as dunning letters, telephone calls and the like. Although there are many exceptions to the very broad scope of the stay, the stay effectively insulates the debtor from any kind of action to collect prebankruptcy debts. The effect of the stay is to require all collection action to be made through or with the consent of the bankruptcy court. Under BC 362(d), a creditor can get relief from the stay in some cases. The importance of the automatic stay cannot be overemphasized. Frequently the primary purpose of the filing of a bankruptcy petition is to obtain the benefit of the stay.

4. TRUSTEE IN BANKRUPTCY

In a Chapter 7 bankruptcy, the bankruptcy estate is administered by a trustee in bankruptcy who can be either an individual or a corporation. BC 321. The duties of the trustee are listed in BC 704. The principal duty of the trustee is to collect the property of the estate, reduce it to money by selling it, and apply the proceeds to payment of expenses of the bankruptcy and claims of creditors. The collecting of the property of the estate sometimes requires the trustee to recover property of the debtor that was transferred before bankruptcy in transactions that are avoidable in bankruptcy because they violate some bankruptcy policy. These "avoidance powers" of the trustee are one of the most important aspects of bankruptcy. In asserting these powers the trustee acts primarily for the benefit of unsecured creditors. The trustee also has wide powers to investigate the financial affairs of the debtor and may oppose discharge of the debtor if the circumstances warrant. The trustee may also examine the validity of claims of creditors and may oppose improper claims.

The trustee, who must be a disinterested person, is a fiduciary although the Bankruptcy Code does not specify the nature of the fiduciary relationship. Its duties, particularly those of collecting, holding and disposing of property of the estate, are exercised on behalf of creditors generally. Sometimes, however, the trustee must oppose some creditors to benefit others. Basically, the job of the trustee is to maximize the value of assets available for payment to general unsecured creditors. Promptly after a Chapter 7 case is commenced, an interim trustee in bankruptcy is appointed by the United States Trustee. In each district there is a panel of persons qualified to serve as trustees. The interim trustee is appointed from this panel. BC 701.

There is a trustee in bankruptcy in a case under Chapter 12 or Chapter 13, but the trustee's duties are somewhat different than in a Chapter 7 case. The only property of the bankruptcy estate that normally comes into the hands of the trustee is the earnings of the debtor that are the source of the payments under the plan. The primary duty of the trustee is to disburse to creditors payments due under the plan. The trustee is either appointed by the bankruptcy court to serve in the particular case or is a "standing trustee" appointed by the court to act generally in Chapter 12 or Chapter 13 cases filed in the district. Normally there is no trustee in bankruptcy in a Chapter 11 case. Rather, the debtor continues in possession of its property as a "debtor in possession" that exercises the powers of a trustee in bankruptcy. BC 1107(a) and BC 1108. A trustee in bankruptcy is appointed in a Chapter 11 case only in unusual cases such as those involving fraud or gross mismanagement by the debtor. BC 1104(a). An exception is when the debtor files for Chapter 11 as a small business debtor. See 101(51D), 1181 et seq. In this case a bankruptcy trustee is appointed by the court. The trustee's role here is to help the debtor develop a reorganization plan and reach agreement with its creditors. In addition, the trustee assures that the debtor is making payments to its creditors under the reorganization plan. BC 1183.

5. CLAIMS IN BANKRUPTCY

In Chapter 7, after the trustee in bankruptcy has collected the bankruptcy estate and has sold it, the proceeds are applied to the payment of bankruptcy expenses and the claims of creditors. A claim is the basis for a distribution from the bankruptcy estate. A "proof of claim," which is a written statement setting forth a creditor's claim, is normally filed by the creditor. BC 501 and Bankruptcy Rule 3001. "Creditor" is defined by BC 101(10) to mean an entity (also defined in BC 101(15)) holding a claim that arose before the filing of the petition in a voluntary case. Thus, rights against the debtor that arise after bankruptcy are not treated as claims in bankruptcy. There are a few exceptions to this statement.

A claim can be paid only if it is "allowed." Allowance of a claim means simply that it has been recognized by the court as valid in the amount claimed. If there is a dispute concerning a claim, the court must determine whether the claim should be allowed. BC 502 contains detailed provisions governing allowance and disallowance. Any claim can be paid within bankruptcy except to the extent that a claim is specifically excepted. The exceptions are stated in BC 502(b), (d), and (e).

Claims are classified as either secured or unsecured. Suppose the debtor owes Bank $20,000 and the debt is secured by a security interest in collateral of the debtor on which there are no other liens. The collateral, because it was owned by the debtor, is part of the bankruptcy estate. BC 541(a)(1). If Bank's security interest is valid in bankruptcy, Bank has a secured claim to the extent that its debt is covered by value of the collateral. To the extent that its debt is not covered by value of the collateral, Bank has an unsecured claim. BC 506(a)(1). For example, if the collateral has a value of $30,000 Bank is oversecured and it has a secured claim of $20,000; if the collateral has a value of $15,000 Bank is undersecured and it has a secured claim of $15,000 and an unsecured claim of $5,000. The value of the collateral is determined by the bankruptcy court.

6. DISTRIBUTION OF ASSETS TO UNSECURED CREDITORS

In Chapter 7, after the trustee has disposed of property of the estate in satisfaction of secured claims, the remaining property will be distributed pursuant to BC 726, which states an order of priority among the various claimants. First to be paid are the ten priority claims set out in BC 507 in the order of priority prescribed in that provision. The first priority is domestic support obligations, defined in BC 101(14A). Second priority is administrative expenses described in BC 503. Other priority claims are ranked in an ever-growing list of additional categories by BC 507(a)(3)–(10). The most important are certain claims of employees of the debtor that have a fourth and fifth priority and taxes with an eighth priority. After all priority claims have been paid in their order of priority, distribution is made pursuant to BC 726 to the remaining creditors. With some exceptions these claims are paid on a pro rata basis to the extent of the property available. Almost all Chapter 7 consumer cases are "no asset" cases, meaning that there are no nonexempt assets to distribute to creditors.

The BC 507 priorities also apply to cases under Chapters 11, 12 and 13. Under Chapters 12 and 13, the plan must provide for payment in full of all priority claims, but deferred payment can be made, with interest, over the period of the plan. A Chapter 11 plan must provide for payment in full of all priority claims. Some priority claims must be paid in cash on the effective date of the plan and some can be paid, with interest, over time.

7. DISCHARGE

In Chapter 7, a debtor who is an individual will normally receive a discharge from pre-bankruptcy debts. BC 727(b). For individuals the primary purpose of filing a petition in Chapter 7 bankruptcy is to obtain this discharge. In some cases, however, the debtor is not entitled to a discharge. The various grounds for denying a discharge to a debtor in Chapter 7 are set forth in BC 727(a). A debtor is not entitled to a discharge if the debtor has received a discharge under Chapter 7 in a case commenced within eight years of the time when the current case was commenced. The other grounds stated for denying discharge refer to misconduct by the debtor. This reflects the fact that bankruptcy is an equitable proceeding and that a debtor guilty of certain inequitable conduct should not enjoy the benefit of a discharge.

Even in cases in which the debtor is entitled to discharge, not all debts are dischargeable. Discharge is a benefit to the debtor and a concomitant loss to the creditor. Although a debtor is generally entitled to a discharge of prepetition debts, in some cases the creditor may have equities that are greater than those of the debtor. In those cases, the law provides that the debt of that creditor is nondischargeable. In effect, that creditor can participate in the distribution of the debtor's property, but to the extent that the creditor's debt has not been satisfied, the creditor will have a claim against the debtor that survives bankruptcy. Debts that are excepted from a Chapter 7 discharge are described in BC 523(a). Chapters 11, 12 and 13 have their own discharge provisions. Corporations and partnerships may be discharged in Chapter 11 and Chapter 12, but not in Chapter 7. They don't need the discharge in Chapter 7 because they can be dissolved after their assets have been liquidated and distributed. The Chapter 11 discharge for non-individual debtors is extremely broad and is not subject to the special exceptions to dischargeability applicable under BC 523(a).

B. SECURED CLAIMS IN BANKRUPTCY

1. MEANING OF "SECURED CLAIM"

As is apparent from the previous section, when a debtor whose property is subject to an Article 9 security interest files in bankruptcy, the secured party enters a new legal world. The governing law is now federal law, the Bankruptcy Code, and all cases and controversies in bankruptcy are heard by bankruptcy judges. Even the creditor's label changes: instead of being a secured party it is now the holder of a "secured claim" under BC 506(a)(1). The collateral is now property of the debtor's estate under BC 541(a) and subject to the jurisdiction of the bankruptcy court. In fact, BC 506(a)(1) defines a "secured claim" broadly to include claims secured by any lien on property, not just consensually created liens. The preceding Chapters have described the creation, perfection and enforcement of security interests under Article 9. This Chapter describes how bankruptcy law modifies the rights of the secured parties under Article 9. No business lawyer working with secured transactions can competently plan them without an understanding of the effect of bankruptcy law.

In the competition among creditors to share in the debtor's assets in bankruptcy, a secured claim is the gold standard, for it is prior to unsecured claims, however meritorious those claims may be. Secured claims "take off the top." This priority is recognized in BC 725, which says that before final distribution of the estate to the unsecured creditors when "the trustee. . .shall dispose of any property in which an entity other than the estate has an interest, such as a lien. . . ." That entity is the secured party. Article 9 makes it very easy for a creditor to take a perfected security interest in all of the tangible and intangible personal property that a debtor now owns or will acquire in the future, leaving nothing for unsecured creditors. As noted in Chapter 2, the only public notice a secured party need give to establish this powerful priority is a brief indication in a financing statement that it may claim a security interest in all of the debtor's personal property. But bankruptcy lawyers have been battling with the holders of secured claims for a long time, and, as discussed below, the "avoidance powers" of the Bankruptcy Code give them some ammunition to work with.

Before going further in this chapter, be sure that you understand BC 506(a)(1). By way of review, suppose that at the time D files in bankruptcy, SP has a perfected security interest in an item of D's personal property securing a debt of $100,000.

Case #1. If the collateral has a value of $150,000, what is the amount of SP's secured claim? Of its unsecured claim?

Case #2. If the collateral has a value of $50,000, what is the amount of SP's secured claim? Of its unsecured claim?

PROBLEM

At the time D files in bankruptcy, SP has a perfected security interest in an item of D's personal property securing a debt of $100,000 that has a value of only $50,000. After D's trustee in bankruptcy (T) examined the collateral, T chose not to take possession of the collateral and, pursuant to BC 554(a), abandoned the property and left it in D's possession, subject to SP's existing security interest. Under BC 704(1), the duty of a trustee is to "collect and reduce to money the property of the estate." In view of this provision, was T's action in abandoning the property appropriate?

2.   THE AUTOMATIC STAY

The first barrier facing the holder of a secured claim who wishes to enforce its security interest against a debtor's property in bankruptcy is BC 362(a)'s automatic stay. The filing of the bankruptcy petition automatically operates as a stay; no formal order of a stay need be entered. The automatic stay is a form of an injunction: violators may in the discretion of the court be held in contempt and assessed damages. In a special provision, BC 362(k)(1) allows an "individual" injured by a willful violation of the stay to recover actual damages, costs and attorney's fees, and, under appropriate circumstances, punitive damages. Although the courts are divided on its meaning in BC 362(k)(1), the term "individual" is consistently used elsewhere in the Bankruptcy Code to refer to natural persons in contrast to legal entities such as corporations and partnerships.

BC 362(a)(5) stays any act of a prepetition secured creditor to enforce its security interest in property of the estate or of the debtor. For its part, BC 362(a)(3) stays that any act by the secured creditor to exercise control over property of the estate. Under both provisions, a creditor having an Article 9 security interest in personal property is barred by the stay from availing itself of its rights under 9–609 to repossess by either self-help or judicial process. If the creditor is a pledgee or has retaken possession of the collateral before the debtor's petition, it may not realize on the collateral by either a judicial sale or nonjudicial creditor's sale under Article 9 after the petition. If the sale of the property had already been completed before the petition, the debtor has no right under 9–623 to redeem. In this case the stay is inapplicable because property sold is no longer property of the estate or of the debtor, and the stay with respect to that property has ended. BC 362(c)(1).

The automatic stay ends when the case is closed or dismissed (BC 362(c)(2)) but, as just noted, it may end earlier with respect to property that is no longer property of the estate. BC 362(c)(1). The holder of a secured claim may seek relief from the stay under BC 362(d), which allows the court to terminate or modify the stay on certain grounds.

PROBLEMS

1.   SP has a perfected security interest in an item of D's personal property securing a debt of $100,000. On Day 1, SP sent to D, who was in default, a notice that the collateral would be sold at a public sale to be held on Day 21. D received the notice and called SP, urging that the sale be postponed. SP declined. On Day 20, D filed in Chapter 7 bankruptcy without notifying SP, who conducted the sale on Day 21 and purchased at its own sale by making a credit bid of $100,000. The sale was well advertised but no bid exceeded SP's bid, and you may assume that the sale was commercially reasonable in every respect. D's trustee in bankruptcy attacked the sale as void in violation of BC 362(a). The sale did not involve the action of any court or judicial officer. Is the trustee correct?

2. Debtor Corporation (D) sought a loan from Bank, which agreed to make the loan only if D granted a security interest in all its assets to Bank and obtained the signature of Garrison, who was the CEO and principal stockholder in D, as a guarantor. D complied with Bank's conditions. D ultimately defaulted on the loan and filed a petition in Chapter 7. Since Bank was stayed from proceeding against D by BC 362(a), it proceeded against Garrison, as D's guarantor. Does BC 362(a) prevent Bank from suing Garrison on her guaranty? Does it stay only claims against the debtor and property of the estate, or does it protect others? You may assume that if Garrison has to pay Bank, she will have recourse against D for reimbursement.

3.   EFFECT OF DISCHARGE ON SECURED CLAIMS

Under 9–601(a), a secured party has two rights after default of the debtor: to hold the debtor personally liable on the secured obligation and to enforce its security interest by proceeding against the collateral. If an individual debtor in Chapter 7 is granted a discharge under BC 727(b), the effect is to discharge the debtor from any further personal liability on the obligation, but the security interest in the collateral remains unaffected. In other words, a discharge in effect transforms a recourse into a nonrecourse debt. BC 524(a). The theory of discharge has always been that it affects only the personal liability of the debtor. It does not affect the debt itself, which remains unpaid. If third parties were liable on the debt, they remain liable. For example, a surety or other guarantor is liable even though the principal debtor is released as a result of the discharge. This is specifically recognized in BC 524(e). Nor is an insurance carrier's liability affected by the discharge of the insured. Similarly, if the debt is secured by property of a third party, that property can be reached to the full extent of the security agreement.

The same rule applies if the discharged debt was secured by a lien in the debtor's property. The debt and the lien continue to exist after bankruptcy even though the debtor may have been discharged from personal liability to pay the debt and even though the creditor did not file a proof of claim in bankruptcy. This principle was recognized in Long v. Bullard, 117 U.S. 617 (1886), a case antedating the Bankruptcy Act of 1898. In that case, Long received a discharge in bankruptcy and retained as exempt property a homestead that was subject to a mortgage in favor of Bullard, who did not file proof of the mortgage debt in the bankruptcy. After bankruptcy, Bullard brought a foreclosure action. Long defended on the ground that the discharge prevented foreclosure under the mortgage. This defense was rejected in the state court, which stated that "there could be no personal recovery against [Long] upon the note, but that the property could be subjected to the payment of the amount due, as the discharge of Long in bankruptcy did not release the lien of the mortgage." 117 U.S. at 619. The court entered a decree for sale of the property. The Supreme Court of the United States affirmed the decree.

BC 506(d), which was amended in the 1984 Amendments, is meant to preserve the rule of Long v. Bullard, but its wording is difficult to follow. The House Report on the Bankruptcy Reform Act of 1978 states with respect to the original version of BC 506(d): "Subsection (d) permits liens to pass through the bankruptcy case unaffected. However, if a party in interest requests the court to determine and allow or disallow the claim secured by the lien under section 502 and the claim is not allowed, then the lien is void to the extent that the claim is not allowed." 1978 U.S.C.C.A.N. 5963, 6313. BC 506(d), in both its original and amended form, is phrased negatively. It states when a lien is void. Only by negative inference does it indicate that a lien not void under BC 506(d) will survive bankruptcy. It assumes that the rule of Long v. Bullard preserves a lien if the lien is not void under BC 506(d) and is not avoided by some other provision of the Code. The text of BC 506(d) follows:

(d)   To the extent that a lien secures a claim against the debtor that is not an allowed secured claim, such lien is void, unless—

(1)   Such claim was disallowed only under section 502(b)(5) [an unmatured claim for spousal or child support, etc.] or 502(e) [a claim for reimbursement or contribution] of this title; or

(2)   Such claim is not an allowed secured claim due only to the failure of any entity to file a proof of such claim under section 501 of this title.

PROBLEMS

1.   Debtor (D), an individual, borrowed $100,000 from Bank to buy equipment and granted Bank a security interest in the equipment to secure the obligation. Later D defaulted on the obligation and filed Chapter 7 bankruptcy. At the time of D's bankruptcy, her obligation to Bank was $90,000, but the equipment was valued at only $60,000. D's trustee in bankruptcy (T) abandoned the equipment to D under BC 554. Bank filed an unsecured claim in D's bankruptcy for the $30,000 deficiency. After T had liquidated all D's other assets, unsecured claims, including Bank's deficiency claim, were paid 10% of the amount of the claims. Bank received $3,000. What are Bank's rights against D and the equipment after D receives a discharge?

2.   If D were a corporation in Problem 1, it could not be granted a discharge under BC 727(a)(1). What is the policy basis for denying D a discharge in Chapter 7 but allowing it in Chapter 11? See BC 1141(d). What are Bank's rights in this case against D and the collateral?

C. TREATMENT OF SECURED CLAIMS IN CHAPTERS 7, 11 AND 13

Bankruptcy law alters some important rights nonbankruptcy law gives secured creditors. Under 9–601(a), if the debtor has defaulted on its obligations to the secured creditor, the creditor can elect to reduce its claim to judgment or pursue the collateral. Bankruptcy's automatic stay prevents the secured creditor from pursuing both remedies after its debtor has filed a bankruptcy petition. Beyond the automatic stay, bankruptcy law alters other rights nonbankruptcy law gives the secured creditor. If a secured creditor has repossessed collateral after its debtor's default, the debtor can redeem the collateral only if it pays the principal owed plus accrued interest. 9–623(b). The secured creditor is not required to turn over the collateral to the debtor until it is repaid in full. It need not accept a lesser amount equal to the assessed value of the collateral. Under nonbankruptcy law a security interest secures the entire obligation secured. Cf. 1–201(b)(35). The secured creditor's security interest is not limited to the value of the collateral as determined by a court. Finally, an effective after-acquired clause in a security agreement enables a creditor's security interest to extend to assets acquired by the debtor and covered by the clause, whenever the debtor acquires the assets. 9–204(a). In this section some specific examples are used to show how bankruptcy law changes these rights depending on which Chapter of the Bankruptcy Code the debtor chooses for relief.

1. CONSUMER DEBTORS

Assume in the following discussion that Debtor owns a car that is subject to a security interest in favor of Bank. The balance of the debt is $20,000 but the car is worth only $13,000. Debtor's financial position is precarious. She owes a good deal on her three credit cards and is in default on several other unsecured debts. She is two payments behind on her vehicle but desperately needs to retain it to drive to work; there is no available public transportation, and, if she loses her car, she loses her job.

a. IN CHAPTER 7

If the car were property that Debtor did not wish to retain, the procedure in Chapter 7 would be simple. The trustee has two choices. It can sell the vehicle for, say, $13,000, free of Bank's security interest (BC 363(f)), and turn the money over to Bank. Bank may credit bid at the trustee's sale (BC 363(k)), that is, offset the balance of the debt against the purchase price and, if no one bids more, Bank will own the car. Bank will have an unsecured claim (BC 506(a)(1)) for the $7,000 deficiency and can share with the other unsecured creditors in Debtor's unencumbered assets. The other alternative is more likely to be chosen by the trustee in this case. Since Bank has a secured claim equal to the value of the car

($13,000), the foreclosure sale is entirely for the benefit of Bank. The unsecured creditors will not benefit from it, and thus the trustee has no incentive to spend the time and money necessary to conduct the foreclosure sale. Hence, the court may grant a motion by Bank to lift the stay (BC 362(d)) or allow the trustee to abandon the auto to Debtor under BC 554(a). In either case, Bank may then proceed to repossess and conduct a creditor's sale under Article 9. If the car is sold for $13,000, Bank may file a claim in Debtor's bankruptcy for the $7,000 deficiency. Bank may receive little or nothing for this claim, but Debtor will be discharged from any further liability to Bank.

If Debtor wishes to retain the car, Chapter 7 offers two alternatives, neither of which is particularly appealing to Debtor. BC 722 empowers Debtor to redeem the property from Bank by paying only the amount of the allowed secured claim (which under 506(a)(1) is the value of the collateral), $13,000, leaving Bank with an unsecured claim for the balance. Although this is not a happy result for Bank because Debtor will be able to retain her car by paying less than the contract obligation, it is unattractive to the cash-strapped Debtor as well, for it offers her a remedy that she can avail herself of only if she can come up with the amount of the secured claim, $13,000, "in full at the time of redemption." BC 722.

The alternative for Debtor is to make a postpetition agreement with Bank to reaffirm the debt under BC 524(c). By this agreement, Debtor undertakes to comply with the terms of the original contract—pay the balance owing on the $20,000 obligation—and, in effect, gives up her right to be discharged with respect to the debt reaffirmed. If Debtor again defaults and the property is resold for less than the amount of the debt then owed, Debtor is liable for the deficiency as though there had been no bankruptcy. Whether a debtor should be allowed to relinquish the right to a discharge with respect to a reaffirmed debt is a controversial policy matter. BC 524 was extensively amended by BAPCPA to provide better disclosure and enforcement for the protection of debtors in reaffirmation cases. Perhaps the very case that moved the drafters to allow reaffirmations to continue under the 1978 Code is the one we consider here: Debtor wishes to keep the car more than she wishes to be discharged from the debt.

Understandably, what debtors usually want in these cases is to keep the car without either redeeming or reaffirming. Debtor would like to get back into the good graces of Bank by making up any back payments and to continue to use the auto while staying current on its payments. This is called a "ride-through" in bankruptcy: the debtor current on its secured debt retains the collateral without redeeming it or reaffirming the debt, while receiving a discharge on the debt. Although the obligation to stay current on the secured debt "rides through" bankruptcy, the discharge eliminates the debtor's personal liability on the obligation. Ride-through therefore makes the debt nonrecourse. There has been a long-running battle between debtors and secured creditors in the courts over whether a debtor who is not in default on an installment contract can hold onto the car in a Chapter 7 bankruptcy without the creditor's consent and without either reaffirming or redeeming. The following case discusses the effect of BAPCPA on this controversy.

In re Jones

United States Court of Appeals, Fourth Circuit, 2010
591 F.3d 308

■ SHEDD, CIRCUIT JUDGE.

David Douglas Jones and Kirsten M. Jones appeal an order of the district court which held that DaimlerChrysler Financial Services Americas, LLC, had the right to repossess their vehicle pursuant to 11 U.S.C. §§ 362(h) and 521(a)(2), and West Virginia Code § 46A–2–106. For the following reasons, we affirm.

I

The Joneses purchased a vehicle under a Retail Installment Contract with DaimlerChrysler that granted DaimlerChrysler a security interest in the vehicle to secure payment; the security interest was later perfected. The contract contains a clause which provides that the Joneses will be in default if they file a bankruptcy petition or if one is filed against them. Subsequently, David Jones filed a petition for relief under Chapter 7 of the Bankruptcy Code. Kirsten M. Jones did not file for bankruptcy but brought this adversary proceeding as the co-owner of the vehicle.

In filing for bankruptcy, Mr. Jones filed a statement of intention with respect to the contract for purchase of the Joneses' vehicle that indicated that he would "Continue Payments" on the vehicle but did not state whether he intended to redeem the vehicle or reaffirm the debt as required by 11 U.S.C. §§ 362(h) and 521(a)(2).[1] He also failed to redeem the vehicle or enter into a reaffirmation agreement with DaimlerChrysler within 45 days of the first meeting of creditors held on June 16, 2006. *See* 11 U.S.C. § 521(a)(6). Mr. Jones made a payment on August 28, 2006, through DaimlerChrysler's automated telephone payment system. This was the only payment made after the § 521(a)(6) 45-day period to either redeem or reaffirm expired on July 31, 2006.

DaimlerChrysler thereafter moved to confirm termination of the automatic stay so that it could enforce its security interest by repossessing the vehicle pursuant to the default-upon-bankruptcy clause,

---

[1] These sections require a debtor intending to retain the collateral to file a statement of intention which states the intent to either reaffirm the debt in a reaffirmation agreement or redeem the property. Then, a creditor and a debtor enter into a reaffirmation agreement prior to discharge, and the consideration for the agreement is the debt which is dischargeable under the Bankruptcy Code; the agreement must be filed with the court. 11 U.S.C. § 524(c). Alternatively, a debtor may redeem property from a secured lien by paying the lienholder the full amount of the lien. 11 U.S.C. § 722. An individual debtor has 45 days after the first meeting of creditors to either reaffirm or redeem. § 521(a)(6).

also called an "*ipso facto*" clause. *See In re Husain,* 364 B.R. 211, 217 n. 7 (Bankr.E.D.Va.2007). After a hearing, the bankruptcy court entered an agreed order confirming that the automatic stay was terminated. Thereafter, without providing written notice of default and right to cure, DaimlerChrysler repossessed the vehicle pursuant to the *ipso facto* clause. The Joneses then commenced this adversary proceeding.

As part of the adversary proceeding, the bankruptcy court enjoined the sale of the vehicle and required its return. The bankruptcy court held that DaimlerChrysler did not have the right under the Bankruptcy Code to repossess the Joneses' vehicle even though Mr. Jones failed to indicate either his intent to redeem the vehicle or reaffirm the debt on his statement of intention. The bankruptcy court relied on the "ride-through" option recognized in *Home Owners Funding Corp. of Am. v. Belanger (In Re Belanger),* 962 F.2d 345, 347–49 (4th Cir.1992). The ride-through option permitted Chapter 7 debtors who were current on their installment payments to continue making payments and retain collateral after discharge without redeeming the collateral or reaffirming the debt. The bankruptcy court also held that West Virginia Code § 46A–2–106 required DaimlerChrysler to first give the Joneses notice of the right to cure default before repossessing the vehicle.

On appeal, the district court reversed both rulings and held that DaimlerChrysler had the right to repossess the vehicle. *In re Jones,* 397 B.R. 775 (S.D.W.Va.2008). Specifically, the court held that the Bankruptcy Abuse Prevention and Consumer Protection Act of 2005 (BAPCPA), Pub.L. No. 109–8, 119 Stat. 23, eliminated the ride-through option recognized in *In re Belanger. In re Jones,* 397 B.R. at 787. The district court also held that § 46A–2–106 is inapplicable here. The Joneses now appeal the order of the district court, challenging both of these rulings. For the following reasons, we reject their contentions and affirm.

II

* * *

A

We initially consider whether the district court erred in holding that BAPCPA eliminated the ride-through option recognized in *In Re Belanger,* 962 F.2d at 347–49. *In re Belanger* analyzed the language of former § 521(2)(A), which required a debtor to file a statement of intention which, "if applicable," indicated the debtor's intent to either redeem the collateral or reaffirm the debt secured by the collateral. We interpreted the language "if applicable" to mean that the options of redeeming or reaffirming were not exclusive and, therefore, the property could ride through the bankruptcy unaffected if the debtor chose to retain the property and continue making payments. 962 F.2d at 347.

Although the text of the former § 521(2)(A) remains largely the same under BAPCPA, former § 521(2)(C) has been amended as follows:

"nothing in subparagraphs (A) and (B) of this paragraph shall alter the debtor's or the trustee's rights with regard to such property under this title, *except as provided in section 362(h)*." § 521(a)(2)(C)(emphasis added). . . .

Sections 521(a)(2)(C) and 362(h) significantly alter the pre-BAPCPA analysis by explicitly requiring a debtor to indicate on the statement of intention an intent to either (1) redeem the property or (2) reaffirm the debt, in order to retain the property. If the debtor fails to so indicate, the stay terminates with respect to the property, and the property will no longer be part of the estate. . . .

Section 521(a)(6), added by BAPCPA, also evidences that the ride-through option has been eliminated. That section provides that a debtor may not retain possession of personal property which is subject to a secured claim unless the debtor either reaffirms the debt or redeems the property, according to the debtor's statement of intention required by §§ 521(a)(2) and 362(h), within 45 days of the first meeting of creditors. This section further provides that if the debtor fails to so act within the 45-day period, the stay is terminated, the property is no longer considered part of the estate, and "the creditor may take whatever action as to such property as is permitted by applicable nonbankruptcy law." § 521(a).

Therefore, BAPCPA amended Title 11 to eliminate the ride-through option that we recognized in *In re Belanger,* at least as applied to these facts. Although our holding is at odds with *In re Belanger,* that decision has been superseded by BAPCPA. . . .

When Mr. Jones failed to timely redeem the vehicle or reaffirm the contract, the automatic stay was terminated and the vehicle was no longer part of the bankruptcy estate. The Joneses were not entitled to retain the vehicle pursuant to the Bankruptcy Code, and DaimlerChrysler was free to take whatever action was permitted under West Virginia law and its contract.

B

We next turn to the question of whether DaimlerChrysler had authority to repossess the vehicle pursuant to the contract's *ipso facto* clause without giving the Joneses prior notice of a right to cure the default under state law. The general rule is that an *ipso facto* clause in an installment loan contract is unenforceable as a matter of law. *See Riggs Nat. Bank of Washington, D.C. v. Perry,* 729 F.2d 982, 984–85 (4th Cir.1984) (explaining that these clauses deprive a debtor of the advantages of bankruptcy proceedings by causing him to default immediately upon his filing a bankruptcy petition). However, BAPCPA created an exception to this general prohibition by adding § 521(d), which permits creditors to enforce *ipso facto* clauses in consumer loan agreements secured by personal property if the debtor fails to comply with the provisions of §§ 521(a)(6) or 362(h). . . . Specifically, § 521(d) provides that upon the debtor's failure to comply with these provisions,

> [N]othing in this title shall prevent or limit the operation of a provision in the underlying lease or agreement that has the effect of placing the debtor in default under such lease or agreement by reason of the occurrence, pendency, or existence of a proceeding under this title or the insolvency of the debtor. Nothing in this subsection shall be deemed to justify limiting such a provision in any other circumstance.

Therefore, the filing of the bankruptcy petition constituted default, and Mr. Jones's failure to redeem the vehicle or reaffirm the debt permitted DaimlerChrysler to take action under its contract and § 521(d) as permitted by West Virginia law. § 521(a)(6). * * *

III

Accordingly, the judgment of the district court is affirmed.

AFFIRMED

NOTE

In concluding that ride-through does not survive enactment of the BAPCA, In re Dumont, 581 F.3d 1104, 1110 (9th Cir.2009), acknowledges that the BAPCPA is "hardly the very model of a well-drafted statute." Some courts find that the BAPCPA does not eliminate ride-through completely. They allow ride-through in a limited circumstance: when the debtor offers a reaffirmation agreement that the court rejects. BC 521(a)(6)(A)–(B) requires the debtor planning to retain personal property to redeem the property or enter into a reaffirmation agreement with the secured creditor with respect to the property. BC 524(c) imposes significant disclosure requirements on the creditor, and BC 524(d) allows a court to reject a reaffirmation agreement that it finds imposes an undue hardship on the debtor or is not in the debtor's best interests. A debtor that is a party to a reaffirmation agreement that is rejected arguably still has "entered into" one for purposes of BC 521(a)(6)(A). Thus, most courts conclude, BC 521(a)(6) does not prevent the debtor from retaining the personal property subject to the rejected reaffirmation agreement. The debtor's obligations to stay current on her payments continue or "ride-through" her bankruptcy. For cases that accept this argument, see In re Rhodes, 635 B.R. 849 (Bankr. S.D. Cal. 2021); Coastal Federal Credit Union v. Hardiman, 398 B.R. 161 (E.D.N.C.2008).

PROBLEM

What does Bank have to lose in allowing Debtor a "ride-through"? If Debtor defaults again, Bank may repossess and dispose of the car. If Debtor doesn't default, Bank is paid the contract amount. So what's the cost to Bank in being big-hearted? In considering the question, realize that the Chapter 7 discharge extinguishes Debtor's personal liability on its obligations to Bank. See BC 727(b), 524(a)(2).

b. IN CHAPTER 13

Before 2005 Chapter 13 gave Debtor what she wanted, that is, the right to retain the car, without Bank's consent, and to pay Bank in installments from her postpetition income. She could retain all her property, including her indispensable car, if she proposed a confirmable plan calling for her to pay all her disposable earnings over a three-year period to a standing trustee to be distributed to her creditors. The plan had to be approved by the court, but the consent of creditors was not necessary. In order for the plan to be approved by the court, Bank, as a secured creditor, had to receive payment of the present value of its secured claim ($13,000) in installments over the three-year life of the plan. Former BC 1325(a)(5). Debtor's unsecured creditors shared in what was left, but they had to receive as much in Chapter 13 as they would have received in Chapter 7, taking into account the fact that payment in Chapter 13 is on a deferred basis. Former BC 1325(a)(4). Thus, if Debtor's earnings were enough to pay off in installments the $13,000 secured claim with interest over a three-year period, she could hold on to her car. The $7,000 deficiency claim, along with other unsecured claims, would be paid only to the extent that Debtor had disposable income in excess of the amount needed to pay off the secured claims relating to property that Debtor wished to retain. Usually these payments were minimal. At the end of the three-year period, Debtor received a broad discharge. The power of debtors to strip-down security interests in assets they wished to retain, as in this case, was a major attraction of Chapter 13 for debtors: a debtor could keep her car by paying only its depreciated value in monthly installments and discharge her deficiency debt by paying pennies on the dollar. Good deal.

Motor vehicle lenders found the result too generous to the debtor, and the BAPCPA made major changes that substantially reduced the attraction of Chapter 13 for debtors. It limits lien-stripping with respect to purchase-money security interests in motor vehicles, as well as certain other collateral, by making inapplicable the bifurcation effect of BC 506(a)(1), in which an undersecured claim is divided into a secured claim for the value of the collateral and an unsecured claim for the remainder of the debt. The following language was added at the end of BC 1325(a):

> For the purposes of paragraph (5), section 506 shall not apply to a claim described in that paragraph if the creditor has a purchase money security interest securing the debt that is the subject of the claim, the debt was incurred within the 910-day [period] preceding the filing of the petition, and the collateral for that debtor consists of a motor vehicle. . .acquired for the personal use of the debtor, or if collateral for that debt consists of any other thing of value, if the debt was incurred during the 1-year period preceding that filing.

"Purchase money security interest" being undefined under the paragraph, courts rely on the 9–103's definition of the term.

The effect of this paragraph is that a debtor can no longer bifurcate a "910" debt under a Chapter 13 cramdown plan. Thus, according to most courts, the paragraph deems the full amount of the claim to be secured. This means that the debtor must pay over the period of the plan the entire amount of the creditor's claim in order to retain the collateral. No longer can a "910" debtor retain a vehicle by paying the stripped down value of the vehicle in installments. If Debtor wishes to retain her car by making installment payments to Bank under a Chapter 13 plan, the balance she must pay (with interest) over the life of the plan is $20,000 rather than $13,000, the value of the secured claim under BC 506(a). Treating undersecured purchase-money automobile loans as fully secured reduces the amount of debtor's income payable to unsecured creditors to the great advantage of secured auto lenders. The effect is similar to reaffirmation of such debts. Moreover, under BC 1325(a)(5)(B)(iii), unless the debtor completes her plan (something that happens in only about one-third of the cases), the secured creditor retains a lien for the remaining unpaid balance. There is little incentive for buyers to retain their cars under such circumstances, and these measures remove a major incentive for debtors to opt for Chapter 13.

One of the most common issues arising with respect to secured claims in Chapter 13 cases concerns the rights of the parties when the debtor's car has been repossessed. Does the creditor have to return the car upon request of the debtor and sue for adequate protection of its collateral? Courts have divided on the question. In *Fulton*, reproduced below, the Supreme Court decided whether a creditor's retention of possession of the debtor's property violates 362(a)(3). Although the creditor in *Fulton* was a lien creditor, not a secured creditor, the Court's ruling applies to secured creditors.

City of Chicago v. Fulton
Supreme Court of the United States, 2021
141 S. Ct. 585

■ JUSTICE ALITO delivered the opinion of the Court.

When a debtor files a petition for bankruptcy, the Bankruptcy Code protects the debtor's interests by imposing an automatic stay on efforts to collect prepetition debts outside the bankruptcy forum. Those prohibited efforts include "any act . . . to exercise control over property" of the bankruptcy estate. 11 U. S. C. § 362(a)(3). The question in this case is whether an entity violates that prohibition by retaining possession of a debtor's property after a bankruptcy petition is filed. We hold that mere retention of property does not violate § 362(a)(3).

I

Under the Bankruptcy Code, the filing of a bankruptcy petition has certain immediate consequences. For one thing, a petition "creates an estate" that, with some exceptions, comprises "all legal or equitable interests of the debtor in property as of the commencement of the case." § 541(a)(1). Section 541 "is intended to include in the estate any property made available to the estate by other provisions of the Bankruptcy Code." *United States* v. *Whiting Pools, Inc.*, 462 U. S. 198, 205, 103 S. Ct. 2309, 76 L. Ed. 2d 515 (1983). One such provision, § 542, is important for present purposes. Titled "Turnover of property to the estate," § 542 provides, with just a few exceptions, that an entity (other than a custodian) in possession of property of the bankruptcy estate "shall deliver to the trustee, and account for" that property.

A second automatic consequence of the filing of a bankruptcy petition is that, with certain exceptions, the petition "operates as a stay, applicable to all entities," of efforts to collect from the debtor outside of the bankruptcy forum. § 362(a). The automatic stay serves the debtor's interests by protecting the estate from dismemberment, and it also benefits creditors as a group by preventing individual creditors from pursuing their own interests to the detriment of the others. Under the Code, an individual injured by any willful violation of the stay "shall recover actual damages, including costs and attorneys' fees, and in appropriate circumstances, may recover punitive damages." § 362(k)(1).

Among the many collection efforts prohibited by the stay is "any act to obtain possession of property of the estate or of property from the estate or *to exercise control over property of the estate.*" § 362(a)(3) (emphasis added). The prohibition against exercising control over estate property is the subject of the present dispute.

In the case before us, the city of Chicago (City) impounded each respondent's vehicle for failure to pay fines for motor vehicle infractions. Each respondent filed a Chapter 13 bankruptcy petition and requested that the City return his or her vehicle. The City refused, and in each case a bankruptcy court held that the City's refusal violated the automatic stay. The Court of Appeals affirmed all of the judgments in a consolidated opinion. *In re Fulton*, 926 F. 3d 916 (CA7 2019). The court concluded that "by retaining possession of the debtors' vehicles after they declared bankruptcy," the City had acted "to exercise control over" respondents' property in violation of § 362(a)(3). *Id.*, at 924–925. We granted certiorari to resolve a split in the Courts of Appeals over whether an entity that retains possession of the property of a bankruptcy estate violates § 362(a)(3). We now vacate the judgment below.

II

The language used in § 362(a)(3) suggests that merely retaining possession of estate property does not violate the automatic stay. Under that provision, the filing of a bankruptcy petition operates as a "stay" of "any act" to "exercise control" over the property of the estate. Taken together, the most natural reading of these terms—"stay," "act," and "exercise control"—is that § 362(a)(3) prohibits affirmative acts that would disturb the status quo of estate property as of the time when the bankruptcy petition was filed.

Taking the provision's operative words in turn, the term "stay" is commonly used to describe an order that "suspend[s] judicial alteration of the status quo." *Nken* v. *Holder*, 556 U. S. 418, 429, 129 S. Ct. 1749, 173 L. Ed. 2d 550 (2009) (brackets in original; internal quotation marks omitted). An "act" is "[s]omething done or performed . . . ; a deed." Black's Law Dictionary 30 (11th ed. 2019); see also Webster's New International Dictionary 25 (2d ed. 1934) ("that which is done," "the exercise of power," "a deed"). To "exercise" in the sense relevant here means "to bring into play" or "make effective in action." Webster's Third New International Dictionary 795 (1993). And to "exercise" something like control is "to put in practice or carry out in action." Webster's New International Dictionary, at 892. The suggestion conveyed by the combination of these terms is that § 362(a)(3) halts any affirmative act that would alter the status quo as of the time of the filing of a bankruptcy petition.

We do not maintain that these terms definitively rule out the alternative interpretation adopted by the court below and advocated by respondents. As respondents point out, omissions can qualify as "acts" in certain contexts, and the term "'control'" can mean "'to have power over.'" *Thompson* v. *General Motors Acceptance Corp.*, 566 F.3d 699, 702 (CA7 2009) (quoting Merriam-Webster's Collegiate Dictionary 272 (11th ed. 2003)). But saying that a person engages in an "act" to "exercise" his or her power over a thing communicates more than merely "having" that power. [9] Thus the language of § 362(a)(3) implies that something more than merely retaining power is required to violate the disputed provision.

Any ambiguity in the text of § 362(a)(3) is resolved decidedly in the City's favor by the existence of a separate provision, § 542, that expressly governs the turnover of estate property. Section 542(a), with two exceptions, provides as follows:

> "[A]n entity, other than a custodian, in possession, custody, or control, during the case, of property that the trustee may use, sell, or lease under section 363 of this title, or that the debtor may exempt under section 522 of this title, shall deliver to the trustee, and account for, such property or the value of such property, unless such property is of inconsequential value or benefit to the estate."

The exceptions to § 542(a) shield (1) transfers of estate property made from one entity to another in good faith without notice or knowledge of the bankruptcy petition and (2) good-faith transfers to satisfy certain life insurance obligations. See §§ 542(c), (d). Reading § 362(a)(3) to cover mere retention of property, as respondents advocate, would create at least two serious problems.

First, it would render the central command of § 542 largely superfluous. "The canon against surplusage is strongest when an interpretation would render superfluous another part of the same statutory scheme." *Yates* v. *United States*, 574 U. S. 528, 543, 135 S. Ct. 1074, 191 L. Ed. 2d 64 (2015) (plurality opinion; internal quotation marks and brackets omitted). Reading "any act . . . to exercise control" in § 362(a)(3) to include merely retaining possession of a debtor's property would make that section a blanket turnover provision. But as noted, § 542 expressly governs "[t]urnover of property to the estate," and subsection (a) describes the broad range of property that an entity "shall deliver to the trustee." That mandate would be surplusage if § 362(a)(3) already required an entity affirmatively to relinquish control of the debtor's property at the moment a bankruptcy petition is filed.

Respondents and their *amici* contend that § 542(a) would still perform some work by specifying the party to whom the property in question must be turned over and by requiring that an entity "account for . . . the value of "the debtor's property if the property is damaged or lost. But that is a small amount of work for a large amount of text in a section that appears to be the Code provision that is designed to govern the turnover of estate property. Under this alternative interpretation, § 362(a)(3), not § 542, would be the chief provision governing turnover— even though § 362(a)(3) says nothing expressly on that question. And § 542 would be reduced to a footnote—even though it appears on its face to be the governing provision. The better account of the two provisions is that § 362(a)(3) prohibits collection efforts outside the bankruptcy proceeding that would change the status quo, while § 542(a) works within the bankruptcy process to draw far-flung estate property back into the hands of the debtor or trustee.

Second, respondents' reading would render the commands of § 362(a)(3) and § 542 contradictory. Section 542 carves out exceptions to the turnover command, and § 542(a) by its terms does not mandate turnover of property that is "of inconsequential value or benefit to the estate." Under respondents' reading, in cases where those exceptions to turnover under § 542 would apply, § 362(a)(3) would command turnover all the same. But it would be "an odd construction" of § 362(a)(3) to require a creditor to do immediately what §542 specifically excuses. *Citizens Bank of Md.* v. *Strumpf*, 516 U. S. 16, 20, 116 S. Ct. 286, 133 L. Ed. 2d 258 (1995). Respondents would have us resolve the conflicting commands by engrafting § 542's exceptions onto § 362(a)(3), but there is no textual basis for doing so.

The history of the Bankruptcy Code confirms what its text and structure convey. Both § 362(a)(3) and § 542(a) were included in the original Bankruptcy Code in 1978. See Bankruptcy Reform Act of 1978, 92 Stat. 2570, 2595. At the time, § 362(a)(3) applied the stay only to "any act to obtain possession of property of the estate or of property from the estate." *Id.*, at 2570. The phrase "or to exercise control over property of the estate" was not added until 1984. Bankruptcy Amendments and Federal Judgeship Act of 1984, 98 Stat. 371.

Respondents do not seriously dispute that § 362(a)(3) imposed no turnover obligation prior to the 1984 amendment. But transforming the stay in § 362 into an affirmative turnover obligation would have constituted an important change. And it would have been odd for Congress to accomplish that change by simply adding the phrase "exercise control," a phrase that does not naturally comprehend the mere retention of property and that does not admit of the exceptions set out in § 542. Had Congress wanted to make § 362(a)(3) an enforcement arm of sorts for § 542(a), the least one would expect would be a cross-reference to the latter provision, but Congress did not include such a cross-reference or provide any other indication that it was transforming § 362(a)(3). The better account of the statutory history is that the 1984 amendment, by adding the phrase regarding the exercise of control, simply extended the stay to acts that would change the status quo with respect to intangible property and acts that would change the status quo with respect to tangible property without "obtain[ing]" such property. * * *

Though the parties debate the issue at some length, we need not decide how the turnover obligation in § 542 operates. Nor do we settle the meaning of other subsections of § 362(a).[2] We hold only that mere retention of estate property after the filing of a bankruptcy petition does not violate § 362(a)(3) of the Bankruptcy Code. The judgment of the Court of Appeals is vacated, and the case is remanded for further proceedings consistent with this opinion.

It is so ordered.

JUSTICE BARRETT took no part in the consideration or decision of this case.

JUSTICE SOTOMAYOR, concurring.

Section 362(a)(3) of the Bankruptcy Code provides that the filing of a bankruptcy petition "operates as a stay" of "any act . . . to exercise control over property of the [bankruptcy] estate." 11 U. S. C. § 362(a)(3). I join the Court's opinion because I agree that, as used in § 362(a)(3), the phrase "exercise control over" does not cover a creditor's passive retention of property lawfully seized prebankruptcy. Hence, when a creditor has taken possession of a debtor's property, § 362(a)(3) does not require the creditor to return the property upon the filing of a bankruptcy petition.

I write separately to emphasize that the Court has not decided whether and when § 362(a)'s other provisions may require a creditor to return a debtor's property. Those provisions stay, among other things, "any act to create, perfect, or enforce any lien against property of the estate" and "any act to collect, assess, or recover a claim against [a] debtor" that arose prior to bankruptcy proceedings. §§ 362(a)(4), (6); see, *e.g.*, *In re Kuehn*, 563 F. 3d 289, 294 (CA7 2009) (holding that a university's refusal to provide a transcript to a student-debtor "was an act to collect a debt" that violated the automatic stay). Nor has the Court

---

[2] In respondent Shannon's case, the Bankruptcy Court determined that by retaining Shannon's vehicle and demanding payment, the City also had violated §§ 362(a)(4) and (a)(6) . Shannon presented those theories to the Court of Appeals, but the court did not reach them. 926 F. 3d, at 926, n. 1. Neither do we.

addressed how bankruptcy courts should go about enforcing creditors' separate obligation to "deliver" estate property to the trustee or debtor under § 542(a). The City's conduct may very well violate one or both of these other provisions. The Court does not decide one way or the other.

Regardless of whether the City's policy of refusing to return impounded vehicles satisfies the letter of the Code, it hardly comports with its spirit. "The principal purpose of the Bankruptcy Code is to grant a "fresh start" to debtors. *Marrama* v. *Citizens Bank of Mass.*, 549 U. S. 365, 367, 127 S. Ct. 1105, 166 L. Ed. 2d 956 (2007) (quoting *Grogan* v. *Garner*, 498 U. S. 279, 286, 111 S. Ct. 654, 112 L. Ed. 2d 755 (1991)). When a debtor files for Chapter 13 bankruptcy, as respondents did here, "the debtor retains possession of his property" and works toward completing a court-approved repayment plan. 549 U. S., at 367, 367, 127 S. Ct. 1105, 166 L. Ed. 2d 956. For a Chapter 13 bankruptcy to succeed, therefore, the debtor must continue earning an income so he can pay his creditors. Indeed, Chapter 13 bankruptcy is available only to "individual[s] with regular income." 11 U. S. C. § 109(e).

For many, having a car is essential to maintaining employment. Take, for example, respondent George Peake. Before the City seized his car, Peake relied on his 200,000-mile 2007 Lincoln MKZ to travel 45 miles each day from his home on the South Side of Chicago to his job in Joliet, Illinois. In June 2018, when the City impounded Peake's car for unpaid parking and red-light tickets, the vehicle was worth just around $4,300 (and was already serving as collateral for a roughly $7,300 debt). Without his car, Peake had to pay for rides to Joliet. He filed for bankruptcy, hoping to recover his vehicle and repay his $5,393.27 debt to the City through a Chapter 13 plan. The City, however, refused to return the car until either Peake paid $1,250 upfront or after the court confirmed Peake's bankruptcy plan. As a result, Peake's car remained in the City's possession for months. By denying Peake access to the vehicle he needed to commute to work, the City jeopardized Peake's ability to make payments to *all* his creditors, the City included. Surely, Peake's vehicle would have been more valuable in the hands of its owner than parked in the City's impound lot.

Peake's situation is far too common. Drivers in low-income communities across the country face similar vicious cycles: A driver is assessed a fine she cannot immediately pay; the balance balloons as late fees accrue; the local government seizes the driver's vehicle, adding impounding and storage fees to the growing debt; and the driver, now without reliable transportation to and from work, finds it all but impossible to repay her debt and recover her vehicle. Such drivers may turn to Chapter 13 bankruptcy for a "fresh start." *Marrama*, 549 U. S., at 367, 367, 127 S. Ct. 1105, 166 L. Ed. 2d 956 (internal quotation marks omitted). But without their vehicles, many debtors quickly find themselves unable to make their Chapter 13 payments. The cycle thus continues, disproportionately burdening communities of color, and interfering not only with debtors' ability to earn an income and pay their creditors but also with their access to childcare, groceries, medical appointments, and other necessities.

Although the Court today holds that § 362(a)(3) does not require creditors to turn over impounded vehicles, bankruptcy courts are not powerless to facilitate the return of debtors' vehicles to their owners. Most obviously, the Court leaves open the possibility of relief under § 542(a). That section requires any "entity," subject to some exceptions, to turn over "property" belonging to the bankruptcy estate. 11 U. S. C. § 542(a). The debtor, in turn, must be able to provide the creditor with "adequate protection" of its interest in the returned property, § 363(e); for example, the debtor may need to demonstrate that her car is sufficiently insured. In this way, § 542(a) maximizes value for all parties involved in a bankruptcy: The debtor is able to use her asset, which makes it easier to earn an income; the debtor's unsecured creditors, in turn, receive timely payments from the debtor; and the debtor's secured creditor, for its part, receives "adequate protection [to] replace the protection afforded by possession." *United States* v. *Whiting Pools, Inc.*, 462 U. S. 198, 207, 103 S. Ct. 2309, 76 L. Ed. 2d 515 (1983). Secured creditors cannot opt out of this arrangement. As even the City acknowledges, § 542(a) "impose[s] a duty of turnover that is mandatory when the statute's conditions . . . are met." Brief for Petitioner 37.

The trouble with § 542(a), however, is that turnover proceedings can be quite slow. The Federal Rules of Bankruptcy Procedure treat most "proceeding[s] to recover . . . property" as "adversary proceedings." Rule 7001(1). Such actions are, in simplified terms, "essentially full civil lawsuits carried out under the umbrella of [a] bankruptcy case." *Bullard* v. *Blue Hills Bank*, 575 U. S. 496, 505, 135 S. Ct. 1686, 191 L. Ed. 2d 621 (2015). Because adversary proceedings require more process, they take more time. Of the turnover proceedings filed after July 2019 and concluding before June 2020, the average case was pending for over 100 days.

One hundred days is a long time to wait for a creditor to return your car, especially when you need that car to get to work so you can earn an income and make your bankruptcy-plan payments. To address this problem, some courts have adopted strategies to hurry things along. At least one bankruptcy court has held that § 542(a)'s turnover obligation is automatic even absent a court order. See *In re Larimer*, 27 B. R. 514, 516 (Idaho 1983). Other courts apparently will permit debtors to seek turnover by simple motion, in lieu of filing a full adversary proceeding, at least where the creditor has received adequate notice. Similarly, even when a turnover request does take the form of an adversary proceeding, bankruptcy courts may find it prudent to expedite proceedings or order preliminary relief requiring temporary turnover.

Ultimately, however, any gap left by the Court's ruling today is best addressed by rule drafters and policymakers, not bankruptcy judges. It is up to the Advisory Committee on Rules of Bankruptcy Procedure to consider amendments to the Rules that ensure prompt resolution of debtors' requests for turnover under § 542(a), especially where debtors' vehicles are concerned. Congress, too, could offer a statutory fix, either by ensuring that expedited review is available for § 542(a) proceedings seeking turnover of a vehicle or by enacting entirely new statutory mechanisms that require creditors to return cars to debtors in a timely manner.

Nothing in today's opinion forecloses these alternative solutions. With that understanding, I concur.

NOTE

Fulton resolves the question of 362(a)(3)'s interpretation that had divided the circuits. However, the case leaves unaddressed other questions about the automatic stay's application to a creditor's refusal to turnover collateral at the start of its debtor's bankruptcy cases. The Supreme Court's ruling construes only BC 362(a)(3) and not 362(a)'s other subsections or BC 542(a)'s interaction with BC 362(a), as both the Court's opinion acknowledges and Justice Sotomayor's concurrence emphasizes. Accordingly, a creditor's retention of collateral might violate BC 362(a)(4) (acts to enforce a lien) or (a)(6) (acts to collect or recover a claim against the debtor), depending on how these provisions are construed. Separately, the refusal might violate 542(a)'s turnover requirement. To date the few cases taking *Fulton* into account have reached different conclusions about its extension to 362(a)'s subsections beyond 362(a)(3). In re Stuart 632 B.R. 531 (B.A.P. 9th Cir. 2021) and In re Margavitch 2021 WL 4597760 (Bankr. W.D. Pa. Oct. 6, 2021) ruled, in light of *Fulton*, that a creditor's retention of collateral does not violate any of BC 362(a)'s subsections. In contrast, Cordova v. City of Chicago, 2021 WL 5774400 (Bankr. N.D. Ill. Dec. 6, 2021) ruled that BC 362(a)(4) and (a)(6), as well as BC 542(a), might apply in the same circumstances.

2. BUSINESS DEBTORS

Assume in the following discussion that Hospital, a corporation, is unsuccessfully struggling with the exigencies of the new managed care regime that governmental agencies and insurance companies have imposed on it. Hospital's cash flow is inadequate to meet its obligations and its creditors are pressing for payment. One of the creditors is Lender, which holds a purchase-money security interest in Hospital's only Magnetic Resonance Imaging (MRI) machine, an important diagnostic device. Although the value of the machine has shrunk to $1 million, Hospital's obligation to Lender that is secured by the machine is $1.5. Lender is threatening to repossess. Hospital owes several hundred thousand dollars to various unsecured trade creditors, as well as to unpaid attending physicians who have performed services for Hospital.

a.   IN CHAPTER 7

Assume that Hospital is hopelessly insolvent and has been attempting, without success, to sell its business for some time. Hospital's aging management has decided to give up and liquidate in Chapter 7. The analysis here is not unlike that above for the consumer debtor, except that, for the reasons discussed above, Hospital cannot be discharged in Chapter 7. So there is no issue in corporate Chapter 7s of a debtor's retaining assets of the estate; the business must dissolve, and everything must go to its creditors. Here again the trustee has the choice of conducting the foreclosure sale of the collateral or, as is likely here, of lifting the stay or abandoning the property to Hospital and leaving it to Lender to proceed under Article 9. In either instance, Lender can credit bid the amount of its debt and file an unsecured claim for the deficiency.

b.   IN CHAPTER 11: AFTER-ACQUIRED PROPERTY AND DIP FINANCING

Suppose Hospital's board of directors won't give up; they hire new management and try to reorganize under Chapter 11. Usually no trustee will be appointed and Hospital, meaning its board, will serve as debtor in possession with the powers of a trustee in bankruptcy. BC 1107. Hospital will have two major tasks in the months following filing. First, it must improve its business operations so that it can create cash flow adequate to meet its current expenses of operation. If Hospital is unable to right the sinking ship, it will have to go into Chapter 7, as a very large percentage of small enterprises that attempt to reorganize under Chapter 11 ultimately do. Second, Hospital must deal with its unhappy prepetition creditors by seeking to achieve confirmation of a plan of reorganization. It has the exclusive right to propose a plan for 120 days after filing (BC 1121(b)) and to obtain acceptance of the proposed plan within an additional 60 days (BC 1121(c)). The court has discretionary authority to grant extensions of these periods (BC 1121(d)), and often does, but since 2005 the period of exclusivity has been limited to 18 months after filing. After the period of exclusivity has ended, creditors and others may propose their own plans. In a small case like this one, it's likely that only the debtor in possession will propose a plan and that the 18-month limitation on exclusivity will not pose difficulties.

To continue its operations, a debtor reorganizing under Chapter 11 often needs to borrow money before it can emerge from bankruptcy. This requires postpetition or debtor in possession ("DIP") financing. In this case, the debtor, exercising the trustee's powers as the debtor in possession, must find a lender willing to make a loan on terms the DIP lender finds acceptable. The interest rates lenders charge for DIP financing reflect the seniority of the security interests securing their loans. DIP lenders usually prefer taking security interests in assets unencumbered with security interests, unless the security interests securing their loans otherwise have priority. The Bankruptcy Code gives the trustee, with court approval, the authority to secure a postpetition loan with assets not subject to a lien. BC 364(c)(2). The problem is that financially distressed debtors likely will have concluded prepetition security agreements with broad after-acquired property clauses. Under 9–204(a), these clauses can encumber virtually all of the debtor's personal property, whenever the debtor acquires it, with a security interest.

To free the collateral base of encumbrances, Bankruptcy Code section 552 in effect invalidates after-acquired property clauses in bankruptcy. Section 552(a) states the general rule that property that the debtor or the estate acquires after the commencement of the case is not subject to a prepetition lien granted by the debtor. By invalidating after-acquired property clauses in prepetition security agreements, the rule prevents these clauses from creating security interests in postpetition assets acquired by the estate. This enables the debtor in possession to offer as collateral for a postpetition loan assets acquired by the estate unencumbered with prepetition security interests.

Section 552(a)'s general rule is subject to two exceptions contained in 552(b). Section 552(b)(1) provides that, with certain exceptions, if a secured creditor and the debtor entered into a prepetition security agreement that granted a security interest in prepetition property as well as "proceeds, products, offspring or profits" of such property, then the secured creditor's security interest extends to such "proceeds, products, offspring or profits" acquired by the estate postpetition to the extent provided by applicable nonbankruptcy law. Section 552(b)(2) provides a comparable exception for rents of prepetition collateral and postpetition "fees, charges, accounts or other payments for the use or occupancy of hotel and motel rooms.

Section 552's application requires a firm distinction between postpetition after-acquired property obtained by the estate (in which 552(a)'s general rule voids a security interest) and postpetition proceeds of prepetition collateral (to which 552(b)(1)'s exception applies to continue a prepetition security interest). The trouble is that sometimes an asset acquired by the estate is both after-acquired property and proceeds of prepetition collateral. For example, suppose inventory item 1 is prepetition collateral under a prepetition security agreement covering all of the debtor's existing and after-acquired inventory. After the debtor goes into bankruptcy the DIP exchanges inventory item 1 for inventory item 2. Inventory item 2 is both postpetition after-acquired property and postpetition proceeds of prepetition collateral. Another difficulty with 552(b)(1)'s application is attributing the contribution of prepetition collateral to the production of postpetition assets. For example, assume that prepetition collateral is used by the estate along with unencumbered estate assets to produce a product. Assume also that the product is sold. To what extent, if any, are the sale revenues "proceeds, products, offspring or profit" of the prepetition collateral? The following case deals with this question.

In re Premier Golf Properties, LP

United States Bankruptcy Appellate Panel, Ninth Circuit, 2012
477 B.R. 767

■ **Opinion by:** HOLLOWELL, BANKRUPTCY JUDGE.

Far East National Bank (the Bank) filed a motion to prohibit the debtor from using cash collateral. The bankruptcy court denied the motion because it determined that revenue from the debtor's postpetition green fees and driving range fees did not constitute the Bank's cash collateral. The Bank appealed. For the reasons given below, we AFFIRM.

I.   FACTS

Premier Golf Properties, L.P. (the Golf Club) owns and operates the Cottonwood Golf Club in El Cajon, California. The Golf Club has two 18-hole golf courses, a driving range, pro shop, and club house restaurant. The Golf Club maintains the golf courses and operates a golf course business on the real property (Land). Its income comes from green fees, range fees, annual membership sales, golf lessons, golf cart rentals, pro shop clothing and equipment sales, and food and beverage services.

The Bank financed the Golf Club's business. In December 2007, the Bank loaned the Golf Club $11,500,000. The loan is secured by a Deed of Trust, Security Agreement, Assignment of Leases and Rents and Fixture Filing (Security Documents). According to the Security Documents, the Bank was granted a blanket security interest in all of the Golf Club's real and personal property. The Security Documents state, in part, that the Bank holds a security interest in all of the following described property "and all proceeds thereof":

> All accounts, contract rights, general intangibles, chattel paper, documents, instruments, inventory, goods, equipment . . . , including without limitation . . . all revenues, receipts, income, accounts, customer obligations, installment payment obligations . . . accounts receivable and other receivables, including without limitation license fees, golf club and membership initiation fees, green fees, driving range fees, golf cart fees, membership fees and dues, revenues, receipts, . . . and profits . . . arising from (i) rentals, . . . license, concession, or other grant of right of possession, use or occupancy of all or any portion of the Land, and . . . (ii) the provision or sale of any goods and services . . . .

Additionally, the Security Documents included an Assignment of Rents and Leases assigning the Bank an interest in "all agreements affecting the use, enjoyment or occupancy of the Land now or hereafter entered into (the "Leases") and all rents, prepayments, security deposits, termination payments, royalties, profits, issues and revenues from the Land . . . accruing under the Leases . . . ." The Bank filed UCC-1 Financing Statements listing the same collateral as that in the Security Documents.

On May 2, 2011, the Golf Club filed a Chapter 11 bankruptcy petition. It continued to operate its business as debtor in possession. The Golf Club opened a new bank account designated for cash collateral and segregated in that account its prepetition cash and receivables from goods and inventory sold but did not segregate the revenue received from green fees and driving range fees. On May 13, 2011, the Bank filed an emergency motion to prohibit the Golf Club from using cash collateral. The Bank asserted that the Golf Club was using the Bank's cash collateral in its ordinary course of business without the Bank's consent and without providing adequate protection. On May 22, 2011, the Golf Club filed an opposition, asserting that it was not using the Bank's cash collateral but was operating the estate from its own postpetition income. The Golf Club argued that the postpetition income from the sale of golf memberships, green fees, cart rentals, the sale of buckets of balls for the driving range, and food and beverage service was not the proceeds, profits, or products of the Bank's collateral.

In its reply, the Bank focused its argument on the revenue from the green fees and driving range fees. It argued the fees were cash collateral because they were rents derived from the use of the Land. Alternatively, the Bank argued that if the green fees and driving range fees were not rents, they were still cash collateral because they were proceeds or profits of its personal property collateral. A hearing was held June 2, 2011. The bankruptcy court took the matter under advisement. On September 1, 2011, the bankruptcy court entered a written decision and order denying the Bank's Motion to Prohibit Use of Cash Collateral. The bankruptcy court held that the revenue received by the Golf Club for green fees and driving range fees was not the rents or proceeds of the Bank's security and therefore, was not cash collateral. The Bank timely appealed. * * *

III. ISSUE

Did the bankruptcy court err in determining that postpetition revenue from the Golf Club's green fees and driving range fees was not rents, proceeds, or profits of the Bank's prepetition security, and therefore, did not constitute cash collateral?

IV. STANDARDS OF REVIEW

We review de novo whether the funds in question are cash collateral.

V. DISCUSSION

A. Cash Collateral

A debtor in possession is prohibited from using cash collateral absent authorization by the court or consent from the entity that has an interest in the collateral. 11 U.S.C. § 363(c)(2). Cash collateral consists of "cash, negotiable instruments . . . deposit accounts, or other cash equivalents whenever acquired in which the estate and an entity other than the estate have an interest." 11 U.S.C. § 363(a). As a general rule, postpetition revenue is not cash collateral. Under § 552(a), a creditor's prepetition security interest does not extend to property acquired by the debtor postpetition even if there is an "after acquired" clause in the security agreement. The purpose of § 552(a) is "to allow a debtor to gather into the estate as much money as possible to satisfy the claims of all creditors." *Philip Morris Capital Corp. v. Bering Trader, Inc. (In re Bering Trader, Inc.)*, 944 F.2d 500, 502 (9th Cir. 1991).

Section 552(b) provides an exception to this rule. Section 552(b)(1) allows a prepetition security interest to extend to the postpetition "proceeds, products, offspring, or profits" of collateral to be covered by a security interest if the security agreement expressly provides for an interest in such property and the interest has been perfected under applicable nonbankruptcy law. Additionally, § 552(b)(2) provides similar treatment for "amounts paid as rents of such property or the fees, charges, accounts, or other payments for the use or occupancy of rooms and other public facilities in hotels, motels, or other lodging properties." Read together, the provisions of § 363(c)(2) and § 552(b) protect a creditor's collateral from being used by a debtor postpetition if the creditor's security interest extends to one of the categories set out in § 552(b). Put another way, a creditor is not entitled to the protections of § 363(c)(2) unless its security interest satisfies § 552(b). Section 552(b) "balances the Code's interest in freeing the debtor of prepetition obligations with a secured creditor's rights to maintain a bargained-for interest in certain items of collateral." *In re Bering Trader, Inc.*, 944 F.2d at 502. It provides "a *narrow* exception to the general rule of 552(a)." Id. (emphasis in original).

The Bank has the burden of establishing the existence and the extent of its interest in the property it claims as cash collateral. 11 U.S.C. § 363(p)(2). Thus, the Bank was required to show that (1) its security agreement extended to the Golf Club's postpetition revenue from green fees and driving range fees and (2) the green fees and driving range fees were proceeds, products, rents or profits of its prepetition collateral.

B. Rents

In 1987, the Ninth Circuit Bankruptcy Appellate Panel (BAP) articulated a general test for determining whether income from real property constitutes rents: If the income is produced by the real property, it is considered rents; but if the income is the result of services rendered or the result of the specific business conducted on the property, then it does not constitute rents. *In re Zeeway Corp.*, 71 B.R. 210, 211–12 (9th Cir. BAP 1987). In applying its test, the BAP concluded that gate receipts generated by postpetition races at the debtor's racetrack were not within the scope of rents subject to the creditor's deed of trust because the income was not produced by the occupancy or use of the real property, but by the services that the raceway provided. Id.

Courts have applied the *Zeeway* test in deciding if a debtor's income from its business operations is rents within § 552(b). Prior to 1994, "rents" was included in the § 552(b)(1) exception and there was a long-running dispute in the courts about whether hotel revenues were rents.

However, the addition of § 552(b)(2) resolved the dispute by treating hotel room revenue the same as rents. Nevertheless, courts continue to confront the question of what constitutes rents in non-hotel cases and refer to pre-1994 case law analysis regarding whether a debtor's income was produced by the real property or by the services on the property.

Courts have used the *Zeeway* test to determine whether revenue from green fees and similar use fees is rents constituting cash collateral. The first of those decisions, *In re GGVXX, Ltd.*, 130 B.R. 322, 326 (Bankr. D. Colo. 1991), held that revenue from green fees and use fees was not directly tied to or wholly dependent on the use of the real property, but was the result of the operation of the golf course business, and therefore, was not rents. The court determined that "a temporary right to enter upon real property and partake of the services offered thereon is not the same as an interest in real property." Id. Thus, it concluded that the relationship to the real property was "too attenuated from the actual real estate to reasonably be considered as directly derived from the use of the land." Id. Similarly, the court in *In re Everett Home Town Ltd. P'ship*, 146 B.R. 453, 456 (Bankr. D. Ariz. 1992) held that although revenue from green fees was produced in part by the use of the real property, the income was the result of the services provided by the golf club business. However, it further held that revenue from suite fees was rents because, like a hotel room, the main charge was for the occupancy of the suite. *Id.* at 457. * * *

The bankruptcy court noted that the key to a golf club's generation of income is due to the regular planting, seeding, mowing, repositioning holes, watering, fertilizing, and maintaining the golf course. Based on *Zeeway* and *In re Days Cal. Riverside Ltd. P'ship*, 27 F.3d 374 (9th Cir. 1994), we agree with the bankruptcy court and conclude that the Golf Club's revenue from green fees and driving range fees is not produced from the Land as much as generated by other services that are performed on the Land, and therefore, is not rents. Unlike hotel cases where the revenue from room rental derives primarily from the usage of real property as shelter or occupancy, a golf course derives its revenue primarily from the usage of real property as entertainment. As a result, the bankruptcy court did not err in determining that the Golf Club's green fees and driving range fees were not rents subject to the Bank's real property security interest.

C. Proceeds

The Bank alternatively argues that if the Golf Club's postpetition green fees and driving range fees are not rents, they are proceeds of the Bank's security interest in the Golf Club's intangible property. As discussed above, distinguishing between after-acquired property and what may fall within § 552(b)'s exceptions is key to determining what is cash collateral. A creditor's interest in proceeds, products, offspring, or profits are secured "to the extent provided by . . . applicable nonbankruptcy law." Thus, Congress intended to defer to state law, namely, the Uniform Commercial Code (UCC), in making the determination of what constitutes proceeds. UCC § 9–102(a)(64) defines proceeds as:

> (A) whatever is acquired upon the sale, lease, license, exchange, or other disposition of collateral;
>
> (B) whatever is collected on, or distributed on account of, collateral;
>
> (C) rights arising out of collateral . . .

Accordingly, postpetition proceeds, products, offspring, or profits are subject to an after-acquired *property clause* only if they derive from prepetition collateral. Here, the Bank holds a perfected security interest in general intangibles, including the Golf Club's personal property, licenses, payment obligations and receipts. A "general intangible" means:

> any personal property, including things in action, other than accounts, chattel paper, commercial tort claims, deposit accounts, documents, goods, instruments, investment property, letter-of-credit rights, letters of credit, money, and oil, gas, or other minerals before extraction. The term includes payment intangibles and software.

UCC § 9–102(a)(42). "General intangibles" is a "residual" category of personal property, and includes rights that arise under a license and payment intangibles. See Official Comment 5(d). The question we must answer is whether the revenue from the Golf Club's green fees and driving range fees was acquired on the disposition of, or collected on, the Golf Club's general intangible property making them proceeds of the Bank's collateral.

a) Licenses

A license is a contract that authorizes the use of an asset without an accompanying transfer of ownership. There is no real dispute that the Golf Club licenses the use of the Land to golfers who pay for "a temporary right to enter upon real property and partake of the services offered thereon." *In re GGVXX, Ltd.*, 130 B.R. at 326; *In re The Wright Group, Inc.*, 443 B.R. 795, 800 (Bankr. N.D. Indiana 2011) (transaction between miniature golf operation and its customers consists of a license for access to real property). Thus, "[g]olfers, by paying a greens fee, become mere licensees, entitled to the non-exclusive use of the golf course for a short period of time." *In re GGVXX, Ltd.*, 130 B.R. at 326.

The bankruptcy court addressed the Bank's argument that green fees and driving range fees were revenue from licenses to use the Land. However, the bankruptcy court concluded the UCC was inapplicable. We disagree. A license or access to golf premises is not an interest in real estate. Id. Therefore, proceeds received from a license are not subject to a security interest perfected under real property law. Instead, proceeds from a license are considered personal property.

The Golf Club asserts that because the licenses belonged to the golfers, not the Golf Club, they were not part of the Bank's security interest. That argument is unpersuasive. The Golf Club, as licensor, collects payment in exchange for providing a license to golfers to use its facilities. It is akin to a software license, where a security interest covers the proceeds generated by the owner's grant of a license to the users of the software. A bank's security interest in the software company's licenses would extend to the payments generated by the sale of the licenses to customers. However, the BAP has noted that "revenue generated by the operation of a debtor's business, post-petition, is not considered proceeds if such revenue represents compensation for goods and services rendered by the debtor in its everyday business performance . . . . Revenue generated post-petition solely as a result of a debtor's labor is not subject to a creditor's pre-petition interest." *In re Skagit Pac. Corp.*, 316 B.R. 330, 336 (BAP 9th Cir. 2003). Section 552(b) is "intended to cover after-acquired property that is directly attributable to prepetition collateral, *without addition of estate resources*." Alan N. Resnick & Henry J. Sommer eds., COLLIER ON BANKRUPTCY, ¶ 552.02[2] (16th ed. 2012) (emphasis added).

The Golf Club must maintain the Land regularly as part of its business operation by mowing, planting, watering, fertilizing, and repairing the grass, raking sand traps, re-positioning the holes, and retrieving golf balls from the range. Thus, the revenue that the Golf Club generates postpetition on the licenses is not merely from issuing a license to its customers but is largely the result of the Golf Club's labor and own operational resources, which make the license valuable to golfers. Consequently, although the green fees and driving range fees may be "collected on" the Golf Club's licenses, they are not proceeds generated from the Bank's collateral.

b)   Payment Intangibles

We next determine whether the revenue from the Golf Club's green fees and driving range fees constitute proceeds of the Bank's security interests in other general intangible property. Although case law on this issue is sparse, we do have the benefit of an Indiana bankruptcy court's analysis of whether income derived from a debtor's operation of a miniature golf course facility constituted proceeds of the creditor's security interest in intangible property. *In re Wright Group, Inc.*, 443 B.R. 802–803 (Bankr. N.D. Ind. 2011). There, the court determined that the transaction between the debtor and its customers was a simultaneous transaction by which the debtor granted a license for use of the course at the same time that the customer paid the fee for the license. Because there was no debt or monetary obligation created, there was no account or payment intangible, and consequently, no proceeds of the collateral was generated.

Instead, the court determined that the postpetition revenue from the miniature golf customers constituted "money," which did not fall under the definition of a general intangible and could only be perfected by possession. *Id.* at 805–06; The court determined that since "implicit in the concept of 'cash collateral' is that a creditor has an enforceable security interest," the receipts did not constitute cash collateral because the creditor did not have possession of the cash receipts paid by the customers. *Id.* at 805. The reasoning of the court in *In re The Wright Group, Inc.*, is sound: the payment of green fees and driving range fees by golfers to use the golf course is a simultaneous transaction that does not produce a monetary obligation. As a result, the revenue is not derived from a creditor's security interest in general intangibles. Therefore, we conclude that the green fees and driving range fees are not proceeds of the Bank's security interest and do not constitute the Bank's cash collateral.

D. Profits

In *In re Northview Corp.*, 130 B.R. 543, 548 (B.A.P. 9th Cir. 1991), the BAP noted that the term "profits" in § 552(b) refers to the sale of real property to which a perfected security interest attached. Thus, profits arise out of the ownership of real property and derive from conversion of the property into some other property. Id. We already concluded that the green fees and driving range fees are not derivative of the Bank's security interest in the Land when we determined that the fees were not in the nature of rents. As a result, the green fees and driving range fees are not profits of the Bank's security interest in the Land.

VI. CONCLUSION

The postpetition revenue from the Golf Club's green fees and driving range fees is not the rents, proceeds or profits of the Bank's security interest within the exceptions of § 522(b). Accordingly, we conclude that the green fees and driving range fees are not the Bank's cash collateral. Therefore, we AFFIRM.

NOTES

1.   The majority of courts follow *Premier Golf* in construing "proceeds" in 552(b)(1)'s exception according to 9–102(a)(64)'s definition of the term. Their stated rationale is that 552(b)(1)'s reference to "applicable nonbankruptcy law" signals Congress' intent to rely on Article 9's definition. Is *Premier Golf*'s analysis of the estate's green and driving range fee income consistent with the court's stated deference to this state law definition? The court acknowledged that these revenues required realty and the grant of a license to customers to use the facilities, and that the secured creditor had a prepetition security interest in both assets. Applying the standard close the one stated in *Zeeway Corp.*, however, the court asked whether the postpetition green and driving range fees represents compensation for goods and services rendered by the debtor in its "everyday business performance." It concluded that the fee income was "largely the result" of the debtor's labor and the estate's unencumbered assets, and therefore was not proceeds of prepetition collateral. Section 9–102(a)(64)'s definition of proceeds, however,

SECTION C TREATMENT OF SECURED CLAIMS IN CHAPTERS 7, 11 AND 13 561

seems to require a different analysis. The definition counts as proceeds whatever is acquired on the disposition of the collateral or collected on account of it. 9–102(a)(64)(A), (B). It doesn't matter how much value the collateral contributes to the value of what is collected, as long as what is collected is "on account" of the collateral. The postpetition fee revenues were "collected on account" of the license the debtor granted its customers. Thus, because a license is a general intangible in which the secured creditor had a prepetition security interest, the fee income was proceeds under 9–102(a)(64)(B).

2. Section 552(b)(1)'s exception is itself subject to an exception: a security interest in prepetition collateral extends to postpetition proceeds except to the extent that the court orders otherwise based on "the equities of the case." The "equities of the case" exception is flexible (and vague) enough to allow courts to apportion the proceeds resulting from use of both prepetition collateral and estate assets. Courts have apportioned proceeds differently. In re Cafeteria Operators, L.P. 299 B.R. 400 (Bankr. N.D. Tex. 2003), limited a security interest in proceeds to the collateral's value; the rest of the proceeds from sales of the collateral represented estate assets and was allocated to the estate. By contrast, the court in Delbridge v. Production Credit Ass'n, 104 B.R. 824 (E.D. Mich.1989) apportioned the proceeds in proportion to the value of the relative contributions of the security interest and estate assets. The ABI Commission studying reforms to Chapter 11 recommended that the "equities of the case" exception be construed broadly: "The basic premise should be that, if the estate creates value through any means during the [C]hapter 11 case and such value enhances the secured creditor's collateral, the estate should receive the benefit of such value." ABI Commission to Study the Reform of Chapter 11: Final Report and Recommendations 232 (2014).

3. VALUING COLLATERAL IN BANKRUPTCY

Collateral must be valued in a bankruptcy proceeding for a number of purposes. For instance, the amount of a secured claim is the value of the collateral securing the claim. BC 506(a)(1). And whether a secured creditors' security interest is adequately protected depends on the whether the debtor's use of collateral affects its value. More controversial is whether adequate protection requires compensating the secured creditor for the time value of the money: in this case the returns on proceeds the creditor could have realized had it foreclosed and disposed of the collateral. BC 362(d). For each of these purposes, the value of collateral must be determined. Finally, to be confirmable, repayment plans under Chapter 11 and Chapter 13 plans must promise secured creditors amounts at least equal to their secured claims. BC 1129(b)(2)(A), 1325(a)(5). BC 506(a)(1), in turn, defines a secured claim by the value of collateral securing the claim ("to the extent of the value of such creditor's interest in the estate's interest in such property"). Thus, the confirmation of a repayment plan depends indirectly on valuations of the collateral.

There are two questions in play here: what is the secured creditor's "interest" in the collateral? And how is the value of that interest measured? In United States Savings Ass'n v. Timbers of Inwood Forest Assoc., Ltd., 484 U.S. 365 (1988), the Supreme Court answered the first question by holding that the secured creditor's interest in collateral did not include returns on the reinvestment of proceeds of collateral. Focusing on the first sentence of BC 506(a)(1), the Court construed the secured creditor's "interest in property" to exclude its right to repossess and dispose of collateral on default. Thus, BC 506(a)(1) doesn't protect the secured creditor's right to compensation for foregone interest on proceeds of collateral over the course of the bankruptcy case. BC 506(b) protects an oversecured creditor's right to postfiling interest on collateral to the extent that its value is enough to cover the interest claim. According to *Timbers of Inwood*, the Bankruptcy Code doesn't do the same for an undersecured creditor.

The second question asks how the security interest in collateral is valued. In a Chapter 7 case, collateral value is easy to determine because liquidation provides a market test of value. The collateral is disposed of, often by sale at auction, and the winning bid establishes the value of the asset purchased. In these circumstances the value of the collateral is the amount the secured creditor realizes from its orderly disposal. In Chapter 11 and Chapter 13 cases, where the debtor's plan proposes to retain the collateral, market tests of value aren't available. The Bankruptcy Code still requires that the collateral be valued, and some measure of value must be set. BC 506(a)(1) doesn't explicitly set the measure of value. The first sentence of 506(a)(1) only defines the secured creditor's interest in collateral, as *Timbers of Inwood* found. It doesn't measure that value. BC 506(a)(1)'s second sentence instead measures the value of collateral: "Such value shall be determined in light of the purpose of the valuation and of the proposed disposition or use of such property, and in conjunction with any hearing on such disposition or use or on a plan affecting such creditor's interest." Chapter 11 or 13 plans often propose that the debtor "use" the collateral by retaining it. How is the value of the collateral measured in these cases?

The Supreme Court answers the question in the following case. In reading *Rash* consider whether the Court's interpretation of BC 506(a)(1) gives the secured creditor more than it is entitled to outside of bankruptcy. Also consider, taking into account footnote 6 of the opinion, whether the "replacement value" measure adopted by the Court is easily applied by bankruptcy courts.

Associates Commercial Corp. v. Rash

Supreme Court of the United States, 1997
520 U.S. 953

■ JUSTICE GINSBURG delivered the opinion of the Court.*

We resolve in this case a dispute concerning the proper application of § 506(a) of the Bankruptcy Code when a bankrupt debtor has exercised the "cram down" option for which Code § 1325(a)(5)(B) provides. Specifically, when a debtor, over a secured creditor's objection, seeks to retain and use the creditor's collateral in a Chapter 13 plan, is the value of the collateral to be determined by (1) what the secured creditor could obtain through foreclosure sale of the property (the "foreclosure-value" standard); (2) what the debtor would have to pay for comparable property (the "replacement-value" standard); or (3) the midpoint between these two measurements? We hold that § 506(a) directs application of the replacement-value standard.

I

In 1989, respondent Elray Rash purchased for $73,700 a Kenworth tractor truck for use in his freight-hauling business. Rash made a downpayment on the truck, agreed to pay the seller the remainder in 60 monthly installments, and pledged the truck as collateral on the unpaid balance. The seller assigned the loan, and its lien on the truck, to petitioner Associates Commercial Corporation (ACC).

In March 1992, Elray and Jean Rash filed a joint petition and a repayment plan under Chapter 13 of the Bankruptcy Code (Code), 11 U.S.C. §§ 1301–1330. At the time of the bankruptcy filing, the balance owed to ACC on the truck loan was $41,171. Because it held a valid lien on the truck, ACC was listed in the bankruptcy petition as a creditor holding a secured claim. Under the Code, ACC's claim for the balance owed on the truck was secured only to the extent of the value of the collateral; its claim over and above the value of the truck was unsecured. See 11 U.S.C. § 506(a).

To qualify for confirmation under Chapter 13, the Rashes' plan had to satisfy the requirements set forth in § 1325(a) of the Code. The Rashes' treatment of ACC's secured claim, in particular, is governed by subsection (a)(5). Under this provision, a plan's proposed treatment of secured claims can be confirmed if one of three conditions is satisfied: The secured creditor accepts the plan, see 11 U.S.C. § 1325(a)(5)(A); the debtor surrenders the property securing the claim to the creditor, see § 1325(a)(5)(C); or the debtor invokes the so-called "cram down" power, see § 1325(a)(5)(B). Under the cram down option, the debtor is permitted to keep the property over the objection of the creditor; the creditor retains the lien securing the claim, see § 1325(a)(5)(B)(i), and the debtor is required to provide the creditor with payments, over the life of the plan,

---

* Justice Scalia joins all but footnote 4 of this opinion [omitted].

that will total the present value of the allowed secured claim, *i.e.,* the present value of the collateral, see § 1325(a)(5)(B)(ii). The value of the allowed secured claim is governed by § 506(a) of the Code.

The Rashes' Chapter 13 plan invoked the cram down power. It proposed that the Rashes retain the truck for use in the freight-hauling business and pay ACC, over 58 months, an amount equal to the present value of the truck. That value, the Rashes' petition alleged, was $28,500. ACC objected to the plan and asked the Bankruptcy Court to lift the automatic stay so ACC could repossess the truck. ACC also filed a proof of claim alleging that its claim was fully secured in the amount of $41,171. The Rashes filed an objection to ACC's claim.

The Bankruptcy Court held an evidentiary hearing to resolve the dispute over the truck's value. At the hearing, ACC and the Rashes urged different valuation benchmarks. ACC maintained that the proper valuation was the price the Rashes would have to pay to purchase a like vehicle, an amount ACC's expert estimated to be $41,000. The Rashes, however, maintained that the proper valuation was the net amount ACC would realize upon foreclosure and sale of the collateral, an amount their expert estimated to be $31,875. The Bankruptcy Court agreed with the Rashes and fixed the amount of ACC's secured claim at $31,875; that sum, the court found, was the net amount ACC would realize if it exercised its right to repossess and sell the truck. See In re Rash, 149 B.R. 430, 431–432 (Bkrtcy.Ct.E.D.Tex.1993). The Bankruptcy Court thereafter approved the plan, and the United States District Court for the Eastern District of Texas affirmed.

A panel of the Court of Appeals for the Fifth Circuit reversed. In re Rash, 31 F.3d 325 (1994). On rehearing en banc, however, the Fifth Circuit affirmed the District Court, holding that ACC's allowed secured claim was limited to $31,875, the net foreclosure value of the truck. In re Rash, 90 F.3d 1036 (1996). In reaching its decision, the Fifth Circuit highlighted, first, a conflict it perceived between the method of valuation ACC advanced, and the law of Texas defining the rights of secured creditors. See *id.,* at 1041–1042 (citing Tex. Bus. & Com.Code Ann. §§ 9.504(a), (c), 9.505 (1991)). In the Fifth Circuit's view, valuing collateral in a federal bankruptcy proceeding under a replacement-value standard—thereby setting an amount generally higher than what a secured creditor could realize pursuing its state-law foreclosure remedy—would "chang[e] the extent to which ACC is secured from what obtained under state law prior to the bankruptcy filing." 90 F.3d, at 1041. Such a departure from state law, the Fifth Circuit said, should be resisted by the federal forum unless "clearly compel[led]" by the Code. *Id.,* at 1042.

The Fifth Circuit then determined that the Code provision governing valuation of security interests, § 506(a), does not compel a replacement-value approach. Instead, the court reasoned, the first sentence of § 506(a) requires that collateral be valued from the creditor's perspective. See *id.,* at 1044. And because "the creditor's interest is in the nature of a security interest, giving the creditor the right to repossess and sell the collateral and nothing more[,] . . . the valuation should start with what the creditor could realize by exercising that right." *Ibid.* This foreclosure-value standard, the Fifth Circuit found, was consistent with the other relevant provisions of the Code, economic analysis, and the legislative history of the pertinent provisions. See *id.,* at 1045–1059. Judge Smith, joined by five other judges, dissented, urging that the Code dictates a replacement-value standard. See *id.,* at 1061–1075.

Courts of Appeals have adopted three different standards for valuing a security interest in a bankruptcy proceeding when the debtor invokes the cram down power to retain the collateral over the creditor's objection. In contrast to the Fifth Circuit's foreclosure-value standard, a number of Circuits have followed a replacement-value approach. See, *e.g., In re Taffi,* 96 F.3d 1190, 1191–1192 (C.A.9 1996) (en banc), cert. pending *sub nom. Taffi v. United States,* No. 96–881;[2] Other courts have settled on the midpoint between foreclosure value and replacement value. See *In re Hoskins,* 102 F.3d 311, 316 (C.A.7 1996). We granted certiorari to resolve this conflict among the Courts of Appeals, and we now reverse the Fifth Circuit's judgment.

II

The Code provision central to the resolution of this case is § 506(a), which states:

> "An allowed claim of a creditor secured by a lien on property in which the estate has an interest. . . is a secured claim to the extent of the value of such creditor's interest in the estate's interest in such property, . . . and is an unsecured claim to the extent that the value of such creditor's interest. . . is less than the amount of such allowed claim. Such value shall be determined in light of the purpose of the valuation and of the proposed disposition or use of such property. . . ." 11 U.S.C. § 506(a).

Over ACC's objection, the Rashes' repayment plan proposed, pursuant to § 1325(a)(5)(B), continued use of the property in question, *i.e.,* the truck, in the debtor's trade or business. In such a "cram down" case, we hold, the value of the property (and thus the amount of the secured claim under § 506(a)) is the price a willing buyer in the debtor's trade, business, or situation would pay to obtain like property from a willing seller.

---

[2] In *In re Taffi,* the Ninth Circuit contrasted replacement value with fair-market value and adopted the latter standard, apparently viewing the two standards as incompatible. See 96 F.3d, at 1192. By using the term "replacement value," we do not suggest that a creditor is entitled to recover what it would cost the debtor to purchase the collateral brand new. Rather, our use of the term replacement value is consistent with the Ninth Circuit's understanding of the meaning of fair-market value; by replacement value, we mean the price a willing buyer in the debtor's trade, business, or situation would pay a willing seller to obtain property of like age and condition. See also *infra,* at 1886–1887, n. 6.

Rejecting this replacement-value standard, and selecting instead the typically lower foreclosure-value standard, the Fifth Circuit trained its attention on the first sentence of § 506(a). In particular, the Fifth Circuit relied on these first sentence words: A claim is secured "to the extent of the value of such *creditor's interest* in the estate's interest in such property." See 90 F.3d, at 1044 (emphasis added) (citing § 506(a)). The Fifth Circuit read this phrase to instruct that the "starting point for the valuation [is] what the creditor could realize if it sold the estate's interest in the property according to the security agreement," namely, through "repossess[ing] and sell [ing] the collateral." *Ibid.*

We do not find in the § 506(a) first sentence words—"the creditor's interest in the estate's interest in such property"—the foreclosure-value meaning advanced by the Fifth Circuit. Even read in isolation, the phrase imparts no valuation standard: A direction simply to consider the "value of such creditor's interest" does not expressly reveal *how* that interest is to be valued.

Reading the first sentence of § 506(a) as a whole, we are satisfied that the phrase the Fifth Circuit considered key is not an instruction to equate a "creditor's interest" with the net value a creditor could realize through a foreclosure sale. The first sentence, in its entirety, tells us that a secured creditor's claim is to be divided into secured and unsecured portions, with the secured portion of the claim limited to the value of the collateral. To separate the secured from the unsecured portion of a claim, a court must compare the creditor's claim to the value of "such property," *i.e.,* the collateral. That comparison is sometimes complicated. A debtor may own only a part interest in the property pledged as collateral, in which case the court will be required to ascertain the "estate's interest" in the collateral. Or, a creditor may hold a junior or subordinate lien, which would require the court to ascertain the creditor's interest in the collateral. The § 506(a) phrase referring to the "creditor's interest in the estate's interest in such property" thus recognizes that a court may encounter, and in such instances must evaluate, limited or partial interests in collateral. The full first sentence of § 506(a), in short, tells a court what it must evaluate, but it does not say more; it is not enlightening on how to value collateral.

The second sentence of § 506(a) does speak to the *how* question. "Such value," that sentence provides, "shall be determined in light of the purpose of the valuation and of the proposed disposition or use of such property." § 506(a). By deriving a foreclosure-value standard from § 506(a)'s first sentence, the Fifth Circuit rendered inconsequential the sentence that expressly addresses how "value shall be determined."

As we comprehend § 506(a), the "proposed disposition or use" of the collateral is of paramount importance to the valuation question. If a secured creditor does not accept a debtor's Chapter 13 plan, the debtor has two options for handling allowed secured claims: surrender the collateral to the creditor, see § 1325(a)(5)(C); or, under the cram down option, keep the collateral over the creditor's objection and provide the creditor, over the life of the plan, with the equivalent of the present value of the collateral, see § 1325(a)(5)(B). The "disposition or use" of the collateral thus turns on the alternative the debtor chooses—in one case the collateral will be surrendered to the creditor, and in the other, the collateral will be retained and used by the debtor. Applying a foreclosure-value standard when the cram down option is invoked attributes no significance to the different consequences of the debtor's choice to surrender the property or retain it. A replacement-value standard, on the other hand, distinguishes retention from surrender and renders meaningful the key words "disposition or use."

Tying valuation to the actual "disposition or use" of the property points away from a foreclosure-value standard when a Chapter 13 debtor, invoking cram down power, retains and uses the property. Under that option, foreclosure is averted by the debtor's choice and over the creditor's objection. From the creditor's perspective as well as the debtor's, surrender and retention are not equivalent acts.

When a debtor surrenders the property, a creditor obtains it immediately, and is free to sell it and reinvest the proceeds. We recall here that ACC sought that very advantage. See *supra,* at 1882. If a debtor keeps the property and continues to use it, the creditor obtains at once neither the property nor its value and is exposed to double risks: The debtor may again default and the property may deteriorate from extended use. Adjustments in the interest rate and secured creditor demands for more "adequate protection," 11 U.S.C. § 361, do not fully offset these risks. See 90 F.3d, at 1066 (Smith, J., dissenting) ("vast majority of reorganizations fail. . . leaving creditors with only a fraction of the compensation due them"; where, as here, "collateral depreciates rapidly, the secured creditor may receive far less in a failed reorganization than in a prompt foreclosure" (internal cross-reference omitted)); accord, *In re Taffi,* 96 F.3d, at 1192–1193.

Of prime significance, the replacement-value standard accurately gauges the debtor's "use" of the property. It values "the creditor's interest in the collateral in light of the proposed [repayment plan] reality: no foreclosure sale and economic benefit for the debtor derived from the collateral equal to. . . its [replacement] value." *In re Winthrop Old Farm Nurseries,* 50 F.3d, at 75. The debtor in this case elected to use the collateral to generate an income stream. That actual use, rather than a foreclosure sale that will not take place, is the proper guide under a prescription hinged to the property's "disposition or use." See *ibid*

The Fifth Circuit considered the replacement-value standard disrespectful of state law, which permits the secured creditor to sell the collateral, thereby obtaining its net foreclosure value "and nothing more." See 90 F.3d at 1044. In allowing Chapter 13 debtors to retain and use collateral over the objection of secured creditors, however, the Code has reshaped debtor and creditor rights in marked departure from state law.

The Code's cram down option displaces a secured creditor's state-law right to obtain immediate foreclosure upon a debtor's default. That change, ordered by federal law, is attended by a direction that courts look to the "proposed disposition or use" of the collateral in determining its value. It no more disrupts state law to make "disposition or use" the guide for valuation than to authorize the rearrangement of rights the cram down power entails.

Nor are we persuaded that the split-the-difference approach adopted by the Seventh Circuit provides the appropriate solution. See *In re Hoskins,* 102 F.3d, at 316. Whatever the attractiveness of a standard that picks the midpoint between foreclosure and replacement values, there is no warrant for it in the Code.[5] Section 506(a) calls for the value the property possesses in light of the "disposition or use" in fact "proposed," not the various dispositions or uses that might have been proposed. The Seventh Circuit rested on the "economics of the situation," *In re Hoskins,* 102 F.3d, at 316, only after concluding that the statute suggests no particular valuation method. We agree with the Seventh Circuit that "a simple rule of valuation is needed" to serve the interests of predictability and uniformity. *Id.,* at 314. We conclude, however, that § 506(a) supplies a governing instruction less complex than the Seventh Circuit's "make two valuations, then split the difference" formulation.

In sum, under § 506(a), the value of property retained because the debtor has exercised the § 1325(a)(5)(B) "cram down" option is the cost the debtor would incur to obtain a like asset for the same "proposed. . . use."[6] * * *

For the foregoing reasons, the judgment of the Court of Appeals is reversed, and the case is remanded for further proceedings consistent with this opinion.

It is so ordered.

NOTES

1. How would *Rash* be decided under the current version of BC 506(a)(2) quoted below?

---

[5] As our reading of § 506(a) makes plain, we also reject a ruleless approach allowing use of different valuation standards based on the facts and circumstances of individual cases.

[6] Our recognition that the replacement-value standard, not the foreclosure-value standard, governs in cram down cases leaves to bankruptcy courts, as triers of fact, identification of the best way of ascertaining replacement value on the basis of the evidence presented. Whether replacement value is the equivalent of retail value, wholesale value, or some other value will depend on the type of debtor and the nature of the property. We note, however, that replacement value, in this context, should not include certain items. For example, where the proper measure of the replacement value of a vehicle is its retail value, an adjustment to that value may be necessary: A creditor should not receive portions of the retail price, if any, that reflect the value of items the debtor does not receive when he retains his vehicle, items such as warranties, inventory storage, and reconditioning. Cf. 90 F.3d, at 1051–1052. Nor should the creditor gain from modifications to the property—*e.g.,* the addition of accessories to a vehicle—to which a creditor's lien would not extend under state law.

(2)   If the debtor in an individual in a case under Chapter 7 or 13, such value with respect to personal property securing an allowed claim shall be determined based on the replacement value of such property as of the date of filing the petition without deduction for costs of sale or marketing. With respect to property acquired for personal, family, or household purpose, replacement value shall mean the price a retail merchant would charge for property of that kind considering the age and condition of the property at the time value is determined.

Since BC 506(a)(2) doesn't apply to cases concerning corporate or partnership debtors or to Chapter 11 or 12 cases, *Rash* presumably remains good authority in commercial cases. What guidance does that case offer on how to determine the "replacement value" of important types of collateral in business reorganization cases involving inventory or accounts?

2.   In footnote 5 of the opinion, the Court rejects a "ruleless approach" and adopts the "replacement value" measure of value when the debtor's repayment plan proposes to retain the collateral. The Court in footnote 6 refuses to identify replacement value with retail or wholesale price, or some other prevalent measure. However, in the same note, the Court finds in the context of the case that replacement cost should not include the cost of such items as warranty coverage, inventory storage and reconditioning. According to the Court, these costs should be deducted from the retail price. The Court's refusal to identify replacement value with wholesale price is questionable. The difference between retail and wholesale price is the additional costs of items such as inventory storage, advertising and the like, which the Court finds should not be included in replacement value. Isn't the Court in fact finding that replacement value is wholesale price? If replacement value can vary with the context of a case, sometimes being retail price and sometimes wholesale, has the Court announced a "rule" for valuation of collateral at all?

3.   In dissent, Justice Stevens acknowledged that BC 506(a)(1) wasn't "entirely clear" but on policy grounds found that ". . .the foreclosure standard best comports with economic reality. Allowing any more than the foreclosure value simply grants a general windfall to undersecured creditors at the expense of unsecured creditors." *Rash*, 520 U.S. at 967. To understand the "windfall" the replacement value measure gives undersecured creditors, consider what the secured creditor would receive outside bankruptcy. Outside bankruptcy, if the debtor defaults, the creditor has a choice. It can elect to foreclose on the collateral. In a foreclosure sale the creditor receives the collateral's foreclosure value, which is its liquidation value. This is less than the replacement value of collateral. Alternatively, the secured creditor can allow the debtor to retain the collateral. In doing so the creditor foregoes foreclosing on the collateral and receiving the collateral's foreclosure value. The creditor therefore will insist on an increased interest rate at least sufficient to compensate it for the loss of foreclosure value and the risk to the collateral while the collateral remains with the debtor. The increased interest rate charge will be less than the replacement value of the collateral, at least where the debtor has some bargaining power. Thus, both options give the secured creditor less than it receives under the replacement measure of value. Compared to what the secured creditor would get outside bankruptcy, the replacement measure of value therefore gives the secured creditor a windfall.

PROBLEM

Bank repossessed Sally Smith's car after she defaulted on a $10,000 loan secured by it. Although pressed financially, Sally wants to keep her car and is considering two alternatives. One is to redeem it from Bank. The other alternative is to file for bankruptcy under Chapter 7 (for which Sally qualifies). Sally knows that her bankruptcy trustee will decide to abandon the car by returning it to Bank. Used car dealers sell cars of the age and condition of Sally's car for $8,000. Sally's car would sell for $6,000 at a properly conducted foreclosure sale. How much must Sally pay Bank to redeem her car if she does not file for bankruptcy? See 9–623(b). How much must she pay Bank to redeem it if she files a Chapter 7 bankruptcy petition? See BC 722, 506(a)(2).

D. AVOIDANCE POWERS OF THE TRUSTEE

The purpose of this Chapter is to offer an introduction to what business lawyers should know about how security interests in personal property are treated under the Bankruptcy Code. Lawyers planning secured transactions must know how to structure those transactions so that they will stand up in bankruptcy. This requires an understanding of the trustee's powers to avoid transfers of the debtor. The trustee not only succeeds to the assets owned by the debtor at the time of filing (BC 541(a)(1)) but also has the power to enhance the value of the debtor's estate by reaching back and nullifying prepetition transfers of the debtor that are subject to some infirmity (BC 550(a))). If the trustee elects to nullify these transfers, the property transferred or its value becomes part of the debtor's estate (BC 541(a)(3)).

The most important of the trustee's avoidance powers can be summarized in simple terms: Under BC 544(a)(1), the "strong arm power," if the security interest isn't perfected at the time the debtor files in bankruptcy, it may be set aside in its totality. Under BC 547(b), if an insolvent debtor pays an unsecured creditor in preference to other creditors within 90 days before filing in bankruptcy, the payment may be recovered as a voidable preference. Under BC 548(a), if an insolvent debtor within two years of filing in bankruptcy transfers property to another person without receiving reasonably equivalent value in exchange, the property transferred may be recovered as a fraudulent transfer, even though no true fraud was involved. And under 544(b), fraudulent transfers are recoverable by the trustee using state fraudulent transfer law. These may seem simple rules, but even in the brief treatment below their complexity and potentially pervasive application will be apparent.

1.   THE TRUSTEE'S STRONG ARM POWER: BC 544(a)

BC 544(a)(1) empowers the trustee to avoid unperfected security interests. This provision is commonly called the "strong arm" clause, and the term is appropriate, for the trustee can use it to turn secured creditors, who are otherwise entitled to the economic value of their collateral in bankruptcy, into unsecured creditors, who often take little or nothing from the debtor's estate. Section 544(a)(1) arms a trustee with the power to avoid any transfer of property of the debtor that is "voidable" by a hypothetical judicial lien creditor on the date the bankruptcy case commences. There does not have to be a judicial lien creditor as of that date ("whether or not such a creditor exists"). The rights of a lien creditor are not determined by the Bankruptcy Code. State law, in this case 9–317(a)(2), instead determines the lien creditor's rights. But that section doesn't speak of avoiding; it says that an unperfected security interest is "subordinate" to the rights of a lien creditor. This has been treated by courts as allowing the trustee, invoking the powers of a lien creditor, to set aside a security interest in its entirety that is subordinated to a judicial lien by 9–317(a)(2). BC 546(b) allows perfection after bankruptcy to defeat the rights of the trustee under BC 544(a)(1) in cases in which the applicable nonbankruptcy law, Article 9, gives retroactive effect to the perfection.

PROBLEMS

1.   On Day 1, SP, after having examined D's finances, was sufficiently interested in accepting D's application for a loan to have D sign a security agreement and for SP to file a financing statement. After checking the UCC filings, on Day 9 SP advanced the funds to D that were called for in the agreement. Later, SP was astonished to learn from D's trustee in bankruptcy (T) that D had filed in bankruptcy on Day 8 without informing SP of that fact. Can T set aside SP's security interest under BC 544(a)(1)? See 9–317(a)(2)(B). Why the change in law? See Comment 4. Are you convinced that the reason given justifies the change in law?

2.   On Day 1, Seller sold and delivered to D several units of equipment. On that date, D signed a security agreement granting a security interest in the equipment to Seller to secure the unpaid balance of the purchase price. On Day 10, D filed in bankruptcy. When Seller learned of D's bankruptcy, it perfected its security interest by filing on Day 19.

(a)   Can D's trustee in bankruptcy set aside Seller's security interest under BC 544(a)(1)? See 9–317(e) and 546(b)(1).

(b)   Did Seller violate the automatic stay by filing a financing statement? See BC 362(b)(3).

2.   SUBROGATION OF TRUSTEE UNDER BC 544(b)

BC 544(b) provides:

(1)   . . .[T]he trustee may avoid any transfer of an interest of the debtor in property or any obligation incurred by the debtor that is voidable under applicable law by a creditor holding an unsecured claim that is allowable under section 502 of this title or that is not allowable only under section 502(e) of this title.

This provision means that if the trustee can find one *actual unsecured creditor* at the time of bankruptcy against whom the debtor's transfer is voidable, the trustee can set aside the entire transfer for the benefit of all the debtor's estate under BC 541(a)(3) and BC 550(a). In effect, the trustee is subrogated to the rights of an unpaid creditor in existence at the time of the debtor's filing against whom the transfer is voidable under state law.

The origin of BC 544(b) is found in the celebrated case of Moore v. Bay, 284 U.S. 4 (1931) (Holmes, J.). Moore v. Bay involved the validity of a chattel mortgage that had not been promptly recorded. Under the applicable state law some unsecured intervening creditors of the mortgagor had priority over the mortgagee's claim because of its late recording and the failure to give advance public notice of the mortgage required by existing law. Some of these creditors had claims in bankruptcy. Other unsecured creditors with claims in the bankruptcy did not, under the state law, have priority over the mortgagee. The Supreme Court held that the chattel mortgage was void in its entirety in bankruptcy. By this decision, all creditors, whether or not they had rights under the state law, got the benefit of the avoidance. Although the opinion in Moore v. Bay is cryptic, the case is understood to articulate a two-part principle: a right voidable under state law is voidable in its entirety under bankruptcy law, and all creditors share in the benefit if the right is avoided. The principle of Moore v. Bay—often described as "void against one, void against all"—was first codified by the enactment of § 70e of the Bankruptcy Act, and subsequently by the enactment of BC 544(b) and BC 550(a) of the Bankruptcy Code.

Potentially the principle of Moore v. Bay, as codified by BC 544(b), can have devastating effects for a transferee. Assume the debtor makes a transfer of property worth $1 million and that under the state law one creditor, with a claim of $100, can avoid the transfer because some duty to that creditor had not been performed. Assume no other creditor has the right under the state law to attack the transfer, that under the state law the creditor with the $100 claim is entitled to have that claim paid from the property transferred, and that the transfer is otherwise valid. The effect in bankruptcy, if the $100 debt exists at the time of bankruptcy, is that the entire $1,000,000 transfer is voidable by the trustee under BC 544(b). Under BC 550(a), the $1,000,000 worth of property recovered benefits the entire estate. This means that all creditors share in the $1,000,000 recovered, including the creditor whose interest in the property was avoided. The following Problem raises the crucial issue of whether BC 544(b) acts to avoid Article 9 security interests.

PROBLEMS

On Day 1 Debtor (D) granted a security interest in personal property to Secured Party (SP) to secure a loan of $1,000,000 made by SP to D. Although SP's security interest attached on Day 1, it did not file a financing statement until Day 30. On Day 25, Creditor (C), having checked the filings on D's property, granted unsecured credit to D in the amount of $1,000 in the belief that there were no security interests in D's property. On Day 180 D defaulted on both loans, which remain unpaid.

1. If D is not in bankruptcy, what are C's rights with respect to SP's collateral on which C relied when it made its unsecured loan? See 9–201(a) and 9–317(a).

2. If D is in bankruptcy, what are the rights of D's trustee in bankruptcy to avoid SP's security interest under BC 544(b)? You may assume that C has an allowed unsecured claim for $1,000 at the time D files in bankruptcy.

E. PREFERENCES: BC 547

1. ELEMENTS OF A PREFERENCE

An insolvent debtor who is unable to pay all unsecured creditors in full may prefer one over the others by paying that creditor or granting it a security interest in the debtor's property. Consumer debtors, skating on the edge of insolvency, make preferential payments every month when they choose, for obvious reasons, to pay the utilities bill or the landlord and leave the bill from the health club until next month. Sometimes the preferential transfer is involuntary. This might occur if one of the creditors acquires a judicial lien in the debtor's property under a writ of execution or pursuant to a statute allowing prejudgment attachment; the creditor is paying itself out of the debtor's property. For the most part, preferences are valid under state law. Under the common law a transfer by an insolvent debtor in payment of a debt was not a fraudulent conveyance even if the effect or the purpose of the transfer was to make it more difficult for other creditors to obtain payment of their debts. See, e.g., Shelley v. Boothe, 73 Mo. 74, 77 (1880). A preferential payment of a bona fide debt does not violate Uniform Voidable Transactions Act (UVTA) § 4(a)(1) (actual fraud). Nor does it violate UVTA § 4(a)(2) (without reasonably equivalent value) because satisfaction of an antecedent debt is "value." UVTA § 3(a).

State debt collection law is a race of diligence among creditors. Priority goes to the first creditor to receive payment or obtain a judicial lien in the debtor's property. But the rule in bankruptcy is different: for the most part unsecured claims are paid on a pro rata basis. Preference law prevents debtors from frustrating this "equality of distribution" rule by making payments to preferred creditors on the eve of bankruptcy. BC 547(b) allows the trustee in bankruptcy to avoid these prebankruptcy transfers of the debtor's property, known as voidable preferences. BC 550(a) allows the trustee to recover the payment or property transferred.

The five elements of a voidable preference are set forth in subsection (b) of BC 547.

Except as provided in subsections (c) and (i) of this section, the trustee may avoid any transfer of an interest of the debtor in property

(1)   to or for the benefit of a creditor;

(2)   for or on account of an antecedent debt owed by the debtor before such transfer was made;

(3)   made while the debtor was insolvent;

(4)   made

    (A)   on or within 90 days before the date of the filing of the petition; or

    (B)   between 90 days and one year before the date of the filing of the petition, if such creditor at the time of such transfer was an insider; and

(5)   that enables such creditor to receive more than such creditor would receive if

    (A)   the case were a case under chapter 7 of this title;

    (B)   the transfer had not been made; and

    (C)   such creditor received payment of such debt to the extent provided by the provisions of this title.

2.   BASIC APPLICATIONS OF PREFERENCE LAW

The fundamental principles of voidable preference law are illustrated by the following Problems. Study them carefully. Problem 2 is very important for its illustration of the operation of BC 547(b)(5).

PROBLEMS

1.   May 1, Debtor was indebted to Creditor on an overdue unsecured loan made the previous year. On that date, Debtor paid Creditor cash equal to the amount due on the loan. At the time of payment Debtor had other debts that were not being paid and that exceeded Debtor's assets. On July 15, Debtor filed a petition in bankruptcy under Chapter 7. Answer the following questions on the basis of BC 547(b) without considering whether an exception under BC 547(c) applies.

(a)   Is the trustee in bankruptcy entitled to recover from Creditor the amount received from Debtor? BC 547(b) and 550(a). Does it matter whether or not Creditor knew of Debtor's financial condition at the time payment was received? Who has the burden of proving that Debtor was insolvent? BC 101 ("insolvent"), and BC 547(f) and (g)?

(b)   Would your answers to (a) be different if Debtor had filed in bankruptcy on August 15? BC 101(31) ("insider"), (45) ("relative").

(c)   Suppose that on May 1 Debtor had not paid the loan and that on that date Creditor had obtained a prejudgment attachment lien on business property of Debtor with a value exceeding the amount due on the loan. When the petition in bankruptcy was filed on July 15, Debtor's assets included the property on which Creditor had an attachment lien. What are the rights of the trustee in bankruptcy? BC 547(b) and 101 ("transfer").

2.   Bank made a one-year loan of $10,000 to Debtor on September 1, 2016, and to secure the loan, Debtor granted Bank a security interest in equipment owned by Debtor. Bank promptly perfected by filing a financing statement. On November 1, 2017, Debtor paid Bank $10,000 plus interest in discharge of the debt. Debtor filed a petition in bankruptcy on December 1, 2017. Debtor was insolvent on November 1, 2017 and at all times thereafter. Was the payment to Bank on November 1, 2017 a transfer on account of an antecedent debt? BC 547(b)(2). Can the transfer be avoided by the trustee in bankruptcy under BC 547(b)? What is the effect of BC 547(b)(5)? Assume that the value of the equipment was greater than the payment made to Bank and that there were no other security interests or liens in the equipment superior to the security interest of Bank. Would the outcome of the case be different if Bank had been undersecured at the time it received payment from Debtor?

3.   WHY PREFERENCE LAW?

Questions arise with respect to the justification of the large and intrusive body of law that has grown up around preferences. Why does the Bankruptcy Code invalidate transfers that are valid outside bankruptcy? Why have a provision such as BC 547 that operates to disadvantage efficient creditors who are able to receive voluntary payment from a debtor before that debtor files in bankruptcy and to benefit less efficient creditors who have not collected their claims? There are basically two different sorts of policies that might underlie preference law. One is equality among creditors when their debtor goes into bankruptcy. A creditor receives an unequal distribution when a prebankruptcy preferential transfer benefits the preferred creditor at the expense of other creditors. Undoing the preference assures that each creditor with the same sort of claim receives a pro rata distribution on its claim from the debtor's bankruptcy estate. This is the rationale adopted by Congress in the excerpt below. Egalitarian notions, such as the pro rata distribution rule, are not common in business transactions. In addition, preferences are not barred outside of bankruptcy. Questions can be raised about the egalitarian rationale. What are the transaction costs of allowing trustees to reopen completed transactions and grab back payments on which the creditor had relied? Why is equality among creditors important in bankruptcy while not outside bankruptcy?

Equality is an ex post rationale: it is concerned with the distribution to creditors after the debtor's bankruptcy case has commenced. A different rationale is an ex ante one: to discourage creditors from financing a debtor in financial trouble. The trustee's power to avoid preferential transfers, other things being equal, can dissuade creditors from financing debtors they know or expect to become financially distressed. After all, what incentive is there for creditors to help debtors stay in business through workout agreements calling for rescheduling of overdue debts if payments made pursuant to those agreements can be recovered under BC 547 if the debtor files in bankruptcy within 90 days after the payment? Perhaps if the policies underlying BC 547 are better understood, it might be easier to predict how this provision will apply to the myriad situations in which preference law has been invoked.

The often-quoted House Committee Report explanation follows. Although the policy goal Congress invokes is one of equality of distribution, this quotation shows that Congress had more in mind.

> A preference is a transfer that enables a creditor to receive payment of a greater percentage of his claim against the debtor than he would have received if the transfer had not been made and he had participated in the distribution of the assets of the bankrupt estate. The purpose of the preference section is two-fold. First, by permitting the trustee to avoid prebankruptcy transfers that occur within a short period before bankruptcy, creditors are discouraged from racing to the courthouse to dismember the debtor during his slide into bankruptcy. The protection thus afforded the debtor often enables him to work his way out of a difficult financial situation through cooperation with all of his creditors. Second, and more important, the preference provisions facilitate the prime bankruptcy policy of equality of distribution among creditors of the debtor. Any creditor that received a greater payment than others of his class is required to disgorge so that all may share equally. The operation of the preference section to deter "the race of diligence" of creditors to dismember the debtor before bankruptcy furthers the second goal of the preference section-that of equality of distribution.

H.R. Rep. No. 95–595, at 177–78 (1977), reprinted in 1978 U.S.C.C.A.N. 5963, 6138.

Congress apparently believed that preference law discourages creditors from racing to the courthouse to satisfy their claims from the debtor's assets on the eve of the debtor's bankruptcy. The Supreme Court agrees; see Union Bank v. Wolas, 502 U.S. 151 (1991). However, it is hard to see how preference law has this effect. A creditor might take a preference on the expectation that the transfer won't be discovered. Even if discovered, the trustee might elect not to recover the preference. Separately, the creditor might have a defense that prevents recovery; see, e.g., BC 547(c)(2), infra *National Gas Distributors*. And even if the trustee discovers the preference and recovers it from the creditor, there is no sanction for receiving a preference. Cf. BC 502(d). For all these reasons, a creditor is not dissuaded from receiving a preference on the eve of the debtor's bankruptcy.

An ex ante consideration might better able to justify preference law. Preference law provides a disincentive for the creditor to make a loan to the debtor in the first place, when it expects that the debtor is likely to be in bankruptcy shortly. A secured loan to a debtor approaching bankruptcy can harm other creditors while not affecting the secured lender if the debtor later goes into bankruptcy. This is because the loan enables the debtor to continue in business when its assets would be worth more if the debtor ceased operations. By allowing recovery of certain prebankruptcy transfers to the secured creditor, preference law discourages the secured lender from making inefficient loans to the debtor.

Congress is telling the creditor of a failing debtor not to worry if it sees other creditors dismembering the debtor; BC 547 will come to the rescue. But this is true only if the debtor files in bankruptcy within 90 days after making its transfers to the preferred creditors or within one year if the preferred creditors are insiders. The Bankruptcy Code offers creditors a remedy in these cases by allowing them to force the debtor into involuntary bankruptcy under BC 303 in cases in which the debtor is "generally not paying" its debts. BC 303(h)(1). In Problem 1(c) above, if Debtor doesn't voluntarily file in bankruptcy within the 90-day period, the other creditors can get rid of Creditor's judicial lien only by forcing Debtor into involuntary bankruptcy before the end of that period. Throughout this section, consider whether the applications of the provisions of BC 547 described there bear any discernible relation to different policies described above.

4. EFFECT OF AVOIDANCE

If the trustee in bankruptcy avoids a preferential transfer under BC 547(b), as mentioned above, the property transferred by the debtor to the creditor or its value can be recovered for the benefit of the estate. BC 550(a). If the preference occurred when the debtor paid a debt in cash, the trustee is entitled to recover an equivalent amount, which then becomes part of the bankruptcy estate. BC 541(a)(3). Suppose the preference occurred when the creditor obtained a lien in the debtor's property to secure the debt either by voluntary act of the debtor or against the will of the debtor, as in the case of a judicial lien. Assume that the property to which the lien applies is property of the bankruptcy estate. In that case, avoidance of the preference usually means that the creditor's lien is nullified. The effect of nullification is to increase the value of property of the estate in the amount of the value of the nullified lien. But sometimes simple nullification of a lien will not benefit the estate.

PROBLEM

Suppose property of the estate worth $10,000 is burdened by two liens, valid outside of bankruptcy, in favor of Creditor A and Creditor B, each of whom is owed $10,000. Assume that under the nonbankruptcy law the lien of Creditor A has priority over the lien of Creditor B, but that the lien of Creditor A is avoidable under BC 547(b) while the lien of Creditor B is indefeasible in bankruptcy. If the lien of Creditor A is nullified, the effect is to benefit Creditor B. The junior lien of Creditor B had no value before nullification, but it has a value of $10,000 after nullification. We have seen that the purpose of allowing the trustee to recover preferential transfers is to benefit the estate, i.e., to increase the value of the estate for the benefit of creditors generally. If the effect of avoidance of a lien is simply to shift the benefit of the preference from one creditor to another creditor, this bankruptcy purpose is frustrated. How does BC 551 prevent this result?

5.   PREFERENCE PERIOD

Under BC 547(b)(4), a transfer cannot be a voidable preference unless it occurs within what is called the "preference period." The preference period can be one of two lengths depending upon the identity of the recipient of the transfer. If the transferee is an insider, defined in BC 101, the preference period is one year before the date of the filing of the petition in bankruptcy. If the transferee is not an insider, the preference period is only 90 days before the filing of the petition. Why does BC 547(b)(4)(A) extend the preference period to one year for transfers to insiders? Judge Easterbrook explains:

> How long should [the] preference-recovery period be? If one outside creditor knows that the firm is in trouble, others will too. Each major lender monitors both the firm and fellow lenders. If it perceives that some other lender is being paid preferentially, a major lender can propel Firm into bankruptcy. Reasonably alert lenders can act with sufficient dispatch to ensure that the perceived preference is recoverable even when the preference period is short. Section 547(b) makes 90 days the rule, time enough (Congress concluded) for careful creditors to protect themselves (and when one does, small unsecured trade creditors get the benefits too).
>
> Insiders pose special problems. Insiders will be the first to recognize that the firm is in a downward spiral. If insiders and outsiders had the same preference-recovery period, insiders who lent money to the firm could use their knowledge to advantage by paying their own loans preferentially, then putting off filing the petition in bankruptcy until the preference period had

passed. Outside creditors, aware of this risk, would monitor more closely, or grab assets themselves (fearing that the reciprocity that is important to the pooling scheme has been destroyed), or precipitate bankruptcy at the smallest sign of trouble, hoping to "catch" inside preferences before it is too late. All of these devices could be costly. An alternative device is to make the preference-recovery period for insiders longer than that for outsiders. With a long period for insiders, even the prescient managers who first see the end coming are unlikely to be able to prefer themselves in distribution.

Levit v. Ingersoll Rand Fin. Corp., 874 F.2d 1186, 1194–1195 (7th Cir.1989). Before 1984, the one-year period applied only if the insider transferee had "reasonable cause to believe that the debtor was insolvent at the time of such transfer." This discarded requirement is briefly discussed later.

Uniform Voidable Transactions Act (UVTA) § 5(b) treats insider preferences as fraudulent transfers. The term "insider" is defined in UVTA § 1(8) to "include" the persons stated. The definition is based on BC 101 ("insider") although there are minor differences between the two sections. The official comment to UVTA § 1 makes clear that this section, like BC 101(31) ("insider"), is not meant to be limited to the persons stated. A court would be free to find that other persons are insiders if they "have the kind of close relationship intended to be covered by the term 'insider.'" Avoidability under UVTA § 5(b) depends upon the insider's having had "reasonable cause to believe that the debtor was insolvent," and there being a creditor whose claim arose before the transfer was made, requirements that no longer exist under BC 547(b). Since the statute of limitations for causes of action arising under § 5(b) is only one year (§ 9(c)), it adds nothing to the rights that a trustee enjoys under BC 547 with respect to insider preferences.

6. TRANSFERS TO OR FOR BENEFIT OF A CREDITOR

a. TRANSFER OF DEBTOR'S PROPERTY

Cutting through the complexities of BC 547, preference law is designed to prevent an insolvent debtor from depleting its estate on the eve of bankruptcy by transfers to particular creditors at the expense of other creditors. Thus, a basic requirement of BC 547(b) is that the property transferred must be that of the debtor. A simple illustration of the kinds of problems that can arise in determining whose property has been transferred follows.

PROBLEM

Debtor's obligation to Creditor was guaranteed by Guarantor. Under the law of the jurisdiction, if Guarantor had to make good on its guaranty by paying Creditor, it had a right to reimbursement from Debtor. When Debtor became insolvent and defaulted on its obligation, Guarantor paid Creditor. Within 90 days of the payment, Debtor filed in bankruptcy. Guarantor promptly filed a claim in Debtor's bankruptcy for reimbursement of the amount of the payment. Since Creditor was paid when other creditors of Debtor were not, Debtor's trustee sought to avoid the transfer to Creditor. BC 547(b) allows avoidance of "any transfer of an interest of the debtor in property. . . ." Was there a voidable preference in this case? Matter of Corland Corporation, 967 F.2d 1069 (5th Cir.1992).

b.   TO OR FOR THE BENEFIT OF A CREDITOR

Preference law differs from fraudulent transfer law in that a fraudulent transfer is voidable whoever the recipient is, but a preference is voidable only if the transfer is made to or for the benefit of a creditor of the debtor-transferor. BC 547(b)(1). Take the guaranty hypothetical in the previous problem. Change the facts so that Debtor, instead of Guarantor, pays the obligation within 90 days of bankruptcy. Can Debtor's trustee pursue Guarantor as the recipient of a voidable preference? Clearly there has been a preference in favor of Creditor, but Debtor's payment also benefited Guarantor, who is now released from the guaranty because Creditor has been paid. Thus, although Debtor's payment is *to* Creditor, there is no voidable preference to Guarantor unless Guarantor is a creditor of Debtor. Under BC 101(10)(A), a "creditor" is person with a "claim" against a debtor, and BC 101(5)(A) defines claim broadly to include a contingent right to payment. Guarantor has a contingent right to be reimbursed by Debtor because if Creditor collects from Guarantor, Guarantor can collect from Debtor. Hence, Debtor's payment to Creditor is voidable under BC 547(b), and Debtor's trustee has a choice under BC 550(a)(1) of recovering the money from either "the initial transferee of such transfer [Creditor] or the entity for whose benefit such transfer was made [Guarantor]."

7.   CONTEMPORANEOUS EXCHANGES

BC 547(b) expands preference law so broadly that virtually every payment or other transfer made by an insolvent debtor to a creditor within the preference period is called into question. BC 547(c) sets out nine exceptions that limit the reach of preference law and bring it more into harmony with its professed purposes. The more important of these exceptions are described in sections 8 and 9 below.

BC 547(b)(2) states as one element of a voidable preference that the transfer be "for or on account of an antecedent debt." Thus, if an insolvent buyer buys goods and pays for them at the time of sale by transferring money or other property to the seller, there is no preference because the buyer's obligation to pay for the goods and the transfer of the property to satisfy the obligation arise contemporaneously. But suppose there is a short delay between the time the obligation is incurred and the transfer of property in payment of the obligation. Does the short delay make the debt antecedent? The issue was considered by the Supreme Court in the case of Dean v. Davis, 242 U.S. 438 (1917). On September 3, the debtor obtained a loan from Dean on the debtor's promise to secure the loan by a mortgage on all of his property. The proceeds of the loan were used by the debtor to pay a debt owed to a bank. The mortgage was executed on September 10 and recorded the next day. Within a few days, a petition for involuntary bankruptcy was filed against the debtor. The trustee in bankruptcy brought an action to set aside the mortgage.

Both the district court and the court of appeals held that the mortgage was voidable as a fraudulent conveyance. The court of appeals also held that the mortgage could be avoided as a preference under § 60b of the Bankruptcy Act. The Supreme Court, in reversing the court of appeals on the latter point, stated: "The mortgage was not voidable as a preference under § 60b. Preference implies paying or securing a pre-existing debt of the person preferred. The mortgage was given to secure Dean for a substantially contemporary advance. The bank, not Dean, was preferred. The use of Dean's money to accomplish this purpose could not convert the transaction into a preferring of Dean, although he knew of the debtor's insolvency." 242 U.S. at 443.

BC 547(c)(1) codifies the part of this holding concerning the timing of the transfer. If a bank advances funds to a debtor who intends to secure the loan by granting the bank a security interest in the debtor's property, and the granting of the security interest is delayed only a short time, the exchange is substantially contemporaneous and the security interest cannot be avoided. If a buyer gives a seller an ordinary check in payment, the exchange is contemporaneous even though the seller doesn't actually receive the funds until a few days later when the check clears. Does this analysis apply to the problems that follow?

PROBLEMS

1. Bank made an unsecured demand loan to Debtor on the morning of April 1. Bank believed that Debtor was financially sound. Later that day, Bank received a credit report indicating that Debtor was in financial difficulty and might be insolvent. Bank immediately spoke to Debtor who acknowledged the truth of the credit report. When Bank demanded immediate repayment of the loan, Debtor offered instead to secure the loan by a mortgage on real property worth more than the amount of the loan. Bank agreed and the mortgage was executed on the evening of April 1 and recorded the next day. If Debtor was insolvent on April 1 and filed a petition in bankruptcy on June 1, can the mortgage be avoided as a preference? BC 547(b) and (c)(1); Nat'l City Bank v. Hotchkiss, 231 U.S. 50 (1913).

2. On April 1, Bank lent $10,000 to Debtor by crediting that amount to Debtor's checking account. The loan agreement signed on that day provided that the $10,000 would be used to buy certain described equipment in which Debtor granted a security interest to Bank. Bank filed a financing statement covering equipment of Debtor on April 1. On April 7, Debtor

bought the equipment described in the loan agreement. On June 20, Debtor filed a petition in bankruptcy. Under BC 547(e)(2) and (3), when did a transfer of property of Debtor occur? If Debtor was insolvent on April 1 and at all times thereafter, can Bank's security interest be avoided under BC 547(b)? Is avoidance prevented by BC 547(c)(1)? Is avoidance prevented by BC 547(c)(3)? Would your answers be different if Debtor had acquired the equipment on April 30?

8. ORDINARY COURSE PAYMENTS

An important goal of any commercial law regime is certainty and finality of transactions. If large numbers of ordinary commercial transactions are subject to being upset by later legal proceedings, all transactions of that type become more expensive. Creditors must charge for the increased risk and expense incident to those transactions. There is general consensus in favor of avoiding preferences made in out-of-the-ordinary transactions in which a creditor seeks, and is given, favored treatment by a debtor in obvious financial difficulty. It is not so clear that transactions by an insolvent debtor in paying debts as they mature should be avoided solely because an incidental result is that the creditors have been preferred over others who did not have the good fortune of being paid before bankruptcy. If a doctrine designed to obtain equality for all creditors interferes with normal commercial practices and significantly adds to the cost of ordinary commercial transactions, the cost of the equality may be too high.

A traditional limitation on avoidance of preferences was to allow avoidance only if the transferee had reasonable cause to believe that the debtor was insolvent. This principle stemmed from the early characterization of preferences in terms of unconscionability or fraud, as in the case in which a preferred creditor relies on a special relationship with the debtor to obtain an advantage not obtainable by others. Another limitation was to allow payments made to trade creditors on short term credit to remain unassailable under preference law. Both these limitations are rejected in BC 547(c). Instead, reliance is placed on one very specific provision, BC 547(c)(8), to cover small consumer debts, and one very general one, BC 547(c)(2), which has been broadly interpreted to cover both long-term and short-term credit. See Union Bank v. Wolas, 502 U.S. 151 (1991).

BC 547(c)(2) bars the trustee from avoiding a transfer:

(2) to the extent that such transfer was in payment of a debt incurred by the debtor in the ordinary course of business or financial affairs of the debtor and such transfer was—

(A) made in the ordinary course of business or financial affairs of the debtor and the transferee; or

(B) made according to ordinary business terms;

This is a major limitation on voidable preference law, and the question that has puzzled courts is when are transfers not in ordinary course. Are payments in ordinary course when made by a business debtor that is struggling to stay in business by paying only essential creditors during the preference period? Suppose the recipients of these payments know of the debtor's financial condition. Is any policy served by taking payments back from creditors who are willing to work with a debtor trying to save its business? These are troublesome issues.

In re National Gas Distributors, L.L.C.

United States Bankruptcy Court for the Eastern District of North Carolina, 2006
346 B.R. 394

■ A. Thomas Small.

The matter before the court is the motion for summary judgment filed by the plaintiff, Richard M. Hutson II, trustee for the chapter 11 debtor National Gas Distributors, LLC ("NGD"). The trustee seeks to avoid and to recover, pursuant to 11 U.S.C. §§ 547 and 550, preferential transfers aggregating $3,263,516.15 made by NGD to the defendant, Branch Banking and Trust Company ("BB&T"). BB&T's defense under § 547(c)(2)(B) is that the transfers, two loan payments in the amounts of $755,329.80 and $2,508,186.35, are not avoidable because they were "made according to ordinary business terms." It is not disputed that the two loan payments meet the requirements of § 547(b) and may be avoided unless BB&T prevails on its "ordinary business terms" defense under § 547(c)(2)(B).

The phrase "ordinary business terms" has been analyzed and interpreted many times by many courts in connection with, and as a part of, what has been known as the "ordinary course of business" defense under § 547(c)(2). Section 547(c)(2), however, was amended by the Bankruptcy Abuse Prevention and Consumer Protection Act of 2005 ("BAPCPA"), Pub. L. No. 109–8, 119 Stat. 23, § 409. That section now includes both an "ordinary course of business" defense under § 547(c)(2)(A) and a separate, independent "ordinary business terms" defense under § 547(c)(2)(B).

Prior to BAPCPA, these two defenses were dual components of a single defense. Now the phrase "ordinary business terms" included in § 547(c)(2)(B), is no longer part of the "ordinary course of business" defense in § 547(c)(2)(A). So, although the words "ordinary business terms" were not changed by BAPCPA, the context in which they appear in § 547(c)(2) has substantially changed. Whether the words "ordinary business terms" acquired new meaning in their new context, and what that meaning might be, are the primary issues before the court. . . .

National Gas Distributors, LLC was a purchaser and distributor of natural gas, propane and other energy commodities, and in January 2006 it became subject to a North Carolina state court receivership. NGD filed a petition for relief under chapter 11 of the Bankruptcy Code on January 20, 2006. On January 24, at the request of the state court receiver and without objection from the debtor, Mr. Hutson was appointed chapter 11 trustee.

NGD, which is owned by Paul Lawing, had several ongoing credit transactions with BB&T including a line of credit, a working capital loan, and letters of credit. None of NGD's obligations to BB&T were secured by NGD's assets, but all of the obligations were subject to the guaranties of Mr. Lawing and his wife, Ann Lawing, and all of the obligations were secured by assets owned by Mrs. Lawing. Two credit facilities were paid with transfers that are the subjects of this proceeding: the revolving line of credit, and the working capital loan.

The line of credit was evidenced by a promissory note dated March 31, 2003, in the principal amount of $1,000,000. The line of credit obligation was to mature on November 5, 2003, but the maturity was extended to November 5, 2004, and later extended to November 8, 2005, and then to December 23, 2005. On December 15, 2005, NGD transferred $755,329.80 to BB&T to pay the balance outstanding under the line of credit note.

The working capital loan was evidenced by a promissory note dated September 27, 2004, in the principal amount of $2,500,000. The working capital note was to mature on March 27, 2005, but the maturity was extended to August 5, 2005, and later extended to October 16, 2005, and then to December 23, 2005. On December 19, 2005, NGD transferred $2,508,186.35 to BB&T to pay the balance outstanding under the working capital note.

On December 20, 2005, about the same time that NGD was paying the line of credit and the working capital loan, NGD transferred $850,000 to BB&T to collateralize NGD's obligations with respect to two letters of credit in the amounts of $600,000 and $250,000. As a result of that transfer, BB&T released property owned by Mrs. Lawing that BB&T held as collateral to secure NGD's liability regarding the letters of credit. The trustee does not seek to recover the $850,000 transfer, but the transfer is relevant to the course of dealing between NGD and BB&T. The trustee, by letter dated February 10, 2006, made demand upon BB&T to repay the transfers.

For a transfer to be avoidable, it must satisfy the requirements of § 547(b). * * *

It is not disputed that the payments of $755,329.80 and $2,508,186.35 were transfers of the debtor's property made to or for the benefit of BB&T on account of antecedent debts, while NGD was insolvent, and within ninety days of date of NGD's bankruptcy petition. It is also not disputed that the payments enabled BB&T to receive more that BB&T would have received had the payments not been made and NGD was a debtor in a case under chapter 7. The trustee has met his burden of establishing the elements of § 547(b), and may avoid the two payments unless BB&T can establish its defense under § 547(c)(2)(B).

11 U.S.C. § 547(c)(2) as amended by BAPCPA provides as follows:

(c)   The trustee may not avoid under this section a transfer—

   (1)   . . .

   (2)   to the extent that such transfer was in payment of a debt incurred by the debtor in the ordinary course of business or financial affairs of the debtor and the transferee, and such transfer was—

      (A)   made in the ordinary course of business or financial affairs of the debtor and the transferee; or

      (B)   made according to ordinary business terms.

The trustee concedes that the transfers were in payment of debts that were incurred by NGD in the ordinary course of business of NGD and BB&T, but disagrees that the payments were made according to "ordinary business terms." BB&T has the burden of proving all of the elements of its defense, Advo-System, Inc. v. Maxway Corp., 37 F.3d 1044, 1047 (4th Cir. 1994), and in support of its defense that the payments were made according to ordinary business terms, it submitted the affidavit of BB&T Vice President Stephen G. Smith.

Mr. Smith, the BB&T loan officer who handled the NGD transactions, stated that BB&T as a matter of routine practice extended the maturity dates of the line of credit note and the working capital note and would have extended the maturity date of December 23, 2005, for each of the notes if requested by NGD. At the time the notes were paid, BB&T and NGD were discussing a $20,000,000 revolving line of credit that would have paid the BB&T notes as well those with another lender. Mr. Smith states that neither note was ever in default, and BB&T had no knowledge of NGD's financial difficulties. BB&T "did not demand, request, or in any way suggest that the Line of Credit Note or the Working Capital Note be paid," and "BB&T made no attempts to collect" on the notes. According to Mr. Smith, he was told by Mr. Lawing that the notes were paid in full as "part of Mr. and Mrs. Lawing's end-of-the-year estate planning."

Mr. Smith, who has been employed with BB&T for approximately 15 years and has been working in the banking industry for approximately 30 years, states that he is "familiar with the standard and ordinary terms used at BB&T and in the banking industry in general for commercial loans, including line of credit loans and working capital loans." The following statements from Mr. Smith's affidavit are in the nature of Mr. Smith's expert opinion regarding "ordinary business terms":

"The terms of the Line of Credit Note and the Working Capital Note are typical of those normally extended to similar businesses that borrow money from BB&T."

"It is a customary practice within BB&T and in the banking industry for a lender to execute modification agreements extending maturity dates of promissory notes for borrowers. The Line of Credit Note and the Working Capital Note and the modifications to these notes were done on standard BB&T documents and contain terms that are standard and ordinary at BB&T and in the banking industry."

"When a promissory note becomes due, it is typical and customary at BB&T and in the banking industry for a borrower to pay the note in full on the maturity date or within several weeks before the maturity date."

"The payment of the Line of Credit Note on December 15, 2005 and the Working Capital Note on December 18, 2005 were made within the terms of the Notes, as modified. These payments were well within the standard terms and practice at BB&T, as well as a standard practice in the banking industry in general."

These four statements capture the heart of BB&T's evidence in support of its defense.

The trustee submitted an affidavit in support of his motion for summary judgment that supports the requirements of § 547(b), but the affidavit does not address BB&T's "ordinary business terms" defense. . . .

The trustee's entitlement to summary judgment depends on whether BB&T has set forth sufficient evidence to establish its "ordinary business terms" defense. In making that determination, the court must first ascertain the meaning of "ordinary business terms." As already mentioned "ordinary business terms" has been interpreted by many courts as a part of the "ordinary course of business" defense under § 547(c)(2). However, that section was amended and reconfigured by BAPCPA. The change was accomplished "by the simple expedient of changing an 'and' to an 'or,' but the defense "changed dramatically." Charles J. Tabb, The Brave New World of Bankruptcy Preferences, 13 Am. Bankr. Inst. L. Rev. 425, 428 (2005). Prior case law provides the answers to some of the "ordinary business terms" questions, but after BAPCPA, those answers may no longer be complete.

After the amendments made by BAPCPA, § 547(c)(2) is, in effect, a new statute, and, as with any new statute, its interpretation starts with the statute's plain meaning. Unfortunately, the phrase "ordinary business terms" is so inclusive that a plain meaning analysis is not helpful. Neither is the legislative history to the BAPCPA amendments.

The legislative history regarding BAPCPA § 409 provides as follows:

[S]ection 547(c)(2) of the Bankruptcy Code [is amended] to provide that a trustee may not avoid a transfer to the extent such transfer was in payment of a debt incurred by the debtor in the ordinary course of the business or financial affairs of the debtor and the transferee and such transfer was made either: (1) in the ordinary course of the debtor's and the transferee's business or financial affairs; or (2) in accordance with ordinary business terms. Present law requires the recipient of a preferential transfer to establish both of these grounds in order to sustain a defense to a preferential transfer proceeding. . . .

E-2 Collier on Bankruptcy App. Pt. 10(b) at App. Pt. 10–355 (Alan N. Resnick and Henry J. Sommer, eds., 15th ed. rev. 2005). The legislative history emphasizes that "or" is to be read in the disjunctive but otherwise imparts no insight into how the reconstructed statute should be interpreted. . . .

To best understand how the statutory language should be interpreted in its new capacity as a separate "stand alone" statutory requirement rather than as a distinct but secondary requirement in a series of others, it is helpful to review the development of the extensive pre-BAPCPA case law interpreting "ordinary business terms."

Section 547(c)(2) of the Bankruptcy Code was enacted as part of the Bankruptcy Reform Act of 1978, Pub. L. No. 95–598, 92 Stat. 2549 (1978). "During the first decade of the Bankruptcy Code, most courts concentrated solely on the relationship between the debtor and the creditor in determining whether the defendant had satisfied its burden of proof under *both* subparagraphs (B) and (C) [of § 547(c)(2)]. Only in the absence of a history between the parties did these courts look to transactions involving third parties." 5 Collier P 547.04[2][a][i] at 547–56.

Then, in the late 1980s to 1990s, developing precedent required "an independent inquiry into whether the payment practice at issue comport[ed] with industry standards." 5 Collier P 547.04[2][a][i] at 547–56. The United States Court of Appeals for the Fourth Circuit in Advo-System, Inc. v. Maxway Corp., 37 F.3d 1044, 1048 (4th Cir. 1994), "refuse[d] to say that Congress wrote a separate subsection for no reason at all," and observed that subsection (C) must be analyzed objectively because "the use of subsection B's subjective approach under subsection C would render subsection C superfluous."

Courts endeavored to construe the second and third subsections in a way that minimized overlap between them. The "march of the circuits to the holding that [former] subparagraph (C) requires an independent analysis of the standard of the industry was based partially upon a principle of statutory construction that '[a]n interpretation of § 547(c)(2)(C) which focuses exclusively on the relationship between the creditor and the debtor, would deprive subsection (c)(2)(C) of any independent meaning because (c)(2)(B) already requires that the payment be evaluated in the context of the ongoing relationship between the debtor and the creditor.'" 5 Collier P 547.04[2][a] at 547–56–7 (quoting Miller v. Florida Mining & Materials (In re A.W. & Assocs., Inc.), 136 F.3d 1439, 1442 (11th Cir. 1998)).

The result of all this was that subsection (C) was perceived as somewhat less important because it focused on objective, larger-scale industry standards instead of the more immediate facts of the parties' relationship, which were reserved for discussion under the umbrella of subsection (B). The required division of focus regarding the two prongs thus shaped the courts' development of the standard to be proved under each as well as the comparative weight to be given to each in differing cases. . . .

The yolk between the "ordinary course of business" defense and the "ordinary business terms" components of § 547(c)(2) has been removed by BAPCPA, and "ordinary business terms" has been released from the controlling influence of the ordinary course of business subsection. The "ordinary business terms" defense is now the equal of the "ordinary course of business" defense, and that change affects pre-BAPCPA case law construing the meaning of "ordinary business terms."

Most courts agreed that an "ordinary business terms" analysis under pre-BAPCPA § 547(c)(2) required an objective application of industry standards. The objective analysis served two important functions, according to the Court of Appeals for the Fourth Circuit: "'One is evidentiary. If the debtor and creditor dealt on terms that the creditor testifies were normal for them but that are wholly unknown in the industry, this casts some doubt on his (self-serving) testimony. . . . The second possible function of the subsection is to allay the concerns of creditors that one or more of their number may have worked out a special deal with the debtor, before the preference period, designed to put that creditor ahead of the others in the event of bankruptcy.'" Advo-System, 37 F.3d at 1048 (quoting Tolona Pizza, 3 F.3d at 1032).

Frequently, both the debtor and the creditor, especially where the creditor was a trade creditor, were involved in the same or related industries. E.g., Tolona Pizza, 3 F.3d at 1031 (debtor was pizza maker and creditor was sausage supplier). . . .

At least one Circuit Court has held that it is the debtor's industry that is the focus of the "ordinary business terms" analysis. See In re Accessair, Inc., 314 B.R. 386, 394 (8th Cir. BAP 2004) ("Section 547(c)(2)(C) requires the transferee to demonstrate that the debtor made the preferential transfer according to the ordinary business terms prevailing within the debtor's industry."), aff'd, 163 Fed. Appx. 445 (8th Cir. 2006). But, the Court of Appeals for the Fourth Circuit has held that the industry standard to be applied when examining "ordinary business terms" is that of the creditor's industry. Advo-System, 37 F.3d at 1048 (courts must "look to the norm in the creditor's industry").

BB&T maintains, consistent with the court's ruling in Advo-System, that the applicable industry standard is that of the banking industry. According to BB&T, it is standard banking practice for a bank to receive payment on a note shortly before the note matures. BB&T argues that both the Line of Credit Note and the Working Capital Note matured on December 23, 2005, and that payments received on December 15, 2005 (Line of Credit Note) and on December 19, 2005 (Working Capital Note) were according to "ordinary business terms." There are several problems with that argument.

Notwithstanding the holding of the Court of Appeals for the Fourth Circuit in Advo-System, the BAPCPA changes to § 547(c)(2) now require an examination of more than just the standards of the creditor's industry. Many courts have observed many times that the purpose of the ordinary course of business defense is to "leave undisturbed normal financial relations, because it does not detract from the general policy of the section to discourage unusual action by either the debtor or its creditors during the debtor's slide into bankruptcy." E.g., Union Bank. v. Wolas, 502 U.S. 151, 160, 112 S. Ct. 527, 532, 116 L. Ed. 2d 514 (1991) (quoting H.R. Rep. No. 95–595, at 373, U.S. Code Cong. & Admin. News 1978, p. 6329). If the "ordinary business terms" defense only requires examination of the industry standards of the creditor, there would be no review or check on the debtor's conduct.

Now that "ordinary business terms" is a separate defense, the court must consider the industry standards of both the debtor and its creditors. Furthermore, there are general business standards that are common to all business transactions in all industries that must be met. Based on the uncontroverted facts in this case, the transfers to BB&T cannot meet those standards.

BB&T contends that the payment of the two notes was consistent with banking industry standards. However, the proffered evidence is not sufficient to support that contention. BB&T's affidavit, which states, for example, that "[w]hen a promissory note becomes due, it is typical and customary at BB&T and in the banking industry for a borrower to pay the note in full on the maturity date or within several weeks before the maturity date," does not establish the industry standard. Such a statement is too general to establish industry norms, or to support the "ordinary business terms" defense. The Court of Appeals for the Fourth Circuit explained in Advo-System, that a creditor may not characterize the industry norm "at too high a level of generality," because generality would render the subsection "virtually meaningless." Advo-System, 37 F.3d at 1051. BB&T's general statement that a payment meets banking standards is not sufficient.

The industry standards must be applied to the factual circumstances of the transfer. It may be standard practice for borrowers to pay loans close to the time that the loans mature, but is it standard in the banking industry for a borrower with a multi-million dollar enterprise to pay all of its corporate loans based upon the owner's end-of-the-year personal financial planning, especially where the corporation has not arranged for financing to continue the business? If that conduct is standard within the banking industry, it is certainly not ordinary from the debtor's perspective and is not consistent with sound business practice in general.

From BB&T'S point of view, it did nothing out of the ordinary. BB&T had no knowledge that NGD was having financial difficulties, did not pursue any collection activity against NGD, and merely received payment on its loans when those loans became due. The court must accept those assertions as true, but that does not entitle BB&T to prevail on its preference defense. The "ordinary business terms" defense also involves consideration of the debtor's industry standards and the standards applicable to business in general. When those standards are examined, the conduct of the debtor in paying its loans was not in accordance with "ordinary business terms." It is clear what was going on here: NGD was going out of business and was paying off those debts which Mr. and Mrs. Lawing guaranteed and for which Mrs. Lawing's assets stood as collateral. These payments were not made "according to ordinary business terms" and are not the type of transfers that the "ordinary business terms" defense is designed to protect. Consequently, BB&T may not prevail on its "ordinary business terms" defense.

The change made by the BAPCPA amendments "substantially lightens the creditor's burden of proof, by allowing the creditor protection from preference recovery if the transfer meets industry standards, regardless of whether it was in the ordinary course of business of the debtor and the creditor." Richard Levin & Alesia Ranney-Marinelli, The Creeping Repeal of Chapter 11: The Significant Business Provisions of the Bankruptcy Abuse Prevention and Consumer Protection Act of 2005, 79 Am. Bankr. L. J. 603, 637 (2005). Although the creditor's burden has been lightened by BAPCPA, it still has some weight, and it has not been lightened to the extent that BB&T can prevail in this proceeding. The trustee is entitled to avoid and to recover from BB&T preferential payments totaling $3,263,516.15 plus interest at the federal judgment rate of 4.67% from the date of demand, February 10, 2006, until paid. Accordingly, the trustee's motion for summary judgment is GRANTED, and a separate judgment will be entered.

NOTES

1.   The BAPCPA amendment to BC 547(c)(2) gives the creditor the option of proving *either* that payment was made in ordinary course of the debtor's business *or* that it was made according to ordinary business terms. Is this a good change? Under what circumstances should a trustee be able to claw back payments in the ordinary course of business between debtors and creditors that are on terms that are not customary in the industry? Why should extraordinary payments between debtor and creditor be shielded from avoidance so long as they are made in accordance with ordinary

business terms? What answer does the court in *National Gas* give to these questions?

2.   Not all courts agree with the *National Gas Distributors* court's ruling that 547(c)(2)(B)'s "ordinary business terms" prong requires the transaction to be ordinary in both the creditor and debtors' industries. Some construe that prong to require only that the transaction be ordinary in the creditor's industry. See, e.g., In re American Home Mortgage Holdings, Inc., 476 B.R. 124 (Bankr. D. Del. 2012); In re Globe Holdings, Inc., 366 B.R. 186 (Bankr. N.D. Ala. 2007). Other courts continue to apply pre-BAPCPA caselaw to 547(c)(2)(B)'s interpretation; see, e.g., In re M. Fabricant & Sons, 2010 WL 4622449 (Bankr. S.D.N.Y. Nov. 12, 2010); In re Horob Livestock, Inc., 382 B.R. 457 (Bankr. D. Mont. 2007). These courts can rely on pre-BAPCPA caselaw to find that (c)(2)(B)'s prong refers to what is ordinary only in the creditor's industry.

3.   The standard of "ordinary business terms" on which the court relies is one that creditors will often find hard to satisfy. According to the court, an industry standard characterized at a high level of generality is insufficient to meet 547(c)(2)(B). The creditor instead must prove that in the industry the transfer was standard practice in the debtor's particular circumstances. Some industry standards might be general practices, not fine-tuned to specific transactions or debtors. In such cases the creditor will be unable to meet the evidentiary burden of proving "ordinary business terms." Other courts might use a less demanding standard than the one used in *National Gas Distributors*. In In re American Camshaft Specialties Inc., 444 B.R. 347 (Bankr. Mich.2011), the court found payment of an invoice was made according to ordinary business terms when it was made within the time given within the 75th percentile of survey responses in the relevant industry.

9.   FLOATING LIEN AS A PREFERENCE

Controversy over the validity of floating liens in bankruptcy arose in the years immediately after enactment of the UCC. The bankruptcy bar had stood by, largely ignored, while Article 9 was drafted in a manner that seemed to give every advantage to the secured creditor: abrogation in 9–205 of the prohibition on the debtor's retention of unrestricted dominion over collateral; automatic future advance and after-acquired property clauses in 9–204; first-to-file priority rule in 9–322; notice filing in 9–502. Taken together, these provisions allowed the secured party to take a security interest in all of a debtor's personal property now owned or thereafter acquired to secure both present and future advances. If the floating lien were upheld in bankruptcy without limitations, there would be nothing left in a debtor's estate to distribute among unsecured trade creditors who had provided goods and services to the failed debtor.

But bankruptcy counsel believed that the drafters of the 1962 version of Article 9 had unknowingly made security interests in inventory acquired and accounts that arose during the preference period potentially to be voidable as preferences. This view if accepted would have destroyed the inventory and accounts financing industry. And these lawyers had a solid basis for their opinion. Test cases followed.

As described in more detail in the following section, the time of the transfer for security interests in bankruptcy is the time of perfection of the security interest, not its attachment. BC 547(e). Suppose Debtor, an appliance retailer, signed a security agreement on February 1 granting a security interest to Bank to secure a loan made at the same time. The collateral was all of Debtor's inventory then owned or thereafter acquired. Bank immediately filed a financing statement covering inventory. Under Article 9, the security interest attached, with respect to any item of inventory, when all of the following conditions were met: (1) Debtor signed a security agreement; (2) Bank gave value to Debtor; and (3) Debtor had rights in the item of inventory. 9–203(b). The first two conditions were satisfied on February 1 when the loan was made and the agreement signed. The third condition was satisfied at various times. With respect to inventory owned on February 1, it was satisfied on that date. With respect to after-acquired inventory, it was satisfied when the inventory was acquired. Section 9–308(a) states that a security interest is perfected when it has attached and when all of the applicable steps required for perfection have been taken. The step normally taken to perfect a security interest in inventory is the filing of a financing statement. Thus, under Article 9, whenever Debtor acquired an item of inventory after February 1, a security interest in that item attached and was perfected. Filing of the financing statement occurred on February 1, but perfection with respect to the inventory covered by the financing statement could not occur until the inventory was acquired.

Suppose in the example that Debtor's inventory completely turned over every 60 days and that Debtor filed in bankruptcy on December 1. Under this assumption, all inventory on hand at the date of bankruptcy had been acquired during the preference period. Assume further that Bank did not make additional loans to Debtor after February 1 and that the original loan was unpaid at the date of bankruptcy. Under Article 9 the security interest of Bank in inventory at the date of bankruptcy attached and was perfected during the preference period and secured a debt that arose on February 1. Under Bankruptcy Act § 60a(2) (now found in BC 547(e)), the apparent result was that the transfer of Debtor's property represented by the security interest was made when the security interest attached and was perfected during the preference period. Thus, if Debtor was insolvent at the time of the transfer, the security interest was voidable as a preferential transfer under Bankruptcy Act § 60b.

For present purposes, it is enough to say that in Grain Merchants of Indiana, Inc. v. Union Bank & Savings Co., 408 F.2d 209 (7th Cir.1969), the court, in a highly unorthodox reading of the law, upheld the validity of floating lien security interests in inventory and accounts in bankruptcy. The reasoning of this opinion was sufficiently questionable to drive all parties to resolve the issue by a compromise amendment to the Bankruptcy Code. This provision is now BC 547(c)(5). It was drafted against a background that assumed the following: accounts receivable and inventory normally turn over within a short period of time. It is likely that at the date of bankruptcy some receivables or inventory on hand were acquired by the debtor within the 90-day period. Since a security interest in this new collateral was, by virtue of BC 547(e)(3), a transfer to the secured party when it was acquired by the debtor, there might have been a voidable preference under BC 547(b)(3) if the debtor was insolvent at the time. BC 547(c)(5), set out below, is a limited exemption from this rule.

 (c) The trustee may not avoid under this section a transfer. . .

  (5) that creates a perfected security interest in inventory or a receivable or the proceeds of either, except to the extent that the aggregate of all such transfers to the transferee caused a reduction, as of the date of the filing of the petition and to the prejudice of other creditors holding unsecured claims, of any amount by which the debt secured by such security interest exceeded the value of all security interests for such debt on the later of

   (A) (i) with respect to a transfer to which subsection (b)(4)(A) of this section applies, 90 days before the date of the filing of the petition; or

    (ii) with respect to a transfer to which (b)(4)(B) of this section applies, one year before the date of the filing of the petition; or

   (B) the date on which new value was first given under the security agreement creating such security interest; . . .

PROBLEM

Secured Party is secured by all Debtor's accounts receivables. Ninety days before Debtor's bankruptcy filing, Debtor owed Secured Party $100,000. As of the date of Debtor's bankruptcy filing Debtor owed Secured Party $90,000; at the beginning of the 90-day period, there were $60,000 in accounts receivable. During the 90-day period, Debtor increased its accounts receivable so that on the date of its bankruptcy they amounted to $70,000. None of Debtor's accounts receivable at the time of its bankruptcy filing were held by Debtor throughout the 90 days before its filing.

 (a) What would be the result in this case?

 (b) What would be the result if Secured Party's $100,000 debt was secured by $120,000 in accounts receivable at the beginning of the 90-day period and $70,000 in receivables on the date of bankruptcy all obtained by Debtor within the 90-day period?

Section 547(c)(5) is a variation of the substitution theory, which was one of the more persuasive bases of the *Grain Merchants* decision. It says, in effect, that it is not important whether the items making up the mass of inventory or account receivables at bankruptcy were identical to the items making up the mass at the beginning of the 90-day period so long as the volume has not changed. Within that limitation, any new item that came into existence within the 90-day period is treated as a substitute for an item that was disposed of by the debtor during the same period.

10. FALSE PREFERENCES: DELAYED PERFECTION OF SECURITY INTERESTS

Delayed Attachment. Section 7 on contemporaneous exchange dealt with cases in which there is a delay between the time when credit is granted and the security interest intended to secure that credit attaches. Since the subsequent attaching of the security interest is a transfer of property of the debtor on account of the antecedent debt arising from the credit, there is a prima facie voidable preference if the other elements of BC 547(b) are present. If the delay is very short, the security interest may, under some circumstances, be saved by BC 547(c)(1). If the credit was for the purpose of enabling the debtor to acquire the collateral which secures the debt the security interest may be saved if there was compliance with BC 547(c)(3). In all of these cases the problem arises because of a delay in the creation of the security interest.

Delayed Perfection. A superficially similar but entirely distinct problem arises when the granting of the credit and the creation of the security interest are contemporaneous, but there is a delay between the creation, or attachment, of the security interest and the subsequent perfection of the security interest by filing. There is no true preference in these cases because the grant of the security interest to the creditor was not on account of an antecedent debt. The problem of delayed perfection is the evil of the secret lien. The classic case is that of a debtor in financial difficulty who wishes to conceal from general creditors the true state of its financial condition. The debtor obtains an emergency loan from a creditor and grants to that creditor a mortgage on real property or a security interest in personal property to secure the loan. The property involved might well be most of the debtor's previously unencumbered assets. If public notice of the transaction were given by recording the mortgage or filing a financing statement with respect to the security interest, the result might be that other creditors would be deterred from giving to the debtor further unsecured credit because of the absence of unencumbered assets. To avoid this result, the creditor might be induced not to record the mortgage or file the financing statement.

Essentially the issue is fraud on creditors, not preference. Usually, an unrecorded mortgage of real property has priority over the claim of a creditor who subsequently levies on the property. The holder of an unperfected security interest in personal property takes a greater risk by not promptly perfecting because an unperfected Article 9 security interest does not have priority over a subsequent judicial lien. But in either case the creditor can protect the lien by promptly perfecting at the first sign that other creditors may either levy on assets of the debtor or file a petition for involuntary bankruptcy against the debtor. In the classic case, the creditor is an insider with access to information that provides some assurance that the creditor will have sufficient advance notice of facts that will allow the creditor to perfect in time.

It is understandable that there should be a policy against secret liens, and such a policy was expressed in the Bankruptcy Act. However, the technique used in the Bankruptcy Act to address the evil was unusual. Instead of dealing with the problem directly as a case of fraud on creditors, Congress discouraged the secret lien by a provision in the Bankruptcy Act preference section. This 1950 provision was the culmination of a series of amendments dating as far back as 1903, designed to deal with the problem of secret liens. The effect was to convert what was not in fact a preferential lien into a preferential lien by a conclusive presumption that the lien became effective at the time it was perfected rather than at the time it was actually created. Certain grace periods were allowed for the creditor to perfect. If the creditor didn't perfect within these periods, the lien was treated as having been given for an antecedent debt. This technique of turning secret liens into false preferences was carried over into the Bankruptcy Code. The relevant provision is BC 547(e)(2). The meaning of BC 547(e)(2) is clarified in BC 547(e)(1), which defines the term "perfected," and limited in BC 547(e)(3), which defines the earliest time a transfer can occur.

BC 547(e)(2) was designed to eliminate the evils of the secret lien, and it is effective in that regard. Unfortunately, it also ensnared many hapless secured creditors who, through no fault of their own, were unable to perfect within the former ten-day time limit. This is particularly true in cases involving motor vehicles. Unhappy with the harsh results in these cases, several states have attempted to deal with the problem by making special rules for security interests in motor vehicles by providing that if proper documentation is presented to the relevant state agency within a given period of time (usually from 15 to 30 days) after the security interest has attached, the security interest is deemed to have been perfected at the time it attached. Courts divided over whether an extended relation-back period under a state statute could prevail over the former ten-day period in BC 547(e)(2). The Supreme Court resolved the issue in Fidelity Financial Services, Inc. v. Fink, 522 U.S. 211 (1998), by holding that the time period provided in BC 547(e)(2) trumped any more expansive relation-back period under state law. In BAPCPA, the periods in BC 547(e)(2)(A), (B) and (C) for refinancing transactions and in BC 547(c)(3)(B) for purchase-money transactions are extended to 30 days. These amendments should lessen the difficulties posed for secured creditors by the Code's policy of dating the time of transfer at the time of perfection. Article 9 has extended the relation-back period for purchase-money security interests to 20 days. 9–317(e).

F. FRAUDULENT TRANSFERS: BC 548

1. BASIC RULES

The ancient law of fraudulent transfers is codified at the federal level by BC 548 and at the state level in almost every state by the Uniform Fraudulent Transfer Act (UFTA) or Uniform Voidable Transactions Act (UVTA). Bankruptcy Code 548 provides that trustees may avoid certain transfers or obligations deemed fraudulent that are made or entered into by debtors within two years of bankruptcy. Similarly, state fraudulent transfer law provides for the avoidance of fraudulent transfers or obligations, typically with a four-year statute of limitations. The Uniform Voidable Transactions Act (2014), enacted in approximately half the states to date, renames and modestly amends the UFTA. "Transfer" in BC 101(54) includes the grant of a security interest. The UVTA contains provisions similar to those in BC 548. These laws are not as important in personal property secured transactions as are BC 544(a)(1), the strong arm power, or BC 547, voidable preference law. Thus, the treatment of fraudulent transfer law below is limited to the few instances in which it affects Article 9 secured transactions.

a. ACTUAL FRAUD

BC 548(a)(1)

The trustee may avoid any transfer of an interest of the debtor in property, or any obligation incurred by the debtor, that was made or incurred on or within two years before the date of filing of the petition, if the debtor voluntarily or involuntarily

(A) made such transfer or incurred such obligation with actual intent to hinder, delay, or defraud any entity to which the debtor was or became, on or after the date that such transfer was made or such obligation was incurred, indebted. . . .

Courts have sought for centuries to decide the illusive issue of when the transferor has "actual intent to hinder, delay, or defraud" another. Sometimes it is obvious, as in the case in which a debtor attempts to shield her assets from her unsecured creditors by granting a phony security interest in her assets to a relative. But in other cases it is not so obvious, and in these cases, the First Circuit, like many other courts, relies on factors known as the "badges of fraud" announced in a famous decision of the Star Chamber, Twyne's Case, (1601) 76 Eng. Rep. 234 (1601), which was decided under the Act Against Fraudulent Deeds,

Gifts, Alienations, [etc.] 13 Elizabeth c. 5 (1570) (Eng.). Most courts subject a showing of actual fraud to an enhanced standard of proof.

Given the practical difficulty of mounting direct evidence of the debtor's intent, few cases turn on such proof. Instead, looking to the circumstances surrounding the transfer, courts have identified several objective indicia that, taken together, strongly indicate fraudulent intent. Those indicia include: (1) insider relationships between the parties; (2) the retention of possession, benefit or use of the property in question; (3) the lack or inadequacy of consideration for the transfer; (4) the financial condition of the party sought to be charged both before and after the transaction at issue; (5) the existence or cumulative effect of the pattern or series of transactions or course of conduct after the incurring of debt, onset of financial difficulties, or pendency or threat of suits by creditors; (6) the general chronology of the events and transactions under inquiry;. . . and (7) an attempt by the debtor to keep the transfer a secret; In re Watman, 301 F.3d 3, 8 (1st Cir.2002). That court adds a 21st century factor to these 17th century indicia: "The shifting of assets by the debtor to a corporation wholly controlled by him is another badge of fraud." UVTA § 4(b) includes a list of the traditional badges of fraud.

b. CONSTRUCTIVE FRAUD

Of greater significance to secured transactions law is what is generally called "constructive fraud," which requires no fraudulent intent. BC 548(a)(1)(B) states this alternative ground for avoiding a transfer or obligation. It provides that the trustee may do so if the debtor:

(B) (i) received less than a reasonably equivalent value in exchange for such transfer or obligation; and

     (ii) (I)   was insolvent on the date that such transfer was made or such obligation was incurred, or became insolvent as a result of such transfer or obligation;

        (II)   was engaged in business or a transaction, or was about to engage in business or a transaction, for which any property remaining with the debtor was an unreasonably small capital; or

        (III) intended to incur, or believed that the debtor would incur, debts that would be beyond the debtor's ability to pay as such debts matured.

        (IV) made such transfer to or for the benefit of an insider or incurred such obligation to or for the benefit of an insider under an employment contract and not in the ordinary course of business.

This ground for avoidance has nothing to do with actual fraud. It states a simple rule that an insolvent debtor must receive "reasonably equivalent value" in exchange for a transfer or obligation.

Subparagraphs (II) and (III) are proxies for insolvency. As is sometimes said, an insolvent debtor must be just before it can be generous. Such a debtor cannot deplete its estate at the expense of its creditors in order to benefit others. An insolvent debtor may transfer its assets or enter into obligations so long as it doesn't prejudice its creditors in doing so. If it receives reasonably equivalent value, its creditors are not harmed.

2. REASONABLY EQUIVALENT VALUE

In most secured transactions, there is no issue regarding whether a debtor who grants a security interest in its property receives reasonably equivalent value. Suppose Debtor has an estate consisting of personal property valued at $500,000. Debtor grants Secured Party a security interest in this property to secure a $100,000 advance made by Secured Party to Debtor. Debtor's estate has not been reduced: after the transaction, it has $100,000 in cash and a $400,000 interest—its "equity," in common parlance—in the personal property. The value of the property available to Debtor's creditors is the same.

However, the reasonably equivalent value issue does arise when the loan proceeds go to a person other than one granting the security interest in its own property. Throughout the discussion of Article 9, it has been assumed in most cases that the "obligor" (9–102(a)(59)), the person who owes the debt, and the "debtor" (9–102(a)(28)), the person who owns the collateral in which the security interest is created, are the same person, as they usually are. When they are different persons, and the loan proceeds go to the obligor rather than to the debtor creating the security interest, there are fraudulent transfer implications that can subject the transaction to avoidance under BC 548.

a. INDIRECT BENEFIT

What if the debtor is the indirect beneficiary of the loan proceeds that went to the obligor, as in the following case?

In re Northern Merchandise, Inc.

United States Court of Appeals, Ninth Circuit, 2004
371 F.3d 1056

■ WARDLAW, CIRCUIT JUDGE.

Frontier Bank ("Frontier") appeals a decision of the Bankruptcy Appellate Panel ("BAP") affirming in part the bankruptcy court's summary judgment in favor of Ronald G. Brown, Chapter 7 Trustee ("Trustee"), in the Trustee's action alleging that Frontier received a fraudulent transfer from Chapter 7 Debtor Northern Merchandise, Inc. ("Debtor"). Specifically, Frontier challenges the BAP's ruling that Debtor did not receive reasonably equivalent value under 11 U.S.C. § 548(a)(1)(B) in exchange for a security interest it granted to Frontier and, thus, Frontier was not protected under 11 U.S.C. § 548(c). We have jurisdiction pursuant to 28 U.S.C. § 1291. Reviewing the bankruptcy court's decision to grant summary judgment de novo. . . we reverse.

I.   Background

In 1997, Debtor, a company that sold general merchandise to grocery stores, was incorporated by Paul Weingartner, Gary David, and Paul Benjamin. In February 1998, Frontier loaned $60,000 to the newly formed company. The loan was evidenced by a promissory note in the amount of $60,000, secured by a commercial financing agreement granting Frontier a security interest in Debtor's inventory, chattel paper, accounts, equipment, and general intangibles. The security interest was later perfected by the filing of a Uniform Commercial Code financing statement on February 24, 1998.

In October 1998, Debtor sought a second loan of $150,000 from Frontier to provide Debtor with working capital. Frontier refused to give such a loan to Debtor after determining that Debtor's financial performance did not support an additional direct loan to the company. However, Frontier agreed to loan $150,000 (the "October Loan") to Paul Weingartner, Paul Benjamin, and Stephen Comer, Debtor's shareholders (collectively, "Shareholders"), whose credit warranted such a loan.[1] Frontier understood that the Shareholders would, in turn, allow Debtor to utilize the money to fund its business operations. In fact, the loan transaction was structured so that Frontier deposited the proceeds of the October Loan directly into Debtor's checking account. However, while the funds themselves were transferred directly from Frontier to Debtor, the transaction was documented as a loan to Shareholders, who then turned the funds over to Debtor. The October Loan was evidenced by a promissory note in favor of Frontier executed by Shareholders. However, on the same day that Shareholders entered into the October Loan with Frontier, Debtor executed a commercial security agreement granting Frontier a security interest in its inventory, chattel paper, accounts, equipment, and general intangibles.

On March 5, 1999, Debtor ceased doing business, leaving approximately $875,000 in unsecured debt. At the time, Debtor had approximately $400,000 worth of inventory. Debtor transferred the $400,000 worth of inventory to Benjamin News Group, a company owned by shareholder Paul Benjamin, for $125,000.[2] On March 19, 1999, Benjamin News Group paid Frontier, not Debtor, the $125,000, which amount was credited to the October Loan. The remaining $25,000 due on the October Loan was paid to Frontier by the Safeway Corporation from the proceeds of prior sales of inventory to the Safeway Corporation.

On March 22, 1999, creditors filed an involuntary Chapter 7 petition against Debtor, and a trustee was appointed. Debtor scheduled assets of

---

[1]   Shareholders were also officers and/or directors of Debtor.

[2]   Trustee filed a fraudulent conveyance action against Benjamin News Group and ultimately recovered $45,000.

$4,116.17 and debts of $875,847.32. On February 9, 2001, Trustee filed a complaint against Frontier, and thereafter a motion for partial summary judgment, arguing that the grant of the security interest and the $125,000 transfer were fraudulent conveyances under 11 U.S.C. § 548(a). The bankruptcy court granted the motion for summary judgment, holding that a fraudulent conveyance had occurred. On appeal before the BAP, Frontier argued, *inter alia*, that the bankruptcy court erred in finding a fraudulent conveyance because (1) Debtor received reasonably equivalent value for the security interest and (2) Frontier was a good faith transferee with respect to receipt of the security interest. The BAP ruled in favor of Trustee on both issues.

II.   Reasonably Equivalent Value

§ 548(a)(1) provides:

> The trustee may avoid any transfer of an interest of the debtor in property, or any obligation incurred by the debtor, that was made or incurred on or within one year before the date of the filing of the petition, if the debtor voluntarily or involuntarily. . . received less than a reasonably equivalent value in exchange for such transfer or obligation.

It is well settled that "reasonably equivalent value can come from one other than the recipient of the payments, a rule which has become known as the indirect benefit rule." *Harman v. First Am. Bank (In re Jeffrey Bigelow Design Group, Inc.)*, 956 F.2d 479, 485 (4th Cir.1992). For example, in *Rubin v. Manufacturers Hanover Trust Co.*, the court explained:

> a debtor may sometimes receive "fair" consideration even though the consideration given for his property or obligation goes initially to a third person. . . although transfers solely for the benefit of third parties do not furnish fair consideration. . . the transaction's benefit to the debtor need not be direct; it may come indirectly through benefit to a third person. . . . If the consideration given to the third person has ultimately landed in the debtor's hands, or if the giving of the consideration to the third person otherwise confers an economic benefit upon the debtor, then the debtor's net worth has been preserved, and [the statute] has been satisfied-provided, of course, that the value of the benefit received by the debtor approximates the value of the property or obligation he has given up.

661 F.2d 979, 991–92 (2d Cir.1981) (internal quotation marks and citations omitted).

Jeffrey Bigelow is such an example. In Jeffrey Bigelow, shareholders of a debtor entered into a line of credit agreement with First American Bank for $1,000,000. 956 F.2d at 481. Although the shareholders were the makers of the line of credit, "only the debtor received the draws and all payments were made directly from the debtor to First American." *Id.*

Subsequently, "the debtor executed a note for $1,000,000 to [the shareholders] with substantially the same terms as the line of credit between First American and [the shareholders]." *Id.* As the debtor directly repaid First American, its liability on the note to the shareholders likewise decreased. *Id.* Holding that the payments made by the debtor on the shareholders' line of credit did not constitute fraudulent conveyances, the Fourth Circuit reasoned:

> [T]he proper focus is on the net effect of the transfers on the debtor's estate, the funds available to the unsecured creditors. As long as the unsecured creditors are no worse off because the debtor, and consequently the estate, has received an amount reasonably equivalent to what it paid, no fraudulent transfer has occurred.

Id. at 484. Because it was "apparent that the transfers [had] not resulted in the depletion of the bankruptcy estate," but rather "served simply as repayment for money received," the Fourth Circuit held that "no fraudulent transfer occurred." *Id.* at 485.

As *Jeffrey Bigelow* illustrates, the primary focus of Section 548 is on the net effect of the transaction on the debtor's estate and the funds available to the unsecured creditors. Trustee contends that Debtor's grant of the security interest to Frontier resulted in a $150,000 loss to Debtor's estate and thus the funds available to the unsecured creditors. Trustee reasons that because the transfer of $150,000 from Shareholders to Debtor was technically a capital contribution, rather than a loan, Debtor was under no legal obligation to grant a security interest to Frontier. Therefore, Trustee argues, Debtor would have been justified to not grant the security interest to Frontier, which would have resulted in an additional $150,000 in Debtor's estate.

We reject this formalistic view. Although Debtor was not a party to the October loan, it clearly received a benefit from that loan. In fact, Frontier deposited the $150,000 proceeds of the October Loan directly into Debtor's checking account. Because Debtor benefited from the October Loan in the amount of $150,000, its grant of a security interest to Frontier to secure Shareholder's indebtedness on that loan, which totaled $150,000, resulted in no net loss to Debtor's estate nor the funds available to the unsecured creditors. To hold otherwise would result in an unintended $150,000 windfall to Debtor's estate. Accordingly, Debtor received reasonably equivalent value in exchange for the security interest it granted to Frontier. . . .

IV. Conclusion

For the foregoing reasons, the BAP erred in holding that Debtor did not receive reasonably equivalent value under § 548(a)(1)(B) in exchange for the security interest it granted to Frontier and that Frontier was not protected under § 548(c).

REVERSED

b. LEVERAGED BUYOUT

A person may want to buy a corporation but lacks the money or collateral necessary to finance the purchase. If the target corporation has unencumbered assets, it may be possible to use those assets to provide most of the capital necessary to make the purchase. Doing so, however, may violate fraudulent transfer law with serious consequences if the acquired firm subsequently files in bankruptcy. Corporate acquisitions in which assets of the acquired firm are encumbered require careful attention to the fraudulent transfer issues raised by the transaction.

PROBLEMS

1.   Shareholder agrees to sell the stock of Target Corporation to Acquirer who is unable to pay for the stock out of its own assets. Acquirer offers Shareholder a security interest in the stock of Target to secure the unpaid amount of the purchase price. Shareholder isn't interested in this because under the absolute priority rule debt must be paid before equity, and creditors of Target would come ahead of Shareholder in any liquidation. Shareholder will sell on credit only if it can have a security interest in Target's assets. Acquirer agrees, and Target grants Shareholder a security interest in Target's assets to secure Acquirer's debt to Shareholder. If the transfer rendered Target insolvent or left it with unreasonably small capital to engage in business and Target filed in bankruptcy within a year, may the trustee of Target avoid the security interest under BC 548?

2.   The same facts, except that instead of Shareholder financing the deal Acquirer borrows the money to buy the stock from Bank and causes Target to grant Bank a security interest in its assets to secure the loan. Bank advances the loan proceeds to Acquirer who pays the money to Shareholder for the stock. Has Acquirer avoided the infirmity present in Problem 1?

3.   The same facts, except that Bank is wise to the problem posed by the transaction in Problem 2, and its loan officers are taught to be sure that the loan proceeds go to the entity that grants Bank the security interest. The transaction is structured so that the loan goes to Target, which grants Bank a security interest in its assets. Target then re-lends the money to Acquirer, an acquisition entity without significant assets, and Acquirer uses the money to pay Shareholder for the stock in Target. Now Bank believes that it is safe; it received a security interest in Target's assets and gave Target hard cash in exchange. What Target does with the loan proceeds is its own business. Surely this meets the requirements of "reasonably equivalent value" under BC 548(a)(1)(B)(i). Does it?

When United States v. Tabor Court Realty Corp., 803 F.2d 1288 (3d Cir.1986) (often referred to by its district court title, *"Gleneagles"*), held that under the facts of Problem 3 Bank was the recipient of a fraudulent transfer, the ancient law of fraudulent transfers became required reading for mergers and acquisitions lawyers throughout the land. The court invalidated Bank's security interest as a fraudulent transfer on the ground that although Bank had given value to Target at the time it received the security interest, the money "merely passed through" Target to Acquirer and ultimately to the shareholders of Target. Acquirer's note to Target was worthless because Acquirer had virtually no assets other than the stock of now insolvent Target; hence, Target's loan to Acquirer was a gratuitous transfer. Bank countered by insisting that there were two separate transactions; first, its loan to Target and, second, Target's loan to Acquirer. Bank gave good value to Target and what Target chose to do with the proceeds of the loan was a decision that should not affect the legitimacy of Bank's security interest. The court rejected this argument; since Bank knew the purpose of the loan, the two transactions were in fact "part of one integrated transaction." This holding made leveraged buy-out transactions more risky and focused the attention of lenders on the solvency of the entities being acquired.

c.   SECURITIZATION

Chapter 3 discussed asset securitization with respect to sale of rights to payment. The following Problem addresses the fraudulent transfer risk that may be present in these transactions.

PROBLEM

At the urging of its shareholders, Originator Corporation decided to securitize some of its intangible assets. Accordingly, it created a separately incorporated special purpose vehicle (SPV) whose only assets are those to be transferred to it by Originator. Originator subsequently transfers to the SPV its existing account receivables in exchange for an agreed price. The SPV undertakes to bear all the risks of payment by the account debtors of the accounts transferred as well as the responsibility for collecting payments from them. The SPV pays Originator for the transferred accounts with funds received from the issuance and sale of securities in it to investors. At the same time, the SPV files a proper financing statement covering Originator's account receivables, listing Originator as "debtor" and itself as "creditor." Originator pays out to its shareholders as a dividend the sum received from the SPV. If Originator files a bankruptcy petition within two years of the transaction, may Originator's trustee avoid the SPV's interest in the account receivables? May the trustee recover amounts from Originator's shareholders?

CHAPTER 10

LETTERS OF CREDIT

A. INTRODUCTION

Letters of credit are important and versatile financial instruments. They frequently are involved in a wide range of different transactions and play different roles in them. Letters of credit customarily are used to pay for goods or services in cross-border and sometimes in domestic transactions. But they also increasingly are used as a credit enhancement to secure the performance of leases, insurance, construction projects or financial obligations. Simply put, a letter of credit is an undertaking by one person to pay a specified person a stated amount of money or other value if that person presents documents that comply with the conditions specified by the undertaking. See 5–102(a)(10). In its most basic form the instrument involves three parties: the issuer, the applicant (or "customer") and the beneficiary. The issuer is the party making the undertaking, often but not always a bank. The applicant is the party requesting the issuer, for a fee, to make the undertaking, and the beneficiary is the party entitled to payment if it satisfies the documentary conditions stated in the undertaking.

To understand the letter of credit's function, consider its role in a contract for the sale of goods. Sales contracts very often are made an open account basis. In these contracts the seller relies on the buyer to meet its payment obligation. Four sorts of risks affect whether the seller receives the purchase price from the buyer. One is commercial risk: the prospect that the buyer will refuse or be unable to pay the price. Even if the contract requires payment against the seller's presentation of negotiable documents covering the goods, the seller is left with the documents if the buyer does not or cannot pay against them. Negotiating them another buyer does not guarantee the seller the purchase price in the breached contract. Political risk is a second risk. Political instability might prevent the buyer from paying the purchase price or the seller from receiving payment. A third risk is legal: capital controls or other regulatory restrictions might prevent the buyer from paying for the goods. Litigation is a fourth risk. This is the prospect that the seller will have to sue the buyer to recover the purchase price.

When a letter of credit is used to pay the purchase price, the issuer undertakes to pay the seller on the seller's presentation of specified documents. The credit represents the issuer's own undertaking to the seller. It therefore gives the seller a (usually) reliably solvent source of payment of the purchase price. This shifts the four payment risks identified from the seller to the issuer. Because the credit entitles the seller to payment from the issuer if it presents specified documents, the seller looks to the issuer to be paid, not the buyer. It therefore no longer bears the risk that the buyer will refuse or be unable to pay. For the same reason, the seller also does not bear political or legal risk. Intervening events or legal restrictions that might prevent the buyer from paying the purchase price do not by themselves prevent the issuer from paying the seller. Finally, the issuer's undertaking relieves the seller of the burden of having to litigate to recover the purchase price from the buyer. The seller gets the purchase price by drawing on the credit. The buyer instead must sue the seller to recover damages for the seller's breach of the underlying sales contract. Although the buyer ultimately risks receiving goods that do not conform to the contract, the documents called for by the letter of credit can provide reliable evidence of the seller's performance of the contract, including the condition of the goods delivered.

The letter of credit also shifts the four risks identified when it secures performance of a contract. This is the case where the credit obligates the issuer to pay the beneficiary upon the party's documentary certification that the issuer's applicant has defaulted on its obligation to the beneficiary. Because the beneficiary is entitled to payment from the issuer in these circumstances, the credit secures the applicant's performance of its obligation. The issuer, not the beneficiary, therefore bears the commercial or financial risk of its applicant's default. Political and legal risks that affect the applicant's performance of its obligation by themselves have no effect on the issuer's obligation or ability to pay the beneficiary. Litigation risk also is not borne by the beneficiary, because it obtains payment on documentary certification of default. The beneficiary therefore does not have to sue the applicant on the applicant's default on its obligation.

B. THE LETTER OF CREDIT RELATIONSHIP AND TYPES OF CREDITS

When a letter of credit is issued, three separate relationships are present. One is the agreement between the beneficiary and the applicant that calls for the establishment of the credit or gives rise to it. This is the underlying transaction. A sale of goods contract or loan agreement are examples. A second relationship is the agreement between the issuer and applicant which states the terms of the credit and provides for the issuer's reimbursement by the applicant. This is the reimbursement agreement. The third is the relationship between the issuer and the beneficiary in which the issuer makes the credit undertaking to the beneficiary. Some courts and scholars refer to this relationship as the letter of credit "contract." Strictly, the letter of credit relationship is not a contract at all. There is no bargained-for exchange between the beneficiary and the issuer, and the beneficiary owes no obligation to the issuer, as a contract requires. Instead, the issuer's undertaking to the beneficiary gives the beneficiary certain rights against the issuer.

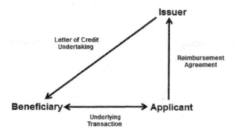

Frequently two other parties are involved in a letter of credit. One is an advisor. 5–102(a). Beneficiaries often want assurance that the credit is authentic and its terms are accurately communicated. To provide assurance, the issuer engages a person familiar to the beneficiary, usually a local bank, which verifies the credit through a secure communication system. The advising bank in turn notifies the beneficiary of the credit and its terms. The obligations of the advising bank are modest. It must satisfy itself that the credit is authentic and that the advice accurately reflects the credit's terms. See 5–107(c). The advisor's responsibilities are limited to those of communication. Importantly, by advising the beneficiary the advisor does not obligate itself under the credit. Thus, it is not obligated to honor documentary presentations that comply with the terms of the credit. The other party sometimes involved in the letter of credit is a confirmer, usually a bank. The confirming bank, at the issuer's request, adds its own undertaking to the beneficiary to that of the issuer. 5–102(a)(4). By adding its confirmation the confirmer undertakes to honor documentary presentations that comply with the terms of the main credit. See 5–107(a). The confirmer may also advise as to the existence and terms of the credit. In doing so it takes on two different obligations: to confirm and to advise. A confirmed letter of credit gives the beneficiary two sources of payment: the issuer and the confirmer. Beneficiaries worried about the issuer's own solvency or political and legal risks affecting the issuer may insist that the letter of credit be confirmed. In 2014 about 10% of international letters of credit were confirmed; see ICC 2105 Global Survey of Trade Finance 62 (Fig. 59) (2015).

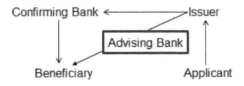

There are two types of letters of credit: commercial (or "documentary") credits and standby credits. They are distinguished by their financial purposes and the sorts of documentary conditions specified by them. Commercial credits are issued to pay for goods or services obtained by the applicant. For instance, the sales contract might require the buyer-applicant to establish a credit naming the seller as the beneficiary. The terms of credit established in turn will require the issuer to pay a stated sum equal to the contract price to the beneficiary if the beneficiary presents documents described in the credit. The described documents can be of any sort. Usually the commercial credit requires some documents that evidence the beneficiary's performance of the underlying sales or services contract. In the case of a sale of goods, the documents typically include a draft drawn by the seller on the buyer, a commercial invoice, a negotiable bill of lading or other document of title, a certificate or origin and an inspection certificate. Where the underlying contract involves a sale of assets other than goods, such as real estate or securities, different documentation will be required. The issuer pays the seller-beneficiary the contract price if it presents document that comply with the terms of the credit.

A standby letter of credit serves as security for the applicant's performance of the underlying contract or transaction with the beneficiary. It is not a mechanism for payment of the contract price. Typically a standby credit provides that the issuer will pay the beneficiary if the beneficiary presents specified documentary evidence of default by the applicant or other party in the underlying contract or transaction. Thus, presentation of these documents allows the beneficiary to obtain payment from the issuer. In this way the issuer's obligation to the beneficiary guarantees the applicant's or another's obligation under the underlying contract or transaction. The standby credit thereby shifts the risk of the applicant's default from the beneficiary to the issuer. Standby credits in turn are of two sorts: "payment" (or "financial") and "performance" standbys. A "payment" standby credit calls for payment on presentation of documentary certification of default on a financial obligation. A "performance" standby credit calls for payment on presentation of documentary certification of default on a non-financial obligation. Sometimes a credit is issued that requires no documents certifying default to be presented or requires merely a certificated demand for payment. These are "clean" credits.

Standby credits serve a guarantee function in a wide range of different underlying transactions. Issuers of commercial paper can market the paper at a higher price by backing it up with a standby letter of credit. Purchasers of limited partnerships on credit can guarantee their partnership interests by having a standby credit issued that undertakes to pay the beneficiaries-sellers on documentary certification of the purchasers' default on their payment obligations. In securitization transactions a standby credit serves to guarantee the payment of interest and principal on debt securities issued by the securitization vehicle. This enhances the credit rating of these securities. A standby credit can play a guarantee role in a sale of goods contract too. There, the credit might allow the seller-beneficiary to draw on its certification that the buyer has failed to pay the invoice price of the goods. A standby credit can be used even when the buyer prepays for the goods. The credit here might entitle the buyer-beneficiary to draw on the credit on documentary presentation of the seller-applicant's breach of the underlying sales contract, such as a breach of warranty. The wide range of uses for standby credits and comparatively low fees charged to issue them make the standby credit an attractive financial instrument. Standby credits dwarf commercial credits in their financial importance in the U.S. In 2021 U.S. FDIC-insured depository banks issued approximately $550.5 billion in standby credits. During the same period they issued about $18.3 billion in commercial credits. FDIC BankFind Suite: Letter of Credit Peer Group Comparison Report, https://banks.data.fdic.gov/bankfind-suite. A form standby letter of credit and reimbursement agreement appear at the end of this Chapter.

C. LEGAL CHARACTER AND SOURCES OF LAW

Letters of credit have a unique or at least peculiar legal character. They are subject to special legal rules, not to the ordinary rules that apply to contracts. For instance, unlike a contract, the issuer's undertaking to the beneficiary is enforceable without consideration. 5–105. Other rules of general contract law also do not apply to the letter of credit. For example, the issuer's obligation to the beneficiary is not created by the beneficiary's acceptance of an offer by the issuer. Rules about third party beneficiaries do not apply to the letter of credit beneficiary, because the issuer cannot raise defenses the applicant might have against the beneficiary to resist paying it. In addition, the letter of credit is not subject to legal rules applicable to special sorts of contracts. For instance, because a credit does not satisfy the requirement of negotiability for such instruments under the UCC, it is not a negotiable instrument. See 3–104. Letters of credit therefore are not governed by negotiable instruments law. The legal principles applicable to guarantees also are inapplicable to letters of credit. A guarantor's liability on its guarantee is secondary. It is liable on the guarantee only if the principal obligor has defaulted. See Restatement (Third) of Suretyship and Guaranty § 34 (1996). The guarantor also may rely on the defenses to payment available to the principal obligor.

By contrast, the issuer's liability under the credit is "primary." Its payment obligation is conditioned only on the documentary terms described in the credit. Those terms alone govern the issuer's obligation. Facts extrinsic to the documents, including default, therefore can have no effect on the issuer's obligation to the beneficiary. For same reason, the issuer cannot rely on defenses available to the applicant against the beneficiary to resist honoring its undertaking to the beneficiary. A letter of credit therefore is not a guarantee because the issuer's payment obligation is not conditional on the applicant's default; the issuer's liability is not secondary. In short, the legal rules central to letter of credit law cannot be assimilated to rules that operate in other areas of law.

Most letter of credit law consists of domestic law and institutional rules, and much of the law is uniform across jurisdictions. It has five potential sources: (1) In the United States Article 5 of the UCC and common law; (2) the Uniform Customs and Practice for Documentary Credits (International Chamber of Commerce, Publication 600) ("UCP 600" or "UCP"); (3) the International Standby Practices (International Chamber of Commerce, Publication 590) ("ISP 98"); (4) the Uniform Rules for Demand Guarantees (International Chamber of Commerce, Publication 758) ("URDG"); and (5) the United Nations Convention on Independent Guarantees and Standby Letters of Credit ("U.N. Convention"). Although eight countries have ratified the U.N. Convention, neither the United States nor other countries with large financial sectors have done so. Thus, domestic law such as Article 5 of the UCC and the International Chamber of Commerce's rules remain the most important sources of letter of credit law.

Article 5 of the UCC governs both commercial and standby letters of credit. The UCP 600 and ISP 98 are the institutional rules most frequently incorporated into credits. By its terms, the UCP 600 applies only to credits issued by banks, although non-bank issuers can make its rules applicable by incorporating the UCP into the credits they issue. Because the International Chamber of Commerce has no legislative authority and therefore does not produce law, its rules apply only if the credit make them applicable. International credits usually incorporate the UCP, as do many domestic credits. To govern the credit, the UCP 600, ISP 98 and the URDG all require that the incorporation be express. UCP 600 art. 1; ISP 98 Rule 1.01(b); URDG art. 1. The ISP 98 and the URDG are made applicable only to standby credits; the UCP 600 is incorporated into both commercial and standby credits. Standby credits increasingly incorporate the ISP 98 rather than to the UCP 600. Several courts have held that the UCP can govern the credit as a matter of trade usage, even when the credit does not expressly provide for the UCP's application.

In most cases the UCP 600, ISP 98 and URDG 758's rules are consistent with UCC Article 5's provisions. They usually either say the same thing or address a matter that Article 5 does not address. However, there are a few instances in which Article 5 and the International Chamber of Commerce's rules conflict. UCC 5–116(c) is clear about which rule controls in these cases. The subsection provides that if the credit is subject to the UCP or other "rules of custom or practice," the UCP or other rules of custom or practice displace UCC Article 5 if the conflicting rule is not a mandatory rule under Article 5. If the conflicting rule is mandatory, Article 5's rule continues to apply.

Very few of Article 5's rules are mandatory; almost all can be varied by the terms of the credit. Section 5–103(c) lists the following mandatory rules: the definition of a letter of credit, formal requirements, restrictions on the stipulation of an expiration date, the independence principle, limits on the issuer's ability to withhold its consent to the assignment of letter of credit proceeds, rights of subrogation, and obligations of good faith. See UCC 5–102(a)(9), (10), 5–106(d), 5–103(d), 5–114(d), 5–117(d), 1–302(b). In every other matter the issuer and applicant are free to set the terms of the credit. In fact, even Article 5's mandatory rules in effect are default rules too. This is because 5–116(a) allows the parties to select the law of the jurisdiction that governs the liability of the issuer, nominated person or adviser. Section 5–116(a) adds that the law selected "need not bear any relation to the transaction." Thus, parties can select applicable law that does not contain Article 5's mandatory rules. Put another way, Article 5's mandatory rules therefore apply only if affected parties fail to select the law of a jurisdiction that does not contain the same rules. See Comment 2 to 5–103 (second paragraph). This makes these rules in effect only default rules.

There are instances in which domestic law must supplement the International Chamber of Commerce's sets of rules. These occur when the rules incorporated into a credit are silent about a particular matter bearing on the credit. For example, the UCP 600 says nothing about when the letter of credit becomes effective. It also has nothing to say about implied warranties the beneficiary or other presenter of documents makes to issuer, the remedies for wrongful dishonor of a documentary presentation, the issuer or applicant's rights of subrogation, or the effect of fraud on the issuer's obligations to the beneficiary. And the UCP 600 is silent about the circumstances in which an applicant can enjoin an issuer from honoring a documentary presentation or the beneficiary from making one. Article 5 has provisions that address these matters. See 5–106(a), 5–110, 5–111, 5–117, 5–109.

D. FORMAL REQUIREMENTS

1. FORM

To be a letter of credit, a financial instrument must take a certain form. Section 5–104 requires that the letter of credit be a signed record. However, to be a letter of credit in the first place, the record must contain a particular sort of undertaking. Since the essential feature of a letter of credit is that the credit is independent of the underlying contract, the instrument must reflect this fact. Form must reflect function. Thus, an instrument is a letter of credit only if it conditions the issuer's obligation on satisfaction of documentary conditions. Section 5–102(a)(10) defines a letter of credit as a "definite undertaking. . . to honor a documentary presentation by payment. . . ." This definition describes a mandatory rule ((5–103(c)), and an agreement to treat an instrument that is not a letter of credit under 5–102(a)(10) therefore is ineffective. In Notes to the following case inquire about the conditions in a written undertaking that, if present, undermine the writing's character as a letter of credit.

Wichita Eagle and Beacon Publishing Co., Inc. v. Pacific National Bank of San Francisco

United States Court of Appeal, Ninth Circuit, 1974
493 F.2d 1285

■ Before CHAMBERS and BROWNING, CIRCUIT JUDGES, and KING, DISTRICT JUDGE.

■ PER CURIAM.

The facts are summarized in the district court's opinion, 343 F.Supp. 332 (N.D.Cal.1971). . . .

[Ed.—Lessors leased a site on which Lessee (Circular Ramp Garages), under the terms of the lease, undertook to build a parking garage. In order to assure Lessors that Lessee would perform, Lessee obtained from Bank (Pacific National Bank) a writing addressed to Lessors in which Bank established its "Letter of Credit No. 17084" in favor of Lessors for payment of $250,000 "available by drafts drawn at sight on the Pacific National Bank providing that all of the following conditions are met at the time said draft is received by the undersigned." The conditions were (1) that Lessee has failed to perform the terms of the lease; (2) that Lessors have given Bank an affidavit stating that it has given notice to Lessee and its contractor specifying how Lessee has failed to perform its lease; and (3) that either Lessee or its contractor has failed to cure defaults under the lease during a period of thirty days after receiving Lessor's notice. Lessee failed to obtain the financing necessary to build the parking garage and defaulted on the lease. Lessors' assignee (Plaintiff) presented to Bank a draft for $250,000 drawn upon Letter of Credit No. 17084, together with the required documents. When Bank refused payment, Plaintiff brought suit against Bank. The district court concluded that "Although the question is not free from doubt, the Instrument denominated 'Letter of Credit No. 17084' should be treated as a letter of credit and be subject to the law respecting letters of credit to the extent applicable and appropriate." Id. at 339.]

We do not agree with the district court that the instrument sued upon is a letter of credit, though it is so labeled. Rather, the instrument is an ordinary guaranty contract, obliging the defendant bank to pay whatever the lessee Circular Ramp Garages, Inc., owed on the underlying lease, up to the face amount of the guaranty. Since the underlying lease clearly contemplated the payment of $250,000 in case of default, and since this provision appears to be a valid liquidated damages clause, the judgment below must be modified to award the plaintiff $250,000 plus interest.

We do not base our holding that the instrument is not a letter of credit on the fact that payment was triggered by default rather than performance or on the fact that the instrument was written in a lease context, for we recognize that the commercial use of letters of credit has expanded far beyond the international sales context in which it originally developed. . . .

The instrument involved here strays too far from the basic purpose of letters of credit, namely, providing a means of assuring payment cheaply by eliminating the need for the issuer to police the underlying contract. . . . The instrument neither evidences an intent that payment be made merely on presentation on a draft nor specifies the documents required for termination or payment. To the contrary, it requires the actual existence in fact of most of the conditions specified:. . .for payment, that the lessee have failed to perform the terms of the lease and have failed to correct that default, in addition to an affidavit of notice.

True, in the text of the instrument itself the instruments is referred to as a "letter of credit," and we should, as the district court notes, "giv[e] effect wherever possible to the intent of the contracting parties." 343 F.Supp. at 338. But the relevant intent is manifested by the terms of the agreement, not by its label. . . . And where, as here, the substantive provisions require the issuer to deal not simply in documents alone, but in facts relating to the performance of a separate contract (the lease, in this case), all distinction between a letter of credit and an ordinary guaranty contract would be obliterated by regarding the instrument as a letter of credit.

It would hamper rather than advance the extension of the letter of credit concept to new situations if an instrument such as this were held to be a letter of credit. The loose terms of this instrument invited the very evil that letters of credit are meant to avoid—protracted, expensive litigation. If the letter of credit concept is to have value in new situations, the instrument must be tightly drawn to strictly and clearly limit the responsibility of the issuer.

NOTES

1. The conceptual issue presented in *Wichita Eagle* concerns the character of the instrument issued by the Bank: is it a guarantee or a standby letter of credit? The issue is important as a matter of bank regulation. Banks in the United States generally are not permitted to issue guarantees. They are permitted, however, to issue letters of credit, subject to regulation. As noted above, in function guarantees and standby letters of credit are indistinguishable, both involving the enhancement of an obligor's promise by adding the promise of a creditworthy third party. In fact, European banking terminology sometimes refers to standby credit as "bank guarantees." Conceptually they are distinguishable by the nature of the issuer's obligation and the conditions under which its obligation attaches. As to the issuer's obligation, it is primary: the issuer cannot invoke defenses against the beneficiary available to the applicant to resist honoring the credit. A guarantor's obligation is secondary: it can invoke defenses available to the obligor to resist payment to the obligee. Because banks generally can

only issue letters of credit, the conceptual distinction between credits and guarantees is crucial.

The Office of the Comptroller of the Currency regulates the issuance of letters of credit by focusing on documentary conditions. By the Comptroller's interpretive ruling, national banks may issue letters of credit, including standby letters of credit, only if the obligation to honor "depends upon the presentation of specified documents and not upon nondocumentary conditions or resolution of questions of fact or law at issue between the applicant and the beneficiary." 12 C.F.R. 7.1016(a) (1998). State chartered banks usually are subject to a similar sort of regulation.

2.   An important question is the effect of a bank issuing a guarantee in violation of bank regulations. Issuing banks or applicants sometimes adopt the odd litigation posture of urging the illegal issuance of a guarantee as a defense to enforcement of the guarantee. This is the "ultra vires" defense to honor. See Republic Nat'l Bank v. Northwest Nat'l Bank, 578 S.W.2d 109 (Tex.1978); *Wichita Eagle.* Although a few courts have accepted the ultra vires defense, the majority of case law has rejected it. See, e.g., Federal Dep. Ins. Corp. v. Freudenfeld, 492 F.Supp. 763 (E.D. Wis.1980); First Am. Nat'l Bank v. Alcorn, Inc., 361 So.2d 481 (Miss.1978); 1 John F. Dolan, The Law of Letters of Credit ¶ 12.03[2] (4th ed. 2007). In *Wichita Eagle,* for instance, the court enforced the instrument as a guarantee. The rejection of the ultra vires defense makes a good deal of sense. The issuer or applicant almost always is in a better position than the beneficiary to avoid violating applicable bank regulations or detecting their violation. Bank regulating agencies also are better positioned than beneficiaries to monitor issuers and applicants. Accordingly, not allowing the defense to enforcement increases the cost to issuers of violating the regulation against the issuance of guarantees. It serves as a partial substitute for closer monitoring of a bank's investment activities by bank regulating agencies.

3.   *Wichita Eagle* was decided under the version of Article 5 in effect before its revision in 1995. How would this case be decided under the current version of Article 5? See 5–102(a)(10) ("letter of credit") and Comment 6 to 5–102. How could the document in *Wichita Eagle* be rewritten to remove all doubt about its status as a letter of credit? Does 5–108(g) allow the court in this case to find that the writing is a valid letter of credit by disregarding the two nondocumentary conditions? Comment 9 to 5–108. If the undertaking is a letter of credit, the disregard of nondocumentary conditions does not mean that the issuer can ignore them. As a matter of the reimbursement agreement between the applicant and the issuer, their honor might be required. Section 5–108(g)'s injunction only means that the issuer's obligations to the beneficiary under the letter of credit do not depend on the satisfaction of nondocumentary conditions. See Comment 9 to 5–108.

4.   Section 5–104 recognizes that the day of an exclusively paper-based system of letter of credit transactions has long since passed. Comment 3 notes: "Many banking transactions, including the issuance of many letters of credit, are now conducted mostly by electronic means. . . . By declining to specify any particular medium in which the letter of credit must be established or communicated, Section 5–104 leaves room for future developments." See the definitions of "document" (5–102(a)(6)) and "record" (5–102(a)(14)).

5. The documents to be presented to the issuer of the letter of credit to obtain payment usually include a draft drawn by the beneficiary (5–102(a)(3)) on the issuing bank (5–102(a)(9)) payable "at sight" (that is on presentment) to the order of the beneficiary. A sight draft is merely a demand for payment that may be negotiable in form, thus conferring upon the beneficiary the power to transfer the draft to a third person who may take the rights of a holder in due course. Comment 11 to 5–102. Some letters of credit either do not require presentation of a draft or do not call for a draft in negotiable form.

PROBLEMS

1. Paysaver Credit Union executed the following writing at the request of Wells and Titan Tool, which owed Transparent Products $33,000 on open account:

Transparent Products Corporation

Bensenville, IL 60101

RE: Thomas Wells

Gentlemen:

We hereby establish our letter of credit at the request of Thomas Wells of 1315 South 3rd Avenue, Maywood up to the aggregate amount of fifty-thousand dollars ($50,000).

Titan wanted to buy more plastics from Transparent and obtained Paysaver's issuance of the writing directed to Transparent to bolster Titan's creditworthiness. Wells is an employee of Titan who was not indebted to Transparent. It was Wells' $50,000 certificate of deposit with Paysaver that apparently persuaded Paysaver to issue this writing. Transparent ultimately declined to extend more credit to Titan, and when the latter filed in bankruptcy, Transparent demanded payment under Paysaver's "letter of credit" to defray the remaining $33,000 debt. Is the quoted writing sufficiently "definite" to be a letter of credit under 5–102(a)(10)? See Comment 6 to Rev. 5–102. If it is not, is the instrument effective as a guaranty? A guarantor undertakes to pay the debt of another and can raise the principal debtor's defenses; the issuer of a letter of credit is primarily liable and cannot set up defenses of the applicant. The facts are based on Transparent Products Corp. v. Paysaver Credit Union, 864 F.2d 60 (7th Cir.1988). Comment 1 to 5–104 states: ". . . . a letter of credit will typically specify the amount available, the expiration date, the place where presentation should be made, and the documents that must be presented to entitle a person to honor."

2. (a) What would be the result in Problem 1 if the body of the writing had said: "We hereby establish our letter of credit at the request of Thomas Wells of 1315 South 3rd Avenue, Maywood up to the aggregate amount of fifty-thousand dollars ($50,000) on which Transparent Products Corporation may draw at any time within the next year by presentation of a draft payable at sight for any amount up to the credit limit"? See 5–102(a)(6) ("document"), (10) ("letter of credit") and (12) ("presentation").

(b)   What would be the result in Problem 1 if the body of the writing had said: "This is a guarantee, not a letter of credit. At the request of Thomas Wells of 1315 South 3rd Avenue, Maywood, we hereby undertake to pay Transparent Products Corporation up to the aggregate amount of fifty-thousand dollars ($50,000) at any time within the next year upon the following three conditions: (1) Transparent presents a written demand for payment; (2) Transparent not make the presentation before 1 p.m. eastern standard time; and (3) Transparent recites to our representative that the writing represented is a written demand for payment"?

2.   DURATION

Under 5–106(a), a letter of credit is enforceable when issued. The credit, in turn, is issued when the issuer sends or transmits the credit to the beneficiary. Because a credit is "sent" when it is mailed or delivered for transmission by the usual means (1–201(36)(A)), the credit becomes enforceable upon dispatch. Article 5 does not explicitly provide when a confirmed credit becomes enforceable. However, Comment 1 to 5–107 instructs us to treat the terms "confirmation" and "letter of credit" interchangeably throughout Article 5. Thus, the same rules concerning issuance and dispatch apply to confirmed letters of credit. Under 5–106(a), UCP 600 art. 7b, and ISP 98 Rule 1.06(a), a letter of credit is irrevocable unless it states otherwise. Irrevocability means that the issuer cannot cancel or amend the credit without the beneficiary's consent. 5–106(b). This default rule makes sense for the vast majority of beneficiaries, who might want to rely on the credit in advance of drawing on it. Section 5–106(c) provides that if there is no stated expiration date in a credit, it expires one year after issuance, and 5–106(d) provides that if the credit purports to be perpetual, it expires five years after issuance. The latter is a mandatory rule.

PROBLEM

The credit issued by Bank to Company in 2008 stated:

This credit shall expire one year from date provided that it shall be deemed automatically renewed without amendment for additional one year period from the present or any future expiration date hereof, unless at least 30 days prior to any such date(s), Company shall have sent Bank notice that Company elects not to require this credit renewed for any such additional period.

Company drew on the credit in 2014. Bank dishonored on the ground that the effect of the duration clause was to make the duration period "perpetual," even though that term was not used; hence, the duration was limited to five years under 5–106(d): "A letter of credit that states that it is perpetual expires five years after its stated date of issuance, or if none is stated, after the date on which it is issued." Credits renewable at the option of the issuer bank are common and are not considered perpetual. See Comment 4 to 5–106. Should this be true in cases like this in which the option to renew is that of the beneficiary? See Golden West Refining Co. v. Suntrust Bank, 538 F.3d 1233 (9th Cir.2008); accord Michigan Commerce Bank v. TDY Industries, Inc., 76 UCC Rep. Serv.2d 279 (W.D. Mich.2011).

NOTE

Letters of credit sometimes contain an "evergreen clause": a provision automatically extending the credit past its expiration date unless the issuer or beneficiary gives notice that is not to be extended. The evergreen clause in the credit in *Golden West* gave Company alone the right to elect not to have the credit renewed. Unless Company elected not to require Bank to renew the credit, the credit would be renewed annually, in perpetuity. The issue in the case was whether the credit was in form (not function) a perpetual letter of credit. This is a simple case: the credit by its terms was not perpetual, as 5–106(d) requires, and thus did not expire five years after its stated date of issue pursuant to 5–106(d). The plain language of the statute requires that the credit state that it is perpetual to qualify as a perpetual credit. The court held for Company.

Should the court have drawn a negative inference from the last sentence of Comment 4? No, for three reasons. First, Comment 4's last sentence makes a limited exception to (d)'s formal requirement to the effect that credits stated to be perpetual are perpetual. The Comment deems a credit non-perpetual (even if stated to be perpetual) if it gives the issuer a right to revoke the credit. As the court notes, the Comment doesn't address the converse situation: when a credit, stated to be non-perpetual, is *perpetual*. Second, and more important, the language of (d) doesn't support the relevant sentence in the Comment. The relevant sentence of the Comment and the language of 5–106(d) instead are in conflict. Although courts frequently treat Comments as part of the UCC text, text controls Comments. Third, (d) recites a sensible rule. It adopts a formal test for "perpetuality;" Comment 4 states a functional test. From an operational perspective, (d)'s formal test has a lot going for it. The test allows parties to the credit to determine easily whether the credit is perpetual or not. By contrast, a functional test makes things harder for them. For instance, qualifying language bearing on revocation of the credit might be complex enough to make it hard to determine whether the credit is perpetual or not. Formal requirements make letters of credit cheaper to administer and therefore more attractive to potential users.

E. ISSUER'S DUTY TO HONOR OR DISHONOR

1. THE STRICT COMPLIANCE STANDARD

A letter of credit is a highly efficient instrument in which banks or others issue suitably definite undertakings to honor complying documentary presentations and the beneficiaries present the prescribed documents and are paid. Indirect evidence of the credit's efficiency is the comparatively low fees issuers charge compared to fees charged for other comparable financial instruments. Central to the credit's cost advantage is the issuer's duty to honor complying documentary presentations. Under 5–108(a), the standard of documentary compliance is strict: ". . . [A]n issuer shall honor a presentation that, as determined by the standard practice referred to in subsection (e), appears on its face strictly to comply with the terms and conditions of the letter of credit." The domestic law of most legal systems apparently also adopts the strict compliance standard. See Boris Kozolchyk, Commercial Letters of Credit in the Americas 72, 259 (1966). Neither the UCP nor ISP 98 expressly adopts a standard of documentary compliance. UCP 600 art. 14a states merely that "the issuing bank must examine a presentation to determine, on the basis of the documents alone, whether or not the documents appear on their face to constitute a complying presentation." See ISP 98 Rule 4.01. Accordingly, in credits governed by the UCP or ISP 98 that otherwise do not address the standard of compliance, domestic law standards continue to apply. The strict compliance standard, therefore, likely will control under applicable law in these cases.

The importance of a documentary discrepancy is irrelevant under the standard. As a Law Lord put it in Equitable Trust Co. of New York v. Dawson Partners Ltd., (1927) 27 L.L.Rep. 49, 52, a leading letter of credit case, "[t]here is no room for documents which are almost the same, or which will do just as well." Of course, facts about the underlying transaction also are irrelevant to the issuer's duty to the beneficiary. If the documents presented correspond to the terms of the credit, the issuer must pay. Otherwise, not. As discussed below, an issuer who honors a noncomplying documentary presentation risks not being reimbursed by the applicant.

The strict compliance standard resists an informative and precise statement. Strict compliance does not require literal, letter-for-letter correspondence between the contents of prescribed documents and the credit's terms. Comment 1 to 5–108 states that the standard does not mean "slavish conformity to the terms of the credit." On the other hand, both the strict compliance standard and Comment 1 reject a substantial compliance standard, which judges compliance by an undefined measure of the degree to which documents comply with the credit's terms. Thus, the standard seems to treat documents as complying if they less than literally, but more than substantially, comply with the credit's terms. Courts and commentators have had trouble identifying the permissible range of less-than-perfect compliance. Even courts that do not insist on absolute compliance sometimes disagree on what is strict but less than literal compliance. A rough working notion of compliance under 5–108(a) finds that documents strictly comply when the issuer, using standard practices of issuers, determines that they correspond on their face with the credit's terms. Put another way, the notion is that the documents comply if a reasonable issuer, examining only the documents and the credit and charged with knowledge of the practices of issuers, would decide that a documentary discrepancy is not substantial. For a brief history of applications of the standard, see Peter Ellinger, The Doctrine of Strict Compliance: Its Development and Current Construction, in Lex Mercatoria: Essays on International Commercial Law in Honour of Francis Reynolds 187–198 (Francis D. Rose ed. 2000). The strict compliance standard and related issues are extensively discussed in 2 Barkley Clark & Barbara Clark, The Law of Bank Deposits, Collections and Credit Cards 14.05 (Rev. ed. 2009); 1 John F. Dolan, The Law of Letters of Credit, Ch. 6 (4th ed. 2007); and 3 White & Summers, Uniform Commercial Code § 26–5a.

Perhaps the most litigated issue in the letter of credit law is the duty of the issuer to both the beneficiary and applicant to honor or dishonor a presentation. At issue in most of the litigation is the application of the strict compliance standard in the face of documentary discrepancies. Strict compliance tests documentary presentations by the standard practice of financial institutions that regularly issue credits. Using slightly different terms, 5–108(a) and (e), UCP 600 art. 14d and ISP 98 Rule 4.01(b) refer to such practice. Did the court in the following case rely on evidence of the standard practice of financial institutions to determine the appropriate compliance standard?

Carter Petroleum Products, Inc. v. Brotherhood Bank & Trust Co.

Court of Appeals of Kansas, 2004
97 P.3d 505

■ GREEN, P.J.

This action involves a bank's wrongful refusal to honor a letter of credit. Carter Petroleum Products, Inc. (Carter) sued Brotherhood Bank & Trust Company (Bank) for its failure to honor a letter of credit. The Bank appeals from a judgment of the trial court granting summary judgment in favor of Carter on the letter of credit. On appeal, the Bank contends that the untimely presentment of the letter of credit and the noncompliance of the submitted documents with the letter of credit relieved the Bank of its duty to honor the letter of credit. We disagree and affirm.

Carter is in the petroleum business and sells fuel products to Highway 210, LLC (Highway 210), which operates a gas station. Highway 210 is also a customer of the Bank. On October 19, 2001, the Bank issued a letter of credit, No. 2001–270, in the aggregate amount of $175,000, for the benefit of Carter on the account of Highway 210.

By its terms, the letter of credit authorized Carter to draw on the Bank on the account of Highway 210, to the aggregate amount of $175,000 available by Carter's draft at sight accompanied by the following document: "STATEMENT SIGNED BY CARTER PETROLEUM PRODUCTS STATING THAT HIGHWAY 210, LLC HAS

FAILED TO PAY OUTSTANDING INVOICES IN ACCORDANCE WITH TERMS OF PAYMENT."

The letter of credit further provided that "[e]ach draft must state that it is 'Drawn under Brotherhood Bank & Trust Company's Letter of Credit #2001–270 dated July 26, 2001.' This credit must accompany the draft(s)." The date of "July 26, 2001" in the aforementioned quotation was a typographical error because the letter of credit at issue was dated October 19, 2001. This letter of credit was a renewal of one of a series of previous letters of credit which were referenced in the lower margin of the letter of credit. The October letter of credit replaced the letter of credit dated July 26, 2001, in the amount of $125,000.

Additionally, the letter of credit stated "that all draft(s) drawn under and in compliance with the terms of this credit will be duly honored on delivery of documents as specified if presented at this office in Shawnee, KS no later than June 26, 2002." The letter of credit was also subject to the Uniform Customs and Practice for Documentary Credits, International Chamber of Commerce Publication No. 500 (1993 Revision) (UCP).

Hal O'Donnell, Carter's credit manager, delivered a draft request to the Bank for payment on June 26, 2002. Carter's draft request contained the following statement:

> "Pursuant to the terms stated in the Letter of Credit #2001–270 dated October 19, 2001 (copy attached), Carter Petroleum Products, Inc., hereby exercises its option to draw against said Brotherhood Bank and Trust Company's Letter of Credit in the amount of $175,000 due to non-payment of invoices in accordance with terms of payment (copies also attached)."

The account name listed on the draft request was Highway 210 Texaco Travel Plaza, LLC, not Highway 210, LLC, as listed on the letter of credit. In addition, the draft request contained a statement that Highway 210 had failed to pay outstanding invoices and contained a statement that Carter was exercising its rights under the letter of credit. Carter's draft request was accompanied by the letter of credit and copies of Carter's outstanding invoices to Highway 210.

O'Donnell arrived at the Bank at approximately 5 p.m. on June 26, 2002, to present the draft request. When O'Donnell arrived at the Bank, the lobby doors were locked, but after O'Donnell knocked on the door, an employee of the Bank admitted O'Donnell into the lobby. O'Donnell indicated he was there to see Ward Kerby, the assistant vice president of the Bank. Upon meeting Kerby, O'Donnell handed him the draft request accompanied by the letter of credit and unpaid Carter invoices of Highway 210. The draft request was then stamped received on June 26, 2002, and was signed by Kerby with a notation that it was received at 5:05 p.m.

When O'Donnell delivered Carter's draft request to the Bank, the drive-through window was still open for business. O'Donnell maintained that had the employee of the Bank not opened the lobby, he would have delivered the draft request along with the attachments to the drive-through window attendant.

June 26, 2002, was a Wednesday. There is no dispute that the lobby of the Bank closed at 5 p.m. on Wednesdays. Similarly, there is no dispute that the drive-through lane at the Bank was open until 7 p.m. on Wednesdays. Additionally, inside the Bank there were several signs which alerted customers that any transactions occurring after 2 p.m. would be posted on the next business day.

The Bank dishonored Carter's draft request on the letter of credit on June 28, 2002. The Bank's dishonor notice stated two reasons: (1) The draft request was presented to the Bank after regular banking hours of the Bank on the date the letter of credit expired, and (2) the request failed to contain the specific language required by the letter of credit: "Drawn under Brotherhood Bank & Trust Company's Letter of Credit #2001–270 dated July 26, 2001."

Carter sued the Bank for its failure to honor the letter of credit. Both parties moved for summary judgment. The trial court ruled in favor of Carter and granted its motion for summary judgment. The Bank requested time to conduct further discovery concerning Highway 210's current debt to Carter. Carter furnished the Bank's counsel with copies of documents including an acknowledgment by Highway 210 that its debt to Carter exceeded the $175,000 face amount of the letter of credit. Later, the trial court entered its judgment in favor of Carter in the amount of $175,000, plus interest, costs, and attorney fees. . . .

On appeal, the Bank relies on two theories. First, the Bank contends that the attempted presentment of the draft request was untimely. The Bank makes two separate arguments. It argues that the presentment was untimely either because it occurred past 2 p.m. and, thus, should be considered on the next day's business or because the presentment occurred past 5 p.m., after the regular banking hours of the Bank. Second, the Bank argues that the draft request did not strictly comply with the terms of the letter of credit.

Letters of credit are governed by Article 5 of the Uniform Commercial Code (UCC), K.S.A. 84–5–101 *et seq.* The pertinent statute is K.S.A. 84–5–108. It states, in relevant part:

> "(a) Except as otherwise provided in K.S.A. 84–5–109, an issuer shall honor a presentation that, as determined by the standard practice referred to in subsection (e), appears on its face strictly to comply with the terms and conditions of the letter of credit. Except as otherwise provided in K.S.A. 84–5–113 and unless otherwise agreed with the applicant, an issuer shall dishonor a presentation that does not appear so to comply.

. . . .

"(e) An issuer shall observe standard practice of financial institutions that regularly issue letters of credit. Determination of the issuer's observance of the standard practice is a matter of interpretation for the court. The court shall offer the parties a reasonable opportunity to present evidence of the standard practice."

Strict compliance and standard practice are explained in the Official UCC Comment 1 to K.S.A. 84–5–108. The comment states:

"The standard of strict compliance governs the issuer's obligation to the beneficiary and to the applicant. By requiring that a 'presentation' appear strictly to comply, the section requires not only that the documents themselves appear on their face strictly to comply, but also that the other terms of the letter of credit such as those dealing with the time and place of presentation are strictly complied with. . . .

. . . .

"The section adopts strict compliance, rather than the standard that commentators have called 'substantial compliance[.]'. . . Strict compliance does not mean slavish conformity to the terms of the letter of credit. For example, standard practice (what issuers do) may recognize certain presentations as complying that an unschooled layman would regard as discrepant. . . .

"Identifying and determining compliance with standard practice are matters of interpretation for the court, not for the jury. . . . Granting the court authority to make these decisions will also encourage the salutary practice of courts' granting summary judgment in circumstances where there are no significant factual disputes."

The Kansas Comment to K.S.A. 84–5–108, as it pertains to strict compliance and standard practice, mirrors the sentiments presented in the official comment.

Turning first to the issue of timeliness, we notice that there is no dispute that the letter of credit was subject to the UCP. Both parties agree that Article 45 of the UCP provides that "[b]anks are under no obligation to accept presentation of documents outside their banking hours."

Letters of credit are governed by the rules applicable to the construction of ordinary contracts. *Sports, Inc. v. The Sportshop, Inc.*, 14 Kan.App.2d 141, 142, 783 P.2d 1318 (1989). The document must be construed from its four corners and all provisions must be considered together and not in isolation. When an ambiguity appears in a document, the language is construed against the party who prepared the instrument. *Amoco Production Co. v. Wilson, Inc.*, 266 Kan. 1084, 1088,

976 P.2d 941 (1999). In the instant case, the Bank prepared the letter of credit.

The letter of credit first stated that $175,000 was available by Carter's draft at "sight" accompanied by certain documents. It then stated that the letter of credit would be honored "if presented at this office in Shawnee, KS no later than June 26, 2002." The only office referred to in the letter of credit is the Bank's office at 7499 Quivira, Shawnee, Kansas.

O'Donnell arrived at the Bank just after 5 p.m., and the lobby was closed. The drive-through window at the Bank, located at 7499 Quivira, was still open. The letter of credit made no reference that the sight draft must be presented before the lobby closed on June 26, 2002. Similarly, it did not state that the draft needed to be presented before 2 p.m. or before 5 p.m. The letter of credit did not state that the draft needed to be presented to a loan officer, a vice president, or any particular person. The letter of credit simply stated that the money was available by draft at "sight" and would be honored "if presented at this office in Shawnee, KS no later than June 26, 2002."

Under the rules of construction, the presentment of the draft did comply with the requirements set forth for the time and place of presentment. The draft was presented at the Bank on June 26, 2002, at a time when the Bank was still open for business. Although the lobby was closed, by the terms of the letter of credit, anyone working at the Bank was authorized and could have accepted the draft, including the drive-through teller who was open for business.

Although the Bank may have intended to limit the presentment of a sight draft to either before 2 p.m. or 5 p.m. on June 26, 2002, the Bank did not specify in the letter of credit that presentment was to be conducted in this way. This was the source of the confusion; other than the date, no specific time of day was mentioned as to when it must be presented. For example, the letter of credit could have stated that it must be presented "no later than 5 p.m., June 26, 2002, at which date and time the letter of credit expires." The letter of credit failed to contain such language or any similar language to that effect. "Any ambiguity in a letter of credit must be resolved against the party drafting it." *East Girard Sav. Ass'n v. Citizens Nat. Bank & Trust Co. of Baytown*, 593 F.2d 598, 602 (5th Cir.1979). The Bank was the sole drafter of the letter of credit. Accordingly, if the Bank wanted more specificity as to when and where Carter had to make presentment, the Bank could have included such provisions in its letter of credit. The ambiguities or lack of explicitness in the letter of credit stemmed from the Bank's own pen. As a result, the Bank's argument fails.

Next, we must consider whether the draft request strictly complied with the terms of the letter of credit. When do documents comply with the terms of the letter of credit so that a bank is forced to pay the draft is a difficult legal question. The UCC furnishes no easy answer to this question.

The Bank was to make funds available to Carter under its sight draft when it was accompanied by a "statement signed by Carter Petroleum Products stating that Highway 210, LLC has failed to pay outstanding invoices in accordance with terms of payment."

Additionally, the letter of credit required that "[e]ach draft must state that it is 'Drawn under Brotherhood Bank & Trust Company's Letter of Credit #2001–270 dated July 26, 2001.' This credit must accompany the draft(s)."

On June 26, 2002, Carter presented to the Bank a sight draft in the amount of $175,000. The account name on the draft was Highway 210 Texaco Travel Plaza, LLC. The draft contained the following statement:

> "Pursuant to the terms stated in the Letter of Credit #2001–270 dated October 19, 2001 (copy attached), Carter Petroleum Products, Inc., hereby exercises its option to draw against said Brotherhood Bank and Trust Company's Letter of Credit in the amount of $175,000 due to non-payment of invoices in accordance with terms of payment (copies also attached)."

The draft was accompanied by the letter of credit and Carter's outstanding invoices to Highway 210.

On appeal, the Bank contends that the demand was not in strict compliance because (1) the draft request stated the account name as "Highway 210 Texaco Travel Plaza, LLC," not "Highway 210, LLC," and (2) the draft request did not contain the exact language from the letter of credit.

In support of its contentions, the Bank cites *American Coleman v. Intrawest Bank of Southglenn*, 887 F.2d 1382 (10th Cir.1989). The defendant bank in *Coleman* was to make funds available to plaintiff under its sight drafts to be accompanied by the " '[o]riginal Letter of Credit and your signed written statement that Jim Gammon and Associates is in default on the Note and Security Agreement dated November 21, 1984, between American Coleman and Jim Gammon and Associates.' " 887 F.2d at 1383. Plaintiff tendered to the bank a sight draft with the following attached statement: "[T]he American Coleman Company informs you that Jim Gammon and Associates is in default on the Note and Security Agreement dated November 21, 1984, *and the Promissory Note dated November 16, 1984,* between American Coleman and Jim Gammon and Associates." (Emphasis added.) 887 F.2d at 1384.

The bank dishonored the draft. In finding in favor of the bank, the trial judge stated:

> "In the present case, it is clear that [plaintiff's] request for payment presented November 13, 1986 was not in technical or literal compliance with the terms of the letter of credit.

[Plaintiff's] reference to two different notes could easily have caused the bank's documents examiner some confusion. Accordingly, because I conclude that the rule of strict compliance, as it is applied in Colorado, requires literal compliance with the terms and requirements set forth in the letter of credit, and there was no such literal compliance in this case." 887 F.2d at 1385.

In affirming the decision of the trial court, the Tenth Circuit Court of Appeals stated:

"While it is apparent from the cases that minute discrepancies which could not possibly mislead a document examiner are usually disregarded, this does not constitute a retreat from the strict compliance standard applicable in this case inasmuch as the district court found that '[plaintiff's] reference to two different notes could easily have caused the bank's documents examiner some confusion.' " 887 F.2d at 1386.

The *Coleman* court then held that the trial court did not err in applying the strict compliance standard. 887 F.2d at 1386. In rejecting plaintiff's argument that reference to the second note was mere surplusage, the *Coleman* court declared:

"The apparent existence of two promissory notes supports the district court's finding that Bank could have been misled by [plaintiff's] November 13, 1986, draft. [Plaintiff's] contention that Bank could not have been misled by the draft because Bank drafted the letter of credit is without support in this record." 887 F.2d at 1386–87.

Thus, the *Coleman* court's decision was largely based upon whether the defendant bank could have been misled by the discrepancy in the draft.

In *American Airlines, Inc. v. Federal Deposit Ins.*, 610 F.Supp. 199 (D.Kan.1985), a bank had issued a letter of credit No. G-301, to American Airlines, Inc. (American). Unfortunately, American delivered a sight draft to the bank referring to the letter of credit No. G0391. The cover letter, however, correctly referred to the letter of credit as G-301. The bank refused to pay on the letter of credit. The bank maintained that the typographical error on the sight draft indicated that American had failed to strictly comply with the terms of the letter of credit. As a result, American was not entitled to payment.

In ruling in favor of American, the *American Airlines* court stated:

"In the case at hand, we conclude that there was no possibility that the Bank could have been misled by the documents submitted to it by [plaintiff]. Even under the rule of strict compliance, a beneficiary may establish compliance with the terms of a letter of credit via documents submitted in conjunction with the disputed draft. [Citation omitted.] Here, the documents submitted along with [plaintiff's] draft clearly indicated the correct letter of credit reference number and the proper drawee (the Bank)." 610 F.Supp. at 202.

Because the bank could not have been misled, even with the typographical error, the *American Airlines* court determined that the documents did strictly comply with the terms of the letter of credit. As a result, American was entitled to payment. 610 F.Supp. at 202.

In the instant case, although the draft request submitted by Carter was not in complete conformity with the letter of credit issued by the Bank, it did contain all the necessary information requested by the letter of credit. Moreover, the Bank could not have been misled by the nonconformity.

Although the draft request listed the account name as "Highway 210 Texaco Travel Plaza, LLC," not "Highway 210, LLC" as requested in the letter of credit, the draw request was accompanied by the letter of credit which properly named the account. Obviously, there was no confusion caused by the different name referred to in the draft request because the Bank did not rely on this ground in rejecting the letter of credit. Moreover, the Bank failed to raise this particular argument before the trial court. Issues not raised before the trial court cannot be raised on appeal. *Board of Lincoln County Comm'rs v. Nielander,* 275 Kan. 257, 268, 62 P.3d 247 (2003).

The draft request also contained all of the other pertinent information requested in the letter of credit. The letter of credit accompanied the draft, the draft stated it was drawn under Brotherhood Bank and Trust Company's letter of credit, and the draft contained the correct letter of credit number: #2001–270. Additionally, as required by the letter of credit, the draft stated that Carter was exercising its option to draw against the Bank due to nonpayment of invoices in accordance with the terms of payment.

The draft request differed from the requirements stated in the letter of credit in that the letter of credit mistakenly referred to the letter of credit dated July 26, 2001. In its draft request, Carter properly referred to the letter of credit dated October 19, 2001. Had Carter referred to the incorrect date as specified in the letter of credit, it would have been likely to cause confusion on the part of the Bank because the October 19, 2001, letter of credit was for a different amount and superceded [sic] the July 26, 2001, letter of credit. As a result, the Bank's argument fails. . . .

Affirmed.

NOTES

1.   With respect to the timeliness issue, is the court saying that presentation of the $175,000 letter of credit in *Carter Petroleum* would have been timely if made to the bank's drive-through teller at 6:59 on June 26, 2002? Might the court have found the presentation untimely had Carter

Petroleum drafted the letter of credit? What does this case teach banks to do in drafting letters of credit with respect to time and place of presentation?

With respect to the compliance issue, is the court saying that, in the absence of proof of standard practice to the contrary, the test of compliance under 5–108(a) is whether the error in compliance (here "October 19, 2001" in the draft instead of "July 26, 2001") is "misleading"? How does a "misleading" test vary from a substantial compliance standard? See Comment 1 to 5–108. The court says that it takes this standard from *American Coleman*, in which the triggering event for the bank's obligation to pay was presentation to the bank of a sight draft accompanied by a written statement by the beneficiary that the "Note and Security Agreement dated November 21, 1984" were in default. Even though there was no such note, the beneficiary's statement contained the required representation. However, out of an abundance of caution and because of its unease about representing that the customers were in default on a nonexistent note, the beneficiary *added* the fatal words "and the Promissory Note dated November 16, 1984," which described the true note on which the customers were actually in default. The court held that under former Article 5, the documentary presentation was not in compliance owing to the additional language, which could have caused the bank's documents examiner some confusion and misled the bank. Wasn't the potential for confusion just as great in *Carter Petroleum*?

2.   Section 5–108(a)'s strict compliance standard is a default rule. As with most aspects of the letter of credit, it can be varied by the reimbursement agreement between the applicant and the issuer when their interests and capabilities favor doing so. See 5–103(c); Comment 2 to 5–103; Comment 1 to 5–108. Reimbursement agreements sometimes are altered accordingly. For example, see ¶ 8 of the Letter of Credit Agreement form reprinted at the end of this chapter. Another example is ISP 98 Rule 4.09(c), which requires exact compliance in the documentary presentation when the credit calls for "exact" or "identical" wording in documents. Even when the parties do not opt out of the default rule, 1–103 allows the reimbursement agreement to set standards of documentary compliance. Thus, whether a strict compliance standard is preferable to an alternative compliance standard depends on the preferences and capacities of typical parties to a letter of credit. Which rule is likely to minimize the costs of effecting payment under a credit for the typical applicant?

The strict compliance rule is essential to the efficient operation of the letter of credit department of banks. See, e.g., Albert J. Givray, Letters of Credit, 44 Bus. Law. 1567, 1589 (1989). The document examiner must lay the draft against the letter of credit in the bank's files. If there is a discrepancy the examiner is ill-equipped to deal with it: she is not a lawyer and may know nothing of the circumstances surrounding the transaction. The examiner's task should merely be to ask: do the presented documents *on their face* meet all the letter of credit's requirements?

3.   Section 5–108(e) states that "[a]n issuer shall observe standard practice of financial institutions that regularly issue letters of credit. Determination of the issuer's observance of the standard practice is a matter

of interpretation for the court." Under both 5–108(a) and UCP 600 art. 14d, the degree of documentary compliance is determined by "standard practice." However, although close in meaning, the two provisions are not identical. They differ in the "practice" referred to: 5–108(e)'s "standard practice" is that of financial institutions that regularly issue credits; UCP 600 art. 14d refers to "international standard banking practice." Comment 8 to 5–108 discusses the intended meaning of "standard practice."

What standard practice considers an insubstantial documentary discrepancy might not be obvious to those who do not deal with letters of credit. For example, the International Chamber of Commerce has attempted to describe some of the specific "best practices" for examining documents among international banks. See ICC, International Standard Banking Practice for the Examination of Documents Under UCP 600 (Pub. No. 745, 2013) ("ISBP 2013"). The ISBP 2013 finds that a document issued in more than one original and marked "duplicate" does not disqualify the document as an original. ISBP 2013 A28. It also considers a credit that calls for "one invoice" or "invoice in 1 copy," without more, to require an original invoice rather than a copy. ISBP 2013 A29(d)(i). Neither discrepancy likely would be regarded as insubstantial by non-issuers. Under 5–108(e) the determination of the standard practice of letter of credit issuers is to be decided by the court, not a jury.

Section 5–108(e) does not allow the issuer to take into account practices other than those of letter of credit issuers. As a result, the issuer is not charged with knowledge of practices in the trade or industry involved in the underlying transaction. This means that a reference in a document that differs from the reference required by the credit may not satisfy the strict compliance standard, even if the relevant trade considers them synonyms. J.H. Rayner & Co. v. Hambros Bank, Ltd., [1943] 1 K.B. 37 (C.A.), a classic English letter of credit case, illustrates the point. There, the credit called for bills lading covering "about 1400 tons Coromandel groundnuts." The bills of lading presented described the goods as "bags machine-shelled groundnuts" and referred to them as "O.T.C. C.R.S. Aarhus." In the nut trade in London "C.R.S." was an abbreviation for "Coromandel." The beneficiary sued for wrongful dishonor after the issuing bank refused to pay the draft drawn under the credit. In ruling that the documents presented did not strictly comply with the terms of the credit, the court found it "quite impossible" that the issuer is charged with knowledge of the trades involved in the transactions from which letters of credit arises. The court therefore concluded that the bank was not required to take into account in determining documentary compliance the practice of those who deal in nuts in Mincing Lane.

Section 5–108(e) allocates to the court the determination of the issuer's observance of standard practice. Comment 1 explains, ". . .it is hoped that there will be more consistency in the outcomes and speedier resolution of disputes if the responsibility for determining the nature and scope of standard practice is granted to the court, not to a jury." Does this unconstitutionally deprive the parties of a jury trial? See Margaret L. Moses, The Uniform Commercial Code Meets the Seventh Amendment: The Demise of Jury Trials Under Article 5?, 72 Ind. L.J. 681 (1997). Compare also 1–205(b), 2–202, 2–302 and 4A–202(c), which use a similar approach. Section 5–108(e)'s treatment of the issue of standard practice as a question of law is controversial. Two states have adopted nonuniform amendments to the subsection eliminating the offending portion of subsection (e). See N.Y. U.C.C. § 5–108(e) (McKinney 2003); Wyo. Stat. Ann. § 34.1–5–108(e) (2003).

4. Does the strict compliance standard enhance the reliability of letters of credit as payment mechanisms? Or does it encourage an issuing bank to find a minor defect in the documents in cases in which the bank doesn't want to pay, such as cases in which the applicant has gone into bankruptcy and reimbursement of the bank's claim against the applicant may be difficult?

In assessing the wisdom of the strict compliance standard, recognize three points. First, in most commercial credits the beneficiary doesn't care if the documents presented contain discrepancies because the issuer will honor the presentation anyway. Where the market price of goods contracted for in the underlying transaction is stable or rising, the applicant-buyer will want the goods and, therefore, will have the issuer waive its right to insist on conforming documents. Alternatively, under these market conditions, the issuer may waive the discrepancy at its own risk. Thus, most of the time, obtaining conforming documents isn't cost-justified for beneficiary-sellers. See John F. Dolan, Why High Discrepancy Rates Do Not Discourage L/C Use, 2003 Ann. Survey Letter Credit L. & Prac. 36. The few beneficiaries who are concerned about the prospect of a falling market can opt-out of strict compliance by insisting that the reimbursement agreement provide a more forgiving standard of compliance.

Second, there is a powerful market mechanism controlling strategic rejections of discrepant documents by issuers. Issuers operate in a market in which reputation matters. Because issuance fees are comparatively low, an issuer's profit from operating a credit department depends on generating a high volume of credits. The issuer, therefore, must both obtain repeat business and attract potential applicants and beneficiaries. The number of issuers is relatively small, and information about their handling of credits often can be obtained from other issuers. An issuer may seize on a discrepancy to avoid honor because it fears not being reimbursed or is undercollateralized or wants to avoid involvement in the applicant's bankruptcy or simply wants to placate its applicant. But doing so risks a loss of credit business since potential beneficiaries will insist that credits be issued by issuers that are reliable sources of payment. The presenting beneficiary also is unlikely to do business with the issuer again. Thus, prospect of a loss in reputation often suffices to prevent issuers from strategic rejections even under a strict compliance standard.

Third, less stringent standards of compliance require judicial intervention, and courts are poorly positioned to intervene effectively. For instance, the court in Voest-Alpine Trading USA Corp. v. Bank of China, 167 F.Supp.2d 940 (S.D.Tex.2000), considers and rejects a standard that finds documentary discrepancies when the deviation in the document risks harming the applicant in the underlying transaction. Application of this standard encourages parties to litigate the issuer's decision to honor or dishonor a documentary presentation. Courts and issuers may be unfamiliar with the facts necessary to make this determination of harm at the time the issuer must decide to honor the presentation. They may know nothing about industry practices bearing on the underlying transaction. Standards less stringent than strict compliance, therefore, undermine the credit's efficient payment function. Professors White and Summers reach the same conclusion and state, without remorse, that "the issuer may examine the documents microscopically and may assert small discrepancies to excuse its duty to pay." 3 White & Summers, Uniform Commercial Code § 26–5, at 164.

5. Under 5–108(a), an issuing bank must honor a conforming presentation. Must it dishonor a nonconforming presentation? Suppose in the case of questionable documentation like that in *American Coleman*, the bank called the applicant and asked its consent to the bank's payment of the credit. If the applicant gave its consent, (1) may the bank safely pay the credit? (2) May it safely decline to pay the credit? 5–108(a) and Comment 7 to 5–108. (3) Does the issuer have a duty to seek a waiver from the applicant in the case of a nonconforming presentation? Comment 2 to 5–108; see Bombay Indus., Inc. v. Bank of N.Y., 649 N.Y.S.2d 784 (N.Y. App. Div.1996).

6. Matter of Coral Petroleum, Inc., 878 F.2d 830 (5th Cir.1989), presented the issue of whether impossibility excuses strict compliance with a letter of credit. Seller sold Buyer 31,000 barrels of West Texas Intermediate crude oil for $880,400 and required Buyer to obtain a standby letter of credit in a form acceptable to Seller for the price. Bank issued the letter of credit under Buyer's instructions that the credit would be payable upon receipt of certain documents including (1) a statement by Seller that West Texas Intermediate oil had been delivered to Buyer and (2) a copy of the shipper's transfer order showing transfer to Buyer of 31,000 barrels of "WTNM SO or SR." Buyer's instructions were mistaken. West Texas Intermediate crude is a sweet oil (meaning not containing certain undesirable elements found in sour oil), but "WTNM SO or SR" refers to sour oil. Thus, the letter of credit required two documents that were contradictory: a shipper's order showing transfer of sour oil to Buyer and a statement that sweet oil had been delivered to Buyer. After Buyer filed in bankruptcy under Chapter 11, Seller demanded payment under the letter of credit. Bank refused to pay because Seller's demand was accompanied by a shipper's order showing transfer of sweet oil to Buyer. Seller had inspected the letter of credit before accepting it and did not ask that the erroneous description be corrected. Seller argued that the terms of the credit were impossible to perform. Seller could not deliver sweet oil to Buyer and procure a shipper's transfer order showing that sour oil had been delivered. Seller also argued that the letter of credit was ambiguous and the ambiguity should be construed against Bank. The court held that the letter of credit was not ambiguous. The fact that it was impossible for Seller to comply did not excuse compliance by Seller. Bank is not required to know the meaning of technical trade terms used in the letter of credit. If Seller finds the terms of a shipping agreement impossible to fulfill, it should attempt to renegotiate them beforehand or refuse to sign the letter of credit. BM Electronics Corp. v. LaSalle, 59 UCC Rep. Serv.2d 280

(N.D. Ill.2006). See also In re Sanders-Langsam Tobacco Co., Inc., 224 B.R. 1 (Bankr. E.D.N.Y.1998). Moreover, Seller was negligent in accepting a letter of credit with requirements that could not be met. Accord First State Bank v. Diamond Plastics Corp., 891 P.2d 1262 (Okla.1995).

Observers have consistently found a high frequency of noncomplying documentary presentations, typically exceeding 50%. A 2003 informal survey of selected banks issuing credits reported that between 60% and 70% of presentations were rejected as discrepant on first presentation. See International Chamber of Commerce, ICC Moves to Cut Documentary Credit Rejections (February 3, 2003). Concerned about the number of discrepant presentations, the ICC has tried to reduce their incidence by publishing a description of international banking practices for handling documentary discrepancies. See ISBP 2013, Introduction.

The high rate of discrepant presentations has encouraged the recent development of a new financial instrument: the bank payment obligation. A bank payment obligation (BPO) is an irrevocable undertaking by one bank to another bank to make a specified payment on a specified date after the successful matching of electronic data provided by the other bank to it. In addition, the bank's payment undertaking is independent of the underlying transaction. See ICC Uniform Rules for Bank Payment Obligations art. 6(a) (Pub. No. 751E 2013). In this respect a BPO is similar to a letter of credit, However, a BPO differs from a letter of credit in two ways. One is that the beneficiary of a BPO is the bank to which the undertaking to pay is made. It is not the seller or another party to the underlying transaction associated with the BPO. The other, more important difference is that the BPO calls for payment against the communication of electronic data from the underlying transaction. By contrast, the letter of credit requires presentation of documents. See 5–102(a)(10). The comparison of data presented with the data required by the BPO is to determine whether the two sets of data match is automated, without a document examiner's scrutiny.

The bank undertaking the payment obligation is called the "obligor bank" and the bank to which the undertaking is made the "recipient bank." In a sales transaction using a BPO for payment of the purchase price, the buyer's bank is the obligor bank and the seller's bank the recipient bank. The buyer and sellers' banks submit specified data about the underlying sales transaction provided by their respective clients to a transaction matching platform. The specified data typically includes data about the purchase order, commercial invoice, transport documents and inspection certificates. The matching platform maintains a "transaction matching application": an automated data comparison program. If the data submitted by the banks match, the BPO is established and obligor bank is irrevocably bound to pay according to the terms of the BPO. The matched data set is called the "matching baseline." To be paid by the obligor bank, the recipient bank must provide data that meet the matching baseline. Once the seller has shipped the goods, it provides the data to the recipient bank called for by the BPO. The recipient bank in turn uploads the data received onto the matching platform. If the data meet the matching baseline, the platform informs the banks of this fact and the obligor bank is obligated to pay the recipient bank by the specified date.

A BPO potentially is a cheaper financial product than a letter of credit. Because the credit risk of the obligor bank and the issuing bank is the same, the potential savings in a BPO come from the lower cost of machine processing and matching data as compared to the cost of human document examination with the letter of credit. However, a BPO requires an additional transaction and transaction cost for the seller not present with the letter of credit. This is because the BPO is a bank-to-bank transaction in which the recipient bank is the beneficiary. Thus, the obligor bank owes no payment obligation to the seller. Accordingly, to assure payment, the seller must contract separately with the recipient bank for the right to receive the proceeds of the BPO. By contrast, in the commercial letter of credit the seller is the beneficiary and the issuer is obligated directly to it. To determine whether a BPO is a cheaper financial product than a letter of credit, both the savings in operational costs and the additional transaction costs of assuring the seller payment must be taken into account. The increased customer demand for BPOs reported by some banks suggests that a BPO sometimes can be a cheaper financing instrument than the letter of credit. See ICC 2015 Global Survey on Trade Finance 42 (Fig. 22) (2015).

BPO's future is unclear. A BPO relies on a platform that offers software for matching submitted data with the baseline data. In 2019 SWIFT. which offered the matching platform underpinning BPOs, announced that it planned to withdraw the messaging service due to insufficient demand. To date no matching platform has emerged to replace SWIFT's platform. A separate development is the rise of blockchain technology, which threatens to make centralized data matching programs outdated. Both developments potentially limit future demand for BPOs.

2.   NOTICE OF DISCREPANCIES: WAIVER AND PRECLUSION

An issuer can respond to a documentary presentation in either of two ways: by honoring or dishonoring it. Both Article 5 and the UCP describe the steps that an issuer must take when documents are presented under a letter of credit and the consequence of failing to take them. The two sets of rules prescribe the same steps. If the documents appear to comply with the credit's terms, both 5–108(a) and UCP 600 art. 8a. require the issuer to honor the presentation. If the documents are discrepant and the discrepancy allows the issuer to refuse honor, the issuer has a choice: it can waive its right to insist on a complying presentation and honor the discrepant presentation or it can dishonor the presentation. An issuer who waives the discrepancy does so at its own risk, unless the customer has agreed to the waiver.

When the beneficiary of a letter of credit seeks payment, it presents the letter of credit and other documents, which will include a draft demanding payment, usually on sight. When we speak of the issuer honoring a letter of credit, we mean that the issuer pays the draft within the statutory period. If the issuer does not pay the draft within the statutory period, it has dishonored. Wrongful dishonor of the draft may subject the issuer to damages. Issues that have troubled courts and law drafters are (i) how long an issuer has to examine the documents presented before deciding whether to honor or dishonor and (ii) the extent to which the issuer must disclose the reasons why it dishonored. We raise these issues in the following problem based on Esso Petroleum Canada v. Security Pacific Bank, 710 F. Supp. 275 (D. Or.1989).

PROBLEM

Esso would not sell aviation fuel to Valley Oil unless the buyer obtained a standby letter of credit for the price of the oil. After Bank issued the requisite letter of credit, Esso shipped the oil. The expiry date for the letter of credit was Monday, November 16. At 1 p.m. on Friday, November 13, Esso presented its draft drawn on Bank pursuant to the letter of credit, which was accompanied by what Esso believed were documents fulfilling the terms and conditions of the letter of credit. At that time, Esso demanded immediate payment, and well it might have done so for within two months Valley Oil filed in bankruptcy. Bank informed Esso at 5:15 on Friday that it would dishonor because of discrepancies in the presentation, but, despite Esso's strong demand for more information, refused to state the discrepancies at that time. It promised a written response stating the discrepancies by 9 a.m. Monday when the officer who had to sign the letter relating the discrepancies would be back in the office. After receiving Bank's written statement of discrepancies on Monday, Esso made another presentation in which it attempted to correct its prior presentation. Bank again dishonored because of uncorrected discrepancies. No payment was made by Bank. Esso sued Bank for the amount of the credit, plus interest and costs. The lower court granted Esso summary judgment on its claims that Bank had wrongfully dishonored its letter of credit and had failed to notify Esso of the discrepancies in a timely manner.

On appeal, what decision should the court reach:

(a) If UCC Article 5 governed the letter of credit? See Comment 4 to 5–108.

Section 5–108(b) and (c) state:

(b) An issuer has a reasonable time after presentation, but not beyond the end of the seventh business day of the issuer after the day of its receipt of documents:

(1) to honor,

    (2) if the letter of credit provides for honor to be completed more than seven business days after presentation, to accept a draft or incur a deferred obligation, or

    (3) to give notice to the presenter of discrepancies in the presentation.

(c) Except as otherwise provided in subsection (d), an issuer is precluded from asserting as a basis for dishonor any discrepancy if timely notice is not given, or any discrepancy not stated in the notice if timely notice is given.

Comment 2 to 5–108 states that the 7-day period is not a safe harbor: the issuer must act within a reasonable time but that period may not exceed seven days. Thus the time within which the issuer must give notice is the lesser of a reasonable time or seven business days.

(b) If UCP 600 governed the letter of credit?

Art. 14b. states: "[An] issuing bank shall. . .have a maximum of five banking days following the day of presentation to determine if a presentation is complying. This period is not curtailed or otherwise affected by the occurrence on or after the date of presentation or any expiry date or last day for presentation."

Art. 16 states:

a. When. . .the issuing bank determines that a presentation does not comply, it may refuse to honour. . . .

b. When an issuing bank determines that a presentation does not comply, it may in its sole judgment approach the applicant for a waiver of the discrepancies. This does not, however, extend the period mentioned in sub-article 14b.

c. When. . . the issuing bank decides to refuse to honour. . . , it must give a single notice to that effect to the presenter.

The notice must state:

i. that the bank is refusing to honour. . . ; and

ii. each discrepancy in respect of which the bank refuses to honour. . . ; and

iii. a) that the bank is holding the documents until it receives a waiver from the applicant and agrees to accept it, or receives further instructions from the presenter prior to agreeing to accept a waiver; or

    b) that the issuing bank is holding the documents until it receives a waiver from the applicant and agrees to accept it, or receives further instructions from the presenter prior to agreeing to accept a waiver; or

    c) that the bank is returning the documents; or

    d)   that the bank is acting in accordance with instructions previously received from the presenter.

  d.   The notice required in sub-article 16c must be given by telecommunication or, if that is not possible, by other expeditious means no later than the close of the fifth banking day following the day of presentation.

NOTE

How would the following case be decided under 5–108? See Comments 2 and 4 to 5–108. In Rhode Island Hospital Trust Nat'l Bank v. Eastern General Contractors, Inc., 674 A.2d 1227 (R.I.1996), a UCP case, the beneficiary made presentation on Thursday, September 26, 1985. On Friday, September 27, the bank did not open for business owing to Hurricane Gloria. Monday, September 30 was the expiry date. On Tuesday, October 1, the bank notified the beneficiary of certain discrepancies and stated that it would hold the documents for beneficiary's disposal. The court concluded that the trial court erred in directing a verdict for the bank. Expert testimony was to the effect that the bank did not act within a reasonable time; if the date of receipt of the presentation to the issuing bank is close to the expiry date of the credit, common banking procedure is to act expeditiously, presumably so that any discrepancy can be cured before expiration of the credit. Article 13b of UCP 500, the then-current version of the UCP relied on by the *Rhode Island Hospital* court, gave the issuer a "reasonable time" in which to examine documents, not to exceed seven banking days following the day they are presented. Article 14b of UCP 600 gives the issuer "a maximum" of five banking days following that day in which to do so. It does not contain a reference to a "reasonable time" in which a documentary examination is to occur within the five day period. How would the *Rhode Island Hospital* be decided under article 14b of UCP 600? Under Rule 5.01 of the ISP 98?

Waiver is an intentional relinquishment of a known legal right and applies to Article 5 via 1–103(a), as a supplementing principle of extra-UCC common law. It is not an amendment of the credit. An amendment requires the agreement of all parties (5–106(b); UCP 600 art. 10a); waiver requires the consent only of the party relinquishing its rights. Unlike an amendment of the credit, a waiver can be oral, unless the reimbursement agreement requires otherwise. Cf. 5–104. Paragraph 11 of the Letter of Credit Agreement Form at the end of this chapter requires that waivers be in writing. UCP 600 art. 16b allows the issuer to approach the applicant for a waiver. The UCP is silent as to the issuer's waiver against the beneficiary. A few courts have divided over whether common law doctrines such as waiver apply to credits subject to the UCP. Compare Banco General Runinahui, S.A. v. Citibank Int'l, 97 F.3d 480 (11th Cir.1996), with Alaska Textile Co., Inc. v. Chase Manhattan Bank, N.A., 982 F.2d 813 (2d Cir.1992).

In deciding whether to waive a documentary discrepancy, prudent issuers usually approach their applicants to obtain their consent. This is because the applicant's consent relinquishes its right to insist on a condition of the credit, so as to allow for the issuer's reimbursement if the issuer honors the presentation. Sometimes issuers waive discrepancies at their own risk, without the consent of their applicants. In all cases, waiver is a right of the issuer that it can exercise within its discretion. The issuer has no obligation to waive a discrepancy, even if the applicant consents to the waiver. See Suntex Industrial Corp., Ltd. v. The CIT Group/BBC, Inc., 2001 WL 34401367 (D. Del.2001). It need not even approach the applicant to elicit the applicant's consent. See Note 6 above. ISP 98 Rules 5.05 and 5.06(a) are to the same effect. Comment 7 to 5–108 construes waiver narrowly, so that waiver of one or more presentations does not waive subsequent discrepant presentations.

The issuer's second alternative is to dishonor a discrepant documentary presentation. Article 5 follows the UCP's approach both to the sufficiency of notice that must be given to the presenter and the effect of the failure to give timely notice and sufficient notice of dishonor. Section 5–108(b) requires that, in the case of dishonor, the issuer must communicate both the fact and grounds of dishonor to the presenter. See Comment 2 to 5–108 (second paragraph); cf. UCP 600 art. 16d.i and ii. Thus, 5–108(b) contemplates two possibilities: either the issuer fails to make a timely decision to honor or dishonor, or the issuer's timely decision fails to give timely notice of the grounds for dishonor. In both cases, 5–108(c) precludes the issuer from relying as a ground for dishonor on discrepancies it has delayed communicating to the presenter within 5–108(b)'s prescribed time limit.

Section 5–108(b)'s preclusion rule is not a rule concerning waiver or estoppel. Courts tend to mix waiver and estoppel together, and sometimes treat both as preclusion. See, e.g., *American Coleman*, 887 F.2d at 1387 ("waiver-estoppel rule"); *Banco General Runinahui, S.A.*, 97 F.3d at 485 n.11 (preclusion as "strict estoppel"). The notions are distinct. Preclusion isn't waiver because it doesn't require the issuer to intentionally relinquish its right to a complying presentation. Section 5–108(b)'s preclusion rule applies when the issuer simply fails to give timely notice of the grounds for dishonor within the prescribed period. Preclusion also isn't estoppel because estoppel requires detrimental reliance and 5–108(b)'s rule does not require reliance. It, therefore, requires no showing that the presenter has been harmed by the issuer's failure to give timely notice of the fact or grounds of dishonor. Unlike waiver and estoppel, Article 5's preclusion rules avoid the proof costs associated with litigating over relinquishment of a right to a complying presentation (waiver) or detrimental reliance on a failure to give timely notice of a discrepancy (estoppel). The UCP's rules are similar.

PROBLEMS

1.   Over the period of a year, Beneficiary presented three drafts for payment to Issuer. Each presentation contained the same discrepancy. The first two times Issuer paid the draft without objection after receiving permission of the Applicant to pay despite the nonconformity. The third time Applicant refused to consent to payment and Issuer dishonored the draft on the ground that the presentation was nonconforming. Has Issuer wrongfully dishonored? Comment 7 to 5–108. 3 White & Summers, Uniform Commercial Code § 26–5(a).

2. Bank issued a letter of credit subject to UCP 600. The credit recited that it was also "subject to provisions of Article 5 of the UCC to the extent that they are consistent with UCP 600." Among the documents required was a commercial invoice covering "toys." Beneficiary presented to Bank documents, including a commercial invoice covering "construction equipment," on Day 1. Bank delayed examining the documents until Day 4. On that date, it properly notified Beneficiary of the documentary discrepancy and stated that it was refusing to honor Beneficiary's presentation. Assume that issuing banks in these circumstances always examine documents the day after they are presented. May Bank nonetheless rely on the documentary discrepancy to dishonor Beneficiary's presentation? If not, why?

3. Bank issued a letter of credit subject to UCP 600 and with an expiration date of January 9. The credit obligated Bank to pay Beneficiary $100,000 (U.S.) upon Beneficiary's presentation of three documents: a commercial invoice, a bill of lading and a certificate of inspection. The terms of the credit required the documents to cover "100 pounds of widgets," and invoice and certificate of inspection to state that the widgets were "quality 100%." On January 1, Beneficiary presented all three documents to Bank. The commercial invoice described the goods as "105 pounds of widgets of 95% quality." The bill of lading described the goods as "105 pounds of widgit. . . all received on board for shipment." The certificate of origin described them as "105 pounds of WGS," "WGS" being an abbreviation for widgets commonly used in the widget trade.

Bank notified Beneficiary on January 2 to the effect that it "finds discrepancies in the invoice presented by you going to the quantity and quality of widgets described." On January 5, it notified Beneficiary that it "rejects the bill of lading based on the failure of the description of the goods in the bill ('105 pounds of widgit') to conform to the terms of the credit." Bank gave notice to Beneficiary on January 6 that it "rejects the certificate of inspection because the description of goods ('WGS') fail to conform to the terms of the credit." Each notice was accompanied by Bank's statement that it was returning the documents to Beneficiary, and Bank did so. This did Beneficiary no good because Beneficiary was unable to make another presentation by January 9, the date on which the credit expired. Bank refused to pay Beneficiary $100,000.

(a) Did Beneficiary's documentary presentation comply with the terms of the credit? Consult ISBP paras. A23 and C13 reproduced below.

(b) If not, is Bank entitled to dishonor Beneficiary's noncomplying documentary presentation? See UCP 600 arts. 16d.i, ii, f.

ICC, International Standard Banking Practice (ISBP) (2013):

A23 A misspelling or typing error that does not affect the meaning of a word or the sentence in which it occurs does not make a document discrepant. . . . However, a description as "model 123" instead of "model 321" would not be regarded as a typing error and would constitute a discrepancy.

C13 The quantity of the goods required in the credit may be indicated on an invoice within a tolerance of +/–5%. . . . The tolerance of +/–5% in the quantity of the goods will not apply when:

> a. a credit states that the quantity in terms of a stipulated number of packing units or individual items.

3. THE INDEPENDENCE PRINCIPLE

Basic to letter of credit law is the principle that the letter of credit undertaking is separate from and independent of all other relationships, including the relationships out of which it arises. This is the independence (or "autonomy") principle. Given the principle, the issuer's obligations are completely unaffected by facts concerning the performance or breach of the underlying transaction or the reimbursement agreement. Section 5–103(d) states the independence principle: "[r]ights and obligations of an issue to a beneficiary . . . under a letter of credit are independent of the existence, performance, or nonperformance of a contract or arrangement out of which the letter of credit arises or which underlies it . . . ." UCP 600 article 4a states the principle more succinctly: "A credit by its nature is a separate transaction from the sale or other contract on which it may be based." The other sets of rules produced by the International Chamber of Commerce governing letters of credit have similar provisions; see, e.g., ISP 98 Rule 1.07; URDG 758 art. 5.

The independence principle is a mandatory rule under Article 5. See 5–103(c), (d). Accordingly, the issuer's undertaking to the beneficiary may not qualify or eliminate the principle. A financial product that purports to do so destroys its character as a letter of credit. The independence principle has a number of implications both outside and within letter of credit law. Outside letter of credit law, the Comptroller of the Currency's Interpretive Ruling 7.1016 relies on the principle to regulate the issuance of letters of credit. The Ruling permits national banks, subject to other conditions, to issue letters of credit "and other independent undertakings." 12 C.F.R. § 7.1016(a). Thus, the Ruling regulates a national bank's permissible engagements by their separateness ("independence") from other relationships. Where a standby credit obeys the independence principle, the Ruling permits its issuance. A national bank generally cannot issue a guarantee because it is not an "independent undertaking."

As important are the implications of the independence principle within letter of credit law. The principle makes the credit a distinct financial product, different from a guarantee or negotiable instrument. The credit issuer's obligation to the beneficiary is primary in part because it does not depend on any other relationships or transactions, or facts about them. Thus, the issuer's obligation is unaffected by whether the underlying transaction has been performed or breached. It therefore cannot rely on defenses to the applicant arising from the underlying transaction to refuse to honor its obligation under the credit. Given the independence principle, the credit issuer's payment obligation depends only on the presentation of documents called for in the issuer's undertaking. As a result, there are fewer circumstances under which the beneficiary will not be paid by the issuer. This makes the credit more valuable to the beneficiary than a guarantee. Without the independence principle, letters of credit would not be legally distinctive instruments.

Innovations in contractual provisions sometimes implicate the independence principle. This is true of certain "sanctions clauses" that banks involved in international trade increasingly include in their credits. For reasons of foreign policy or national security, countries enforce economic and trade boycotts. U.S. sanction regulations, administered by the Treasury Department's Office of Foreign Assets Control, prohibit trade or its facilitation with designated countries, assets or persons. The prohibition is broad enough to include the issuance or honor of a letter of credit made in connection with an underlying transaction that violates U.S. sanctions. In response banks issuing international credits sometimes include in their engagement to their credit beneficiaries wording to the effect that applicable sanctions laws override the conditions of the credit and might prevent honor of their obligations under the credit.

The application of sanctions laws to the letter of credit does not by itself threaten the independence principle. Sanction laws that prohibit the issuer from honoring a complying documentary presentation have priority over the duties imposed on the issuer under Article 5 of the UCC or other rules. Their priority no more compromises the independence principle than do criminal laws that prohibit the issuer from murdering its competitors or stealing their property. However, some sanctions clauses give the issuer the discretion to pay under the credit based on its internal policy or its belief that payment might violate a sanctions law, whether or not that law applies to the payment. These clauses condition the issuer's payment obligation on facts extrinsic to documents required by the credit—facts about its internal policy or beliefs—even when applicable law allows payment. Clauses of this sort therefore violate the independence principle. Because the independence principle is a mandatory rule under Article 5 of the UCC, inclusion of such clauses in an instrument has one of two consequences: either the clause describes a nonfundamental nondocumentary condition that must be ignored or the instrument is not a letter of credit. The International Chamber of Commerce has become concerned enough about the use of sanctions clauses to recommend that issuers incorporating the UCP into their credits omit them. See ICC Banking Commission, Guidance Paper on Sanctions Clauses for Trade Related Products (e.g., Letters of Credit, Documentary Collections and Guarantees) Subject to ICC Rules (470/1129, March 2010). Perhaps understandably, issuing banks apparently have been reluctant to act on the recommendation.

4. ISSUER'S RIGHT TO REIMBURSEMENT AND OTHER REMEDIES

a. REIMBURSEMENT

Section 5–108(i) arms the issuer with a statutory right of reimbursement against the applicant. Credits usually also provide for reimbursement, as in the opening paragraph of the Letter of Credit Agreement at the end of this chapter.

The credit risk that an issuer takes with respect to payment of a letter of credit depends on whether the transaction involves a commercial or a standby letter of credit. Commercial letters of credit are payment mechanisms and are meant to be paid in every case, usually upon presentation of the seller-beneficiary's bill of lading covering the goods sold to the buyer-applicant. When the issuer has paid, it receives possession of the bill of lading which the applicant must obtain from the issuer in order to receive the goods from the carrier that issued the bill of lading. 5–108(i)(2). The issuer can secure its claim for reimbursement by holding the bill of lading until the applicant either pays or arranges for credit.

A standby letter of credit functions as a guaranty and is usually meant to be paid only in case of the applicant's failure to perform the underlying contract. When the issuer pays a standby letter of credit, it receives no bill of lading or similar document that can be used to induce the applicant to pay. Functionally, a letter of credit is a conditional loan made to the applicant by the issuer, and issuing banks treat it as such. Since it is a loan that will usually not have to be funded unless the applicant is in financial difficulty, as when the applicant is in bankruptcy, the statutory reimbursement right under 5–108(i) is invariably supplemented with an express reimbursement agreement between the issuer and applicant containing the usual terms of commercial loans with respect to security, interest rates, set-off, and the like. See ¶¶ 4, 5 and 9 of the Letter of Credit Agreement form reprinted at the end of this chapter.

As mentioned before, if obligees are able to obtain standby letters of credit from their obligors, they are in a position far superior to that of secured parties under Article 9. Upon default by their obligor, they can go to the issuing bank and obtain prompt payment of the obligation. They do not need to engage in the expensive and time-consuming exercise of collecting the debt by repossessing and foreclosing on collateral, with all the attendant problems raised in the preceding Chapters of this book, problems that are exacerbated by the obligor's bankruptcy. If no rational obligee would take a security interest in preference to a standby letter of credit, does this mean the death of security interests? Not at all; it merely changes the identity of the secured party from the obligee to the bank issuing the letter of credit. Unless the applicant is a customer who could borrow money on unsecured credit, banks will usually not issue standby letters of credit without receiving a security interest in the applicant's property. Efficiencies flowing from this tripartite arrangement have contributed to the great popularity of standby letters of credit. The creditworthiness of the obligor is determined by the bank, a professional credit grantor, rather than by the obligee who may be a seller of goods, a centerfielder, or others who are not in the business of credit granting. In this respect, the efficiency of the standby letter of credit resembles that present in the consumer bank credit card transaction. Retail stores, hotels, restaurants and others who sell goods and services can rely on a credit card issued by a bank that will guarantee payment on transactions made pursuant to the card; they don't need to maintain credit departments making costly credit evaluations of their customers. Banks will make the determination of the consumer's creditworthiness in deciding whether to issue the credit card.

b.   STANDARD OF COMPLIANCE

Under 5–108(i), an issuer is entitled to reimbursement from the applicant only if it "has honored a presentation as permitted or required by this article." Under 5–108(a), an issuer must dishonor a presentation that does not strictly comply with the terms of the letter of credit. Comment 1 to 5–108 says that "[t]he standard of strict compliance governs the issuer's obligation to the beneficiary and to the applicant." The view adopted by Article 5 that an issuing bank that pays on a presentation that does not strictly comply with the terms of the letter of credit cannot receive reimbursement from the applicant was rejected by some cases under the old law which applied a "bifurcated" standard of compliance. This approach applied a strict compliance standard for the issuer's liability to the beneficiary for wrongful dishonor but a substantial compliance standard for the issuer's liability to the applicant for wrongful honor. The bifurcation view was thought to be justified by an appreciation of the difficulty an issuing bank experiences in a case in which the applicant is demanding that the bank dishonor while the beneficiary is threatening suit if the bank does not pay.

In rejecting the bifurcated approach, Article 5 takes the realistic position that institutions issuing letters of credit, usually commercial banks, are sophisticated parties that are eminently capable of looking out for themselves. Section 5–108(a) recognizes that an issuing bank can safely pay on a noncomplying presentation if the applicant will waive the discrepancy and consent to the payment. But what if the bank is uncertain about whether there is a discrepancy in the presentation and the applicant will not waive the potential discrepancy? Section 5–103(c) allows the parties to contract around 5–108(a)'s standard of compliance as it applies to the issuer's right to reimbursement. Prudent issuers will safeguard themselves against liability for wrongful payment by including exculpatory clauses in the reimbursement agreement designed to allow them to obtain reimbursement, even when they honor a credit in which a discrepant presentation has been made. See ¶ 8 of the Letter of Credit Agreement form reprinted at the end of this chapter. Provisions imposing a standard of only substantial compliance on issuing banks with respect to their duty to dishonor are clearly enforceable. Comment 2 to 5–103. However, under the last sentence of 5–103(c), terms "generally excusing liability or generally limiting remedies for failure to perform obligations" are unenforceable.

c. SUBROGATION, RESTITUTION AND BREACH OF WARRANTY

As noted above, the prudent issuer of a standby letter of credit makes sure that if it has to pay the credit the applicant will be able to reimburse it. This is usually done by requiring that the applicant give security for its reimbursement obligation. However, if the security proves worthless and the applicant is insolvent, the issuer is unable to obtain reimbursement from the applicant. In these cases, the issuer will explore alternative remedies. If the applicant has given the beneficiary security, the issuer may seek to be subrogated to the beneficiary's rights to the security. If the issuer can claim to have paid because of fraud or mistake, it may demand restitution from the beneficiary, or the issuer may claim that the beneficiary has breached its presentation warranties to the issuer.

Whether an issuer, having paid the beneficiary of a letter of credit, is entitled to the equitable remedy of subrogation has been much litigated. Courts divided on the question. Some took the view that equitable subrogation is available to issuers of standby credits, as standby credits serve the same function as guarantees, and subrogation is available to guarantors. Other courts denied equitable subrogation to issuers of standby credits on the ground that the issuer's payment obligation is primary while the guarantor's obligation is secondary. For reasons noted in *JPMorgan Chase Bank* below, a majority of courts have denied issuers the right to subrogation. Section 5–117(a), in a change in law, recognizes subrogation for issuers: "An issuer that honors a beneficiary's presentation is subrogated to the rights of the beneficiary to the same extent as if the issuer were a secondary obligor of the underlying obligation owed to the beneficiary and of the applicant to the same extent as if the issuer were the secondary obligor of the underlying obligation owed to the applicant." The subsection does not itself give an issuer a right of subrogation. It instead gives the issuer whatever rights a secondary obligor would have in the same circumstances "as if the issuer were a secondary obligor. . . ." Thus, 5–117(a) removes a doctrinal barrier based on the issuer's "primary obligation" to granting issuers rights of subrogation. Whether the issuer has rights against the applicant or beneficiary depends on whether a secondary obligor would be subrogated in the circumstances and whether the applicant or beneficiary has defenses it could assert against the primary obligor. See In re B.C. Roger's Poultry, Inc., 455 B.R. 524 (S.D. Miss.2011).

JPMorgan Chase Bank v. Cook

District Court, Southern District of New York, 2004
318 F. Supp.2d 159

■ GERARD E. LYNCH, DISTRICT JUDGE:

[Ed.—Cook was an executive at Global Crossing, which was in bankruptcy. He borrowed $7.5 million pursuant to a promissory note from Private Bank, a division of JPMorgan Chase (JPM). The promissory note was secured by a $7.5 million standby letter of credit issued by JPM. The letter of credit, which was issued at Global Crossing's request, guaranteed that Global Crossing's revolving credit facility would pay Private Bank's loan if Cook defaulted. Before JPM issued the letter of credit, Cook signed a reimbursement agreement promising to reimburse Global Crossing for any amount drawn on the letter of credit. When Cook's promissory note matured, he failed to repay Private Bank and Private Bank drew on the letter of credit. JPM was reimbursed by the consortium of lending banks participating in Global Crossing's revolving credit facility in accordance with their own reimbursement agreement with JPM. JPM was also acting as the administrative agent for the consortium of lending banks. Although Global Crossing was obligated to reimburse JPM as the administrative agent for the consortium, Global Crossing's bankruptcy prevented JPM from collecting from it. JPM instead sued to collect $7.5 million from Cook.]

JPM argues that under the doctrine of equitable subrogation it stands in the shoes of Private Bank and can pursue claims against Cook for breach of the promissory note. Underlying JPM's claims is the fact that JPM was a member of, as well as administrative agent for, the lender consortium that ultimately had to cover the $ 7.5 million under the terms of the letter of credit issued pursuant to Global Crossing's revolving credit facility. Private Bank drew down $ 7.5 million on the letter of credit, and was thus made whole for the defaulted loan. However, the revolving credit facility took the loss and now JPM, as issuer and/or administrative representative of the consortium of lender banks participating in the facility, seeks to recover $ 7.5 million directly from Cook. As a practical matter, Global Crossing cannot be sued owing to the automatic stay in place as a result of its bankruptcy. Cook has moved to dismiss the complaint, arguing primarily that JPM was made whole for the loss, and that JPM has no standing to sue. JPM cross-moves for summary judgment on the ground that it is equitably subrogated to Private Bank, and that Cook breached the promissory note. The parties appeared for oral argument on the motions on July 22, 2003. For the reasons that follow, the motion to dismiss will be denied, and the cross motion for summary judgment will be granted. * * *

II. Equitable Subrogation

Subrogation "simply means substitution of one person for another; that is, one person is allowed to stand in the shoes of another and assert that person's rights against the defendant. Factually, the case arises because, for some justifiable reason, the subrogation plaintiff has paid a debt owed by defendant." Black's Law Dictionary 1440 (7th ed. 1999), quoting Dan B. Dobbs, Law of Remedies § 4.3, at 404 (2d ed. 1993). "In short, one party known as the subrogee is substituted for and succeeds to the rights of another party, known as the subrogor. The doctrine of subrogation . . . is based upon principles of equity." Allstate Insurance Co. v. Mazzola, 175 F.3d 255, 258 (2d Cir. 1999). The right of subrogation is rooted in the common law, and "does not depend upon contract, but is created simply from the equities of the situation." Aetna Casualty and Surety Company v. Norwalk Foods, Inc., 125 Misc. 2d 986, 480 N.Y.S.2d 851, 852–853 (1984).

Equitable subrogation essentially provides that the guarantor of another's obligation may seek reimbursement from the obligor. It is relevant in the context of standby letters of credit, such as the Letter of Credit at issue here, because a standby letter of credit resembles, in some ways, a guarantee for another's loan. That is because a beneficiary of a standby letter of credit (here, Private Bank) may normally draw on the letter of credit issued by the issuer (here, JPM) only after a third party (here, Cook) defaults on a loan. In such cases, issuers have sought to recover, not from the party that requested the letter of credit, but from the defaulting borrower. Courts grappling with this issue in the absence of a controlling statute have generally found that equitable subrogation does *not* apply to this situation because guarantees and letters of credit remain distinct in that an issuer's obligation under a letter of credit is primary, whereas a guarantor's obligation is secondary. Unlike a guarantor, who becomes subject to liability only if the borrower fails to fulfill its obligation to the borrower's creditor, an issuer of a letter of credit has a primary contractual obligation to the beneficiary, which is independent of the relationship between the beneficiary and its customer. Thus, "having paid its own debt, as it has contractually undertaken to do, the issuer 'cannot then step into the shoes of the creditor to seek subrogation, reimbursement or contribution from the [beneficiary's customer].'" Tudor Development Group, Inc. v. United States Fidelity & Guarantee Co., 968 F.2d 357 (3d Cir. 1992).

In 2000, in response to the widely-accepted conclusion that the common-law remedy of equitable subrogation does not apply to standby letters of credit, the New York Legislature amended the Uniform Commercial Code provision on Letters of Credit to provide for subrogation in certain circumstances. See N.Y.S.B.A. Committee Report on N.Y. U.C.C. § 5–117, McKinney's Uniform Commercial Code (2001). Section 5–117 provides that: "(a) An issuer that honors a beneficiary's presentation is subrogated to the rights of the beneficiary to the same extent as if the issuer were a secondary obligor of the underlying obligation owed to the beneficiary . . . . (d) . . . The rights of subrogation stated in subsection[ ] (a) . . . of this section do not arise until the issuer honors the letter of credit . . . ." N.Y. UCC § 5–117(a), (d).

The question presented on these motions is whether this statutory remedy permits JPM (as Issuing Bank and/or as Administrative Agent of the Facility) to subrogate to the rights of Private Bank (as Beneficiary), to pursue Cook for the defaulted $7.5 million. It is uncontested that the Issuer in this case is JPM and the Beneficiary is Private Bank. It is uncontested that JPM disbursed $7.5 million as a draw on a Letter of Credit which completely satisfied Cook's outstanding obligation to Private Bank. And the structure of the entire deal reveals that the Letter of Credit functioned like a guarantee of Cook's underlying obligation. In other words, the transactions contemplated that if Cook defaulted on the Promissory Note, then Private Bank would present the Letter of Credit and receive $7.5 million from JPM. Therefore, JPM acted like a secondary obligor (or guarantor) of the underlying obligation. The statutory remedy will thus permit JPM to subrogate *if* the other requirements of the subrogation remedy are met.

Cook argues that the requirements of subrogation are not met. First, he claims that JPM was made whole for the draw down because the Revolving Credit Facility reimbursed JPM for the disbursement. Thus, any further recovery from Cook would, according to defendant, constitute a double recovery for the Issuer and thereby violate a well-established principle of equity prohibiting double recovery. However, there is no danger that subrogation will unjustly award JPM a *double* recovery, because neither JPM nor anyone else ever received a *primary* recovery from Cook. Cook simply never paid back the loan principal to anyone, ever. If the issuer of a letter of credit has some way of covering its exposure to a draw that does not involve the underlying obligor, that is independent of the underlying obligor's obligation to pay back the loan. For instance, if an issuer borrowed money to cover its losses incurred as a result of a draw on a letter of credit, that would not mean what the issuer could not subrogate to the beneficiary's rights because the issuer had been made whole. Such an issuer would not have been made whole; it would simply owe money to different parties that would need to be repaid, and it would still be entitled to proceed against the obligor. Similarly, to the extent JPM's arrangements with other banks in the consortium required those banks to pay their pro rata shares of the money advanced to cover Cook's default, any money obtained by JPM from Cook in this lawsuit will be held in constructive trust for those banks to prevent unjust enrichment of JPM. But these are matters between JPM and the other banks; they do not affect *Cook's* obligation to repay the $7.5 million he borrowed. Thus, double recovery is not a barrier to JPM subrogating to Private Bank in its capacity as Issuer of the Letter of Credit.

In a second and related argument, Cook contends that JPM has no standing to sue as Administrative Agent of the Facility because the Lenders were not issuers. This argument ignores the economic realities of the transactions. As the documents reveal, JPM issued the Letter of Credit on behalf of all forty-four Lenders in the Facility. The Letter of Credit was supported by a collective line of credit extended to Global Crossing by the consortium of forty-four Lenders, each of whom had a pro rata participation in the Letter of Credit and thus shared in its issuance and the risk of non-reimbursement. While the funds disbursed immediately upon presentment came from JPM, the Letter of Credit, by its very terms, draws upon the Revolving Credit Facility, and *not* upon JPM alone. Thus, Cook's mantra that JPM is the sole issuer repeats a misleading formalism, because in reality JPM is the Issuer on behalf of all forty-four Lenders who each support a specific percentage of the $7.5 million Letter of Credit.

The Lenders who participated in the Facility chose JPM to act on their behalf. However, JPM did not thereby agree to assume the risk for the entire $7.5 million, because the Credit Agreement provides that immediately upon issuance of a letter of credit under the Facility, all Lenders participate in the letter of credit to their percentage share of the Facility. When the Letter of Credit was presented for payment, JPM made the entire $7.5 million disbursement, and then, when no reimbursement was forthcoming from Global Crossing, JPM called upon the other Lenders to accept their contractual burden to share the loss. In sum, the Letter of Credit was supported by the entire Facility, and the entire Facility is still missing $7.5 million. The allocation of that loss among the different Lenders within the Facility is irrelevant to Cook. That the Facility is still entitled to recover for the draw down regardless of the internal bookkeeping is clear from the language of Credit Agreement § 2.05(e), providing that in the event the Lenders make pro rata reimbursements to the Issuer when Global Crossing fails to reimburse the Facility for the draw down, such payments "shall not relieve [Global Crossing] of their obligation to reimburse such [Letter of Credit] Disbursement." To the extent JPM as Agent recovers funds from Global Crossing, or by extrapolation, from Cook, to cover the draw down, it is obligated to adhere to the Credit Agreement and whatever internal allocation the Lenders in the Facility have agreed to. Therefore, not only does JPM have standing as agent of the Facility to subrogate to Private Bank, but any recovery by JPM would be a primary recovery of the Facility's loss, and not a double recovery.

To find otherwise would penalize the Lenders for participating in a line of credit created by multiple participating banks. For example, had JPM issued a letter of credit drawing, not on a collective line of credit such as the Revolving Credit Facility, but solely on credit advanced by JPM, it is clear that after JPM honored a draw down on such letter of credit, JPM could be statutorily subrogated to the rights of the beneficiary. There is no reason why the conclusion should be different when the line of credit supporting the Letter of Credit is extended by multiple banks, rather than a single bank.

To disallow statutory subrogation here would take the § 5–117 remedy beyond the reach of collective lines of credit such as this Facility, and would discourage the creation of such loan participation agreements, which are regular features of commercial life. There is no indication that the New York Legislature intended any such commercially undesirable result. Global Crossing benefitted from the multiple lender Facility because it had access to a line of credit far larger than a single lender could provide. The Lenders received the benefit of diversifying the risk for any single draw on the Facility (as here, where all forty-four have shared in the loss of the $7.5 million draw). As a practical matter, in the context of a multiple-lender facility it is more efficient to call upon one bank to issue a letter of credit on behalf of all multiple lenders, rather than have, as would be necessary here if Cook's argument were accepted, forty-four transactions to issue the letter, then forty-four more transactions to present and honor the letter. To avoid such needless complexity, the Lenders in the Facility chose JPM to issue the letter of credit on behalf of all, and agreed to share the risk of non-repayment by covering the draw down once it became clear no reimbursement was forthcoming. The Facility can only act though its contractually-created agents, in contractually-mandated ways. There is no reason why JPM should not be permitted to act as agent for the Lenders in bringing this lawsuit. Accordingly, JPM has standing as Administrative Agent of the Facility to subrogate to Private Bank's right to pursue Cook for breach of the Promissory Note.

Cook's final argument against subrogation is that he did not profit from the $ 7.5 million Loan, and therefore it would not serve equity to subrogate plaintiff to Private Bank's rights of recovery on the Promissory Note. At oral argument, Cook attempted to bolster this contention by describing his participation int the Guaranteed Loan Program as motivated, not by economic self-interest, but rather by a "team player" spirit. Rather than liquidate his GX shares (at the time supposedly worth considerably more than $7.5 million) to the possible detriment of GX, Cook opted to weather the storm of share price decline by borrowing $7.5 million to offset the losses caused by the stock depreciation, in the hope that the share price would eventually recover and he could pay back the Loan from gains on the recovered stock price. Moreover, under the terms of the Collateral Agreement, Cook was unable to liquidate his GX stock as long as the Promissory Note was outstanding. Cook argues that he did all of this to benefit Global Crossing, and not for himself. As events transpired, this turned out to be an unprofitable gamble for Cook. The GX stock price never recovered, and he was left with GX stock worth considerably less than $7.5 million, and a debt to Private Bank in that amount.

However, this argument amounts to nothing more than that Cook assumed a risk, and made what turned out to be a series of ill-advised business decisions. Cook, a principal executive of Global Crossing, took actions he hoped would better the price of its stock, in which he held a major position, rather than to liquidate that stock to cover a margin call. Had GX stock increased in value, he would have profited by being able to repay the Loan, and preserve his investment. As it happened, the strategy failed. But, the Facility did not underwrite the risk of Cook's financial strategy, it merely guaranteed Private Bank that it would recover whatever portion of the $7.5 million Loan Cook might fail to repay on the maturity date.

CONCLUSION

For the foregoing reasons, defendant's motion to dismiss is denied, and plaintiff's motion for summary judgment is granted. Plaintiff is directed to submit a proposed Order of Judgment to the Court within ten days of the issuance of this Opinion.

NOTE

The most common case in which the subrogation issue is litigated concerns the applicability of Bankruptcy Code 509(a), which states: "Except as provided in subsection (b) or (c) of this section, an entity that is *liable with the debtor* on, or that has secured, a claim of a creditor against the debtor, and that pays such claim, is subrogated to the rights of such creditor to the extent of such payment" (emphasis added). In In re Slamans, 69 F.3d 468 (10th Cir.1995), the court held that the independence principle under which an issuer is not "liable with the debtor" precluded subrogating an issuer to the beneficiary's right to setoff against funds of the applicant that the beneficiary had collected on behalf of the applicant. Accord In re Hamada, 291 F.3d 645 (9th Cir.2002); but cf. In re Dow Corning Corp., 244 B.R. 705 (Bankr. E.D. Mich.1999). Although 5–117 was not yet law in the jurisdiction in question, the court was aware of it and said: "Although the revised Article Five provides an issuer with the remedy of subrogation, the UCC does not determine the availability of subrogation in a bankruptcy proceeding. Rather, 509 of the Bankruptcy Code governs an entity's eligibility for subrogation in a bankruptcy proceeding. Thus, the effect of the Rev. 5–117 on 509 subrogation is presently undecided, and suitable for resolution by a future court." In re Slamans, at 476 n.7.

Courts remain uncertain about whether BC 509 provides the exclusive source of subrogation in bankruptcy or whether equitable subrogation instead continues to be available. The issue is one of bankruptcy law and is unaffected by nonbankruptcy law such as 5–117(a). In concluding that the issuer lacked subrogation rights in bankruptcy, the *Hamada* court analyzed the issuer's rights under both BC 509 and state law of equitable subrogation. In re AGF Direct Gas Sales & Servicing, Inc., 47 UCC Rep. Serv.2d 445 (D. N.H.2002), offered the same analysis, adding in passing that it is not "apparent" that a ruling to the effect that BC 509 preempted state law of equitable subrogation would constitute legal error. Id. at 449. The court's analysis didn't rely on this observation.

NOTE: RESTITUTION AND BREACH OF WARRANTY

Issuers who have honored a draft drawn under a letter of credit but have been unable to obtain reimbursement from the applicant may attempt to get their money back from the beneficiary under doctrines of restitution or breach of warranty. The applicable common law of restitution may allow one who has paid out under mistake or who has honored a forged or fraudulent presentation to recover the payment. Former Article 5 was silent on the subject. Section 5–108(i)(4) provides that an issuer who has honored a presentation is "except as otherwise provided in Sections 5–110 and 5–117, is precluded from restitution of money paid or other value given by mistake to the extent the mistake concerns discrepancies in the documents or tender which are apparent on the face of the presentation. . . ." Section 5–110 states: "(a) If its presentation is honored, the beneficiary warrants: (1) to the issuer, any other person to whom presentation is made, and the applicant that there is no fraud or forgery of the kind described in § 5–109(a); and (2) to the applicant that the drawing does not violate any agreement between the applicant and beneficiary or any other agreement intended by them to be augmented by the letter of credit."

Under 5–110, after its presentation has been honored, the beneficiary makes two warranties. One warranty, created by 5–110(a)(1), is to the applicant, issuer and persons who received the presentation. The beneficiary warrants that there is no forgery or material fraud. As is made clear below, forgery involves a document presented whereas material fraud need not. Material fraud may involve fraud in the nondocumentary aspects of the underlying transaction. A party protected by 5–110(a)(1)'s warranty might prefer to recover under it even when the party can recover on some other basis, such as in tort. This is because forgery or documentary fraud typically presents fewer problems of proof than other bases of recovery.

A second warranty, created by 5–110(a)(2), runs only to the applicant. The beneficiary warrants that the drawing did not violate either an agreement between the applicant and beneficiary or any other agreement underlying the credit. Section 5–110(a)(2)'s warranty is more complicated than 5–110(a)(1)'s warranty, and leaves some uncertainty. It applies to any agreement that is part of the transaction underlying the letter of credit. Thus, even if the applicant isn't a party to the underlying agreement, the beneficiary breaches its 5–110(a)(2) warranty to the applicant if its draw "violates" the agreement. For instance, the warranty applies when an applicant has a credit issued at the request of a party to an underlying agreement other than the beneficiary. Usually, of course, the applicant has no need for 5–110(a)(2)'s warranty when it is a party to the agreement with the beneficiary. It can rely on warranties created by the underlying agreement. See Comment 2 to 5–110.

An uncertainty remains with respect to the "violations" referred to in 5–110(a)(2). Does a draw following any breach of the underlying agreement constitute a "violation" or must the breach rise to the level of seriousness on par with forgery or material fraud? Comment 2 (last sentence) to 5–110 suggests the former: the beneficiary warrants that it has performed all acts under the underlying agreement necessary for it to demand honor. If so, a beneficiary's draw upon presentation of documents indicating "due performance" of the underlying contract breaches the beneficiary's 5–110(a)(2) warranty to the applicant when the beneficiary has breached the underlying contract. Professor White agrees; 3 White & Summers § 26–7 (Prac. ed. 2008). The position has a lot going for it. After the issuer has honored a presentation and paid, none of the concerns about disturbing the credit's payment function apply. Finality of payment by the issuer isn't jeopardized by the beneficiary's warranty against "violations" because the warranty runs only to the applicant against the beneficiary. In any case, finality of payment isn't a first principle of letter of credit law. Its principle, if any, is "pay first, litigate later." Both of 5–110's warranties arise only if honor has occurred. Thus, there seems to be no good reason to restrict 5–110(a)(2)'s warranty to breaches ("violations") of the underlying agreement on the order of forgery or material fraud. For an argument reaching the opposite conclusion, see Richard F. Dole, Jr., Warranties by Beneficiaries of Letters of Credit Under Revised Article 5 of the UCC: The Truth and Nothing But the Truth, 39 Houston L. Rev. 375, 394–97 (2002).

The UCP contains no warranties. Professor White, the Reporter for Revised Article 5, notes that of the "hotly debated issues" in Article 5's drafting, 5–110(a)'s warranty provision was the only one that "went against" the UCP. See James J. White, The Influence of International Practice on the Revision of Article 5 of the UCC, 16 Nw. J. Int'l L. & Bus. 189, 207 (1995). This does not mean that the UCP conflicts with 5–110(a)'s warranties. It merely means that the ICC's representatives preferred that warranty provisions not apply to a credit also subject to the UCP. They were disappointed. Given 5–110(a), its warranties apply to credits subject to the UCP, unless Article 5 is otherwise inapplicable or the credit excludes 5–110(a)'s application.

PROBLEMS

In the Problems below assume the following facts: Applicant, a movie producer with limited assets, engaged Beneficiary to appear in a new film, entitled "Legal Nights." In order to induce Beneficiary to agree to perform, Applicant caused Bank to issue a standby letter of credit to her payable on presentation to Bank of the letter of credit, a draft drawn on Bank payable 15 days after the date of presentation, and an affidavit that Beneficiary had satisfactorily completed the film and had not been paid by Applicant. Upon presentation by Beneficiary, Bank honored the draft but was unable to obtain reimbursement from Applicant. Bank proceeded against Beneficiary invoking the remedies of restitution and breach of warranty. What result in the following two cases under Article 5? The issues in these Problems are discussed in 3 White & Summers, Uniform Commercial Code § 26–7 (warranties), § 26–8(c) (restitution).

1. The documents presented by Beneficiary included a draft drawn on Bank "at sight," meaning at the time of presentation. Bank did not notice that the draft did not comply with the documents specified by the letter of credit and paid the draft according to its terms. Had the draft complied with the terms of the credit, Bank might not have paid it at all because during the 15-day period Applicant filed in bankruptcy and Bank's right of reimbursement became virtually worthless.

2. The documents presented by Beneficiary complied with the requirements of the credit, including the affidavit of completion. After honoring the draft, Bank learned that Beneficiary had not completed the film and had breached her contract with Applicant.

5. DAMAGES FOR WRONGFUL DISHONOR

As emphasized above, it is fundamental that the letter of credit undertaking between an issuer and a beneficiary is independent of the underlying contract between the beneficiary and the applicant. 5–103(d). It follows that if the issuer wrongfully dishonors a draft presented under a letter of credit, the beneficiary can recover the full amount of the draw from the issuer, leaving the applicant to litigate with the beneficiary in a separate action over any amount the beneficiary has received in excess of its rights on the underlying contract. Under 5–111(a), the beneficiary or any other presenter can recover from the issuer the face amount of the draw under the credit if the issuer wrongfully dishonors the draw. The presenter also can recover incidental damages, but not consequential damages. Section 5–111(a) doesn't require the presenter to mitigate its damages in these circumstances. Because the issuer will have paid the presenter according to the credit's terms, as required by 5–111(a) (the dishonor was wrongful), the issuer's reimbursement agreement requires the applicant to reimburse it. The applicant, in turn, is left to recover from the beneficiary or other presenter in a separate action.

Section 5–111(b) governs the remedies of an applicant against the issuer. Under 5–111(b), the applicant can recover damages from the issuer who wrongfully dishonors a draft or other presentation under the credit. As under 5–111(a), incidental damages are recoverable but not consequential damages. Unlike 5–111(a)'s recovery, the applicant is required to mitigate its damages under 5–111(b). Article 5 does not provide a remedy in cases of improper honor by the issuer. Instead, recoverable damages are left to the courts. See Comment 2 to 5–111.

Section 5–111(e) requires courts to award reasonable attorney's fees and other litigation expenses to the prevailing party for any action in which a remedy is obtained under Article 5. The subsection overrules the "American rule" under which each party bears its own litigation costs. Section 5–111(e)'s mandatory award is not limited to remedies available under 5–111. The operative language of 5–111(e) is "under this Article." Thus, a party prevailing on a breach of warranty claim against a beneficiary under 5–110, for instance, must be awarded reasonable attorney's fees and other litigation expenses. Would an injunction issued to prevent a materially fraudulent draw, discussed below, be a "remedy. . .obtained under Article 5"? Unsurprisingly, both 5–111(e) and the exclusion of consequential damages have proven controversial. Connecticut and Louisiana have adopted nonuniform amendments to 5–111 allowing recovery of consequential damages, and several states have enacted nonuniform versions of 5–111(e). New Jersey and Texas, for instance, simply allow the award of attorney's fees and litigation expenses. New York's enactment of Article 5, significantly, omits 5–111(e) entirely. See 2B U.L.A. § 5–111 (2003). How would you apply 5–111 to the following Problems?

PROBLEMS

1.   Seller in New York agreed to sell goods to Buyer in Los Angeles by rail shipment with payment to be made pursuant to a commercial letter of credit. Buyer obtained issuance of a letter of credit by Issuer, Buyer's bank. The credit was payable to Seller on presentation to Issuer of a bill of lading, invoice, inspection and insurance certificates, sight draft drawn on Issuer, and the letter of credit. Issuer sent the letter of credit to Seller in New York (this is usually done through an "adviser" bank (5–102(a)(1)). Seller shipped the goods and obtained an order bill of lading from the carrier. Seller then assembled the required documents and sent them through banking channels to Issuer for payment. Buyer decided that it had made a bad bargain and urged Issuer to dishonor the credit. Buyer threatened that if Issuer honored the letter of credit, Buyer would take its business elsewhere. Issuer reluctantly dishonored. When the goods arrived in Los Angeles, Seller ordered the carrier to store them in a warehouse. Several months later, Seller sold the goods for only a fraction of their invoice price. Seller sued Issuer for wrongful dishonor and sought the face amount of the draft drawn pursuant to the letter of credit in damages. Issuer contended that Seller should have mitigated damages, and that the goods should have been sold for a much higher price; moreover, at the very least, Seller must offset the amount actually recovered from the resale against its claim on the letter of credit.

(a)   What result under 5–111(a)? See Comment 1 to 5–111.

(b)   What incentive does Issuer have not to dishonor wrongfully? Comment 6 to 5–111. The explanation of the phrase "expenses of litigation" in that comment should be enough to chill the blood of any banker.

(c)   When might Seller have an incentive to seek recovery under law other than Article 5? See 5–111(e).

2.   Applicant planned to develop a recreational community. County approval of Applicant's subdivision was conditional on Applicant's agreement to provide a standby letter of credit payable to the County as beneficiary to ensure that Applicant would complete roads and related improvements in accordance with subdivision design specifications. The required letter of credit was obtained from Issuer. Applicant never

commenced construction of the roads or other improvements. Issuer wrongfully dishonored the letter of credit upon presentation. The County sued Issuer for the face amount of the credit plus interest from the date of the demand for payment. Issuer defended on the ground that the County would receive a windfall since it had not expended or committed itself to expend any funds to complete the improvements. The facts are based on Colorado National Bank v. Board of County Commissioners, 634 P.2d 32 (Colo.1981). What result under 5–111(a)? 1 John F. Dolan, The Law of Letters of Credit ¶ 9.02[5][b][ii] and 3 White & Summers, Uniform Commercial Code § 26–13(b), discuss the existing law.

3. Sport manufactured running shoes for various retail chains. It made the shoes to the specifications of retailers who sold the shoes under their own brand names. Sport was thinly capitalized and the business was highly competitive. Sport had contracts for large deliveries to Retailer A on March 1, Retailer B on June 1, and Retailer C on September 1. Sport required A to obtain a standby letter of credit for the invoice price of the goods on which Sport could draw if A failed to pay for the goods within 15 days of delivery. When the shoes arrived, A contended that they were defective and ordered Issuer not to honor the letter of credit. Sport made timely presentation to Issuer of the required documents and Issuer wrongfully dishonored. Sport immediately implored Issuer to pay, explaining that without the proceeds of this large sale it would be unable to fulfill its obligations to B and C and would lose the profits that it anticipated making on these contracts. When Issuer continued to refuse payment, Sport sued Issuer for wrongful dishonor and claimed damages measured by the face amount of the credit plus the amount of lost profits on its contracts with B and C. What result under 5–111(a)? Do you believe that this is a desirable result? See Comment 4 to 5–111.

F. FORGERY AND FRAUD

Fraud is the single exception to the independence principle described in Section 3. above. It is recognized in decisional law and 5–109(a). Section 5–109(a) allows an issuer to dishonor an apparently complying documentary prestation if a required document would facilitate a material fraud by the beneficiary. Under 5–109(b), a court may enjoin the issuer from enjoin the issuer from honoring an apparently complying presentation or the beneficiary from making the presentation ("other persons") if the applicant claims that a required document is materially fraudulent. The injunction can be issued only if the court finds that the standards for injunctive relief described in 5–109(b)(1)–(4) are met. Issuers seldom raise 5–109(a)'s defense of fraud to refuse honor, probably because doing so harms their reputation as a reliable letter of credit processor. More frequent are instances in which an applicant, alleging a material fraud by the beneficiary, seeks to enjoin the issuer from honoring an apparently complying documentary presentation or the beneficiary from presenting them for honor.

In an influential pre-Code case, Sztejn v. J. Henry Schroder Banking Corp., 31 N.Y.S.2d 631 (N.Y. Sup. Ct.1941), the court made a concession to the reality that the independence principle, however important, must have limits. The facts of *Sztejn* are summarized as follows: In brief, the contract of sale between the applicant and beneficiary was for the beneficiary to ship bristles to the applicant. Payment was to be made by a letter of credit calling for presentation of a draft along with a bill of lading describing the goods as bristles. The beneficiary's agent presented these documents to the issuer. However, the applicant discovered that the beneficiary had actually shipped what the court described as worthless "rubbish" before the issuer honored the draft. It sought to enjoin the issuer from honoring the draft on the ground of fraud. On the pleadings, assuming the applicant was correct about the fraud, the court held for the applicant. Although the documents were in compliance on their face, they were fraudulent in that the beneficiary had shipped worthless rubbish rather than bristles. The issuer therefore did not have to honor the beneficiary's presentation.

This case seemed to undermine the independence principle in that it allowed the court to look outside the documents presented to determine whether the issuer must honor. Would this mean that honor could be enjoined if the applicant could make a showing that the goods shipped by the beneficiary were defective in a degree amounting to a breach of warranty of quality? Or if the applicant could show that it had been induced to enter into the underlying sale transaction by misrepresentations by the beneficiary about the goods? Former 5–114 attempted to codify and delimit *Sztejn*. It allowed the applicant to obtain an injunction against honor even though the documents appear on their face to be in compliance so long as a required document "is forged or fraudulent or there is fraud in the transaction." The breadth of the "fraud in the transaction" test seemed to place the independence principle in peril.

Intraworld Industries, Inc. v. Girard Trust Bank, 336 A.2d 316 (Penn.1975), is the leading case in interpreting former 5–114 in a manner that preserved the independence principle by limiting "fraud in the transaction" to cases in which the beneficiary had no bona fide claim to payment or that its claim had absolutely no basis in fact. It required that the beneficiary's alleged wrongdoings had so vitiated the transaction that the legitimate ends of the independence principle would no longer be served. Comment 1 to 5–109 incorporates the *Intraworld Industries* standard as the intended meaning of "material fraud."

In part to clarify the "fraud in the transaction" test, 5–109 to Revised Article 5 redrafts former 5–114. Section 5–109(a) adopts the standard of "material fraud." Comment 1 states: "Material fraud by the beneficiary occurs only when the beneficiary has no colorable right to expect honor and where there is no basis in fact to support such a right to honor." There are two conceptual problems inherent in the material fraud test:

describing behavior that constitutes fraud and identifying the transaction in which fraud occurs. Consider these problems in turn. Professor White concedes that the Drafting Committee for Revised Article 5 was unable to agree on a definition of fraud. See James J. White, The Influence of International Practice on the Revision of Article 5 of the UCC, 16 Nw. J. Int'l L. & Bus. 189, 192 n.11 (1995). However, without a working notion of fraud, 5–109(a)'s requirement that the fraud be material is imprecise. Adding an adjective does not make the fraud inquiry more manageable.

The *Sztejn* court distinguished between what it called "active fraud" and a "mere" breach of warranty without precisely characterizing the distinction. See *Sztejn*, 31 N.Y.S.2d at 634–635. To see the difficulty in making the distinction, consider a sales contract calling for Seller to deliver new widgets and a letter of credit requiring documents describing the goods delivered as "new widgets." Is there fraud in Seller's performance of the sales contract in the following four circumstances? (1) Seller intentionally delivers an automobile, not new widgets. (2) Seller intentionally delivers new widgets with very minor scratches. (3) The same as (2) except the market price for widgets has increased so that scratched widgets sell for more than new widgets were previously sold. (4) Seller intentionally delivers seriously malfunctioning new widgets. Seller has breached an express warranty in all four circumstances. Circumstance (4) arguably is an easy case: deliberately delivering seriously defective goods is egregious behavior characteristic of fraud. The extent of breach differs in the other three circumstances, and a standard is needed to find fraud nonarbitrarily in one or more of them. Article 5's drafters apparently decided not to provide one.

Consider next the transactions to which the material fraud standard applies. Section 5–109(a) abandons the "fraud in the transaction" formulation in former 5–114 that had led courts and scholars to differ on whether the transaction referred to was only the credit transaction or whether it extended to the underlying transaction as well. With the addition of "or honor of the presentation would facilitate a material fraud by the beneficiary on the issuer or applicant," 5–109(a) expressly applies to fraud in the underlying transaction. Section 5–109's fraud provision also is not limited to forgery or fraud by the beneficiary. By its terms, 5–109(a) applies when "a required document is forged or materially fraudulent." Thus, if 5–109(b)'s conditions for injunctive relief are satisfied, an applicant can enjoin an issuer from honoring a draw by the beneficiary even if the beneficiary has not perpetrated the forgery or fraud. Prevailing authority finds that Article 5's fraud exception continues to apply to credits governed by the UCP. See Mid-Am. Tire, Inc. v. PTZ Trading Ltd., 768 N.E.2d 619 (Ohio 2002).

In some cases, applicants have attempted to forestall payment under a letter of credit by seeking to enjoin the beneficiary from making a presentation to the issuer. An occasional opinion has applied a lesser standard for granting an injunction in such a case than in the usual case of an injunction against the issuer. 1 John F. Dolan, The Law of Letters of Credit ¶ 7.04[4][f]. Section 5–109(b) makes clear that the same standards must apply to limit injunctions in both cases by the addition of the language: "or grant similar relief against the issuer or other persons." Comment 5 to 5–109.

The following case discusses and applies the material fraud test in connection with a request for a preliminary injunction against honor. For an extensive discussion of fraud in the transaction, see 1 John F. Dolan, The Law of Letters of Credit ¶ 7.04.

Hook Point, LLC v. Branch Banking & Trust Co.

Supreme Court of South Carolina, 2012
725 S.E.2d 681

■ **Opinion by:** JUSTICE PLEICONES.

Respondent Hook Point, LLC (Hook Point) was granted a preliminary injunction preventing Appellant Branch Banking and Trust Company (BB&T) from drawing on, and defendant First Reliance Bank (First Reliance) from honoring, a $1.5 million letter of credit. BB&T appeals. We reverse.

FACTS

In late 2007, Hook Point sought a loan from BB&T for the purpose of developing a subdivision on property Hook Point owned on Lake Murray called Panama Pointe. BB&T issued a commitment letter to Hook Point in September 2007 indicating that it would loan the company $5.1 million and establish a $2 million line of credit to enable Hook Point to develop the subdivision. Security for the loan included a first mortgage on the Panama Pointe property, personal guarantees of Hook Point's four principals, and a $1.5 million standby letter of credit issued by First Reliance in favor of BB&T.

Hook Point applied to and obtained a letter of credit (LC) from First Reliance that named BB&T as beneficiary. The LC was secured by a cash deposit at First Reliance of approximately $310,000, several real properties owned by a Hook Point affiliate, and personal guarantees of the Hook Point principals. Under the terms of the LC, BB&T was permitted to make draws upon presentation of a draft accompanied by

> 1) The original letter of credit. 2) A notarized, sworn statement by the Beneficiary, or an officer thereof, that: a) The Borrower has failed to perform its obligations to the Beneficiary under the Loan Agreement and Promissory Note dated November 16, 2007, executed by and between [Hook Point and BB&T] b) The amount of the draft does not exceed the amount due to the Beneficiary under the obligations; and; [sic] c) The signer has

the authority to act for the Beneficiary with regard to the Letter of Credit.

The loan from BB&T to Hook Point was finalized in a loan agreement on the same day the LC was issued. Hook Point proceeded to complete infrastructure work in the development and began construction on the first home before determining that market conditions had become unfavorable to the project as originally contemplated. Hook Point defaulted on the Loan Agreement and related notes and loan documents by, among other things, failing to pay property taxes, to make interest payments due under the notes, or to pay the principal due under one note. BB&T gave Hook Point notice of default in September 2010 and accelerated the loans under the terms of the Loan Agreement on December 21, 2010. On the same day, BB&T tendered a demand letter to First Reliance, seeking to draw the full amount of the LC.

On December 23, Hook Point filed suit alleging several causes of action against BB&T, including for fraudulent misrepresentation by which BB&T induced Hook Point to enter the loan agreement. Hook Point admitted to being $70,000 in arrears on interest but argued that the terms of the agreement did not permit BB&T to draw the full amount of the LC if that exceeded the amount of interest due. It also sought an ex parte temporary restraining order preventing First Reliance from honoring a draft on the LC by BB&T, which the court granted. After a hearing, the court also granted a preliminary injunction against drafts on or honor of the LC beyond amounts of accrued interest, requiring extension of the LC for one year, and requiring Hook Point to post a $50,000 bond with the court. This appeal followed, and the case was transferred to this Court pursuant to Rule 204(b), SCACR.

ISSUE

Did the circuit court err when it granted a preliminary injunction?

STANDARD OF REVIEW

The grant of an injunction is reviewed for abuse of discretion. "An abuse of discretion occurs when the decision of the trial court is unsupported by the evidence or controlled by an error of law." *Peek v. Spartanburg Reg'l Healthcare Sys.*, 626 S.E.2d 34, 36 (S.C. Ct. App. 2005).

DISCUSSION

BB&T contends that the circuit court erred when it granted the preliminary injunction. We agree.

"A preliminary injunction should issue only if necessary to preserve the status quo ante, and only upon a showing by the moving party that without such relief it will suffer irreparable harm, that it has a likelihood of success on the merits, and that there is no adequate remedy at law." *Poynter Investments, Inc.*

v. Century Builders of Piedmont, Inc., 694 S.E.2d 15, 17 (S.C. 2010).

On the second element, likelihood of success on the merits, BB&T argues that the grounds for refusing to honor a letter of credit are exceedingly narrow and that Hook Point has failed to show it is likely to succeed on the merits under that standard. Thus, BB&T argues that the circuit court erred when it found that Hook Point had sufficiently established this element. We agree.

A letter of credit is a financial instrument designed to reduce the need for counterparties in a transaction to trust one another by adding an intermediary bank to the transaction. This intermediary bank extends credit to one party (typically the buyer in a sales transaction) so that the other need not do so. In a sales transaction, the letter of credit typically requires a seller to represent that he has shipped goods under a sales contract and to document this representation with a bill of lading in order to draw on the LC provided by the buyer. This arrangement entails risk to the buyer, who is vulnerable to loss should the seller present fraudulent documents or deliberately ship nonconforming goods. Nevertheless, the usefulness of a letter of credit depends on its being the virtual equivalent of cash. The judicial doctrine that has developed around letters of credit reflects courts' understanding of this background and the importance to commerce of respecting the terms of this financial instrument so that it remains available as a reliable means of shifting financial risk.

Specifically, this understanding is embodied in the independence principle, under which courts recognize that the obligations created in the letter of credit are independent of the obligations of the underlying contract. See, e.g., *Intraworld Industries, Inc. v. Girard Trust Bank*, 336 A.2d 316, 323 (Pa. 1975) ("The primary purpose of a letter of credit is to provide assurance to the seller of goods . . . of prompt payment upon presentation of documents. A seller who would otherwise have only the solvency and good faith of his buyer as assurance of payment may, with a letter of credit, rely on the full responsibility of a bank. Promptness is assured by the engagement of the bank to honor drafts upon the presentation of documents. The great utility of letters of credit flows from the independence of the issuer-bank's engagement from the underlying contract between beneficiary and customer. Long-standing case law has established that, unless otherwise agreed, the issuer deals only in documents. If the documents presented conform to the requirements of the credit, the issuer may and must honor demands for payment, regardless of whether the goods conform to the underlying contract between beneficiary and customer."); *Itek Corp. v. First Nat'l Bank of Boston*, 730 F.2d 19 (1st Cir. 1984) (Breyer, J.) "Parties to a contract may use a letter of credit in order to make certain that contractual disputes wend their way towards resolution with money in the beneficiary's pocket rather than in the pocket of the contracting party. Thus, courts typically have asserted that such letters of credit are 'independent' of the underlying contract. . . . And they have recognized that examining the rights and wrongs of a contract dispute to determine whether a letter of credit should be paid risks depriving its beneficiary of the very advantage for which he bargained, namely that the dispute would be resolved while he is in possession of the money." (citations omitted)).

Nevertheless, courts have carved out a very narrow exception to the independence principle. Aside from permitting the intermediary bank to refuse to honor forged documents presented in order to draw on the letter of credit, courts enjoin the payment of LCs for "fraud in the transaction" when "the beneficiary's conduct has so vitiated the entire transaction that the legitimate purposes of the independence of the issuer's obligation would no longer be served." *Itek*, 730 F.2d at 25 (internal quotation marks and citations omitted).

Put simply, the cases in which the "fraud in the transaction" exception has been applied are those in which the underlying transaction or the demand for payment is clearly a sham, and it is apparent that rigid adherence to the independence principle would facilitate what amounts to a scheme to defraud. In the case that established the fraud in the transaction exception, the beneficiary made an actual shipment so that the shipping documents were real, but substituted "rubbish" in place of salable bristles. *Sztejn v. J. Henry Schroder Banking Corp.*, 31 N.Y.S.2d 631 (Sup. Ct. 1941). In another leading case, the beneficiary was not permitted to collect on the LC because the fall of the Iranian government so altered conditions that the contract for military equipment could not be completed, and thus there was no possibility that the original purpose of the transaction of which the LC was a part could be accomplished. In addition, no other legal recourse was available to the applicant, and the applicant had cancelled the underlying contract in compliance with its force majeure provisions, which called for cancellation of the LC upon cancellation of the underlying contract. *Itek, supra.*

Several other cases also illustrate the narrowness of the fraud in the transaction exception. See *Intraworld Industries, Inc. v. Girard Trust Bank*, 336 A.2d 316 (Pa. 1975) ("We conclude that, if the documents presented by [the beneficiary of the LC] are genuine in the sense of having some basis in fact, an injunction must be refused. . . . [N]either the trial court nor this Court may attempt to determine [the beneficiary's] actual entitlement to payment under the lease."); see also *Roman Ceramics Corp. v. Peoples Nat. Bank*, 714 F.2d 1207, 1209 (3d Cir. 1983) (permitting issuing bank to dishonor LC when it knew underlying invoice had been paid and that contrary certification was false); *Dynamics Corp. of Am. v. Citizens & S. Nat. Bank*, 356 F.Supp. 991, 999 (D.C. Ga. 1973) (describing court's role as limited to ensuring that the defendant could not "run off with plaintiff's money on a *pro forma* declaration which has absolutely no basis in fact"); *Mid-America Tire, Inc. v. PTZ Trading Ltd.*, 768 N.E.2d 619, 641 (Ohio, 2002) (affirming injunction against honor of LC where defendants repeatedly lied to and misled plaintiffs about the tires available for sale in order to pressure them into making the LC available before they "could discover the truth").

The Uniform Commercial Code (UCC) incorporated this judicially developed doctrine into Article 5, the UCC formulation of the law governing letters of credit. Thus, South Carolina's adoption of the UCC incorporated into South Carolina law the same independence principle and narrow exception limiting the enjoinment of payment of LCs to instances of egregious fraud that operates to vitiate the entire transaction. In particular, UCC Article 5, S.C. Code §§ 36–5–101 through –119, governs letters of credit. S.C. Code Ann. § 36–5–109(b) (2003) sets forth the conditions under which a court may enjoin honor of a letter of credit as follows, in relevant part:

> If an applicant claims that a required document is forged or materially fraudulent or that honor of the presentation would facilitate a material fraud by the beneficiary on the issuer or applicant, a court of competent jurisdiction may temporarily or permanently enjoin the issuer from honoring a presentation or grant similar relief against the issuer or other persons only if the court finds that:
>
> . . .
>
> (3) all of the conditions to entitle a person to the relief under the law of this State have been met; and
>
> (4) on the basis of the information submitted to the court, the applicant is more likely than not to succeed under its claim of forgery or material fraud . . . .

For purposes of a preliminary injunction, subsection (3) effectively incorporates the requirements of the common law related to injunctions generally: that the movant show that irreparable harm will result and that no adequate remedy at law exists if the court refuses the injunction. Subsection (4) codifies not only the general common law requirement that the movant show a likelihood of success on the merits but also the special rule for letters of credit allowing only a narrow exception for fraud in the transaction, as discussed above. The Official Comment makes this codification explicit.

In the present case, Hook Point argues that BB&T is not entitled to draw on the LC because the commitment letter described the LC as "to be used as last resort for interest carry." Hook Point also seeks to construe as fraudulent BB&T's demand on the LC. The LC, however, by its terms requires only that BB&T represent that "[t]he Borrower has failed to perform its obligations . . . under the Loan Agreement and Promissory Note" and that "[t]he amount of the draft does not exceed the amount due to the Beneficiary under the obligation." Thus, contrary to Hook Point's arguments, the plain language of the LC permitted BB&T

to use it if Hook Point defaulted under any obligation of the loan agreement and note, including an acceleration clause. Furthermore, no term in the loan agreement or note to which the LC refers limits BB&T's use of the LC to interest due. Thus, it is incontrovertible that BB&T had some basis in fact for the representations it made when it drew on the LC.

If there is any validity to Hook Point's argument that the commitment letter limited the utilization of the LC exclusively to interest, that is an ordinary contract dispute that raises no implication of fraud by BB&T sufficient to trigger the narrow fraud exception. In fact, $500,000 had been reserved by BB&T from the original $5.1 million loan for the purpose of drawing down interest carry. A more plausible explanation for the "last resort" language in the commitment letter is that it was intended merely as an accommodation to the principals that BB&T would not seek to draw on the LC for interest until the reserve had been exhausted. That language, whatever it meant, is a red herring in this case as the draw on the LC was sought not only to recoup interest but as a result of multiple defaults that caused BB&T to invoke the acceleration of the entire debt.

Indeed, Hook Point's admission that BB&T was entitled to any draw on the LC for past due interest was conclusive as to the issue whether honor of the LC should be enjoined, since BB&T's entitlement to past due interest is alone some basis in fact on which BB&T could demand payment under the LC. Moreover, the strict standard required under § 36–5–109(b)(4) is that the alleged fraud vitiate the entire transaction, that is, it deprives Hook Point of any benefit from the transaction. In this case, there is no dispute that Hook Point received $5.1 million from BB&T. These facts hardly parallel the receipt of "rubbish" instead of bargained-for salable bristles. See *Sztejn v. J. Henry Schroder Banking Corp., supra*. Thus, there is no evidence Hook Point is more likely than not to succeed on a claim of material fraud so egregious as to vitiate the entire transaction as required under § 36–5–109(b)(4), and the circuit court failed to evaluate the evidence under the strict standard required for injunctions against the honor of LCs. Under the proper standard, it is clear that BB&T had a sufficient basis in fact upon which to demand payment under the LC. Thus, the circuit court's finding was based upon an error of law.

CONCLUSION

The standard under which a fraud in the transaction claim must be measured when deciding whether to enjoin honor of a letter of credit requires that the beneficiary have no colorable claim or basis in fact for asserting its rights under the letter of credit. In this case BB&T has, in our view, not only a colorable claim but an undeniable basis in fact for asserting its rights under the letter of credit. Therefore, the circuit court erred when it granted the preliminary injunction. **REVERSED.**

■ TOAL, C.J., BEATTY, HEARN, JJ., and ACTING JUSTICE JAMES E. MOORE, concur.

NOTES

1.   As *Hook Point* shows, an applicant seeking to enjoin honor by issuers has more than the tough *Intraworld* standard to contend with. The applicant also must show that it is more likely than not to succeed on the merits of the fraud or forgery issue (5–109(b)(4)), and it must also comply with the law of the jurisdiction on granting injunctions (5–109(b)(3)). Applied to 5–109(b)(4), the *Intraworld* standard requires the application to establish that it is more likely than not that the beneficiary's claim to payment has absolutely no basis in fact. Section 5–109(b)(3) normally requires a showing of irreparable harm. An equitable suit for an injunction is not appropriate if there is an adequate remedy at law. Since the remedy would usually be an action by the applicant against the beneficiary for a money judgment, an injunction would usually be inappropriate if the beneficiary were solvent and subject to service of process. See Archer Daniels Midland Corp. v. JP Morgan Chase Bank, N.A., 74 UCC Rep. Serv.2d 107 (S.D.N.Y.2011) (injunction granted on finding that Iraqi courts were inadequate fora in which the issuer could pursue its post-honor claims); Hendricks v. Bank of America, 408 F.3d 1127 (9th Cir.2004) (injunction granted where beneficiary is insolvent).

2.   As noted above, 5–109(a)(2) allows an issuer acting in good faith to honor a presentation made by an unprotected presenter, even when the presentation involves forgery or material fraud. "Good faith" is defined in 5–102(a)(7) as "honesty in fact." This is a subjective standard. Section 1–201(b)(20) contains the operative standard of good faith in the Articles of the UCC: " 'Good faith,' except as otherwise provided in Article 5, means honesty in fact and the observance of reasonable commercial standards of fair dealing." The generally applicable definition includes both subjective and objective elements. Why is the "commercially reasonable standards" language not included in the Article 5 definition of good faith? See Comment 3 to 5–102. Professor White reports that in Article 5's drafting, representatives of a banking industry trade group argued that "Europeans and other non-Americans were frightened by the threat of a runaway good faith doctrine, particularly by American courts' applying good faith in unforeseen cases." James J. White, The Influence of International Practice on the Revision of Article 5 of the UCC, 16 Nw. J. Int'l L. & Bus. 189, 205 (1995).

Comment 3 finds 5–102(a)(7)'s subjective standard of good faith appropriate because it creates greater certainty in the issuer's obligations. The finding goes against the usual assessment of the effects of subjective standards. Standards such as "honesty in fact" make potentially relevant large bodies of evidence, encourage prelitigation coaching of witnesses, and potentially extend the course of judicial proceedings going to the issue of good faith. Objective standards of good faith, by contrast, typically involve more limited evidence, less prelitigation jockeying, and more truncated proceedings. The usual assessment is that subjective standards produce indeterminacy and high costs in the application of otherwise clear rules. See, e.g., Richard A. Epstein, Simple Rules for a Complex World (1995); Robert D. Cooter & Edward L. Rubin, A Theory of Loss Allocation for Consumer Payments, 66 Tex. L. Rev. 63 (1987). Comment 3's different assessment depends on a confidence that the requisite showing of "honesty in fact" is so easy (and a showing of "dishonesty in fact" so hard) as to discourage investment in litigation of the issue.

   3.   Section 5–109(a) distinguishes between two classes of presenters: presenters whose conforming documentary presentations the issuer must honor even if there is fraud in the transaction and presenters whose conforming presentations the issuer in good faith is permitted to honor or dishonor when there is fraud. See 5–109(a)(1), (2). The former class of presenters are protected against dishonor: fraud does not allow the issuer to dishonor their conforming presentations. Under 5–109(b)(4), the issuer also cannot be enjoined from honoring the draw. Protected presenters are all transferees of documents under the letter of credit. See 5–109(a)(1)(i)–(iv). (Recognizing developments in letter of credit practice, 5–109(a)(1)(iv) protects an assignee under a deferred obligation credit, a relatively recent type of credit first issued in Southeast Asia.) For instance, a negotiating bank, holder of a draft, or good faith purchaser of documents can be protected purchasers. To be protected, the presenter must take the documents or draft in good faith and without notice of the fraud. See 5–109(a)(1). All other presenters are not protected, and the issuer, therefore, in good faith can dishonor conforming presentations by them. Because a beneficiary under the credit does not purchase the draft or documents, it is a not transferee and, therefore, not a protected presenter.

   Section 5–109(a)(2) deals with the rights of the issuer against unprotected presenters. It allows the issuer to honor ("may honor") presentations by them, even when the presentation involves forgery or material fraud, as long as the issuer does so in good faith. Is an issuer acting in good faith if it honors after the applicant has given it notice of the fraud or forgery? A common tactic used by applicants is to send a barrage of evidence to the issuer in advance of honor documenting the alleged fraud. The purpose is to present a risk to the issuer that a judge or jury ex post will find the issuer to have honored the draw in bad faith. Prudent practice sometimes leads issuers to resort to interpleader in these and other circumstances. See 1 John F. Dolan, The Law of Letters of Credit ¶ 7.04[4][g]; White & Summers, Uniform Commercial Code § 26–9, at 203 disapproves of the practice.

   Note how 5–109 allocates the risk of the beneficiary's fraud. In the case of a protected presenter, the applicant bears this risk. This is because the issuer honoring the draw is entitled to be reimbursed by the applicant either by contract or by statute, or both. 5–108(i)(1). The applicant therefore must recover from the beneficiary. Because the issuer can dishonor an unprotected presenter's conforming presentation, the presenter bears the risk of the beneficiary's fraud when dishonor occurs. It must recover from the beneficiary (or its transferor, who ultimately must recover from the beneficiary). Thus, the unprotected presenter bears the risk of the beneficiary's fraud. Article 5's implicit judgment is that protected presenters are in an inferior position to the applicant or issuer to detect the beneficiary's fraud.

Allocating fraud risk to either the applicant or unprotected presenters but never to protected presenters is thought to be the cost-minimizing solution. Is this judgment sound? In support, it is usually observed that the applicant has dealt with the beneficiary whereas a presenter may have purchased a draft or documents from a remote transferor and never have dealt directly with the applicant. See United Bank Ltd. v. Cambridge Sporting Goods Corp., 360 N.E.2d 943, 949 n. 6 (N.Y.1976). The applicant's costs in taking appropriate precautions, therefore, are thought generally to be lower than those facing the ultimate transferee's precaution costs. The observation has no force when the presenter purchases directly from the beneficiary. Consider also that often issuers or confirmers are local banks who know the beneficiary or can easily acquire information about it. Article 5's allocation of fraud risk is justifiable only if most documentary drafts are discounted in markets to strangers to the underlying contract. Neither the Comments to 5–109 nor its drafting history discuss this assumed empirical generalization.

PROBLEM

At Buyer's request, Bank One issued a letter of credit in Beneficiary's favor. At Beneficiary's-Seller's insistence, Buyer also asked Bank One to have a bank known to Beneficiary, Bank Two, confirm the credit, and Bank One did so. Bank Two accordingly notified Beneficiary of its confirmation. Later, Buyer learns that Beneficiary has intentionally breached the underlying sales contract by shipping nothing but will present documents to Bank Two for payment under Bank Two's credit. The documents will evidence shipment in accordance with the sales contract, as required under the credit. (a) At Buyer's urging, can Bank One obtain an injunction to prevent Bank Two from honoring Beneficiary's presentation? See 5–107(a), 5–109(b). (b) Can Buyer obtain an injunction against Bank Two in these circumstances? See 5–109(b); 5–107(a); Comment 1 to 5–107 (third paragraph); International Trade Relationship & Export v. Citibank, N.A., 41 UCC Rep. Serv.2d 626 (S.D.N.Y.2000).

G. TRANSFER, ASSIGNMENT AND SECURITY INTERESTS

1. TRANSFER AND ASSIGNMENT

There are two ways to transfer rights in a letter of credit: by "transferring" the credit and by assigning the proceeds of the credit. The two notions are different. To transfer a letter of credit is to convey the right to perform the conditions of the credit and demand honor to a third party. See Comment 1 to 5–115, 5–112(a). Letter of credit law calls this right the "right to draw" on the credit. Transferring the credit changes the party who is entitled to present documents to the issuer for honor. See also UCP 600 art. 38b. It is analogous to a novation. Section 5–114(a) defines "proceeds of a letter of credit" to mean cash, checks or other items of value paid by the issuer upon honor of the letter of credit. Thus, assignment of the proceeds merely changes the party entitled to receive them. Assignment doesn't change the party who must present the documents for honor. Letter of credit law treats transfer of the credit very differently from assignment of the credit's proceeds.

Transfer of the right to draw is a radical change in the original deal in which an applicant obtained an issuer's undertaking to pay a beneficiary, who is usually a party to whom the applicant is or will be indebted for performance. In the commercial letter of credit setting, the applicant is usually a buyer and the beneficiary a seller. Since after the transfer the issuer's undertaking is to pay another person who may perform the beneficiary's contract, how are the applicant's rights protected in transfer cases? A letter of credit can be transferred only if the credit provides that it is transferable. 5–112(a); see also UCP 600 art. 38a. Section 5–112(a) sets the default rule against transfer, reflecting the preferences of most applicants and issuers.

If the applicant doesn't want to give the beneficiary the right to transfer, it must be sure that the credit it procures from the issuer does not permit transfer. In this case, the issuing bank must dishonor any presentation of invoices of third persons; the applicant bargained for performance by its beneficiary and only its invoices will do. But if the credit is transferable on its face, Comment 2 to 5–112 states: "The issuance of a transferable letter of credit with the concurrence of the applicant is ipso facto an agreement by the issuer and applicant to permit a beneficiary to transfer its drawing right and permit a nominated person to recognize and carry out that transfer without further notice to them." Issuing banks may counter this by a requirement in the letter of credit that the beneficiary obtain the bank's permission before transfer so that the bank can anticipate who will make the presentation. 5–112(b)(2).

Transferable credits often are used by intermediate sellers to finance sales to their buyers. In the simplest form of such transactions, the intermediate seller has its buyer issue a transferable credit in the amount of the contract price naming the seller as the beneficiary. Typically, the credit requires the seller to present its invoice and draft. The seller, in turn. asks the issuer to transfer part of the credit to the supplier of the goods it is selling to its buyer. This is called a "partial transfer" of the credit because the issuer is being asked to allow the transferee to draw less than the full amount payable under the credit. The issuer notifies the supplier of the terms of the transfer, agreeing to pay the amount of the supplier's invoice and draft upon the supplier's presentation of conforming documents. If the documents comply with the notice of transfer, the issuer pays the supplier the face amount of the supplier's draft. It also pays over to the intermediate seller the difference between the amount it paid to the supplier and the amount of the credit—the seller's profit from the sale to its buyer. The issuer substitutes the intermediate seller's invoice, draft and other documents it has received from the seller for the supplier's documents. This is done in order to avoid disclosing to the buyer the supplier's identity and its lower invoice price. See UCP 600 art. 38i. The issuer then delivers the substituted documents to the buyer. Transferable credits usually involve more parties, such as advisers of the credit, who may themselves undertake to allow transfer.

Proceeds of the letter of credit are always assignable. The beneficiary may assign its rights to part or all of the proceeds, and it may do so after the credit is established but before presentation. Presumably, the beneficiary may also assign the proceeds even after presentation if the issuer wrongfully dishonors. In re XYZ Options, Inc., 154 F.3d 1276 (11th Cir.1998), so held, interpreting former Article 5. Comment 1 to 5–114 appears to support this sensible holding by its statement that assignments of proceeds are valid if made after the credit is established "but before the proceeds are realized." Section 5–114(a)'s default rule allowing assignment presumably reflects the preferences of most beneficiaries under credits.

Section 5–114(c) provides that an issuing bank can ignore an assignment of proceeds "until it consents to the assignment." The common practice is for the beneficiary to sign an assignment form giving the issuer notice of the assignment and instructing the issuer to pay the assignee directly upon presentation. The assignment form both provides evidence that the issuer has consented to the assignment and allows the issuer to keep track of assignments of the letter of credit proceeds so that it knows whom to pay in the event the beneficiary makes a complying documentary presentation. Noting that it is always advisable for assignees to obtain the consent of the issuer, the Comment 3 to 5–114 states: "By unconditionally consenting to such an assignment, the issuer or nominated person becomes bound . . .to pay the assignee the assigned letter of credit proceeds that the issuer or nominated person would otherwise pay to the beneficiary or another assignee."

Thus, does banking practice become law. Some amelioration is found in 5–114(d), which provides that though an issuer is not obliged to consent, "consent may not be unreasonably withheld if the assignee possesses and exhibits the letter of credit and presentation of the letter of credit is a condition to honor." The assignee's exhibition to the issuer of a letter of credit presumably gives the issuer sufficient evidence of the assignment to make unreasonable its refusal to consent. Presumably, the issuer may consent in advance to assignments by a provision in the letter of credit.

2. SECURITY INTERESTS

The most common reason a beneficiary assigns the proceeds of a letter of credit is to secure the beneficiary's obligation to a creditor.

Security interests in the proceeds of a credit fall within Article 9. Section 5–114(f) provides that "[t]he mode of creating and perfecting a security interest in or granting an assignment of a beneficiary's rights to proceeds is governed by Article 9 or other law." Article 9 governs only the right to proceeds of the credit; it does not control rights in the letter of credit itself. Article 9 calls the right to proceeds of the credit "a letter-of-credit right." Comment 5e to 9–102. Under 9–102(a)(51), a letter-of-credit right is "a right to payment or performance under a letter of credit. . . The term does not include the right of a beneficiary to demand payment or performance under a letter of credit." Thus, the term does not include the right to draw on the credit. The transfer of rights to draw is controlled by Article 5. 5–114(e).

Article 9 rules governing security interests apply to letter-of-credit rights as collateral. To obtain a property right in a letter-of-credit right, the creditor's security interest must attach to it. Attachment allows enforcement of the right against the debtor. It occurs when three conditions are satisfied. § 9–203(b)(3)(D). Two of the conditions are easily met in letter of credit contexts involving a loan or other value provided to the beneficiary: that the creditor give value to the debtor-beneficiary, and that the debtor-beneficiary have a right to the letter of credit proceeds. The third condition is disjunctive: the debtor must either authenticate a security agreement describing the letter-of-credit right or the secured creditor obtain "control" of the right pursuant to the debtor's security agreement or the secured creditor obtain a security interest in collateral for which the letter-of-credit right is a "supporting obligation." 9–203(f).

Thus, under the third condition, a security interest can attach to the letter-of-credit right in either of two different ways. Attachment occurs if the right is described in a security agreement signed by the debtor or the creditor obtains control of the letter-of-credit right pursuant to the debtor's security agreement. Alternatively, the security interest attaches to the letter-of-credit right if it attaches to collateral for which the letter-of-credit right is a "supporting obligation." The next section discusses the letter-of-credit right as a "supporting obligation." Section 9–409(a) treats as ineffective restrictions on the creation of security interests in letter of credit proceeds. This allows a security interest to attach when the restriction otherwise would prevent attachment. Comment 2 to 9–409.

Perfection of a security interest allows enforcement of a security interest against third parties. It requires attachment plus the secured creditor to take steps, usually acts of public notice, prescribed by Article 9. 9–308(a), 9–310. Under 9–312(b)(2), a security interest in a letter-of-credit right as original collateral may be perfected only by "control." Thus, control is a particularly effective (but sometimes costly) means of attachment because a security interest that attaches by control also is perfected. Control, according to 9–107, occurs when the issuer "has consented to an assignment of proceeds of the letter of credit under

Section 5–114(c)." Section 5–114(c), in turn, provides that an issuer need not recognize an assignment of credit proceeds until it consents to the assignment. Where the assignee possesses and exhibits the credit to the issuer, the issuer cannot withhold its consent unreasonably. Article 5 gives no further guidance on obtaining the issuer's consent, and Comment 2 to 9–107 states that the details of the consenting issuer's duty to pay the assignee are left to the parties' agreement.

Article 9's use of the concept of control is borrowed from Article 8. First used in Article 8 to govern the rights of purchasers and secured parties in investment property, Article 9 adapts and applies the concept to security interests in deposit accounts, electronic chattel paper, letter-of-credit rights, and investment property. It replaces the old system of requiring possession of the credit by the assignee in order to perfect a security interest in the credit proceeds. The requirement of possession was cumbersome, contrary to industry practice and, in the case of partial assignments of the credit, sometimes impossible to satisfy.

PROBLEM

Determine whether the secured parties have control over the described letter-of-credit proceeds.

1. Beneficiary assigned 1/3 of the credit proceeds to A1, its secured creditor, and delivered possession of the letter of credit to A1. Subsequently, Beneficiary assigned 1/3 of the letter-of-credit proceeds to each A2 and A3. Beneficiary notified the issuer of all three assignments.

2. On Foreign Buyer's application, Foreign Issuer issued a letter of credit payable to US Seller. Issuer sent the letter of credit to its US correspondent bank to serve as an advising and confirming bank, which delivered Issuer's letter of credit to Seller. Seller granted a security interest to SP Bank in the credit proceeds to secure a loan of $500,000, and a second security interest in the proceeds to US Distributor to secure an existing $250,000 obligation. Advising Bank's invariable practice when notified of assignments of letter-of-credit rights was to demand and retain possession of the credit and note on it the terms of the assignment. It followed the practice in this case. When Seller filed a bankruptcy petition, its trustee sought to avoid the security interests of SP Bank and Distributor in the proceeds of the letter of credit. Seller's trustee can avoid their security interests if the interests are unperfected.

Article 9 leaves unaddressed the rights and priority of a secured creditor when it becomes the transferee of a letter of credit. A transferee acquires all of the beneficiary's rights under the letter of credit, and, therefore, transferring the credit is a good way to secure the beneficiary's obligations. Section 9–109(c)(4) makes Article 9 inapplicable to the rights of a transferee beneficiary given priority under 5–114(e). And Section 5–114(e), in turn, gives the transferee priority over the assignee's right to credit proceeds as well as over claims of competing secured creditors in the proceeds. See Comment 3 to 9–329. Thus, Article 9 leaves undisturbed 5–114(e)'s grant of paramount rights in the letter of credit proceeds to the transferee beneficiary, even when the transferee is a secured creditor.

Article 9 therefore does not govern at least two situations: (1) the rights of a beneficiary-debtor against the transferee beneficiary-secured creditor; and (2) the priority of the transferee beneficiary-secured creditor against competing secured creditors. In situation (1), a distinction between an outright transfer and the grant of a security interest has to be made. In situation (2), a conflict between Article 9's priority rules and 5–114(e)'s priority rule is possible. Section 9–329's "control priority" rule gives priority to the security party first obtaining control of the letter-of-credit right. Section 5–114(e), however, gives priority to the transferee beneficiary over competing claimants to the letter of credit proceeds. Suppose Secured Creditor 1 obtains control over credit proceeds of a transferable letter of credit. Later, Secured Creditor 2 becomes a transferee beneficiary under the same letter. It never obtains control over the credit proceeds. Section 9–329(1) awards priority to Secured Creditor 1. Section 5–114(e) awards it to Secured Creditor 2. Comment 4 to 9–329 recognizes the two unaddressed situations and simply counsels courts to give "appropriate consideration to the policies and provisions of Article 5 and letter-of-credit practice as well as Article 9."

3. LETTERS OF CREDIT AS SUPPORTING OBLIGATIONS

Article 9 has special rules that apply to letter-of-credit rights when the letter of credit is a "supporting obligation" under 9–102(a)(78). This term "means a letter-of-credit right or secondary obligation that supports the payment or performance of an account, chattel paper, a document, a general intangible, an instrument, or investment property." Collateral described in (a)(78) is the "supported obligation," and the letter-of-credit right is the "supporting obligation." When a letter-of-credit right "supports" the sort of collateral described in 9–102(a)(78), it serves to enhance the value of the supported collateral. Given the frequent use of standby credits as credit enhancement devices, it is highly unlikely that in the great majority of cases letter-of-credit rights will be supporting obligations. If a sports franchise assures a basketball player that if its promissory note for the athlete's salary is not paid, the athlete can rely on a standby letter of credit, the letter of credit is a supporting obligation. The same is true when a dealer assigns its accounts to a financer and backs the accounts by a letter of credit. The examples are endless. Supporting obligations are discussed in Chapter 1.

Article 9's special rules for attachment, perfection and priority of a security interest in a letter-of-credit right treat the right as an incident of the collateral it supports. Comment 5f. to 9–102. Accordingly, the secured creditor's rights in the credit proceeds derive from its rights in the collateral supported by the credit proceeds. Thus, under 9–203(f), a security interest automatically attaches to the letter-of-credit right when it attaches to the supported collateral. So, for example, there is no need for a signed security agreement describing the supported obligation to describe or contain any reference to the letter-of-credit right supporting it. Under 9–308(d) perfection in the supported collateral is perfection in the letter-of-credit right. And under 9–322(c), with one significant exception, priority in the supported collateral is priority in the letter-of-credit right.

Article 9's control concept must be understood taking into account its special rules for supporting obligations. Two points are important. First, the role of control is significantly qualified for letter-of-credit rights when they are supporting obligations. If a letter-of-credit right is not a supporting obligation, 9–312(b)(2) provides that perfection may be achieved only by control. But the requirement doesn't apply to supporting obligations. In this case, perfection of the security interest in the supported collateral automatically perfects a security interest in the supported obligation. See 9–308(d). Some commercial and most standby transactions letter-of-credit rights are supporting obligations. Thus, in many cases, attachment and perfection in these rights is automatic. Control isn't necessary and will be a more expensive alternative.

Second, and by far more important, are Article 9's special priority rule for supporting obligations. Section 9–322(b)(2) describes Article 9's basic priority rule for supporting obligations. Under it the time for filing and perfection as to the supported obligation is also the time of filing and perfection as to the supported obligation. This priority rule treats priority in the supporting obligation as derivative: the priority of the supporting obligation is the priority of the supported collateral. However, 9–322(b)(2)'s basic rule is subject to an important exception contained in 9–322(c). Section 9–322(c)(1) provides in relevant part that the rule that a security interest in the supporting obligation takes the priority of a security interest in the supported collateral, subject to 9–329(1). Section 9–329(1), in turn, provides that if there are conflicting security interests in the same letter-of-credit right, the security interest of the secured party having control has priority over a security interest of a secured party that does not have control. Thus, to be sure of their priority, secured parties claiming security interests in letter-of-credit rights that are supporting obligations must obtain control. Control remains the central tenet of the law of secured transactions in letter-of-credit rights.

PROBLEM

On September 1 SP-1 acquired a security interest in Debtor's accounts, which are backed by Debtor's letter-of-credit rights in a letter of credit issued by Issuer. SP-1 perfected in Debtor's accounts the same day by filing a financing statement covering the accounts. On November 1 SP-2 perfected a security interest is Debtor's letter-of-credit rights by having Issuer consent to the assignment to SP-2 of the proceeds of the letter of credit. What are the relative priorities in the Debtor's letter-of-credit rights? See 9–107, 9–203(f), 9–329(1); cf. 9–322(a)(1). What result if the credit were transferable and Debtor transferred the credit to Finance on October 1? See 9–109(c)(4), 5–114(e).

H. LETTERS OF CREDIT IN BANKRUPTCY

If a standby letter of credit is to be useful as the functional equivalent of a guaranty, it must pass muster in bankruptcy. So far, it has. Discharge of the applicant in bankruptcy does not effect the liability of the issuer on a letter of credit. BC 524(e). The initial question is whether the automatic stay of BC 362(a) restrains the beneficiary from drawing on the issuer after the applicant's bankruptcy. If it does, the utility of letters of credit is greatly impaired because the beneficiary would be forced to go through the expensive and time-consuming procedure to lift the stay under BC 362(d). As described earlier in the Chapter, the usual letter of credit transaction involves three undertakings: the letter of credit between the issuer and the beneficiary; the underlying contract between the applicant and the beneficiary; and the reimbursement contract between the applicant and the issuer. There is no question that the automatic stay precludes any action by the beneficiary against the applicant on the underlying contract as well as any action by the issuer against the applicant on the reimbursement agreement.

That BC 362(a) does not stay the beneficiary's draw against the issuer was decided in In re Page, 18 B.R. 713 (D.D.C.1982), and has been widely accepted. Accord In re Williams, 2010 WL 2670801 (Bankr. N.D. Ala. June 10, 2010). The applicant in *Page* granted security interests in its assets to issuer to secure its obligation to reimburse the issuer if the issuer had to pay the letter of credit. Later, the applicant filed in bankruptcy and the beneficiary presented the letter of credit for honor. The bankruptcy court held that unless payment of the letter of credit were stayed, the issuer, after payment, would be able to realize on its security interest in debtor's property, thereby reducing the assets available to the other creditors. The district court reversed on the ground that before the applicant had filed in bankruptcy the issuer already had a perfected security interest in the applicant's assets to secure its contingent claim for reimbursement. In its payment of the letter of credit, the issuer merely liquidated its claim against the applicant for reimbursement, and applicant's other creditors are no worse off because the property of the applicant's bankruptcy estate has not been depleted. The letter of credit was not, of course, property of the applicant's estate. The court demonstrated its respect for the importance of the independence principle of letter of credit law: "Moreover, enjoining the payment of the letter of credit, even temporarily, would frustrate the commercial purposes of letters of credit to the detriment of financial institutions as well as their customers. . . . If payment on a letter of credit could be routinely delayed by the filing of a Chapter 11 petition, the intended substitution of a bank for its less credit-worthy customer would be defeated." 18 B.R. at 717.

The more difficult problems concerning letters of credit in bankruptcy have arisen in the area of voidable preference law. Sometimes clients come to believe that obtaining a letter of credit fully insulates them from the risks attending the bankruptcy of their obligors. But under preference law, this view may not be true in certain situations.

In the common case, there is no preference because the letter of credit is given for contemporaneous consideration. Usually, a letter of credit is issued at the inception of a credit sale transaction. To assure payment, the seller requires the buyer to obtain a letter of credit obliging the issuing bank to pay the sale price if the buyer doesn't pay when it becomes due. To induce the bank to issue the letter of credit, the buyer grants the bank a security interest in the buyer's property to secure the buyer's obligation to reimburse the bank if the bank is required to pay the seller. The letter of credit transaction is a substitute for a secured transaction between the seller and buyer. After the letter of credit is issued, the seller delivers the goods to the buyer. If the buyer doesn't pay and files in bankruptcy, the seller obtains payment from the bank. The bank has a secured claim in bankruptcy. There is no preference to either the seller or the bank in this kind of case. Although the security interest granted to the bank is a transfer of property by the buyer for the benefit of the seller, it is not a preference to the seller because the transfer is not on account of an antecedent debt. Rather, it is a contemporaneous exchange for new value by the seller. The seller obligates itself to make a credit sale of goods to the buyer in exchange for issuance of the letter of credit. There is no preference to the bank because the security interest does not secure an antecedent debt owed to the bank. The transfer of property to the bank is a contemporaneous exchange for new value by the bank, the bank's issuance of the letter of credit.

The result may be different if the letter of credit is given to the creditor for antecedent consideration. Suppose that Debtor, an insolvent company, owed Creditor $500,000, and Creditor was pressing Debtor for payment. When it became convinced that Debtor was unable to pay at that time, Creditor accepted a letter of credit issued by Bank for $500,000 payable to Creditor a year later if Debtor had not paid Creditor its debt by that time. To induce Bank to issue the letter of credit, Debtor granted Bank a security interest in its property to secure its obligation to reimburse Bank for any payment Bank has to make on the letter of credit to Creditor. Debtor failed to pay its obligation to Creditor within the one-year deadline, and Bank paid Creditor the amount owing on the letter of credit. Debtor filed in bankruptcy and its assets were liquidated. Bank received full payment from Debtor's estate on its secured claim. Debtor's trustee brought an action against Creditor to recover the amount paid to Bank on the secured claim on the ground that Creditor had received a voidable preference.

If Debtor had granted Creditor a security interest in its property rather than a letter of credit, there clearly would have been an avoidable preference: there would be a transfer of an interest in Debtor's property for the benefit of a creditor for the account of an antecedent debt made while Debtor was insolvent. The use by Debtor of a letter of credit does not change this result. The court in Matter of Compton Corp., 831 F.2d 586 (5th Cir.1987), held that there was a preferential transfer to Creditor even though Debtor transferred no property to Creditor. There is no requirement that the transfer of Debtor's property be to Creditor. A transfer of Debtor's property "to or for the benefit of" Creditor is sufficient under BC 547(b)(1). Since the transfer was made on account of the past-due debt to Creditor, 547(b)(2) is satisfied as well. Thus, there was a voidable preference to Creditor. However, there was no preference to the Bank because the transfer of the security interest to the Bank was a contemporaneous exchange for new value by Bank, the Bank's undertaking on the letter of credit.

FORM. LETTER OF CREDIT APPLICATION AND AGREEMENT

When an applicant requests a standby letter of credit, banks require completion of the following form which states the agreement between the applicant and issuing bank and the terms under which the bank must honor upon presentation of the letter of credit.

 CITY NATIONAL BANK

INTERNATIONAL OPERATIONS CENTER

606 South Olive Street, Suite 300   Date:_____

CABLE ADDRESS "CINABANK LSA"   Los Angeles, California 90014

TELEX 825717

IRREVOCABLE STANDBY LETTER OF CREDIT APPLICATION AND LETTER OF CREDIT AGREEMENT

TO: CITY NATIONAL BANK (CNB)

☐ Cable

We (Applicant) request you to establish by   ☐ Overnight courier service   an irrevocable standby
                                              ☐ Same day messenger service   Letter of Credit on

the following terms and conditions:

ADVISING BANK	APPLICANT
(name and address)	(name and address)
BENEFICIARY	**AMOUNT**
(name and address)	indicate currency—i.e., U.S. $— and specify amount in figures and words
EXCEPT SO FAR AS OTHERWISE EXPRESSLY STATED THIS CREDIT WILL BE SUBJECT TO INTERNATIONAL STANDBY PRACTICES 1998 (ISP98), INTERNATIONAL CHAMBER OF COMMERCE PUBLICATION AS IN FORCE AS OF THE DATE OF ISSUANCE OF THE LETTER OF CREDIT	Expiry Date At CNB's Issuing Office

available by Draft(s) at sight on CNB and accompanied by the following:

APPLICANT'S AGREEMENT TO PAY CNB

Applicant agrees immediately upon CNB's demand or if no demand is made then on_____, to repay to CNB the total amount of each disbursement by CNB under this Letter of Credit, together with interest thereon at the rate of____ percent per year in excess of the Prime Rate. The "Prime Rate" shall mean the floating loan rate of CNB announced from time to time as its "Prime Rate". Any change in the interest rate resulting from a change in the Prime Rate shall be effective on the effective date of change in the Prime Rate. Interest shall be calculated on a basis of a 360-day year and actual days elapsed. We further authorize you to charge, without further notice, our account, (or an account of any of us) for all such amounts when and as such are due and payable.

THE OPENING OF THIS CREDIT IS SUBJECT TO THE TERMS AND CONDITIONS AS SET FORTH IN THE LETTER OF CREDIT AGREEMENT APPEARING ON THE REVERSE HEREOF TO WHICH WE AGREE. WE FURTHER AGREE THAT THE CREDIT AS ISSUED SHALL INCLUDE SUCH REVISIONS OF THE LANGUAGE SET FORTH ABOVE AS YOU DEEM NECESSARY.

(APPLICANT)

FOR BANK USE ONLY:
APPROVAL OF CREDIT:
    Lending Officer
    Sr. Loan Officer (when applicable)
    Branch
ACCOUNT TO BE DEBITED:
( ) Branch G/L No. 11305000
( ) Customer Acct. No.

FIRM NAME
AUTHORIZED SIGNATURE
SOCIAL SECURITY/TAXPAYER I.D. NO.

LETTER OF CREDIT AGREEMENT

In consideration of your opening, at our request, a letter of Credit (herein called "the Credit"), the terms and conditions of which appear on the reverse side hereof we hereby agree as follows:

1. As to drafts under or purporting to be under the Credit, which are payable in lawful United States funds, we agree to pay you on demand at your issuing office in lawful United States funds, the amount of such draft(s) on the presentment to you thereof or, at your request in advance.

2. As to drafts under or purporting to be under the Credit, which are payable in foreign currency, we agree to pay you at your office on demand, the equivalent of each such draft in lawful United States funds at your then prevailing rate of exchange effective for sales of that other currency for cable transfer to the country of which it is the currency.

3. We also agree to pay to you any attorneys' fees incurred in the enforcement of this Letter of Credit Agreement, your service charge in accordance with your Schedule of Fees and Charges now existing or as hereafter adopted, and all other charges and expenses paid or incurred by you in connection therewith.

4. We agree to reimburse you for any losses and charges incurred by you or made against you in connection with this Agreement and related to the reevaluation or fluctuations in the exchange rate of any currency whether United States or any other.

5. We hereby convey and transfer to you a security interest in all goods, documents and instruments which shall come into your control or into your possession or that of any of your correspondents as the result of opening or in connection with any transactions under the Credit, which goods, documents and instruments are and shall be granted to you as security (a) for all payments made or to be made by you or your correspondents under the Credit; (b) for any interest, commission or other customary charges in relation to the Credit and (c) for any other obligations or liabilities (absolute or contingent) of us to you, which now exist or are hereafter created. Upon any default by us in any of the undertakings set forth in this Letter of Credit Agreement, you are authorized to sell, under the provisions of the Commercial Code of the State of California, any or all goods, documents and instruments; in the event of any deficiency, we will pay the same to you immediately or in the event of any surplus, you shall pay the same to us or to the persons entitled thereto. In the event such described property should suffer any decline in value we will upon demand, deliver to you additional collateral to your satisfaction.

6. We agree that your rights and duties under the Credit are, except as otherwise provided herein, governed by the International Standby Practices 1998 (ISP98), International Chamber of Commerce Publication as in force on the date of issuance of the Credit.

7. We agree that in the event of any amendments or modifications of the terms of the Credit, this Agreement shall be binding upon us with regard to the Credit so amended. You may (at your option) issue the requested Credit through a correspondent of your choice.

8. The users of the Letter of Credit shall be deemed our agents and we assume all risks of their acts of omissions. Neither you nor your correspondents shall be responsible for/or: the validity, sufficiency, or genuineness of documents, even if such documents should in fact prove to be in any or all respects invalid, insufficient, fraudulent or forged; the solvency or responsibility of any party issuing any documents; delay in arrival or failure to arrive of any documents; delay in giving or failure to give notice of arrival or any other notice; failure of any draft to bear adequate reference to the Credit; failure of documents to accompany any draft at negotiation, or failure of any person to note the amount of any draft on the reverse of the Credit, to surrender or take up the Credit or to send documents apart from drafts as required by the terms of the Credit, each of which provisions, if contained in the Credit itself, it is agreed may be waived by you; errors, or omissions, or interruptions or delays in transmission or delivery of any message by mail, cable, telegraph, wireless or otherwise; nor shall you be responsible for any error, neglect, or default of any of your correspondents; and none of the above shall affect, impair, or prevent the vesting of any of your rights or powers hereunder. In furtherance and extension and not in limitation of the specific provisions hereinbefore set forth, we agree that any action taken by you or any correspondent of you under or in connection with the Credit or relative drafts or documents, if taken in good faith, shall be binding on us and shall not put you or your correspondent under any resulting liability to us.

9. We agree at any time and from time to time, on demand, to deliver, convey, transfer, or assign to you, as security for any and all of our obligations and liabilities hereunder, and also for any and all other obligations and liabilities, absolute or contingent, due or to become due, which are or may at any time hereafter be owing to you, additional security of a value and character satisfactory to you, or to make such cash payment as you may require. We agree that all property belonging to us, or in which we may have an interest, conveyed, transferred, assigned, or paid to you, or coming into your possession or into the possession of anyone for you in any manner whatsoever, whether expressly as security, or for safekeeping or otherwise including any items received for collection or transmission and the proceeds thereof, whether or not such property is in whole or in part released to us on trust of bailee receipt, is security for each and all such obligations and liabilities. We agree that upon our failure at all times to keep a margin of security with you satisfactory to you, or upon the making by us of any assignments for the benefit of creditors, or upon the filing of any voluntary or involuntary petition in bankruptcy by or against us, or upon any application for the appointment of a receiver of any of our property, or upon any act of bankruptcy or state of insolvency of us, or if you in good faith deem yourself insecure at any time, or upon the death of any of us, all of such obligations and liabilities shall become and be immediately due and payable without demand or notice notwithstanding any credit or time allowed to us, or any instrument evidencing any such obligation or otherwise; and each of us, and all of us, as to property in which we may have any interest, expressly authorize you in any such event, or upon our failure to pay any of such obligations or liabilities when it or they shall become or be made due, to sell all such property, in accordance with the Commercial Code of the State of California and to apply the net proceeds of such sale or sales, together with any balance of deposits and any sum credited by or due from you to us, in general accounts or otherwise, to the payment of all of our obligations or liabilities to you however arising.

10. Your rights specified in this Agreement are in addition to any created by statute or rule of law. You are expressly given the right to execute and file and record endorsements, assignments, financing statements, and other instruments in the name of any of us with respect to documents, property and interests relative to the Credit or any property of any of us in which you have a security interest which may at any time come into your possession under the Credit or by virtue of this Agreement. We agree to pay all expenses, filing fees and other charges incurred by you relative to the perfection or enforcement of your rights and security interests hereunder.

11.   You shall not be deemed to have waived any of your rights hereunder, unless you or your authorized agent shall have signed such waiver, in writing. No such waiver unless expressly stated therein shall be effective as to any transaction which occurs subsequent to the date of such waiver, nor as to any continuance of a breach after such waiver.

12.   We understand that any credit issued pursuant to this Agreement is the direct obligation of you established in favor of our designated beneficiaries. Once established, such credit is irrevocable and is not subject to recall or stop payment, and any claim or demand by us to stop payment thereunder is void and of no effect.

13.   The word "property" as used in this Agreement includes goods, merchandise, securities, funds, choses in action, and any and all other forms of property, whether real, personal or mixed and any right or interest therein.

14.   This Agreement incorporates the provisions on the reverse hereof. Time is of the essence. Acceptance by you of partial or delinquent payments or your failure to exercise any right, power or remedy shall not waive any obligation of us or modify this Agreement. You, your successors and assigns have all rights, powers and remedies herein and as provided by law, and may exercise the same and effect any set-off and proceed against any security for the obligations of us at any time notwithstanding any cessation of our liability or running of any statute of limitations, which we hereby waive to the fullest extent permitted by law. Notice to you must be given at the office of City National Bank to which this Credit and Agreement is addressed.

15.   We hereby agree to pay all reasonable fees and costs incurred by you and arising out of any act or action you may take to enforce any provision of this Agreement or to enforce collection of any sums, payments or obligations owing from us to you.

16.   If this Agreement is signed by one individual the terms, "we", "our", "us", shall be read throughout as "I", "my", "me", as the case may be. If this Agreement is signed by two or more parties, it shall be the joint and several Agreement of such parties.

APPENDIX I

ACCOUNTS RECEIVABLE/LOAN AGREEMENT

This Accounts Receivable and Inventory Loan Agreement ("Agreement") is entered into as of October 30, 2013, by and between XYZ. Inc., a California corporation ("Borrower"), and City National Bank, a national banking association ("CNB").

1. **DEFINITIONS. As used in this Agreement, these terms have the following meanings:**

   1.1 "Account" or "Accounts" has the meaning given in the Code, and includes, but is not limited to, any right to payment for goods sold or leased or for services rendered which is not evidenced by an instrument or chattel paper from any Person, whether now existing or hereafter arising or acquired, whether or not it has been earned by performance.

   1.2 "Account Debtor" means the Person obligated on an Account.

   1.3 "Affiliate" means any Person directly or indirectly controlling, controlled by, or under common control with Borrower, and includes any employee stock ownership plan of Borrower or an Affiliate. "Control" (including with correlative meaning, the terms "controlling," "controlled by" and "under common control with"), as applied to any Person, means the possession, directly or indirectly, of the power to direct or cause the direction of the management and policies of that Person, whether through the ownership of voting securities, by contract or otherwise.

   1.4 "Audit Fee" is $500.00 per day for each field examination and audit of Borrower's operations, books and records and the Collateral.

   1.5 "Banker's Acceptance Commitment" is $1,000,000.00.

   1.6 "Borrower's Loan Account" means the statement of daily balances on the books of CNB in which will be recorded Revolving Credit Loans made by CNB to Borrower, payments made on such loans, and other appropriate debits and credits as provided by this Agreement. CNB will provide a statement of account for Borrower's Loan Account at least once each month on a date established by CNB, which statement will be accepted by and conclusively binding upon Borrower unless it notifies CNB in writing to the contrary, within five (5) days of receipt of such statement, or ten (10) days after sending of such statement if Borrower does not notify CNB of its non-receipt of the statement. Statements regarding other credit extended to Borrower will be provided separately.

1.7   "Borrowing Base" will be in an amount, determined by CNB, equal to the sum of:

    1.7.1   Eighty percent (80%) of the Eligible Accounts ("Accounts Borrowing Base"); and

    1.7.2   Twenty five percent (25%) of the Eligible Inventory ("Inventory Borrowing Base");

In no event will (a) the Inventory Borrowing Base exceed the lesser of (i) $2,000,000.00 or (ii) the Accounts Borrowing Base or (b) the Borrowing Base exceed the Revolving Credit Commitment.

1.8   "Borrowing Base Certificate" means the certificate, in form and satisfactory to CNB, executed by Borrower to evidence the Borrowing Base.

1.9   "Business Day" means a day that CNB's Head Office is open and conducts a substantial portion of its business.

1.10   "Cash Flow from Operations" will be determined on a consolidated basis for Borrower and the Subsidiaries and means the sum of (a) net income after taxes and before extraordinary items in accordance with GAAP, plus (b) amortization of intangible assets, plus (c) interest expense, plus (d) depreciation, each of such items computed on an annualized basis.

1.11   "Code" means the Uniform Commercial Code of California, as currently in effect and as amended and replaced from time to time, except where the Uniform Commercial Code of another state governs the perfection of a security interest in Collateral located in that state.

1.12   "Collateral" means all property securing the Obligations, as described in Section 8.

1.13   "Commercial Letters of Credit" means letters of credit issued pursuant to this Agreement and in response to Borrower's submission of an Irrevocable Letter of Credit Application and Security Agreement.

1.14   "Commitment" means CNB's commitment to make the Loans, issue Letters of Credit and create Banker's Acceptances in the aggregate principal amount outstanding at any one time of up to Twelve Million Dollars ($12,000,000.00).

1.15   "Current Assets" will be determined on a consolidated basis for Borrower and the Subsidiaries in accordance with GAAP excluding, however, loans to stockholders, management or employees, amounts due from Subsidiaries or Affiliates, deferred costs and other intangible assets.

1.16 "Current Liabilities" will be determined on a consolidated basis for Borrower and the Subsidiaries in accordance with GAAP and will include, without limitation: (a) all payments on Subordinated Debt required to be made within one (1) year after the date on which the determination is made, and (b) all indebtedness payable to stockholders, Affiliates, Subsidiaries or officers regardless of maturity, unless such indebtedness has been subordinated, on terms satisfactory to CNB, to the Obligations.

1.17 "Debt" means, at any date, the aggregate amount of, without duplication, (a) all obligations of Borrower or any Subsidiary for borrowed money, or reimbursement for open letters of credit and banker's acceptances, (b) all obligations of Borrower or any Subsidiary evidenced by bonds, debentures, notes or other similar instruments, (c) all obligations of Borrower or any Subsidiary to pay the deferred purchase price of property or services, (d) all capitalized lease obligations of Borrower or any Subsidiary, (e) all obligations or liabilities of others secured by a lien on any asset of Borrower or any Subsidiary, whether or not such obligation or liability is assumed, (f) all obligations guaranteed by Borrower or any Subsidiary, (g) all obligations, direct or indirect, for letters of credit, and (h) any other obligations or liabilities which are required by GAAP to be shown as liabilities on the balance sheet of Borrower or any Subsidiary.

1.18 "Debt Service" means (a) the aggregate amount of Current Maturity of Long-Term Debt plus (b) all interest incurred on borrowed money, computed on an annualized basis. "Current Maturity of Long-Term Debt" means that portion of Borrower's consolidated long-term liabilities, determined in accordance with GAAP, which will, by the terms thereof, become due and payable within one (1) year following the date of the balance sheet upon which such calculations are based.

1.19 "Demand Deposit Account" means Borrower's demand deposit account no. 001 895 037 maintained with CNB.

1.20 "Dilution" will be determined at the end of each month by CNB for the preceding three-month period by dividing total reductions, excluding cash collections of Accounts, by gross sales which gave rise to the Accounts for such three-month period.

1.21 "Documentation Fee" is $1,000.00.

1.22 "Eligible Account" means an Account of Borrower:

1.22.1 Upon which Borrower's right to receive payment is absolute and not contingent upon the fulfillment of any condition;

1.22.2 Against which is asserted no defense, counterclaim, discount or set-off, whether well-founded or otherwise;

1.22.3 That is a true and correct statement of a bona fide indebtedness incurred in the amount of the Account with respect to a money obligation owed by the Account Debtor, including but not limited to obligations arising, for goods sold or leased and delivered to, or for services rendered to and accepted by, the Account Debtor;

1.22.4 That is owned by Borrower free and clear of all liens, encumbrances, charges, interests and rights of others, except the security interests granted to CNB;

1.22.5 That does not arise from a sale or lease to or for services rendered to an employee, stockholder, director, Subsidiary or Affiliate of Borrower or any entity in which any employee, stockholder, director, Subsidiary or Affiliate of Borrower has any interest;

1.22.6 That is not the obligation of an Account Debtor that is the federal government unless perfected under the Federal Assignment of Claims Act of 1940, as amended;

1.22.7 That is not the obligation of an Account Debtor located in a foreign country, except Canada, unless the obligation is insured by foreign credit insurance satisfactory to CNB or through a letter of credit negotiated through CNB with drawing documents in order;

1.22.8 That is due and payable not more than thirty (30) days from the original invoice date unless otherwise agreed to in writing by CNB;

1.22.9 As to which not more than ninety (90) days has elapsed since the original invoice date;

1.22.10 As to which the Account Debtor has not:

(a) died, suspended business, made a general assignment for the benefit of creditors, become the subject of a petition under the Bankruptcy Code or consented to or applied for the appointment of a receiver, trustee, custodian or liquidator for itself or any of its property;

(b) become more than sixty (60) days past due, under the original terms of sale, with respect to 20% or more of the amounts owed by such Account Debtor to Borrower;

(c) had its check in payment of an Account returned unpaid; or

(d) become or appear to have become unable, in the opinion of CNB, to pay the Account in accord with its terms;

1.22.11 That does not, when added to all other Accounts that are obligations of the Account Debtor to Borrower, result in a total sum that exceeds twenty percent (20%) of the total balance then due on all Accounts; and

1.22.12 That is not an obligation owed by the Account Debtor which is evidenced by chattel paper or an instrument as those terms are defined in the Code.

1.23 "Eligible Inventory" means Inventory, excluding work-in-process, raw materials, packing materials and supplies which (a) is owned by Borrower free and clear of all liens, encumbrances and rights of others, except the security interests granted to CNB; (b) is permanently located in the United States of America and in the physical possession of Borrower; (c) if not in the physical possession of Borrower, is in transit and covered by negotiable documents of title or air bills which have been presented for a drawing under a Letter of Credit issued pursuant to this Agreement; (d) if not in the physical possession of Borrower or in transit, is referred to in an open and unexpired Letter of Credit which has been issued pursuant to this Agreement; and (e) is not, in CNB's opinion, obsolete, unsalable, damaged, unfit for further processing or otherwise unacceptable to CNB. Eligible Inventory will be valued, in the case of finished goods, at the lower of cost or market in accordance with GAAP and, in the case of raw materials, at the lower of Borrower's cost, market or CNB's independent determination of the resale value of raw materials in such quantities and on such terms as CNB deems appropriate.

1.24 "Equipment Acquisition Commitment" is $500,000.00.

1.25 "Eurocurrency Reserve Requirement" means the aggregate (without duplication) of the rates (expressed as a decimal) of reserves (including, without limitation, any basic, marginal, supplemental, or emergency reserves) that are required to be maintained by banks during the Interest Period under any regulations of the Board of Governors of the Federal Reserve System, or any other governmental authority having jurisdiction with respect thereto, applicable to funding based on so-called "Eurocurrency Liabilities", including Regulation D (12 CFR 224).

1.26 "Facility Fee" is $20,000.00.

1.27 "GAAP" means generally accepted accounting principles, consistently applied.

1.28 "Guarantors" are Joe XYZ and Mabel XYZ.

1.29 "Inventory" means goods held for sale or lease in the ordinary course of business, work in process and any and all raw materials used in connection with the foregoing.

1.30 "Interest Period" means the period commencing on the date the LIBOR Loan is made (including the date a Prime Loan is converted to a LIBOR Loan, or a LIBOR Loan is renewed as a LIBOR Loan, which, in the latter case, will be the last day of the expiring Interest Period) and ending on the last day of the month occurring prior to or on the date which is one (1), two (2), three (3), six (6), nine (9) or twelve (12)] months thereafter, as selected by the Borrower; provided, however, no Interest Period may extend beyond the Termination Date.

1.31 "Letters of Credit" means Commercial Letters of Credit and Standby Letters of Credit.

1.32 "Letters of Credit Commitment" is $2,500,000.00.

1.33 "LIBOR Base Rate" means the British Banker's Association definition of the London InterBank Offered Rates as made available by Bloomberg LP, or such other information service available to CNB, for the applicable monthly period upon which the Interest Period is based for the LIBOR Loan selected by Borrower and as quoted by CNB on the Business Day Borrower requests a LIBOR Loan or on the last Business Day of an expiring Interest Period.

1.34 "LIBOR Interest Rate" means the rate per year (rounded upward to the next one-sixteenth (1/16th) of one percent (0.0625%), if necessary) determined by CNB to be the quotient of (a) the LIBOR Base Rate divided by (b) one minus the Eurocurrency Reserve Requirement for the Interest Period; which is expressed by the following formula:

LIBOR Base Rate

1. Eurocurrency Reserve Requirement

1.35 "LIBOR Loan" means any Loan tied to the LIBOR Interest Rate.

1.36 "Loan" or "Loans" means the loans extended by CNB to Borrower pursuant to Section 2.

1.37 "Loan Documents" means, individually and collectively, this Agreement, any note, guaranty, security or pledge agreement, financing statement and all other contracts, instruments, addenda and documents executed in connection with or related to extensions of credit under this Agreement.

1.38 "Obligations" means all present and future liabilities and obligations of Borrower to CNB hereunder and all other liabilities and obligations of Borrower to CNB of every kind, now existing or hereafter owing, matured or unmatured, direct or indirect, absolute or contingent, joint or several, including any extensions and renewals thereof and substitutions therefor.

1.39 "Person" means any individual or entity.

1.40 "Potential Event of Default" means any condition that with the giving of notice or passage of time or both would, unless cured or waived, become an Event of Default.

1.41 "Prime Rate" means the rate most recently announced by CNB at its principal office in Beverly Hills, California as its "Prime Rate." Any change in the interest rate resulting from a change in the Prime Rate will become effective on the day on which each change in the Prime Rate is announced by CNB.

1.42 "Quick Assets" means the sum of cash, plus cash equivalents, plus Accounts, plus securities classified as short-term marketable securities according to GAAP, as such items appear on Borrower's consolidated balance sheet, determined in accordance with GAAP.

1.43 "Revolving Credit Commitment" means CNB's commitment to make the Revolving Credit Loans, issue Letters of Credit and create Banker's Acceptances in the aggregate principal amount at any one time of up to Ten Million Dollars ($10,000,000.00).

1.44 "Standby Letters of Credit" means standby letters of credit issued pursuant to this Agreement and in response to Borrower's submission of an Irrevocable Standby Letter of Credit Application and Letter of Credit Agreement.

1.45 "Subordinated Debt" means Debt of Borrower or any Subsidiary, the repayment of which is subordinated, on terms satisfactory to CNB, to the Obligations. The holders of Subordinated Debt, as of the date of this Agreement, are: Joe XYZ.

1.46 "Subsidiary" means any corporation, the majority of whose voting shares are at any time owned, directly or indirectly, by Borrower and/or by one or more Subsidiaries.

1.47 "Tangible Net Worth" means the total of all assets appearing on a balance sheet prepared in accordance with GAAP for Borrower and the Subsidiaries on a consolidated basis, minus (a) all intangible assets, including, without limitation, unamortized debt discount, Affiliate, employee, officer and stockholder receivables or advances, goodwill, research and development costs, patents, trademarks, the excess of purchase price over underlying values of acquired companies, any covenants not to compete, deferred charges, copyrights, franchises and appraisal surplus; minus (b) the amount, if any, at which shares of stock of a non-wholly owned Subsidiary appear on the asset side of Borrower's consolidated balance sheet, as determined in accordance with GAAP; minus (c) all obligations which are required by GAAP to be classified as a liability on the consolidated balance sheet of Borrower and the Subsidiaries; minus (d) minority interests; and minus (e) deferred income and reserves not otherwise classified as a liability on the consolidated balance sheet of Borrower and the Subsidiaries.

1.48   "Term Loan Commitment" is $1,500,000.00.

1.49   "Termination Date" means December 31, 2014, unless the term of this Agreement is renewed by CNB for an additional period under Section 3, or such earlier termination date under Section 9.3 upon the occurrence of an Event of Default. Upon any renewal, the Termination Date will be the renewed maturity date determined by CNB.

1.50   "Total Senior Liabilities" means, as of any date of determination, the amount of all liabilities that should be reflected as a liability on a consolidated balance sheet of Borrower and the Subsidiaries prepared in accordance with GAAP, less Subordinated Debt.

1.51   "Unused Facility Fee" will be equal to one quarter of one percent (1/4%) of the average daily difference between the Borrowing Base and the Revolving Credit Loans, Letters of Credit and Banker's Acceptances outstanding.

2.   THE CREDIT.

2.1   Revolving Credit Loan. Subject to the terms of this Agreement, CNB agrees to make loans ("Revolving Credit Loans") to Borrower, from the date of this Agreement up to but not including the Termination Date, at such times as Borrower may request, up to the amount of the Borrowing Base, less the amount of outstanding Letters of Credit and Banker's Acceptances. The Revolving Credit Loans may be repaid and reborrowed at any time up to the Termination Date; provided, however, that the aggregate unpaid principal amount of outstanding Revolving Credit Loans will at no time exceed the Borrowing Base less the amount of outstanding Letters of Credit and Banker's Acceptances.

2.1.1   Interest. The Revolving Credit Loans will bear interest from disbursement until due (whether at stated maturity, by acceleration on otherwise) at a rate equal to, at Borrower's option, either (a) for a LIBOR Revolving Loan, the LIBOR Interest Rate plus three percent (3%) per year, or (b) for a Prime Revolving Loan, the fluctuating Prime Rate plus one half of one percent (1/2%) per year. Interest on the Revolving Credit Loans and other charges incurred under this Agreement will accrue daily and be payable (a) monthly in arrears, on the last day of each month, commencing on the first such date following disbursement; (b) if a LIBOR Revolving Loan, upon any prepayment of any LIBOR Revolving Loan (to the extent accrued on the amount prepaid); and (c) at the Termination Date. A Revolving Credit Loan tied to the LIBOR Interest Rate is called a "LIBOR Revolving Loan," and a Revolving Credit Loan tied to the Prime Rate is called a "Prime Revolving Loan." A Revolving Credit Loan will be a Prime Revolving Loan any time it is not a LIBOR Revolving Loan.

2.1.2   Minimum Monthly Payments. Borrower will pay CNB a monthly fee from the date hereof until the next Termination Date, whether or not the Obligations have been repaid, equal to $1,000.00 less the amount of interest paid by Borrower for Revolving Credit Loans for such month.

2.1.3   Payment for Amounts Exceeding Borrowing Base. Borrower will, immediately upon demand, repay the amount by which the unpaid principal amount of Borrower's Loan Account exceeds the amount CNB has agreed to lend under Section 2.1. The portion of the Revolving Credit Loans exceeding the Borrowing Base will bear additional interest of three percent (3.0%) per year over the rate set forth in Section 2.1.1 for Prime Loans.

2.1.4   Application to Borrower's Loan Account. Borrower agrees that CNB may make a charge equal to two (2) days' collection time at the interest rate set forth in Section 2.1.1 for Prime Loans, payable monthly in arrears on the first day of each month for the previous month for all uncollected funds as to which immediate credit is given by application to Borrower's Loan Account.

2.2   Letter of Credit and Banker's Acceptance Facility. CNB will, at the request of Borrower any time up to the Termination Date, issue Letters of Credit and create Banker's Acceptances, in connection with drawings thereunder, for the account of Borrower. The aggregate face amount of outstanding Letters of Credit at any time will not exceed the lesser of (a) the Letter of Credit Commitment or (b) the Borrowing Base less outstanding Revolving Credit Loans and Banker's Acceptances. The aggregate face amount of outstanding Banker's Acceptances at any time will not exceed the lesser of (a) the Banker's Acceptance Commitment or (b) the Borrowing Base less Revolving Credit Loans and Letters of Credit outstanding.

2.2.1   Issuance of Letters of Credit. Commercial Letters of Credit will be issued to finance the import of merchandise in accordance with an Irrevocable Letter of Credit Application and Security Agreement submitted by Borrower and incorporated herein by this reference, subject to the terms of this Agreement in the event of any conflict herewith. Standby Letters of Credit will be issued in accordance with an Irrevocable Standby Letter of Credit Application and Letter of Credit Agreement submitted by Borrower and incorporated herein by this reference, subject to the terms of this Agreement in the event of any conflict herewith. Letters of Credit will be issued on the normal documentation used by CNB from time to time in accord with the Uniform Customs and Practices for Documentary Credits (1993 Revision) International Chamber of Commerce Publication No. 500, or the International Standby Practices 1998, whichever is applicable. Commercial Letters of Credit will expire no more than 90 days after issuance. Unless CNB otherwise agrees in writing, no Standby Letter of Credit may expire after the Termination Date. Standard CNB fees and charges will apply to the issuance of Letters of Credit.

2.2.2   Creation of Banker's Acceptances. Banker's Acceptances will be created in response to Borrower's request or the acceptance by CNB of a draft drawn against a Letter of Credit not payable at sight, on the normal documentation used by CNB, and will mature within 60 days. Creation of Banker's Acceptances will be subject to standard CNB fees and charges plus, if applicable, a payment equal to the CNB Banker's Acceptance Discount Rate plus two percent. There will be no obligation to accept drafts which would:

(a)   not be eligible for discount by a Federal Reserve Bank;

(b)   become a liability subject to reserve requirements under any regulation of the Board of Governors of the Federal Reserve System; or

     (c) cause CNB to violate any lending limit imposed upon CNB by any law, regulation or administrative order.

2.2.3 Reimbursement for Funding Letter of Credit. Any sight drawing under a Letter of Credit will be deemed to be an irrevocable request for a Revolving Credit Loan under this Agreement. Borrower's obligation to reimburse CNB may also be satisfied by charging Borrower's Demand Deposit Account if requested by Borrower. All drawings under Letters of Credit which are not payable at sight will be deemed to be requests for the creation of Banker's Acceptances hereunder. CNB's obligation under this Subsection to make a Revolving Credit Loan or create a Banker's Acceptance will exist irrespective of the existence of any Potential Event of Default or Event of Default.

2.2.4 Reimbursement for Payment of Banker's Acceptances. The creation of a Banker's Acceptance will be deemed to be an irrevocable request for a Revolving Credit Loan made at the maturity date of the Banker's Acceptance. Borrower's obligation to pay such accepted draft may, at Borrower's request, be satisfied by charging Borrower's Demand Deposit Account. CNB's obligation under this Subsection to make a Revolving Credit Loan will exist irrespective of the existence of any Potential Event of Default or Event of Default.

2.3 Term Loan Facility. CNB agrees to make a term loan ("Term Loan") to Borrower, on or before November 30, 2013, in the amount of the Term Loan Commitment. The Term Loan will be evidenced by a promissory note ("Term Note") consistent with the terms of this Agreement.

2.3.1 Interest on Term Loan. The Term Loan will bear interest on the unpaid principal amount thereof at a fluctuating annual rate equal to the Prime Rate of CNB plus one half of one percent (1/2%). Interest on the Term Loan will be payable monthly on the first day of each month, commencing on the first such date after the date hereof and on the date the Term Loan is paid in full.

2.3.2 Payment of Term Loan. The principal amount of the Term Loan will be repaid by Borrower to CNB in forty eight (48) equal consecutive monthly installments, payable on the first day of each month commencing on January 1, 2004. All unpaid principal and interest will be due and payable forty eight (48) months after the funding of the Term Loan, or on the Termination Date, whichever first occurs.

2.4   Equipment Acquisition Facility. Prior to June 30, 2014, and provided that no Event of Default or Potential Event of Default exists at the time of Borrower's request, CNB agrees to make loans ("Equipment Acquisition Loans") to Borrower up to the amount of the Equipment Acquisition Commitment, for the acquisition of new fixed assets consisting of machinery and equipment. Each Equipment Acquisition Loan will be made (a) in an amount equal to eighty percent (80%) of the invoice purchase price for such assets, excluding sales taxes, delivery and set-up charges, and (b) when Borrower submits an appropriate purchase invoice and executes and delivers to CNB its promissory note, in form and substance satisfactory to CNB (the "Equipment Acquisition Note"). The Equipment Acquisition Note will provide for interest payable monthly at a fluctuating annual rate equal to the Prime Rate plus one half of one percent (1/2%), and principal payable at the same time as interest in sixty (60) equal monthly payments. Borrower will submit such further documents as are required to perfect a first lien in the purchased assets in favor of CNB. All unpaid principal and interest will be due and payable sixty (60) months after the funding of the Equipment Acquisition Loan or on the Termination Date, whichever first occurs. The Equipment Acquisition Loans may be repaid and reborrowed at any time up to the Termination Date; provided, however, that the aggregate unpaid principal amount of outstanding Equipment Acquisition Loans will at no time exceed the Equipment Acquisition Commitment.

2.5   LIBOR Loan Terms and Conditions

2.5.1   Procedure for LIBOR Loans. Borrower may request that a Revolving Credit Loan be a LIBOR Loan (including conversion of a Prime Revolving Loan to a LIBOR Revolving Loan, or continuation of a LIBOR Revolving Loan as a LIBOR Revolving Loan upon the expiration of the Interest Period). Borrower's request will be irrevocable, will be made to CNB using the "Notice of Borrowing" form attached hereto as Exhibit "A," no earlier than two (2) Business Days before and no later than 1:00 p.m. Pacific Time on the day the LIBOR Loan is to be made. If Borrower fails to select a LIBOR Loan in accordance herewith, the Loan will be a Prime Loan, and any outstanding LIBOR Loan will be deemed a Prime Loan upon expiration of the Interest Period.

2.5.2   Availability of LIBOR Loans. Notwithstanding anything herein to the contrary, each LIBOR Loan must be in the minimum amount of $500,000.00 and increments of $100,000.00. Borrower may not have more than five (5) LIBOR Loans outstanding at any one time under this Agreement. Borrower may have Prime Loans and LIBOR Loans outstanding simultaneously.

2.5.3   Prepayment of Principal. Borrower may not make a partial principal prepayment on a LIBOR Loan. Borrower may prepay the full outstanding principal balance on a LIBOR Loan prior to the end of the Interest Period, provided, however, that such prepayment is accompanied by a fee ("LIBOR Prepayment Fee") equal to the amount, if any, by which (a) the additional interest which would have been earned by CNB had the LIBOR Loan not been prepaid exceeds (b) the interest which would have been recoverable by CNB by placing the amount of the LIBOR Loan on deposit in the LIBOR market for a period starting on the date on which it was prepaid and ending on the last day of the applicable Interest Period. CNB's calculation of the LIBOR Prepayment Fee will be deemed conclusive absent manifest error.

2.5.4   Suspension of LIBOR Loans. If CNB, on any Business Day, is unable to determine the LIBOR Base Rate applicable for a new, continued, or converted LIBOR Loan for any reason, or any law, regulation, or governmental order, rule or determination, makes it unlawful for CNB to make a LIBOR Loan, Borrower's right to select LIBOR Loans will be suspended until CNB is again able to determine the LIBOR Base Rate or make LIBOR Loans, as the case may be. During such suspension, new Loans, outstanding Prime Loans, and LIBOR Loans whose Interest Periods terminate may only be Prime Loans.

2.6   Optional Prepayments. Subject to the provisions of Section 2.5.3, Borrower will have the right to prepay any Term Loan or Equipment Acquisition Loan provided that (a) each partial payment will be in an amount equal to the amount of the normal monthly payment or an integral multiple thereof, (b) on each prepayment, Borrower will pay the accrued interest on the prepaid principal, to the date of such prepayment, and (c) all prepayments will be applied to principal installments in the inverse order of their maturities.

2.7 Default Interest Rate. From and after written notice by CNB to Borrower of the occurrence of an Event of Default (and without constituting a waiver of such Event of Default), the Loans and any other amounts due CNB hereunder (and interest to the extent permitted by law) will bear additional interest at a fluctuating rate equal to five percent (5.0%) per year higher than the interest rate as determined in Sections 2.1.1 and 2.1.3, until the Event of Default has been cured; provided, however, for purposes of this Section, a LIBOR Loan will be treated as a Prime Loan upon the termination of the Interest Period. All interest provided for in this Section will be compounded monthly and payable on demand.

2.8 Payments. All payments will be in United States Dollars and in immediately available funds. Interest will accrue daily and will be computed on the basis of a 360-day year, actual days elapsed. All payments of principal, interest, fees and other charges incurred under this Agreement will be made by charging, and Borrower hereby authorizes CNB to charge, Borrower's Demand Deposit Account or Borrower's Loan Account. All loan disbursements made pursuant to this Agreement shall be made by direct deposit to Borrower's Demand Deposit Account. Borrower also authorizes CNB to charge to Borrower's Demand Deposit Account or Borrower's Loan Account any payment credited against the Obligations which is dishonored by the drawee or maker thereof.

2.9 Audit Fee and Unused Facility Fee. Borrower will pay the Unused Facility Fee on the last day of each calendar quarter; such fee will be non-refundable and fully earned when paid. Further, Borrower will pay the Audit Fee annually. Borrower hereby authorizes CNB to charge Borrower's Demand Deposit Account or Borrower's Loan Account for the amount of each such fee.

3. TERM AND TERMINATION.

3.1 Establishment of Termination Date. The term of this Agreement will begin as of the date hereof and continue until the Termination Date, unless the term is renewed for an additional period by CNB giving Borrower prior written notice, in which event the Termination Date will mean the renewed maturity date set forth in such notice. Notwithstanding the foregoing, CNB may, at its option, terminate this Agreement pursuant to Section 9.3; the date of any such termination will become the Termination Date as that term is used in this Agreement. Upon renewal, Borrower authorizes CNB to charge Borrower's Loan Account with the amount of the Facility Fee and any applicable Audit Fee.

3.2   Obligations Upon the Termination Date. Borrower will, upon the Termination Date:

     3.2.1   Repay the amount of the balance due as set forth in Borrower's Loan Account plus any accrued interest, fees and charges; and

     3.2.2   Pay CNB cash in the aggregate face amount of the Letters of Credit outstanding to be held as cash collateral for Borrower's obligation to reimburse CNB upon the funding of such Letters of Credit; and

     3.2.3   Pay CNB cash in the aggregate face amount of the Banker's Acceptances outstanding to be held by CNB to make payment under the drafts which have been accepted; and

     3.2.4   Pay the amounts due on all other Obligations owing to CNB. In this connection and notwithstanding anything to the contrary contained in the instruments evidencing such Obligations, the Termination Date hereunder will constitute the maturity date of such other Obligations.

3.3   Survival of Rights. Any termination of this Agreement will not affect the rights, liabilities and obligations of the parties with respect to any Obligations outstanding on the date of such termination. Until all Obligations have been fully repaid, CNB will retain its security interest in all existing Collateral and Collateral arising thereafter, and Borrower will continue to assign all Accounts to CNB and to immediately turn over to CNB, in kind, all collections received on the Accounts.

4. CONDITIONS PRECEDENT.

4.1   Extension of Credit. The obligation of CNB to make any Loan or other extension of credit hereunder is subject to CNB's receipt of each of the following, in form and substance satisfactory to CNB, and duly executed as required by CNB:

     4.1.1   All Loan Documents required by CNB, including but not limited to this Agreement and any guaranties required hereunder;

     4.1.2   A subordination agreement ("Subordination Agreement") duly executed and delivered by Joe XYZ in the form customarily used by CNB;

     4.1.3   (a) a copy of Borrower's Articles of Incorporation; (b) a Resolution of Borrower's Board of Directors approving and authorizing the execution, delivery and performance of this Agreement and any other documents required pursuant to this Agreement, certified by Borrower's corporate secretary; and, (c) a copy of the last certificate filed on behalf of Borrower containing the information required by California Corporations Code Section 1502(a) or Section 2117(a), as applicable;

4.1.4   (a) copies (and acknowledgement copies to the extent reasonably available) of financing statements (Form UCC-1) duly filed under the Code in all such jurisdictions as may be necessary or, in CNB's opinion, desirable to perfect CNB's security interests created under this Agreement; and (b) evidence that all filings, recordings and other actions that are necessary or advisable, in CNB's opinion, to establish, preserve and perfect CNB's security interests and liens as legal, valid and enforceable first security interests and liens in the Collateral have been effected;

4.1.5   Evidence that the insurance required by Section 6.6 hereof is in effect;

4.1.6   A complete list of claims made against Borrower together with an opinion of Borrower's counsel with respect to such claims, that the representations contained in Section 5.5 are true and correct as of the date of this Agreement;

4.1.7   Borrower's detailed and comprehensive statement of projected cash flows ("Cash Flow Statement"), a projected balance sheet ("Balance Sheet") and a projected income statement ("Income Statement") (collectively, the "Budget") for the period from January 1, 2014, through December 31, 2014. The Budget will be prepared in accordance with FASB 95, will be realistic and conservative, will be based upon considered analysis and diligent investigation of Borrower, and will disclose all material liabilities or expenses which Borrower expects to incur during said period;

4.1.8   The Documentation Fee and the pro-rated portion of the first Facility Fee through the initial Termination Date equal to $12,000.00; and

4.1.9   An assignment issued by an insurance company acceptable to CNB, of a key-man life insurance policy upon the life of Joe XYZ with the cash surrender value and with death benefits in the minimum amount of Five Million Dollars ($5,000,000.00).

4.2   Conditions to Each Extension of Credit. The obligation of CNB to make any Loan or other extension of credit hereunder will be subject to the fulfillment of each of the following conditions to CNB's satisfaction:

4.2.1   The representations and warranties of Borrower set forth in Section 5 will be true and correct on the date of the making of each Loan or other extension of credit with the same effect as though such representations and warranties had been made on and as of such date;

4.2.2   No Guarantor will have revoked his, her or its guaranty and no such guaranty will have become otherwise unenforceable with respect to future advances;

4.2.3   No holder of Subordinated Debt will be in violation of his, her or its Subordination Agreement executed in favor of CNB, and such Subordination Agreement is enforceable with respect to future advances;

4.2.4   There will be in full force and effect in favor of CNB a legal, valid and enforceable first security interest in, and a valid and binding first lien on the Collateral; and CNB will have received evidence, in form and substance acceptable to CNB, that all filings, recordings and other actions that are necessary or advisable, in the opinion of CNB, in order to establish, protect, preserve and perfect CNB's security interests and liens as legal, valid and enforceable first security interests and liens in the Collateral have been effected;

4.2.5   There will have occurred no Event of Default or Potential Event of Default; and

4.2.6   All other documents and legal matters in connection with the transactions described in this Agreement will be satisfactory in form and substance to CNB.

5.   **REPRESENTATIONS AND WARRANTIES. Borrower makes the following representations and warranties, which will survive the making and repayment of the Loans and other extensions of credit:**

5.1   Corporate Existence, Power and Authorization. Borrower and each Subsidiary is duly organized, validly existing and in good standing under the laws of the state of its organization, and is duly qualified to conduct business in each jurisdiction in which its business is conducted. The execution, delivery and performance of all Loan Documents executed by Borrower are within Borrower's powers and have been duly authorized by the Board of Directors of Borrower and do not require any consent or approval of the stockholders of Borrower.

5.2   Binding Agreement. The Loan Documents constitute the valid and legally binding obligations of Borrower, enforceable against Borrower in accordance with their terms.

5.3   Ancillary Documents. To the extent that any security agreement, subordination agreement or guaranty is required to be executed by a Subsidiary or Affiliate, the representations and warranties set forth in Sections 5.1 and 5.2 are also true and correct with respect to such Subsidiary and Affiliate and such document.

5.4   Other Agreements. The execution and performance of the Loan Documents will not violate any provision of law or regulation (including, without limitation, Regulations X and U of the Federal Reserve Board) or any order of any governmental authority, court or arbitration board or the Articles of Incorporation or Bylaws of Borrower, or result in the breach of or a default under any provisions of any agreement to which Borrower is a party.

5.5   Litigation. There is no litigation, tax claim, investigation or proceeding pending, threatened against or affecting Borrower, any Subsidiary or Guarantor, or any of their respective properties which, if adversely determined, would have a material adverse effect on the business, operation or condition, financial or otherwise, of Borrower or any Subsidiary or Guarantor.

5.6   Financial Condition. The most recent financial statements of Borrower and each Guarantor, if any, copies of which have been delivered to CNB, have been prepared in accordance with GAAP and are true, complete and correct and fairly present the financial condition of Borrower, its Subsidiaries and each Guarantor, including operating results, as of the accounting period referenced therein. There has been no material adverse change in the financial condition or business of Borrower or any Subsidiary or Guarantor since the date of such financial statements. Neither Borrower nor any Subsidiary or Guarantor has any material liabilities for taxes or long-term leases or commitments, except as disclosed in the financial statements.

5.7   No Violations. Borrower is not, nor is any Subsidiary, in violation of any law, ordinance, rule or regulation to which it or any of its properties is subject.

5.8   Collateral. Borrower owns and has possession of and has the right and power to grant a security interest in the Collateral, and the Collateral is genuine and free from liens, adverse claims, set-offs, defaults, prepayments, defenses and encumbrances except those in favor of CNB. No bills of lading, warehouse receipts or other documents or instruments of title are outstanding with respect to the Collateral or any portion of the Collateral, in favor of a Person other than Borrower. The office where Borrower keeps its records concerning all Accounts and where it keeps the bulk of its Inventory is 606 South Olive St. Suite 4800, Los Angeles, CA and all of its other places of business are as follows: 9701 Wilshire Blvd., 20th Floor, Beverly Hills, CA.

5.9   ERISA. Borrower is in compliance in all material respects with all applicable provisions of the Employee Retirement Income Security Act of 1974 ("ERISA"). No "Reportable Event" (as defined in ERISA and the regulations issued thereunder [other than a "Reportable Event" not subject to the provision for thirty (30) day notice to the Pension Benefit Guaranty Corporation ("PBGC") under such regulations]) has occurred with respect to any benefit plan of Borrower nor are there any unfunded vested liabilities under any benefit plan of Borrower. Borrower has met its minimum funding requirements under ERISA with respect to each of its plans and has not incurred any material liability to the PBGC in connection with any such plan.

5.10   Consents. No consent, license, permit, or authorization of, exemption by, notice or report to, or registration, filing or declaration with, any governmental authority or agency is required in connection with the execution, delivery and performance by Borrower of this Agreement or the transactions contemplated hereby.

5.11   Use of Proceeds. The proceeds of the Revolving Credit Loans will be used by Borrower solely for working capital purposes in the normal course of business. The proceeds of the Term Loan will be used by Borrower solely for a trip to Tahiti.

5.12   Regulation U. Borrower is not engaged principally, or as one of its principal activities, in the business of extending credit for the purpose of purchasing or carrying margin stock (within the meaning of Regulations U or X of the Federal Reserve Board). No part of the proceeds of the Loans will be used by Borrower to purchase or carry any such margin stock or to extend credit to others for the purpose of purchasing or carrying such margin stock.

5.13   Environmental Matters.

     5.13.1 The operations of Borrower and each Subsidiary comply in all material respects with all applicable federal, state and local environmental, health and safety statutes, regulations and ordinances and fully comply with all terms of all required permits and licenses.

5.13.2 Borrower and each Subsidiary have received no notices of threatened or pending governmental or private civil, criminal or administrative proceeding regarding any environmental or health and safety statute, regulation or ordinance and have not been subject to any federal, state or local investigations, inspections or orders regarding any environmental or health and safety statute, regulation or ordinance.

5.13.3 Neither Borrower nor any Subsidiary knows of any facts or conditions which may exist which may subject Borrower or any Subsidiary to liability or contingent liability and neither Borrower nor any Subsidiary is presently liable or contingently liable for any removal, remedial, response or other costs or damages in connection with any release into the environment of toxic or hazardous substances or waste included on any federal, state or local hazardous chemical or substance lists under any federal, state or local statute, regulation or ordinance.

5.13.4 Borrower will, at all times, indemnify and hold CNB (which for purposes of this Section and Section 10.8 includes CNB's parent company and subsidiaries and all of their respective shareholders, directors, officers, employees, agents, representatives, successors, attorneys and assigns) harmless from and against any liabilities, claims, demands, causes of action, losses, damages, expenses (including without limitation reasonable attorneys' fees [which attorneys may be employees of CNB, or may be outside counsel]), costs, settlements, judgments or recoveries directly or indirectly arising out of or attributable to the use, generation, manufacture, production, storage, release, threatened release, discharge, disposal or presence of a hazardous substance on, under, or about Borrower's property or operations or property leased to or used by Borrower. For these purposes, the term "hazardous substances" means any substance which is or becomes designated as "hazardous" or "toxic" under any Federal, state, or local law. This indemnity will survive the Termination Date and the repayment of all Obligations of Borrower to CNB.

6. AFFIRMATIVE COVENANTS. Borrower agrees that until payment in full of all Obligations, Borrower will comply with the following covenants:

6.1 Collateral.

6.1.1 Borrower will, on demand of CNB, make available to CNB, shipping and delivery receipts evidencing the shipment of the goods which gave rise to an Account; completion certificates or other proof of the satisfactory performance of services which gave rise to an Account; a copy of the invoice for each Account; and Borrower's copy of any written contract or order from which an Account arose. Unless previously requested by Borrower in writing to return such documents, CNB will be authorized to destroy any such documentation six (6) months after its receipt by CNB;

6.1.2 Borrower will advise CNB within ten (10) days whenever an Account Debtor refuses to retain, or returns, any goods from the sale of which an Account arose, when the sale exceeds $10,000.00, and will comply with any instructions which CNB may give regarding the sale or other disposition of such returns;

6.1.3 Borrower will give CNB, upon request, specific assignments of Accounts after they come into existence, and schedules of Accounts, the form and content of such assignments and schedules to be satisfactory to CNB; but, despite this provision for express assignments to CNB, CNB will have a continuing security interest in all Accounts irrespective of whether some Accounts are omitted from such assignments or whether any assignments are ever given; and Borrower will execute and deliver to CNB any instrument, document, financing statement, assignment or other writing which CNB may deem necessary or desirable to carry out on the terms of this Agreement, to perfect CNB's security interest in the Accounts, and any other Collateral for the Obligations, or to enable CNB to enforce its security interest in any of the foregoing;

6.1.4 Borrower will maintain, in accord with sound accounting practices, accurate records and books of account showing, among other things, all Inventory and Accounts, the proceeds of the sale or other disposition thereof and the collections therefrom. Borrower will not change the accounting method used to determine Borrower's Inventory cost without CNB's prior written approval. Borrower will permit representative(s) of CNB, at any reasonable time, to inspect, audit, examine and make extracts or copies from all books, records and other data relating to the Collateral, to inspect any of Borrower's properties and to confirm balances due on Accounts by direct inquiry to Account Debtors, and will give CNB, promptly upon request, all information regarding the business or finances of Borrower;

6.1.5   Borrower will, if requested by CNB, mark its records concerning its Inventory and Accounts in a manner satisfactory to CNB to show CNB's security interest therein;

6.1.6   Borrower will, if requested by CNB, provide CNB with a current physical count of its Inventory in the manner specified by CNB;

6.1.7   Borrower will endorse to the order of and deliver to CNB any negotiable instrument accepted by Borrower in lieu of payment in accord with the original terms of sale;

6.1.8   Borrower will pay CNB, upon demand, the cost, including, but not limited to reasonable attorneys' fees and expenses (which counsel may be CNB employees) expended or incurred by CNB (or allocable to CNB's in-house counsel) in the collection or enforcement of any Accounts or other Collateral if CNB itself undertakes such collection or enforcement, together with all taxes, charges and expenses of every kind or description paid or incurred by CNB under or with respect to loans hereunder or any Collateral therefor and Borrower authorizes CNB to charge the same to any deposit account of Borrower or Borrower's Loan Account maintained with CNB;

6.1.9   Borrower will promptly notify CNB of any occurrence or discovery of any event which would cause or has caused a previously Eligible Account to become ineligible;

6.1.10   Borrower will maintain the tangible Collateral in good condition and promptly notify CNB of any event causing loss or reduction of value of Collateral and the amount of such loss or reduction; and

6.1.11   Borrower will, upon request by CNB, but in no event less than once every six (6) months, supply CNB with a current list of the names and addresses of all Account Debtors.

6.2   Financial Statements. Borrower will furnish to CNB on a continuing basis:

6.2.1   Within thirty (30) days after the end of each month, or sooner if available, a financial statement consisting of not less than a balance sheet, income statement, reconciliation of net worth and statement of cash flows, with notes thereto, prepared in accordance with GAAP, which financial statement may be internally prepared;

6.2.2   Within forty-five (45) days after the end of each quarterly accounting period of each fiscal year, a financial statement consisting of not less than a balance sheet, income statement, reconciliation of net worth and statement of cash flows, with notes thereto, prepared in accordance with GAAP and accompanied by the following: (a) supporting schedules of costs of goods sold, operating expenses and other income and expense items, and (b) Borrower's certification as to whether any event has occurred which constitutes an Event of Default or Potential Event of Default, and if so, stating the facts with respect thereto, which financial statement may be internally prepared;

6.2.3   Within ninety (90) days after the close of Borrower's fiscal year, a copy of the annual audit report for Borrower and the Subsidiaries, including therein a balance sheet, income statement, reconciliation of net worth and statement of cash flows, with notes thereto, the balance sheet, income statement and statement of cash flows to be audited by a certified public accountant acceptable to CNB, certified by such accountant to have been prepared in accordance with GAAP and accompanied by the following: (a) supporting schedules of costs of goods sold, operating expenses and other income and expense items, and (b) Borrower's certification as to whether any event has occurred which constitutes an Event of Default or Potential Event of Default, and if so, stating the facts with respect thereto;

6.2.4   Contemporaneously with each annual review report required by Section 6.2.3 above, a copy of the representation letter from Borrower to its independent certified public accountant, in form and substance satisfactory to CNB, confirming in writing the oral representations made by Borrower to the accountant during the review process;

6.2.5   As soon as available, any written report pertaining to material items involving Borrower's internal controls submitted to Borrower by Borrower's independent public accountants in connection with each annual or interim special audit of the financial condition of Borrower and the Subsidiaries made by such accountants;

6.2.6   As soon as available, a copy of the letter to Borrower from its independent public accountants, in form and substance satisfactory to CNB, setting forth the scope of such accountants' engagement;

6.2.7   A proforma Budget as described in Section 4.1.7 prior to the end of each of Borrower's fiscal years for the next fiscal year;

6.2.8   Upon request by CNB, a copy of the Federal Income Tax Return of Borrower; and

6.2.9   Within ten (10) days of filing, a copy of the Federal Income Tax Return of each Guarantor, if any.

6.3   Collateral Reports. Borrower will supply the following collateral reports, together with such additional information, reports and/or statements as CNB may reasonably request, within fifteen (15) days after the end of each month:

6.3.1   A listing and aging by invoice date of all accounts receivable and accounts payable (together with sales and payment terms, and detail of outstanding balances due by invoice date from all Account Debtors);

6.3.2   A reconciliation of such aging with the previous aging delivered to CNB and CNB account records;

6.3.3   A listing of all Inventory, setting out types, locations and dollar value, which dollar value is in conformity with GAAP, in form acceptable to CNB; and

6.3.4   A Borrowing Base Certificate.

6.4   Financial Statements of Guarantors. No later than ninety (90) days after Borrower's fiscal year end of each year, Borrower will provide CNB with the financial statement, in form and substance satisfactory to CNB, of each Guarantor certified by such Guarantor to be true and correct.

6.5   Taxes and Premiums. Borrower will, and will cause each Subsidiary to, pay and discharge all taxes, assessments, governmental charges, and real and personal taxes including, but not limited to, federal and state income taxes, employee withholding taxes and payroll taxes, and all premiums for insurance required hereunder, prior to the date upon which penalties are attached thereto. CNB may pay, for the account of Borrower, any of the foregoing which Borrower fails to pay; any such amounts will be debited to Borrower's Loan Account and will be paid by Borrower to CNB, with interest thereon at the rate stated in Section 2.1.1 (exclusive of LIBOR Loans), upon demand.

6.6 Insurance.

6.6.1 Borrower will, and will cause each Subsidiary to, (a) keep its Inventory, equipment and any other tangible personal property which is Collateral insured for the benefit of CNB under a standard mortgagee protection clause (to whom any loss will be payable) in such amounts, by such companies and against such risks as may be satisfactory to CNB; (b) pay the cost of all such insurance; and (c) deliver certificates evidencing such insurance to CNB (and copies of policies if requested); and Borrower hereby assigns to CNB all right to receive proceeds of such insurance, and agrees to direct any insurer to pay all proceeds directly to CNB, and authorizes CNB to endorse Borrower's name to any draft or check for such proceeds;

6.6.2 In addition to the insurance required above, Borrower will, and will cause each Subsidiary to, maintain insurance of the types and in amounts customarily carried in its lines of business, including, but not limited to, fire, public liability, property damage, business interruption and worker's compensation, such insurance to be carried with companies and in amounts satisfactory to CNB, and deliver to CNB, upon request, schedules setting forth all insurance then in effect; and

6.6.3 If Borrower fails to provide and maintain the policies of insurance required hereunder, CNB may, but is not obligated to, procure such insurance, and Borrower will pay all premiums thereon promptly upon demand by CNB, together with interest thereon at the rate set forth in Section 2.1.1 hereof (exclusive of LIBOR Loans) from the date of expenditure until reimbursement by Borrower; and

6.6.4 Within sixty (60) days of the date hereof, Borrower will cause all issuers of key-man life insurance policies, to acknowledge the assignment to CNB of such policies, and monies payable thereunder, and furnish evidence thereof to CNB.

6.7 Notice. Borrower will promptly advise CNB in writing of (a) the opening of any new, or the closing of any existing, places of business, each location at which Inventory or equipment is or will be kept, and any change of Borrower's name, trade name or other name under which it does business or of any such new or additional name; (b) the occurrence of any Event of Default or Potential Event of Default; (c) any litigation pending or threatened where the amount or amounts in controversy exceed $50,000.00; (d) any unpaid taxes which are more than fifteen (15) days delinquent; and (e) any other matter which might materially or adversely affect Borrower's or any Subsidiary's or Guarantor's financial condition, property or business.

6.8   Fair Labor Standards Act. Borrower will, and will cause each Subsidiary to, comply with the requirements of, and all regulations promulgated under, the Fair Labor Standards Act.

6.9   Corporate Existence. Borrower will, and will cause each Subsidiary to, maintain its corporate existence and all of its rights, privileges and franchises necessary or desirable in the normal course of its business.

6.10   Compliance with Law. Borrower will, and will cause each Subsidiary to, comply with all requirements of all applicable laws, rules, regulations (including, but not limited to, ERISA with respect to each of their benefit plans, and all environmental and hazardous materials laws), orders of any governmental agency and all material agreements to which they are a party.

6.11   Financial Tests. Borrower will maintain at all times:

6.11.1   Tangible Net Worth plus Subordinated Debt of not less than $5,000,000.00;

6.11.2   A ratio of Total Senior Liabilities to Tangible Net Worth plus Subordinated Debt of not more than 5.0 to 1;

6.11.3   A ratio of Cash Flow from Operations to Debt Service of not less than 2.0 to 1;

6.11.4   Current Assets less Current Liabilities of not less than $1,000,000.00;

6.11.5   A ratio of Current Assets to Current Liabilities of not less than 2.5 to 1; and

6.11.6   A ratio of Quick Assets to Current Liabilities of not less than 1.5 to 1.

6.12   Proforma Budget. Borrower will maintain the actual financial results measured on a cumulative basis, monthly, equal to no greater than 20% variation from the corresponding item of the proforma Budget (as defined in Section 4.1.7), unless otherwise agreed to by CNB.

7. **NEGATIVE COVENANTS. Borrower agrees that until payment in full of all the Obligations, Borrower will not, nor will it permit any Subsidiary to, do any of the following, without CNB's prior written consent:**

7.1 Borrowing. Create, incur, assume or permit to exist any Debt except (a) Debt to CNB, (b) Subordinated Debt, and (c) trade Debt in the ordinary course of Borrower's business and (d) purchase money debt in an aggregate amount not to exceed $200,000.00 per Borrower's fiscal year incurred in connection with the acquisition of capital assets (including capitalized lease expenditures).

7.2 Sale of Assets. Sell, lease or otherwise dispose of any of Borrower's or any Subsidiary's assets, other than merchandise Inventory in the ordinary course of business.

7.3 Loans. Make loans or advances to any Person, except credit extended to employees or to customers in the ordinary course of business.

7.4 Contingent Liabilities. Assume, guarantee, endorse, contingently agree to purchase or otherwise become liable for the obligation of any Person, including Borrower, a Subsidiary or Affiliate, except (a) by the endorsement of negotiable instruments for deposit or collection or similar transactions in the ordinary course of business, and (b) contingent liabilities in favor of CNB.

7.5 Investments. Purchase or acquire the obligations or stock of, or any other interest in, any partnership, joint venture, limited liability company or corporation, except (a) direct obligations of the United States of America; or (b) investments in certificates of deposit issued by, and other deposits with, commercial banks organized under the United States or a State thereof having capital of at least One Hundred Million Dollars ($100,000,000.00).

7.6 Mortgages, Liens, etc. Mortgage, pledge, hypothecate, grant or contract to grant any security interest of any kind in any property or assets, to anyone except CNB.

7.7 Involuntary Liens. Permit any involuntary liens to arise with respect to any property or assets including but not limited to those arising from the levy of a writ of attachment or execution, or the levy of any state or federal tax lien which lien will not be removed within a period of thirty (30) days.

7.8 Sale and Leaseback. Enter into any sale-leaseback transaction.

7.9 Mergers and Acquisitions. Enter into any merger or consolidation, or acquire all or substantially all the assets of any Person, except a Subsidiary may be merged into or consolidated with another Subsidiary or with Borrower.

7.10   Executive Compensation. (a) Make any loan or advance to any shareholder of Borrower or any Subsidiary; or (b) pay salary, wages, bonus or other remuneration directly or indirectly to the shareholders in the aggregate of more than 60% of Borrower's pre-tax and pre-compensation profits for any fiscal year. Provided, however, that any amounts paid to or as compensation which are reloaned to Borrower as Subordinate Debt will not be governed by this limitation. Provided, however, if Borrower for any tax year elects to file as a Sub-Chapter S corporation under the federal and state income tax laws, distributions may be made to Borrower's shareholders in proportion to their holdings, in an aggregate amount equal to that payable by an individual in the highest tax bracket upon Borrower's taxable income computed as if Borrower were a tax-paying entity.

7.11   Capital Expenditures. Make or commit to make expenditures for capital assets (including capitalized lease expenditures) amounting, in the aggregate for Borrower and all Subsidiaries in any fiscal year of Borrower, to more than $100,000.00.

7.12   Dividends and Purchase of Stock. Redeem or repurchase stock or partnership interests, declare or pay any dividends or make any distribution, whether of capital, income or otherwise, and whether in cash or other property, except that any Subsidiary may declare distributions to Borrower; provided, however, if Borrower for any tax year elects to file as a Sub-Chapter S corporation under the federal or state income tax laws, distributions may be made to Borrower's shareholders during any current or subsequent tax year in proportion to their holdings, in an aggregate amount equal to that payable by an individual in the highest tax bracket upon Borrower's taxable income computed as if Borrower were a taxpaying entity.

7.13   Obligations as Lessee. Enter into any arrangement as owner or lessee of real or personal property if the aggregate of all debt service secured by Borrower's real or personal property and rental payments, with respect to real or personal property leased by Borrower, will exceed $200,000.00 in each fiscal year.

7.14   Event of Default. Permit a default to occur under any document or instrument evidencing Debt incurred under any indenture, agreement or other instrument under which such Debt may be issued, or any event to occur under any of the foregoing which would permit any holder of the Debt outstanding thereunder to declare the same due and payable before its stated maturity, whether or not such acceleration occurs or such default be waived.

8.   SECURITY AGREEMENT.

8.1   Grant of Security Interest. To secure all Obligations hereunder as well as all other Obligations to CNB, Borrower hereby grants and transfers to CNB a continuing security interest in the following property whether now owned or hereafter acquired:

8.1.1   All of Borrower's Inventory;

8.1.2   All of Borrower's Accounts;

8.1.3   All of Borrower's general intangibles as that term is defined in the Code;

8.1.4   All of Borrower's equipment, as that term is defined in the Code;

8.1.5   All of Borrower's interest in any patents (now existing or pending), copyrights, trade names, trademarks and service marks useful to the operation of Borrower's business;

8.1.6   All notes, drafts, acceptances, instruments, documents of title, policies and certificates of insurance, chattel paper, guaranties and securities now or hereafter received by Borrower or in which Borrower has or acquires an interest;

8.1.7   All cash and noncash proceeds of the foregoing property, including, without limitation, proceeds of policies of fire, credit or other insurance;

8.1.8   All of Borrower's books and records pertaining to any of the Collateral described in this Section 8.1; and

8.1.9   Any other Collateral which CNB and Borrower may designate as additional security from time to time by separate instruments including but not limited to the key-man life insurance policies on the lives of Joe XYZ.

8.2   Notification of Account Debtors. CNB will have the right to notify any Account Debtor to make payments directly to CNB, take control of the cash and noncash proceeds of any Account, and settle any Account, which right CNB may exercise at any time whether or not an Event of Default has occurred or whether Borrower was theretofore making collections thereon. Until CNB elects to exercise such right, Borrower is authorized on behalf of CNB to collect and enforce the Accounts. Immediately upon CNB's request, Borrower will deliver to CNB for application in accord with this Agreement, all checks, drafts, cash and other remittances in payment or on account of payment of its Accounts on the banking day following the receipt thereof, and in precisely the form received, except for the endorsement of Borrower where necessary to permit collection of the items, which endorsement Borrower hereby agrees to make. Pending such delivery, Borrower will not commingle any such checks, cash, drafts and other remittances with any of its other funds or property, but will hold them separate and apart therefrom expressly in trust for CNB. All such remittances will be accompanied by such statements and reports of collections and adjustments as CNB may specify.

8.3   Attorney-In-Fact. CNB or any of its officers is hereby irrevocably made the true and lawful attorney for Borrower with full power of substitution to do the following: (a) endorse the name of Borrower upon any and all checks, drafts, money orders and other instruments for the payment of moneys which are payable to Borrower and constitute collections on Accounts; (b) execute in the name of Borrower any schedules, assignments, instruments, documents and statements which Borrower is obligated to give CNB hereunder; (c) receive, open and dispose of all mail addressed to Borrower; (d) notify the Post Office authorities to change the address for delivery of mail addressed to Borrower to such address as CNB will designate; and (e) do such other acts in the name of Borrower which CNB may deem necessary or desirable to enforce any Account or other Collateral. The powers granted CNB hereunder are solely to protect its interests in the Collateral and will not impose any duty upon CNB to exercise any such powers.

9. EVENTS OF DEFAULT AND PROCEEDINGS UPON DEFAULT.

9.1   Events of Default. After expiration of any applicable cure period set forth in Section 9.2, the following will constitute Events of Default under this Agreement:

9.1.1   Borrower fails to pay when due any installment of principal or interest or any other amount payable under this Agreement, including but not limited to amounts payable under Section 2.1.3;

9.1.2   Any Person, or any Subsidiary of any Person, which is a party to any Loan Document fails to perform or observe any of the terms, provisions, covenants, agreements or obligations;

9.1.3   Any financial statement, representation or warranty made or furnished by Borrower or any Subsidiary or

Guarantor in connection with the Loan Documents proves to be in any material respect incorrect;

9.1.4   The entry of an order for relief or the filing of an involuntary petition with respect to Borrower or any Subsidiary or Guarantor under the United States Bankruptcy Code; the appointment of a receiver, trustee, custodian or liquidator of or for any part of the assets or property of Borrower or any Subsidiary or Guarantor; or Borrower or any Subsidiary or Guarantor makes a general assignment for the benefit of creditors;

9.1.5   CNB's security interest in or lien on any portion of the Collateral becomes impaired or otherwise unenforceable;

9.1.6   Any Person obtains an order or decree in any court of competent jurisdiction enjoining or prohibiting Borrower or CNB from performing this Agreement, and such proceedings are not dismissed or such decree is not vacated within ten (10) days after the granting thereof;

9.1.7   Borrower or any Subsidiary neglects, fails or refuses to keep in full force and effect any governmental permit, license or approval which is necessary to the operation of its business;

9.1.8   All or substantially all of the property of Borrower or any Guarantor or Subsidiary is condemned, seized or otherwise appropriated;

9.1.9   The occurrence of (a) a Reportable Event (as defined in ERISA) which CNB determines in good faith constitutes grounds for the institution of proceedings to terminate any pension plan by the PBGC, (b) an appointment of a trustee to administer any pension plan of Borrower, or (c) any other event or condition which might constitute grounds under ERISA for the involuntary termination of any pension plan of Borrower, where such event set forth in (a), (b) or (c) results in a significant monetary liability to Borrower;

9.1.10   Dilution exceeds five percent (5%); or

9.1.11   Joe XYZ and Mabel XYZ no longer control at least eighty percent (%) of the stock of Borrower; or

9.1.12   Any obligee of Subordinated Debt fails to comply with the provisions of the documents evidencing such Subordinated Debt or any Subordination Agreement; or

9.1.13 Any Guarantor dies, becomes incapacitated, or revokes his or its Guaranty, or such Guaranty becomes otherwise unenforceable with respect to future advances; or

9.1.14 The Termination Date is not extended.

9.2 Notice of Default and Cure of Potential Events of Default. Except with respect to the Events of Default specified in Sections 9.1.1, 9.1.4, or 9.1.5 above, and subject to the provisions of Section 9.4, CNB will give Borrower at least ten (10) days' written notice of any event which constitutes, or with the lapse of time would become, an Event of Default, during which time Borrower will be entitled to cure same.

9.3 CNB's Remedies. Upon the occurrence of an Event of Default, at the sole and exclusive option of CNB, and upon written notice to Borrower, CNB may (a) declare the principal of and accrued interest on the Loans immediately due and payable in full, whereupon the same will immediately become due and payable; (b) terminate this Agreement as to any future liability or obligation of CNB, but without affecting CNB's rights and security interest in the Collateral and without affecting the Obligations owing by Borrower to CNB; and/or (c) exercise its rights and remedies under the Loan Documents and all rights and remedies of a secured party under the Code and other applicable laws with respect to the Collateral.

9.4 Additional Remedies. Notwithstanding any other provision of this Agreement, upon the occurrence of any event, action or inaction by Borrower, or if any action or inaction is threatened which CNB reasonably believes will materially affect the value of the Collateral, CNB may take such legal actions as it deems necessary to protect the Collateral, including, but not limited to, seeking injunctive relief and the appointment of a receiver, whether an Event of Default or Potential Event of Default has occurred under this Agreement.

10. MISCELLANEOUS.

10.1 Reimbursement of Costs and Expenses. Borrower will reimburse CNB for all costs and expenses relating to this Agreement including, but not limited to, filing, recording or search fees, audit or verification fees, appraisals of the Collateral and other out-of-pocket expenses, and reasonable attorneys' fees and expenses expended or incurred by CNB (or allocable to CNB's in-house counsel) in documenting or administering the Loan Documents or collecting any sum which becomes due CNB under the Loan Documents, irrespective of whether suit is filed, or in the protection, perfection, preservation or enforcement of any and all rights of

CNB in connection with the Loan Documents, including, without limitation, the fees and costs incurred in any out-of-court workout or a bankruptcy or reorganization proceeding.

10.2 Dispute Resolution.

    10.2.1 Mandatory Arbitration. At the request of CNB or Borrower, any dispute, claim or controversy of any kind (whether in contract or tort, statutory or common law, legal or equitable) now existing or hereafter arising between CNB and Borrower and in any way arising out of, pertaining to or in connection with: (1) this Agreement, and/or any renewals, extensions, or amendments thereto; (2) any of the Loan Documents; (3) any violation of this Agreement or the Loan Documents; (4) all past, present and future loans; (5) any incidents, omissions, acts, practices or occurrences arising out of or related to this Agreement or the Loan Documents causing injury to either party whereby the other party or its agents, employees or representatives may be liable, in whole or in part, or (6) any aspect of the present or future relationships of the parties, will be resolved through final and binding arbitration conducted at a location determined by the arbitrator in Los Angeles County, California, and administered by the American Arbitration Association ("AAA") in accordance with the California Arbitration Act (Title 9, California Code of Civil Procedure Section 1280 et. seq.) and the then existing Commercial Rules of the AAA. Judgment upon any award rendered by the arbitrator(s) may be entered in any state or federal court having jurisdiction thereof.

    10.2.2 Real Property Collateral. Notwithstanding the provisions of Section 10.2.1, no controversy or claim will be submitted to arbitration without the consent of all the parties if, at the time of the proposed submission, such controversy or claim arises from or relates to an obligation owed to CNB which is secured in whole or in part by real property collateral. If all parties do not consent to submission of such a controversy or claim to arbitration, the controversy or claim will be determined as provided in Section 10.2.3.

    10.2.3 Judicial Reference. At the request of any party, a controversy or claim which is not submitted to arbitration as provided and limited in Sections 10.2.1 and 10.2.2 will be determined by a reference in accordance with California Code of Civil Procedure Sections 638 et. seq. If such an election is made, the parties will designate to the court a referee or referees selected under the auspices of the AAA in the same manner as arbitrators are selected in AAA-sponsored proceedings. The presiding referee of the panel, or the referee if there is a single referee, will be an active attorney or retired judge. Judgment upon the award rendered by such referee or referees will be entered in the court in which such proceeding was commenced in accordance with California Code of Civil Procedure Sections 644 and 645.

10.2.4 Provisional Remedies, Self Help and Foreclosure. No provision of this Agreement will limit the right of any party to: (1) foreclose against any real property collateral by the exercise of a power of sale under a deed of trust, mortgage or other security agreement or instrument, or applicable law, (2) exercise any rights or remedies as a secured party against any personal property collateral pursuant to the terms of a security agreement or pledge agreement, or applicable law, (3) exercise self help remedies such as setoff, or (4) obtain provisional or ancillary remedies such as injunctive relief or the appointment of a receiver from a court having jurisdiction before, during or after the pendency of any arbitration or referral. The institution and maintenance of an action for judicial relief or pursuit of provisional or ancillary remedies, or exercise of self help remedies will not constitute a waiver of the right of any party, including the plaintiff, to submit any dispute to arbitration or judicial reference.

10.2.5 Powers and Qualifications of Arbitrators. The arbitrator(s) will give effect to statutes of limitation, waiver and estoppel and other affirmative defenses in determining any claim. Any controversy concerning whether an issue is arbitratable will be determined by the arbitrator(s). The laws of the State of California will govern. The arbitration award may include equitable and declaratory relief. All arbitrator(s) selected will be required to be a practicing attorney or retired judge licensed to practice law in the State of California and will be required to be experienced and knowledgeable in the substantive laws applicable to the subject matter of the controversy or claim at issue.

10.2.6 Discovery. The provisions of California Code of Civil Procedure Section 1283.05 or its successor section(s) are incorporated herein and made a part of this Agreement. Depositions may be taken and discovery may be obtained in any arbitration under this Agreement in accordance with said section(s).

10.2.7 Miscellaneous. The arbitrator(s) will determine which is the prevailing party and will include in the award that party's reasonable attorneys' fees and costs (including allocated costs of in-house legal counsel). Each party agrees to keep all controversies and claims and the arbitration proceedings strictly confidential, except for disclosures of information required in the ordinary course of business of the parties or by applicable law or regulation.

10.3 Cumulative Rights and No Waiver. All rights and remedies granted to CNB under the Loan Documents are cumulative and no one such right or remedy is exclusive of any other. No failure or delay on the part of CNB in exercising any right or remedy will operate as a waiver thereof, and no single or partial exercise or waiver by CNB of any such right or remedy will preclude any further exercise thereof or the exercise of any other right or remedy.

10.4 Applicable Law. This Agreement will be governed by California law.

10.5 Lien and Right of Set-off. Borrower grants to CNB a continuing lien for all Obligations of Borrower to CNB upon any and all moneys, securities and other property of Borrower and the proceeds thereof, now or hereafter held or received by or in transit to CNB from or for Borrower, whether for safekeeping, custody, pledge, transmission, collection or otherwise, and also upon any and all deposits (general or special) and credits of Borrower with, and any and all claims of Borrower against, CNB at any time existing. Upon the occurrence of any Event of Default, CNB is hereby authorized at any time and from time to time, without notice to Borrower or any other Person to setoff, appropriate and apply any or all items hereinabove referred to against all Obligations of Borrower whether under this Agreement or otherwise, and whether now existing or hereafter arising.

10.6 Notices. Any notice required or permitted under any Loan Document will be given in writing and will be deemed to have been given when personally delivered or when sent by the U.S. mail, postage prepaid, certified, return receipt requested, properly addressed. For the purposes hereof, the addresses of the parties will, until further notice given as herein provided, be as follows:

CNB:	City National Bank
	Special Assets Department
	606 South Olive Street, Suite 2000,
	Los Angeles, CA 90014
	Attention: Greg Meis, SVP
with copy to:	City National Bank, Legal Department
	400 North Roxbury Drive
	Beverly Hills, California 90210-5021
	Attention: Managing Counsel, Credit Unit
Borrower:	XYZ Corp.
	1900 Olympic Blvd.,
	Los Angeles, CA 90001
	Attention: Joe XYZ

10.7 Assignments. The provisions of this Agreement are hereby made applicable to and will inure to the benefit of CNB's successors and assigns and Borrower's successors and assigns; provided, however, that Borrower may not assign or transfer its rights or obligations under this Agreement without the prior written consent of CNB. CNB may assign this Agreement and its rights and duties hereunder. CNB reserves the right to sell, assign, transfer, negotiate, or grant participations in all or any part of, or any interest in CNB's rights and benefits hereunder. In connection therewith, CNB may disclose all documents and information which CNB now or hereafter may have relating to Borrower or Borrower's business.

10.8 Indemnification. Borrower will, at all times, defend and indemnify and hold CNB harmless from and against any and all liabilities, claims, demands, causes of action, losses, damages, expenses (including without limitation reasonable attorneys' fees [Which attorneys may be employees of CNB, or may be outside counsel]), costs, settlements, judgements or recoveries arising out of or resulting from (a) any breach of the representations, warranties, agreements or covenants made by Borrower herein; (b) any suit or proceeding of any kind or nature whatsoever against CNB arising from or connected with the transactions contemplated by this Agreement, the Loan Documents or any of the rights and properties assigned to CNB hereunder; and/or (c) any suit or proceeding that CNB may deem necessary or advisable to institute, in the name of CNB, Borrower or both, against any other Person, for any reason whatsoever to protect the rights of CNB hereunder or under any of the documents, instruments or agreements executed or to be executed pursuant hereto, including attorneys' fees and court costs and all other costs and expenses incurred by CNB (or allocable to CNB's in-house counsel), all of which will be charged to and paid by Borrower and will be secured by the Collateral. Any obligation or liability of Borrower to CNB under this Section will survive the Termination Date and the repayment of all Loans and other extensions of credit and the payment or performance of all other Obligations of Borrower to CNB.

10.9 Complete Agreement. This Agreement, together with other Loan Documents, constitutes the entire agreement of the parties and supersedes any prior or contemporaneous oral or written agreements or understandings, if any, which are merged into this Agreement. This Agreement may be amended only in a writing signed by Borrower and CNB.

10.10 Headings. Section headings in this Agreement are included for convenience of reference only and do not constitute a part of the Agreement for any purpose.

10.11 Accounting Terms. Except as otherwise stated in this Agreement, all accounting terms and financial covenants and information will be construed in conformity with, and all financial data required to be submitted will be prepared in conformity with, GAAP as in effect on the date hereof.

10.12 Severability. Any provision of the Loan Documents which is prohibited or unenforceable in any jurisdiction, will be, only as to such jurisdiction, ineffective to the extent of such prohibition or unenforceability, but all the remaining provisions of the Loan Documents will remain valid.

10.13 Counterparts. This Agreement may be signed in any number of counterparts which, when taken together, will constitute but one agreement.

10.14 Joint and Several. Should more than one Person sign this Agreement, the obligations of each signer will be joint and several.

IN WITNESS WHEREOF, CNB and Borrower have caused this Agreement to be executed as of the date first specified at the beginning of this Agreement.

Borrower   XYZ Corp.

                    A California corporation

                    By: _____

                    Joe XYZ, President

CNB   City National Bank, a

                    national banking association

                    By: _____

                    Sarah Davies, Chief Communicator

LOCKBOX AGREEMENT

This LOCKBOX AGREEMENT (the "Agreement") is between CITY NATIONAL BANK, a national banking association ("BANK"), and ("SUBSCRIBER"), with reference to the following lockbox services (the "Service") to be provided by BANK to SUBSCRIBER:

1. **SERVICE COMMENCEMENT.**

   (a) The Service shall commence on the Commencement Date shown on Schedule A. The Commencement Date may be extended by BANK by reason of delay caused by SUBSCRIBER or a cause beyond BANK'S reasonable control. BANK shall incur no liability for a delay in the Projected Commencement Date

   (b) On or before the date requested by BANK, SUBSCRIBER shall furnish BANK with copies of SUBSCRIBER'S invoice and envelope forms and such other forms and information as BANK may require to perform the Service.

   (c) On or before the date requested by BANK, SUBSCRIBER will open in the name of SUBSCRIBER a Post Office Box with the United States Postal Service or a private box for the receipt of mail with a private box provider (either such box is referred to herein as "Box") at the location set forth in Schedule A. The location shall be acceptable to BANK. SUBSCRIBER will grant BANK exclusive and unrestricted access to the Box on such form as shall be acceptable to the Box provider. At its option SUBSCRIBER may authorize BANK to open a Box in the name of SUBSCRIBER to which BANK shall have exclusive and unrestricted access. Such authorization shall be in such form as shall be acceptable to the Box provider. SUBSCRIBER shall be responsible to pay the Box rental fee. Upon termination of the Service, at the direction of SUBSCRIBER BANK will either close the Box or transfer it to SUBSCRIBER. and BANK shall have no further responsibility hereunder.

   (d) On or before the Commencement Date, SUBSCRIBER will open a demand deposit account with BANK as identified in Schedule A (the "Collection Account") and will maintain the Collection Account in good standing throughout the period of the Service.

   (e) SUBSCRIBER will direct its customers or debtors to mail invoices and remittances to be processed by the Service to the Box.

2.   **REMITTANCE PROCESSING.**

(a)   BANK will collect all mail received at the Box which is properly addressed to the Box on business days, which are days other than Saturdays, Sundays and holidays when either BANK or the Box provider is closed, according to a schedule established by BANK, which may be changed from time to time. BANK will return to the Box provider mail incorrectly delivered to the Box.

(b)   BANK will open all correctly addressed mail and examine it for invoices, cash, checks and other remittances, correspondence and other materials. All cash will be removed, held in double custody and a memorandum of the amount thereof made on the invoice and Collection Report (if any—see Schedule A). The contents of mail not containing an invoice, remittance or cash will be delivered to SUBSCRIBER without further processing.

(c)   Remittances, including checks, drafts, money orders and other instruments (collectively "checks"), will be processed according to the following, unless otherwise specified in Schedule A. Checks will be reviewed for date, payee, signature, amount (written and numerical) and endorsements, if any. Unless otherwise specified in Schedule A, checks will not be reconciled to accompanying invoices. The following items will be delivered to SUBSCRIBER without further, processing:

   (i)   Any check not drawn to the order of SUBSCRIBER, any others authorized payee designated on Schedule A or any recognizable variation thereof in BANK'S sole discretion.

   (ii)   Any check bearing a restrictive notation or endorsement, or accompanied by correspondence stating "paid in full," reserving rights or remedies, or containing any other restrictive language.

   (iii) Any stale-dated check or post-dated check unless in BANK's sole discretion the post-dated check would not reach the drawee bank through normal clearing channels until after the date thereof.

   (iv)   Any check the endorsement and deposit of which by BANK might, in BANK'S sole judgment, subject BANK to unacceptable claim or liability.

Unless otherwise specified in Schedule A, the following extraordinary items will be processed as described below:

   (v)   Unsigned checks may, in BANK's sole discretion, be delivered to SUBSCRIBER without further processing or deposited with a request to the drawee bank to obtain the payor's signature or other authority to pay. If returned, the Collection Account will be charged and the check will be delivered to SUBSCRIBER.

(vi)   Undated checks will be deposited.

(vii) Checks without accompanying invoices will be deposited.

(viii) Checks with a discrepancy between the written and numerical amounts will be deposited at the written amount.

(ix)   Checks returned for insufficient funds may, in BANK's sole discretion, be presented to the drawee bank for payment a second time. If unpaid, the Collection Account will be charged and the check will be delivered to SUBSCRIBER.

(x)   Checks returned for special endorsement will be endorsed "Pay to the Order of City National Bank" and BANK is hereby authorized to insert such endorsement. Checks returned for any other reason will be charged to the Collection Account and delivered to SUBSCRIBER.

(xi)   Checks which are payable in foreign currency or are drawn on a bank outside the United States will not be credited to the Collection Account unless and until payment is received by BANK.

All checks in proper form will be endorsed "Credit the Account of the Within Named Payee, Absence of Endorsement Guaranteed by City National Bank" and, together with all cash, will be deposited to the Collection Account of the day processed and, unless otherwise specified in Schedule A, written advice of the credit will be delivered to SUBSCRIBER daily. Except as otherwise specified in this Agreement and the Schedules hereto, the processing of checks and the availability of funds will be subject to the terms and conditions of the deposit agreement applicable to the Collection Account and BANK'S normal procedures and regulations for deposits.

(d)   Unless otherwise specified in Schedule A, SUBSCRIBER will furnish, at its expense, all invoices, envelopes and other forms requiring any special logo or imprint, and BANK will furnish, at its expense, all internal BANK forms, Collection Reports, advices of credit and similar forms.

3.   FEES AND CHARGES.

SUBSCRIBER shall compensate BANK for the Service hereunder as provided in Schedule B and reimburse BANK for its out-of-pocket expenses.

4.   MISCELLANEOUS.

(a)   SUBSCRIBER agrees that this Agreement, including without limitation the fees in Schedule B, may be amended by BANK effective upon the earlier of the written acknowledgment thereof by SUBSCRIBER or 30 calendar days after written notice to SUBSCRIBER by BANK of the amendment.

(b) When performing the Service BANK shall exercise at least the same degree of care commonly exercised by banks and other service providers of similar size when providing similar services to customers in California. BANK MAKES NO WARRANTY, EXPRESS OR IMPLIED, CONCERNING THE SERVICE INCLUDING BUT NOT LIMITED TO THE IMPLIED WARRANTIES OF MERCHANTABILITY AND FITNESS FOR A PARTICULAR PURPOSE. BANK will not be liable for any loss, expense, error or delay, including but not limited to any delay or inability to provide access to the Service, caused by accidents, strikes, flood, fire, electrical or mechanical failures, software defects, computer failure, acts or omissions by you, the Box provider or any third party (including but not limited to acts or omissions of any telephone or telecommunications carrier, legal constraints, acts of God or any other causes or conditions which are beyond BANK's reasonable control). BANK will not be liable to SUBSCRIBER for any damage arising out of or related to BANK's performance of the Service other than damage actually incurred resulting directly form BANK's failure to exercise reasonable care. As a condition precedent to BANK's liability hereunder, SUBSCRIBER must notify BANK in writing of any alleged negligence or breach by BANK as promptly as reasonably possible, but in no event later than five (5) business days following the day on which such alleged negligence or breach was, or could reasonably have been, discovered by SUBSCRIBER. BANK's entire liability and SUBSCRIBER's sole remedy, including but not limited to liability for negligence, will not exceed the fees actually paid to BANK by SUBSCRIBER for the Service during the six (6) month period preceding the date of the alleged negligence or breach. IN NO EVENT WILL BANK BE LIABLE FOR SPECIAL, GENERAL, CONSEQUENTIAL, INCIDENTAL, EXEMPLARY OR SIMILAR DAMAGES, INCLUDING BUT NOT LIMITED TO LOST PROFITS, EVEN IF BANK HAS BEEN ADVISED OF THE POSSIBILITY THEREOF. This provision also limits the liability of BANK's agents, employees, affiliates and vendors and will survive termination of the Service.

(c) SUBSCRIBER will at all times, defend, indemnify and hold BANK (which includes BANK's shareholders, officers, directors, other employees, agents, affiliates and vendors) harmless from and against any and all liabilities, claims, demands, causes of action, losses, damages, costs, expenses and attorneys' fees (including those fees allocable to in-house counsel), settlements, judgments or recoveries of third parties, other than SUBSCRIBER or BANK, arising out of or relating, directly or indirectly, to SUBSCRIBER's use of the Service or BANK's performance of BANK's obligations hereunder provided that BANK exercised reasonable care, as stated herein, and acted in good faith. This provision will survive the termination of the Service.

(d) Nothing in this Agreement shall be deemed to constitute either party the agent or partner of the other, and the relationship between the parties shall be that of independent contractors.

(e) All specifications, records, software, forms, systems and programs utilized or developed by BANK in connection with the Service are and will remain the sole property of BANK, unless supplied to BANK by SUBSCRIBER.

(f) Subject to any minimum term set forth in Schedule B, this Agreement will remain in effect until terminated by either party upon 30 calendar days' written notice to the other party, provided that SUBSCRIBER may terminate this Agreement on shorter notice (but not less than 10 days) at any time within 30 days after notice from BANK of any amendment to this Agreement or any-Schedules hereto. If BANK terminates this Agreement, it will allow SUBSCRIBER a reasonable period of time beyond said 30 days, if necessary to make other arrangements, not to exceed 60 calendar days after such written notice of termination. SUBSCRIBER will reimburse BANK for any out-of-pocket costs incurred by reason of any termination hereunder.

(g) This Agreement supersedes any and all agreements entered into between BANK and SUBSCRIBER prior to the date of this Agreement relating to the Service. This Agreement is intended as a final expression of the parties' agreement with respect to the Service and such other terms are included herein, and as a complete and exclusive statement of such terms. This Agreement may not be amended or waived, in whole or in part, except as provided in Section 4(a) above or in a writing executed by both of the parties hereto.

(h) This Agreement is governed by the laws of the State of California.

(i) Any dispute arising out of or relating to this Agreement and the Service which the parties are unable to resolve informally shall be submitted for resolution in accordance with the terms of the City National Bank Standard Dispute Resolution Clause for Cash Management, a copy of which is attached hereto and which is incorporated herein by this reference. BY THIS AGREEMENT EACH PARTY WAIVES THE CONSTITUTIONAL RIGHT TO A JURY TRIAL TO RESOLVE CERTAIN DISPUTES ARISING UNDER THIS AGREEMENT.

(j) SUBSCRIBER represents and warrants to BANK that the signers of this Agreement have the corporate power and authority to execute, deliver and perform this Agreement and that when executed this Agreement is binding on SUBSCRIBER.

(k) Any notice required or permitted to be given under this Agreement will be in writing and will be deemed effective if to BANK, upon receipt, and if to SUBSCRIBER when placed in the United States mail postage prepaid to the address set forth in records of BANK, or such other address subsequently provided to BANK by written notice.

(l) This Agreement will inure to the benefit of and be binding upon both parties, their successors and assigns. No assignment may be made by SUBSCRIBER without the prior written consent of BANK. Nothing in this Agreement restricts the right of BANK to effect an assignment by merger, reorganization, sale of corporate assets or other corporate change.

(m) If any provision of this Agreement, or part of a provision, is held to be invalid, illegal, void or unenforceable, the remainder of the Agreement, or other parts or application of such provision, will not affected thereby.

CITY NATIONAL BANK, a national banking association

Date: _____   By: _____

Its: _____

_____

("SUBSCRIBER")

_____

_____

_____

(Address)

Date: _____   By: _____

Its: _____

INDEX

References are to Pages

ADVANCES
Future Advances, this index

AFTER-ACQUIRED PROPERTY
Bankruptcy, this index
Collateral descriptions in security
     agreements
     Business lending, 34
     Consumer lending, 39
Future advances distinguished, 153
Priorities, 153, 159

AGRICULTURAL LIENS
Attachment and perfection, 55
Livestock priorities, 163
Priorities, 151
Security interests distinguished, 55

ASSIGNMENTS
Letters of credit, 664
Recourse rights of assignees, 521, 522
Security interests, assignment
     restrictions, 385

**ATTACHMENT OF SECURITY
     INTERESTS**
          Generally, 13 et seq.
After-acquired collateral descriptions in
     security agreements
     Business lending, 34
     Consumer lending, 39
Agreements. *See* Security Agreements,
     this index
Agricultural liens, 55
"All assets" collateral descriptions, 27
Authentication of security agreements,
     14, 21, 22
Authority of debtor to transfer rights in
     collateral, 43
Bankruptcy proceeding, testing of
     attachment in, 21
Collateral, this index
Composite document rule, 15
Conditions
          Generally, 13
          Rights-in-collateral test, 13, 41
          Value given as, 13, 41
Descriptions of collateral, 23
Disclosure functions of security
     agreements, 26
Enforceability-attachment relationship,
     13, 53
Intent vs agreement to create, 20, 21
Investment securities, security interests
     in, 396
Power of debtor to transfer rights in
     collateral, 43
Proceeds references in security
     agreements, 49
Rights of debtor in collateral as condition,
     41

Rights-in-collateral test, 13
Security Agreements, this index
Signing of security agreement as
     condition, 13
Supergeneric descriptions of collateral, 25
Value given as condition, 13, 41

AUTHORITY
Creditor's authority to file financing
     statement, 100
Debtor's authority to transfer rights in
     collateral, 43

**BANK PAYMENT OBLIGATION
     (BPO)**
As alternative to letter of credit, 631

BANKRUPTCY
          Generally, 525 et seq.
Accounts collateral, preference issues, 591
After-acquired property, business debtors,
     552
"All assets" collateral descriptions, 27
Attachment of security interests, testing
     of, 21
Automatic stay
          Generally, 529
          Secured claims, 534
Avoidance powers of trustees
          Generally, 570
          Fraudulent transfers, 570, 596
          Unperfected security interests, 53
Benefit of a creditor transfers as
     preferences, 579
Business debtors
          After-acquired property, 552
          Debtor in possession financing, 552
          Discharge of secured claims, below
Claims of creditors, 530
Collateral valuation, 561
Delayed perfection of security interests,
     preferences, 594
Discharge of secured claims
          Generally, 535 et seq.
          Business debtors
               Generally, 551 et seq.
               Chapter 7 bankruptcies, 552
               Chapter 11 bankruptcies, 552
               Reorganization plans, 552
          Chapter 7 bankruptcies, 537
          Chapter 11 bankruptcies, 552
          Chapter 13 bankruptcies, 543
          Consumer debtors, 543
               Chapter 7 bankruptcies, 537
               Reorganization plans, 543
          Fraudulent transfers, below
          Preferences, below
          Reorganization plans
               Business debtors, 528, 552
               Consumer debtors, 543
Discharge, effects of, 532

Distribution of assets
    Discharge of secured claims, above
    Secured creditors, distributions to
    Unsecured creditors, distributions
       to, 531
False preferences, 594
Floating liens as preferences, 591
Fraudulent transfers
    Generally, 596
    Actual fraud, 596
    Avoidance powers of trustees, 570,
       596
    Constructive fraud, 597
    Indirect benefits debtors, 598
    Leveraged buyouts, 602
    Payment rights securitization, 603
    Preferences distinguished, 573
    Reasonably equivalent value issue,
       598, 602, 603
    Securitization transfers as, 603
Indirect benefit, debtor as receiving, 598
Inventory collateral, preference issues,
    591
Letters of credit in bankruptcy, 671
Leveraged buyouts as fraudulent
    transfers, 602
Liquidation vs reorganization, 526, 527
Means test limitations on liquidation, 527
Ordinary course payments, preferences,
    582 et seq.
Payment rights collateral, preference
    issues, 591
Perfection of security interests
    Delayed, preferences, 594
    Effect of, 53
Petitions, 529
Preferences
    Generally, 573 et seq.
    Accounts collateral, 591
    Avoidance, effect of, 577
    Benefit of a creditor transfers, 579
    Contemporaneous exchanges, 580
    Delayed perfection, 594
    Effect of avoidance, 577
    Elements of voidable preferences,
       574
    Exceptions limiting reach of
       preference law, 580
    False preferences, 594
    Floating liens, 591
    Fraudulent conveyances
       distinguished, 573
    Inventory collateral, 591
    Ordinary course payments, 582 et
       seq.
    Payment rights collateral, 591
    Perfection of security interests,
       delayed, 594
    Period, preference, 578
    Policy considerations, 575
    Transfers to or for benefit of a
       creditor, 579
    Unsecured creditors, 573
Reasonably equivalent value issue,
    fraudulent transfers, 598, 602, 603
Redemption of repossessed goods, 523

Secured creditors, distributions to
    Generally, 532 et seq.
    Automatic stays, 534
    Avoidance powers of trustees, above
    Definitions, 532
    Discharge of secured claims, above
Strong arm powers
    Definition, 146
    Subrogation of trustee, 571
Subrogation of trustee, 571
Transfers to or for benefit of a creditor as
    preferences, 579
Trustees in bankruptcy
    Generally, 529
    Avoidance powers of trustees, above
    Subrogation of, 571
Unperfected security interests, avoidance
    of, 53
Unsecured creditors, preferences, 573
Valuing collateral, 561

BANKS
Deposit Accounts, this index
Letters of Credit, this index
Setoff rights, 241

BONDING EXPLANATIONS
Secured vs unsecured lending, 7

BREACH OF WARRANTY
Letters of credit, 642

BRIGHT-LINE TEST
True lease vs financing devices, 285 et
    seq.

BUSINESS LENDING
    Generally, 1
After-acquired collateral descriptions in
    security agreements, 34
Consumer lending compared, 2

CASH PROCEEDS
See also Proceeds, this index

**CERTIFICATED STOCKS AND
    BONDS**
Investment Securities, Security Interests
    in, this index

CERTIFICATES OF TITLE GOODS
    See also Motor Vehicles, this index
Enforcement of security interests, 508
Foreign certificates, choice of law issues,
    144 et seq.
Perfection of security interests
    Generally, 21
    Choice of law issues, 144
True lease vs financing device, certificate
    of title rules, 318

CHATTEL PAPER
Payment Rights, this index
Security interests, chattel mortgages
    compared, 10

COLLATERAL
Accounts, after-acquired collateral
    descriptions reaching, 34

After-Acquired Property, this index
"All assets"
    Generally, 27
    Financing statement requirements,
        67
Authority of debtor to transfer rights in,
    43
Bankruptcy, valuing collateral in, 561
Cash proceeds. *See* Proceeds, this index
Categories of, 22
Certificates of Title Goods, this index
Commercial tort claims treated as, 39
Cross-collateralization by dragnet clauses,
    154
Deposit accounts, collateral use problems,
    240
Descriptions of, 22
Disablement of collateral, enforcement of
    security interests by, 471
Dragnet clauses covering future advances,
    154
Federal tax liens, collateral subject to, 268
Fixtures as, state laws affecting
    characterizations, 431
Future Advances, this index
Generic descriptions in financing
    statements
        Generally, 22
        Searchers' vs filers' requirements,
            68
Indication of collateral covered in
    financing statements
        Original collateral, 67
        Proceeds, 76
Inventory financing, after-acquired
    collateral descriptions reaching, 34
Investment securities, collateral
    designations issues, 420
Power of debtor to transfer rights in, 43
Priorities, this index
Proceeds, this index
Searchers' vs filers' requirements as to
    generic descriptions, 68
Supergeneric descriptions of collateral, 25,
    69
Tangible vs intangible items, perfection of
    security interests in, 54
Valuing collateral in bankruptcy, 561

COMMERCIAL REASONABILITY
Enforcement of Security Interests, this
    index

COMPOSITE DOCUMENT RULE, 15,
    31

CONDITIONAL SALES
Security interests compared, 10

CONSIGNMENTS
    Generally, 320 et seq.
Commercial consignment as financing
    device, 321
Common law consignments, 320
Debtor's retailer status, knowledge of
    creditors as to, 333

Financing device, commercial
    consignment as, 321
Knowledge of creditors as to debtor's
    retailer status, 333
Motor vehicles, floor financing, 332
Ostensible ownership issues, 321, 333
Perfection issues, 325, 333
Priorities, 325, 339
Security consignment exclusion, 323 et
    seq.
True consignments, 321, 325
UCC Article 9 consignments
        Generally, 321
        Non-Article 9 consignments and
            non-Article 9 law, 339

CONSUMER LAW
Business and consumer lending
    compared, 2
Buyers of consumer goods, priorities. *See*
    Priorities, this index
Enforcement of security interests,
    redemption rights disclosures, 523
Leases, this index
Payment rights priority issues of sellers of
    consumer goods, 228
Perfection of security interests
        Generally, 131, 132
        Filing requirements, 133
Purchase-money security interests. *See*
    Priorities, this index
Redemption rights disclosures, 523
Repossession breaches of peace, creditor
    liability, 472
Retailers, payment rights priorities, 228
UCC Article 9 provisions, original vs
    revised, 131, 132
Wrongful repossession, 472

CONTROL
Deposit accounts, control based priority,
    241
Investment securities certificates
        Held by owners, control in pledge
            transactions, 397
        Held by securities intermediaries
            Control agreements, 420
            Control test, 410
Perfection of security interests by, 129,
    241

CONTROLLABLE ACCOUNT, 13, 24,
    25, 54, 129, 226, 413

**CONTROLLABLE ELECTRONIC
    RECORD**, 12, 13, 24, 25, 43, 130,
    131, 225, 522

**CONTROLLABLE PAYMENT
    INTANGIBLE**, 13, 24, 25, 43, 54,
    129, 225, 226, 413

**CREATION OF SECURITY
    INTERESTS**
        Generally, 1 et seq.
    See also Security Interests, this index
Electronic vs written communications as
    records, 14

Intent vs agreement to create, 20, 21

DEFAULT
Rights of secured lenders
  Generally, 455 et seq.
  Bankruptcy, this index
  Definitions, 456
  Enforcement of Security Interests,
    this index
  Waivers, effect of nonwaiver
    clauses, 458
Workout agreements to avoid, 495
Wrongful declaration of default, 520, 521

DEPOSIT ACCOUNTS
Collateral use problems, 240
Creditor status of depositors, 240
Definitions, 239
Original collateral priority treatment of
  security interests in, 245
Payment rights of depositors, 240, 241
Priorities, policy considerations, 250
Proceeds of other collateral, treatment as
  for priorities purposes,
Setoff rights of banks, 241
Subordination agreements, 250

DIGITAL ASSETS
See Controllable Electronic Record, this
  index

DOUBLE DEBTOR CONUNDRUM,
  195

ELECTRONIC FILING, 100

ENFORCEMENT OF SECURITY
  INTERESTS
    Generally, 465 et seq.
    See also Bankruptcy, this index
Acceptance of collateral in satisfaction of
  debt, 511
Attachment-enforceability relationship,
  13, 53
Breach of peace by repossession, 471
Certificates of title transfers in sales, 508
Commercial reasonability
  Collections to enforce payment
    rights security interests, 521,
    522
  Delayed sale, 495
  Disposition requirement,
    compliance with, 499
  Liability for deficiency, 507
  Payment rights security interests
    collections, 521, 522
  Policy considerations, 494
  Public vs private sales, 485, 493, 496
  Safe harbor definition, 494
  Sale preparation requirements, 501
Conditions of enforceability
  Generally, 13, 53
  See also Attachment of Security
    Interests, this index
Consent of debtor to repossession, 477
Constructive strict foreclosure, 512
Consumer goods, redemption rights
  disclosures, 523

Damages caused by repossession, 479
Delayed sales
  Commercial reasonableness, 495
  Liability, 495
Disablement of collateral, 471
Disposition of repossessed collateral
  Generally, 482 et seq.
  Acceptance of collateral in
    satisfaction of debt, 511
  Effect of disposition or acceptance
    on third parties, 517
  Junior security interests or liens,
    effects on, 517
  Notification requirements, 483
  Priorities of junior claimants and
    lienors, effect on, 517
  Public vs private sales, below
  Secondary obligors, 509
Election of remedies doctrine, 466
Estoppel defenses, 458
Extra-judicial remedies, 465
Fairness of secured credit practices, 6
Federal tax liens, 268
Fixtures, security interests in, 445
In personam judgment rights, 465
Intellectual property security interests,
  assignment restrictions, 385
Judicial repossession, 479
Junior security interests or liens, effects
  of dispositions of, 517
Liability for deficiency
  Generally, 504
  Commercial reasonability
    limitation, 502
  Consumer transactions, 506
  Nonconsumer transactions, 504
Marshaling, public vs private sales, 493
Motor vehicle repossession, 473, 474
Notification requirements prior to
  disposition, 483
Public vs private sales, 496
  Commercial reasonability, 485, 491,
    496
  Delayed sale liability, 495
  Distinctions, 490
  Liability for deficiency, above
  Marshaling, 493
  Notification requirements, 485
Redemption after repossession, 523
Removals of fixtures, 445
Repossessed collateral, effect of
  disposition or acceptance on third
  parties, 517
Repossession
  Breach of peace, 471
  Consent of debtor, 477
  Damages caused by, 479
  Fixtures, security interests in, 445
  Judicial, 479
  Liability for deficiency, above
  Motor vehicles, 473, 474
  Redemption, 523
  Self-help, 470
  Trespass to accomplish, 473
  Vicarious liability of creditor, 473,
    474, 481, 482

Wrongful repossession, 472
Rights of secured vs unsecured creditors, 3
Rights to payment, collection of, 520
Sales
    Certificates of title transfers, 508
    Commercial reasonability, above
    Effect of disposition or acceptance on third parties, 517
    Priorities of junior claimants and lienors, effect on, 517
    Public vs private sales, above
    Transfer statements, 508
    Transferees, 517
Secondary obligors, noticed as to disposition of repossessed collateral, 509
Self-help repossession, 470
Strict foreclosure, 511
Transferees of sales, 517
Trespass to accomplish repossession, 473
Waivers of rights, 458
Workout agreements to avoid, 495
Wrongful repossession, 472

EQUITABLE SUBROGATION, 161

FEDERAL TAX LIEN ACT
    Generally, 266 et seq., 274
Choateness doctrine, priorities, 267
Collateral subject to federal tax liens, 268
Creation, 268
Enforceability, 268
Future advances and floating liens, priorities, 277
Notice requirements, 269
Post-lien proceeds, priorities exceptions, 279
Priorities
    Generally, 274
    Choateness doctrine, 267
    Exceptions for purchase-money security interests and post-lien proceeds, 279
    Future advances and floating liens, 277
    Post-lien transactions, 277
    Purchase-money security interests and post-lien proceeds, 279
Purchase-money security interests priorities exceptions, 279
Transactions post-lien, priorities, 277

FILINGS
    See also Financing Statements, this index
Electronic filings, 100
Federal Tax Lien Act, filing issues, 269
Fixtures filings, 432
Unauthorized filings, liabilities, 101

FINANCING STATEMENT
Accuracy of names and addresses of creditors, 60 et seq.
Addendum forms, 114
Addresses of creditors, accuracy of, 60 et seq.

All assets collateral descriptions, 27, 67
Amendment forms, 114
Amendments, 64, 65
Authorization by debtor, 100
Basic requirements, 59
Burden of proof as to name issues, searchers vs filers, 93, 96
Business structure changes, post-filing, 119
Changes of debtor names, post-filing, 118
Collateral covered, indication of
    Original collateral, 67
    Proceeds, 76
Collateral transfers, post-filing, 116
Consumer goods, filing requirements, 133
D/b/a name uses by debtors, 94, 99
Disclosure purposes of filing, 56, 57
Duty of filing office to accept or reject, 115
Effective date of filing, 114, 115
Electronic filing, 100
Errors in debtors' names, 80, 81
Estoppel to challenge accuracy of, 64
Filing
    Consumer goods, 133
    Disclosure purposes, 56, 57
    Duty of filing office to accept or reject, 115
    Indexing errors in filing office, 114
    Necessity of, 55
    Notice filing, 56
    Perfection by, possession as alternative, 125
    Priorities, 56
    Purposes of filing system, 56
    Sufficiency, 59
    Systems, 102 et seq.
Generic descriptions of collateral, searchers' vs filers' requirements, 68
Indexing errors in filing office, 114
Kinds of records filed, 103 et seq.
Liabilities for unauthorized filings, 101
Local vs central filing systems, 102
Names of creditors, accuracy of, 60 et seq.
Names of debtors
    Generally, 77 et seq.
    Burden of proof, searchers vs filers, 93, 96
    Changes, post-filing, 118
    D/b/a names, 94, 99
    Organizational names, 79
    Trade names, 92
National safe harbor form, 113
Necessity of filing, 55
New debtor issues, post-filing, 121
Notice filing, 56
Omissions of debtors' names, 80, 81
Post-filing changes, 116
Purposes, 96
Safe harbors, 95, 98, 113
Search procedures
    Generally, 95
    Noise words, 98
Searchers vs filers
    Burden of proof as to name issues, 93, 96
    Generic descriptions of collateral, 68

Security agreements distinguished, 25, 26
Seriously misleading standard of name
    issue determinations, 95, 98
Signatures of debtors, 100
State promulgated filing forms, 114
Sufficiency, 59
Supergeneric descriptions of collateral, 69
Trade names, debtors use of, 92
Transfers of collateral, post-filing, 116
Umbrella, financing statement as for
    priorities determinations, 156
When filing becomes effective, 114

**FIXTURES, SECURITY INTERESTS
    IN**
    Generally, 431
Circular priorities problems, 438
Collateral characterizations, state laws
    affecting, 431
Definitions, 431
Enforcement, 445
Priorities
    Generally, 434
    Circular priorities problems, 438
State laws affecting fixture
    characterizations, 431
Three element test of fixture status, 432

FLOATING LIENS
Bankruptcy preferences, 591

FORECLOSURE
Enforcement of Security Interests, this
    index

**FRAUD, FORGERY, AND
    ALTERATION**
Bankruptcy, this index
Letters of credit, 653

FUTURE ADVANCES
After-acquired property distinguished,
    153
Dragnet clauses covering, 154
Lien creditors, priorities conflicts vs
    unperfected security interest, 182
Priority position of first-to-file secured
    party, 159
Umbrella, financing statement as for
    priorities determinations, 156

**HONOR OR DISHONOR RESPONSES
    TO PRESENTMENT**
Letters of credit, issuer duties, 617

INDEPENDENCE PRINCIPLE
Letters of Credit, this index

INTANGIBLES
Pledgeable and nonpledgeable, 228

**INTELLECTUAL PROPERTY,
    SECURITY INTERESTS IN**
Generally, 343
Copyrights
    Generally, 344 et seq.
    License fees, payment rights issues,
        356
    Recordation of interests, 354

Registration
    Generally, 344
    Perfection of security interests
        in, 54
    Unregistered copyrights, priorities,
        358 et seq.
Enforcement, assignment restrictions, 385
Federal statutes, preemptive, 343, 374
General intangibles, treatment as, 343
Patents, 374
Perfection of security interests, registered
    copyrights, 54
Priorities, unregistered copyrights, 358 et
    seq.
Software, 343
Trademarks, 369
UCC Article 9, step-back provisions, 345,
    353

INVENTORY
After-acquired collateral descriptions
    reaching, 34
Bankruptcy preference issues, 591
Dual status rule, 179
Notice requirement, purchase-money
    security interests exception, 174
Ordinary course of business buyers,
    priorities vs secured creditors, 185
Priorities, this index
Securitization, 2
Waivers of priorities by secured creditors
    vs buyers and lessees, 193

**INVESTMENT SECURITIES,
    SECURITY INTERESTS IN**
Generally, 389 et seq.
Asset management accounts, 421
Attachment, 396
Certificate in possession of securities
    intermediary
    Generally, 410 et seq.
    Asset management accounts, 421
    Control agreements, 420
    Control test, 410
Certificated securities held by owners
    Generally, 397
    Control in pledge transactions, 398
    Dividends, 401
    Pledgee's duty of reasonable care,
        401
Collateral designations issues, 420
Control, this index
Definitions, 397
Direct vs indirect holding systems, 389
Dividends, certificated securities held by
    owners, 401
Government bonds, 429
Mutual funds, 422
Perfection, 396
Pledgee's duty of reasonable care, 401
Priorities, 396
Treasury securities, 429
UCC Article 8
    Generally, 389
    Securities subject to, 393
Uncertificated securities, 422

LEASES
    Generally, 281 et seq.
Accounting, 281
Alternatives to secured transactions, use as, 281 et seq.
Bright Line Test, true lease vs financing devices, 282 et seq., 285 et seq.
Certificate of title rules, true lease vs financing devices, 318
Consideration test, true lease vs financing devices, 306
Consumer leases
    Generally, 319
    Rent-to-own leases, 300
Intent of parties, true lease vs financing device, 304
Meaningful residual interest test, true lease vs financing device, 299, 311
Open-end leases, 312
Per se test, true lease vs financing devices, 316
Priorities, this index
Purchase or renew options
    Leases with, 282 et seq., 285 et seq.
    Leases without, 301 et seq.
Rent-to-own leases, 300
Sales distinguished, 281
Secured transaction alternatives, use as, 281 et seq.
Tax treatment, 281, 282
Terminal rent adjustment clause, true lease vs financing devices, 312
True lease vs financing device
    Bright Line Test, 282 et seq., 285 et seq.
    Certificate of title rules, 318
    Consideration test, 306
    Economic realities as determining, 301
    Intent of parties, 304
    Meaningful residual interest test, 299, 311
    Payment rights issues compared, 319
    Per se test, 316
    Rent-to-own leases, 300
    Terminal rent adjustment clause, 312

LETTERS OF CREDIT
    Generally, 605 et seq.
Advisors' roles, 607
Applicants, 605
Assignments, 664
Bank regulations affecting issuers, 613
Bankruptcy treatment, 671
Beneficiaries, 605
Breach of warranty, 642
Confirmers' roles, 607
Credit enhancement uses, 605
Damages for wrongful dishonor, 651
Defenses and liabilities, 609
Discrepancies in instructions
    Notice of discrepancies, 632
    Preclusion rule, 636

    Strict compliance standard, 617 et seq.
    Waiver options of issuers, 632
Documentary credits, 607, 613
Duration of enforceability, 616
Forgery or fraud, 653
Form of letter of credit application and agreement, 673
Formal requirements, 611
Honor or dishonor duty of issuers, 617 et seq.
Independence principle
    Generally, 638
    Forgery or fraud exception, 653
    Mandatory rules, 610, 639
Issuers
    Bank regulations affecting, 613
    Definition, 605
    Duty to honor or dishonor, 617 et seq.
    Right to reimbursement, 640
Liabilities and defenses, 609
Negotiable instruments distinguished, 609
Notice of discrepancies, 632
Payment uses, 605
Preclusion rule, discrepancies in instructions, 636
Reimbursement and other remedies, issuer's right to, 640
Relationships created by, 606
Restitution, 642
Risk shifting functions, 605
Security interests in, 666, 667
Sources of applicable law, 609
Standby credits
    Generally, 607, 613
    Bankruptcy treatment, 671
Strict compliance standard, 617 et seq.
Subrogation, 642
Transfers, 664
Waiver options of issuers, discrepancies in instructions, 632
Wrongful dishonor
    Generally, 633
    Damages, 651

LIENS
Agricultural Liens, this index
Choate liens, 267
Federal Tax Lien Act, this index
Floating liens, bankruptcy preferences, 591
Future advances, lien creditors priorities, 182
Priorities vs unperfected security interests, 182

LIVESTOCK
Purchase-money security interests priorities, 162, 163

MONEY
Electronic money, 13, 24, 54, 129
Perfection of security interests in, 55

MONITORING OF LENDING COSTS
Secured vs unsecured lending, 7

MOTOR VEHICLES
Generally, 55
See also Certificates of Title Goods,
this index
Enforcement of security interests,
certificates of title transfers, 508
Floor financing
Generally, 332
Priorities, 233
Leases, this index
Perfection of security interests, 55
Repossession, 473, 474
Sales transfers of certificates of title, 508

NEGOTIABLE INSTRUMENTS
Generally, 237
Holders in due course, priorities, 266
Letters of credit distinguished, 609
Security interests in, perfection by
possession, 124

PAYMENT RIGHTS
Generally, 228
See also Securitization, this index
Accounts
After-acquired collateral
descriptions reaching, 34
Automatic perfection of casual or
isolated assignments, 220, 221
Bankruptcy preference issues, 591
Casual or isolated assignments,
automatic perfection, 220, 221
Loans secured by payment rights vs
sales of payment rights, 216,
521
Priorities, this index
Purchase-money security interests
priorities exception, 162
Securitization, 2
After-acquired collateral descriptions
reaching, 34
Automatic perfection of casual or isolated
assignments, 220, 221
Bankruptcy
Preference issues, 591
Securitization, fraudulent transfers,
603
Casual or isolated assignments, automatic
perfection, 220, 221, 222
Chattel paper
Generally, 228
Electronic chattel paper, 229
Loans secured by payment rights vs
sales of payment rights, 216
Naming history, 228
Priorities, this index
Proceeds treatment for priority
purposes, 233
Collections to enforce security interests
Generally, 520 et seq.
Commercial reasonableness, 521,
522
Duties of secured party to debtor, 521
Nonnotification financing, 521

Notification, 520, 521
Recourse rights of assignees, 521,
522
Copyright license fees, payment rights
issues, 356
Deposit accounts, payment rights of
depositors, 240, 241
Development of financing based on, 9
Direct payment to secured party, 520, 521
Dual status rule inventory, purchase-
money security interests exception,
179
Duties of secured party to debtor,
collections to enforce security
interests, 521
Floor planning motor vehicle financing
Generally, 332
Priorities, 233
Historical background, 228
Instruments as, 228
Inventory securitization, 2
Letters of credit securing, 666, 667
Loans secured by payment rights vs sales
of payment rights, 216
Nonnotification financing, 521
Notification of collections to enforce
security interests, 520, 521
Payment intangibles distinguished, 206 et
seq.
Perfection of security interests in, 222
Priorities, this index
Proceeds
Accounts and general intangibles
priorities, 218
Inventory priorities, 174
Treatment for priority purposes, 233
Purchase-money security interests
exception
Dual status rule inventory, 179
Priorities, 162
Recourse rights of assignees, 521, 522
Sales of payment rights vs loans secured
by payment rights, 216
True lease vs financing devices, payment
rights issues compared, 319
Wrongful declaration of default, 520, 521

PAYMENT SYSTEMS
Letters of Credit, this index

**PERFECTION OF SECURITY
INTERESTS**
Generally, 53 et seq.
Agent, perfection by possession of, 123
Agricultural liens, 55
Automatic perfection
Attachment, 53
Casual or isolated assignments of
accounts, 220, 221
Consumer goods, 53, 133
Proceeds, 76
Avoidance of unperfected security
interests in bankruptcy, 53
Bailee's possession, perfection by, 127
Bankruptcy
Effect of perfection in, 53

Preferences, delayed perfection, 594
Casual assignments of accounts,
    automatic perfection, 220, 221
Choice of law issues
        Generally, 135 et seq.
        Certificate of title goods, 144
        Change in debtor's location, 145
        Debtor location, 137
        Foreign certificates of title, 144 et
            seq.
        Tangible and intangible collateral,
            136
Consignments, perfection issues, 325, 333
Consumer goods, 132
Control, perfection by
        Generally, 55, 129
        Deposit accounts, 241
Copyrights, registered, 55
Debtor location, choice of law issues, 137
Definitions, 53
Delayed perfection, bankruptcy
    preferences, 594
Effect of perfection, 53
Filing
        Generally, 56 et seq.
        See also Financing Statements, this
            index
Fixtures, 432
Floor planning motor vehicle financing,
    233
Foreign certificates of title, choice of law
    issues, 144 et seq.
Intellectual Property, Security Interests
    in, this index
Investment securities, security interests
    in, 396
Isolated assignments of accounts,
    automatic perfection, 220, 221
Money, 55
Motor vehicles, 55
        Certificates of title, 21
        Floor-planning financing, 233
Negotiable instruments, perfection by
    possession, 124
Notice effect of possession by secured
    creditor, 124
Notice filing, 56
Other law, perfection of security interests
    subject to, 55
Payment rights, 222
Possession, perfection by
        Generally, 53, 123
        Agent's possession, 123
        Bailee's possession, 127
        Negotiable instruments, 124
        Notice effect of possession by
            secured creditor, 124
        Pledges, 123
Priorities, filing to establish, 56
Purchase-money security interests, 162
Tangible vs intangible items of collateral
        Generally, 54
        Choice of law issues, 136

PLEDGES
Intangibles, pledgeable and
    nonpledgeable, 228

POSSESSION
Bankruptcy, debtor in possession
    financing, 552
Perfection by. See Perfection of Security
    Interests, this index

PRIORITIES
        Generally, 151 et seq.
Accounts
        Payment rights, below
        Priority in proceeds, 218
        Purchase-money security interests
            exception, 162
After-Acquired Property, this index
Agricultural liens, 151
Avoidance of unperfected security
    interests, 53
Buyers and lessees
        Generally, 184
        Consumer goods buyers, below
        Double debtor conundrum, 195
        Non-inventory goods, 184
        Payment rights, sales of
                Generally, 204
                Sold payment rights, priorities
                    in, 217
        Waivers of priorities vs secured
            creditors, 193
Cash proceeds. Proceeds, below
Chattel paper
        Generally, 228 et seq.
        Payment rights, below
        Proceeds treatment, 233
Circular priorities in fixtures, 438
Commingling of cash proceeds, 263, 264
Conflicting security interests, 152
Consignments, 325, 339
Consumer goods
        Buyers, 193
        Purchase-money security interests,
            179
        Sellers, payment rights priority
            issues, 228
Control based priority in deposit accounts,
    241
Controllable Electronic Record, 225–227
Deposit accounts
        Generally, 239
        Collateral use problems, 240
        Control based priority, 241
        Original collateral, security
            interests in deposit accounts
            as, 245
        Policy considerations, 250
        Proceeds of other collateral,
            treatment as, 244
        Security interests in deposit
            accounts as original collateral,
            245
        Subordination agreements, 250
Double debtor conundrum, 195

Dragnet clauses covering future advances,
          effectiveness, 153
Electronic chattel paper, 229
Federal Tax Lien Act, this index
Filing to establish, 56
Financing statement as an umbrella, 156
First-to-file-or-perfect creditor status,
          policy considerations, 160
First-to-file-or-perfect rule
          Junior secured creditors, 160
          Purchase-money security interests
                    as exception, 162
          Secured creditor vs secured creditor,
                    151, 152
          Secured creditor vs unsecured
                    creditor, 159, 160
Floor planning motor vehicle financing,
          233
Future Advances, this index
General intangibles, priority in proceeds,
          218
Holders in due course of negotiable
          instruments, 266
Instruments
          Generally, 228 et seq., 237
          Holders in due course of negotiable
                    instruments, 266
          Payment rights, below
          Purchasers for value, 266
          Transferees, 265
Intangibles. Payment rights, below
Intellectual Property, Security Interests
          in, this index
Inventory
          Generally, 163 et seq.
          Buyers and lessees, priorities vs
                    secured creditors
                    Generally, 185
                    Certificate of title goods, 191
                    Ordinary course of business,
                              185
                    Waivers, 193
          Dual status rule, 179
          Notice requirement, purchase-
                    money security interests
                    exception, 174
          Proceeds, 174, 218, 219, 233
          Proceeds treatment, 233
          Purchase-money security interests
                    exception
                    Generally, 162
                    Dual status rule, 179
                    Notice requirement, 174
                    Proceeds treatment, 174
Investment securities, security interests
          in, 396
Junior secured creditors
          Effect of sales of repossessed
                    collateral on, 517
          First-to-file-or-perfect rule, 160
          Security agreements covenants
                    precluding, 160
Lessees. Buyers and lessees, above
Lien creditors, unperfected security
          interest
          Generally, 182

Future advance conflicts, 182
Livestock, purchase-money security
          interests exception, 163
Negotiable instruments, holders in due
          course of, 266
Noninventory goods
          Buyers and lessees vs secured
                    creditors, 184
          Purchase-money priority
                    Generally, 167
                    Transformation rule, 172
Ordinary course of business buyers of
          inventory vs secured creditors, 185
Original collateral, security interests in
          deposit accounts as, 245
Payment intangibles
          Payment rights distinguished, 206
                    et seq.
Payment rights
          Generally, 202 et seq., 228
          Chattel paper, 228 et seq.
          Floor planning motor vehicle
                    financing, 233
          Instruments, 228 et seq., 237
          Retailers of consumer goods, 228
          Sales
                    Generally, 204
                    Sold payment rights, priorities
                              in, 217
Policy considerations
          First-to-file-or-perfect creditor
                    status, 160
          Purchase-money security interests,
                    162
Position of first-to-file secured party, 159
Priorities of junior claimants and lienors,
          effect of sales of repossessed
          collateral, 517
Proceeds
          Generally, 252
          Accounts and general intangibles,
                    218
          Chattel paper, proceeds treatment,
                    233
          Commingling, 263, 264
          Deposit accounts, treatment as, 244
          Tracing, 261
          Transferees
                    Generally, 252
Promissory notes. Payment rights, above
Purchase-money security interests
          Generally, 162 et seq.
          Accounts exception, 162
          Consumer goods, 179
          Definitions, 162, 163, 176
          Federal tax lien exceptions, 279
          First-to-file-or-perfect rule
                    exception, 162
          Livestock exception, 163
          Noninventory goods
                    Generally, 167
                    Transformation rule, 172
          Perfection, 162
          Policy considerations, 162
Purchase-money security interests. See
          Inventory, this index

Purchasers for value of instruments, 266
Purchasers vs secured creditors, 151
Retailers of consumer goods, payment
    rights, 228
Sales affecting priority status. Buyers and
    lessees, above
Sales of repossessed collateral, priorities
    of junior claimants and lienors, 517
Secured creditor vs secured creditor
        Generally, 151, 152
        Subordination agreements, 160, 161
Secured creditor vs tort creditor, 7
Secured creditor vs unsecured creditor,
    159, 160
Security agreement covenants precluding
    junior secured creditors, 160
Sold payment rights, priorities in, 217
Subordination agreements
        Deposit accounts, 250
        Secured vs secured creditors, 160,
            161
Taxes. *See* Federal Tax Lien Act, this
    index
Time of transaction issues, consumer
    goods buyers, 194
Transferees as to cash proceeds
        Generally, 252
        Tracing, 261
Transferees of instruments, 265
Transformation rule, purchase-money
    security interests in noninventory
    goods, 172
Umbrella, financing statement as, 156
Unperfected security interests
        Generally, 53
        Secured creditors vs, 151
        Versus lien creditors, future
            advance conflicts, 182
Waivers of secured creditor priorities to
    buyers of inventory, 193

PROCEEDS OF COLLATERAL
Attachment, 49
Perfection, 76
Priorities, this index
Tracing issues, 261

**PURCHASE-MONEY SECURITY
    INTERESTS (PMSIs)**
Priorities, this index

REPAYMENT RISK
Secured vs unsecured lending, 8

REPOSSESSION
Enforcement of Security Interests, this
    index

RESTITUTION
Letters of credit, 642

SECURITIES, INVESTMENT
Investment Securities, Security Interests
    in, this index

SECURITIZATION
    Generally, 2, 203, 204
Accounts receivable, 2

Bankruptcy, fraudulent transfers, 603
Chattel paper treatment, 206
Inventory, 2
Special purpose vehicles, 603
UCC Article 9 treatment, 205

SECURITY AGREEMENTS
After-acquired collateral descriptions
        Business lending, 34
        Consumer lending, 39
Authentication of, 21, 22
Composite document rule, 15
Covenants precluding junior secured
        creditors, 160
Definition, 13
Disclosure functions of, 26
Financing statements distinguished, 25,
    26
Intent to create distinguished, 20, 21
Junior secured creditors, covenants
        precluding, 160
Proceeds of collateral, references to, 49
Supergeneric descriptions of collateral, 25

SECURITY INTERESTS
Agricultural liens distinguished, 55
Attachment of Security Interests, this
    index
Chattel mortgages compared, 10
Conditional sales compared, 10
Default, this index
Enforcement of Security Interests, this
    index
Fixtures, Security Interests in, this index
Intellectual Property, Security Interests
    in, this index
Investment Securities, Security Interests
    in, this index
Leases, this index
Letters of credit, security interests in,
    666, 667
Perfection of Security Interests, this index
Priorities, this index
UCC Article 9
        Drafting history, 9
        Fairness and efficiency of secured
            lending, 8
        Legitimization of nonpossessory
            personal property financing, 9
        Revisions, 12

SETOFF RIGHTS OF BANKS, 241

SIGNALING OF DEBTOR QUALITY
Secured vs unsecured lending, 7

SIGNATURES
Electronic and manual, 13, 14
Financing statements, signatures of
    debtors, 100

STRONG ARM POWERS, 146
See Bankruptcy, this index

SUBORDINATION
Agreements
        Deposit accounts priorities, 250

Secured vs secured creditors, 160,
161

SUBROGATION
See Equitable Subrogation, this
index
Letters of credit, 642

**TANGIBLE AND INTANGIBLE
COLLATERAL**
General intangibles, priority in proceeds,
218
Intellectual property treatment as general
intangibles, 343
Payment rights, payment intangibles
distinguished, 206 et seq.
Perfection of security interests
Generally, 54
Choice of law issues, 136
Pledgeable and nonpledgeable
intangibles, 228
Pledges, 228
Proceeds of accounts and general
intangibles, priorities, 218

TAXES
Federal Tax Lien Act, this index
Financing leases, tax treatment, 281, 282

TITLE CERTIFICATES
Certificates of Title Goods, this index

TORTS
Collateral, commercial tort claims treated
as, 39
Wrongful repossession, 472

TRACING
Cash proceeds, priorities, 261

TRANSFERS
Collateral transfers, post-filing
Generally, 116
Motor vehicles, 508
Fraudulent transfers. *See* Bankruptcy,
this index
Letters of credit, 664
Priorities, this index

WRONGFUL DISHONOR
Letters of Credit, this index